For more resources, visit the Web site for
The Making of the West: A Concise History

bedfordstmartins.com/huntconcise

FREE Online Study Guide

Get instant feedback on your progress with

- Chapter self-tests
- Key terms review
- Map quizzes
- Timeline activities
- Note-taking outlines

FREE History research and writing help

Refine your research skills and find plenty of good sources with

- A database of useful images, maps, documents, and more at *Make History*
- A guide to online sources for history
- Help with writing history papers
- A tool for building a bibliography
- Tips on avoiding plagiarism

FOURTH EDITION

The Making of the West

Peoples and Cultures

A Concise History

Lynn Hunt
University of California, Los Angeles

Thomas R. Martin
College of the Holy Cross

Barbara H. Rosenwein
Loyola University Chicago

Bonnie G. Smith
Rutgers University

Bedford / St. Martin's
Boston ▪ *New York*

For Bedford/St. Martin's

Publisher for History: Mary V. Dougherty
Director of Development for History: Jane Knetzger
Senior Developmental Editor: Leah R. Strauss
Senior Production Editor: Karen S. Baart
Senior Production Supervisors: Jennifer L. Peterson and Dennis J. Conroy
Senior Marketing Manager: Paul Stillitano
Editorial Assistant: Victoria Royal
Production Assistant: Elise Keller
Copyeditor: Janet Renard
Indexer: Leoni Z. McVey, McVey & Associates, Inc.
Cartography: Mapping Specialists, Limited
Photo Researcher: Bruce Carson
Permissions Manager: Kalina K. Ingham
Senior Art Director: Anna Palchik
Text Designer: Lisa Buckley
Cover Designer: Billy Boardman
Cover Art: Parisian Street Scene, Jean Béraud (1849–1935) / Private Collection /
   The Bridgman Art Library
Composition: Jouve
Printing and Binding: RR Donnelley and Sons

President, Bedford/St. Martin's: Denise B. Wydra
Presidents, Macmillan Higher Education: Joan E. Feinberg and Tom Scotty
Director of Marketing: Karen R. Soeltz
Production Director: Susan W. Brown
Associate Production Director: Elise S. Kaiser
Managing Editor: Elizabeth M. Schaaf

Library of Congress Control Number: 2012937001

Manufactured in the United States of America.

7 6 5 4 3 2
f e d c b a

For information, write: Bedford/St. Martin's, 75 Arlington Street, Boston, MA 02116 (617-399-4000)

ISBN 978–0–312–67272–0 (Combined Edition)
ISBN 978–0–312–67273–7 (Volume I)
ISBN 978–0–312–67274–4 (Volume II)

At the time of publication all Internet URLs published in this text were found to accurately link to their intended Web site. If you do find a broken link, please forward the information to history@bedfordstmartins.com so that it can be corrected for the next printing.

Preface

WE ARE DELIGHTED TO PRESENT this revision of *The Making of the West: Peoples and Cultures, A Concise History.* There are many reasons to revisit a history text. First, history requires constant rethinking and rewriting because new perspectives and new evidence can shake up our preconceptions about the past. Textbooks, in particular, require revision as the needs of students and their instructors also change over time. In keeping with change, instructors will welcome this edition's enhanced digital resources (see page x). In this edition of the Concise, a revised chapter organization makes it easier for students to follow the narrative by presenting it in slightly shorter segments. At the same time, our continuing emphasis on chronological integration and the generous use of full-color art and maps encourage readers to engage with the events and processes that went into the making of the West.

Second, current events force us to see the past in a new light. The fall of the Berlin Wall in 1989; the attacks of September 11, 2001; and the world economic crisis that began in 2008 are dramatic examples of how events shift our perspective. As a result of these events, communism, Islam, and globalization all have taken on different meanings — not just for the present but also in ways that compel us to reconsider the past. To take just one example, Islam has been part of the history of the West since its founding as a religion in the seventh century, and yet until the last two decades most textbooks of the history of the West gave it relatively little attention. No one would think of limiting its coverage now.

As this book goes into its fourth edition, we authors feel confident that our fundamental approach is well suited to incorporating changes in perspective. We have always linked the history of the West to wider developments in the world. A new edition gives us the opportunity to make those links even stronger and more global, and thereby help students better understand the world in which they live. Instructors who have read and used our book also confirm that the synthesis of approaches we offer — from military to gender history — enables them to bring the most up-to-date conceptualizations of the West into their classroom. We aim to integrate different approaches rather than privileging any one of them.

The Concise edition offers this integration of approaches in a shorter narrative than the parent text. In response to feedback from instructors, the Concise has been reorganized from 24 to 29 chapters — the same number as in the parent text and the companion sourcebook. We believe that by creating more but shorter chapters, while keeping the overall book length the same, we have made the narrative even more integrated and comprehensible than ever before. Our primary goal remains the same: to demonstrate that the history of the West is the story of an ongoing process, not a finished result with one fixed meaning. No one Western people or culture has existed from the beginning until now. Instead, the history of the West includes many different peoples and cultures. To convey these ideas, we have written a sustained story of the West's development in a broad, global context that reveals the cross-cultural interactions fundamental to the shaping of Western politics, societies, cultures, and economies. Indeed, the first chapter opens with a section on the origins and contested meaning of the term *Western civilization*.

We know from our own teaching that introductory students need a solid chronological framework, one with enough familiar benchmarks to make the material easy to grasp. Each chapter is organized around the main events, people, and themes of a period in which the West significantly changed; thus, students learn about political and military events and social and cultural developments as they unfolded. This chronological integration also makes it possible for students to see the interconnections among varieties of historical experience — between politics and cultures, between public events and private experiences, between wars and diplomacy and everyday life. For teachers, our chronological approach ensures a balanced account and provides the opportunity to present themes within their greater context. But perhaps best of all, this approach provides a text that reveals history as a process that is constantly alive, subject to pressures, and able to surprise us.

Cultural borrowing between the peoples of Europe and their neighbors has characterized Western civilization from the beginning. Thus, we have insisted on an expanded vision of the West that includes the United States and fully incorporates Scandinavia, eastern Europe, and the Ottoman Empire. Now this vision encompasses an even wider global context than before, as Latin America, Africa, China, Japan, and India also come into the story. We have been able to offer sustained treatment of crucial topics such as Islam and to provide a more thorough examination of globalization than any competing text. Study of Western history provides essential background to today's events, from debates over immigration to conflicts in the Middle East. Instructors have found this synthesis essential for helping students understand the West amid today's globalization.

In this edition, we have enhanced our coverage of Western interactions with other parts of the world and the cross-cultural exchanges that influenced the making of the West. Chapter 2, for example, demonstrates that despite the Dark Age, Greek civilization stayed in contact with civilization in the Near East as it reinvented itself — and that this cultural interaction produced a reemergence with profound differences from the social and political traditions that had existed in Greece before. Chapter 14 shows how the gold and silver discovered in the New World combined with growing confrontations over religion within Europe to reshape the long-standing rivalries among princes, treat-

ing these topics together to illustrate how such early forms of globalization influenced daily life, religious beliefs, and the ways wars were fought. Chapter 27 features a revised, updated discussion of decolonization and the end of empire in Asia, Africa, and the Middle East. Chapter 29 includes current coverage of recent events in the Middle East, the global economic crisis, the rise of economies in the Pacific and the Southern Hemisphere, and globalized culture and communications.

As always, we have also incorporated the latest scholarly findings throughout the book so that students and instructors alike have a text on which they can confidently rely. In the fourth edition, we have included new and updated discussions of topics such as fresh archaeological evidence for the possible role of religion in stimulating the major changes of the Neolithic Revolution; the dating of the Great Sphinx in Egypt, the scholarly debate that could radically change our ideas of the earliest Egyptian history; the newest thinking on the origins of Islam; the crucial issues in the Investiture Conflict between pope and emperor; the impact of the Great Famine of the fourteenth century; the slave trade, especially its continuation into the nineteenth century; and the ways in which scholars are considering recent events within the context of the new digital world.

Aided by new multimedia offerings that give students and instructors interactive tools for study and teaching (see "Versions and Supplements," page xi), the new edition is, we believe, even better suited to today's Western civilization courses. In writing *The Making of the West: Peoples and Cultures, A Concise History,* we have aimed to communicate the vitality and excitement as well as the fundamental importance of history. Students should be enthusiastic about history; we hope we have conveyed some of our own enthusiasm and love for the study of history in these pages.

Pedagogy and Features

We know from our own teaching that students need all the help they can get in absorbing and making sense of information, thinking analytically, and understanding that history itself is often debated and constantly revised. With these goals in mind, we retained the class-tested learning and teaching aids that worked well in the previous editions, but we have also done more to help students distill the central story of each age.

Each chapter begins with a vivid *anecdote* that draws readers into the atmosphere of the period and introduces the chapter's main themes, accompanied by a full-page illustration. The *Chapter Focus* poses an overarching question at the start of the narrative to help guide students' reading. Strategically placed at the end of each major section, a *Review Question* helps students assimilate core points in digestible increments. *Key Terms* and names that appear in boldface in the text have been updated to concentrate on likely test items; these terms are defined in the *Glossary of Key Terms and People* at the end of the book.

At the end of each chapter, the *Conclusion* further reinforces the central developments covered in the chapter. The *Review Questions* are then presented again so that students can revisit the chapter's core points. We have also added new *Making Connections* questions that prompt students to think across the sections of a given

chapter. A graphical *Timeline* enables students to see the sequence and overlap of important events in a given period. And a list of author-selected *Suggested References* directs students to print and online resources for further investigation.

The map program of *A Concise History* has been praised as the most comprehensive of any brief survey text. In each chapter, we offer three types of maps, each with a distinct role in conveying information to students. Up to five **full-size maps** show major developments, up to four **"spot" maps** — small maps positioned within the discussion right where students need them — serve as immediate locators, and *Mapping the West* **summary maps** at the end of each chapter provide a snapshot of the West at the close of a transformative period and help students visualize the West's changing contours over time. In this edition, we have added new maps and carefully considered each of the existing maps, simplifying where possible to better highlight essential information, and clarifying and updating borders and labels where needed. In addition to the more than 150 maps, *Taking Measure* **features** introduce students to the intriguing stories revealed by quantitative analysis. Each feature highlights a chart, table, graph, or map of historical statistics that illuminates an important political, social, or cultural development.

We have integrated art as fully as possible into the narrative. Over 240 illustrations — a quarter of which are new — were carefully chosen to reflect this edition's broad topical coverage and geographic inclusion, reinforce the text, and show the varieties of visual sources from which historians build their narratives and interpretations. All artifacts, illustrations, paintings, and photographs are contemporaneous with the chapter; there are no anachronistic illustrations. The captions for the maps and art help students learn how to read visuals, and we have frequently included specific questions or suggestions for comparisons that might be developed.

Acknowledgments

In the vital process of revision, the authors have benefited from repeated critical readings by many talented scholars and teachers. Our sincere thanks go to the following instructors, whose comments often challenged us to rethink or justify our interpretations and who always provided a check on accuracy down to the smallest detail.

John H. Ball, *Hillsborough Community College*
Caroline Barton, *Holmes Community College*
James T. Carroll, *Iona College*
Heidi Chretien, *Dominican University of California*
Jason Coy, *College of Charleston*
Laura A. Endicott, *Southwestern Oklahoma State University*
Kevin Grant, *Hamilton College*
Martin P. Johnson, *Miami University at Hamilton*
William Krend, *West Hills College*
James Lenaghan, *The Ohio State University*

Erika L. Lindgren, *Wartburg College*

Rebecca Livingstone, *Simpson College*

Matthew Lungerhausen, *Winona State University*

Benjamin G. Martin, *San Francisco State University*

Roger L. Martinez, *Saint Joseph's University*

Martin Menke, *Boston College*

William A. Pelz, *Elgin Community College*

Craig W. Pilant, *County College of Morris*

Matthew M. Stith, *The University of Texas at Tyler*

Rachelle Wadsworth, *Florida State College at Jacksonville*

Janet M. C. Walmsley, *George Mason University*

Aaron Wilson, *Creighton University*

Dolly Smith Wilson, *Texas Tech University*

Matthew Donald Zarzeczny, *Ashland University*

Many colleagues, friends, and family members have made contributions to this work. They know how grateful we are. We also wish to acknowledge and thank the publishing team at Bedford/St. Martin's who did so much to bring this revised edition to completion: co-president of Macmillan Higher Education, Joan Feinberg; president Denise Wydra; publisher for history Mary Dougherty; director of development for history Jane Knetzger; senior editor Leah Strauss; assistant editor Robin Soule; editorial assistant Victoria Royal; senior marketing manager Paul Stillitano; senior production editor Karen Baart; managing editor Elizabeth Schaaf; art researcher Bruce Carson; text designer Lisa Buckley; cover designer Billy Boardman; and copyeditor Janet Renard.

Our students' questions and concerns have shaped much of this work, and we welcome all our readers' suggestions, queries, and criticisms. Please contact us at our respective institutions or via history@bedfordstmartins.com.

Versions and Supplements

ADOPTERS OF *The Making of the West: A Concise History* and their students have access to abundant extra resources, including documents, presentation and testing materials, volumes in the acclaimed Bedford Series in History and Culture volumes, and much more.

To Learn More

For more information on the offerings described below, visit the book's catalog site at **bedfordstmartins.com/huntconcise/catalog**, or contact your local Bedford/St. Martin's sales representative.

Get the Right Version for Your Class

To accommodate different course lengths and course budgets, *The Making of the West: A Concise History* is available in several different formats, including e-books, which are available at a substantial discount.

- Combined edition (Chapters 1–29) — available in paperback and e-book formats
- Volume I: To 1750 (Chapters 1–17) — available in paperback and e-book formats
- Volume II: Since 1500 (Chapters 14–29) — available in paperback and e-book formats

NEW Assign the online, interactive Bedford x-Book. With all the content of the print book plus the companion documents reader, the *x-Book for The Making of the West: A Concise History* features a robust search engine, navigation tools, easy ways to take and share notes, and interactive exercises. And with fast ways to rearrange chapters and add new pages, sections, or links, it lets teachers build just the right book for their course.

Let students choose their e-book format. Students can purchase the downloadable *Bedford e-Book to Go for The Making of the West: A Concise History* from our Web site or find other PDF versions of the e-book at our publishing partners' sites: CourseSmart, Barnes & Noble NookStudy, Kno, CafeScribe, or Chegg.

Send Students to Free Online Resources

The book's companion site at **bedfordstmartins.com/huntconcise** gives students a way to read, write, and study by providing plentiful quizzes and activities, study aids, and history research and writing help.

FREE **Online Study Guide.** Available at the companion site, this popular resource provides students with quizzes and activities for each chapter, including multiple-choice self-tests that focus on important concepts; flashcards that test students' knowledge of key terms; timeline activities that emphasize causal relationships; and map quizzes intended to strengthen students' geography skills. Instructors can monitor students' progress through an online Quiz Gradebook or receive e-mail updates.

FREE **Research, Writing, and Anti-plagiarism Advice.** Available at the companion site, Bedford's **History Research and Writing Help** includes **History Research and Reference Sources**, with links to history-related databases, indexes, and journals; **More Sources and How to Format a History Paper**, with clear advice on how to integrate primary and secondary sources into research papers and how to cite and format sources correctly; **Build a Bibliography**, a simple Web-based tool known as *The Bedford Bibliographer* that generates bibliographies in four commonly used documentation styles; and **Tips on Avoiding Plagiarism**, an online tutorial that reviews the consequences of plagiarism and features exercises to help students practice integrating sources and recognize acceptable summaries.

Take Advantage of Instructor Resources

Bedford/St. Martin's has developed a wide range of teaching resources for this book and for this course. They range from lecture and presentation materials and assessment tools to course management options. Most can be downloaded or ordered at **bedfordstmartins.com/huntconcise/catalog**.

NEW *HistoryClass for The Making of the West: A Concise History.* *HistoryClass*, a Bedford/ St. Martin's Online Course Space, puts the online resources available with this textbook in one convenient and completely customizable course space. There you and your students can access the interactive x-Book and primary sources reader; maps, images, additional documents, and links; chapter review quizzes; and research and writing help. In *HistoryClass* you can get all of our premium content and tools and

assign, rearrange, and mix them with your own resources. For more information, visit yourhistoryclass.com.

Instructor's Resource Manual. The instructor's manual offers both experienced and first-time instructors tools for preparing lectures and running discussions. It includes chapter review material, teaching strategies, and a guide to chapter-specific supplements available for the text.

Guide to Changing Editions. Designed to facilitate an instructor's transition from the previous edition of *The Making of the West: A Concise History* to the current edition, this guide presents an overview of major changes as well as changes in each chapter.

Computerized Test Bank. The test bank includes a mix of fresh, carefully crafted multiple-choice, matching, short-answer, and essay questions for each chapter. It also contains the Chapter Focus, Review, Making Connections, and Map and Visual Activity questions from the textbook and model answers for each. All questions appear in Microsoft Word format and in easy-to-use test bank software that allows instructors to add, edit, re-sequence, and print questions and answers. Instructors can also export questions into a variety of formats, including WebCT and Blackboard.

NEW *The Bedford Lecture Kit:* **PowerPoint Maps, Images, Lecture Outlines, and i>clicker Content.** These presentation materials are downloadable individually from the Instructor Resources tab at bedfordstmartins.com/huntconcise/catalog and are available on *The Bedford Lecture Kit* **Instructor's Resource CD-ROM.** They provide ready-made and fully customizable PowerPoint multimedia presentations that include lecture outlines with embedded maps, figures, and selected images from the textbook and extra background for instructors. Also available are maps and selected images in JPEG and PowerPoint formats; content for i>clicker, a classroom response system, in Microsoft Word and PowerPoint formats; and outline maps in PDF format for quizzing or handing out. All files are suitable for copying onto transparency acetates.

Make History — **Free Documents, Maps, Images, and Web Sites.** *Make History* combines the best Web resources with hundreds of maps and images, to make it simple to find the source material you need. Browse the collection of thousands of resources by course or by topic, date, and type. Each item has been carefully chosen and helpfully annotated to make it easy to find exactly what you need. Available at bedfordstmartins.com/makehistory.

Videos and Multimedia. A wide assortment of videos and multimedia CD-ROMs on various topics in Western civilization is available to qualified adopters through your Bedford/St. Martin's sales representative.

Package and Save Your Students Money

For information on free packages and discounts up to 50%, visit **bedfordstmartins.com/huntconcise/catalog** or contact your local Bedford/St. Martin's sales representative.

Sources of The Making of the West, **Fourth Edition.** This companion sourcebook provides written and visual sources to accompany each chapter of *The Making of the West: A Concise History.* Political, social, and cultural documents offer a variety of perspectives that complement the textbook and encourage students to make connections between narrative history and primary sources. Over thirty new documents and visual sources highlight the diversity of historical voices that shaped each period. To aid students in approaching and interpreting documents, each chapter contains an introduction, document headnotes, and questions for discussion. Now with a chapter organization that matches the textbook, this reader is available free when packaged with the print text.

Sources of The Making of the West e-Book. The reader is also available as an e-book. When packaged with the print or electronic version of the textbook, it is available for free.

The Bedford Series in History and Culture. More than one hundred fifty titles in this highly praised series combine first-rate scholarship, historical narrative, and important primary documents for undergraduate courses. Each book is brief, inexpensive, and focused on a specific topic or period. For a complete list of titles, visit **bedfordstmartins .com/history/series**. Package discounts are available.

Rand McNally Atlas of Western Civilization. This collection of over fifty full-color maps highlights social, political, and cross-cultural change and interaction from classical Greece and Rome to the postindustrial Western world. Each map is thoroughly indexed for fast reference. Available for $3.00 when packaged with the print text.

The Bedford Glossary for European History. This handy supplement for the survey course gives students historically contextualized definitions for hundreds of terms — from *Abbasids* to *Zionism* — that they will encounter in lectures, reading, and exams. Available free when packaged with the print text.

Trade Books. Titles published by sister companies Hill and Wang; Farrar, Straus and Giroux; Henry Holt and Company; St. Martin's Press; Picador; and Palgrave Macmillan are available at a 50% discount when packaged with Bedford/St. Martin's textbooks. For more information, visit **bedfordstmartins.com/tradeup**.

A Pocket Guide to Writing in History. This portable and affordable reference tool by Mary Lynn Rampolla, now also available as a searchable e-book, provides reading, writing,

and research advice useful to students in all history courses. Concise yet comprehensive advice on approaching typical history assignments, developing critical reading skills, writing effective history papers, conducting research, using and documenting sources, and avoiding plagiarism — enhanced with practical tips and examples throughout — have made this slim reference a best seller. Package discounts are available.

A Student's Guide to History. This complete guide to success in any history course provides the practical help students need to be effective. In addition to introducing students to the nature of the discipline, author Jules Benjamin teaches a wide range of skills, from preparing for exams to approaching common writing assignments, and explains the research and documentation process with plentiful examples. Package discounts are available.

The Social Dimension of Western Civilization. Combining current scholarship with classic pieces, this reader's forty-eight secondary sources, compiled by Richard M. Golden, hook students with the fascinating and often surprising details of how everyday Western people worked, ate, played, celebrated, worshipped, married, procreated, fought, persecuted, and died. Package discounts are available.

The West in the Wider World: Sources and Perspectives. Edited by Richard Lim and David Kammerling Smith, this first college reader to focus on the central historical question "How did the West become the West?" offers a wealth of written and visual source materials to reveal the influence of non-European regions on the origins and development of Western Civilization. Package discounts are available.

Brief Contents

1 Early Western Civilization, 400,000–1000 B.C.E.   3

2 Near East Empires and the Reemergence of Civilization in Greece, 1000–500 B.C.E.   39

3 The Greek Golden Age, c. 500–c. 400 B.C.E.   75

4 From the Classical to the Hellenistic World, 400–30 B.C.E.   109

5 The Rise of Rome and Its Republic, 753–44 B.C.E.   139

6 The Creation of the Roman Empire, 44 B.C.E–284 C.E.   169

7 The Transformation of the Roman Empire, 284–600 C.E.   203

8 The Heirs of Rome: Islam, Byzantium, and Europe, 600–750   239

9 From Centralization to Fragmentation, 750–1050   269

10 Commercial Quickening and Religious Reform, 1050–1150   305

11 The Flowering of the Middle Ages, 1150–1215   337

12 The Medieval Synthesis — and Its Cracks, 1215–1340   369

13 Crisis and Renaissance, 1340–1492   399

14 Global Encounters and the Shock of the Reformation, 1492–1560   431

15 Wars of Religion and the Clash of Worldviews, 1560–1648   461

16 Absolutism, Constitutionalism, and the Search for Order, 1640–1700   493

17 The Atlantic System and Its Consequences, 1700–1750   529

18 The Promise of Enlightenment, 1750–1789   563

19 The Cataclysm of Revolution, 1789–1799   595

20 Napoleon and the Revolutionary Legacy, 1800–1830   627

21 Industrialization and Social Ferment, 1830–1850   659

22 Politics and Culture of the Nation-State, 1850–1870   695

23 Empire, Industry, and Everyday Life, 1870–1890   731

24 Modernity and the Road to War, 1890–1914   767

25 World War I and Its Aftermath, 1914–1929   803

26 The Great Depression and World War II, 1929–1945   841

27 The Cold War and the Remaking of Europe, 1945–1960s   881

28 Postindustrial Society and the End of the Cold War Order, 1960s–1989   917

29 A New Globalism, 1989 to the Present   953

Contents

Preface   *v*

Versions and Supplements   *x*

Brief Contents   *xv*

Maps and Figures   *xlvi*

Authors' Note: The B.C.E./C.E. Dating System   *lii*

Map of Europe   *liv*

Chapter 1

Early Western Civilization, 400,000–1000 B.C.E. 3

From the Stone Age to Mesopotamian Civilization, 400,000–1000 B.C.E. 4
Life and Change in the Stone Age *4* ▪ The Emergence of Cities in
Mesopotamia, 4000–2350 B.C.E. *8* ▪ Metals and Empire Making: The
Akkadians and the Ur III Dynasty, c. 2350–c. 2000 B.C.E. *12* ▪ The
Achievements of the Assyrians, the Babylonians, and the Canaanites,
2000–1000 B.C.E. *13*

Egypt, the First Unified Country, 3050–1000 B.C.E. 15
From the Unification of Egypt to the Old Kingdom, 3050–2190 B.C.E. *15*
▪ The Middle and New Kingdoms in Egypt, 2061–1081 B.C.E. *22*

The Hittites, the Minoans, and the Mycenaeans, 2200–1000 B.C.E. 25
The Hittites, 1750–1200 B.C.E. *26* ▪ The Minoans, 2200–1400 B.C.E. *28*
▪ The Mycenaeans, 1800–1000 B.C.E. *30* ▪ The Violent End to Early
Western Civilization, 1200–1000 B.C.E. *32*

Conclusion 35

Chapter 2

Near East Empires and the Reemergence of Civilization in Greece, 1000–500 B.C.E. *39*

From Dark Age to Empire in the Near East, 1000–500 B.C.E. *40*

The New Empire of Assyria, 900–600 B.C.E. *41* ▪ The Neo-Babylonian Empire, 600–539 B.C.E. *41* ▪ The Persian Empire, 557–500 B.C.E. *42* ▪ The Israelites, Origins to 539 B.C.E. *44*

The Reemergence of Greek Civilization, 1000–750 B.C.E. *47*

The Greek Dark Age *48* ▪ The Values of the Olympic Games *49* ▪ Homer, Hesiod, and Divine Justice in Greek Myth *51*

The Creation of the Greek City-State, 750–500 B.C.E. *52*

The Physical Environment of the Greek City-State *52* ▪ Trade and "Colonization," 800–580 B.C.E. *52* ▪ Citizenship and Freedom in the Greek City-State *53*

New Directions for the Greek City-State, 750–500 B.C.E. *61*

Oligarchy in the City-State of Sparta, 700–500 B.C.E. *61* ▪ Tyranny in the City-State of Corinth, 657–585 B.C.E. *64* ▪ Democracy in the City-State of Athens, 632–500 B.C.E. *65* ▪ New Ways of Thought and Expression in Greece, 630–500 B.C.E. *67*

Conclusion *71*

Chapter 3

The Greek Golden Age, c. 500–c. 400 B.C.E. *75*

Wars between Persia and Greece, 499–479 B.C.E. *76*
From the Ionian Revolt to the Battle of Marathon, 499–490 B.C.E. *76*
- The Great Persian Invasion, 480–479 B.C.E. *77*

Athenian Confidence in the Golden Age, 478–431 B.C.E. *79*
The Establishment of the Athenian Empire *79* ▪ Radical Democracy and
Pericles' Leadership, 461–431 B.C.E. *81* ▪ The Urban Landscape in Athens *82*

Tradition and Innovation in Athens's Golden Age *86*
Religious Tradition in a Period of Change *86* ▪ Women, Slaves,
and Metics *87* ▪ Innovative Ideas in Education, Philosophy, History,
and Medicine *90* ▪ The Development of Greek Tragedy *96*
▪ The Development of Greek Comedy *99*

The End of Athens's Golden Age, 431–403 B.C.E. *100*
The Peloponnesian War, 431–404 B.C.E. *100* ▪ Athens Defeated:
Tyranny and Civil War, 404–403 B.C.E. *104*

Conclusion *104*

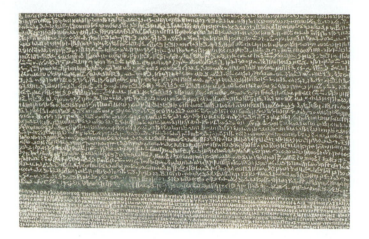

Chapter 4

From the Classical to the Hellenistic World, 400–30 B.C.E. *109*

Classical Greece after the Peloponnesian War, 400–350 B.C.E. *110*
Athens's Recovery after the Peloponnesian War *110* ▪ The Execution of Socrates, 399 B.C.E. *112* ▪ The Philosophy of Plato *112* ▪ Aristotle, Scientist and Philosopher *113* ▪ Greek Political Disunity *114*

The Rise of Macedonia, 359–323 B.C.E. *115*
Macedonian Power and Philip II, 359–336 B.C.E. *115* ▪ The Rule of Alexander the Great, 336–323 B.C.E. *116*

The Hellenistic Kingdoms, 323–30 B.C.E. *118*
Creating New Kingdoms *119* ▪ The Layers of Hellenistic Society *122* ▪ The End of the Hellenistic Kingdoms *124*

Hellenistic Culture *124*
The Arts under Royal Support *124* ▪ Philosophy for a New Age *126* ▪ Scientific Innovation *129* ▪ Cultural and Religious Transformations *130*

Conclusion *134*

Chapter 5

The Rise of Rome and Its Republic, 753–44 B.C.E. *139*

Roman Social and Religious Traditions *140*
Roman Moral Values *140* ▪ The Patron-Client System *141* ▪ The Roman Family *142* ▪ Education for Public Life *144* ▪ Public and Private Religion *144*

From Monarchy to Republic *145*
Roman Society under the Kings, 753–509 B.C.E. *146* ▪ The Early Roman Republic, 509–287 B.C.E. *148*

Roman Imperialism and Its Consequences *150*
Expansion in Italy, 500–220 B.C.E. *151* ▪ Wars with Carthage and in the East, 264–121 B.C.E. *152* ▪ Greek Influence on Roman Literature and the Arts *155* ▪ Stresses on Society from Imperialism *156*

Civil War and the Destruction of the Republic *158*
The Gracchus Brothers and Violence in Politics, 133–121 B.C.E. *158* ▪ Marius and the Origin of Client Armies, 107–100 B.C.E. *159* ▪ Sulla and Civil War, 91–78 B.C.E. *160* ▪ Julius Caesar and the Collapse of the Republic, 83–44 B.C.E. *161*

Conclusion *165*

Chapter 6

The Creation of the Roman Empire, 44 B.C.E.–284 C.E. *169*

From Republic to Empire, 44 B.C.E.–14 C.E. *170*
  Civil War, 44–27 B.C.E. *170* ■ The Creation of the Principate, 27 B.C.E.–14 C.E. *171* ■ Daily Life in the Rome of Augustus *173* ■ Changes in Education, Literature, and Art in Augustus's Rome *175*

Politics and Society in the Early Roman Empire *177*
  The Perpetuation of the Principate after Augustus, 14–180 C.E. *178* ■ Life in the Roman Golden Age, 96–180 C.E. *180*

The Emergence of Christianity in the Early Roman Empire *186*
  Jesus and His Teachings *186* ■ Growth of a New Religion *188* ■ Competing Religious Beliefs *191*

From Stability to Crisis in the Third Century C.E. *194*
  Threats to the Northern and Eastern Frontiers of the Early Roman Empire *194* ■ Uncontrolled Spending, Natural Disasters, and Political Crisis, 193–284 C.E. *195*

Conclusion *198*

Chapter 7

The Transformation of the Roman Empire, 284–600 C.E. *203*

From Principate to Dominate in the Late Roman Empire, 284–395 *204*
The Political Transformation and Division of the Roman Empire *204*
■ The Social Consequences of Financial Pressures *207* ■ From the
Great Persecution to Religious Freedom *209*

The Official Christianization of the Empire, 312–c. 540 *210*
Polytheism and Christianity in Competition *211* ■ The Struggle for
Clarification in Christian Belief *214* ■ The Emergence of Christian
Monks *218*

Non-Roman Kingdoms in the Western Roman Empire, c. 370–550s *220*
Non-Roman Migrations into the Western Roman Empire *221*
■ Social and Cultural Transformation in the Western Roman Empire *225*

The Roman Empire in the East, c. 500–565 *227*
Imperial Society in the Eastern Roman Empire *227* ■ The Reign of Emperor
Justinian, 527–565 *230* ■ The Preservation of Classical Traditions in the Late
Roman Empire *232*

Conclusion *234*

Chapter 8

The Heirs of Rome: Islam, Byzantium, and Europe, 600–750 *239*

Islam: A New Religion and a New Empire *240*
Nomads and City Dwellers *240* ▪ The Prophet Muhammad and the Faith of Islam *241* ▪ Growth of Islam, c. 610–632 *242* ▪ The Caliphs, Muhammad's Successors, 632–750 *243* ▪ Peace and Prosperity in Islamic Lands *245*

Byzantium Besieged *246*
Wars on the Frontiers, c. 570–750 *246* ▪ From an Urban to a Rural Way of Life *248* ▪ New Military and Cultural Forms *249* ▪ Religion, Politics, and Iconoclasm *250*

Western Europe: A Medley of Kingdoms *251*
Frankish Kingdoms with Roman Roots *252* ▪ Economic Activity in a Peasant Society *256* ▪ The Powerful in Merovingian Society *257* ▪ Christianity and Classical Culture in the British Isles *260* ▪ Unity in Spain, Division in Italy *262* ▪ Political Tensions and the Power of the Pope *263*

Conclusion *264*

Chapter 9

From Centralization to Fragmentation, 750–1050 *269*

The Byzantine Emperor and Local Elites *270*
Imperial Power *270* ▪ The Macedonian Renaissance, c. 870–c. 1025 *272*
▪ The *Dynatoi*: A New Landowning Elite *273* ▪ The Formation of Eastern
Europe and Kievan Rus *274*

The Rise and Fall of the Abbasid Caliphate *275*
The Abbasid Caliphate, 750–936 *275* ▪ Regional Diversity in Islamic
Lands *276* ▪ Unity of Commerce and Language *278* ▪ The Islamic
Renaissance, c. 790–c. 1050 *278*

The Carolingian Empire *280*
The Rise of the Carolingians *280* ▪ Charlemagne and His Kingdom,
768–814 *281* ▪ The Carolingian Renaissance, c. 790–c. 900 *284*
▪ Charlemagne's Successors, 814–911 *285* ▪ Land and Power *286*
▪ Viking, Muslim, and Magyar Invasions, c. 790–955 *288*

After the Carolingians: The Emergence of Local Rule *289*
Public Power and Private Relationships *290* ▪ Warriors and Warfare *293*
▪ Efforts to Contain Violence *294* ▪ Political Communities in Italy,
England, and France *295* ▪ Emperors and Kings in Central and
Eastern Europe *297*

Conclusion *301*

Chapter 10

Commercial Quickening and Religious Reform, 1050–1150 *305*

The Commercial Revolution *306*
Fairs, Towns, and Cities *306* ▪ Organizing Crafts and Commerce *309* ▪ Communes: Self-Government for the Towns *310* ▪ The Commercial Revolution in the Countryside *311*

Church Reform *312*
Beginnings of Reform *313* ▪ The Gregorian Reform and the Investiture Conflict, 1075–1122 *315* ▪ The Sweep of Reform *318* ▪ New Monastic Orders of Poverty *319*

The Crusades *322*
Calling the Crusade *323* ▪ The First Crusade *324* ▪ The Crusader States *326* ▪ The Disastrous Second Crusade *326* ▪ The Long-Term Impact of the Crusades *327*

The Revival of Monarchies *328*
Reconstructing the Empire at Byzantium *328* ▪ England under Norman Rule *328* ▪ Praising the King of France *331* ▪ Surviving as Emperor *332*

Conclusion *332*

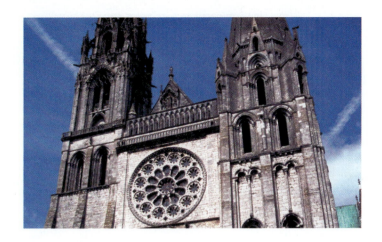

Chapter 11

The Flowering of the Middle Ages, 1150–1215 *337*

New Schools and Churches 338

The New Learning and the Rise of the University *338* ▪ Architectural Style: From Romanesque to Gothic *341*

Governments as Institutions 344

England: Unity through Common Law *345* ▪ France: Consolidation and Conquest *349* ▪ Germany: The Revived Monarchy of Frederick Barbarossa *350* ▪ Eastern Europe and Byzantium: Fragmenting Realms *353*

The Growth of a Vernacular High Culture 354

The Troubadours: Poets of Love and Play *354* ▪ The Birth of Epic and Romance Literature *356*

Religious Fervor and Crusade 357

New Religious Orders in the Cities *357* ▪ Disastrous Crusades to the Holy Land *359* ▪ Victorious Crusades in Europe and on Its Frontiers *360*

Conclusion 364

Chapter 12

The Medieval Synthesis — and Its Cracks, 1215–1340 *369*

The Church's Mission 370
> Innocent III and the Fourth Lateran Council *370* ▪ The Inquisition *372*
> ▪ Lay Piety *372* ▪ Jews and Lepers as Outcasts *373*

Reconciling This World and the Next 375
> The Achievement of Scholasticism *375* ▪ New Syntheses in Writing
> and Music *376* ▪ Gothic Art *378*

The Politics of Control 380
> The Weakening of the Empire *381* ▪ Louis IX and a New Ideal of
> Kingship *382* ▪ The Birth of Representative Institutions *385*
> ▪ The Weakening of the Papacy *386* ▪ The Rise of the *Signori* *388*
> ▪ The Mongol Takeover *389* ▪ The Great Famine *390*

Conclusion 393

Chapter 13

Crisis and Renaissance, 1340–1492 *399*

Crisis: Disease, War, and Schism *400*
The Black Death, 1347–1352 *400* ▪ The Hundred Years' War, 1337–1453 *404* ▪ The Ottoman Conquest of Constantinople, 1453 *407* ▪ The Great Schism, 1378–1417 *408*

The Renaissance: New Forms of Thought and Expression *411*
Renaissance Humanism *412* ▪ The Arts *414*

Consolidating Power *418*
New Political Formations in Eastern Europe *419* ▪ Powerful States in Western Europe *419* ▪ Power in the Republics *422* ▪ The Tools of Power *424*

Conclusion *427*

Chapter 14

Global Encounters and the Shock of the Reformation, 1492–1560 *431*

The Discovery of New Worlds 432

Portuguese Explorations *432* ▪ The Voyages of Columbus *433* ▪ A New Era in Slavery *434* ▪ Conquering the New World *435* ▪ The Columbian Exchange *436*

The Protestant Reformation 436

The Invention of Printing *437* ▪ Popular Piety and Christian Humanism *438* ▪ Martin Luther's Challenge *440* ▪ Protestantism Spreads and Divides *441* ▪ The Contested Church of England *443*

Reshaping Society through Religion 444

Protestant Challenges to the Social Order *445* ▪ New Forms of Discipline *447* ▪ Catholic Renewal *448*

Striving for Mastery 450

Courtiers and Princes *450* ▪ Dynastic Wars *452* ▪ Financing War *453* ▪ Divided Realms *455*

Conclusion 458

Chapter 15

Wars of Religion and the Clash of Worldviews, 1560–1648 *461*

Religious Conflicts Threaten State Power, 1560–1618 *462*
French Wars of Religion, 1562–1598 *462* ▪ Dutch Revolt against Spain *464*
▪ Elizabeth I's Defense of English Protestantism *467* ▪ The Clash of Faiths and Empires in Eastern Europe *469*

The Thirty Years' War, 1618–1648 *470*
Origins and Course of the War *470* ▪ The Effects of Constant Fighting *472*
▪ The Peace of Westphalia, 1648 *472*

Economic Crisis and Realignment *475*
From Growth to Recession *475* ▪ Consequences for Daily Life *477*
▪ The Economic Balance of Power *479*

The Rise of Science and a Scientific Worldview *481*
The Scientific Revolution *481* ▪ The Natural Laws of Politics *485*
▪ The Arts in an Age of Crisis *486* ▪ Magic and Witchcraft *487*

Conclusion *489*

Chapter 16

Absolutism, Constitutionalism, and the Search for Order, 1640–1700 *493*

Louis XIV: Absolutism and Its Limits *494*

The Fronde, 1648–1653 *494* ▪ Court Culture as an Element of Absolutism *495* ▪ Enforcing Religious Orthodoxy *497* ▪ Extending State Authority at Home and Abroad *498*

Constitutionalism in England *502*

England Turned Upside Down, 1642–1660 *502* ▪ Restoration and Revolution Again *506* ▪ Social Contract Theory: Hobbes and Locke *508*

Outposts of Constitutionalism *509*

The Dutch Republic *509* ▪ Freedom and Slavery in the New World *511*

Absolutism in Central and Eastern Europe *513*

Poland-Lithuania Overwhelmed *513* ▪ Brandenburg-Prussia: Militaristic Absolutism *514* ▪ An Uneasy Balance: Austrian Habsburgs and Ottoman Turks *515* ▪ Russia: Setting the Foundations of Bureaucratic Absolutism *517*

The Search for Order in Elite and Popular Culture *518*

Freedom and Constraint in the Arts and Sciences *518* ▪ Women and Manners *521* ▪ Reforming Popular Culture *523*

Conclusion *525*

Chapter 17

The Atlantic System and Its Consequences, 1700–1750 *529*

The Atlantic System and the World Economy *530*
Slavery and the Atlantic System *530* ▪ World Trade and Settlement *535*
▪ The Birth of Consumer Society *537*

New Social and Cultural Patterns *538*
Agricultural Revolution *538* ▪ Social Life in the Cities *540* ▪ New Tastes
in the Arts *542* ▪ Religious Revivals *544*

Consolidation of the European State System *545*
A New Power Alignment *545* ▪ British Rise and Dutch Decline *547*
▪ Russia's Emergence as a European Power *549* ▪ Continuing Dynastic
Struggles *552* ▪ The Power of Diplomacy and the Importance of
Population *553*

The Birth of the Enlightenment *554*
Popularization of Science and Challenges to Religion *555* ▪ Travel Literature
and the Challenge to Custom and Tradition *557* ▪ Raising the Woman
Question *558*

Conclusion *559*

Chapter 18

The Promise of Enlightenment, 1750–1789 *563*

The Enlightenment at Its Height 564

Men and Women of the Republic of Letters *564* ▪ Conflicts with Church and State *566* ▪ The Individual and Society *568* ▪ Spreading the Enlightenment *570* ▪ The Limits of Reason: Roots of Romanticism and Religious Revival *571*

Society and Culture in an Age of Enlightenment 573

The Nobility's Reassertion of Privilege *573* ▪ The Middle Class and the Making of a New Elite *575* ▪ Life on the Margins *577*

State Power in an Era of Reform 580

War and Diplomacy *580* ▪ State-Sponsored Reform *583* ▪ Limits of Reform *585*

Rebellions against State Power 586

Food Riots and Peasant Uprisings *586* ▪ Public Opinion and Political Opposition *587* ▪ Revolution in North America *588*

Conclusion 590

Chapter 19

The Cataclysm of Revolution, 1789–1799 *595*

The Revolutionary Wave, 1787–1789 *596*
  Protesters in the Low Countries and Poland *596* ▪ Origins of the French Revolution, 1787–1789 *597*

From Monarchy to Republic, 1789–1793 *602*
  The Revolution of Rights and Reason *602* ▪ The End of Monarchy *604*

Terror and Resistance *607*
  Robespierre and the Committee of Public Safety *608* ▪ The Republic of Virtue, 1793–1794 *609* ▪ Resisting the Revolution *611* ▪ The Fall of Robespierre and the End of the Terror *612*

Revolution on the March *615*
  Arms and Conquests *616* ▪ Poland Extinguished, 1793–1795 *618* ▪ Revolution in the Colonies *618* ▪ Worldwide Reactions to Revolutionary Change *619*

Conclusion *623*

Chapter 20

Napoleon and the Revolutionary Legacy, 1800–1830 *627*

The Rise of Napoleon Bonaparte *628*

A General Takes Over *628* ■ From Republic to Empire *629* ■ The New Paternalism: The Civil Code *632* ■ Patronage of Science and Intellectual Life *632*

"Europe Was at My Feet": Napoleon's Conquests *634*

The Grand Army and Its Victories, 1800–1807 *635* ■ The Impact of French Victories *637* ■ From Russian Winter to Final Defeat, 1812–1815 *640*

The "Restoration" of Europe *641*

The Congress of Vienna, 1814–1815 *642* ■ The Emergence of Conservatism *644* ■ The Revival of Religion *646*

Challenges to the Conservative Order *646*

Romanticism *647* ■ Political Revolts in the 1820s *650* ■ Revolution and Reform, 1830–1832 *653*

Conclusion *655*

Chapter 21

Industrialization and Social Ferment, 1830–1850 *659*

The Industrial Revolution *660*
Roots of Industrialization *660* ▪ Engines of Change *661* ▪ Urbanization and Its Consequences *666* ▪ Agricultural Perils and Prosperity *668*

Reforming the Social Order *670*
Cultural Responses to the Social Question *670* ▪ The Varieties of Social Reform *673* ▪ Abuses and Reforms Overseas *676*

Ideologies and Political Movements *677*
The Spell of Nationalism *678* ▪ Liberalism in Economics and Politics *680* ▪ Socialism and the Early Labor Movement *681*

The Revolutions of 1848 *684*
The Hungry Forties *684* ▪ Another French Revolution *684* ▪ Nationalist Revolution in Italy *686* ▪ Revolt and Reaction in Central Europe *687* ▪ Aftermath to 1848: Reimposing Authority *688*

Conclusion *689*

Chapter 22

Politics and Culture of the Nation-State, 1850–1870 *695*

The End of the Concert of Europe 696
Napoleon III and the Quest for French Glory *697* ▪ The Crimean War, 1853–1856: Turning Point in European Affairs *698* ▪ Reform in Russia *699*

War and Nation Building 702
Cavour, Garibaldi, and the Process of Italian Unification *702* ▪ Bismarck and the Realpolitik of German Unification *705* ▪ Francis Joseph and the Creation of the Austro-Hungarian Monarchy *708* ▪ Political Stability through Gradual Reform in Great Britain *709* ▪ Nation Building in North America *710*

Nation Building through Social Order 712
Bringing Order to the Cities *712* ▪ Expanding Government Bureaucracy *713* ▪ Schooling and Professionalizing Society *714* ▪ Spreading National Power and Order beyond the West *715* ▪ Contesting the Nation-State's Order at Home *717*

The Culture of Social Order 719
The Arts Confront Social Reality *719* ▪ Religion and National Order *722* ▪ From the Natural Sciences to Social Science *724*

Conclusion 725

Chapter 23

Empire, Industry, and Everyday Life, 1870–1890 *731*

The New Imperialism *732*
> The Scramble for Africa — North and South *733* ▪ Acquiring Territory in Asia *736* ▪ Japan's Imperial Agenda *737* ▪ The Paradoxes of Imperialism *738*

The Industry of Empire *740*
> Industrial Innovation *740* ▪ Facing Economic Crisis *743* ▪ Revolution in Business Practices *744*

Imperial Society and Culture *746*
> The "Best Circles" and the Expanding Middle Class *746* ▪ Working People's Strategies *747* ▪ National Fitness: Reform, Sports, and Leisure *749* ▪ Artistic Responses to Empire and Industry *751*

The Birth of Mass Politics *753*
> Workers, Politics, and Protest *754* ▪ Expanding Political Participation in Western Europe *756* ▪ Power Politics in Central and Eastern Europe *758*

Conclusion *763*

Chapter 24

Modernity and the Road to War, 1890–1914 *767*

Public Debate over Private Life 768
Population Pressure *769* ▪ Reforming Marriage *770* ▪ New Women,
New Men, and the Politics of Sexual Identity *771* ▪ Sciences of the
Modern Self *773*

Modernity and the Revolt in Ideas 774
The Opposition to Positivism *774* ▪ The Revolution in Science *775*
▪ Modern Art *776* ▪ The Revolt in Music and Dance *777*

Growing Tensions in Mass Politics 778
The Expanding Power of Labor *778* ▪ Rights for Women and the Battle for
Suffrage *779* ▪ Liberalism Tested *781* ▪ Anti-Semitism, Nationalism,
and Zionism in Mass Politics *782*

European Imperialism Challenged 786
The Trials of Empire *786* ▪ The Russian Empire Threatened *789*
▪ Growing Resistance to Colonial Domination *791*

Roads to War 793
Competing Alliances and Clashing Ambitions *793* ▪ The Race to Arms *794*
▪ 1914: War Erupts *796*

Conclusion 799

Chapter 25

World War I and Its Aftermath, 1914–1929 *803*

The Great War, 1914–1918 *804*
Blueprints for War *804* ▪ The Battlefronts *806* ▪ The Home Front *809*

Protest, Revolution, and War's End, 1917–1918 *812*
War Protest *812* ▪ Revolution in Russia *812* ▪ Ending the War, 1918 *816*

The Search for Peace in an Era of Revolution *817*
Europe in Turmoil *817* ▪ The Paris Peace Conference, 1919–1920 *818*
▪ Economic and Diplomatic Consequences of the Peace *821*

A Decade of Recovery: Europe in the 1920s *823*
Changes in the Political Landscape *823* ▪ Reconstructing the Economy *826*
▪ Restoring Society *827*

Mass Culture and the Rise of Modern Dictators *829*
Culture for the Masses *829* ▪ Cultural Debates over the Future *830*
▪ The Communist Utopia *832* ▪ Fascism on the March in Italy *834*

Conclusion *836*

Chapter 26

The Great Depression and World War II, 1929–1945 *841*

The Great Depression *842*
> Economic Disaster Strikes *842* ▪ Social Effects of the Depression *844*
> ▪ The Great Depression beyond the West *844*

Totalitarian Triumph *846*
> The Rise of Stalinism *846* ▪ Hitler's Rise to Power *849* ▪ The Nazification
> of German Politics *850* ▪ Nazi Racism *851*

Democracies on the Defensive *852*
> Confronting the Economic Crisis *853* ▪ Cultural Visions in Hard Times *856*

The Road to Global War *857*
> A Surge in Global Imperialism *857* ▪ The Spanish Civil War, 1936–1939 *859*
> ▪ Hitler's Conquest of Central Europe, 1938–1939 *860*

World War II, 1939–1945 *863*
> The German Onslaught *863* ▪ War Expands: The Pacific and Beyond *864*
> ▪ The War against Civilians *865* ▪ Societies at War *868* ▪ From Resistance
> to Allied Victory *869* ▪ An Uneasy Postwar Settlement *872*

Conclusion *875*

Chapter 27

The Cold War and the Remaking of Europe, 1945–1960s *881*

World Politics Transformed 882
Chaos in Europe *883* ▪ New Superpowers: The United States and the Soviet Union *883* ▪ Origins of the Cold War *885* ▪ The Division of Germany *888*

Political and Economic Recovery in Europe 890
Dealing with Nazism *890* ▪ Rebirth of the West *891* ▪ The Welfare State: Common Ground East and West *894* ▪ Recovery in the East *896*

Decolonization in a Cold War Climate 899
The End of Empire in Asia *899* ▪ The Struggle for Identity in the Middle East *901* ▪ New Nations in Africa *902* ▪ Newcomers Arrive in Europe *904*

Daily Life and Culture in the Shadow of Nuclear War 906
Restoring "Western" Values *906* ▪ Cold War Consumerism and Shifting Gender Norms *908* ▪ The Culture of Cold War *910* ▪ The Atomic Brink *911*

Conclusion 912

Chapter 28

Postindustrial Society and the End of the Cold War Order, 1960s–1989 *917*

The Revolution in Technology *918*

The Information Age: Television and Computers *918* ▪ The Space Age *920* ▪ The Nuclear Age *921* ▪ Revolutions in Biology and Reproductive Technology *922*

Postindustrial Society and Culture *923*

Multinational Corporations *923* ▪ The New Worker *924* ▪ The Boom in Education and Research *926* ▪ Changing Family Life and the Generation Gap *926* ▪ Art, Ideas, and Religion in a Technocratic Society *927*

Protesting Cold War Conditions *929*

Cracks in the Cold War Order *929* ▪ The Growth of Citizen Activism *931* ▪ 1968: Year of Crisis *933*

The Testing of Superpower Domination and the End of the Cold War *937*

A Changing Balance of World Power *937* ▪ The Western Bloc Meets Challenges with Reform *939* ▪ Collapse of Communism in the Soviet Bloc *943*

Conclusion *947*

Chapter 29

A New Globalism, 1989 to the Present *953*

Collapse of the Soviet Union and Its Aftermath 954
The Breakup of Yugoslavia *955* ▪ The Soviet Union Comes Apart *956* ▪ Toward a Market Economy *959* ▪ International Politics and the New Russia *960*

The Nation-State in a Global Age 962
Europe Looks beyond the Nation-State *962* ▪ Globalizing Cities and Fragmenting Nations *964* ▪ Global Organizations *966*

An Interconnected World's New Challenges 966
The Problems of Pollution *967* ▪ Population, Health, and Disease *969* ▪ North versus South? *970* ▪ Radical Islam Meets the West *971* ▪ The Promise and Problems of a World Economy *974*

Global Culture and Society in the Twenty-First Century 977
Redefining the West: The Impact of Global Migration *977* ▪ Global Networks and Social Change *979* ▪ A New Global Culture? *980*

Conclusion 986

Glossary of Key Terms and People *G-1*

Index *I-1*

Map of the World *I-76*

century C.E., while 395 C.E. is a date late in the same century. When numbers are given without either B.C.E. or C.E., they are presumed to be dates C.E. For example, the term *eighteenth century* with no abbreviation accompanying it refers to the years 1701 C.E. to 1800 C.E.

No standard system of numbering years, such as B.C.E./C.E., existed in antiquity. Different people in different places identified years with varying names and numbers. Consequently, it was difficult to match up the years in any particular local system with those in a different system. Each city of ancient Greece, for example, had its own method for keeping track of the years. The ancient Greek historian Thucydides, therefore, faced a problem in presenting a chronology for the famous Peloponnesian War between Athens and Sparta, which began (by our reckoning) in 431 B.C.E. To try to explain to as many of his readers as possible the date the war had begun, he described its first year by three different local systems: "the year when Chrysis was in the forty-eighth year of her priesthood at Argos, and Aenesias was overseer at Sparta, and Pythodorus was magistrate at Athens."

A Catholic monk named Dionysius, who lived in Rome in the sixth century C.E., invented the system of reckoning dates forward from the birth of Jesus. Calling himself *Exiguus* (Latin for "the little" or "the small") as a mark of humility, he placed Jesus's birth 754 years after the foundation of ancient Rome. Others then and now believe his date for Jesus's birth was in fact several years too late. Many scholars today calculate that Jesus was born in what would be 4 B.C.E. according to Dionysius's system, although a date a year or so earlier also seems possible.

Counting backward from the supposed date of Jesus's birth to indicate dates earlier than that event represented a natural complement to reckoning forward for dates after it. The English historian and theologian Bede in the early eighth century was the first to use both forward and backward reckoning from the birth of Jesus in a historical work, and this system gradually gained wider acceptance because it provided a basis for standardizing the many local calendars used in the Western Christian world. Nevertheless, B.C. and A.D. were not used regularly until the end of the eighteenth century. B.C.E. and C.E. became common in the late twentieth century.

The system of numbering years from the birth of Jesus is far from the only one in use today. The Jewish calendar of years, for example, counts forward from the date given to the creation of the world, which would be calculated as 3761 B.C.E. under the B.C.E./C.E. system. Under this system, years are designated A.M., an abbreviation of the Latin *anno mundi*, "in the year of the world." The Islamic calendar counts forward from the date of the Prophet Muhammad's flight from Mecca, called the *Hijra*, in what is the year 622 C.E. The abbreviation A.H. (standing for the Latin phrase *anno Hegirae*, "in the year of the Hijra") indicates dates calculated by this system. Anthropology commonly reckons distant dates as "before the present" (abbreviated B.P.).

History is often defined as the study of change over time; hence the importance of dates for the historian. But just as historians argue over which dates are most significant, they disagree over which dating system to follow. Their debate reveals perhaps the most enduring fact about history—its vitality.

Authors' Note
The B.C.E./C.E. Dating System

WHEN WERE YOU BORN? What year is it? We customarily answer questions like these with a number, such as "1991" or "2008." Our replies are usually automatic, taking for granted the numerous assumptions Westerners make about how dates indicate chronology. But to what do numbers such as 1991 and 2008 actually refer? In this book the numbers used to specify dates follow a recent revision of the system most common in the Western secular world. This system reckons the dates of solar years by counting backward and forward from the traditional date of the birth of Jesus Christ, over two thousand years ago.

Using this method, numbers followed by the abbreviation B.C.E., standing for "before the common era" (or, as some would say, "before the Christian era"), indicate the number of years counting backward from the assumed date of the birth of Jesus Christ. B.C.E. therefore indicates the same chronology marked by the traditional abbreviation B.C. ("before Christ"). The larger the number preceding B.C.E. (or B.C.), the earlier in history is the year to which it refers. The date 431 B.C.E., for example, refers to a year 431 years before the birth of Jesus and therefore comes earlier in time than the dates 430 B.C.E., 429 B.C.E., and so on. The same calculation applies to numbering other time intervals calculated on the decimal system: those of ten years (a decade), of one hundred years (a century), and of one thousand years (a millennium). For example, the decade of the 440s B.C.E. (449 B.C.E. to 440 B.C.E.) is earlier than the decade of the 430s B.C.E. (439 B.C.E. to 430 B.C.E.). "Fifth century B.C.E." refers to the fifth period of 100 years reckoning backward from the birth of Jesus and covers the years 500 B.C.E. to 401 B.C.E. It is earlier in history than the fourth century B.C.E. (400 B.C.E. to 301 B.C.E.), which followed the fifth century B.C.E. Because this system has no year "zero," the first century B.C.E. covers the years 100 B.C.E. to 1 B.C.E. Dating millennia works similarly: the second millennium B.C.E. refers to the years 2000 B.C.E. to 1001 B.C.E., the third millennium to the years 3000 B.C.E. to 2001 B.C.E., and so on.

To indicate years counted forward from the traditional date of Jesus's birth, numbers are followed by the abbreviation C.E., standing for "of the common era" (or "of the Christian era"). C.E. therefore indicates the same chronology marked by the traditional abbreviation A.D., which stands for the Latin phrase *anno Domini* ("in the year of the Lord"). A.D. properly comes before the date being marked. The date A.D. 1492, for example, translates as "in the year of the Lord 1492," meaning 1492 years after the birth of Jesus. Under the B.C.E./C.E. system, this date would be written as 1492 C.E. For dating centuries, the term "first century C.E." refers to the period from 1 C.E. to 100 C.E. (which is the same period as A.D. 1 to A.D. 100). For dates C.E., the smaller the number, the earlier the date in history. The fourth century C.E. (301 C.E. to 400 C.E.) comes before the fifth century C.E. (401 C.E. to 500 C.E.). The year 312 C.E. is a date in the early fourth

TAKING MEASURE Census Records during the First and Second Punic Wars   *153*

FIGURE 6.1 Cutaway Reconstruction of the Forum of Augustus   *172*

TAKING MEASURE The Value of Roman Imperial Coinage, 27 B.C.E.–300 C.E.   *195*

TAKING MEASURE Peasants' Use of Farm Produce in the Roman Empire   *208*

TAKING MEASURE Papal Letters Sent from Rome to Northern Europe, c. 600–c. 700   *254*

FIGURE 9.1 Diagram of a Manor and Its Three-Field System   *287*

TAKING MEASURE Sellers, Buyers, and Donors, 800–1000   *291*

FIGURE 10.1 Floor Plan of a Cistercian Monastery   *321*

TAKING MEASURE English Livestock in 1086   *331*

FIGURE 11.1 Floor Plan of a Romanesque Church   *342*

FIGURE 11.2 Troubadour Song: "I Never Died for Love"   *356*

TAKING MEASURE Grain Prices during the Great Famine   *391*

TAKING MEASURE Population Losses and the Black Death   *401*

FIGURE 13.1 The Valois Succession   *404*

TAKING MEASURE Precious Metals and the Spanish Colonies, 1550–1800   *476*

TAKING MEASURE The Seventeenth-Century Army   *514*

FIGURE 17.1 African Slaves Imported into American Territories, 1701–1810   *532*

FIGURE 17.2 Annual Imports in the Atlantic Slave Trade, 1450–1870   *533*

TAKING MEASURE Relationship of Crop Harvested to Seed Used, 1400–1800   *539*

TAKING MEASURE European Urbanization, 1750–1800   *575*

TAKING MEASURE Railroad Lines, 1830–1850   *662*

TAKING MEASURE European Emigration, 1870–1890   *749*

TAKING MEASURE The Growth in Armaments, 1890–1914   *797*

TAKING MEASURE The Victims of Influenza, 1918–1919   *816*

TAKING MEASURE Postindustrial Occupational Structure, 1984   *925*

FIGURE 28.1 Fluctuating Oil Prices, 1955–1985   *939*

TAKING MEASURE World Population Growth, 1950–2010   *969*

SPOT MAP National Minorities in Postwar Poland *824*

SPOT MAP The Irish Free State and Ulster, 1921 *826*

MAPPING THE WEST Europe and the World in 1929 *837*

Chapter 26

MAP 26.1 The Spanish Civil War, 1936–1939 *860*

MAP 26.2 The Growth of Nazi Germany, 1933–1939 *862*

SPOT MAP The Division of France, 1940 *863*

MAP 26.3 Concentration Camps and Extermination Sites in Europe *866*

MAP 26.4 World War II in Europe and Africa *870*

MAP 26.5 World War II in the Pacific *873*

MAPPING THE WEST Europe at War's End, 1945 *876*

Chapter 27

MAP 27.1 The Impact of World War II on Europe *884*

SPOT MAP Yugoslavia after the Revolution *887*

MAP 27.2 Divided Germany and the Berlin Airlift, 1946–1949 *888*

MAP 27.3 European NATO Members and the Warsaw Pact in the 1950s *889*

SPOT MAP The Korean War, 1950–1953 *900*

SPOT MAP Indochina, 1954 *900*

MAP 27.4 The Partition of Palestine and the Creation of Israel, 1947–1948 *901*

MAP 27.5 The Decolonization of Africa, 1951–1990 *903*

MAPPING THE WEST The Cold War World, c. 1960 *913*

Chapter 28

MAP 28.1 The Vietnam War, 1954–1975 *932*

SPOT MAP Prague Spring, 1968 *935*

SPOT MAP Israel after the Six-Day War, 1967 *938*

SPOT MAP Nationalist Movements of the 1970s *940*

MAPPING THE WEST The Collapse of Communism in Europe, 1989–1990 *948*

Chapter 29

MAP 29.1 The Former Yugoslavia, c. 2000 *956*

MAP 29.2 Countries of the Former Soviet Union, c. 2000 *958*

MAP 29.3 The European Union in 2011 *963*

MAP 29.4 The Middle East in the Twenty-First Century *972*

SPOT MAP Tigers of the Pacific Rim, c. 1995 *975*

MAPPING THE WEST The World's Top Fifteen Economies as of 2010 *987*

FIGURES

FIGURE 1.1 Cuneiform Writing *11*

FIGURE 1.2 Egyptian Hieroglyphs *19*

TAKING MEASURE Greek Family Size and Agricultural Labor in the Archaic Age *57*

FIGURE 3.1 Triremes, the Foremost Classical Greek Warships *80*

FIGURE 3.2 Styles of Greek Capitals *85*

TAKING MEASURE Military Forces of Athens and Sparta at the Beginning of the Peloponnesian War (431 B.C.E.) *103*

MAP 19.3 The Second and Third Partitions of Poland, 1793 and 1795   *618*

SPOT MAP St. Domingue on the Eve of the Revolt, 1791   *619*

MAPPING THE WEST Europe in 1799   *622*

Chapter 20

MAP 20.1 Napoleon's Empire at Its Height, 1812   *634*

MAP 20.2 Europe after the Congress of Vienna, 1815   *644*

MAP 20.3 Revolutionary Movements of the 1820s   *650*

SPOT MAP Nationalistic Movements in the Balkans, 1815–1830   *651*

MAP 20.4 Latin American Independence, 1804–1830   *653*

MAPPING THE WEST Europe in 1830   *657*

Chapter 21

MAP 21.1 Industrialization in Europe, c. 1850   *663*

MAP 21.2 The Spread of Cholera, 1826–1855   *668*

SPOT MAP The Opium War, 1839–1842   *677*

MAP 21.3 Languages of Nineteenth-Century Europe   *678*

SPOT MAP The Divisions of Italy, 1848   *686*

MAPPING THE WEST Europe in 1850   *691*

Chapter 22

MAP 22.1 The Crimean War, 1853–1856   *698*

MAP 22.2 Unification of Italy, 1859–1870   *703*

MAP 22.3 Unification of Germany, 1862–1871   *707*

SPOT MAP The Austro-Hungarian Monarchy, 1867   *709*

MAP 22.4 U.S. Expansion, 1850–1870   *711*

MAPPING THE WEST Europe and the Mediterranean, 1871   *727*

Chapter 23

MAP 23.1 Africa, c. 1890   *734*

SPOT MAP British Colonialism in the Malay Peninsula and Burma, 1826–1890   *736*

MAP 23.2 Expansion of Russia in Asia, 1865–1895   *737*

MAP 23.3 Expansion of Berlin to 1914   *759*

MAP 23.4 The Balkans, c. 1878   *761*

MAPPING THE WEST The West and the World, c. 1890   *763*

Chapter 24

MAP 24.1 Jewish Migrations in the Late Nineteenth Century   *785*

SPOT MAP The Struggle for Ethiopia, 1896   *786*

MAP 24.2 Africa in 1914   *787*

MAP 24.3 Imperialism in Asia, 1894–1914   *789*

MAP 24.4 The Balkans, 1908–1914   *795*

MAPPING THE WEST Europe at the Outbreak of World War I, August 1914   *799*

Chapter 25

MAP 25.1 The Fronts of World War I, 1914–1918   *805*

MAP 25.2 The Russian Civil War, 1917–1922   *815*

MAP 25.3 Europe and the Middle East after the Peace Settlements of 1919–1920   *820*

Chapter 12

SPOT MAP Italy at the End of the
Thirteenth Century *381*

MAP 12.1 France under Louis IX,
r. 1226–1270 *384*

MAP 12.2 The Mongol Invasions
to 1259 *389*

MAPPING THE WEST Europe,
c. 1340 *394*

Chapter 13

MAP 13.1 Advance of the Black Death,
1346–1353 *402*

MAP 13.2 The Hundred Years' War,
1337–1453 *405*

MAP 13.3 Ottoman Expansion in the
Fourteenth and Fifteenth
Centuries *407*

SPOT MAP Italy at the Peace of Lodi,
1454 *422*

MAPPING THE WEST Europe,
c. 1492 *426*

Chapter 14

MAP 14.1 Early Voyages of World
Exploration *433*

MAP 14.2 The Peasants' War
of 1525 *446*

MAPPING THE WEST Reformation
Europe, c. 1560 *457*

Chapter 15

MAP 15.1 The Empire of Philip II,
r. 1556–1598 *464*

SPOT MAP Retreat of the Spanish
Armada, 1588 *468*

SPOT MAP Russia, Poland-
Lithuania, and Sweden in the Late
1500s *469*

MAP 15.2 The Thirty Years' War
and the Peace of Westphalia,
1648 *473*

MAP 15.3 European Colonization of the
Americas, c. 1640 *480*

MAPPING THE WEST The Religious
Divisions of Europe, c. 1648 *489*

Chapter 16

MAP 16.1 Louis XIV's Acquisitions,
1668–1697 *501*

MAP 16.2 Dutch Commerce in the
Seventeenth Century *510*

SPOT MAP Poland-Lithuania in the
Seventeenth Century *513*

MAP 16.3 State Building in Central and
Eastern Europe, 1648–1699 *516*

MAPPING THE WEST Europe at the End
of the Seventeenth Century *525*

Chapter 17

MAP 17.1 European Trade Patterns,
c. 1740 *531*

MAP 17.2 Europe, c. 1715 *546*

MAP 17.3 Russia and Sweden after the
Great Northern War, 1721 *551*

SPOT MAP Austrian Conquest of
Hungary, 1657–1730 *552*

MAPPING THE WEST Europe
in 1750 *561*

Chapter 18

MAP 18.1 The Seven Years' War,
1756–1763 *581*

SPOT MAP The First Partition of
Poland, 1772 *582*

SPOT MAP The Pugachev
Rebellion, 1773 *587*

MAPPING THE WEST Europe and the
World, c. 1780 *591*

Chapter 19

MAP 19.1 Redrawing the Map of
France, 1789–1791 *604*

MAP 19.2 French Expansion,
1791–1799 *617*

Chapter 6

MAP 6.1 The Expansion of the Roman Empire, 30 B.C.E.–117 C.E.   *181*

MAP 6.2 Natural Features and Languages of the Roman World   *183*

MAP 6.3 Christian Populations in the Late Third Century C.E.   *190*

SPOT MAP The Fragmented Roman Empire of the Third Century   *197*

MAPPING THE WEST The Roman Empire in Crisis, 284 C.E.   *198*

Chapter 7

MAP 7.1 Diocletian's Reorganization of 293   *206*

SPOT MAP The Empire's East/West Division, 395   *207*

MAP 7.2 The Spread of Christianity, 300–600   *213*

MAP 7.3 Migrations and Invasions of the Fourth and Fifth Centuries   *223*

MAPPING THE WEST Western Europe and the Eastern Roman Empire, c. 600   *235*

Chapter 8

MAP 8.1 Expansion of Islam to 750   *244*

MAP 8.2 Byzantine and Sasanid Empires, c. 600   *247*

MAP 8.3 The Merovingian Kingdoms in the Seventh Century   *252*

SPOT MAP Tours, c. 600   *255*

SPOT MAP The British Isles   *260*

SPOT MAP Lombard Italy, Early Eighth Century   *263*

MAPPING THE WEST Rome's Heirs, c. 750   *265*

Chapter 9

MAP 9.1 The Byzantine Empire, 1025   *271*

MAP 9.2 Islamic States, c. 1000   *277*

MAP 9.3 Expansion of the Carolingian Empire under Charlemagne   *282*

SPOT MAP England in the Age of King Alfred, 871–899   *295*

SPOT MAP The Kingdom of the Franks under Hugh Capet, 987–996   *296*

MAPPING THE WEST Europe and the Mediterranean, c. 1050   *300*

Chapter 10

SPOT MAP The Walls of Piacenza   *308*

SPOT MAP The World of the Investiture Conflict, c. 1070–1122   *312*

MAP 10.1 The First Crusade, 1096–1099   *323*

SPOT MAP The Crusader States in 1109   *326*

SPOT MAP Norman Conquest of England, 1066   *329*

MAPPING THE WEST Europe and the Mediterranean, c. 1150   *333*

Chapter 11

MAP 11.1 Europe in the Age of Henry II and Frederick Barbarossa, 1150–1190   *346*

SPOT MAP The Consolidation of France under Philip Augustus, 1180–1223   *350*

MAP 11.2 Crusades and Anti-Heretic Campaigns, 1150–1215   *361*

MAP 11.3 The Reconquista, 1150–1212   *362*

SPOT MAP The Albigensian Crusade, 1209–1229   *364*

MAPPING THE WEST Europe and Byzantium, c. 1215   *365*

Chapter 29

A New Globalism, 1989 to the Present *953*

Collapse of the Soviet Union and Its Aftermath 954
The Breakup of Yugoslavia *955* ▪ The Soviet Union Comes Apart *956* ▪ Toward a Market Economy *959* ▪ International Politics and the New Russia *960*

The Nation-State in a Global Age 962
Europe Looks beyond the Nation-State *962* ▪ Globalizing Cities and Fragmenting Nations *964* ▪ Global Organizations *966*

An Interconnected World's New Challenges 966
The Problems of Pollution *967* ▪ Population, Health, and Disease *969* ▪ North versus South? *970* ▪ Radical Islam Meets the West *971* ▪ The Promise and Problems of a World Economy *974*

Global Culture and Society in the Twenty-First Century 977
Redefining the West: The Impact of Global Migration *977* ▪ Global Networks and Social Change *979* ▪ A New Global Culture? *980*

Conclusion 986

Glossary of Key Terms and People   *G-1*

Index   *I-1*

Map of the World   *I-76*

Maps and Figures

MAPS

Chapter 1

MAP 1.1 The Ancient Near East, 4000–3000 B.C.E.   *6*

SPOT MAP The Akkadian Empire, 2350–2200 B.C.E.   *12*

MAP 1.2 Ancient Egypt   *16*

MAP 1.3 Greece and the Aegean Sea, 1500 B.C.E.   *26*

MAPPING THE WEST The Violent End to Early Western Civilization, 1200–1000 B.C.E.   *34*

Chapter 2

MAP 2.1 Expansion of the Persian Empire, c. 550–490 B.C.E.   *43*

MAP 2.2 Phoenician and Greek Expansion, 750–500 B.C.E.   *54*

SPOT MAP Sparta and Corinth, 750–500 B.C.E.   *61*

SPOT MAP Ionia and the Aegean, 750–500 B.C.E.   *69*

MAPPING THE WEST Mediterranean Civilizations, c. 500 B.C.E.   *70*

Chapter 3

MAP 3.1 The Persian Wars, 499–479 B.C.E.   *78*

MAP 3.2 Fifth-Century B.C.E. Athens   *83*

MAP 3.3 The Peloponnesian War, 431–404 B.C.E.   *101*

MAPPING THE WEST Greece, Europe, and the Mediterranean, 400 B.C.E.   *105*

Chapter 4

SPOT MAP Athens's Long Walls as Rebuilt after the Peloponnesian War   *111*

MAP 4.1 Conquests of Alexander the Great, r. 336–323 B.C.E.   *117*

MAP 4.2 Hellenistic Kingdoms, 240 B.C.E.   *119*

MAPPING THE WEST Roman Takeover of the Hellenistic World, to 30 B.C.E.   *134*

Chapter 5

MAP 5.1 Ancient Italy, 500 B.C.E.   *146*

MAP 5.2 The City of Rome during the Republic   *149*

SPOT MAP Roman Roads, 110 B.C.E.   *151*

MAP 5.3 Roman Expansion, 500–44 B.C.E.   *154*

MAPPING THE WEST The Roman World at the End of the Republic, 44 B.C.E.   *166*

The Making of the West

Peoples and Cultures

A Concise History

Early Western Civilization

400,000–1000 B.C.E.

KINGS IN ANCIENT EGYPT BELIEVED the gods judged them in the afterlife. In *Instructions for Merikare,* written around 2100–2000 B.C.E., a king gives his son advice: "Secure your place in the cemetery by being upright, by doing justice, upon which people's hearts rely. . . . When a man is buried and mourned, his deeds are piled up next to him as treasure." Being judged pure of heart led to an eternal reward: "abiding [in the afterlife] like a god, roaming [free] like the lords of time."

Ordinary Egyptians, too, believed they should live justly, which meant worshipping the gods and obeying the king. A guidebook instructing mummies about the underworld, the *Book of the Dead,* said the jackal-headed god Anubis would weigh the dead person's heart against the goddess Maat and her feather of Truth, with the bird-headed god Thoth recording the result. Pictures in the book show the Swallower of the Damned — with a crocodile's head, a lion's body, and a hippopotamus's hind end — crouching ready to eat the heart of anyone who failed. Egyptian mythology thus taught that living a just life was the most important human goal because it won a blessed existence after death.

This belief — that there is a divine world more powerful than the human — goes back to the time before civilization, when people in the Stone Age lived as hunter-gatherers. Ten to twelve thousand years ago, when a global warming led to the invention of agriculture and the domestication of animals, human life changed in revolutionary ways that affect us to this day. Civilization first emerged around 4000–3000 B.C.E. in cities in Mesopotamia (the region between the Euphrates and Tigris Rivers, today Iraq). Historians define **civilization** as a way of life based on agriculture and trade, with cities containing large buildings for religion and government; technology to produce metals, textiles, pottery, and other

The Afterlife in Egyptian Religion
This illustration comes from the ancient Egyptian *Book of the Dead,* a collection of illustrated instructions and magic spells buried with dead people to help them in the afterlife. It shows the deceased standing in front of offerings made to Osiris, the god of the underworld. He is seated on a throne with his sister and wife, the goddess Isis, and her sister standing behind him. The myth of Osiris, who died and was cut up into pieces but then reassembled and resurrected by Isis, expressed Egyptians' belief in an eternal life after death. (Egyptian Museum, Cairo / Alfredo Dagli Orti / The Art Archive at Art Resource, NY.)

manufactured objects; and knowledge of writing. So far as current archaeological research reveals, those conditions first existed in Mesopotamia.

Civilization always arose with a religious core. In Mesopotamian civilization, rulers believed they were judged for maintaining order on earth and honoring the gods. Egyptian civilization, which began about 3100–3000 B.C.E., built enormous temples and pyramids. Civilizations emerged starting about 2500 B.C.E. in India, China, and the Americas. By 2000 B.C.E., civilizations appeared in Anatolia (today Turkey), on islands in the eastern Mediterranean Sea, and in Greece. The formation of civilizations produced intended and unintended consequences. The spread of metallurgy (using high heat to extract metals from ores), for example, created better tools and weapons but also increased preexisting social **hierarchy** (ranking people as superiors or inferiors).

The peoples of Mesopotamia, Egypt, the eastern Mediterranean, and Greece created Western civilization by exchanging ideas, technologies, and objects through trade, travel, and war. Building on concepts from the Near East, Greeks originated the idea of the West as a separate region, identifying Europe as the West (where the sun sets) and different from the East (where the sun rises). The making of the West depended on cultural, political, and economic interaction among diverse groups. The West remains an evolving concept, not a fixed region with unchanging borders and members.

CHAPTER FOCUS What changes did Western civilization bring to human life?

From the Stone Age to Mesopotamian Civilization, 400,000–1000 B.C.E.

People in the Stone Age developed patterns of life that have persisted ever since. The most significant of those early developments were (1) the evolution of hierarchy in society and (2) the invention of agriculture and the domestication of animals. Those inventions allowed people to stay in one place and raise their own food instead of wandering around to find things to eat in the wild. This change in how human beings met their most basic need — nutrition — led them to settle down in permanent communities for the first time. Eventually, some of these communities grew large enough in population and area to be considered cities. The conditions of life in these populous settlements incubated civilization, beginning in the fertile plains of the two great rivers of the Near East, the Euphrates and the Tigris. There, the Mesopotamians learned to work metals, and their rulers' desire to acquire and control the sources of these increasingly precious resources generated the drive to create empires. That drive in turn set the world on a course that extends to the modern age.

Life and Change in the Stone Age

About four hundred thousand years ago, people whose brains and bodies resembled ours appeared first in Africa. Called *Homo sapiens* ("wise human beings"), they were the immediate ancestors of modern people. Spreading out from Africa, they gradually

populated the rest of the earth. Anthropologists call this time the Stone Age because people made tools and weapons from stone as well as from bone and wood; they did not yet know how to work metals. The Stone Age is divided into an early part, the Paleolithic ("Old Stone"), and a later part, the Neolithic ("New Stone").

In the Paleolithic Age, people existed as **hunter-gatherers** who originally lived in mostly egalitarian bands (meaning all adults enjoyed a rough equality in making group decisions). They roamed in groups of twenty to fifty, hunting animals, catching fish and shellfish, and gathering plants, fruits, and nuts. Women with young children foraged for plants close to camp; they provided the group's most reliable supply of nourishment. Men did most of the hunting of dangerous wild animals far from camp, although recent archaeological evidence shows that women also participated, especially in hunting with nets. Objects from distant regions found in burials show that hunter-gatherer bands traded with one another. Trade spread knowledge — especially technology, such as techniques for improving tools, and art for creating beauty and expressing beliefs. The use of fire for cooking was a major innovation because it allowed people to eat wild grains that they could not digest raw.

Evidence from graves shows that hierarchy eventually emerged in Paleolithic times. Some Paleolithic burial sites contain weapons, tools, animal figurines, ivory beads, seashells, and bracelets alongside the corpses, which indicate that certain dead persons had greater status and wealth than others. Hierarchy probably emerged as men acquired prestige from bringing back meat after long hunts and from fighting in wars. (The many traumatic wounds seen in male skeletons show warfare was frequent.) Older women and men also earned status from their experience and longevity, in an age when illness or accidents killed most people before age thirty. The decoration of corpses with red paint and valuable objects suggests that Paleolithic people wondered about the mystery of death and perhaps believed in an afterlife. Paleolithic artists also sculpted statuettes of human figures, probably for religious purposes.

Climate and geography — the fundamental features of the natural environment — defined a new way of life for human beings beginning about 10,000 B.C.E. A slow process of transformation started when climate change in the late Paleolithic period brought warmer temperatures and more rainfall at higher elevations. This weather increased the amount of wild grains people could gather in the foothills of the Near East's Fertile Crescent, an arc of territory that curved up from the Jordan valley in Israel, through eastern Turkey, and down into the foothills and plains of Iraq and Iran (Map 1.1).* Paleolithic hunter-gatherers came to settle where wild grains grew abundantly and game animals grazed. Recent archaeological excavation in Turkey suggests that around eleven thousand years ago, groups organized to erect stone monuments to worship gods whom they believed helped them to survive, and they started growing food nearby. A more reliable food supply allowed people to raise more children, and increased social organization

---

*In this book, we observe the common usage of the term *Near East* to mean the lands of southwestern Asia and Egypt.

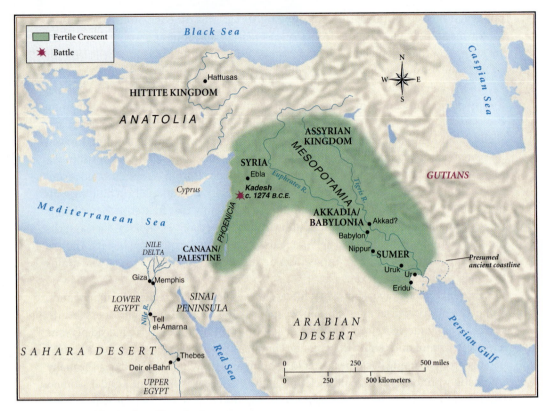

Map 1.1 The Ancient Near East, 4000–3000 B.C.E.
The diverse region we call the ancient Near East included many different landscapes, climates, peoples, and languages. Kings ruled its independent city-states, the centers of the world's first civilizations, beginning around 4000–3000 B.C.E. Trade by land and sea for natural resources, especially metals, and wars of conquest kept the peoples of the region in constant contact and conflict with one another. How did geography facilitate — or hinder — the development of civilization in the Near East?

promoted larger settlements. The more hungry mouths that were born, however, the greater the need for food became.

After thousands of years of trial and error, people in the Fertile Crescent invented reliable agriculture by sowing seeds from wild grains to produce harvests year after year. This marked the start of the Neolithic Age. Since women had more experience gathering plants than men did, they probably played the major role in developing farming, while men continued to hunt. Recent research suggests that people also learned to domesticate animals about the same time. By nine thousand years ago, keeping herds for food was widespread in the Near East, which was home to wild animals that could be domesticated, such as sheep, goats, pigs, and cattle.

Historians call agriculture and the domestication of animals the "farming package," and it was this package that created the Neolithic Revolution. The farming package had revolutionary effects because it produced many permanent settlements and food

Model of a House at Çatalhöyük
Archaeologists built this model of a house to show how Neolithic villagers lived in Çatalhöyük (today in central Turkey) from around 6500 to 5500 B.C.E. The wall paintings and bull-head sculpture had religious meaning, perhaps linked to the graves that the residents dug under the floor for their dead. The main entrance to the house was through the ceiling, as the houses were built right next to one another without streets in between, only some space for dumping refuse; the roofs served as walkways. Why do you think the villagers chose this arrangement for their settlement? (Çatalhöyük Research Project.)

surpluses. Some Neolithic people lived as pastoralists (herders moving around to find grazing land for their animals), while others were farmers who had to reside in a settled location to raise crops. Fixed settlements marked a turning point in the relation between human beings and the environment, as farmers increasingly diverted streams for irrigation. DNA evidence from ancient bones and modern populations shows that by 4000 B.C.E., immigrants and traders from the Fertile Crescent had helped spread knowledge of agriculture and domestication as far as the European shores of the Atlantic Ocean. When farmers began producing more food than they needed, the surpluses allowed other people in the settlement to specialize in architecture, art, crafts, metalwork, textile production, and trade.

The Neolithic Revolution generated more hierarchy because positions of authority were needed to allow some people to supervise the complex irrigation system that supported agricultural surpluses, and because greater economic activity created a stricter

division of labor by gender. Men began to dominate agriculture following the invention of heavy wooden plows pulled by oxen, sometime after 4000 B.C.E. Not having to bear and nurse babies, men took over long-distance trade. Women and older children mastered new domestic tasks such as turning milk from domesticated animals into cheese and yogurt and making clothing for themselves and their families. This gendered division of labor arose as an efficient response to the conditions and technologies of the time, but it had the unintended consequence of increasing men's status.

The Emergence of Cities in Mesopotamia, 4000–2350 B.C.E.

Additional significant changes in human society took place when the first cities — and therefore the first civilization — emerged in Mesopotamia about 4000–3000 B.C.E. on the plains bordering the Tigris and Euphrates Rivers (Map 1.1, page 6). Cities developed there because the climate and the land could support large populations. Mesopotamian farmers operated in a challenging environment: temperatures soared to 120 degrees Fahrenheit and little rain fell in the low-lying plains, yet the rivers flooded unpredictably. They maximized agricultural production by devising the technology and administrative arrangements necessary to irrigate the arid flatlands with water channeled from the rivers. A vast system of canals controlled flooding and turned the former desert green with food crops. The need to construct and maintain a system of irrigation canals in turn led to the centralization of authority in Mesopotamian cities, which controlled the farmland and irrigation canals lying outside their fortified walls. This political arrangement — an urban center exercising control over the surrounding countryside — is called a **city-state**. Mesopotamian city-states were independent communities competing with each other for land and resources.

The people of Sumer (southern Mesopotamia) established the earliest city-states. Unlike other Mesopotamians, the Sumerians did not speak a Semitic language (the group of languages from which Hebrew and Arabic came); the origins of their language remain a mystery. By 3000 B.C.E., the Sumerians had created twelve independent city-states — including Uruk, Eridu, and Ur — which repeatedly battled each other for territory. By 2500 B.C.E., most of the cities had expanded to twenty thousand residents or more. The rooms in Sumerians' mud-brick houses surrounded open courts. Large homes had a dozen rooms or more.

Agricultural surpluses and trade in commodities and manufactured goods made the Sumerian city-states prosperous. Their residents bartered grain, vegetable oil, woolens, and leather with one another, and they acquired metal, timber, and precious stones from foreign trade. The invention of the wheel for use on transport wagons around 3000 B.C.E. strengthened the Mesopotamian economy. Traders traveled as far as India, where the cities of Indus civilization emerged about 2500 B.C.E. Two groups dominated the Sumerian economy: religious officials controlled the temples, and ruling families controlled large farms and gangs of laborers. However, some private households also became rich.

The Ziggurat at Ur in Sumer

Sumerian royalty built this massive temple (called a ziggurat) in the twenty-first century B.C.E. To construct its three huge terraces (connected with stairways), workers glued bricks together with tar around a central core. The walls had to be more than seven feet thick to hold the weight of the building, whose original height is uncertain. The first terrace reached forty-five feet above the ground. Still, the Great Pyramid in Egypt dwarfed even this large monument. (© Michael S. Yamashita / Corbis.)

Increasingly rigid forms of hierarchy evolved in Sumerian society. Slaves, owned by temple officials and by individuals, had the lowest status. People became slaves by being captured in war, by being born to slaves, by voluntarily selling themselves or their children (usually to escape starvation), or by being sold by their creditors when they could not repay loans (debt slavery). Children whose parents dedicated them as slaves to the gods could rise to prominent positions in temple administration. In general, however, slaves existed in near-total dependence on other people and were excluded from normal social relations. They usually worked without pay and lacked almost all legal rights. Considered as property, they could be bought, sold, beaten, or even killed by their masters.

Slaves worked in domestic service, craft production, and farming, but scholars dispute whether they or free laborers were more important to the economy. Free persons performed most government labor, paying their taxes with work rather than with money, which was measured in amounts of food or precious metal (coins were not invented until much later). Although some owners liberated slaves in their wills and others allowed some slaves to keep enough earnings to purchase their freedom, most slaves had little chance of becoming free.

Hierarchy became so strong in Mesopotamian society that it led to monarchy — the political system that became the most widespread form of government in the ancient world. In a monarchy, the king was at the top of the hierarchy, like the ruler of the gods. His male descendants inherited his position. To display their exalted status, royal

families lived in elaborate palaces that served as administrative centers and treasure houses. Archaeologists excavating royal graves in Ur have revealed the rulers' dazzling riches — spectacular possessions crafted in gold, silver, and precious stones. These graves also have yielded grisly evidence of the top-ranking status of the king and queen: servants killed to care for their royal masters after death.

Patriarchy — domination by men in political, social, and economic life — already existed in Mesopotamian city-states, probably as an inheritance from the development of hierarchy in Paleolithic times. A Sumerian queen was respected because she was the king's wife and the mother of the royal children, but her husband held supreme power. The king formed a council of older men as his advisers, but he publicly acknowledged the gods as his rulers; this concept made the state a theocracy (government by gods) and gave priests and priestesses public influence. The king's greatest responsibility was to keep the gods happy and to defeat attacks from rival cities. The king demanded taxes from the working population to support his family, court, palace, army, and officials. The kings, along with the priests of the large temples, regulated most of the economy in their kingdoms by controlling the exchange of food and goods between farmers and craft producers in a system known as a **redistributive economy**.

In religion, Mesopotamians continued earlier traditions by practicing **polytheism**: worshipping many gods who were thought to control different aspects of life, including the weather, fertility, and war. People believed that their safety depended on the goodwill of the gods, and each city-state honored one deity as its special protector. To please their gods, city dwellers offered sacrifices and built ziggurats (temple towers) soaring as high as ten stories. Mesopotamians believed that if human beings angered the gods, divinities such as the sky god, Enlil, and the goddess of love and war, Inanna (also called Ishtar), would punish them by sending disease, floods, famine, and defeats in war.

Myths told in long poems such as the *Epic of Creation* and the *Epic of Gilgamesh* expressed Mesopotamian ideas about the challenges and violence that human beings faced in struggling with the natural environment and creating civilization. Gilgamesh was a legendary king of Uruk who forced the young men of Uruk to labor like slaves and the young women to sleep with him. When his subjects begged the mother of the gods to grant them a protector, she created Enkidu, "hairy all over . . . dressed as cattle are." A week of sex with a prostitute tamed this brute, preparing him for civilization: "Enkidu was weaker; he ran slower than before. But he had gained judgment, was wiser." After wrestling to a draw, Gilgamesh and Enkidu became friends; together they defeated Humbaba (the ugly giant of the Pine Forest) and the Bull of Heaven. The gods doomed Enkidu to die soon after these triumphs. Depressed about the human condition and longing to cheat death, Gilgamesh sought the secret of immortality, but a thieving snake ruined his quest. He decided that the only immortality for mortals was winning fame for deeds. Only memory and gods could live forever.

Mesopotamian myths, living on in poetry, song, and art, greatly influenced other peoples. A late version of the Gilgamesh story recounted how the gods sent a huge flood over the earth. They warned one man, instructing him to build a boat. He loaded his

vessel with his relatives, workers, possessions; domesticated and wild animals; and "everything there was." After a week of torrential rains, they left the boat to repopulate the earth and regenerate civilization. This story recalled the frequent floods of the Mesopotamian environment and was echoed later in the biblical account of the great flood covering the globe and Noah's ark.

The invention of writing in Mesopotamia transformed the way people exchanged stories and ideas. Sumerians originally invented this new technology to do accounting. Before writing, people drew small pictures on clay tablets to keep count of objects or animals. Writing developed when people created symbols to represent the sounds of speech instead of pictures to represent concrete things. Sumerian writing did not use an alphabet (a system in which each symbol represents the sound of a letter), but rather a system of wedge-shaped marks pressed into clay tablets to represent the sounds of syllables and entire words (Figure 1.1). Today this form of writing is called **cuneiform** (from *cuneus,* Latin for "wedge"). For a long time, writing was a professional skill for accounting mastered by only a few men and women known as scribes.

The possibilities for communication over time and space exploded when people began writing down nature lore, mathematics, foreign languages, and literature. In the

c. 3100 B.C.E.	c. 3000 B.C.E.	c. 2500 B.C.E.	c. 2100 B.C.E.	c. 700 B.C.E. (Neo-Assyrian)	Sumerian reading + meaning
					SAG Head
					NINDA bread
					GU$_7$ eat
					AB$_2$ cow
					APIN plough
					SUHUR carp

Figure 1.1 Cuneiform Writing
The earliest known form of writing developed in different locations in Mesopotamia in 4000–3000 B.C.E. when people began linking meaning and sound to signs such as those shown in the chart. Some scribes who mastered the system used sticks or reeds to press dense rows of small wedge-shaped marks into damp clay tablets; others used chisels to engrave them on stone. Cuneiform was used for at least fifteen Near Eastern languages and continued to be written for three thousand years.

twenty-third century B.C.E., Enheduanna, the daughter of King Sargon of the city of Akkad, composed the oldest written poetry whose author is known. Written in Sumerian, her poetry praised the life-giving goddess of love, Inanna: "The great gods scattered from you like fluttering bats, unable to face your intimidating gaze . . . knowing and wise queen of all the lands, who makes all creatures and people multiply." Later princesses who wrote love songs, lullabies, dirges, and prayers continued the Mesopotamian tradition of royal women becoming authors.

Metals and Empire Making: The Akkadians and the Ur III Dynasty, c. 2350–c. 2000 B.C.E.

The riches for which people now fought had a new component: metal. Early metallurgy demonstrates how technological innovation can generate social and political change. Pure copper, which people had long been using, lost its shape and edge quickly. So craftsmen were motivated to invent ways to smelt ore and to make metal alloys at high temperatures. The invention of bronze, a copper-tin alloy hard enough to hold a razor edge, enabled metalsmiths to produce durable and deadly swords, daggers, and spearheads. Historians label the period from about 4000 to 1000 B.C.E. the Bronze Age because at this time bronze was the most important metal for weapons and tools; iron was not yet in common use. The ownership of metal objects strengthened visible status divisions in society between men and women and rich and poor. This new technology made the Mesopotamian social elite want new luxury goods in metal, improved tools for agriculture and construction, and bronze weapons. The desire to accumulate wealth and status symbols stimulated demand for decorated weapons and elaborate jewelry. Rich men ordered bronze swords and daggers with expensive inlays. Such weapons increased visible social differences between men and women because they marked the status of the masculine roles of hunter and warrior.

Mesopotamian rulers fought to capture territory containing ore mines. The desire to acquire metals led the kings of Akkad to create by force the world's first **empire** (a political state in which a single power rules formerly independent peoples). It began around 2350 B.C.E., when Sargon, king of Akkad, launched invasions north and south of his central Mesopotamian homeland. He conquered Sumer and the regions all the way westward to the Mediterranean Sea, creating the Akkadian Empire. A poet of around 2000 B.C.E. credited Sargon's success to the favor of the god Enlil: "To Sargon the king of Akkad, from below to above, Enlil had given him lordship and kingship."

Sargon's grandson Naram-Sin also conquered distant places to gain resources and glory. By around 2250 B.C.E., he had reached Ebla, a large city in Syria. Archaeologists have unearthed many cuneiform tablets at Ebla; these discoveries suggest that the city was a center for learning and trade.

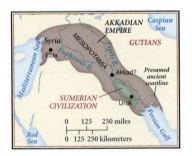

The Akkadian Empire, 2350–2200 B.C.E.

The process of building an empire by force had the unintended consequence of spreading Mesopotamian literature and art and promoting cultural interaction. The Akkadians spoke a language unrelated to Sumerian, but in conquering Sumer they adopted much of that region's religion, literature, and culture. Other peoples conquered by the Akkadians were then exposed to Sumerian beliefs and traditions, which they in turn adapted to suit their own purposes.

Civil war ended the Akkadian Empire. A newly resurgent Sumerian dynasty called Ur III (2112–2004 B.C.E.) seized power in Sumer and presided over a flourishing of Sumerian literature. The Ur III rulers created a centralized economy, published the earliest preserved law code, and justified their rule by proclaiming their king to be divine. The best-preserved ziggurat was built in their era. Royal hymns, a new literary form, glorified the king; one example reads: "Your commands, like the word of a god, cannot be reversed; your words, like rain pouring down from heaven, are without number."

Mesopotamia remained politically unstable, however. When civil war weakened the Ur III kingdom, nearby Amorite marauders conducted damaging raids. The Ur III dynasty collapsed after only a century of rule.

The Achievements of the Assyrians, the Babylonians, and the Canaanites, 2000–1000 B.C.E.

New kingdoms emerged in Assyria and Babylonia in the second millennium B.C.E. At the time, Mesopotamia was experiencing extended economic troubles caused by climate change and agricultural pollution. By around 2000 B.C.E., intensive irrigation had unintentionally raised the soil's salt level so high that crop yields declined. When decreased rainfall made the situation worse, economic stress generated political instability that lasted for centuries.

The Assyrians, who inhabited northern Mesopotamia, took advantage of their geography to create a kingdom whose rulers permitted long-distance trade conducted by private entrepreneurs. Acting as intermediaries in the trade for wood and metals between Anatolia and Mesopotamia, Assyrians became prosperous. They exported woolen textiles to Anatolia in exchange for raw materials, which they sold to the rest of Mesopotamia.

Centralized state monopolies in which the government controlled international trade and redistributed goods had previously dominated the Mesopotamian economy. This kind of redistributive economy persisted in Mesopotamia, but by 1900 B.C.E. Assyrian kings were allowing individuals to transact commerce. This market-based system let private entrepreneurs maximize profits if their ventures succeeded. Private Assyrian investors, for example, financed traders to export cloth. The traders then formed donkey caravans to travel hundreds of miles to Anatolia, where, if they survived the dangerous journey, they could make huge profits to be split with their investors. Royal regulators settled any complaints of trader fraud or losses in transit.

To maintain social order, Mesopotamians established written laws made known to the people. Private commerce and property created a need to guarantee fairness in contracts. Mesopotamians believed that the king had a sacred duty to make divine justice

known to his subjects by rendering judgments in all sorts of cases, from commercial disputes to crime. Once written down, the record of the king's decisions became what historians today call a law code. **Hammurabi** (r. c. 1792–c. 1750 B.C.E.), king of Babylon, on the Euphrates River, became the most famous lawgiver in Mesopotamia. His laws drew on earlier Mesopotamian codes, such as that of the Ur III dynasty.

Hammurabi proclaimed that he was supporting "the principles of truth and equity" and protecting the weak. He emphasized relieving the poor's burdens as crucial to royal justice. His code divided society into free persons, commoners, and slaves. These categories reflected a social hierarchy in which some people were assigned a higher value than others. An attacker who caused a pregnant woman of the free class to miscarry, for example, paid twice the fine levied for the same offense against a commoner. Between social equals, the code specified "an eye for an eye." A member of the free class who killed a commoner, however, was not executed, only fined.

Many of Hammurabi's laws concerned the king's interests as a property owner leasing land to tenants. His laws were harsh for offenses against property, including mutilation or a gruesome death for crimes ranging from theft to wrongful sales and careless construction. Women had limited legal rights, but they could make contracts and appear in court. A wife could divorce her husband for cruelty; a husband could divorce his wife for any reason. The law protected the wife's interests by requiring a husband to restore his divorced wife's property.

Hammurabi's law code was based on an ideal of justice. The eye-for-an-eye principle matched the crime and punishment as literally as possible. The code punished bad-faith prosecutions by imposing the death penalty on anyone who failed to prove a serious accusation. It also relied on "nature-decided justice" by allowing an accused person to leap into a river: if the accused person sank, he was guilty; if he floated, he was innocent.

Hammurabi's laws were not always strictly followed, and penalties were often less severe than specified. The people themselves assembled in courts to determine most cases by their own judgments. Why, then, did Hammurabi have his laws written down? He explained that it was to show Shamash, the Babylonian sun god and god of justice, that he had fulfilled his responsibility as a divinely installed king — to ensure justice and the moral and material welfare of his people: "So that the powerful may not oppress the powerless, to provide justice for the orphan and the widow . . . let the victim of injustice see the law which applies to him, let his heart be put at ease."

Hammurabi's code suggests that crimes of burglary and assault were common in cities, and it reveals that marriages were arranged by the bride's father and the groom, and sealed with a legal contract. The laws on surgery show that doctors practiced in the cities. Because people believed that angry gods or evil spirits caused serious diseases, Mesopotamian medicine included magic: a doctor might prescribe an incantation along with potions and diet recommendations. Magicians or exorcists offered medical treatment that depended on spells and interpreting signs, such as the patient's dreams or hallucinations.

Babylonian cities had many taverns and wine shops, often run by women proprietors. Contaminated drinking water caused many illnesses because sewage disposal was rudimentary. Citizens found relief from a city's odors and crowding in its open

spaces. The world's oldest known map, an inscribed clay tablet showing the outlines of the city of Nippur about 1500 B.C.E., indicates a large park.

Cities involved large numbers of people from different places in many different interactions, which stimulated intellectual developments. Mesopotamian achievements in mathematics and astronomy had an enduring effect. Mathematicians devised algebra, including the derivation of roots of numbers. They invented place-value notation, which makes a numeral's position in a number indicate ones, tens, hundreds, and so on. The system of reckoning based on sixty, still used in the division of hours and minutes and in the degrees of a circle, also comes from Mesopotamia. Mesopotamian expertise in recording the paths of the stars and planets probably arose from the desire to make predictions about the future, following the astrological belief that the movement of celestial bodies directly affects human life. The charts and tables compiled by Mesopotamian stargazers underlay later advances in astronomy.

The people of Canaan (ancient Palestine) expanded their population by absorbing foreign merchants. The interaction of traders and travelers from many different cultures encouraged innovation in recording business transactions. This multilingual business environment produced the alphabet about 1600 B.C.E. In this new writing system, a simplified picture — a letter — stood for only one sound in the language, a large change from cuneiform. The Canaanite alphabet later became the basis for the Greek and Roman alphabets and therefore of modern Western alphabets.

> **REVIEW QUESTION**   How did life change for people in Mesopotamia, first after the Neolithic Revolution and then when they began to live in cities?

Egypt, the First Unified Country, 3050–1000 B.C.E.

The other earliest example of Western civilization arose in Egypt, in northeastern Africa. The Egyptians built a wealthy, profoundly religious, and strongly centralized society ruled by kings. Unlike the separate Mesopotamian city-states, Egypt became unified. Its prosperity and stability depended on the king maintaining strong central authority and defeating enemies. Egypt was located close enough to Mesopotamia to learn from peoples there but was geographically protected enough to develop its own distinct culture, which Egyptians believed was superior to any other. The Egyptians believed that a just society respected the gods, preserved hierarchy, and obeyed the king. The Egyptian rulers' belief in the soul's immortality and a happy afterlife motivated them to construct the most imposing tombs in history, the pyramids. Egyptian architecture, art, and religious ideas influenced later Mediterranean peoples, especially the Greeks.

From the Unification of Egypt to the Old Kingdom, 3050–2190 B.C.E.

When climate change dried up the grasslands of the Sahara region of Africa about 5000–4000 B.C.E., people slowly migrated from there to the northeast corner of the continent, settling along the Nile River. They had formed a large political state by about 3050 B.C.E.,

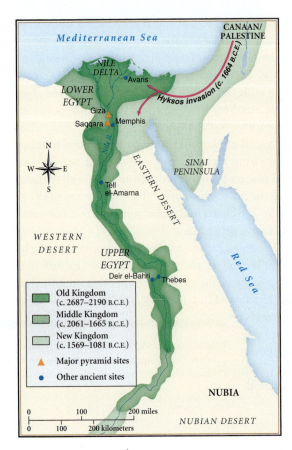

Map 1.2 Ancient Egypt
Large deserts enclosed the Nile River on the west and the east. The Nile provided Egyptians with water to irrigate their fields and a highway for traveling north to the Mediterranean Sea and south to Nubia. The only easy land route into and out of Egypt lay through the northern Sinai peninsula into the coastal area of the eastern Mediterranean; Egyptian kings always fought to control this region to secure their land.

when King Narmer (also called Menes)* united the previously separate territories of Upper (southern) Egypt and Lower (northern) Egypt. (*Upper* and *Lower* refer to the direction of the Nile River, which begins south of Egypt and flows northward to the Mediterranean.) The Egyptian ruler therefore referred to himself as King of the Two Lands. By around 2687 B.C.E., the monarchs had created a large centralized state, called the Old Kingdom. It lasted until around 2190 B.C.E. (Map 1.2). Egyptian kings built only a few large cities. The first capital, Memphis (south of modern Cairo), grew into a metropolis packed with mammoth structures.

The most spectacular — and most mysterious — of the Old Kingdom architectural marvels is the so-called Great Sphinx. The world's oldest monumental sculpture, this

---

*Since the Egyptians did not include vowel sounds in their writing, we are not sure how to spell their names. The spelling of names here is taken from *The Oxford Encyclopedia of Ancient Egypt,* edited by Donald B. Redford (2001), with alternate names given in cases where they seem more familiar. Dates are approximate and uncertain, and scholars bitterly disagree about them. (For an explanation of the problems, see Redford, "Chronology and Periodization," *The Oxford Encyclopedia,* vol. 1, 264–68.) The dates appearing in this book are compiled with as much consistency as possible from articles in *The Oxford Encyclopedia* and in the "Egyptian King List" given at the back of each of its volumes.

The Great Sphinx of Egypt
This enormous stone sculpture of a sphinx, a mythical female creature with a human head and torso and lion's body, was built near the Great Pyramid in Egypt. Since no inscriptions tell us which king or kings ordered it built, or when or why, scholars still debate its place in ancient Egyptian history and thought. It remains the largest stone monument in the world. (Gianni Dagli Orti / The Art Archive at Art Resource, NY.)

stone statue has a human head on the body of a lion lying on its four paws. It is nearly 250 feet long and almost 70 feet high. A temple was built in front of it, perhaps to worship the sun as a god. The Sphinx's purpose and date remain hotly debated. No records exist to explain its original meaning. Most scholars believe that it was erected sometime in the Old Kingdom. A few, however, citing its weathering and erosion patterns, argue that it is as old as 5000 B.C.E. If clear evidence supporting this date is ever discovered, then the history of early Egypt will have to be completely rewritten. This is just one of the many controversies about ancient Egypt that archaeology may someday settle.

The Old Kingdom's costly architecture demonstrates the prosperity and power of Narmer's unified state. Its territory consisted of a narrow strip of fertile land running along both sides of the Nile River. This ribbon of green fields zigzagged for seven hundred miles southward from the Mediterranean Sea. The deserts flanking the fields on the west and the east protected Egypt; invasion was possible only through the northern Nile delta and from Nubia in the south. The deserts also were sources of wealth because they

contained large deposits of metal ores. Egypt's geography additionally contributed to its prosperity by supporting seaborne commerce in the Mediterranean Sea and the Indian Ocean as well as overland trade with central Africa.

Agriculture was Egypt's most important economic resource. Usually, the Nile River overflowed its channel for several weeks each year, when melting snow from central African mountains swelled its waters. This predictable annual flood enriched the soil with nutrients from the river's silt and diluted harmful mineral salts, thereby making farming more productive and supporting strong population growth. In sharp contrast to the unpredictable floods that harmed Mesopotamia, the regular flooding of the Nile benefited Egyptians. Trouble came in Egypt only if the usual flood did not take place, as happened when too little winter precipitation fell in the mountains.

The plants and animals raised by Egypt's farmers fed a fast-growing population. Egypt had expanded to perhaps several million people by around 1500 B.C.E. Date palms, vegetables, grass for pasturing animals, and grain grew in abundance. The Egyptians loved beer, which people of all ages consumed. Thicker and more nutritious than modern brews, Egyptian beer was such an important food that it could be used to pay workmen's wages. Egyptians, like other ancient societies, often flavored their beer with fruits.

Egypt's population included people whose skin color ranged from light to dark. Although many ancient Egyptians would be regarded as black by modern racial classification, ancient peoples did not observe such distinctions. The modern controversy over whether Egyptians were people of color is therefore not an issue that ancient Egyptians would have considered. If asked, they would probably have identified themselves by geography, language, religion, or traditions rather than skin color. Like many other ancient groups, the Egyptians called themselves simply The People. Later peoples, especially the Greeks, recognized the ethnic and cultural differences between themselves and the Egyptians, but they deeply admired Egyptian civilization for its long history and strongly religious character.

Although Egyptians absorbed knowledge from both the Mesopotamians and the Nubians, their African neighbors to the south, they developed their own written scripts. For official documents they used a pictographic script known as **hieroglyphic** (Figure 1.2). They developed other, simpler scripts for everyday purposes.

Some scholars believe that Nubian society was the outside influence that most deeply influenced early Egypt. A Nubian social elite lived in dwellings much grander than the small huts housing most of the population. Egyptians interacted with Nubians while trading for raw materials such as gold, ivory, and animal skins, and scholars argue that Nubia's hierarchical political and social organization influenced the development of Egypt's politically centralized Old Kingdom. Eventually, however, Egypt's greater power led it to dominate its southern neighbor.

Keeping Egypt unified and stable was difficult. When the kings were strong, as during the Old Kingdom, the country was peaceful, with flourishing international trade. Regional governors rebelling against weak kings, however, could create political turmoil. Kings gained strength by fulfilling their public religious obligations. Egyptians worshipped

Hieroglyph	Meaning	Sound value
	vulture	glottal stop
	flowering reed	consonantal I
	forearm and hand	ayin
	quail chick	W
	foot	B
	stool	P
	horned viper	F
	owl	M
	water	N
	mouth	R
	reed shelter	H
	twisted flax	slightly guttural
	placenta (?)	H as in "loch"
	animal's belly	slightly softer than h
	door bolt	S
	folded cloth	S
	pool	SH
	hill	Q
	basket with handle	K
	jar stand	G
	loaf	T

Figure 1.2 Egyptian Hieroglyphs

Ancient Egyptians used pictures such as these to develop their own system of writing around 3000 B.C.E. Egyptian hieroglyphs include around seven hundred pictures in three categories: ideograms (signs indicating things or ideas), phonograms (signs indicating sounds), and determinatives (signs clarifying the meaning of the other signs). Because Egyptians employed this formal script mainly for religious inscriptions on buildings and sacred objects, Greeks referred to it as *ta hieroglyphica* ("the sacred carved letters"), from which comes the modern word *hieroglyphic,* used to designate this system of writing. Eventually, Egyptians also developed the handwritten cursive script called demotic (Greek for "of the people"), a much simpler and quicker form of writing. The hieroglyphic writing system continued until about 400 C.E., when it was replaced by the Coptic alphabet. Compare hieroglyphs with cuneiform shapes (see page 11).

a great variety of gods, often shown in paintings and sculptures as creatures with both human and animal features, such as the head of a jackal or a bird atop a human body. These images reflected the belief that the gods each had a particular animal through which they revealed themselves to human beings. Egyptian gods were associated with powerful natural objects, emotions, qualities, and technologies — examples are Re, the sun god; Isis, the goddess of love and fertility; and Thoth, the god of wisdom and the

inventor of writing. People worshipped the gods with rituals, prayers, and festivals that expressed their respect and devotion to these divine powers.

Egyptians regarded their king as a helpful divinity in human form, identified with the hawk-headed god Horus. They saw the king's rule as divine because he helped generate *maat* ("what is right"), the supernatural force that brought order and harmony to human beings if they maintained a stable hierarchy. The goddess **Maat** embodied this force, the source of justice in a world that the Egyptians believed would fall apart violently if the king ruled unjustly. The king therefore had the duties of making law, keeping the forces of nature in balance to ensure the Nile flood, and waging war on enemies.

Art expressed the king's legitimacy as ruler by representing him doing his religious and military duties. The requirement to show piety (proper religious belief and behavior) demanded strict regulation of the king's daily activities: he had specific times to take a bath, go for a walk, and make love to his wife. Most important, he had to ensure the country's fertility and prosperity. If the Nile flood failed to occur, this weakened the king's authority by leaving many people hungry and angry, thus encouraging rebellions by rivals.

Successful Old Kingdom rulers used expensive building programs to demonstrate their piety and status. They erected huge tombs — the pyramids (see the illustration below) — in the desert outside Memphis. Temples and halls accompanied the tombs for religious ceremonies and royal funerals. Although the pyramids were not the first monuments built from enormous worked stones (the temples, admittedly much smaller in scale, on the Mediterranean island of Malta are earlier), they rank as the grandest, much larger even than the Great Sphinx.

The Pyramids at Giza in Egypt

The kings of the Egyptian Old Kingdom constructed massive stone pyramids for their tombs, the centerpieces of large complexes of temples and courtyards stretching down to the banks of the Nile or along a canal leading to the river. The inner burial chambers lay at the end of long, narrow tunnels snaking through the pyramids' interiors. The biggest pyramid shown here is the so-called Great Pyramid of King Khufu (Cheops). Erected at Giza (in the desert outside what is today Cairo) in the twenty-sixth century B.C.E., it soars almost 480 feet high, several times taller than the famous Parthenon of fifth-century B.C.E. Athens (see page 84). (Travel Pix Ltd. / SuperStock.)

Old Kingdom rulers spent vast resources on these huge complexes to proclaim their divine status and protect their mummified bodies for existence in the afterlife. King Khufu (r. 2609–2584 B.C.E.; also known as Cheops) commissioned the hugest monument of all — the Great Pyramid at Giza. Taller than a forty-story skyscraper at 480 feet high, it covered thirteen acres and stretched 760 feet long on each side. It required more than two million blocks of limestone, some of which weighed fifteen tons. Its exterior blocks were quarried along the Nile and then floated to the site on barges. Free workers dragged the blocks up ramps into position using rollers and sleds.

The Old Kingdom rulers' expensive preparations for death reflected their belief in the afterlife. As one text says: "O [god] Atum, put your arms around King Neferkare Pepy II [r. c. 2300–2206 B.C.E.], around this construction work, around this pyramid. . . . May you guard lest anything happen to him evilly throughout the course of eternity." The royal family equipped their tombs with many comforts to use in the underworld. The kings had gilded furniture, sparkling jewelry, and precious objects placed alongside the coffins holding their mummies. Archaeologists have even uncovered two full-sized cedar ships buried next to the Great Pyramid, meant to carry King Khufu on his journey into eternity.

The Old Kingdom ranked Egyptians in a strict hierarchy to preserve their kings' authority and support what they regarded as the proper order of a just society. Egyptians believed that their ordered society was superior to any other, and they despised foreigners. The king and queen headed the hierarchy. Brothers and sisters in the royal family could marry each other, perhaps because such matches were thought to preserve the purity of the royal line and imitate the gods' marriages. The priests, royal administrators, provincial governors, and army commanders ranked second. Then came the free common people, most of whom worked in agriculture. Free workers had heavy obligations to the state. In a system called corvée labor, the kings commanded commoners to work on the pyramids during slack times in farming. The state fed, housed, and clothed the workers while they performed this seasonal work; their labor was a way of paying taxes. Taxation reached 20 percent on the farmers' produce. Slaves captured in foreign wars served the royal family and the priests; privately owned slaves became numerous only after the Old Kingdom. The king hired mercenaries, many from Nubia, to form the majority of the army.

Egyptians preserved more of the gender equality of the early Stone Age than did their neighbors. Women generally enjoyed the same legal rights as free men. They could own land and slaves, inherit property, pursue lawsuits, transact business, and initiate divorces. Portrait statues show the equal status of wife and husband: each figure is the same size and sits on the same kind of chair. Men dominated public life, while women devoted themselves mainly to private life, managing their households and property. When their husbands went to war or were killed in battle, however, women often took on men's work. Women could serve as priestesses, farm managers, or healers in times of crisis.

The formal style of Egyptian art illustrates the high value placed on order and predictability. Statues represent the subject either standing stiffly with the left leg advanced

or sitting on a chair or throne, stable and poised. The concern for decorum (suitable be-havior) also appears in the Old Kingdom literature called **wisdom literature**. These texts gave officials instructions for appropriate behavior. One text instructs a young man to seek advice from ignorant people as well as the wise, and to avoid arrogant overconfi-dence. This kind of literature had a strong influence on later civilizations, especially the ancient Israelites.

The Middle and New Kingdoms in Egypt, 2061–1081 B.C.E.

The Old Kingdom began to disintegrate in the late third millennium B.C.E. Climate change perhaps caused the annual Nile flood to shrink, making people believe the kings had betrayed Maat. Rivalry for power erupted among leading families, and civil war between a northern and a southern dynasty ripped the country apart. This disunity al-lowed regional governors to increase their power, and some now seized independence for their regions. Famine and civil unrest during the so-called First Intermediate Period (2190–2061 B.C.E.) prevented the reestablishment of political unity.

The kings of what historians label the Middle Kingdom (2061–1665 B.C.E.) restored the strong central authority their Old Kingdom predecessors had lost. They waged war to extend Egypt's southern boundaries, and they expanded diplomatic and trade con-tacts in the eastern Mediterranean region and with the island of Crete. Middle King-dom literature reveals that restored unity contributed to a deeply felt pride in the home-land. The Egyptian narrator of *The Story of Sinuhe,* for example, reports that he lived luxuriously during a forced stay in Syria but still longed to return: "Whichever god you are who ordered my exile, have mercy and bring me home! Please allow me to see the land where my heart dwells! Nothing is more important than that my body be buried in the country where I was born!" For this lost soul, love for Egypt outranked personal riches and comfort in a foreign land.

The Middle Kingdom lost its unity during the Second Intermediate Period (1664–1570 B.C.E.), when the kings proved too weak to control foreign migrants who had es-tablished independent communities in Egypt. By 1664 B.C.E., diverse bands of a Semitic people originally from the eastern Mediterranean coast seized power. The Egyptians called these foreigners Hyksos ("rulers of the foreign countries"). Hyksos settlers trans-planted foreign cultural elements to Egypt: their capital, Avaris, boasted wall paintings done in the Minoan style of the island of Crete. Hyksos possibly also introduced bronze-making technology, new musical instruments, humpbacked cattle, and olive trees; they certainly promoted frequent contact between Egypt and other Near Eastern states. Hyksos rulers also strengthened Egypt's military capacity by expanding the use of war chariots and more powerful bows.

The leaders of Thebes, in southern Egypt, reunited the kingdom after long struggles with the Hyksos. The series of dynasties they founded is called the New Kingdom (1569–1081 B.C.E.). Thebes may have drawn strength from its connections with prosperous settlements that emerged far out in the western desert, such as at Kharga Oasis. Oases featured abundant water from underground aquifers in the middle of a scorching en-

vironment. Oasis settlements flourished by providing stopping points for the caravans of merchants who endured dangerously harsh desert conditions to profit from commerce. Thebes's expansion of contact with the western desert settlements reveals that Egyptian society did not remain unchanged over time, shutting itself off behind its natural boundaries along the Nile. Similarly, contacts with peoples to the east across the Red Sea and along the Indian Ocean increased in the New Kingdom.

The kings of the New Kingdom, known as pharaohs, rebuilt central authority by restricting the power of regional governors and promoting national identity. To prevent invasions, the pharaohs created a standing army, another significant change in Egyptian society. These kings still employed mercenaries, but they formed an Egyptian military elite as commanders. Recognizing that knowledge of the rest of the world was necessary for safety, the pharaohs engaged in regular diplomacy with neighboring monarchs to increase their international contacts. The pharaohs exchanged official letters with their "brother kings," as they called them, in Mesopotamia, Anatolia, and the eastern Mediterranean region.

The New Kingdom pharaohs sent their army into foreign wars to gain territory and show their superiority. Their imperialism has earned them the title *warrior pharaohs*. They waged many campaigns abroad and presented themselves in official propaganda and art as the incarnations of warrior gods. They invaded lands to the south to win access to gold and other precious materials, and they fought up and down the eastern Mediterranean coast to control that crucial land route into Egypt.

Massive riches supported the power of the warrior pharaohs. Egyptian traders exchanged local fine goods, such as ivory, for foreign luxury goods, such as wine and olive oil transported in painted pottery from Greece. Egyptian rulers displayed their wealth most conspicuously in the enormous sums spent to build stone temples. Queen Hatshepsut (r. 1502–1482 B.C.E.), for example, built her massive mortuary temple at Deir el-Bahri, near Thebes, including

Hatshepsut as Pharaoh Offering Maat

This granite statue, eight and a half feet tall, portrayed Hatshepsut, queen of Egypt in the early fifteenth century B.C.E., as pharaoh wearing a beard and male clothing. She is performing her royal duty of offering *maat* (the divine principle of order and justice) to the gods. Egyptian religion taught that the gods "lived on maat" and that the land's rulers were responsible for providing it. Hatshepsut had this statue, and many others, placed in a huge temple she built outside Thebes, in Upper Egypt. Why do you think Hatshepsut is shown as calm and relaxed, despite having her toes severely flexed? (Egypt, 18th dynasty, c. 1473–1458 B.C.E. Granite. h. 261.5 cm [102¹⁵⁄₁₆ in.]; w. 80 cm [31½ in.]; d. 137 cm [53¹⁵⁄₁₆ in.]. Rogers Fund, 1929 [29.3.1]. The Metropolitan Museum of Art, New York, NY, USA. Image copyright © The Metropolitan Museum of Art, New York, NY, USA / Art Resource, NY.)

a temple dedicated to the god Amun (or Amen), to express her claim to divine birth and the right to rule. After her husband (who was also her half brother) died, Hatshepsut proclaimed herself "female king" as co-ruler with her young stepson. In this way, she sidestepped the restrictions of Egyptian political tradition, which did not recognize the right of a queen to reign by herself. Hatshepsut also had herself represented in official art as a king, with a royal beard and male clothing. Hatshepsut succeeded in her unusual rule because she demonstrated that a woman could ensure safety and prosperity by maintaining the goodwill of the gods toward the country and its people.

Egyptians believed that their gods oversaw all aspects of life and death. Many large temples and festivals honored the gods. A calendar based on the moon governed the dates of religious ceremonies. (The Egyptians also developed a calendar for administrative and fiscal purposes that had 365 days, divided into 12 months of 30 days each, with the extra 5 days added before the start of the next year. Our modern calendar comes from this source.) The early New Kingdom pharaohs promoted their state god Amun-Re (a combination of Thebes's patron god and the sun god) so energetically that he became far more important than the other gods. This Theban cult subordinated the other gods, without denying their existence or the continued importance of their priests. The pharaoh Akhenaten (r. 1372–1355 B.C.E.) went a step further, however: he proclaimed that official religion would concentrate on worshipping Aten, who represented the sun. Akhenaten made the king and the queen the only people with direct access to the cult of Aten; ordinary people had no part in it. Some scholars identify Akhenaten's religious reform as a step toward monotheism, with Aten meant to be the state's sole god.

To showcase the royal family and the concentration of power that he desired, Akhenaten built a new capital for his favorite god at Tell el-Amarna (Map 1.2, page 16). He tried to force his revised religion on the priests of the old cults, but they resisted. Historians have blamed Akhenaten's religious zeal for leading him to neglect practical affairs and thus weakening his kingdom's defense, but recent research on international correspondence found at Tell el-Amarna has shown that the pharaoh tried to use diplomacy to turn foreign enemies against one another so that they would not become strong enough to threaten Egypt. His policy failed, however, when the Hittites from Anatolia defeated the Mitanni, Egypt's allies in eastern Syria. Akhenaten's religious reform also died with him. During the reign of his successor, Tutankhamun (r. 1355–1346 B.C.E.) — famous today through the discovery in 1922 of his rich, unlooted tomb — the cult of Amun-Re reclaimed its leading role. The crisis created by Akhenaten's attempted reform emphasizes the overwhelming importance of religious conservatism in Egyptian life and the control of religion by the ruling power.

Most New Kingdom Egyptians' lives revolved around their labor and the annual flood of the Nile. During the months when the river stayed between its banks, they worked their fields, rising early in the morning to avoid the searing heat. When the flooding halted agricultural work, the king required laborers to work on his building projects. They lived in workers' quarters erected next to the construction sites. Although slaves became more common as household workers in the New Kingdom than they had been before, free workers — who were obliged to perform a certain amount of labor

for the king — did most of the work on this period's mammoth royal construction projects. Workers lightened their burden by singing songs, telling adventure stories, and drinking a lot of beer. They accomplished a great deal: the majority of the ancient temples remaining in Egypt today were built during the New Kingdom.

Ordinary people worshipped many different gods, especially those believed to protect them in their daily existence. They venerated Bes, for instance, a dwarf with the features of a lion, as a protector of the household. They carved his image on amulets, beds, headrests, and mirror handles. By this time, ordinary people believed that they could have a blessed afterlife and put great effort into preparing for it. Those who could afford it arranged to have their tombs outfitted with all the goods needed for the journey in the underworld. Most important, they paid burial experts to turn their corpses into mummies so that they could have a complete body for eternity. Making a mummy required removing the brain (through the nose with a long-handled spoon), cutting out the internal organs to store separately in stone jars, drying the body with mineral salts to the consistency of old leather, and wrapping the shrunken flesh in linen soaked with ointments.

Every mummy had to travel to the afterlife with a copy of the *Book of the Dead*, which included magic spells for avoiding dangers along the way as well as instructions on how to prepare for the judgment-day trial before the gods. To prove that they deserved a good fate, the dead had to convincingly recite claims such as the following: "I have not committed crimes against people; I have not mistreated cattle; I have not robbed the poor; I have not caused pain; I have not caused tears."

Magic played a large role in the lives of Egyptians. Professional magicians sold spells and charms, both written and oral, which the buyers used to promote eternal salvation, protect against demons, smooth the rocky course of love, exact revenge on enemies, and find relief from disease and injury. Egyptian doctors knew many medicinal herbs (knowledge they passed on to later civilizations) and could perform major surgeries, including opening the skull. Still, no doctor could cure severe infections; as in the past, sick people continued to rely on the help of supernatural forces through prayers and spells.

> **REVIEW QUESTION**   How did religion guide the lives of both rulers and ordinary people in ancient Egypt?

The Hittites, the Minoans, and the Mycenaeans, 2200–1000 B.C.E.

The first examples of Western civilization to emerge in the central Mediterranean region were located in Anatolia, dominated by the warlike Hittite kingdom (Map 1.1, page 6); on the large island of Crete and nearby islands, home to the Minoans; and on the Greek mainland, where the Mycenaeans grew rich from raiding and trade (Map 1.3). As early as 6000 B.C.E., people from southwestern Asia, especially Anatolia, began migrating westward and southward to inhabit islands in the Mediterranean Sea. From this migration, the rich civilization of the Minoans gradually emerged on Crete and other islands in the Aegean Sea by around 2200 B.C.E. In mainland Greece, civilization eventually arose among

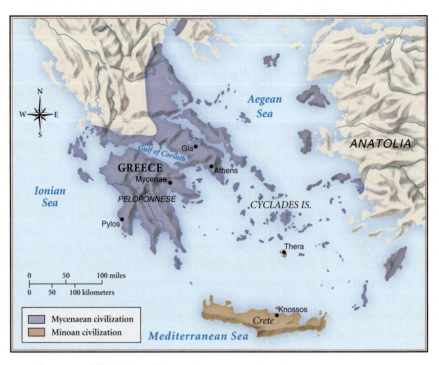

Map 1.3 Greece and the Aegean Sea, 1500 B.C.E.
A varied landscape of mountains, islands, and seas defined the geography of Greece. The distances between settlements were mostly short, but rough terrain and seasonally stormy sailing made travel a chore. The distance from the mainland to the largest island in this region, Crete, where Minoan civilization arose, was long enough to keep Cretans isolated from the wars of most of later Greek history.

peoples who had moved into the area thousands of years before, again most likely from southwestern Asia.

The Hittites, the Minoans, and the Mycenaeans had advanced military technologies, elaborate architecture, striking art, a marked taste for luxury, and extensive trade contacts with Egypt and the Near East. The Hittites, like the Egyptians, created a unified state under a single central authority. The Minoans and the Mycenaeans, like the Mesopotamians, established separate city-states. All three peoples inhabited a dangerous world in which repeated raids and violent disruptions lasting from around 1200 to 1000 B.C.E. ultimately destroyed their prosperous cultures. Nevertheless, their accomplishments paved the way for the later civilization of Greece, which greatly influenced Western civilization.

The Hittites, 1750–1200 B.C.E.

By around 1750 B.C.E., the Hittites had made themselves the most powerful people of central Anatolia. They had migrated from the Caucasus area, between the Black and Caspian Seas, and defeated indigenous Anatolian peoples to set up their centralized king-

dom. It flourished because they inhabited a fertile upland plateau in the peninsula's center, excelled in war and diplomacy, and controlled trade in their region and southward. The Hittites' southward-knifing military campaigns eventually threatened Egypt's possessions on the eastern Mediterranean coast, bringing them into conflict with the warrior pharaohs of the New Kingdom.

Since the Hittites spoke an Indo-European language, they belonged to the linguistic family that over time populated most of Europe. The original Indo-European speakers, who were pastoralists and raiders, had migrated as separate groups into Anatolia and Europe, including Greece, most likely from western Asia. Recent archaeological discoveries in that general region have revealed graves of women buried with weapons. These burials suggest that women in these groups originally occupied positions of leadership in war and peace alongside men; the prominence of Hittite queens in documents, royal letters, and foreign treaties perhaps sprang from that tradition.

As in other early civilizations, rule in the Hittite kingdom depended on religion for its justification and structuring of authority. Hittite religion combined worship of Indo-European gods with worship of deities inherited from the original Anatolian population. The king served as high priest of the storm god, and Hittite belief demanded that he maintain a strict purity in his life as a demonstration of his justice and guardianship of social order. His drinking water, for example, always had to be strained. The king's water carrier was executed if so much as one hair was found in the water. Like Egyptian kings, Hittite rulers felt responsible for maintaining the gods' goodwill toward their subjects. King Mursili II (r. 1321–1295 B.C.E.), for example, issued a set of prayers begging the gods to end a plague: "What is this, o gods, that you have done? Our land is dying. . . . We have lost our wits, and we can do nothing right. O gods, whatever sin you behold, either let a prophet come forth to identify it . . . or let us see it in a dream!"

The kings conducted many religious ceremonies in their capital, Hattusas. Ringed by massive defensive walls and stone towers, it featured huge palaces aligned along straight, gravel-paved streets. Sculptures of animals, warriors, and, especially, the royal rulers decorated public spaces. Hittite kings maintained their rule by forging personal alliances — cemented by marriages and oaths of loyalty — with the noble families of the kingdom.

These rulers aggressively employed their troops to expand their power. In periods when ties between kings and nobles remained strong and the kingdom therefore preserved its unity, they launched extremely ambitious military campaigns. In 1595 B.C.E., for example, the royal army raided as far southeast as Babylon in Mesopotamia, destroying that kingdom. Scholars no longer accept the once popular idea that the Hittites owed their success in war to a special knowledge of making weapons from iron, although their craftsmen did smelt iron, from which they made ceremonial implements. (Weapons made from iron did not become common in the Mediterranean world until well after 1200 B.C.E. — at the end of the Hittite kingdom.) The Hittite army excelled in the use of chariots, and perhaps this skill gave it an edge.

The economic strength of the Hittite kingdom came from control over long-distance trade routes for raw materials, especially metals. The Hittites dominated the lucrative

trade moving between the Mediterranean coast and inland northern Syria, despite the New Kingdom pharaohs' resistance against Hittite expansion and power. The Anatolian kingdom proved too strong, however, and in the bloody battle of Kadesh, around 1274 B.C.E., the Hittites fought the Egyptians to a standstill in Syria, leading to a political stalemate in the eastern Mediterranean. Fear of neighboring Assyria eventually led the Hittite king to negotiate with his Egyptian rival, and the two war-weary kingdoms became allies sixteen years after the battle of Kadesh by agreeing to a treaty that is a landmark in the history of international diplomacy. In it, the two monarchs pledged to be "at peace and brothers forever." The alliance lasted, and thirteen years later the Hittite king gave his daughter in marriage to his Egyptian "brother."

The Minoans, 2200–1400 B.C.E.

Study of early Greek civilization traditionally begins with the people today known as Minoans, who inhabited Crete and other islands in the Aegean Sea by the late third millennium B.C.E. The word *Minoan* was applied after the archaeologist Arthur Evans (1851–1941) searched the island for traces of King Minos, famous in Greek myth for building the first great navy and keeping the half-human/half-bull Minotaur in a labyrinth at his palace. Scholars today are not sure whether to count the Minoans as the earliest Greeks because they are uncertain whether the Minoan language, whose decipherment remains controversial, was related to Greek or belongs to another linguistic tradition.

Minoans had no written literature, only official records, which they wrote in a script called Linear A. If research confirms that Minoan was a member of the Indo-European family of languages (the ancestor of many languages, including Greek, Latin, and, much later, English), then Minoans can be seen as the earliest Greeks. In any case, their interactions with the mainland deeply influenced later Greek civilization.

By around 2200 B.C.E., Minoans on Crete and nearby islands had created a **palace society**, so named in recognition of its sprawling multichambered buildings that housed not only the rulers, their families, and their servants but also the political, economic, and religious administrative offices of the state. Minoan rulers combined the functions of ruler and priest, dominating both politics and religion. The palaces seem to have been independent, with no one Minoan community imposing unity on the others. The general population clustered around each palace in houses adjacent to one another; some of these settlements reached the size and density of small cities. The Cretan site Knossos is the most famous such palace complex. Other, smaller settlements dotted outlying areas of the island, especially on the coast. The Minoans' numerous ports supported extensive international trade, above all with the Egyptians and the Hittites.

The most surprising feature of Minoan communities is that they did not build elaborate defensive walls. Palaces, towns, and even isolated country houses had no fortifications. The remains of the newer palaces — such as the one at Knossos, with its hundreds of rooms in five stories, indoor plumbing, and colorful scenes painted on the walls — have led some historians to the controversial conclusion that Minoans avoided war among

Wall Painting from Knossos, Crete
Minoan artists painted with vivid colors on plaster to enliven the walls of buildings. Unfortunately, time and earthquakes have severely damaged most Minoan wall paintings, and the versions we see today are largely reconstructions painted around surviving fragments of the originals. This painting from the palace at Knossos depicted an acrobatic performance in which a youth somersaulted over the back of a charging bull. Some scholars speculate this dangerous activity was a religious ritual instead of just a circus act. If it was a part of Minoan religion, what do you think this performance could symbolize? (Archeological Museum of Heraklion, Crete, Greece / Bernard Cox / The Bridgeman Art Library International.)

themselves, despite their having no single central authority over their independent settlements. Others object to this vision of peaceful Minoans as mistaken, arguing that the most powerful Minoans on Crete dominated some neighboring islands. Recent discoveries of tombs on Crete have revealed weapons caches, and a find of bones cut by knives has even raised the possibility of human sacrifice. The prominence of women in palace frescoes and the numerous figurines of large-breasted goddesses found on Minoan sites have also prompted speculation that women dominated Minoan society, but no texts so far discovered have verified this. Minoan art certainly depicts women prominently and respectfully, but the same is true of other civilizations of the time controlled by men. More research is needed to resolve the controversies concerning gender roles in Minoan civilization.

Scholars agree, however, that the development of **Mediterranean polyculture** — the cultivation of olives, grapes, and grains in a single, interrelated agricultural system — greatly increased the health and wealth of Minoan society. This innovation made the most efficient use of a farmer's labor by combining crops that required intense work at different seasons. This system of farming, which still characterizes Mediterranean agriculture, had two major consequences. First, the combination of crops provided a healthy way of eating (the "Mediterranean diet"), which in turn stimulated population growth. Second, agriculture became both more diversified and more specialized, increasing production of the valuable products olive oil and wine.

Agricultural surpluses on Crete and nearby islands spurred the growth of specialized crafts. To store and transport surplus food, Minoan artisans manufactured huge storage jars (the size of a modern refrigerator) and in the process created another specialized industry. Craft workers, producing sophisticated goods using time-consuming techniques, no longer had time to grow their own food or make the things, such as clothes and lamps, they needed for everyday life. Instead, they exchanged the products they made for food and other goods. In this way, Minoan society experienced increasing economic interdependence.

The vast storage areas in their palaces suggest that the Minoan rulers, like some Mesopotamian kings before them, controlled their society's interdependence through a redistributive economic system. The Knossos palace, for example, held hundreds of gigantic jars capable of storing 240,000 gallons of olive oil and wine. Bowls, cups, and dippers crammed storerooms nearby. Palace officials would have decided how much each farmer or craft producer had to contribute to the palace storehouse and how much of those contributions would then be redistributed to each person in the community for basic subsistence or as an extra reward. In this way, people gave the products of their labor to the central authority, which redistributed them according to its own priorities.

The Mycenaeans, 1800–1000 B.C.E.

Ancestors of the Greeks had moved into the mainland region of Greece by perhaps 8000 B.C.E., yet the first civilization definitely identified as Greek because of its Indo-European language arose only in the early second millennium B.C.E. These first Greeks are called Mycenaeans, a name derived from the hilltop site of Mycenae, famous for its many-roomed palace, rich graves, and massive fortification walls. Located in the Peloponnese (the large peninsula forming southern Greece; Map 1.3, page 26), Mycenae dominated its local area, but neither it nor any other settlement ever ruled all of Bronze Age Greece. Instead, the independent communities of Mycenaean civilization vied with one another in a fierce competition for natural resources and territory.

The nineteenth-century German millionaire Heinrich Schliemann was the first to discover treasure-filled graves at Mycenae. The burial objects revealed a warrior culture organized in independent settlements and ruled by aggressive kings. Constructed as stone-lined shafts, the graves contained entombed dead who had taken hordes of valuables with them: golden jewelry, including heavy necklaces loaded with pendants; gold and silver vessels; bronze weapons decorated with scenes of wild animals inlaid in precious metals; and delicately painted pottery.

In his excitement at finding treasure, Schliemann proudly announced that he had found the grave of Agamemnon, the legendary king who commanded the Greek army against Troy, a city in northwestern Anatolia, in the Trojan War. Homer, Greece's first and most famous poet, immortalized this war in his epic poem *The Iliad*. Archaeologists now know the shaft graves date to around 1700–1600 B.C.E., long before the Trojan War could have taken place. Schliemann, who paid for his own excavation at Troy to prove

Decorated Dagger from Mycenae
The hilltop fortress and palace at Mycenae was the capital of Bronze Age Greece's most famous kingdom. The picture of a lion hunt inlaid in gold and silver on this sixteenth-century B.C.E. dagger expressed how wealthy Mycenaean men saw their roles in society: as courageous hunters and warriors overcoming the hostile forces of nature. The nine-inch blade was found in a circle of graves inside Mycenae's walls, where the highest-ranking people were buried with their treasures as evidence of their status. (Nimatallah / Art Resource, NY.)

to skeptics that the city had really existed, was wrong on this point, but his discoveries provided the most spectacular evidence for mainland Greece's earliest civilization.

Since the hilly terrain of Greece had little fertile land but many useful ports, settlements tended to spring up near the coast. Mycenaean rulers enriched themselves by dominating local farmers, conducting naval raids, and participating in seaborne trade. Palace records inscribed on clay tablets reveal that the Mycenaeans operated under a redistributive economy. On the tablets scribes made detailed lists of goods received and goods paid out, recording everything from chariots to livestock, landholdings, personnel, and perfumes, even broken equipment taken out of service. Like the Minoans, the Mycenaeans did not use writing to record the oral literature that scholars believe they created.

The existence of *tholos* tombs — massive underground burial chambers built in beehive shapes with closely fitted stones — shows that some Mycenaeans had become very rich by about 1500 B.C.E. The architectural details of the tholos tombs and the style of the burial goods placed in them testify to the far-flung expeditions for trade and war that Mycenaean rulers conducted throughout the eastern Mediterranean. Above all, however, their many decorative patterns clearly inspired by Minoan art indicate a close connection with Minoan civilization.

Underwater archaeology has revealed the influence of international commerce during this period in (unintentionally) promoting cultural interaction. Divers have discovered, for example, that a late-fourteenth-century B.C.E. shipwreck off Uluburun in Turkey carried a mixed cargo and varied personal possessions from many locations in the eastern Mediterranean, including Canaan, Cyprus, Greece, Egypt, and Babylon. The variety confirms that merchants and consumers involved in this sort of trade were exposed directly to the goods produced by others and indirectly to their ideas.

The sea brought the Mycenaean and Minoan civilizations into close contact, but they remained different in significant ways. The Mycenaeans spoke Greek and made burnt offerings to the gods; the Minoans did neither. The Minoans extended their religious

worship outside their centers, establishing sacred places in caves, on mountaintops, and in country villas, while the mainlanders concentrated the worship of their gods inside their walled communities. When the Mycenaeans started building palaces in the four-teenth century B.C.E., they (unlike the palace-society Minoans) designed them around *megarons* — rooms with prominent ceremonial hearths and thrones for the rulers. Some Mycenaean palaces had more than one megaron, which could soar two stories high with columns to support a roof above the second-floor balconies.

Documents found in the palace at Knossos reveal that by around 1400 B.C.E. the Mycenaeans had acquired dominance over Crete, possibly in a war over commerce in the Mediterranean. The documents were tablets written in **Linear B**, a pictographic script based on Linear A (which scholars still cannot fully decipher). The twentieth-century architect Michael Ventris proved that Linear B was used to write not Minoan, but Greek. Because the Linear B tablets date from before the final destruction of Knossos in about 1370 B.C.E., they show that the palace administration had been keeping its rec-ords in a foreign language for some time and therefore that Mycenaeans were control-ling Crete well before the end of Minoan civilization. By the middle of the fourteenth century B.C.E., then, the Mycenaeans had displaced the Minoans as the Aegean region's preeminent civilization.

By the time Mycenaeans took over Crete, war at home and abroad was the princi-pal concern of well-off Mycenaean men, a tradition that they passed on to later Greek civilization. Contents of Bronze Age tombs in Greece reveal that no wealthy man went to his grave without his war equipment. Armor and weapons were so central to a Myce-naean man's identity that he could not do without them, even in death. Warriors rode into battle on revolutionary transport — lightweight two-wheeled chariots pulled by horses. These expensive vehicles, perhaps introduced by Indo-Europeans migrating from Central Asia, first appeared in various Mediterranean and Near Eastern societies not long after 2000 B.C.E.; the first picture of such a chariot in the Aegean region occurs on a Mycenaean grave marker from about 1500 B.C.E. Wealthy people evidently desired this new and costly equipment not only for war but also as proof of their social status.

The Mycenaeans seem to have spent more on war than on religion. In any case, they did not construct any giant religious buildings like Mesopotamia's ziggurats or Egypt's pyramids. Their most important deities were male gods concerned with war. The names of gods found in the Linear B tablets reveal that Mycenaeans passed down many divini-ties to the Greeks of later times, such as Dionysus, the god of wine.

The Violent End to Early Western Civilization, 1200–1000 B.C.E.

A state of political equilibrium, in which kings corresponded with one another and trad-ers traveled all over the area, characterized the Mediterranean and Near Eastern world around 1300 B.C.E. Within a century, however, violence had destroyed or weakened al-most every major political state in the region, including Egypt, some kingdoms of Meso-potamia, and the Hittite and Mycenaean kingdoms. Neither the civilizations united under

a single central authority nor the ones with independent states survived. This period of international violence from about 1200 to 1000 B.C.E. remains one of the most fascinating and disturbing puzzles in the history of Western civilization.

The best clue to what happened comes from Egyptian and Hittite records. They document many foreign attacks in this period, especially from the sea. According to one inscription, in about 1190 B.C.E. a warrior pharaoh defeated a powerful coalition of seaborne invaders from the north, who had fought their way to the edge of Egypt. These **Sea Peoples**, as historians call them, were made up of many different groups operating separately. No single, unified group of peoples originated the tidal wave of violence starting around 1200 B.C.E. Rather, many different bands devastated the region. A chain reaction of attacks and flights in a recurring and expanding cycle put even more bands on the move. Some were mercenary soldiers who had deserted the rulers who had employed them; some were raiders by profession. Many may have been Greeks. The story of the Trojan War probably recalls this period of repeated violent attacks from abroad: it portrays an army from Greece crossing the Aegean Sea to attack and plunder Troy and the surrounding coastal region. The attacks also reached far inland. As a result, the Babylonian kingdom collapsed, the Assyrians were confined to their homeland, and much of western Asia and Syria was devastated.

It remains mysterious how so many attackers could be so successful over such a long time, but the consequences for the eastern Mediterranean region are clear. The once mighty Hittite kingdom fell around 1200 B.C.E., when raiders cut off its trade routes for raw materials. Invaders razed its capital city, Hattusas, which never revived. Egypt's New Kingdom turned back the Sea Peoples after a tremendous military effort, but the raiders destroyed the Egyptian long-distance trade network. By the end of the New Kingdom, around 1081 B.C.E., Egypt had shrunk to its original territorial core along the Nile's banks. These problems ruined the Egyptian state's credit. For example, when an eleventh-century B.C.E. Theban temple official traveled to Phoenicia to buy cedar for a ceremonial boat, the city's ruler demanded cash in advance. Although the Egyptian monarchy hung on, power struggles between pharaohs and priests, made worse by frequent attacks from abroad, prevented the reestablishment of centralized authority. No Egyptian dynasty ever again became an aggressive international power.

In Greece, homegrown conflict apparently led to the tipping point for Mycenaean civilization at the time when the Sea Peoples became a threat. The Mycenaeans reached the zenith of their power around 1400–1250 B.C.E. The enormous domed tomb at Mycenae, called the Treasury of Atreus, testifies to the riches of this period. The tomb's elaborately decorated front and soaring roof reveal the pride and wealth of the Mycenaean warrior princes. The last phase of the extensive palace at Pylos on the west coast of the Peloponnese also dates from this time. It boasted vivid wall paintings, storerooms bursting with food, and a royal bathroom with a built-in tub and intricate plumbing. But these prosperous Mycenaeans did not escape the widespread violence that began around 1200 B.C.E. Linear B tablets record the disposition of troops to the coast to guard the palace at Pylos from raids from the sea. The palace inhabitants of eastern

Greece constructed defensive walls so massive that the later Greeks thought giants had built them. These fortifications would have protected coastal palaces against seafaring attackers, who could have been either outsiders or Greeks. The wall around the inland palace at Gla in central Greece, however, which foreign raiders could not easily reach, confirms that Mycenaean communities also had to defend themselves against other Mycenaean communities.

The internal conflict probably did more damage to Mycenaean civilization than the raids of the Sea Peoples. Major earthquakes also struck at this time, spreading further destruction among the Mycenaeans. Archaeology offers no evidence for the ancient

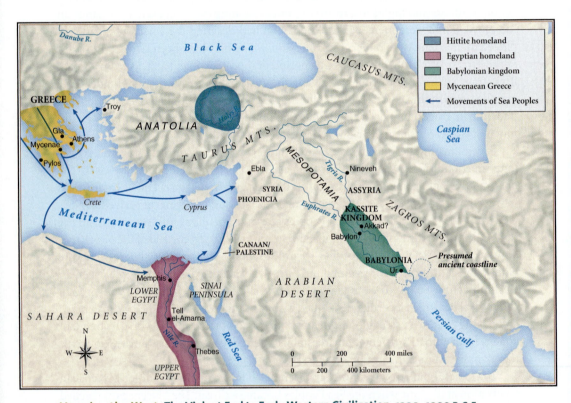

Mapping the West The Violent End to Early Western Civilization, 1200–1000 B.C.E.

Bands of wandering warriors and raiders set the eastern Mediterranean aflame at the end of the Bronze Age. This violence displaced many people and ended the power of the Egyptian, Hittite, and Mycenaean kingdoms. Even some of the Near Eastern states well inland from the eastern Mediterranean coast felt the effects of this period of unrest, whose causes remain mysterious. The Mediterranean Sea was a two-edged sword for the early civilizations that grew up around and near it: as a highway for transporting goods and ideas, it was a benefit; as an easy access corridor for attackers, it was a danger. The raids of the Sea Peoples smashed the prosperity of the eastern Mediterranean region around 1200–1000 B.C.E. and set in motion the forces that led to the next step in our story, the reestablishment of civilization in Greece. Internal conflict among Mycenaean rulers turned the regional unrest of those centuries into a local catastrophe; fighting each other for dominance, they so weakened their monarchies that their societies could not recover from the effects of battles and earthquakes.

tradition that Dorian Greeks invading from the north caused this damage. Rather, near-constant civil war by jealous local Mycenaean rulers overburdened the complicated administrative balancing system necessary for the palaces' redistributive economies and hindered recovery from earthquake damage. The violence killed many Mycenaeans, and the disappearance of the palace-based redistributive economy put many others on the road to starvation. The rulers' loss of power left most Greeks with no organized way to defend or feed themselves and forced them not only to wander abroad in search of new places to settle but also to learn to farm. Like people from the earliest times, they had to move to build a better life.

> **REVIEW QUESTION** How did war determine the fate of early Western civilization in Anatolia, Crete, and Greece?

Conclusion

The best way to create a meaningful definition of Western civilization is to study its history, which begins in Mesopotamia and Egypt; early societies there influenced the later civilization of Greece. Cities first arose in Mesopotamia around 4000 to 3000 B.C.E. Hierarchy had characterized society to some degree from the very beginning, but it, along with patriarchy, grew more prominent once civilization and political states with centralized authority became widespread.

Trade and war were constants, both aiming in different ways at profit and glory. Indirectly, they often generated cultural interaction by putting civilizations into close contact. Technological innovation was also a prominent characteristic of this long period. The invention of metallurgy, monumental architecture, mathematics, and alphabetic writing greatly affected people's lives. Religion was at the center of society; people believed that the gods demanded everyone, from king to worker, to display just and righteous conduct. But not even their faith could protect the people of the early civilizations of the Mediterranean from the destruction inflicted by the Sea Peoples and from their own internal conflicts in a period of prolonged violence. Neither hierarchy nor central authority could preserve their prosperity, and a Dark Age began around 1000 B.C.E.

Review Questions
1. How did life change for people in Mesopotamia, first after the Neolithic Revolution and then when they began to live in cities?
2. How did religion guide the lives of both rulers and ordinary people in ancient Egypt?
3. How did war determine the fate of early Western civilization in Anatolia, Crete, and Greece?

Making Connections
1. Compare and contrast the environmental factors in Mesopotamia and Egypt with regard to how they affected the emergence of the world's first civilizations.
2. What were the advantages and disadvantages of living in a unified country under a single central authority compared to living in a region with separate city-states?
3. Which were more important in influencing the development of early Western civilization: the intentional or the unintentional consequences of change?

- For practice quizzes and other study tools, visit the **Online Study Guide** at bedfordstmartins.com/huntconcise.

- For primary-source material from this period, see *Sources of the Making of the West,* Fourth Edition.

- For Web sites, images, and documents related to topics in this chapter, visit *Make History* at bedfordstmartins.com/huntconcise.

Suggested References

The combination of archaeological and linguistic research informs scholarship on the history of the ancient Near East, Egypt, and Greece. New discoveries and new ideas both help historians achieve a clearer understanding of these earliest societies of Western civilization.

Bertman, Stephen. *Handbook to Life in Ancient Mesopotamia.* 2003.

Bryce, Trevor. *Life and Society in the Hittite World.* 2004.

———, and Adam Hook. *Hittite Warrior.* 2007.

*Chavalas, Mark W., ed. *The Ancient Near East. Historical Sources in Translation.* 2006.

Cline, Eric H. *Oxford Handbook of the Bronze Age Aegean.* 2010.

Crouch, Carly L. *War and Ethics in the Ancient Near East.* 2009.

*Dalley, Stephanie, trans. *Myths from Mesopotamia: Creation, the Flood, Gilgamesh, and Others.* 1991.

Ikram, Salima. *Ancient Egypt: An Introduction.* 2010.

TIMELINE

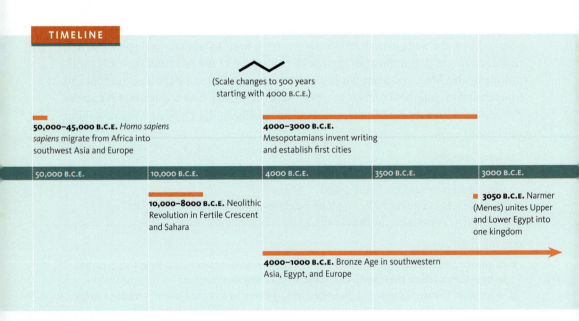

(Scale changes to 500 years starting with 4000 B.C.E.)

50,000–45,000 B.C.E. *Homo sapiens sapiens* migrate from Africa into southwest Asia and Europe

4000–3000 B.C.E. Mesopotamians invent writing and establish first cities

| 50,000 B.C.E. | 10,000 B.C.E. | 4000 B.C.E. | 3500 B.C.E. | 3000 B.C.E. |

10,000–8000 B.C.E. Neolithic Revolution in Fertile Crescent and Sahara

3050 B.C.E. Narmer (Menes) unites Upper and Lower Egypt into one kingdom

4000–1000 B.C.E. Bronze Age in southwestern Asia, Egypt, and Europe

Mieroop, Marc Van De. *King Hammurabi of Babylon: A Biography*. 2005.

Partridge, Robert B. *Fighting Pharaohs: Weapons and Warfare in Ancient Egypt*. 2002.

Podany, Amanda H. *Brotherhood of Kings: How International Relations Shaped the Ancient Near East*. 2010.

Sanders, N. K. *The Sea Peoples: Warriors of the Ancient Mediterranean, 1250–1150 B.C.* Rev. ed. 1985.

Scarre, Chris. *The Human Past: World Prehistory and the Development of Human Societies*. 2009.

*Simpson, William Kelly, ed. *The Literature of Ancient Egypt. An Anthology of Stories, Instructions, and Poetry*. 3rd ed. 2003.

Szapakowska, Kasia. *Daily Life in Ancient Egypt: Recreating Lahun*. 2008.

Tyldesley, Joyce. *Hatchepsut: The Female Pharaoh*. 1998.

Primary source.

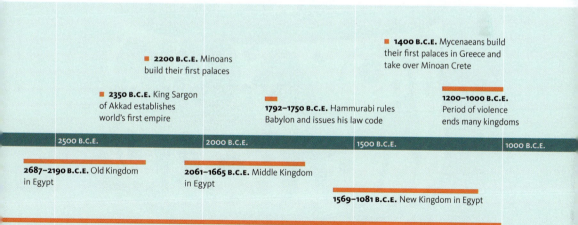

2200 B.C.E. Minoans build their first palaces

1400 B.C.E. Mycenaeans build their first palaces in Greece and take over Minoan Crete

2350 B.C.E. King Sargon of Akkad establishes world's first empire

1792–1750 B.C.E. Hammurabi rules Babylon and issues his law code

1200–1000 B.C.E. Period of violence ends many kingdoms

2500 B.C.E. 2000 B.C.E. 1500 B.C.E. 1000 B.C.E.

2687–2190 B.C.E. Old Kingdom in Egypt

2061–1665 B.C.E. Middle Kingdom in Egypt

1569–1081 B.C.E. New Kingdom in Egypt

Near East Empires and the Reemergence of Civilization in Greece

1000–500 B.C.E.

I N *THE ILIAD*, the eighth-century B.C.E. Greek poet Homer narrates bloody tales of the Trojan War. The story is rich with legends born from Greek and Near Eastern traditions, such as that of the Greek hero Bellerophon. Driven from his home by a false charge of sexual assault, Bellerophon has to serve as "enforcer" for a foreign king, fighting his most dangerous enemies. In his most famous combat, Bellerophon is pitted against "the Chimera, an inhuman freak created by the gods, horrible with its lion's head, goat's body, and dragon's tail, breathing fire all the time." Bellerophon triumphs by mounting the winged horse Pegasus and swooping down on the Chimera with an aerial attack. For such amazing heroics, the king gives Bellerophon his daughter in marriage and half his kingdom.

Homer's story provides evidence for the intercultural contact between the Near East and Greece that helped Greek civilization reemerge after 1000 B.C.E. Both the Chimera and the winged beast painted on the vase from Corinth shown in the chapter-opening illustration were creatures from Near Eastern myth that Greeks adapted. Greece's geography allowed it many ports, which promoted contacts by sea through trade, travel, and war with the Near East. From 1000 to 500 B.C.E., these contacts — combined with the Greeks' value of competitive individual excellence, their sense of a communal identity, and their belief that people in general were responsible for maintaining justice

Black-Figure Vase from Corinth

This vase was made in Corinth about 600 B.C.E., painted in the so-called black-figure style in which artists carved details into the dark-baked clay. In the late sixth century B.C.E., this style gave way to red-figure, in which artists painted details in black on a reddish background instead of engraving them; the result was finer detail (compare this vase painting with that on page 55). The animals and mythical creatures on the vase shown here follow Near Eastern models, which inspired Archaic Age Greek artists to put people and animals into their designs again after their absence during the Dark Age. Why do you think the artist depicted the animal at the lower right with two bodies but only one head? (© The Trustees of the British Museum / Art Resource, NY.)

and the goodwill of the gods toward the community—aided Greeks in reinventing their civilization.

Western peoples' desire for trade and cross-cultural contact increased as conditions improved after 1000 B.C.E. The Near East, retaining monarchy as its traditional form of government, recovered more quickly than Greece. Near Eastern kings extracted surpluses from subject populations to fund their palaces and their armies. They also pursued new conquests to win glory, exploit the labor of conquered peoples, seize raw materials, and conduct long-distance trade.

During Greece's initial recovery from poverty and depopulation from 1000 to 750 B.C.E., new political and social traditions arose that rejected the rule of kings. In this period, Greeks maintained trade and cross-cultural contact with the Near East. Their mythology, as in Homer, and their art, as on the Corinthian vase, reveal that Greeks imported ideas and technology from that part of the world. By the eighth century B.C.E., Greeks had begun to create their own kind of city-state, the polis. The polis was a radical innovation because it made citizenship—not subjection to kings—the basis for society and politics, and included the poor as citizens. Women in the polis had legal, though not political, rights; slaves still had neither. With the exception of occasional tyrannies, Greek city-states governed themselves by having male citizens share political power. In some places, small groups of upper-class men dominated, but in other city-states the polis shared power among all free men, even the poor, eventually creating the world's first democracy. The Greeks' invention of democratic politics, limited though it might have been by modern standards, stands as a landmark in the history of Western civilization.

New ways of belief and thought also developed in the Near East and Greece that deeply influenced Western civilization. In religion, the Persians developed beliefs that saw human life as a struggle between good and evil, and the Israelites evolved their monotheism. In philosophy, the Greeks began to use reason and logic to replace mythological explanations of nature.

CHAPTER FOCUS   How did the forms of political and social organization that Greece developed after 1000 B.C.E. differ from those of the Near East?

From Dark Age to Empire in the Near East, 1000–500 B.C.E.

The widespread violence in 1200–1000 B.C.E. had damaged many communities and populations in the eastern Mediterranean. Historians have traditionally used the term *Dark Age* to refer to the times following the period of violence, both because economic conditions were so gloomy for so many people and because the surviving evidence is so limited.

By 900 B.C.E., the Neo-Assyrian Empire had emerged in Mesopotamia. It inspired first the Babylonians and then the Persians to form empires after Assyrian power collapsed. By comparison, the Israelites had little military power, but they established a new path for civilization during this period by changing their religion. They developed monotheism and produced the Hebrew Bible (as it is known today), later called the Old Testament by Christians.

The New Empire of Assyria, 900–600 B.C.E.

By 900 B.C.E., Assyrian armies had punched westward all the way to the Mediterranean coast. The Neo-Assyrian kings conquered Babylon and then Egypt. Foot soldiers were the Assyrians' main strike force. They deployed siege towers and battering rams, while chariots carried archers. Foreign wars brought in revenues to supplement agriculture, herding, and long-distance trade.

Neo-Assyrian kings treated conquered peoples brutally. Those allowed to stay in their homelands had to make annual payments to the Assyrians. The kings also deported many defeated people to Assyria for work on huge building projects. One unexpected consequence of this policy was the undermining of the kings' native language: so many Aramaeans, for example, were deported from Canaan to Assyria that Aramaic had largely replaced Assyrian as the land's everyday language by the eighth century B.C.E.

Neo-Assyrian men displayed their status and masculinity in waging war and in hunting wild animals. The king hunted lions to demonstrate his vigor and power and thus his capacity to rule. Practical technology and knowledge also mattered to the kings. One boasted that he invented new irrigation equipment and a novel method of metal casting. Another one proclaimed, "I have read complicated texts, whose versions in Sumerian are obscure and in Akkadian hard to understand. I do research on the cuneiform texts on stone from before the Flood." Women of the social elite could become literate, but they were excluded from the male dominions of war and hunting.

Public religion reflected the prominence of war in Assyrian culture: the cult of Ishtar, the goddess of love and war, glorified warfare. The Neo-Assyrian rulers' desire to demonstrate their respect for the gods motivated them to build huge temples. These shrines' staffs of priests and slaves grew so large that the revenues from temple lands were insufficient; the kings had to supply extra funds from the spoils of conquest.

The Neo-Assyrian kings' demand for revenue and harsh rule made their own people, especially the social elite, resentful. Rebellions therefore became common, and a seventh-century B.C.E. revolt fatally weakened the kingdom. The Medes, an Iranian people, and the Chaldeans, a Semitic people who had driven the Assyrians from Babylonia, combined forces to defeat the Neo-Assyrian Empire.

The Neo-Babylonian Empire, 600–539 B.C.E.

The Chaldeans seized the lion's share of territory. Originating among semi-nomadic herders along the Persian Gulf, the Chaldeans had by 600 B.C.E. established the Neo-Babylonian Empire. The Neo-Babylonians increased the splendor of Babylon, rebuilding the great temple of Marduk, the chief god, and constructing an elaborate city gate dedicated to the goddess Ishtar. Blue-glazed bricks and lions molded in yellow, red, and white decorated the gate's walls, which soared thirty-six feet high.

The Neo-Babylonians preserved much Mesopotamian literature, such as the *Epic of Gilgamesh*. They also created many new works of prose and poetry, which the educated minority would often read aloud publicly to the illiterate. Particularly popular were

fables, proverbs, essays, and prophecies teaching morality and proper behavior. This so-called wisdom literature, a tradition going back at least to the Egyptian Old Kingdom, was a Near Eastern tradition that was also prominent in the religious writings of the Israelites.

The Neo-Babylonians passed their knowledge to others outside their region. Their advances in astronomy became so influential that the Greeks later used the word *Chaldean* to mean "astronomer." The primary motivation for observing the stars was the belief that the gods communicated their will to humans through natural phenomena like celestial movements and eclipses. (Other such phenomena included abnormal births, patterns of smoke curling upward from a fire, and the trails of ants.)

The Persian Empire, 557–500 B.C.E.

Cyrus (r. 557–530 B.C.E.) founded the Persian Empire in what is today Iran through his skills as a general and a diplomat who saw respect for others' religious practices as good imperial policy. He conquered Babylon in 539 B.C.E. Cyrus won support by proclaiming himself the restorer of traditional religion.

Cyrus's successors expanded Persian rule via the same principles of military strength and cultural tolerance. At its height, the Persian Empire extended from Anatolia (today Turkey), the eastern Mediterranean coast, and Egypt on the west to present-day Pakistan on the east (Map 2.1). Believing they had a divine right to rule everyone in the world, Persian kings continually tried to expand their empire.

Everything about the king emphasized his magnificence. His robes of purple outshone everyone else's; only he could step on the red carpets spread for him; his servants held their hands before their mouths so that he would not have to breathe the same air as they. As in other Near Eastern royal art, the Persian king was shown as larger than any other person in the sculpture adorning his immense palace at Persepolis. To display his concern for his loyal subjects as well as the gigantic scale of his resources, the king provided meals for fifteen thousand nobles and other guests every day — although he ate hidden from their view. The king punished criminals by mutilating their bodies and executing their families.

So long as his subjects — numbering in the millions and of many different ethnicities — remained peaceful, the king let them live and worship as they pleased. The empire's satraps (regional governors) ruled enormous territories with little interference from the kings. In this decentralized system, the governors' duties included keeping order, enrolling troops when needed, and sending revenues to the royal treasury.

Darius I (r. 522–486 B.C.E.) extended Persian power eastward to the western edge of India and westward to Thrace, northeast of Greece, creating the Near East's greatest empire. Darius assigned each region taxes payable in precious metals, grain, horses, and slaves. Royal roads and a courier system provided communication among the far-flung provincial centers. The Greek historian Herodotus reported that neither snow, rain, heat, nor darkness slowed the couriers from completing their routes as swiftly as possible.

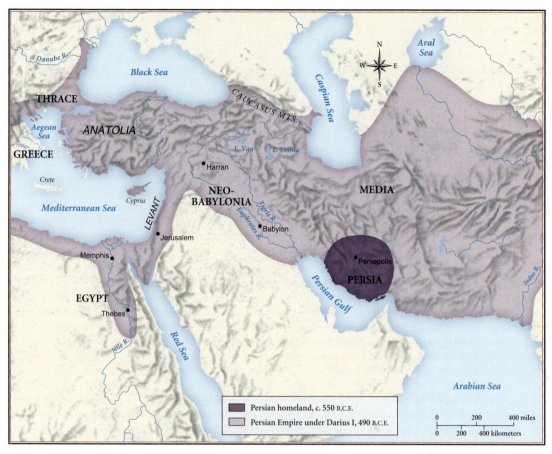

Map 2.1 Expansion of the Persian Empire, c. 550–490 B.C.E.
Cyrus (r. c. 557–530 B.C.E.) founded the Persian Empire, which his successors expanded to be even larger than the Neo-Assyrian Empire that it replaced. The Persian kings made war outward from their inland center to gain coastal possessions for access to seaborne trade and naval bases. By late in the reign of Darius I (r. 522–486 B.C.E.), the Persian Empire had expanded eastward as far as the western edge of India, while to the west it reached Thrace, the eastern edge of Europe. Unlike their imperial predecessors, the Persian kings won their subjects' loyalty with tolerance of local customs and religion, although they treated rebels harshly.

Persian kings ruled as the agents of Ahura Mazda, the supreme god of Persia. Persian religion, Zoroastrianism, made Ahura Mazda the center of its devotion and took its doctrines from the teachings of the legendary prophet Zarathustra. Zarathustra taught that Ahura Mazda demanded purity from his worshippers and helped those who lived truthfully and justly. The most important doctrine of Zoroastrianism was **moral dualism**, which saw the world as a battlefield between the divine forces of good and evil. Ahura Mazda, the embodiment of good and light, struggled against the evil darkness represented by the Satan-like figure Ahriman. Human beings had to choose between the way of the truth and the way of the lie, between purity and impurity. In Persian religion only

The Great King of Persia
Like their Assyrian predecessors, the Persian kings decorated their palaces with large relief sculptures emphasizing royal dignity and success. This one from Persepolis shows officials and petitioners giving the king proper respect when entering his presence. To symbolize their elevated status, the king and his son, who stands behind the throne, are shown larger than everyone else, as also in other Near Eastern royal art. Do you think the way the sculptors portrayed the figures from the side is more or less artistic than the technique used by the Egyptian painters in the image from the *Book of the Dead* on page 2? Why? (Courtesy of the Oriental Institute of the University of Chicago.)

those judged righteous after death made it across "the bridge of separation" to heaven and avoided falling from its narrow span into hell. Persian religion's emphasis on ethical behavior and on a supreme god had a lasting influence on others, especially the Israelites.

The Israelites, Origins to 539 B.C.E.

The Israelites never rivaled the political and military power of the great empires in the Near East. Their influence on Western civilization comes from their religion, Judaism. It originally reflected influences from the Israelites' polytheistic neighbors in Canaan (ancient Palestine), but the Israelites' development of monotheism became a turning point in the history of religions.

The Israelites' scripture, the Hebrew Bible, deeply affected not only Judaism but also Christianity and, later, Islam. No source provides definitive evidence for the historical background of the Israelites. According to the Bible's account, Abraham and his followers migrated from the Mesopotamian city of Ur to Canaan, perhaps around 1900 B.C.E. Traditionally believed to have been divided into twelve tribes, the Israelites never formed a political state in this period. The Canaanites remained the political and military power in the region.

Abraham's grandson Jacob, the story continues, moved to Egypt when his son Joseph brought his family there to escape famine. Joseph had previously used his intel-

ligence and charisma to rise to an important position in the Egyptian administration. In fact, Israelites had probably drifted into Egypt during the seventeenth or sixteenth century B.C.E. as part of the movement of peoples there under Hyksos rule. By the thirteenth century B.C.E., the pharaohs had forced the Israelite men into slave-labor gangs.

According to the biblical Book of Exodus, the Israelite deity, Yahweh, instructed Moses to lead the Israelites out of bondage in Egypt against the will of the king, perhaps around the mid-thirteenth century B.C.E. Yahweh sent ten plagues to compel the pharaoh to free the Israelites, but the king still tried to recapture them during their flight. Yahweh therefore miraculously parted the sea to allow them to escape eastward; the water swirled back together and drowned the pharaoh's army as it tried to follow.

Next in the biblical narrative comes the crucial event in the history of the Israelites: the formalizing of a contractual agreement (a covenant) between them and their deity, who revealed himself to Moses on Mount Sinai in the desert northeast of Egypt. This contract between the Israelites and Yahweh specified that, in return for their worshipping him exclusively as their only god and living by his laws, Yahweh would make them his chosen people and lead them into a promised land of safety and prosperity. The form of the covenant with Yahweh followed the ancient Near Eastern tradition of treaties between a superior and subordinates, but its content differed from that of other ancient Near Eastern religions because it made Yahweh the exclusive deity of his people.

This binding agreement demanded human obedience to divine law and promised punishment for unrighteousness. Yahweh described himself to Moses as "compassionate and gracious, patient, ever constant and true . . . forgiving wickedness, rebellion, and sin," yet he also declared that he was "one who punishes sons and grandsons to the third and fourth generation for their fathers' iniquity" (Exod. 34:6–7).

The Hebrew Bible sets forth the religious and moral code the Israelites had to follow. The **Torah** (the first five books of the Hebrew Bible, called the Pentateuch by Christians) recorded laws for righteous living. Most famous are the Ten Commandments, which required Israelites to worship Yahweh exclusively; make no idols; keep from misusing Yahweh's name; honor their parents; refrain from work on the seventh day of the week (the Sabbath); and abstain from murder, adultery, theft, lying, and covetousness. Many of the Israelites' laws shared the traditional form and content of earlier Mesopotamian laws, such as those of Hammurabi. Like his code, Israelite law protected the lower classes and people without power, including strangers, widows, and orphans.

Israelite law and thus Israelite justice differed significantly from their Mesopotamian precedent, however, in applying the same rules and punishments to everyone regardless of social rank. Israelite law also eliminated eye-for-an-eye punishment — a Mesopotamian tradition ordering, for example, that a rapist's wife be raped, or that the son of a builder be killed if his father's negligent work caused the death of someone else's son. Crimes against property did not carry the death penalty, as in other Near Eastern societies. Israelite laws also protected slaves against flagrant mistreatment. Slaves who lost an eye or a tooth from a beating were to be freed. Like free people, slaves enjoyed the right to rest on the Sabbath. Israelite women and children, however, had fewer legal rights than men did.

According to the Bible, the Israelites who fled from Egypt with Moses made their way back to Canaan, joining their relatives who had remained there and somehow carving out separate territories for themselves. The twelve Israelite tribes remained politically distinct under the direction of separate leaders, called judges, until the eleventh century B.C.E., when according to tradition their first monarchy emerged. Their monotheism gradually developed over the succeeding centuries.

Controversy rages about the accuracy of the biblical account, which reports that the Israelites created a monarchy in the late eleventh century B.C.E. when Saul became the Israelites' first king. His successors David (r. 1010–970 B.C.E.) and Solomon (r. c. 961–922 B.C.E.) brought the Israelite kingdom to the height of its prosperity. The kingdom's wealth, based on international commerce, supported the great temple that Solomon built in Jerusalem as the house of Yahweh. The temple, richly decorated with gold leaf, and the daily animal sacrifices to God that priests performed on the altar there became the center of the Israelites' religion.

After Solomon's death, the monarchy split into two kingdoms: Israel in the north and Judah in the south. The Assyrians destroyed Israel in 722 B.C.E. and deported its population to Assyria. In 597 B.C.E., the Babylonians conquered Judah and captured its capital, Jerusalem. In 586 B.C.E., they destroyed the temple to Yahweh and banished the Israelite leaders, along with much of the population, to Babylon. In exile the Israelites learned about Persian religion. Zoroastrianism and Judaism came to share ideas, such as the existence of God and Satan, angels and demons, God's day of judgment, and the arrival of a messiah (an "anointed one," that is, a divinely chosen leader with special powers).

When the Persian king Cyrus overthrew the Babylonians in 539 B.C.E., he permitted the Israelites to return to their part of Canaan. The Bible proclaimed Cyrus a messiah of the Israelites chosen by Yahweh as his "shepherd . . . to accomplish all his purpose" in restoring his people to their previous home (Isa. 44:28–45:1). This region was called Yehud, from the name of the southern Israelite kingdom, Judah. From this geographical term came the word *Jew*, a designation for the Israelites after their Babylonian exile. Cyrus allowed them to rebuild their main temple in Jerusalem and to practice their religion.

Jewish prophets, both men and women, preached that their defeats were divine punishment for neglecting the Sinai covenant and mistreating their poor. Some prophets also predicted the end of the present world following a great crisis, a judgment by Yahweh, and salvation leading to a new and better world. This apocalypticism ("uncovering," or revelation), recalling Babylonian prophetic wisdom literature, would later provide the worldview of Christianity.

Jewish leaders developed complex religious laws to maintain ritual and ethical purity. Marrying non-Jews and working on the Sabbath were forbidden. Fathers had legal power over the household, subject to intervention by the male elders of the community; women gained honor as mothers. Only men could initiate divorce proceedings. Jews had to pay taxes and offerings to support and honor the sanctuary of Yahweh, and they had to forgive debts every seventh year.

Goddess Figurines from Judah
Many small statues of this type, called Astarte figurines after a goddess of Canaan, have been found in private houses in Judah dating from about 800 to 600 B.C.E. Israelites evidently kept them as magical tokens to promote fertility and prosperity. The prophets fiercely condemned the worship of such figures as part of the development of Israelite monotheism and the abandoning of polytheism. (Collection of the Israel Antiquities Authority and Collection of The Israel Museum, Jerusalem. Photo © The Israel Museum, Jerusalem.)

Gradually, Jews created their monotheism by accepting that Yahweh was the only god and that they had to obey his laws. Jews retained their identity by following this religion regardless of their personal fate or their geographical location. Therefore, Jews who did not return to their homeland could maintain their Jewish identity by following Jewish law while living among foreigners. In this way, the **Diaspora** ("dispersion of population") came to characterize the history of the Jewish people.

Israelite monotheism made the preservation and understanding of a sacred text, the Hebrew Bible, the center of religious life. Making scripture the focus of religion proved the most crucial development for the history not only of Judaism but also of Christianity and Islam, because these later religions made their own sacred texts — the Christian Bible and the Qur'an, respectively — the centers of their belief and practice. Through the continuing vitality of Judaism and its impact on the doctrines of Christianity and Islam, the early Jews passed on ideas — chiefly monotheism and the notion of a covenant bestowing a divinely ordained destiny on a people if they obey divine will — whose effects have endured to this day.

> **REVIEW QUESTION**   In what ways was religion important in the Near East from c. 1000 B.C.E. to c. 500 B.C.E.?

The Reemergence of Greek Civilization, 1000–750 B.C.E.

The period of violence in 1200–1000 B.C.E. destroyed the prosperous large settlements of the Greeks and erased their knowledge of how to write. They therefore had to remake their civilization in Greece's Dark Age (c. 1000–750 B.C.E.). Trade, cultural interaction,

and technological innovation led to recovery: contact with the Near East promoted intellectual, artistic, and economic revival, while the introduction of metallurgy for making iron made farming more efficient. As conditions improved, a social elite distinguished by wealth and the competitive pursuit of individual excellence replaced the hierarchy of Mycenaean times. In the eighth century B.C.E., communal values helped create a radically new form of political organization in which central authority was based on citizenship.

The Greek Dark Age

Greeks apparently lost their knowledge of writing when Mycenaean civilization fell. The Linear B script they had used was probably known only by a few scribes, who used writing to track the redistribution of goods. When the Mycenaean palaces collapsed, scribes and writing disappeared. Only oral transmission kept Greek cultural traditions alive.

Compared with their forebears, Greeks in the early Dark Age cultivated much less land and had many fewer settlements. There was no redistributive economy. The number of ships carrying Greek adventurers, raiders, and traders dwindled. People scratched out an existence as herders, shepherds, and subsistence farmers bunched in tiny settlements as small as twenty people. As agriculture declined, more Greeks than ever before made their living by herding animals. In this transient lifestyle, people built only simple huts and kept few possessions. Unlike their Bronze Age ancestors, Greeks in the Dark Age had no monumental architecture. They also stopped painting people and animals on their ceramics (their principal art form), instead putting only abstract designs on their pots.

Geography allowed the Greeks to continue seaborne trade with the civilizations of the eastern Mediterranean even during their Dark Age. Trade promoted cultural interaction, and the Greeks learned to write again about 800 B.C.E., adopting and adapting the alphabet from the Phoenicians, seafaring traders from Canaan. Near Eastern art inspired Greeks to resume the production of ceramics with figural designs (as on the Corinthian vase on page 38). Seaborne commerce encouraged better-off Greeks to produce agricultural surpluses and goods they could trade for luxuries such as gold jewelry and gems from Egypt and Syria.

Most important, trade brought the new technology of iron metallurgy. Greeks learned this skill through their eastern trade contacts and mined their own iron ore, which was common in Greece. Iron eventually replaced bronze in agricultural tools, swords, and spear points. (The Greeks still used bronze for shields and armor, however, because it was easier to shape into thin, curved pieces.) The iron tools' lower cost allowed more people to acquire them. Because iron is harder than bronze, implements kept their sharp edges longer. Better and more plentiful farming implements of iron helped increase food production, which sustained population growth. In this way, technology imported from the Near East improved people's chances for survival and thus helped Greece recover from the Dark Age's depopulation.

With the Mycenaean rulers gone, leadership became an open competition in Dark Age Greece. Individuals who proved themselves excellent in action, words, charisma, and religious knowledge joined the social elite, enjoying higher prestige and authority in society. Excellence — *aretê* in Greek — was earned by competing. Men competed with others for aretê as warriors and persuasive public speakers. Women won their highest aretê by managing a household of children, slaves, and storerooms. Members of the elite accumulated wealth by controlling agricultural land, which people of lower status worked for them as tenants or slaves.

The Iliad and The Odyssey, the eighth-century B.C.E. poems of **Homer**, reflect the social elite's ideals. Homer was the last in a long line of poets who, influenced by Near Eastern mythology, had been singing these stories for centuries, orally transmitting cultural values from one generation to the next. In telling the story of the Greek army in the Trojan War, *The Iliad* focuses on the greatest Greek warrior, Achilles, who proves his aretê by choosing to die in battle rather than accept the gods' offer to return home safely but without glory. *The Odyssey* recounts not only the hero Odysseus's ten-year adventure sailing home after the fall of Troy but also the struggle of his wife, Penelope, to protect their household from the schemes of rivals.

Homer reveals that the white-hot emotions inflamed by the competition for excellence could provoke a disturbing level of inhumanity. Achilles, in preparing to duel Hector, the prince of Troy, brutally rejects the Trojan's proposal that the winner return the loser's corpse to his family and friends: "Do wolves and lambs agree to cooperate? No, they hate each other to the roots of their being." The victor, Achilles, mutilates Hector's body. When Hecuba, the queen of Troy, sees this outrage, she bitterly shouts, "I wish I could sink my teeth into his liver to eat it raw." The endings of Homer's poems suggest that the gods could sometimes help people achieve reconciliation after violent conflict, but human suffering in his stories shows that the pursuit of excellence is painful.

As in Homer, Dark Age Greece had a small but wealthy social elite. On the island of Euboea, for example, archaeologists have discovered the tenth-century B.C.E. grave of a couple who took such enormous riches with them to the next world that the woman's body was covered in gold ornaments. They had done well in the competition for prestige and wealth; most people of the time were, by comparison, desperately poor.

The Values of the Olympic Games

Greece had recovered enough population and prosperity by the eighth century B.C.E. to begin creating new forms of social and political organization. The most vivid evidence is the founding of the Olympic Games, traditionally dated to 776 B.C.E. This international religious festival showcased the competitive value of aretê.

Every four years, the games took place in a huge sanctuary dedicated to Zeus, the king of the gods, at Olympia, in the northwestern Peloponnese. Male athletes from elite families vied in sports, imitating the aretê needed for war: running, wrestling, jumping, and throwing. Horse and chariot racing were added to the program later, but the main event remained a two-hundred-yard sprint, the *stadion* (hence our word *stadium*).

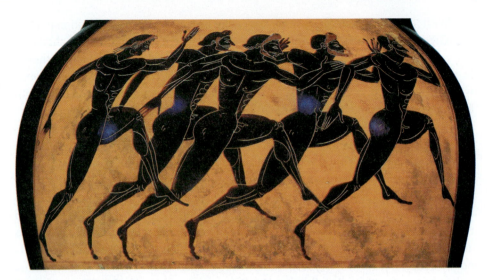

Athletic Competition
Greek vase painters often showed male athletes in action or training, perhaps in part because athletes were customers who would buy pottery with such scenes. As in this painting of an Athenian foot race from around 530 B.C.E., the athletes were usually shown nude, which is how they competed, revealing their superb physical condition and strong musculature. Being in excellent shape was a man's ideal for several reasons: it was regarded as beautiful, it enabled him to compete for individual glory in athletic contests, and it allowed him to fulfill his community responsibility by fighting as a well-conditioned soldier in the city-state's citizen militia. Why do you think the figure at the far left does not have a full beard? (See the caption on page 68 for a hint.) (Euphiletos Painter [sixth century B.C.E.], Panathenaic prize amphora, c. 530 B.C.E. Reverse. Terracotta, h. 24½ in. [62.2 cm]. Archaic Greek, Attic. Rogers Fund, 1914. [14.130.12]. The Metropolitan Museum of Art, New York, U.S.A. Image copyright © The Metropolitan Museum of Art / Art Resource, NY.)

The athletes competed as individuals, not on national teams. Winners received only a garland made from wild olive leaves to symbolize the prestige of victory.

The Olympics illustrate Greek notions of proper behavior for each gender: crowds of men flocked to the games, but women were prohibited on pain of death. Women had their own separate Olympic festival on a different date in honor of Hera, queen of the gods. Only unmarried women could compete. In later times, professional athletes dominated the Olympics, earning their living from appearance fees and prizes at games held throughout the Greek world.

Once every four years an international truce of several weeks was declared so that competitors and fans from all Greek communities could safely travel to and from Olympia. The games were open to any socially elite Greek male. These rules represented beginning steps toward a concept of collective Greek identity. The Olympics helped channel the competition for individual excellence into a new context of social cooperation and community values, essential preconditions for the creation of Greece's new political form, the city-state ruled by citizens.

Homer, Hesiod, and Divine Justice in Greek Myth

The Greeks' belief in divine justice inspired them to develop the cooperative values that remade their civilization. This idea came not from scripture — Greeks had none — but from poetry that told myths about the gods and goddesses and their relationships to humans. Different myths often provided different lessons, teaching that human beings could not expect to have a clear understanding of the gods and had to make choices by themselves about how to live.

Homer's poems reveal that the gods had plans for human existence but did not guarantee justice. Bellerophon, for example, the hero whose brave efforts won him a princess bride and a kingdom, ended up losing everything. He became, in Homer's words, "hated by the gods and wandering the land alone, eating his heart out, a refugee fleeing from the haunts of men." The poem gives no explanation for this tragedy.

Hesiod's poetry from the eighth century B.C.E., by contrast, reveals how other myths describing divine support for justice contributed to the Greek feeling of community. Hesiod's vivid stories, which originated in Near Eastern creation myths, show that deities experienced struggle, sorrow, and violence but that the divine order of the universe included a concern for justice.

Hesiod's epic poem *Theogony* (whose title means "genealogy of the gods") recounted the birth of the race of gods — including Sky and numerous others — from the intercourse of primeval Chaos and Earth. Hesiod explained that when Sky began to imprison his siblings, Earth persuaded her fiercest son, Kronos, to overthrow him violently because "Sky first schemed to do shameful things." When Kronos later began to swallow his own children to avoid sharing power with them, his wife, Rhea (who was also his sister), had their son Zeus violently force his father from power.

In *Works and Days,* his poem on conditions in his own time, Hesiod identified Zeus as the source of justice in human affairs: "Zeus commanded that fishes and wild beasts and birds should eat each other, for they have no justice; but to human beings he has given justice, which is far the best." People were responsible for administering justice, and in the eighth century B.C.E. this meant the male social elite. They controlled their family members and household servants. Hesiod insisted that a leader should demonstrate aretê by employing persuasion instead of force: "When his people in their assembly get on the wrong track, he gently sets matters right, persuading them with soft words."

Hesiod complained that many elite leaders in his time failed to exercise their power in this way, instead creating conflict between themselves and the peasants — free proprietors of small farms owning a slave or two, oxen to work their fields, and a limited amount of goods acquired by trading the surplus of their crops. Peasants' outrage at unjust treatment helped push the gradual movement toward a new form of social and political organization in Greece.

REVIEW QUESTION What factors proved most important in the Greek recovery from the troubles of the Dark Age?

The Creation of the Greek City-State, 750–500 B.C.E.

The Archaic Age (c. 750–500 B.C.E.) saw the creation of the Greek city-state — the **polis** — an independent community of citizens inhabiting a city and the countryside around it. Greece's geography, dominated by mountains and islands, promoted the creation of hundreds of independent city-states around the Aegean Sea. From there, Greeks dispersed around the Mediterranean to settle hundreds more trading communities that often grew into new city-states. Individuals' drive for profit from trade, especially in raw materials, and for free farmland probably started this process of founding new settlements.

Though it took varying forms, the Greek polis differed from the Mesopotamian city-state primarily in being a community of citizens making laws and administering justice among themselves instead of being the subjects of a king. Another difference was that poor citizens of Greek city-states enjoyed a rough legal and political equality with the rich. Not different, however, were the subordination of women and the subjugation of slaves.

The Physical Environment of the Greek City-State

Culturally, Greeks identified with one another because they spoke the same language and worshipped the same gods. Still, the ancient Greeks never unified into a single political state. Mountains separated independent and often mutually hostile Greek communities. Because few city-states had enough farmland to support many people, most of them had populations of only several hundred to several thousand. A few, prosperous from international trade, grew to have a hundred thousand or more inhabitants.

Long-distance transportation in Greece overwhelmingly occurred by sea. Land travel was slow and expensive because roads were mostly just dirt paths. The most plentiful resource was timber from the mountains for building houses and ships. Deposits of metal ore were scattered throughout Greek territory, as were clays suitable for pottery and sculpture. Various quarries of fine stone such as marble provided material for special buildings and works of art.

Only 20 to 30 percent of Greece's mountainous terrain could be farmed, making it impossible to raise large herds of cattle and horses. Pigs, sheep, goats, and chickens were the common livestock. Because the amount of annual precipitation varied greatly, farming was a precarious business of boom and bust. People preferred wheat, but since that grain was expensive to cultivate, the cereal staple of the Greek diet became barley. Wine grapes and olives were the other most important crops.

Trade and "Colonization," 800–580 B.C.E.

Greece's jagged coastline made sea travel practical: almost every community lay within forty miles of the Mediterranean Sea. But seaborne commerce faced dangers from pirates and, especially, storms. As Hesiod commented, merchants took to the sea "because an income means life to poor mortals, but it is a terrible fate to die among the waves."

The Odyssey describes the basic strategy of Greek long-distance trade in commodities, when the goddess Athena appears disguised as a metal trader: "I am here . . . with my ship and crew on our way across the wine-dark sea to foreign lands in search of copper; I am carrying iron now." By 800 B.C.E., the Mediterranean swarmed with entrepreneurs of many nationalities. The Phoenicians established settlements as far west as Spain's Atlantic coast to gain access to inland mines there. Their North African settlement at Carthage (modern Tunis) would become one of the Mediterranean's most powerful cities in later times.

The scale of trade soared near the end of the Dark Age: archaeologists have found only two tenth-century B.C.E. Greek pots that were carried abroad, but eighth-century pottery has turned up at more than eighty foreign sites. By 750 B.C.E., Greeks were settling far from home, sometimes living in others' settlements, especially those of the Phoenicians, and sometimes establishing trading posts of their own, as on an island in the Bay of Naples. Everywhere they traded with the local populations, such as the Etruscans in central Italy, who imported large amounts of Greek goods. Traders were not the only Greeks to emigrate. As the population expanded following the Dark Age, a shortage of farmland in Greece drove some poor farmers abroad to find fields they could work. Apparently only males left home on trading and land-hunting expeditions, so they had to find wives wherever they settled, either through peaceful negotiation or by kidnapping.

By about 580 B.C.E., Greek settlements had spread westward to Spain, present-day southern France, southern Italy, and Sicily; southward to North Africa; and eastward to the Black Sea coast (Map 2.2). The settlements in southern Italy and Sicily, such as Naples and Syracuse, eventually became so large and powerful that this region was called Magna Graecia ("Great Greece").

A Greek trading station had sprung up in Syria by 800 B.C.E., and in the seventh century B.C.E. the Egyptians permitted Greek merchants to settle in a coastal town. These close contacts with eastern Mediterranean peoples paid cultural as well as economic dividends. Near Eastern art inspired Greeks to reintroduce figures into their painting and provided models for statues that stood stiffly and stared straight ahead. When the improving economy of the later Archaic Age allowed Greeks again to afford monumental architecture in stone, their rectangular temples on platforms with columns reflected Egyptian architectural designs.

Historians have traditionally called the Greeks' settlement process in this era colonization, but recent research questions this term's accuracy because the word *colonization* implies the process by which modern European governments officially installed dependent settlements and regimes abroad. The evidence for these Greek settlements suggests rather that private entrepreneurship created most of them. Official state involvement was minimal, at least in the beginning.

Citizenship and Freedom in the Greek City-State

The creation of the polis filled the political vacuum left by Mycenaean civilization's fall. The Greek city-state was unique because it was based on the concept of citizenship for

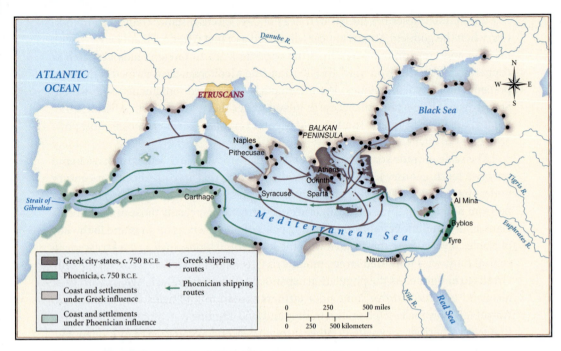

Map 2.2 Phoenician and Greek Expansion, 750–500 B.C.E.

The Phoenicians were early explorers and settlers of the western Mediterranean. By 800 B.C.E., they had already founded the city of Carthage, which would become the main commercial power in the region. During the Archaic Age, groups of adventurous Greeks followed the Phoenicians' lead and settled all around the Mediterranean, hoping to improve their economic prospects by trade and farming. Some-times they moved into previously established Phoenician settlements; sometimes they founded their own. Some Greek city-states established formal ties with new settlements or sent out their own expeditions to try to establish loyal colonies. Where did Phoenicians predominantly settle, and where did Greeks?

all its free inhabitants, rejected monarchy as its central authority, and made justice the responsibility of the citizens. Moreover, except in tyrannies (in which one man seized control of the city-state), at least some degree of shared governing was normal.

Power sharing reached its widest form in democratic Greek city-states. The most famous ancient analyst of Greek politics and society, the philosopher Aristotle (384–322 B.C.E.), argued, "Humans are beings who by nature live in a city-state." Anyone who existed outside such a community, Aristotle remarked, must be either a simple fool or superhuman. The polis's innovation in making shared power the basis of government did not immediately change the course of history — monarchy later became once again the most common form of government in ancient Western civilization — but it was im-portant as proof that power sharing was a workable system of political organization.

Greek city-states were officially religious communities. As well as worshipping many deities, each city-state honored a particular god or goddess as its special protector, such as Athena at Athens. Different communities could choose the same deity: Sparta, Athens's chief rival in later times, also chose Athena as its defender. Greeks envisioned the twelve

most important gods banqueting atop Mount Olympus, the highest peak in mainland Greece. Zeus headed this pantheon; the others were Hera, his wife; Aphrodite, goddess of love; Apollo, sun god; Ares, war god; Artemis, moon goddess; Athena, goddess of wisdom and war; Demeter, earth goddess; Dionysus, god of pleasure, wine, and disorder; Hephaestus, fire god; Hermes, messenger god; and Poseidon, sea god. The Greeks believed that their gods occasionally experienced temporary pain or sadness but were immune to permanent suffering because they were immortal.

Greek religion's core beliefs were that humans must honor the gods to thank them for blessings received and to receive more blessings in return, and that the gods sent both good and bad into the world. Gods could punish offenders by sending disasters such as floods, famines, earthquakes, epidemic diseases, and defeats in battle. The relationship between gods and humans generated sorrow as well as joy, and only a limited hope for favored treatment in this life and in the underworld after death even for the god's favorites. Ordinary Greeks did not expect the gods to take them to a paradise at some future time when evil forces would be eliminated forever. An inscription on a seventh-century B.C.E. bronze statuette sums up the reciprocity that characterized Greek religious ideas: "Mantiklos gave this from his share to [the god Apollo] the Far Darter of the Silver Bow; now you, Apollo, do something for me in return."

Mythology hinted at the gods' expectations of proper human behavior. For example, gods demanded hospitality for strangers and proper burial for family members. Other acts such as performing a sacrifice improperly, violating the sanctity of a temple area, or breaking an oath or sworn agreement counted as disrespect for the gods. Humans had to police most crimes themselves. Homicide was such a serious offense, however, that the gods were thought to punish it by casting a miasma (ritual contamination) on the

A Greek Woman at an Altar

This red-figure vase painting (contrast the black-figure vase on page 38) from the center of a large drinking cup shows a woman in rich clothing pouring a libation to the gods onto a flaming altar. In her other arm, she carries a religious object that has not been securely identified. This scene illustrates the most important and frequent role of women in Greek public life: participating in religious ceremonies, both at home and in community festivals. Greek women (and men) commonly wore sandals; why do you think they are usually depicted without shoes in vase paintings? (Attributed to Makron [painter] and Hieron [potter], [Greek, from Athens], Kylix [Drinking Vessel], detail, *Tondo: Woman Sacrificing at an Altar*, c. 490–480 B.C.E., wheel-thrown, slip-decorated earthenware, red-figure technique, h. 4⁷⁄₁₆ in. [11.3 cm]; diam. at lip 11⁵⁄₁₆ in. [28.7 cm]; diam. with handles 14¼ in. [36.2 cm]. Toledo Museum of Art [Toledo, Ohio], Purchased with funds from the Libbey Endowment, Gift of Edward Drummond Libbey [1972.55].)

murderer and on all those around. Unless the members of the affected group purified themselves by punishing the murderer, they could all expect to suffer divine punishment, such as bad harvests or disease.

Oracles, dreams, divination, and the interpretations of prophets provided clues about what humans might have done to anger the gods. The most important oracle was at Delphi, in central Greece, where a priestess in a trance provided Apollo's answers — in the form of riddles that had to be interpreted — to questions posed by city-states as well as individuals.

City-states honored gods by sacrificing animals such as cattle, sheep, goats, and pigs; decorating their sanctuaries with works of art; and celebrating festivals with songs, dances, prayers, and processions. Both city-states and individuals worshipped each god and goddess through a **cult**, a set of official, publicly funded religious activities overseen by priests and priestesses. People prayed, sang hymns of praise, offered sacrifices, and presented gifts at the deity's sanctuary. In these holy places a person could honor and thank the deities for blessings and beg them for relief when misfortune struck the community or the individual. People could also offer sacrifices at home with the household gathered around; sometimes the family's slaves were allowed to participate.

Priests and priestesses chosen from the citizen body performed the sacrifices of public cults; they did not use their positions to influence political or social matters. They were not guardians of correct religious thinking because Greek polytheism had no scripture or uniform set of beliefs and practices. It required its worshippers only to support the community's local rituals and to avoid religious pollution.

The concept of citizenship in the Greek city-state meant free people agreeing to form a political community that was a partnership of privileges and duties in common affairs under the rule of law. Citizenship was a remarkable political concept because, even in Greek city-states organized as tyrannies or oligarchies (rule by a small group), it meant a basic level of political equality among citizens. Most important, it carried the expectation of equal treatment under the law for male citizens regardless of their social status or wealth. The degree of power sharing varied. In oligarchic city-states, small groups from the social elite or even a single family could dominate the process of legislating. Women had the protection of the law, but they were barred from participation in politics on the grounds that female judgment was inferior to male. Regulations governing sexual behavior and control of property were stricter for women than for men. (See "Taking Measure," page 57.)

In democratic city-states, all free adult male citizens shared in governing by attending and voting in a political assembly, where the laws and policies of the community were decided, and by serving on juries. Citizens did not enjoy perfect political equality. The right to hold office, for example, could be restricted to citizens possessing a certain amount of property. Equality prevailed most strongly in the justice system, in which all male citizens were treated the same, regardless of wealth or status. Making equality of male citizens the principle for the reorganization of Greek society and politics in the Archaic Age was a radical innovation. The polis — with its emphasis on equal protection

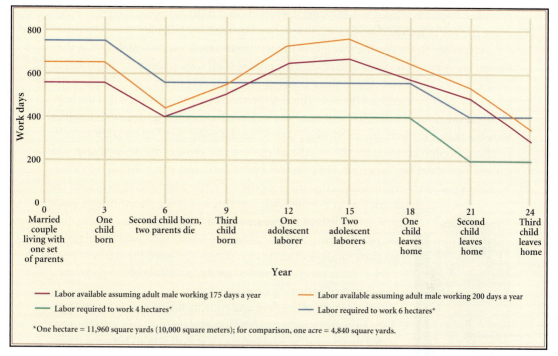

Taking Measure **Greek Family Size and Agricultural Labor in the Archaic Age**

Using archaeological surveys and estimates of population size, modern demographers have calculated the changing relationship in the Archaic Age between the number of people in a farming family and the amount of land that the family could cultivate successfully. The graph shows how valuable healthy teenage children were to the family's prosperity. For example, when the family had two children old enough to work in the fields, it could farm over 50 percent more land, increasing its productivity significantly and thus making the family better off. (Adapted from Thomas W. Gallant, *Risk and Survival in Ancient Greece: Reconstructing the Rural Domestic Economy*, 1991, Fig. 4.10.)

of the laws for rich and poor alike — remained the preeminent form of political and social organization in Greece until the beginning of Roman control six centuries later.

How the poor originally gained the privileges of citizenship remains a mystery. The population increase in the late Dark Age and the Archaic Age was greatest among the poor. These families raised more children to help farm more land, which had been vacant after the depopulation brought on by the worst of the Dark Age. There was no precedent in Western civilization for extending even limited political and legal equality to the poor.

Historians have customarily believed that a hoplite revolution was the reason for expanded political rights. A **hoplite** was an infantryman who wore metal body armor and attacked with a thrusting spear. Hoplites formed the basis of the citizen militias that defended Greek city-states. Staying in line and working together were the secrets to successful hoplite tactics. In the eighth century B.C.E., a growing number of men

became prosperous enough to buy metal weapons and train as hoplites, especially because the use of iron had made such weapons more readily available.

According to the hoplite revolution theory, these new hoplites — feeling that they should enjoy political rights in exchange for buying their own equipment and training hard — forced the social elite to share political power by threatening to refuse to fight, which would cripple military defense. This interpretation correctly assumes that the hoplites had the power to demand and receive a voice in politics but ignores that hoplites were not poor. Furthermore, archaeology shows that not many men were wealthy enough to afford hoplite armor until the middle of the seventh century B.C.E., well after the earliest city-states had emerged. How then did poor men, too, win political rights?

The most likely explanation is that the poor earned respect by fighting to defend the community, just as hoplites did. Fighting as lightly armed troops, poor men could disrupt an enemy's line by slinging rocks and shooting arrows. It is also possible that tyrants — sole rulers who seized power for their families in some city-states — boosted the status of poor men. Tyrants may have granted greater political rights to poor men as a means of gathering popular support.

The growth of freedom and equality for citizens in Greece produced a corresponding expansion of slavery, as free citizens protected their status by establishing clear distinctions between themselves and slaves. Many slaves were war captives. Pirates or raiders also seized people from non-Greek regions to sell into slavery. Rich families prized educated Greek-speaking slaves, who could tutor their children (no public schools existed yet).

City-states as well as individuals owned slaves. Publicly owned slaves enjoyed limited independence, living on their own and performing specialized tasks. In Athens, for example, special slaves were trained to detect counterfeit coinage. Temple slaves belonged to the deity of the sanctuary, for whom they worked as servants.

Slaves made up about one-third of the total population in some city-states by the fifth century B.C.E. They became cheap enough that even middle-class people could afford one or two. Still, small landowners and their families continued to do much work themselves. Not even wealthy Greek landowners acquired large numbers of agricultural slaves because maintaining gangs

Grave Monument of a Greek Warrior
This inscribed flat pillar stood above the grave of a Greek warrior from Athens who died in the late sixth century B.C.E. An inscription preserves his name for future generations to remember: Aristion. The sculpture shows him with the muscular build that Greek hoplites (heavily armed infantry) worked to develop so that they could fight effectively while wearing metal armor. He holds the thrusting spear that was a hoplite's main battle weapon. (© AISA / Everett Collection.)

of hundreds of enslaved workers year-round was too expensive. Most crops required short periods of intense labor punctuated by long stretches of inactivity, and owners did not want to feed slaves who had no work.

Slaves did all kinds of jobs. Household slaves, often women, cleaned, cooked, fetched water from public fountains, helped the wife with the weaving, watched the children, accompanied the husband as he did the marketing, and performed other domestic chores. Neither female nor male slaves could refuse if their masters demanded sexual favors. Owners often labored alongside their slaves in small manufacturing businesses and on farms. Slaves toiling in the narrow, landslide-prone tunnels of Greece's silver and gold mines had the most dangerous work.

Since slaves existed as property, not people, owners could legally beat or even kill them. But injuring or executing slaves made no economic sense — the master would have been damaging or destroying his own property. Under the best conditions, household workers could live free of violent punishment. They sometimes were allowed to join their owners' families on excursions and attend religious rituals. However, without families of their own, without property, and without legal or political rights, slaves remained alienated from regular society. Sometimes owners freed their slaves, and some promised freedom at a future date to encourage their slaves to work hard. Those slaves who gained their freedom did not become citizens in Greek city-states but instead mixed into the population of noncitizens officially allowed to live in the community.

Greek slaves rarely rebelled on a large scale, except in Sparta, because they were usually of too many different origins and nationalities and too scattered to organize. No Greeks called for the abolition of slavery. The expansion of slavery in the Archaic Age reduced more and more people to a state of absolute dependence.

Although only free men had the right to participate in city-state politics and to vote, free women counted as citizens legally, socially, and religiously. Citizenship gave women security and status because it guaranteed them access to the justice system and a respected role in a cult. Free women had legal protection against being kidnapped for sale into slavery and access to the courts in disputes over property, although they usually had to have a man speak for them. The traditional paternalism of Greek society required that all women have male guardians to regulate their lives and safeguard their interests (as defined by men). Before a woman's marriage, her father served as her legal guardian; after marriage, her husband took over that duty.

The expansion of slavery added new responsibilities for women. While their husbands farmed, participated in politics, and met with their male friends, well-off wives managed the household: raising the children, supervising the preservation and preparation of food, keeping the family's financial accounts, weaving fabric for clothing, directing the work of the slaves, and tending them when they were ill. Poor women worked outside the home, laboring in the fields or selling produce and small goods such as ribbons and trinkets in the market. Women's labor ensured the family's economic self-sufficiency and allowed male citizens the time to participate in public life.

Women's religious functions gave them prestige and freedom of movement. Women left the home to attend funerals, state festivals, and public rituals. They had access, for

example, to the initiation rights of the popular cult of Demeter at Eleusis, near Athens. Women had control over cults reserved exclusively for them and also performed important duties in other official cults. In fifth-century B.C.E. Athens, for example, women officiated as priestesses for more than forty different deities, with benefits including salaries paid by the state.

Marriages were arranged, and everyone was expected to marry. A woman's guardian would often engage her to another man's son while she was still a child, perhaps as young as five. The engagement was a public event conducted in the presence of witnesses. The guardian on this occasion repeated the phrase that expressed the primary aim of the marriage: "I give you this woman for the plowing [procreation] of legitimate children." The wedding took place when the girl was in her early teens and the groom ten to fifteen years older.

A legal wedding consisted of the bride moving to her husband's dwelling; the procession to his house served as the ceremony. The bride's father bestowed on her a dowry (a certain amount of family property a daughter received at marriage); if she was wealthy, this could include land yielding an income as well as personal possessions that formed part of her new household's assets and could be inherited by her children. The husband was legally obliged to preserve the dowry, use it to support his wife and their children, and return it in case of a divorce.

Except in certain cases in Sparta, monogamy was the rule, as was a nuclear family (husband, wife, and children living together without other relatives in the same house). Citizen men, married or not, were free to have sexual relations with slaves, foreign concubines, female prostitutes, or willing pre-adult citizen males. Citizen women, single or married, had no such freedom. Sex between a wife and anyone other than her husband carried harsh penalties for both parties.

A Bride's Preparation

This special piece of pottery was designed to fit over a woman's thigh to protect it while she sat down to spin wool. As a woman's tool, it appropriately carried a picture from a woman's life: a bride being helped to prepare for her wedding by her family, friends, and servants. The inscriptions indicate that this fifth-century B.C.E. piece shows the mythological bride Alcestis, famous for sacrificing herself to save her husband and then being rescued from Death by the hero Heracles. (Deutsches Archeologisches Institut-Athens, Neg. Nr. DAI-ATHEN-NM 5126. Photo: E. M. Czako.)

Greek citizen men placed Greek citizen women under their guardianship both to regulate marriage and procreation and to maintain family property. According to Greek mythology, women were a necessary evil. Zeus supposedly ordered the creation of the first woman, Pandora, as a punishment for men in retaliation against Prometheus, who had stolen fire from Zeus and given it to humans. To see what was in a container that had come as a gift from the gods, Pandora lifted its lid and accidentally released into a previously trouble-free world the evils that had been locked inside. When she finally slammed the lid back down, only hope still remained in the container. Hesiod described women as "big trouble" but thought any man who refused to marry to escape the "troublesome deeds of women" would come to "destructive old age" alone, with no heirs. In other words, a man needed a wife so that he could father children who would later care for him and preserve the family property after his death. This paternalistic attitude allowed Greek men to control human reproduction and consequently the distribution of property.

> **REVIEW QUESTION**   How did the physical, social, and intellectual conditions of life in the Archaic Age promote the emergence of the Greek city-state?

New Directions for the Greek City-State, 750–500 B.C.E.

Greek city-states developed three forms of social and political organization based on citizenship: oligarchy, tyranny, and democracy. Sparta provided Greece's most famous example of an oligarchy, in which a small number of men dominated policymaking in an assembly of male citizens. For a time Corinth had the best-known tyranny, in which one man seized control of the city-state, ruling it for the advantage of his family and loyal supporters, while acknowledging the citizenship of all (thereby distinguishing a tyrant from a king, who ruled over subjects). Athens developed Greece's best-known democracy.

Greeks in the Archaic Age also created new forms of artistic expression and new ways of thought. In this period they developed innovative ways of using reason to understand the physical world, their relations to it, and their relationships with one another. This intellectual innovation laid the foundation for the gradual emergence of scientific thought and logic in Western civilization.

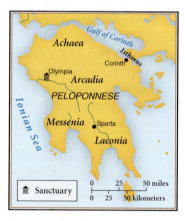

Sparta and Corinth, 750–500 B.C.E.

Oligarchy in the City-State of Sparta, 700–500 B.C.E.

Sparta organized its society for military readiness. This oligarchic city-state developed the mightiest infantry force in Greece during the Archaic Age. Its citizens were famous for their militaristic self-discipline. Sparta's urban center nestled in an easily defended

valley on the Peloponnesian peninsula twenty-five miles from the Mediterranean coast. This separation from the sea kept the Spartans focused on being a land power.

The Spartan oligarchy included three components of rule. First came the two hereditary, prestigious military leaders called kings, who served as the state's religious heads and the generals of its army. Despite their title, they were not monarchs but just one part of the ruling oligarchy. The second part was a council of twenty-eight men over sixty years old (the elders), and the third part consisted of five annually elected officials called *ephors* ("overseers"), who made policy and enforced the laws.

In principle, legislation had to be approved by an assembly of all Sparta's free adult males, who were called the Alike to stress their common status and purpose. The assembly had only limited power to amend the proposals put before it, however, and the council would withdraw a proposal when the assembly's reaction proved negative. Spartan society demanded strict obedience to all laws. When the ephors took office, they issued an official proclamation to Sparta's males: "Shave your mustache and obey the laws." Unlike other Greeks, the Spartans never wrote down their laws. Instead, they preserved their system with a unique, highly structured way of life. All Spartan citizens were expected to put service to their city-state before personal concerns because their state's survival was continually threatened by its own economic foundation: the great mass of Greek slaves, called helots, who did almost all the work for Spartan citizens.

A **helot** was a slave owned by the Spartan city-state. Helots were Greeks captured in neighboring parts of Greece that the Spartans defeated in war. Most helots lived in Messenia, to the west, which Sparta had conquered by around 700 B.C.E. The helots outnumbered Sparta's free citizens. Harshly treated by their Spartan masters, helots constantly looked for chances to revolt.

Helots had some family life because they were expected to produce children to maintain their population, and they could own some personal possessions and practice their religion. They labored as farmers and household slaves so that Spartan citizens would not have to do nonmilitary work. Spartan men wore their hair very long to show they were warriors rather than laborers.

Helots lived under the constant threat of officially approved violence by Spartan citizens. Every year the ephors formally declared war between Sparta and the helots, allowing any Spartan to kill a helot without legal penalty or fear of offending the gods. By beating the helots frequently, forcing them to get drunk in public as an object lesson to young Spartans, and humiliating them by making them wear dog-skin caps, the Spartans emphasized their slaves' "otherness." In this way Spartans created a justification for their harsh abuse of fellow Greeks. A later Athenian observed, "Sparta is the home of the freest of the Greeks, and of the most enslaved."

With helots to work the fields, male citizens could devote themselves full-time to preparation for war, training to protect their state both from hostile neighbors and its own slaves. Boys lived at home until their seventh year, when they were sent to live in barracks with other males until they were thirty. They spent most of their time exercising, hunting, practicing with weapons, and learning Spartan values by listening to tales of bravery and heroism at shared meals, where adult males in groups of about fifteen

usually ate instead of at home. Discipline was strict, and the boys were purposely under-fed so that they would learn stealth tactics by stealing food. If they were caught, pun-ishment and disgrace followed immediately. One famous Spartan tale reported that a boy hid a stolen fox under his clothing and let the panicked animal rip out his insides rather than allow himself to be detected in the theft. A Spartan male who could not sur-vive the tough training was publicly disgraced and denied the status of being an Alike.

Spending so much time in shared quarters schooled Sparta's young men in their society's values. The community took the place of a Spartan boy's family when he was growing up and remained his main social environment even after he reached adult-hood. There he learned to call all older men Father, to emphasize that his primary loy-alty was to the group instead of his biological family. This way of life trained him for the one honorable occupation for Spartan men: obedient soldier. A seventh-century B.C.E. poet expressed the Spartan male ideal: "Know that it is good for the city-state and the whole people when a man takes his place in the front row of warriors and stands his ground without flinching."

An adolescent boy's life often involved what in today's terminology would be called a homosexual relationship, although the ancient concepts of heterosexuality and homo-sexuality did not match modern notions. An older male would choose a teenager as a special favorite, in many cases engaging him in sexual relations. Their bond was meant to make each ready to die for the other in battle. Numerous Greek city-states included this form of sexuality among their customs, although some thought it disgraceful and made it illegal. The Athenian author Xenophon (c. 430–355 B.C.E.) wrote a work on the Spartan way of life denying that sex with boys existed there because he thought it a stain on the Spartans' reputation for vir-tue. However, other sources testify that such relationships did exist in Sparta and elsewhere.

In such relationships the elder partner (the "lover") was supposed to help educate the young man (the "beloved") in politics and community values, and not just exploit him for physical pleasure. Beloveds were expected

Bronze Sculpture of a Spartan Youth

This sculpted handle of a bronze water jar from sixth-century B.C.E. Sparta shows a young male holding two lions by the tail on his shoulders. That spectacular pose portrayed the fearlessness and control over fierce nature that Sparta expected of its citizens. His hair is long in the self-conscious style of Spartan warriors, who prided themselves on not having the short hair that was common for laborers. (Greek, Archaic, about 540 B.C.E. Place of manufacture: Greece, Laconia, Sparta. Bronze. H. 12.8 cm [5¹⁄₁₆ in.]. Museum of Fine Arts, Boston; Museum purchase with funds donated by contributions, 85.515. Photograph © 2013 Museum of Fine Arts, Boston.)

to get married after they became adults and later become the older member of a new pair. Sex between adult males was considered disgraceful, as was sex between females of all ages (at least according to men).

Spartan women were known throughout the Greek world for their personal freedom. Since their husbands were so rarely at home, women controlled the households, which included servants, daughters, and sons who had not yet left for their communal training. Consequently, Spartan women exercised even more power at home than did women elsewhere in Greece. They could own property, including land. Wives were expected to stay physically fit so that they could bear healthy children to keep up the population. They were also expected to drum Spartan values into their children. One mother became legendary for handing her son his shield on the eve of battle and sternly telling him, "Come back with it or [lying dead] on it."

Demographics determined Sparta's long-term fate. The population of Sparta was never large. Adult males — who made up the army — numbered between eight and ten thousand in the Archaic period. Over time, the problem of producing enough children to keep the Spartan army from shrinking became desperate, probably because losses in war far outnumbered births. Men became legally required to marry, with bachelors punished by fines and public ridicule. A woman could legitimately have children by a man other than her husband, if all three agreed.

Because the Spartans' survival depended on the exploitation of enslaved Greeks, they believed changes in their way of life must be avoided because any change might make them vulnerable to internal revolts. Some Greeks criticized the Spartan way of life as repressive and monotonous, but the Spartans' discipline and respect for their laws also gained them widespread admiration.

Tyranny in the City-State of Corinth, 657–585 B.C.E.

In some city-states, competition among the social elite became so bitter that a single family would suppress all its rivals and establish itself in rule. The family's leader thus became a tyrant, a dictator who gained political dominance by force. Tyrants usually rallied support by promising support for poor citizens, such as public employment schemes. Since few tyrants successfully passed their dominance on to their heirs, tyrannies tended to be short-lived.

Tyrants usually preserved their city-states' existing laws and political institutions. If a city-state had an assembly, for example, the tyrant would allow it to continue to meet, expecting it to follow his direction. Although today the word *tyrant* indicates a brutal or unwanted leader, tyrants in Archaic Greece did not always fit that description. Ordinary Greeks evaluated tyrants according to their behavior, opposing the ruthless and violent ones but accepting the fair and generous ones.

The most famous early tyranny arose at Corinth in 657 B.C.E., when the family of Cypselus rebelled against the city's harsh oligarchic leadership. Corinth's location on the isthmus controlling land access to the Peloponnese and a huge amount of seaborne trade made it the most prosperous city-state of the Archaic Age. Cypselus "became one

of the most admired of Corinth's citizens because he was courageous, prudent, and helpful to the people, unlike the oligarchs in power, who were insolent and violent," according to a later historian. Cypselus's son succeeded him at his death in 625 B.C.E. and aggressively continued Corinth's economic expansion by founding colonies to increase trade. He also pursued commercial contacts with Egypt. Unlike his father, the son lost popular support by ruling harshly. He held on to power until his death in 585 B.C.E., but the hostility he had provoked soon led to the overthrow of his own heir. The social elite, to prevent tyranny, then installed an oligarchic government based on a board of officials and a council.

Democracy in the City-State of Athens, 632–500 B.C.E.

Athens, located at the southeastern corner of central Greece, became the most famous of the democratic city-states because its government gave political rights to the greatest number of people; financed magnificent temples and public buildings; and, in the fifth century B.C.E., became militarily strong enough to force numerous other city-states to follow Athenian leadership in a maritime empire. Athenian democracy did not reach its full development until the mid-fifth century B.C.E., but its first steps in the Archaic Age allowed all male citizens to participate in making laws and administering justice.

Athens's early development of a large middle class was a crucial factor in opening this new path for Western civilization. The Athenian population apparently expanded at a phenomenal rate when economic conditions improved rapidly from about 800 to 700 B.C.E. The ready availability of good farmland in Athenian territory and opportunities for seaborne trade allowed many families to improve their standing. These hard-working entrepreneurs felt that their self-won economic success entitled them to a say in government. The democratic unity forged by the Athenian masses was evident as early as 632 B.C.E., when the people rallied to block an elite Athenian's attempt to install a tyranny.

By the seventh century B.C.E., all freeborn adult Athenian male citizens had the right to vote on public matters in the assembly. They also elected officials called archons, who ran the judicial system by rendering verdicts in disputes and criminal accusations. Members of the elite dominated these offices; because archons received no pay, poor men could not afford to serve.

An extended economic crisis beginning in the late seventh century B.C.E. almost destroyed Athens's infant democracy. The first attempt to solve the crisis was the emergency appointment around 621 B.C.E. of a man named Draco to revise the laws. Draco's changes, which made death the penalty for even minor crimes, proved too harsh to work. Later Greeks said Draco (whose harshness inspired the word *draconian*) had written his laws in blood, not ink. By 600 B.C.E., economic conditions had become so terrible that poor farmers had to borrow constantly from richer neighbors and deeply mortgage their land. As the crisis grew worse, impoverished citizens were sold into slavery to pay off debts.

Desperate, Athenians appointed another emergency official in 594 B.C.E., a war hero named **Solon**. To head off violence, Solon gave both rich and poor something of what they wanted, a compromise called the "shaking off of obligations." He canceled private debts, which helped the poor but displeased the rich; he decided not to redistribute land, which pleased the wealthy but disappointed the poor. He banned selling citizens into slavery to settle debts and liberated citizens who had become slaves in this way. His elimination of debt slavery was a significant recognition of citizen rights.

Solon balanced political power between rich and poor by reordering Athens's traditional ranking of citizens into four groups. Most important, he made the top-ranking group depend solely on wealth, not birth. This change eliminated inherited aristocracy at Athens. The groupings did not affect a man's treatment at law, only his eligibility for government office. The higher a man's ranking, the higher the post to which he could be elected, but higher also was the contribution he was expected to make to the community with his service and his money. Men at the poorest level, called laborers, were not eligible for any office. Solon did, however, confirm the laborers' right to vote in the legislative assembly. His classification scheme was consistent with democratic principles because it allowed for upward social mobility: a man who increased his wealth could move up the scale of eligibility for office.

The creation of a smaller council to prepare the agenda for the assembly was a crucial development in making Athenian democracy efficient. Four hundred council members were chosen annually from the adult male citizenry by lottery—the most democratic method possible—which prevented the social elite from capturing too many seats.

Solon's two reforms in the judicial system promoted democratic principles of equality. First, he directed that any male citizen could start a prosecution on behalf of any crime victim. Second, he gave people the right to appeal an archon's judgment to the assembly. With these two measures, Solon empowered ordinary citizens in the administration of justice. Characteristically, he balanced these democratic reforms by granting broader powers to the Areopagus Council ("council that meets on the hill of the god of war Ares"). This select body, limited to ex-archons, held great power because its members judged the most important cases—accusations against archons themselves.

Solon's reforms extended power through the citizen body and created a system of law that applied more equally than before to all the community's free men. A critic once challenged Solon, "Do you actually believe your fellow citizens' injustice and greed can be kept in check this way? Written laws are more like spiders' webs than anything else: they tie up the weak and the small fry who get stuck in them, but the rich and the powerful tear them to shreds." Solon replied that communal values ensure the rule of law: "People abide by their agreements when neither side has anything to gain by breaking them. I am writing laws for the Athenians in such a way that they will clearly see it is to everyone's advantage to obey the laws rather than to break them."

Some elite Athenians wanted oligarchy and therefore bitterly disagreed with Solon. The unrest they caused opened the door to tyranny at Athens. Peisistratus, helped by his upper-class friends and the poor whose interests he championed, made himself ty-

rant in 546 B.C.E. Like the Corinthian tyrants, he promoted the economic, cultural, and architectural development of Athens and bought the masses' support. He helped poorer men, for example, by hiring them to build roads, a huge temple to Zeus, and fountains to increase the supply of drinking water. He boosted Athens's economy and its image by minting new coins stamped with Athena's owl (a symbol of the goddess of wisdom; see the illustration on page 111) and organizing a great annual festival honoring the god Dionysus that attracted people from near and far to see its musical and dramatic performances.

Peisistratus's eldest son, Hippias, ruled harshly and was denounced as unjust by a rival elite family. These rivals convinced the Spartans, the self-proclaimed champions of Greek freedom, to "liberate" Athens from tyranny by expelling Hippias and his family in 510 B.C.E.

Peisistratus's support of ordinary people evidently had the unintended consequence of making them think that they deserved political equality. Tyranny at Athens thus opened the way to the most important step in developing Athenian democracy, the reforms of Cleisthenes. A member of the social elite, Cleisthenes found himself losing against rivals for election to office in 508 B.C.E. He turned his electoral campaign around by offering more political participation to the masses; he called his program "equality through law." Ordinary people so strongly favored his plan that they spontaneously rallied to repel a Spartan army that Cleisthenes' bitterest rival had convinced Sparta's leaders to send to block his reforms.

By about 500 B.C.E., Cleisthenes had engineered direct participation in Athens's democracy by as many adult male citizens as possible. First he created constituent units for the city-state's new political organization by grouping country villages and urban neighborhoods into units called **demes**. The demes chose council members annually by lottery in proportion to the size of their populations. To allow for greater participation, Solon's Council of Four Hundred was expanded to five hundred members. Finally, Cleisthenes required candidates for public office to be spread widely throughout the demes.

The creation of demes suggests that Greek democratic notions stemmed from traditions of small-community life, in which each man was entitled to his say in running local affairs and had to persuade — not force — others to agree. It took another fifty years of political struggle, however, before Athenian democracy reached its full development with the democratization of its judicial system.

New Ways of Thought and Expression in Greece, 630–500 B.C.E.

The idea that persuasion, rather than force or status, should drive political decisions matched the spirit of intellectual change rippling through Greece in the late Archaic Age. In city-states all over the Greek world, artists, poets, and philosophers pursued new ways of thought and new forms of expression. Through their contacts with the Near East, the Greeks encountered traditions to learn from and alter for their own purposes. By the sixth century B.C.E., Greeks were introducing innovations of their own into art.

In ceramics, painters experimented with different clays and colors to depict vivid scenes from mythology and daily life. Sculptors gave their statues balanced poses and calm, smiling faces.

Building on the Near Eastern tradition of poetry expressing personal emotions, Greeks created a new poetic form. This poetry, which sprang from popular song, was performed to the accompaniment of a lyre (a kind of harp) and thus called lyric poetry. Greek lyric poems were short, rhythmic, and diverse in subject. Lyric poets wrote songs both for choruses and for individual performers. Choral poems honored gods on public occasions, celebrated famous events in a city-state's history, praised victors in athletic contests, and enlivened weddings.

Solo lyric poems generated controversy because they valued individual expression and opinion over conventional views. Solon wrote poems justifying his reforms. Other poets criticized traditional values, such as strength in war. **Sappho**, a lyric poet from Lesbos born about 630 B.C.E. and famous for her poems on love, wrote, "Some would say the most beautiful thing on our dark earth is an army of cavalry, others of infantry, others of ships, but I say it's whatever a person loves." In this poem Sappho was expressing her longing for a woman she loved, who was now far away. Archilochus of Paros,

Vase Painting of a Music Lesson
This sixth-century B.C.E. red-figure vase shows a young man (seated on the left, without a beard) holding a lyre and watching an older, bearded man play the same instrument, while an adolescent boy and an older man listen. They all wear wreaths to show they are in a festive mood. The youth is evidently a pupil learning to play. Instruction in performing music and singing lyric poetry was considered an essential part of an upper-class Greek male's education. The teacher's lyre has a sounding board made from a turtle shell, as was customary for this instrument. (Foto Marburg / Art Resource, NY.)

who probably lived in the early seventh century B.C.E., became famous for poems mocking militarism, lamenting friends lost at sea, and regretting love affairs gone wrong. He became infamous for his lines about throwing away his shield in battle so that he could run away to save his life: "Oh, the hell with it; I can get another one just as good." When he taunted a family in verse after the father had ended Archilochus's affair with one of his daughters, the power of his ridicule reportedly caused the father and his two daughters to commit suicide.

The study of philosophy ("love of wisdom") began in the seventh and sixth centuries B.C.E. when Greek thinkers created prose writing to express their innovative ideas, above all their new explanations of the human world and its relation to the gods. Most of these philosophers lived in Ionia, on Anatolia's western coast, where they came in contact with Near Eastern knowledge in astronomy, mathematics, and myth. Because there were no formal schools, philosophers communicated their ideas by teaching privately and giving public lectures. Some also composed poetry to explain their theories. People who studied with these philosophers or heard their presentations helped spread the new ideas.

Ionia and the Aegean, 750–500 B.C.E.

Working from Babylonian discoveries about the regular movements of the stars and planets, Ionian philosophers such as Thales (c. 625–545 B.C.E.) and Anaximander (c. 610–540 B.C.E.), both of Miletus, reached the revolutionary conclusion that unchanging laws of nature (rather than gods' wishes) governed the universe. Pythagoras, who emigrated from the island of Samos to the Greek city-state Croton in southern Italy about 530 B.C.E., taught that numerical relationships explained the world. He began the Greek study of high-level mathematics and the numerical aspects of musical harmony.

Ionian philosophers insisted that natural phenomena were neither random nor arbitrary. They applied the word *cosmos* — meaning "an orderly arrangement that is beautiful"— to the universe. The cosmos included not only the motions of heavenly bodies but also the weather, the growth of plants and animals, and human health. Because the universe was ordered, it was knowable; because it was knowable, thought and research could explain it. Philosophers therefore looked for the first or universal cause of all things, a quest that scientists still pursue. These first philosophers believed they needed to give reasons for their conclusions and to persuade others by arguments based on evidence. That is, they believed in logic. This new way of thought, called **rationalism**, became the foundation for the study of science and philosophy. This rule-based view of the causes of events and physical phenomena contrasted sharply with the traditional mythological view. Many people had difficulty accepting such a startling change in their

understanding of the world, and the older tradition of explaining events as the work of deities lived on alongside the new approach.

The early Greek philosophers deeply influenced later times by being the first to clearly separate scientific thinking from myth and religion. Their idea that people must give reasons to justify their beliefs, rather than simply make assertions that others must accept without evidence, was their most important achievement. This insistence on rationalism, coupled with the belief that the world could be understood as something other than the plaything of the gods, gave people hope that they could improve their lives through their own efforts. Xenophanes of Colophon (c. 570–c. 478 B.C.E.) concluded, "The gods have not revealed all things from the beginning to mortals, but, by seeking, human beings find out, in time, what is better." This saying expressed the value Archaic Age philosophers gave to intellectual freedom, corresponding to the value that citizens gave to political freedom in the city-state.

REVIEW QUESTION What were the main differences among the various forms of government in the Greek city-states?

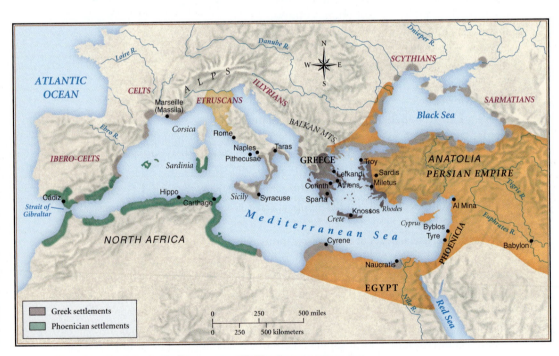

Mapping the West **Mediterranean Civilizations, c. 500 B.C.E.**

At the end of the sixth century B.C.E., the Persian Empire was by far the most powerful civilization touching the Mediterranean. Its riches and its unity gave it resources that no Phoenician or Greek city could match. The Phoenicians dominated economically in the western Mediterranean, while the Greek city-states in Sicily and southern Italy rivaled the power of those in the heartland. In Italy, the Etruscans were the most powerful civilization; the Romans were still a small community struggling to replace monarchy with a republic.

Conclusion

After its Dark Age, the Near East revived its traditional pattern of social and political organization: empire under a strong central authority. The Neo-Assyrians, the Neo-Babylonians, and the Persians succeeded one another as imperial powers. The moral dualism of Persian religion, Zoroastrianism, influenced later religions. The Israelites' development of monotheism based on scripture changed the course of religious history in Western civilization.

Greece's recovery from its Dark Age produced a new form of political and social organization: the polis, a city-state based on citizenship and shared governance. The growing population of the Archaic Age developed a communal sense of identity, personal freedom, and justice administered by citizens. The degree of power sharing varied in the Greek city-states. Some, like Sparta, were oligarchies; in others, like Corinth, rule was by tyranny. Over time, Athens developed the most extensive democracy, in which political power extended to all male citizens.

Greeks in the Archaic Age also developed new methods of artistic expression and new ways of thought. Building on Near Eastern traditions, Greek poets created lyric poetry to express personal emotion. Greek philosophers argued that laws of nature controlled the universe and that humans could discover these laws through reason and research, thereby establishing rationalism as the conceptual basis for science and philosophy.

Review Questions

1. In what ways was religion important in the Near East from c. 1000 B.C.E. to c. 500 B.C.E.?

2. What factors proved most important in the Greek recovery from the troubles of the Dark Age?

3. How did the physical, social, and intellectual conditions of life in the Archaic Age promote the emergence of the Greek city-state?

4. What were the main differences among the various forms of government in the Greek city-states?

Making Connections

1. What characteristics made the Greek city-state differ in political and social organization from the Near Eastern city-state?

2. How were the ideas of the Ionian philosophers different from mythic traditions?

3. To what extent were the most important changes in Western civilization in this period intentional or unintentional?

- For practice quizzes and other study tools, visit the **Online Study Guide** at bedfordstmartins.com/huntconcise.

- For primary-source material from this period, see *Sources of the Making of the West,* Fourth Edition.

- For Web sites, images, and documents related to topics in this chapter, visit *Make History* at bedfordstmartins.com/huntconcise.

Suggested References

Scholars today emphasize the importance of contact and intercultural influence among different peoples around the Mediterranean in helping us understand the history of the region as it recovered from the economic troubles and depopulation of the Dark Age.

Ancient Olympic Games: http://www.perseus.tufts.edu/Olympics/

*Barnes, Jonathan. *Early Greek Philosophy*. Rev. ed. 2002.

*Boyce, Mary, trans. *Textual Sources for the Study of Zoroastrianism*. 1990.

Bright, John. *A History of Israel*. 4th ed. 2000.

Brosius, Maria. *The Persians*. New ed. 2006.

Bryce, Trevor. *Life and Society in the Hittite World*. 2004.

*Dalley, Stephanie, trans. *Myths from Mesopotamia: Creation, the Flood, Gilgamesh, and Others*. Rev. ed. 2009.

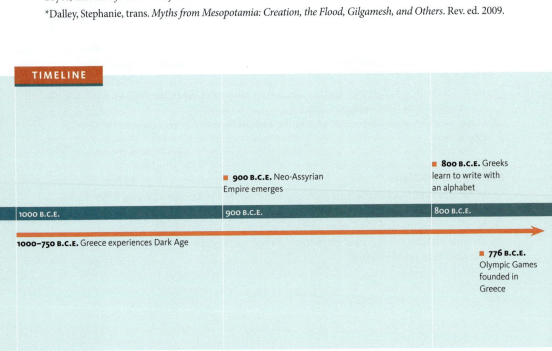

TIMELINE

■ **900 B.C.E.** Neo-Assyrian Empire emerges

■ **800 B.C.E.** Greeks learn to write with an alphabet

1000 B.C.E.   900 B.C.E.   800 B.C.E.

1000–750 B.C.E. Greece experiences Dark Age

■ **776 B.C.E.** Olympic Games founded in Greece

Finkelstein, Israel, and Amihai Mazar. *The Quest for the Historical Israel: Debating Archaeology and the History of Early Israel*. Brian B. Schmidt, ed. 2007.

Hurwitt, Jeffrey M. *The Art and Culture of Early Greece, 1100–480 B.C.* 1985.

Kugel, James. *The God of Old: Inside the Lost World of the Bible*. 2003.

Lewis, John. *Solon the Thinker: Political Thought in Archaic Athens*. 2008.

*Malandra, William W. *An Introduction to Ancient Iranian Religion: Readings from the Avesta and the Achaemenid Inscriptions*. 1983.

Osborne, Robin. *Greece in the Making, 1200–479 B.C.* 2nd ed. 2009.

Shapiro, H. A. *The Cambridge Companion to Archaic Greece*. 2007.

Primary source.

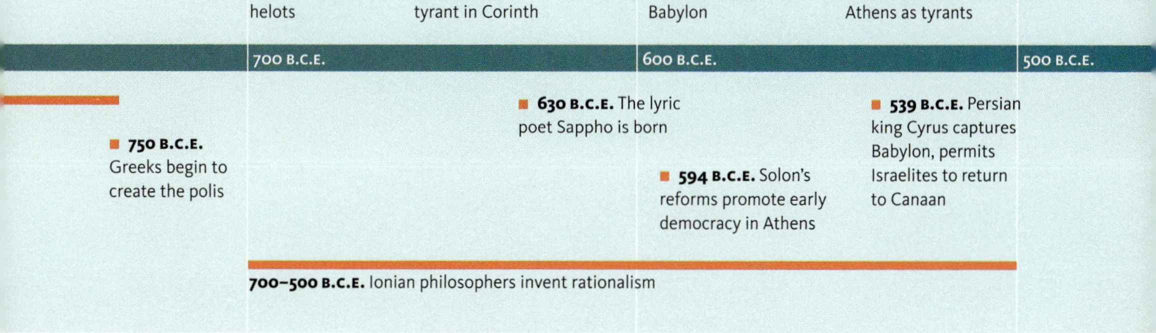

508–500 B.C.E.
Cleisthenes' reforms
extend democracy
in Athens

700 B.C.E.
Spartans conquer
Messenia, enslave
its inhabitants as
helots

657 B.C.E.
Cypselus becomes
tyrant in Corinth

597 AND 586 B.C.E.
Israelites exiled to
Babylon

546–510 B.C.E.
Peisistratus's family rules
Athens as tyrants

700 B.C.E.   600 B.C.E.   500 B.C.E.

630 B.C.E. The lyric
poet Sappho is born

539 B.C.E. Persian
king Cyrus captures
Babylon, permits
Israelites to return
to Canaan

750 B.C.E.
Greeks begin to
create the polis

594 B.C.E. Solon's
reforms promote early
democracy in Athens

700–500 B.C.E. Ionian philosophers invent rationalism

The Greek Golden Age

C. 500–C. 400 B.C.E.

N 507 B.C.E., ATHENS FEARED an attack from Sparta (its more powerful rival) and therefore sent ambassadors to the Persian king Darius I (r. 522–486 B.C.E.) to ask for help. Athens and Sparta so mistrusted each other that the Athenians chose to appeal to foreigners for help against fellow Greeks. Darius's representative asked, "But who in the world are these people and where do they live that they are begging for an alliance with the Persians?" Even so, the Persian king offered the Athenians help on his standard terms: that they acknowledge his superiority. Darius was eager to make more Greek city-states his subjects because their trade and growing wealth made them desirable prizes. The Athenian democratic assembly rejected his offer.

This incident reveals why war dominated Greece's history throughout the fifth century B.C.E., first with Greeks fighting Persians and then with Greeks fighting Greeks. Conflicting interests and misunderstandings between Persia and Greece at the start of the century ignited a great conflict: the Persian Wars (499–479 B.C.E.), which culminated with Persia invading mainland Greece. Some Greek states temporarily laid aside their competition and united to defeat the Persians, surprising the world. In victory, however, they lost their unity and fought one another. Despite nearly constant warfare, fifth-century B.C.E. Greeks (especially in Athens) created their most famous innovations in architecture, art, and theater. This Golden Age, as historians later named it, is the first part of the period called the Classical Age of Greece, which lasted from around 500 B.C.E. to the death of Alexander the Great in 323 B.C.E.

New ideas in education and philosophy that were deeply controversial in the fifth century B.C.E.

Greek against Persian in Hand-to-Hand Combat (detail)

This red-figure painting appears on the interior of a Greek wine cup. Painted about 480 B.C.E. (during the Persian Wars), it shows a Greek hoplite (armored infantryman) striking a Persian warrior in hand-to-hand combat with swords. The Greek has lost his principal weapon, a spear, and the Persian can no longer shoot his, the bow and arrow. The Greek artist has designed the painting to express multiple messages: the Persian's colorful outfit with sleeves and pants stresses the "otherness" of the enemy in Greek eyes, and the soldiers' serene expressions at such a desperate moment dignify the horror of killing in war. Greek warriors often had heroic symbols painted on their shields, such as the winged horse Pegasus, an allusion to the brave exploits of Bellerophon. (© National Museums of Scotland / The Bridgeman Art Library International.)

have had a lasting influence on Western civilization. The controversies arose because many people saw the changes as attacks on ancient traditions, especially religion; they feared the gods would punish their communities for abandoning ancestral beliefs. Political change also characterized the Athenian Golden Age. First, Athenian citizens made their city-state government more democratic than ever. Second, Athens grew internationally powerful by using its navy to establish rule over other Greeks in a system dubbed "empire" by modern scholars. This naval power also promoted seaborne trade, and revenues from rule and trade brought Athens enormous prosperity. Athens's citizens voted to use the funds to finance new public buildings, art, and competitive theater festivals, and to pay for poorer men to serve as officials and jurors in an expanded democratic government.

The Golden Age ended when Sparta defeated Athens in the Peloponnesian War (431–404 B.C.E.) and the Athenians then fought a brief but bloody civil war (404–403 B.C.E.). The Peloponnesian War and its aftermath bankrupted and divided Athens.

CHAPTER FOCUS Did war bring more benefit or more harm — politically, socially, and intellectually — to Golden Age Athens?

Wars between Persia and Greece, 499–479 B.C.E.

The Athenian ambassadors in 507 B.C.E. agreed to the Persian requirement for an alliance: presenting tokens of earth and water to acknowledge submission to the Persian king. However, the Athenian assembly failed to inform King Darius that it had rejected his terms; he continued to believe that Athens had agreed to obey him in return for support. This misunderstanding planted the seed for two Persian attacks on Greece. Since the Persian Empire far outweighed the Greek city-states in soldiers and money, the conflict pitted the equivalent of a huge bear against a pack of undersized dogs.

From the Ionian Revolt to the Battle of Marathon, 499–490 B.C.E.

In 499 B.C.E., the Greek city-states in Ionia rebelled against their Persian-installed tyrants. The Athenians sent troops because they saw the Ionians as close kin. By 494 B.C.E., a Persian counterattack had crushed the revolt (Map 3.1). Darius exploded in anger when he learned that the Athenians had helped the Ionian rebels. He even ordered a slave to repeat three times at every meal, "Lord, remember the Athenians."

In 490 B.C.E., Darius sent a small fleet to punish Athens and install a puppet tyrant. The Athenians confronted the invaders at the town of Marathon, on their coast. The Athenian soldiers were stunned by the Persians' strange garb — colorful pants instead of the short tunics and bare legs that Greeks regarded as proper dress (see the chapter-opening photo) — but the Greek commanders had their infantry charge the enemy at a dead run. The soldiers in their heavy armor clanked across the plain through a hail of Persian arrows. In the hand-to-hand combat, the Greek hoplites used their long spears to overwhelm the Persian infantry.

A Cylindrical Signet of Persia's King Darius
Like other kings in the ancient Mediterranean region, the Persian king hunted lions to show his courage and his ability to overcome nature's threats. Here on this cylindrical signet, used to impress the royal seal into wet clay to verify documents, Darius I (r. 522–486 B.C.E.) shoots arrows from a chariot driven for him by a charioteer. He is depicted wearing his crown so that his status as ruler would be obvious. The symbol of Ahura Mazda, the chief god of Persian religion, hovers in the sky to indicate that the king enjoys divine favor. (The British Museum / akg-images.)

The Athenian infantry then hurried the twenty-six miles to Athens to guard the city against the Persian navy. (Today's marathon races commemorate the legend of a runner speeding ahead to announce the victory, and then dropping dead.) Their unexpected success strengthened the Athenians' sense of community. When a rich strike was made in Athens's publicly owned silver mines in 483 B.C.E., a far-sighted leader named **Themistocles** convinced the assembly to spend the money on doubling the size of the navy instead of on distributing it to the citizens.

The Great Persian Invasion, 480–479 B.C.E.

Themistocles' foresight proved valuable when Darius's son Xerxes I (r. 486–465 B.C.E.) assembled an immense force to avenge his father's defeat by invading Greece and adding the mainland city-states to the many lands paying him taxes. So huge was Xerxes' army, the Greeks claimed, that when the invasion began in 480 B.C.E. it took seven days and seven nights for it to cross the strip of sea between Asia and Europe. Thirty-one Greek city-states (out of hundreds) allied to defend their political freedom.

Their coalition represented only a small sample of the Greek world. The allies desperately wanted the major Greek city-states in Italy and Sicily to join the coalition because they were rich naval powers, but they refused. Syracuse, for example, the most

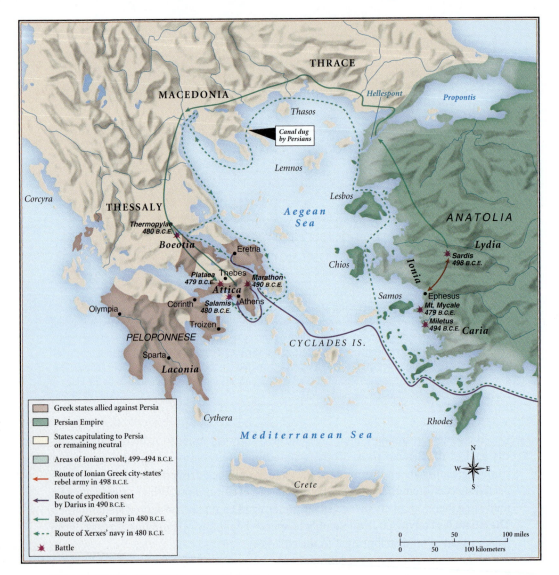

Map 3.1 The Persian Wars, 499–479 B.C.E.

Following the example of King Cyrus (r. 557–530 B.C.E.), who founded the Persian Empire, his successors on the throne expanded the empire eastward and westward. King Darius I (r. 522–486 B.C.E.) invaded Thrace more than fifteen years before the conflict against the Greeks that we call the Persian Wars. The Persians' unexpected defeat in Greece put an end to their attempt to extend their power into Europe.

powerful Greek state at the time, controlled a regional empire built on agriculture in Sicily's plains and seaborne commerce through its harbors on the Mediterranean's western trading routes. The tyrant ruling Syracuse rejected the allies' appeal for help because he was fighting his own war against Carthage, a Phoenician city in North Africa, over control of the trade routes.

The Greek allies chose Sparta as their leader because of its military excellence. The Spartans demonstrated their courage in 480 B.C.E. when three hundred of their infantry (and a few hundred other troops) blocked Xerxes' army for several days at the pass called Thermopylae in central Greece. Told the Persian archers were so numerous that their arrows darkened the sun, one Spartan reportedly remarked, "That's good news; we'll get to fight in the shade." They did — to the death. Their tomb's memorial proclaimed, "Go tell the Spartans that we lie buried here obedient to their orders."

When the Persians marched south, the Athenians, knowing they could not defend the city, evacuated their residents to the Peloponnese region rather than surrender. The Persians then burned Athens. Themistocles and his political rival Aristides cooperated to convince the other city-states' generals to fight a naval battle. Themistocles tricked the Persian king into attacking the Greek fleet in the narrow channel between the island of Salamis and the west coast of Athens, where Xerxes could not send all his fleet (twice the size of the Greeks') into battle simultaneously. The heavier Greek warships won the battle by ramming the flimsier Persian craft. The battle of Salamis induced Xerxes to return home. In 479 B.C.E., the Spartans commanded victories over the Persian land forces.

The Greeks won their battles against the Persians because their generals had better strategic foresight, their soldiers had stronger weapons, and their warships were more effective. Above all, the Greeks won the war because enough of them took the innovative step of uniting to fight together to keep their independence. Because the Greek forces included both the social elites and the poorer men who rowed the warships, their success showed that rich and poor Greeks alike treasured political freedom.

> **REVIEW QUESTION**   How did the Greeks overcome the dangers of the Persian invasions?

Athenian Confidence in the Golden Age, 478–431 B.C.E.

Victory fractured the Greek alliance because the allies resented the Spartans' harshness and the Athenians now competed with them to lead Greece. This competition created the Athenian Empire. The growth of Athens's power inspired its citizens to broaden their democracy and spend vast amounts to fund officials and jurors, public buildings, art, and religious festivals.

The Establishment of the Athenian Empire

Sparta and Athens built up separate alliances to strengthen their own positions, believing that their security depended on winning a competition for power. Sparta led strong infantry forces from the Peloponnese region, and its ally Corinth had a sizable navy. The Spartan alliance had an assembly to decide policy, but Sparta dominated.

Athens allied with city-states in northern Greece, on the islands of the Aegean Sea, and along the Ionian coast — the places most threatened by Persia. This alliance, the **Delian League**, was built on naval power. It began as a democratic alliance, but Athens

soon controlled it because the allies allowed the Athenians to command and to set the financing arrangements for the league's fleet. At its height, the league included some three hundred city-states. Each paid dues according to its size; Athens determined how the dues were spent. Larger city-states paid their dues by sending **triremes** — warships propelled by 170 rowers on three levels and equipped with a battering ram at the bow (Figure 3.1) — complete with trained crews and their pay. Smaller states could share in building one ship or contribute cash instead.

Over time, more and more Delian League members voluntarily paid cash because it was easier. Athens then used this money to construct triremes and pay men to row them; oarsmen who brought a slave to row alongside them earned double pay. Drawn primarily from the poorest citizens, rowers gained both income and political influence in Athenian democracy because the navy became the city-state's main force. These benefits made poor citizens eager to expand Athens's power over other Greeks. The increase in Athenian naval power thus promoted the development of a wider democracy at home, but it undermined the democracy of the Delian League.

The Athenian assembly could use the league fleet to force disobedient allies to pay cash dues. Athens's dominance of the Delian League has led historians to use the label *Athenian Empire*. By about 460 b.c.e., the Delian League's fleet had expelled all Persian garrisons from northern Greece and driven the enemy fleet from the Aegean Sea. This sweep eliminated the Persian threat for the next fifty years.

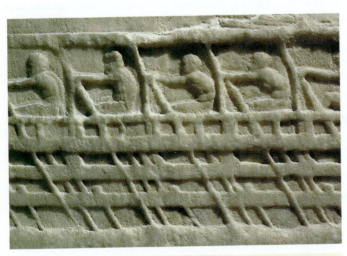

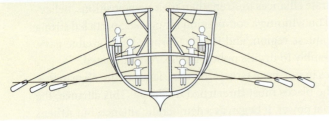

Figure 3.1 Triremes, the Foremost Classical Greek Warships

Innovations in military technology and training propelled a naval arms race in the fifth century b.c.e. when Greek shipbuilders designed larger and faster ramming ships powered by 170 rowers seated in three rows, each above the other. (See the line illustration of the rowers from behind.) Called triremes, these ships were expensive to build and required extensive crew training. Only wealthy and populous city-states such as Athens could afford to build and man large fleets of triremes. The relief sculpture found on the Athenian acropolis and dating from about 400 b.c.e. gives a glimpse of what a trireme looked like from the side when being rowed into battle. (Sails were used for power only when the ship was not in combat.) (Acropolis Museum, Athens / Gianni Dagli Orti / The Art Archive at Art Resource, NY.)

Military success made Athens prosperous by bringing in spoils and cash dues from the Delian League and making seaborne trade safe. The prosperity benefited rich and poor alike — the poor rowers earned good pay, while elite commanders enhanced their chances for election to high office by spending their spoils on public festivals and buildings. In this way, the democracy of Golden Age Athens supported imperialism.

Radical Democracy and Pericles' Leadership, 461–431 b.c.e.

In the late 460s b.c.e., the trireme rowers decided that in their own interest they should make Athens's court system as democratic as its legislative assembly, in which all free adult male citizens could already participate. They wanted to be free of unfair verdicts rendered by the elite in legal cases. Hoping to win popular support for election to high office, members of the elite pushed this judicial reform, which was accomplished in 461 b.c.e. **Pericles** (c. 495–429 b.c.e.), a member of one of Athens's most distinguished families, became Golden Age Athens's dominant politician by spearheading reforms to democratize its judicial system and provide pay for many public offices.

Historians have labeled the changes to Athenian democracy in the 460s and 450s b.c.e. *radical* ("from the roots") because the new system gave direct political and judicial power to all adult male citizens (the "roots" of democracy, in the Greek view). The government consisted of the assembly, the Council of Five Hundred chosen annually by lottery, the Council of the Areopagus of ex-archons serving for life, an executive board of ten "generals" elected annually, nine archons chosen by lottery, hundreds of other annual minor officials (most chosen by lottery), and the court system.

Athens's **radical democracy** balanced two competing goals: (1) participation by as many ordinary male citizens as possible in direct (not representative) democracy with term limits on service in office and (2) selective leadership by elite citizens. To achieve the second goal, the highest-level officials were elected and received no pay. A successful general could be reelected indefinitely.

The changes in the judicial system did the most to create radical democracy. To make the system more democratic and prevent bribery, Athenians selected jurors by lottery from male citizens over thirty years old. Juries, whose members all received pay, numbered from several hundred to several thousand members. No judges or lawyers existed, and jurors voted by secret ballot after hearing speeches from the persons involved in a case. As in the assembly, a majority vote decided matters; no appeals of verdicts were allowed.

In Athenian radical democracy the majority could overrule the legal protections for individuals. In **ostracism**, all male citizens could cast a ballot on which they scratched the name of one man they thought should be exiled for ten years. If at least six thousand ballots were cast, the man whose name appeared on the greatest number was expelled from Athens. He suffered no other penalty; his family and property remained undisturbed. Usually a man was ostracized because a majority feared he would overthrow the democracy to rule as a tyrant. There was no guarantee of voters' motives in an ostracism, as a story about Aristides illustrates. He was nicknamed "the Just" because he had

proved himself so fair-minded in setting the original level of dues for Delian League members. On the day of an ostracism, an illiterate citizen handed him a pottery fragment and asked him to scratch a name on it:

> "Certainly," said Aristides. "Which name shall I write?" "Aristides," replied the man. "All right," said Aristides as he inscribed his own name, "but why do you want to ostracize Aristides? What has he done to you?" "Oh, nothing. I don't even know him," sputtered the man. "I just can't stand hearing everybody refer to him as 'the Just.'"

True or not, this tale demonstrates that most Athenians believed the right way to support democracy was to trust a majority vote.

Some socially elite citizens bitterly criticized Athens's democracy for giving political power to the poor. These critics insisted that oligarchy — the rule of the few — was morally superior to radical democracy because they believed that the poor lacked the education and moral values needed for leadership and would use their majority rule to strip the rich of their wealth by making them pay for public works.

Pericles convinced the assembly to pass reforms to strengthen citizens' equality, making him the most influential leader of his era. He introduced pay for the offices filled by lottery and for jury service so that the poor could serve as well as the wealthy. In 451 b.c.e., Pericles sponsored a law restricting citizenship to those whose mother and father were both Athenian by birth. Previously, wealthy men had often married foreign women from elite families. This change both increased the status of Athenian women, rich or poor, as potential mothers of citizens and made Athenian citizenship more valuable by reducing the number of people eligible for its legal and financial benefits. Thousands had their citizenship revoked.

Pericles also convinced the assembly to launch naval campaigns when war with Sparta broke out in the 450s b.c.e. The assembly was so eager to compete for power and plunder against other Greeks and against Persians in the eastern Mediterranean that it voted for up to three major expeditions at once. These efforts slowed in the late 450s b.c.e. after a large naval force sent to aid an Egyptian rebellion against Persian rule suffered a horrendous defeat, losing tens of thousands of oarsmen. In 446–445 b.c.e., Pericles arranged a peace treaty with Sparta for thirty years, to preserve Athenian control of the Delian League.

The Urban Landscape in Athens

Golden Age Athens prospered from Delian League dues, war spoils, and taxes on seaborne trade. Its artisans produced goods traded far and wide; the Etruscans in central Italy, for example, imported countless painted vases. All these activities boosted Athens to its greatest prosperity.

Athenians spent their new riches on pay for citizens participating in its democracy and on public buildings, art, and religious festivals. In private life, rich urban dwellers splurged on luxury goods influenced by Persian designs, but most houses remained mod-

est and plain. Archaeology at the city of Olynthus in northeastern Greece shows homes that grouped bedrooms, storerooms, and dining rooms around open-air courtyards. Poor city residents rented small apartments. Toilets consisted of pots and a pit outside the front door. The city paid collectors to dump the waste in the countryside.

Generals won votes by spending their spoils on public running tracks, shade trees, and buildings. The super-rich commander Cimon, for example, paid for the Painted Stoa to be built on the edge of Athens's **agora**, the central market square. There, shoppers could admire the building's paintings of Cimon's family's military achievements. This sort of contribution was voluntary, but the laws required wealthy citizens to pay for festivals and warship equipment. This financial obligation on the rich was essential because Athens, as usual in ancient Greece, had no regular property or income taxes.

On Athens's acropolis (the rocky hill at the city's center, Map 3.2), Pericles had the two most famous buildings of Golden Age Athens erected during the 440s and 430s B.C.E.: a mammoth gateway and an enormous marble temple of Athena called the **Parthenon** ("virgin goddess's house"). These two buildings cost more than the equivalent of a billion dollars, a phenomenal sum for a Greek city-state. Pericles' political rivals slammed him for spending too much public money on the project and diverting Delian League funds to beautify Athens.

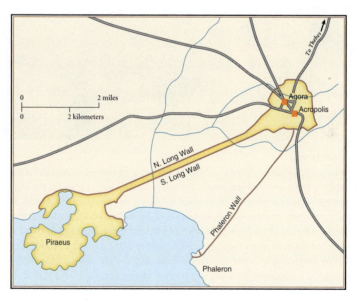

Map 3.2 Fifth-Century B.C.E. Athens
The urban center of Athens, with the agora and acropolis at its heart, measured about one square mile; it was surrounded by a stone wall with a circuit of some four miles. Gates guarded by towers and various smaller entries allowed traffic in and out of the city. Much of the Athenian population lived in the many demes (villages) of the surrounding countryside. Most of the city's water supply came from wells and springs inside the walls, but, unusual for a Greek city, Athens also had water piped in from outside. The Long Walls provided a protected corridor connecting the city to its harbor at Piraeus, where the Athenian navy was anchored and grain was imported to feed the people.

The Acropolis of Athens

Most Greek city-states, including Athens, sprang up around a prominent rocky hill, called an acropolis ("height of the city"). The summit of the acropolis usually housed sanctuaries for the city's protective deities and could serve as a fortress for the population during an enemy attack. Athens's acropolis boasted several elaborately decorated marble temples honoring the goddess Athena; the largest one was the Parthenon, seen here from its west (back) side. Recent research suggests that the ruins of a temple burned by the Persians when they captured Athens in 480 b.c.e. remained in place right next to the Parthenon. The Athenians left its charred remains to remind themselves of the sacrifices they had made in defending their freedom. (The walls in the lower foreground are from a theater built in Roman times.) (akg-images.)

The Parthenon is the foremost symbol of Athens's Golden Age. It honored Athena, the city's chief deity. Inside the temple, a gold-and-ivory statue nearly forty feet high depicted the goddess in armor, holding a six-foot statue of Nike, the goddess of victory.

Like all other Greek temples, the Parthenon was a divinity's residence, not a hall for worshippers. Its design was standard: a rectangular box on a raised platform lined

with columns, a plan probably taken from Egypt. The Parthenon's soaring columns fenced in a porch surrounding the interior chamber. They were carved in the simple style called Doric, in contrast to the more elaborate Ionic and Corinthian styles (Figure 3.2).

The Parthenon's massive size and innovative style proclaimed the self-confidence of Golden Age Athens and its competitive drive to build a monument more spectacular than any other in Greece. Constructed from twenty thousand tons of local marble, the temple stretched 230 feet long and 100 feet wide. Its complex architecture demonstrated the Athenian ambition to use human skill to improve nature: because perfectly rectilinear architecture appears curved to the human eye, subtle curves and inclines were built into the Parthenon to produce an illusion of completely straight lines and emphasize its massiveness.

The Parthenon's many sculptures communicated confident messages: the gods ensure triumph over the forces of chaos, and Athenians enjoy the gods' goodwill more than anyone else. The sculptures in each pediment (the triangular space atop the columns at either end of the temple) portrayed Athena as the city-state's benefactor. The metopes (panels sculpted in relief above the outer columns around all four sides) portrayed victories over hostile centaurs (creatures with the body of a horse but torso and head of a man) and other enemies of civilization. Most strikingly of all, a frieze (a continuous band of figures carved in relief) ran around the top of the walls inside the porch and was painted in bright colors to make it more visible. The Parthenon's frieze was special because usually only Ionic-style buildings had one. The frieze showed Athenian men, women, and children parading before the gods, the procession shown in motion like the pictures in a graphic novel today.

No other Greeks had ever adorned a temple with representations of themselves. The Parthenon staked a claim of unique closeness between the city-state and the gods, reflecting the Athenians' confidence after helping turn back the Persians, achieving

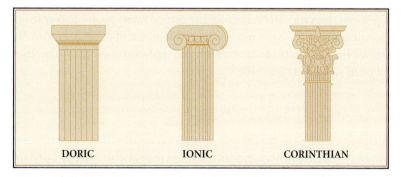

Figure 3.2 Styles of Greek Capitals
The Greeks decorated the capitals, or tops, of columns in these three styles to fit the different architectural "canons" (their word for precise mathematical systems of proportions) that they devised for designing buildings. These styles were much imitated in later times, as on many U.S. state capitols and the U.S. Supreme Court Building in Washington, D.C.

leadership of a powerful naval alliance, and accumulating great wealth. Their success, the Athenians believed, proved that the gods were on their side, and their fabulous buildings displayed their gratitude.

Like the unique Parthenon frieze, the innovations that Golden Age artists made in representing the human body shattered tradition. By the time of the Persian Wars, Greek sculptors had begun replacing the stiffly balanced style of Archaic Age statues with statues in motion in new poses. This style of movement in stone expressed an energetic balancing of competing forces, echoing radical democracy's principles.

Sculptors began carving anatomically realistic but perfect-looking bodies, suggesting that humans could be confident about achieving beauty and perfection. Female statues now displayed the shape of the curves underneath clothing, while male ones showed bodybuilders' muscles. The faces showed a more relaxed and self-confident look in place of the rigid smiles of Archaic Age statues.

Freestanding Golden Age statues, whether paid for with private or government funds, were erected to be seen by the public. Privately commissioned statues of gods were placed in sanctuaries as symbols of devotion. Wealthy families paid for statues of their deceased relatives, especially if they had died young in war, to be placed above their graves as memorials of their excellence and signs of the family's social status.

REVIEW QUESTION   What factors produced political change in fifth-century b.c.e. Athens?

Tradition and Innovation in Athens's Golden Age

Golden Age Athens's prosperity and international contacts created unprecedented innovations in architecture, art, drama, education, and philosophy, but the desire to innovate sometimes conflicted with traditional ways. In keeping with tradition, women were expected to limit their public role to participation in religious ceremonies. The new ideas of philosophers and teachers called Sophists and the Athenian philosopher Socrates' views on personal morality and responsibility caused many people to fear that the gods would become angry at the community. The development of publicly funded drama festivals reflected the clash between innovation and tradition; their tragic and comic plays examined problems in city-state life.

Religious Tradition in a Period of Change

Greeks maintained religious tradition as protection against life's dangers. They participated in the city-state's sacrifices and festivals, and they also worshipped privately. Each public and private cult had its own rituals, including everything from large-animal sacrifices to offerings of fruits, vegetables, and small cakes. State-funded sacrifices of large animals gathered the community to reaffirm its ties to the divine world and to feast on the roasted meat of the sacrificed beast. For poor people, the free food provided at religious festivals might be the only meat they ever tasted.

The biggest festivals featured parades and contests in music, dancing, poetry, and athletics. Laborers' contracts specified how many days off they received to attend such ceremonies. Some festivals were for women only, such as the three-day festival for married women in honor of Demeter, goddess of agriculture and fertility.

Families marked significant events such as birth, marriage, and death with prayers, rituals, and sacrifices. They honored their ancestors with offerings made at their tombs, consulted seers about the meanings of dreams and omens, and paid magicians for spells to improve their love lives or curses to harm their enemies. Hero cults included rituals performed at the tomb of an extraordinarily famous man or woman. Heroes' remains were thought to retain special power to provide oracles, heal sickness, and protect the army. The strongman Herakles (or Hercules, as the Romans spelled his name) had cults all over the Greek world because his superhuman reputation gave him international appeal. **Mystery cults** initiated members into "secret knowledge" about the divine and human worlds. Initiates believed that they gained divine protection from the cult's god or gods.

The Athenian mystery cult of Demeter and her daughter Persephone offered hope for protection on earth and in the afterlife. The cult's central rite was the Mysteries, a series of initiation ceremonies. So important were these Mysteries that an international truce — as with the Olympic Games — allowed people to travel from distant places to attend them. The Mysteries were open to any free Greek-speaking individuals — women and men, adults and children — if they were clear of ritual pollution (for example, if they had not committed sacrilege, been convicted of murder, or had recent contact with a corpse or blood from a birth). Some slaves who worked in the sanctuary were also eligible to participate. The main stage of initiation took almost two weeks. A sixth-century B.C.E. poem explained the initiation's benefits: "Richly blessed is the mortal who has seen these rites; but whoever is not an initiate and has no share in them, that one never has an equal portion after death, down in the gloomy darkness."

Women, Slaves, and Metics

Women, slaves, and **metics** (foreigners granted permanent residence status in return for taxes and military service) made up the majority of Athens's population, but they lacked political rights. Citizen women enjoyed legal privileges and social status, earning respect through their family roles and religious activities. Upper-class women managed their households, visited female friends, and participated in religious cults. Poor women worked as small-scale merchants, crafts producers, and agricultural laborers. Slaves and metics performed a variety of jobs in agriculture and commerce.

Bearing children in marriage earned women public and family status. Men were expected to respect and support their wives. Childbirth was dangerous under the medical conditions of the time. In *Medea*, a play of 431 B.C.E. by Euripides, the heroine shouts in anger at her husband, who has selfishly betrayed her: "People say that we women lead a safe life at home, while men have to go to war. What fools they are! I would much rather fight in battle three times than give birth to a child even once."

Wives were partners with their husbands in owning and managing the household's property to help the family thrive. Rich women acquired property, including land — the most valued possession in Greek society because it could be farmed or rented out for income — through inheritance and dowry. A husband often had to put up valuable land of his own as collateral to guarantee repayment to his wife of the amount of her dowry if he squandered it.

Like fathers, mothers were expected to hand down property to their children to keep it in the family through male heirs, since only sons could maintain their father's family line; married daughters became members of their husband's family. The goal of keeping property in the possession of male heirs shows up most clearly in Athenian law about heiresses (daughters whose fathers died without any sons, which happened in about one of every five families): the closest male relative of the heiress's father — her official guardian after her father's death — was required to marry her. The goal was to produce a son to inherit the father's property. This rule applied regardless of whether either party was already married (unless the heiress had sons); the heiress and the male relative were both supposed to divorce their present spouses and marry each other. In real life, however, people often used legal technicalities to get around this requirement so that they could remain with their chosen partners.

Tradition restricted women's freedom of movement to protect them, men said, from seducers and rapists. Men wanted to ensure that their family property went only to their biological children. Well-off city women were expected to avoid contact with male strangers. Recent research has discredited the idea that Greek homes had a defined "women's quarter" to which women were confined. Rather, women were granted privacy in certain rooms. In their homes women would spin wool for clothing, converse with visiting friends, direct their children, supervise the slaves, and present opinions on everything, including politics, to their male relatives. Poor women had to leave the house, usually a crowded rental apartment, to sell bread, vegetables, simple clothing, or trinkets they had made.

An elite woman left home for religious festivals, funerals, childbirths at the houses of relatives and friends, and shopping. Often her husband escorted her, but sometimes she took only a slave, setting her own itinerary. Most upper-class women probably viewed their limited contact with men as a badge of superior social status. For example, a pale complexion, from staying inside so much, was much admired as a sign of an enviable life of leisure and wealth.

Women who bore legitimate children gained increased respect and freedom, as an Athenian man explained in his speech defending himself for having killed his wife's lover:

> After my marriage, I at first didn't interfere with my wife very much, but neither did I allow her too much independence. I kept an eye on her. . . . But after she had a baby, I started to trust her more and put her in charge of all my things, believing we now had the closest of relationships.

Vase Painting of a Woman Buying Shoes (detail)
Greek vases frequently displayed scenes from daily life instead of mythological stories. Here, a woman is being fitted for a pair of custom-made shoes by a craftsman and his apprentice. Her husband has accompanied her, as was often the case for shopping, and he appears to be participating in the discussion of the purchase. This vase was painted in so-called black-figure technique, in which the figures are dark and have their details incised on a background of red clay. (The Plousios Painter, Two-handled jar [amphora], Greek, Late Archaic Period, about 500–490 b.c.e. Place of manufacture: Greece, Attica, Athens. Ceramic, Black Figure. H: 36.1 cm [14³⁄₁₆ in.]; diameter: 25.9 cm [10³⁄₁₆ in.]. Museum of Fine Arts, Boston, Henry Lillie Pierce Fund, 01.8035. Photograph © 2013 Museum of Fine Arts, Boston.)

Bearing male children brought a woman special honor because sons meant security. Sons could appear in court to support their parents in lawsuits and protect them in the streets of Athens, which for most of its history had no regular police force. By law, sons were required to support elderly parents.

Some women escaped traditional restrictions by working as a **hetaira** ("companion"). Hetairas, usually foreigners, were unmarried, physically attractive, witty in speech, and skilled in music and poetry. Men hired them to entertain at a symposium (a drinking party to which wives were not invited). Their skill at clever teasing and joking with men gave hetairas a freedom of speech denied to "proper" women. Hetairas nevertheless lacked the social status and respectability that wives and mothers possessed.

Sometimes hetairas also sold sex for a high price, and they could control their own sexuality by choosing their clients. Athenian men (but not women) could buy sex as they pleased without legal hindrance. Men (but not women) could also have sex freely with female or male slaves, who could not refuse their masters.

The most skilled hetairas earned enough to live in luxury on their own. The most famous hetaira in Athens was Aspasia from Miletus, who became Pericles' lover and bore him a son. She dazzled men with her brilliant talk and wide knowledge. Pericles fell so

deeply in love with her that he wanted to marry her, despite his own law of 451 B.C.E. restricting citizenship to the children of two Athenian parents.

Great riches also freed a woman from tradition. The most outspoken rich Athenian woman was Elpinike. She once publicly criticized Pericles by sarcastically remarking in front of a group of women who were praising him for an attack on a rebellious Delian League ally, "This really is wonderful, Pericles. . . . You have caused the loss of many good citizens, not in battle against Phoenicians or Persians . . . but in suppressing an allied city of fellow Greeks."

Slaves and metics were considered outsiders. Both individuals and the city-state owned slaves, who could be purchased from traders or bred in the household. Some people picked up unwanted newborns abandoned by their parents (in an accepted practice called infant exposure) and raised them as slaves. Athens's commercial growth increased the demand for slaves, who in Pericles' time made up around 100,000 of the city-state's total of perhaps 250,000 inhabitants. Slaves worked in homes, on farms, and in crafts shops; rowed alongside their owners in the navy; and toiled in Athens's dangerous silver mines. Unlike those in Sparta, slaves in Athens almost never rebelled, probably because they originated from too many different places to be able to unite.

Golden Age Athens's wealth and cultural activities attracted many metics from all around the Mediterranean. By the late fifth century B.C.E., metics constituted perhaps 50,000 to 75,000 of the estimated 150,000 free men, women, and children in the city-state. Metics paid for the privilege of living and working in Athens through a special foreigners' tax and army service, but they did not become citizens.

Innovative Ideas in Education, Philosophy, History, and Medicine

Thinkers in the Greek Golden Age developed innovative ideas in education, philosophy, history, and medicine. These innovations deeply upset some people, who feared that such departures from tradition would undermine society, especially in religion, thereby provoking punishment from angry gods. However, the changes opened the way to the development of scientific study as an enduring characteristic of Western civilization.

Education and philosophy provided the hottest battles between tradition and innovation. Parents had traditionally controlled their children's education, which occurred in the home and included hired tutors (there were still no public schools). Controversy erupted when men known as Sophists appeared in the mid-fifth century B.C.E. and offered, for pay, classes to young males on nontraditional philosophy and religious doctrines as well as new techniques for public speaking. Some philosophers' ideas challenged traditional religious views. The philosopher Socrates' views on personal morality provoked another fierce controversy. In history, innovators created novel models of interpretation to help in understanding human experience; in medicine, they developed a scientific method to help in understanding the body.

Disagreement over whether these intellectual changes were dangerous for Athenian society added to the political tension that had arisen at Athens by the 430s B.C.E. concerning Athens's harsh treatment of its own allies and its economic sanctions against

Sparta's allies. Athenians connected philosophic ideas about the nature of justice with their decisions about the city-state's domestic and foreign policy, while also worrying about the attitude of the gods toward the community.

Wealthy families sent their sons to private teachers to learn to read, write, play a musical instrument or sing, and to develop athletic skills. Physical training was considered vital because it made men's bodies beautiful and prepared them to fight in the militia (they could be summoned to war anytime between ages eighteen and sixty). Men exercised nude every day in gymnasia, public open-air facilities paid for by wealthy families. The daughters of wealthy families usually received instruction at home from educated slaves. Young girls learned reading, writing, and arithmetic to be able to help their future husbands by managing the household.

Poor girls and boys learned a trade and perhaps a little reading, writing, and calculating by assisting their parents in their daily work or by serving as apprentices to skilled craft workers. Most people probably were weak readers, but they could always find someone to read written texts aloud. Oral communication remained central to Greek life, in political speeches, songs, plays, and stories about the past.

Prosperous young men learned to participate in public life by observing their fathers, uncles, and other older men as they debated in the Council of Five Hundred and the assembly, served in public office, and spoke in court. Often an older man would choose an adolescent boy as his special favorite to educate. The teenager would learn about public life by spending time with the older man. During the day the boy would listen to his mentor talking politics in the agora, help him perform his duties in public office, and work out with him in a gymnasium. They would spend their evenings at a symposium, whose agenda could range from serious political and philosophical discussion to riotous partying.

This older mentor/younger favorite relationship could lead to sexual relations between the youth and the older (married) male. Sex between mentors and favorites was considered acceptable in elite circles in many city-states, including Athens, Sparta, and Thebes. Other city-states banned this behavior because they believed that it reflected an adult man's shameful inability to control his lustful desires.

By the time radical democracy emerged in Athens, young men could obtain higher education in a new way: paying expensive professional teachers called **Sophists** ("men of wisdom"). Sophists challenged tradition by teaching new skills of persuasion in speaking and new ways of thinking based on rational arguments. Sophists became notorious for using complex reasoning to make deceptive arguments.

By 450 B.C.E., Athens was attracting Sophists from around the Greek world. These entrepreneurs competed with one another to pull in pupils who could pay the hefty tuitions they charged. Sophists strove for excellence by offering specialized training in rhetoric — the skill of speaking persuasively. Every ambitious man wanted rhetorical training because it promised power in Athens's assembly, councils, and courts. The Sophists alarmed those who feared their teachings would destroy the tradition that preserved democracy. Speakers trained by silver-tongued Sophists, they believed, might be able to mislead the assembly while promoting their personal interests.

The most notorious Sophist was Protagoras, a contemporary of Pericles. Emigrating to Athens from Abdera, in northern Greece, around 450 b.c.e., Protagoras expressed views on the nature of truth and morality that outraged many Athenians. He argued that there could be no absolute standard of truth because every issue had two irreconcilable sides. For example, if one person feeling a breeze thinks it warm whereas another person thinks it cool, neither judgment can be absolutely correct because the wind simply is warm to one and cool to the other. Protagoras summed up this subjectivism — the belief that there is no absolute reality behind and independent of appearances — in his work *Truth:* "The human being is the measure of all things, of the things that are that they are, and of the things that are not that they are not."

The subjectivism of Protagoras and other Sophists contained two main ideas: (1) human institutions and values are only matters of convention, custom, or *nomos* ("law") and not creations of *physis* ("nature"), and (2) since truth is subjective, speakers should be able to argue either side of a question with equal persuasiveness and rationality. The first view implied that traditional human institutions were arbitrary and changing rather than natural and permanent, while the second seemed to many people to make questions of right and wrong irrelevant.

The Sophists' critics accused them of teaching moral relativism and threatening the shared public values of the democratic city-state. Aristophanes, author of comic plays, satirized Sophists for harming Athens by instructing students in persuasive techniques "to make the weaker argument the stronger." Protagoras, for one, energetically responded that his doctrines were not hostile to democracy, arguing that every person had a natural capability for excellence and that human society depended on the rule of law based on a sense of justice. Members of a community, he explained, must be persuaded to obey the laws, not because laws were based on absolute truth, which did not exist, but because rationally it was advantageous for everyone to be law-abiding. A thief, for example, who might claim that stealing was a part of nature, would have to be persuaded by reason that a man-made law forbidding theft was to his advantage because it protected his own property and the community in which he, like all humans, had to live in order to survive.

Even more disturbing to Athenians than the Sophists' ideas about truth were their ideas about religion. Protagoras angered people with his agnosticism (the belief that supernatural phenomena are unknowable): "Whether the gods exist I cannot discover, nor what their form is like, for there are many impediments to knowledge, [such as] the obscurity of the subject and the brevity of human life." He upset those who thought he was saying that conventional religion had no meaning. They worried that his words would provoke divine anger against the community where he now lived.

Other fifth-century b.c.e. philosophers and thinkers also proposed controversial new scientific theories about the nature of the cosmos and the origin of religion. A philosopher friend of Pericles, for example, argued that the sun was a lump of flaming rock, not a god. Another philosopher invented an atomic theory of matter to explain how change was constant in the universe. Everything, he argued, consisted of tiny, invisible particles in eternal motion. Their random collisions caused them to combine and re-

combine in an infinite variety of forms, with no divine purpose guiding their collisions and combinations. These ideas seemed to invalidate traditional religion, which explained events as governed by the gods' will. Even more provocative was a play written by the wealthy aristocrat Critias that denounced religion as a clever but false system invented by powerful men to fool ordinary people into obeying moral standards through fear of divine punishment.

Since only wealthy men could afford their classes or spend time conversing with them, thereby gaining yet more advantages by learning to speak persuasively in the assembly's debates or in court speeches, poorer people saw the Sophists and the philosophers as threats to Athenian democracy. Moral relativism and the physical explanation of the universe also struck many Athenians as dangerous: they feared such teachings would destroy the gods' goodwill toward their city-state. These ideas so infuriated some Athenians that in the 430s B.C.E. they sponsored a law allowing citizens to bring charges of impiety against "those who fail to respect divine things or teach theories about the cosmos." Not even Pericles could prevent his philosopher friend from being convicted on this charge and expelled from Athens.

Socrates (469–399 B.C.E.), the most famous philosopher of the Golden Age, became well-known during this troubled time of the 430s, when people were anxious not just about new ways of thinking but also about war with Sparta. Socrates devoted his life to questioning people about their beliefs, but he insisted he was not a Sophist because he took no pay. Above all, he rejected the view that justice in fact amounted to power over others. Insisting that true justice was always better than injustice,

Statuette of the Philosopher Socrates
The controversial Socrates, the most famous philosopher of Athens in the fifth century B.C.E., joked that he had a homely face and a bulging stomach. This small statue is an artist's impression of Socrates; we cannot be sure what the philosopher actually looked like. Socrates was renowned for his irony, and he may have purposely exaggerated his physical unattractiveness to show his disdain for ordinary standards of beauty and his own emphasis on the quality of one's soul as the true measure of one's worth. Compare his body to that of the athletes shown in the vase painting on page 50. (Erich Lessing / Art Resource, NY.)

he created an emphasis on ethics (the study of ideal human values and moral duties) in Greek philosophy.

Socrates lived an eccentric life attracting constant attention. Sporting a stomach that he called "a bit too big to be convenient," he wore the same cheap cloak summer and winter and always went barefoot no matter how cold the weather. His physical stamina — including both his tirelessness as a soldier and his ability to outdrink anyone — was legendary. He lived in poverty and disdained material possessions, though he supported a wife and several children by accepting gifts from wealthy admirers.

Socrates spent his time in conversations all over Athens: participating in symposia, strolling in the agora, or watching young men exercise in a gymnasium. He wrote nothing. Our knowledge of his ideas comes from others' writings, especially those of his famous follower Plato (c. 428–348 B.C.E.). Plato portrays Socrates as a relentless questioner of his fellow citizens, foreign friends, and leading Sophists. Socrates pushed his conversational partners to examine their basic assumptions about life. Giving few answers, Socrates never directly instructed anyone. Instead, he led people to draw conclusions in response to his probing questions and refutations of their unexamined beliefs. Today this procedure is called the **Socratic method**.

Socrates frequently outraged people because his method made them feel ignorant and baffled. His questions forced them to admit that they did not in fact know what they had assumed they knew very well. Even more painful to them was Socrates' fiercely argued view that the way they lived their lives — pursuing success in politics or business or art — was merely an excuse for avoiding the hard work of understanding and developing genuine *aretê* ("excellence"). Socrates insisted that he was ignorant of the definition of excellence and what was best for human beings, but that his wisdom consisted of knowing that he did not know. He vowed he wanted to improve, not undermine, people's ethical beliefs, even though, as a friend put it, a conversation with Socrates made a man feel numb — as if a jellyfish had stung him.

Socrates especially wanted to use reasoning to discover universal, objective standards for individual ethics. He attacked the Sophists for their relativistic claim that conventional standards of right and wrong were merely "the chains that handcuff nature." This view, he protested, equated human happiness with power and "getting more."

Socrates insisted that the only way to achieve true happiness was to behave according to a universal, transcendent standard of just behavior that people could understand rationally. He argued that just behavior and excellence were identical to knowledge, and that true knowledge of justice would inevitably lead people to choose good over evil. They would therefore have truly happy lives, regardless of how rich or poor they were. Since Socrates believed that ethical knowledge was all a person needed for the good life, he argued that no one knowingly behaved unjustly and that behaving justly was always in the individual's interest. It was simply ignorant to believe that the best life was the life of unlimited power to pursue whatever one desired. The most desirable human life was concerned with excellence and guided by reason, not by dreams of personal gain.

Though very different from the Sophists' doctrines, Socrates' ideas proved just as disturbing to the masses because they rejected the Athenians' traditional way of life.

His ridicule of commonly accepted ideas about the importance of wealth and public success angered many people. Unhappiest of all were the fathers whose sons, after listening to Socrates' questions reduce someone to utter bewilderment, came home to try the same technique on their parents, employing rational arguments to criticize their parents' values as old-fashioned and worthless. Men who experienced this reversal of the traditional educational hierarchy — the father was supposed to educate the son — felt that Socrates was undermining the stability of society by making young men question Athenian traditions. Socrates evidently did not teach women, but Plato portrays him as ready to learn from exceptional women, such as Pericles' companion Aspasia.

The worry that Socrates' ideas presented a danger to conventional society inspired Aristophanes to write his comedy *The Clouds* (423 B.C.E.). This play portrays Socrates as a cynical Sophist who, for a fee, offers instruction in Protagoras's technique of making the weaker argument the stronger. When Socrates' school transforms a youth into a public speaker arguing persuasively that a son has the right to beat his parents, his father burns the place down. None of these plot details was real, but people did have a genuine fear that Socrates' radical views on individual morality endangered the city-state's traditional practices.

Just as the Sophists and Socrates antagonized many people with their new ideas, the men who first wrote Greek history created controversy because they took a critical attitude in their descriptions of the past. Herodotus of Halicarnassus (c. 485–425 B.C.E.) and Thucydides of Athens (c. 455–399 B.C.E.) became Greece's most famous historians and established Western civilization's tradition of writing history. The fifth-century B.C.E.'s unprecedented events — a coalition Greek victory over the world's greatest power and then the longest war ever between Greeks — inspired them to create history as a subject based on strenuous research. They explained that they wrote histories because they wanted people to remember the past and to understand why wars had taken place.

Herodotus's long, groundbreaking work *The Histories* ("Inquiries" in Greek) explained the Persian Wars as a clash between the cultures of the East and West. A typically competitive Greek intellectual, Herodotus — who by Roman times had become known as the Father of History — made the justifiable claim that he surpassed all those who had previously recorded the past by taking an in-depth and investigative approach to evidence, examining the culture of non-Greeks as well as Greeks, and expressing explicit and implicit judgments about people's actions. Because Herodotus recognized the necessity (and the delight) of studying other cultures with respect, he pushed his inquiries deep into the past, looking for long-standing cultural differences to help explain the Persian-Greek conflict. He showed that Greeks and non-Greeks were equally capable of good and evil. Unlike poets and playwrights, he focused on human psychology and interactions, not the gods, as the driving forces in history.

Thucydides innovated — and competed with Herodotus — by writing contemporary history and creating the kind of analysis of power that today underlies political science. His *History of the Peloponnesian War* made power politics, not divine intervention, history's primary force. Deeply affected by the war's brutality, Thucydides used his experiences as a politician and failed military commander (he was exiled for losing a

key outpost) to make his narrative vivid and frank in describing human moral failings. His insistence that historians should energetically seek out the most reliable sources and evaluate their testimony with objectivity set a high standard for later writers. Like Herodotus, he challenged tradition by revealing that Greek history included not just glorious achievements but also some share of shameful acts (such as the Athenian punishment of the Melians in the Peloponnesian War — see pages 102–03).

Hippocrates of Cos, a fifth-century B.C.E. contemporary of Thucydides, challenged tradition by grounding medical diagnosis and treatment in clinical observation. His fame continues today in the oath bearing his name (the Hippocratic Oath), which doctors swear at the beginning of their professional careers. Previously, medicine had depended on magic and ritual. People believed that evil spirits caused diseases, and various cults offered healing to patients through divine intervention. Competing to refute these earlier doctors' theories, Hippocrates insisted that only physical factors caused illnesses. He may have been the author of the view, dominant in later medicine, that four humors (fluids) made up the human body: blood, phlegm, black bile, and yellow bile. Health depended on keeping the proper balance among them; being healthy was to be "in good humor." This system for understanding the body corresponded to the division of the inanimate world into four elements: earth, air, fire, and water.

Hippocrates taught that the physician's most important duty was to base his knowledge on careful observation of patients and their response to different treatments. Clinical experience, not abstract theory or religious belief, was the proper foundation for establishing effective cures. By putting his innovative ideas and practices to the test in competition with those of traditional medicine, Hippocrates established the truth of his principle, which later became a cornerstone of scientific medicine.

The Development of Greek Tragedy

Ideas about the problematic relationship between gods and humans inspired Golden Age Athens's most prominent cultural innovation: tragic drama. Plays called tragedies were presented over three days at the major annual festival of the god Dionysus in a contest for playwrights, reflecting the competitive spirit of Greek life. Tragedies presented shocking stories involving fierce conflict among powerful men and women, usually from myth but occasionally from recent history. The plots involved themes relevant to controversial issues in contemporary Athens. Therefore, these plays stimulated their large audiences to consider the dangers to their democracy from ignorance, arrogance, and violence. Golden Age playwrights explored topics ranging from the roots of good and evil to the nature of individual freedom and responsibility in the family and the political community. As with other ancient texts, most Greek tragedies have not survived: only thirty-three still exist of the hundreds that were produced at Athens.

Tax revenues and mandatory contributions by the rich paid for Athenian dramas. The competition in this public art took place at an annual religious festival honoring the god Dionysus, with an official choosing three authors from a pool of applicants. Each of

the finalists presented four plays during the festival: three tragedies in a row (a trilogy), followed by a semicomic play featuring satyrs (mythical half-man, half-animal beings) to end the day on a lighter note. Tragedies were written in verses of solemn language, and many were based on stories about the violent possibilities when gods and humans interacted. The plots often ended with a resolution to the trouble — but only after enormous suffering.

The performances of tragedies in Athens, as in many other cities in Greece, took place during the daytime in an outdoor theater. The theater at Athens was built into the southern slope of the acropolis; it held about fourteen thousand spectators overlooking an open, circular area in front of a slightly raised stage. A tragedy had eighteen cast members, all of whom were men: three actors to play the speaking roles (both male and female characters) and fifteen chorus members. Although the chorus leader sometimes engaged in dialogue with the actors, the chorus primarily performed songs and dances in the circular area in front of the stage, called the orchestra.

A successful tragedy offered a vivid spectacle. The chorus wore elaborate costumes and performed intricate dance routines. The actors, who wore masks, used broad gestures and booming voices to reach the upper tier of seats. A powerful voice was crucial to a tragic actor because words represented the heart of the plays, which featured extensive dialogue and long speeches. Special effects were popular. Actors playing the roles of gods swung from a crane to fly suddenly onto the stage. Actors playing lead roles, called the protagonists ("first competitors"), competed to win the "Best Actor" award. A skilled protagonist was so important to a play's success that actors were assigned by lottery to the competing playwrights so that all three had an equal chance to have a winning cast. Great protagonists became enormously popular.

Playwrights came from the social elite because only men with wealth could afford the amount of time and learning this work demanded. They served as authors, directors, producers, musical composers, choreographers, and sometimes even actors for their own plays. In their lives as citizens, playwrights fulfilled the military and political obligations of Athenian men. The best-known Athenian tragedians — Aeschylus (525–456 B.C.E.), Sophocles (c. 496–406 B.C.E.), and Euripides (c. 485–406 B.C.E.) — all served in the army, and Sophocles was elected to Athens's highest board of officials. Authors of plays competed from a love of honor, not money. The prizes, determined by a board of judges, awarded high prestige but little cash. The competition was regarded as so important that any judge who took a bribe in awarding prizes was put to death.

Tragedy's plots set out the difficulties of telling right from wrong when humans came into conflict and the gods became involved. Even though most tragedies were based on stories that referred to a legendary time before city-states existed, such as the period of the Trojan War, the plays' moral issues were relevant to the society and obligations of citizens in a city-state. The plays suggest that human beings learn only by suffering but that the gods provide justice in the long run. For example, Aeschylus's trilogy *Oresteia* (458 B.C.E.) explains the divine origins of democratic Athens's court system through the story of the gods finally stopping the murderous violence in the family of Orestes, son of King Agamemnon, the Greek leader against Troy.

Greek Vase Painting of the Murder of King Agamemnon

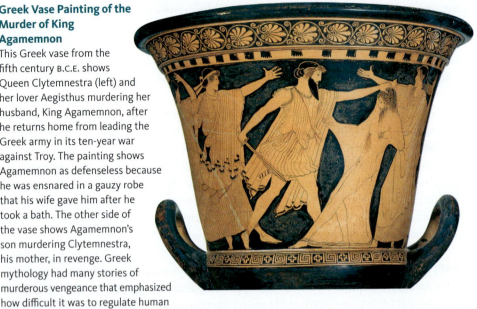

This Greek vase from the fifth century B.C.E. shows Queen Clytemnestra (left) and her lover Aegisthus murdering her husband, King Agamemnon, after he returns home from leading the Greek army in its ten-year war against Troy. The painting shows Agamemnon as defenseless because he was ensnared in a gauzy robe that his wife gave him after he took a bath. The other side of the vase shows Agamemnon's son murdering Clytemnestra, his mother, in revenge. Greek mythology had many stories of murderous vengeance that emphasized how difficult it was to regulate human passions with social norms and laws. (Greek, Early Classical Period, about 460 B.C.E. Place of manufacture: Greece, Attica, Athens. Ceramic, Red Figure. H: 51 cm [20⅕₆ in.]; diameter: 51 cm [20⅕ in.]. Museum of Fine Arts, Boston; William Francis Warden Fund, 63.1246. Photograph © 2013 Museum of Fine Arts, Boston.)

Sophocles' *Antigone* (441 B.C.E.) presents the story of the cursed family of Oedipus of Thebes as a drama of harsh conflict between a courageous woman, Antigone, and the city-state's stern male leader, her uncle Creon. After her brother dies in a failed rebellion, Antigone insists on her family's moral obligation to bury its dead in obedience to divine command. Creon, however, takes harsh action to preserve order and protect community values by prohibiting the burial of his traitorous nephew. In a horrifying story of raging anger and suicide that features one of the most famous heroines of Western literature, Sophocles exposes the right and wrong on each side of the conflict. His play offers no easy resolution of the competing interests of divinely sanctioned moral tradition and the state's political rules.

Ancient sources report that audiences reacted strongly to the messages of these tragedies. For one thing, spectators realized that the plays' central characters were figures who fell into disaster even though they held positions of power and prestige. The characters' reversals of fortune came about not because they were absolute villains but because, as humans, they were susceptible to a lethal mixture of error, ignorance, and **hubris** (violent arrogance that transformed one's competitive spirit into a self-destructive force). The Athenian Empire was at its height when audiences at Athens attended the tragedies written by competing playwrights. Thoughtful playgoers could reflect on the possibility that Athens's current power and prestige, managed as they were by humans, might fall victim to the same kinds of mistakes and conflicts that brought down the heroes and heroines of tragedy. Thus, these publicly funded plays both entertained through their

spectacle and educated through their stories and words. In particular, they reminded male citizens — who governed the city-state in its assembly, council, and courts — that success created complex moral problems that self-righteous arrogance turned into community-wide catastrophes.

The Development of Greek Comedy

Golden Age Athens developed comedy as its second distinctive form of public theater. Like tragedies, comedies were written in verse, performed in Dionysus festivals, and subsidized with public funds and contributions from the rich. Unlike tragedies, comedies commented directly on public policy and criticized current politicians and intellectuals. Their plots and casts presented outrageous fantasies of contemporary life. Comic choruses, which had twenty-four dancing singers, could be colorfully costumed as talking birds or dancing clouds, or an actor could fly on a giant dung beetle to visit the gods.

Authors competed to win the award for the festival's best comedy by creating beautiful poetry, raising laughs with constant jokes and puns, and mocking self-important citizens and political leaders. The humor, delivered in a stream of imaginative profanity, frequently concerned sex and bodily functions. Well-known men of the day were targets for insults as cowards or weaklings. Women characters portrayed as figures of fun and ridicule seem to have been fictional, to protect the dignity of actual female citizens.

Athenian comedies often made fun of political leaders. As the leading politician of radical democracy, Pericles was the subject of fierce criticism in comedy. Comic playwrights ridiculed his policies, his love life, even the shape of his skull ("Old Turnip Head" was a favorite insult). Aristophanes (c. 455–385 b.c.e.), Athens's most famous comic playwright, so fiercely satirized Cleon, the city's most prominent leader early in the Peloponnesian War, that Cleon sued him. A citizen jury ruled in Aristophanes' favor, upholding the Athenian tradition of free speech.

In several of Aristophanes' comedies, the main characters are powerful women who force the men of Athens to change their policy to preserve family life and the city-state. These plays even criticize the assembly's policy during wartime. Most famous is *Lysistrata* (411 b.c.e.), named after the female lead character of the play. In this fantasy, the women of Athens and Sparta unite to force their husbands to end the Peloponnesian War. To make the men agree to a peace treaty, they first seize the acropolis, where Athens's financial reserves are kept, to prevent the men from squandering them further on the war. They then use sarcasm and pitchers of cold water to beat back an attack on their position by the old men who have remained in Athens while the younger men are away at war with Sparta. Above all, the women steel themselves to refuse to sleep with their husbands returning from battle. The effects of their sex strike on the men, portrayed in a series of explicit episodes, finally drive the warriors to make peace.

Lysistrata presents women acting bravely and aggressively against men who seem bent on destroying traditional family life — the men are absent from home for long stretches while on military campaigns and ruin the city-state by prolonging a pointless war. Lysistrata insists that women have the intelligence and judgment to make political

decisions: "I am a woman, and, yes, I have brains. And I'm pretty good in my judgment. My education hasn't been bad: it came from my listening often to the conversations of my father and the elders among the men." Lysistrata's old-fashioned training and good sense allow her to see what needs to be done to protect the community. Like the heroines of tragedy, Lysistrata is a conservative, even a reactionary. She wants to put things back the way they were before the war fractured family life. To do that, she has to act like an impatient revolutionary. That irony sums up the challenge that fifth-century B.C.E. Athens faced in trying to resolve the tension between the dynamic innovation of its Golden Age and the importance of tradition in Greek life.

The remarkable freedom of speech of Athenian comedy allowed frank, even brutal, commentary on current issues and personalities. It cannot be an accident that this energetic, critical drama emerged in Athens at the same time as radical democracy, in the mid-fifth century B.C.E. The feeling that all citizens should have a stake in determining their government's policies evidently fueled a passion for using biting humor to keep the community's leaders from becoming arrogant and aloof.

REVIEW QUESTION   How did new ways of thinking in the Golden Age change traditional ways of life?

The End of Athens's Golden Age, 431–403 B.C.E.

A war between Athens and Sparta (431–404 B.C.E.) ended the Golden Age. This long conflict is called the Peloponnesian War because it matched Sparta's Peloponnese-based alliance against Athens and the Delian League. The war started, according to Thucydides, because the growth of Athenian power alarmed the Spartans, who feared that their interests and allies would fall to the Athenians' relentless drive. Pericles persuaded Athens's assembly to take a hard line when the Spartans demanded that Athens ease restrictions on city-states allied with Sparta. Corinth and Megara, crucial Spartan allies, complained bitterly to Sparta about Athens. Finally, Corinth told Sparta to attack Athens, or else Corinth and its navy would change sides to the Athenian alliance. Sparta's leaders therefore gave Athens an ultimatum — stop mistreating our allies. Pericles convinced the Athenian voters to reject the ultimatum on the grounds that Sparta had refused to settle the dispute through the third-party arbitration process called for by the 446–445 B.C.E. treaty. Pericles' critics claimed he was insisting on war against Sparta to revive his fading popularity. His supporters replied that he was defending Athenian honor and protecting foreign trade, a key to the economy. By 431 B.C.E., these disputes had shattered the peace treaty between Athens and Sparta that Pericles had negotiated fifteen years before.

The Peloponnesian War, 431–404 B.C.E.

Lasting longer than any previous war in Greek history, the Peloponnesian War (Map 3.3) took place above all because Spartan leaders believed they had to fight now to keep the Athenians from using their superior long-distance offensive power — the Delian League's

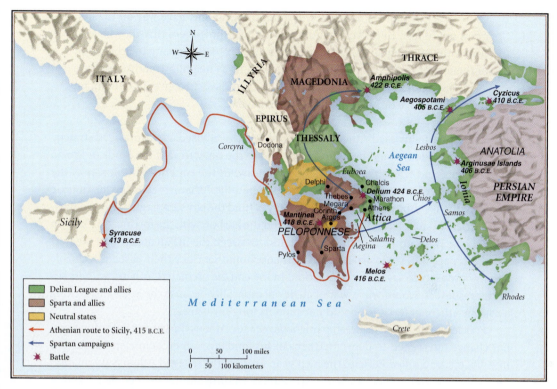

Map 3.3 The Peloponnesian War, 431–404 B.C.E.

For the first ten years, the Peloponnesian War's battles took place largely in mainland Greece. Sparta, whose armies usually avoided distant campaigns, shocked Athens when its general Brasidas led successful attacks against Athenian forces in northeast Greece. Athens stunned the entire Greek world in the war's next phase by launching a huge naval expedition against Spartan allies in far-off Sicily. The last ten years of the war saw the action move to the east, on and along the western coast of Anatolia and its islands, on the boundary of the Persian Empire. Feeling threatened, the Persian king helped the Spartans build a navy there to defeat the famous Athenian fleet. Look at the route of Athens's expedition to Sicily; why do you think the Athenians took this longer voyage, rather than a more direct route?

naval forces — to destroy Sparta's control of their Peloponnesian League. Sparta made the first strike of the war, but the conflict dragged on so long because the Athenian assembly failed to negotiate peace with Sparta when it had the chance and because the Spartans were willing to make a deal with Persia to secure money to build a fleet to win the war.

Dramatic evidence for the anger that fueled the war comes from Thucydides' version of Pericles' stern oration to the Athenian assembly about not yielding to Spartan pressure:

> If we do go to war, have no thought that you went to war over a trivial affair.
> For you this trifling matter is the assurance and the proof of your determination. If you yield to their demands, they will immediately confront you with

some larger demand, since they will think that you only gave way on the first point out of fear. But if you stand firm, you will show them that they have to deal with you as equals. . . . When our equals, without agreeing to arbitration of the matter under dispute, make claims on us as neighbors and state those claims as commands, it would be no better than slavery to give in to them, no matter how large or how small the claim may be.

When Sparta invaded Athenian territory, Pericles advised a two-pronged strategy to win what he saw would be a long war: (1) use the navy to raid the lands of Sparta and its allies, and (2) avoid large infantry battles with the superior land forces of the Spartans, even when the enemy hoplites plundered the Athenian countryside outside the city. Athens's citizens could retreat to safety behind the city's impregnable walls, massive barriers of stone that encircled the city and the harbor, with the fortification known as the Long Walls protecting the land corridor between the urban center and the port (Map 3.2, page 83). He insisted that Athenians should sacrifice their vast and valuable country property to save their population. In the end, he predicted, Athens, with its superior resources, would win a war of attrition, especially because the Spartans, lacking a base in Athenian territory, could not support long invasions.

Pericles' strategy and leadership might have made Athens the winner in the long run, but chance intervened to deprive Athens of his guidance: an epidemic struck Athens in 430 b.c.e. and killed Pericles the next year. This plague ravaged Athens's population for four years, killing thousands as it spread like wildfire among the people packed in behind the walls to avoid Spartan attacks. Despite their losses and their fears that the gods had sent the disease to punish them, the Athenians fought on. Over time, however, they abandoned the disciplined strategy that Pericles' prudent plan had required. The generals elected after his death, especially Cleon, pursued a much more aggressive strategy. At first this succeeded, especially when a group of Spartan hoplites surrendered after being blockaded by Cleon's forces at Pylos in 425 b.c.e. Their giving up shocked the Greek world and led Sparta to ask for a truce, but the Athenian assembly refused, believing their army could now crush their enemy. When the daring Spartan general Brasidas captured Athens's possessions in northern Greece in 424 and 423 b.c.e., however, he turned the tide of war in the other direction by crippling the Athenian supply of timber and precious metals from this crucial region. When Brasidas and Cleon were both killed in 422 b.c.e., Sparta and Athens made peace in 421 b.c.e. out of mutual exhaustion.

Athens's most innovative and confident new general, Alcibiades, soon persuaded the assembly to reject the peace and to attack Spartan allies in 418 b.c.e. In 416–415 b.c.e., the Athenians and their allies overpowered the tiny and strategically meaningless Aegean island of Melos because it refused to abandon its allegiance to Sparta. Thucydides in his history of the Peloponnesian War dramatically represents Athenian messengers telling the Melians they had to be conquered to show that Athens permitted no defiance to its dominance. Following their victory the Athenians executed the Melian men, sold the

women and children into slavery, and colonized the island. (See "Taking Measure," below.)

The turning point in the war came soon thereafter when, in 415 B.C.E., Alcibiades persuaded the Athenian assembly to launch the greatest and most expensive campaign in Greek history. The expedition of 415 B.C.E. was directed against Sparta's allies in Sicily, far to the west. Alcibiades had dazzled his fellow citizens with the dream of conquering that rich island and especially its greatest city, Syracuse. Alcibiades' political rivals had him removed from his command, however, and the other generals blundered into catastrophic defeat in Sicily in 413 B.C.E. (Map 3.3, page 101). The victorious Syracusans destroyed the allied invasion fleet and packed the survivors like sardines into quarries under the blazing sun, with no toilets and only half a pint of drinking water and a handful of food a day.

On the advice of Alcibiades, who had deserted to their side in anger at having lost his command, the Spartans in 413 B.C.E. seized a permanent base of operations in the Athenian countryside for year-round raids, now that Athens was too weak to drive them out. Constant Spartan attacks devastated Athenian agriculture, and twenty thousand slave workers crippled production in Athens's silver mines by deserting to the enemy. The democratic assembly became so upset over these losses that in 411 B.C.E. it voted itself out of existence in favor of an emergency government run by the wealthier citizens. When an oligarchic group illegally took charge, however, the citizens restored the radical democracy and kept fighting for another seven years. They even recalled Alcibiades, seeking better generalship, but the end came when Persia gave the Spartans money to

Taking Measure **Military Forces of Athens and Sparta at the Beginning of the Peloponnesian War (431 B.C.E.)**

This chart compares the military forces of the Athenian side and the Spartan side when the Peloponnesian War broke out in 431 B.C.E. The numbers come from ancient sources, above all the Athenian general and historian Thucydides, who fought in the war. The bar graph starkly reveals the different characteristics of the competing forces: Athens relied on its navy of triremes and its archers (the fifth-century B.C.E. equivalent of artillery and snipers), while Sparta was superior in the forces needed for pitched land battles — hoplites (heavily armed infantry) and cavalry (shock troops used to disrupt opposing phalanxes). These differences dictated the differing strategies and tactics of the two sides: Athens in guerrilla fashion launching surprise raids from the sea, and Sparta trying to force decisive confrontations on the battlefield.

(From Pamela Bradley, *Ancient Greece: Using Evidence*, 1990, 229.)

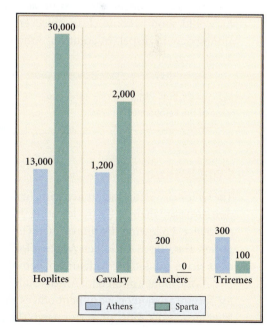

build a navy. The Persian king thought it served his interests to have Athens defeated. Aggressive Spartan naval action forced Athens to surrender in 404 B.C.E. After twenty-seven years of near-continuous war, the Athenians were at their enemy's mercy.

Athens Defeated: Tyranny and Civil War, 404–403 B.C.E.

Following Athens's surrender, the Spartans installed a regime of antidemocratic Athenians known as the Thirty Tyrants who collaborated with the victors. The collaborators were members of the social elite; some, including the violent leader Critias, infamous for his criticism of religion, had been well-known pupils of the Sophists. Brutally suppressing democratic opposition, these oligarchs embarked on an eight-month period of murder and plunder in 404–403 B.C.E. The speechwriter Lysias, for example, reported that Spartan henchmen murdered his brother in order to steal the family's valuables, even ripping the gold rings from the ears of his brother's wife. Outraged at the violence and greed of the Thirty Tyrants, citizens who wanted to restore democracy banded together outside the city to fight to regain control of Athens. A feud between Sparta's two most important leaders paralyzed the Spartans, and they failed to send help to the Athenian collaborators. The democratic rebels defeated the forces of the Thirty Tyrants in a series of bloody street battles in Athens.

Democracy was thereby restored, but the citizens still seethed with anger and unrest. To settle the internal strife that threatened to tear Athens apart, the newly restored democratic assembly voted the first known amnesty in Western history, a truce agreement forbidding any official charges or recriminations from crimes committed in 404–403 B.C.E. Agreeing not to pursue grievances in court was the price of peace. As would soon become clear, however, some Athenians harbored grudges that no amnesty could dispel. In addition, Athens's financial and military strength had been shattered. At the end of the Golden Age, Athenians worried about how to remake their lives and restore the reputation that their city-state's innovative accomplishments had produced.

REVIEW QUESTION What factors determined the course of the Peloponnesian War?

Conclusion

The Greek city-states that united early in the fifth century B.C.E. to resist the Persian Empire surprised themselves by defeating the invaders and preserving their political independence. Following the unexpected Greek victory, Athens competed with Sparta for power. The Athenian Golden Age that followed was based on empire and trade, and the city's riches funded the widening of democracy and famous cultural accomplishments.

As the money poured in, Athens built glorious and expensive temples, legislated pay for service in many government offices to strengthen democracy, and assembled the Mediterranean's most powerful navy. The poor men who rowed the ships demanded

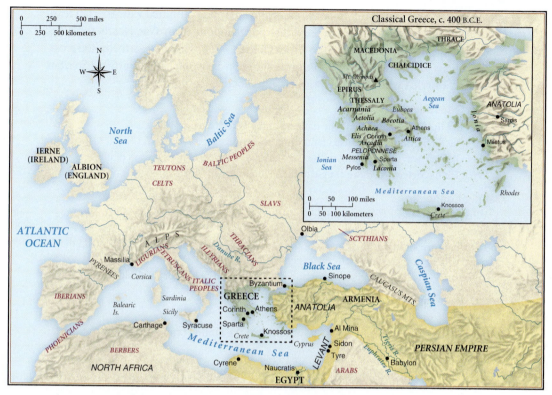

Mapping the West Greece, Europe, and the Mediterranean, 400 B.C.E.

No single power controlled the Mediterranean region at the end of the fifth century B.C.E. In the west, the Phoenician city of Carthage and the Greek cities on Sicily and in southern Italy were rivals for the riches to be won by trade. In the east, the Spartans, confident after their recent victory over Athens in the Peloponnesian War, tried to become an international power outside the mainland for the first time in their history by sending campaigns into Anatolia. This aggressive action aroused stiff opposition from the Persians because it was a threat to their westernmost imperial provinces. There was to be no peace and quiet in the Mediterranean even after the twenty-seven years of the Peloponnesian War.

greater democracy; such demands led to political and legal reforms that guaranteed fairer treatment for all. Pericles became the most famous politician of the Golden Age by leading the drive for radical democracy.

Religious practice and women's lives reflected the strong grip of tradition on everyday life, but dramatic innovations in education and philosophy created social tension. The Sophists' moral relativism disturbed tradition-minded people, as did Socrates' definition of virtue, which questioned ordinary people's love of wealth and success. Art and architecture broke out of old forms, promoting an impression of balanced motion rather than stability, while medicine gained a more scientific basis. Tragedy and comedy developed at Athens as competitive public theater commenting on contemporary social and political issues.

The Athenians' harsh treatment of allies and enemies combined with Spartan fears about Athenian power to bring on the disastrous Peloponnesian War. Nearly three decades of battle brought the stars of the Greek Golden Age crashing to earth: by 400 B.C.E. the Athenians found themselves in the same situation as in 500 B.C.E., fearful of Spartan power and worried whether the world's first democracy could survive.

Review Questions

1. How did the Greeks overcome the dangers of the Persian invasions?
2. What factors produced political change in fifth-century B.C.E. Athens?
3. How did new ways of thinking in the Golden Age change traditional ways of life?
4. What factors determined the course of the Peloponnesian War?

Making Connections

1. What were the most significant differences between Archaic Age Greece and Golden Age Greece?
2. For what sorts of things did Greeks of the Golden Age spend public funds? Why did they believe these things were worth the expense?
3. What price, in all senses, did Athens and the rest of Greece pay for the Golden Age? Was it worth it?

- For practice quizzes and other study tools, visit the **Online Study Guide** at bedfordstmartins.com/huntconcise.

- For primary-source material from this period, see *Sources of the Making of the West,* Fourth Edition.

- For Web sites, images, and documents related to topics in this chapter, visit *Make History* at bedfordstmartins.com/huntconcise.

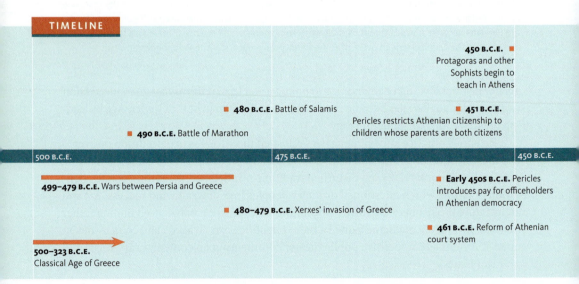

TIMELINE

450 B.C.E. ■
Protagoras and other
Sophists begin to
teach in Athens

■ **480 B.C.E.** Battle of Salamis   ■ **451 B.C.E.**
Pericles restricts Athenian citizenship to
■ **490 B.C.E.** Battle of Marathon   children whose parents are both citizens

| 500 B.C.E. | 475 B.C.E. | 450 B.C.E. |

499–479 B.C.E. Wars between Persia and Greece

■ **Early 450s B.C.E.** Pericles
introduces pay for officeholders
in Athenian democracy

■ **480–479 B.C.E.** Xerxes' invasion of Greece

■ **461 B.C.E.** Reform of Athenian
court system

500–323 B.C.E.
Classical Age of Greece

Suggested References

The Greek city-states, especially Athens, reached the height of their political, economic, and military power in the fifth century B.C.E. following the defeat of the Persian invasion of mainland Greece; scholars continue to investigate how the frequent wars of this period influenced not only the democracy of Athens but also the famous dramatists and philosophers of this so-called Golden Age.

Blundell, Sue. *Women in Ancient Greece*. 1995.

Briant, Pierre. *From Cyrus to Alexander: History of the Persian Empire*. Trans. Peter Daniels. 2006.

Camp, John M. *The Archaeology of Athens*. 2004.

*Dillon, John, and Tania Gergel. *The Greek Sophists*. 2003.

*Grene, David, and Richmond Lattimore, eds. *The Complete Greek Tragedies*. 1992.

Herman, Gabriel. *Morality and Behavior in Democratic Athens*. 2006.

*Herodotus. *The Histories*. Trans. Aubrey de Sélincourt. Revised by John Marincola. Rev. ed. 2003.

Mitchell-Boyask, Robin. *Plague and the Athenian Imagination: Drama, History, and the Cult of Asclepius*. 2008.

Parker, Robert. *Athenian Religion: A History*. 1996.

Parthenon: http://www.perseus.tufts.edu/cgi-bin/vor?x=16&y=13&lookup=parthenon

Patterson, Cynthia B. *The Family in Greek History*. 1998.

*Strassler, Robert B., ed. *The Landmark Thucydides. A Comprehensive Guide to the Peloponnesian War*. 1996.

Strauss, Barry. *The Battle of Salamis: The Naval Encounter That Saved Greece — and Western Civilization*. 2005.

Thorley, John. *Athenian Democracy*. 2004.

Wees, Han van, ed. *War and Violence in Ancient Greece*. 2000.

Primary source.

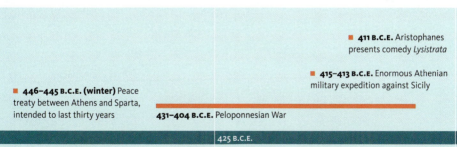

■ **411 B.C.E.** Aristophanes presents comedy *Lysistrata*

■ **415–413 B.C.E.** Enormous Athenian military expedition against Sicily

■ **446–445 B.C.E. (winter)** Peace treaty between Athens and Sparta, intended to last thirty years

431–404 B.C.E. Peloponnesian War

425 B.C.E.   400 B.C.E.

■ **441 B.C.E.** Sophocles presents tragedy *Antigone*

■ **420S B.C.E.** Herodotus finishes *Histories*

■ **404–403 B.C.E.** Rule of Thirty Tyrants at Athens

■ **403 B.C.E.** Restoration of democracy in Athens

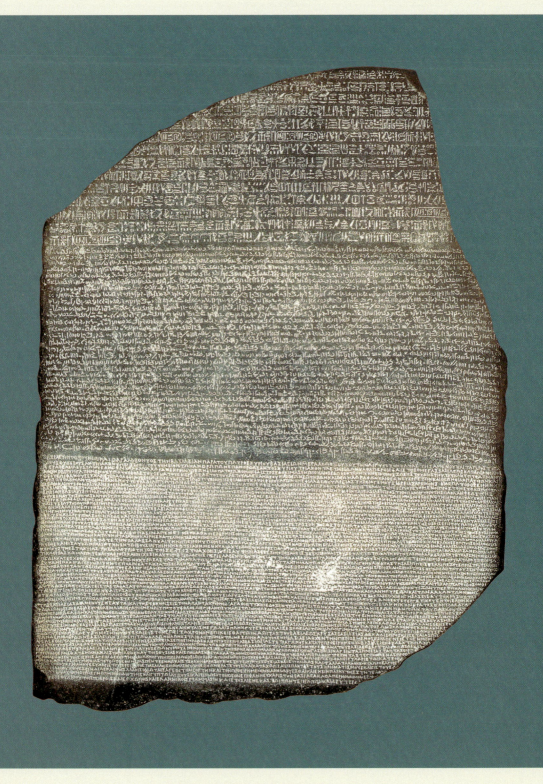

4

From the Classical to the Hellenistic World

ABOUT 255 B.C.E., AN EGYPTIAN CAMEL TRADER far from home sent a letter of complaint to his Greek employer back in Egypt:

> You know that when you left me in Syria with Krotos I followed all your instructions concerning the camels and behaved blamelessly towards you. But Krotos has ignored your orders to pay me my salary; I've received nothing despite asking him for my money over and over. He just tells me to go away. I waited a long time for you to come, but when I no longer had life's necessities and couldn't get help anywhere, I had to run away . . . to keep from starving to death. . . . I am desperate summer and winter. . . . They have treated me like dirt because I am not a Greek. I therefore beg you, please, command them to pay me so that I won't go hungry just because I don't know how to speak Greek.

The Rosetta Stone

Dug out of the wall of a fort in 1799 by a soldier in Napoleon's army near Rosetta, in the Nile River delta, this Hellenistic inscription in two different languages and three different forms of writing unlocked the lost secrets of how to read Egyptian hieroglyphs. The bands of text repeat the same message (priests praising King Ptolemy V in 196 B.C.E.) in hieroglyphs, demotic (a cursive form of Egyptian invented around 600 B.C.E.), and Greek. Bilingual texts were necessary to reach the mixed population of Hellenistic Egypt. Scholars deciphered the hieroglyphs by comparing them to the Greek version. They started with the hieroglyphs surrounded by an oval, which they guessed were royal names. (Art Resource, NY.)

The trader's plea for help from a foreigner who held power in his homeland reflects the changes in the eastern Mediterranean world during the Hellenistic Age (323–30 B.C.E.). The movement of Greeks into the Near East increased the cultural interaction between the Greek and the Near Eastern worlds and set a new course for Western civilization in politics, art, philosophy, science, and religion. Above all, Alexander the Great (356–323 B.C.E.) changed the course of history by conquering the Persian Empire,

leading an army of Greeks and Macedonians to the border of India, taking Near Eastern-ers into his army and imperial administration, and planting colonies of Greeks as far east as Afghanistan. His amazing expedition shocked the world and spurred great change in Western civilization by combining Near Eastern and Greek traditions as never before.

Politics changed in the Greek world when Alexander's successors (who had been commanders in his army) created new kingdoms that became the dominant powers of the Hellenistic Age. The existing Greek city-states retained local rule but lost their in-dependence in international affairs. The Hellenistic kings imported Greeks to fill royal offices, man their armies, and run businesses, generating tension with their non-Greek subjects. Egyptians, Syrians, or Mesopotamians who wanted to rise in Hellenistic society had to win the support of these Greeks and learn their language.

The Near East's local cultures interacted with the Greek overlords' culture to spawn a multicultural synthesis. Although Hellenistic royal society always remained hierar-chical, its kings and queens did finance innovations in art, philosophy, religion, and science that combined Near Eastern and Greek traditions. The Hellenistic kingdoms fell in the second and first centuries B.C.E. when the Romans overthrew them one by one. But the cultural interaction between diverse peoples and the emergence of new ideas — unintended consequences of Alexander's military campaigns — would strongly influence Roman civilization.

CHAPTER FOCUS   What were the major political and cultural changes in the Hellenistic Age?

Classical Greece after the Peloponnesian War, 400–350 B.C.E.

The Greek city-states restored their economic and political stability after the Pelopon-nesian War (431–404 B.C.E.), but daily life remained hard for many. The war's aftermath dramatically affected Greek philosophy. At Athens, citizens who blamed Socrates for inspiring the Thirty Tyrants' crimes brought him to trial; the jury condemned him to death. His execution helped persuade the philosophers Plato and Aristotle to detest de-mocracy and develop new ways of thinking about right versus wrong and how human beings should live.

The Greek city-states' continuing competition for power in the fourth century B.C.E. drained their resources. Sparta's attempt to dominate central Greece and western Ana-tolia by collaborating with the Persians provoked violent resistance from Thebes and Athens. By the 350s B.C.E., the Greek city-states had so weakened themselves that they were unable to prevent the Macedonian kingdom from taking control of Greece.

Athens's Recovery after the Peloponnesian War

The devastation of Athens's economy in the Peloponnesian War and overcrowding of refugees from the country in the wartime city produced social conflict. Life became difficult for middle-class women whose male relatives had been killed. With no man to

Silver Coins of Athens

The city-state of ancient Athens owned rich silver mines that financed its silver coinage, famous around the Greek world for purity and reliability. This coin from the fifth century B.C.E. was a tetra-drachm ("four drachmas"), which was the amount that a worker or rower in the Athenian navy earned in four days. The images show Athena, the city-state's main goddess, and an owl with an olive branch, also symbols of Athena. The style of the images was kept old-fashioned and mostly unchanging so as not to harm the trust that people in foreign lands had in accepting Athenian coins in trade and commerce as a form of international currency. (© C. M. Dixon / Ancient Art & Architecture Collection, Ltd.)

provide for them and their children, many war widows had to work outside the home. The only jobs open to them — such as wet-nursing, weaving, or laboring in vineyards — were low-paying.

Resourceful Athenians found ways to profit from women's skills. The family of one of Socrates' friends, for example, fell into poverty when several widowed sisters, nieces, and female cousins moved in. The friend complained to Socrates that he was too poor to support his new family of fourteen plus their slaves. Socrates replied that the women knew how to make clothing, so they should sell it. This plan succeeded financially, but the women then complained that Socrates' friend was the household's only member who ate without working. Socrates advised the man to reply that the women should think of him as sheep did a guard dog — he earned his share of the food by keeping the wolves away.

Athens's postwar economy recovered as international trade was revived once its Long Walls, which protected the transportation corridor from the city to the port, were rebuilt and mining for silver to produce the city's coinage resumed. Greek businesses producing manufactured goods were small and usually family-run; the largest known was a shield-making company with 120 slave workers. Some changes occurred in occupations formerly defined by gender. For example, men began working alongside women in cloth production when the first commercial weaving shops outside the home sprang up. Some women made careers in the arts, especially painting and music, which men had traditionally dominated.

Daily life remained difficult for working people. Most workers earned barely enough to feed and clothe their families. They ate two meals a day, with bread baked from barley as their main food; only rich people could afford wheat bread. A family bought bread from small bakery stands, often run by women, or made it at home, with the wife directing the slaves

Athens's Long Walls as Rebuilt after the Peloponnesian War

in grinding the grain, shaping the dough, and baking it in a clay oven heated by charcoal. People topped their bread with greens, beans, onions, garlic, olives, fruit, and cheese. The few households rich enough to afford meat boiled or grilled it over a fire. Everyone of all ages drank wine, diluted with water, with every meal.

The Execution of Socrates, 399 B.C.E.

Socrates, Athens's most famous philosopher in the Golden Age, fell victim to the bitterness many Athenians felt about the rule of the Thirty Tyrants following the Peloponnesian War. Some prominent Athenians hated Socrates because his follower Critias had been one of the Thirty Tyrants' most violent leaders. These citizens charged Socrates with impiety, claiming he rejected the city-state's gods, introduced new divinities, and lured young men away from Athenian moral traditions. Speaking to a jury of 501 male cititzens, Socrates refused to beg for sympathy, as was customary in trials, and repeated his dedication to goading his fellow citizens into examining how to live justly. He vowed to remain their stinging gadfly.

When the jurors narrowly voted to convict Socrates, Athenian law required them to decide between the penalty proposed by the prosecutors and that proposed by the defendant. The prosecutors proposed death. Socrates said he deserved a reward rather than punishment, but his friends made him propose a fine as his penalty. The jury chose death, requiring him to drink a poison concocted from powdered hemlock. Socrates accepted his sentence calmly, saying that "no evil can befall a good man either in life or in death." Ancient sources report that many Athenians soon came to regret Socrates' punishment as a tragic mistake and a severe blow to their reputation.

The Philosophy of Plato

Socrates' death made his follower and Greece's most famous philosopher, **Plato** (429–348 B.C.E.), hate democracy. Plato started out as a political consultant supporting philosopher-tyrants as the best form of government, but he gave up hope that political action could stop violence and greed. Instead, he turned to talking and writing about philosophy as the guide to life and established a school, the Academy, in Athens around 386 B.C.E. The Academy was an informal association of people who studied philosophy, mathematics, and theoretical astronomy under the leader's guidance. It attracted intellectuals to Athens for the next nine hundred years, and Plato's ideas about the nature of reality, ethics, and politics have remained central to philosophy and political science to this day.

Plato's intellectual interests covered astronomy, mathematics, political philosophy, ethics, and **metaphysics** (ideas about the ultimate nature of reality beyond the reach of the human senses). Plato wrote dialogues, to provoke readers into thoughtful reflection, not to prescribe a set of beliefs. Nevertheless, he always maintained one essential idea based on his view of reality: ultimate moral qualities are universal, unchanging, and absolute, not relative.

Plato's dialogues explore his theory that justice, goodness, beauty, and equality exist on their own in a higher realm beyond the daily world. He used the word *Forms* (or *Ideas*) to describe the abstract, invariable, and ultimate realities of such ethical qualities. According to Plato, the Forms are the only genuine reality. All things that humans perceive with their senses on earth are only dim and imperfect copies of these metaphysical, ultimate realities.

Plato believed that humans possess immortal souls distinct from their bodies; this idea established the concept of **dualism**, a separation between soul (or mind) and body. Plato further explained that the human soul possesses preexisting knowledge put there by a god. Humans' present, impure existence is only a temporary stage in cosmic existence because, while the body does not last, the soul is immortal. Plato argued that people must seek perfect order and purity in their souls by using rational thought to control irrational and therefore harmful desires. People who yield to irrational desires fail to consider the future of their body and soul. The desire to drink too much alcohol, for example, is irrational because the binge drinker fails to consider the painful hangover that will follow.

Plato presented his most famous ideas on politics and justice in his dialogue *The Republic*. This work, whose Greek title means "system of government," discusses the nature of justice and the reasons people should never commit injustice. Democracy, Plato wrote, does not produce justice because people cannot rise above their own self-interest to knowledge of the transcendent reality of universal truth. Justice can come only under the rule of an enlightened oligarchy or monarchy.

Plato's *Republic* describes an ideal society with a hierarchy of three classes distinguished by their ability to grasp the truth of Forms. Plato did not think humans could actually create the ideal society as described in *The Republic,* but he did believe that imagining it was an important way to help people learn to live justly. The highest class in his envisioned hierarchy is the rulers, or "guardians," who must be educated in mathematics, astronomy, and metaphysics. Next come the "auxiliaries," who defend the community. "Producers" make up the bottom class; they grow food and make objects for everyone. According to Plato's *Republic,* women can be guardians because they possess the same virtues and abilities as men, except that the average woman has less physical strength than the average man. To minimize distraction, guardians are to have neither private property nor nuclear families. Male and female guardians are to live in houses shared in common, eat in the same dining halls, and exercise in the same gymnasia. They are to have sex with various partners so that the best women can mate with the best men to produce the best children. The children are to be raised together by special caretakers, not their parents. Guardians who achieve the highest level of knowledge can rule as philosopher-kings.

Aristotle, Scientist and Philosopher

After studying with Plato, **Aristotle** (384–322 B.C.E.) founded his own school, the **Lyceum** in Athens. He taught his own life-guiding philosophy, emphasizing practical reasoning. Like Plato, he thought Athenian democracy was a bad system because it did not restrict

decision making to the most educated and moderate citizens. His vast writings made him one of the world's most influential thinkers.

Aristotle's achievements included scientific investigation of the natural world, development of systems of logical argument, and practical ethics based on experience. He believed that the search for knowledge brought the good life and genuine happiness. His teachings covered biology, botany, zoology, medicine, anatomy, psychology, meteorology, physics, chemistry, mathematics, music, metaphysics, rhetoric, literary criticism, political science, and ethics. By creating a system of logic for precise argumentation, Aristotle also established grounds for determining whether an argument was logically valid. Aristotle's thought process stressed rationality and common sense, not metaphysics. He rejected Plato's theory of Forms and insisted that understanding depended on observation. He coupled detailed investigation with careful reasoning in biology, botany, and zoology. He collected information on more than five hundred different kinds of animals, including insects. His recognition that whales and dolphins are mammals was not rediscovered for another two thousand years.

Some of Aristotle's observations justified inequalities that were characteristic of his time. He argued that some people were slaves by nature because their souls lacked the rationality to be fully human. Mistaken biological information led Aristotle to evaluate females as incomplete males, judging them as inferior. At the same time, he believed that human communities could be successful and happy only if women and men both contributed.

In ethics, Aristotle emphasized the need to develop practical habits of just behavior in order to achieve happiness. Ethics, he taught, cannot work if they consist only of abstract reasons for just behavior. People should achieve self-control by training their minds to overcome instincts and passions. Self-control meant finding "the mean," or balance, between denying and indulging physical pleasures.

Greek Political Disunity

In the same period that Plato and Aristotle were developing their philosophies as guides to life, the Greek city-states were in a constant state of war. Sparta, Thebes, and Athens competed to dominate Greece in this period. None succeeded. Their endless fighting weakened their morale and their finances.

Thebes, Athens, Corinth, and Argos formed an anti-Spartan coalition, but the Spartans checkmated the alliance by negotiating with the Persian king. Betraying their traditional claim to defend Greek freedom, the Spartans acknowledged the Persian ruler's right to control the Greek city-states of Anatolia — in return for permission to wage war in Greece without Persian interference. This agreement of 386 B.C.E., called the King's Peace, sold out the Greeks of Anatolia, returning them to submission to the Persian Empire. Athens rebuilt its navy, again becoming the leader of a naval alliance. In the 370s B.C.E., Thebes attacked Sparta and freed many helots to weaken the enemy. The Theban success alarmed the Athenians, who allied with their hated enemies, the Spartans. The allied armies confronted the Thebans in the battle of Mantinea in the Peloponnese in

362 B.C.E. Thebes won the battle but lost the war when its best general was killed and no capable replacement could be found. This stalemate left the Greek city-states disunified and weak. By the 350s B.C.E., no Greek city-state controlled anything except its own territory. By failing to cooperate with one another, the Greeks opened the way for the rise of a new power — the kingdom of Macedonia.

> **REVIEW QUESTION**   How did daily life, philosophy, and the political situation change in Greece during the period 400–350 B.C.E.?

The Rise of Macedonia, 359–323 B.C.E.

The kingdom of Macedonia's rise to superpower status counts as one of the greatest surprises in ancient military and political history. Located north of central Greece, Macedonia rocketed from being a minor state to ruling the Greek and Near Eastern worlds. Two aggressive and charismatic Macedonian kings produced this transformation: Philip II (r. 359–336 B.C.E.) and his son **Alexander the Great** (r. 336–323 B.C.E.). Their conquests ended the Greek Classical Age and set in motion the Hellenistic Age's cultural changes.

Macedonian Power and Philip II, 359–336 B.C.E.

The Macedonian kings governed by maintaining the support of the elite, who ranked as their social equals and controlled many followers. Men spent their time training for war, hunting, and drinking heavily. The king had to excel in these activities to show that he deserved to lead the state. Queens and royal mothers received respect because they came from powerful families or the ruling houses of neighboring regions.

Macedonian kings thought of themselves as ethnically Greek; they spoke Greek as well as they did their native Macedonian. Macedonians as a whole, however, looked down on the Greeks as too soft to survive life in their northern land. The Greeks regarded Macedonians as barbarians.

In 359 B.C.E., the Illyrians, neighbors to the west, slaughtered Macedonia's king and four thousand troops. Philip, the new king, restored the troops' confidence by teaching them to use thrusting spears sixteen feet long. He trained them to maneuver in battle while maintaining formation. Deploying cavalry as a strike force, Philip routed the Illyrians. During the 340s B.C.E., Philip persuaded or forced most of northern and central Greece into alliance with him. Seeking glory for Greece and fearing the instability his strengthened army would create in his kingdom if the soldiers had nothing to do, he decided to lead a united Macedonian and Greek army to conquer the Persian Empire. He justified attacking Persia as revenge for its invasion of Greece 150 years earlier.

Athens and Thebes rallied a coalition of southern Greek city-states to combat Philip, but in 338 B.C.E. the Macedonian king and his Greek allies crushed the coalition's forces at the battle of Chaeronea in Greece. The defeated city-states retained their internal freedom, but Philip forced them to join his alliance. The battle of Chaeronea marked a

turning point in Greek history: never again would the city-states of Greece be independent agents in international affairs.

The Rule of Alexander the Great, 336–323 B.C.E.

Philip was murdered in 336 B.C.E. Some scholars think his son Alexander and his son's mother, Olympias, arranged the killing to seize power for the twenty-year-old Alexander, but the murderer was a bodyguard probably motivated by personal anger at the king. Alexander secured his rule by eliminating rivals and defeating Macedonia's enemies to the west and north with swift attacks. He forced the southern Greeks, who had defected from the alliance at the news of Philip's death, to rejoin. To demonstrate the cost of disloyalty, in 335 B.C.E. Alexander destroyed Thebes for having rebelled.

In 334 B.C.E., Alexander launched the most astonishing military campaign in ancient history, leading a Macedonian and Greek army against the Persian Empire to fulfill Philip's dream of avenging Greece. Alexander's conquest of all the lands from Turkey to Egypt to Uzbekistan while still in his twenties led later peoples to call him Alexander the Great. Alexander inspired his troops by leading charges against the enemy, riding his warhorse Bucephalas ("oxhead"). Everyone saw him speeding ahead in his plumed helmet, polished armor, and vividly colored cloak. He was so intent on conquest that he rejected advice to delay the war until he had fathered an heir. He gave away nearly all of his land to strengthen ties with his army officers. Alexander aimed at becoming more famous even than Achilles; he always kept a copy of Homer's *Iliad* under his pillow — along with a dagger.

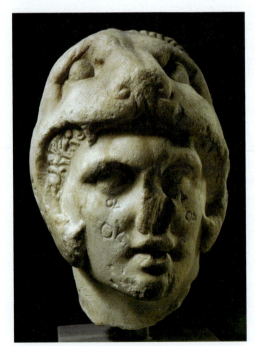

Building on Near Eastern traditions of siege technology and Philip's innovations, Alexander developed even better military technology. When Tyre, a heavily fortified city on an island off the eastern Mediterranean coast, refused to surrender to him in 332 B.C.E., he built a massive stone pier as a platform for

Alexander the Great
This marble portrait of Alexander (a copy of a bronze original) has him wearing a lion's head as a helmet to recall the hero Herakles (Hercules), whose myth said he killed the fiercest beast in Greece and wore its head as proof. Alexander gazes into the distance; he commanded that his portraits show him with this visionary expression. Why do you think he wanted the world to see him with these attributes? (National Archeological Museum, Athens / Dagli Orti Collection / The Art Archive at Art Resource, NY.)

artillery towers, armored battering rams, and catapults flinging boulders to breach Tyre's walls. Knowing that Alexander could overcome their fortifications made enemies much readier to negotiate a deal.

In his conquest of Egypt and the Persian heartland, Alexander revealed his strategy for ruling a vast empire: keep an area's traditional administrative system in place while founding cities of Greeks and Macedonians in the conquered territory. In Egypt, he established his first new city, naming it Alexandria after himself. In Persia, he proclaimed himself the king of Asia and relied on Persian administrators.

Alexander led his army past the Persian heartland farther east into territory hardly known to the Greeks (Map 4.1). He aimed to outdo the heroes of legend by marching to the end of the world. Shrinking his army to reduce the need for supplies, he marched northeast into what is today Afghanistan and Uzbekistan. Unable to subdue the local guerrilla forces, Alexander settled for an alliance sealed by his marriage to the Bactrian princess Roxane.

Alexander then headed east into India. Seventy days of marching through monsoon rains extinguished his soldiers' fire for conquest. In the spring of 326 B.C.E., they mutinied, forcing Alexander to turn back. The return journey through southeastern

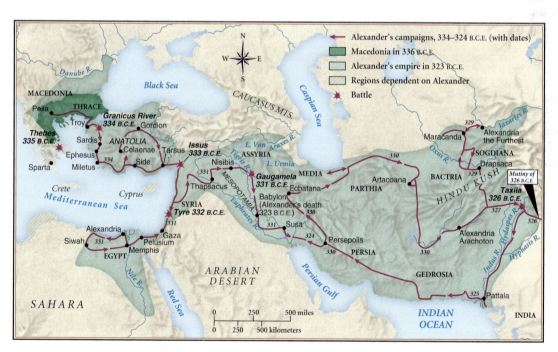

Map 4.1　Conquests of Alexander the Great, r. 336–323 B.C.E.
From the time Alexander led his army against Persia in 334 B.C.E. until his death in 323 B.C.E., he was continually fighting military campaigns. His charismatic and fearless generalship, combined with effective intelligence gathering about his targets, generated an unbroken string of victories and made him a legend. His founding of garrison cities and preservation of local governments kept his conquests largely stable during his lifetime.

Iran's deserts cost many casualties from hunger and thirst; the survivors finally reached safety in the Persian heartland in 324 B.C.E. Alexander immediately began planning an invasion of the Arabian peninsula and, after that, of North Africa. He also announced that he wished to receive the honors due a god. Most Greek city-states obeyed by sending religious delegations to him. Personal motives best explain Alexander's announcement: he had come to believe he was truly the son of Zeus and that his superhuman accomplishments demonstrated that he must himself be a god.

Alexander died from a fever in 323 B.C.E. Unfortunately for the stability of his immense conquests, he had no heir ready to take over his rule. Roxane gave birth to their son only after Alexander's death. The story goes that, when at Alexander's deathbed his commanders asked him to whom he left his kingdom, he replied, "To the most powerful."

Scholars disagree on almost everything about Alexander. Was he a bloodthirsty monster obsessed with war, or a romantic visionary intent on creating a multiethnic world open to all cultures? The ancient sources suggest that Alexander had interlinked goals reflecting his restless and ruthless nature: to conquer and administer the known world, to outdo the exploits and glory of legendary heroes, and to earn the status no living human had ever achieved—that of a god on earth.

Alexander's explorations benefited scientific fields from geography to botany because he took along knowledgeable writers to collect and catalog new knowledge. He had vast quantities of scientific observations dispatched to his old tutor Aristotle. Alexander's new cities promoted trade between Greece and the Near East. Most of all, his career brought the two cultures into closer contact than ever before. This contact represented his career's most enduring impact.

REVIEW QUESTION   What were the accomplishments of Alexander the Great, and what were their effects both for the ancient world and for later Western civilization?

The Hellenistic Kingdoms, 323–30 B.C.E.

New kingdoms arose when Alexander's empire fragmented after his death. The time from Alexander's death in 323 B.C.E. to the death of Cleopatra VII, the last Macedonian queen of Egypt, in 30 B.C.E. is the Hellenistic Age. The term **Hellenistic** ("Greek-like") conveys the most significant characteristic of this period: the emergence in the eastern Mediterranean world of a mixture of Near Eastern and Greek traditions generating innovations in politics, literature, art, philosophy, and religion. War stirred up this cultural mixing, and tension persisted between conquerors and subjects.

The Hellenistic period reintroduced monarchy into Greek culture for the first time in a thousand years. Commanders from Alexander's army created the kingdoms by seizing portions of his empire and proclaiming themselves kings. This process of state formation took more than fifty years of war. The self-proclaimed kings—called Alexander's successors—had to transform their families into dynasties and accumulate enough power to force the Greek city-states to obey them. Eventually, wars with the Romans ended the Hellenistic kingdoms.

Creating New Kingdoms

Alexander's successors divided his conquests among themselves. Antigonus (c. 382–301 B.C.E.) took over Anatolia, the Near East, Macedonia, and Greece; Seleucus (c. 358–281 B.C.E.) seized Babylonia and the East as far as India; and Ptolemy (c. 367–282 B.C.E.) took over Egypt. These successors had to create their own form of monarchy based on military power and personal prestige because they were self-proclaimed rulers with no connection to Alexander's royal line.

The kingdoms' territories were never completely stable because the Hellenistic monarchs never stopped competing (Map 4.2). Conflicts repeatedly arose over border areas. The Ptolemies and the Seleucids, for example, fought to control the eastern Mediterranean coast, just like the Egyptians and Hittites. The wars between the major kingdoms created openings for smaller kingdoms to establish themselves. The most famous of these smaller kingdoms was that of the Attalids in western Anatolia, with the wealthy city of Pergamum as its capital. In Bactria in Central Asia, the Greeks — originally colonists settled by Alexander — broke off from the Seleucid kingdom in the mid-third century B.C.E. to found their own regional kingdom, which flourished for a time from the trade in luxury goods between India and China and the Mediterranean world.

The Hellenistic kingdoms imposed foreign rule by Macedonian kings and queens on indigenous populations. The kings incorporated local traditions into their rule to build

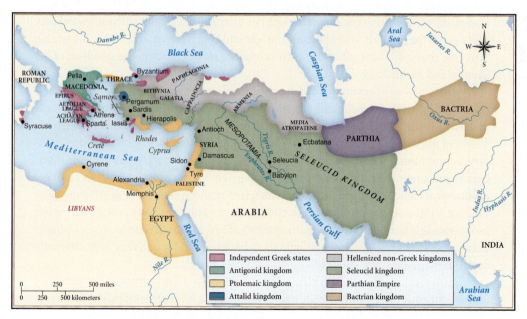

Map 4.2 Hellenistic Kingdoms, 240 B.C.E.

Monarchy became the dominant political system in the areas of Alexander's conquests. By about eighty years after his death, the three major kingdoms established by his successors had settled their boundaries, after the Seleucids gave up their easternmost territories to an Indian king and the Attalids carved out their kingdom in western Anatolia.

Royal Silver Coin of Bactria

Bactria, in central Asia (today part of Afghanistan, Pakistan, and Tajikistan), had been a province of the Persian Empire and then of the empire of Alexander the Great. After the fragmentation of Alexander's empire in the century after his death, Greeks established what scholars call Indo-Greek kingdoms there. This coin of King Demetrius I

shows him wearing an elephant headdress, a symbol of his ambitions to conquer India. The other side shows the Greek mythological hero Herakles, who was said to have been the first Greek to visit this part of the world.

legitimacy. The Ptolemaic royal family, for example, observed the Egyptian royal tradition of brother-sister marriage. Royal power was the ultimate source of control over the kingdoms' subjects, in keeping with the Near Eastern monarchical tradition that Hellenistic kings adopted. Seleucus justified his rule on what he claimed as a universal truth of monarchy: "It is not the customs of the Persians and other people that I impose upon you, but the law which is common to everyone, that what is decreed by the king is always just." The survival of these dynasties depended on their ability to create strong armies, effective administrations, and close ties to urban elites. A letter from a Greek city summed up the situation while praising the Seleucid king Antiochus I (c. 324–261 B.C.E.): "His rule depends above all on his own excellence [aretê], and on the goodwill of his friends, and on his forces."

Professional soldiers manned Hellenistic royal armies and navies. To develop their military might, the Seleucid and Ptolemaic kings encouraged immigration by Greeks and Macedonians, who received land grants in return for military service. When this source of manpower gave out, the kings had to employ more local men as troops. Military competition put tremendous financial pressure on the kings to pay growing numbers of mercenaries and to purchase expensive new military technology. To compete effectively, a Hellenistic king had to provide giant artillery, such as catapults capable of flinging a 170-pound projectile up to two hundred yards. His navy cost a fortune because warships were now huge, requiring crews of several hundred men. War elephants became popular after Alexander brought them back from India, and they were extremely costly to maintain.

Hellenistic kings needed effective administrations to collect revenues. Initially, they recruited mostly Greek and Macedonian immigrants to fill high-level posts. The Seleucids and the Ptolemies also employed non-Greeks for middle- and low-level positions, where officials had to be able to deal with the subject populations and speak their languages. Local men who wanted a government job bettered their chances if they could read and write Greek in addition to their native language. Bilingualism qualified them to fill positions communicating the orders of the highest-ranking officials, all Greeks

and Macedonians, to local farmers, builders, and crafts producers. Non-Greeks who had successful government careers were rarely admitted to royal society because Greeks and Macedonians saw themselves as too superior to mix with locals. Greeks and non-Greeks therefore tended to live in separate communities.

Administrators' principal responsibilities were to maintain order and to direct the kingdoms' tax systems. The Ptolemaic administration used methods of central planning and control inherited from earlier Egyptian history. Its officials continued to administer royal monopolies, such as that on vegetable oil, to maximize the king's revenue. They decided how much land farmers could sow in oil-bearing plants, supervised production and distribution of the oil, and set prices for every stage of the oil business. The king, through his officials, also often entered into partnerships with private investors to produce more revenue.

Cities were the Hellenistic kingdoms' economic and social hubs. Many Greeks and Macedonians lived in new cities founded by Alexander and the Hellenistic kings in Egypt and the Near East, and they also immigrated to existing cities there. Hellenistic kings promoted this urban immigration by adorning their new cities with the features of classical Greek city-states, such as gymnasia and theaters. Although these cities often retained the city-state's political institutions, such as councils and assemblies for citizen men, the need to follow royal policy limited their freedom; they made no independent decisions on foreign policy. The cities taxed their populations to send money demanded by the king.

The crucial element in the Hellenistic kingdoms' political and social structure was the system of mutual rewards by which the kings and their leading urban subjects became partners in government and public finance. Wealthy people in the cities were responsible for collecting taxes from the people in the surrounding countryside as well as from the city dwellers and sending the money on to the royal treasury. The kings honored and flattered the cities' Greek and Macedonian social elites because they needed their cooperation to ensure a steady flow of tax revenues. When writing to a city's council, a king would issue polite requests, but the recipients knew he was giving commands.

This system thus continued the Greek tradition of requiring the wealthy elite to contribute financially to the common good. Cooperative cities received gifts from the king to pay for expensive public works like theaters and temples or for reconstruction after natural disasters such as earthquakes. Wealthy men and women in turn helped keep the general population peaceful by subsidizing teachers and doctors, financing public works, and providing donations and loans to ensure a reliable supply of grain to feed the city's residents.

To keep their vast kingdoms peaceful and profitable, the kings established relationships with well-to-do non-Greeks living in the old cities of Anatolia and the Near East. In addition, non-Greeks and non-Macedonians from eastern regions began moving westward to the new Hellenistic Greek cities in increasing numbers. Jews in particular moved from their ancestral homeland to Anatolia, Greece, and Egypt. The Jewish community eventually became an influential minority in Egyptian Alexandria, the most important Hellenistic city. In Egypt, as the Rosetta stone shows, the king also had to

build good relationships with the priests who controlled the temples of the traditional Egyptian gods because the temples owned large tracts of rich land worked by tenant farmers.

The Layers of Hellenistic Society

The royal family and the king's friends had the highest social rank. The Greek and Macedonian elites of the major cities came next. Then came indigenous urban elites, leaders of large minority urban populations, and local lords in rural regions. Merchants, artisans, and laborers made up the free population's bottom layer. Slaves remained without any social status.

The kingdoms' growth increased the demand for slave labor throughout the eastern Mediterranean; a market on the island of Delos sold up to ten thousand slaves a day. The fortunate ones were purchased as servants for the royal court or elite households and lived physically comfortable lives, so long as they pleased their owners. The luckless ones labored, and often died, in the mines. Enslaved children could be taken far from home to work. For example, a sales contract from 259 B.C.E. records that a Greek bought a seven-year-old girl named Gemstone to work in an Egyptian textile factory. Originally from an eastern Mediterranean town, she had previously labored as the slave of a Greek mercenary soldier employed by a Jewish cavalry commander in the Transjordan region.

Poor people — the majority of the population — mostly labored in agriculture, the foundation of the Hellenistic kingdoms' economies. There were some large cities, above all Alexandria in Egypt, but most people lived in country villages. Many of the poor were employed on the royal family's huge estates, but free peasants still worked their own small fields in addition to laboring for wealthy landowners. Perhaps as many as 80 percent of all adult men and women had to work the land to produce enough food to sustain the population. In cities, poor women and men worked as small merchants, peddlers, and artisans, producing and selling goods such as tools, pottery, clothing, and furniture. Men could sign on as deckhands on the merchant ships that sailed the Mediterranean Sea and Indian Ocean.

Many country people in the Seleucid and Ptolemaic kingdoms existed in a state of dependency between free and slave. The peoples, as they were called, were tenants who farmed the estates belonging to the king. Although they could not be sold like slaves, they were not allowed to move away or abandon their tenancies. They owed a large quota of produce to the king, and this compulsory rent gave these tenant farmers little chance to escape poverty.

Hellenistic queens had great social status and commanded enormous riches and honors. They exercised power as the representatives of distinguished families, as the mothers of a line of royal descendants, and as patrons of artists, thinkers, and even entire cities. Later Ptolemaic queens essentially co-ruled with their husbands. Queens ruled on their own when no male heir existed. For example, Arsinoe II (c. 316–270 B.C.E.),

the daughter of Ptolemy I, first married the Macedonian successor Lysimachus, who gave her four towns as her personal domain. After his death she married her brother Ptolemy II of Egypt and was his partner in making policy. Public praise for a queen reflected traditional Greek values for women. A city decree from about 165 B.C.E. honored Queen Apollonis of Pergamum by praising her piety toward the gods, her reverence toward her parents, her distinguished conduct toward her husband, and her harmonious relations with her "beautiful children born in wedlock."

Some queens paid special attention to the condition of women. About 195 B.C.E., for example, the Seleucid queen Laodice gave a ten-year endowment to a city to provide dowries for needy girls. Laodice's gift shows that she recognized the importance to women of controlling property, which was the surest guarantee of respect.

Most women remained under the control of men. A common saying by men was "Who can judge better than a father what is to his daughter's interest?" Most of the time, elite women continued to be separated from men outside their families, while poor women worked in public. Greeks continued to abandon infants they did not want to raise — girls more often than boys — but other populations, such as the Egyptians and the Jews, did not practice infant exposure. Exposure differed from infanticide in that the parents expected someone to find the child and rear it, usually as a slave. A third-century B.C.E. comic poet overstated the case by saying, "A son, one always raises even if one is poor; a daughter, one exposes, even if one is rich." Daughters of wealthy parents were not usually abandoned, but scholars have estimated that up to 10 percent of other infant girls were.

A woman of exceptional wealth could enter public life by making donations or loans to her city and in return be rewarded with an official post in local government. In Egypt, women of all classes acquired greater say in married life as the marriage contract evolved from an agreement between the bride's parents and the groom to one in which the bride made her own arrangements with the groom.

Rich people showed increasing concern for the welfare of the less fortunate during the Hellenistic period. They were following the lead of the royal families, who emphasized philanthropy to build a reputation for generosity that would support their legitimacy in ruling. Sometimes wealthy citizens funded a foundation to distribute free grain to eliminate food shortages, and they also funded schools for children in various Hellenistic cities, the first public schools in the Greek world. In some places, girls as well as boys could attend school. Many cities also began sponsoring doctors to improve medical care: patients still had to pay, but at least they could count on finding a doctor.

The donors funding these services were repaid by the respect and honor they earned from their fellow citizens. When an earthquake devastated Rhodes, many cities joined kings and queens in sending donations to help the residents recover. In return, they showered honors on their benefactors by appointing them to prestigious municipal offices and erecting inscriptions expressing the city's gratitude. In this system, the masses' welfare depended more and more on the generosity of the rich. Lacking democracy, the poor had no political power to demand support.

The End of the Hellenistic Kingdoms

All the Hellenistic kingdoms eventually lost their riches and power, mostly through internal disunity in their ruling families. Thus weakened, they could not prevent takeovers by the Romans, who over time intervened forcefully in conflicts among kingdoms and Greek city-states in the eastern Mediterranean.

The Roman interventions caused wars. Rome first established dominance over the Antigonid kingdom by the middle of the second century B.C.E. Next, the Seleucid kingdom fell to the Romans in 64 B.C.E. The Ptolemaic kingdom in Egypt survived a bit longer; by the 50s B.C.E., however, its royal family had split into warring factions, and the resulting weakness forced the rivals for the throne to seek Roman support. The end came when the famous queen Cleopatra VII, the last Macedonian to rule Egypt, chose the losing side in the civil war between Mark Antony and the future emperor Augustus in the late first century B.C.E. An invading Roman army ended Ptolemaic rule in 30 B.C.E. Rome then became the heir to all the Hellenistic kingdoms (see Mapping the West, page 134).

> **REVIEW QUESTION**   How did the political and social organization of the new Hellenistic kingdoms compare with that of the earlier Greek city-states?

Hellenistic Culture

Hellenistic culture reflected three principal influences: (1) the overwhelming impact of royal wealth, (2) increased emphasis on private life and emotion, and (3) greater interaction of diverse peoples. The kings drove developments in literature, art, science, and philosophy by deciding which scholars and artists to put on the royal payroll. The obligation of authors and artists to the kings meant that they did not have freedom to criticize public policy; their works mostly concentrated on everyday life and personal feelings.

Cultural interaction between Near Eastern and Greek traditions occurred most prominently in language and religion. These developments deeply influenced the Romans as they took over the Hellenistic world. The Roman poet Horace (65–8 B.C.E.) described the effect of Hellenistic culture on his own Roman culture by saying that "captive Greece captured its fierce victor."

The Arts under Royal Support

Hellenistic kings became the supporters of scholarship and the arts on a vast scale, competing with one another to lure the best scholars and artists to their capitals with lavish salaries. They funded intellectuals and artists because they wanted to boost their reputations by having these famous people produce books, poems, sculptures, and other prestigious creations at their courts.

The Ptolemies turned Alexandria into the Mediterranean's leading arts and sciences center, establishing the world's first scholarly research institute and a massive library.

The librarians were instructed to collect all the books in the world. The library grew to hold half a million scrolls, an enormous number for the time. Linked to it was the building in which the hired research scholars dined together and produced encyclopedias of knowledge such as *The Wonders of the World* and *On the Rivers of Europe.* We still use the name of the research institute's building, the Museum ("place of the Muses," the Greek goddesses of learning and the arts), to designate institutions preserving knowledge.

The writers and artists paid by Hellenistic kings had to please their paymasters. The poet Theocritus (c. 300–260 B.C.E.) spelled out the deal underlying royal support in a poem flattering King Ptolemy II: "The spokesmen of the Muses [that is, poets] celebrate Ptolemy in return for his benefactions." Poets such as Theocritus avoided political topics and exploited the social gap that existed between the intellectual elite — to which the kings belonged — and the uneducated masses. They filled their new poetry with erudite references to make it difficult to understand and therefore exclusive. Only people with a deep literary education could appreciate the mythological allusions that studded these authors' elaborate poems.

No Hellenistic women poets seem to have enjoyed royal financial support; rather, they created their art independently. They excelled in writing **epigrams**, short poems in the style of those originally used on tombstones to remember the dead. Highly literary poems by women from diverse regions of the Hellenistic world still survive. Many epigrams were about women, from courtesans to respectable matrons, and the writer's personal feelings. No other Hellenistic literature better conveys the depth of human emotion than the epigrams written by women poets.

Hellenistic comedies also emphasized stories about emotions and stayed away from politics. Comic playwrights presented plays concerning the troubles of fictional lovers. These comedies became enormously popular because, like modern situation comedies (sitcoms), they offered humorous views of daily life. Papyrus discoveries have restored previously lost comedies of Menander (c. 342–289 B.C.E.), the most famous Hellenistic comic poet, noted for his

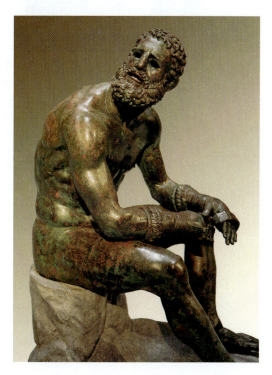

Seated Boxer

This Hellenistic-era sculpture in bronze shows an obviously tired boxer after a bout. He is still wearing the hard-edged leather gloves that made Greek and Roman boxing so brutal and dangerous. His pose, showing him looking up at the sky in weariness, or perhaps listening to his trainer or a fan, is characteristic of the tendency of Hellenistic artists to portray people in realistic rather than idealized ways. (Museo Nazionale Romano delle Terme / akg-images / Jürgen Raible.)

Praxiteles' Statue of Aphrodite

The fourth-century B.C.E. Athenian sculptor Praxiteles excelled at carving stone to resemble flesh and producing perfect surfaces, which he had a painter make lively with color. His masterpiece was the Aphrodite made for the city-state of Cnidos in southwestern Anatolia; the original is lost, but many Hellenistic-era copies like this one were made. Praxiteles was the first to show the goddess of love nude, and rumor said his lover was the model. Given that there was a long tradition of nude male statues, why do you think it took until the Hellenistic period for Greek sculptors to produce female nudes? (Nimatallah / Art Resource, NY.)

skill in depicting human personality. Hellenistic tragedy could take a multicultural approach: Ezechiel, a Jew living in Alexandria, wrote *Exodus,* a tragedy in Greek about Moses leading the Hebrews out of captivity in Egypt.

Hellenistic sculptors and painters featured emotions in their works as well. Classical artists had given their subjects' faces an idealized serenity, but now Hellenistic sculptures depicted intense personal feelings. Athletes, for example, could be shown realistically as exhausted and scarred by the exertion required to compete at a high level.

The increasing diversity of subjects that emerged in Hellenistic art presumably represented a trend approved by kings, queens, and the elites. Sculpture best reveals this new preference for depicting people who had never before appeared in art: heartbreaking victims of war, drunkards, battered athletes, wrinkled old people. The female nude became common. A statue of Aphrodite by Praxiteles, which portrayed the goddess completely nude for the first time, became renowned as a religious object and also a tourist attraction in the city of Cnidos, which had commissioned it. The king of Bithynia offered to pay off the citizens' entire public debt if he could have the work of art. They refused.

Philosophy for a New Age

New philosophies arose in the Hellenistic period, all asking the same question: "What is the best way to live?" They recommended different paths to the same answer: individuals must achieve inner personal tranquillity to achieve freedom from the disruptive effects of outside forces, especially chance. It is easy to see why these philosophies

had appeal: outside forces — the Hellenistic kings — had robbed the Greek city-states of their independence in foreign policy, and their citizens' fates ultimately rested in the hands of unpredictable monarchs. More than ever, human life seemed out of individuals' control. It therefore was appealing to look to philosophy for personal solutions to the unsettling new conditions of Hellenistic life.

Hellenistic philosophers concentrated on **materialism**, the doctrine that only things made of matter truly exist. This idea corresponded to Aristotle's teaching that only things identified through logic or observation exist. Hellenistic philosophy was divided into three areas: (1) logic, the process for discovering truth; (2) physics, the fundamental truth about the nature of existence; and (3) ethics, how humans should achieve happiness and well-being through logic and physics.

One of the two most significant new Hellenistic philosophies was **Epicureanism**, named for its founder, Epicurus (341–271 B.C.E.). He settled his followers around 307 B.C.E. in an Athenian house surrounded by greenery — hence, his school came to be known as the Garden. Epicurus broke tradition by admitting women and slaves to study philosophy in his group.

Epicurus's key idea was that people should be free of worry about death. Because all matter consists of tiny, invisible, and irreducible pieces called atoms in random movement, he said, death is nothing more than the painless separating of the body's atoms. Moreover, all human knowledge must be empirical, that is, derived from experience and perception. Phenomena that most people perceive as the work of the gods, such as thunder, do not result from divine intervention in the world. The gods live far away in perfect tranquillity, ignoring human affairs. People therefore have nothing to fear from the gods.

Epicurus believed people should pursue true pleasure, meaning an "absence of disturbance." Thus, people should live free from the turmoil, passions, and desires of ordinary existence. A sober life spent with friends and separated from the cares of the common world provided Epicurean pleasure. Epicureanism thus challenged the Greek tradition of political participation by citizens.

The other important new Hellenistic philosophy, **Stoicism**, prohibited an isolationist life. Its name derives from the Painted Stoa in Athens, where Stoic philosophers discussed their ideas. Stoics believed that fate controls people's lives but that individuals should still make the pursuit of excellence their goal. Stoic excellence meant putting oneself in harmony with the divine, rational force of universal nature by cultivating good sense, justice, courage, and temperance. These doctrines applied to women as well as men. Some Stoics advocated equal citizenship for women, unisex clothing, and abolition of marriage and families.

The Stoic belief in fate raised the question of whether humans have free will. Stoic philosophers concluded that purposeful human actions do have significance even if fate rules. Nature, itself good, does not prevent evil from occurring, because excellence would otherwise have no meaning. What matters in life is striving for good. A person should therefore take action against evil by, for example, participating in politics. To be a Stoic also meant to shun desire and anger while calmly enduring pain and sorrow, an attitude

that yields the modern meaning of the word *stoic*. Through endurance and self-control, Stoics gained inner tranquillity. They did not fear death because they believed that people live the same life over and over again. This repetition occurred because the world is periodically destroyed by fire and then re-formed.

Several other Hellenistic philosophies competed with Epicureanism and Stoicism. Philosophers called Skeptics aimed for a state of personal calm, as did Epicureans, but from a completely different basis. They believed that secure knowledge about anything was impossible because the human senses perceive contradictory information about the world. All people can do, the Skeptics insisted, is depend on perceptions and appearances while suspending judgment about their ultimate reality. These ideas had been influenced by the Indian ascetics (who practiced self-denial as part of their spiritual discipline) encountered on Alexander the Great's expedition.

Cynics rejected every convention of ordinary life, especially wealth and material comfort. The name *Cynic,* which means "like a dog," came from the notion that dogs had no shame. Cynics believed that humans should aim for complete self-sufficiency and that whatever was natural was good and could be done without shame before anyone. Therefore, such things as bowel movements and sex acts in public were acceptable. Above all, Cynics rejected life's comforts. The most famous early Cynic, Diogenes (d. 323 B.C.E.), wore borrowed clothing and slept in a storage jar. Also notorious was Hipparchia, a female Cynic of the late fourth century B.C.E. who once defeated a philosophical opponent named Theodorus the Atheist with the following remarks: "That which would not be considered wrong if done by Theodorus would also not be considered wrong if done by Hipparchia. Now if Theodorus punches himself, he does no wrong. Therefore, if Hipparchia punches Theodorus, she does no wrong."

Philosophy in the Hellenistic Age reached a wider audience than ever before. Although the working poor were too busy to attend philosophers' lectures, many well-off members of society studied philosophy. Greek settlers took their interest in philosophy

Gemstone Showing Diogenes in His Jar

This engraved gem from the Roman period shows the famous philosopher Diogenes (c. 412–c. 324 B.C.E.) living in a storage jar and talking with a man holding a scroll. Diogenes was born at Sinope on the Black Sea but was exiled in a dispute over monetary fraud. He then lived at Athens and Corinth, becoming infamous as the founder of Cynic ("doglike") philosophy. To defy social convention, he lived as shamelessly as a dog, hence the name given to his philosophical views and the dog usually shown beside him in art. What kind of person do you think would have wanted this gemstone as a piece of jewelry? (Inv. No. I 977, Diogenes in his pithos, in dispute with a seated man. Roman Republican ringstone, 100 B.C.E.–30 B.C.E. Thorvaldsens Museum.)

with them to even the most remote Hellenistic cities. Archaeologists excavating a city in Afghanistan — thousands of miles from Greece — uncovered a Greek philosophical text and inscriptions of moral advice recording Apollo's oracle at Delphi as their source. Sadly, this site, called Ai-Khanoum, was devastated in the twentieth century during the Soviet war in Afghanistan.

Scientific Innovation

Historians have called the Hellenistic period the golden age of ancient science. Scientific innovation flourished because Alexander's expedition had encouraged curiosity and increased knowledge about the world's extent and diversity, royal families supported scientists financially, and the concentration of scientists in Alexandria promoted the exchange of ideas.

The greatest advances in scientific knowledge came in geometry and mathematics. Euclid, who taught at Alexandria around 300 B.C.E., made revolutionary discoveries in analyzing two- and three-dimensional space. The utility of Euclidean geometry still endures. Archimedes of Syracuse (287–212 B.C.E.) calculated the approximate value of pi and invented a way to manipulate very large numbers. He also invented hydrostatics (the science of the equilibrium of fluid systems) and mechanical devices, such as a screw for lifting water to a higher elevation and cranes to disable enemy warships. Archimedes' shout of delight when he solved a problem while soaking in his bathtub has been immortalized in the expression *Eureka!* meaning "I have found it!"

Advances in Hellenistic mathematics energized other fields that required complex computation. Early in the third century B.C.E., Aristarchus was the first to propose the correct model of the solar system: the earth revolving around the sun. Later astronomers rejected Aristarchus's heliocentric model in favor of the traditional geocentric one (with the earth at the center) because conclusions drawn from his calculations of the earth's orbit failed to correspond to the observed positions of celestial objects. Aristarchus had assumed a circular orbit instead of an elliptical one, an assumption not corrected until much later. Eratosthenes (c. 275–194 B.C.E.) pioneered mathematical geography. He calculated the circumference of the earth with astonishing accuracy by measuring the length of the shadows cast by widely separated but identically tall structures. Together, these researchers gave Western scientific thought an important start toward its fundamental procedure of reconciling theory with observed data through measurement and experimentation.

Hellenistic science and medicine made gains even though no technology existed to measure very small amounts of time or matter. The science of the age was as quantitative as it could be given these limitations. Ctesibius invented pneumatics by creating machines operated by air pressure. He also built a working water pump, an organ powered by water, and the first accurate water clock. Hero of Alexandria also built a rotating sphere powered by steam. As in most of Hellenistic science, these inventions did not lead to usable applications in daily life. The scientists and their royal patrons were more interested in new theoretical discoveries than in practical results, and the

technology did not exist to produce the pipes, fittings, and screws needed to build metal machines.

Hellenistic science produced impressive military technology, such as more powerful catapults and huge siege towers on wheels. The most famous large-scale application of technology for nonmilitary purposes was the construction of the Pharos, a lighthouse three hundred feet tall, for the harbor at Alexandria. Using polished metal mirrors to reflect the light from a large bonfire, the Pharos shone many miles out over the sea. Awe-struck sailors called it one of the wonders of the world.

Medicine also benefited from the Hellenistic quest for new knowledge. Increased contact between Greeks and people of the Near East made Mesopotamian and Egyptian medical knowledge better known in the West and promoted research on what made people ill. Hellenistic medical researchers discovered the value of measuring the pulse in diagnosing illness and studied anatomy by dissecting human corpses. It was rumored that they also dissected condemned criminals while they were still alive; they had access to these subjects because the king authorized the research. Some of the terms then invented are still used, such as *diastolic* and *systolic* for blood pressure. Other Hellenistic advances in anatomy included the discovery of the nerves and nervous system.

Cultural and Religious Transformations

Cultural transformations also shaped Hellenistic society. Wealthy non-Greeks increasingly adopted a Greek lifestyle to conform to the Hellenistic world's social hierarchy. Greek became the common language for international commerce and cultural exchange. The widespread use of the simplified form of the Greek language called **Koine** ("shared" or "common") reflected the emergence of an international culture based on Greek models; this was the reason the Egyptian camel trader stranded in Syria (recall the story at the beginning of this chapter) was at a disadvantage because he did not speak Greek. The most striking evidence of this cultural development comes from Afghanistan. There, King Ashoka (r. c. 268–232 B.C.E.), who ruled most of the Indian subcontinent, used Greek as one of the languages in his public inscriptions. These texts announced his plan to teach his subjects Buddhist self-control, such as abstinence from eating meat. Local languages did not disappear in the Hellenistic kingdoms, however. In one region of Anatolia, for example, people spoke twenty-two different languages.

Religious diversity also grew. Traditional Greek cults (as described in Chapter 3) remained popular, but new cults, especially those deifying kings, reflected changing political and social conditions. Preexisting cults that previously had only local significance gained adherents all over the Hellenistic world. In many cases, Greek cults and local cults from the eastern Mediterranean influenced each other. Sometimes, local cults and Greek cults existed side by side and even overlapped. Some Egyptian villagers, for example, continued worshipping their traditional crocodile god and mummifying their dead but also paid honor to Greek deities. As polytheists (believers in multiple gods), people could worship in both old and new cults.

Greek-Style Buddha

The style of this statue of the founder of Buddhism, who expounded his doctrines in India, shows the mingling of eastern and western art. The Buddha's appearance, gaze, and posture stem from Indian artistic traditions, while the flowing folds of his garment recall Greek traditions. Compare the garment that Socrates is wearing on page 93. This combination of styles is called Gandhara, after the region in northwestern India where it began. What do you think are the possible motives for combining different artistic traditions? (Borromeo / Art Resource, NY.)

New cults incorporated a concern for the relationship between the individual and what seemed the arbitrary power of divinities such as Tychê ("chance" or "luck"). Since advances in astronomy had furthered knowledge about the movement of the universe's celestial bodies, religion now had to address the disconnect between "heavenly uniformity" and the "shapeless chaos of earthly life." One increasingly popular approach to bridging that gap was to rely on astrology, which was based on the movement of the stars and planets, thought of as divinities. Another common choice was to worship Tychê in the hope of securing good luck in life.

The most revolutionary approach in seeking protection from Tychê's unpredictable tricks was to pray for salvation from deified kings, who expressed their divine power in **ruler cults**. Various populations established these cults in recognition of great benefactions. The Athenians, for example, deified the Macedonian Antigonus and his son Demetrius as savior gods in 307 B.C.E., when they liberated the city and bestowed magnificent gifts on it. Like most ruler cults, this one expressed the population's spontaneous gratitude to the rulers in hopes of flattering them and obtaining additional favors (working in conjunction with the rulers' own wish to have their power respected). Many cities in the Ptolemaic and Seleucid kingdoms set up ruler cults for their kings and queens. An inscription put up by Egyptian priests in 238 B.C.E. concretely described the qualities appropriate for a divine king and queen:

> King Ptolemy III and Queen Berenice, his sister and wife, the Benefactor Gods, . . . have provided good government . . . and [after a drought] sacrificed a large amount of their revenues for the salvation of the population, and by importing grain . . . they saved the inhabitants of Egypt.

The Hellenistic monarchs' tremendous power and wealth gave them the status of gods to the ordinary people who depended on their generosity and protection. The idea that a human being could be a god, present on earth to save people from evils, was now firmly established and would prove influential later in Roman imperial religion and Christianity.

Healing divinities offered another form of protection to anxious individuals. The cult of the god Asclepius, who offered cures for illness and injury at his many shrines, grew in popularity during the Hellenistic period. Suppliants seeking Asclepius's help would sleep in special locations at his shrines to await dreams in which he prescribed healing treatments. These prescriptions emphasized diet and exercise, but numerous inscriptions commissioned by grateful patients also testified to miraculous cures and surgery performed while the sufferer slept. The following example is typical:

> Ambrosia of Athens was blind in one eye. . . . She . . . ridiculed some of the cures [described in inscriptions in the sanctuary] as being incredible and impossible. . . . But when she went to sleep, she saw a vision; she thought the god was standing next to her. . . . He split open the diseased eye and poured in a medicine. When day came she left cured.

People's faith in divine healing gave them hope that they could overcome the constant danger of illness, which appeared to strike at random; there was no knowledge of germs as causing infections.

Mystery cults promised initiates secret knowledge for salvation. The cults of the Greek god Dionysus and the Egyptian goddess Isis attracted many people. Isis became the most popular female divinity in the Mediterranean because her powers protected her worshippers in all aspects of their lives. Her cult involved rituals and festivals mixing Egyptian religion with Greek elements. Disciples of Isis strove to achieve personal purification and the goddess's aid in overcoming the demonic power of Tychê. This popularity of an Egyptian deity among Greeks (and, later, Romans) is clear evidence of the cultural interaction of the Hellenistic world.

Cultural interaction between Greeks and Jews influenced Judaism during the Hellenistic period. King Ptolemy II made the Hebrew Bible accessible to a wide audience by having his Alexandrian scholars produce a Greek translation — the Septuagint. Many Jews, especially those in the large Jewish communities that had grown up in Hellenistic cities outside their homeland, began to speak Greek and adopt Greek culture. These Greek-style Jews mixed Jewish and Greek customs, while retaining Judaism's rituals and rules and not worshipping Greek gods.

Internal conflict among Jews erupted in second-century B.C.E. Palestine over how much Greek tradition was acceptable for traditional Jews. The Seleucid king Antiochus IV (r. 175–164 B.C.E.) intervened to support Greek-style Jews in Jerusalem, who had taken over the high priesthood that ruled the Jewish community. In 167 B.C.E., Antiochus converted the great Jewish temple in Jerusalem into a Greek temple and outlawed Jewish religious rites such as observing the Sabbath and performing circumcision. This

Underground Labyrinth for Healing

This underground stone labyrinth formed part of the enormous healing sanctuary of the god Asclepius at Epidaurus in Greece. Patients flocked to the site from all over the Mediterranean world. They descended into the labyrinth, which was covered and dark, as part of their treatment, which centered on reaching a trance state to receive dreams that would provide instructions on their healing and, sometimes, miraculous surgery. Do you think such treatment could be effective? (Gianni Dagli Orti / The Art Archive at Art Resource, NY.)

action provoked a revolt led by Judah the Maccabee, which won Jewish independence from Seleucid control after twenty-five years of war. The most famous episode in this revolt was the retaking of the Jerusalem temple and its rededication to the worship of the Jewish god, Yahweh, commemorated by the Hanukkah holiday.

That Greek culture attracted some Jews in the first place provides a striking example of the transformations that affected many—though far from all—people of the Hellenistic world. By the time of the Roman Empire, one of those transformations would be Christianity, whose theology had roots in the cultural interaction of Hellenistic Jews and Greeks and their ideas on apocalypticism (religious ideas revealing the future) and divine human beings.

REVIEW QUESTION How did the political changes of the Hellenistic period affect art, science, and religion?

Conclusion

The aftermath of the Peloponnesian War led ordinary people as well as philosophers like Plato and Aristotle to question the basis of morality. The disunity of Greek international politics allowed Macedonia's aggressive leaders Philip II (r. 359–336 B.C.E.) and Alexander the Great (r. 336–323 B.C.E.) to make themselves the masters of the competing city-states. Inspired by Greek heroic ideals, Alexander the Great conquered the Persian Empire and set in motion the Hellenistic period's enormous political, social, and cultural changes.

When Alexander's commanders transformed themselves into Hellenistic kings after his death, they reintroduced monarchy into the Greek world, adding an administrative layer of Greek and Macedonian officials to the conquered lands' existing governments. Local elites cooperated with the new Hellenistic monarchs in governing and financing

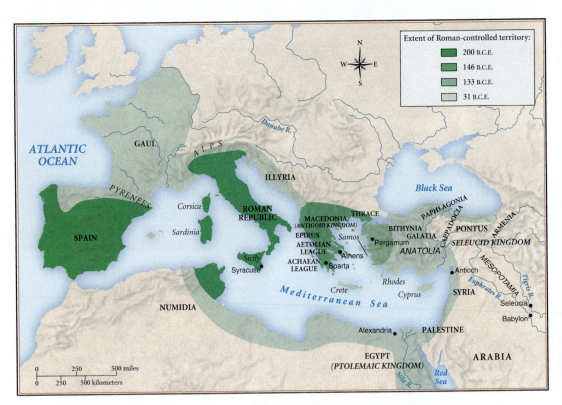

Mapping the West   Roman Takeover of the Hellenistic World, to 30 B.C.E.
By the death of Cleopatra VII of Egypt in 30 B.C.E., the Romans had taken over the Hellenistic kingdoms of the eastern Mediterranean. This territory became the eastern half of the Roman Empire. Compare the political divisions on this map with those on the map at the end of Chapter 3 (page 105) to see the differences from the Classical Age.

their hierarchical society, which was divided along ethnic lines, with the Greek and Macedonian elite ranking above local elites. To enhance their own reputations, Hellenistic kings and queens funded writers, artists, scholars, philosophers, and scientists, thereby energizing intellectual life. The traditional city-states continued to exist in Hellenistic Greece, but their freedom extended only to local governance; the Hellenistic kings controlled foreign policy.

Increased contacts between diverse peoples promoted greater cultural interaction in the Hellenistic world. Artists and writers expressed emotion in their works, philosophers discussed how to achieve true happiness, and scientists conducted research with royal support. More anxious than ever about the role of chance in life, many people looked for new religious experiences, especially in cults promising secret knowledge to initiates. What changed most of all was the Romans' culture once they took over the Hellenistic kingdoms' territory and came into close contact with their diverse peoples' traditions. Rome's rise to power took centuries, however, because Rome originated as a tiny, insignificant place that no one except Romans ever expected to amount to anything in the wider world.

Review Questions

1. How did daily life, philosophy, and the political situation change in Greece during the period 400–350 B.C.E.?
2. What were the accomplishments of Alexander the Great, and what were their effects both for the ancient world and for later Western civilization?
3. How did the political and social organization of the new Hellenistic kingdoms compare with that of the earlier Greek city-states?
4. How did the political changes of the Hellenistic period affect art, science, and religion?

Making Connections

1. What made ancient people see Alexander as "great"? Would he be regarded as "great" in today's world?
2. What are the advantages and disadvantages of governmental support of the arts and sciences? Compare such support in the Hellenistic kingdoms to that in the United States today (e.g., through the National Endowment for the Humanities, the National Endowment for the Arts, and the National Science Foundation).
3. Is inner personal tranquillity powerful enough to make a difficult or painful life bearable?

- For practice quizzes and other study tools, visit the **Online Study Guide** at bedfordstmartins.com/huntconcise.

- For primary-source material from this period, see *Sources of the Making of the West,* Fourth Edition.

- For Web sites, images, and documents related to topics in this chapter, visit *Make History* at bedfordstmartins.com/huntconcise.

Suggested References

After the Peloponnesian War, the structure of international relations changed radically in the Greek world as the city-states became secondary in political power to the kingdom of Macedonia, and then to the kingdoms of the Hellenistic period. Long-lasting cultural changes accompanied this political transformation.

*Aristotle. *Complete Works.* Ed. Jonathan Barnes. 1985.

Briant, Pierre. *Alexander the Great and His Empire: A Short Introduction.* Trans. Amélie Kuhrt. 2010.

Chaniotis, Angelos. *War in the Hellenistic World.* 2005.

Collins, John Joseph. *Between Athens and Jerusalem: Jewish Identity in the Hellenistic Diaspora.* 1999.

Evans, J. A. S. *Daily Life in the Hellenistic Age: From Alexander to Cleopatra.* 2008.

Mikalson, Jon D. *Religion in Hellenistic Athens.* 1998.

TIMELINE

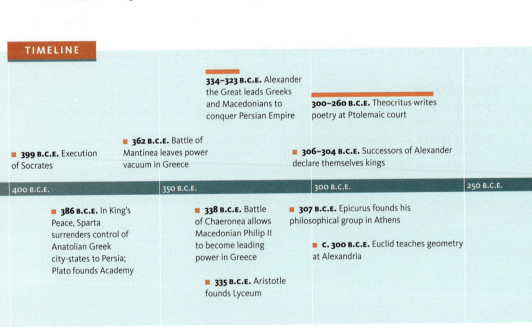

334–323 B.C.E. Alexander the Great leads Greeks and Macedonians to conquer Persian Empire

300–260 B.C.E. Theocritus writes poetry at Ptolemaic court

362 B.C.E. Battle of Mantinea leaves power vacuum in Greece

399 B.C.E. Execution of Socrates

306–304 B.C.E. Successors of Alexander declare themselves kings

400 B.C.E.   350 B.C.E.   300 B.C.E.   250 B.C.E.

386 B.C.E. In King's Peace, Sparta surrenders control of Anatolian Greek city-states to Persia; Plato founds Academy

338 B.C.E. Battle of Chaeronea allows Macedonian Philip II to become leading power in Greece

307 B.C.E. Epicurus founds his philosophical group in Athens

C. 300 B.C.E. Euclid teaches geometry at Alexandria

335 B.C.E. Aristotle founds Lyceum

*Plato. *The Collected Dialogues*. Ed. Edith Hamilton and Huntington Cairns. 1963.

*Plutarch. *The Age of Alexander*. Trans. Ian Scott-Kilvert. 1973.

Pollitt, J. J. *Art in the Hellenistic Age*. 1986.

Ptolemaic Egypt: http://www.houseofptolemy.org/

Rogers, Guy MacLean. *Alexander: The Ambiguity of Greatness*. 2004.

Sharples, R. W. *Stoics, Epicureans, and Sceptics: An Introduction to Hellenistic Philosophy*. 1996.

Shipley, Graham. *The Greek World after Alexander 323–30 B.C.* 1999.

Snyder, Jane M. *The Woman and the Lyre: Women Writers in Classical Greece and Rome*. 1989.

Primary source.

■ **195 B.C.E.** Seleucid queen Laodice endows dowries for girls

■ **30 B.C.E.** Cleopatra VII dies; Rome takes over Ptolemaic Empire

200 B.C.E.   150 B.C.E.   100 B.C.E.   50 B.C.E.

■ **167 B.C.E.** Maccabee revolt after Antiochus IV turns temple in Jerusalem into Greek sanctuary

The Rise of Rome and Its Republic

753–44 B.C.E.

THE ROMANS TREASURED LEGENDS about their state's transformation from a tiny village to a world power. They especially loved stories about their city's legendary first king, Romulus. When early Rome needed more women to bear children to increase its population and build a strong army, Romulus begged Rome's neighbors for permission for Roman men to marry their women. Everyone turned him down, mocking Rome's poverty and weakness. Enraged, Romulus hatched a plan to use force where diplomacy had failed. Inviting the neighboring Sabines to a religious festival, he had his men kidnap the unmarried Sabine women. The Roman kidnappers immediately married the women, promising to cherish them as beloved wives and new citizens. When the Sabine men attacked Rome to rescue their kin, the women rushed into the midst of the bloody battle, begging their brothers, fathers, and new husbands either to stop slaughtering one another or to kill them — their devoted sisters, daughters, and wives — to end the war. The men made peace on the spot and agreed to merge their populations under Roman rule.

This legend emphasizes that Rome, unlike the city-states of Greece, expanded by absorbing outsiders into its citizen body. Rome's growth was the ancient world's greatest expansion of population and territory, as a people originally housed in a few huts gradually created a state that fought countless wars and relocated an unprecedented number of citizens to gain control of most of Europe, North Africa, Egypt, and the eastern Mediterranean region. The social, cultural, political, legal, and economic traditions that Romans developed to

The Wolf Suckling Romulus and Remus

This bronze statue relates to the myth that a she-wolf nursed the twin brothers Romulus and Remus, the offspring of the war god Mars and the future founders of Rome. Romans treasured this story because it meant that Mars loved their city so dearly that he sent a wild animal to nurse its founders after a cruel tyrant had forced their mother to abandon the infants. The myth also taught Romans that their state had been born in violence: Romulus killed Remus in an argument over who would lead their new settlement. The wolf is an Etruscan sculpture from the fifth century B.C.E.; the babies were added in the Renaissance. (Scala / Art Resource, NY.)

rule this vast area created greater connections between diverse peoples than had ever existed before. Unlike the Greeks and Macedonians, the Romans maintained the unity of their state for centuries. The empire's long existence allowed many Roman values and traditions to become essential components of Western civilization.

Greek literature, art, and philosophy influenced Rome's culture greatly. Romans learned from their neighbors, adapting foreign traditions to their own purposes and forging their own cultural identity.

The legend about Romulus belongs to Rome's earliest history, when kings ruled (753–509 B.C.E.). Rome's later history is divided into the republic and the empire. Under the republic (founded 509 B.C.E.), men elected their officials and passed laws (although an oligarchy of the social elite controlled politics). Under the empire, monarchs once again ruled. Rome's greatest expansion came during the republic. Romans' belief in a divine destiny fueled this tremendous growth. They believed that the gods wanted them to rule the world and improve it by making everyone adhere to their social and moral values.

Roman values emphasized family loyalty, selfless political and military service to the community, individual honor and public status, the importance of the law, and shared decision making. By the first century B.C.E., power-hungry leaders such as Sulla and Julius Caesar had plunged Rome into civil war. By putting their personal ambition before the good of the state, they destroyed the republic.

CHAPTER FOCUS   How did traditional Roman values affect both the rise and the downfall of the Roman republic?

Roman Social and Religious Traditions

Rome's citizens believed that eternal moral values connected them to one another and required them to honor the gods in return for divine support. Hierarchy affected everyone: people at all social levels were obligated to patrons or clients; in families, fathers dominated; in religion, people at all levels of society owed sacrifices, rituals, and prayers to the gods who protected the family and the state.

Roman Moral Values

Roman values defined relationships with other people and with the gods. Romans guided their lives by the **mos maiorum** ("the way of the elders"), values from their ancestors. The Romans preserved these values because, for them, *old* equaled "tested by time," while *new* meant "dangerous." Roman morality emphasized virtue, faithfulness, and respect. A reputation for behaving morally was crucial to Romans because it earned them the respect of others.

Virtus ("manly virtue") meant strength, loyalty, and courage, especially in war. It also included wisdom and moral purity; in this broader sense, women, too, could possess virtus. In the second century B.C.E., the Roman poet Lucilius defined it this way:

Virtus is to know the human relevance of each thing,
To know what is humanly right and useful and honorable,
And what things are good and what are bad, useless, shameful, and
    dishonorable. . . .
And, in addition, *virtus* is putting the country's interests first,
Then our parents', with our own interests third and last.

Fides (FEE dehs, "faithfulness") meant keeping one's obligations no matter the cost. Failing to meet an obligation offended the community and the gods. Faithful women remained virgins before marriage and monogamous afterward. Faithful men kept their word, paid their debts, and treated everyone with justice — which did not mean treating everyone equally, but rather appropriately, according to whether the person was a social superior, an equal, or an inferior. Showing respect and devotion to the gods and to one's family was the supreme form of faithfulness. Romans believed they had to worship the gods faithfully to maintain the divine favor that protected their community.

Roman values required that each person maintain self-control and limit displays of emotion. So strict was this value that not even wives and husbands could kiss in public without seeming emotionally out of control. It also meant that a person should never give up no matter how hard the situation.

The reward for living these values was respect from others. Women earned respect by bearing legitimate children and educating them morally. Respected men relied on their reputations to help them win election to government posts. A man of the highest reputation commanded so much respect that others would obey him regardless of whether he held an office with formal power over them. A man with this much prestige was said to possess authority. The concept of authority based on respect reflected the Roman belief that some people were by nature superior to others and that society had to be hierarchical to be just. Romans believed that aristocrats, people born into the "best" families, automatically deserved high respect. In return, aristocrats were supposed to live strictly by the highest values to serve the community.

In legends about the early days of Rome, a person could be poor and still remain a proud aristocrat. Over time, however, money became overwhelmingly important to the Roman elite, to spend on showy luxuries, large-scale entertaining, and costly gifts to the community. In this way, wealth became necessary to maintain high social status.

The Patron-Client System

The **patron-client system** was an interlocking network of personal relationships that obligated people to one another. A patron was a man of superior status who could provide benefits to lower-status people; these were his clients, who in return owed him duties and paid him special attention. In this hierarchical system, a patron was often himself the client of a higher-status man.

Benefits and duties created mutual exchanges of financial and political help. Patrons would help their clients get started in business by giving them a gift or a loan and connecting them with others who could help them. In politics, a patron would promote a client's candidacy for elective office and provide money for campaigning. Patrons also supported clients if they had legal trouble.

Clients had to support their patrons' campaigns for public office and lend them money to build public works and to fund their daughters' dowries. A patron expected his clients to gather at his house at dawn to accompany him to the forum, the city's public center, to show his great status. A Roman leader needed a large house to hold this throng and to entertain his social equals.

Patrons' and clients' mutual obligations endured for generations. Ex-slaves, who became the clients for life of the masters who freed them, often passed this relationship on to their children. Romans with contacts abroad could acquire clients among foreigners; Roman generals sometimes had entire foreign communities obligated to them. The patron-client system demonstrated the Roman idea that social stability and well-being were achieved by faithfully maintaining established ties.

The Roman Family

The family was Roman society's bedrock because it taught values and determined the ownership of property. Men and women shared the duty of teaching their children values, though by law the father possessed the ***patria potestas*** ("father's power") over his children — no matter how old — and his slaves. This power made him the sole owner of all his dependents' property. As long as he was alive, no son or daughter could officially own anything, accumulate money, or possess any independent legal standing. Unofficially, however, adult children did control personal property and money, and favored slaves could build up savings. Fathers also held legal power of life and death over these members of their households, but they rarely exercised this power except through exposure of newborns, an accepted practice to limit family size and dispose of physically imperfect infants.

Patria potestas did not allow a husband to control his wife; instead, under the common arrangement called a "free" marriage, the wife formally remained under her father's power as long as the father lived. But in the ancient world, few fathers lived long enough to oversee the lives of their married daughters or sons; four out of five parents died before their children reached age thirty. A Roman woman without a living father was relatively independent. Legally she needed a male guardian to conduct her business, but guardianship was largely an empty formality by the first century B.C.E. As a commentator explained, "The common belief, that because of their instability of judgment women are often deceived and that it is only fair to have them controlled by the authority of guardians, seems more false than true. For women of full age manage their affairs themselves."

A Roman woman had to grow up fast. Tullia (c. 79–45 B.C.E.), daughter of Rome's most famous politician and orator, Cicero, was engaged at twelve, married at sixteen,

Sculpture of a Woman Running a Store

This sculpture portrays a woman selling food from a small shop while customers make purchases or chat. Since Roman women could own property, it is possible that the woman is the store owner. The man standing behind her could be her husband or a servant. Much like malls of today, markets in Roman towns were packed with small stores. (Art Resource, NY.)

and widowed by twenty-two. Like every other wealthy married Roman woman, she managed the household slaves, monitored the nurturing of the young children by wet nurses, kept account books to track the property she personally owned, and accompanied her husband to dinner parties — something a Greek wife never did.

A mother's responsibility for shaping her children's values constituted the foundation of female virtue. Women like Cornelia, a famous aristocrat of the second century B.C.E., won enormous respect for loyalty to family. When her husband died, Cornelia refused an offer of marriage from King Ptolemy VIII of Egypt so that she could continue to oversee the family estate and educate her surviving daughter and two sons. (Her other nine children had died.) The boys, Tiberius and Gaius Gracchus, grew up to be among the most influential political leaders in the late republic. The number of children Cornelia bore reveals the fertility and stamina required of a Roman wife to ensure the survival of her husband's family line. Cornelia also became famous for her stylishly worded letters, which were still being read a century later.

Roman women could not vote or hold political office, but wealthy women like Cornelia influenced politics by expressing their opinions to men at home and at dinner parties. Marcus Porcius Cato (234–149 B.C.E.), a famous politician and author, described this clout: "All mankind rule their wives, we [Roman men] rule all mankind, and our wives rule us."

Women could acquire property through inheritance and entrepreneurship. Archaeological discoveries reveal that by the end of the republic some women owned large businesses. Prenuptial agreements determining the property rights of husband and wife were common. In divorce fathers kept the children. Most poor women worked

as field laborers or in shops. Women and men both worked in manufacturing, which mostly happened in the home. The men worked the raw materials — cutting, fitting, and polishing wood, leather, and metal — while the women sold the finished goods. The poorest women earned money through prostitution, which was legal but considered disgraceful.

Education for Public Life

Roman education aimed to make men and women effective speakers and exponents of traditional values. Most children received their education at home; there were no public schools; the rich hired private teachers. Wealthy parents bought literate slaves called pedagogues to educate their children, especially to teach them Greek. In upper-class families, both daughters and sons learned to read. The girls were taught literature and music, and how to make educated conversation at dinner parties. The aim of women's education was to prepare them to teach traditional social and moral values to their children.

Sons received physical training and learned to fight with weapons, but rhetorical training dominated an upper-class Roman boy's education because a successful political career depended on the ability to speak persuasively in public. A boy would learn winning techniques by listening to speeches in political meetings and arguments in court cases. The orator Cicero said, "[Young men must learn to] excel in public speaking. It is the tool for controlling men at Rome."

Public and Private Religion

Romans followed Greek models of religion. Their chief deity, Jupiter, corresponded to the Greek god Zeus and was seen as a powerful, stern father. Juno (Greek Hera), queen of the gods, and Minerva (Greek Athena), goddess of wisdom, joined Jupiter to form the state religion's central triad. These three deities shared Rome's most revered temple.

Protecting Rome's safety and prosperity was the gods' major function. They were supposed to help Rome defeat enemies in war and to support agriculture. Prayers requested the gods' aid in growing abundant crops, healing disease, and promoting reproduction for animals and people. In times of crisis, Romans sought foreign gods for help, such as when the government imported the cult of the healing god Asclepius from Greece in 293 B.C.E., praying he would stop an epidemic.

The republic supported many other cults, including that of Vesta, goddess of the hearth and protector of the family. Her shrine housed Rome's official eternal flame, which guaranteed the state's permanent existence. The Vestal Virgins, six unmarried women sworn to chastity and Rome's only female priests, tended Vesta's shrine. They earned high status and freedom from their fathers' control by performing their most important duty: keeping the flame from going out. If the flame went out, the Romans assumed that one of the Vestal Virgins had had sex and buried her alive.

Religion was important in Roman family life. Each household maintained small indoor shrines that housed statuettes of the spirits of the household and those of the ancestors, protectors' of the family's health and morality. Upper-class families kept death masks of famous ancestors hanging in the main room and wore them at funerals to display their status.

Religious rituals accompanied everyday activities such as breast-feeding babies or fertilizing crops. Many public religious gatherings promoted the community's health and stability. For example, during the Lupercalia festival (whose name recalled the wolf, *luper* in Latin, that had reared Romulus and his twin, Remus, according to legend), near-naked young men streaked around the Palatine hill, lashing any woman they met with strips of goatskin. Women who had not yet borne children would run out to be struck, believing this would help them become fertile.

The Romans did not regard the gods as guardians of human morality. As Cicero explained, "We call Jupiter the Best and Greatest not because he makes us just or sober or wise but, rather, healthy, unharmed, rich, and prosperous." Roman officials preceded important actions with the ritual called taking the auspices, in which they sought Jupiter's approval by observing natural signs such as birds' flight direction or eating habits, or the appearance of thunder and lightning.

Romans regarded values as divine forces. *Pietas* ("piety"), for example, meant devotion and duty to family, friends, the state, and the gods; a temple at Rome held a statue personifying pietas as a female divinity. The personification of abstract moral qualities provided a focus for cult rituals.

The duty of Roman religious officials was to maintain peace with the gods. Socially prominent men served as priests, conducting sacrifices, festivals, and prayers. Priests were citizens performing public service, not religious professionals. The chief priest, the *pontifex maximus* ("greatest bridge-builder"), served as the head of state religion, a position carrying political prominence.

Disrespect for religious tradition brought punishment. Admirals, for example, took the auspices by feeding sacred chickens on their warships: if the birds ate energetically, Jupiter favored the Romans and an attack could begin. In 249 B.C.E., the commander Publius Claudius Pulcher grew frustrated when his chickens, probably seasick, refused to eat. Determined to attack, he finally hurled the birds overboard in a rage, sputtering, "Well then, let them drink!" When he promptly suffered a huge defeat, he was fined heavily.

REVIEW QUESTION What common themes underlay Roman values, and how did Romans' behavior reflect those values?

From Monarchy to Republic

Romans' values and their belief in a divine destiny fueled their astounding growth from a tiny settlement into the Mediterranean's greatest power. The Romans spilled much blood as they gradually expanded their territory through war. From the eighth to the sixth century B.C.E., they were ruled by kings, but the later kings' violence provoked

members of the social elite to overthrow the monarchy and create the republic, which lasted until the first century B.C.E. The republic — ***res publica*** ("the people's matter" or "the public business") — distributed power among elected officials and assemblies of voters. This model of republican government, rather than Athens's direct democracy, influenced the founders of the United States in organizing their new nation as a federal republic. Rome gained land and population by winning aggressive wars and by absorbing other peoples. Its economic and cultural growth depended on contact with many other peoples around the Mediterranean.

Roman Society under the Kings, 753–509 B.C.E.

Seven kings ruled from 753 to 509 B.C.E. and created Rome's most famous and enduring government body: the Senate, a group of distinguished men chosen as the king's personal council. This council played the same role — advising government leaders — for a thousand years, as Rome changed from a monarchy to a republic and back to a monarchy (the empire). It was always a Roman tradition that one should never make decisions by oneself but only after consulting advisers and friends.

Rome's expansion depended on taking in outsiders conquered in war and, uniquely in the ancient world, freed slaves. Though freedmen and freedwomen owed special obligations to their former owners and could not hold elective office or serve in the army, they enjoyed all other citizens' rights, such as legal marriage. Their children possessed citizenship without any limits. By the late republic, many Roman citizens were descendants of freed slaves.

Map 5.1 Ancient Italy, 500 B.C.E.
When the Romans removed the monarchy to found a republic in 509 B.C.E., they inhabited a relatively small territory in central Italy. Many different peoples lived in Italy at this time, with the most prosperous occupying fertile agricultural land and sheltered harbors on the peninsula's west side. The early republic's most urbanized neighbors were the Etruscans to the north and the Greeks in the city-states to the south, including on the island of Sicily. Immediately adjacent to Rome were the people of Latium, called Latins. How did geography aid Roman expansion?

By 550 B.C.E., Rome had grown to some forty thousand people and, through war and diplomacy, had won control of three hundred square miles of surrounding territory. Rome's geography propelled its further expansion. The Romans originated in central Italy, a long peninsula with a mountain range down its middle like a spine and fertile plains on either side. Rome also controlled a river crossing on a major north–south route. Most important, Rome was ideally situated for international trade: the Italian peninsula stuck so far out into the Mediterranean that east–west seaborne traffic naturally encountered it (Map 5.1), and the city had a good port nearby.

The Italian ancestors of the Romans lived by herding animals, farming, and hunting. They became skilled metalworkers, especially in iron. The earliest Romans' neighbors in central Italy were poor villagers, too, and spoke the same language, Latin. Greeks lived to the south in Italy and Sicily, and contact with them deeply affected Roman cultural development. Romans developed a love-hate relationship with Greece, admiring its literature and art but looking down on its lack of military unity. Romans adopted many elements from Greek culture — from the deities for their national cults to the models for their poetry, prose, and architectural styles.

The Etruscans, a people to the north, also influenced Roman culture. Brightly colored wall paintings in tombs, portraying funeral banquets and festive games, reveal the splendor of Etruscan society. In addition to producing their own art, jewelry, and sculpture, the Etruscans imported luxurious objects from Greece and the Near East. Most of the intact Greek vases known today were found in Etruscan tombs, and Etruscan culture was deeply influenced by that of Greece.

Romans adopted ceremonial features of Etruscan culture, such as musical instruments, religious rituals, and lictors (attendants who walked before the highest officials carrying the

Etruscan Painting of a Musician

This Etruscan painting, characteristically done with bright colors (now faded), shows a man playing the double pipe, a reed wind instrument with holes in both tubes that the player fingered simultaneously. This instrument originated in Greece, as did the designs above and below the central figure. The Etruscans adopted many cultural traditions from the Greeks, some of which they then passed on to the Romans. (Italic, Etruscan, Late Archaic period or early Classical period, about 470 B.C.E. Terracotta, overall dimensions: 112.5 × 52 cm (44⁵⁄₁₆ × 20½ in.). Museum of Fine Arts, Boston, William Francis Warden Fund, 62.363. Photograph © 2013 Museum of Fine Arts, Boston.)

fasces, a bundle of rods around an ax, symbolizing the officials' right to command and punish). The Romans also borrowed from the Etruscans the ritual of divination — determining the will of the gods by examining organs of slaughtered animals. Other prominent features of Roman culture were probably part of the ancient Mediterranean's shared practices, such as the organization of the Roman army (a citizen militia of heavily armed infantry troops fighting in formation) and the use of an alphabet.

The Early Roman Republic, 509–287 B.C.E.

The Roman social elite's hatred of monarchy motivated the creation of the republic. In 509 B.C.E., when the son of the king raped the virtuous Roman woman Lucretia, who committed suicide to preserve her honor, her relatives and friends from the social elite overthrew the king and founded the republic. Thereafter, the Romans prided themselves on having a political system based on sharing political power among (male) citizens.

The Romans struggled for 250 years to shape a stable government for the republic. Roman social hierarchy split the population into two **orders**: the **patricians** (a small group of the most aristocratic families) and the **plebeians** (the rest of the citizens). These two groups' conflicts over power created the so-called struggle of the orders. The struggle finally ended in 287 B.C.E. when plebeians won the right to make laws in their own assembly.

Patricians constituted a tiny percentage of the population — numbering only about 130 families — but in the beginning of the republic their inherited status entitled them to control public religion and to monopolize political office. Many patricians were much wealthier than most plebeians. Some plebeians, however, were also rich, and they resented the patricians' dominance, especially their ban on intermarriage with plebeians. Poor plebeians demanded farmland and relief from crushing debts. Patricians inflamed tensions by wearing special red shoes to set themselves apart; later they changed to black shoes adorned with a small metal crescent. To pressure the patricians, the plebeians periodically refused military service. This tactic worked because Rome's army depended on plebeian manpower.

In response to plebeian unrest, the patricians agreed to the earliest Roman law code. This code, enacted between 451 and 449 B.C.E. and known as the **Twelve Tables**, guaranteed greater equality and social mobility. The Twelve Tables prevented patrician judges from giving judgments in legal cases only according to their own wishes. The Roman belief in fair laws as the best protection against social strife helped keep the republic united until the late second century B.C.E.

The voting to elect officials took place around the forum in the city center (Map 5.2). All officials worked as part of committees, to ensure power sharing. The highest officials, two elected each year, were called consuls. Their most important duty was to command the army.

To be elected consul, a man had to win elections all the way up a **ladder of offices** (*cursus honorum*). Before politics, however, came ten years of military service from about age twenty. The ladder's first step was getting elected quaestor (a financial administrator).

Map 5.2 The City of Rome during the Republic

Roman tradition said that a king built Rome's first defensive wall in the sixth century B.C.E., but archaeology shows that the first wall encircling the city's center and seven hills on the east bank of the Tiber River belongs to the fourth century B.C.E.; this wall covered a circuit of about seven miles. By the second century B.C.E., the wall had been extended to soar fifty-two feet high and had been fitted with catapults to protect the large gates. Like the open agora surrounded by buildings at the heart of a Greek city, the forum remained Rome's political and social heart. How might modern cities benefit from having a large public space at their center?

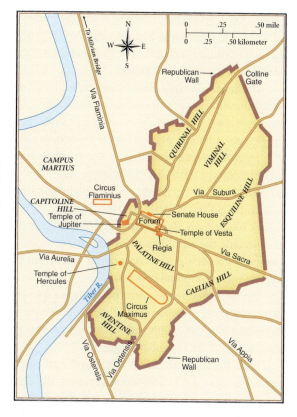

Next was election as an aedile (supervisors of Rome's streets, sewers, aqueducts, temples, and markets). The third step was election as praetor (a powerful office with judicial and military duties). The most successful praetors competed to be one of the two consuls elected each year. Praetors and consuls held imperium (the power to command and punish) and served as army generals. Families with a consul among their ancestors were honored as nobles. By 367 B.C.E., the plebeians had forced passage of a law requiring that at least one of the two consuls be a plebeian. Ex-consuls competed to become one of the censors, elected every five years to conduct censuses of the citizen body and to appoint new senators. To be eligible for selection to the Senate, a man had to have been at least a quaestor.

The patricians tried to monopolize the highest offices, but after violent struggle from about 500 to 450 B.C.E., the plebeians forced the patricians to create ten annually elected plebeian officials, called tribunes, who could stop actions that would harm plebeians or their property. The tribunate did not count as a regular ladder office. Tribunes based their special power on the plebeians' sworn oath to protect them, and their authority to block officials' actions, prevent laws from being passed, suspend elections, and contradict the Senate's advice. The tribunes' extraordinary power to veto government action often made them agents of political conflict.

Men competed in elections to win respect and glory, not money. Only well-off men could serve in government because officials earned no salaries and were expected to spend their own money to pay for public works and for expensive shows featuring gladiators and wild animals. In the early republic, officials' only reward was respect, but as Romans

conquered overseas territory, the desire for money from plunder overcame many men's adherence to traditional Roman values of faithfulness and honesty. By the second century B.C.E., military officers were also enriching themselves by extorting bribes as administrators of conquered territories.

The Senate directed government policy by giving advice to the consuls. The senators' social standing gave their opinions great weight. To make their status visible, the senators wore black high-top shoes and robes with a broad purple stripe. If a consul rejected the Senate's advice, a political crisis ensued.

Three different assemblies made legislation, conducted elections, and rendered judgment in certain trials. The Centuriate Assembly, which elected praetors and consuls, was dominated by patricians and rich plebeians. The Plebeian Assembly, which excluded patricians, elected the tribunes. In 287 B.C.E., its resolutions, called **plebiscites**, became legally binding on all Romans. The Tribal Assembly mixed patricians with plebeians and became the republic's most important assembly. Each assembly was divided into groups, with each group comprising a different number of men based on status and wealth; each group had one vote.

Before assembly meetings, orators gave speeches about issues. Everyone, including women and noncitizens, could listen to these pre-vote speeches. The crowd expressed its opinions by either applauding or hissing. This process mixed a small measure of democracy with the republic's oligarchy.

Early on, the praetors decided most legal cases. A separate jury system arose in the second century B.C.E., and senators repeatedly clashed with other upper-class Romans over whether these juries should consist exclusively of senators. Accusers and accused had to speak for themselves in court or have friends speak for them. Priests dominated in legal knowledge until the third century B.C.E., when senators with legal expertise, called jurists, began to offer advice about cases.

The republic's complex political and judicial system evolved in response to conflicts over power. Laws could emerge from different assemblies, and legal cases could be decided by various institutions. Rome had no single highest court, such as the U.S. Supreme Court, to give final verdicts. The republic's stability therefore depended on maintaining the *mos maiorum*. Because they defined this tradition, the most socially prominent and richest Romans dominated politics and the courts.

REVIEW QUESTION   How and why did the Roman republic develop its complicated political and judicial systems?

Roman Imperialism and Its Consequences

From the fifth to the third century B.C.E., the Romans fought war after war in Italy until Rome became the most powerful state on the peninsula. In the third and second centuries B.C.E., Romans warred far from home in every direction, above all against Carthage to the south. Their success in these campaigns made Rome the premier power in the Mediterranean by the first century B.C.E.

Fear of enemies and the desire for wealth propelled Roman imperialism. The senators' worries about national security spurred them to recommend preemptive attacks against foreign powers. Poor soldiers hoped to pull their families out of poverty; the elite, who commanded the armies, wanted to strengthen their campaigns for office by acquiring glory and greater wealth.

The state of being at war transformed Roman life. Romans had no literature until around 240 B.C.E., when contact with conquered peoples stimulated their first written history and poetry. War's harshness also influenced Roman art. Repeated military service away from home created stresses on small farmers and undermined the stability of Roman society; so, too, did the relocation of numerous citizens and the importation of countless war captives to work as slaves on wealthy people's estates. Rome's great conquests turned out to be a double-edged sword: they brought expansion and wealth, but their unexpected social and political consequences disrupted the traditional values and stability of the community.

Expansion in Italy, 500–220 B.C.E.

After defeating their Latin neighbors in the 490s B.C.E., the Romans spent the next hundred years warring with the nearby Etruscan town of Veii. Their 396 B.C.E. victory doubled their territory. By the fourth century B.C.E., the Roman infantry legion of five thousand men had surpassed the Greek and Macedonian infantry phalanx as an effective fighting force because in the legion's more flexible battle line the soldiers were trained to throw javelins from behind their long shields and then rush in to finish off the enemy with swords. A devastating sack of Rome in 387 B.C.E. by marauding Gauls (Celts) from beyond the Alps made Romans forever fearful of foreign invasion. By around 220 B.C.E., Rome controlled all of Italy south of the Po River, at the northern end of the peninsula.

The Romans combined brutality with diplomacy to control conquered peoples. Sometimes they enslaved the defeated or forced them to surrender large parcels of land. Other times they offered generous peace terms to former enemies but required them to join in fighting against other foes, for which they received a share of the spoils, namely, slaves and land.

To increase homeland security, the Romans planted numerous colonies of relocated citizens and constructed roads up and down the peninsula to allow troops to travel faster. By connecting Italy's diverse peoples, these settlements promoted a unified culture dominated by Rome. Latin became the common language, although some local tongues lived on.

The wealth of its army attracted hordes of people to Rome, where new aqueducts provided fresh, running water and a massive building program employed

Roman Roads, 110 B.C.E.

Aqueduct at Nîmes in France
The Romans excelled at building complex delivery systems of tunnels, channels, bridges, and fountains to transport fresh water from far away. One of the best-preserved sections of a major aqueduct is the so-called Pont-du-Gard near Nîmes (ancient Nemausus) in France, erected in the late first century B.C.E. to serve the flourishing town there. Built of stones fitted together without clamps or mortar, the span soars 160 feet high and 875 feet long, carrying water along its topmost level from thirty-five miles away in a channel constructed to fall only one foot in height for every three thousand feet in length so that the flow would remain steady but gentle. What sort of social and political organization would be necessary to construct such a system? (Hubertus Kanus / Photo Researchers, Inc.)

many. By 300 B.C.E., about 150,000 people lived within Rome's walls (Map 5.2, page 149). Outside the city, around 750,000 free Roman citizens inhabited various parts of Italy on land that had been taken from local peoples. Much conquered territory was declared public land, open to any Roman for grazing cattle.

Rich plebeians and patricians cooperated to exploit the expanding Roman territories, deriving their wealth from agricultural land and war plunder. Since Rome had no regular income or inheritance taxes, families could pass down their wealth from generation to generation freely.

Wars with Carthage and in the East, 264–121 B.C.E.

The republic fought its three most famous foreign wars against the wealthy city of Carthage in North Africa, which Phoenicians had founded around 800 B.C.E. Carthage, governed as a republic like Rome, controlled a powerful empire rich from farming in Africa and seaborne trade in the Mediterranean. Carthage seemed both a dangerous rival and a fine prize. Horror at the Carthaginians' reported tradition of incinerating infants to placate their gods in times of trouble also fed Romans' hostility against people they saw as barbarians.

Rome's wars with Carthage are called the Punic Wars (from the Latin word for "Phoenician"). The first one (264–241 B.C.E.) erupted over Sicily, where Carthage wanted to preserve its trading settlements, while Rome wanted to block Carthaginian power close to Italy. This long conflict revealed why the Romans won wars: the large Italian population provided deep manpower reserves, and the government was prepared to sacrifice as many troops, spend as much money, and fight as long as it took to defeat the enemy. Previously unskilled at naval warfare, the Romans expended vast sums to build warships to combat Carthage's experienced navy; they lost more than five hundred ships and 250,000 men while learning how to win at sea (see "Taking Measure," below).

The Romans' victory in the First Punic War made them masters of Sicily, where they set up their first province (a foreign territory ruled and taxed by Roman officials). This innovation proved so profitable that they soon seized the islands of Sardinia and Corsica from the Carthaginians to create another province. These first successful foreign conquests increased the Romans' appetite for expansion outside Italy (Map 5.3). Fearing

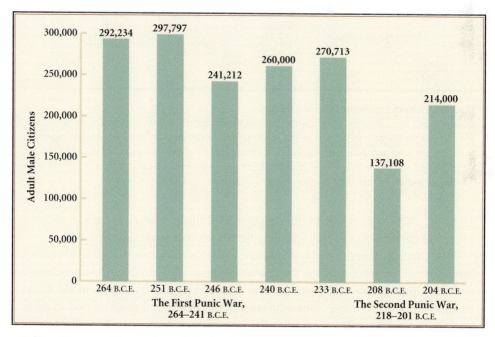

Taking Measure **Census Records during the First and Second Punic Wars**
Writing hundreds of years apart, Livy (59 B.C.E.–17 C.E.) and Jerome (c. 347–420 C.E.) provide these numbers from Rome's censuses, which counted only adult male citizens (the men eligible for Rome's regular army), conducted during and between the first two wars against Carthage. Since the census did not include the Italian allies fighting on Rome's side, the census numbers understate the wars' total casualties; scholars estimate that they took the lives of nearly a third of Italy's adult male population, which would have meant perhaps a quarter of a million soldiers killed. (Tenney Frank, *An Economic Survey of Ancient Rome*, vol. 1 [New York: Farrar, Straus and Giroux, 1959], 56.)

Map 5.3 Roman Expansion, 500–44 B.C.E.
During its first two centuries, the Roman republic used war and diplomacy to extend its power north and south in the Italian peninsula. In the third and second centuries B.C.E., conflict with Carthage in the south and west and the Hellenistic kingdoms in the east extended Roman power outside Italy and led to the creation of provinces from Spain to Greece. The first century B.C.E. saw the conquest of Syria by Pompey and of Gaul by Julius Caesar.

a renewal of Carthage's power, the Romans cemented alliances with local peoples in Spain, where the Carthaginians were expanding from their southern trading posts.

The Carthaginians decided to strike back. In the Second Punic War (218–201 B.C.E.), their general Hannibal terrified the Romans by marching troops and war elephants over the Alps into Italy. Slaughtering thirty thousand Romans at Cannae in 216 B.C.E., Hannibal tried to convince Rome's Italian allies to desert, but most refused to rebel. Hannibal's alliance in 215 B.C.E. with the king of Macedonia forced the Romans to fight on a second front in Greece. Still, they refused to crack despite Hannibal's ravaging of Italy from 218 to 203 B.C.E. Invading the Carthaginians' homeland, the Roman army won the battle of Zama in 202 B.C.E. The Senate forced Carthage to scuttle its navy, pay huge war indemnities, and hand over its Spanish territory, rich with silver mines.

The Third Punic War (149–146 B.C.E.) began when the Carthaginians retaliated against the aggression of the king of Numidia, a Roman ally. After winning the war, the

Romans heeded the senator Cato's demand, "Carthage must be destroyed!" They obliterated the city and converted its territory into a province. This disaster did not destroy Carthaginian culture, however, and under the Roman Empire this part of North Africa flourished economically and intellectually, creating a synthesis of Roman and Carthaginian traditions.

The aftermath of the Punic Wars extended Roman power to Spain, North Africa, Macedonia, Greece, and western Asia Minor. Hannibal's alliance with the king of Macedonia had brought Roman troops east of Italy for the first time. After defeating the Macedonian king for revenge and to prevent any threat of his invading Italy, the Roman commander proclaimed the "freedom of the Greeks" in 196 B.C.E. to show respect for Greece's glorious past. The Greek cities and federal leagues understood the proclamation to mean that they, as "friends" of Rome, could behave as they liked. They were mistaken. The Romans expected them to behave as clients and follow their new patrons' advice.

The Romans repeatedly intervened to make the kingdom of Macedonia and the Greeks observe their obligations as clients. The Senate in 146 B.C.E. ordered Corinth destroyed for asserting its independence and converted Macedonia and Greece into a province. In 133 B.C.E., a Hellenistic king increased Roman power with a stupendous gift: in his will he bequeathed to Rome his kingdom in western Asia Minor. In 121 B.C.E., the Romans made the lower part of Gaul across the Alps (modern southern France) into a province. By the late first century B.C.E., then, Rome governed and profited from two-thirds of the Mediterranean region; only the easternmost Mediterranean lay outside its control (see Map 5.3).

Greek Influence on Roman Literature and the Arts

Roman imperialism generated extensive cross-cultural contact with Greece. Roman authors and artists found inspiration in Greek literature and art. The earliest Latin poetry was a translation of Homer's *Odyssey* by a Greek ex-slave, composed sometime after the First Punic War. About 200 B.C.E., the first Roman historian used Greek to write his narrative of Rome's founding and the wars with Carthage.

Many famous early Latin authors were not native Romans but came from different regions of Italy, Sicily, and even North Africa. All found inspiration in Greek literature. Roman comedies, for example, took their plots and stock characters from Hellenistic comedy such as that of Menander, which featured jokes about family life and stereotyped personalities, such as the braggart warrior and the obsessed lover.

In the mid-second century B.C.E., Cato established Latin prose writing with his history of Rome, *The Origins,* and his instructions on running a large farm, *On Agriculture.* He predicted that if the Romans adopted Greek values, they would lose their power. In fact, early Latin literature reflected traditional Roman values. For example, the pathbreaking Latin epic *Annals,* a poetic version of Roman history by the poet Ennius, shows the influence of the Greek epic but praises ancestral Roman traditions, as in this famous

line: "On the ways and the men of old rests the Roman state." Later Roman writers also took inspiration from Greek literature. The first-century B.C.E. poet Lucretius wrote *On the Nature of Things* to persuade people not to fear death. His ideas reflected Greek philosophy's "atomic theory," which said that matter was composed of tiny, invisible particles. Dying, the poem taught, simply meant the dissolving of the union of atoms, which had come together temporarily to make up a person's body. There could be no eternal punishment or pain after death because a person's soul perished along with the body.

Hellenistic Greek authors inspired Catullus in the first century B.C.E. to write witty poems ridiculing prominent politicians for their sexual behavior and lamenting his own disastrous love life. His most famous love poems revealed his obsession with a married woman named Lesbia. The orator and politician **Cicero** (106–43 B.C.E.) wrote speeches, letters, and treatises on political science, philosophy, ethics, and theology. He adapted Greek philosophy to Roman life and stressed the need to appreciate each person's uniqueness. His doctrine of ***humanitas*** ("humaneness," "the quality of humanity") expressed an ideal for human life based on generous and honest treatment of others and a commitment to morality based on natural law (the rights that belong to all people because they are human beings, independent of the differing laws and customs of different societies).

Greece also influenced Rome's art and architecture. Hellenistic sculptors had pioneered a realistic style showing the ravages of age and infirmity on the human body. They portrayed only stereotypes, however, such as the "old man" or the "drunken woman," not specific people. Their portrait sculpture presented actual individuals in the best possible light, much like a digitally enhanced photograph today. By contrast, Roman artists applied Greek realism to male portraiture, as contemporary Etruscan sculptors also did. They sculpted men without hiding their unflattering features: long noses, receding chins, deep wrinkles, bald heads, and worried looks. Portraits of women, by contrast, were more idealized, probably representing the traditional vision of the bliss of family life. Because the men depicted in the portraits (or their families) paid for the busts, they may have wanted their faces sculpted realistically — showing the damage of age and effort — to emphasize how hard they had worked to serve the republic.

Stresses on Society from Imperialism

The wars of the third and second centuries B.C.E. damaged small farmers, creating grave social and economic difficulties for the republic. The long deployments of troops abroad disrupted Rome's agricultural system, the economy's foundation. A farmer absent during a protracted war had to rely on a hired hand or slave to manage his crops and animals, or have his wife perform farmwork in addition to her usual family responsibilities.

The story of the consul Regulus, who won a great victory in Africa in 256 B.C.E., revealed the problems that prolonged absence caused. When the man who managed Regulus's farm died while the consul was away fighting, a worker stole all the farm's tools and livestock. Regulus begged the Senate to send a replacement fighter so that he could return to save his wife and children from starving. The senators instead sent help

to preserve Regulus's family and property because they wanted to keep him on the battle lines.

Ordinary soldiers received no special aid, and economic troubles hit them hard when, in the second century B.C.E., for unknown reasons, there was no longer enough farmland to support the population. The rich had deprived the poor of land, but recent research suggests that an increase in the number of young people created the crisis. Not all regions of Italy suffered as severely as others, and some impoverished farmers and their families survived by working as agricultural laborers for others. Many homeless people, however, relocated to Rome, where the men begged for work and women made cloth or, in desperation, became prostitutes.

This flood of landless poor created an explosive element in Roman politics by the late second century B.C.E. The government had to feed its poor citizens to avert riots, so Rome needed to import grain. The poor's demand for low-priced (and eventually free) food distributed at state expense became one of the most divisive issues in the late republic.

While the landless poor struggled, imperialism meant political and financial rewards for Rome's social elite. The need for commanders to lead military campaigns abroad

Bedroom in a Rich Roman House

This bedroom from about 40 B.C.E. was in the house of a rich Roman family near Naples; it was buried — and preserved — by the eruption of the volcano Vesuvius in 79 C.E. The bright paintings showed a dazzling variety of outdoor scenes and architecture. The stone floor helped create a sensation of coolness in the summer. (Cubiculum [bedroom] from the Villa of P. Fannius Synistor at Boscoreale, c. 50–40 B.C.E. Fresco, Room: 8 ft. ½ in. × 10 ft. 11½ in. × 19 ft. 7⅛ in. [265.4 × 334 × 583.9 cm]. Rogers Fund, 1903 [03.14.13a-g]. Location: The Metropolitan Museum of Art, New York, NY, U.S.A. Image copyright © The Metropolitan Museum of Art / Art Resource, NY.)

created opportunities for successful generals to enrich their families. The elite enhanced their reputations by spending their gains to finance public works that benefited the general population. Building new temples, for example, won praise because the Romans believed it pleased their gods to have many shrines.

The troubles of small farmers enriched landowners who could buy bankrupt farms to create large estates. Some landowners also illegally occupied public land carved out of territory seized from defeated enemies. The rich worked their huge farms, called *latifundia,* with free laborers as well as slaves who had been taken captive in the same wars that displaced so many farmers. The size of the latifundia slave crews made their periodic revolts so dangerous that the army had to fight hard to suppress them.

The elite profited from Rome's expansion by filling the governing offices in the new provinces. Some governors ruled honestly, but others used their power to squeeze the locals. Since martial law ruled, no one in the provinces could curb a greedy governor's appetite for graft and extortion. Often such offenders escaped punishment because their fellow senators excused their crimes.

The new opportunities for rich living strained the traditional values of moderation and frugality. Previously, a man could become legendary for his life's simplicity: Manius Curius (d. 270 B.C.E.), for example, boiled turnips for his meals in a humble hut despite his glorious military victories. Now the elite acquired showy luxuries, such as large country villas for entertaining friends and clients. Money had become more valuable to them than the republic's ancestral values.

> **REVIEW QUESTION**   What advantages and disadvantages did Rome's victories over foreign peoples create for both rich and poor Romans?

Civil War and the Destruction of the Republic

Conflict among members of the Roman upper class in the late second century B.C.E. turned politics into a violent competition. This conflict exploded into civil wars in the first century that destroyed the republic. Senators introduced violence to politics by murdering the tribunes Tiberius and Gaius Gracchus when the brothers pushed for reforms to help the poor by giving them land. When a would-be member of the elite, Gaius Marius, opened military service to the poor to boost his personal status, his creation of "client armies" undermined faithfulness to the general good of the community. The people's unwillingness to share citizenship with Italian allies sparked a damaging war in Italy. Finally, the competition for power by the "great men" Sulla, Pompey, and Julius Caesar peaked in destructive civil wars.

The Gracchus Brothers and Violence in Politics, 133–121 B.C.E.

Tiberius and Gaius Gracchus based their political careers on pressing the rich to make concessions to strengthen the state. Their policies supporting the poor angered many of their fellow members of the social elite. Tiberius explained the tragic circumstances motivating them:

The wild beasts that roam over Italy have their dens. . . . But the men who fight and die for Italy enjoy nothing but the air and light. They wander about homeless with their wives and children. . . . They fight and die to protect the wealth and luxury of others. They are called masters of the world, and have not a lump of earth they call their own.

When Tiberius became tribune in 133 B.C.E., he took the radical step of blocking the Senate's will by having the Plebeian Assembly vote to redistribute public land to landless Romans and to spend the Attalid king's gift of his kingdom to equip new farms on the land. Tiberius next announced he would run for reelection as tribune for the following year, violating the prohibition against consecutive terms. His opponents therefore led a band of senators and their clients to kill him and many of his clients, shouting, "Save the Republic."

Gaius, elected tribune for 123 B.C.E. and, contrary to tradition, again for the next year, also pushed measures that outraged his fellow elite: more farming reforms, subsidized prices for grain, public works projects to employ the poor, and colonies abroad with farms for the landless. His most revolutionary measures proposed Roman citizenship for many Italians, and new courts to try senators accused of corruption as provincial governors. The new juries would be manned by *equites* ("equestrians" or "knights"). These were wealthy businessmen whose focus on commerce instead of government made their interests different from the senators'. Because they did not serve in the Senate, the equites could convict senators for crimes without having to face peer pressure.

When the senators blocked Gaius's plans in 121 B.C.E., he threatened violent resistance. The senators then advised the consuls "to take all measures necessary to defend the republic," meaning they should kill anyone identified as dangerous to public order. When his enemies came to murder him, Gaius committed suicide by having a slave cut his throat. The senators then killed hundreds of his supporters.

The conflict over reforms introduced factions (aggressive interest groups) into Roman politics. Members of the elite now identified themselves as either supporters of the people, the *populares* faction, or supporters of "the best," the *optimates* faction. Some chose a faction from genuine allegiance to its policies; others supported whichever side better promoted their own political advancement. The elite's splintering into bitterly hostile factions remained a source of murderous political violence until the end of the republic.

Marius and the Origin of Client Armies, 107–100 B.C.E.

A new kind of leader arose to meet the need to combat slave revolts and foreign invasions in the late second and early first centuries B.C.E. The "new man" was an upperclass man without a consul among his ancestors, whose ability led him to fame, fortune, and — his ultimate goal — the consulship.

Gaius Marius (c. 157–86 B.C.E.), from the equites class, set the pattern for the influential "new man." Gaining fame for his brilliant military record, Marius won election as a consul for 107 B.C.E. Marius's success as a commander, first in North Africa and

next against German tribes attacking southern France and Italy, led the people to elect him consul six times, breaking all tradition.

For his victories, the Senate voted Marius a triumph, Rome's ultimate military honor. In this ceremony, crowds cheered as he rode a chariot through Rome's streets. His soldiers shouted obscene jokes about him, to ward off the evil eye at his moment of supreme glory. Despite Marius's triumph, the optimates never accepted him as an equal. His support came from the common people, whom he had won over with his revolutionary reform of entrance requirements for the army. Previously, only men with property could usually enroll as soldiers. Marius opened the ranks to **proletarians**, men who had no property and could not afford weapons. For them, serving in the army meant an opportunity to better their life by acquiring plunder and a grant of land.

Marius's reform created armies that were more loyal to their commander than to the republic. Poor Roman soldiers behaved like clients following their commander as patron, who benefited them with plunder. They in turn supported his political ambitions. Commanders after Marius used client armies to advance their careers more ruthlessly than he had, accelerating the republic's internal conflict.

Sulla and Civil War, 91–78 B.C.E.

One such commander, Lucius Cornelius Sulla (c. 138–78 B.C.E.), took advantage of uprisings by non-Romans in Italy and Asia Minor in the early first century B.C.E. to use his client army to seize Rome's highest offices and force the Senate to support him. His career revealed the dirty secret of politics in the late republic: traditional values no longer restrained commanders who prized their own advancement over peace and the good of the community.

The uprisings in Italy occurred because many of Rome's Italian allies lacked Roman citizenship and therefore had no vote in decisions that affected them. Their upper classes also wanted to share the prosperity that war brought to Rome's citizen elite. The Roman people rejected the allies' demand for citizenship, afraid that sharing such status would lessen their own privileges.

The Italians' discontent erupted in 91–87 B.C.E. in the Social War. They demonstrated their commitment by the number of their casualties — 300,000 dead. Although Rome's army prevailed, the rebels won the political war: the Romans granted citizenship and the vote to all freeborn people in Italy south of the Po River. The Social War's bloodshed therefore reestablished Rome's tradition of strengthening the state by granting citizenship to outsiders.

Sulla's generalship in the war won him election as consul for 88 B.C.E. When Mithridates VI (120–63 B.C.E.), king of Pontus on the Black Sea's southern coast, rebelled against Roman control and high taxation, Sulla seized his chance. Victory against Mithridates would mean capturing unimaginable riches from Asia Minor's cities and allow him to restore his patrician but impoverished family's status. When the Senate gave Sulla the command, Marius had it transferred to himself by plebiscite. Outraged, Sulla marched his client army against Rome. All his officers except one deserted him in

horror at this shameful attack, but his common soldiers followed him. After capturing Rome, Sulla killed or exiled his opponents. He let his men rampage through the city and then led them off to Asia Minor, ignoring a summons to stand trial and sacking Athens on the way. In Sulla's absence, Marius embarked on his own reign of terror in Rome to try to regain his former power. In 83 B.C.E., Sulla returned victorious, having allowed his soldiers to plunder Asia Minor. Civil war erupted for two years until Sulla crushed his enemies at home.

Sulla then exterminated his opponents. He used proscription — posting a list of people accused of being traitors so that anyone could hunt them down and execute them. Because proscribed men's property was confiscated, the victors fraudulently added to the list anyone whose wealth they coveted. The terrorized Senate appointed Sulla dictator — an emergency office supposed to be held only temporarily — and gave him permanent immunity from prosecution. Sulla reorganized the government to favor the optimates — his social class — by making senators the only ones allowed to judge cases against their colleagues and forbidding tribunes from sponsoring legislation or holding any other office after their term.

Sulla's career revealed the strengths and weaknesses of Roman values. First, the purpose of war had changed from defending the community to accumulating plunder for common soldiers as well as commanders. Second, the patron-client system led proletarian soldiers to feel stronger ties of loyalty to their generals than to the republic.

Finally, the traditional competition for status worked both for and against political stability. When that value motivated men to seek office to promote the community's welfare, it promoted social unity and prosperity. But pushed to its extreme, the contest for individual prestige and wealth destroyed the republic.

Julius Caesar and the Collapse of the Republic, 83–44 B.C.E.

Powerful generals after Sulla proclaimed their loyalty to the community while in reality ruthlessly pursuing their own advancement. The competition for power and money between Gnaeus Pompey and Julius Caesar, two Roman aristocrats, generated the civil war that ended the republic and led to the return of monarchy.

Escape from Troy on a Coin of Julius Caesar
This coin minted for Julius Caesar in 47/46 B.C.E. shows the hero Aeneas escaping from Troy, which the victorious Greeks were burning down. He carries his elderly father on his shoulder and the city's wooden statue of the goddess Athena in his right hand. This myth was a famous example of the Roman value of faithfulness, a quality that Caesar wanted to claim for himself at the time, when he was still fighting other Romans for control of the state as the republic was being torn apart by the violent conflict among upper-class leaders. (bpk, Berlin / Muenzkabinett, Staatliche Museen, Berlin, Germany / Art Resource, NY.)

Pompey (106–48 B.C.E.) was a brilliant general. In his early twenties he won victories supporting Sulla. In 71 B.C.E., he won the mop-up battles defeating a massive slave rebellion led by a gladiator named Spartacus, stealing the glory from the real victor, Marcus Licinius Crassus. (Spartacus had terrorized southern Italy for two years and defeated consuls with his army of 100,000 escaped slaves.) Pompey shattered tradition by demanding and receiving a consulship for 70 B.C.E., even though he was nowhere near the legal age of forty-two and had not been elected to any lower post on the ladder of offices. Three years later, he received a command to exterminate the pirates who were then infesting the Mediterranean, a task he accomplished in a matter of months. This success made him wildly popular with many groups: the urban poor, who depended on a steady flow of imported grain; merchants, who depended on safe sea lanes; and coastal communities, which were vulnerable to pirates' raids. In 66 B.C.E., he defeated Mithridates, who was still stirring up trouble in Asia Minor. By annexing Syria as a province in 64 B.C.E., Pompey ended the Seleucid kingdom and extended Rome's power to the Mediterranean's eastern coast.

People compared Pompey to Alexander the Great and added *Magnus* ("the Great") to his name. He ignored the tradition of consulting the Senate about conquering and administering foreign territories, and behaved like an independent king. He summed up his attitude by replying to some foreigners who criticized his actions as unjust: "Stop quoting the laws to us," he told them. "We carry swords."

Pompey's enemies at Rome undermined his popularity by seeking the people's support, declaring sympathy for the problems of citizens in financial trouble. By the 60s B.C.E., Rome's urban population had soared to more than half a million. Hundreds of thousands of the poor lived crowded together in slum apartments, surviving on subsidized food distributions. Jobs were scarce. Danger haunted the streets because the city had no police force. Even many formerly wealthy property owners were in trouble: Sulla's confiscations had caused land values to plummet and produced a credit crunch by flooding the real estate market with properties for sale.

The senators, jealous of Pompey's glory, blocked his reorganization of the former Seleucid kingdom and his distribution of land to his army veterans. He then negotiated with his fiercest political rivals, Crassus and Caesar (100–44 B.C.E.). In 60 B.C.E., they formed an unofficial arrangement called the **First Triumvirate** ("group of three"). Pompey forced through laws confirming his plans, reinforcing his status as a great patron. Caesar got the consulship for 59 B.C.E. and a special command in Gaul, where he could build his own client army. Crassus received financial breaks for the Roman tax collectors in Asia Minor, who supported him politically and financially.

This coalition of political rivals revealed how private relationships had largely replaced communal values in politics. To cement their political bond, Caesar arranged to have his daughter, Julia, marry Pompey in 59 B.C.E., even though she had been engaged to another man. Pompey soothed Julia's jilted fiancé by offering the hand of his own daughter, who had been engaged to yet somebody else. Through these marital machinations, the two powerful antagonists now had a common interest: the fate of Julia, Caesar's only daughter and Pompey's new wife. (Pompey had earlier divorced his second

wife after Caesar allegedly seduced her.) Pompey and Julia apparently fell deeply in love in their arranged marriage. As long as Julia lived, Pompey's affection for her kept him from breaking his alliance with her father.

During the 50s B.C.E., Caesar won his soldiers' loyalty with victories and plunder in Gaul, which he added to the Roman provinces. His political enemies in Rome dreaded his return, and the bond allying him to Pompey shattered in 54 B.C.E. when Julia died in childbirth. The two leaders' rivalry exploded into violence: gangs of their supporters battled each other in Rome's streets. The violence became so bad in 53 B.C.E. that it prevented elections. The First Triumvirate dissolved, and in 52 B.C.E. Caesar's enemies convinced the Senate to make Pompey consul alone, breaking the republic's long tradition of two consuls sharing power at the head of the state.

Civil war exploded when the Senate ordered Caesar to surrender his command. Like Sulla, Caesar led his army against Rome. In 49 B.C.E., when he crossed the Rubicon River, the official northern boundary of Italy, he uttered the famous words signaling there was now no turning back: "We have rolled the dice." His troops and the people in the countryside cheered him on. He had many backers in Rome, with the masses counting on his legendary generosity for handouts and impoverished members of the elite hoping to regain their fortunes.

The support for Caesar convinced Pompey and most senators to flee to Greece. Caesar entered Rome peacefully, left soon thereafter to defeat enemies in Spain, and then sailed to Greece. There he nearly lost the war when his supplies ran out, but his soldiers stayed loyal even when they were reduced to eating bread made from roots. When Pompey saw what Caesar's men were willing to live on, he cried, "I am fighting wild beasts." Caesar defeated Pompey and the Senate at the battle of Pharsalus in central Greece in 48 B.C.E. Pompey fled to Egypt, where the pharaoh's ministers treacherously murdered him.

Caesar then invaded Egypt, winning a difficult campaign that ended when he restored Cleopatra VII (69–30 B.C.E.) to the Egyptian throne. As ruthless as she was intelligent, Cleopatra charmed Caesar into sharing her bed and supporting her rule. Their love affair shocked the general's friends and enemies alike: they thought Rome should seize power from foreigners, not share it with them.

By 45 B.C.E., Caesar had won the civil war. He apparently believed that only a sole ruler could end the chaotic violence of the factions, but the republic's oldest tradition prohibited monarchy. So Caesar decided to rule as a king without the title, taking instead the traditional Roman title of *dictator,* used for a temporary emergency ruler. In 44 B.C.E., he announced he would continue as dictator without a term limit. "I am not a king," he insisted. The distinction, however, was meaningless. As ongoing dictator, he controlled the government. Elections for offices continued, but Caesar manipulated the results by recommending candidates to the assemblies, which his supporters dominated.

As sole ruler, Caesar imposed a moderate cancellation of debts; a cap on the number of people eligible for subsidized grain; a large program of public works, including public libraries; colonies for his veterans in Italy and abroad; plans to rebuild Corinth and Carthage as commercial centers; and citizenship for more non-Romans. Caesar

Relief Carving of Cleopatra and Her Son Caesarion
This relief carving appears on the wall of a temple at Dendera in Egypt. It depicts Cleopatra VII, queen of Egypt, and her son by Julius Caesar, Caesarion ("Little Caesar"). They are shown wearing the traditional ceremonial clothing and crowns of Egyptian pharaohs, a sign of the claim of the Ptolemaic ruling family to be the legitimate rulers of Egypt despite their Macedonian ethnic origins. Both died in 30 B.C.E. when Octavian, the adopted son of Julius Caesar and soon to become Augustus and the ruler of Rome, conquered Egypt and made it a Roman province. (© Ancient Art and Architecture Collection, Ltd.)

treated his opponents mildly, thereby obligating them to become his grateful clients. Caesar's decision not to seek revenge earned him unheard-of honors, such as a special golden seat in the Senate house and the renaming of the seventh month of the year after him (July). He also regularized the Roman calendar by having each year include 365 days, a calculation based on an ancient Egyptian calendar that forms the basis for our modern one.

Caesar's dictatorship satisfied the people but outraged the optimates. They resented being dominated by one of their own, a "traitor" who had deserted to the people's faction. Some senators, led by Caesar's former close friend Marcus Junius Brutus (85–42 B.C.E.), conspired to murder him. They stabbed Caesar repeatedly in the Senate house on March 15 (the Ides of March), 44 B.C.E. When Brutus struck him, Caesar gasped his last words — in Greek: "You, too, son?" He collapsed dead at the foot of a statue of Pompey.

The liberators, as they called themselves, had no new plans for government. They apparently expected the republic to revive automatically after Caesar's murder, ignoring the political violence of the past century and the deadly imbalance in Roman values, with "great men" placing their competitive private interests above the community's well-being. The liberators were stunned when the people rioted at Caesar's funeral to vent their anger against the upper class that had robbed them of their generous patron. Instead of then forming a united front, the elite resumed their personal vendettas. The traditional values of the republic failed to save it.

REVIEW QUESTION What factors generated the conflicts that caused the Roman republic's destruction?

Ides of March Coin Celebrating Caesar's Murder
Coins were the most widely distributed form of art and communication in the Roman world. Their messages became topical and contemporary during the crisis of the late republic. Caesar's assassins, led by Marcus Junius Brutus, issued this coin celebrating the murder and their claim to be liberators. The daggers refer to their method, while the conical cap stands for liberation — it was the kind of headgear worn by slaves who had won their freedom. The inscription gives the date of the assassination, the Ides of March (March 15). What political message was intended by putting pictures of murder weapons on a coin? (© The Trustees of the British Museum / Art Resource, NY.)

Conclusion

The two most remarkable features of the Roman republic's history were its tremendous expansion and its violent disintegration. Rome expanded to control vast territories because it incorporated outsiders, its small farmers produced agricultural surpluses to support a growing population and army, and its leaders respected the traditional values stressing the common good. The Romans' willingness to endure great loss of life and property — the proof of faithfulness — made their army unstoppable: Rome might lose battles, but never wars. Because wars of conquest brought profits to leaders and the common people alike, peace seemed a wasted opportunity.

But the victories over Carthage and in Macedonia and Greece had unexpected consequences. Long military service ruined many farming families, and poor people flocked to Rome to live on subsidized food, becoming an unstable political force. Members of the upper class increased their competition with one another for the career opportunities presented by constant war. These rivalries became dangerous to the state when successful generals began acting as patrons to client armies of poor troops. Violence and murder became common in political disputes. Communal values submerged in the blood of civil war. No one could have been optimistic about the chances for an enduring peace following Caesar's assassination in 44 B.C.E. It would have seemed an impossible dream to imagine that Caesar's grandnephew and adopted son, Octavian — a teenage student at the time of the murder — would eventually bring peace by creating a new political system disguised as the restoration of the old republic.

Review Questions

1. What common themes underlay Roman values, and how did Romans' behavior reflect those values?
2. How and why did the Roman republic develop its complicated political and judicial systems?
3. What advantages and disadvantages did Rome's victories over foreign peoples create for both rich and poor Romans?
4. What factors generated the conflicts that caused the Roman republic's destruction?

Making Connections

1. How did the political and social values of the Roman republic compare to those of the Greek city-state in the Classical Age?
2. What were the positive and the negative consequences of war for the Roman republic?
3. How can people decide what is the best balance between individual advancement and communal stability?

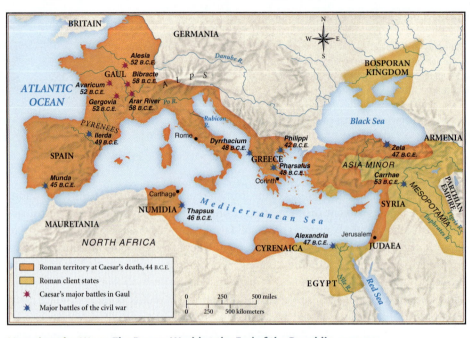

Mapping the West The Roman World at the End of the Republic, 44 B.C.E.
By the time of Julius Caesar's assassination in 44 B.C.E., the territory that would be the Roman Empire was almost complete. Caesar's young relative Octavian (the future Augustus) would conquer and add Egypt in 30 B.C.E. Geography, distance, and formidable enemies were the primary factors inhibiting further expansion—which Romans never stopped wanting, even when lack of money and political discord rendered it purely theoretical. The deserts of Africa and the once again powerful Persian kingdom in the Near East worked against expansion southward or eastward, while trackless forests and fierce resistance from local inhabitants made expansion into central Europe and the British Isles impossible to maintain.

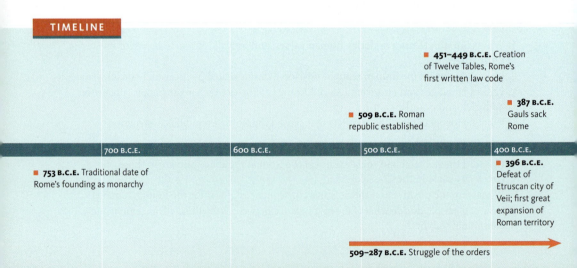

TIMELINE

451–449 B.C.E. Creation of Twelve Tables, Rome's first written law code

387 B.C.E. Gauls sack Rome

509 B.C.E. Roman republic established

700 B.C.E.   600 B.C.E.   500 B.C.E.   400 B.C.E.

753 B.C.E. Traditional date of Rome's founding as monarchy

396 B.C.E. Defeat of Etruscan city of Veii; first great expansion of Roman territory

509–287 B.C.E. Struggle of the orders

- For practice quizzes and other study tools, visit the **Online Study Guide** at bedfordstmartins.com/huntconcise.

- For primary-source material from this period, see *Sources of the Making of the West,* Fourth Edition.

- For Web sites, images, and documents related to topics in this chapter, visit *Make History* at bedfordstmartins.com/huntconcise.

Suggested References

Scholars continue to debate the causes and the effects of the rise and fall of the Roman republic, focusing in particular on the intended and unintended political, social, and cultural consequences of the many wars that the Romans fought in this period.

Beard, Mary, et al. *Religions of Rome*. 2 vols. 1998.

Billows, Richard. *Julius Caesar: The Colossus of Rome*. 2008.

*Caesar. *The Civil War*. Trans. John Carter. 1997.

*Cicero. *On the Good Life*. Trans. Michael Grant. 1971.

Cornell, Tim. *The Beginnings of Rome: Italy and Rome from the Bronze Age to the Punic Wars (c. 1000–264 B.C.)*. 1995.

Daily life (and more): http://www.vroma.org/~bmcmanus/romanpages.html

Earl, Donald. *The Moral and Political Tradition of Rome*. 1967.

Flower, Harriet. *Roman Republics*. 2009.

Gardner, Jane. *Women in Roman Law and Society*. 1986.

Goldsworthy, Adrian. *The Punic Wars*. 2000.

Haynes, Sybill. *Etruscan Civilization: A Cultural History*. 2005.

Hoyos, Dexter. *The Carthaginians*. 2010.

*Plutarch. *The Fall of the Roman Republic*. Trans. Rex Warner. Rev. ed. 2006.

Ramage, Nancy H., and Andrew Ramage. *Roman Art*. 2008.

Roller, Duane W. *Cleopatra: A Biography*. 2010.

*Primary source.

264–241 B.C.E. Rome and Carthage fight First Punic War

218–201 B.C.E. Rome and Carthage fight Second Punic War

220 B.C.E. Rome controls Italy south of Po River

168–149 B.C.E. Cato writes The Origins, first history of Rome in Latin

149–146 B.C.E. Rome and Carthage fight Third Punic War

133 B.C.E. Tiberius Gracchus elected tribune; assassinated in same year

146 B.C.E. Carthage and Corinth destroyed

60 B.C.E. First Triumvirate of Caesar, Pompey, and Crassus

91–87 B.C.E. Social War between Rome and its Italian allies

44 B.C.E. Caesar appointed dictator with no term limit; assassinated in same year

49–45 B.C.E. Civil war, with Caesar the victor

45–44 B.C.E. Cicero writes his philosophical works on *humanitas*

300 B.C.E.   200 B.C.E.   100 B.C.E.   0

6

The Creation of the Roman Empire

44 B.C.E.–284 C.E.

I N 203 C.E., VIBIA PERPETUA, wealthy and twenty-two years old, sat in a Carthage jail, nursing her infant. She was condemned to death for treason, having refused to sacrifice to the gods for the Roman emperor's health and safety. Perpetua recorded what happened when the local governor tried to persuade her to save her life:

> My father came carrying my son, shouting "Perform the sacrifice; take pity on your baby!" Then the governor said, "Think of your old father; show pity for your little child! Offer the sacrifice for the imperial family's well being." "I refuse," I answered. "Are you a Christian?" asked the governor. "Yes." When my father would not stop trying to change my mind, the governor ordered him thrown to the earth and whipped with a rod. I felt sorry for my father; it seemed they were beating me. I pitied his pathetic old age.

Gored by a wild cow and stabbed by a gladiator, Perpetua died because she placed her faith above her duty of loyalty to her family and the state.

Rome's rulers during what we call the Roman Empire punished disloyalty because it threatened to reignite the civil wars that had destroyed the Roman republic. The refusal of Christians such as Perpetua to perform traditional sacrifice was considered treason because Romans believed the gods would punish them for sheltering people who refused to worship them and rejected the traditional religion.

Mosaic of Chariot Racing

Racing four-horse chariots was the most popular — and most expensive — sport in the Roman Empire. This mosaic, a picture made from thousands of tiny colored tiles put together like a giant jigsaw puzzle, shows a driver holding a branch signifying that he has just won a big race. Two attendants or race officials are in the background. Hundreds of thousands of spectators attended the largest races at the Circus Maximus in Rome, but many cities across the empire had tracks. Romans loved the races' action and potential violence, as chariots swerved at top speed around and around the tight turns of the track and sometimes collided in bloody accidents.

(National Museum of Archeology, Madrid, Spain / ullstein bild / AISA.)

The transformation from republic to empire opened with seventeen years of civil war after Julius Caesar's death in 44 B.C.E. Finally, in 27 B.C.E., his adopted son, Octavian (thereafter known as Augustus), created a disguised monarchy to end the violence, declaring that he had restored the republic. Augustus's new system retained traditional institutions for sharing power — the Senate, the consuls, the courts — but in reality he and his successors governed like kings ruling an empire.

Augustus's innovations brought peace for two hundred years, except for a struggle between generals for rule in 69 C.E. This **Pax Romana** ("Roman Peace") allowed agriculture and trade to flourish in the provinces, but paying for the military eventually weakened Rome. Previously, foreign wars had won Romans huge amounts of land and money, but now the distances were too great and the enemies too strong. The army was no longer an offensive weapon for expansion that brought in new taxes but instead a defense force that had to be paid for out of existing revenues. The financial strain drained the treasury and destabilized the government. Christianity emerged as a new religion that would slowly transform the Roman world, but it also created tension because the growing presence of Christians made other Romans worry about punishment from the gods. In the third century C.E., a crisis developed when generals competing to rule reignited civil war that lasted fifty years.

CHAPTER FOCUS   How did Augustus's "restored republic" successfully keep the peace for more than two centuries, and why did it fail in the third century?

From Republic to Empire, 44 B.C.E.–14 C.E.

It takes time for a new tradition to take hold. Augustus created his new political system gradually; following his favorite saying, Augustus "made haste slowly." He succeeded because he reinvented government, guaranteed the army's support, did not hesitate to use violence to win power, and built political legitimacy by communicating an image of himself as a dedicated leader and patron. He announced his respect for tradition and established his disguised monarchy as Rome's political system, thereby saving the state from anarchy. Succeeding where Caesar had failed, Augustus preserved his power by making the new look old.

Civil War, 44–27 B.C.E.

The main competitors in the civil war after Caesar's death were his friend Mark Antony and Caesar's eighteen-year-old grandnephew and adopted son, Octavian (the future Augustus). Octavian won over Caesar's soldiers by promising them money he had inherited from their general. Marching them to Rome, the teenager Octavian forced the Senate to make him consul in 43 B.C.E., ignoring the ladder of offices.

Octavian and Mark Antony joined with a general named Lepidus to eliminate rivals. In 43 B.C.E., they formed the Second Triumvirate to reorganize the government.

They murdered many of their enemies, including some of their own relatives, and seized their property.

Octavian and Antony then forced Lepidus out and fought each other. Antony controlled the eastern provinces by allying with the ruler of Egypt, Queen Cleopatra VII (69–30 B.C.E.), who had earlier allied with Caesar. Dazzled by her intelligence and magnetism, Antony, who was married to Octavian's sister, fell in love with Cleopatra. Octavian rallied support by claiming that Antony planned to make this foreign queen Rome's ruler. He made the residents of Italy and the western provinces swear an oath of allegiance to him. Octavian's victory in the naval battle of Actium in northwest Greece in 31 B.C.E. won the war. Cleopatra and Antony fled to Egypt, where they both committed suicide in 30 B.C.E. The general Mark Antony first stabbed himself, bleeding to death in his lover's embrace. Queen Cleopatra then ended her life by allowing a poisonous snake to bite her. Octavian's revenues from the capture of Egypt made him Rome's richest citizen.

The Creation of the Principate, 27 B.C.E.–14 C.E.

In 27 B.C.E., Octavian proclaimed that he "gave back the state from [his] own power to the control of the Roman Senate and the people" and announced they should decide how to preserve it. Recognizing Octavian's power, the senators asked him to safeguard the state, granted him special civil and military powers, and bestowed on him the honorary title **Augustus**, meaning "divinely favored."

Augustus changed Rome's political system, but he retained the name *republic* and maintained the appearance of representative government. Citizens elected consuls, the Senate gave advice, and the assemblies met. Augustus occasionally served as consul, but mostly he let others hold that office. He concealed his monarchy by referring to himself only with the honorary title *princeps,* meaning "first man" (among social equals), a term of status from the republic. The Romans used the term *princeps* to describe the position that we call emperor, and so the Roman government in the early empire after 27 B.C.E. is best described as the *principate*. Each new princeps was supposed to be chosen only with the Senate's approval, but in practice each ruler chose his own successor, like a royal family decides who will be king. To preserve the tradition that no official should hold more than one post at a time, Augustus as princeps had the Senate grant him the powers, though not the office, of a tribune. In 23 B.C.E., the Senate agreed that Augustus should also have a consul's power to command (*imperium*): in fact, his power would be superior to that held by the actual consuls.

Holding the power of a tribune and a power even greater than that of a consul meant that Augustus could rule the state without filling any formal executive political office. Augustus insisted that people obeyed him not out of fear but out of respect for his *auctoritas* ("moral authority"). Since Augustus realized that symbols affect people's perception of reality, he dressed and acted modestly, like a regular citizen, not an arrogant king. Livia, his wife, played a prominent role as his political adviser and partner

in publicly upholding old-fashioned values. In fact, Augustus and the emperors who came after him were able to exercise supreme power because they controlled the army and the treasury. Later Roman emperors held the same power but continued to refer to the state as the republic; the senators and the consuls continued to exist, and the rulers continued to pretend to respect them.

Augustus made the military the foundation of the emperor's power by turning the republic's citizen militia into a professional, full-time army and navy. He established regular lengths of service and retirement benefits, thereby making the emperor the troops' patron and solidifying their loyalty to him. To pay the added costs, Augustus imposed Rome's first inheritance tax on citizens, angering the rich. He also stationed several thousand soldiers in Rome for the first time ever. These soldiers — the **praetorian guard** — would later play a crucial role in selecting the next emperor when the current one died. Augustus meant them to provide security for him and prevent rebellion in the capital by serving as a visible reminder that the superiority of the princeps was backed by the threat of armed force.

Augustus constantly promoted his image as patron and public benefactor. He used media as small as coins and as large as buildings. As a mass-produced medium for official messages, Roman coins functioned like modern political advertising. They proclaimed slogans such as "Father of His Country" to stress Augustus's moral authority, or "Roads have been built" to emphasize his generosity.

Augustus used his personal fortune to erect spectacular public buildings in Rome. The huge Forum of Augustus, dedicated in 2 B.C.E., best illustrates his skill at communicating messages through architecture (Figure 6.1). This public gathering space centered on a temple to Mars, the god of war. Two-story colonnades held statues of famous Roman heroes to serve as inspirations to the young. Augustus's forum hosted religious rituals

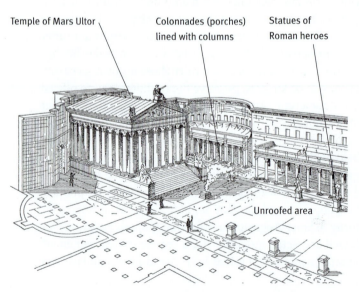

Temple of Mars Ultor

Colonnades (porches) lined with columns

Statues of Roman heroes

Unroofed area

Figure 6.1 Cutaway Reconstruction of the Forum of Augustus

Augustus built this large forum (120 × 90 yards) to commemorate his victory over the assassins of Julius Caesar. The centerpiece was a marble temple to Mars Ultor ("Mars the Avenger"), and inside the temple were statues of Mars, Venus (the divine ancestor of Julius Caesar), and Julius Caesar (as a god), as well as works of art and Caesar's sword. The two spaces flanking the temple featured statues of Aeneas and Romulus, Rome's founders. The high stone wall behind the temple protected it from fire, a constant threat in the crowded neighborhood behind.

and the coming-of-age ceremonies of upper-class boys. As a symbol, it demonstrated his justifications for ruling: a new age of peace and security through military power, devotion to the gods protecting Rome, respect for tradition, and generosity in spending money on public works.

Augustus used the paternalism of the patron-client system to make the princeps everyone's most important patron, possessing the moral authority to guide their lives. When in 2 B.C.E. the Senate and the people proclaimed Augustus "Father of His Country," the title emphasized that the emperor governed like a father: stern but caring, expecting obedience and loyalty from his children, and taking care of them in return. The goal was stability and order, not freedom.

Augustus ruled until his death at age seventy-five in 14 C.E. As the historian Tacitus (c. 56–120 C.E.) remarked, by the time Augustus died after a reign of forty-one years, "almost no one was still alive who had seen the republic." His longevity, military innovations, support for the masses, and manipulation of political symbols had allowed Augustus to create the Roman Empire.

Daily Life in the Rome of Augustus

In Augustan Rome's population of nearly one million, many had no regular jobs and too little to eat. The streets were packed: "One man jabs me with his elbow, another whacks me with a pole; my legs are smeared with mud, and big feet step on me from all sides," one poet wrote of walking in Rome. To ease congestion in the narrow streets, the city banned wagons in the daytime.

Most residents lived in small apartments in multistoried buildings called islands. The first floors housed shops, bars, and restaurants. The higher the floor, the cheaper the rent. The wealthy, who lived at ground level, had piped-in water. The less fortunate had to fill water jugs at public fountains, to which aqueducts delivered fresh water, and then lug the heavy jugs up the stairs. Most people had to use the public latrines or keep buckets for toilets at home and then carry the waste down to the streets for sewage collectors. Sanitation was a problem in this city that generated sixty tons of human waste daily.

However, low fees for public baths meant that almost everyone could bathe regularly. Baths were centers for exercising and socializing. Bathers progressed through a series of increasingly warm areas until they reached a sauna-like room. They swam naked in their choice of either hot or cold pools. Men and women bathed apart.

Augustus improved public safety and health. He instituted the first public fire department in Western history. He also established Rome's first permanent police force. He greatly enlarged the city's main sewer, but its contents still emptied untreated into the Tiber River. Also, poor people often left human and animal corpses in the streets, to be gnawed by birds and dogs. Flies and no refrigeration contributed to frequent gastrointestinal ailments. The wealthy splurged on luxuries such as snow rushed from the mountains to ice their drinks and slaves to clean their houses, which were built around courtyards and gardens. Roman architects built public structures with concrete, brick, and stone that lasted centuries, but crooked contractors cheated on materials for

A Roman Street

Like Pompeii, the town of Herculaneum on the Bay of Naples was frozen in time by the volcanic eruption of Mount Vesuvius in 79 C.E. Mud from the eruption buried the town and preserved its buildings. Herculaneum's straight roads paved with flat stones and sidewalks were typical for a Roman town. Balconies jutted from the houses, offering a shady viewing point for life in the streets. Roman houses often enclosed a garden courtyard instead of having yards in front or back. Why do you think urban homes had this arrangement? (Scala / Art Resource, NY.)

private buildings; therefore, apartment buildings sometimes collapsed. Augustus imposed a height limit of seventy feet on new apartment buildings to limit the danger.

As the people's patron, Augustus paid for grain to feed the poor, extending the government's traditional distribution of food to 250,000 heads of households. From this grain, people made bread or soup, adding beans, leeks, or cheese if they could afford them; they washed down these meals with cheap wine. The rich ate more costly food, such as roast pork or seafood with honey and vinegar sauce.

Wealthy Romans increasingly spent money on luxuries and political careers instead of raising families. Fearing the falling birthrate would destroy the social elite on whom Rome relied for public service, Augustus granted privileges to the parents of three or more children. He criminalized adultery, even exiling his own daughter — his only child — and a granddaughter for sex scandals. His legislation failed, however, and the prestigious old families dwindled over time. With each generation three-quarters of senatorial families lost their official status by either spending all their money or dying off without having children. The emperors filled the open places in the social hierarchy and the Senate with equites and provincials.

Since imperial Rome still gave citizenship to freed slaves, all slaves hoped someday to become a free Roman citizen, regardless of how they had originally become enslaved (by being captured in war, stolen from their home region by slave traders, or born to slave women as the owner's property). Freed slaves' descendants, if they became wealthy, could become members of the social elite. This policy of giving citizenship to former slaves meant that eventually most Romans had slave ancestors.

The harshness of slaves' lives varied widely. Slaves in agriculture and manufacturing had a grueling existence, while household slaves lived better. Modestly prosperous families owned one or two slaves, while rich houses and the imperial palace owned large numbers. Domestic slaves were often women, working as nurses, maids, kitchen helpers, and clothes makers. Some male slaves ran businesses for their masters and were often allowed to keep part of the profits, which they could save to purchase their freedom. Women had less opportunity to earn money, though masters sometimes granted tips for sexual favors to both female and male slaves. Many female prostitutes were slaves working for their owner in a brothel. Slaves with savings would sometimes buy other slaves, especially to have a mate; they were barred from legal marriage, because they and their children remained their master's property, but they could live as a shadow family. Some masters' tomb inscriptions express affection for a slave, but if slaves attacked their owner, the punishment was death.

Violence featured in much of Roman public entertainment. The emperors provided shows featuring hunters killing wild beasts, animals mangling condemned criminals, mock naval battles in flooded arenas, gladiatorial combats, and wreck-filled chariot races. Spectators were seated according to their social rank and gender. The emperor and senators sat up front, while women and the poor were in the upper tiers.

Criminals and slaves could be forced to fight as gladiators, but free people also voluntarily competed, hoping to become celebrities and win prizes. Most gladiators were men, though women could fight other women until such matches were banned around 200 C.E. Gladiators were often wounded or killed, but their contests rarely required a fight to the death, unless they were captives or criminals. To make the fights unpredictable, pairs of gladiators often competed with different weapons. One favorite bout pitted a lightly armored "net man" with a net and a trident against a heavily armored "fish man," so named from his helmet design. Betting was popular, and the crowds were rowdy.

Public entertainment supported communication between the ruler and the ruled. Emperors provided gladiatorial combats, chariot races, and theater productions for the masses, and ordinary citizens staged protests at them to express their wishes. Poor Romans, for example, rioted to protest shortfalls in the free grain supply.

Changes in Education, Literature, and Art in Augustus's Rome

Elite culture changed in the Augustan period to serve the same goal as public entertainment: legitimizing the transformed political system. Orators — who developed the skill to speak persuasively and critically — lost their freedom of expression, as did artists. Under the republic, the ability to make critical speeches about political opponents had been such a powerful weapon that it could catapult a "new man" like Cicero to a leadership role. Now, the emperor's dominance limited frank political debate or subversive art. Criticism of the ruler was very dangerous.

With no public schools, only wealthy Romans received formal education. Most people learned only through working. As a character in a novel said, "I didn't study geometry and literary criticism and worthless junk like that. I just learned how to read

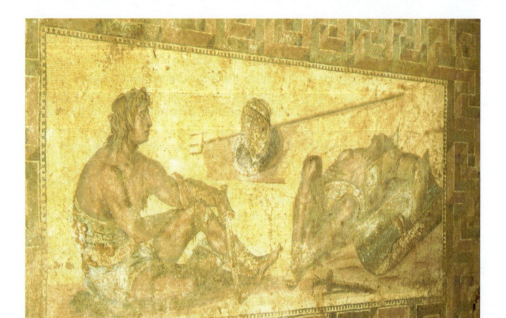

Gladiator after a Kill
This first-century C.E. mosaic covered a villa floor in North Africa. It shows a gladiator staring at the opponent he has just killed. What feelings do you think his expression conveys? Gladiatorial combats originated as part of wealthy people's funeral ceremonies, symbolizing the human struggle to avoid death. Training an expert gladiator took many years and great expense. Like boxers today, gladiators fought only a couple of times a year. Because it cost so much to replace a dead gladiator, most fights were not to the death intentionally; however, kills often happened in the fury of combat. (Photo courtesy Helmut Ziegert / University of Hamburg.)

the letters on signs and how to work out percentages, and I learned weights, measures, and the values of the different kinds of coins." Rich boys and girls attended private elementary schools to learn reading, writing, and arithmetic. Some went on to study literature, history, and grammar. Only a few boys then proceeded to study advanced literature and history, rhetoric, ethical philosophy, law, and dialectic (reasoned argument). Mathematics and science were rarely studied as separate subjects, but engineers and architects became proficient at calculation.

Scholars call the Augustan period the Golden Age of Latin literature. The emperor was the patron for writers and artists. Augustus's favorite authors were Horace (65–8 B.C.E.) and Virgil (70–19 B.C.E.). Horace's poem celebrating Augustus's victory at Actium became famous for its opening line: "Now we have to drink!" Virgil's epic poem *The Aeneid* became Rome's most famous work of literature. Inspired by Homer, Virgil told the story of the Trojan Aeneas, the original founder of Rome. Virgil balanced his praise

Marble Statue of Augustus from Prima Porta

At six feet eight inches high, this statue of Augustus stood a foot taller than he did. Found at his wife Livia's country villa at Prima Porta ("First Gate"), the portrait was probably done about 20 B.C.E., when Augustus was in his forties; however, it shows him as younger, using the idealizing techniques of classical Greek art. Compare his smooth face to the realistic portraiture in Chapter 5. The statue's symbols communicate Augustus's image: his bare feet hint he is a near-divine hero, the Cupid refers to the Julian family's descent from the goddess Venus (the Roman equivalent of Aphrodite, Greek goddess of love), and the breastplate's design shows a Parthian surrendering to a Roman soldier under the gaze of personified cosmic forces admiring the peace Augustus's regime has created. (Scala / Art Resource, NY.)

for Roman civilization with the acknowledgment that peace existed at the cost of freedom.

Livy (54 B.C.E.–17 C.E.) wrote a history of Rome recording Augustus's ruthlessness in the civil war after Caesar's murder. The emperor only scolded him, because Livy's work proclaimed that stability and prosperity depended on traditional values of loyalty and self-sacrifice. The poet Ovid (43 B.C.E.–17 C.E.), however, wrote *Art of Love* and *Love Affairs* to mock the emperor's moral legislation with witty advice on sexual affairs and adultery. Ovid's work *Metamorphoses* undermined the idea of natural hierarchy with stories of supernatural shape-changes, with people becoming animals and mixing the human and the divine. Augustus exiled the poet in 8 B.C.E. for his alleged involvement in the scandal involving the emperor's granddaughter.

Changes in public sculpture also reflected the emperor's supremacy. Augustus preferred sculpture that had an idealized style. In the Prima Porta statue, Augustus had himself portrayed as serene and dignified, not weary and sick, as he often was. As with architecture, Augustus used sculpture to project a calm and competent image of himself as the "Restorer of the Roman Republic" and founder of a new age for Rome.

> **REVIEW QUESTION** How did the peace gained through Augustus's "restoration of the Roman republic" affect Romans' lives in all social classes?

Politics and Society in the Early Roman Empire

Since Augustus claimed his system was not a monarchy, his successor could inherit his power only with the Senate's approval. Augustus therefore decided to identify an heir for the Senate to recognize as princeps after his death. This strategy succeeded and

kept rule in his family, called the **Julio-Claudians**, until the death in 68 C.E. of Nero, Augustus's last descendent. It established the tradition that family dynasties ruled the principate.

The Julio-Claudian emperors worked to prevent unrest, maintain loyalty, finance the administration and army, and govern the provinces. Augustus set the pattern for effective imperial rule: take special care of the army, communicate the emperor's image as a just ruler and generous patron, and promote Roman law and culture as universal standards. The citizens, in return for their loyalty, expected the emperors to be generous patrons — but the difficulties of long-range communication imposed practical limits on imperial support of or intervention in the lives of the residents of the provinces.

The Perpetuation of the Principate after Augustus, 14–180 C.E.

Augustus needed the Senate to bestow legitimacy on his successor to continue his disguised monarchy. Having no son, he adopted Livia's son by a previous marriage, Tiberius (42 B.C.E.–37 C.E.). Since Tiberius had a brilliant career as a general, the army supported Augustus's choice. Augustus had the Senate grant Tiberius the power of a tribune and the power of a consul equal to his own; his hope was that the senators would recognize Tiberius as emperor after his death. The senators did just that when Augustus died in 14 C.E.

Tiberius (r. 14–37 C.E.) was able to stay in power for twenty-three years because he retained the army's loyalty. He built the praetorian guard a fortified camp in Rome to help its soldiers protect the emperor. The guards would influence all future successions — no emperor could come to power without their support.

Tiberius's long reign made permanent the compromise between the elite and the emperor that promoted political stability. The offices of consul, senator, and provincial governor continued, with elite Romans filling them and enjoying their prestige, but the emperors not only decided who received the offices but also controlled law and government policy. The social elite supported the regime by staying loyal and managing the collection of taxes while governing provinces. (The emperor used his own assistants to govern the provinces that housed strong military forces.) Everyone saved face by pretending that the republic's traditional offices retained their original power.

Tiberius paid a bitter price to rule. To strengthen their family tie, Augustus had forced Tiberius to divorce his beloved wife, Vipsania, to marry Augustus's daughter, Julia — a marriage that proved disastrously unhappy. When Tiberius's sadness led him to spend his reign's last decade in seclusion far from Rome, his neglect of the government permitted abuses in the capital and kept him from training a decent successor.

Tiberius designated Gaius, better known as Caligula (r. 37–41 C.E.), to be the next emperor, and the Senate approved him because the young man was Augustus's great-grandson. The third Julio-Claudian emperor might have been successful because he knew about soldiering: *Caligula* means "baby boots," the nickname the soldiers gave him as a child because he wore little leather shoes like theirs when he was growing up in the military garrisons his father commanded. Caligula, however, bankrupted the

treasury to satisfy his desires. His biographer labeled him a monster for his murders and sexual crimes, which some said included incest with his sisters. He outraged the elite by fighting in mock gladiatorial combats and appearing in public in women's clothing or costumes imitating gods. He once said, "I'm allowed to do anything." The praetorian commanders murdered him in his fourth year of rule to avenge personal insults.

The senators then debated the idea of truly restoring the republic by refusing to approve a new emperor. They backed down, however, when Claudius (r. 41–54 C.E.), Augustus's grandnephew, bribed the praetorian guard to support him. The soldiers' insistence on having an emperor so that they would have a patron signaled that the original republic was never coming back.

Claudius was an active emperor, commanding a successful invasion of Britain in 43 C.E. that made much of the island into a Roman province. He promoted provincial elites' participation in government by enrolling men from Gaul in the Senate. In return for keeping their regions peaceful and ensuring tax payments, upper-class provincials received offices and prestige at Rome. Claudius also transformed imperial bureaucracy by employing freed slaves as powerful administrators who owed loyalty only to the emperor.

Claudius's successor, Nero (r. 54–68 C.E.), became emperor at sixteen. He loved music and acting, not governing. The poor loved him for his public entertainments and distributions of cash. His generals suppressed a revolt in Britain led by the woman commander Boudica in 60 C.E. and fought the Jewish rebels against Roman rule in Judaea in 66 C.E., but he had no military career. A giant fire in 64 C.E. (the event behind the legend that Nero fiddled while Rome burned) aroused suspicions that he ordered the city burned to make space for a new palace. Nero emptied the treasury by building a huge palace. To raise money, he faked treason charges against senators and equites to seize their property. When his generals toppled his regime in 68 C.E., Nero had a servant help him cut his own throat.

Nero's death sparked a civil war in 69 C.E. during which four generals competed for power. Vespasian (r. 69–79 C.E.) won. To give his new dynasty (the Flavians) legitimacy, Vespasian had a law passed granting him the powers of previous good emperors, pointedly leaving Caligula and Nero off the list. He encouraged the imperial cult (worship of the emperor as a living god and sacrifices for his household's welfare) in the provinces beyond Italy but not in Italy itself, where it would have disturbed traditional Romans. The imperial cult communicated the image of the emperor as a superhuman who provided benefactions and deserved loyalty.

Vespasian's sons, Titus (r. 79–81 C.E.) and Domitian (r. 81–96 C.E.), conducted hardheaded fiscal policy and wars. Titus had suppressed the Jewish revolt, capturing Jerusalem in 70 C.E. He sent relief to Pompeii and Herculaneum when, in 79 C.E., Mount Vesuvius's volcanic eruption buried these towns. He built Rome's **Colosseum**, outfitting the fifty-thousand-seat amphitheater with awnings to shade the crowd. The Colosseum was constructed on the site of the private fishpond in Nero's palace to demonstrate the Flavian dynasty's commitment to the people.

When Titus died suddenly after only two years as emperor, his brother, Domitian, stepped in. Domitian balanced the budget and campaigned against the Germanic tribes threatening the empire's northern frontiers. Domitian's arrogance turned the senators against him; once he sent them a letter announcing, "Our lord god, myself, orders you to do this." Domitian executed numerous upper-class citizens as disloyal. Fearful that they, too, would become victims, his wife and members of his court murdered him in 96 C.E.

The next five emperors gained reputations for ruling well: Nerva (r. 96–98 C.E.), Trajan (r. 98–117 C.E.), Hadrian (r. 117–138 C.E.), Antoninus Pius (r. 138–161 C.E.), and Marcus Aurelius (r. 161–180 C.E.). Historians call this period the Roman political Golden Age because it had peaceful successions for nearly a century. Wars and rivalry among the elite continued, however. Trajan fought to expand Roman control across the Danube River into Dacia (today Romania) and eastward into Mesopotamia (Map 6.1); Hadrian executed several senators as alleged conspirators, punished a Jewish revolt by turning Jerusalem into a military colony, and withdrew Roman forces from Mesopotamia; and Marcus Aurelius fought off invaders from the Danube region as the dangers to imperial territory along the northern frontiers kept increasing.

Still, the five "good emperors" did preside over a political and economic Golden Age. They succeeded one another without murder or conspiracy — the first four, having no surviving sons, used adoption to find the best possible successor. The economy provided enough money to finance building projects such as the fortification wall Hadrian built across Britain. Most important, the army remained obedient. These reigns marked Rome's longest stretch without a civil war since the second century B.C.E.

Life in the Roman Golden Age, 96–180 C.E.

Peace and prosperity in Rome's Golden Age depended on defense by a loyal military, service by provincial elites in local administration and tax collection, common laws enforced throughout the empire, and a healthy population reproducing itself. The empire's vast size and the relatively small numbers of soldiers and imperial officials in the provinces meant that emperors had only limited control over these factors.

In theory, Rome's military goal was to expand perpetually because conquest brought land, money, and glory. In reality, the emperors lacked the resources to expand the empire much beyond the territory that Augustus had controlled, and they had to concentrate on defending imperial territory.

Most provinces were peaceful, housing few troops. Most legions (units of five thousand troops) were stationed on frontiers to prevent invasions from Germanic tribes to the north and Persians to the east. The peace allowed long-distance trade to import luxury goods, such as spices and silk, from as far away as India and China. Roman merchants regularly sailed from Egypt to India and back.

The army of both Romans and noncitizens reflected the population's diversity. Serving under Roman officers, the non-Romans learned to speak Latin and follow Roman customs. Upon discharge, they received Roman citizenship. Thus the army helped spread a common way of life.

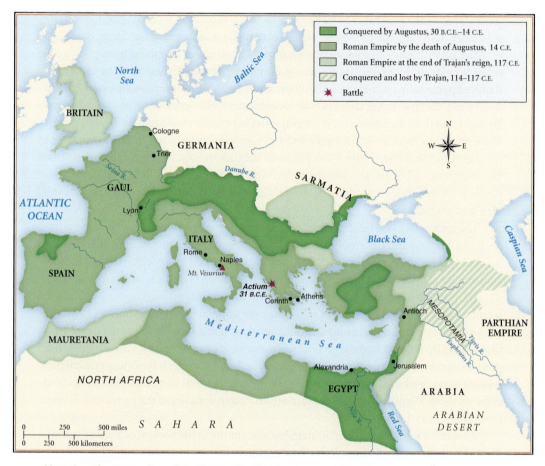

Map 6.1 The Expansion of the Roman Empire, 30 B.C.E.–117 C.E.
When Octavian (the future Augustus) captured Egypt in 30 B.C.E. after the suicides of Mark Antony and Cleopatra, he greatly boosted Rome's economic strength. The land produced enormous amounts of grain and metals, and Roman power now almost encircled the Mediterranean Sea. When Emperor Trajan took over the southern part of Mesopotamia in 114–117 C.E., imperial conquest reached its height; Rome's control had never extended so far east. Egypt remained part of the empire until the Arab conquest in 642 C.E., but Mesopotamia was immediately abandoned by Hadrian, Trajan's successor, probably because it seemed too distant to defend. How did territorial expansion both strengthen and weaken the Roman Empire?

Paying for defense became an impossible problem. Previously, foreign wars had brought in revenue from riches and prisoners of war sold as slaves. Conquered territory also provided regular income from taxes. Now the army was no longer making conquests, but the soldiers had to be paid well to maintain discipline. This made a soldier's career desirable but cost the emperors dearly.

A tax on agriculture in the provinces (Italy was exempt) now provided the principal source of revenue. The bureaucracy was inexpensive because it was small: only several hundred officials governed a population of about fifty million. Most locally collected

taxes stayed in the provinces to pay expenses there, especially soldiers' pay. Governors with small staffs ran the provinces, which eventually numbered about forty.

The government's finances depended on tax collection carried out by provincial elites. Serving as **decurions** (members of municipal Senates), these wealthy men were required personally to guarantee that their area's financial responsibilities were met. If there was a shortfall in tax collection or local finances, the decurions had to pay the difference from their own pockets. Wise emperors kept taxes moderate. As Tiberius put it when refusing a request for tax increases from provincial governors, "I want you to shear my sheep, not skin them alive." The financial liability in holding civic office made that honor expensive, but the accompanying prestige made the elite willing to take the risk. Rewards for decurions included priesthoods in the imperial cult, an honor open to both men and women.

The system worked because it observed tradition: the local elites were their communities' patrons and the emperor's clients. As long as there were enough rich, public-spirited provincials participating, the principate functioned by fostering the old ideal of community service by the upper class in return for respect and social status.

The provinces contained diverse peoples who spoke different languages, observed different customs, dressed in different styles, and worshipped different divinities (Map 6.2). In the countryside, Roman conquest only lightly affected local customs. In new towns that sprang up around Roman forts or settlements of army veterans, Roman influence predominated. Roman culture had the greatest effect on western Europe, permanently rooting Latin (and the languages that would emerge from it) as well as Roman law and customs there. Eventually, emperors came from citizen-families in the provinces; Trajan, from Spain, was the first.

Romanization, the spread of Roman law and culture in the provinces, raised the standard of living by providing roads and bridges, increasing trade, and establishing peaceful conditions for agriculture. The army's need for supplies created business for farmers and merchants. The prosperity that provincials enjoyed under Roman rule made Romanization acceptable. In addition, Romanization was not a one-way street. In western regions as diverse as Gaul, Britain, and North Africa, interaction between the local people and Romans produced mixed cultural traditions, especially in religion and art. Therefore, Romanization merged Roman and local culture. (See the illustration on page 184.)

The eastern provinces, however, largely retained their Greek and Near Eastern characteristics. Huge Hellenistic cities such as Alexandria (in Egypt) and Antioch (in Syria) rivaled Rome in size and splendor. The eastern provincial elites readily accepted Roman governance because Hellenistic royal traditions had prepared them to see the emperor as their patron and themselves as his clients.

The continuing vitality of Greek language and culture contributed to new trends in Roman literature. Lucian (c. 117–180 C.E.) composed satirical dialogues in Greek mocking stuffy and superstitious people. The essayist and philosopher Plutarch (c. 50–120 C.E.) also used Greek to write paired biographies of Greek and Roman men. His exciting stories made him favorite reading for centuries; William Shakespeare based several plays on Plutarch's biographies.

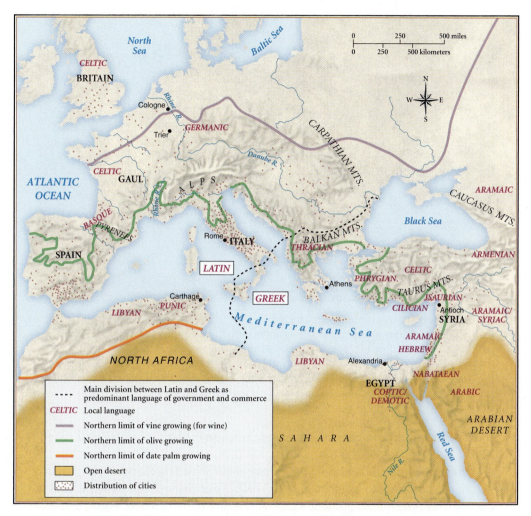

Map 6.2 Natural Features and Languages of the Roman World

The environment of the Roman world included a large variety of topography, climate, and languages. The inhabitants of the Roman Empire, estimated to have numbered as many as fifty million, spoke dozens of different tongues, many of which survived well into the late empire. The two predominant languages were Latin in the western part of the empire and Greek in the eastern. Latin remained the language of law even in the eastern empire. Vineyards and olive groves were important agricultural resources because wine was regarded as an essential beverage, and olive oil was the principal source of fat for most people as well as being used to make soap, perfume, and other products for daily life. Dates and figs were popular sweets in the Roman world, which had no refined sugar.

The late first century and early to mid-second century C.E. can be called the Silver Age of Latin literature. Tacitus (c. 56–120 C.E.) wrote historical works that exposed the Julio-Claudian emperors' ruthlessness. Juvenal (c. 65–130 C.E.) wrote poems ridiculing pretentious Romans while complaining about living broke in the capital. Apuleius (c. 125–170 C.E.) excited readers with a sexually explicit novel called *The Golden Ass,*

Roman Theater at Sabratha in North Africa
This theater, with its three-story scene building at the back of the stage, was built in the late third century C.E. at the coastal city of Sabratha in Libya. Phoenicians had founded Sabratha as a trading station some eight hundred years earlier; it was still flourishing under the Roman Empire. The size of this very expensive building shows the importance that Romans attached to public entertainment for large numbers of people. (Frans Lemmens / The Image Bank / Getty Images.)

about a man turned into a donkey who regains his body and his soul through the kindness of the Egyptian goddess Isis.

The emperors made the laws for the entire empire based on the principle of equity. This meant doing what was "good and fair" even if that required ignoring the letter of the law. This principle taught that a contract's intent outweighed its words, and that accusers should prove the accused guilty because it was unfair to make defendants prove their innocence. The emperor Trajan ruled that no one should be convicted on the grounds of suspicion alone because it was better for a guilty person to go unpunished than for an innocent person to be condemned.

The importance of hierarchy led Romans to continue formal distinctions in society based on wealth. The elites constituted a tiny portion of the population. Only about one in every fifty thousand had enough money to qualify for the senatorial order, the highest-ranking class, while about one in a thousand belonged to the equestrian order, the second-ranking class. Different purple stripes on clothing identified these orders. The third-highest order consisted of decurions, the local Senate members in provincial towns.

The legal distinction between the elite and the rest of the population now became stricter. "Better people" included senators, equites, decurions, and retired army veterans. Everybody else — except slaves, who counted as property — made up the vastly larger group of "humbler people." The law imposed harsher penalties on them than on "better

people" for the same crime. "Humbler people" convicted of serious crimes were regularly executed by being crucified or torn apart by wild animals before a crowd of spectators. "Better people" rarely received the death penalty, and those who did were allowed a quicker and more dignified execution by the sword. "Humbler people" could also be tortured in criminal investigations, even if they were citizens. Romans regarded these differences as fair on the grounds that an elite person's higher status required of him or her a higher level of responsibility for the common good. As one provincial governor expressed it, "Nothing is less equitable than mere equality itself."

Nothing mattered more to the empire's strength than steady population levels. Concerns about marriage and reproduction thus filled Roman society; remaining single and childless represented social failure for both women and men. The propertied classes usually arranged marriages. Girls often married in their early teens, to have as many years as possible to bear children. Because so many babies died young, families had to produce numerous offspring to keep from disappearing. The tombstone of Veturia, a soldier's wife, tells a typical story: "Here I lie, having lived for twenty-seven years. I was married to the same man for sixteen years and bore six children, five of whom died before I did."

The social pressure to bear numerous children created many health hazards for women. Doctors possessed metal instruments for surgery and physical examinations,

Midwife's Sign
Childbirth carried the danger of death from infection or internal hemorrhage. This terra-cotta sign from Ostia, the ancient port city of Rome, probably hung outside a midwife's room to announce her expertise in helping women give birth. It shows a pregnant woman clutching the sides of her chair, with an assistant supporting her from behind and the midwife crouched in front to help deliver the baby. Why do you think the woman is seated for delivery instead of lying down? Such signs were especially effective for people who were illiterate; a person did not have to read to understand the services that the specialist inside could provide. (Scala / Art Resource, NY.)

but many were poorly educated former slaves with only informal training. There was no official licensing of medical personnel. Complications in childbirth could easily kill the mother because doctors and midwives could not stop internal bleeding or cure infections. Romans controlled reproduction with contraception (by obstructing the vagina or by administering drugs to the female partner) or by abandoning unwanted infants.

The emperors tried to support reproduction. They gave money to feed needy children, hoping they would grow up to have families. Wealthy people often adopted children in their communities. One North African man supported three hundred boys and three hundred girls each year until they grew up.

REVIEW QUESTION   In the early Roman Empire, what was life like in the cities and in the country for the elite and for ordinary people?

The Emergence of Christianity in the Early Roman Empire

Christianity began as what scholars call "the Jesus movement," a Jewish splinter group in Judaea (today Israel and the Palestinian Territories). There, as elsewhere under Roman rule, Jews were allowed to worship in their ancestral religion. The emergence of the new religion was gradual: three centuries after the death of Jesus, Christians were still a minority in the Roman Empire. Moreover, Roman officials suspected that Christians' beliefs made them disloyal. Christianity grew because of the attraction of Jesus's charismatic career, its message of salvation, its early members' sense of mission, and the strong bonds of community it inspired. Ultimately, Christianity's emergence proved the most significant development in Roman history.

Jesus and His Teachings

Jesus (c. 4 B.C.E.–30 C.E.) grew up in a troubled region. Harsh Roman rule in Judaea had angered the Jews, and Rome's provincial governors worried about rebellion. Jesus's execution reflected the Roman policy of eliminating any threat to social order. In the two decades after his crucifixion, his followers, particularly Paul of Tarsus, elaborated on and spread his teachings beyond his region's Jewish community to the wider Roman world.

Christianity offered an answer to the question about divine justice raised by the Jews' long history of oppression under the kingdoms of the ancient and Hellenistic Near East: If God was just, as Hebrew monotheism taught, how could he allow the wicked to prosper and the righteous to suffer? Nearly two hundred years before Jesus's birth, persecution by the Seleucid king Antiochus IV (r. 175–164 B.C.E.) had provoked the Jews into revolt, a struggle that generated the concept of apocalypticism (see Chapter 2, page 46).

According to this doctrine, evil powers controlled the world, but God would end their rule by sending the Messiah ("anointed one," *Mashiach* in Hebrew, **Christ** in Greek) to conquer them. A final judgment would follow, punishing the wicked and rewarding the righteous for eternity. Apocalypticism especially influenced the Jews living in Judaea under Roman rule and later inspired Christians and Muslims.

During Jesus's life, Jews disagreed among themselves about what form Judaism should take in such troubled times. Some favored cooperation with Rome, while others preached rejection of the non-Jewish world. Unrest in Judaea led Augustus to install a Roman governor to suppress disorder.

The writings that would later become the New Testament Gospels, composed around 70 to 90 C.E., offer the earliest accounts of Jesus's life. Jesus wrote nothing down, and others' accounts of his words and deeds are often inconsistent. He began his career as a teacher and healer during the reign of Emperor Tiberius. He taught through stories and parables that challenged his followers to reflect on what he meant.

Jesus's public ministry began with his baptism by John the Baptist, who preached a message of repentance before the approaching final judgment. After John was executed as a rebel, Jesus traveled around Judaea's countryside teaching that God's kingdom was coming and that people needed to prepare spiritually for it. Some saw Jesus as the Messiah, but his apocalypticism did not call for immediate revolt against the Romans. Instead, he taught that God's true kingdom was to be found not on earth but in heaven. He stressed that this kingdom was open to believers regardless of their social status or sinfulness. His emphasis on God's love for humanity and people's responsibility to love one another reflected Jewish religious teachings, such as the scriptural interpretations and moral teachings of the scholar Hillel, who lived in Jesus's time.

Realizing that he had to reach more than country people, Jesus took his message to the Jewish population of Jerusalem, the region's main city. His miraculous healings and exorcisms, combined with his powerful preaching, created a sensation. So popular was he that his followers created the Jesus movement; it was not yet Christianity but rather a Jewish sect, of which there were several, such as the Saducees and Pharisees, competing for authority at the time. Jesus attracted the attention of Jewish leaders, who assumed that he wanted to replace them. Fearing Jesus might lead a Jewish revolt, the Roman governor Pontius Pilate ordered his crucifixion in Jerusalem in 30 C.E.

Jesus's followers reported that they had seen him in person after his death, proclaiming that God had raised him from the dead. They convinced a few other Jews that he would soon return to judge the world and begin God's kingdom. At this time, his closest disciples, the twelve Apostles (Greek for "messengers"), still considered themselves faithful Jews and continued to follow the commandments of Jewish law. Their leader was Peter, who won acclaim as the greatest miracle worker of the Apostles, an ambassador to Jews interested in the Jesus movement, and the most important messenger proclaiming Jesus's teachings in the imperial capital. The later Christian church called him the first bishop of Rome.

A turning point came with the conversion of Paul of Tarsus (c. 10–65 C.E.), a pious Jew and a Roman citizen who had violently opposed Jews who accepted Jesus as the Messiah. A spiritual vision on the road to Damascus in Syria, which Paul interpreted as a divine revelation, inspired him to become a follower of Jesus as the Messiah, or Christ — a Christian, as members of the movement came to be known. Paul taught that accepting Jesus as divine and his crucifixion as the ultimate sacrifice for the sins of humanity was the only way of becoming righteous in the eyes of God. In this way alone could one

expect to attain salvation in the new world to come. Paul's mission opened the way for Christianity to become a new religion separate from Judaism.

Seeking converts outside Judaea, Paul traveled to preach to Jews and Gentiles (non-Jews) who had adopted some Jewish practices in Asia Minor (today Turkey), Syria, and Greece. Although he stressed the necessity of ethical behavior as defined by Jewish tradition, especially the rejection of sexual immorality and polytheism, Paul also taught that converts did not have to live strictly according to Jewish law. To make conversion easier, he did not require male converts to undergo the Jewish initiation rite of circumcision. He also told his congregations that they did not have to observe Jewish dietary restrictions or festivals. These teachings generated tensions with Jewish authorities in Jerusalem as well as with followers of Jesus living there, who still believed that Christians had to follow Jewish law. Roman authorities arrested Paul as a troublemaker and executed him in 65 C.E.

Hatred of Roman rule provoked Jews to revolt in 66 C.E. After crushing the rebels in 70 C.E., the Roman emperor Titus destroyed the Jerusalem temple and sold most of the city's population into slavery. Following this catastrophe, which cost Jews their religious center, Christianity began to separate more and more clearly from Judaism.

Paul's importance in early Christianity shows in the number of letters — thirteen — attributed to him among the twenty-seven Christian writings that were eventually put together as the New Testament. Christians came to regard the New Testament as having equal authority with the Jewish Bible, which they then called the Old Testament. Since teachers like Paul preached mainly in the cities, congregations of Christians sprang up in urban areas. In early Christianity, women in some locations could be leaders — such as Lydia, a businesswoman who founded the congregation in Philippi in Greece — but many men, including Paul, opposed women's leadership.

Growth of a New Religion

Christianity faced serious obstacles as a new religion. Imperial officials, suspecting Christians of being traitors, could prosecute them for refusing to perform traditional sacrifices. Christian leaders had to build an organization from scratch to administer their growing congregations. Finally, Christians had to decide whether women could continue as leaders in their congregations.

The Roman emperors found Christians baffling and troublesome. Unlike Jews, Christians professed a new faith rather than their ancestors' traditional religion. Roman law therefore granted them no special treatment, as it did Jews out of respect for the great age of Judaism. Most Romans feared that Christians' denial of the old gods and the imperial cult would bring divine punishment upon the empire. Secret rituals in which Christians symbolically ate the body and drank the blood of Jesus during communal dinners, called Love Feasts, led to accusations of cannibalism and sexual promiscuity.

Romans were quick to blame Christians for disasters. Nero declared that Christian arsonists set Rome's great fire, and he covered Christians in animal skins to be torn to

Catacomb Painting of Christ as the Good Shepherd

Catacombs (tunnels with underground rooms) cut deep into soft rock outside major cities in the Roman Empire served as meeting places and burial chambers for Jews and Christians. Rome had 340 miles of catacombs. This painting from the catacomb at Rome named after Priscilla, who was probably a Christian from the first century C.E., shows Jesus as the Good Shepherd (John 10:10–11). He is carrying an animal back to the flock, symbolizing his role as savior; he is dressed in the traditional fashion for a Roman man on a special occasion. Catacomb paintings such as this one were the earliest form of Christian art. (Catacomb of Priscilla, Rome, Italy / photograph by Erich Lessing / Art Resource, NY.)

pieces by dogs or fastened to crosses and set on fire at night. Nero's cruelty, however, earned Christians sympathy from Rome's population.

Persecutions like Nero's were infrequent. There was no law against Christianity, but officials could punish Christians, as they could anyone, to protect public order. Pliny's actions as a provincial governor in Asia Minor illustrated the situation. In about 112 C.E., Pliny asked a group of people accused of following this new religion if they were really Christians. When some said yes, he asked them to reconsider. He freed those who denied Christianity, so long as they sacrificed to the gods, swore loyalty to the imperial cult, and cursed Christ. He executed those who refused these actions. Christians argued that Romans had nothing to fear from their faith. Christianity, they insisted, taught morality and respect for authority. It was the true philosophy, combining the best features of Judaism and Greek thought.

The occasional persecutions in the early empire did not stop Christianity. Christians like Vibia Perpetua regarded public executions as an opportunity to become a **martyr** (Greek for "witness"), someone who dies for his or her religious faith. Martyrs' belief that their deaths would send them directly to paradise allowed them to face torture. Some Christians actively sought to become martyrs. Tertullian (c. 160–240 C.E.) proclaimed that "martyrs' blood is the seed of the Church." Ignatius (c. 35–107 C.E.), bishop of Antioch, begged Rome's congregation, which was becoming the most prominent Christian group, not to ask the emperor to show him mercy after his arrest: "Let me be food for the wild animals [in the arena] through which I can reach God," he pleaded. "I am God's wheat, to be ground up by the teeth of beasts so that I may be found pure

bread of Christ." Stories reporting the martyrs' courage showed that the new religion gave its believers spiritual power to endure suffering.

First-century C.E. Christians expected Jesus to return to pass judgment on the world during their lifetimes. When that did not happen, they began transforming their religion from an apocalyptic Jewish sect expecting the immediate end of the world into one that could survive indefinitely. This transformation was painful because early Christians fiercely disagreed about what they should believe, how they should live, and who had the authority to decide these questions. Some insisted Christians should withdraw from the everyday world to escape its evil, abandoning their families and shunning sex and reproduction. Others believed they could follow Christ's teachings while living ordinary lives. Many Christians worried they could not serve as soldiers without betraying their faith because the army participated in the imperial cult. This dilemma raised the further issue of whether Christians could remain loyal subjects of the emperor. Disagreement over these doctrinal questions raged in the many congregations that arose in the early empire around the Mediterranean, from Gaul to Africa to the Near East (Map 6.3).

The need to deal with such tensions, to administer the congregations, and to promote spiritual communion among believers led Christians to create an official hierarchy

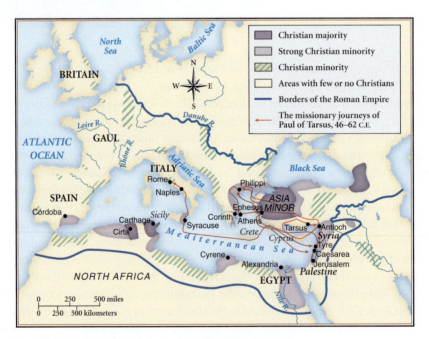

Map 6.3 Christian Populations in the Late Third Century C.E.
Christians were still a minority in the Roman world three hundred years after Jesus's crucifixion. However, certain areas of the empire—especially Asia Minor, where Paul had preached—had a concentration of Christians. Most Christians lived in cities and towns, where the missionaries had gone to find crowds to hear their message. *Paganus*, a Latin word for "country person" or "rural villager," came to mean a believer in traditional polytheistic cults—hence the word *pagan* that modern historians sometimes use to indicate traditional polytheism. Paganism lived on in rural areas for centuries.

of men, headed by bishops. They spearheaded the drive to build the connection between congregations and Christ that promised salvation to believers. Bishops possessed authority to define Christian doctrine and administer practical affairs for congregations. The emergence of bishops became the most important institutional development in early Christianity. Bishops received their positions according to the principle later called **apostolic succession**, which states that the Apostles appointed the first bishops as their successors, granting these new officials the authority Jesus had originally given to the Apostles. Those designated by the Apostles in turn appointed their own successors. Bishops had authority to ordain ministers with the holy power to administer the sacraments, above all baptism and communion, which believers regarded as necessary for achieving eternal life. Bishops also controlled their congregations' memberships and finances. The money financing the early church came from members' donations.

The bishops tried to suppress the disagreements that arose in the new religion. They used their authority to define **orthodoxy** (true doctrine) and **heresy** (false doctrine). The meetings of the bishops of different cities constituted the church's organization in this period. Today this loose organization is referred to as the early Catholic (Greek for "universal") church. Since the bishops often disagreed about doctrine and about which bishops should have greater authority than others, unity remained impossible to achieve.

When the male bishops came to power, they demoted women from positions of leadership. This change reflected their view that in Christianity women should be subordinate to men, just as in Roman imperial society in general.

Some congregations took a long time to accept this shift, however, and women still claimed authority in some groups in the second and third centuries C.E. In late-second-century C.E. Asia Minor, for example, Prisca and Maximilla declared themselves prophetesses with the power to baptize believers in anticipation of the coming end of the world. They spread the apocalyptic message that the heavenly Jerusalem would soon descend in their region.

Excluded from leadership posts, many women chose a life without sex to demonstrate their devotion to Christ. Their commitment to celibacy gave these women the power to control their own bodies. Other Christians regarded women who reached this special closeness to God as holy and socially superior. By rejecting the traditional roles of wife and mother in favor of spiritual excellence, celibate Christian women achieved independence and status otherwise denied them.

Competing Religious Beliefs

Three centuries after Jesus's death, traditional polytheism was still the religion of the overwhelming majority of the Roman Empire's population. Polytheists, who worshipped a variety of gods in different ways in diverse kinds of sanctuaries, often reflecting regional religious rituals and traditions, never created a unified religion. Nevertheless, the stability and prosperity of the early empire gave traditional believers confidence that the old gods and the imperial cult protected them. Even those who preferred religious philosophy, such as Stoicism's idea of divine providence, respected the old cults because

they embodied Roman tradition. By the third century C.E., the growth of Christianity, along with the persistence of Judaism and polytheistic cults, meant that people could choose from a number of competing beliefs. Especially appealing were beliefs that offered people hope that they could change their present lives for the better and also look forward to an afterlife.

Polytheistic religion aimed at winning the goodwill of all the divinities who could affect human life. Its deities ranged from the state cults' major gods, such as Jupiter and Minerva, to spirits thought to inhabit groves and springs. International cults such as the mystery cults of Demeter and Persephone outside Athens remained popular.

The cults of Isis and Mithras demonstrate how polytheism could provide a religious experience arousing strong emotions and demanding a moral way of life. The Egyptian goddess Isis had already attracted Romans by the time of Augustus, who tried to suppress her cult because it was Cleopatra's religion. But the fame of Isis as a kind, compassionate goddess who cared for her followers made her cult too popular to crush: the Egyptians said it was her tears for starving humans that caused the Nile to flood every year and bring them good harvests. Her image was that of a loving mother, and in art she was often depicted nursing her son. Her cult's central doctrine concerned the death and resurrection of her husband, Osiris. Isis also promised her believers a life after death.

Isis required her followers to behave righteously. Many inscriptions expressed her high moral standards by listing her own civilizing accomplishments: "I broke down the rule of tyrants; I put an end to murders; I caused what is right to be mightier than gold and silver." The hero of Apuleius's novel *The Golden Ass* shouts out his intense joy after his rescue and spiritual rebirth through Isis: "O holy and eternal guardian of the human race, who always cherishes mortals and blesses them, you care for the troubles of miserable humans with a sweet mother's love. Neither day nor night, nor any moment of time, ever passes by without your blessings." Other cults also required worshippers to lead upright lives. Inscriptions from Asia Minor, for example, record people's confessions to sins such as sexual transgressions for which their local god had imposed severe penance.

Archaeology reveals that the cult of Mithras had many shrines under the Roman Empire, but no texts survive to explain its mysterious rituals and symbols, which Romans believed had originated in Persia. Mithras's legend said that he killed a bull in a cave, apparently as a sacrifice for the benefit of his worshippers. As pictures show (see the illustration on page 193), this was an unusual sacrifice because the animal was allowed to struggle as it was killed. Initiates in Mithras's cult proceeded through rankings named, from bottom to top, Raven, Male Bride, Soldier, Lion, Persian, Sun-runner, and Father — the latter a title of great honor.

Many upper-class Romans also guided their lives by Greek philosophy. Most popular was Stoicism, which presented philosophy as the "science of living" and required self-discipline and duty from men and women alike. (See Chapter 4, page 127.) Philosophic individuals put together their own set of beliefs, such as those on duty expressed by the emperor Marcus Aurelius in his memoirs, entitled *To Myself* (or *Meditations*).

Christian and polytheist intellectuals debated Christianity's relationship to Greek philosophy. Origen (c. 185–255 C.E.) argued that Christianity was superior to Greek philo-

Mithras Slaying the Bull

Hundreds of shrines to the mysterious god Mithras have been found in the Roman Empire. Scholars debate the symbolic meaning of the bull slaying that is prominent in art connected to Mithras's cult, as in this wall painting of about 200 C.E. from the shrine at Marino, south of Rome. Here, a snake and a dog lick the sacrificial animal's blood, while a scorpion pinches its testicles as it dies in agony. The ancient sources do not clarify the scene's meaning. What do you think could be the explanation for this type of sacrifice? (Scala / Art Resource, NY.)

sophical doctrines as a guide to correct living. At about the same time, Plotinus (c. 205–270 C.E.) developed the philosophy that had the greatest influence on religion. His spiritual philosophy was influenced by Persian religious ideas and, above all, Plato's philosophy, for which reason it is called **Neoplatonism**. Plotinus's ideas deeply influenced many Christian thinkers as well as polytheists. He wrote that ultimate reality is a trinity of The One, of Mind, and of Soul. By rejecting the life of the body and relying on reason,

individual souls could achieve a mystic union with The One, who in Christian thought would be God. To succeed in this spiritual quest required strenuous self-discipline in personal morality and spiritual purity as well as in philosophical contemplation.

REVIEW QUESTION   Which aspects of social, cultural, and political life in the early Roman Empire supported the growth of Christianity, and which opposed it?

From Stability to Crisis in the Third Century C.E.

In the third century C.E., military expenses provoked a financial crisis that fed a political crisis lasting from the 230s to the 280s C.E. Invasions on the northern and eastern frontiers had forced the Roman emperors to expand the army for defense, but no new revenues came in to meet the increased costs. The emperors' desperate schemes to pay for defense damaged the economy and infuriated the population. This anger at the regime encouraged generals to repeat the behavior that had destroyed the republic: commanding client armies to seize power in a prolonged civil war. Earthquakes and regional epidemics added to people's misery. By 284 C.E., this combination of troubles had destroyed the Pax Romana.

Threats to the Northern and Eastern Frontiers of the Early Roman Empire

Emperors since Domitian in the first century had combated invaders. The most aggressive attackers were the multiethnic bands from northern Europe that crossed the Danube and Rhine Rivers to raid Roman territory. These attacks perhaps resulted from pressure on the northerners caused by wars in central Asia that disrupted trade and the economy. These originally poorly organized northerners developed military discipline through their frequent fighting against the Roman army. They mounted especially damaging invasions during the reign of Marcus Aurelius (r. 161–180 C.E.). A major threat also appeared at the eastern edge of the empire, when a new Persian dynasty, the Sasanids, defeated the Parthian Empire and fought to re-create the ancient Persian Empire. By the early third century C.E., Persia's renewed military power forced the Roman emperors to deploy a large part of the army to protect the rich eastern provinces, which took troops away from defense of the northern frontiers.

Recognizing the northern warriors' bravery, the emperors had begun hiring them as auxiliary soldiers for the Roman army in the late first century C.E. and settling them on the frontiers as buffers against other invaders. By the early third century, the army had expanded to enroll perhaps as many as 450,000 troops (the size of the navy remains unknown). Training constantly, soldiers had to be able to carry forty-pound packs twenty miles in five hours, swimming rivers on the way. Since the early second century C.E., the emperors had built stone camps for permanent garrisons, but while on the march an army constructed a fortified camp every night. Soldiers transported all the makings of a wooden walled city everywhere they went. As one ancient commentator noted, "Infantrymen were little different from loaded pack mules." At one temporary fort in a frontier area, archaeologists found a supply of a million iron nails — ten tons' worth. The same encampment required seventeen miles of timber for its barracks' walls. To outfit a single legion with tents required fifty-four thousand calves' hides.

The increased demand for pay and supplies strained imperial finances. The army had become a source of negative instead of positive cash flow to the treasury, and the economy had not expanded to make up the difference. To make matters worse, inflation

had driven up prices. The principate's long period of peace promoted inflation by increasing demand for goods and services to a level that outstripped the supply.

In desperation, some emperors attempted to curb inflation by debasing imperial coinage. **Debasement of coinage** meant putting less silver in each coin without changing its face value. In this way, the emperors created more cash from the same amount of precious metal. (See "Taking Measure," below.) But merchants soon raised prices to make up for the debased coinage's reduced value; this in turn produced more inflation, causing prices to rise even more. Still, the soldiers demanded that their patrons, the emperors, pay them well. This pressure drove imperial finances into collapse by the 250s C.E.

Uncontrolled Spending, Natural Disasters, and Political Crisis, 193–284 C.E.

The emperors Septimius Severus (r. 193–211 C.E.) and his son Caracalla (r. 211–217 C.E.) made financial crisis unavoidable when they drained the treasury to satisfy the army and their own dreams of glory. A soldier's soldier from North Africa, Severus became emperor when his predecessor's incompetence caused a government crisis and civil war. Seeking to restore imperial prestige and acquire money from foreign conquest, Severus campaigned beyond the frontiers of the provinces in Mesopotamia and Scotland.

Since inflation had reduced their wages to almost nothing, soldiers expected the emperors to provide gifts of extra money. Severus spent large sums on gifts and raised soldiers' pay by a third. The army's expanded size made this raise more expensive than the treasury could handle. The out-of-control spending did not trouble Severus. His

Taking Measure **The Value of Roman Imperial Coinage, 27 B.C.E.–300 C.E.**
Ancient silver coinage got its value from its metallic content; the less silver in a coin, the less the coin was worth. When government and military expenses rose but revenues fell because no conquests were being made, emperors debased the coinage by reducing the amount of silver and increasing the amount of other, cheaper metals in each coin. These pie charts reveal that devaluation of the coinage was gradual until the third century C.E., when military expenses skyrocketed. By 300 C.E., coins contained only a trace amount of silver. Debasement fueled inflation because merchants and producers had to raise their prices for goods and services when they were paid with currency that was increasingly less valuable. (Adapted from Kevin Greene, *The Archeology of the Roman Empire* [London: B. T. Batsford, Ltd., 1986], 60.)

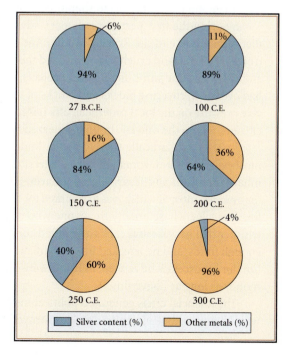

27 B.C.E. — 94%, 6%
100 C.E. — 89%, 11%
150 C.E. — 84%, 16%
200 C.E. — 64%, 36%
250 C.E. — 40%, 60%
300 C.E. — 96%, 4%

Silver content (%)   Other metals (%)

Emperor Severus and His Family

This portrait of the emperor Septimius Severus; his wife, Julia Domna; and their sons, Caracalla (on the right) and Geta (with his face obliterated), was painted in Egypt about 200 C.E. The males hold scepters, symbolic of rule, but all four family members wear bejeweled golden crowns fit for royalty. Severus arranged to marry Julia without ever meeting her because her horoscope predicted she would become a queen, and she served as her husband's valued adviser. They hoped their sons would share rule, but when Severus died in 211 C.E., Caracalla murdered Geta so that he could rule alone. Why do you think the portrait's owner rubbed out Geta's face? (bpk, Berlin / Antikensammlung, Staatliche Museen, Berlin, Germany / photo by Johannes Laurentius / Art Resource, NY.)

deathbed advice to his sons, Caracalla and Geta, in 211 C.E. was to "stay on good terms with each other, be generous to the soldiers, and pay no attention to anyone else."

Ignoring the first part of his father's advice, Caracalla murdered his brother. He then went on to end the Roman Golden Age of peace and prosperity with his uncontrolled spending and cruelty. He increased the soldiers' pay by another 40 to 50 percent and spent gigantic sums on building projects, including the largest public baths Rome had ever seen, covering blocks and blocks of the city. These huge expenses put unbearable pressure on the local provincial officials responsible for collecting taxes and on the citizens, whom the officials in turn squeezed for ever larger payments.

In 212 C.E., Caracalla tried to fix the budget by granting Roman citizenship to almost every man and woman in imperial territory except slaves. Since only citizens paid inheritance taxes and fees for freeing slaves, an increase in citizens meant an increase in revenues, most of which was earmarked for the army. But too much was never enough for Caracalla, whose cruelty to anyone who displeased him made his contemporaries whisper that he was insane. His attempted conquests of new territory failed to bring in enough funds, and he wrecked imperial finances. Once when his mother reprimanded him for his excesses he replied, as he drew his sword, "Never mind, we won't run out of money as long as I have this."

The financial crisis generated political instability that led to a half century of civil war. This period of violent struggle destroyed the principate. More than two dozen

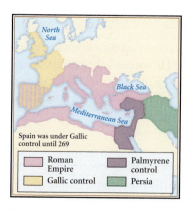

North
Sea

Black Sea

Mediterranean Sea

Spain was under Gallic
control until 269

☐ Roman
Empire
☐ Gallic control

☐ Palmyrene
control
☐ Persia

**The Fragmented Roman Empire
of the Third Century**

men, often several at once, held or claimed power in this period. Their only qualification was their ability to command a frontier army and to reward the troops for loyalty to their general instead of to the state.

The civil war devastated the population and the economy. Violence and hyperinflation made life miserable in many regions. Agriculture withered as farmers could not keep up normal production when armies searching for food ravaged their crops. City council members faced constantly escalating demands for tax revenues from the swiftly changing emperors. The endless financial pressure destroyed members' will to serve their communities.

Earthquakes and epidemics also struck the provinces in the mid-third century. In some regions, the population declined significantly as food supplies became less dependable, civil war killed soldiers and civilians alike, and infection raged. The loss of population meant fewer soldiers for the army, whose strength as a defense and police force had been gutted by political and financial chaos. This weakness made frontier areas more vulnerable to raids and allowed roving bands of robbers to range unchecked inside the borders.

Foreign enemies to the north and east took advantage of the third-century crisis to attack. Roman fortunes hit bottom when Shapur I, king of the Sasanid Empire of Persia, invaded the province of Syria and captured the emperor Valerian (r. 253–260 C.E.). By this time, Roman imperial territory was in constant danger of being captured. Zenobia, the warrior queen of Palmyra in Syria, for example, seized Egypt and Asia Minor. Emperor Aurelian (r. 270–275 C.E.) won back these provinces only with great difficulty. He also had to encircle Rome with a larger wall to ward off attacks from northern raiders, who were smashing their way into Italy.

Polytheists explained the third-century crisis in the traditional way: the state gods were angry about something. But what? To them, the obvious answer was the presence of Christians, who denied the existence of the Roman gods and refused to worship them. Emperor Decius (r. 249–251 C.E.) therefore launched a systematic persecution to eliminate Christians and restore the goodwill of the gods. He ordered all the empire's inhabitants to prove their loyalty to the state by sacrificing to its gods. Christians who refused were killed. This persecution did not stop the civil war, economic failure, and natural disasters that threatened Rome's empire, and Emperor Gallienus (r. 253–268 C.E.) ordered Christians to be left alone and their property restored. The crisis in government continued, however, and by the 280s C.E. the principate had reached a political dead end.

REVIEW QUESTION What were the causes and the effects of the Roman crisis in the third century C.E.?

Conclusion

Augustus created the principate and the Pax Romana by constructing a disguised monarchy while insisting that he was restoring the republic. He succeeded by ensuring the loyalty of both the army and the people to him by becoming their patron. He bought off the upper class by letting them keep their traditional offices and status. The imperial cult provided a focus for building and displaying loyalty to the emperor.

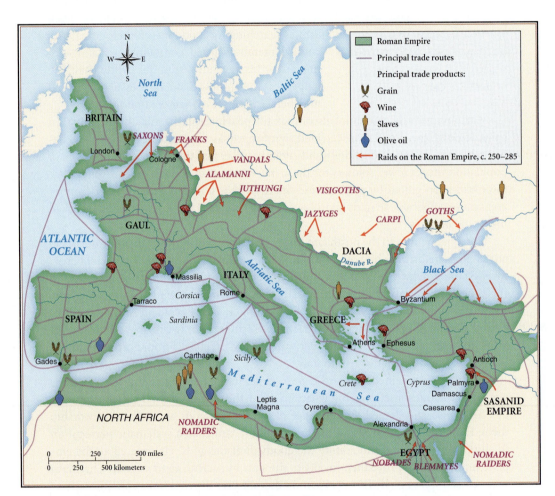

Mapping the West   The Roman Empire in Crisis, 284 C.E.

By the 280s C.E., fifty years of civil war had torn the principate apart. Imperial territory retained the outlines inherited from the time of Augustus (compare Map 6.1, on page 181), except for the loss of Dacia to the Goths a few years before. Attacks from the north and east had repeatedly penetrated the frontiers, however. Long-distance trade had always been important to the empire's prosperity, but the decades of violence had made transport riskier and therefore more expensive, contributing to the crisis. What do you think would have been the greatest challenges in ruling such a vast empire in an age without swift communications or fast travel?

The emperors provided food to the poor, built baths and arenas for public entertainment, paid their troops well, and gave privileges to the elite. By the second century, peace and prosperity created a Golden Age. Long-term financial difficulties set in, however, because the army, now concentrating on defense, no longer brought in money from conquests. Severe inflation made the situation desperate. Ruined by the demand for more tax revenues, provincial elites lost their public-spiritedness and avoided their communal responsibilities.

The emergence of Christianity generated tension because Romans doubted Christians' loyalty. The new religion had evolved from Jewish apocalypticism to a hierarchical organization. Its believers argued with one another and with the authorities. Martyrs such as Vibia Perpetua worried the government by placing their beliefs ahead of loyalty to the state.

When financial ruin, natural disasters, and civil war combined to create a political crisis in the mid-third century C.E., the emperors lacked the money and the popular support to solve it. Not even their persecution of Christians had convinced the gods to restore Rome's good fortunes. Threatened with the loss of peace, prosperity, and territory, the empire needed a political transformation to survive. That process began under the emperor Diocletian (r. 284–305 C.E.). Under his successor, Constantine (r. 306–337 C.E.), the Roman Empire also began the slow process of becoming officially Christian.

Review Questions

1. How did the peace gained through Augustus's "restoration of the Roman republic" affect Romans' lives in all social classes?
2. In the early Roman Empire, what was life like in the cities and in the country for the elite and for ordinary people?
3. Which aspects of social, cultural, and political life in the early Roman Empire supported the growth of Christianity, and which opposed it?
4. What were the causes and the effects of the Roman crisis in the third century C.E.?

Making Connections

1. What were the similarities and differences between the crisis in the first century B.C.E. that undermined the Roman republic and the crisis in the third century C.E. that undermined the principate?
2. If you had been a first-century Roman emperor under the principate, what would you have done about the Christians and why? What if you had been a third-century emperor?
3. Do you think that the factors that caused the crisis in the Roman Empire could cause a similar crisis in the Western world of today?

- For practice quizzes and other study tools, visit the **Online Study Guide** at bedfordstmartins.com/huntconcise.

- For primary-source material from this period, see *Sources of the Making of the West,* Fourth Edition.

- For Web sites, images, and documents related to topics in this chapter, visit *Make History* at bedfordstmartins.com/huntconcise.

Suggested References

Scholars continue to debate the nature and the significance of the many social, cultural, and (especially) religious changes that occurred under the early Roman Empire. Perhaps the most difficult question to answer is to what extent life became better or worse for most people — and indeed how to define *better* and *worse* in this context — once the empire stopped expanding into new territories.

Ando, Clifford. *The Matter of the Gods: Religion and the Roman Empire*. 2008.

Crossan, Dominic, and Jonathan Reed. *In Search of Paul: How Jesus's Apostle Opposed Rome's Empire with God's Kingdom*. 2005.

Denzey, Nicola. *The Bone Gatherers: The Lost Worlds of Early Christian Women*. 2007.

*Futrell, Allison. *The Roman Games: Historical Sources in Translation*. 2006.

TIMELINE

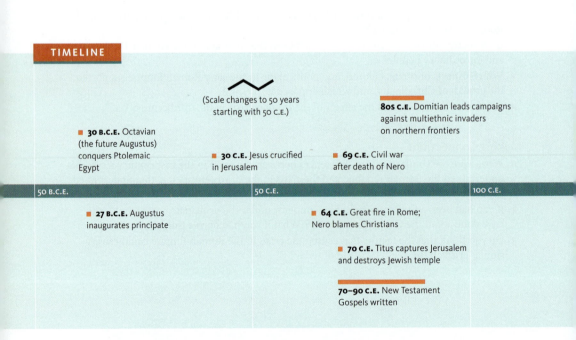

(Scale changes to 50 years starting with 50 C.E.)

80s C.E. Domitian leads campaigns against multiethnic invaders on northern frontiers

30 B.C.E. Octavian (the future Augustus) conquers Ptolemaic Egypt

30 C.E. Jesus crucified in Jerusalem

69 C.E. Civil war after death of Nero

50 B.C.E.   50 C.E.   100 C.E.

27 B.C.E. Augustus inaugurates principate

64 C.E. Great fire in Rome; Nero blames Christians

70 C.E. Titus captures Jerusalem and destroys Jewish temple

70–90 C.E. New Testament Gospels written

Galinsky, Karl, ed. *The Cambridge Companion to the Age of Augustus.* 2005.

Goldsworthy, Adrian. *The Complete Roman Army.* 2003.

Green, Bernard. *Christianity in Ancient Rome: The First Three Centuries.* 2010.

Harris, W. V. *Rome's Imperial Economy.* 2010.

*Kraemer, Ross Shephard. *Her Share of the Blessings: Women's Religion among Pagans, Jews, and Christians in the Greco-Roman World.* 1992.

Mattingly, David J. *Imperialism, Power, and Identity: Experiencing the Roman Empire.* 2010.

Matz, David. *Life of the Ancient Romans: Daily Life through History.* 2008.

Roman emperors: http://www.roman-emperors.org/startup.htm

*Suetonius. *Lives of the Caesars.* Trans. Catharine Edwards. 2009.

*Tacitus. *The Complete Works.* Trans. Alfred John Church and William Jackson Brodribb. 1964.

Primary source.

230s–280s C.E.
Third-century financial and political crisis

150 C.E. 200 C.E. 250 C.E.

161–180 C.E. Marcus Aurelius battles multiethnic bands attacking northern frontiers

212 C.E. Caracalla extends Roman citizenship to almost all free inhabitants of the provinces

249–251 C.E. Decius persecutes Christians

The Transformation of the Roman Empire

AROUND 300,* EMPEROR DIOCLETIAN (r. 284–305) proclaimed the reason why the Roman Empire was endangered: "The immortal gods in their foresight have taken care to proclaim and prescribe what is good and true, which the sayings of many good and distinguished men have approved and confirmed, along with the reasoned judgments of the wisest. It is wrong to oppose and resist these traditions, and a new cult should not find fault with ancient religion. It is a serious crime to question matters that our ancestors established and fixed once and for all. . . . Therefore, we are eager to punish the obstinate and perverse thinking of these utterly worthless people."

Diocletian had ended the third-century political crisis and kept the Roman Empire from breaking into warring parts by appointing a co-emperor and two assistant emperors. Still, suspicions endured that nontraditional worshippers were responsible for the divine anger that, everyone believed, had sent the crisis. Diocletian convinced his co-rulers first to persecute the pagan Manichaeans (followers of the Iranian prophet Mani and the objects of his proclamation) and then the Christians. His successor Constantine (r. 306–337) ended the persecution by converting to Christianity and supporting his new faith with imperial funds and a policy of religious freedom.

Vandal General Stilicho and His Family

This ivory diptych ("folding tablet") from around 400 C.E. shows Stilicho, the top general in the Roman army in Europe and close adviser to the western Roman emperor, with his wife, Serena, and their son Eucherius. Stilicho's life reveals the mixing of cultures in the later Roman Empire: his father was from the Vandal tribe in Germany, and his mother was Roman; he himself rose to prominence in Roman imperial government and society. Serena was the adoptive daughter of the emperor, and Stilicho and Serena's daughter Maria married the emperor's son. Stilicho is shown dressed in the richly decorated clothing appropriate for a member of the Roman elite, and he wears a metal clasp to fasten his robe, a symbol of his father's ethnicity. The images on his shield of the two emperors then ruling the divided Roman Empire proclaim his loyalty even as they point to the political and geographic fragmentation of the time. (Basilica di San Giovanni Battista, Monza, Italy / The Bridgeman Art Library International.)

---

*From this point on, dates are C.E. unless otherwise indicated.

Nevetheless, it took a century more for Christianity to become the state religion. The social and cultural transformations produced by the Christianization of the Roman Empire came slowly because many Romans clung to their ancestral beliefs.

Diocletian's reform of government only postponed the division of imperial territory. In 395, Emperor Theodosius I split the empire in two to try to provide better defense against the barbarians pressing into Roman territory, especially from the north. He appointed one of his sons to rule the west and the other the east. The two emperors were supposed to cooperate, but in the long run this system of divided rule could not cope with the different pressures affecting the two regions.

In the western Roman Empire, military and political events provoked social and cultural change when barbarian immigrants began living side by side with Romans. Both groups underwent changes: the barbarians created kingdoms and laws based on Roman traditions yet adopted Christianity, and the wealthy Romans fled from cities to seek safety in country estates when the western government became ineffective. These changes in turn transformed the political landscape of western Europe in ways that foreshadowed the later development of nations there. In the east, however, the empire lived on for another thousand years, passing on the memory of classical traditions to later Western civilization. The eastern half endured as the continuation of the Roman Empire until Turkish invaders conquered it in 1453.

CHAPTER FOCUS What were the most important sources of unity and of division in the Roman Empire from the reign of Diocletian to the reign of Justinian, and why?

From Principate to Dominate in the Late Roman Empire, 284–395

Diocletian and Constantine pulled Roman government out of its extended crisis by increasing the emperors' authority, reorganizing the empire's defense, restricting workers' freedom, and changing the tax system to try to increase revenues. The two emperors firmly believed they had to win back divine favor to ensure their people's safety.

Diocletian and Constantine believed that they could solve the empire's problems by becoming more autocratic. They transformed their appearance as rulers to make their power seem awesome beyond compare, taking ideas from the self-presentation of their most powerful rivals, the rulers of the Persian Empire. Diocletian and Constantine hoped that their assertion of supremacy would keep their empire united; in the long run, however, it proved impossible to preserve Roman imperial territory on the scale once ruled by Augustus.

The Political Transformation and Division of the Roman Empire

No one could have predicted Diocletian's rise to power: he began life as an uneducated peasant in the Balkans, but his leadership, courage, and intelligence propelled him

through the ranks until the army made him emperor in 284. He ended a half a century of civil war by imposing the most autocratic system of rule in Roman history.

Historians refer to Roman rule from Diocletian onward as the **dominate** because he took the title *dominus* ("lord" or "master") — what slaves called their owners. The emperors of the dominate continued to refer to their government as the Roman republic, but in truth they ruled autocratically. This new system eliminated the principate's ideal of the princeps ("first man") as the social equal of the senators. The emperors of the dominate now recognized no equals. The offices of senator, consul, and so on continued, but only as posts of honor. These officials had the responsibility to pay for public services, especially chariot races and festivals, but no power to govern. Imperial administrators were increasingly chosen from lower ranks of society according to their competence and their loyalty to the emperor.

The dominate's emperors took ideas for emphasizing their superiority from the Sasanids in Persia, whose empire (224–651) they recognized as equal to their own in power and whose king and queen they addressed as "our brother" and "our sister." The Roman Empire's masters broadcast their majesty by surrounding themselves with courtiers and ceremony, presiding from a raised platform, and sparkling in jeweled crowns, robes, and shoes. Constantine took from Persia the tradition that emperors set themselves apart by wearing a diadem, a purple gem-studded headband. In another echo of Persian monarchy, a series of veils separated the palace's waiting rooms from the interior room where the emperor listened to people's pleas for help or justice. Officials marked their rank by wearing special shoes and belts and claiming grandiose titles such as "Most Perfect."

The dominate's emperors also asserted their supreme power through laws and punishments. They alone made law. To impose order, they raised punishments to brutal levels. New punishments included Constantine's order that the "greedy hands" of officials who took bribes "shall be cut off by the sword." The guardians of a young girl who allowed a lover to seduce her were executed by having molten lead poured into their mouths. Penalties grew ever harsher for the majority of the population, legally designated as "humbler people," who were punished more severely than the "better people" for comparable offenses. In this way, the dominate strengthened the divisions between ordinary people and the rich.

Diocletian appointed three "partners" (a co-emperor, Maximian, and two assistant emperors, Constantius and Galerius, who were the designated successors) to join him in ruling the empire in a **tetrarchy** ("rule by four"). Each ruler controlled one of four districts. Diocletian served as supreme ruler and was supposed to receive the loyalty of the others. He also created smaller administrative units, called dioceses, under separate governors, who reported to the four emperors' assistants, the praetorian prefects (Map 7.1). This system was Diocletian's attempt to put imperial government into closer contact with the empire's frontier regions, where the dangers of invasion and rebellious troops loomed.

Diocletian's reforms ended Rome's thousand years as the empire's most important city. Diocletian did not even visit Rome until 303, nearly twenty years after becoming

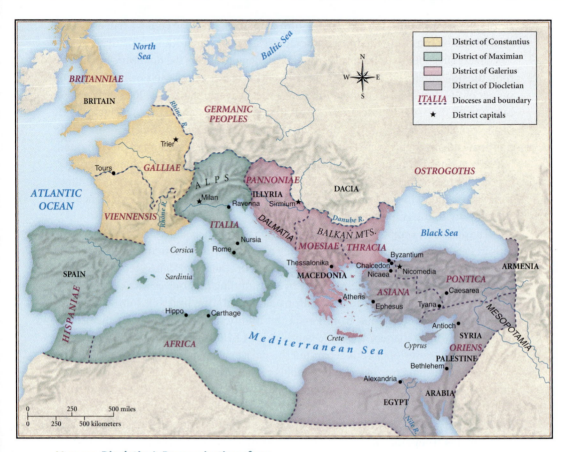

Map 7.1 Diocletian's Reorganization of 293

Trying to prevent civil war, Emperor Diocletian reorganized Rome's imperial territory into a tetrarchy, to be ruled by himself, his co-emperor Maximian, and assistant emperors Constantius and Galerius, each the head of a large district. He subdivided the preexisting provinces into smaller units and grouped them into twelve dioceses, each overseen by a regional administrator. The four districts as shown here reflect the arrangement recorded by the imperial official Sextus Aurelius Victor in about 360. What were the advantages and disadvantages of subdividing the empire?

emperor. Italy became just another section of the empire, now subject to the same taxation as everywhere else.

Diocletian resigned in 305 for unknown reasons, after which rivals for power abandoned the tetrarchy and fought a civil war until 324, when Constantine finally won. At the end of his reign in 337, Constantine designated his three sons to rule as co-emperors. Failing to cooperate, they waged war against one another.

Constantine's warring sons unofficially split the empire on a north–south line along the Balkan peninsula, a division that Theodosius made permanent in 395. In the long run, the empire's halves would be governed largely as separate territories despite the emperors' insistence that the empire remained one state.

The Empire's East/West Division, 395

Each half had its own capital city. Constantinople ("Constantine's City") — formerly the ancient city of Byzantium (today Istanbul, Turkey) — was the eastern capital. Constantine made it his capital, a "new Rome," because of its strategic military and commercial location: it lay at the mouth of the Black Sea guarding principal routes for trade and troop movements. To recall the glory of Rome, Constantine constructed a forum, an imperial palace, a hippodrome for chariot races, and monumental statues of the traditional gods in his refounded city. Constantinople grew to be the most important city in the Roman Empire.

Honorius, Theodosius's son and successor in the west, wanted a headquarters that was easy to defend. In 404, he chose the port of Ravenna, a commercial center on Italy's northeastern coast housing a naval base. Marshes and walls protected Ravenna by land, while its harbor kept it from being starved out in a siege. Though the emperors enhanced Ravenna with churches covered in multicolored mosaics, it never rivaled Constantinople in size or splendor.

The Social Consequences of Financial Pressures

To try to control inflation and support his huge army, Diocletian imposed price and wage controls and a new taxation system. Putting great financial pressures on both rich and poor, these measures failed. Diocletian also placed restrictions on many people's rights to choose their occupations.

Diocletian was desperate to reduce the hyperinflation resulting from the third-century crisis. As prices escalated, people hoarded whatever they could buy. "Hurry and spend all my money you have; buy me any kinds of goods at whatever prices they are available," wrote one official to his servant. Hoarding only worsened the inflation.

In 301, the inflation was so severe that Diocletian imposed harsh price and wage controls in the worst-hit areas. This mandate, which blamed high prices on merchants' "unlimited and frenzied avarice," forbade hoarding of goods and set cost ceilings for about a thousand goods and services. The mandate failed to change people's behavior, despite penalties of exile or death. Diocletian's price and wage controls thus only increased financial pressure on everyone.

The emperors increased taxes mostly to support the army, which required enormous amounts of grain, meat, salt, wine, vegetable oil, horses, camels, and mules. The major sources of revenue were a tax on land, assessed according to its productivity, and a head tax on individuals. To supplement taxes paid in coin, the emperors began collecting some payments in goods and services.

The empire was too large to enforce the tax system uniformly. In some areas both men and women ages twelve to sixty-five paid the full tax, but in others women paid only half the tax assessment or none at all. The reasons for such differences are not recorded. Workers in cities periodically paid "in kind," that is, by laboring without pay on public works projects such as cleaning municipal drains or repairing buildings. People in commerce, from shopkeepers to prostitutes, still paid taxes in money, while members of the senatorial class were exempt from ordinary taxes but had to pay special levies.

The new tax system could work only if agricultural production remained stable and the government kept track of the people who were liable for the head tax (see "Taking Measure," below). Diocletian therefore restricted the movement of tenant farmers, called **coloni** ("cultivators"), whose work provided the empire's economic base. Now male coloni, as well as their wives in areas where women were assessed for taxes, were increasingly tied to a particular plot of land. Their children were also bound to the family plot, making farming a hereditary obligation.

The government also regulated other occupations deemed essential. Bakers, who were required to produce free bread for Rome's poor, a tradition begun under the republic to prevent food riots, could not leave their jobs. Under Constantine, the sons of military veterans were obliged to serve in the army. However, conditions were not the same everywhere in the empire. Free workers who earned wages apparently remained important in the economy of Egypt in the late Roman Empire, and archaeological evidence suggests that some regions may actually have become more prosperous.

The emperors also decreed oppressive regulations for the **curials**, the social elite in the cities and towns. During this period, many men in the curial class were obliged to

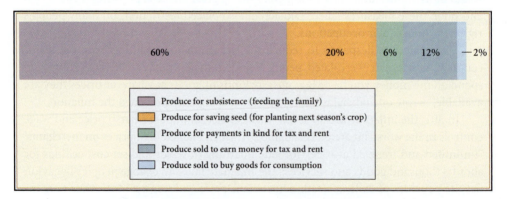

| 60% | 20% | 6% | 12% | ─2% |

Produce for subsistence (feeding the family)
Produce for saving seed (for planting next season's crop)
Produce for payments in kind for tax and rent
Produce sold to earn money for tax and rent
Produce sold to buy goods for consumption

Taking Measure Peasants' Use of Farm Produce in the Roman Empire
This graph offers a speculative model (precise statistics have not survived) of how peasants during the Roman Empire perhaps used what they produced as farmers and herders to maintain their families, pay rent and taxes, and buy things they did not produce themselves. Individual families would have had widely varying experiences and there were definitely strong regional differences in the vast empire, but it is nevertheless likely that most families had to use most of their production just to maintain a subsistence level — a description of poverty by modern standards. (Adapted from Keith Hopkins, *Conquerors and Slaves: Sociological Studies in Roman History* [New York: Cambridge University Press, 1978], 17.)

serve as decurions (unsalaried members of their city Senate) and to spend their own funds to support the community. Their financial responsibilities ranged from maintaining the water supply to feeding troops, but their most expensive duty was paying for shortfalls in tax collection. The emperors' demands for revenue made this a crushing obligation.

The empire had always depended on property owners to fill local offices in return for honor and the emperor's favor. Now this tradition broke down as some wealthy people avoided public service to escape financial ruin. Service on a municipal council could even be imposed as punishment for a crime. Eventually, to prevent curials from escaping their obligations, imperial policy decreed that they could not move away from the town where they had been born. Members of the elite sought exemptions from public service by petitioning the emperor, bribing imperial officials, or taking up an occupation that freed them from curial obligations (the military, imperial administration, or church governance). The most desperate simply abandoned their homes and property.

These restrictions eroded the communal values motivating wealthy Romans. The drive to increase revenues also produced social discontent among poorer citizens: the tax rate on land eventually reached one-third of the land's gross yield, impoverishing small farmers. Financial troubles, especially severe in the west, kept the empire from ever regaining the prosperity of its Golden Age.

From the Great Persecution to Religious Freedom

To eliminate what he saw as a threat to national security, Diocletian in 303 launched the so-called **Great Persecution** to please the gods by suppressing Christianity. He expelled Christians from official posts, seized their property, tore down churches, and executed anyone who refused to participate in official religious rituals.

His three partners in the tetrarchy applied the policy unevenly. In the western empire, official violence against Christians stopped after about a year; in the east, it continued for a decade. The public executions of Christians were so gruesome that they aroused the sympathy of some polytheists. The Great Persecution ultimately failed: it undermined social stability without destroying Christianity.

Constantine changed the world's religious history forever by converting to the new faith. During the civil war after Diocletian's resignation, before the crucial battle of the Milvian Bridge in Rome in 312, Constantine reportedly experienced a dream promising him God's support and saw Jesus's cross in the sky surrounded by the words "In this sign you will be the victor." Constantine ordered his soldiers to paint "the sign of the cross of Christ" on their shields. When his soldiers won a great victory in that battle, Constantine attributed his success to the Christian God and declared himself a Christian.

However, Constantine did not make polytheism illegal and did not make Christianity the official state religion. Instead, he and his polytheist co-emperor Licinius enforced religious freedom, as shown by the **Edict of Milan** of 313. The edict proclaimed

Coin Portrait of Emperor Constantine
Constantine had these special, extra-large coins minted to depict him for the first time as an overtly Christian emperor. The jewels on his helmet and crown, the fancy bridle on the horse, and the scepter indicate his status as emperor, while his armor and shield signify his military accomplishments. He proclaims his Christian rule with his scepter's new design — a cross with a globe — and the round badge sticking up from his helmet that carries the monogram signifying "Christ" that he had his soldiers paint on their shields to win God's favor in battle. (The Art Archive at Art Resource, NY.)

free choice of religion for everyone and referred to protection of the empire by "the highest divinity" — a general term meant to satisfy both polytheists and Christians.

Constantine promoted his newly chosen religion while trying to placate traditional polytheists, who still greatly outnumbered Christians. For example, he returned all property confiscated from Christians during the Great Persecution, but he had the treasury compensate those who had bought it. When in 321 he made the Lord's Day of each week a holy occasion on which no official business or manufacturing work could be performed, he called it Sunday to blend Christian and traditional notions in honoring two divinities, God and the sun. He decorated his new capital of Constantinople with statues of traditional gods. Above all, he respected tradition by continuing to hold the office of *pontifex maximus* ("chief priest"), which emperors had filled ever since Augustus.

REVIEW QUESTION What were Diocletian's policies to end the third-century crisis, and how successful were they?

The Official Christianization of the Empire, 312–c. 540

The process of Christianization of the Roman Empire was gradual: not until the end of the fourth century was Christianity proclaimed the state religion, and even then many people continued to worship the traditional gods in private. Eventually, Christianity became the religion of most people by attracting converts among women and men of all classes, assuring believers of personal salvation, offering the social advantages and security of belonging to the emperors' religion, nourishing a strong sense of shared identity and community, developing a hierarchy to govern the church, and creating communities of devoted monks (male and female). The transformation from a polytheist into a Christian state was the Roman Empire's most important influence on Western civilization.

Polytheism and Christianity in Competition

Polytheism and Christianity competed for people's faith. They shared some similar beliefs. Both, for example, regarded spirits and demons as powerful and ever-present forces in life. Some polytheists focused their beliefs on a supreme god who seemed almost monotheistic; some Christians took ideas from Neoplatonist philosophy, which was based on Plato's ideas about God and spirituality.

Unbridgeable differences remained, however, between the beliefs of traditional polytheists and Christians. People disagreed over whether there was one God or many, and what degree of interest the divinity (or divinities) paid to the human world. Polytheists could not accept a divine savior who promised eternal salvation for believers but had apparently lacked the will or the power to overthrow Roman rule and prevent his own execution. The traditional gods by contrast, they believed, had given their worshippers a world empire. Moreover, polytheists could say, cults such as that of the goddess Isis and philosophies such as Stoicism insisted that only the pure of heart and mind could be admitted to their fellowship. Christians, by contrast, embraced sinners. Why, wondered perplexed polytheists, would anyone want to associate with such people? In short, as the Greek philosopher Porphyry argued, Christians had no right to claim they possessed the sole version of religious truth, for no one had ever discovered a doctrine that provided "the sole path to the liberation of the soul."

The slow pace of Christianization revealed how strong polytheism remained in this period, especially at the highest social levels. In fact, the emperor known as **Julian the Apostate** (r. 361–363) rebelled against his family's Christianity — the word *apostate* means "renegade from the faith" — by trying to reverse official support of the new religion in favor of his own less traditional and more philosophical interpretation of polytheism. Like Christians, he believed in a supreme deity, but he based his religious beliefs on Greek philosophy when he said, "This divine and completely beautiful universe, from heaven's highest arch to earth's lowest limit, is tied together by the continuous providence of god, has existed ungenerated eternally, and is imperishable forever."

Emperors after Julian provided financial support for Christianity, dropped the title *pontifex maximus,* and stopped paying for sacrifices. Symmachus (c. 340–402), a polytheist senator who also served as prefect (mayor) of Rome, objected to the suppression of religious diversity: "We all have our own way of life and our own way of worship. . . . So vast a mystery cannot be approached by only one path."

Christianity officially replaced polytheism as the state religion in 391 when **Theodosius I** (r. 379–395) enforced a ban on privately funded polytheist sacrifices. In 395, he also announced that all polytheist temples had to close. Nevertheless, some famous shrines, such as the Parthenon in Athens, remained open for a long time. Pagan temples were gradually converted to churches during the fifth and sixth centuries. Non-Christian schools were not forced to close — the Academy, founded by Plato in Athens in the early fourth century b.c.e., endured for 140 years more.

Jews posed a special problem for the Christian emperors. They seemed entitled to special treatment because Jesus had been a Jew. Previous emperors had allowed Jews

to practice their religion, but the rulers now imposed legal restrictions. They banned Jews from holding office but still required them to assume the financial burdens of curials without the status. By the late sixth century, the law barred Jews from marrying Christians, making wills, receiving inheritances, or testifying in court.

These restrictions began the long process that turned Jews into second-class citizens in later European history, but they did not destroy Judaism. Magnificent synagogues had appeared in Palestine, though most Jews had been dispersed throughout the cities of the empire and the lands to the east. Jewish scholarship flourished in this period, culminating in the vast fifth-century C.E. texts known as the Palestinian and the Babylonian Talmuds (learned opinions on the Mishnah, a collection of Jewish law) and the Midrash (commentaries on parts of Hebrew Scripture).

As the official religion, Christianity attracted more believers, especially in the military. Soldiers could convert and still serve in the army. Previously, some Christians had felt a conflict between the military oath and their allegiance to Christ. Once the emperors were Christians, however, soldiers viewed military duty as serving Christ's regime.

Christianity's social values contributed to its appeal by offering believers a strong sense of shared identity and community. When Christians traveled, they could find a warm welcome in the local congregation (Map 7.2). The faith also won converts by promoting the tradition of charitable works characteristic of Judaism and some polytheist cults, which emphasized caring for poor people, widows, and orphans. By the mid-third century, Rome's Christian congregation was supporting fifteen hundred widows and poor people.

Women were deeply involved in the new faith. **Augustine** (354–430), bishop of Hippo, in North Africa, and perhaps the most influential theologian in Western civilization, recognized women's contribution to the strengthening of Christianity in a letter he wrote to the unbaptized husband of a baptized woman: "O you men, who fear all the burdens imposed by baptism! Your women easily best you. Chaste and devoted to the faith, it is their presence in large numbers that causes the church to grow." Women could earn respect by giving their property to their congregation or by renouncing marriage to dedicate themselves to Christ. Consecrated virgins who rejected marriage and widows who did not remarry joined large donors as especially admired women. Their choices challenged the traditional social order, in which women were supposed to devote themselves to raising families. Even these sanctified women, however, were largely excluded from leadership positions as the church's hierarchy came more closely to resemble the male-dominated world of imperial rule. There were still some women leaders in the church even in the fourth century, but they were a small minority.

The hierarchy of male bishops replaced early Christianity's relatively loose communal organization, in which women held leadership posts. Over time, the bishops replaced the curials as the emperors' partners in local rule, taking control of the distribution of imperial subsidies to the people. Regional councils of bishops appointed new bishops and addressed doctrinal disputes. Bishops in the largest cities became the most powerful leaders in the church. The bishop of Rome eventually emerged as the church's supreme leader in the western empire, claiming for himself a title previously applied to

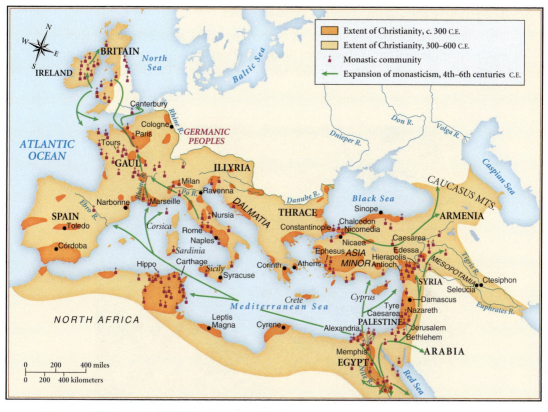

Map 7.2 The Spread of Christianity, 300–600

Christians were a minority in the Roman Empire in 300, although congregations existed in many cities and towns, especially in the eastern provinces. The emperor Constantine's conversion to Christianity in the early fourth century gave a boost to the new religion. It gained further strength during that century as the Christian emperors supported it financially and eliminated subsidies for the polytheist cults that had previously made up the religion of the state. By 600, Christians were numerous in all parts of the empire. (From Henry Chadwick and G. R. Evans, *Atlas of the Christian Church* [Oxford: Andromeda Oxford Ltd., 1987], 28. Reproduced by permission of Andromeda Oxford Limited.)

many bishops: pope (from *pappas,* a child's word for "father" in Greek), the designation still used for the head of the Roman Catholic church. Christians in the eastern empire never conceded this title to the bishop of Rome.

The bishops of Rome claimed they had leadership over other bishops on the basis of the New Testament, where Jesus addresses Peter, his head apostle: "You are Peter, and upon this rock I will build my church. . . . I will entrust to you the keys of the kingdom of heaven. Whatever you bind on earth shall be bound in heaven. Whatever you loose on earth shall be loosed in heaven" (Matt. 16:18–19). Noting that Peter's name in Greek means "rock" and that Peter had founded the Roman church, bishops in Rome eventually argued that they had the right to command the church as Peter's successors.

The Struggle for Clarification in Christian Belief

The bishops struggled to establish clarity concerning what Christians should believe to ensure their spiritual purity. They often disagreed about theology, however, as did ordinary Christians, and doctrinal disputes repeatedly threatened the church's unity.

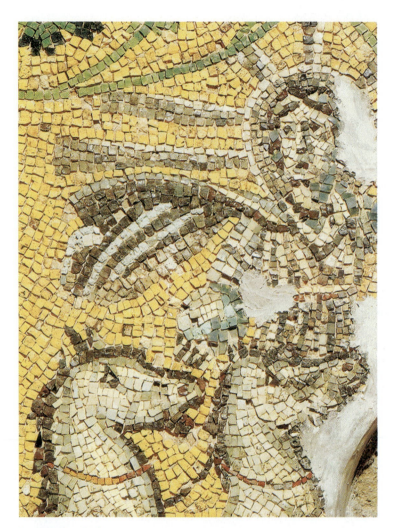

Jesus as Sun God

This heavily damaged mosaic, perhaps from the mid-third century, depicts Jesus like the Greek god of the sun, Apollo, riding in a chariot pulled by horses with rays of light shining forth around his head. This symbolism — God is light — reached back to ancient Egypt. Christian artists used it to portray Jesus because he had said, "I am the light of the world" (John 8:12). The mosaic artist arranged the sunbeams to suggest the shape of the Christian cross. The cloak flaring from Jesus's shoulder suggests the spread of his motion across the heavens. (Scala / Art Resource, NY.)

Controversy centered on what was orthodoxy and what was heresy. (See Chapter 6, page 191.) The emperor was ultimately responsible for enforcing orthodox creed (a summary of correct beliefs) and could use force to compel agreement when disputes led to violence.

Theological questions about the nature of the Christian Trinity — Father, Son, and Holy Spirit, three seemingly separate deities nevertheless conceived by orthodox believers to be a unified, co-eternal, and identical divinity — proved the hardest to clarify. The doctrine called **Arianism** generated fierce controversy for centuries. Named after its founder, Arius (c. 260–336), a priest from Alexandria, it maintained that God the Father begot (created) his son Jesus from nothing and gave him his special status. Thus, Jesus was not identical with God the Father and was, in fact, dependent on him. Arianism found widespread support — the emperor Valens and his barbarian opponents were Arian Christians. Many people found Arianism appealing because it eliminated the difficulty of understanding how a son could be the equal of his father and because its subordination of son to father corresponded to the norms of family life. Arius used popular songs to make his views known, and people everywhere became engaged in the controversy. "When you ask for your change from a shopkeeper," one observer remarked in describing Constantinople, "he harangues you about the Begotten and the Unbegotten. If you inquire how much bread costs, the reply is that 'the Father is superior and the Son inferior.'"

Disputes such as this led Constantine to try to determine religious truth. In 325, he convened 220 bishops at the Council of Nicaea to discuss Arianism. The majority voted to banish Arius to the Balkans and declared in the **Nicene Creed** that the Father and the Son were *homoousion* ("of one substance") and co-eternal. So difficult were the issues, however, that Constantine later changed his mind twice, first recalling Arius from exile and then reproaching him again not long after.

Numerous other disputes divided believers. Orthodoxy taught that Jesus's divine and human natures commingled within his person but remained distinct. Monophysites (a Greek term for "single-nature believers") argued that the divine took precedence over the human in Jesus and that he therefore had essentially only a single nature. They split from the orthodox hierarchy in the sixth century to found independent churches in Egypt (the Coptic church), Ethiopia, Syria, and Armenia.

Nestorius, made bishop of Constantinople in 428, argued that Mary, in giving birth to Jesus, had produced the human being who became the temple for God dwelling within him. Nestorianism therefore offended Christians who accepted the designation of *theotokos* (Greek for "bearer of God") for Mary. The bishops of Alexandria and Rome had Nestorius deposed and his doctrines officially rejected at councils held in 430 and 431. Nestorian bishops then established a separate church centered in the Persian Empire, where for centuries Nestorian Christians flourished under the tolerance of non-Christian rulers. They later became important agents of cultural diffusion by establishing communities that still endure in Arabia, India, and China.

The heresy of Donatism best illustrates the ferocity that Christian disputes could generate. A conflict erupted in North Africa over whether to readmit to their old

Mosaic of a Family from Edessa
This mosaic, found in a cave tomb from c. 218–238 C.E., depicts an elite family from Edessa in the late Roman Empire. Their names are given in Syriac, the dialect of Aramaic spoken in their region, and their colorful clothing reflects local Iranian traditions. The mosaic's border uses decorative patterns from Roman art, illustrating the combining of cultural traditions in the Roman Empire. Edessa was the capital of the small kingdom of Osrhoëne, annexed by Rome in 216. It became famous in Christian history because its king Abgar (r. 179–216) was the first monarch to convert to Christianity, well before Constantine. The eastern Roman emperors proclaimed themselves the heirs of King Abgar. (Photo by J. B. Segal, one of the authors, from *Vanished Civilizations: Forgotten Peoples of the Ancient World*, ed. Edward Bacon [London: Thames and Hudson, 1967].)

congregations Christians who had cooperated with imperial authorities during the Great Persecution. The Donatists (followers of the North African priest Donatus) insisted that the church should not be polluted with such "traitors." So bitter was the clash that it even broke apart Christian families. One son threatened his mother, "I will join Donatus's followers, and I will drink your blood."

A council organized in Chalcedon (a suburb of Constantinople) in 451 to settle the still-raging disagreement over Nestorius's views was the most important attempt to clarify orthodoxy. The conclusions of the Council of Chalcedon form the basis of the doctrine of most Christians in the West today. At the time, however, it failed to create unanimity, especially in the eastern empire, where Monophysites flourished.

By around 500, Augustine and other influential theologians such as Ambrose (c. 339–397) and Jerome (c. 345–420) earned the informal title *church fathers* because their views were cited as authoritative in disputes over orthodoxy. Augustine became the most famous of this group of patristic (from *pater,* Greek for "father") authors, and for the next thousand years his many works would be the most influential texts in western Christianity aside from the Bible.

In *The City of God,* Augustine expressed his views on the need for order in human life and asserted that the basic human dilemma lay in the conflict between desiring earthly pleasures and desiring spiritual purity. Emotion, especially love, was natural and commendable, but only when directed toward God. Humans were misguided to look for any value in life on earth. Only life in God's eternal city at the end of time had meaning.

Nevertheless, Augustine wrote, law and government are required on earth because humans are imperfect. God's original creation was perfect, but after Adam and Eve disobeyed God, humans lost their initial perfection and inherited a permanently flawed nature. According to this doctrine of original sin — a subject of theological debate since at least the second century — Adam and Eve's disobedience passed down to human beings a hereditary moral disease that made the human will a divisive force. This corruption necessitated governments that could suppress evil. The state therefore had a duty to compel people to remain loyal to the church, by force if necessary.

Christians, he argued, had a duty to obey the emperor and participate in political life. Soldiers, too, had to follow their orders. Order was so essential, Augustine argued, that it even justified what he admitted was the unjust institution of slavery. Although he detested slavery, he believed it was a lesser evil than the social disorder that he thought its abolition would create.

In *The City of God,* Augustine argued that history has a divine purpose, even if people could not see it. History progressed toward an ultimate goal, but only God knew the meaning of his creation:

> To be truthful, I myself fail to understand why God created mice and frogs, flies and worms. Nevertheless, I recognize that each of these creatures is beautiful in its own way. For when I contemplate the body and limbs of any living creature, where do I not find proportion, number, and order exhibiting the unity of concord? Where one discovers proportion, number, and order, one should look for the craftsman.

The question of how to understand and regulate sexual desire perplexed Christians in the search for religious truth. Augustine wrote that sex trapped human beings in evil and that they should therefore strive for **asceticism**, the practice of self-denial and spiritual discipline. Augustine knew from personal experience how difficult it was to accept this doctrine. In his autobiographical work *Confessions,* written about 397, he described the deep conflict he felt between his sexual desires and his religious beliefs. Only after a long period of reflection and doubt, he wrote, did he find the inner strength to commit to chastity as part of his conversion to Christianity.

He advocated sexual abstinence as the highest course for Christians because he believed that Adam and Eve's disobedience had forever ruined the perfect harmony God created between the human will and human passions. According to Augustine, God punished his disobedient children by making sexual desire a disruptive force that human will would always struggle to control. He reaffirmed the value of marriage in God's plan, but he insisted that sexual intercourse even between loving spouses carried the unhappy reminder of humanity's fall from grace. Reproduction, not pleasure, was the only acceptable reason for sex.

This doctrine ennobled virginity and sexual renunciation as the highest virtues. By the end of the fourth century, Christians valued virginity so highly that congregations began to request virgin ministers and bishops.

The Emergence of Christian Monks

Christian asceticism peaked with the emergence of monks: men and women who withdrew from everyday society to live a life of extreme self-denial imitating Jesus's suffering, while praying for divine mercy on the world. In monasticism, monks originally lived alone, but soon they formed communities for mutual support in the pursuit of holiness.

Polytheists and Jews had strong ascetic traditions, but Christian monasticism was distinctive for the huge numbers of people drawn to it and the high status that they earned in the Christian population. Monks' fame came from their rejection of ordinary pleasures and comforts. They left their families and congregations, renounced sex, worshipped almost constantly, wore rough clothes, and ate so little they were always starving. To achieve inner peace, monks fought a constant spiritual battle against fantasies of earthly delights — plentiful, tasty food and the joys of sex.

The earliest monks emerged in Egypt in the second half of the third century. Antony (c. 251–356), the son of a well-to-do family, was among the first to renounce regular existence. After hearing a sermon stressing Jesus's command to a rich young man to sell his possessions and give the proceeds to the poor (Matt. 19:21), he left his property in about 285 and withdrew into the desert to devote the rest of his life to worshipping God through extreme self-denial.

The opportunity to gain fame as a monk seemed especially valuable after the end of the Great Persecution. Becoming a monk — a living martyrdom — not only served as the substitute for dying a martyr's death but also emulated the sacrifice of Christ. In Syria, "holy women" and "holy men" sought fame through feats of pious endurance; Symeon (390–459), for example, lived atop a tall pillar for thirty years, preaching to the people gathered at the foot of his perch. Egyptian Christians came to believe that their monks' supreme piety made them living heroes who ensured the annual flooding of the Nile (which enriched the soil, aiding agriculture), an event once associated with the pharaohs' religious power.

In a Christian tradition originating with martyrs, the relics of dead holy men and women — body parts or clothing — became treasured sources of protection and healing. The power associated with the relics of saints (people venerated after their deaths for their holiness) gave believers faith in divine favor.

In about 323, an Egyptian Christian named Pachomius organized the first monastic community, establishing the tradition of single-sex settlements of male or female monks. This communal monasticism dominated Christian asceticism ever after. Communities of men and women were often built close together to share labor, with women making clothing, for example, while men farmed.

Some monasteries imposed military-style discipline, but there were large differences in the degree of control of the monks and the extent of contact allowed with the outside world (see the illustration on page 219). Some groups strove for complete self-sufficiency and strict rules to avoid transactions with outsiders. Basil of Caesarea (c. 330–379), in Asia Minor, started an alternative tradition of monasteries in service to society. Basil (later dubbed "the Great") required monks to perform charitable deeds, especially

ministering to the sick, a development that led to the foundation of the first hospitals, which were attached to monasteries.

A milder code of monastic conduct became the standard in the west beginning about 540. Called the Benedictine rule after its creator, Benedict of Nursia (c. 480–553), it mandated the monastery's daily routine of prayer, scriptural readings, and manual labor. This was the first time in Greek and Roman history that physical work was seen as noble, even godly. The rule divided the day into seven parts, each with a compulsory service of prayers and lessons, called the office. Unlike the harsh regulations of other monastic communities, Benedict's code did not isolate the monks from the outside world or deprive them of sleep, adequate food, or warm clothing. Although it gave the abbot (the head monk) full authority, it instructed him to listen to other members of the community before deciding important matters. He was not allowed to beat disobedient monks. Communities of women, such as those founded by Basil's sister Macrina and Benedict's sister Scholastica, generally followed the rules of the male monasteries, with an emphasis on the decorum thought necessary for women.

Monastic piety held special appeal for women and the rich, because women could achieve greater status and respect for their holiness than ordinary life allowed them,

Monastery of St. Catherine at Mount Sinai

The sixth-century eastern Roman emperor Justinian built a wall to protect this monastery in the desert at the foot of Mount Sinai (on the peninsula between Egypt and Arabia). Justinian fortified the monastery to promote orthodoxy in a region dominated by Monophysite Christians. The monastery gained its name in the ninth century when the story was circulated that angels had recently brought the body of Catherine of Alexandria there. Catherine was said to have been martyred in the fourth century for refusing to marry the emperor because, in her words, she was the bride of Christ. (Erich Lessing / Art Resource, NY.)

while the rich could win fame on earth and hope for favor in heaven by endowing monasteries with large gifts of money. Jerome wrote, "[As monks,] we evaluate people's virtue not by their gender but by their character, and deem those to be worthy of the greatest glory who have renounced both status and riches." Some monks did not choose their life; monasteries took in children from parents who could not raise them or who, in a practice called oblation, gave them up to fulfill pious vows. Jerome once advised a mother regarding her young daughter:

> Let her be brought up in a monastery, let her live among virgins, let her learn to avoid swearing, let her regard lying as an offense against God, let her be ignorant of the world, let her live the angelic life, while in the flesh let her be without the flesh, and let her suppose that all human beings are like herself.

When the girl reached adulthood as a virgin, he added, she should avoid the baths so that she would not be seen naked or give her body pleasure by dipping in the warm pools. Jerome emphasized traditional values favoring males when he promised that God would reward the mother with the birth of sons in compensation for the dedication of her daughter.

Monasteries could come into conflict with the church leadership. Bishops resented members of their congregations who withdrew into monasteries, especially because they then gave money and property to their new community instead of to their local churches. Monks represented a threat to bishops' authority because holy men and women earned their special status not by having it bestowed from the church hierarchy but through their own actions.

REVIEW QUESTION   How did Christianity both unite and divide the Roman Empire?

Non-Roman Kingdoms in the Western Roman Empire, c. 370–550s

The western Roman Empire came under great pressure from the incursions of non-Roman peoples — barbarians, the Romans called them, meaning "brave but uncivilized" — that took place in the fourth and fifth centuries. The emperors had traditionally admitted some multiethnic groups from east of the Rhine River and north of the Danube River into the empire to fight in the Roman army, but eventually other barbarians fought their way in from the northeast. The barbarians wanted to flee attacks by the Huns (nomadic warriors from central Asia) and share in Roman prosperity. By the 370s, this human tide provoked violence and a loss of order in the western empire.

The immigrants slowly transformed themselves from loosely organized tribes into kingdoms with newly defined identities. By the 470s, one of their commanders ruled Italy — the political change that has been said to mark the fall of the Roman Empire. However, the interactions of these non-Roman peoples with the empire's residents in western Europe and North Africa seem closer to a political, social, and cultural trans-

formation — based on force more than cooperation — that made the immigrants the heirs of the western Roman Empire and led to the formation of medieval Europe.

Non-Roman Migrations into the Western Roman Empire

The non-Roman peoples who flooded into the empire had diverse origins; simply labeling them "Germanic peoples" misrepresents the diversity of their multiethnic languages and customs. What we must remember is that the diverse barbarian peoples had no previously established sense of ethnic identity, and many of them had had long-term contact with Romans through trade across the frontiers and service in the Roman army. By encouraging this contact, the emperors unwittingly set in motion forces that they could not in the end control. By late in the fourth century, attacks by the Huns had destabilized life for these bands across the Roman frontiers, and the families of the warriors followed them into the empire seeking safety. Hordes of men, women, and children crossed into the empire as refugees, fleeing the Huns. They came with no political or military unity and no clear plan. They shared only their terror of the Huns and their custom of conducting raids for a living in addition to farming small plots.

The inability to prevent immigrants from crossing the border or to integrate them into Roman society once they had crossed put great stress on the western central government. Persistent economic weakness rooted in the third-century crisis worsened this pressure. Tenant farmers and landlords fleeing crushing taxes had left as much as 20 percent of farmland unworked in the most seriously affected areas. The loss of revenue made the government unable to afford enough soldiers to control the frontiers. Over time, the immigrating non-Roman peoples forced the Roman government to grant them territory in the empire. Remarkably, they then began to develop separate ethnic identities and create new societies for themselves and the Romans living under their control.

In their homelands the barbarians had lived in chiefdom societies, whose members could only be persuaded, not ordered, to follow the chief. Chiefs maintained their status by giving gifts to their followers and leading raids to capture cattle and slaves. They led clans — groups of households organized by kinship lines, following maternal as well as paternal descent. Violence against a fellow clan member was the worst possible offense. Clans in turn grouped themselves into tribes — fluctuating coalitions that anyone could join. Tribes differentiated themselves by their clothing, hairstyles, jewelry, weapons, religious cults, and oral stories.

Family life was patriarchal: men headed households and held authority over women, children, and slaves. Warfare preoccupied men, as their ritual sacrifices of weapons preserved in northern European bogs have shown. Women were valued for their ability to bear children, and rich men could have more than one wife and perhaps concubines as well. A division of labor made women responsible for growing crops, making pottery, and producing textiles, while men worked iron and herded cattle. Women enjoyed certain rights of inheritance and could control property, and married women received a dowry of one-third of their husband's property.

Assemblies of free male warriors made major decisions in the tribes. Their leaders' authority was restricted mostly to religious and military matters. Tribes could be unstable and prone to internal conflict—clans frequently feuded, with bloody consequences. Tribal law tried to determine what forms of violence were and were not acceptable in seeking revenge, but laws were oral, not written, and thus open to wide dispute. Tribes frequently attacked other tribes.

The migrations became a flood of people when the Huns invaded eastern Europe in the fourth century. The Huns arrived on the Russian steppes shortly before 370 as the vanguard of Turkish-speaking nomads moving west. Their warriors' appearance terrified their victims, who reported skulls elongated from having been bound between boards in infancy, faces grooved with decorative scars, and arms fearsome with elaborate tattoos. Huns excelled as raiders, launching cavalry attacks without warning. Skilled as horsemen, they could shoot their powerful bows accurately while riding full tilt and stay mounted for days, sleeping atop their horses and carrying snacks of raw meat between their thighs and the animal's back.

By later in the fourth century the Huns had moved as far west as the Hungarian plain north of the Danube, terrifying the peoples there and launching raids southward into the Balkans. The emperors in Constantinople began paying the Huns to spare their territory, so the most ambitious Hunnic leader, Attila (r. c. 440–453), pushed his domain westward toward the Alps. He led his forces as far west as central France and into northern Italy. At Attila's death in 453, the Huns lost their fragile unity and faded from history. By this time, however, the terror that they had inspired in the peoples living in eastern Europe had provoked the migrations that eventually transformed the western empire.

The first non-Roman group that created a new identity and society inside the empire were barbarians from the north. Their history illustrates the pattern of the migrations: desperate barbarians in barely organized groups with no uniform ethnic identity, who sought protection in the Roman Empire in return for military service but were brutalized, and then rebelled to form their own, new kingdom. Abused by the officers of the emperor Valens, these barbarians defeated and killed him at the battle of Adrianople in 378 (Map 7.3).

When the emperor Theodosius died in 395, the barbarians whom he had allowed to settle in the empire rebelled. United by the Gothic chief Alaric into a tribe known as the **Visigoths**, they fought their way into the western empire. In 410, they stunned the world by sacking Rome itself. For the first time since the Gauls eight hundred years before, a foreign force occupied the ancient capital. They terrorized the population: "What will be left to us?" the Romans asked when Alaric demanded all the citizens' goods. "Your lives," he replied.

Too weak to fend off the invaders, the western emperor Honorius in 418 reluctantly agreed to settle the newcomers in southwestern Gaul (present-day France), where they completed their unprecedented transition from tribe to kingdom, organizing a political state and creating their identity as Visigoths. They had no precedents to follow from their previous existence, so they adapted the only model available: Roman tradition, especially having a code of law. The Visigoths established mutually beneficial relations

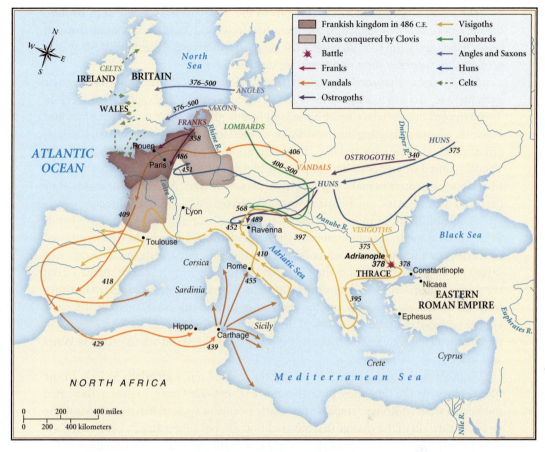

Map 7.3 Migrations and Invasions of the Fourth and Fifth Centuries
The movements of non-Roman peoples into imperial territory transformed the Roman Empire. These migrations had begun as early as the reign of Domitian (r. 81–96), but in the fourth century they increased greatly when the Huns' attacks pushed numerous barbarian bands into the empire's northern provinces. Print maps offer only a static representation of dynamic processes such as movements of populations, but this map helps illustrate the variety of peoples involved, the wide extent of imperial territory that they affected, and their prominence in the western empire.

with local Roman elites, who used time-tested ways of flattering their new superiors to gain advantages. Sidonius Apollinaris (c. 430–479), for example, a well-connected noble from Lyon, once purposely lost a backgammon game to the Visigothic king as a way of winning a favor.

How the new non-Roman kingdoms raised revenues is uncertain. Did the newcomers become landlords by forcing Roman property owners to redistribute a portion of their lands, slaves, and movable property as "ransom" to them? Or did Romans directly pay the expenses of the kingdom's soldiers, who lived mostly in urban garrisons? Whatever the new arrangements were, the Visigoths found them profitable enough to expand into Spain within a century of establishing themselves in southwestern Gaul.

The western government's concessions to the Visigoths led other groups to seize territory and create new kingdoms and identities. In 406, the Vandals cut a swath through Gaul all the way to the Spanish coast. (The modern word *vandal,* meaning "destroyer of property," perpetuates their reputation for destruction.)

In 429, eighty thousand Vandals ferried to North Africa, where they broke their agreement to become federate allies with the western empire and captured the region. They crippled the western empire by seizing North Africa's tax payments of grain and vegetable oil and disrupting the importation of food to Rome. They threatened the eastern empire with their navy and in 455 sailed to Rome, plundering the city. In Africa the Vandals caused tremendous hardship for local people by confiscating property rather than allowing owners to make regular payments on the land. As Arian Christians, they persecuted North African Christians whose doctrines they considered heresy.

Small non-Roman groups took advantage of the disruption caused by bigger bands to break off distant pieces of the empire. The Anglo-Saxons, for example, were composed of Angles from what is now Denmark and Saxons from northwestern Germany. This mixed group invaded Britain in the 440s after the Roman army had been recalled from the province to defend Italy against the Visigoths. The Anglo-Saxons captured territory from the local Celtic peoples and the remaining Roman inhabitants. Gradually, their culture replaced the local traditions of the island's eastern regions. The Celts there lost most of their language, and Christianity gave way to Anglo-Saxon beliefs except in Wales and Ireland.

Another barbarian group, the Ostrogoths, carved out a kingdom in Italy in the fifth century. By the time their king Theodoric (r. 493–526) came to power, there had not been a western Roman emperor for nearly twenty years, and there never would be again. The details of the change that has traditionally, but simplistically, been called the fall of the Roman Empire reveal the complexity of the political transformation of the western empire under the new kingdoms. The weakness of the western emperors' army had obliged them to hire foreign officers to lead the defense of Italy. By the middle of the fifth century, one non-Roman general after another had come to decide who would serve as a puppet emperor under his control.

The last such unfortunate puppet was only a child. His father, a former aide to Attila, tried to establish a royal house by proclaiming his young son as western emperor in 475. He gave the boy ruler the name Romulus Augustulus ("Romulus the Little Augustus") to match his young age and to recall both Rome's founder and its first emperor. In 476, following a dispute over pay, the boy emperor's non-Roman soldiers murdered his father and deposed him. Little Augustus was given refuge and a pension. The rebels' leader, Odoacer, had the Roman Senate petition Zeno, the eastern emperor, to recognize his leadership in return for his acknowledging Zeno as sole emperor over west and east. Odoacer thereafter oversaw Italy nominally as the eastern emperor's subordinate, but he ruled on his own.

Theodoric established the Ostrogothic kingdom in Italy by eliminating Odoacer. He and his nobles wanted to enjoy the luxurious life of the empire's elite and to preserve the empire's prestige; they therefore left the Senate and consulships intact. An Arian

Christian, Theodoric announced a policy of religious freedom. Like the other non-Romans, the Ostrogoths adopted and adapted Roman traditions that supported the stability of their own rule.

The Franks were especially significant in the reshaping of the western Roman Empire because they transformed Roman Gaul into Francia (from which comes the name *France*). In 507, their king Clovis (r. 485–511), with support from the eastern Roman emperor, overthrew the Visigothic king in Gaul. When the emperor named Clovis an honorary consul, Clovis celebrated this honor by having himself crowned with a diadem in the style of the emperors. He established western Europe's largest new kingdom in what is today mostly France, overshadowing the neighboring and rival kingdoms of the Burgundians and Alemanni in eastern Gaul. Probably persuaded by his wife, Clotilda, a Christian, to believe that God had helped him defeat the Alemanni, Clovis proclaimed himself an orthodox Christian and renounced Arianism. To build stability, he carefully fostered good relations with the bishops as the regime's intermediaries with the population.

Clovis's dynasty, called Merovingian after the legendary Frankish ancestor Merovech, endured for another two hundred years, foreshadowing the kingdom that would emerge much later as the forerunner of modern France. The Merovingians survived so long because they successfully combined their own traditions of military bravery with Roman social and legal traditions. In addition, their location in far western Europe kept them out of the reach of the destructive invasions sent against Italy by the eastern emperor Justinian in the sixth century to reunite the Roman world.

Social and Cultural Transformation in the Western Roman Empire

The gradual replacement of government in the western Roman Empire by barbarian kingdoms set in motion social and cultural transformations. The newcomers and their Roman subjects created novel ways of life by combining old traditions, as the Visigoth king Athaulf (r. 410–415) explained after marrying a Roman noblewoman:

> At the start I wanted to erase the Romans' name and turn their land into a Gothic empire, doing myself what Augustus had done. But I have learned that the Goths' freewheeling wildness will never accept the rule of law, and that state with no law is no state. Thus, I have more wisely chosen another path to glory: reviving the Roman name with Gothic vigor. I pray that future generations will remember me as the founder of a Roman restoration.

This process of social and cultural transformation promoted stability by producing new law codes but undermined long-term security by weakening the economic situation.

Roman law was the most influential precedent for the new kings in constructing states. Their tribes had never possessed written laws, but their new states required legal codes to create a sense of justice and keep order. The Visigothic kings issued the first "barbarian law code." Published in Latin in about 475, it made fines and compensation the primary method for resolving disputes. Clovis also emphasized written law for the

Merovingian kingdom. His code, also published in Latin between about 507 and 511, promoted social order through clear penalties for specific crimes, formalizing a system of fines intended to defuse feuds and vendettas between individuals and clans. The most prominent component of this system was **wergild**, the payment a murderer had to make as compensation for his crime, to prevent endless cycles of revenge. The king received about one-third of the fine, with the rest paid to the victim's family.

Since laws indicate social values, the differing amounts of wergild in Clovis's code suggest the relative values of different categories of people in his kingdom. Murdering a woman of childbearing age, a boy under twelve, or a man in the king's retinue brought a massive fine of six hundred gold coins, enough to buy six hundred cattle. A woman past childbearing age (specified as sixty years), a young girl, or a freeborn man was valued at two hundred gold coins. Ordinary slaves rated thirty-five.

The migrations of new groups into Roman territory had the unintended consequence of harming the empire's already weakened economy. The Vandals' violence battered many towns in Gaul, hastening a decline in urban population. In the countryside, now beyond the control of any central government, wealthy Romans built sprawling

Mosaic of Women Exercising
This picture covered a floor in a fourth-century country villa in Sicily that had more than forty rooms decorated with thirty-five hundred square meters of mosaics. The women shown in this mosaic were perhaps dancers getting in shape for public appearances, or athletes performing as part of a show. Members of the Roman elite built such enormous and expensive houses as the centerpieces of estates meant to insulate them from increasingly dismal conditions in cities and protect them from barbarian attack. In this case, the strategy apparently failed: the villa was likely seriously damaged by Vandal invaders. (Erich Lessing / Art Resource, NY.)

villas on extensive estates, staffed by tenants bound to the land like slaves. These establishments aimed to operate as self-sufficient units by producing all they needed, defending themselves against barbarian raids, and keeping their distance from any authorities. The owners shunned municipal offices and tax collection, the public services that had supplied the lifeblood of Roman administration. Provincial government slowly disappeared.

In some areas now outside reach of the central government, the infrastructure of trade — roads and bridges — fell into disrepair with no public-spirited elite to maintain them. The elite holed up in their fortress-like households. They could afford to protect themselves: the annual income of the richest of them rivaled the revenue of an entire province in the old western empire.

In some cases, these fortunate few helped pass down Roman learning to later ages. Cassiodorus (c. 490–585) founded a monastery on his ancestral estate in Italy in the 550s after a career in imperial administration. He gave the monks the task of copying manuscripts to keep their contents from disappearing as old ones disintegrated. His own book, *Institutions,* summed up what he saw as the foundation of ancient Greek and Roman culture by listing the books an educated person should read; it included ancient classical literature as well as Christian texts.

> **REVIEW QUESTION** How did their migrations and invasions change the barbarians themselves and the Roman Empire?

The Roman Empire in the East, c. 500–565

The eastern Roman Empire (later called the Byzantine Empire — see Chapter 8) avoided the massive transformations that reshaped the western Roman Empire. Trade and agriculture kept the eastern empire from poverty, while its emperors used force, diplomacy, and bribery to prevent invasions from the north and repel attacks by the powerful Sasanid Empire in Persia.

The eastern emperors believed it was their duty to rule a united Roman Empire and prevent barbarians from degrading its culture. The most famous eastern Roman emperor, **Justinian** (r. 527–565), and his wife and partner in rule, **Theodora** (500–548), waged war against the barbarian kingdoms in the west, aiming to reunite the empire and restore the imperial glory of the Augustan period. Justinian increased imperial authority and tried to purify religion to satisfy what he saw as his duty to provide strong leadership and God's favor. He and his successors in the eastern empire contributed to the preservation of the memory of classical Greek and Roman culture by preserving a great deal of earlier literature, non-Christian and Christian.

Imperial Society in the Eastern Roman Empire

The sixth-century eastern empire enjoyed a vitality that had vanished in the west. Its social elite spent freely on luxuries such as silk, precious stones, and pepper and other spices imported from India and China. Markets in its large cities teemed with merchants

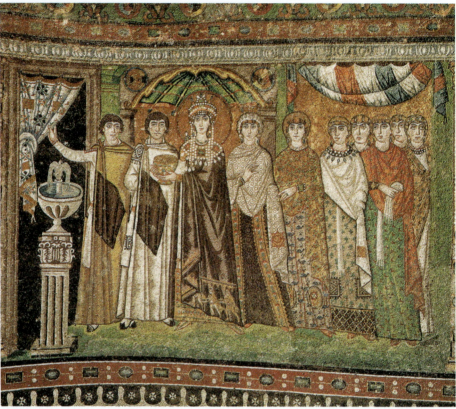

Theodora and Her Court in Ravenna
This mosaic shows the empress Theodora and members of her court presenting a gift to the church
at San Vitale in Ravenna. It faced the matching scene of her husband Justinian and his attendants
(page 229). Theodora wears the jewels, pearls, and rich robes characteristic of eastern Roman monarchs.
Theodora extends in her hands a gem-encrusted wine cup as her present. Her gesture imitates the
gift-giving of the Magi to the baby Jesus, the scene illustrated on the hem of her garment. The circle
around her head, called a nimbus (Latin for "cloud"), indicates special holiness. (Scala / Art Resource, NY.)

from abroad. Its churches' soaring domes testified to its confidence in the Christian God
as its divine protector.

The eastern emperors sponsored religious festivals and entertainments on a massive
scale to rally public support. Rich and poor alike crowded city squares, theaters, and
hippodromes on these lively occasions. Chariot racing aroused the hottest passions.
Constantinople's residents divided themselves into competitive factions called Blues
and Greens after the racing colors of their favorite charioteers. Emperors sometimes
backed one gang or the other to intimidate potential rivals.

The eastern emperors worked to maintain Roman tradition and identity, believing
that "Romanness" was the best defense against what they saw as the barbarization of the
western empire. They hired foreign mercenaries but also tried to keep their subjects

Justinian and His Court in Ravenna
This mosaic scene dominated by the eastern Roman emperor Justinian stands opposite Theodora's mosaic (page 228) in San Vitale's Church in Ravenna. The emperor is shown presenting a gift to the church. Justinian and Theodora finished building the church, which the Ostrogothic king Theodoric had started, to commemorate their successful campaign to restore Italy to the Roman Empire and reassert control of the western capital, Ravenna. The inclusion of the portrait of Maximianus, bishop of Ravenna, standing on Justinian's left and identified by name, stresses the theme of cooperation between bishops and emperors in ruling the world. What do you think the inclusion of the soldiers at the left is meant to indicate? (Scala / Art Resource, NY.)

from adopting foreign ways. The emperors ordered Constantinople's residents not to wear barbarian-style clothing (especially heavy boots and furs, which the chariot racing fans favored) instead of traditional Roman attire (sandals or light shoes and cloth robes).

The push for cultural unity was hopeless because society in the eastern empire was widely multilingual and multiethnic. The inhabitants referred to themselves as Romans, but most of them spoke Greek as their native language and used Latin only for government and military communication. Many people retained their traditional languages, such as Phrygian and Cappadocian in western Asia Minor, Armenian farther east, and Syriac and other Aramaic dialects along the eastern Mediterranean coast. The streets of Constantinople reportedly rang with seventy-two languages.

Romanness definitely included Christianity, but the eastern empire's theological diversity rivaled its ethnic and linguistic complexity. Bitter controversies over doctrine divided eastern Christians; emperors used violence against Christians with different beliefs — heretics they called them — when persuasion failed. They had to employ force, they believed, to save lost souls and preserve the empire's religious purity and divine goodwill.

Most women in eastern Roman society lived according to ancient Mediterranean tradition, concentrating on their households and minimizing contact with men outside that circle. Law barred them from performing many public functions, such as witnessing wills. Subject to the authority of their fathers and husbands, women veiled their heads (though not their faces) to show modesty. The strict views of Christian theologians on sexuality and reproduction made divorce more difficult and discouraged remarriage even for widows. Sexual offenses carried harsher legal penalties. Female prostitution remained legal and common, but emperors raised the penalties for those who forced girls or female slaves under their control into prostitution.

Women in the imperial family could achieve prominence unattainable for ordinary women. Empress Theodora demonstrated the influence high-ranking women could have in the eastern empire. Uninhibited by her humble origins (she was the daughter of a bear trainer and had been an actress with a scandalous reputation), she came to rival anyone in influence and wealth (see the illustration on page 228). She participated in every aspect of Justinian's rule, advising him on personnel for his administration, advocating for her doctrinal views in Christian disputes, and rallying Justinian's courage at times of crisis. A contemporary called her "superior in intelligence to any man."

Government in the eastern empire increased social divisions because it provided services according to people's wealth. Officials received fees for activities from commercial permits to legal grievances. People with money and status certainly found this situation useful: they relied on their social connections and wealth to get what they wanted. The poor had trouble affording the payments that government officials expected.

This fee-based system allowed the emperors to pay their civil servants tiny salaries and spend imperial funds for other purposes. One top official reported that he earned thirty times his annual salary in payments from people seeking services. To keep the system from destroying itself through extortion, the emperors published an official list of the maximum fees that their employees could charge.

The Reign of Emperor Justinian, 527–565

Justinian became the most famous eastern emperor by waging war to reunite the empire as it had been in the days of Augustus, making imperial rule more autocratic, constructing costly buildings in Constantinople, and instituting legal and religious reforms. Justinian had the same aims as all his predecessors: to preserve social order based on hierarchy and maintain divine goodwill (see the illustration on page 229). The cost of his plans, however, forced him to raise taxes, generating civil strife.

Justinian's unpopular taxes provoked the Nika Riot in 532, when the Blue and Green factions, gathering to watch chariot races, united against the emperor, shouting "Nika! Nika!" ("Win! Win!"). After nine days of violence had left much of Constantinople in ashes, Justinian prepared to flee in panic. But Theodora sternly rebuked him: "Once born, no one can escape dying, but for one who has held imperial power it would be unbearable to be a fugitive. May I never take off my imperial robes of purple, nor live to see the day when those who meet me will not greet me as their ruler." Her husband then sent in troops, who ended the rioting by slaughtering thirty thousand rioters trapped in the racetrack.

Justinian's most ambitious goal was to restore the empire to a unified territory, religion, and culture. Invading the former western provinces, his generals defeated the Vandals and Ostrogoths after campaigns that in some cases took decades to complete. At an enormous cost in lives and money, Justinian's armies restored the boundaries of the Roman Empire as in the time of Augustus, with its territory stretching from the Atlantic to the western edge of Mesopotamia. His successors, however, would not be able to retain these reconquests.

Justinian's success in reuniting the western and eastern empires had unintended consequences: severe damage to the west's infrastructure and the east's finances. Italy endured the most physical destruction, while the eastern empire suffered because Justinian demanded even more taxes to finance his wars and pay the Persian kingdom not to attack. The tax burden crippled the economy, leading to constant banditry in the countryside. Crowds poured into the capital from rural areas, seeking relief from poverty and robbers.

Natural disaster compounded Justinian's problems. In the 540s, a horrific epidemic killed a third of his empire's inhabitants; a quarter of a million, half the capital's population, died in Constantinople alone. This was the first of many pandemics that erased millions of people in the eastern empire over the next two centuries. Serious earthquakes increased the death toll. The loss of so many people created a shortage of army recruits, requiring the emperor to hire expensive mercenaries, and left countless farms vacant, reducing tax revenues.

Justinian sought stability by emphasizing his closeness to God and increasing the autocratic power of his rule. Moreover, he proclaimed the emperor the "living law," recalling the Hellenistic royal doctrine that the ruler's decisions defined law.

He communicated his supremacy and piety through his building program in Constantinople, especially in Hagia Sophia ("Church of the Holy Wisdom"). Creating a new design for churches, Justinian's architects erected a huge building on a square plan capped by a dome 107 feet across and 160 feet high. Its interior walls glowed like the sun from the light reflecting off their four acres of gold mosaics. Imported marble of every color added to the sparkling effect. When he first entered his masterpiece, dedicated in 538, Justinian exclaimed, "I have defeated you, Solomon," claiming to have bested the glorious temple that the ancient king built for the Hebrews.

Justinian's autocratic rule reduced the autonomy of cities: imperial officials governed instead of their councils. Provincial elites still had to ensure full payment of their area's

taxes, but they no longer controlled local matters or social status. Men of property from the provinces who aspired to power and prestige could satisfy their ambitions only by joining the imperial administration in the capital.

To streamline the mass of decisions that earlier emperors had made, Justinian codified the laws. His *Codex* appeared in 529, with a revised version completed in 534. A team of scholars also condensed millions of words of regulations to produce the *Digest* in 533, intended to expedite legal cases and provide a syllabus for law schools. This collection, like the *Codex* written in Latin and therefore readable in the western empire, influenced legal scholars for centuries. Justinian's legal experts also compiled a textbook for students, the *Institutes,* which appeared in 533 and remained on law-school reading lists until modern times.

To fulfill the emperor's sacred duty to the welfare of his people, Justinian acted to enforce religious purity. He believed his world could not flourish if its god became angered by the presence of religious offenders. As emperor, Justinian decided who the offenders were. Zealously enforcing laws against polytheists, he compelled them to be baptized or forfeit their lands and official positions. He also purged heretical Christians opposing his version of orthodoxy.

Justinian's laws made male homosexual relations illegal for the first time in Roman history. Male same-sex unions had apparently been allowed, or at least officially ignored, until they were prohibited in 342 after Christianity became the emperors' religion. There had never before been any civil penalties imposed on men engaging in homosexual activity, perhaps because previous rulers considered it impractical to regulate men's sexuality, given that adult men lived their private lives free of direct oversight. All the previous emperors had, for example, simply taxed male prostitutes. The legal status of homosexual activity between women is uncertain, but homosexual activity between married women probably counted as adultery and thus as a crime.

Justinian tried to reconcile orthodox and Monophysite Christians by revising the creed of the Council of Chalcedon. But the church leaders in Rome and Constantinople could not agree. The eastern and western churches were therefore launched on diverging courses that would result in formal schism five hundred years later. Justinian's own ecumenical council in Constantinople ended in conflict in 553 when it jailed Rome's defiant pope Vigilius while also managing to alienate Monophysite bishops. Justinian's efforts to impose religious unity only drove Christians further apart and undermined his vision of a restored Roman world.

The Preservation of Classical Traditions in the Late Roman Empire

Christianization of the late Roman Empire endangered the memory of classical traditions. The plays, histories, philosophical works, poems, speeches, and novels of classical Greece and Rome were polytheist and therefore potentially subversive of Christian belief, but the threat to their survival stemmed more from neglect than suppression. As many Christians became authors, their works displaced ancient Greek and Roman texts as the most important literature of the age.

Some classical texts survived, however, because Christian education and literature depended on non-Christian models, both Latin and Greek. Latin scholarship in the east received a boost when Justinian's Italian wars caused Latin-speaking scholars to flee to Constantinople. There they helped conserve many ancient Roman texts. Scholars preserved classical literature because they regarded it as a crucial part of an elite education. Some knowledge of pre-Christian classics was required for a successful career in government service, the goal of every ambitious student. An imperial decree from 360 stated, "No person shall obtain a post of the first rank unless it shall be shown that he excels in long practice of liberal studies, and that he is so polished in literary matters that words flow from his pen faultlessly."

Another factor promoting the preservation of classical literature was the use of classical rhetoric and its techniques for making persuasive arguments to present Christian theology. When Ambrose, bishop of Milan from 374 to 397, composed the first systematic description of Christian ethics for young ministers, he imitated the great Roman orator Cicero. Theologians refuted heresies among Christians by employing the dialogue form pioneered by Plato. Authors of the biographies of saints found inspiration in ancient literature that praised the heroes of traditional polytheist religion. Choricius, a Christian who held the official position of professor of rhetoric in Gaza, wrote works based on subjects from pre-Christian Greek mythology and history, such as the Trojan War or the Athenian general Miltiades. Similarly, Christian artists incorporated polytheist traditions in communicating their beliefs and emotions in paintings, mosaics, and carved reliefs. A favorite artistic motif of Christ with a sunburst surrounding his head, for example, took its inspiration from polytheist depictions of the radiant Sun as a god. (See the illustration on page 214.)

The growth of Christian literature generated a technological innovation that helped preserve classical literature. Polytheist scribes had written books on sheets of parchment (made from animal skin) or paper (made from papyrus). They then glued the sheets together and attached rods at both ends to form a scroll. Readers faced an awkward task in unrolling scrolls to read. For ease of use, Christians produced their literature in the form of the codex — a book with bound pages. Eventually the codex became the standard form of book production.

Despite its continuing importance in education and rhetoric, classical Greek and Latin literature barely survived the war-torn world dominated by Christians. Knowledge of Greek in the west faded so drastically that by the sixth century almost no one there could read the original versions of Homer's *Iliad* and *Odyssey,* the foundations of a classical literary education. Latin fared better, and scholars such as Augustine and Jerome knew Rome's ancient literature extremely well. But they also saw its classics as potentially too seductive for a pious Christian because the pleasure that came from reading them could be a distraction from the worship of God. Jerome in fact once had a nightmare of being condemned on Judgment Day for having been more dedicated to Cicero than to Christ.

The closing around 530 of the Academy, founded in Athens by Plato more than nine hundred years earlier, demonstrated the dangers for classical learning in the later

An Author or Scribe at Work

This illustration from a book produced in late Roman/early medieval times shows either an author writing a book or a scribe making a copy of a book by hand. This was the painstaking and slow process necessary to produce books in antiquity; mechanical printing had not yet been invented, and therefore mass production of books was not possible. As a result, books were expensive and precious objects, as indicated in the painting by their being carefully placed on their sides in the cabinet behind the writer to keep their weight from warping their spines and pages.

Roman Empire. This most famous of classical schools finally went out of business when many of its scholars emigrated to Persia to escape Justinian's tightened restrictions on polytheist teachers and its revenues dwindled because the Athenian elite, its traditional supporters, were increasingly Christianized. The Neoplatonist school at Alexandria, by contrast, continued. Its leader John Philoponus (c. 490–570) was a Christian. In addition to Christian theology, Philoponus wrote commentaries on the works of Aristotle. Some of his ideas anticipated those of Galileo a thousand years later. He achieved the kind of synthesis of old and new that was one of the innovative outcomes of the cultural transformation of the late Roman world — he was a Christian subject of the eastern Roman Empire in sixth-century Egypt, heading a school founded long before by polytheists, studying the works of an ancient Greek philosopher as the inspiration for his forward-looking scholarship. The strong possibility that present generations could learn from the past would continue as Western civilization once again remade itself in medieval times.

> **REVIEW QUESTION** What policies did Justinian undertake to try to restore and strengthen the Roman Empire?

Conclusion

Diocletian ended the third-century crisis of the Roman Empire, but his reforms only delayed its fragmentation. In the late fourth century, migrations of barbarians fleeing the Huns weakened the Roman imperial government. Emperor Theodosius I divided

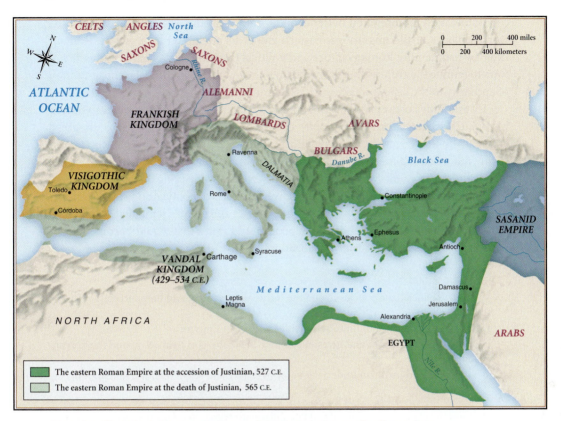

Mapping the West Western Europe and the Eastern Roman Empire, c. 600

The eastern Roman emperor Justinian employed brilliant generals and expended huge sums of money to reconquer Italy, North Africa, and part of Spain to reunite the western and eastern halves of the former Roman Empire. His wars to regain Italy and North Africa eliminated the Ostrogothic and Vandal kingdoms, respectively, but at a huge cost in effort, time — the war in Italy took twenty years — and expense. The resources of the eastern empire were so depleted that his successors could not maintain the reunification. By the early seventh century, the Visigoths had taken back all of Spain. Africa, despite serious revolts by indigenous Berber tribes, remained under imperial control until the Arab conquest of the seventh century. Within five years of Justinian's death, however, the Lombards had set up a new kingdom controlling a large section of Italy. Never again would anyone in the ancient world attempt to reestablish a universal Roman Empire.

the empire into western and eastern halves in 395 to try to improve its administration and defense. When Roman authorities bungled the task of integrating barbarian tribes into Roman society, the newcomers created kingdoms that eventually replaced Roman rule in the west.

Large-scale and violent immigration transformed the western empire's politics, society, and economy. The political changes and economic deterioration accompanying this transformation destroyed the public-spiritedness of the elite, as wealthy nobles retreated to self-sufficient country estates and shunned municipal office.

The eastern empire fared better economically than the western and avoided the worst violence of the migrations. Eastern emperors attempted to preserve "Roman-ness" by maintaining Roman culture and political traditions. The financial pressure of wars to reunite the empire drove tax rates to unbearable levels, while the concentration of authority in the capital weakened local communities.

Constantine's conversion to Christianity in 312 marked a turning point in Western history. Christianization of the empire occurred gradually, and Christians disagreed among themselves over doctrines of faith, even to the point of deadly violence. Monastic life redefined the meaning of holiness by creating communities of "God's heroes" who withdrew from this world to devote their service to glorifying the next. In the end, the quest for unity fell short through the powerful effects of political and social transformation. Nevertheless, the memory of Roman power and culture remained potent, providing an influential inheritance to the peoples and states that would become Rome's heirs in the next stage of Western civilization.

Review Questions

1. What were Diocletian's policies to end the third-century crisis, and how successful were they?
2. How did Christianity both unite and divide the Roman Empire?
3. How did their migrations and invasions change the barbarians themselves and the Roman Empire?
4. What policies did Justinian undertake to try to restore and strengthen the Roman Empire?

Making Connections

1. How did the principate and the dominate differ with regard to political appearance versus political reality?
2. What were the main similarities and differences between polytheism and Christianity as official state religions in the late Roman Empire?
3. What developments in the late Roman Empire would support the idea that it is possible for a state to be too large to be well governed and to remain united indefinitely?

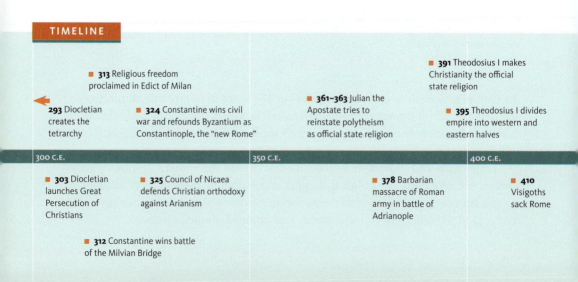

TIMELINE

391 Theodosius I makes Christianity the official state religion

313 Religious freedom proclaimed in Edict of Milan

361–363 Julian the Apostate tries to reinstate polytheism as official state religion

293 Diocletian creates the tetrarchy

324 Constantine wins civil war and refounds Byzantium as Constantinople, the "new Rome"

395 Theodosius I divides empire into western and eastern halves

300 C.E.　　　　350 C.E.　　　　400 C.E.

303 Diocletian launches Great Persecution of Christians

325 Council of Nicaea defends Christian orthodoxy against Arianism

378 Barbarian massacre of Roman army in battle of Adrianople

410 Visigoths sack Rome

312 Constantine wins battle of the Milvian Bridge

- For practice quizzes and other study tools, visit the **Online Study Guide** at
  bedfordstmartins.com/huntconcise.

- For primary-source material from this period, see *Sources of the Making of the West,* Fourth Edition.

- For Web sites, images, and documents related to topics in this chapter, visit *Make History* at bedfordstmartins.com/huntconcise.

Suggested References

Some scholars regard the political, social, and cultural changes in the late Roman Empire as evidence of a sad "decline and fall"; others judge them to have had mixed positive and negative consequences. The rise of Christianity to the status of an official religion also changed Roman life in complex ways that are still being investigated.

Brown, Peter. *The Body and Society: Men, Women, and Sexual Renunciation in Early Christianity*. 1988.

Daryaee, Touraj. *Sasanian Iran (224–651 C.E.): Portrait of a Late Antique Empire*. 2008.

*Drew, Katherine Fischer, ed. *The Laws of the Salian Franks*. 1991.

Elsner, Jas. *Imperial Rome and Christian Triumph: The Art of the Roman Empire, A.D. 100–450*. 1998.

*Grubbs, Judith Evans. *Women and Law in the Roman Empire: A Sourcebook on Marriage, Divorce, and Widowhood*. 2002.

Heather, Peter. *Empires and Barbarians: The Fall of Rome and the Birth of Europe*. 2010.

Kelly, Christopher. *Ruling the Later Roman Empire*. 2006.

*Lee, A. D. *Pagans and Christians in Late Antiquity: A Sourcebook*. 2000.

MacMullen, Ramsay. *Christianity and Paganism in the Fourth to Eighth Centuries*. 1997.

Odahl, Charles. *Constantine and the Christian Empire*. 2nd ed. 2010.

*Procopius. *The Secret History*. Trans. G. A. Williamson and Peter Sarris. 2007.

*Procopius. *The Wars*. Vols. I–V. Trans. H. B. Dewing. 1914–1928.

Rosen, William. *Justinian's Flea: The First Great Plague and the End of the Roman Empire*. 2008.

Southern, Pat, and Karen R. Dixon. *The Late Roman Army*. 1996.

Wickham, Chris. *Framing the Early Middle Ages: Europe and the Mediterranean*. 2007.

*Primary source.

527–565 Reign of eastern Roman emperor Justinian

475 Visigoths publish law code

493–526 Ostrogothic kingdom in Italy

450 C.E.   500 C.E.   550 C.E.

426 Augustine publishes *The City of God*

476 German commander Odoacer deposes final western emperor, Romulus Augustulus ("fall of Rome")

507 Clovis establishes Frankish kingdom in Gaul

540 Benedict devises his rule for monasteries

The Heirs of Rome: Islam, Byzantium, and Europe

600–750

I N THE EIGHTH CENTURY, JOSHUA, a Syrian monk, wrote about the first appearance of Islam in Roman territory. "The Arabs conquered the land of Palestine and the land as far as the great river Euphrates. The Romans fled," he marveled, and then continued:

> The first king was a man among them named Muhammad, whom they also called Prophet because he turned them away from cults of all kinds and taught them that there was only one God, creator of the universe. He also instituted laws for them because they were much entangled in the worship of demons.

The Dome of the Rock at Jerusalem (691)

Rivaling the great churches of Christendom, the mosque in Jerusalem called Dome of the Rock borrowed from late Roman and Byzantine forms even while asserting its Islamic identity. The columns and the capitals atop them, the round arches, the dome, and the mosaics are all from Byzantine models. In fact, the columns were taken from older buildings at Jerusalem. But the strips of Arabic writing on the dome itself — and in many other parts of the building — assert Islamic doctrine. (Erich Lessing / Art Resource, NY.)

Joshua was wrong about Muhammad leading the conquest of Palestine — Muhammad had died in 632, six years before that event. But he was right to see the Arab movement as a momentous development. In the course of a few decades the Arabs conquered much of the Persian and Roman Empires. Joshua was also right to emphasize Muhammad's teachings, for it was Islam's fervor that brought the Arabs out of the Arabian peninsula and into the regions that hugged the Mediterranean in one direction and led to the Indus River in the other.

In the sixth century, as the western and eastern parts of the Roman Empire went their separate ways, a third power — Arab and Muslim — took shape. These three powers have continued in various forms to the present day: the western Roman Empire became western Europe, the eastern Roman Empire became eastern Europe and Turkey and helped create Russia, and the Arab world endures in North Africa and the Middle East.

Diverse as these cultures are today, they share many of the same roots. All were heirs of Rome. All adhered to monotheism. The western and eastern halves of the Roman

Empire had Christianity in common, although they differed at times in interpreting it. Adherents of Islam, the Arab world's religion, believed in the same one God as the Jews and Christians.

The seventh and eighth centuries illustrate the Roman Empire's persistence and transformation. Changes in the eastern half of the empire were so important that historians have given it a new name — Byzantine Empire. The term *Byzantine Empire* or *Byzantium,* which comes from the old Greek name for Constantinople, rightly implies that the center of power and culture in the eastern Roman Empire was now concentrated in this one city. Over the centuries, the empire expanded, shrank, and even nearly disappeared — but it hung on in one form or another until 1453.

During the period 600–750, which historians consider the beginning of the Middle Ages, all three heirs of the Roman Empire combined elements of their heritage with new values, interests, and conditions. Their differences should not obscure the fact that the Byzantine, Muslim, and western European cultures were related.

CHAPTER FOCUS What three cultures took the place of the Roman Empire, and to what extent did each of them both draw on and reject Roman traditions?

Islam: A New Religion and a New Empire

In the early seventh century, a religion that called on all to believe in one God began in Arabia (today Saudi Arabia). Islam ("submission to God") took shape under **Muhammad** (c. 570–632). While many of the people living in Arabia were polytheists, Muhammad recognized the one God of the Jews and Christians. He saw himself as God's final prophet and thus became known as the Prophet. Invited by the people of Medina, in western Arabia, to come and act as a mediator in their disputes, Muhammad exercised the powers of both a religious and a secular leader. This dual role became the model for his successors, known as caliphs. Through a combination of persuasion and force, Muhammad and his co-religionists, the Muslims ("those who submit to Islam"), converted most of the Arabian peninsula. By the time Muhammad died in 632, Muslims had begun to conquer Byzantine and Persian territories. In the next generation, they expanded both east- and westward. Yet within the territories they conquered, daily life went on much as before.

Nomads and City Dwellers

In the seventh century, the vast deserts of the Arabian peninsula were populated by both sedentary (settled) and nomadic peoples. The sedentary peoples, sometimes farmers, sometimes merchants and artisans, lived in oases. They far outnumbered the nomads, known as Bedouins, who herded livestock and raided one another for plunder, slaves, and wives (men practiced polygyny — having more than one wife at a time). Their poetry, oral rather than written, expressed their esteem for honor, friendship, bravery, and love.

Islam began as a religion of the sedentary, but it soon found support and military strength among the nomads. It started in Mecca, an important commercial and religious center south of Medina. Mecca was the home of the Ka'ba, a shrine that contained the images of many gods and a sacred place within which war and violence were prohibited. The tribe that dominated Mecca, the Quraysh, controlled access to the shrine, taxing the pilgrims who flocked there. Visitors, assured of their safety, bartered on the sacred grounds, transforming the plunder from raids into trade.

The Prophet Muhammad and the Faith of Islam

Muhammad was born in Mecca. Orphaned at the age of six, he went to live with his uncle, a leader of the Quraysh tribe. Eventually, he became a trader and married Khadija, a rich widow. They lived (to all appearances) happily and comfortably. Yet Muhammad sometimes left home to pray in a nearby cave, practicing a type of piety similar to that of the early Christians.

Around 610, on one of these retreats, Muhammad heard a voice and had a vision that summoned him to worship the God of the Jews and Christians, Allah ("the God" in Arabic). Over the next years, he received messages that he understood to be divine revelations. Later, when these messages had been written down and compiled — a process completed in the seventh century, but after Muhammad's death — they became the **Qur'an**, the holy book of Islam. *Qur'an* means "recitation"; each of the book's parts, called suras, is understood to be God's revelation as told to Muhammad by the archangel Gabriel — the very Gabriel of the Hebrew and Christian Bibles — and then recited by Muhammad to others. Written entirely in verse and focused on the divine, the Qur'an stood apart from traditional Bedouin poetry, which had emphasized the here and now.

Beginning with the Fatihah, which praises God as the "lord sustainer of the worlds," the Qur'an continues with suras of gradually decreasing length. They cover the gamut of human experience and the life to come after death. For Muslims, the Qur'an contains

Qur'an
More than a holy book, the Qur'an represents for Muslims the very words of God that were dictated to Muhammad by the archangel Gabriel. In the Umayyad period, the Qur'an was written, as here, on pages wider than long. The first four lines on the top give the last verses of Sura 21. (Freer Gallery of Art, Smithsonian Institution, Washington, D.C., Purchase F1945.16.)

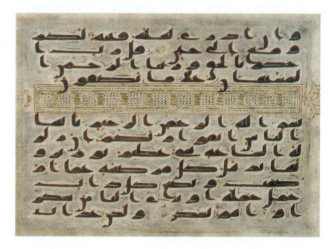

the legal and moral code by which men and women should live: "Do not set up another god with God. . . . Do not worship anyone but Him, and be good to your parents." It emphasizes the family — a man, his wife (or wives), and children — as the basic unit of Muslim society. Islam replaced the identity and protection of the tribe with a new identity: the *ummah,* the community of believers, who share both a belief in one God and a set of religious practices. Stressing individual belief in God and adherence to the Qur'an, Islam had no priests or sacraments, though in time it came to have authoritative religious leaders who interpreted the Qur'an and related texts.

Growth of Islam, c. 610–632

The first convert to Muhammad's faith was his wife. Eventually, as Muhammad preached the new faith, others became adherents. But Muhammad's insistence that the cults of all other gods be abandoned in favor of one brought him into conflict with leading members of the Quraysh tribe, whose control over the Ka'ba had given them prestige and wealth. Perceiving Muhammad as a threat, they insulted him and harassed his followers.

Disillusioned with the people of Mecca, Muhammad looked elsewhere for converts. In particular, he expected support from Jews because he thought their monotheism prepared them for his own faith. He eagerly accepted an invitation to go to Medina, in part because of its significant Jewish population. Muhammad's journey to Medina — called the **Hijra** — proved to be a crucial event for the new faith, and the year in which it occurred, 622, became the first year of the Islamic calendar.*

Although he was disappointed not to find much support among the Jews at Medina, Muhammad did find others there ready to listen to his religious message and to accept him as the leader of their community. Muhammad's political position in the community set the pattern by which Islamic society would be governed afterward; rather than simply adding a church to political and cultural life, Muslims made their political and religious institutions inseparable.

Yet Muhammad felt threatened by the Quraysh tribe at Mecca, and he led raids against their caravans. At the battle of Badr in 624, the Muslims killed forty-nine of the Meccan enemy, took numerous prisoners, and confiscated considerable treasure. From the time of this conflict, the Bedouin tradition of plundering was grafted onto the Muslim duty of **jihad** ("striving in the way of God").

The battle of Badr was a great triumph for Muhammad, who now secured his position at Medina, gaining new adherents and silencing all doubters, including Jews. Turning against those who refused to convert, he expelled two Jewish tribes from Medina and executed the male members of another. Although Muslims had originally prayed in the direction of Jerusalem, the center of Jewish worship, Muhammad now had them turn in the direction of Mecca.

Around the same time, Muhammad instituted new religious obligations. Among these were the *zakat,* a tax on possessions to be used for alms; the fast of Ramadan, which

---

*Thus, 1 anno Hegirae (1 A.H.) on the Muslim calendar is equivalent to 622 C.E.

took place during the ninth month of the Islamic year, the month in which the battle of Badr had been fought; the *hajj,* the pilgrimage to Mecca during the last month of the year, which each Muslim was to make at least once in his or her lifetime; and the *salat,* formal worship at least three times a day (later increased to five). The salat could include the *shahadah,* or profession of faith: "There is no divinity but God, and Muhammad is the messenger of God." Detailed regulations for these practices, sometimes called the **Five Pillars of Islam**, were worked out in the eighth and early ninth centuries.

Meanwhile, Muhammad sent troops to subdue Arabs north and south. In 630, he entered Mecca with ten thousand men and took over the city. As the prestige of Islam grew, clans elsewhere converted. Through a combination of force, conversion, and negotiation, Muhammad was able to unite many, though not all, Arabic-speaking tribes under his leadership by the time of his death in 632.

Muhammad was responsible for social as well as religious change. The ummah included both men and women; Islam thus enhanced women's status. At first, Muslim women joined men during the prayer periods that punctuated the day, but beginning in the eighth century, women began to pray apart from men. Men were allowed to have up to four wives at one time but were obliged to treat them equally; wives received dowries and had certain inheritance rights. Islam prohibited all infanticide, a practice that Arabs had long used largely against female infants. Like Judaism and Christianity, however, Islam retained the practices of a patriarchal society in which women's participation in community life was limited.

The ummah functioned in many ways as a "supertribe," obligated to fight common enemies, share plunder, and peacefully resolve any internal disputes. Bedouin converts to Islam turned their traditional warrior culture to its cause. Unlike intertribal fighting, warfare was now the jihad of people who were carrying out God's command against unbelievers as recorded in the Qur'an: "Strive, O Prophet, against the unbelievers and the hypocrites, and deal with them firmly. Their final abode is Hell: And what a wretched destination!"

The Caliphs, Muhammad's Successors, 632–750

In the new political community he founded in Arabia, Muhammad reorganized traditional Arab society by cutting across clan allegiances and welcoming converts from every tribe. He forged the Muslims into a formidable military force, and his successors, the caliphs, took the Byzantine and Persian worlds by storm. They quickly conquered Byzantine territory in Syria and Egypt and invaded the Sasanid Empire, conquering the whole of Persia by 651 (Map 8.1). During the last half of the seventh century and the beginning of the eighth, Islamic warriors extended their sway westward to Spain and eastward to India.

How were such widespread conquests possible, especially in so short a time? First, the Islamic forces came up against weakened empires. The Byzantine and Sasanid states were exhausted from fighting each other. Second, discontented Christians and Jews welcomed Muslims into both Byzantine and Persian territories. The Monophysite

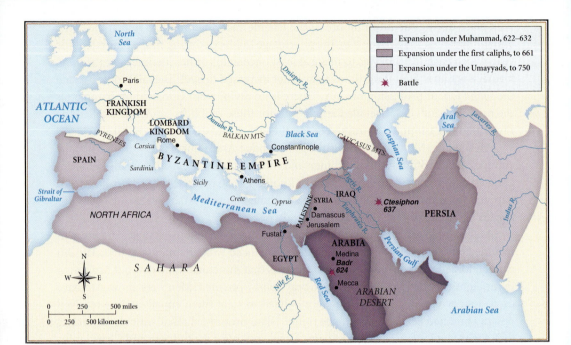

Map 8.1 Expansion of Islam to 750

In little more than a century, Islamic armies conquered a vast region that included numerous different people, cultures, climates, and living conditions. Yet under the Umayyads these disparate territories were administered by one ruler from the capital city at Damascus. The uniting force was the religion of Islam, which gathered all believers into one community, the *ummah*.

Christians in Syria and Egypt, for example, had suffered persecution under the Byzantines and were glad to have new, Islamic overlords. There were also internal reasons for Islam's success. Inspired by jihad, Arab fighters were well prepared: fully armed and mounted on horseback, using camel convoys to carry supplies and provide protection, they conquered with amazing ease. To secure their victories, they built garrison cities from which their soldiers requisitioned taxes and goods.

Yet the solidarity of the Muslim community was threatened by disputes over the successors to Muhammad, the caliphs. While the first two caliphs came to power without serious opposition, the third, Uthman (r. 644–656), a member of the Umayyad clan and son-in-law of Muhammad, aroused discontent among other members of the inner circle and soldiers unhappy with his distribution of high offices and revenues. Accusing Uthman of favoritism, they supported his rival, Ali, a member of the Hashim clan (to which Muhammad had belonged) and the husband of Muhammad's only surviving child, Fatimah. After a group of discontented soldiers murdered Uthman, civil war broke out between the Umayyads and Ali's faction. It ended when Ali was killed by one of his own former supporters, and the caliphate remained in Umayyad hands from 661 to 750.

Despite defeat, the Shi'at Ali ("Ali's faction"), did not fade away. Ali's memory lived on among **Shi'ite** Muslims, who saw in him a symbol of justice and righteousness. For

them, Ali's death was the martyrdom of the true successor to Muhammad. They remained faithful to his dynasty, shunning the mainstream caliphs of Sunni Muslims (whose name derived from the word *sunna,* the practices of Muhammad). They awaited the arrival of the true leader — the imam — who in their view could come only from the house of Ali.

Peace and Prosperity in Islamic Lands

Ironically, the definitive victories of the Muslim warriors in the seventh and early eighth centuries ushered in a time of peace. While the conquerors stayed within their fortified cities or built magnificent hunting lodges in the deserts of Syria, the conquered, including Christian and Jews, went back to work, to study, to play, and to worship. Under the **Umayyad caliphate**, which lasted from 661 to 750, the Muslim world became a state, its capital at Damascus, in Syria.

Borrowing from institutions well known to the civilizations they had just conquered, the Muslims issued coins and hired Byzantine and Persian officials as civil servants. They made Arabic a tool of centralization, imposing it as the language of government.

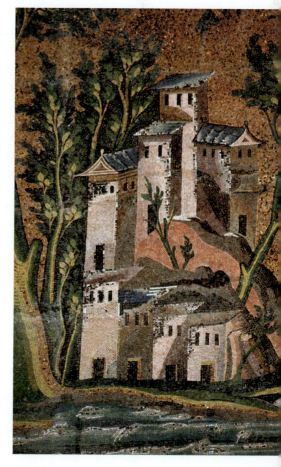

The Umayyads took advantage of the vigorous economy in both the cities and the countryside to preside over a literary and artistic flowering. At Damascus, local artists and craftspeople worked on the lavish decorations for a mosque that used Roman motifs. At Jerusalem, the mosque called the Dome of the Rock used Christian building models for its octagonal form and its interior arches (see the chapter-opening photo). Muslim scholars determined the definitive form for the Qur'an and compiled pious narratives about Muhammad, called hadith literature. A literate class — consisting mainly of the old

Mosaic from the Great Mosque at Damascus
Like the Dome of the Rock, the Umayyad mosque at Damascus in Syria, built at the beginning of the eighth century, drew on Byzantine forms. In this mosaic, which is one of many that decorate the interior of the mosque, the style is Byzantine. But the harmonious intertwining of trees, buildings, rocks, and water picks up on an Islamic theme: the new faith's conquest over both civilization and nature.
(Umayyad Mosque, Damascus, Syria / Bildarchiv Steffens / The Bridgeman Art Library International.)

Persian and Syrian elites, now converted to Islam — created new forms of prose and poetry in Arabic. Supported by the caliphs, these writers reached a wide audience that delighted in their clever use of words, their satire, and their verses celebrating courage, piety, and sometimes erotic love:

> I spent the night as her bed-companion, each enamored of the other,
> And I made her laugh and cry, and stripped her of her clothes.

Poetry like this scandalized conservative Muslims, brought up on the ascetic tenets of the Qur'an. But it was a by-product of the new urban civilization of the Umayyad period, during which wealth, cultural mix, and the confidence born of conquest inspired diverse and experimental literary forms. By the time the Umayyad caliphate ended in 750, Islamic civilization was multiethnic, urban, and sophisticated — a true heir of Roman and Persian traditions.

REVIEW QUESTION How and why did the Muslims conquer so many lands in the period 632–750?

Byzantium Besieged

The eastern Romans (the Byzantines) saw themselves as the direct heirs of Rome. In fact, as we have seen, Emperor Justinian (r. 527–565) had tried to re-create the old Roman Empire territorially. Under Justinian, vestiges of classical Roman society persisted: an educated elite, town governments, and old myths and legends, which were depicted in literature and art. Around 600, however, Byzantium began to undergo a transformation as striking as the one that had earlier remade the western half of the Roman Empire.

Constant war shrank the eastern empire's territory drastically. Cultural and political change followed. Cities decayed, and the countryside became the focus of government and military administration. In the wake of these shifts, the old elite largely disappeared and classical learning gave way to new forms of education, mainly religious in content. The traditional styles of urban life, dependent on public gathering places and community spirit, faded away.

Nevertheless, the transformations should not be exaggerated. A powerful emperor continued to rule at Constantinople (today Istanbul, Turkey). Roman laws and taxes remained in place. The cities, while shrunken, nevertheless survived, and Constantinople itself had a flourishing economic and cultural life even in Byzantium's darkest hours. The Byzantines continued to call themselves Romans. For them, the empire never ended: it just moved to Constantinople.

Wars on the Frontiers, c. 570–750

From about 570 to 750, the Byzantines waged war against invaders. One key challenge came from an old enemy, Persia. Another involved many new groups — Lombards, Slavs, Avars, Bulgars, and Muslims. In the wake of these onslaughts, Byzantium became smaller but tougher.

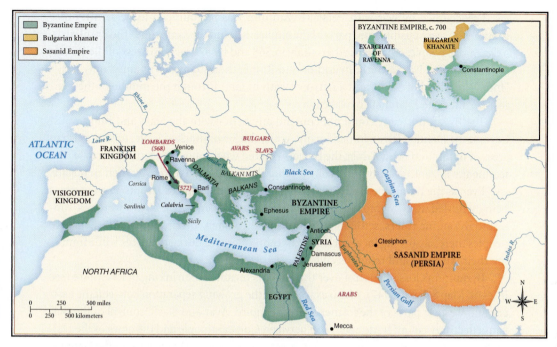

Map 8.2 Byzantine and Sasanid Empires, c. 600
The emperor Justinian (r. 527–565) hoped to re-create the old Roman Empire, but just a century after his death Italy was largely conquered by the Lombards. Meanwhile, the Byzantine Empire had to contend with the Sasanid Empire to its east. In 600, these two major powers faced each other uneasily. Three years later, the Sasanid king attacked Byzantine territory. The resulting wars, which lasted until 627, exhausted both empires and left them open to invasion by the Arabs. By 700, the Byzantine Empire was quite small. Compare the inset map here with Map 8.1, on page 244. Where had the Muslims made significant conquests of Byzantine territory?

Before the Muslims came on the scene, the principal challenge to Byzantine power came from the Sasanid Empire of Persia (Map 8.2). From their capital city at Ctesiphon, where they built a grand palace complex, the Sasanid kings promoted an exalted view of themselves: they took the title *King of Kings* and gave the men at their court titles such as *priest of priests* and *scribe of scribes*. With dreams of military glory, they invaded major areas of the Roman Empire, using the revenues from new taxes to strengthen the army. King Chosroes II (r. 591–628) took Syria and Jerusalem between 611 and 614, and he conquered Egypt in 620.

Responding to these attacks, the Byzantine emperor **Heraclius** reorganized his army and inspired his troops to avenge the sack of Jerusalem. By 627, the Byzantines had regained all their lost territory. But the wars had changed much: Syrian, Egyptian, and Palestinian cities had grown used to being under Persian rule, and Christians who did not adhere to the orthodoxy at Byzantium preferred their Persian overlords. Even more important, the constant wars and plundering sapped the wealth of the region and the energy of the people who lived under Byzantine rule.

Preoccupied by war with Persia, Byzantium was ill equipped to deal with other groups who were pushing into parts of the empire at about the same time. The **Lombards**, a Germanic people, entered northern Italy in 568 and by 572 were masters of the Po valley and parts of Italy's south. In addition to Rome, the Byzantines retained only Italy's "foot," the island of Sicily, and a narrow swath of land through the middle of the peninsula called the Exarchate of Ravenna.

The Byzantine army could not contend any better with the Slavs and Bulgars just beyond the Danube River. Joined by the Avars, the Slavs attacked both rural and urban areas of Byzantium. Meanwhile, the Bulgars entered what is now Bulgaria in the 670s, defeating the Byzantine army and in 681 forcing the emperor to recognize their new state.

Even as the Byzantine Empire was facing military attacks on all fronts, its power was being whittled away by more peaceful means. As Slavs and Avars, who were not subject to Byzantine rulers, settled in the Balkans, they often intermingled with the native peoples there, absorbing local agricultural techniques and burial practices while imposing their language and religious cults.

Byzantium's loss of control over the Balkans meant the shrinking of its empire (see inset on Map 8.2, page 247). It also exacerbated the growing separation between the eastern and western parts of the former Roman Empire. Avar and Slavic control of the Balkans effectively cut off trade and travel between Constantinople and the cities of the Dalmatian coast, while the new Bulgarian state served as a political barrier across the Danube. The two halves of the former Roman Empire communicated very little in the seventh century, a fact reflected in their different languages: Greek in the East, Latin in the West.

From an Urban to a Rural Way of Life

As Byzantium shrank, the conquered regions had to adjust to new rulers. Byzantine subjects in Syria and Egypt who came under Arab rule adapted to the new conditions, paying a special tax to their conquerors and practicing their Christian and Jewish religions in peace. Cities remained centers of government, scholarship, and business, and peasants were permitted to keep and farm their lands. In the Balkans, as Slavs and Bulgars came to dominate the peninsula, some cities disappeared when people fled to hilltop settlements. Nevertheless, the newcomers recognized the Byzantine emperor's authority and soon began to flirt with Christianity.

Some of the most radical transformations for seventh- and eighth-century Byzantines occurred not in the territories lost but in the shrunken empire itself. Under the ceaseless barrage of invaders, many towns, formerly bustling centers of trade and the imperial bureaucracy, vanished or became unrecognizable. The public activity of open marketplaces, theaters, and town squares largely ended. City baths, once places where people gossiped, made deals, and talked politics and philosophy, disappeared in most Byzantine towns — with the significant exception of Constantinople. Warfare reduced some cities to rubble, and the limited resources available for rebuilding went to construct thick city walls and solid churches instead of spacious marketplaces and baths.

Despite the general urban decay, Constantinople and a few other urban centers retained some of their old vitality. The manufacture and trade of fine silk textiles continued. Even though Byzantium's economic life became increasingly rural and barter-based in the seventh and eighth centuries, the skills, knowledge, and institutions of urban workers remained.

As urban life declined, agriculture, always the basis of the Byzantine economy, became the center of its social life as well. Unlike Europe, where peasants often depended on aristocratic landlords, the Byzantine Empire had many free peasants; they grew food, herded cattle, and tended vineyards on their own small plots of land. As Byzantine cities declined, the curials (town councilors), the elite who for centuries had mediated between the emperor and the people, disappeared. Now on those occasions when farmers came into contact with the state — to pay taxes, for example — they felt the impact of the emperor or his representatives directly.

Byzantine emperors, drawing on the still-vigorous Roman legal tradition, promoted domestic life with new imperial legislation, strengthening the nuclear family by narrowing the grounds for divorce and setting new punishments for marital infidelity. Abortion was prohibited, and new protections were set in place against incest. Mothers were given equal power with fathers over their offspring; if widowed, they became the legal guardians of their minor children and controlled the household property.

New Military and Cultural Forms

The shift from an urban to a rural-centered society meant changes not only in daily life and the economy but also in the empire's military and cultural institutions. The Byzantine navy fought successfully at sea with its powerful weapon of "Greek fire," a mixture of crude oil and resin that was heated and shot via a tube over the water, engulfing enemy ships in flames. Determined to win wars on land as well, the imperial government tightened its control over the military by wresting power from elite families and encouraging the formation of a middle class of farmer-soldiers. In the seventh century, the empire was divided into military districts called **themes**. All civil and military authority in each theme was held by a general, a *strategos*. Landless men were lured to join the army with the promise of land and low taxes; they fought side by side with local farmers, who provided their own weapons and horses. The new organization effectively countered frontier attacks.

The disappearance of the old cultural elite meant a shift in the focus of education. Whereas the curial class had cultivated the study of the pagan classics, eighth-century parents showed far more interest in a religious education. Even with the decay of urban centers, cities and villages often retained an elementary school. There, teachers used the Book of Psalms (the Psalter) as their primer. Secular, classical learning remained decidedly out of favor throughout the seventh and eighth centuries; dogmatic writings, biographies of saints, and devotional works took center stage.

Religion, Politics, and Iconoclasm

The new stress on religious learning in the seventh century complemented both the autocratic imperial ideal and the powers of the bishops. While in theory imperial and church powers were separate, in practice they were interdependent. The emperor exercised considerable power over the church: he influenced the appointment of the chief religious official, the patriarch of Constantinople; he called church councils to determine dogma; and he regularly used bishops as local governors.

Bishops and their clergy, whose seats were in the cities, formed a rich and powerful upper class. They distributed food to the needy, sat as judges, functioned as tax collectors, and built military fortifications. They owed their appointment to metropolitans (bishops who headed an entire province), who in turn were appointed by the patriarchs (bishops with authority over whole regions).

Theoretically, monasteries were under the limited control of the local bishop, but in practice they were enormously powerful institutions that often defied the authority of bishops and even emperors. Because monks commanded immense prestige as the holiest of God's faithful, they could influence the many issues of doctrine that racked the Byzantine church.

The most important of these issues involved **icons** — images of holy people, such as Jesus; his mother, Mary; and the saints. To the Byzantines, icons were more than mere representations: they were like Christ's incarnation, manifesting in physical form the holy person depicted.

Icons were the focus of many people's religious devotion. Some Byzantines actually worshipped icons; others, particularly monks, considered icons a necessary part of Christian piety. Other Byzan-

Icon of the Virgin and Child
Surrounded by two angels in the back and two soldier-saints at either side, the Virgin Mary and the Christ Child are depicted with still, otherworldly dignity. The sixth-century artist gave the angels transparent halos to emphasize their spiritual natures, while depicting the saints as earthly men, with hair and beards, and feet planted firmly on the ground. Icons like this were used for worship both in private homes and in Byzantine monasteries. (Erich Lessing / Art Resource, NY.)

tines, however, abhorred icons. Many of these were the soldiers on the frontiers. Unnerved by Arab triumphs, they attributed their misfortunes to disregard of the biblical command against graven (carved) images. When they compared their defeats to Muslim successes, Byzantine soldiers could not help but notice that Islam prohibited all visual images of the divine. To these soldiers and others who shared their view, icons revived pagan idolatry and desecrated Christian divinity. As the movement toward **iconoclasm** ("icon breaking") grew, some churchmen became outspoken in their opposition to icons.

Byzantine emperors shared these religious objections, and they also had important political reasons for opposing icons. Icons diluted loyalties because they created intermediaries between worshippers and God that undermined the emperor's exclusive place in the divine and temporal order. In addition, the emphasis on icons in monastic communities made the monks potential threats to imperial power; the emperors hoped to use this issue to weaken the monasteries. Above all, the emperors opposed icons because the army did, and they needed to retain the loyalty of their troops.

After Emperor Leo III the Isaurian (r. 717–741) defeated the Arabs besieging Constantinople at the beginning of his reign, he turned his attention to consolidating his political position. In 726, he ordered all icons destroyed, a ban that remained in effect until 787. This is known as the period of iconoclasm in Byzantine history. (A modified ban was imposed in 815 and last until 843.)

Iconoclasm had an enormous impact on Byzantium. The devout had to destroy their personal icons or worship them in secret. Iconoclasts (who were especially numerous at Constantinople itself) whitewashed the walls of churches, erasing all the images. They smashed portable icons. Artists largely ceased depicting the human form, and artistic production in general dwindled during this time. The power and prestige of the monasteries, which were associated with icons, diminished. As the tide of battle turned in favor of the Byzantines, imperial supporters and soldiers credited iconoclasm for their victories.

> **REVIEW QUESTION** What stresses did the Byzantine Empire endure in the seventh and eighth centuries, and how was iconoclasm a response to those stresses?

Western Europe: A Medley of Kingdoms

In contrast to Byzantium — where an emperor still ruled as the successor to Augustus and Constantine — western Europe saw a dispersal of political power. With the end of Roman imperial government there, independent monarchs ruled in Spain, Italy, England, and Gaul. The European kings relied on the support of powerful men who attended them at court, kinship networks, the prestige that came from church patronage, and wealth derived from land and plunder.

In some places churchmen and rich magnates were even more powerful than royalty. So were saintly relics. Icons were not very important in the West, but in their place was the power of the saints as exercised through their relics — their bodies and body parts, even clothes and dust from their tombs. Relics represented and wielded the divine forces of God.

Frankish Kingdoms with Roman Roots

The most important kingdoms in post-Roman Europe were Frankish. The Franks dominated Gaul during the sixth century, and by the seventh century their kingdoms roughly approximated the eastern borders of present-day France, Belgium, the Netherlands, and Luxembourg (Map 8.3). Moreover, the Frankish kings who constituted the **Merovingian dynasty** (c. 486–751) subjugated many of the peoples beyond the Rhine River, foreshadowing the contours of the western half of modern Germany.

Where there were cities, there were reminders of Rome. Elsewhere, the Roman heritage was less obvious. Imagine, then, travelers going from Rome to Trier (near what is now Bonn, Germany) in the early eighth century, perhaps to visit its bishop and check up on his piety. They would have relied on river travel: water routes were preferable to roads because land travel was slow, even though some Roman roads were still in fair repair, and because even large groups of travelers on the roads were vulnerable to attacks

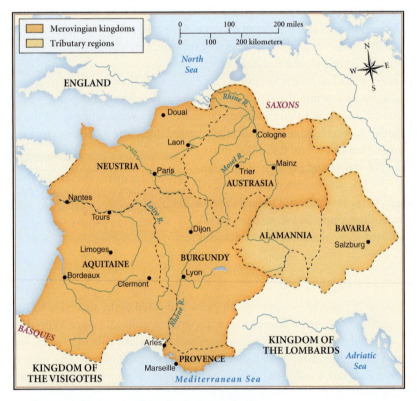

Map 8.3 The Merovingian Kingdoms in the Seventh Century
By the seventh century, there were three powerful Merovingian kingdoms: Neustria, Austrasia, and Burgundy. The important cities of Aquitaine were assigned to these major kingdoms, while Aquitaine as a whole was assigned to a duke or other governor. Kings did not establish capital cities; they did not even stay in one place. Rather, they continually traveled throughout their kingdoms, making their power felt in person.

by robbers. Traveling northward on the Rhône River, our voyagers would have passed Roman walled cities and farmlands neatly and squarely laid out by Roman land surveyors. The great stone palaces of villas would still have dotted the countryside. Once at Trier, the travelers would have felt at home seeing the city's great gate (now called the Porta Nigra; see the illustration below), its monumental baths (some still standing today), and its cathedral, built on the site of a Roman palace. Being in Trier was almost like being in Rome.

Nevertheless, these travelers would have noticed that the cities that they passed through were not what they had been in the heyday of the Roman Empire. True, cities still served as the centers of church administration. Bishops lived in them, and so did clergymen, servants, and others who helped the bishops. Cathedrals (the churches presided over by bishops) remained within city walls, and people were drawn to them for important rituals such as baptism. Nevertheless, many urban centers had lost their commercial and cultural vitality. Largely depopulated, they survived as skeletons of their former selves.

The Porta Nigra at Trier

Although in Germania, Trier became one of Rome's capitals in the fourth century. The Porta Nigra was originally the northern gate of the city. During the course of the fifth century, the Porta Nigra came to be considered at best useless and at worst pagan, so bits and pieces of it were pillaged to be used in other building projects. However, this practice stopped when a hermit named Simeon moved into its eastern tower. After Simeon's death in 1035, the Porta Nigra was turned into a two-story church, which it remained until the early nineteenth century, when Napoleon, who conquered Trier, ordered the church to be dismantled and the site returned (more or less) to its original shape. (Gianni Dagli Orti / The Art Archive at Art Resource, NY.)

Whereas the chief feature of the Roman landscape had been cities, the Frankish landscape was characterized by dense forests, acres of marshes and bogs, patches of cleared farmland, and pastures for animals. These areas were not much influenced by Rome; they more closely represented the farming and village settlement patterns of the Franks.

On the vast plains between Paris and Trier, most peasants were only semi-free. They were settled in family groups on small holdings called manses, which included a house, a garden, and cultivable land. The peasants paid dues and sometimes owed labor services to a lord (an aristocrat who owned the land). Some of the peasants were descendants of the *coloni* (tenant farmers) of the late Roman Empire; others were the sons and daughters of slaves, now provided with a small plot of land; and a few were people of free Frankish origin who for various reasons had come down in the world. At the lower end of the social scale, the status of Franks and Romans had become identical.

Romans (or, more precisely, Gallo-Romans) and Franks had also merged at the elite level. Although people south of the Loire River continued to be called Romans and people to the north Franks, their cultures — their languages, their settlement patterns, their newly military way of life — were strikingly similar. (See "Taking Measure," below.)

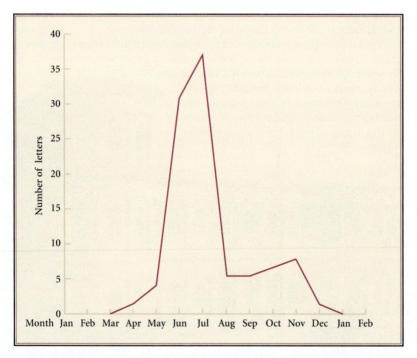

Taking Measure **Papal Letters Sent from Rome to Northern Europe, c. 600–c. 700**
Between 600 and 700, the pope at Rome sent many letters to kings, queens, aristocrats, and members of the clergy in northern Europe. But he didn't send the same number every month. This graph shows that papal communications were never sent in January and February, whereas their numbers peaked in June and July. The explanation? Very likely the popes had to wait for fine sailing weather to get their letters to their destination, since land routes were too uncertain. (Adapted from Michael McCormick, *Origins of the European Economy: Communications and Commerce, AD 300–900* [Cambridge: Cambridge University Press, 2001], chart 3.1, 80.)

The language that aristocrats spoke and (often) read depended on location, not ethnicity. Among the many dialects in the Frankish kingdoms, some were Germanic, especially to the east and north, but most were derived from Latin, yet no longer the Latin of Cicero. At the end of the sixth century, the bishop **Gregory of Tours** (r. 573–c. 594), wrote, "Though my speech is rude, . . . to my surprise, it has often been said by men of our day, that few understand the learned words of the rhetorician but many the rude language of the common people." This beginning to Gregory's *Histories,* a valuable source for the Merovingian period, testifies to Latin's transformation; Gregory expected that his "rude" Latin — the plain Latin of everyday speech — would be understood and welcomed by the general public.

The Frankish elites, like Frankish peasants, tended to live in the countryside rather than cities. In fact, peasants and aristocrats tended to live together in villages. In many cases, a village consisted of a large central building (probably for the aristocratic household to use), sometimes with stone foundations. Surrounding the central building were smaller buildings, some of which were houses for peasant families, who lived with their livestock. Such villages might boast populations a bit over a hundred.

The elites of the Merovingian period cultivated military — rather than civilian — skills. They went on hunts and wore military-style clothing: the men wore trousers, a heavy belt, and a long cloak; both men and women bedecked themselves with jewelry. As hardened warriors, or wanting to appear so, aristocrats no longer lived in grand villas, choosing instead modest wooden structures without baths or heating systems. That explains why the village great house and the smaller ones nearby looked very much alike.

Sometimes villages formed around old villas. In other instances they clustered around sacred sites. Tours — where Gregory was bishop — exemplified this new-style settlement. In Roman times, Tours was a thriving city; around 400, its population diminished, and it constructed walls around its shrunken perimeter. By Gregory's day, however, it had gained a new center *outside* the city walls. There a church had been built to house the remains of the most important and venerated person in the locale: St. Martin. This fourth-century soldier-turned-monk was long dead, but his relics remained at Tours, where he had served as bishop. The population of the surrounding countryside was pulled to his church as if to a magnet. Seen as a miracle worker, Martin acted as the representative of God's power: a protector, healer, and avenger. In Gregory's view, Martin's relics (or rather God *through* Martin's relics) not only cured the lame and sick but even prevented armies from plundering local peasants.

The veneration of saints and their relics marked a major departure from practices of the classical age, in which the dead had been banished from the presence of the living. In the medieval world, the holy dead held the place of highest esteem. The church had no formal procedures

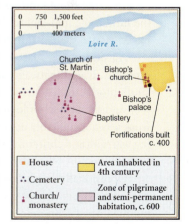

Tours, c. 600 (Nancy Gauthier and Henri Galinié, eds., *Gregoire de Tours et l'espace gaulois* [Tours: Actes du congrès internationale, 1997], 70.)

Reliquary

The cult of relics necessitated housing the precious parts of the saints in equally precious containers. This reliquary — made of cloisonné enamel (bits of enamel framed by metal), garnets, glass gems, and a cameo — is in the shape of a miniature sarcophagus. It was made in honor of St. Maurice, a venerated martyr, and was given to a monastery dedicated to Maurice, Saint-Maurice d'Agaune (today in Switzerland). Note the side hinges, which allowed the casket to be worn on a chain. No doubt the abbot of Saint-Maurice wore it when he traveled outside the monastery, to ensure him of the power and protection of the saint. (Erich Lessing / Art Resource, NY.)

for proclaiming saints in the early Middle Ages, but holiness was "recognized" by influential local people and the local bishop. Everyone at Tours recognized Martin as a saint, and to tap into the power of his relics, the local bishop built a church directly over his tomb. For a man like Gregory of Tours and his flock, the church building was above all a home for the relics of the saints.

Economic Activity in a Peasant Society

Gregory wrote about some sophisticated forms of economic activity that existed in early medieval Europe, such as long-distance trade, which depended on surpluses. But he also wrote about famines. Most people in his day lived on the edge of survival. From the fifth to the mid-eighth century the mean temperature in Europe dropped. This climatic change spelled shortages in crops and the likelihood of famine and disease.

An underlying reason for these calamities was the weakness of the agricultural economy. Even the meager population of the Merovingian world was too large for the land's productive capacities. The heavy, wet soils of northern Europe were difficult to turn and aerate. Technological limitations meant a limited food supply, and agricultural work was not equitably or efficiently allocated and managed. A leisure class of landowning warriors and churchmen lived off the work of peasant men, who tilled the fields, and peasant women, who wove cloth, gardened, brewed, and baked.

Occasionally surpluses developed, either from good harvests in peacetime or plunder in warfare, and these changed hands, although rarely in an impersonal, commercial manner. Most economic transactions of the seventh and eighth centuries were part of a gift economy, a system of give-and-take: the rich took plunder, demanded tribute, hoarded harvests, and minted coins — all to be redistributed to friends, followers, and dependents. Powerful men and women amassed gold, silver, ornaments, and jewelry

in their treasuries and grain in their storehouses to mark their power, add to their pres-tige, and demonstrate their generosity. Those benefiting from the gifts of the rich in-cluded monasteries and churches. The gift economy was the dynamic behind most of the exchanges of goods and money in the Merovingian period.

However, some economic activity in this period was purely commercial and im-personal. Long-distance traders transported slaves and raw materials such as furs and honey from areas of northern Europe such as the British Isles and Sweden. These they sold to traders in Byzantium and the Islamic world, returning home with luxuries and manufactured goods such as silks and papyrus. Byzantine, Islamic, and western Euro-pean descendants of the Roman Empire kept in tenuous contact with one another by making voyages for trade, diplomatic ventures, and pilgrimages. Seventh- and eighth-century sources speak of Byzantines, Syrians, and Jews as the chief intermediaries of such long-distance trade. Many of these merchants lived in the still-thriving port cities of the Mediterranean. Gregory of Tours associated Jews with commerce, complaining that they sold things "at a higher price than they were worth."

Although the population of the Merovingian world was overwhelmingly Christian, Jews were integrated into every aspect of secular life. They used Hebrew in worship, but otherwise they spoke the same languages as Christians and used Latin in their legal docu-ments. Jews dressed as everyone else did, and they engaged in the same occupations. Many Jews planted and tended vineyards, partly because of the importance of wine in synagogue services and partly because they could easily sell the surplus. Some Jews were rich landowners, with slaves and dependent peasants working for them; others were independent peasants of modest means. Some Jews lived in towns with a small Jewish quarter that included both homes and synagogues, but most Jews, like their Christian neighbors, lived on the land.

The Powerful in Merovingian Society

The Merovingian elite — who included monks and bishops as well as kings and lay aristocrats — obtained their power through hereditary wealth, status, and personal in-fluence. Many of them were extremely wealthy. The will drawn up by a bishop and aris-tocrat named Bertram of Le Mans, for example, shows that he owned estates — some from his family, others given him as gifts — scattered all over Gaul.

Along with administering their estates, many male aristocrats spent their time hon-ing their proficiency as warriors. To be a great warrior in Merovingian society meant perfecting the virtues necessary for leading armed men. Merovingian warriors affirmed their skills and comradeship in the hunt: they proved their worth in the regular taking of plunder, and they rewarded their followers afterward at generous banquets.

Merovingian aristocrats also spent time with their families. The focus of marriage was procreation. Important both to the survival of aristocratic families and to the trans-mission of their property and power, marriage was an expensive institution. It had two forms: in the most formal, the man gave a generous dowry of clothes, livestock, and

land to his bride; after the marriage was consummated, he gave her a "morning gift" of furniture. Very wealthy men also might support one or more concubines, who enjoyed a less formal type of marriage, receiving a morning gift but no dowry. Churchmen in this period had many ideas about the value of marriages, but in practice they had little to do with the matter. Marriage was a family decision and a family matter: the couple exchanged rings before witnesses, and later the girl moved to the house of the groom.

In the sixth century, some aristocrats still patterned their lives on the old Roman model, teaching their children classical Latin poetry and writing to one another in phrases borrowed from Virgil. But this changed in the seventh century. The spoken language had become very different from classical Latin, and written Latin was learned mainly to read the Psalms. Just as in Byzantium, a religious culture that emphasized Christian piety over the classics was developing in Europe.

The arrival on the continent around 590 of the Irish monk St. Columbanus (c. 543– 615) heightened this emphasis on religion. Columbanus's brand of monasticism — which stressed exile, devotion, and discipline — found much favor among the Merovingian elite. The monasteries St. Columbanus established in both Gaul and Italy attracted local recruits from the aristocracy. Some were grown men and women; others were young children, given to the monastery by their parents in the ritual called oblation. This practice was not only accepted but also often considered essential for the spiritual well-being of both the children and their families.

Alongside monks, bishops ranked among the most powerful men in Merovingian society. Gregory of Tours, for example, considered himself the protector of "his citizens." When representatives of the king came to collect taxes in Tours, Gregory stopped them in their tracks, warning them that St. Martin would punish anyone who tried to tax his people. "That very day," Gregory reported, "the man who had produced the tax rolls caught a fever and died." Little wonder that Frankish kings let the old Roman land tax die out.

Like other aristocrats, many bishops were married, even though church councils demanded celibacy. As the overseers of priests and guardians of morality, bishops were expected to refrain from sexual relations with their wives. Since bishops were ordinarily appointed late in life, long after they had raised a family, this restriction did not threaten the ideal of a procreative marriage.

Noble parents generally decided whom their daughters would marry, for such unions bound together not only husbands and wives but entire extended families as well. Aristocratic brides received a dowry from their families in addition to their husband's gift. This was often land, over which they had some control; if they were widowed without children, they were allowed to sell, give away, exchange, or rent out their dowry estates as they wished. Moreover, people could give property to their women kinfolk outright in written testaments. Many aristocratic women were very rich, and like rich men, they frequently gave generous gifts to the church from their vast possessions.

Though legally under the authority of her husband, a Merovingian married woman often found ways to exercise some power and control over her life. Tetradia, wife of Count

Eulalius, left her husband, taking all his gold and silver, because, as Gregory of Tours tells us,

> he was in the habit of sleeping with the women-servants in his household. As a result he neglected his wife. . . . As a result of his excesses, he ran into serious debt, and to meet this he stole his wife's jewelry and money.

A court of law ordered Tetradia to repay Eulalius four times the amount she had taken from him, but she was allowed to keep and live on her own property.

Other women were able to exercise behind-the-scenes control through their sons. A woman named Artemia, for example, used the prophecy that her son Nicetius would become a bishop to prevent her husband from becoming a bishop himself. After Nicetius fulfilled the prophecy, he nevertheless remained at home with his mother well into his thirties, working alongside the servants and teaching the younger children to read the Psalms.

Some women exercised direct power. Rich widows with fortunes to bestow wielded enormous influence. Some Merovingian women were abbesses, rulers in their own right over female monasteries and sometimes over "double monasteries," with separate facilities for men and women. Monasteries under the control of abbesses could be substantial centers of population: the convent at Laon, for example, had three hundred nuns in the seventh century. Because women lived in populous convents or were monopolized by rich men able to support several wives or mistresses at one time, unattached aristocratic women were scarce.

Atop the aristocracy were the Merovingian kings, rulers of the Frankish kingdoms. The Merovingian dynasty (c. 486–751) owed its longevity to good political sense: from the start it allied itself with local lay aristocrats and ecclesiastical (church) authorities. Bishops and abbots bolstered the power that kings also gained from their leadership in war, their access to the lion's share of plunder, and their takeover of the public lands and legal framework of Roman administration. The kings' courts functioned as schools for the sons of the elite. When kings sent officials — counts and dukes — to rule in their name in various regions of their kingdoms, these regional governors worked with and married into the aristocratic families who had long controlled local affairs.

Both kings and aristocrats benefited from a powerful royal authority. The king acted as arbitrator and intermediary for the competing interests of the aristocrats. Gregory of Tours's history of the sixth century is filled with stories of bitter battles between Merovingian kings, as royal brothers fought continuously. Yet what seemed to the bishop like royal weakness and violent chaos was in fact one way the kings contained local aristocratic tensions, organizing them on one side or another, and preventing them from spinning out of royal control. By the beginning of the seventh century, three relatively stable Frankish kingdoms had emerged: Austrasia to the northeast; Neustria to the west, with its capital city at Paris; and Burgundy, incorporating the southeast (Map 8.3, page 252).

As the power of the kings in the seventh century increased, however, so did the might of their chief court official, the mayor of the palace. As we shall see, one mayoral

family allied with the Austrasian aristocracy would in the following century displace the Merovingian dynasty and establish a new royal line, the Carolingians.

Christianity and Classical Culture in the British Isles

The Merovingian kingdoms exemplify some of the ways in which Roman and non-Roman traditions combined; the British Isles show others. Ireland had never been part of the Roman Empire, but the Irish people were early converts to Christianity, as were people in Roman Britain and parts of Scotland. Invasions by various Celtic and Germanic groups — particularly the Anglo-Saxons, who gave their name to England ("land of the Angles") — redrew the religious boundaries. Ireland, largely free of invaders, remained Christian. Scotland, also relatively untouched by invaders, had been slowly Christianized by the Irish from the west and in early years by the British from the south. England, which emerged from the invasions as a mosaic of about a dozen kingdoms ruled by separate Anglo-Saxon kings, became largely pagan until it was actively converted in the seventh century.

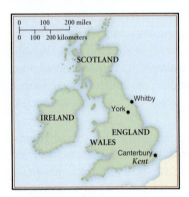

The British Isles

Christianity was introduced to Anglo-Saxon England from two directions. To the north, Irish monks brought their own brand of Christianity. Converted in the fifth century by St. Patrick and other missionaries, the Irish had evolved a church organization that corresponded to its rural clan organization. Abbots and abbesses were more powerful than bishops there. The Irish missionaries to England were monks, and they set up monasteries modeled on those at home — out in the countryside.

In the south, Christianity came to England in 597 via missionaries sent by the pope known as **Gregory the Great** (r. 590–604). These men, led by Augustine (not the same Augustine as the bishop of Hippo; see page 212), intended to convert the king and people of Kent, the southernmost kingdom, and then work their way northward. Augustine and his party brought with them Roman practices at odds with those of Irish Christianity, stressing ties to the pope and the authority of bishops. Using the Roman model, they divided England into territorial units, called dioceses, headed by an archbishop and bishops. Augustine became archbishop of Canterbury. Because he was a monk, he set up a monastery right next to his cathedral, and having a community of monks attached to the bishop's church became a characteristic of the English church. Later a second archbishopric was added at York.

A major bone of contention between the Roman and Irish churches involved the calculation of the date of Easter, celebrated by Christians as the day on which Christ rose from the dead. Because everyone agreed that believers could not be saved unless they observed Christ's resurrection properly and on the right date, the conflict was bitter. It was resolved by Oswy, king of Northumbria, who organized a meeting of churchmen,

the **Synod of Whitby**, in 664. Convinced that Rome spoke with the voice of St. Peter, who was said in the New Testament to hold the keys of the kingdom of heaven, Oswy chose the Roman date. His decision paved the way for the triumph of the Roman brand of Christianity in England.

The authority of St. Peter was only one of the attractions of Roman Christianity. Rome had great prestige as a treasure trove of knowledge, piety, and holy objects. Benedict Biscop (c. 630–690), the founder of two important English monasteries, made many difficult trips to Rome, bringing back relics, liturgical vestments, and even a cantor to teach his monks the proper melodies in a time before written musical notation. Above all, he went to Rome to get books. At his monasteries in the north of England, he built up a grand library. In Anglo-Saxon England, as in Scotland and Ireland, all of which lacked a strong classical tradition from Roman times, a book was considered a precious object, to be decorated as finely as a jewel-studded reliquary.

The Anglo-Saxons and Irish Celts had a thriving oral culture but extremely limited uses for writing. Books became valuable only when these societies converted to Christianity. Just as Islamic reliance on the Qur'an made possible a literary culture under the Umayyads, so Christian dependence on the Bible, liturgy, and the writings of the church fathers helped make England and Ireland centers of literature and learning in the seventh and eighth centuries. Men like Benedict Biscop soon sponsored other centers of learning, using texts from the classical past. Although women did not establish famous schools, many abbesses ruled over monasteries that stressed Christian learning. Latin writings, even pagan texts, were studied diligently, in part because Latin was so foreign a language on the British Isles that mastering it required systematic and formal study.

One of Benedict Biscop's pupils was Bede ("the Venerable," 673–735), an Anglo-Saxon monk and a historian of extraordinary breadth. Bede in turn taught a new generation of monks who became advisers to eighth-century rulers.

Page from the Lindisfarne Gospels
The lavishly illuminated manuscript known as the Lindisfarne Gospels, of which this is one page, was probably produced in the first third of the eighth century. For the monks at Lindisfarne (a tidal island off the northeast coast of England) and elsewhere in the British Isles, books were precious objects. The page shown here depicts the Evangelist St. Mark, writing while also holding a book. Above his halo is his symbol, a winged lion; it is blowing a trumpet while its front paws rest on a book. What books might St. Mark and the lion be holding? (© The British Library / HIP / The Image Works.)

Much of the vigorous pagan Anglo-Saxon oral tradition was adapted to Christian culture. Bede encouraged and supported the use of the Anglo-Saxon language, urging priests, for example, to use it when they instructed their flocks. In contrast to other European regions, where Latin was the primary written language in the seventh and eighth centuries, England made use of the vernacular — the language normally spoken by the people. Written Anglo-Saxon (or Old English) was used in every aspect of English life, from government to entertainment.

The decision at the Synod of Whitby to favor Roman Christianity tied the English church to Rome by doctrine, friendship, and conviction. The Anglo-Saxon monk and bishop Wynfrith took the Latin name Boniface to symbolize his loyalty to the Roman church. Preaching on the continent, Boniface (680–754) set up churches in Germany and Gaul that, like those in England, looked to Rome for leadership and guidance. Boniface was one of those travelers from Rome who went to Trier to check on the bishop's piety. He found it badly wanting! Boniface's efforts to reform the Frankish church gave the papacy new importance in Europe.

Unity in Spain, Division in Italy

Southern Gaul, Spain, and Italy, unlike the British Isles, had long been part of the Roman Empire and preserved many of its traditions. Nevertheless, as these areas were settled and fought over by new peoples, their histories diverged dramatically. When the Merovingian king Clovis (r. 485–511) defeated the Visigoths in 507, the Visigothic kingdom, which had sprawled across southern Gaul into Spain, was dismembered. By midcentury, the Franks had come into possession of most of its remnants in southern Gaul.

In Spain, the Visigothic king Leovigild (r. 569–586) established territorial control by military might. But no ruler could hope to maintain his position in Visigothic Spain without the support of the Hispano-Roman population, which included both the great landowners and leading bishops — and their backing was unattainable while the Visigoths remained Arian Christians, who maintained that Christ was not identical with God (see page 215). Leovigild's son Reccared (r. 586–601) took the necessary step in 587, converting to Roman Catholic Christianity. Two years later, at the Third Council of Toledo, most of the Arian bishops followed their king by announcing their conversion to Catholicism.

Thereafter, the bishops and kings of Spain cooperated to a degree unprecedented in other regions. While the king gave the churchmen free rein to set up their own hierarchy (with the bishop of Toledo at the top) and to meet regularly at synods to regulate and reform the church, the bishops in turn supported their Visigothic king, who ruled as a minister of the Christian people. Rebellion against him was tantamount to rebellion against Christ. The Spanish bishops reinforced this idea by anointing the king, daubing him with holy oil in a ritual that paralleled the ordination of priests and demonstrated divine favor. Toledo, the city where the highest bishop presided, was also where the kings were "made" through anointment. While the bishops in this way made the king's cause their own, their lay counterparts, the great landowners, helped

supply the king with troops, allowing him to maintain internal order and repel his external enemies.

Ironically, it was precisely the centralization and unification of the Visigothic kingdom that proved its undoing. When the Arabs arrived in 711, they needed only to kill the king, defeat his army, and capture Toledo to take the kingdom.

By contrast, in Italy the Lombard king faced a hostile papacy in the center of the peninsula and insubordinate dukes in the south. Theoretically the dukes of Benevento and Spoleto were royal officers, but in fact they ruled independently. Although many Lombards were Catholics, others were Arian. The "official" religion of Lombards in Italy varied with the ruler in power. The conversion of the Lombards to Catholic Christianity occurred gradually, ending only around the mid-seventh century. Partly as a result of this slow development, the Lombard kings never gained the full support of the church.

Lombard Italy, Early Eighth Century

Nevertheless, Lombard kings had strengths. Chief among these were the traditions of leadership associated with the royal dynasty, the kings' military ability, their control over large estates in northern Italy, and their hold on surviving Roman institutions. Lombard kings took advantage of the still-urban organization of Italian society and the economy, assigning dukes to city bases and setting up a royal capital at Pavia. Recalling emperors like Constantine and Justinian, the kings built churches, monasteries, and other places of worship in the royal capital; they maintained the city walls, issued laws, and minted coins. Revenues from tolls, sales taxes, port duties, and court fines filled their treasuries, although their inability to revive the Roman land tax was a major weakness. The greatest challenge for the Lombard kings came from sharing the peninsula with Rome. As soon as the kings began to make serious headway into southern Italy against the duchies of Spoleto and Benevento, the pope began to fear for his own position and called on the Franks for help.

Political Tensions and the Power of the Pope

Around 600, the pope's position was ambiguous: he was both a ruler — successor of St. Peter and head of the church — and a subordinate, subject to the Byzantine emperor. Pope Gregory the Great in many ways laid the foundations for the papacy's spiritual and temporal ascendancy. During Gregory's reign, the papacy became the greatest landowner in Italy. Gregory organized the defenses of Rome and paid for its army; he heard court cases, made treaties, and provided welfare services. The missionary expedition Gregory sent to England was only a small part of his involvement in the rest of Europe.

A prolific author of spiritual works and biblical commentaries, Gregory digested and simplified the ideas of church fathers like St. Augustine of Hippo, making them

accessible to a wider audience. His book *Pastoral Rule* was used as a guide for bishops throughout Europe.

Yet even Gregory was not independent, for he was subordinate to the emperor. For a long time the Byzantine views on dogma, discipline, and church administration prevailed at Rome. This authority began to unravel in the seventh century. Sheer distance, as well as diminishing imperial power in Italy, meant that the popes became, in effect, the leaders of the parts of Italy not controlled by the Lombards.

The gap between Byzantium and Rome widened in the early eighth century as Emperor Leo III tried to increase the taxes on papal property to pay for his war against the Arab invaders. The pope responded by leading a general tax revolt. Meanwhile, Leo's fierce policy of iconoclasm collided with the pope's tolerance of images. In Italy, as in other European regions, Christian piety focused more on relics than on icons. Nevertheless, the papacy would not allow sacred images and icons to be destroyed. The pope argued that holy images should be respected, though not worshipped.

These disputes with the emperor were matched by increasing friction between the pope and the Lombards. The Lombard kings had gradually managed to bring under their control the duchies of Spoleto and Benevento as well as part of the Exarchate of Ravenna. By the mid-eighth century, the popes feared that Rome would fall to the Lombards, and Pope Zachary (r. 741–752) looked northward for friends. He created an ally by giving his approval to the removal of the last Merovingian king and his replacement by the first Carolingian king, Pippin III (r. 751–768). In 753, Pope Stephen II (r. 752–757) called on Pippin to march to Italy with an army to fight the Lombards.

REVIEW QUESTION   What were the similarities and differences among the kingdoms that emerged in western Europe, and how did their histories combine and diverge?

Conclusion

The Islamic world, Byzantium, and western Europe were heirs of the Roman Empire, but they built on its legacies in different ways. Muslims were the newcomers to the Roman world, but their religion, Islam, was influenced by both Jewish and Christian monotheism, each with roots in Roman culture. Under the guidance of Muhammad the Prophet, Islam became both a coherent theology and a way of life. Once the Muslim Arabs embarked on military conquests, they became the heirs of Rome in other ways: preserving Byzantine cities, hiring Syrian civil servants, and adopting Mediterranean artistic styles. Drawing on Roman and Persian traditions, the Umayyad dynasty created a powerful Islamic state, with a capital city in Syria and a culture that generally tolerated a wide variety of economic, religious, and social institutions so long as the conquered paid taxes to their Muslim overlords.

Byzantium directly inherited the central political institutions of Rome: its people called themselves Romans; its emperor was the Roman emperor; and its capital, Constantinople, was considered to be the new Rome. Byzantium also inherited the taxes, cities, laws, and Christian religion of Rome. The changes of the seventh and eighth

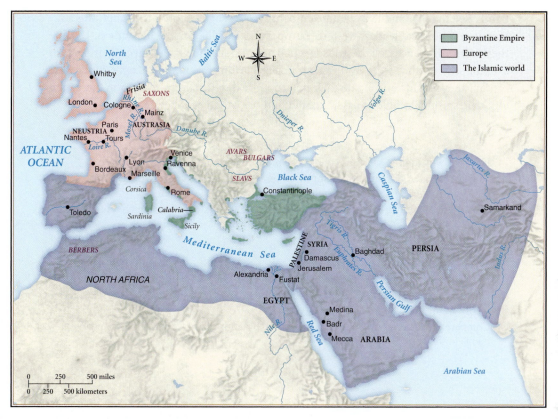

Mapping the West Rome's Heirs, c. 750

The major political fact of the period 600–750 was the emergence of Islam and the creation of an Islamic state that reached from Spain to the Indus River. The Byzantine Empire, once a great power, was dwarfed — and half swallowed up — by its Islamic neighbor. To the west were fledgling European kingdoms, mere trifles on the world stage. The next centuries, however, would prove their resourcefulness and durability.

centuries — contraction of territory, urban decline, disappearance of the old elite, and a ban on icons — whittled away at this Roman character. By 750, Byzantium was less Roman than it was a new, resilient political and cultural entity, a Christian state.

Western Europe also inherited — and transformed — Roman institutions. The Frankish kings built on Roman traditions that had earlier been modified by provincial and Germanic custom. In the seventh century, Anglo-Saxon England reimported the Roman legacy through Latin learning and the Christian religion. Visigothic kings in Spain converted from Arian to Roman Christianity and allied themselves with the Hispano-Roman elite. In Italy and at Rome itself, the traditions of the classical past endured. The roads remained, the cities of Italy survived (although depopulated), and both the popes and the Lombard kings ruled according to the traditions of Roman government.

Muslim, Byzantine, and western European societies all suffered the ravages of war. Social hierarchies became simpler, with the loss of "middle" groups like the curials at Byzantium and the near suppression of tribal affiliations among Muslims. Politics were

tightly tied to religion: the Byzantine emperor was a religious force; the caliph was a religious and political leader; western European kings allied with churchmen. Despite their many differences, all these leaders had a common understanding of their place in a divine scheme: they were God's agents on earth, ruling over God's people. In the next century they would consolidate their power. Little did they know that, soon thereafter, local elites would be able to assert greater authority than ever before.

Review Questions

1. How and why did the Muslims conquer so many lands in the period 632–750?
2. What stresses did the Byzantine Empire endure in the seventh and eighth centuries, and how was iconoclasm a response to those stresses?
3. What were the similarities and differences among the kingdoms that emerged in western Europe, and how did their histories combine and diverge?

Making Connections

1. What were the similarities and the differences in political organizations of the Islamic, Byzantine, and western European societies in the period 600–750?
2. Compare and contrast the roles of religion in the Islamic, Byzantine, and western European worlds in the period 600–750.
3. Compare the material resources of the Islamic, Byzantine, and western European governments in the period 600–750.

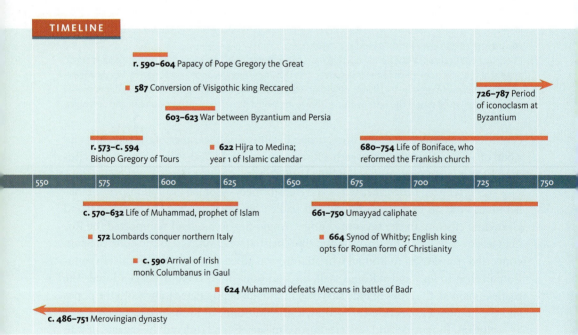

TIMELINE

r. 590–604 Papacy of Pope Gregory the Great

587 Conversion of Visigothic king Reccared

726–787 Period of iconoclasm at Byzantium

603–623 War between Byzantium and Persia

r. 573–c. 594 Bishop Gregory of Tours

622 Hijra to Medina; year 1 of Islamic calendar

680–754 Life of Boniface, who reformed the Frankish church

| 550 | 575 | 600 | 625 | 650 | 675 | 700 | 725 | 750 |

c. 570–632 Life of Muhammad, prophet of Islam

661–750 Umayyad caliphate

572 Lombards conquer northern Italy

664 Synod of Whitby; English king opts for Roman form of Christianity

c. 590 Arrival of Irish monk Columbanus in Gaul

624 Muhammad defeats Meccans in battle of Badr

c. 486–751 Merovingian dynasty

- For practice quizzes and other study tools, visit the **Online Study Guide** at bedfordstmartins.com/huntconcise.

- For primary-source material from this period, see *Sources of the Making of the West*, Fourth Edition.

- For Web sites, images, and documents related to topics in this chapter, visit *Make History* at bedfordstmartins.com/huntconcise.

Suggested References

Donner's book is insightful on the origins of Islam. Herrin gives a dazzling overview of Byzantine history. Smith's and Wickham's books are essential for understanding the early medieval West.

*Bede. *A History of the English Church and People*. Trans. Leo Sherley-Price. 1991.

Berkey, Jonathan P. *The Formation of Islam: Religion and Society in the Near East, 600–1800*. 2003.

*Byzantine Sourcebook: http://www.fordham.edu/halsall/sbook1c.html

Cameron, Averil. *The Byzantines*. 2006.

Donner, Fred McGraw. *Muhammad and the Believers: At the Origins of Islam*. 2010.

*Geanakoplos, Deno John, ed. and trans. *Byzantium: Church, Society, and Civilization Seen through Contemporary Eyes*. 1984.

Geary, Patrick. *Before France and Germany: The Creation and Transformation of the Merovingian World*. 1988.

*Gregory of Tours. *The History of the Franks*. Trans. Lewis Thorpe. 1976.

Haldon, J. F. *Byzantium in the Seventh Century: The Transformation of a Culture*. 1990.

Herrin, Judith. *Byzantium: The Surprising Life of a Medieval Empire*. 2007.

*Islamic Sourcebook: http://www.fordham.edu/halsall/islam/islamsbook.html

Kennedy, Hugh. *The Prophet and the Age of the Caliphates: The Islamic Near East from the Sixth to the Eleventh Century*. 2nd ed. 2004.

Smith, Julia M. H. *Europe after Rome: A New Cultural History 500–1000*. 2005.

Whittow, Mark. *The Making of Byzantium, 600–1025*. 1996.

Wickham, Chris. *Framing the Early Middle Ages: Europe and the Mediterranean, 400–800*. 2005.

Primary source.

From Centralization to Fragmentation

I N 841, A FIFTEEN-YEAR-OLD BOY named William went to serve at the court of Charles the Bald, king of the Franks. William's father, Bernard, was an extremely powerful noble. His mother, Dhuoda, was a well-educated, pious, and able woman; she administered the family's estates in the south of France while her husband was occupied with politics at court. In 841, however, politics had become a dangerous business. King Charles was fighting with his brothers over his portion of the Frankish Empire, and he doubted Bernard's loyalty. In fact, William was sent to Charles's court as a kind of hostage, to ensure Bernard's fidelity. Anxious about her son, Dhuoda wrote a handbook of advice for William, outlining his moral obligations. She emphasized duty to his father even over loyalty to the king:

> Royal and imperial . . . power seem pre-eminent in the world, and the custom of men is to [put] their names ahead of all others. . . . But despite all this, I caution you to render first to him whose son you are special, faithful, steadfast loyalty as long as you shall live. . . . So I urge you . . . that first of all you love God. . . . Then love, fear, and cherish your father.

William heeded his mother's words, with tragic results: when Bernard ran afoul of Charles and was executed, William died in a failed attempt to avenge his father.

Dhuoda's handbook reveals the volatile political atmosphere of the mid-ninth century, and her advice to her son points to one of its causes: a crisis of loyalty. Loyalty to emperors, caliphs, and kings competed with allegiances to local authorities, which, in

The Kiss of Judas

According to the Gospels, Judas, one of the original twelve Apostles, betrayed Jesus by giving him a kiss, in that way identifying him to the Roman and Hebrew authorities. In this depiction of the scene from the late tenth century, Judas is almost dancing with Jesus. Soldiers and the servants of the Hebrew high priest grab his arms from both sides. Meanwhile, St. Peter, the chief of the Apostles, has grabbed one of the priest's servants and is cutting off his ear. In the tenth century, people knew a great deal about loyalty and betrayal. Most of the institutions of government relied on oaths of fidelity, but these turned out to be fragile instruments for cohesion. (Stadtbibliothek / Stadtarchiv, Trier.)

turn, vied with family loyalties. The period 600–750 had seen the startling rise of Islam, the whittling away of Byzantium, and the beginnings of stable political and economic development in an impoverished Europe. The period 750–1050 would see all three societies contend with internal issues of diversity even as they became increasingly conscious of their unity and uniqueness. At the beginning of this period, rulers built up and dominated strong, united political communities. By the end, these realms had fragmented into smaller, more local units.

In Byzantium, military triumphs brought emperors enormous prestige. A renaissance (French for "rebirth") — that is, an important revival — of culture and art took place at Constantinople. Yet at the same time new elites began to dominate the Byzantine countryside. In the Islamic world, a dynastic revolution in 750 ousted the Umayyads from the caliphate and replaced them with a new family, the Abbasids. The Abbasid caliphs moved their capital to the east, from Damascus to Baghdad. Even though the Abbasids' power began to ebb as regional Islamic rulers came to the fore, the Islamic world, too, saw a renaissance. In western Europe, Charlemagne — a Frankish king from a new dynasty, the Carolingians — forged a huge empire and presided over yet another cultural renaissance. Yet this newly unified kingdom was fragile, disintegrating within a generation of Charlemagne's death. In western Europe, even more than in the Byzantine and Islamic worlds, power fell into the hands of local lords.

Along the borders of these realms, new political entities began to develop, shaped by the religion and culture of their more dominant neighbors. Rus, the ancestor of Russia, grew up in the shadow of Byzantium, as did Bulgaria and Serbia. Western Europe cast its influence over central European states. In the west, the borders of the Islamic world remained stable or were pushed back. By the year 1050, the contours of what were to become modern Europe and the Middle East were dimly visible.

CHAPTER FOCUS What forces led to the dissolution — or weakening — of centralized governments in the period 750–1050, and what institutions took their place?

The Byzantine Emperor and Local Elites

Between 750 and 850, Byzantium staved off Muslim attacks and began to rebuild. After 850, it expanded. Military victories brought new wealth and power to the imperial court, and the emperors supported a vast program of literary and artistic revival at Constantinople. But while the emperor dominated at the capital, a new landowning elite began to control the countryside. On its northern frontier, Byzantium helped create new Slavic realms.

Imperial Power

While the *themes,* with their territorial military organization, took care of attacks on Byzantine territory, *tagmata* — new mobile armies made up of the best troops — moved aggressively outward, beginning around 850. By 1025, the Byzantine Empire extended from the Danube in the north to the Euphrates in the south (Map 9.1).

Map 9.1 The Byzantine Empire, 1025
Under Emperor Basil II, the Byzantine Empire once again embraced the entire area of the Balkans, while its eastern arm extended around the Black Sea and its southern fringe reached nearly to Tripoli. The year 1025 marked the Byzantine Empire's greatest size after the rise of Islam.

Military victories gave new prestige and wealth to the army and to the imperial court. The Byzantine emperors drew revenues from vast and growing imperial estates. They could demand services and money from the general population at will, and they used their wealth to create a lavish court culture, surrounding themselves with servants, slaves, family members, and civil servants. From their powerful position, the emperors negotiated with other rulers, exchanging ambassadors and receiving and entertaining diplomats with elaborate ceremonies to express the serious, sacred, concentrated power of imperial majesty.

Some of the emperors' wealth derived from a prosperous agricultural economy organized for trade. Byzantine commerce depended on a careful balance of state regulation and individual enterprise. The emperor controlled craft and commercial guilds, while entrepreneurs organized most of the markets held throughout the empire. Foreign merchants were welcomed, but because international trade intertwined with foreign policy, the Byzantine government insisted on controlling it, issuing privileges to certain

"nations" (as the Venetians, Genoese, and Jews, among others, were called), regulating the fees they were obliged to pay and the services they had to render.

The emperors also negotiated privileges for their own traders in foreign lands. Byzantine merchants were guaranteed protection in Syria, for example, while the two governments split the income on sales taxes. Thus, Byzantine trade flourished in the Middle East and, thanks to Venetian intermediaries, with western Europe. Equally significant was trade to the north; from the conquerors of the area around the outpost of Kiev, known as the Kievan Rus, the Byzantines imported furs, slaves, wax, and honey.

The Macedonian Renaissance, c. 870–c. 1025

Flush with victory and recalling Byzantium's past glory, the emperors of the late ninth century revived classical intellectual pursuits. Basil I (r. 867–886) from Macedonia founded the imperial dynasty that presided over the so-called Macedonian renaissance. Basil's dynasty drew on an intellectual elite who came from families that — even in the anxious years of the eighth century — had persisted in studying the classics. Now, with the empire slowly regaining its military eminence and with icons permanently restored in 843, this scholarly elite thrived again.

Under the patronage of the emperor and other members of the imperial court, scholars wrote summaries of classical literature, encyclopedias of ancient knowledge, and commentaries on classical authors. Some copied religious manuscripts and theologi-

A Depiction of David from the Macedonian Renaissance
This manuscript illumination, made at Constantinople in the mid-ninth century, combines Christian and classical elements in a harmonious composition. David, author of the Psalms, sits in the center. Like the classical Orpheus, he plays music that attracts and tames the beasts. In the right-hand corner, a figure labeled "Bethlehem" is modeled on a lounging river or mountain god. (Bibliothèque nationale, Paris, France / The Bridgeman Art Library International.)

The Crowning of Constantine Porphyrogenitos

This ivory relief was carved at Constantinople in the mid-tenth century. The artist wanted to emphasize hierarchy and symbolism, not nature. Christ is shown crowning Emperor Constantine Porphyrogenitos (r. 913–959). What message do you suppose the artist wanted to telegraph by making Christ higher than the emperor and by having the emperor slightly incline his head and upper torso to receive the crown? (Pushkin Museum, Moscow, Russia / The Bridgeman Art Library International.)

cal commentaries such as Bibles, Psalters, homilies, and liturgical texts. But the merging of classical and Christian traditions is clearest in manuscript illuminations (painted illustrations or embellishments in hand-copied manuscripts). Here Byzantine artists showed how liberated they were from the sober taboos of the iconoclastic period. For example, to depict King David, the supposed poet of the Psalms, an artist illuminating a Psalter turned to a model of Orpheus, the enchanting musician of ancient Greek mythology. (See the illustration on page 272.) Other artists worked in a less classical style, as in the depiction of Christ crowning Emperor Constantine Porphyrogenitos.

The *Dynatoi*: A New Landowning Elite

At Constantinople the emperor reigned supreme. But outside the capital, extremely powerful military families began to compete with imperial power. The **dynatoi** ("powerful men"), as this new hereditary elite was called, got rich on plunder and new lands taken in the aggressive wars of the tenth century. They took over or bought up whole villages, turning the peasants' labor to their benefit. For the most part they exercised their power locally, but they also sometimes occupied the imperial throne.

The Phocas family exemplifies the strengths as well as the weaknesses of the dynatoi. Probably originally from Armenia, they possessed military skills and exhibited loyalty to the emperor that together brought them high positions in both the army and at court in the last decades of the ninth century. In the tenth century, with new successes in the east, the Phocas family gained independent power. After some particularly brilliant victories, Nicephorus Phocas was declared emperor by his armies and ruled (as Nicephorus II Phocas) at Constantinople from 963 to 969. But opposing factions of the dynatoi brought him down. The mainstay of Phocas family power, as of that of all the dynatoi, was outside the capital, on the family's great estates.

As the dynatoi gained power, the social hierarchy of Byzantium began to resemble that of western Europe, where land owned by aristocratic lords was farmed by peasants bound by tax and service obligations to the fields they cultivated.

The Formation of Eastern Europe and Kievan Rus

The contours of modern eastern Europe took shape during the period 850–950. By 800, Slavic settlements dotted the area from the Danube River down to Greece and from the Black Sea to Croatia. The ruler of the Bulgarians, called a *khagan,* presided over the largest realm. In the ninth century, Bulgarian rule stretched west to the Tisza River in modern Hungary. At about the same, however, the Byzantine Empire began its own campaigns to conquer, convert, and control these Slavic regions, today known as the Balkans.

The Byzantine offensive began under Emperor Nicephorus I (r. 802–811), who waged war against the Slavs of Greece in the Peloponnese, set up a new Christian diocese there, organized it as a new military *theme,* and forcibly resettled Christians in the area to counteract Slavic paganism. The Byzantines followed this pattern of conquest as they pushed northward. By 900, Byzantium ruled all of Greece.

Still under Nicephorus I, the Byzantines launched a massive attack against the Bulgarians, took the chief city of Pliska, plundered it, burned it to the ground, and then marched against the khagan's encampment in the Balkan Mountains. But the Bulgarians successfully parried this attack. In 816, the two sides agreed to a temporary peace — though it was punctuated by hostilities — that lasted for most of the tenth century. Then Emperor **Basil II** (r. 976–1025) led the Byzantines in a slow, methodical conquest. Aptly known as the Bulgar-Slayer, Basil brought the entire region under Byzantine control and forced its ruler to accept the Byzantine form of Christianity. Around the same time, the Serbs, encouraged by Byzantium to oppose the Bulgarians, began to form the political community that would become Serbia.

Religion played an important role in the Byzantine conquest of the Balkans. In 863, the brothers Cyril and Methodius were sent as Christian missionaries from the Byzantines to the Slavs. Well educated in both classical and religious texts, they devised an alphabet for Slavic (until then an oral language) based on Greek forms. It was the ancestor of the modern Cyrillic alphabet used in Bulgaria, Serbia, and Russia today.

The region that would eventually become Russia lay outside the sphere of direct Byzantine rule in the ninth and tenth centuries. Like Serbia and Bulgaria, however, it came under increasingly strong Byzantine influence. In the ninth century, the Vikings — Scandinavian adventurers who ranged over vast stretches of ninth-century Europe seeking trade, riches, and land — penetrated the region below the Gulf of Finland, where they imposed their rule. By the end of the century, they had moved southward and had conquered the region around Kiev, a key commercial emporium. From there the Rus, as the Viking conquerors were called, sailed the Dnieper River and crossed the Black Sea in search of markets for their slaves and furs.

The relationship between Rus and Byzantium began with trade, continued with war, and ended with a common religion. By the beginning of the tenth century, the Rus had

special trade privileges at Constantinople. But relations deteriorated, and the Rus unsuccessfully attacked Constantinople in 941. Soon they resumed trading with Byzantium.

Few Rus were Christian (most were polytheists, others Muslims or Jews), but that changed at the end of the tenth century, when good relations between the Rus and the Byzantines were sealed by the conversion of the Rus ruler Vladimir (r. c. 978–1015). In 988, Emperor Basil II sent his sister Anna to marry Vladimir in exchange for an army of Rus. To seal the alliance, Vladimir was baptized and took his brother-in-law's name. The general population seems to have quickly adopted the new religion.

Vladimir's conversion represented a wider pattern: the Christianization of Europe. In the southeast, orthodox Byzantine Christianity dominated, while in the west and northwest, Roman Catholicism tended to be most important. Slavic realms such as Moravia, Serbia, and Bulgaria adopted the Byzantine form of Christianity, while the rulers and peoples of Poland, Hungary, Denmark, and Norway were converted under the auspices of the Roman church. The conversion of the Rus was especially significant, because they were geographically as close to the Islamic world as to the Christian and could conceivably have become Muslims. By converting to Byzantine Christianity, the Rus made themselves heir to Byzantium and its church, customs, art, and political ideology. However, choosing the Byzantine form of Christianity, rather than the Roman Catholic, later served to isolate the region from western Europe.

For over fifty years, Rus remained united under one ruler. But after 1054, civil wars broke out. Invasions by outsiders, particularly from the east, further weakened the Kievan rulers, who were eventually displaced by princes from the north. At the crossroads of East and West, Rus could meet and absorb a great variety of traditions, but its geographical position also opened it to unremitting military pressures.

> **REVIEW QUESTION** In what ways did the Byzantine emperor expand his power, and in what ways was that power checked?

The Rise and Fall of the Abbasid Caliphate

A new dynasty of caliphs — the Abbasids — first brought unity and then, in their decline, fragmentation to the Islamic world as regional rulers took over. Local traditions based on religious and political differences played an increasingly important role in people's lives. Yet, even in the eleventh century, the Islamic world had a clear sense of its own unity, based on language, commerce, and artistic and intellectual achievements that transcended regional boundaries.

The Abbasid Caliphate, 750–936

In 750, a civil war ousted the Umayyads and raised the **Abbasids** to the caliphate. The Abbasids found support in an uneasy coalition of Shi'ites (the faction of Islam loyal to Ali's memory; see Chapter 8, page 244) and non-Arabs who had been excluded from the Umayyad government. Under the Abbasids, the center of Islamic rule shifted from Damascus, with its roots in the Roman tradition, to the newly founded city of Baghdad

in Iraq. Here the Abbasid caliphs adhered even more firmly than the Umayyads to Persian courtly models, with a centralized administration, a large staff, and control over the appointment of regional governors.

The Abbasid caliph Harun al-Rashid (r. 786–809) presided over a flourishing empire. His contemporary Frankish ruler, Charlemagne, was impressed with the elephant Harun sent him as a gift, along with monkeys, spices, and medicines. Such items were mainstays of everyday commerce in Harun's Iraq. A mid-ninth-century catalog of imports listed "tigers, panthers, elephants, panther skins, rubies, white sandal[wood], ebony, and coconuts" from India as well as "silk, chinaware, paper, ink, peacocks, racing horses, saddles, felts [and] cinnamon" from China.

The Abbasid dynasty began to decline after Harun's death. While his sons waged war against each other, the caliphs lost control over many regions, including Syria and Egypt. They needed to recruit an army that would be loyal to them alone. This they found in "outsiders," many of them Turks from east of the Caspian Sea (today Kazakhstan). Many of the Turks, later called Mamluks, were bought as slaves. Once purchased, the Turks were freed and paid a salary. They were expert fighters, but the Abbasids needed a good tax base to be able to pay them. This they did not have. Serious uprisings just south of Baghdad kept huge swaths of territory outside the control of the caliphs. Other regions of the Islamic world easily went their own way when the caliphs lacked the money to keep them in line. In the tenth century, the caliphs became figureheads only, while independent regional rulers collected taxes and hired their own armies.

Thus, in the Islamic world, as in the Byzantine, new regional lords challenged the power of the central ruler. But the process advanced quicker in Islamic than in Byzantine territories. Map 9.1 (page 271) correctly omits any indication of regional dynatoi because the key center of power in the Byzantine Empire continued to be Constantinople. Map 9.2, in contrast, shows how the Abbasid caliphate fragmented as local dynasties established themselves.

Regional Diversity in Islamic Lands

The splintering of the Islamic world was to be expected, since central power there was based on the conquest of many diverse regions, each with its own deeply rooted traditions and culture. The Islamic religion, with its Sunni/Shi'ite split, also became a source of polarization.* Western Europeans knew almost nothing about Muslims, calling all of them Saracens (from the Latin word for "Arabs") without distinction. But, as is still true today, Muslims were of different ethnicities, practiced different customs, and identified with different regions. With the fragmentation of political and religious unity, each of the tenth- and early-eleventh-century Islamic states built on local traditions under local rulers.

---

*The Shi'ites, originally followers of Ali, had by this time come to practice Islam differently from the Sunni. Each faction adhered to its own interpretation of the Prophet Muhammad's life and message.

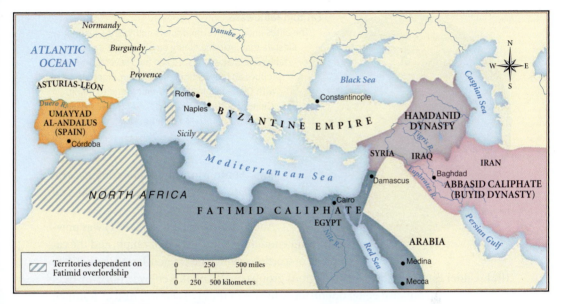

Map 9.2 Islamic States, c. 1000

Comparing this map with Map 8.1 (page 244) will quickly demonstrate the fragmentation of the once united Islamic caliphate. In 750, one caliph ruled territory stretching from Spain to India. In 1000, there was more than one caliphate as well as several other ruling dynasties. The most important of those dynasties were the Fatimids, who began as organizers of a movement to overthrow the Abbasids. By 1000, the Fatimids had conquered Egypt and claimed hegemony over all of North Africa.

A good example of this trend was the Shi'ite group known as the **Fatimids**. Taking their name from Fatimah, daughter of Muhammad and wife of Ali, they established themselves in 909 as rulers in the region of North Africa now called Tunisia. The Fatimid ruler claimed to be not only the true imam — the descendant of Ali — but also the *mahdi,* the "divinely guided" messiah, come to bring justice on earth. In 969, the Fatimids declared themselves rulers of Egypt. Their dynasty lasted for about two hundred years. Fatimid leaders also controlled North Africa, Arabia, and even Syria for a time. They established a lavish court culture that rivaled the one at Baghdad, and they supported industries such as lusterware that had once been a monopoly of the Abbasids.

While the Shi'ites dominated Egypt, Sunni Muslims ruled al-Andalus, the Islamic central and southern heart of Spain. The emirate of Córdoba (so called because its ruler took the secular title *emir,* "commander," and fixed his capital at Córdoba) was created early, near the start of the Abbasid caliphate. During the Abbasid revolution of 750, a member of the Umayyad family gathered an army, invaded Spain, and after only one battle was declared emir in 756, becoming Abd al-Rahman I. He and his successors ruled a broad range of peoples, including many Jews and Christians. After the initial Islamic conquest of Spain, the Christians had adopted so much of the new Arabic language and so many of the customs that they were called Mozarabs ("like Arabs"). The Muslims allowed them freedom of worship and let them live according to their own

Fatimid Tableware
The elites under the Fatimid rulers cultivated a luxurious lifestyle that included dining on lusterware — porcelain tableware that was glazed and fired several times to produce an iridescent metallic sheen. Trade contacts with China inspired the Islamic world to mimic Chinese pottery. (Museum of Fine Arts, Cleveland / photo © Werner Forman / HIP / The Image Works.)

laws. Some Mozarabs were content with their status, others converted to Islam, and still others intermarried.

Abd al-Rahman III (r. 912–961) was powerful enough to take the title of caliph, and the caliphate of Córdoba, which he created, lasted from 929 to 1031. Under him, members of all religious groups in al-Andalus enjoyed not only freedom of worship but also equal opportunity to rise in the civil service. Abd al-Rahman enjoyed diplomatic relations with European and Byzantine rulers. Yet under later caliphs, al-Andalus experienced the same political fragmentation that was occurring everywhere else. The caliphate of Córdoba broke up in 1031, and rulers of small, independent regions, called *taifas,* took power.

Unity of Commerce and Language

Although the regions of the Islamic world were culturally and politically diverse, they maintained a measure of unity through trade networks and language. Their principal bond was Arabic, the language of the Qur'an. At once poetic and sacred, Arabic was also the language of commerce and government from Baghdad to Córdoba. Moreover, despite political differences, borders were open. The primary reason for these open borders was Islam itself, but the openness extended to non-Muslims as well.

The commercial activities of the Tustari brothers, Jewish merchants from southern Iran, are a good example. By 1026, they had established a flourishing business in Egypt. Informal contacts with friends and family allowed them to import fine textiles from Iran to sell in Egypt and to export Egyptian fabrics to sell in Iran. The Tustari brothers held the highest rank in Jewish society and had contacts with Muslim rulers. At the same time, commercial networks even more vast than those of the Tustari family were common. Muslim merchants brought tin from England; salt and gold from Timbuktu in west-central Africa; amber, gold, and copper from Rus; and slaves from every region.

The Islamic Renaissance, c. 790–c. 1050

Unlike the Macedonian renaissance, which was concentrated in Constantinople, the Islamic renaissance occurred throughout the Islamic world. In fact, the dissolution of the caliphate into separate political entities multiplied the centers of learning and intellec-

A Princely Pyxis

A pyxis is a small container, and this one, about six inches high and carved out of ivory, was made for the younger son of Abd al-Rahman III, the caliph of Córdoba. The prince is depicted in a decorative lozenge, sitting on a rug and holding a bottle and a flower. One servant sits beside him to cool him with a fan; another stands and plays the lute. Underneath the rug are lions, symbols of power. Outside the princely enclosure, falconers stand by, ready to accompany the prince to the hunt. The whole scene suggests order, skill, and elegance, all important features of the Islamic renaissance. (Louvre, Paris, France / Peter Willi / The Bridgeman Art Library International.)

tual productivity. The Islamic renaissance was particularly dazzling in capital cities such as Córdoba (a city in southern Spain today), where tenth-century rulers presided over a brilliant court culture, patronizing scholars, poets, and artists.

Islamic scholarship was diverse. Some scholars read, translated, and commented on the works of ancient philosophers. Others studied astronomy or wrote on mathematical matters. Ibn Sina (980–1037), known in Christian Europe as Avicenna, wrote books on logic, the natural sciences, and physics. His *Canon of Medicine* systematized earlier treatises and reconciled them with his own experience as a physician.

Long before there were universities in Europe, there were institutions of higher learning in the Islamic world. A rich Muslim might demonstrate his piety and charity by establishing a madrasa, a school located within or attached to a mosque. Professors at madrasas held classes throughout the day on the interpretation of the Qur'an and literary or legal texts. Students, all male, attended the classes that suited their achievement level and interest. Most students paid a fee for learning, but there were also scholarship students. One tenth-century court official was so solicitous of the welfare of the scholars he supported that each day he set out iced refreshments, candles, and paper for them in his own kitchen.

The use of paper, made from flax and hemp or rags and vegetable fiber, points to a major difference among the Islamic, Byzantine, and (as we shall see) Carolingian renaissances. Byzantine scholars worked to enhance the prestige of the ruling classes. Their work, written on expensive parchment (made from animal skins), kept manuscripts out of the hands of all but the very rich. This was true of scholarship in Europe as well. By contrast, Islamic scholars wrote on paper, which was cheap, and they spoke to a broad audience.

REVIEW QUESTION What forces contributed to the fragmentation of the Islamic world in the tenth and eleventh centuries, and what forces held it together?

The Carolingian Empire

Just as in the Byzantine and Islamic worlds, in Europe the period 750–1050 saw first the formation of a strong empire, ruled by one man, and then its fragmentation as local rulers took power into their own hands. A new dynasty, the Carolingian, came to rule in the Frankish kingdom at almost the very moment (c. 750) that the Abbasids gained the caliphate. Charlemagne, the most powerful Carolingian monarch, conquered new territory, took the title of emperor, and presided over a revival of Christian classical culture known as the Carolingian renaissance. He ruled at the local level through counts and other military men. Nevertheless, the unity of the Carolingian Empire — based largely on conquest, a measure of prosperity, and personal allegiance to Charlemagne — was shaky. Its weaknesses were exacerbated by attacks from Viking, Muslim, and Magyar invaders. Charlemagne's successors divided his empire among themselves and saw it divided further as local leaders took defense — and rule — into their own hands.

The Rise of the Carolingians

The Carolingians were among many aristocratic families on the rise during the Merovingian period (see Chapter 8, page 252), but they gained exceptional power by monopolizing the position of "palace mayor" — a sort of prime minister — under the Merovingian kings. Charles Martel ("Charles the Hammer"), mayor 714–741, gave the name **Carolingian** (from *Carolus*, Latin for "Charles") to the dynasty. Renowned for defeating an invading army of Muslims from al-Andalus near Poitiers in 732, he also contended vigorously against other aristocrats who were carving out independent lordships for themselves. Charles Martel and his family turned aristocratic factions against one another, rewarded supporters, crushed enemies, and dominated whole regions by supporting monasteries that served as focal points for both religious piety and land donations.

The Carolingians also allied themselves with the Roman papacy. They supported Anglo-Saxon missionaries like Boniface (see page 262) who went to areas on the fringes of the Carolingian realm as the pope's ambassador. Reforming the Christianity that these regions had adopted, Boniface set up a hierarchical church organization and founded new monasteries. His newly appointed bishops were loyal to Rome and the Carolingians.

Pippin III (d. 768), Charles Martel's son, turned to the pope directly. When he deposed the Merovingian king in 751, taking over the kingship himself, Pippin petitioned Pope Zachary to legitimize the act; the pope agreed. The Carolingians returned the favor a few years later when the pope asked for their help against hostile Lombards. That papal request signaled a major shift. Before 754, the papacy had been part of the Byzantine Empire; after that, it turned to Europe for protection.

Pippin launched a successful campaign against the Lombard king that ended in 756 with the so-called Donation of Pippin, a peace accord between the Lombards and the pope. The treaty gave back to the pope cities that had been taken by the Lombard

king. The new arrangement recognized what the papacy had long before created: a territorial "republic of St. Peter" ruled by the pope, not by the Byzantine emperor. Henceforth, the fate of Italy would be tied largely to the policies of the pope and the Frankish kings to the north, not to the eastern emperors.

Partnership with the Roman church gave the Carolingian dynasty a Christian aura, expressed in symbolic form by anointment. Bishops rubbed holy oil on the foreheads and shoulders of Carolingian kings during the coronation ceremony, imitating the Old Testament kings who had been anointed by God.

Charlemagne and His Kingdom, 768–814

The most famous Carolingian king was Charles, whom his contemporaries called the Great (*le Magne* in Old French) — thus, **Charlemagne** (r. 768–814). Charlemagne was complex, contradictory, and sometimes brutal. He loved listening to St. Augustine's *City of God* as it was read aloud, and he supported major scholarly enterprises, yet he never learned to write. He was devout, yet he flouted the advice of churchmen when they told him to convert pagans rather than force baptism on them. He admired the pope, yet he was furious when a pope placed the imperial crown on his head. He waged many successful wars, yet he thereby destroyed the buffer states surrounding the Frankish kingdoms, unleashing a new round of invasions.

Behind these contradictions, however, lay a unifying vision. Charlemagne dreamed of an empire that would unite the martial and learned traditions of the Roman and Germanic worlds with the legacy of Christianity. This vision lay at the core of his political activity, his building programs, and his support of scholarship and education.

During the early years of his reign, Charlemagne conquered lands in all directions (Map 9.3). He invaded Italy, seizing the crown of the Lombard kings and annexing northern Italy in 774. He then moved northward and began a long and difficult war against the Saxons, during which he annexed their territory and forcibly converted them to Christianity. To the southeast, Charlemagne fought the Avars, bringing home cartloads of plunder. To the southwest, he led an expedition to al-Andalus and there set up a march (a military buffer region).

By the 790s, Charlemagne's kingdom stretched east beyond the Elbe River (today in Germany), southeast to what is today Austria, and south to Spain and Italy. Such power in the West had been unheard of since the time of the Roman Empire, and Charlemagne began to imitate aspects of the imperial model. He sponsored building programs to symbolize his authority, standardized weights and measures, and acted as a patron of intellectual and artistic efforts. He built a capital city at Aachen, complete with a chapel that was patterned on Justinian's church of San Vitale at Ravenna (see the illustrations on pages 228–29 and 283).

To discourage corruption, Charlemagne appointed special officials, called *missi dominici* ("those sent out by the lord king"), to oversee his regional governors — the counts. The missi (lay aristocrats or bishops) traveled in pairs throughout the kingdom to ensure that all, rich and poor alike, had access to royal justice.

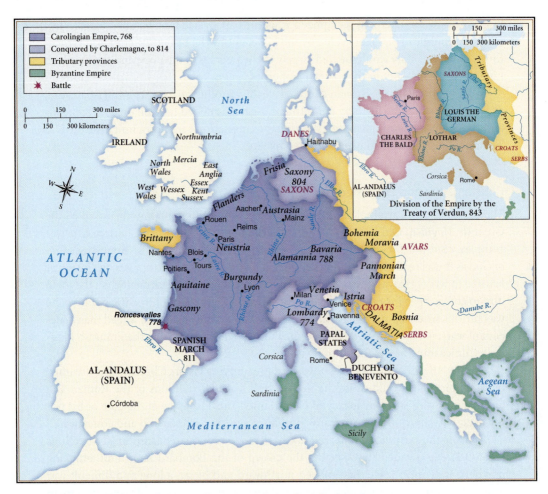

Map 9.3 Expansion of the Carolingian Empire under Charlemagne
The conquests of Charlemagne temporarily united almost all of western Europe under one ruler. Although the great Carolingian Empire broke apart (see the inset showing how the empire was divided by the Treaty of Verdun), the legacy of that unity remained, even serving as one of the inspirations behind today's European Union.

Meanwhile, the papacy was beginning to claim imperial power for itself. At some point, perhaps in the 760s, members of the papal chancery (writing office) created a document called the Donation of Constantine. It declared the pope the recipient of the fourth-century emperor Constantine's crown, cloak, and military rank along with "all provinces, palaces, and districts of the city of Rome and Italy and of the regions of the West." (Only much later was the document proved a forgery.) The tension between the imperial claims of the Carolingians and those of the pope was heightened by the existence of an emperor at Constantinople who also had rights in the west.

Pope Leo III (r. 795–816) upset the delicate balance among these three powers. In 799, accused of adultery and perjury by a faction of the Roman aristocracy, Leo nar-

Charlemagne's Chapel
Charlemagne was the first Frankish king to build a permanent capital city. He decided to do so in 789 and chose Aachen because of its natural warm springs. There he built a palace complex that, besides a grand living area for himself and his retinue, included a chapel (a small semiprivate church). Today the entire chapel is enclosed within Aachen's cathedral. (Aachen Cathedral, Aachen, Germany / Bildarchiv Steffens / The Bridgeman Art Library International.)

rowly escaped being blinded and having his tongue cut out. He fled northward to seek Charlemagne's protection. Charlemagne had the pope escorted back to Rome, and he soon arrived there himself to an imperial welcome orchestrated by Leo. On Christmas Day, 800, Leo put an imperial crown on Charlemagne's head, and the clergy and nobles who were present acclaimed the king Augustus, the title of the first Roman emperor. The pope hoped in this way to exalt the king of the Franks, to downgrade the Byzantine ruler, and to claim for himself the role of "emperor maker."

At first, Charlemagne avoided using the imperial title. He may have hesitated to adopt it because he feared the reaction of the Byzantines. Or perhaps he objected to the papal role in his crowning, since it seemed to give the pope power over the imperial office. When Charlemagne finally did call himself emperor he used a long and revealing title: "Charles, the most serene Augustus, crowned by God, great and peaceful Emperor who governs the Roman Empire and who is, by the mercy of God, king of the Franks and the Lombards." According to this title, Charlemagne was not the Roman

emperor crowned by the pope, but rather God's emperor who governed the Roman Empire along with his many other duties.

The Carolingian Renaissance, c. 790–c. 900

Charlemagne inaugurated a revival of learning designed to enhance the glory of the kings, educate their officials, and purify the faith. Like the renaissances of the Byzantine and Islamic worlds, the Carolingian renaissance resuscitated the learning of the past. Scholars studied Roman imperial writers such as Suetonius and Virgil, read and commented on the works of the church fathers, and worked to establish complete and accurate texts of everything they read and prized.

The English scholar Alcuin (c. 732–804), a member of the circle of scholars whom Charlemagne recruited to form a center of study, brought with him the traditions of Anglo-Saxon scholarship that had been developed by men such as Benedict Biscop and Bede. Invited to Aachen, Alcuin became Charlemagne's chief adviser, writing letters on the king's behalf, counseling him on royal policy, and tutoring the king's household. He also prepared an improved edition of the Vulgate, the Latin Bible used by the clergy in all church services.

Art, like scholarship, served Carolingian political and religious goals. Carolingian artists turned to models from Italy and Byzantium (perhaps some refugees from Byzantine iconoclasm joined them) to illustrate Bibles (see the illustration at left), Psalters, scientific treatises, and literary manuscripts.

Many of the achievements of the Carolingian renaissance endured even after the dynasty itself had faded to a memory. The work of locating, understanding, and transmitting models of the past continued in a number of monastic schools. In the twelfth century,

David in the Carolingian Renaissance
In this sumptuous illustration from a Bible made for Charlemagne's grandson Charles the Bald, the central figure is David, the composer of the Psalms, who is playing the harp and dancing on a cloud. Above and below him are his musicians with their instruments. The influence of earlier models is clear in the two figures flanking David, who are dressed like soldiers in the late Roman Empire. Compare this depiction of David with the one painted during the Macedonian renaissance on page 272. (Scala / White Images / Art Resource, NY.)

scholars would build on the foundations laid by the Carolingian renaissance. The very print of this textbook depends on one achievement of the period: modern typefaces are based on the clear and beautiful letter forms, called Caroline minuscule, invented in the ninth century to standardize manuscript handwriting.

Charlemagne's Successors, 814–911

Charlemagne's successor, Louis the Pious (r. 814–840), took his role as leader of the Christian empire even more seriously than his father did. In 817, he imposed on all the monasteries of the empire a uniform way of life, based on the Benedictine rule. Although some monasteries opposed this legislation, and in the years to come the king was unable to impose his will directly, this moment marked the effective adoption of the Benedictine rule as the monastic standard in Europe.

In a new development of the coronation ritual, Louis's first wife, Ermengard, was crowned empress by the pope in 816. In 817, their firstborn son, Lothar, was named emperor and made co-ruler with Louis. Their other sons, Pippin and Louis (later called Louis the German), were made subkings under imperial rule. Louis the Pious hoped in this way to ensure the unity of the empire while satisfying the claims of all his sons. Should any son die, only his firstborn could succeed him, a measure intended to prevent further splintering. But Louis's hopes were thwarted by events. Ermengard died, and Louis married Judith, reputed to be the most beautiful woman in the kingdom. In 823, she and Louis had a son, Charles (later known as Charles the Bald, to whose court Dhuoda's son William was sent). The sons of Ermengard, bitter over the birth of another royal heir, rebelled against their father and fought one another for more than a decade.

Finally, after Louis the Pious died in 840, the **Treaty of Verdun** (843) divided the empire among his three remaining sons (Pippin had died in 838). The arrangement roughly defined the future political contours of western Europe (see the inset in Map 9.3, page 282). The western third, bequeathed to Charles the Bald (r. 843–877), would eventually become France, and the eastern third, handed to Louis the German (r. 843–876), became Germany. The "Middle Kingdom," which was given to Lothar (r. 840–855) along with the imperial title, had a different fate: parts of it were absorbed by France and Germany, and the rest eventually formed what became the modern states of the Netherlands, Belgium, Luxembourg, Switzerland, and Italy.

Thus, by 843, the European-wide empire of Charlemagne had dissolved. Forged by conquest, it had been supported by a small group of privileged aristocrats with lands and offices stretching across its entire expanse. Their loyalty — based on shared values, friendship, expectations of gain, and sometimes formal ties of vassalage and oaths of fealty (faithfulness) — was crucial to the success of the Carolingians. The empire had also been supported by an ideal, shared by educated laymen and churchmen alike, of conquest and Christian belief working together to bring good order to the earthly state.

But powerful forces operated against the Carolingian Empire. Once the empire's borders were fixed and conquests ceased, the aristocrats could not hope for new lands and offices. They put down roots in particular regions and began to gather their own

followings. Powerful local traditions such as different languages also undermined imperial unity.

Finally, as Dhuoda revealed in the handbook she wrote for her son, some people disagreed with the imperial ideal. By asking her son to put his father before the emperor, Dhuoda demonstrated her belief in the primacy of the family and the personal ties that bound it together. Her ideal represented a new sensibility that saw real value in the breaking apart of Charlemagne's empire into smaller, more intimate local units.

Land and Power

The Carolingian economy, based on war profits, trade, and agriculture, contributed first to the rise and then to the dissolution of the Carolingian Empire. After the spoils of war ceased to pour in, the Carolingians still had access to money and goods. To the north, the Carolingian economy intermingled with that of the Abbasid caliphate. Silver from the Islamic world probably came north up the Volga River through Kievan Rus to the Baltic Sea. There the coins were melted down and the silver was traded to the Carolingians in return for wine, jugs, glasses, and other manufactured goods. The Carolingians turned the silver into coins of their own, to be used throughout the empire for small-scale local trade. The weakening of the Abbasid caliphate in the mid-ninth century, however, disrupted this far-flung trade network and contributed to the weakening of the Carolingians at about the same time.

Land provided the most important source of Carolingian wealth and power. Carolingian aristocrats held many estates, called manors, scattered throughout the Frankish kingdoms and organized for production. The names of the peasants who tilled the soil and the dues and services they owed were even sometimes carefully noted down in registers.

A typical manor was Villeneuve Saint-Georges, which belonged to the monastery of Saint-Germain-des-Prés (today in Paris) in the ninth century. Villeneuve consisted of arable fields, vineyards, meadows where animals could roam, and woodlands, all scattered about the countryside rather than connected in a compact unit. Peasant families did the farming. Each family had its own manse, which consisted of a house, a garden, and small sections of the arable land. Besides farming the land that belonged to them, the families also worked the demesne, the very large manse of the lord, in this case the abbey of Saint-Germain. Grown children would found their own families, and their parents' land would be subdivided to give them a share. In many ways, the peasant household of the Carolingian period was the precursor of the modern nuclear family.

Peasants at Villeneuve practiced the most progressive sort of plowing, known as the three-field system, in which they farmed two-thirds of the arable land at one time (see Figure 9.1). They planted one-third of the arable land in the fall with winter wheat, one-third in the spring with summer crops, and left the remaining third fallow to restore its fertility. The crops sown and the fallow field then rotated so that land use was

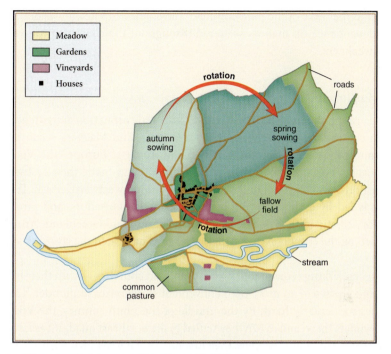

Figure 9.1 Diagram of a Manor and Its Three-Field System

This schematic diagram of a manor shows that peasants lived clustered together in a village that consisted of houses and gardens. One of the buildings was a church. Nearby were vineyards. A bit beyond were the fields, pastureland, and meadows, well connected by dirt roads. The field sown with spring crops (such as oats) this year would have been sown with winter wheat the next year, while the fallow field would get a spring crop. (Based on Map IV in Marc Bloch, *French Rural History: An Esssay on Its Basic Characteristics.* Berkeley: University of California Press, 1966.)

repeated only every three years. This method of organizing the land produced larger yields (because two-thirds of the land was cultivated each year) than the still-prevalent two-field system, in which only half of the arable land was cultivated one year while the other half lay fallow.

All the peasants at Villeneuve were dependents of the monastery and owed dues and services to Saint-Germain. Their status and obligations varied enormously. One family, for example, owed four silver coins, wine, wood, three hens, and fifteen eggs every year, and the men had to plow the fields of the demesne. Another family owed the intensive labor of working the vineyards. Peasant women spent much time at the lord's house in the *gynaeceum* — the workshop where women made and dyed cloth and sewed garments — or in the kitchens, as cooks. Peasant men spent most of their time in the fields.

Manors organized on the model of Villeneuve were profitable. Like other lords, the Carolingians benefited from their extensive landholdings. Nevertheless, farming was still too primitive to return great surpluses, and as the lands belonging to the king were

divided up in the wake of the partitioning of the empire and new invasions, the Carolingians' dependence on manors scattered throughout their kingdom proved to be a source of weakness.

Viking, Muslim, and Magyar Invasions, c. 790–955

Beginning around the time of Charlemagne's imperial coronation and extending to the mid-tenth century, new groups — Vikings, Muslims, and Magyars — confronted the Carolingian Empire and many of the other kingdoms of Europe. The Vikings were the first invaders. About the same time as some Vikings made their eastward forays into the region below the Gulf of Finland, others moved westward as well. Traveling in small bands led by a chief, the Vikings were merchants, sailors, and pirates. Some crossed the Atlantic in their longships to settle Iceland and Greenland. Around 1000, a few landed on the coast of North America. Others navigated the rivers of continental Europe.

As pagans, Vikings considered monasteries and churches — with their reliquaries, chalices, and crosses — no more than convenient storehouses of plunder. They hit the British Isles particularly hard. By the middle of the ninth century, the Vikings were spending winters there, and in 876 they settled in the northeast quadrant as farmers. This region was later called the Danelaw. (See England in the Age of King Alfred, page 295.)

In Wessex, the southernmost kingdom of England, King Alfred the Great bought time and peace from the Vikings by giving them hostages and tribute. The tribute, later called Danegeld, eventually became the basis of a relatively lucrative taxation system in England. After Alfred led his army against the Vikings, set up strongholds, and deployed new warships, the threat of invasions eased.

On the continent, too, the Vikings set up trading stations and settled where originally they had raided. Beginning about 850, their attacks became well-organized expeditions for regional control. At the end of the ninth century, one contingent settled in the region of France that soon took the name Normandy ("land of the Northmen"). In 911, the Frankish king Charles the Simple ceded the region to Rollo, the Viking leader there. In turn, Rollo converted to Christianity.

Normandy was not the only new Christian polity created in the north during the tenth and eleventh centuries. Scandinavia itself was transformed with the creation of the powerful kingdom of Denmark. There had been kings in Scandinavia before the tenth century, but they had been weak, their power challenged by nearby chieftains. Some of these chieftains led the Viking raids, competing with one another for foreign plunder in order to win prestige, land, and power back home. During the course of their raids, they and their followers came into contact with new cultures and learned from them.

Meanwhile the Carolingians and the English supported missionaries in Scandinavia. By the middle of the tenth century, the Danes had become Christian. Following the model of the Christian kings to their south, the kings there built up an effective monarchy, with a royal mint and local agents who depended on them. By about 1000, the

Danish monarch had extended its control to parts of Sweden, Norway, and even England under King Cnut (also spelled Canute) (r. 1017–1035).

Southern Europe largely escaped the Vikings, but parts of it were attacked by Muslim adventurers from North Africa, Sicily, and northeastern al-Andalus who set up bases in the Mediterranean. Meanwhile, the Magyars (or Hungarians) settled in Europe's very center. A nomadic people from the Ural Mountains (today northeastern Russia), they arrived around 899 in the Danube basin, driving a wedge between the Slavs near the Frankish kingdom and those bordering on Byzantium. The Bulgarians, Serbs, and Rus were forced into the Byzantine orbit, while the Slavs nearer the Frankish kingdom came under the influence of Germany.

From their bases in present-day Hungary, the Magyars raided far to the west, attacking Germany, Italy, and even southern Gaul frequently between 899 and 955. Then in 955 the German king Otto I (r. 936–973) defeated a marauding party of Magyars at the battle of Lechfeld. Otto's victory, his subsequent military reorganization of his eastern frontiers, and the cessation of Magyar raids around this time made Otto a great hero to his contemporaries. However, historians today think the containment of the Magyars had more to do with their internal transformation from nomads to farmers than with their military defeat. Soon they converted to the Roman form of Christianity. Hungary's position between East and West made it a frontier region, vulnerable to invasion and immigration but also open to new experiments in assimilation and integration.

The Viking, Muslim, and Magyar invasions were the final onslaught western Europe experienced from outsiders. In some ways they were a continuation of the invasions that had rocked the Roman Empire in the fourth and fifth centuries. Loosely organized in war bands, the new groups entered western Europe looking for wealth but stayed on to become absorbed in the region's post-invasion society.

REVIEW QUESTION What were the strengths and weaknesses of Carolingian institutions of government, warfare, and defense?

After the Carolingians: The Emergence of Local Rule

As royal power diminished, counts and other powerful men stopped looking to the king for new lands and offices; instead, they began to develop and exploit what they already had. Commanding allegiance from vassals, controlling the local peasantry, building castles to dominate the countryside, setting up markets, collecting revenues, and keeping the peace, they regarded themselves as independent regional rulers. In this way, a new warrior class of lords and vassals came to dominate post-Carolingian society.

There were, to be sure, variations on this theme. In northern and central Italy, where urban life had never lost its importance, elites ruled from the cities rather than from rural castles. Everywhere kings retained a certain amount of power; in some places, such as Germany and England, they were extremely effective. Central European monarchies

formed under the influence of Germany.* Still, throughout this period, local allegiances — between lord and vassal, castellan and peasant, bishop and layman — mattered most to the societies of Europe.

Public Power and Private Relationships

Both kings and less powerful men commanded others through institutions designed to ensure personal loyalty. This was true already under Charlemagne, and in the wake of the Viking, Magyar, and Muslim invasions, more and more warriors were drawn into networks of dependency, but not with the king: they became the faithful men — the vassals — of local lords, who often gave them **fiefs** (grants of land) in return for their military service. As sons often took the place of their fathers, this arrangement tended to be permanent. From the Latin *feodum* ("fief") comes the word *feudal,* and some historians use the term **feudalism** to describe the social and economic system created by the relationship among vassals, lords, and fiefs.

Medieval people divided their society into three groups: those who prayed, those who fought, and those who worked. All these groups were involved in hierarchies of dependency and linked by personal bonds, but the upper classes — those who prayed (monks) and those who fought (knights) — were free. Their brand of dependency was prestigious, whether they were vassals, lords, or both. In fact, a typical warrior was lord of several vassals even while serving as the vassal of another lord. Monasteries normally had vassals to fight for them, and their abbots in turn were often vassals of a king or other powerful lord.

Vassalage served both as an alternative to public power and as a way to strengthen what little public power remained. Given the impoverished economic conditions of western Europe, its primitive methods of communication, and its lack of unifying traditions, lords of every sort needed faithful men to protect them and carry out their orders. And vassals needed lords. At the low end of the social scale, poor vassals depended on their lords to feed, clothe, house, and arm them. At the upper end of the social scale, landowning vassals looked to lords to give them still more land. (See "Taking Measure," page 291.)

Many upper-class laywomen participated in the society of "those who fought" as wives and mothers of vassals and lords. A few women were themselves vassals, and some were lords (or, rather, ladies). Other women entered convents and joined the group of those who prayed. Through its abbess or a man standing in for her, a convent often had vassals as well. Many elite women engaged in property transactions, whether alone, with other family members, or as part of a group such as a convent.

Becoming a vassal involved both ritual gestures and verbal promises. In a ceremony witnessed by others, the vassal-to-be knelt and, placing his hands between the hands of

---

*Names such as *Germany, France,* and *Italy* are used here for the sake of convenience. They refer to regions, not to the nation-states that would eventually become associated with those names.

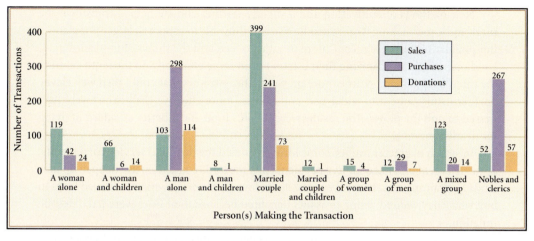

Taking Measure Sellers, Buyers, and Donors, 800–1000

How did ladies get their wealth, and what did they do with it? Two counties in northeastern Spain, Osona and Manresa, are particularly rich in documentation for the period 880–1000. We have 2,121 charters (legal documents) attesting to sales, purchases, and donations of land from this period. As the graph shows, few women purchased property, which suggests that they gained their lands mainly through inheritance. As for what they did with it: by themselves they were more likely to sell property than men alone, and as part of a married couple, they were often involved in sales. They were less likely than men to make donations, many of which went to churches or monasteries. (Lluís to Figueras, "Dot et douaire dans la société rurale de Catalogne," in *Dots et douaires dans le haut moyen âge*, ed. F. Bougard, L. Feller, and R. Le Jan [École française de Rome, 2002], 193, Table 1.)

his lord, said, "I promise to be your man." This act, known as homage, was followed by the promise of fealty — fidelity, trust, and service — which the vassal swore with his hand on relics or a Bible. Then the vassal and the lord kissed. In an age when many people could not read, a public ceremony such as this represented a visual and verbal contract. Vassalage bound the lord and vassal to one another with reciprocal obligations, usually military. Knights, as the premier fighters of the day, were the most desirable vassals.

At the bottom of the social scale were those who worked — the peasants. In the Carolingian period, many peasants were free; they did not live on a manor or, if they did, they owed very little to its lord. (Manors like Villeneuve were the exceptions.) But as power fell into the hands of local rulers, fewer and fewer peasants remained free. Rather, they were made dependent on lords, not as vassals but as serfs. A serf's dependency was completely unlike that of a vassal. Serfdom was not voluntary. No serf did homage or fealty to his lord; no serf kissed his lord as an equal. Whereas vassals served their lords as warriors, serfs worked as laborers on their lord's land and paid taxes and dues to their lord. Peasants constituted the majority of the population, but unlike knights, who were celebrated in song, they were barely noticed by the upper classes — except as a source of revenue. While there were still free peasants who could lease land or till their own soil without paying dues to a lord, serfs — who could not be kicked off their land but who were also not free to leave it — became the norm.

New methods of cultivation and a slightly warmer climate helped transform the rural landscape, making it more productive and thus able to support a larger population. But population increase meant more mouths to feed and the threat of food shortages. Landlords began reorganizing their estates to run more efficiently. In the tenth century, the three-field system became more prevalent; heavy plows that could turn wet, clayey northern soils came into wider use, and horses (more effective than oxen) were harnessed to pull the plows. The results were surplus food and a better standard of living for nearly everyone.

In search of greater profits, some lords lightened the dues and services of peasants, or turned them into fixed money payments that the lords could then use to open up new lands by draining marshes and cutting down forests. Money payments allowed lords to buy what they wanted, while peasants benefited because their dues were fixed despite inflation.

By the tenth century, many peasants had begun living in populous rural settlements, true villages. Surrounded by arable lands, meadows, woods, and wastelands, villages developed a sense of community. Boundaries — sometimes real fortifications, sometimes simple markers — told nonresidents to stay away or to find shelter in huts located outside the village limits.

The church often formed the focal point of village activity. There people met, received the sacraments, drew up contracts, and buried their dead. Religious feasts and festivals joined the rituals of farming to mark the seasons. The church dominated the village in another way: men and women owed it a tax called a tithe (one-tenth of their crops or income, paid in money or in kind), which was first instituted on a regular basis by the Carolingians.

Village peasants developed a sense of common purpose based on their interdependence, as they shared oxen or horses for the teams that pulled the plow or turned to village craftsmen to fix their wheels or shoe their horses. Village solidarity could be compromised, however, by conflicting loyalties and obligations. A peasant in one village might very well have one piece of land connected with a certain manor and another piece on a different estate; and he or she might owe several lords different kinds of dues. Even peasants of one village working for one lord might owe him varied services and taxes.

Obligations differed even more strikingly across the regions of Europe than within particular villages. The principal distinction was between free peasants — such as small landowners in Saxony and other parts of Germany, who had no lords — and serfs, who were especially common in France and England. In Italy, peasants ranged from small independent landowners to leaseholders.

As landlords consolidated their power over their manors, they collected not only dues and services but also fees for the use of their flour mills, bake houses, and breweries. Some built castles, fortified strongholds, collected taxes, heard court cases, levied fines, and mustered men for defense. In France, for example, as the king's power waned, political control fell into the hands of counts and other princes. By 1000, castles had become the key to their power. In the south of France, power was so fragmented that each

man who controlled a castle — a **castellan** — was a virtual ruler, although often with a very limited reach. In northwestern France, territorial princes, basing their rule on the control of many castles, dominated much broader regions.

The development of virtually independent local political units, dominated by a castle and controlled by a military elite, marks an important turning point in western Europe. Although this development did not occur everywhere simultaneously (and in some places it hardly occurred at all), the social, political, and cultural life of Europe was now dominated by landowners who were both military men and regional rulers.

Warriors and Warfare

Not all medieval warriors were alike. At the top of this elite group were the kings, counts, and dukes. Below them, but on the rise, were the castellans; and still further down the social scale were ordinary knights. Yet all shared in a common lifestyle.

Knights and their lords fought on horseback. High astride his steed, wearing a shirt of chain mail and a helmet of flat metal plates riveted together, the knight marked a military revolution. The war season started in May, when the grasses were high enough for horses to forage. Horseshoes allowed armies to move faster than ever before and to negotiate rough terrain previously unsuitable for battle. Stirrups, probably invented by nomadic Asiatic tribes, allowed the mounted warrior to hold his seat while thrusting at the enemy with a heavy lance. The light javelin of ancient Roman warfare was abandoned.

Lords and their vassals often lived together. In the lord's great hall they ate, listened to entertainment, and bedded down for the night. They went out hunting together, competed with one another in military games, and went off to the battlefield as a group. Some powerful vassals — counts, for example — lived on their own fiefs. These vassals hardly ever saw their lord (probably the king), except when doing homage and fealty — once in their lifetime — or serving him in battles, for perhaps forty days a year (as was the custom in eleventh-century France). These powerful vassals were themselves lords of other men — typically unmarried knightly vassals who lived, ate, and hunted together with their lord.

No matter how old they might be, unmarried knights who lived with their lords were called youths by their contemporaries. Such perpetual bachelors were something new, the result of a profound transformation in the organization of families and inheritance. Before about 1000, noble families had recognized all their children as heirs and had divided their estates accordingly. Thereafter, adapting to diminished opportunities for land and office and wary of fragmenting the estates they had, French nobles (in particular) changed both their conception of their family and the way property passed to the next generation. Recognizing the overriding claims of one son, often the eldest, they handed down their entire inheritance to him. (The system of inheritance in which the heir is the eldest son is called **primogeniture**.) The heir, in turn, traced his lineage only through the male line, backward through his father and forward through his own eldest

son. Such **patrilineal** families left many younger sons without an inheritance and therefore without the prospect of marrying and founding a family; instead, the younger sons lived at the courts of the great as youths, or they joined the church as clerics or monks. The development of territorial rule and patrilineal families went hand in hand, as fathers passed down to one son not only manors but also titles, castles, and authority over the peasantry.

Patrilineal inheritance tended to bypass daughters and so worked against aristocratic women, who lost the power that came with inherited wealth. In families without sons, however, widows and daughters did inherit property. And wives often acted as lords of estates when their husbands were at war. Moreover, all aristocratic women played an important role in this warrior society, whether in the monastery (where they prayed for the souls of their families) or through their marriages (where they produced children and helped forge alliances between their own natal families and the families of their husbands).

Efforts to Contain Violence

The rise of the castellans meant an increase in violence. Supported by their knights, castellans were keen to maintain their new authority over the peasants in their vicinity in the face of older regional powers, like counts and dukes. Threatened from below, those higher-ranking authorities looked to the bishops for help. The bishops, themselves resentful of local castellan claims and, moreover, generally members of the same elite families as counts and dukes, were glad to oblige. To do so, they enlisted the lower classes — peasants who were tired of wars that destroyed their crops or forced them to join regional infantries. The result was the **Peace of God**, which united bishops, counts, and peasants in an attempt to contain local violence. The movement began in the south of France around 990 and had spread over a wide region by 1050. At impassioned meetings of bishops, lords, and crowds of enthusiastic men and women, the clergy set forth the provisions of this peace. "No man in the counties or bishoprics shall seize a horse, colt, ox, cow, ass, or the burdens which it carries. . . . No one shall seize a peasant, man or woman," ran the decree of one early council. Anyone who violated this peace was to be excommunicated: cut off from the community of the faithful, denied the services of the church and the hope of salvation.

The Peace of God proclaimed at local councils like this limited some violence but did not address the problem of conflict between armed men. A second set of agreements, the Truce of God, soon supplemented the peace. The truce prohibited fighting between warriors at certain times. Enforcement fell to the local knights and nobles, who swore over saints' relics to uphold it and to fight anyone who broke it.

The Peace of God and the Truce of God were only two of the mechanisms that attempted to contain or defuse violent confrontations in the tenth and eleventh centuries. At times, lords and their vassals mediated wars and feuds at grand judicial assemblies. In other instances, monks or laymen tried to find solutions to disputes that would leave the honor of both parties intact. Rather than establishing guilt or inno-

cence, winners or losers, these methods of adjudication often resulted in compromises on both sides.

Political Communities in Italy, England, and France

The political systems that emerged following the breakup of the Carolingian Empire were as varied as the regions of Europe. In northern and central Italy, cities were the centers of power, still reflecting, if feebly, the political organization of ancient Rome. Italian lords tended to construct their family castles within the walls of cities. From there they the controlled the land and people in the surrounding countryside.

Italian cities also served as marketplaces where peasants sold their surplus goods, artisans and merchants lived, and foreign traders offered their wares. These members of the lower classes were supported by the wealthy elite, who depended, here more than elsewhere, on cash to satisfy their desires. In the course of the ninth and tenth centuries, the peasants in the countryside became renters who paid in currency, helping meet their landlords' need for cash.

Families in Italy organized themselves quite differently from the patrilineal families of France. To prevent dividing its properties among heirs, the Italian family became a kind of economic corporation in which all male members shared the profits of the family's inheritance and all women were excluded. In the coming centuries, this successful model would also serve as the foundation of most early Italian businesses and banks.

In contrast to Italy, most of England was rural. Having successfully repelled the Viking invaders, **Alfred the Great**, king of Wessex (r. 871–899), developed new mechanisms of royal government, instituting reforms that his successors continued. He fortified settlements throughout Wessex and divided the army into two parts, one with the duty of defending these fortifications, the other operating as a mobile unit. Alfred also started a navy. The money to pay for these military innovations came from assessments on peasants' holdings.

Along with its regional fortifications, Alfred sought to strengthen his kingdom's religious integrity. He began his program of religious reform by bringing scholars to his court to translate works by church fathers such as Gregory the Great and St. Augustine into Anglo-Saxon (Old English) so that everyone would understand them. Alfred himself did some of these translations. He had even the Psalms, until now sung only in Hebrew, Greek, and Latin, put into the vernacular — the common spoken language. In most of ninth- and tenth-century Europe,

England in the Age of King Alfred, 871–899

only the Latin language was used in writing. In England, however, the spoken language became a written language as well.

Alfred's reforms strengthened not only defense, education, and religion but also royal power. He consolidated his control over Wessex and fought the Danish kings, who by the mid-870s had taken Northumbria, northeastern Mercia, and East Anglia. Eventually, as he successfully fought the Danes who were pushing south and westward, he was recognized as king of all the English not under Danish rule. He issued a law code for all of the English kingdoms, becoming, in effect, the first king of all the English.

Alfred's successors rolled back the Danish rule in England even though many Vikings remained. Converted to Christianity, their great men joined Anglo-Saxons in attending the English king at court. As peace returned, new administrative subdivisions for judicial and tax purposes were established throughout England: shires (the English equivalent of counties) and hundreds (smaller units). The powerful men of the kingdom swore fealty to the king, promising to be enemies of his enemies, friends of his friends. England was united and organized to support a strong ruler.

Alfred's grandson Edgar (r. 957–975) commanded all the possibilities early medieval kingship offered. He was the sworn lord of all the great men of the kingdom. He controlled appointments to the English church and sponsored monastic reform. In 973, he was anointed king. The fortifications of the kingdom were in his hands, as was the army, and he took responsibility for keeping the peace by proclaiming certain crimes — arson and theft — to be under his special jurisdiction and by mobilizing the machinery of the shire and the hundred to find and punish thieves.

Despite its apparent centralization, England was not a unified state in the modern sense, and the king's control was often tenuous. Many royal officials were great landowners who (as on the European continent) worked for the king because it was in their best interest. When it was not, they allied with different claimants to the throne. This political fragility may have helped the Danish king Cnut to conquer England. As king there from 1017 to 1035, Cnut reinforced the already strong connections between England and Scandinavia while keeping intact much of the administrative, ecclesiastical, and military apparatus already established in England by the Anglo-Saxons. By Cnut's time, Scandinavian traditions had largely merged with those of the rest of Europe and the Vikings were no longer an alien culture.

Across the Channel, French kings had a harder time than the English coping with invasions because their realm was much larger. They had no chance to build their defenses slowly from one powerful base. During most of the tenth century, Carolingian kings alternated on the throne with kings from a family that would later be called the Capetian. As the Caro-

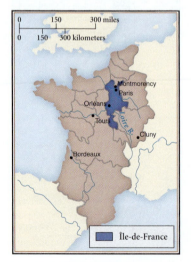

The Kingdom of the Franks under Hugh Capet, 987–996

lingian dynasty waned, the most powerful men of the kingdom — dukes, counts, and important bishops — came together to elect as king Hugh Capet (r. 987–996), a lord of great prestige yet relatively little power. His choice marked the end of Carolingian rule and the beginning of the **Capetian dynasty**, which would hand down the royal title from father to son until the fourteenth century.

In the eleventh century, territorial lordships limited the reach of the Capetian kings. The king's scattered but substantial estates lay in the north of France, in the region around Paris — the Île-de-France ("island of France"). His castles and his vassals were there. Independent castellans, however, controlled areas nearby. In the sense that he was a neighbor of castellans and not much more powerful militarily than they, the king of the Franks — who would only later take the territorial title of king of France — was just another local leader. Yet the Capetian kings had considerable prestige. They were anointed with holy oil, and they represented the idea of unity inherited from Charlemagne. Most of the counts, at least in the north of France, became their vassals. But because they were powerful, these vassals' obligations to the king were minimal.

Emperors and Kings in Central and Eastern Europe

In contrast to the development of territorial lordships in France, Germany's fragmentation had hardly begun before it was reversed. In the late Carolingian period, five large duchies (regions dominated by dukes) emerged in Germany. When the last Carolingian king in Germany died, in 911, the dukes elected one of themselves as king. Then, as the Magyar invasions increased, the dukes gave the royal title to the duke of Saxony, Henry I (r. 919–936), who proceeded to set up fortifications and reorganize his army, crowning his efforts with a major defeat of a Magyar army in 933.

Otto I (r. 936–973), the son of Henry I, was an even greater military hero. In 951, he marched into Italy and took the Lombard crown. His defeat of the Magyar forces in 955 at Lechfeld gave him prestige and helped solidify his dynasty. Against the Slavs, with whom the Germans shared a border, Otto created marches (border regions specifically set up for defense) from which he could make expeditions and stave off counterattacks. After the pope crowned him emperor in 962, Otto claimed the Middle Kingdom carved out by the Treaty of Verdun and cast himself as the agent of Roman imperial renewal. His kingdom was called the Empire, as if it were the old Roman Empire revived. Some historians call it the Holy Roman Empire to distinguish it from the Roman Empire, but Otto and his successors made no such distinction; they considered it a continuation. In this book, it will be called the Empire.

Otto's victories brought tribute and plunder, ensuring him a following but also raising the German nobles' expectations for enrichment. The **Ottonian kings** — including Otto I and his successors Otto II (r. 973–983) and Otto III (r. 983–1002) — were not always able or willing to provide the gifts and inheritances their family members and followers expected. They did not divide their kingdom among their sons; instead, like castellans in France, they created a patrilineal pattern of inheritance. As a consequence,

Otto III Receiving Gifts

These triumphal images are in a book of Gospels made for Otto III (r. 983–1002). The crowned women on the left are personifications of the four parts of Otto's empire: Sclavinia (the Slavic lands), Germania (Germany), Gallia (Gaul), and Roma (Rome). Each offers a gift in tribute and homage to the emperor, who sits on a throne holding the symbols of his power (orb and scepter) and flanked by representatives of the church (on his right) and of the army (on his left). Why do you suppose the artist separated the image of the emperor from that of the women? What does the body language of the women indicate about the relations Otto wanted to portray between himself and the parts of his empire? Can you relate this manuscript, which was made in 997–1000, to Otto's conquest over the Slavs in 997? (bpk, Berlin / Bayerische Staatsbibliothek, Munich, Germany / Art Resource, NY.)

younger sons and other potential heirs felt cheated, and disgruntled royal kin led revolt after revolt against the Ottonian kings.

Relations between the Ottonians and the German clergy were more harmonious. Otto I appointed bishops, gave them extensive lands, and subjected the local peasantry to their overlordship. Like Charlemagne, Otto believed that the well-being of the church in his kingdom depended on him. The Ottonians gave bishops the right to collect revenues and call men to arms. Answering to the king and furnishing him with troops, the bishops became royal officials, while also carrying out their religious duties. German kings claimed the right to select bishops, even the pope at Rome, and to "invest" them (install them in their office) by participating in the ceremony that made them bishops.

Like all strong rulers of the day, the Ottonians presided over a renaissance of learning. They brought learned churchmen to court to write and teach. To an extent unprecedented elsewhere, noblewomen in Germany also acquired an education and participated in the intellectual revival. Living at home with their kinfolk and servants or in

convents that provided them with comfortable private apartments, noblewomen wrote books and supported other artists and scholars.

Despite their military and political strength, the kings of Germany faced resistance from dukes and other powerful princes, who hoped to become regional rulers themselves. The Salians, the dynasty that succeeded the Ottonians, tried to balance the power among the German dukes but could not meld them into a corps of vassals the way the Capetian kings tamed their counts. In Germany, vassalage was considered beneath the dignity of free men. Instead of relying on vassals, the Salian kings and their bishops used ministerials (specially designated men who were legally serfs) to collect taxes, administer justice, and fight on horseback. Ministerials retained their servile status even though they often rose to wealth and high position. Under the Salian kings, ministerials became the mainstay of the royal army and administration.

Hand in hand with the popes, German kings created new, Catholic polities along their eastern frontier. The Czechs, who lived in the region of Bohemia, converted under the rule of Václav (r. 920–929), who thereby gained recognition in Germany as the duke of Bohemia. He and his successors did not become kings, remaining politically within the German sphere. Václav's murder by his younger brother made him a martyr and the patron saint of Bohemia, a symbol around which later movements for independence rallied.

The Poles gained a greater measure of independence than the Czechs. In 966, Mieszko I (r. 963–992), the leader of the Slavic tribe known as the Polanians, accepted baptism to forestall the attack that the Germans were already mounting against pagan Slavic peoples along the Baltic coast and east of the Elbe River. Busily engaged in bringing the other Slavic tribes of Poland under his control, Mieszko adroitly shifted his alliances with various German princes to suit his needs. In 991, he placed his realm under the protection of the pope, establishing a tradition of Polish loyalty to the Roman church. Mieszko's son Boleslaw the Brave (r. 992–1025) greatly extended Poland's boundaries, at one time or another holding sway from the Bohemian border to Kiev. In 1000, he gained a royal crown with papal blessing.

Hungary's case was similar to that of Poland. As we have seen, the Magyars settled in the region known today as Hungary. Under Stephen I (r. 997–1038), they accepted Roman Christianity. According to legend, the crown placed on Stephen's head at his coronation (in late 1000 or early 1001) was sent to him by the pope. Stephen was canonized in 1083, and to this day the crown of St. Stephen remains the most hallowed symbol of Hungarian nationhood.

Symbols of rulership such as crowns, consecrated by Christian priests and accorded a prestige almost akin to saints' relics, were among the most vital sources of royal power in central Europe. The economic basis for the power of central European rulers was largely agricultural. As happened elsewhere, here too centralized rule gradually gave way to regional rulers.

REVIEW QUESTION After the dissolution of the Carolingian Empire, what political systems developed in western, northern, eastern, and central Europe, and how did these systems differ from one another?

Mapping the West **Europe and the Mediterranean, c. 1050**

The clear borders and distinct colors of the "states" on this map distort an essential truth: none of the areas shown had centralized governments that controlled whole territories, as in modern states. Instead, there were numerous regional rulers within each, and there were often competing claims of jurisdiction and conflicting allegiances. Consider Sicily: it was conquered by Muslims in the tenth century, but by 1060 it had been taken over by the Normans — adventurers from Normandy (in France). Its predominantly Greek-speaking population, however, adhered to the Greek Orthodox religion, a legacy of its Byzantine past.

Conclusion

In 800, the three heirs of the Roman Empire all appeared to be organized like their parent: centralized, monarchical, imperial. Byzantine emperors writing their learned books, Abbasid caliphs holding court in their new resplendent palace at Baghdad, and Carolingian emperors issuing their directives for reform all mimicked the Roman emperors. Yet leaders in the three realms confronted tensions and regional pressures that tended to put political power into the hands of local lords. Byzantium felt this fragmentation least, yet even there the emergence of a new elite, the dynatoi, weakened the emperor's control over the countryside. In the Islamic world, quarrels between Abbasid heirs, army disloyalty, economic weakness, and the ambitions of powerful local rulers decisively weakened the caliphate and opened the way to separate successor states. In Europe, powerful independent landowners strove with greater or lesser success (depending on the region) to establish themselves as effective rulers.

Local conditions determined political and economic organizations. Between 900 and 1000, for example, French society was transformed by the rise of castellans, the formation of patrilineal families, and the spread of ties of vassalage. These factors figured less prominently in Germany, where a central monarchy remained, buttressed by churchmen, ministerials, and conquests to the east.

After 1050, however, the German king would lose his supreme position as a storm of church reform whirled around him. The economy changed, becoming more commercial and urban, and the papacy asserted itself with new force in the life of Europe.

Review Questions

1. In what ways did the Byzantine emperor expand his power, and in what ways was that power checked?
2. What forces contributed to the fragmentation of the Islamic world in the tenth and eleventh centuries, and what forces held it together?
3. What were the strengths and weaknesses of Carolingian institutions of government, warfare, and defense?
4. After the dissolution of the Carolingian Empire, what political systems developed in western, northern, eastern, and central Europe, and how did these systems differ from one another?

Making Connections

1. How were the Byzantine, Islamic, and European economies similar? How did they differ? How did these economies interact?
2. How did the powers and ambitions of castellans compare with those of the dynatoi of Byzantium and of Muslim provincial rulers?
3. Compare the effects of the barbarian invasions into the Roman Empire with the effects of the Viking, Muslim, and Magyar invasions into Carolingian Europe.

- For practice quizzes and other study tools, visit the **Online Study Guide** at bedfordstmartins.com/huntconcise.

- For primary-source material from this period, see *Sources of the Making of the West,* Fourth Edition.

- For Web sites, images, and documents related to topics in this chapter, visit *Make History* at bedfordstmartins.com/huntconcise.

Suggested References

A few books, like Brubaker and Smith's, try to bridge the divides between the Byzantine, Islamic, and western European worlds. Nevertheless, for the most part these regions are treated separately. For Byzantium, Whittow is essential. For insight into the Islamic world, see especially Cooperson. For the Carolingian world, De Jong provides a new approach.

Becher, Matthias. *Charlemagne.* 2003.

Berend, Nora. *At the Gate of Christendom: Jews, Muslims, and "Pagans" in Medieval Hungary, c. 1000–c. 1300.* 2001.

Brubaker, Leslie, and Julia M. H. Smith. *Gender in the Early Medieval World: East and West, 300–900.* 2004.

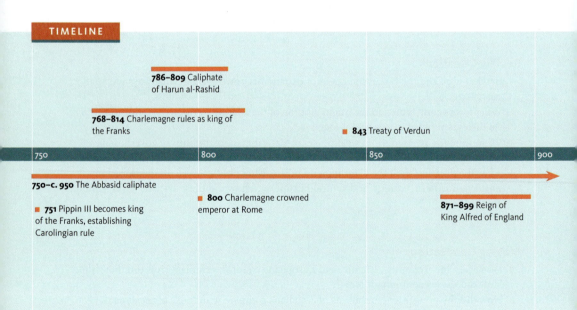

TIMELINE

786–809 Caliphate of Harun al-Rashid

768–814 Charlemagne rules as king of the Franks

843 Treaty of Verdun

| 750 | 800 | 850 | 900 |

750–c. 950 The Abbasid caliphate

751 Pippin III becomes king of the Franks, establishing Carolingian rule

800 Charlemagne crowned emperor at Rome

871–899 Reign of King Alfred of England

Chronicle of Zuqnin, Parts III and IV, A.D. 488–775. Trans. Amir Harrak. 1999.

Cooperson, Michael. *Al Ma'mun*. 2005.

De Jong, Mayke. *The Penitential State: Authority and Atonement in the Age of Louis the Pious, 814–840*. 2009.

*Dutton, Paul Edward, ed. *Carolingian Civilization: A Reader*. 2004.

* ——, ed. and trans. *Charlemagne's Courtier: The Complete Einhard*. 1998.

Franklin, Simon, and Jonathan Shepard. *The Emergence of Rus, 750–1200*. 1996.

Garver, Valerie L. *Women and Aristocratic Culture in the Carolingian World*. 2009.

Jones, Anna Trumbore. *Noble Lord, Good Shepherd: Episcopal Power and Piety in Aquitaine, 877–1050*. 2009.

Kennedy, Hugh. *The Armies of the Caliphs: Military and Society in the Early Islamic State*. 2001.

*Psellus, Michael. *Fourteen Byzantine Rulers: The Chronographia*. Trans. E. R. A. Sewter. 1966.

Whittow, Mark. *The Making of Byzantium, 600–1025*. 1996.

*Primary source.

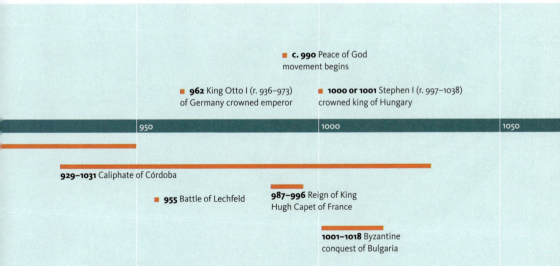

■ **c. 990** Peace of God movement begins

■ **962** King Otto I (r. 936–973) of Germany crowned emperor

■ **1000 or 1001** Stephen I (r. 997–1038) crowned king of Hungary

950   1000   1050

929–1031 Caliphate of Córdoba

■ **955** Battle of Lechfeld

987–996 Reign of King Hugh Capet of France

1001–1018 Byzantine conquest of Bulgaria

Commercial Quickening and Religious Reform

1050–1150

I N THE MID-TWELFTH CENTURY, a sculptor was hired to add some scenes from the Old and New Testaments to the facade of the grand new hilltop cathedral at Lincoln, England. He portrayed in striking fashion the deaths of the poor man Lazarus and the rich man Dives. Their fates could not have been more different. While Lazarus was carried to heaven by two angels, a contented-looking devil poked Dives and two other rich men straight into the mouth of hell — headfirst.

The sculptor's work reflected a widespread change in attitude toward money. In the Carolingian and post-Carolingian period (up to, say, 1050), people generally considered wealth a very good thing. Rich kings were praised for their generosity; expensively produced manuscripts, illuminated with gold leaf and precious colors, were highly prized; and splendid churches like Charlemagne's chapel at Aachen were widely admired. Such views changed over the course of the eleventh century.

The most striking feature of the period 1050–1150 was the rise of a money economy in western Europe. Agricultural production swelled, fueling the growth of trade and the expansion of cities. A new class of well-heeled merchants, bankers, and entrepreneurs emerged. These developments were met with a wide variety of responses. Some people fled the cities and their new wealth altogether, seeking isolation and poverty. Others, even the participants in the new economy, condemned it and emphasized its corrupting influence. Many people, however, embraced the new money economy.

The development of a profit-based economy quickly transformed the landscape and lifestyles of western Europe. Many villages and fortifications became cities where traders,

Dives and Lazarus

At the time this sculpted depiction of Dives and Lazarus was made, the town of Lincoln was expanding both within and without its Roman walls. Within the walls were the precincts of the fishmongers, the grain sellers, and the poultry merchants. Outside the walls were the bakers, the soapmakers, and the salt sellers. The town was highly attuned to moneymaking and well aware of its pleasures and dangers both. (Conway Library, The Courtauld Institute of Art, London.)

merchants, and artisans conducted business. In some places, town dwellers began to determine their own laws and administer their own justice. Although most people still lived in sparsely populated rural areas, the new cash economy touched their lives in many ways. Economic concerns helped drive changes within the church, where a movement for reform gathered steam and exploded in three directions: the Investiture Conflict, new monastic orders emphasizing poverty, and the crusades. Money allowed popes, kings, and princes to redefine the nature of their power.

CHAPTER FOCUS How did the commercial revolution affect religion and politics?

The Commercial Revolution

A growing population, cities, long-distance trade networks, local markets, and new business arrangements meshed to create a profit-based economy. With improvements in agriculture and more land in cultivation, the great estates of the eleventh century produced surpluses that helped feed — and therefore make possible — a new urban population.

Commerce was not new to the history of western Europe, but the **commercial revolution** of the Middle Ages spawned the institutions that would be the direct ancestors of modern businesses: corporations, banks, accounting systems, and above all urban centers that thrived on economic vitality. Whereas ancient cities had primarily religious, social, and political functions, medieval cities were centers of production and economic activity. Wealth meant power: it allowed city dwellers to become self-governing.

Fairs, Towns, and Cities

The commercial revolution took place in three venues: markets, fairs, and permanent centers. In some places, markets met weekly to sell local surplus goods. In others, fairs — which lasted anywhere from several days to a few months — took place once a year and drew traders from longer distances. Some fairs specialized in particular goods: at Saint-Denis, a monastery near Paris that had had a fair since at least the seventh century, the star attraction was wine. Most fairs offered a wide variety of products: at the Champagne fairs in France, there were woolen fabrics from Flanders; silks from Lucca, Italy; leather goods from Spain; and furs from Germany. Bankers attended as well, exchanging coins from one currency into another — and charging for their services. Local inhabitants did not have to pay taxes or tolls, but traders from the outside — protected by guarantees of safe conduct — were charged stall fees as well as entry and exit fees. Local landlords reaped great profits, and as the fairs came under royal control, kings did so as well.

Permanent commercial centers (cities and towns) developed around castles and monasteries and within the walls of ancient Roman towns. Great lords in the countryside — and this included monasteries — were eager to take advantage of the profits that their estates generated. In the late tenth century, they reorganized their lands for greater productivity, encouraged their peasants to cultivate new land, and converted services and dues to money payments. With ready cash, they not only fos-

tered the development of local markets and yearly fairs, where they could sell their surpluses and buy luxury goods, but also encouraged traders and craftspeople to settle down near them.

Some markets formed just outside the walls of older cities; these gradually merged into new and enlarged urban communities as towns built new walls around them to protect their inhabitants. Along the Rhine River and in other river valleys, cities sprang up to service the merchants who traversed the route between Italy and the north. Many long-distance traders were Italians and Jews. They supplied the fine wines, spices, and fabrics beloved by lords and ladies, their families, and their vassals. Italians took up long-distance trade because of Italy's proximity to Byzantine and Islamic ports, their opportunities for plunder and trade on the high seas, and their never entirely extinguished urban traditions.

The Jews of Mediterranean regions — especially Italy and Spain — had been involved in commerce since Roman times. That trade had centered on the Mediterranean; now it extended to the north as well. For Jews living in the port cities of the old Roman Empire, little had changed. But for many Jews in northern Europe, the story was different. They had settled on the land alongside other peasants, and during the Carolingian period their properties bordered those of their Christian neighbors. As political power fragmented over the course of the tenth century and the countryside was reorganized under local lords, many Jews were driven off the land. They found refuge in the new towns and cities. Some became scholars, doctors, and judges within their communities; many became small-time pawnbrokers; and still others became moneylenders and financiers.

By the eleventh century, most Jews lived in cities but were not citizens. They were generally serfs of the king or, in the Rhineland, under the safeguard of the local bishop. This status was ambiguous: the Jews were "protected" but also exploited, since their

Synagogue Inscription from the City of Worms
This inscription is the oldest artifact we have from a synagogue in Europe. It says that Jacob ben David and his wife, Rahel, used their fortune to construct and furnish the synagogue, which was completed in 1034. They express the belief that this act of piety is as pleasing to God as having children. (Jüdisches Museum im Raschihaus, Worms, Germany.)

protectors constantly demanded steep taxes. Regular town trade groups, craft organizations, and town governments often rested on a conception of the common good sealed by an oath among Christians — and thus, by definition, excluded Jews.

Nevertheless, Jews had their own institutions, centered on the synagogue, their place of worship. Although they often lived in a "Jewish quarter," they were not forcibly segregated from other townspeople. In many cities they lived near Christians, purchased products from Christian craftspeople, and hired Christians as servants. In turn, Christians purchased luxury goods from Jewish long-distance traders and often borrowed money from Jewish lenders. The fact that Jews and Christians could live side by side had less to do with tolerance than with lack of planning. Most towns in medieval Europe grew haphazardly. Typically, towns had a center, where the church and town government had their headquarters, and around this were the shops of tradespeople and craftspeople, generally grouped by specialty: butchers, for example, lived and worked on the Street of the Butchers.

The look and feel of such developing cities varied enormously, but nearly all included a marketplace, a castle, and several churches. The streets — made of packed clay or gravel — were often narrow, dirty, dark, and winding. Most people had to adapt to increasingly crowded conditions. Even so, most city dwellers tended a garden and perhaps livestock as well, living largely off the food they raised themselves.

Cities were part of a building boom. Towns put up specialized buildings for trade and city government — charitable houses for the sick and indigent, city halls, and warehouses. They also expanded their walls. Workers at Piacenza, for example, first pulled down the late antique wall and replaced it with a more extensive one in 872. Then, in 1169, Piacenzans took down the ninth-century wall and replaced it with one that was still more expansive. (See The Walls of Piacenza at left.)

Before the eleventh century, Europeans had depended on boats and waterways for bulky long-distance transport. In the twelfth century, carts could haul items overland because new roads through the countryside linked the urban markets and strengthened governments could protect overland travelers. Still, although commercial centers developed throughout western Europe, they grew fastest and most densely in regions along key waterways: the Mediterranean coasts of Italy, France, and Spain; northern Italy along the Po River; the Rhône-Saône-Meuse river system; the Rhineland; the English Channel; the shores of the Baltic Sea. During the eleventh century, these waterways became part of a single interdependent economy.

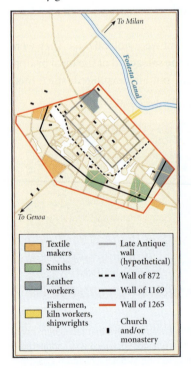

The Walls of Piacenza

Baptismal Font at Liège, 1107–1118
This detail from a large bronze baptismal font cast at Liège (a city today in Belgium) illustrated the words of Luke 3:12–14: "Tax collectors also came to be baptized, and said to [Jesus], 'Teacher, what shall we do?' And he said to them, 'Collect no more than is appointed you.' Soldiers also asked him, 'And we, what shall we do?' And he said to them, 'Rob no one . . . and be content with your wages.'" In this representation, the tax collectors are dressed like twelfth-century city dwellers, while a soldier is dressed like a knight of the period. (akg-images.)

What did townspeople look like? We can get an idea from a twelfth-century baptismal font cast in Liège (see above). It shows Jesus speaking to the soldiers and publicans (tax collectors): the soldier is dressed as a medieval knight, while the publicans wear the caps and clothes of well-to-do city dwellers.

Organizing Crafts and Commerce

In the Middle Ages, most manufactured goods were produced by hand or with primitive machines and tools. Though not mechanized, most medieval industries, crafts, and trades were highly organized. The fundamental unit of organization was the **guild**. Originally guilds were religious and charitable associations of people in the same line of business. In Ferrara, Italy, for example, the shoemakers' guild started as a prayer confraternity, an association whose members gathered and prayed for one another. But soon guilds became professional corporations defined by statutes and rules. They charged dues, negotiated with lords and town governments, set the standards of their trade, and controlled their membership.

The manufacture of finished products often required the cooperation of several guilds. The production of wool cloth, for example, involved numerous guilds — shearers, weavers, fullers (who thickened the cloth), dyers — generally working under the supervision of the merchant guild that imported the raw wool. Within each guild was a hierarchy, starting at the bottom with the **apprentices**, who were learning the trade, moving up to the **journeymen** and **journeywomen** (that is, male or female day laborers — the word comes from the Middle English for "a day's work"), ending with the **masters** at the top.

It was hard to become a master. Young people might spend many years as an apprentice and then as a day laborer hired by masters who needed extra help. But most journeymen and journeywomen aspired to be masters because then they would be able to draw up regulations for the guild and serve as its chief overseers, inspectors, and

treasurers. Most masters eventually had a chance to serve as guild officers. Occasionally they were elected, but more often they were appointed by town governments or local rulers.

In addition to guilds, medieval entrepreneurs created new kinds of business arrangements through partnerships, contracts, and large-scale productive enterprises — the ancestors of modern **capitalism**. Although they took many forms, all of these business agreements had the common purpose of bringing people together to pool their resources and finance larger initiatives. Short-lived partnerships were set up for the term of one sea voyage; longer-term partnerships were created for land trade. In northern and central Italy, for example, long-term ventures took the form of a family corporation formed by extended families. Everyone who contributed to this corporation bore joint and unlimited liability for all losses and debts. This provision enhanced family solidarity, because each member was responsible for the debts of all the others, but it also risked bankrupting everyone in the family.

The commercial revolution also fostered the development of contracts for sales, exchanges, and loans. Loans were the most problematic. In the Middle Ages, as now, interest payments were the chief inducement for an investor to supply money. To circumvent the church's ban on usury (lending money at interest), a contract often disguised interest as a "penalty for late payment." The new willingness to finance business enterprises with loans signaled a changed attitude toward credit: risk was acceptable if it brought profit.

Contracts and partnerships made large-scale productive enterprises possible. In fact, light industry began in the eleventh century. One of the earliest products to benefit from new industrial technologies was cloth. Water mills powered machines such as presses to extract oil from fibers, and flails to clean and thicken cloth. Machines also exploited raw materials more efficiently: new deep-mining technology provided Europeans with hitherto untapped sources of metals. Simultaneously, forging techniques improved, and for the first time since antiquity, iron was regularly used for agricultural tools and plows. Iron tools — which were more durable than wood — made farming more productive, which in turn fed the commercial revolution.

Communes: Self-Government for the Towns

In the eleventh and twelfth centuries, townspeople did not fit into the old categories of medieval types: those who prayed, those who fought, or those who labored on the land. Just knowing they were different from those groups gave townspeople a sense of solidarity. But practical reasons also contributed to their feeling of common purpose: they lived in close quarters, and they shared a mutual interest in laws to facilitate commerce, freedom from servile dues and duties, reliable coinage, and independence to buy and sell as the market dictated. Already in the early twelfth century, the king of England granted to the citizens of Newcastle-upon-Tyne the privilege that any unfree peasant who lived there unclaimed by his lord for a year and a day would thereafter be a free person. This privilege became general. To townspeople, freedom meant having their own

officials and law courts. They petitioned the political powers that ruled them — bishops, kings, counts, castellans — for the right to govern themselves. Often they had to fight for this freedom and, if successful, paid a hefty sum for it. A type of town institution of self-government arose called a **commune**; citizens swore allegiance to the commune, forming a legal corporate body.

Communes were especially common in northern and central Italy, France, and Flanders. Even before the commercial revolution, Italian cities had become centers of regional political power; the commercial revolution swelled them with tradespeople, whose interest in self-government was often fueled by religious as well as economic concerns. At Milan in the second half of the eleventh century, popular discontent with the archbishop, who effectively ruled the city, led to numerous armed clashes. In 1097, the Milanese succeeded in transferring political power from the archbishop and his clergy to a government of leading men of the city, who called themselves consuls, recalling the ancient Roman republic. The consuls' rule extended beyond the town walls into the *contado,* the outlying countryside.

Outside Italy, movements for city independence took place within the framework of larger kingdoms or principalities. Such movements were sometimes violent, as at Milan, but at other times peaceful. For example, William Clito, who claimed the county of Flanders (today in Belgium), willingly granted the citizens of St. Omer the privileges they asked for in 1127; he recognized them as legally free, gave them the right to mint coins, allowed them their own laws and courts, and lifted certain tolls and taxes. In return, the citizens supported his claims to rule Flanders. Whether violently or peacefully, the men and women of many towns and cities gained a measure of self-rule.

The Commercial Revolution in the Countryside

The countryside, too, was caught in the web of trade. By 1150, rural life in many regions was organized for the marketplace. Great lords hired trained, literate agents to administer their estates, calculate profits and losses, and make marketing decisions. Aristocrats needed money not only because they relished luxuries but also because their honor and authority continued to depend on their personal generosity, patronage, and displays of wealth. In the twelfth century, when some townsmen could boast fortunes that rivaled the riches of the landed aristocracy, the economic pressures on the nobles increased as their extravagance exceeded their income. Many went into debt.

The lord's need for money integrated peasants, too, into the developing commercial economy. The increase in population and the resultant greater demand for food required bringing more land under cultivation. Sometimes lords sponsored land clearance. At other times peasants acted on their own to clear land and relieve the pressure of overpopulation, as when the small freeholders in England's Fenland region cooperated to build banks and dikes to reclaim the land that led out to the North Sea. Villages were founded on the drained land, and villagers shared responsibility for repairing and maintaining the dikes even as each peasant family farmed its new holding individually.

On old estates the rise in population strained to the breaking point the Carolingian period's manse organization, in which each household had been settled on the land that supported it. Now, in the twelfth century, twenty peasant families might live on what had been, in the tenth century, the manse of one family. With the manse supporting so many more people, labor services and dues had to be recalculated, and peasants and their lords often turned services and dues into money rents, payable once a year.

The commercial revolution and the resulting money economy brought both benefits and burdens to peasants. They gained from rising prices, which made their fixed rents less onerous. They had access to markets where they could sell their surplus and buy what they lacked. Increases in land under cultivation and the use of iron tools meant greater productivity. Peasants also gained increased personal freedom as they shook off direct control by lords. Nevertheless, these advantages were partially canceled out by their cash obligations. Peasants touched by the commercial revolution ate better than their forebears had eaten, but they also had to spend more money.

> **REVIEW QUESTION** What new institutions resulted from the commercial revolution?

Church Reform

The commercial revolution affected the church no less than it affected other institutions of the time. Typically, kings or powerful local lords appointed bishops, who then ruled over the city. This transaction involved gifts: churchmen gave gifts and money to secular leaders in return for their offices. Soon the same sorts of people who appreciated the fates of Dives and Lazarus were condemning such transactions. The impulse to free the church from "the world" — from rulers, wealth, sex, money, and power — was as old as the origins of monasticism; but, beginning in the tenth century and increasing to fever pitch in the eleventh, reformers demanded that the church as a whole remodel itself and become free of secular entanglements.

The World of the Investiture Conflict, c. 1070–1122

This freedom was, from the start, as much a matter of power as of religion. Most people had long believed that their ruler — whether king, duke, count, or castellan — reigned by the grace of God and had the right to control the churches in his territory. But by the second half of the eleventh century, more and more people saw a great deal wrong with secular power over the church. They looked to the papacy to lead the movement of church reform. The matter came to a head during the so-called Investiture Conflict, when Pope Gregory VII clashed with Emperor Henry IV (whose empire embraced both Germany and Italy). The Investiture Conflict ushered in a major civil war in Germany and a great upheaval in the distribution of power across western Europe. By the

early 1100s, a reformed church — with the pope at its head — was penetrating into areas of life never before touched by churchmen. Church reform began as a way to free the church from the world, but in the end the church was thoroughly involved in the new world it had helped create.

Beginnings of Reform

The project of freeing the church from the world began in the tenth century with no particular plan and only a vague idea of what it might mean. The Benedictine monastery of Cluny (today in France) may serve to represent the early phases of the reform. The duke and duchess of Aquitaine founded Cluny in 910 and endowed it with property. Then they did something new: instead of retaining control over the monastery, like most other monastic founders, they gave it and its worldly possessions to Saints Peter and Paul. In this way, they put control of the monastery into the hands of heaven's two most powerful saints. They designated the pope, as the successor of St. Peter, to be the monastery's worldly protector if anyone should bother or threaten it.

The whole notion of "freedom" at this point was vague. But Cluny's prestige was great because of its status as St. Peter's property and the elaborate round of prayers that the monks carried out there with scrupulous devotion. The Cluniac monks fulfilled the role of "those who pray" in a way that dazzled their contemporaries. Through their prayers, they seemed to guarantee the salvation of all Christians. Rulers, bishops, rich landowners, and even serfs (if they could) donated land to Cluny, joining their lands to the land of St. Peter and the fate of their souls to Cluny's efficacious prayers. Powerful men and women called on the Cluniac monks to reform other monasteries along the Cluniac model.

The abbots of Cluny came to see themselves as reformers of the world as well. They advocated clerical celibacy and argued against the prevailing norm, in which parish priests and even some bishops were married. They thought that the laity (all Christians who were not part of the clergy) could be reformed and become more virtuous. In particular, they sought to curb the oppression of the poor by the rich and powerful. In the eleventh century, the Cluniacs began to link their program of internal monastic and external worldly reform to the papacy. When bishops and laypeople encroached on their lands, they appealed to the popes for help. The causes that the Cluniacs championed were soon taken up by a small group of clerics and monks in the Empire, the political entity created by the Ottonians. They buttressed their arguments with new interpretations of canon law — the laws decreed over the centuries at church councils and by bishops and popes. They concentrated on two breaches of those laws: clerical marriage and **simony** (buying church offices).* Later they added the condemnation of **lay investiture** — the installation of clerics into their offices by lay rulers. In the investiture ritual, the emperor or his representative symbolically gave the church and the land that went with it to the priest or bishop or archbishop chosen for the job.

---

*The word *simony* comes from the name Simon Magus, the magician in the New Testament who wanted to buy the gifts of the Holy Spirit from St. Peter.

At first the emperors supported the reformers. Many of the men who promoted the reform lived in the highly commercialized regions of the empire — Italy and the regions along the northern half of the Rhine River. Familiar with the impersonal practices of a profit economy, they regarded the gifts that churchmen usually gave in return for their offices as no more than crass purchases.

Emperor Henry III (r. 1039–1056) took seriously his position as the anointed of God. He felt responsible for the well-being of the church in his empire. He denounced simony and refused to accept money or gifts when he appointed bishops to their posts. When in 1046 three men, each representing a different faction of the Roman aristocracy, claimed to be pope, Henry, as ruler of Rome, traveled to Italy to settle the matter. There Henry presided over the Synod of Sutri (1046), which deposed all three popes and elected another. In 1049, Henry appointed a bishop from the Rhineland to the papacy as Leo IX (r. 1049–1054). But this appointment did not work out as Henry had expected.

Leo set out to reform the church under his own, not the emperor's, control. Under his rule, the pope's role expanded. He traveled to France and Germany, holding councils to condemn bishops guilty of simony. He sponsored the creation of a canon law textbook — *Collection in 74 Titles* — that emphasized the pope's power. He brought to the papal court the most zealous reformers of his day, including Humbert of Silva Candida and Hildebrand (later Pope Gregory VII).

In 1054, his last year as pope, Leo sent Humbert to Constantinople on a diplomatic mission to argue against the patriarch of Constantinople on behalf of the new, lofty claims of the pope. When the patriarch treated him with contempt, Humbert became furious

Leo IX

This eleventh-century manuscript shows not so much a portrait of Pope Leo IX as an idealized image of his power and position. What might the halo signify? Why do you suppose Leo stands at least three heads taller than the other figure in the picture, Warinus, the abbot of St. Arnulf of Metz? What is Leo doing with his right hand? With his left hand he holds a little church (symbol of a real one) that is being presented to him by Warinus. What did the artist intend to convey about the relationship of this church to papal power? (Burgerbibliothek Bern, Cod. 292, f. 72r.)

and excommunicated him. In retaliation, the patriarch excommunicated Humbert and his party, threatening them with eternal damnation. Clashes between the two churches had occurred before and had been patched up, but this one, the schism between the eastern and western churches (1054), proved insurmountable.* Thereafter, the Roman Catholic and the Greek Orthodox churches were largely separate.

Leo also confronted a new power to his south. Under Count Roger I (c. 1040–1101), the Normans created a county that would eventually stretch from Capua to Sicily (see the map on page 312). Leo, threatened by this great power, tried to curtail it: in 1053 he sent a military force to Apulia, but it was soundly defeated. Leo's successors were obliged to change their policy. In 1058, the reigning pope "invested" — in effect, gave — Apulia, nearby Calabria, and even the still-unconquered Sicily to Roger's brother, even though none of this was the pope's to give. The papacy was particularly keen to see the Normans gain Sicily. Once part of the Byzantine Empire, the island had been taken by Muslims in the tenth century; now the pope hoped to bring it under Catholic control. Thus, the pope's desires to convert Sicily meshed nicely with the territorial ambitions of Roger and his brother. The agreement of 1058 included a promise that all of the churches of southern Italy and Sicily would be placed under papal jurisdiction. No wonder that when the Investiture Conflict broke out, the Normans played an important role as a military arm of the papacy.

The popes were in fact becoming more and more involved in military enterprises. They participated in wars of expansion in Spain, for example. There, political fragmentation into small and weak *taifas* (see page 278) made al-Andalus fair game for the Christians to the north. Slowly the idea of the **reconquista**, the Christian "reconquest" of Spain from the Muslims, took shape, fed by religious fervor as well as by greed for land and power. In 1063, just before a major battle, the pope issued an incentive to all who would fight — an indulgence that lifted the knights' obligation to do penance, although it did not go so far as to forgive all sins.

The Gregorian Reform and the Investiture Conflict, 1075–1122

Historians associate the papal reform movement above all with Gregory VII (r. 1073–1085) and therefore often call it the **Gregorian reform**. Beginning as a lowly Roman cleric named Hildebrand, with the job of administering the papal estates, Gregory rose slowly through the hierarchy. A passionate advocate of papal primacy (the theory that the pope was the head of the church), Gregory was not afraid to clash head-on with **Henry IV** (r. 1056–1106), ruler of Germany and much of Italy, over leadership of the church. As his views crystallized, Gregory came to see an anointed ruler as just another

---

*The mutual excommunications led to a permanent breach between the churches that largely remained in effect until 1965, when Pope Paul VI and Patriarch Athenagoras I made a joint declaration regretting "the offensive words" and sentences of excommunication the two sides had exchanged more than nine hundred years before, deploring "the effective rupture of ecclesiastical communion," and expressing the hope that in time the "differences between the Roman Catholic Church and the Orthodox Church" would be overcome.

layman who had no right to meddle in church affairs. At the time, this was an astonishing position, given the traditional religious and spiritual roles associated with kings and emperors.

Gregory was, and remains, an extraordinarily controversial figure. As pope, he thought that he was acting as the vicar, or representative, of St. Peter on earth. In his view, the reforms he advocated and the upheavals he precipitated were necessary to free the church from the evil rulers of the world. But his great nemesis, Henry IV, had a very different view of Gregory. He considered him an ambitious and evil man who "seduced the world far and wide and stained the Church with the blood of her sons." Modern historians are only a bit less divided in their assessment of Gregory. Few deny his sincerity and deep religious devotion, but many speak of his pride, ambition, and single-mindedness.

Henry IV was less complex. He was raised in the traditions of his father, Henry III. He believed that he and his bishops — who were, at the same time, his most valuable supporters and administrators — were the rightful leaders of the church. He had no intention of allowing the pope to become head of the church; he didn't see that new religious ideals were sweeping away the old traditions. The great confrontation between Gregory and Henry that historians call the **Investiture Conflict*** began in 1075 over the appointment of the archbishop of Milan and a few other Italian prelates. When Henry insisted on appointing these clergymen, Gregory admonished the king. Henry responded by calling on Gregory to step down as pope. In turn, Gregory called a synod that both excommunicated and suspended Henry from office:

> I deprive King Henry [IV], son of the emperor Henry [III], who has rebelled against [God's] Church with unheard-of audacity, of the government over the whole kingdom of Germany and Italy, and I release all Christian men from the allegiance which they have sworn or may swear to him, and I forbid anyone to serve him as king.

It was this last part of the decree that made it politically explosive; it authorized everyone in Henry's kingdom to rebel against him. Henry's enemies, mostly German princes (as German aristocrats were called), now threatened to elect another king. They were motivated partly by religious sentiments and partly by political opportunism. Some bishops joined forces with Gregory's supporters, a great blow to royal power because Henry desperately needed the troops supplied by his churchmen.

Attacked from all sides, Henry traveled to intercept Gregory, who was journeying northward to visit the rebellious princes. In early 1077, king and pope met at a castle belonging to Matilda, countess of Tuscany, at Canossa, high in central Italy's snowy Apennine Mountains. Gregory remained inside the fortress there; Henry stood outside

---

*This movement is also called the Investiture Controversy, Investiture Contest, or Investiture Struggle. The epithets all refer to the same thing: the disagreement and eventually war between the pope and the emperor over the right to invest churchmen in particular and power over the church hierarchy in general.

Matilda of Tuscany

How often is a woman the dominant figure in medieval art? In this illustration made around 1115, Matilda, countess of Tuscany, towers above the king (Henry IV) and upstages the abbot of Cluny (Hugh). Matilda was a key supporter of Pope Gregory VII. It was at her castle at Canossa that Henry IV did penance. The words underneath the picture emphasize Henry's abjection. They read: "The king begs the abbot and supplicates Matilda as well." (Biblioteca Apostolica Vaticana, The Vatican, Italy / Flammarion / The Bridgeman Art Library International.)

as a penitent, begging forgiveness. Henry's move was astute, for no priest could refuse absolution to a penitent; Gregory had to lift the excommunication and receive Henry back into the church. But, as Henry stood in the snow, Gregory had the advantage of enjoying the king's humiliation before the majesty of the pope.

Although Henry was technically back in the church's fold, nothing of substance had been resolved. The princes elected an antiking (a king chosen illegally), and Henry and his supporters elected an antipope. From 1077 until 1122, papal and imperial armies and supporters waged intermittent war in both Germany and Italy.

The Investiture Conflict was finally resolved long after Henry IV and Gregory VII had died. The **Concordat of Worms** of 1122 ended the fighting with a compromise. Henry V, the heir of Henry IV, gave up the right in the investiture ceremony to confer the ring and the pastoral staff — symbols of spiritual power. But he retained, in Germany, the right to be present when bishops were elected. In effect, he would continue to have influence over those elections. In both Germany and Italy he also had the right to give the scepter to the churchman in a gesture meant to indicate the transfer of the temporal, or worldly, powers and possessions of the church (the lands by which it was supported).

Superficially, nothing much had changed; the Concordat of Worms ensured that secular rulers would continue to have a part in choosing and investing churchmen. In fact, however, few people would now claim that a king could act as head of the church. Just as the concordat broke the investiture ritual into two parts — one spiritual, with ring and staff, the other secular, with the scepter — so too it implied a new notion of kingship that separated it from priesthood. The Investiture Conflict did not produce the modern distinction between church and state — that would develop slowly — but it set the wheels in motion.

The most important changes brought about by the Investiture Conflict, however, were on the ground: the political landscape in both Italy and Germany was irrevocably transformed. In Germany, the princes consolidated their lands and their positions at the expense of royal power. In Italy, the emperor lost power to the cities. The northern and central Italian communes were formed in the crucible of the war between the pope and the emperor. In fierce communal struggles, city factions, often created by local grievances but claiming to fight on behalf of the papal or the imperial cause, created their own governing bodies. In the course of the twelfth century, these Italian cities became accustomed to self-government.

The Sweep of Reform

Church reform involved much more than the clash of popes, emperors, and their supporters. It penetrated into the daily lives of ordinary Christians. It inspired new ways to think about church institutions such as the sacraments, brought about a new systemization of church law, changed the way the papacy operated, inspired new monastic orders dedicated to poverty, and led to the crusades.

The **sacraments** were, in the Catholic church's terminology, the regular means by which God's heavenly grace infused mundane existence. They included rites such as baptism, the Eucharist (holy communion), and marriage. But this did not mean that Christians were clear about how many sacraments there were, how they worked, or even what their significance was. Eleventh-century church reformers began the process — which would continue into the thirteenth century — of emphasizing the importance of the sacraments and the special nature of the priest, whose chief role was to administer them.

Marriage, for example, became a sacrament only after the Gregorian reform. Before the twelfth century, priests had little to do with weddings, which were family affairs. After the twelfth century, however, priests were expected to consecrate marriages. Churchmen also began to assume jurisdiction over marital disputes, not simply in cases involving royalty (as they had always done) but also in those involving lesser aristocrats. The clergy's prohibition of marriage partners as distant as seventh cousins (since marriage between cousins was considered incest) had the potential to control dynastic alliances.

At the same time, churchmen began to stress the sanctity of marriage. Hugh of St. Victor, a twelfth-century scholar, dwelled on the sacramental meaning of marriage:

> Can you find anything else in marriage except conjugal society which makes it sacred and by which you can assert that it is holy? . . . Each shall be to the other as a same self in all sincere love, all careful solicitude, every kindness of affection, in constant compassion, unflagging consolation, and faithful devotedness.

In other words, Hugh saw marriage as a matter of Christian love.

The reformers also proclaimed the special importance of the sacrament of the Eucharist, received by eating the wafer (the body of Christ) and drinking wine (the blood

of Christ) during the Mass. Gregory VII called the Mass "the greatest thing in the Christian religion." No layman, regardless of how powerful, and no woman of any class or status at all could perform anything equal to it, for the Mass was the key to salvation.

The new emphasis on the more thoroughly and carefully defined sacraments, along with the desire to set priests clearly apart from the laity, led to vigorous enforcement of an old element of church discipline: the celibacy of priests. The demand for a celibate clergy had far-reaching significance for the history of the church. It distanced western clerics even further from their eastern Orthodox counterparts (who did not practice celibacy), exacerbating the east–west church schism of 1054. It also broke with local practices in places where clerical marriage was customary.

Undaunted, the reformers persisted, and in 1123 the pope proclaimed all clerical marriages invalid. With its new power, the papacy was largely able to enforce the rule.

What were the foundations of this new power? Some of it came from the consolidation and imposition of canon, or church, law. These laws had begun simply as rules determined at church councils. Later they were supplemented with papal declarations. Churchmen had made several attempts to gather together and organize these laws before the eleventh century. But the proliferation of rules during that century, along with the desire of Gregory's followers to clarify church law as they saw it, made a systematic collection of rules even more necessary. Around 1140, a teacher of canon law named Gratian achieved this goal with a landmark synthesis, the *Decretum*. Collecting nearly two thousand passages from the decrees of popes and councils as well as the writings of the church fathers, Gratian intended to demonstrate their essential agreement. In fact, his book's original title was *Harmony of Discordant Canons*. If he found any discord in his sources, Gratian usually imposed the harmony himself by arguing that the passages dealt with different situations. A bit later, another legal scholar revised and expanded the *Decretum,* adding ancient Roman law to the mix.

Even while Gratian was writing, the papal curia (government), centered in Rome, resembled a court of law with its own collection agency. In the course of the eleventh and twelfth centuries, the papacy developed a bureaucracy to hear cases, such as disputed elections of bishops. Churchmen went to the papal curia for other purposes as well: to petition for privileges for their monasteries or to be consecrated by the pope. All these services were expensive, requiring lawyers, judges, hearing officers, notaries, and collectors. The lands owned by the papacy were not sufficient to support the growing cost of its administrative apparatus, so the petitioners and litigants themselves had to pay. The pope, with his law courts, bureaucracy, and financial apparatus, had become a monarch.

New Monastic Orders of Poverty

Like the popes, the monks of Cluny and other Benedictine monasteries were reformers. Unlike the popes, they spent nearly their entire day in large and magnificently outfitted churches singing a long and complex liturgy consisting of Masses, prayers, and psalms. These "black monks" — so called because they dyed their robes black — reached the height of their popularity in the eleventh century. Their monasteries often housed

Cluny (twelfth century)
The church of the monastery of Cluny, built under the abbot Hugh (who appears with Matilda on page 317) was the largest and grandest in all of Christendom in the twelfth century. In its cavernous stone building, the sounds of the liturgy echoed throughout the day. Unfortunately, much of the church was torn down after the French Revolution in 1789. The depiction here is an image of the interior that relies on the best archaeological insights combined with computer-enhanced technologies. (Major Ecclésia © on-situ / Arts et Métiers ParisTech / Centre des Monuments Nationaux — 2010.)

hundreds of monks, though convents for Benedictine nuns were usually less populated. Cluny was one of the largest monasteries, with some four hundred brothers in the mid-eleventh century.

In the twelfth century, the black monks' lifestyle came under attack by groups seeking a religious life of poverty. They considered the opulence of a huge and gorgeous monastery like Cluny to be a sign of greed rather than honor. The Carthusian order founded by Bruno of Cologne in the 1080s was one such group. Each monk took a vow of silence and lived as a hermit in his own small hut. Monks occasionally joined others for prayer in a common prayer room, or oratory. When not engaged in prayer or meditation, the Carthusians copied manuscripts. They considered this task part of their religious vocation, a way to preach God's word with their hands rather than their mouths. The Carthusian order grew slowly. Each monastery was limited to only twelve monks, the number of the Apostles.

The Cistercians, by contrast, expanded rapidly. Their guiding spirit was **St. Bernard** (c. 1090–1153), who arrived at the Burgundian monastery of Cîteaux (in Latin, Cistercium, hence the name of the monks) in 1112 along with about thirty friends and relatives. St. Bernard soon became abbot of Clairvaux, one of a cluster of Cistercian monasteries in Burgundy. By the mid-twelfth century, more than three hundred monasteries spread throughout Europe were following what they took to be the customs of Cîteaux. Nuns, too — as eager as monks to live the life of simplicity and poverty that they believed the Apostles had enjoyed and endured — adopted Cistercian customs. By the end of the twelfth century, the Cistercians were an order: all of their houses followed rules determined at the General Chapter, a meeting at which the abbots met to hammer out legislation.

Although they held up the rule of St. Benedict as the foundation of their monastic life, the Cistercians created a lifestyle all their own, largely governed by the goal of simplicity. Rejecting even the conceit of blackening their robes, they left them undyed (hence their nickname, the "white monks"). Cistercian monasteries were remarkably standardized. As shown in Figure 10.1, there were two halves to each monastery: the eastern half was for the monks, and the western half was for the lay brothers. The lay brothers did the hard manual labor necessary to keep the other monks — the "choir" monks — free to worship.

Cistercian churches reflected the order's emphasis on poverty. The churches were small, made of smoothly hewn, undecorated stone. Wall paintings and sculpture were prohibited. Their buildings cultivated a quiet beauty. Cistercian churches like the one at Le Thoronet (see the illustration on page 322) were bright, cool, and serene.

The white monks dedicated themselves to monastic administration as well as to private prayer and contemplation. Each house had large and highly organized farms and grazing lands called granges. Cistercian monks spent much of their time managing their estates and flocks, both of which were yielding handsome profits by the end

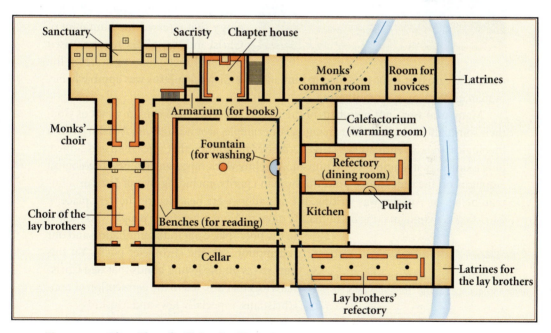

Figure 10.1 Floor Plan of a Cistercian Monastery

Cistercian monasteries seldom deviated much from this standard plan, which perfectly suited their dual nature — one half for the lay brothers, who worked in the fields, the other half for the monks, who performed the devotions. This plan shows the first floor. Above were the dormitories. The lay brothers slept above their cellar and refectory, the monks above their chapter house, common room, and room for novices. No one had a private bedroom, just as the rule of St. Benedict prescribed. (Adapted from Wolfgang Braunfels, *Monasteries of Western Europe* [Princeton, NJ: Princeton University Press, 1972], 75.)

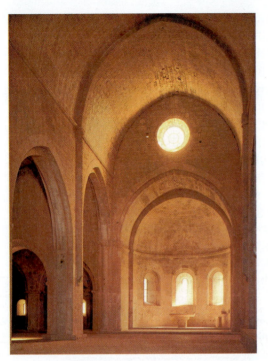

Le Thoronet

Le Thoronet, a Cistercian monastery founded in 1136, boasted a small and plain church devoid of any wall paintings, ornaments, or sculpture. Nothing was to interfere with the contemplative inner lives of the monks worshipping there. (Giraudon / The Bridgeman Art Library International.)

of the twelfth century. Although they had reacted against the wealth of the commercial revolution, the Cistercians became part of it, and managerial expertise was an integral part of their monastic life.

At the same time, the Cistercians emphasized a spirituality of intense emotion. They cultivated a theology that stressed the humanity of Christ and Mary. They regularly used maternal metaphors to describe the nurturing care that Jesus provided to humans. The Cistercian Jesus was approachable, human, protective, even mothering.

Many who were not members of the Cistercian order held similar views of God; their spirituality signaled wider changes. For example, around 1099, St. Anselm wrote a theological treatise entitled *Why God Became Man,* arguing that since man had sinned, only a sinless man could redeem him. St. Anselm's work represented a new theological emphasis on the redemptive power of human charity, including that of Jesus as a human being. As Anselm was writing, the crusaders were heading for the very place of Christ's crucifixion, making his humanity more real and powerful to people who walked in the holy "place of God's humiliation and our redemption," as one chronicler put it. Yet this new stress on the loving bonds that tied Christians together also led to the persecution of non-Christians, especially Jews and Muslims.

REVIEW QUESTION What were the causes and consequences of the Gregorian reform?

The Crusades

The crusades were the culmination of two separate historical movements: pilgrimages and holy wars. Like pilgrimages to the Holy Land, the place where Jesus had lived and died, the crusades drew on a long tradition of making pious voyages to sacred shrines to petition for help or cure. The relics of Jesus's crucifixion in Jerusalem, and even the region around it, attracted pilgrims long before the First Crusade was called in 1095.

As holy wars blessed by church leaders, the crusades had a prehistory. The Truce of God, begun in the late tenth century, depended on knights ready to go to battle to uphold it. The Normans' war against Sicily had the pope's approval. Already, as we have seen, the battle of 1063 in the reconquista of Spain was fought with a papal indulgence.

European crusaders established states in the Middle East that lasted for two hundred years. A tiny strip of crusader states along the eastern Mediterranean survived — perilously — until 1291.

Calling the Crusade

The events leading to the First Crusade began with the entry of the Seljuk Turks into Asia Minor (Map 10.1). As noted in Chapter 9, the Muslim world had splintered into numerous small states during the 900s. Weakened by disunity, those states were easy prey for the fierce Seljuk Turks — Sunni Muslims inspired by religious zeal to take over

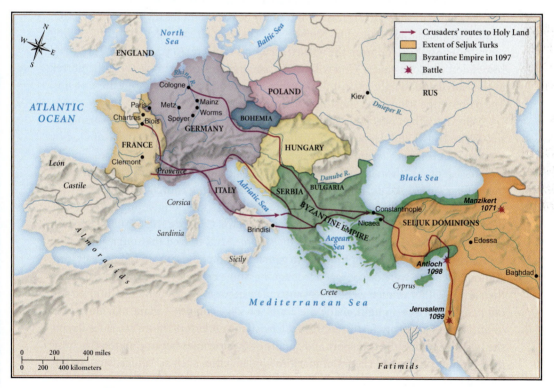

Map 10.1 The First Crusade, 1096–1099

The First Crusade was a major military undertaking that required organization, movement over both land and sea, and enormous resources. Four main groups were responsible for the conquest of Jerusalem. One began at Cologne, in northern Germany; a second group started out from Blois, in France; the third originated just to the west of Provence; and the fourth launched ships from Brindisi, at the heel of Italy. All joined up at Constantinople, where their leaders negotiated with Alexius Comnenus for help and supplies in return for a pledge of vassalage to the emperor.

both Islamic and infidel (unbeliever) regions. By the 1050s, the Seljuks had captured Baghdad, subjugated the Abbasid caliphate, and begun to threaten Byzantium.

The difficulties the Byzantine emperor Romanus IV had in pulling together an army to attack the Turks reveal how weak his position had become. Unable to muster Byzantine troops — which either were busy defending their own districts or were under the control of *dynatoi* (see page 273) wary of sending support to the emperor — Romanus had to rely on a mercenary army made up of Normans, Franks, Slavs, and even Turks. This motley force met the Seljuks at Manzikert in what is today eastern Turkey. The battle was a disaster for Romanus: the Seljuks routed the Byzantine army and captured the emperor. The battle of Manzikert (1071) marked the end of Byzantine domination in the region.

Gradually settling in Asia Minor, the Turks extended their control across the empire and beyond, all the way to Jerusalem, which had been under Muslim control since the seventh century and most recently had been under the rule of the Shi'ite Fatimids. In 1095, the Byzantine emperor **Alexius I (Alexius Comnenus)** (r. 1081–1118) appealed for help to Pope Urban II, hoping to get new mercenary troops for a fresh offensive.

Urban II (r. 1088–1099) chose to interpret the request in his own way. At a church council in Clermont (France) in 1095 he addressed an already excited throng, telling them to "wrest that land from the wicked race, and subject it to yourselves." The crowd responded with one voice: "God wills it." Urban offered all who made the difficult trek to the Holy Land to fight against the Muslims an indulgence — the forgiveness of sins. The pains of the trip would substitute for ordinary penance.

Why did Urban make this call to arms? Certainly he hoped to win Christian control of the Holy Land. He was also anxious to fulfill the goals of the Truce of God by turning the crowd at Clermont into a peace militia dedicated to holy purposes. Finally, Urban's call placed the papacy in a new position of leadership, one that complemented in a military arena the position the popes had gained in the church hierarchy.

Inspired by local preachers, men and women, rich and poor, young and old, laypeople and clerics heeded Urban's call to go on the **First Crusade** (1096–1099). Between 60,000 and 100,000 people abandoned their homes and braved the rough journey to Jerusalem. They went to fight for God, to gain land and plunder, or to follow their lord. Although women were discouraged from going, some crusaders were accompanied by their wives. Other women went as servants; a few may have been fighters. Children and old people, not able to fight, made the cords for siege engines — giant machines used to hurl stones at enemy fortifications. As Christians undertook more crusades during the twelfth century, the transport and supply of these armies became a lucrative business for the commercial classes of maritime Italian cities such as Venice, strategically located on the route eastward.

The First Crusade

The armies of the First Crusade were organized not as one military force but rather as separate militias each commanded by a different individual authorized by the pope. There were also irregular armies. Some of these, not heeding the pope's official depar-

Statuette of a Crusader
This statuette, perhaps made by the Normans in southern Italy,
shows a crusader in his war gear — a coat of mail, a helmet, a
lozenge-shaped shield strapped to his left shoulder, a sword,
and a heavy lance held at the ready under his right arm.
(Réunion des Musées Nationaux / Art Resource, NY.)

ture date in August, left early. Historians call these
loosely affiliated groups the People's (or Peasants')
Crusade. Some of the participants were peasants,
others knights. Inspired by the charismatic
orator Peter the Hermit and others
like him, they took off for the Holy
Land via the Rhineland. This unlikely
route was no mistake: the crusaders
wanted to kill Jews, who, like the Muslims, did not accept Christ's divinity.
By 1095, three cities of the Rhineland —
Speyer, Worms, and Mainz — had especially large and flourishing Jewish populations with long-established relationships
with the local bishops.

The People's Crusade — joined by local nobles, knights, and townspeople — vented
its fury against the Jews of the Rhineland. As one commentator put it, the crusaders
considered it ridiculous to attack Muslims when other infidels lived in their own backyards: "That's doing our work backward." The Rhineland Jews had to choose between
conversion or death. Many Jews in Speyer found refuge in the bishop's castle, but at
Worms and Mainz hundreds were massacred. Similar pogroms — systematic persecutions of Jews — took place a half century later, when the preaching of the Second Crusade led to new attacks on the Jews.

After they had vented their fury in the Rhineland, some members of the People's
Crusade dropped out. The rest continued through Hungary to Constantinople, where
Alexius Comnenus promptly shipped them to Asia Minor, where most of them died. In
the autumn, the main armies of the crusaders began to arrive, their leaders squabbling
with Alexius from the start.

Considering them too weak to bother with, the Turks spared the arriving crusaders,
who made their way south to the Seljuk capital at Nicaea. At first, their armies were uncoordinated and their food supplies uncertain, but soon the crusaders organized themselves. They managed to defeat a Turkish army that attacked from nearby; then, surrounding Nicaea and besieging it with catapults and other war machines, they took the
city on June 18, 1097.

Most of the crusaders then went toward Antioch, which stood in the way of their
conquest of Jerusalem, but one led his followers to Edessa, where they took over the city

and its outlying area, creating the first of the crusader states. Meanwhile, the main body of crusaders took Antioch after a long stalemate. From there, it was only a short march to Jerusalem. Quarrels among Muslim rulers eased the way. In early June 1099, a large force of crusaders amassed before the walls of Jerusalem; in mid-July, they attacked, breaching the walls and entering the city. "Now that our men had possession of the walls and towers, wonderful sights were to be seen," wrote Raymond d'Aguiliers, a priest serving one of the crusade leaders. "Some of our men (and this was the more merciful) cut off the heads of their enemies; others shot them with arrows, so that they fell from the towers; others tortured them longer by casting them into the flames."

The Crusader States

The main objective of the First Crusade — to wrest the Holy Land from the Muslims and subject it to Christian rule — had now been accomplished. The leaders of the expedition did not give the conquered territories to Alexius but held on to them instead. By 1109, they had carved out several tiny states in the Holy Land.

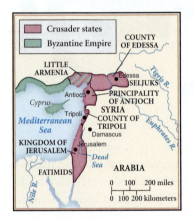

The Crusader States in 1109

Because the crusader states were created by conquest, they were treated as lordships. The rulers granted fiefs to their vassals, and some of these in turn gave portions of their holdings as fiefs to their own vassals. Since most Europeans went home after the First Crusade, the rulers who remained learned to coexist with the indigenous population, which included Muslims, Jews, and Greek Orthodox Christians. They encouraged a lively trade at their ports.

The main concerns of these rulers were military. They set up castles and recruited knights from Europe. So organized for war was this society that it produced a new and militant kind of monasticism: the Knights Templar. The Templars vowed themselves to poverty and chastity. But unlike monks, the Templars, whose name came from their living quarters in the area of the former Jewish Temple at Jerusalem, devoted themselves to warfare. Their first mission — to protect the pilgrimage routes from Palestine to Jerusalem — soon diversified. They manned the town garrisons of the crusader states, and they transported money from Europe to the Holy Land. In this way, the Order of the Templars became enormously wealthy (even though individual monks owned nothing), with branch "banks" in major cities across Europe.

The Disastrous Second Crusade

The presence of the Knights Templar did not prevent the Seljuks from taking the county of Edessa in 1144. This was the beginning of the slow but steady shrinking of the crusader states. It sparked the Second Crusade (1147–1149), which attracted, for the first time, ruling monarchs to the cause: Louis VII of France and Emperor Conrad III in Ger-

many. (The First Crusade had been led by counts and dukes.) St. Bernard, the charismatic and influential Cistercian abbot, was its tireless preacher.

Little organization or planning went into the Second Crusade. The emperor at Byzantium was hardly involved. Louis VII and Conrad had no coordinated strategy. A chronicler of the crusade wryly remarked, "Those whose common will had undertaken a common task should also use a common plan of action." All the armies were badly hurt by Turkish attacks. Furthermore, they largely acted at cross-purposes with the Christian rulers still in the Holy Land.

At last the leaders met at Acre (today in Israel) and agreed to storm Damascus, which was under Muslim control and a thorn in the side of the Christian king of Jerusalem. On July 24, 1148, they were on the city's outskirts, but, encountering a stiff defense, they abandoned the attack after five days, suffering many losses as they retreated. The crusade was over.

The Second Crusade had one decisive outcome: it led Louis VII to divorce his wife, Eleanor, the heiress of Aquitaine. He was disappointed that she had provided him with a daughter but no son, and he suspected her of infidelity. After the pope "dissolved" their marriage — that is, found it to have been uncanonical in the first place — Eleanor promptly married Henry, count of Anjou and duke of Normandy. This marriage had far-reaching consequences, as we shall see, when Henry became King Henry II of England in 1154.

The Long-Term Impact of the Crusades

The success of the First Crusade was a mirage. The European toehold in the Middle East could not last. Numerous new crusades were called, and eight major ones took place between the first in 1096 and the last at the end of the thirteenth century. But most Europeans were not willing to commit the vast resources and personnel that would have been necessary to maintain the crusader states, which fell to the Muslims permanently in 1291. In Europe, the crusades to the Holy Land became a sort of myth — an elusive goal that receded before more pressing ventures nearer to home. Yet they inspired far-flung expeditions like Columbus's in 1492. Although the crusades stimulated trade a bit, especially enhancing the prosperity of Italian cities like Venice, the commercial revolution would have happened without them. On the other hand, modern taxation systems may well have been stimulated by the machinery of revenue collection used to finance the crusades.

In the Middle East, the crusades worsened — but did not cause — Islamic disunity. Before the crusades, Muslims had a complex relationship with the Christians in their midst — taxing but not persecuting them, allowing their churches to stand and be used, permitting pilgrims into Jerusalem to visit the holy sites of Christ's life and death. In many ways, the split between Shi'ite and Sunni Muslims was more serious than the rift between Muslims and Christians. The crusades, and especially the conquest of Jerusalem, shocked and dismayed Muslims: "We have mingled blood with flowing tears," wrote one of their poets, "and there is no room left in us for pity."

REVIEW QUESTION How and why was the First Crusade a success, and how and why was it a failure?

The Revival of Monarchies

Even as the papacy was exercising its authority by annulling marriages and calling crusades, most kings and other rulers were enhancing and consolidating their own power. They created new ideologies and dusted off old theories to justify their hegemony (dominating influence), they hired officials to work for them, and they found vassals and churchmen to support them. Money gave them greater effectiveness, and the new commercial economy supplied them with increased revenues. The exception was the emperor in Germany, who was weakened by the Investiture Conflict.

Reconstructing the Empire at Byzantium

Ten years after the disastrous battle at Manzikert, Alexius Comnenus became the Byzantine emperor. He was an upstart — from a family of dynatoi — who saw the opportunity to seize the throne in a time of crisis. The people of Constantinople were suffering under a combination of high taxes and rising living costs. In addition, the empire was under attack on every side — from Normans in southern Italy, Seljuk Turks in Asia Minor, and new groups in the Balkans. However, the emperor managed to avert the worst dangers.

To wage all the wars he had to fight, Alexius relied on mercenaries and allied dynatoi, armed and mounted like European knights and accompanied by their own troops. In return for their services, he gave these nobles lifetime possession of large imperial estates and their dependent peasants. Meanwhile, Alexius satisfied the urban elite by granting them new offices. He normally got on well with the patriarch and Byzantine clergy, for emperor and church depended on each other to suppress heresy and foster orthodoxy. The emperors of the Comnenian dynasty (1081–1185) thus gained in prestige and military might, but at the price of significant concessions to the nobility.

England under Norman Rule

In the twelfth century, the kings of England were the most powerful monarchs of Europe, in large part because they ruled their whole kingdom by right of conquest. When the Anglo-Saxon king Edward the Confessor (r. 1042–1066) died childless in 1066, three main contenders vied for the English throne: Harold, earl of Wessex, an Englishman close to the king but not of royal blood; Harald Hardrada, the king of Norway, who had unsuccessfully attempted to conquer the Danes and now turned hopefully to England; and William, duke of Normandy, who claimed that Edward had promised him the throne fifteen years earlier. On his deathbed, Edward had named Harold of Wessex to succeed him, and a royal advisory committee that had the right to choose the king had confirmed the nomination. When he learned that Harold had been anointed and crowned, William (1027–1087) prepared for battle. Appealing to the pope, he received the banner of St. Peter and with this symbol of God's approval launched the invasion of England, filling his ships with warriors recruited from many parts of France. Just before William's inva-

sion force landed, Harold defeated Harald Hardrada at Stamford Bridge, near York, in the north of England. When he heard of William's arrival, Harold turned his forces south, marching them 250 miles and picking up new soldiers along the way to meet the Normans.

The two armies clashed at the **battle of Hastings** on October 14, 1066, in one of history's rare decisive battles. Most of Harold's men were on foot, armed with battle-axes and stones tied to sticks, which could be thrown with great force. William's army consisted of perhaps three thousand mounted knights, a thousand archers, and the rest infantry. At first William's knights broke rank, frightened by the deadly battle-axes thrown by the English; but then some of the English also broke rank as they pursued the knights. Gradually Harold's troops were worn down, particularly by William's archers, whose arrows flew a hundred yards, much farther than an Englishman could throw his battle-ax. (Some of the archers are depicted on the lower margin of the Bayeux "Tapestry," page 330.) By dusk, King Harold was dead and his army defeated.

Norman Conquest of England, 1066

Some Anglo-Saxons in England supported William. But William — known to posterity as William the Conqueror — wanted to replace, not assimilate, the Anglo-Saxons. During William's reign, families from the European continent almost totally supplanted the English aristocracy. Although the English peasantry remained — now with new lords — many of them "perished . . . by famine or the sword," as William confessed on his deathbed. Modern historians estimate that one out of five people in England died as a result of the Norman conquest and its immediate aftermath.

Yet, although the Normans destroyed a generation of English men and women, they preserved and extended many Anglo-Saxon institutions. For example, the new kings retained the old administrative divisions and legal system of the shires. At the same time, they drew from continental institutions. They set up a political hierarchy, culminating in the king, whose strength was reinforced by his castles. Because all of England was the king's by conquest, he could treat it as his booty; William kept about 20 percent of the land for himself and divided the rest, distributing it in large but scattered fiefs to a relatively small number of his barons and family members, lay and ecclesiastical, as well as to some lesser men. In turn, these fief-holders maintained their own vassals; they owed the king military service — and the service of a fixed number of their vassals — along with certain dues, such as reliefs (money paid upon inheriting a fief) and aids (payments made on important occasions).

Bayeux "Tapestry" (detail)
This famous "tapestry" is misnamed; it is really an embroidery, 230 feet long and 20 inches wide, created to tell the story of the Norman conquest of England from William's point of view. In this detail, the Norman archers are lined up along the lower margin, in a band below the armies. In the central band, the English warriors are on foot (the one at the farthest right holds a long battle-ax), while the Norman knights are on horseback. Who seems to be winning? (Detail of the Bayeux Tapestry — eleventh century. By special permission of the City of Bayeux.)

In addition to these revenues from the nobles, the king of England made sure that he would get his share from the peasantry. In 1086, William ordered a survey and census of England, popularly called Domesday because, like the reckoning Christians expected at doomsday, it provided facts that could not be appealed. It was the most extensive inventory of land, livestock, taxes, and population that had ever been compiled in Europe. The king's men consulted Anglo-Saxon tax lists and took testimony from local men. From these inquests, scribes drew up reports, which were then summarized in Domesday itself. (See "Taking Measure," page 331.)

William was not just the ruler of England; he was also duke of Normandy. The Norman conquest tied England to the languages, politics, institutions, and culture of the European continent. English commerce was linked to the wool industry in Flanders. St. Anselm, the archbishop of Canterbury and author of *Why God Became Man,* was born in Italy and served as the abbot of a monastery in Normandy before crossing the Channel to England. Modern English is an amalgam of Anglo-Saxon and Norman French.

The barons of England retained their estates in Normandy and elsewhere, and the kings of England often spent more time on the continent than they did on the island. When William's son Henry I (r. 1100–1135) died without male heirs, civil war soon erupted: the throne of England was fought over by two French counts, one married to Henry's daughter, the other to his sister. The story of England after 1066 was, in miniature, the story of Europe.

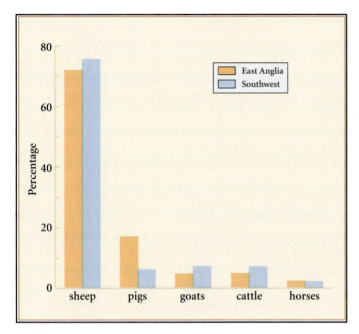

Taking Measure
English Livestock in 1086
Domesday provided important data for the English king in 1086, and those data remain important for historians today. Although relatively few Domesday records discuss livestock — apart from the oxen that pulled the plows — documents from East Anglia and the southwest are exceptions to this rule. They show that the great preponderance of animals raised was sheep. These were grazed on the marshes of both regions. Apart from milk and meat, sheep provided wool. It is no wonder that England soon became the great exporter of raw wool to textile manufacturers in Flanders.
(Robert Bartlett, *England under the Norman and Angevin Kings, 1075–1225* [Oxford: Clarendon Press, 2000], Fig. 7, 306.)

Praising the King of France

The twelfth-century kings of France were much less obviously powerful than their English and Byzantine counterparts. Yet they, too, took part in the monarchical revival. Louis VI, called Louis the Fat (r. 1108–1137), was a tireless defender of royal power. We know a good deal about him and his reputation because a contemporary and close associate, Suger (1081–1152), abbot of Saint-Denis, wrote Louis's biography.

Although a churchman, Suger was a propagandist for his king. When Louis set about consolidating his rule in the Île-de-France, Suger portrayed him as a righteous hero. He thought that the king had rights over the French nobles because they were his vassals. He believed that the king had a religious role as the protector of the church and the poor. To be sure, the Gregorian reform had made its mark: Suger did not claim that Louis was the head of the church. But he nevertheless emphasized the royal dignity and its importance to the papacy. He stressed Louis's piety and active defense of the faith.

When Louis VI died in 1137, Suger's notion of the might and right of the king of France reflected reality in an extremely small area. Nevertheless, Louis laid the groundwork for the gradual extension of royal power in France. As the lord of vassals, the king could call on his men to aid him in times of war, though the most powerful among them sometimes disregarded the summons. As a king and landlord, he could obtain many dues and taxes. He drew revenues from Paris, a thriving city not only of commerce but also of scholarship. Officials called provosts enforced his royal laws and collected taxes. With money and land, Louis dispensed the favors and gave the gifts that added to his prestige and his power. Louis VI and Suger together created the territorial core and royal ideal of the future French monarchy.

Surviving as Emperor

Henry IV lost much of the power over the church and over Italy that his father had wielded. The Investiture Conflict meant that he could no longer control the church hierarchy in Germany and northern Italy, nor could he depend on bishops to work as government officials. The German princes rebelled against him, and the cities of northern Italy found ways to declare their independence of him.

The Concordat of Worms (1122) conceded considerable power within the church to the king, but said nothing about the ruler's relations with the German princes or the Italian cities. When Henry V (r. 1105–1125) died childless, the position of the emperor was extremely uncertain.

When a German king died childless, the great bishops and princes would meet together to elect the next emperor. In 1125, numerous candidates were put forward; the winner, Lothar III (r. 1125–1137), was chosen largely because he was *not* the person designated by Henry V. Lothar had little time to reestablish royal control before he, too, died childless, leaving the princes to elect Conrad III. It was Conrad's nephew, Frederick Barbarossa, who would have a chance to find new sources of imperial power in a post-Gregorian age.

REVIEW QUESTION Which ruler—Alexius Comnenus, William the Conqueror, or Louis VI— was the strongest, which the feeblest, and why?

Conclusion

The commercial revolution and the building boom it spurred profoundly changed Europe. New trade, wealth, and business institutions became common in its thriving cities. Merchants and artisans became important. Mutual and fraternal organizations like the guilds and communes expressed and reinforced the solidarity and economic interests of city dwellers. The countryside became reorganized for the market.

Sensitized by the commercial revolution to the corrupting effects of money and inspired by the model of Cluny, which seemed to "free the church from the world," reformers began to demand a new and purified church. Under Pope Gregory VII, the reform asserted a new vision of the church with the pope at the top. But many people— especially rulers—depended on the old system. Henry IV was particularly affected; for him the Gregorian reform meant war. The Investiture Conflict, though officially ended by a compromise, in fact greatly enhanced the power of the papacy and weakened that of the emperor.

The First Crusade was both cause and effect of the pope's new power. But the crusades were not just papal projects. They were fueled by enormous popular piety as well as by the ambitions of European rulers. They resulted in a ribbon of crusader states along the eastern Mediterranean.

Apart from the emperor, rulers in the period after the Investiture Conflict gained new prestige and, with the wealth of the commercial revolution, the ability to hire civil servants and impose their will as never before. The Norman ruler of England is a good

Mapping the West Europe and the Mediterranean, c. 1150
A comparison with Mapping the West on page 300 reveals the major changes wrought during the century 1050–1150. England was politically tied to the continent with the Norman invasion of 1066. Soon the Seljuk Turks settled most of Anatolia, and the eastern wing of Byzantium was tightly wedged around Constantinople. At the end of the eleventh century, a narrow ribbon of crusader states was set up in the Holy Land. Meanwhile, Sicily and southern Italy came under Norman rule.

example of the new-style king; William the Conqueror was interested not only in waging war but also in setting up the most efficient possible taxation system in times of peace. The successes of these rulers signaled a new era: the flowering of the Middle Ages.

Review Questions

1. What new institutions resulted from the commercial revolution?
2. What were the causes and consequences of the Gregorian reform?
3. How and why was the First Crusade a success, and how and why was it a failure?
4. Which ruler — Alexius Comnenus, William the Conqueror, or Louis VI — was the strongest, which the feeblest, and why?

Making Connections

1. What were the similarities — and what were the differences — between the powers wielded by the Carolingian kings and those wielded by twelfth-century rulers?

2. In what ways was the movement for church reform a consequence of the commercial revolution?

3. How may the First Crusade be understood as a consequence of the Gregorian reform?

- For practice quizzes and other study tools, visit the **Online Study Guide** at bedfordstmartins.com/huntconcise.

- For primary-source material from this period, see *Sources of the Making of the West*, Fourth Edition.

- For Web sites, images, and documents related to topics in this chapter, visit *Make History* at bedfordstmartins.com/huntconcise.

Suggested References

Lopez was the first to recognize the importance of the commercial revolution, and Little makes crucial connections between the new commerce and religious reform. Miller's running narrative and primary sources provide the best introduction to the Investiture Conflict and its aftermath. Asbridge offers a vivid account of the crusades, while Nicholson gives a quick overview along with primary sources. Fuhrmann, Hallam, and Huscroft cover the new western monarchies well, while Waley takes up the Italian republics.

Asbridge, Thomas. *The Crusades: The Authoritative History of the War for the Holy Land.* 2010.

*Bayeux Tapestry: http://www.bayeuxtapestry.org.uk/Index.htm

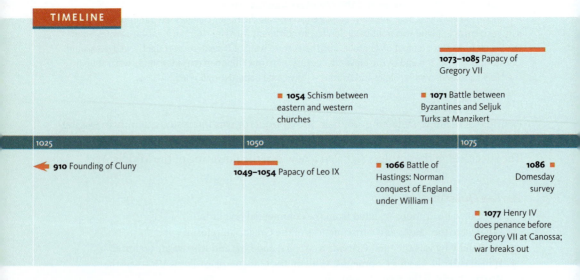

TIMELINE

1073–1085 Papacy of Gregory VII

1054 Schism between eastern and western churches

1071 Battle between Byzantines and Seljuk Turks at Manzikert

1025   1050   1075

910 Founding of Cluny

1049–1054 Papacy of Leo IX

1066 Battle of Hastings: Norman conquest of England under William I

1086 Domesday survey

1077 Henry IV does penance before Gregory VII at Canossa; war breaks out

Clanchy, Michael. *From Memory to Written Record: England 1066–1307*. 3rd ed. 2006.

Fuhrmann, Horst. *Germany in the High Middle Ages, c. 1050–1200*. 2002.

Hallam, Elizabeth M., and Judith Everard. *Capetian France, 987–1328*. 2nd ed. 2001.

Huscroft, Richard. *The Norman Conquest: A New Introduction*. 2009.

Little, Lester K. *Religious Poverty and the Profit Economy in Medieval Europe*. 1978.

Lopez, Robert S. *The Commercial Revolution of the Middle Ages, 950–1350*. 1976.

* ——, and Irving W. Raymond. *Medieval Trade in the Mediterranean World*. 1955.

*Miller, Maureen C. *Power and the Holy in the Age of the Investiture Conflict*. 2005.

Moore, Robert I. *The First European Revolution, c. 970–1215*. 2000.

Morris, Colin. *The Papal Monarchy: The Western Church from 1050 to 1250*. 1989.

Nicholson, Helen. *The Crusades*. 2004.

*Peters, Edward, ed. *The First Crusade: The Chronicle of Fulcher of Chartres and Other Source Materials*. 1971.

*Suger. *The Deeds of Louis the Fat*. Trans. Richard C. Cusimano and John Moorhead. 1992.

Tyerman, Christopher. *God's War: A New History of the Crusades*. 2006.

Waley, Daniel. *The Italian City-Republics*. 1969.

*Primary source.

■ **1097** Establishment of commune at Milan

■ **1095** Council of Clermont; Pope Urban II calls First Crusade

■ **1109** Establishment of crusader states

■ **1122** Concordat of Worms ends Investiture Conflict

■ **c. 1140** Gratian's *Decretum* published

1100   1125   1150

1096–1099 First Crusade

1108–1137 Reign of Louis VI

1147–1149 Second Crusade

Testament figures flanking its western portals were meant to prefigure the kings of France; they demonstrate the extraordinary importance of powerful princes in this period, when monarchies and principalities ceased to be the personal creation of each ruler and became permanent institutions, with professional bureaucratic staffs. The outpouring of popular support that culminated in the building of the cathedral is evidence of a vibrant vernacular (non-Latin-speaking) culture, which expressed itself not only in stone but in literature as well. Finally, the emphasis at Chartres on the divine wisdom echoes the age's fervor about Christian truths, a zeal that led to the creation of new religious movements even as it stoked the fires of intolerance.

CHAPTER FOCUS What tied together the cultural and political achievements of the late twelfth century?

New Schools and Churches

Key to the flowering of the Middle Ages was a new emphasis on learning and a new form of church architecture termed Gothic. In many ways, these developments laid the foundation for other trends of the period. The schools trained men to staff new bureaucracies and at the same time fed religious fervor. The Gothic style gave luster to its rich patrons, the increasingly powerful rulers of the time, who gave needed support both to the schools and to the architects who produced the style.

The New Learning and the Rise of the University

Since the Carolingian period schools had been connected to monasteries and cathedrals, where they trained men to become either monks or priests. Some schools were better endowed with books and masters (or teachers) than others; a few developed a reputation for a certain kind of theological approach or specialized in a particular branch of learning, such as literature, medicine, or law. By the end of the eleventh century, the best schools were generally in the cathedrals of the larger cities: Reims, Paris, and Montpellier in France, and Bologna in Italy.

Finding these schools both exciting and practical, eager students flocked to them. Teachers were forced to search out larger halls to accommodate the crush. Some set up shop by renting a room. If a teacher could prove his mettle in the classroom, he had no trouble finding paying students.

Because schools hitherto had been the training grounds for clergymen, all students were considered clerics, whether or not they had been ordained. Using Latin, Europe's common language, students could drift from, say, Italy and Spain to France and England, wherever a noted master had settled. Students joined crusaders, pilgrims, and merchants to make the roads of Europe crowded indeed as the consolidation of castellanies, counties, and kingdoms made violence against travelers less frequent. Markets, taverns, and lodgings sprang up in urban centers to serve the needs of transients.

What the students sought, above all, was knowledge of the seven liberal arts. Grammar, rhetoric, and logic (or dialectic) belonged to the beginning arts, the so-called

11

The Flowering of the Middle Ages

1150–1215

I N 1194 A RAGING FIRE BURNED most of the town of Chartres, in France — including its cathedral. Worried citizens feared that their most prized relic, the sacred tunic worn by the Virgin Mary when Christ was born, had gone up in flames as well. Had the Virgin abandoned the town? Suddenly the bishop and his clerics emerged from the cathedral crypt carrying the sacred tunic, which had remained unharmed. They took it as a sign that the Virgin had not only *not* abandoned her city but also wanted a new and more magnificent cathedral to house her relic. The town dedicated itself to the task; the bishop, his clerics, and the town guilds all gave generously to pay for stonecutters, carvers, glaziers, countless other workmen, and a master builder. Donations poured in from the counts, dukes, and even the king of France. The new cathedral was finished in twenty-six years — a very short time in an age when such churches usually took a century or more to build. Its vault soared 116 feet high; its length stretched more than 100 yards. Its western portals, which had been spared the flames, retained the sculptural decoration — carved around 1150 — of the old church: three doorways surrounded and surmounted by figures that demonstrated the close relationship between the truths of divine wisdom, the French royal house, and the seven liberal arts — grammar, rhetoric, logic, arithmetic, geometry, music, and astronomy. The rest of the church was built in a new style: Gothic.

Chartres Cathedral
Rebuilt after a fire in 1194, the cathedral of Chartres reconciled old and new. The three doorways of its west end (shown here) were remnants of the former church. But they were crowned by a rose window, a form newly in vogue. (Neil Setchfield / The Art Archive at Art Resource, NY.)

The rebuilt cathedral at Chartres sums up in stone the key features that characterized the period 1150–1215 and would mark the rest of the Middle Ages. Its Gothic style — with its high vault, flying buttresses, and enormous stained-glass windows — became the quintessential style of medieval architecture. The celebration of the liberal arts on one of its doorways mirrored the new schools that flourished in the twelfth century and culminated in the universities of the thirteenth. The twenty-four statues of Old

Testament figures flanking its western portals were meant to prefigure the kings of France; they demonstrate the extraordinary importance of powerful princes in this period, when monarchies and principalities ceased to be the personal creation of each ruler and became permanent institutions, with professional bureaucratic staffs. The outpouring of popular support that culminated in the building of the cathedral is evidence of a vibrant vernacular (non-Latin-speaking) culture, which expressed itself not only in stone but in literature as well. Finally, the emphasis at Chartres on the divine wisdom echoes the age's fervor about Christian truths, a zeal that led to the creation of new religious movements even as it stoked the fires of intolerance.

CHAPTER FOCUS What tied together the cultural and political achievements of the late twelfth century?

New Schools and Churches

Key to the flowering of the Middle Ages was a new emphasis on learning and a new form of church architecture termed Gothic. In many ways, these developments laid the foundation for other trends of the period. The schools trained men to staff new bureaucracies and at the same time fed religious fervor. The Gothic style gave luster to its rich patrons, the increasingly powerful rulers of the time, who gave needed support both to the schools and to the architects who produced the style.

The New Learning and the Rise of the University

Since the Carolingian period schools had been connected to monasteries and cathedrals, where they trained men to become either monks or priests. Some schools were better endowed with books and masters (or teachers) than others; a few developed a reputation for a certain kind of theological approach or specialized in a particular branch of learning, such as literature, medicine, or law. By the end of the eleventh century, the best schools were generally in the cathedrals of the larger cities: Reims, Paris, and Montpellier in France, and Bologna in Italy.

Finding these schools both exciting and practical, eager students flocked to them. Teachers were forced to search out larger halls to accommodate the crush. Some set up shop by renting a room. If a teacher could prove his mettle in the classroom, he had no trouble finding paying students.

Because schools hitherto had been the training grounds for clergymen, all students were considered clerics, whether or not they had been ordained. Using Latin, Europe's common language, students could drift from, say, Italy and Spain to France and England, wherever a noted master had settled. Students joined crusaders, pilgrims, and merchants to make the roads of Europe crowded indeed as the consolidation of castellanies, counties, and kingdoms made violence against travelers less frequent. Markets, taverns, and lodgings sprang up in urban centers to serve the needs of transients.

What the students sought, above all, was knowledge of the seven liberal arts. Grammar, rhetoric, and logic (or dialectic) belonged to the beginning arts, the so-called

Clanchy, Michael. *From Memory to Written Record: England 1066–1307*. 3rd ed. 2006.

Fuhrmann, Horst. *Germany in the High Middle Ages, c. 1050–1200*. 2002.

Hallam, Elizabeth M., and Judith Everard. *Capetian France, 987–1328*. 2nd ed. 2001.

Huscroft, Richard. *The Norman Conquest: A New Introduction*. 2009.

Little, Lester K. *Religious Poverty and the Profit Economy in Medieval Europe*. 1978.

Lopez, Robert S. *The Commercial Revolution of the Middle Ages, 950–1350*. 1976.

* ———, and Irving W. Raymond. *Medieval Trade in the Mediterranean World*. 1955.

*Miller, Maureen C. *Power and the Holy in the Age of the Investiture Conflict*. 2005.

Moore, Robert I. *The First European Revolution, c. 970–1215*. 2000.

Morris, Colin. *The Papal Monarchy: The Western Church from 1050 to 1250*. 1989.

Nicholson, Helen. *The Crusades*. 2004.

*Peters, Edward, ed. *The First Crusade: The Chronicle of Fulcher of Chartres and Other Source Materials*.
     1971.

*Suger. *The Deeds of Louis the Fat*. Trans. Richard C. Cusimano and John Moorhead. 1992.

Tyerman, Christopher. *God's War: A New History of the Crusades*. 2006.

Waley, Daniel. *The Italian City-Republics*. 1969.

*Primary source.

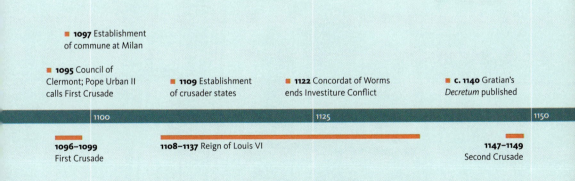

1097 Establishment
of commune at Milan

1095 Council of
Clermont; Pope Urban II
calls First Crusade

1109 Establishment
of crusader states

1122 Concordat of Worms
ends Investiture Conflict

c. 1140 Gratian's
Decretum published

1100

1125

1150

1096–1099
First Crusade

1108–1137 Reign of Louis VI

1147–1149
Second Crusade

trivium. Logic, involving the technical analysis of texts as well as the application and manipulation of mental constructs, was a transitional subject leading to the second part of the liberal arts, the quadrivium. This comprised four areas of study that we might call theoretical math and science: arithmetic, geometry, music (theory), and astronomy. Of all these arts, logic appealed the most to twelfth-century students. Medieval students and masters were convinced that logic could order and clarify every issue, even questions about the nature of God.

After studying the trivium, students went on to schools of medicine, theology, or law. Paris was renowned for theology, Montpellier for medicine, and Bologna for law. All of these schools trained men for jobs. The law schools, for example, taught men who would later serve popes, bishops, kings, princes, and communes. Scholars interested in the quadrivium tended to pursue those studies outside the normal school curriculum, and few gained their living through such pursuits. With books expensive and hard to find, lectures were the chief method of communication. Students committed the lectures to memory.

The remarkable renewal of scholarship in the twelfth century had an unexpected benefit: we know a great deal about the men involved in it — and a few of the women — because they wrote so much, often about themselves. Three important figures may serve to typify the scholars of the period: Abelard and Heloise, who were early examples of the new learning; and Peter the Chanter, the product of a slightly later period.

Although Peter Abelard (1079–1142) was expected to become a lord and warrior, he gave up his inheritance to become one of the twelfth century's greatest thinkers. In his autobiographical account, *The Story of My Misfortunes,* Abelard described how he first studied with one of the best-known teachers of his day in Paris. Soon he began to lecture and to gather students of his own. Around 1122–1123, he composed a textbook for his students, *Sic et Non* (*Yes and No*). It consisted of opposing positions on 156 subjects, among them "That God is one and the contrary" and "That all are permitted to marry and the contrary." Abelard arrayed passages from the Bible, the church fathers, and other authorities on both sides of each question. The juxtaposition of such sources was nothing new; what was new was calling attention to their contradictions. Abelard's students loved the challenge: they were eager to find the origins of the quotes, consider the context of each one carefully, and seek to reconcile the opposing sides by using the tools of logic.*

Abelard's fame as a teacher was such that a Parisian cleric named Fulbert gave Abelard room and board and engaged him as tutor for his niece, Heloise (c. 1100–c. 1163/1164). Brought up under Fulbert's guardianship, Heloise had been sent as a young girl to a convent school, where she received a thorough literary education. Her uncle hoped

---

*Abelard's students did not yet have the sophisticated rules of logic that had been worked out by the ancient philosopher Aristotle (see page 113). Until the middle of the twelfth century, very little of Aristotle's work was available in Europe because it had not been translated from Greek into Latin. By the end of the century, however, that situation had been rectified by translators who traveled to cities such as Córdoba in Spain and Syracuse in Sicily, where they found Islamic scholars who had already translated Aristotle's Greek into Arabic and could help them translate from Arabic to Latin.

to continue her education at home by hiring Abelard. Abelard, however, became Heloise's lover as well as her tutor. "Our desires left no stage of love-making untried," wrote Abelard in his *Misfortunes.*

At first their love affair was secret. But Heloise became pregnant, and Abelard insisted they marry. They did so clandestinely to prevent damaging Abelard's career, for the new emphasis on clerical celibacy meant that Abelard's professional success and prestige would have been compromised if news of his marriage were made public. After they were married, Heloise and Abelard rarely saw one another; Abelard's sister took in their child. Fulbert, suspecting that Abelard had abandoned his niece, plotted a cruel revenge against him: he paid a servant to castrate Abelard. Soon after, Abelard and Heloise entered separate monasteries.

For Heloise, separation from Abelard was a lasting blow. Although she became a successful abbess, carefully tending to the physical and spiritual needs of her nuns, she continued to call on Abelard for "renewal of strength." In a series of letters addressed to him, she poured out her feelings as "his handmaid, or rather his daughter, wife, or rather sister."

For Abelard, however, the loss of Heloise and even his castration were not the worst disasters of his life. The heaviest blow came later, and it was directed at his intellect. He wrote a book that applied "human and logical reasons" (as he put it) to the Trinity; the book was condemned at the Council of Soissons in 1121, and he was forced to throw it, page by page, into the flames. Bitterly weeping at the injustice, Abelard lamented, "This open violence had come upon me only because of the purity of my intentions and love of our Faith, which had compelled me to write."

By the second half of the twelfth century, masters like Abelard had become far more common. Many of them taught in Paris. Peter the Chanter (d. 1197) was one of the most influential and prolific. He studied at the cathedral school at Reims and was given the honorary title of chanter of Notre Dame in Paris in 1183. The chant, as we shall see, consisted of the music and words of the church liturgy. But Peter had his underlings work with the choir singers; he himself was far more interested in lecturing, disputing, and preaching.

Peter's lectures followed the pattern established by other masters. The lecture began with the recitation of a passage from an important text. The master then explained the text, giving his comments. He then "disputed" — mentioning other explanations and refuting them, often drawing on the logic of Aristotle, which by Peter's time was fully available. Sometimes masters held public debates on their interpretations.

Peter chose to comment on biblical texts. There were many ways to interpret the Bible. Some commentators chose to talk about it as an allegory; others preferred to stress its literal meaning. Peter was interested in the morals it taught. While most theology masters commented on just the Psalms and the New Testament, Peter taught all the books of the Bible. He wrote two important treatises and was particularly interested in exploring social issues and the sacrament of penance.

Peter also took the fruits of his classroom experience to the public. His sermons have not survived, but he inspired a whole group of men to preach in and around Paris. One

of his protégés, for example, was renowned for turning prostitutes, usurers, and immoral clerics from their sinful ways.

Around 1200, the pope wrote to the masters of theology, church law, and the liberal arts at Paris. He called them a *universitas* — the Latin word for a corporation or guild. The pope was right: universities were guilds. Like guilds, they had apprentices (students) and masters (schoolmasters). They issued rules to cover their trade (the acquisition and dissemination of knowledge). They had provisions for disciplining, testing, and housing students and regulated the masters in similar detail. For example, masters at the University of Paris were required to wear long black gowns, follow a particular order in their lectures, and set the standards by which students could become masters themselves. The University of Bologna was unique in having two guilds, one of students and one of masters. At Bologna, the students participated in the appointment of masters and paid their salaries.

University curricula differed in content and duration. At the University of Paris in the early thirteenth century, for example, a student had to spend at least six years studying the liberal arts before he could begin to teach. If he wanted to continue his studies with theology, he had to attend lectures on the subject for at least another five years.

Because masters and students were considered clerics, and clerics were male, it meant that women could be neither students nor masters. And because clerics were subject to church courts only, no secular jurisdiction, whether town courts or lords, could touch those who attended the university. For example, in 1200 the king of France promised that "neither our provost nor our judges shall lay hands on a student [at the University of Paris] for any offense whatever." Another king declared that in his territories — Germany and northern Italy — "no one shall be so rash as to venture to inflict any injury on scholars."

The combination of clerical status and special privileges made universities virtually self-governing corporations within the towns. This sometimes led to friction. For example, when a student at Oxford was suspected of killing his mistress and the townspeople tried to punish him, the masters protested by refusing to teach and leaving town. Incidents such as this explain why historians speak of the hostility between "town" and "gown." Yet, as in our own time, university towns depended on scholars to patronize local restaurants, shops, and hostels. Town and gown normally learned to negotiate with each other to their mutual advantage.

Architectural Style: From Romanesque to Gothic

While Peter the Chanter lectured at Notre Dame, the cathedral itself was going up around him — in Gothic style. This was a new architectural style, associated at first with the Île-de-France and the Capetian kings of France. Elsewhere the reigning style was Romanesque. But in the course of the thirteenth century Gothic style took much of Europe by storm, and by the fourteenth it was the quintessential cathedral style.

Romanesque is the term art historians use to describe the massive church buildings of eleventh-century monasteries like Cluny. Heavy, serious, and solid, Romanesque

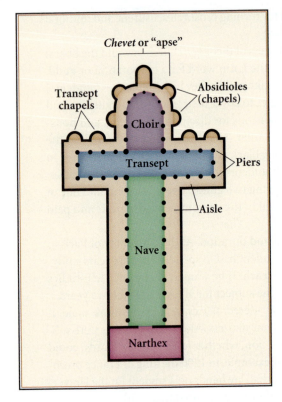

Figure 11.1 Floor Plan of a Romanesque Church

As churchgoers entered a Romanesque church, they passed through the narthex, an anteroom decorated with sculptures depicting scenes from the Bible. Walking through the portal of the narthex, they entered the church's nave, at the east end of which — just after the crossing of the transept and in front of the choir — was the altar. Walking down the nave, they passed tall, massive piers leading up to the vault (the ceiling) of the nave. Each of these piers was decorated with sculpture, and the walls were brightly painted. Romanesque churches were both lively and colorful (because of their decoration) and solemn and somber (because of their heavy stones and massive scale).

churches were decorated with brightly colored wall paintings and sculpture. The various parts of the church — the chapels in the *chevet,* or apse (the east end), for example — were handled as discrete units, with the forms of cubes, cones, and cylinders (Figure 11.1). Inventive sculptural reliefs, both inside and outside the church, enlivened the geometrical forms. Emotional and sometimes frenzied, Romanesque sculpture depicted themes ranging from the beauty of Eve to the horrors of the Last Judgment. (See the frieze depicting Dives and Lazarus on page 304 for an example.)

Romanesque churches were above all houses for prayer, which was neither silent nor private. The musical style for prayer was called plainchant, or Gregorian chant. Monks sang plainchant melodies in unison and without instrumental accompaniment. Rhythmically free and lacking a regular beat, plainchant's melodies ranged from extremely simple to highly ornate and embellished. By the twelfth century, a large repertoire of melodies had grown up, at first composed and transmitted orally and then, starting in the ninth century, using written notation. Echoing within the stone walls and the cavernous choirs, plainchant worked well in a Romanesque church.

Gothic architecture, to the contrary, was a style of the cities, reflecting the self-confidence and wealth of merchants, guildspeople, bishops, and kings.* Usually a cathedral — the bishop's principal church — rather than a monastic church, the Gothic church was the religious, social, and commercial focal point of a city. The style, popular from the twelfth to the fifteenth centuries, was characterized by pointed arches, ribbed vaults, and stained-glass windows. The arches began as architectural motifs but were

*Gothic is a modern term, originally meant to denigrate the style's "barbarity" but now used admiringly.

Saint-Savin-sur-Gartempe

In this view down the nave of a French monastic church built in the late eleventh century, all the elements of Romanesque architecture are visible: a "tunnel" vault, here decorated with scenes from the Bible; round arches; and relatively small windows. Romanesque churches impress by their sober solidity, which is, however, often enlivened by decorative carving above the pillars and paintings, either on the vault (as here) or on the walls. (Giraudon / The Bridgeman Art Library International.)

Bourges

The cathedral (a bishops' church) of Bourges, built about a century after Saint-Savin-sur-Gartempe, illustrates all the elements of a Gothic church: a multistory elevation made to seem even higher by pointed arches; a ribbed, pointed-arch vault; and (taking the place of walls) large lancet windows filled with stained glass. The vault was supported not by walls but by flying buttresses on the church's exterior. (Scala / Art Resource, NY.)

soon adopted in every art form. Flying buttresses permitted much of the wall to be cut away and the open spaces to be filled with glass. Soaring above the west, north, south, and often east ends of many Gothic churches is a rose window: a large round window shaped like a flower. Gothic churches appealed to the senses the way that Peter the Chanter's lectures and disputations appealed to human logic and reason: both were

Sant'Andrea
The church of Sant'Andrea at Vercelli suggests that Italian church architects and patrons adopted what they liked of French Gothic, particularly its pointed arches, while remaining uninterested in soaring heights and grand stained-glass windows. The real interest of the interior of Sant'Andrea is its inventive and lively use of contrasting light and dark stone. (Scala / Art Resource, NY.)

designed to lead people to knowledge that touched the divine. The atmosphere of a Gothic church was a foretaste of heaven.

The style had its beginnings around 1135, with the project of Abbot Suger, the close associate of King Louis the Fat of France (see page 331), to remodel portions of the church of Saint-Denis. Suger's rebuilding was part of the fruitful melding of royal and ecclesiastical interests and ideals in the north of France. At the west end of his church, the place where the faithful entered, Suger decorated the portals with figures of Old Testament kings, queens, and patriarchs, signaling the links between the present king and his illustrious predecessors. At the eastern end, behind the altar, Suger used pointed arches and stained glass to let in light, which Suger believed would transport the worshipper from the "slime of earth" to the "purity of Heaven." Suger said that the father of lights, God himself, "illuminated" the minds of the beholders through the light that filtered through the stained-glass windows.

By the mid-thirteenth century, Gothic architecture had spread from France to other European countries. The style varied by region, most dramatically in Italy. At Sant'Andrea in Vercelli, for example, there are only two stories, and light filters in from small windows. Yet with its pointed arches and ribbed vaulting, Sant'Andrea is considered a Gothic church. At its east end is a rose window.

REVIEW QUESTION What was new about education and church architecture in the twelfth and early thirteenth centuries?

Governments as Institutions

Around the same time that architects, workers, patrons, theologians, and city dwellers were coming together to produce Gothic cathedrals, rulership was becoming institutionalized. By the end of the twelfth century, western Europeans for the first time spoke

of their rulers not as kings of a people (for example, the king of the Franks) but as kings of a territory (for example, the king of France). This new designation reflected an important change in medieval rulership. However strong earlier rulers had been, their political power had been personal (depending on ties of kinship, friendship, and vassalage) rather than territorial (touching all who lived within the borders of their state). Renewed interest in Roman law, a product of the schools, served as a foundation for strong, central rule. Money allowed kings to hire salaried professionals — talented, literate officials, many of whom had been schooled in the new universities cropping up across Europe — to carry out the new ideology. The process of state building had begun.

In England, the governmental system was institutionalized early, with royal officials administering both law and revenues. In other regions, such as France and Germany, bureaucratic administration did not develop that far. In eastern Europe, it hardly existed at all. At Byzantium, the bureaucracy that had long been in place frayed badly, leaving the state open to conquest by western crusaders.

England: Unity through Common Law

In the mid-twelfth century, the government of England was by far the most institutionalized in Europe. The king hardly needed to be present: royal government functioned smoothly without him, since officials handled all the administrative matters and record keeping. The very circumstances of the English king favored the growth of an administrative staff — the king's frequent travels to and from the European continent meant that officials needed to work in his absence, and his enormous wealth meant that he could afford them.

Henry II (r. 1154–1189) was the driving force in extending and strengthening the institutions of English government. He took the throne in the wake of a terrible civil war (1139–1153) between two royal claimants. The chaos had benefited the English barons and high churchmen, who gained new privileges and powers as the monarch's authority waned. Newly built private castles, already familiar on the continent, now appeared in England as symbols of the rising power of the English barons. But when Henry was crowned king of England, ushering in the Angevin (from Anjou) dynasty there, he reversed the trend.*

Even beyond England, Henry had enormous power. His marriage to Eleanor of Aquitaine in 1152, after her marriage to Louis VII of France was annulled, brought the enormous inheritance of the duchy of Aquitaine to the English crown. Although Henry was technically the vassal of the king of France for his continental lands, he effectively ruled a territory that stretched from England to southern France (Map 11.1).

Eleanor gave Henry not only an enormous inheritance but also the sons he needed to maintain his dynasty. He gave her much less. As queen of France, Eleanor had enjoyed

---

*Henry's father, Geoffrey of Anjou, was nicknamed "Plantagenet," from the *genet*, a shrub he liked. Historians sometimes use the name to refer to the entire dynasty, so Henry II was the first Plantagenet as well as the first Angevin king of England.

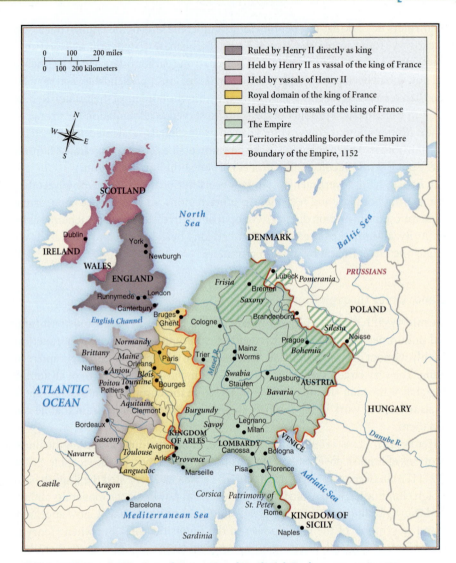

Map 11.1 Europe in the Age of Henry II and Frederick Barbarossa, 1150–1190
The second half of the twelfth century was dominated by two men, King Henry II and Emperor Frederick Barbarossa. Of the two, Frederick seemed to control more land, but this was deceptive. Although he was emperor, he had great difficulty ruling the territory that was theoretically part of the Empire. Frederick's base was in central Germany, and even there he had to contend with powerful vassals. Henry II's territory was more compact but also more surely under his control.

an important position: she disputed with St. Bernard, the Cistercian abbot who was the most renowned churchman of the day, and when she accompanied Louis on the Second Crusade, she brought more troops than he did. Of independent mind, she determined to separate from Louis even before he considered leaving her. But with Henry, she lost much of her power, for he dominated her just as he came to dominate his barons. Turning

Eleanor and Henry Nothing about their side-by-side tombs suggests the stormy relationship of Eleanor of Aquitaine and King Henry II of England. Their effigies, carved of limestone and walnut, suggest peace and piety. How does Eleanor's book help project this image? What do you suppose she is reading? The placement of the

couple's tombs also attests to their religious fervor: they were buried in the powerful monastery of Fontevraud, a "double monastery" that housed (in separate quarters) both monks and nuns. An abbess presided over all. (Hervé Champollion / © Cephas Picture Library / Alamy.)

to her offspring in 1173, Eleanor, disguised as a man, tried to join her eldest son, Henry the Younger, in a plot against his father. But the rebellion was put down, and she spent most of her years thereafter, until her husband's death in 1189, confined under guard at Winchester Castle. (In death, however, she gained dignity, with her tomb next to Henry's.)

As soon as Henry II became king of England, he destroyed or confiscated the new castles and regained crown land. Then he proceeded to extend monarchical power, above all by imposing royal justice. His judicial reforms built on an already well-developed legal system. The Anglo-Saxon kings had royal district courts: the king appointed sheriffs to police the shires, muster military levies, and haul criminals into court. The Norman kings retained these courts and had the right to summon large landowners in the shire to attend them. To these established institutions, Henry II added a system of judicial visitations called eyres (from the Latin *iter,* "journey"). Under this system, royal justices made regular trips to every locality in England to judge those accused of murder, arson, or rape — all defined as crimes against the "king's peace." The justices summoned representatives of the knightly class to meet and either give the sheriff the names of those suspected of committing crimes in the vicinity or arrest the suspects themselves and hand them over to the royal justices.

During the eyres, the justices also heard cases between individuals, today called civil cases. Free men and women (that is, people of the knightly class or above) could bring their disputes over such matters as inheritance, dowries, and property claims to the king's justices. Earlier courts had generally relied on duels between litigants to determine verdicts. Henry's new system offered a different option, an inquest under royal supervision.

The new system of **common law** — law that applied to all of England — was praised for its efficiency, speed, and conclusiveness in a twelfth-century legal treatise known

The Murder of Thomas Becket
Almost immediately after King Henry II's knights murdered Archbishop Thomas Becket in his church at Canterbury, Becket was viewed as a martyr. In this early depiction of the event, one of the murderers knocks off Becket's cap, while another hits the arm of Becket's supporter, who holds the bishop's cross-staff. (British Library, London, UK / © British Library Board. All Rights Reserved. / The Bridgeman Art Library International.)

as *Glanvill* (after its presumed author). *Glanvill* might have added that the king also speedily gained a large treasury. The exchequer, as the financial bureau of England was called, recorded all the fines paid for judgments and the sums collected for writs. The amounts, entered on parchment sewn together and stored as rolls, became the Receipt Rolls and Pipe Rolls, the first of many such records of the English monarchy and an indication that writing had become a mechanism for institutionalizing royal power in England.

The stiffest opposition to Henry's extension of royal courts came from the church, where a separate system of trial and punishment had long been available to the clergy and to others who enjoyed church protection. The punishments for crimes meted out by church courts were generally quite mild. Protective of their special status, churchmen refused to submit to the jurisdiction of Henry's courts. Henry insisted, and the ensuing contest between Henry II and his archbishop, Thomas Becket (1118–1170), became the greatest battle between the church and the state in the twelfth century. The conflict simmered for six years, with Becket refusing to allow "criminous clerics" — clergy suspected of committing a crime — to come before royal courts. Then Henry's henchmen murdered Thomas, right in his own cathedral. The desecration unintentionally turned Becket into a martyr. Henry was forced by a general public outcry to do penance for the deed. In the end, both church and royal courts expanded to address the concerns of an increasingly litigious society.

In England, Henry II made the king's presence felt everywhere through his system of traveling royal courts. On the continent, he maintained his position through a combination of war and negotiation. He bequeathed to his sons Richard I (r. 1189–1199) and John (r. 1199–1216) an omnipresent and wealthy monarchy. Its omnipresence derived largely from its eyre system of justice and its administrative apparatus. Its wealth

came from court fees, income from numerous royal estates both in England and on the continent, taxes from cities, and customary feudal dues (reliefs and aids) collected from barons and knights. Enriched by the commercial economy of the late twelfth century, the English kings encouraged their knights and barons not to serve them personally in battle but, in lieu of service, to pay the king a tax called scutage. The monarchs preferred to hire mercenaries both as troops to fight external enemies and as police to enforce the king's will at home.

Richard I, known as the Lion-Hearted, went on the Third Crusade the very year he was crowned. On his way home, he was captured and held for ransom by political enemies for a long time; he died soon thereafter while defending his possessions on the continent. His successor, John, lived longer but gained no admiring epithet. In fact, he presided over the whittling away of the English empire. In 1204, the king of France confiscated the northern French territories held by John. Between 1204 and 1214, John did everything he could to add to the crown revenues so that he could pay for an army to win back the territories. He forced his vassals to pay ever-increasing scutages, and he extorted money in the form of new feudal dues. He compelled the widows of his vassals either to marry men of his choosing or to pay him a hefty fee. Despite John's heavy investment in the war, his army was defeated in 1214 at the battle of Bouvines. The defeat caused discontented English barons to rebel openly against the king. At Runnymede in June 1215, John was forced to agree to the charter of baronial liberties that has come to be called **Magna Carta** ("Great Charter").

The English barons intended Magna Carta to be a conservative document defining the "customary" obligations and rights of the nobility and forbidding the king to break from these customs without consulting his barons. It maintained that all free men in the land had certain rights that the king was obligated to uphold. In this way, Magna Carta implied that the king was not above the law. In time, as the definition of *free men* expanded to include all the king's subjects, Magna Carta came to be seen as a guarantee of the rights of Englishmen (and eventually Englishwomen) in general.

France: Consolidation and Conquest

John's territorial loss was the gain of the French king **Philip II (Philip Augustus)** (r. 1180–1223). When Philip came to the throne, the royal domain, the Île-de-France, was sandwiched between territory controlled by the counts of Flanders, Champagne, and Anjou. King Henry II and the counts of Flanders and Champagne vied to control the young king. Philip, however, quickly learned to play the three rulers off one another. Contemporaries were astounded when Philip successfully gained territory: he wrested land from Flanders in the 1190s and then, as we have seen, he took Normandy, Anjou, Maine, the Touraine, and Poitou from King John of England in 1204. No wonder he was given the epithet *Augustus,* after the first Roman emperor.

After Philip's army confirmed its triumph over most of John's continental territories in 1214, the French monarch could boast that he was the richest and most powerful

**The Consolidation of France
under Philip Augustus, 1180–1223**

ruler in France. Most important, Philip had sufficient support and resources to keep a tight hold on Normandy.* He received homage and fealty from most of the Norman aristocracy, and his officers carried out their work there in accordance with Norman customs.

Wherever he ruled, Philip instituted new administrative practices. Before Philip's day, most French royal arrangements were committed to memory rather than to writing. If decrees were recorded at all, they were saved by the recipient, not by the government. The king did keep some documents, which he generally carried with him in his travels like personal possessions. But in 1194, in a battle with the king of England, Philip lost his meager cache of documents along with much treasure when he had to abandon his baggage train. After 1194, the king had all his decrees written down, and he established permanent repositories in which to keep them.

Like the English king, Philip relied largely on members of the lesser nobility — knights and clerics, many of whom were masters educated in the city schools of France. They served as officers of his court, tax collectors, and overseers of the royal estates, making the king's power felt locally as never before.

Germany: The Revived Monarchy of Frederick Barbarossa

Theoretically, Henry V and his successors were kings of Germany and Italy, and at Rome they received the crown and title of emperor from the popes as well. But the Investiture Conflict (see page 316) reduced their power and authority. Meanwhile, the German princes strengthened their position, enjoying near independence as they built castles on their properties and established control over whole territories. When they elected a new king, the princes made sure that he would give them new lands and powers. The German kings were in a difficult position: they had to balance the many conflicting interests of their royal and imperial offices, their families, and the German princes, and they had to contend with the increasing power of the papacy and the Italian communes. All this prevented the consolidation of power under a strong German monarch during the first half of the twelfth century.

During the Investiture Conflict, the two sides (imperial and papal) were represented by two noble families. Leading the imperial party were the Staufer, or Hohenstaufen, clan; opposing them were the Welfs. (Two later Italian factions, the Ghibellines and the Guelphs, corresponded, respectively, to the Hohenstaufens and the Welfs.) The enmity

---

*Philip was particularly successful in imposing royal control in Normandy; later French kings gave most of the other territories conquered by Philip to various members of the royal family.

between these families was legendary, and warfare between the groups raged long after the Concordat of Worms in 1122. Decades of constant battles exhausted all parties, who began to long for peace. In an act of rare unanimity, they elected **Frederick I (Barbarossa)**. In Frederick (r. 1152–1190) they seemed to have a candidate who could end the strife: his mother was a Welf, his father a Staufer. Contemporary accounts of the king's career represented Frederick in the image of Christ as the cornerstone that joined two houses and reconciled enemies.

Frederick's very appearance impressed his contemporaries — the name *Barbarossa* referred to his red-blond hair and beard. But beyond appearances, Frederick impressed those around him by what they called his firmness. He affirmed royal rights, even when he handed out duchies and allowed others to name bishops, because in return for these political powers Frederick required the princes to concede formally and publicly that they held their rights and territories from him as their lord. By making them his vassals, although with nearly royal rights within their principalities, Frederick defined the princes' subordinate relationship to the German king.

As the king of Germany, Frederick had the traditional right to claim the imperial crown. When, in 1155, he marched to Rome to be crowned emperor, the fledgling commune there protested that it alone had the right to give him the crown. Frederick interrupted them, asserting that the glory of Rome, together with its crown, came to him by right of conquest. He was equally insistent with the pope, who wrote to tell him that Rome belonged to St. Peter. Frederick replied that his imperial title gave him rights over the city. In part, Frederick was influenced by the revival of Roman law — the laws of Theodosius and Justinian — that was taking place in the schools of Italy. In part, too, he was convinced of the sacred — not just secular — origins of the imperial office. Frederick called his empire *sacer* ("sacred"), asserting that it was in its own way as precious, worthwhile, and God-given as the church.

Frederick buttressed this high view of his imperial right with worldly power. He married Beatrice of Burgundy, whose vast estates in Burgundy and Provence enabled him to establish a powerful political and territorial base centered in Swabia (today southwestern Germany). From Swabia, Frederick looked south to Italy, with its wealthy cities. Swabia and northern Italy together could give Frederick a compact and centrally located territory.

Nevertheless, Frederick's ambitions in Italy were problematic. Since the Investiture Conflict, the emperor had ruled Italy in name only. The communes of the northern cities guarded their liberties jealously, while the pope considered Italy his own sphere of influence. Frederick's territorial base just north of Italy threatened those interests (Map 11.1, page 346).

Despite the opposition of the cities and the pope, Frederick was determined to conquer northern Italy, which he managed to do by 1158. Adopting an Italian solution for governing the communes — appointing outsiders as magistrates — Frederick appointed his own men to these powerful positions. But that was where Frederick made a mistake. He chose German officials who lacked a sense of Italian communal traditions. Their heavy hand created enormous resentment. By 1167, most of the cities of northern Italy

Frederick Barbarossa
In this image of Frederick, made during his lifetime, the emperor is dressed as a crusader, and the inscription tells him to fight the Muslims. The small figure on the right is the abbot of the Monastery of Schäftlarn, who gives Frederick a book that contains an account of the First Crusade. (HIP / Art Resource, NY.)

had joined with the pope to form the Lombard League against Frederick. Defeated by the league at the battle of Legnano in 1176, Frederick made peace and withdrew most of his forces from Italy. The battle marked the triumph of the cities over the crown in Italy, which would not have a centralized government until the nineteenth century; its political history would instead be that of its various regions and their dominant cities.

Frederick was the victim of traditions that were rapidly becoming outmoded. He based much of his rule in Germany on the bond of lord and vassal at the very moment when rulers elsewhere were relying less on such personal ties and more on salaried officials. He lived up to the meaning of *emperor,* with all its obligations to rule Rome and northern Italy, when other leaders were consolidating their territorial rule bit by bit. In addition, as "universal" emperor, he did not recognize the importance of local pride, language, customs, and traditions; he tried to rule Italian communes with his own men from Germany, and he failed.

Frederick also had problems in Germany, where he had to contend with princes of near-royal status who acted as independent rulers of their principalities, though acknowledging Frederick as their feudal lord. One of the most powerful was Henry the Lion (c. 1130–1195), who was duke of Saxony and Bavaria, which gave him important bases in both the north and the south of Germany. A confident and aggressive ruler, Henry dominated his territory by investing bishops (usurping the role of the emperor as outlined in the Concordat of Worms), collecting dues from his estates, and exercising judicial rights over his territories. Henry also actively extended his rule, especially in Slavic regions, pushing northeast past the Elbe River to reestablish dioceses and to build the commercial city of Lübeck (today in northern Germany). He

was lord of many vassals and ministerials (people of unfree status but high prestige). He organized a staff of clerics and ministerials to collect taxes and tolls and to write up his legal acts.

Yet like kings, princes could fall. Henry's growing power so threatened other princes and even Frederick that in 1179 Frederick called Henry to the king's court for violating the peace. When Henry chose not to appear, Frederick exercised his authority as Henry's lord and charged him with violating his duty as a vassal. Because Henry refused the summons to court and avoided serving his lord in Italy, Frederick condemned him, confiscated his holdings, and drove him out of Germany.

However, successfully challenging one recalcitrant prince/vassal meant negotiating costly deals with the others, since their support was vital. Frederick wanted to retain Henry's duchy for himself, as Philip Augustus had managed to do with Normandy. But Frederick was not powerful enough to do so and was forced to divide and distribute it to the supporters he had relied on to enforce his decrees against Henry.

Eastern Europe and Byzantium: Fragmenting Realms

The importance of governmental and bureaucratic institutions such as those developed in England and France is made especially clear by comparing the experience of regions where they were not established. In eastern Europe, the characteristic pattern was for states to form under the leadership of one great ruler and then to fragment under his successor. For example, King Béla III of Hungary (r. 1172–1196) built up a state that looked superficially like a western European kingdom. He married a French princess, sent his officials to Paris to be educated, and built his palace in the French Romanesque style. The annual income from his estates, tolls, dues, and taxes equaled that of the richest western monarchs. But Béla did not set up enduring governmental institutions, and in the decades that followed his death, wars between his sons splintered his monarchical holdings, and aristocratic supporters divided the wealth.

Rus underwent a similar process. Although twelfth-century Kiev was politically fragmented, autocratic princes to the north constructed Vladimir (also known as Suzdalia), the nucleus of the later Muscovite state. Within the clearly defined borders of this principality, well-to-do towns prospered and monasteries and churches flourished; one chronicler wrote that "all lands trembled at the name [of its ruler]." Yet early in the thirteenth century this nascent state began to crumble as princely claimants fought one another for power, much as Béla's sons had done in Hungary. Soon Rus would be conquered by the Mongols (see page 389).

Although the Byzantine Empire was already a consolidated bureaucratic state, after the mid-twelfth century it gradually began to show weaknesses. Traders from the west — the Venetians especially — dominated its commerce. The Byzantine emperors who ruled during the last half of the twelfth century downgraded the old civil servants, elevated imperial relatives to high offices, and favored the military elite, who nevertheless rarely came to the aid of the emperor. As Byzantine rule grew more personal and European rule became more bureaucratic, the two gradually became more alike.

The Byzantine Empire might well have continued like this for a long time. Instead, its heart was knocked out by the warriors of the Fourth Crusade (1202–1204). At the instigation of Venice, the crusaders made a detour to Constantinople on their way to the Holy Land, capturing the city in 1204. Although one of the crusade leaders was named "emperor" and ruled in Constantinople and its surrounding territory, the Byzantine Empire itself continued to exist, though disunited and weak. It retook Constantinople in 1261, but it never regained the power that it had had in the eleventh century.

REVIEW QUESTION What new sources and institutions of power became available to rulers in the second half of the twelfth century?

The Growth of a Vernacular High Culture

With their consolidation of territory, wealth, and power in the last half of the twelfth century, kings, barons, princes, and their wives and daughters supported new kinds of literature and music. For the first time on the continent, though long true in England, poems and songs were written in the vernacular, the spoken language, rather than in Latin. Meant to be read or sung aloud, sometimes with accompanying musical instruments, they celebrated nobles' lives and provided a common experience for aristocrats at court. Patrons and patronesses in the cities of Italy and in the more isolated courts of northern Europe spent the profits from their estates and commerce on the arts. Their support helped develop and enrich the spoken language while it heightened their prestige as aristocrats.

The Troubadours: Poets of Love and Play

Already at the beginning of the twelfth century, Duke William IX of Aquitaine (1071–1126), the grandfather of Eleanor of Aquitaine, had written lyric poems in Occitan, the vernacular of southern France. Perhaps influenced by Arabic and Hebrew love poetry from al-Andalus, his own poetry in turn provided a model for poetic forms that gained popularity through repeated performances. The final four-line stanza of one such poem demonstrates the composer's skill with words:

Per aquesta fri e tremble,	For this one I shiver and tremble,
quar de tan bon' amor l'am;	I love her with such a good love;
qu'anc no cug qu'en nasques semble	I do not think the like of her was ever born
en semblan de gran linh n'Adam.	in the long line of Lord Adam.

The rhyme scheme of this poem appears to be simple — *tremble* goes with *semble*, *l'am* with *n'Adam* — but the entire poem has five earlier verses, all six lines long and all containing the *-am, -am* rhyme in the fourth and sixth lines, while every other line within each verse rhymes as well.

Troubadours, male and sometimes female lyric poets who wrote in Occitan, varied their rhymes and meters endlessly to dazzle their audiences with brilliant originality. Their most common topic, love, echoed the twelfth-century church's emphasis on the emotional relationship between God and humans. But the troubadours concentrated on the various forms of human love and its joys and sorrows. Thus the Contessa de Dia (flourished c. 1160) wrote about her unrequited love for a man:

> So bitter do I feel toward him
> whom I love more than anything.
> With him my mercy and *cortesia* [fine manners] are in vain.

The key to these lines, as to troubadour verse in general, is the idea of *cortesia*. The word refers to courtesy (the refinement of people living at court) and to the struggle to achieve an ideal of virtue.

Historians and literary critics used to use the term *courtly love* to emphasize one of the themes of this literature: overwhelming love for a beautiful married noblewoman who is far above the poet in status and utterly unattainable. But this theme was only one of many aspects of love that the troubadours sang about: some of the songs boasted of sexual conquests, others played with the notion of equality between lovers, and still others preached that love was the source of virtue. The real overall theme of this literature is not courtly love; it is the power of women. And no wonder: there were many powerful ladies (the female counterparts of lords) in southern France. They owned property, had vassals, led battles, decided disputes, and entered into and broke political alliances as their advantage dictated. Both men and women appreciated troubadour poetry, which recognized and praised women's power even as it eroticized it.

Troubadour poetry was not read; it was sung, typically by a *jongleur,* a medieval musician. Manuscripts from the thirteenth century show troubadour music written on four- and five-line staves, so scholars can at least determine relative pitches, and modern musicians can sing some troubadour songs with the hope of sounding reasonably like the original. This popular music is the earliest that can be re-created authentically (Figure 11.2).

From southern France, the troubadours' songs spread to Italy, northern France, England, and Germany. Similar poetry appeared in other vernacular languages: the *minnesingers* ("love singers") sang in German; the *trouvères* sang in the Old French of northern France. One trouvère was the English king Richard the Lion-Hearted. Taken prisoner on his return from the Third Crusade, Richard wrote a poem expressing his longing not for a lady but for the good companions of war, the knightly "youths" he had joined in battle:

> They know well, the men of Anjou and Touraine,
> . . . that I am arrested, far from them, in another's hands.
> There's no lordly fighting now on the barren plains,
> because I am a prisoner.

Clearly some troubadour poetry was about war rather than love.

Figure 11.2 Troubadour Song: "I Never Died for Love"
This music is the first part of a song written by troubadour poet Peire Vidal sometime between 1175 and 1205. It has been adapted here for the treble clef. There is no time signature, but the music may easily be played by calculating one beat for each note, except for the two-note slurs, which fit into one beat together. (From Samuel N. Rosenberg, Margaret Switten, and Gerard Le Vot, eds., *Songs of the Troubadours and Trouvères.* Copyright © 1997 by Samuel N. Rosenberg, Margaret Switten, and Gerard Le Vot. Reprinted by permission of Taylor & Francis / Garland Publishing, http://www.taylorandfrancis.com.)

The Birth of Epic and Romance Literature

War was not as common a topic in lyric poetry as love, but some long vernacular poems, called **chansons de geste** ("songs of heroic deeds") and later termed epic poems, were all about warriors and their battles. They were written down at about the same time as love poems. Like the songs of the troubadours, these epic poems implied a code of behavior for aristocrats, in this case on the battlefield. They served heroic models for nobles and knights, whose positions were being threatened by the newly emerging merchants in the cities on the one hand and newly powerful kings on the other. The knights' ascendancy on the battlefield, where they unhorsed one another with lances and long swords and took prisoners rather than killing their opponents, was also beginning to wane in the face of mercenary infantrymen who wielded long hooks and knives that ripped easily through chain mail. A knightly ethos and sense of group solidarity emerged in the face of these social, political, and military changes. Even while heroic poems celebrated battles, they explored the moral issues that made war tragic, if inevitable.

Other long poems, later called romances, explored the relationships between men and women. Often inspired by the legend of King Arthur, romances reached their zenith of popularity during the late twelfth and early thirteenth centuries. In one romance, for example, the heroic knight Lancelot, who is in love with King Arthur's wife, Queen Guinevere, chooses humiliation over honor because of his love for the queen. When she sees him — the greatest knight in Christendom — fighting in a tournament, she tests him by asking him to do his "worst." The poor knight is obliged to lose all his battles until she changes her mind.

Lancelot was the perfect chivalric knight. The word **chivalry** derives from the French word *cheval* ("horse"); the fact that the knight was a horseman marked him as a warrior of the most prestigious sort. Perched high on his horse, his heavy lance couched in his right arm, the knight was both imposing and menacing. Chivalry made him gentle — except to his enemies on the battlefield. The chivalric hero was a knight constrained by a code of refinement, fair play, piety, and devotion to an ideal. Historians debate whether real knights lived up to the codes implicit in epics and romances, but there is no doubt that knights saw themselves mirrored there. They were the poets' audience.

> **REVIEW QUESTION** What do the works of the troubadours and vernacular poets reveal about the nature of entertainment — its themes, its audience, its performers — in the twelfth century?

Religious Fervor and Crusade

The new vernacular culture was one sign of the growing wealth, sophistication, and self-confidence of the late twelfth century. New forms of religious life were another. Unlike the reformed orders of the early half of the century, which had fled the cities, the new religious groups embraced (and were embraced by) urban populations. Rich and poor, male and female joined these movements. They criticized the existing church as too wealthy, impersonal, and spiritually superficial. Intensely interested in the life of Christ, men and women in the late twelfth century made his childhood, agony, death, and presence in the Eucharist — the bread and wine that became the body and blood of Christ in the Mass — the emotional focus of their own lives.

Religious fervor mixed with greed in new crusades that had little success in the Holy Land but were victorious on the borders of Europe and, as we have already seen, at Constantinople. These were the poisonous flowers of the Middle Ages.

New Religious Orders in the Cities

The quick rebuilding of the cathedral at Chartres reveals the religious fervor of late-twelfth-century city dwellers. This helps explain the new religious orders that appeared in the cities. The church accepted many new orders; some, however, so threatened the established doctrine and hierarchy that they were condemned as heresies.

St. Francis (c. 1182–1226) founded one of the most successful of the movements within the church, the **Franciscans**. Son of a well-to-do trader in the city of Assisi in

Italy, Francis began to experience doubts, dreams, and illnesses that spurred him to religious self-examination. Eventually, he renounced his family's wealth, put on a simple robe, and went about preaching penance to anyone who would listen.

Clinging to poverty as if, in his words, "she" were his "lady" (and thus borrowing the vocabulary of chivalry), Francis accepted no money, walked without shoes, and wore only one coarse tunic. He brought religious devotion out of the monastery and into the streets. Intending to follow the model of Christ, he received, as his biographers put it, a miraculous gift of grace: the stigmata, bleeding sores corresponding to the wounds Christ suffered on the cross.

By all accounts Francis was a spellbinding speaker, and he attracted many followers. Because they went about begging, those followers were called mendicants, from the Latin verb *mendicare* ("to beg"). Recognized as a religious order by the pope, the Brothers of St. Francis (or friars, from the Latin term for "brothers") spent their time preaching, ministering to the sick, and doing manual labor. Eventually they dispersed, setting up fraternal groups throughout Italy and then in France, Spain, Germany, England, and the Holy Land.

Francis converted not only men but women. One of these, Clare, formed the nucleus of a community of pious women, which became the Order of the Sisters of St. Francis. At first, the women worked alongside the friars; but both Francis and the church hierarchy disapproved of their activities in the world, and soon Franciscan sisters were confined to cloisters under the rule of St. Benedict.

Clare was one of many women who sought outlets for religious expression. Some women joined convents; others became recluses, living alone like hermits; still others sought membership in new lay sisterhoods. In northern Europe at the end of the twelfth century, laywomen who lived together in informal pious communities were called Beguines. Without permanent vows or an established rule, the Beguines chose to be celibate (though they were free to leave their Beguinage to marry) and often made their living by weaving cloth or tending to the sick and old. Some of them may have prepared and illustrated their own reading materials. (See the illustration on page 359.) Although their daily occupations were ordinary, the Beguines' spiritual lives were often emotional and ecstatic, infused with the combined imagery of love and religion so pervasive in both monasteries and courts. One renowned Beguine, Mary of Oignies (1177–1213), who like St. Francis was rumored to have received stigmata, said that sometimes "she held [Christ] close to her so that He nestled between her breasts like a baby."

The church tentatively tolerated the Beguines. But other religious movements so contradicted officially accepted ideas that church authorities labeled them heresies. Heresies were not new in the twelfth century. But the eleventh-century Gregorian reform had created for the first time in the West a clear church hierarchy headed by a pope who could enforce a single doctrine and discipline. Clearly defined orthodoxy meant that people in western Europe now perceived deviant religious ideas as a serious problem.

Among the most visible heretics were dualists who saw the world as being torn between two great forces — one good, the other evil. In Languedoc, an area of southern

Beguine Psalter

Although emphasizing labor and caring for others, most Beguines were also literate. The Psalter (book of Psalms) illustrated here was probably made by Beguines. The painting focuses on Mary: in the bottom tier is the Annunciation, when she learns that she will give birth to the Savior. At the top Mary reigns as Queen of Heaven, with a crown on her head and the baby Jesus on her lap.

France, the dualists were called Albigensians, a name derived from the town of Albi. Calling themselves "Christ's poor" — though modern historians have given them the collective name Cathars (from a Greek word meaning "pure") — these men and women believed that the devil had created the material world. They renounced the world, rejecting wealth, meat, and sex. Their repudiation of sex reflected some of the attitudes of eleventh-century church reformers (whose orthodoxy, however, was never in doubt), while their rejection of wealth echoed the same concerns that moved St. Francis to embrace poverty. In many ways, the dualists simply took these attitudes to an extreme; but unlike orthodox reformers, they also challenged the efficacy and legitimacy of the church hierarchy. Attracting both men and women, young and old, literate and unlettered, and giving women access to all but the highest positions in their church, the dualists saw themselves as followers of Christ's original message. But the church called them heretics.

Disastrous Crusades to the Holy Land

Did religious fervor also inspire the crusades of the later twelfth century? Some Europeans thought so. The pope called the Third Crusade "an opportunity for repentance and doing good." This crusade was indirectly a result of the fall of the Seljuk Empire at the hands of Nur al-Din and his successor Saladin (1138–1193), Sunni Muslims eager to impose their brand of Islam in the region. They took Syria and Egypt and, in 1187, Saladin conquered Jerusalem.

The Third Crusade was an unsuccessful bid to retake the Holy City. The greatest rulers of Europe — Emperor Frederick I (Barbarossa), Philip II of France, Leopold of Austria, and Richard I of England — led it. But they spent most of their time quarreling with one another or harassing the Byzantines. After they went home, the crusader states

remained a shadow of themselves — minus Jerusalem — until they were entirely snuffed out in 1291. Islamic hegemony over the Holy Land would remain a fact of life for centuries.

The hostilities that surfaced during the Third Crusade made it a dress rehearsal for the **Fourth Crusade** (1202–1204). Hostility toward the Byzantines had begun long before the thirteenth century. Now it combined with Venetian opportunism. When the pope called the crusade, the Venetians fitted out a fine fleet of ships and galleys for the expedition. But when the crusaders arrived in Venice, there were far fewer fighters to pay for the transport than had been anticipated. To defray the costs of the ships and other expenses, the Venetians convinced the crusaders to do them some favors before taking off against the Muslims. First, they had the crusaders attack Zara, a Christian city in Dalmatia (today's Croatia) that was Venice's competitor in the Adriatic. Then they urged the army to attack Constantinople itself, where they hoped to gain commercial advantage over their rivals (Map 11.2).

Convinced of the superiority of their brand of Christianity over that of the Byzantines, the crusaders killed many inhabitants of Constantinople and ransacked the city for treasure and relics. When one crusader discovered a cache of relics, a chronicler recalled, "he plunged both hands in and, girding up his loins, he filled the folds of his gown with the holy booty of the Church." The pope decried the sack of Constantinople, but he also took advantage of it, ordering the crusaders to stay there for a year to consolidate their gains. Plans to go on to the Holy Land were never carried out. The crusade leaders chose one of themselves — Baldwin of Flanders — to be emperor, and he, the other princes, and the Venetians divided the conquered lands among themselves.

Popes continued to call crusades to the Holy Land until the mid-fifteenth century, but the Fourth Crusade marked the last major mobilization of men and leaders for such an enterprise. Working against these expeditions were the new values of the late twelfth century, which placed a premium on the interior pilgrimage of the soul and valued rulers who stayed home and cared for their people.

Victorious Crusades in Europe and on Its Frontiers

Armed expeditions against those perceived as infidels were launched not only to the Holy Land but also much nearer to home. In Spain, the reconquista continued with increasing success and virulence in the second half of the twelfth century. Christian Spain took on the political configuration that would last for centuries: Aragon in the east, Castile in the middle, and Portugal in the west. The leaders of these polities competed for territory and power, but above all they sought an advantage against the Muslims to the south (Map 11.3, page 362).

Piecemeal conquests — followed by the granting of law codes to regulate relations among new Christian settlers as well as the Muslims, Mozarabs (Christians who had lived under the Muslims), and Jews who remained — gradually brought more territory under northern control. In 1212, a crusading army of Spaniards led by the kings of

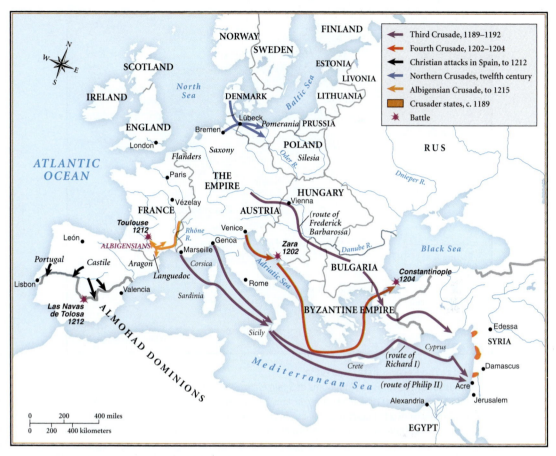

Map 11.2 Crusades and Anti-Heretic Campaigns, 1150–1215
Europeans aggressively expanded their territory during the second half of the twelfth century. To the north, knights pushed into the Baltic Sea region. To the south, warriors pushed against the Muslims in al-Andalus and waged war against the Cathars in southern France. To the east, the new crusades were undertaken to shore up the tiny European outpost in the Holy Land. Although most of these aggressive activities had the establishment of Christianity as at least one motive, the conquest of Constantinople in 1204 had no such justification. It grew in part out of general European hostility toward Byzantium but mainly out of Venice's commercial ambitions.

Aragon and Castile defeated the Muslims decisively at the battle of Las Navas de Tolosa. "On their side 100,000 armed men or more fell in the battle," the king of Castile wrote afterward, "but . . . incredible though it may be, unless it be a miracle, hardly 25 or 30 Christians of our whole army fell. O what happiness! O what thanksgiving!" The decisive turning point in the reconquista had been reached, though all of Spain came under Christian control only in 1492.

    Christians flexed their military muscle along Europe's northern frontiers as well (Map 11.2, above). Already during the Second Crusade a number of campaigns had

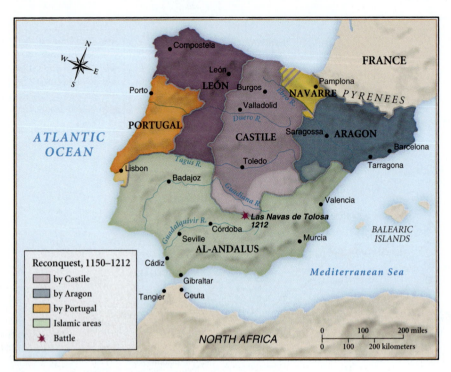

Map 11.3 The Reconquista, 1150–1212
Slowly but surely the Christian kingdoms of Spain encroached on al-Andalus, taking Las
Navas de Tolosa, deep in Islamic territory, in 1212. At the center of this activity was Castile.
It had originally been a tributary of León, but in the twelfth century it became a power in its
own right. (In 1230, León and Castile merged into one kingdom.) Meanwhile, the ruler of Portugal,
who had also been dependent on León, began to claim the title of king, which was recognized
officially in 1179, when he put Portugal under the protection of the papacy. Navarre was joined
to Aragon until 1134, when it became, briefly, an independent kingdom. (In 1234, the count of
Champagne came to the throne of Navarre, and thereafter its history was as much tied to
France as to Spain.)

been launched against the people on the Baltic coast. Those campaigns were the beginnings of the Northern Crusades, which continued intermittently until the early fifteenth
century. The first phase was led by the king of Denmark and the Saxon duke Henry the
Lion. Their initial attacks on the Slavs were uncoordinated, but in the 1160s and 1170s,
the two leaders worked together to bring much of the region west of the Oder River under their control. They took some land outright; even more frequently, they turned Slavic
princes into their vassals. Meanwhile, the Cistercians arrived even before the first phase
of fighting had ended, building monasteries to the very banks of the Oder River. Soon
German traders, craftspeople, and colonists poured in, populating new towns and cities
along the Baltic coast and dominating the shipping that had once been controlled by

Almourol Castle

In the early twelfth century, the papacy recognized the reconquista as equivalent to a crusade, and the rulers of Portugal, Castile, and Aragon persuaded the Templars and other military orders to help them hold on to regions that had formerly been Muslim. When the Portuguese ruler conquered the western end of the Tagus River valley in the mid-twelfth century, he entrusted some of the Muslim strongholds there to the Templars. They rebuilt one of them as Almourol castle, using it to defend Portugal's new frontier. (© Patrick Frilet / Hemis / Corbis.)

non-Christians. The leaders of the crusades gave these townsmen some political independence but demanded a large share of the cities' wealth in return.

Slavic peasants suffered from the conquerors' fire and pillage, but the Slavic ruling classes ultimately benefited from the Northern Crusades. Once converted to Christianity, they found it advantageous for both their eternal salvation and their worldly profit to join new crusades to areas still farther east.

Although less well known than the crusades to the Holy Land, the Northern Crusades had far more lasting effects: they settled the Baltic region with German-speaking lords and peasants and forged a permanent relationship between northeastern Europe and its neighbors to the south and west. With the Baltic dotted with churches and monasteries and its peoples dipped into baptismal waters, the region gradually adopted the institutions of western medieval society — cities, guilds, universities, castles, and

The Albigensian Crusade, 1209–1229

manors. Only the Lithuanians managed to resist western conquest, settlement, and conversion.

Crusades were also launched within Europe itself. The first of these attacked the Cathars in southern France. To be sure, the papacy initially tried conversion, and the Dominican Order had its start as preachers to the heretics. Its founder, St. Dominic (1170–1221), and his followers rejected material riches and went about on foot, preaching and begging and trying to bring the Cathars back into the church. Resembling the Franciscans both organizationally and spiritually, they too were called friars. But their missions did not have much success, and in 1208 the pope called upon northern princes to take up the sword, invade Languedoc, wrest the land from the heretics, and populate it with orthodox Christians.

The Albigensian Crusade (1209–1229) for the first time offered warriors fighting an enemy within Christian Europe all the spiritual and temporal benefits of a crusade to the Holy Land. Like all other crusades, the Albigensian Crusade had political as well as religious dimensions. It pitted southern French princes, who often had heretical sympathies, against northern leaders eager to demonstrate their piety and win new possessions. After sixteen years of warfare, the Capetian kings of France took over leadership of the crusade. By 1229, all resistance was broken, and Languedoc was brought under the French crown.

REVIEW QUESTION How did the idea of crusade change from the time of the original expedition to the Holy Land?

Conclusion

In the second half of the twelfth century, Christian Europe expanded from the Baltic Sea to the southern Iberian peninsula. European settlements in the Holy Land, by contrast, were nearly obliterated. When western Europeans sacked Constantinople in 1204, Europe and the Islamic world became the dominant political forces in the West.

Powerful territorial kings and princes established institutions of bureaucratic authority. They hired staffs to handle their accounts, record acts, collect taxes, issue writs, and preside over courts. A money economy provided the finances necessary to support the new bureaucracy. Cathedral schools and universities became its training ground. A new lay vernacular culture celebrated the achievements and power of the ruling class, while Gothic architecture reflected above all the pride and power of the cities.

New religious groups blossomed — Beguines, Franciscans, Dominicans, and heretics. However dissimilar the particulars, their beliefs and lifestyles all reflected the fact that people, especially city dwellers, yearned for a deeper spirituality.

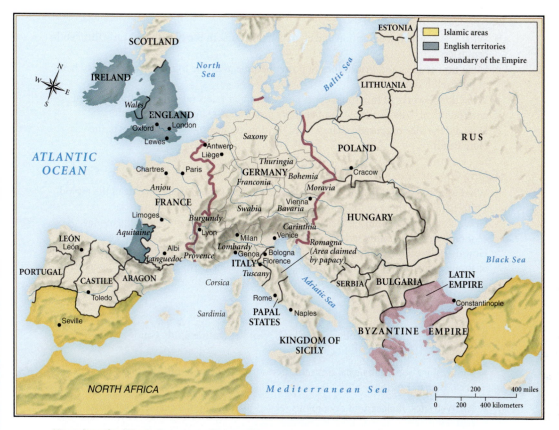

Mapping the West Europe and Byzantium, c. 1215

The major transformation in the map of the West between 1150 and 1215 was the conquest of Constantinople and the setting up of European rule there until 1261. The Byzantine Empire was now split into two parts. Bulgaria once again gained its independence. If Venice had hoped to control the Adriatic by conquering Constantinople, it must have been disappointed, for Hungary became its rival over the ports of the Dalmatian coast.

Intense religiosity helped fuel the flames of crusades, which were now fought more often and against an increasing variety of foes, not only in the Holy Land but also in Spain, in southern France, and on Europe's northern frontiers. The peoples on the Baltic coast became targets for new evangelical zeal; the Byzantines became the butt of envy, hostility, and finally enmity. With heretics voicing criticisms, the church, led by the papacy, now defined orthodoxy and declared dissenters its enemies. European Christians still considered Muslims arrogant heathens, and the deflection of the Fourth Crusade did not stem the zeal of popes to call for new crusades to the Holy Land.

Confident and aggressive, the leaders of Christian Europe in the thirteenth century would attempt to impose their rule, legislate morality, and create a unified worldview impregnable to attack. But this drive for order would be countered by unexpected varieties of thought and action, by political and social tensions, and by intensely personal religious quests.

Review Questions

1. What was new about education and church architecture in the twelfth and early thirteenth centuries?
2. What new sources and institutions of power became available to rulers in the second half of the twelfth century?
3. What do the works of the troubadours and vernacular poets reveal about the nature of entertainment — its themes, its audience, its performers — in the twelfth century?
4. How did the idea of crusade change from the time of the original expedition to the Holy Land?

Making Connections

1. What were the chief differences that separated the ideals of the religious life in the period 1150–1215 from those of the period 1050–1150?
2. How was the gift economy associated with Romanesque architecture and the money economy with the Gothic style?
3. How do political developments — the growth of bureaucratic institutions, the development of strong monarchies, the growth of city governments — help explain the rise and popularity of vernacular literature and song in the twelfth and thirteenth centuries?

- For practice quizzes and other study tools, visit the **Online Study Guide** at bedfordstmartins.com/huntconcise.

- For primary-source material from this period, see *Sources of the Making of the West*, Fourth Edition.

- For Web sites, images, and documents related to topics in this chapter, visit *Make History* at bedfordstmartins.com/huntconcise.

TIMELINE

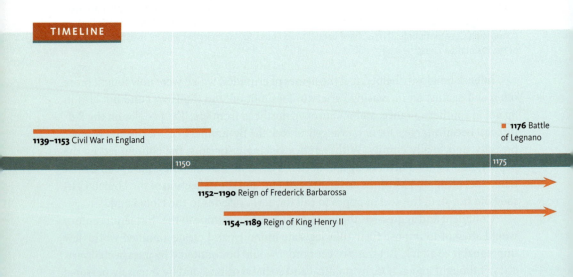

1139–1153 Civil War in England

1176 Battle of Legnano

1150

1175

1152–1190 Reign of Frederick Barbarossa

1154–1189 Reign of King Henry II

Suggested References

For the new schools, Abelard is a key primary source, while Clanchy provides perceptive background. Both Burl and Coldstream discuss cultural and artistic developments. Bartlett and Bradbury are essential for politics.

*Abelard's *The Story of My Misfortunes:* http://www.fordham.edu/halsall/source/abelard-sel.html

Aurell, Martin. *The Plantagenet Empire, 1154–1224.* Trans. David Crouch. 2007.

Bartlett, Robert. *England under the Norman and Angevin Kings, 1075–1225.* 2000.

Bouchard, Constance Brittain. *"Every Valley Shall Be Exalted": The Discourse of Opposites in Twelfth-Century Thought.* 2003.

Bradbury, Jim. *Philip Augustus: King of France.* 1998.

Burl, Aubrey. *Courts of Love, Castles of Hate: Troubadours and Trobairitz in Southern France, 1071–1321.* 2008.

Cheyette, Fredric L. *Ermengard of Narbonne and the World of the Troubadours.* 2001.

Christiansen, Eric. *The Northern Crusades.* 2nd ed. 1998.

Clanchy, Michael. *Abelard: A Medieval Life.* 1997.

Coldstream, Nicola. *Medieval Architecture.* 2002.

Crusade of Frederick Barbarossa: The History of the Expedition of the Emperor Frederick and Related Texts. Trans. G. A. Loud. 2010.

Hudson, John. *The Formation of the English Common Law: Law and Society in England from the Norman Conquest to Magna Carta.* 1996.

Moore, R. I. *The Formation of a Persecuting Society: Power and Deviance in Western Europe, 950–1250.* 2nd ed. 2007.

Paden, William, and Frances Freeman Paden, eds. and trans. *Troubadour Poems from the South of France.* 2007.

Pegg, Mark Gregory. *A Most Holy War: The Albigensian Crusade and the Battle for Christendom.* 2008.

Primary source.

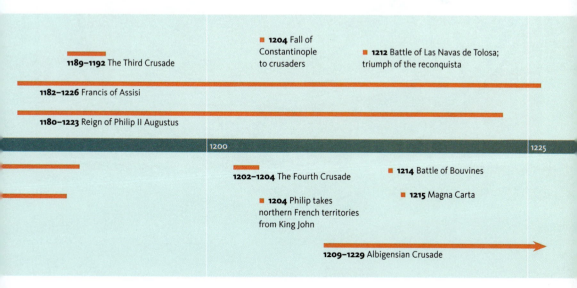

1204 Fall of Constantinople to crusaders

1212 Battle of Las Navas de Tolosa; triumph of the reconquista

1189–1192 The Third Crusade

1182–1226 Francis of Assisi

1180–1223 Reign of Philip II Augustus

1200

1225

1202–1204 The Fourth Crusade

1214 Battle of Bouvines

1204 Philip takes northern French territories from King John

1215 Magna Carta

1209–1229 Albigensian Crusade

The Medieval Synthesis — and Its Cracks

1215–1340

I N THE SECOND HALF of the thirteenth century, a wealthy patron asked a Parisian workshop specializing in manuscript illuminations to decorate Aristotle's *On the Length and Shortness of Life*. Most Parisian illuminators knew very well how to illustrate the Bible, liturgical books, and the writings of the church fathers. But Aristotle was a Greek who had lived before the time of Christ, and he was skeptical about the possibility of an afterlife. His treatise on life ended with death. The workshop's artists did not care about this fact. They illustrated Aristotle's work as if he had been a Christian and had believed in the immortal soul. As shown in the illustration opposite this page, the artists decorated one of the opening letters of the text with a depiction of the Christian Mass for the dead, a rite performed for the eternal salvation of Christians. In this way, the artists subtly but surely incorporated the pagan Aristotle into Christian belief and practice.

Christianizing Aristotle

This illumination was created for a thirteenth-century Latin translation of Aristotle's *On the Length and Shortness of Life*. Although Aristotle did not believe in the eternity of the soul, the artists nevertheless placed a depiction of the Christian Mass for the dead in one of the book's initials, in this way revealing their conviction that the ancient teachings of Aristotle and Christian practice worked together. (© Biblioteca Apostolica Vaticana [Vatican Library] Vat. Lat. 2071, f. 297.)

In the period 1215–1340, Europeans at every level, from workshop artisans to kings and popes, thought that they could harmonize all ideas with Christianity, all aspects of this world with the next, and all of nature with revelation. Sometimes, as in the case of the illumination made for Aristotle's treatise, the synthesis worked. But often it was forced, fragile, or elusive. Not everyone was willing to subordinate his or her beliefs to the tenets of Christianity; kings and popes argued, without resolution, about the limits of their power; and theologians fought over the place of reason in matters of faith. Discord continually threatened expectations of unity and harmony.

Medieval thinkers, writers, musicians, and artists attempted to reconcile faith and reason and to find the commonalities in the sacred and secular realms. At the level of

philosophy, this quest led to a new method of inquiry and study known as scholasti-cism. Yet some scholastic thinkers pointed out cracks and disjunctions in the synthe-ses achieved.

To impose greater order and unity, kings and other rulers found new ways to extend their influence over their subjects. They used the tools of taxes, courts, and even repre-sentative institutions to control their realms. Popes issued new laws for Christians and established courts of inquisition to find and punish heretics (those who dissented from church teachings). Both secular and religious authorities at times persecuted Jews and lepers. Yet none of this prevented dissent, and rulers often did not gain all the power they wanted.

CHAPTER FOCUS In what areas of life did thirteenth-century Europeans try to find harmony and impose order, and how successful were these attempts?

During the period 1215–1340, the Em-pire weakened, the papacy asserted itself but was eventually forced to move out of Rome, and the Mongols challenged Christian rul-ers. Soon natural disasters — crop failures and famine — added to the tension.

The Church's Mission

The church had long sought to reform the secular world. In the eleventh century, dur-ing the Gregorian reform, it focused on the king. In the thirteenth century, it hoped to purify all of society. It tried to strengthen its institutions of law and justice to combat heresy and heretics, and it supported preachers who would bring the official views of the church to the streets. In this way, the church attempted to reorder the world in the image of heaven, with everyone following the laws of God as set forth by the church. It succeeded in this endeavor to some degree, but it also came up against the limits of con-trol as dissident voices and forces clashed with its vision.

Innocent III and the Fourth Lateran Council

Innocent III (r. 1198–1216) was the most powerful, respected, and prestigious of me-dieval popes. As pope, he allowed St. Francis's group of impoverished followers to be-come a new church order, and he called the Fourth Crusade, which mobilized a large force drawn from every level of European society. The first university-trained pope, Innocent studied theology at Paris and law at Bologna. From theology, he learned to tease new meaning out of canonical writings to magnify papal authority: he thought of himself as ruling in the place of Christ the King, with kings and emperors existing to help the pope. From law, Innocent gained his conceptions of the pope as lawmaker and of law as an instrument of moral reformation.

Innocent used the traditional method of declaring church law: a council. Presided over by Innocent, the **Fourth Lateran Council** (1215) attempted to regulate all aspects of Christian life. Its comprehensive legislation aimed at reforming both the clergy and

the laity. Those attending the council expected Christians, clerical and lay alike, to work together harmoniously to achieve the common goal of salvation. They did not anticipate either the sheer variety of responses to their message or the persistence of those who defied it altogether.

For laypeople, perhaps the most important canons (church laws) of the Fourth Lateran Council concerned the sacraments, the rites the church believed Jesus had instituted to confer sanctifying grace. For example, Fourth Lateran required Christians to attend Mass and to confess their sins to a priest at least once a year. It also precisely defined the sacrament of the Eucharist: "[Christ's] body and blood are truly contained in the sacrament of the altar under the forms of bread and wine, the bread and wine having been changed in substance [transubstantiated], by God's power, into his body and blood." The word *transubstantiated* was meant to explain how the Eucharist could *look* like bread and wine even though it had been transformed during the Mass into Christ's body and blood.

Other canons concerned marriage. The church declared that it had the duty to discover any impediments to a union (such as a close relationship by blood), and it claimed jurisdiction over marital disputes. It insisted that children conceived within clandestine or forbidden marriages were illegitimate; they were not to receive inheritances or become priests.

The impact of the council's provisions was perhaps less dramatic than church leaders hoped. All church laws took effect only when local political powers enforced them. Well-to-do London fathers still included their bastard children in their wills. On English manors, sons conceived out of wedlock regularly took over their parents' land. Men and women continued to marry in secret, and even churchmen had to admit that the consent of both parties made any marriage valid. Nevertheless, many men and women accepted the obligation to take communion and confess once a year, and priests proceeded to call out the banns (announcements of marriages) to discover any impediments to them.

The Fourth Lateran Council wanted to control Jews as well as Christians. It required all Jews to advertise their religion by some outward sign: "We decree that [Jews] of either sex in every Christian province at all times shall be distinguished from other people by the character of their dress in public." Eventually Jews almost everywhere had to wear some sign of their second-class status. In southern France and in a few places in Spain, they wore round badges. In England, Oxford required a rectangle, while Salisbury demanded that Jews wear special clothing. In Vienna and Germany, Jews were told to put on pointed hats. (See the illustration on page 372.)

The Fourth Lateran Council's longest decree blasted heretics: "Those condemned as heretics shall be handed over to the secular authorities for punishment." If the secular authority did not carry out the punishment, the heretic was to be excommunicated. If he or she had vassals, they were to be released from their oaths of fealty and their lands taken over by orthodox Christians. Church authorities set up a court of papal inquisitors; this court and its activities, later known as the Inquisition, became permanent in 1233.

Jewish Couple

In this illustration from a Hebrew prayer book, a couple sits in a garden of lilies under a starry sky, illustrating the Bible's Song of Solomon 4:8: "Come with me from Lebanon, my bride." Hebrew commentators on this verse interpreted the bride as standing for Israel, while the speaker, the groom, was God. Here the artist has portrayed the groom wearing a traditional Jewish hat, while Israel is a woman with a crown. There is an irony here: Christians portrayed the church as a crowned female. However, in this case the woman wears a blindfold. This makes her like the Christian depiction of the allegorical figure of the Jewish synagogue. In short, this seemingly innocuous illustration gives the synagogue the status and dignity of the church. (Staats- und Universitäts-bibliothek Hamburg Carl von Ossietzky, Cod. Levy 37, fol. 169.)

The Inquisition

The word *inquisition* simply means "investigation"; secular rulers had long used the method to summon people together, either to discover facts or to uncover and punish crimes. In its zeal to end heresy, the thirteenth-century church used the Inquisition to ferret out "heretical depravity." Calling suspects to testify, inquisitors, aided by secular authorities, rounded up virtually entire villages, first preaching to the throngs and then questioning each man and woman who seemed to know something about heresy: "Have you ever seen any heretics? Have you heard them preach?" Relatively lenient penalties were given to those who were not aware that they held heretical beliefs and to heretics who quickly recanted. But unrepentant heretics were punished severely because the church believed that such people threatened the salvation of all.

Lay Piety

The church's zeal to reform the laity was matched by the desire of many laypeople to become more involved in their religion. Men and women flocked to hear the preaching of friars, who made themselves a permanent feature of the towns. When Berthold, a Franciscan preacher who traveled the length and breadth of Germany giving sermons, came to a town, a high tower was set up for him outside the town walls. A pennant advertised his presence and let people know which way the wind would blow his voice.

Townspeople gathered to hear preachers like Berthold because they wanted to know how the Christian message applied to their daily lives. They were concerned, for ex-

ample, about the ethics of moneymaking, sex in marriage, and family life. The preachers in turn met the laity on their own turf, spoke in the vernacular that all could understand, and taught them to shape their behaviors to church teachings.

Laypeople further tied their lives to the mendicants, particularly the Franciscans, by becoming tertiaries. A tertiary was one who adopted the practices of the friars — prayer and works of charity, for example — while continuing to live in the world, work at his or her usual occupation, raise a family, and tend to the normal tasks of daily life.

Although for many people religion was only one facet of life, for some — especially women — it was a focus. Within the towns and cities, powerful families founded new nunneries for their wealthy daughters. Less well-to-do women sought the life of quiet activity and rapturous mysticism led by the Beguines. Others pursued a life of charity and service in women's mendicant orders. Still others, like Elisabeth of Hungary, raised their children while devoting their free time to fasting, prayer, and service to the poor.

The new emphasis on the holiness of the transformed wine and bread encouraged some pious women to eat nothing but the Eucharist. They believed that Christ's crucifixion was the literal sacrifice of his body, to be eaten by sinful men and women as the way to redeem themselves and others. Some bypassed their priests, receiving the Eucharist (as they explained) directly from Christ. Furthermore, renouncing all other foods became part of a life of charity, because many of these devout women gave the poor the food they refused to eat. Thus, pious women used their control over ordinary food to gain new kinds of social and religious prestige and power.

Jews and Lepers as Outcasts

While Christian women found new roles for themselves, non-Christians were pushed further into the category of "outsiders." To be sure, the First and Second Crusades gave outlet to anti-Jewish feeling. Nevertheless, they were abnormal episodes in the generally stable if tense relationship between Christians and Jews in Europe up to the middle of the twelfth century. Then things changed dramatically as kings became more powerful, popular piety deepened, and church law singled out Jews in particular for discrimination.

Even though Jews had been ousted from manors and banned from town guilds, they were essential to the surrounding Christian community. Although there were some Christian moneylenders (despite the Bible's prohibition against charging interest for loans), lords, especially kings, preferred to borrow from Jews because, along with their newly asserted powers, they claimed the Jews as their serfs and Jewish property as their own. In England, where Jews had arrived with the Norman conquest in 1066, a special exchequer of the Jews was created in 1194 to collect for the king any unpaid debts due after the death of a Jewish creditor. Even before that, the king of England had imposed new and arbitrary taxes on the Jewish community.

Similarly in France, persecuting Jews and confiscating their property benefited both the treasury and the authoritative image of the king. In 1198, the French king declared that Jews must be moneylenders or money changers exclusively. Their activities were

to be taxed and monitored by royal officials. Limiting Jews to moneylending in an increasingly commercial economy clearly served the interests of kings. But lesser lords who needed cash also benefited: they borrowed money from Jews and then, as happened in York, England, in 1190, they orchestrated an attack to rid themselves of their debts and of the Jews to whom they owed money. Churchmen, too, borrowed from Jews but resented having to repay.

Rulers of both church and state exploited and coerced the Jews while drawing on and encouraging a wellspring of elite and popular anti-Jewish feeling. But attacks against Jews were inspired by more than resentment against Jewish money and the desire for power and control: they also grew out of the codification of Christian religious doctrine and the anxieties of Christians about their own institutions. For example, the newly rigorous definition of the Eucharist meant to many pious Christians that the body of Christ literally lay on the altar. Even as some Christians found this thought unsettling, sensational stories (originating in clerical circles but soon widely circulated) told of Jews who secretly sacrificed Christian children in their Passover ritual — a charge that historians have termed **blood libel**. (In truth, of course, Jews had no rituals involving blood sacrifice at all.)

In 1144, in one of the earliest instances of this charge, the body of a young boy named William was found in the woods near Norwich, England. His uncle, a priest, accused local Jews of killing the child. A monk connected to the cathedral at Norwich, Thomas of Monmouth, took up the cause, writing *The Life and Martyrdom of St. William of Norwich*. According to his account, the Jews carefully prepared at Passover for the horrible ritual slaughter of the boy, whom they had chosen "to be mocked and sacrificed in scorn of the Lord's passion." Similar charges were brought against Jews elsewhere in England as well as in France, Spain, and Germany, leading to massacres of the Jewish population. Some communities expelled Jews, and in 1291 the kingdom of England cast them out entirely. Most dispersed to France and Germany, but to a sad welcome. In 1306, for example, King Philip the Fair had Jews driven from France, though they were allowed to reenter, tentatively, in 1315.

Meanwhile, lepers were suffering a similar fate. People afflicted with **leprosy** — a disease that causes skin lesions and attacks the peripheral nerves — were an unimportant minority in medieval society until the eleventh century. Then, beginning around 1075 and extending to the fourteenth century, lepers, though still a small minority, became the objects of both charity and disgust. Houses for lepers were set up both to provide for them and to segregate them from everyone else.

Leprosy delivered three blows: it was horribly disfiguring, it was associated with sin in the Bible, and it was contagious. In 1179, the Third Lateran Council took note of the fact that "lepers cannot dwell with the healthy or come to church with others" and asked that, where possible, special churches and cemeteries be set aside for them. No doubt this inspired a boom in the founding of leper houses, which peaked between 1175 and 1250.

Before the leper went to such a house, he or she was formally expelled from the community of Christians via a ceremony of terrible solemnity. In northern France, for

example, the leper had to stand in a cemetery with his or her face veiled. The priest intoned Mass and threw dirt on the leper as if he or she were being buried. "Be dead to the world, be reborn in God," the priest said, continuing, "I forbid you to ever enter the church or monastery, fair, mill, marketplace, or company of persons. . . . I forbid you to wash your hands or any thing about you in the stream or in the fountain." The pro-hibition against drinking in the stream or fountain gained more sinister meaning in 1321, when false rumors spread that Mus-lims had recruited both Jews and lepers to poison all the wells of Christendom.

> **REVIEW QUESTION** How did people respond to the teachings and laws of the church in the early thirteenth century?

Reconciling This World and the Next

Just as the church in the early thirteenth century wanted to regulate worldly life in ac-cordance with God's plan for salvation, so thinkers, writers, musicians, and artists sought to harmonize the secular and the sacred realms. Scholars wrote treatises that recon-ciled faith with reason, poets and musicians sang of the links between heaven and hu-man life on earth, and artists expressed the same ideas in stone and sculpture and on parchment. In the face of many contradictions, all of these groups were largely success-ful in communicating an orderly image of this world and the next.

The Achievement of Scholasticism

Scholasticism was the culmination of the method of logical inquiry and exposition pio-neered by masters like Peter Abelard and Peter the Chanter (see pages 339–40). In the thirteenth century, the method was used to summarize and reconcile all knowledge. Many of the thirteenth-century scholastics (those who practiced scholasticism) were members of the Dominican or Franciscan Orders and taught in the universities. On the whole, they were confident that knowledge obtained through the senses and reason was compatible with the knowledge derived from faith and revelation.

One of the scholastics' goals was to demonstrate this harmony. The scholas-tic summa, or summary of knowledge, was a systematic exposition of the answer to every possible question about human morality, the physical world, society, belief, ac-tion, and theology. Another goal of the scholastics was to preach the conclusions of these treatises.

The method of the summa borrowed much of the vocabulary and many of the rules of logic outlined by Aristotle in ancient Greece. Even though Aristotle lived before the time of Christ, scholastics considered his coherent and rational body of thought the most perfect that human reason alone could devise. They thought that because they had the benefit of Christ's revelations, they could take Aristotle's philosophy one necessary step further and reconcile human reason with Christian faith. Confident in their method and conclusions, scholastics embraced the world and its issues.

St. Thomas Aquinas (1225–1274) was perhaps the most famous scholastic. When he was about eighteen years old, Thomas thwarted his family's wishes that he become a bishop and joined the Dominicans. He soon became a university master. Like many other scholastics, Thomas considered Aristotle to be "the Philosopher," the authoritative voice of human reason, which he sought to reconcile with divine revelation in a universal and harmonious scheme. In 1273, he published his monumental *Summa Theologiae* (sometimes called *Summa Theologica*), intended to cover all important topics, human and divine. He divided these topics into questions, exploring each one thoroughly and concluding with a decisive position and a refutation of opposing views.

Many of Thomas's questions spoke to the keenest concerns of his day. He asked, for example, whether it was lawful to sell something for more than its worth. Arranging his argument systematically, Thomas first quoted authorities that seemed to declare every sort of selling practice, even deceptive ones, to be lawful; this was the *sic* ("yes") position. Then he quoted an authority that opposed selling something for more than its worth; this was the *non*. Following that, he gave his own argument, prefaced by the words "I answer that." Thomas arrived at clear conclusions that harmonized both the yes and the no responses. In the case of selling something for more than it was worth, he concluded that charging more than a seller had originally paid could be legitimate at times, as, for example, "when a man has great need of a certain thing, while another man will suffer if he is without it."

Scholastics like Thomas were great optimists. They believed that everything had a place in God's scheme of things, that the world was orderly, and that human beings could make rational sense of it. Their logical arguments filled the classrooms, spilled into the friars' convents, found their way into the shops of artisans, and even crept between the sheets of lovers. Scholastic philosophy helped give ordinary people a sense of purpose and a guide to behavior.

Yet even among scholastics, unity was elusive. In his own day, Thomas was accused of placing too much emphasis on reason and relying too fully on Aristotle. Later scholastics argued that reason could not find truth through its own faculties and energies. In the summae of the Franciscan John Duns Scotus (c. 1266–1308), for example, the world and God were less compatible. For John, human reason could know truth only through the "special illumination of the uncreated light," that is, by divine illumination. Unlike Thomas, John believed that this illumination came not as a matter of course, but only when God chose to intervene. John — and others — experienced God as sometimes willful rather than reasonable. Human reason could not soar to God; God's will alone determined whether or not a person could know him. In this way, John separated the divine and secular realms, and the medieval synthesis cracked.

New Syntheses in Writing and Music

Thirteenth-century vernacular writers, like scholastics, synthesized seemingly contradictory ideas. Dante Alighieri (1265–1321) harmonized the mysteries of faith with the poetry of love. Born in Florence in a time of political turmoil, Dante incorporated the

major figures of history and his own day into his most famous poem, *Commedia,* written between 1313 and 1321. Later known as *Divina commedia* (*Divine Comedy*), Dante's poem describes the poet taking an imaginary journey from hell to purgatory and finally to paradise. At the most literal level, the poem is about Dante's travels. At a deeper level, it is about the soul's search for meaning and enlightenment and its ultimate discovery of God in the light of divine love. Just as Thomas Aquinas employed Aristotle's logic to reach important truths, so Dante used the pagan poet Virgil as his guide through hell and purgatory. And just as Thomas believed that faith went beyond reason to even higher truths, so Dante found a new guide representing earthly love to lead him through most of paradise. That guide was Beatrice, a Florentine girl with whom Dante had fallen in love as a boy and whom he never forgot. But only faith, in the form of the divine love of the Virgin Mary, could bring Dante to the culmination of his journey — a blinding and inexpressibly awesome vision of God.

Dante's poem electrified a wide audience. By elevating one dialect of Italian — the language that ordinary Florentines used in their everyday life — to a language of exquisite poetry, Dante was able to communicate an orderly and optimistic vision of the universe in an even more exciting and accessible way than the scholastics had. So influential was his work that it is no exaggeration to say that modern Italian is based on Dante's Florentine dialect.

Other writers of the period used different methods to express the harmony between heaven and earth. The anonymous author of the *Quest of the Holy Grail* (c. 1225), for example, wrote about the adventures of some of the knights of King Arthur's Round Table to convey the doctrine of transubstantiation and the wonder of the vision of God.

Just as vernacular writers asserted the harmony of heavenly and earthly things, so musicians combined sacred and secular music. This was quite new. The music before this time, plainchant (see page 342), had a particular sequence

Singing a Motet

In this fourteenth-century English Psalter, the artist has illustrated the first letter of Psalm 96 — which begins, "O sing to the Lord a new song" — with a depiction of three clerics singing a motet. Its words and musical notation are written on a scroll draped over a lectern. (© The British Library Board, All Rights Reserved. Arundel 83, fol. 63v.)

of notes for a given text. It is true that sometimes a form of harmony was achieved when two voices sang exactly the same melody an interval apart. This was the first form of polyphony, the simultaneous sounding of two or more melodies. In the twelfth century, musicians experimented with freer melodies. One voice might go up the scale, for example, while the other went down, achieving even so a pleasing harmony. Or one voice might hold a pitch while the other danced around it.

Now, in the thirteenth century, some musicians put secular and sacred tunes together. This form of music, which probably originated in Paris, was called the motet (from the French *mot,* meaning "word"). It typically had two or three melody lines, or "voices." The lowest was usually a plainchant melody sung in Latin. The remaining melodies had different texts, either Latin or French (or one of each), which were sung simultaneously. Latin texts were usually sacred, whereas French ones were secular, dealing with themes such as love and springtime. The motet thus wove the sacred (the chant melody in the lowest voice) and the secular (the French texts in the upper voices) into a sophisticated tapestry of words and music.

Like the scholastic summae, motets were written by and for a clerical elite. (See the illustration on page 377.) Yet they incorporated the music of ordinary people, such as the calls of street vendors and the boisterous songs of students. In turn, they touched the lives of everyone, for polyphony influenced every form of music, from the Mass to popular songs that entertained laypeople and churchmen alike.

Complementing the motet's complexity was the development of a new notation for rhythm. Music theorists of the thirteenth century developed increasingly precise methods to indicate rhythm, with each note shape allotted a specific duration. The music of the thirteenth century reflected both the melding of the secular and the sacred and the possibilities of greater order and control.

Gothic Art

Gothic architecture — like philosophy, literature, and music — brought together this world and the next. By the end of

Last Judgment

Stained glass could illustrate complex theological truths. In this thirteenth-century depiction of the Last Judgment from the cathedral at Bourges, in France, two colorful devils force two naked sinners into the toothy mouth of hell. Licks of red flame greet them. While the devils enjoy their task (the green one is smiling), the sinners grimace and seem to cry out in pain. (Saint-Etienne Cathedral, Bourges, France / The Bridgeman Art Library International.)

the thirteenth century, the Gothic style had spread across most of Europe. Some of its elements began to appear as well in other forms of art, like stained glass. Because pointed arches and flying buttresses allowed the walls of a Gothic church to be pierced with large windows, stained glass became a newly important art form. To make this colored glass, workers added chemicals to sand, heated the mixture until it was liquid, and then blew and flattened it. From these colored glass sheets, artists cut shapes, holding them in place with lead strips. The size of the windows allowed the artists to depict complicated themes ranging from heaven to hell. As the sun shone through the finished windows, they glowed like jewels.

The exteriors of Gothic cathedrals were decorated with figures sculpted in the round. The figures evoked motion — turning, moving, and interacting; at times, they even smiled. Like stained glass, Gothic sculptures evoked complex ideas. For example,

the figures on the south portals of the cathedral at Chartres tell the story of the soul's pilgrimage from the suffering of this world to eternal life: on the left doorway are the martyrs (who died for their beliefs), on the right the confessors (who were tortured), and in the center the Last Judgment (when the good receive eternal life and the bad eternal damnation).

The allure of Gothic was so great that painters began to use elements of its style. Manuscript illuminations feature the pointed shapes of Gothic cathedral windows and vaults as common background themes. (See the illustration on page 383 for one example.) The colors of Gothic manuscripts echoed the rich hues of stained

The Annunciation
Figures decorating Gothic churches, such as this one at Reims (in northern France), were carved in the round. Here the angel Gabriel (on the left) turns and smiles joyfully at Mary, who looks down modestly as he announces that she will give birth to Jesus. (Scala / Art Resource, NY.)

Giotto's *Birth of the Virgin*
This depiction of the Virgin Mary's birth pays attention to the homey details of a thirteenth-century Florentine aristocratic household. Those details portray a sequence: the baby is bathed and swaddled by maidservants in the bottom tier, while above she is handed to her mother, St. Anne, who reaches out eagerly for the child. (Scrovegni Chapel, Padua / Collection Dagli Orti / The Art Archive at Art Resource, NY.)

glass. Gothic sculpture inspired painters like Giotto (1266–1337), an Italian artist. When he filled the walls of a private chapel at Padua with paintings depicting scenes of Christ's life, Giotto experimented with the illusion of depth, figures in the round, and emotional expression. By fusing naturalistic forms with religious meaning, Giotto found yet another way to fuse the earthly and divine realms.

REVIEW QUESTION How did artists, musicians, and scholastics in the thirteenth and early fourteenth centuries try to link the physical world with the divine?

The Politics of Control

The quest for order, control, and harmony also became part of the political agendas of princes, popes, and cities. These rulers and institutions imposed — or tried to impose — their authority ever more fully and systematically through taxes, courts, and sometimes

representative institutions. Vestiges of these systems live on in modern European parliaments and in the U.S. Congress.

Louis IX of France is a good example of a ruler whose power increased during this period. In contrast, the emperor had to give up Italy and most of his power in Germany. At first powerful, the papacy was later forced to move from Rome to Avignon, a real blow to its prestige. In Italy the rise of *signori* (lords) meant that the communes, which had long governed many cities, gave way to rule by one strong man.

A new political entity, the Mongols, directly confronted the rulers of Russia, Poland, and Hungary even as they opened up new trade routes to the East. But just as this was taking place, a series of calamities known as the Great Famine hit Europe.

The Weakening of the Empire

During the thirteenth century, both popes and emperors sought to dominate Italy. After Barbarossa failed in his bid for the north (see page 351), his son Henry VI tried a new approach to gain Italy: he married Constance, the heiress of Sicily. With Sicily as a base, Henry hoped to make good his imperial title in Italy. But he died suddenly, leaving as his heir his three-year-old son. It was a perilous moment. The imperial office became the plaything of the German princes and the papacy. But Pope Innocent III miscalculated when, in 1212, he gave the imperial crown to Henry's son, **Frederick II** (r. 1212–1250), now a young man ready to take up the reins of power.

Frederick was an amazing ruler: *stupor mundi* ("wonder of the world") his contemporaries called him. Heir to two cultures, Sicilian on his mother's side and German on his father's, he cut a worldly and sophisticated figure. In Sicily, he moved easily within a diverse culture of Jews, Muslims, and Christians. Here he could play the role of all-powerful ruler. In Germany, he was less at home. There Christian princes, often churchmen with ministerial retinues, were acutely aware of their crucial role in royal elections and jealously guarded their rights and privileges.

Both emperor and pope needed to dominate Italy to maintain their power and position. The papacy under Innocent III was expansionist, gathering money and troops to make good its claim to the Papal States. The pope expected dues and taxes, military service, and the profits of justice from this region. To ensure the survival of the Papal States, the pope refused to tolerate any imperial claims to Italy.

Frederick, in turn, could not imagine ruling as an emperor unless he controlled Italy. To give himself a free hand, he consolidated his rule in Sicily and gave important concessions to the German princes (allowing them

Italy at the End of the Thirteenth Century

to turn their principalities into virtually independent states). Then he tried to enter Italy through Lombardy, as his grandfather Barbarossa had done.

Each of the four popes who ruled after Innocent died in 1216 followed Frederick's every move and excommunicated the emperor a number of times. The most serious of these condemnations came in 1245, when the pope and other churchmen assembled at the Council of Lyon to excommunicate and depose Frederick, absolving his vassals and subjects of their fealty to him and forbidding anyone to support him. By 1248, papal legates were preaching a crusade against Frederick and all his followers. Frederick's death, in 1250, ensured their triumph.

The fact that Frederick's vision of the Empire failed is of less long-term importance than the way it failed. His concessions to the German princes allowed them to divide Germany into discrete principalities. (In fact, Germany would not be united as a nation until the nineteenth century.) Between 1254 and 1273, the princes kept the German throne empty. Splintered into factions, they elected two different foreigners, who spent their time fighting each other.

In one of history's great ironies, it was during this low point of the German monarchy that the term Holy *Roman* Empire was coined, emphasizing, just when he had lost all hope to control Italy, the emperor's power over Rome. In 1273, the princes at last united and elected a German, Rudolf (r. 1273–1291), whose family, the Habsburgs, was new to imperial power. Rudolf used the imperial title to help him consolidate control over his own principality, Swabia, but he did not try to fulfill the meaning of the imperial title elsewhere. For the first time, the word *emperor* was freed from its association with Italy and Rome. For the Habsburgs, the title *Holy Roman Emperor* was a prestigious but otherwise meaningless honorific.

The failure of Frederick II in Italy meant that the Italian cities would continue their independent course. To ensure that Frederick's heirs would not continue their rule in Sicily, the papacy called successively on other rulers to take over the island — first Henry III of England and then Charles of Anjou. Forces loyal to Frederick's family turned to the king of Aragon (Spain). The move left two enduring claimants to Sicily's crown — the kings of Aragon and the house of Anjou — and it spawned a long war that impoverished the region.

The popes won the war against Frederick, but at a cost. Even the king of France criticized the popes for doing "new and unheard-of things." By making its war against Frederick part of its crusade against heresy, the papacy came under attack for using religion as a political tool.

Louis IX and a New Ideal of Kingship

In hindsight, we can see that Frederick's fight for an empire that would stretch from Germany to Sicily was doomed. The successful rulers of medieval Europe were those content with smaller, more compact, more united polities. In France, a new ideal of a stay-at-home monarch started in the thirteenth century with the reign of **Louis IX** (r. 1226–1270). Louis's two crusades to the Holy Land made clear to his subjects just

Louis IX and Blanche of Castile
This miniature shows Louis IX (St. Louis), portrayed as a young boy, sitting opposite his mother, Blanche of Castile. Blanche served as regent twice in Louis's lifetime, once when he was too young to rule and a second time when he was away on crusade. The emphasis on the equality of queen and king may be evidence of Blanche's influence on and patronage of the artist. (Detail from Moralized Bible, France, c. 1230. MS. M. 240, F.8. The Pierpont Morgan Library / Art Resource, NY.)

how much they needed him in France, even though his place was ably filled the first time by his mother, Blanche of Castile.

Louis was revered not because he was a military leader but because he was an administrator, a judge, and a "just father" of his people. On warm summer days, he would sit under a tree in the woods near his castle at Vincennes, on the outskirts of Paris, hearing disputes and dispensing justice personally. Through his administrators, he vigorously imposed his laws and justice over much of France. At Paris he appointed a salaried chief magistrate, who could be supervised and fired if necessary. During Louis's reign, the influence of the parlement of Paris (the royal court of justice) increased significantly. Originally a changeable and movable body, part of the king's personal entourage when he dealt with litigation, the parlement was now permanently housed in Paris and staffed by professional judges who heard cases and recorded their decisions.

Unlike his grandfather Philip Augustus, Louis did not try to expand his territory. He inherited a large kingdom that included Poitou and Languedoc (Map 12.1), and he was content. Although at first Henry III, the king of England, attacked France continually to try to regain territory lost under Philip Augustus, Louis remained unprovoked.

Rather than prolong the fighting, he conceded a bit and made peace. At the same time, Louis was a zealous crusader. He took seriously the need to defend the Holy Land from the Muslims when most of his contemporaries were weary of the idea.

Respectful of the church and the pope, Louis never claimed power over spiritual matters. Nevertheless, he vigorously maintained the dignity of the king and his rights. He expected royal and ecclesiastical power to work in harmony, and he refused to let the church dictate how he should use his temporal authority. For example, French bishops wanted royal officers to support the church's sentences of excommunication. But Louis declared that he would authorize his officials to do so only if he was able to judge each case himself, to see if the excommunication had been justly pronounced or not. The bishops refused, and Louis held his ground. Royal and ecclesiastical power would work side by side, neither subservient to the other.

It would be easy to fault Louis for his policies toward Jews. His hatred of them was well-known. He did not exactly advocate violence against them, but on occasion he subjected Jews to arrest, canceling the debts owed to them (but collecting part into the royal treasury) and confiscating their belongings. In 1253, he ordered Jews to live "by the labor of their hands" or leave France. He meant that they should no longer lend money, in effect taking away their one means of livelihood. Louis's contemporaries did not criticize him for his Jewish policies. If anything, his hatred of Jews enhanced his reputation.

In fact, many of Louis's contemporaries considered him a saint, praising his care for the poor and sick, the pains and penances he inflicted on himself, and his regular participation in church services. In 1297, Pope Boniface VIII canonized him as St. Louis. The result was enormous prestige for the French monarchy. This prestige, joined with the renown of Paris as the center of scholarship and the repute of French courts as the hubs of chivalry, made France the cultural model of Europe.

Map 12.1 France under Louis IX, r. 1226–1270
Louis IX did not expand his kingdom as dramatically as his grandfather Philip Augustus had done. He was greatly admired, nevertheless, for he was seen by contemporaries as a model of Christian piety and justice. After his death, he was recognized as a saint and thus posthumously enhanced the prestige of the French monarchy.

The Birth of Representative Institutions

As thirteenth-century monarchs and princes expanded their powers, they devised a new political tool to enlist more broadly based support: all across Europe, from Spain to Poland, from England to Hungary, rulers summoned parliaments. These grew out of the ad hoc advisory sessions kings had held in the past with men from the two most powerful classes, or orders, of medieval society — the nobility and the clergy. In the thirteenth century, the advisory sessions turned into solemn, formal meetings of representatives of the orders to the kings' chief councils — the precursor of parliamentary sessions. Eventually these groups became institutions through which people not ordinarily present at court could articulate their wishes. In practice, thirteenth-century kings did not so much command representatives of the orders to come to court as they simply summoned the most powerful members of their realm — whether clerics, nobles, or important townsmen — to support their policies.

The *cortes* of Castile-León in Spain were among the earliest representative assemblies called to the king's court and the first to include townsmen. Enriched by plunder, fledgling villages soon burgeoned into major commercial centers. Like the cities of Italy, Spanish towns dominated the countryside. No wonder King Alfonso IX (r. 1188–1230) summoned townsmen to the cortes in the first year of his reign, getting their representatives to agree to his plea for military and financial support and for help in consolidating his rule. Once convened at court, the townsmen joined bishops and noblemen in formally counseling the king and assenting to royal decisions. Beginning with Alfonso X (r. 1252–1284), Castilian monarchs regularly called on the cortes to participate in major political and military decisions and to assent to new taxes to finance them.

The English Parliament also developed as a new tool of royal government.* In this case, however, the king's control was complicated by the power of the barons, manifested, for example, in Magna Carta. In the twelfth century, the king had used great councils of churchmen and barons to ratify and gain support for his policies. Although Magna Carta had nothing to do with such councils, the barons thought the document gave them an important and permanent role in royal government as the king's advisers and a solid guarantee of their customary rights and privileges. In the thirteenth century, while Henry III (r. 1216–1272) was still a child, England was governed by a council consisting of a few barons, some university-trained administrators, and a papal legate. Although not quite "government by Parliament," this council set a precedent for baronial participation in government.

A parliament that included commoners came only in the midst of war and as a result of political weakness. Once in power, Henry III so alienated nobles and commoners

---

*Although *parlement* and *Parliament* are similar words, both deriving from the French word *parler* ("to speak"), the institutions they named were very different. The parlement of France was a law court, whereas the English Parliament, although beginning as a court to redress grievances, had by 1327 become above all a representative institution. The major French representative assembly, the Estates General, first convened at the beginning of the fourteenth century (see page 387).

alike by his wars, debts, choices of advisers, and demands for money that the barons threatened to rebel. At a meeting at Oxford in 1258, they forced Henry to dismiss his foreign advisers. Henceforth he was to rule with the advice of a so-called Council of Fifteen, chosen jointly by the barons and the king. Chief royal officers were to serve for one year only, after which they were to account for their actions to the council. However, this new government was itself plagued by strife among the barons, and civil war erupted in 1264. At the battle of Lewes in the same year, the leader of the baronial opposition, Simon de Montfort (c. 1208–1265), routed the king's forces, captured the king, and became England's de facto ruler.

Because only a minority of the barons followed him, Simon sought new support by convening a parliament in 1265, to which he summoned not only the earls, barons, and churchmen who backed him but also representatives from the towns, the "commons" — and he appealed for their help. Thus, for the first time the commons were given a voice in English government. Even though Simon's brief rule ended that very year and Henry's son Edward I (r. 1272–1307) became a rallying point for royalists, the idea of representative government in England had emerged, born out of the interplay between royal initiatives and baronial revolts.

The Weakening of the Papacy

In contrast with England, representative institutions developed in France out of the conflict between Pope **Boniface VIII** (r. 1294–1303) and King Philip IV (r. 1285–1314), known as Philip the Fair. At the time, this confrontation seemed to be just one more episode in the ongoing struggle between medieval

Portrait of a Pope
Celebrating the power of the papacy, Pope Nicholas III (r. 1277–1280) sponsored a thorough redecoration of Rome's ancient basilica of St. Paul's Outside the Walls (the burial place of St. Paul). In the space above each of the columns running down the nave, he had his artists paint portraits of the popes, linking all to one another and ultimately to St. Peter (whose portrait was nearest the altar). In this image of Anacletus (c. 79–c. 91), the artist asserted the pope's gravity, solemnity, and otherworldliness. Anacletus wears a pallium, a white scarf symbolizing papal power, even though the pallium did not exist in the first century.
(Nimatallah / Art Resource, NY.)

popes and secular rulers for power and authority. Throughout the thirteenth century, the papacy confidently asserted its prerogatives. In fact, however, kings were gradually gaining ground. The conflict between Boniface and Philip signaled the turning point, when royal power trumped papal power.

The conflict began over taxation. Traditionally, clerics were not taxed except in the case of religious wars. But Philip the Fair and the English king Edward I both financed their wars (mainly against one another) by taxing the clergy along with everyone else. The new principle of national sovereignty that they were claiming led them to assert jurisdiction over all people who lived within their borders, even churchmen. For the pope, however, the principle at stake was his role as head of the clergy. Thus, Pope Boniface VIII declared that only the pope could authorize taxes on clerics. Threatening to excommunicate kings who taxed churchmen without papal permission, he called on clerics to disobey any such royal orders.

Edward and Philip reacted swiftly. Taking advantage of the role English courts played in protecting the peace, Edward declared that all clerics who refused to pay his taxes would be considered outlaws — that is, "outside the law." Clergymen who were robbed, for example, would have no recourse against their attackers; if accused of crimes, they would have no defense in court. Relying on a different strategy, Philip forbade the exportation of precious metals, money, or jewels — effectively sealing the French borders. Immediately, the English clergy cried out for legal protection, while the papacy itself cried out for the revenues it had long enjoyed from French pilgrims, litigants, and travelers. Boniface was forced to back down, conceding in 1297 that kings had the right to tax their clergy in emergencies.

But this concession did not end the confrontation. In 1301, Philip the Fair tested his jurisdiction in southern France by arresting Bernard Saisset, the bishop of Pamiers, on a charge of treason for slandering the king by comparing him to an owl. Saisset's imprisonment violated the principle, maintained both by the pope and by French law, that a clergyman was not subject to lay justice. Pope Boniface reacted angrily, and King Philip seized the opportunity to deride and humiliate him, orchestrating a public relations campaign against Boniface. Philip convened representatives of the clergy, nobles, and townspeople to explain, justify, and propagandize his position. This new assembly, which met in 1302, was the ancestor of the French representative institution, the Estates General. The pope's reply, the bull* *Unam Sanctam* (1302), intensified the situation to fever pitch by declaring bluntly that "it is altogether necessary to salvation for every human creature to be subject to the Roman Pontiff." At meetings of the king's inner circle, Philip's agents declared Boniface a false pope, accusing him of sexual perversion, various crimes, and heresy.

In 1303, French royal agents, acting on Philip's orders, invaded Boniface's palace at Anagni (southeast of Rome) to capture the pope, bring him to France, and try him. Fearing for the pope's life, the people of Anagni joined forces and drove the French agents out of town. Yet even after such public support for the pope, the king made his power

---

*An official papal document is called a bull, from the *bulla,* or seal, that was used to authenticate it.

felt. Boniface died very shortly thereafter, and the next two popes quickly pardoned Philip and his agents for their actions.

Just as Frederick II's failure revealed the weakness of the empire, so Boniface's humiliation demonstrated the limits of papal control. The two powers that claimed "universal" authority had very little weight in the face of new, limited, but tightly controlled national states such as France and England. After 1303, popes continued to denounce kings and emperors, but their words had less and less impact. Against newly powerful medieval states — sustained by vast revenues, judicial apparatuses, representative institutions, and even the loyalty of churchmen — the papacy could make little headway. The delicate balance between church and state, reflecting a sense of universal order and harmony and a hallmark of the reign of St. Louis, broke down at the end of the thirteenth century.

The papacy's weakness was dramatically demonstrated by its move to Avignon. In 1309, forced from Rome by civil strife, the papacy settled in this city close to France. Here it remained until 1378, and thus the period 1309–1378 is called the **Avignon papacy**. Europeans ashamed that the pope lived so far from Rome called it the Babylonian captivity. They were thinking of the Old Testament story of the Hebrews captured and brought into slavery in ancient Babylon.*

The Avignon popes, many of them French, established a sober and efficient organization that took in regular revenues and gave the papacy more say than ever before in the appointment of churchmen. Slowly, they abandoned the idea of leading all of Christendom, tacitly recognizing the growing power of the secular states to regulate their internal affairs.

The Rise of the *Signori*

During the thirteenth century, new groups, generally made up of the non-noble classes — the *popolo* ("people"), who fought on foot — attempted to take power from the nobility in many Italian communes. The popolo incorporated members of city associations such as craft and merchant guilds, parishes, and the commune itself. In fact, the popolo was a kind of alternative commune. Armed and militant, the popolo demanded a share in city government. In 1223 at Piacenza, the popolo and the nobles worked out a plan to share the election of their city's government; such power sharing was a typical result of the popolo's struggle. In some cities, however, nobles dissolved the popolo, while in others the popolo virtually excluded the nobles from government. Such factions turned northern Italian cities into centers of civil discord.

Weakened by this constant friction, the communes were tempting prey for great regional nobles who, allying with one or another urban group, often succeeded in establishing themselves as *signori* (singular *signore,* "lord") of the cities, keeping the peace at the price of repression. Thirteenth-century Piacenza was typical: first dominated by

---

*See 2 Kings 24–25.

nobles, the popolo gained a voice by 1225; but then by midcentury both the nobles and the popolo were eclipsed by the power of a signore.

The Mongol Takeover

Europeans were not the only warring society in the thirteenth century: to the east, the Mongols (sometimes called Tatars or Tartars) created an aggressive army under the leadership of Chingiz (or Genghis) Khan (c. 1162–1227) and his sons. In part, economic necessity drove them out of Mongolia: changes in climate had reduced the grasslands that sustained their animals and their nomadic way of life. But they were also inspired by Chingiz's hope of conquering the world. By 1215, the Mongols held Beijing and most of northern China. Some years later, they moved through central Asia and skirted the Caspian Sea (Map 12.2).

In the 1230s, the Mongols began concerted attacks against Rus, Poland, and Hungary, where native princes were weak. Fighting mainly on horseback with heavy lances

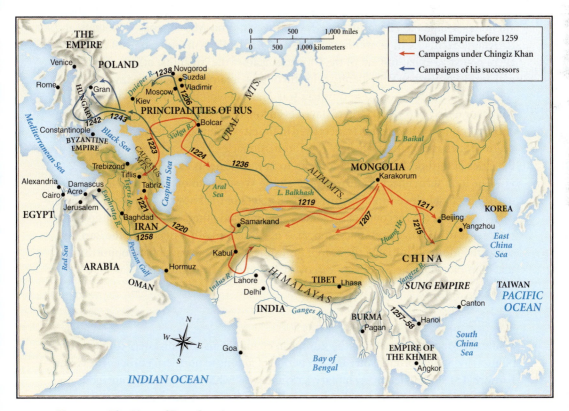

Map 12.2 The Mongol Invasions to 1259
The Mongols tied East Asia to the west. Their conquest of China, which took place at about the same time as their invasions of Russia and Iran, created a Eurasian economy. Compare this map with the Mapping the West map on page 365. Why were the Mongol invasions a threat to the Muslim world?

and powerful bows and arrows whose shots traveled far and penetrated deeply, the Mongols initially pushed through Hungary. Only the death of the second Great Khan, Chingiz's son Ogodei (1186–1241), and disputes over his succession prevented a concentrated assault on Germany. In the 1250s, the Mongols took Iran and Iraq.

Soon retreating from Hungary, the Mongols established themselves in Rus, where in 1240 they had captured Kiev. This remained the center of their power, but they dominated all of Russia for about two hundred years. The Mongol Empire in Rus, later called the **Golden Horde** (*golden* probably from the color of their leader's tent; *horde* from a Turkish word meaning "camp"), adopted much of the local government apparatus and left many of the old institutions in place. The Mongols allowed Rus princes to continue ruling as long as those princes paid homage and tribute to the khan, and they tolerated the Rus church, exempting it from taxes. The Mongols' chief undertaking was a series of population censuses on the basis of which they recalculated taxes and recruited troops.

The Mongol invasion changed the political configuration of Europe and Asia. Because the Mongols were willing to deal with Westerners, one effect of their conquests was to open China to European travelers for the first time. Missionaries, diplomats, and merchants went to China over land routes and via the Persian Gulf. Some of these voyagers hoped to enlist the aid of the Mongols against the Muslims, others expected to make new converts to Christianity, and still others dreamed of lucrative trade routes.

The most famous of these travelers was Marco Polo (1254–1324), who stayed in China for nearly two years. Others stayed even longer. In fact, evidence suggests that an entire community of Venetian traders lived in the city of Yangzhou in the mid-fourteenth century. Such merchants paved the way for missionaries. Friars, who were preachers to the cities of Europe, became missionaries to new continents as well.

The long-term effect of the Mongols on the West was to open up new land routes to the East that helped bind together the two halves of the known world. Travel stories such as Marco Polo's account of his journeys stimulated others to seek out the fabulous riches — textiles, ginger, ceramics, copper — of China and other regions of the East. In a sense, the Mongols initiated the search for exotic goods and missionary opportunities that culminated in the European "discovery" of a new world, the Americas.

The Great Famine

While the Mongols stimulated the European economy, natural disasters coupled with political ineptitude brought on a terrible period of famine in northern Europe. The **Great Famine** (1315–1322) left many hungry, sick, and weak while it fueled social antagonisms. An anonymous chronicler looking back on the events of 1315 wrote:

> The floods of rain have rotted almost all the seed, . . . and in many places the hay lay so long under water that it could neither be mown nor gathered. Sheep generally died and other animals were killed in a sudden plague. . . . [In the next year, 1316,] the dearth of grain was much increased. Such a scarcity has

not been seen in our time in England, nor heard of for a hundred years. For the measure of wheat sold in London and the neighboring places for forty pence [a very high price], and in other less thickly populated parts of the country thirty pence was a common price.

Thus did the writer chronicle the causes and effects of the famine: uncommonly heavy rains, which washed up or drowned the crops; a disease that killed farm animals key to agricultural life not only for their meat and fleeces but also for their labor; and, finally, the economic effects, as scarcity drove up the prices of ordinary foods. All of these led to hunger, disease, and death.

Had the rains gone back to normal, the Europeans might have recovered. But the rains continued, and the crops kept failing. In many regions, the crisis lasted for a full seven years. Hardest hit were the peasants and the poor. In rural areas, wealthy lords, churches, monasteries, and well-to-do peasants profited from the newly high prices they could charge. (See "Taking Measure," below.) In the cities, some merchants and

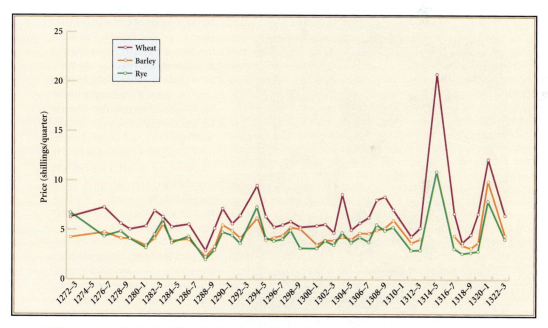

Taking Measure Grain Prices during the Great Famine
Famine was caused not just by a shortage of food but also by spikes in prices that made it impossible for the poor to buy enough to eat. The graph shown here represents the prices of grain produced on the English manor of Hinderclay between 1272 and 1324. It is clear that prices fluctuated greatly and that during the period of the Great Famine, 1315–1322, they rose dramatically, with the years 1316–1317 particularly striking. Note that the price of wheat was always higher than the prices of barley and rye, which were considered inferior grains. (That notion would change as beer, which is made with barley, gained favor.) The spikes in prices suggest that very little charitable distribution of grain was taking place on Hinderclay manor. (Based on Phillipp R. Schofield, "The Social Economy of the Medieval Village in the Early Fourteenth Century," *Economic History Review* 61 [2008]: 44, Figure 1.)

ecclesiastical institutions benefited as well. But on the whole, even the well-to-do suffered: both rural and urban areas lost fully 5 to 10 percent of their population, and loss of population meant erosion of manpower and falling productivity.

To cope with and contain these disasters, the clergy offered up prayers and urged their congregations to do penance. In the countryside, charitable monasteries gave out food, conscientious kings tried to control high interest rates on loans, and hungry peasants migrated from west to east — to Poland, for example, where land was more plentiful. In the cities, where starving refugees from rural areas flocked for food, wealthy men and women sometimes opened their storehouses or distributed coins. Other rich townspeople founded hospitals for the poor. Town councils sold municipal bonds at high rates of interest, gaining some temporary solvency. These towns became the primary charitable institutions of the era, importing grain and selling it at or slightly below cost.

Contributing to the crop failure was population growth that challenged the productive capabilities of the age. The exponential leap in population from the tenth through

A Famine in Florence
Starvation did not end with the last year of the Great Famine. This miniature from a manuscript detailing grain prices shows the effects — and the artist's interpretation — of a famine in 1329. The scene is the Orsanmichele, the Florentine grain market. The market was dominated by an image of the Virgin Mary, here depicted on the right-hand side. Extending beyond the margin on the far left, a mother with two children raises her hands and eyes to heaven in prayer. In the back, soldiers guard the market's entrance. The market itself bustles with rich buyers, who hand over their money and pack their bags with grain. Above flies an angel with broken trumpets, while a demon takes center stage and says, among other things, "I will make you ache with hunger and high prices." (Biblioteca Laurenziana, Florence, Italy / Scala / Art Resource, NY.)

most of the thirteenth century slowed to zero around the year 1300, but all the land that could be cultivated had been settled by this time. No new technology had been developed to increase crop yields. The swollen population demanded a lot from the productive capacities of the land. Just a small shortfall could dislocate the whole system of distribution.

The policies of rulers added to the problems of too many people and too little food. Wars between England and Scotland destroyed crops. So did wars between the kings of Norway, Denmark, and Sweden. These wars also diverted manpower and resources to arms and castles, and they disrupted normal markets and trade routes.

In order to wage wars, rulers imposed heavy taxes and, as the Great Famine became worse, requisitioned grain to support their troops. The effects of the famine grew worse, and in many regions people rose up in protest. In England, peasants resisted tax collectors. In a more violent reaction, poor French shepherds, outcasts, clerics, and artisans entered Paris to storm the prisons. They then marched southward — burning royal castles and attacking officials, Jews, and lepers. The king of France pursued them and succeeded in putting down the movement. But the limits of the politics of control were made clear in this confrontation, which exacerbated the misery of the famine while doing nothing to contain it.

> **REVIEW QUESTION** How did the search for harmony result in cooperation — and confrontation — between the secular rulers of the period 1215–1340 and other institutions, such as the church and the towns?

Conclusion

The thirteenth century sought harmony and synthesis but discovered how elusive these goals could be. Theoretically, the papacy and empire were supposed to work together; instead they clashed in bitter warfare, leaving the government of Germany to the princes and northern Italy to its communes and signori. Theoretically, faith and reason were supposed to arrive at the same truths. They sometimes did so in the hands of scholastics, but not always. Theoretically, all Christians practiced the same rites and followed the teachings of the church. In practice, local enforcement determined which church laws took effect — and to what extent. Moreover, the search for order was never able to bring together all the diverse peoples, ideas, and interests of thirteenth-century society. Heretics and Jews were set apart.

Synthesis was more achievable in the arts. Heaven, earth, and hell were melded harmoniously together in stained glass and sculpture. Musicians wove disparate melodic and poetic lines into motets. Writers melded heroic and romantic themes with theological truths and mystical visions.

Political leaders also aimed at harmony. Via representative institutions, they harnessed the various social orders to their quest for greater order and control. They asserted sovereignty over all the people who lived in their borders, asserting unity while increasing their revenues, expanding their territories, and enhancing their prestige. The

Mapping the West Europe, c. 1340

The Empire, which in the thirteenth century came to be called the Holy Roman Empire, still dominated the map of Europe in 1340, but the emperor himself had less power than ever. Each principality — often each city — was ruled separately and independently. To the east, the Ottoman Turks were just beginning to make themselves felt. In the course of the next century, they would disrupt the Mongol hegemony and become a great power.

kings of England and France and the governments of northern and central Italian cities largely succeeded in these goals, while the king of Germany failed miserably. Germany and Italy remained fragmented until the nineteenth century. Ironically, the Mongols, who began as invaders in the West, helped unify areas that were far apart by opening trade routes.

Events at the end of the thirteenth century thwarted the search for harmony. The mutual respect of church and state achieved under St. Louis in France disintegrated into

irreconcilable claims to power under Pope Boniface VIII and Philip the Fair. The carefully constructed tapestry of St. Thomas's summae began to unravel in the teachings of John Duns Scotus. An economy stretched to the breaking point resulted in a terrible period of famine. Disorder and anxiety — but also extraordinary creativity — would mark the next era.

Review Questions

1. How did people respond to the teachings and laws of the church in the early thirteenth century?
2. How did artists, musicians, and scholastics in the thirteenth and early fourteenth centuries try to link the physical world with the divine?
3. How did the search for harmony result in cooperation — and confrontation — between the secular rulers of the period 1215–1340 and other institutions, such as the church and the towns?

Making Connections

1. Why was Innocent III more successful than Boniface VIII in carrying out his objectives?
2. How did the growth of lay piety help bolster the prestige and power of kings like Louis IX?
3. Comparing the goals and methods of Abelard's scholarship with those of Thomas Aquinas, explain the continuities and the differences between the twelfth-century schools and the scholastic movement.

- For practice quizzes and other study tools, visit the **Online Study Guide** at bedfordstmartins.com/huntconcise.

- For primary-source material from this period, see *Sources of the Making of the West*, Fourth Edition.

- For Web sites, images, and documents related to topics in this chapter, visit *Make History* at bedfordstmartins.com/huntconcise.

Suggested References

For the church's mission, see both Bynum and Sayers. The Inquisition and other forms of persecution are the subjects of the books by Given, Jordan (on the Jews), and Nirenberg. Abulafia, Jones, Maddicott, and O'Callaghan each helpfully cover the political developments of the period.

Abulafia, David. *Frederick II: A Medieval Emperor*. 1988.

Bynum, Caroline Walker. *Holy Feast and Holy Fast: The Religious Significance of Food to Medieval Women*. 1987.

*Fourth Lateran Council: http://www.fordham.edu/halsall/source/lat4-select.asp

Gaposchkin, M. Cecilia. *The Making of Saint Louis: Kingship, Sanctity, and Crusade in the Later Middle Ages*. 2008.

Given, James Buchanan. *Inquisition and Medieval Society*. 2001.

Jackson, Peter. *The Mongols and the West*. 2005.

*Joinville, Jean de, and Geoffroy de Villehardouin. *Chronicles of the Crusades*. Trans. M. R. B. Shaw. 1963.

Jones, Philip. *The Italian City-State: From Commune to Signoria*. 1997.

Jordan, William Chester. *The French Monarchy and the Jews: From Philip Augustus to the Last Capetians*. 1989.

Maddicott, J. R. *Simon De Montfort*. 1994.

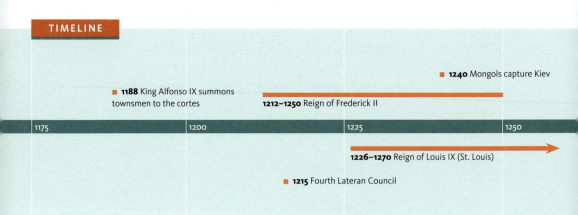

TIMELINE

1240 Mongols capture Kiev

1188 King Alfonso IX summons townsmen to the cortes

1212–1250 Reign of Frederick II

1175   1200   1225   1250

1226–1270 Reign of Louis IX (St. Louis)

1215 Fourth Lateran Council

Nichols, Aidan. *Discovering Aquinas: An Introduction to His Life, Work and Influence*. 2003.

Nirenberg, David. *Communities of Violence: Persecution of Minorities in the Middle Ages*. 1996.

O'Callaghan, Joseph F. *The Cortes of Castille-León, 1188–1350*. 1989.

Richardson, H. G., and G. O. Sayles. *The English Parliament in the Middle Ages*. 1981.

Sayers, Jane. *Innocent III: Leader of Europe, 1198–1216*. 1994.

Strayer, Joseph R. *The Reign of Philip the Fair*. 1980.

*Thomas Aquinas: http://www.newadvent.org/summa

*Primary source.

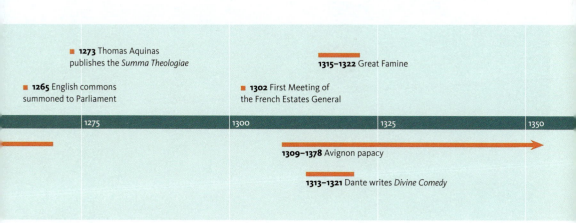

1273 Thomas Aquinas publishes the *Summa Theologiae*

1315–1322 Great Famine

1265 English commons summoned to Parliament

1302 First Meeting of the French Estates General

| 1275 | 1300 | 1325 | 1350 |

1309–1378 Avignon papacy

1313–1321 Dante writes *Divine Comedy*

Crisis and Renaissance

I N 1453, THE OTTOMAN TURKS turned their cannons on Constantinople and blasted the city's walls. The fall of Constantinople, which spelled the end of the Byzantine Empire, was an enormous shock to Europeans. Some, like the pope, called for a crusade against the Ottomans; others, like the writer Lauro Quirini, sneered, calling the Ottomans "a barbaric, uncultivated race, without established customs, or laws, [who lived] a careless, vagrant, arbitrary life."

But the Turks didn't consider themselves uncultivated or arbitrary. They saw themselves as the true heirs of the Roman Empire, and they shared many of the values and tastes of the very Europeans who were so hostile to them. Sultan Mehmed II employed European architects to construct his new palace — the Topkapi Saray — in the city once known as Constantinople and now popularly called Istanbul. He commissioned the Venetian artist Gentile Bellini to paint his portrait, a genre invented in Burgundy to celebrate the status and individuality of important and wealthy patrons.

Portrait of Mehmed II

The Ottoman ruler Mehmed II saw himself as a Renaissance patron of the arts, and he called on the most famous artists and architects of the day to work for him. The painter of this portrait, Gentile Bellini, was from a well-known family of artists in Venice and served at Mehmed's court in 1479–1480. The revival of portraiture, so characteristic of Renaissance tastes, was as important to the Turkish sultans as to European rulers. (Erich Lessing / Art Resource, NY.)

Mehmed's actions sum up the dual features of the period of crisis and Renaissance that took place from the middle of the fourteenth century to the late fifteenth century. What was a crisis from one point of view — the fall of the Byzantine Empire — was at the same time stimulus for what historians call the Renaissance. Both to confront and to mask the crises of the day, people discovered new value in ancient, classical culture; they created a new vocabulary drawn from classical literature as well as astonishing new forms of art and music based on ancient precedents. The classical revival provided the stimulus for new styles of living, ruling, and thinking.

Along with the fall of the Byzantine Empire, other crises marked the period from 1340 to 1492. These were matched by equally significant gains. The plague, or Black Death, tore at the fabric of communities and families; but the survivors and their

children reaped the benefits of higher wages and better living standards. The Hundred Years' War, fought between France and England, involved many smaller states in its slaughter and brought untold misery to the French countryside; but it also helped create the glittering court of Burgundy. By the war's end, both the French and the English kings were more powerful than ever. Following their conquest of Constantinople, the Ottoman Turks penetrated far into the Balkans; but this was a calamity only from the European point of view. Well into the sixteenth century, the Ottomans were part of the culture that nourished the artistic achievements of the Renaissance. A crisis in the church overlapped with the crises of disease and war as a schism within the papacy — pitting pope against pope — divided Europe into separate camps. But a church council whose members included Renaissance humanists eventually resolved the papal schism by reestablishing the old system: a single pope who presided over the church from Rome.

CHAPTER FOCUS How were the crises of 1340–1492 and the Renaissance related?

Crisis: Disease, War, and Schism

In the mid-fourteenth century, a series of crises shook the West. The Black Death swept through Europe and decimated the population, especially in the cities. Two major wars redrew the map of Europe between 1340 and 1492. The first was the Hundred Years' War, fought from 1337 to 1453 (thus actually lasting 116 years). The second was the Ottoman conquest of Constantinople in 1453. As the wars raged and attacks of the plague came and went, a crisis in the church also weighed on Europeans. Attempts to return the papacy from Avignon to Rome resulted in the Great Schism (1378–1417), when first two and then three rival popes asserted universal authority. In the wake of these crises, many ordinary folk sought solace in new forms of piety, some of them condemned by the church as heretical.

The Black Death, 1347–1352

The **Black Death**, so named by later historians, was a calamitous disease. It decimated the population wherever it struck and wreaked havoc on social and economic structures (see "Taking Measure," page 401). Yet in the wake of this plague, those fortunate enough to survive benefited from an improved standard of living. Birthrates climbed, and new universities were established to educate the post-plague generations.

Already in 1346, the Byzantine scholar Nicephorus Gregoras noted a new disease and described its symptoms, including "tumorous outgrowths at the roots of thighs and arms and simultaneously bleeding ulcerations." Scientists now ascribe the Black Death to the bacterium *Yersinia pestis,* the same organism responsible for outbreaks of plague today.

Carried by fleas traveling on the backs of rats, the Black Death hitched boat rides with spices, silks, and porcelain. It hit the Genoese colony in Caffa in 1347 and soon ar-

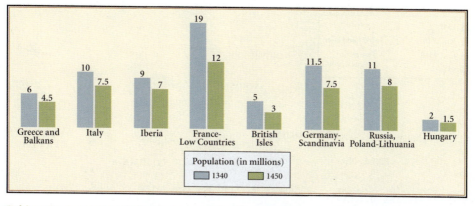

Taking Measure **Population Losses and the Black Death**

The bar chart dramatically represents the impact of the Black Death and the recurrent epidemics that hit Europe between 1340 and 1450. More than a century after the Black Death, none of the regions of Europe had made up for the losses of population. The population of 1450 stood at about 75–80 percent of the pre-plague population. The areas hardest hit were France and the Low Countries, which also suffered from the devastation of the Hundred Years' War. (From Carlo M. Cipolla, ed., *Fontana Economic History of Europe: The Middle Ages* [Great Britain: Collins/Fontana Books, 1974], 36.)

rived in Constantinople and southern Europe. It then crept northward to Germany, England, Scandinavia, and the state that now was starting to be called Russia.* Meanwhile, it attacked the Islamic world as well (Map 13.1). Recurring every ten to twelve years throughout the fourteenth century (though only the outbreak of 1347–1352 is called the Black Death), the disease attacked, with decreasing frequency, until the eighteenth century.

The effects of the Black Death were spread across Europe yet oddly localized. At Florence, in Italy, nearly half of the population died, yet two hundred miles to the north, Milan suffered very little. Conservative estimates put the death toll in Europe anywhere between 30 and 50 percent of the entire population, but some historians put the mortality rate as high as 60 percent. Already weakened by the Great Famine as well as by local food shortages and epidemic diseases like smallpox, Europeans were devastated by the arrival of *Yersinia*.

Many localities sought remedies. The government of the Italian city of Pistoia, for example, set up a quarantine and demanded better sanitation. Elsewhere reactions were religious. In England, the archbishop of York tried to prevent the plague from entering his diocese by ordering "devout processions." Some people took more extreme measures. Lamenting their sins — which they believed had brought on the plague — and attempting to placate God, flagellants, both men and women, wandered from city to city whipping themselves. Religious enthusiasm often culminated in violence against the Jews, who were blamed for the Black Death. In Germany, thousands of Jews were slaughtered.

---

*The Russian Orthodox church had always used the term *Russia*. In the fourteenth century, the princes who ruled the northern parts, called Muscovy, started to do so as well.

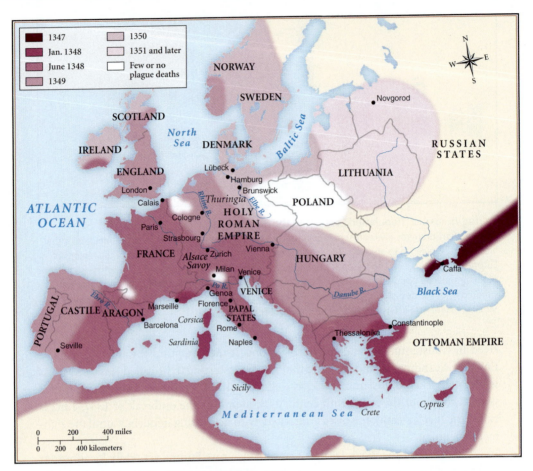

Map 13.1 Advance of the Black Death, 1346–1353
Hitting the Mediterranean area first, the Black Death quickly worked its way northward, generally following waterways and roads. With the exception of a few regions that were spared, it killed between one-third and one-half of the population of western Europe. However, in eastern Europe its impact was far less. The plague recurred—at first every ten to twelve years and then at longer intervals.

Many Jews fled to Poland, where the epidemic affected fewer people and where the authorities welcomed Jews as productive taxpayers.

Preoccupation with death led to the popularity of a theme called the Dance of Death as a subject of art, literature, and performance. It featured a procession of people of every age, sex, and rank making their way to the grave. In works of art, skeletal figures of Death, whirling about, laughed as they abducted their prey. Preachers, poets, and playwrights relished the theme.

At the same time that it helped inspire this bleak view of the world, the Black Death brought new opportunities for those who survived its murderous path. With a smaller population to feed, less land was needed for cultivation. Landlords allowed marginal land that had been cultivated to return to pasture, meadow, or forest, and they diversi-

Dance of Death

This fresco, painted in 1474 on a wall of a cemetery church in Croatia, depicts figures meant to represent all the "types" in medieval society. It should be read from right to left. Not pictured here, but first in line, is the pope, followed by a cardinal and a bishop. The portion shown here comes next: the king, who holds a scepter; the queen; and a landlord, carrying a small barrel. At the far left is a child. Even farther to the left (but not shown here) come a beggar, a knight, and a shopkeeper. All the figures are flanked by gleeful, dancing skeletons. The message is clear: everyone, even the most exalted, ends up in the grave. (Alfredo Dagli Orti / Art Resource, NY.)

fied their products. Wheat had been the favored crop before the plague, but barley — the key ingredient of beer — turned out to be more profitable afterward. Animal products continued to fetch a high price, and some landlords switched from raising crops to raising animals.

These changes in agriculture meant a better standard of living. The peasants and urban workers who survived the plague were able to negotiate better conditions or higher wages from their landlords or employers. With more money to spend, people could afford a better and more varied diet that included beer and meat. Birthrates jumped as people could afford to marry at younger ages.

The Black Death, which spared neither professors nor students, also affected patterns of education. The survivors built new local colleges and universities, partly to train a new generation for the priesthood and partly to satisfy local donors — many of them princes — who, riding on a sea of wealth left behind by the dead, wanted to be known as

patrons of education. Thus, in 1348, in the midst of the Black Death, Holy Roman Emperor Charles IV chartered a university at Prague. The king of Poland founded Cracow University, and a Habsburg duke created a university at Vienna. Rather than traveling to Paris or Bologna, young men living east of the Rhine River now tended to study nearer home.

The Hundred Years' War, 1337–1453

Adding to people's miseries during the Black Death were the ravages of war. One of the most brutal was the **Hundred Years' War**, which pitted England against France. Since the Norman conquest of England in 1066, the king of England had held land on the continent. The French kings continually chipped away at it, however, and by the beginning of the fourteenth century England retained only the area around Bordeaux, called Guyenne. In 1337, after a series of challenges and skirmishes, King Philip VI of France (whose dynasty, the Valois, took over when the Capetians had no male heir) declared Guyenne to be his. In turn, King Edward III of England, son of Philip the Fair's daughter, declared himself king of France (Figure 13.1). The Hundred Years' War had begun.

The war had two major phases. In the first, the English gained ground, and a new political entity, the duchy of Burgundy, allied itself with England. This phase culmi-

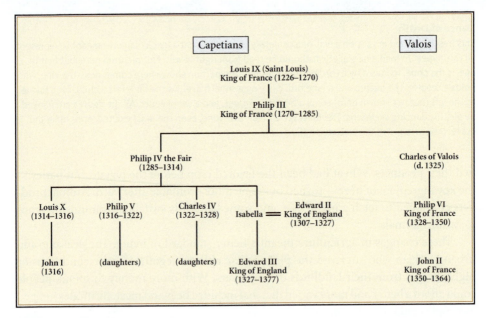

Figure 13.1 The Valois Succession
When the Capetian king Charles IV died in 1328, his daughter was next in line for the French throne, but prejudice in France against female succession was so strong that the crown went to the Valois branch of the family. Meanwhile the English king Edward III, as son of the French princess Isabella, claimed to be the rightful king of France.

nated in 1415, when the English achieved a great victory at the battle of Agincourt and took over northern France. In the second phase, however, fortunes reversed entirely after a sixteen-year-old peasant girl inspired the dauphin (the yet-uncrowned heir to the throne) and his troops. Prompted by visions in which God told her to lead the war against the English, and calling herself "the Maid" (a virgin), **Joan of Arc** (1412–1431) arrived at court in 1429 wearing armor, riding a horse, and leading a small army. Full of charisma and confidence at a desperate hour, Joan convinced the French that she had been sent by God when she fought courageously (and was wounded) in the successful battle of Orléans. Soon, with Joan at his side, the dauphin traveled deep into enemy territory to be anointed and crowned as King Charles VII at the cathedral in Reims, following the tradition of French monarchs. Although Joan herself was captured by the English and put to death, the French went on to oust the English (Map 13.2).

As it unfolded, the Hundred Years' War drew people from much of Europe into its vortex. Both the English and the French hired mercenaries from Germany, Switzerland, and the Netherlands; the best crossbowmen came from Genoa.

The duchy of Burgundy became involved in the war when the marriage of the heiress to Flanders and the duke of Burgundy in 1369 created a powerful new state. Calculating shrewdly which side — England or France — to support and cannily entering the fray when it suited them, the dukes of Burgundy created a glittering court, a center of art and culture. Had Burgundy maintained its alliance with England, the map of Europe would be entirely different today. But, sensing France's new strength, the duke of Burgundy broke off with England in 1435. The duchy continued to prosper until

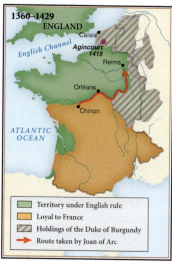

Map 13.2 The Hundred Years' War, 1337–1453
During the Hundred Years' War, English kings — aided by the new state of Burgundy — contested the French monarchy for the domination of France. For many decades, the English seemed to be winning, but the French monarchy prevailed in the end.

its expansionist policies led to the formation of a coalition against it. The last duke, Charles the Bold, died fighting in 1477. His daughter, his only heir, tried to save Burgundy by marrying the Holy Roman Emperor, but the move was to little avail. The duchy broke up, with France absorbing its western bits.

Flanders, too, got drawn into the war. Its cities depended on England for the raw wool that they turned into cloth. This is why, at the beginning of the war, Flemish townsmen allied with England against their count, who supported the French king. But discord among the cities and within each town soon ended the rebellion. Although revolts continued to flare up, the count thereafter allowed a measure of self-government to the towns, maintained some distance from French influence, and managed on the whole to keep the peace.

The nature of warfare changed during the Hundred Years' War. At its start, the chronicler Jean Froissart (d. c. 1405) considered it a chivalric adventure, expecting it to display the gallantry and bravery of the medieval nobility. But even Froissart could not help but notice that most of the men who went to battle were not wealthy nobles and knights. They were not even ordinary foot soldiers, who previously had made up a large portion of all medieval armies. The soldiers of the Hundred Years' War were primarily mercenaries: men who fought for pay and plunder, heedless of the king for whom they were supposed to be fighting. During lulls in the war, these so-called Free Companies lived off the French countryside, terrorizing the peasants and exacting "protection" money.

The ideal chivalric knight fought on horseback with other armed horsemen. But in the Hundred Years' War, foot soldiers and archers were far more important than swordsmen. The French tended to use crossbows, whose heavy, deadly arrows were released by a mechanism that even a townsman could master. The English employed longbows, which could shoot five arrows for every one launched on the crossbow. Meanwhile, gunpowder was slowly being introduced and cannons forged. Handguns were beginning to be used, their effect about equal to that of crossbows.

By the end of the war, chivalry was only a dream — though one that continued to inspire soldiers even up to the First World War. Heavy artillery and foot soldiers, tightly massed together in formations of many thousands of men, were the face of the new military. Moreover, the army was becoming more professional and centralized. In the 1440s, the French king created a permanent army of mounted soldiers. He paid them a wage and subjected them to regular inspection.

In addition to changing the face of warfare, the Hundred Years' War gave a new voice — however temporary — to the lower classes in France and England. When the English captured the French king John at the battle of Poitiers in 1358, Étienne Marcel, provost of the Paris merchants, and other disillusioned members of the estates of France (the representatives of the clergy, nobility, and commons) met to discuss political reform, the incompetence of the French army, and the high taxes they paid to finance the war. Under Marcel's leadership, a crowd of Parisians killed some nobles and for a short while took control of the city. But troops soon blockaded Paris and cut off its food supply. Later that year, Marcel was assassinated and the Parisian revolt came to an end.

In the same year, peasants weary of the Free Companies (who were ravaging the countryside) and disgusted by the military incompetence of the nobility rose up in protest. The French nobility called the peasant rebellion the **Jacquerie**, probably taken from a derisive name for male peasants: Jacques Bonhomme ("Jack Goodfellow"). The peasants committed atrocities against local nobles, but the nobles soon gave as good as they got, putting down the Jacquerie with exceptional brutality.

Similar revolts took place in England. The movement known as Wat Tyler's Rebellion started in much of southern and central England when royal agents tried to collect poll taxes (a tax on each household) to finance the Hundred Years' War. Refusing to pay and refusing to be arrested, the commons — peasants and small householders — rose up in rebellion in 1381. They massed in various groups, vowing "to slay all lawyers, and all jurors, and all the servants of the King whom they could find." Marching to London to see the king, they began to make a more radical demand: an end to serfdom. Although the rebellion was put down and its leaders executed, peasants returned home to bargain with their lords for better terms. The death knell of serfdom in England had been sounded.

The Ottoman Conquest of Constantinople, 1453

The end of the Hundred Years' War coincided with an event that was even more decisive for all of Europe: the conquest of Constantinople by the Ottoman Turks. The Ottomans, who were converts to Islam, were one of several tribal confederations in central Asia. Starting as a small enclave between the Mongol Empire and Byzantium, and taking their name from a potent early leader, Osman I (r. 1280–1324), the Ottomans began to expand in the fourteenth century in a quest to wage holy war against infidels, or unbelievers.

During the next two centuries, the Ottomans took over the Balkans and Anatolia by both negotiations and arms (Map 13.3). They reduced the Byzantine Empire to the city of Constantinople and treated it as a vassal state. Under the sultan **Mehmed II** (r. 1451–1481), they besieged the city of Constantinople itself in 1453. Perhaps eighty thousand men confronted some three thousand defenders (the entire population of Constantinople was no more than fifty thousand) and a fleet from Genoa. The city held out until the end of May but was forced

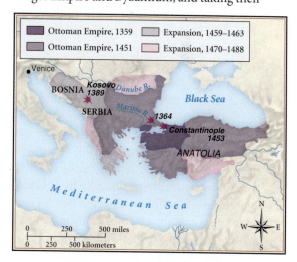

Map 13.3 Ottoman Expansion in the Fourteenth and Fifteenth Centuries
The Balkans were the major theater of expansion for the Ottoman Empire. The Byzantine Empire was reduced to the city of Constantinople and surrounded by the Ottomans before its final fall in 1453.

to capitulate when the sultan's cannons breached the city's land walls. Mehmed's troops entered the city and plundered it thoroughly, killing the emperor and displaying his head in triumph.

The conquest of Constantinople marked the end of the Byzantine Empire. But that was not the way Mehmed saw the matter. He conquered Constantinople in part to be a successor to the Roman emperors — a Muslim successor, to be sure. He turned Hagia Sophia (the great church built by the emperor Justinian in 538) into a mosque, as he did with most of the other Byzantine churches. He retained the city's name, the City of Constantine — Qustantiniyya in Turkish — though it was popularly referred to as Istanbul, meaning, simply, "the city."

Like the French and English kings after the Hundred Years' War, the Ottoman sultans were centralizing monarchs who guaranteed law and order. The core of their army consisted of European Christian boys, who were requisitioned as tribute every five years. Trained in arms and converted to Islam, these young fighters made up the Janissaries — a highly disciplined military force also used to supervise local administrators throughout formerly Byzantine regions. Building a system of roads that crisscrossed their empire, the sultans made long-distance trade easy and profitable.

Once Constantinople was his, Mehmed embarked on an ambitious program of expansion and conquest. By 1500, the Ottoman Empire was a new and powerful state bridging Europe and the Middle East.

The Great Schism, 1378–1417

Even as war and disease threatened Europeans' material and physical well-being, a crisis in the church, precipitated by a scandal in the papacy, tore at their spiritual life. The move of the papacy from Rome to Avignon in 1309 had caused an outcry, and some critics, such as Marsilius of Padua, became disillusioned with the institution of the papacy itself. In *The Defender of the Peace* (1324), Marsilius argued that the source of all power lay with the people: Christians themselves formed the church; the pope should be elected by a general council representing all Christians.

William of Ockham (c. 1285–1349), an English Franciscan, was an even more thoroughgoing critic of the papacy. Not only did he believe that church power derived from the congregation of the faithful, but he rejected the confident synthesis of Christian doctrine and Aristotelian philosophy by Thomas Aquinas. William argued that universal concepts, such as "human being," had no reality in nature but instead existed only as mere representations, names in the mind — a philosophy that came to be called nominalism. The principle that simple explanations were superior to complex ones became known as Ockham's razor (to suggest the idea of shaving away unnecessary hypotheses).

Stung by his critics, Pope Gregory XI (r. 1370–1378) left Avignon to return to Rome in 1377. The scandal of the Avignon papacy seemed to be over. Glad to have the papacy back, the Romans were determined never to lose it again. But when the cardinals chose an Italian (who took the name Urban VI), he immediately exalted the power of the pope and began to reduce the cardinals' wealth and privileges. The cardinals from France

decided that they had made a big mistake. Many left Rome for a meeting at Anagni, where they claimed that Urban's election had been irregular and called on him to resign. When he refused, they elected a Frenchman as pope; he took the name Clement VII and soon moved his papal court to Avignon, but not before he and Urban had excommunicated each other. The **Great Schism** (1378–1417), which split the loyalties of all of Europe, had begun.

The king of France supported Clement; the king of England favored Urban. Some European states lined up on the side of France, while others supported Urban. Each pope declared that those who followed the other were to be deprived of the rights of church membership; in effect, everyone in Europe was excommunicated by one pope or the other. Church law said that only a pope could summon a general council of the church. But given the state of confusion in Christendom, many intellectuals argued that the crisis justified calling a general council to represent the body of the faithful, even against the wishes of an unwilling pope — or popes. They spearheaded the conciliar movement — a movement to have the cardinals or the emperor call a council.

In 1408, long after Urban and Clement had passed away and new popes had followed, the conciliar movement succeeded when cardinals from both sides met and declared their resolve "to pursue the union of the Church . . . by way of abdication of both papal contenders." With support from both England and France, the cardinals called for a council to be held at Pisa in 1409. Both popes refused to attend, and the council deposed them, electing a new pope.

But the "deposed" popes refused to budge, even though most of the European powers abandoned them. There were now three popes. The successor of the newest one, John XXIII, turned to the emperor to arrange for another council.

The Council of Constance (1414–1418) met to resolve the papal crisis as well as to institute church reforms. The delegates deposed John XXIII and accepted the resignation of the pope at Rome. After long negotiations with rulers still supporting the Avignon pope, all allegiance to him was withdrawn and he was deposed. The council then elected Martin V, whom every important ruler of Europe recognized as pope. Finally, the Great Schism had come to an end.

Nevertheless, the schism had worked changes in the religious sensibilities of Europeans. Worried about the salvation of their souls now that the church was fractured by multiple popes, pious men and women eagerly sought new forms of religious solace. The church offered the plenary indulgence — full forgiveness of sins, which had been originally offered to crusaders who died while fighting for the cause — to those who made a pilgrimage to Rome and other designated holy places during declared Holy Years. People could wipe away their sins through confession and contrition, but they retained some guilt that they could remove only through good deeds or in purgatory. The idea of purgatory — the place where sins were fully purged — took precise form at this time, and with it **indulgences** became popular. These remissions of sin were offered for good works to reduce the time in purgatory.

Both clergy and laity became more interested than ever in the education of young people as a way to deepen their faith and spiritual life. The Brethren of the Common

Life — laypeople, mainly in the Low Countries (the region comprising today's Belgium, Luxembourg, and the Netherlands), who devoted themselves to pious works — set up a model school at Deventer. In Italy, humanists (see page 412) emphasized primary school education. Priests were expected to teach the faithful the basics of the Christian religion.

Home was equally a place for devotion. Portable images of Mary, the mother of God, and of the life and passion of Christ proliferated. Ordinary Christians contemplated them at convenient moments throughout the day. People purchased or commissioned copies of Books of Hours, which contained prayers to be said at the same hours of the day that monks chanted their liturgy. Books of Hours included calendars, sometimes splendidly illustrated with depictions of the seasons and labors of the year. Other illustrations reminded their users of the life and suffering of Christ.

On the streets of towns, priests marched in dignified processions, carrying the sanctified bread of the Mass — the very body of Christ — in tall and splendid monstrances that trumpeted the importance and dignity of the Eucharistic wafer. The image of a bleeding, crucified Christ was repeated over and over in depictions of the day. Viewers were meant to think about Christ's pain and feel it themselves, mentally participating in his death on the cross.

Religious anxieties, intellectual dissent, and social unrest combined to create new heretical movements in England and Bohemia. In England were the Lollards, a term that was derogatory in the hands of their opponents and yet a proud title when used by the Lollards themselves. Inspired by the Oxford scholar John Wycliffe (c. 1330–1384), who taught that the true church was the community of believers rather than the clerical hierarchy, Lollards

Book of Hours

This illustration for June in a Book of Hours made for the duke of Berry was meant for the contemplation of a nobleman. In the background is a fairy-tale depiction of the duke's palace and the tower of a Gothic church, while in the foreground graceful women rake the hay and well-muscled men swing their scythes. (Réunion des Musées Nationaux / Art Resource, NY.)

emphasized Bible reading in the vernacular. Although suffering widespread hostility and persecution into the sixteenth century, the Lollards were extremely active, setting up schools for children (girls as well as boys), translating the Bible from Latin into English, preaching numerous sermons, and inspiring new recruits.

On the other side of Europe were the Bohemian Hussites — named after one of their leaders, Jan Hus (1372?–1415), an admirer of Wycliffe. When priests celebrated Mass, they had the privilege of drinking the wine (the blood of Christ); the faithful received only the bread (the body). The Hussites, who were largely Czech laity, wanted the privilege of drinking the wine as well and, with it, recognition of their dignity and worth. Their demand brought together several passionately held desires and beliefs: it reflected a focus on the redemptive power of Christ's blood. Furthermore, the call for communion with *both* bread and wine signified a desire for equality. Bohemia was an exceptionally divided country, with an urban German-speaking elite, including merchants, artisans, bishops, and scholars, and a Czech-speaking nobility and peasantry that was beginning to seek better opportunities. (Hus himself was a Czech of peasant stock who became a professor at the University of Prague.)

The Bohemian nobility protected Hus after the church condemned him as a heretic, but the Holy Roman Emperor Sigismund lured him to the Council of Constance, promising him safe conduct. Nevertheless, Hus was arrested when he arrived. When he refused to recant his views, the church leaders burned him at the stake.

Hus's death caused an uproar, and his movement became a full-scale national revolt of Czechs against Germans. Sigismund called crusades against the Hussites, but all of his expeditions were soundly defeated. Radical groups of Hussites organized several new communities in southern Bohemia, attempting to live according to the example of the first apostles. They recognized no lord, gave women some political rights, and created a simple liturgy that was carried out in the Czech language. Negotiations with Sigismund and his successor led to the Hussites' incorporation into the Bohemian political system by 1450. Though the Hussites were largely marginalized, they had won the right to receive communion in "both kinds" (wine and bread) and they had made Bohemia intensely aware of its Czech, rather than German, identity.

REVIEW QUESTION What crises did Europeans confront in the fourteenth and fifteenth centuries, and how did they handle them?

The Renaissance: New Forms of Thought and Expression

Some Europeans confronted the crises they faced by creating the culture of the Renaissance (French for "rebirth"). The period associated with the Renaissance, about 1350 to 1600, revived elements of the classical past — the Greek philosophers before Aristotle, Hellenistic artists, and Roman rhetoricians. Disillusioned with present institutions, many people looked back to the ancient world; in Greece and Rome they found models of thought, language, power, prestige, and the arts that they could apply to their own circumstances. Humanists modeled their writing on the Latin of Cicero, architects embraced ancient notions of public space, artists adopted classical forms, and musicians

used classical texts. In reality, Renaissance writers and artists built much of their work on medieval precedents, but they rarely acknowledged this fact. They found great satisfaction in believing that they were resuscitating the glories of the ancient world — and that everything between them and the classical past was a contemptible "Middle Age."

Renaissance Humanism

Three of the delegates at the Council of Constance — Cincius Romanus, Poggius Bracciolinus, and Bartholomaeus Politianus — reveal the attitudes of the Renaissance. Although busy with church work, they decided to take time off for a "rescue mission." Cincius described the escapade to one of his Latin teachers back in Italy:

> In Germany there are many monasteries with libraries full of Latin books. This aroused the hope in me that some of the works of Cicero, Varro, Livy, and other great men of learning, which seem to have completely vanished, might come to light, if a careful search were instituted. A few days ago, [we] went by agreement to the town of St. Gall. As soon as we went into the library [of the monastery there], we found *Jason's Argonauticon,* written by C. Valerius Flaccus in verse that is both splendid and dignified and not far removed from poetic majesty. Then we found some discussion in prose of a number of Cicero's orations.

Cicero, Varro, Livy, and Valerius Flaccus were pagan Latin writers. Even though Cincius and his friends were working for Pope John XXIII, they loved the writings of the ancients, whose Latin was, in their view, "splendid and dignified," unlike the Latin used in their own time, which they found debased and faulty. They saw themselves as the resuscitators of ancient language, literature, and culture, and they congratulated themselves on rescuing captive books from the "barbarian" monks of the monastery of St. Gall.

Humanism was a literary and linguistic movement — an attempt to revive classical Latin (and later Greek) as well as the values and sensibilities that came with the language. It began among men and women who, like Cincius, lived in the Italian city-states. The humanists saw parallels between their urban, independent lives and the experiences of the city-states of the ancient world. Humanism was a way to confront the crises — and praise the advances — of the fourteenth through sixteenth centuries. Humanists wrote poetry, history, moral philosophy, and grammar books, all patterned on classical models, especially the writings of Cicero.

That Cincius was employed by the pope yet considered the monks of St. Gall barbarians was no oddity. Most humanists combined sincere Christian piety with a new appreciation of the pagan past. Besides, they needed to work in order to live, and they took employment where they found it. Some humanists worked for the church, others were civil servants, and still others were notaries. A few were rich men who had a taste for literary subjects.

The first humanist, most historians agree, was **Francis Petrarch** (1304–1374). He was born in Arezzo, a town about fifty miles southeast of Florence. As a boy, he moved around a lot (his father was exiled from Florence), ending up in the region of Avignon, where he received his earliest schooling and fell in love with classical literature. He became a poet, writing in both Italian and Latin. When writing in Italian, he drew on the traditions of the troubadours, dedicating poems of longing to an unattainable and idealized woman named Laura; who she really was, we do not know. When writing in Latin, Petrarch was much influenced by classical poetry.

On the one hand, a boyhood in Avignon made Petrarch sensitive to the failings of the church: he was the writer who coined the phrase "Babylonian captivity" to liken the Avignon papacy to the Bible's account of the Hebrews' captivity in Babylonia. On the other hand, he took minor religious orders there, which gave him a modest living. Struggling between what he considered a life of dissipation (he fathered two children out of wedlock) and a religious vocation, he resolved the conflict at last in his book *On the Solitary Life,* in which he claimed that the solitude needed for reading the classics was akin to the solitude practiced by those who devoted themselves to God. For Petrarch, humanism was a vocation, a calling.

Less famous, but for that reason perhaps more representative of humanists in general, was Lauro Quirini (1420–1475?), the man who (as we saw at the start of this chapter) wrote disparagingly about the Turks as barbarians. Educated at the University of Padua, Quirini eventually got a law degree there. He wrote numerous letters and essays, and corresponded with other humanists. He spent the last half of his life in Crete, where he traded various commodities — alum, cloth, wine, and Greek books.

If Quirini represents the ordinary humanist, Giovanni Pico della Mirandola (1463–1494) was perhaps the most flamboyant. Born near Ferrara of a noble family, Pico received a humanist education at home before going on to Bologna to study law and to Padua to study philosophy. Soon he was picking up Hebrew, Aramaic, and Arabic. A convinced eclectic (one who selects the best from various doctrines), he thought that Jewish mystical writings supported Christian scriptures, and in 1486 he proposed that he publicly defend at Rome nine hundred theses drawn from diverse sources. The church found some of the theses heretical, however, and banned the whole affair. But Pico's *Oration on the Dignity of Man,* which he intended to deliver before his defense, summed up the humanist view: the creative individual, armed only with his (or her) "desires and judgment," could choose to become a boor or an angel. Humanity's potential was unlimited.

Christine de Pisan (c. 1365–c. 1430) exemplifies a humanist who chose to fashion herself into a writer and courtier. Born in Venice and educated in France, Christine was married and then soon widowed. Forced to support herself, her mother, and her three young children, she began to write poems inspired by classical models, depending on patrons to admire her work and pay her to write more. Many members of the upper nobility supported her, including Duke Philip the Bold of Burgundy, Queen Isabelle of Bavaria, and the English earl of Salisbury.

The Arts

The lure of the classical past was as strong in the visual arts as in literature — and for many of the same reasons. Architects and artists admired ancient Athens and Rome, but they also modified these classical models, melding them with medieval artistic traditions.

The Florentine architect Leon Battista Alberti (1404–1472) looked at the unplanned medieval city with dismay. He proposed that each building in a city be proportioned to fit harmoniously with all the others and that city spaces allow for all necessary public activities — there should be market squares, play areas, grounds for military exercises. In Renaissance cities, the agora and the forum (the open, public spaces of the classical world) appeared once again, but in a new guise: the piazza — a plaza or open square. Architects carved out spaces around their new buildings, and they rimmed them with porticoes — graceful covered walkways of columns and arches.

The Gothic cathedral of the Middle Ages was a cluster of graceful spikes and soaring arches. While Renaissance architects appreciated its vigor and energy, they tamed it with regular geometrical forms inspired by classical buildings. Classical forms were applied to previously built structures as well as new ones. Florence's Santa Maria Novella, for example, had been a typical Gothic church when it was first built. But when Alberti, the man who believed in public spaces and harmonious buildings, was commissioned to replace its facade, he drew on Roman temple forms.

The classical world inspired artists as well. This explains the style Lorenzo Ghiberti (1378?–1455) chose when he competed to produce the doors of Florence's baptistery in 1400. His entry showed the sacrifice of Isaac from the Old Testament: the young, nude Isaac was modeled on the masculine ideal of ancient Greek sculpture. At the same time, Ghiberti drew on medieval models for his depiction of Abraham and for his quatrefoil frame. In this way, he gracefully melded old and new elements — and won the contest.

The Renaissance Facade at Santa Maria Novella

When Italians wished to transform their churches into the Renaissance style, they did not tear them down; they gave them a new facade. At Santa Maria Novella in Florence, the architect Leon Battista Alberti designed a facade that was inspired by classical models — hence the round-arched entranceway and columns. At the same time he paid tribute to the original Gothic church by including a round window. (Scala / Art Resource, NY.)

Lorenzo Ghiberti, *The Sacrifice of Isaac*

This bronze relief, which was entered into the competition to decorate the doors of the San Giovanni Baptistery in Florence, captures (on the right-hand side) the dramatic moment when the angel intervenes as Abraham prepares to kill Isaac, a story told in the Hebrew Scriptures. (Museo Nazionale del Bargello / akg-images / Rabatti-Domingie.)

In addition to using the forms of classical art, Renaissance artists also mined the ancient world for new subjects. Venus, the Roman goddess of love and beauty, had numerous stories attached to her name. At first glance, *The Birth of Venus* by Sandro Botticelli (c. 1445–1510) seems simply an illustration of the tale of Venus's rise from the sea (see page 416). A closer look, however, shows that Botticelli borrowed from the poetry of Angelo Poliziano (1454–1494), who wrote of "fair Venus, mother of the cupids":

> Zephyr bathes the meadow with dew
> spreading a thousand lovely fragrances:
> wherever he flies he clothes the countryside
> in roses, lilies, violets, and other flowers.

In Botticelli's painting, Zephyr — one of the winds — blows while Venus herself is about to be clothed in a fine robe embroidered with leaves and flowers.

The Sacrifice of Isaac and *The Birth of Venus* show some of the ways in which Renaissance artists used ancient models. Other Renaissance artists perfected perspective — the illusion of three-dimensional space — to a degree that even classical antiquity had not anticipated. The development of the laws of perspective accompanied the introduction of long-range weaponry, such as cannons. In fact, some of perspective's practitioners — Leonardo da Vinci (1452–1519), for example — were military engineers as well as artists. In Leonardo's painting *The Annunciation,* sight lines meeting at a point on the horizon open wide precisely where the angel kneels and Mary responds in surprise.

Ghiberti, Botticelli, and Leonardo were all Italian artists. While they were creating their works, a northern Renaissance was taking place as well. At the court of Burgundy during the Hundred Years' War, the dukes commissioned portraits of themselves — sometimes unflattering ones — just as Roman leaders had once commissioned their own busts. Soon it was the fashion for those who could afford it to have a portrait made, showing them as naturalistically as possible. Around 1433, the chancellor Nicolas Rolin,

Sandro Botticelli, *The Birth of Venus*
Other artists had depicted Venus, but Botticelli was the first since antiquity to portray her in the nude.
(Galleria degli Uffizi, Florence, Italy / The Bridgeman Art Library International.)

Leonardo da Vinci, *The Annunciation*
Working with a traditional Christian theme — the moment when the angel Gabriel announced to the
Virgin Mary that she would give birth to Christ — Leonardo produced a work of great originality, draw-
ing the viewer's eye from a vanishing point in the distance to the subject of the painting. The ability to
subordinate the background to the foreground was the key contribution of Renaissance perspective.
(Scala / Ministero per i Beni e le Attività culturali / Art Resource, NY.)

Jan van Eyck, *The Virgin of Chancellor Rolin*
Van Eyck portrays the Virgin and Chancellor Nicolas Rolin as if they were contemporaries sharing a nice chat. Only the angel, who is placing a crown on the Virgin's head, suggests that something out of the ordinary is happening. (Erich Lessing / Art Resource, NY.)

for example, commissioned the Dutch artist Jan van Eyck to paint his portrait. Though opposite the Virgin and the baby Jesus, Rolin, in a pious pose, is the key figure in the picture. The grand view of a city behind the figures was meant to underscore Rolin's prominence in the community. In fact Rolin *was* an important man: he worked for the duke of Burgundy and was also the founder of a hospital at Beaune and a religious order of nurses to serve it. Van Eyck's portrait emphasized not only Rolin's dignity and status but also his individuality. The artist took pains to show even the wrinkles of his neck and the furrows on his brow.

In music, Renaissance composers incorporated classical texts and allusions into songs that were based on the motet and other forms of polyphony. Working for patrons — whether churchmen, secular rulers, or republican governments — they expressed the glory, religious piety, and prestige of their benefactors. In fact, Renaissance rulers spent as much as 6 percent of their annual revenue to support musicians and composers.

Every proper court had its own musicians. Some served as chaplains, writing music for the ruler's private chapel — the place where his court and household heard Mass. When Josquin Desprez (1440–1521) served as the duke of Ferrara's chaplain, he wrote

a Mass that used the musical equivalents of the letters of the duke's name (the Italian version of *do re mi*) as its theme. Isabella d'Este (1474–1539), the daughter of the duke, employed her own musicians — singers, woodwind and string players, percussionists, and keyboard players — while her husband, the duke of Mantua, had his own band. Humanism and music came together: because Isabella loved Petrarch's poems, she had the composer Bartolomeo Tromboncino set them to music.

The church, too, was a major sponsor of music. Every feast required music, and the papal schism inadvertently encouraged more musical production than usual, as rival popes tried to best one another in the realm of pageantry and sound. Churches needed choirs of singers, and many choirboys went on to become composers, while others sang well into adulthood: in the fourteenth century, the men who sang in the choir at Reims received a yearly stipend and an extra fee every time they sang the Mass and the liturgical offices of the day.

When the composer Johannes Ockeghem — chaplain for three French kings — died in 1497, his fellow musicians vied in expressing their grief in song. Josquin Desprez was among them, and his composition illustrates how the addition of classical elements to traditional musical forms enhanced music's emotive power. Josquin's work combines personal grief with religious liturgy and the feelings expressed in classical elegies. The piece uses five voices. Inspired by classical mythology, four of the voices sing in the vernacular French about the "nymphs of the wood" coming together to mourn. But the fifth voice intones the words of the liturgy: *Requiescat in pace* ("May he rest in peace"). At the very moment in the song that the four vernacular voices lament Ockeghem's burial in the dark ground, the liturgical voice sings of the heavenly light. The contrast makes the song more moving. By drawing on the classical past, Renaissance musicians found new ways in which to express emotion.

REVIEW QUESTION How and why did Renaissance humanists, artists, and musicians revive classical traditions?

Consolidating Power

The shape of Europe changed between 1340 and 1492. In eastern Europe, the Ottoman Empire took the place (though not the role) of Byzantium. The capital of the Holy Roman Empire moved to Prague, bringing Bohemia to the fore. Meanwhile, the duke of Lithuania married the queen of Poland, uniting those two states. In western Europe, a few places organized and maintained themselves as republics; the Swiss, for example, consolidated their informal alliances in the Swiss Confederation. Italy, which at the beginning of the period was dotted with numerous small city-states, was by the end dominated by five major powers: Milan, the papacy, Naples, and the republics of Venice and Florence. Most western European states — England and France, for example — became centralized monarchies. The union of Aragon and Castile via the marriage of their respective rulers created Spain. Whether monarchies, principalities, or republics, states throughout Europe used their new powers to finance humanists, artists, and musicians — and to persecute heretics, Muslims, and Jews with new vigor.

New Political Formations in Eastern Europe

In the eastern half of the Holy Roman Empire, Bohemia gained new status as the seat of the Luxembourg imperial dynasty, whose last representative was Emperor Sigismund. This development led to a religious and political crisis when the Hussites clashed with Sigismund (see page 411). The chief beneficiaries of the violence were the nobles, both Catholic and Hussite, but they quarreled among themselves, especially about who should be king. There was no Joan of Arc to galvanize the national will, and most of Europe considered Bohemia a heretic state.

Farther north, the cities (rather than the landed nobility) held power. Allied cities, known as *Hanse,* were common. The most successful alliance was the **Hanseatic League**, a loose federation of mainly north German cities formed to protect their mutual interests in defense and trade — and art. For example, the artist Bernt Notke, who hailed from the Hanse town of Lübeck, painted a famous Dance of Death at Reval (today Tallinn, Estonia), another Hanse town. The Hanseatic League linked the Baltic coast with Russia, Norway, the British Isles, France, and even (via imperial cities like Augsburg and Nuremberg) the cities of Italy. When threatened by rival powers in Denmark and Norway in 1367–1370, the league waged war and usually won. But in the fifteenth century it confronted new rivals and began a long, slow decline.

To the east of the Hanseatic cities, two new monarchies took shape in northeastern Europe: Poland and Lithuania. Poland had begun to form in the tenth century. Powerful nobles soon dominated it, and Mongol invasions devastated the land. But recovery was under way by 1300. Unlike almost every other part of Europe, Poland expanded demographically and economically during the fourteenth century. Jews migrated there to escape persecutions in western Europe, and both Jewish and German settlers helped build thriving towns like Cracow. Monarchical consolidation began thereafter.

On Poland's eastern flank was Lithuania, the only major holdout from Christianity in eastern Europe. But as it expanded into southern Russia, its grand dukes flirted with both the Roman Catholic and Orthodox varieties. Grand Duke Jogailo (c. 1351–1434), taking advantage of a hiatus in the Polish ruling dynasty, united both states in 1386 when he married Queen Jadwiga of Poland, received a Catholic baptism, and was elected by the Polish nobility as King Wladyslaw II Jagiello. As part of the negotiations prior to these events, he promised to convert Lithuania, and after his coronation he sent churchmen there to begin the long, slow process. The union of Poland and Lithuania lasted, with some interruptions, until 1772. (See Mapping the West, page 426.)

Powerful States in Western Europe

Four powerful states dominated western Europe during the fifteenth century: Spain, the duchy of Burgundy, France, and England. By the end of the century, however, Burgundy had disappeared, leaving three exceptionally powerful monarchies.

The kingdom of Spain was created by marriage. Decades of violence on the Iberian peninsula ended when Isabella of Castile and Ferdinand of Aragon married in 1469

and restored law and order in the decades that followed. Castile was the powerhouse, with Aragon its lesser neighbor and Navarre a pawn between the two. When the king and queen joined forces, they ruled together over their separate dominions, allowing each to retain its traditional laws and privileges. The union of Castile and Aragon was the first step toward a united Spain and a centralized monarchy there.

Relying on a lucrative taxation system, pliant meetings of the *cortes* (the representative institution that voted on taxes), and an ideology that glorified the monarchy, Ferdinand and Isabella consolidated their power. They had an extensive bureaucracy for financial matters and a well-staffed writing office. They sent their own officials to rule over towns that had previously been self-governing, and they established regional courts of law.

Created, like Spain, by marriage, the duchy of Burgundy was disunited linguistically and geographically. Through purchases, inheritance, and conquests, the dukes ruled over French-, Dutch-, and German-speaking subjects, creating a state that resembled a patchwork of provinces and regions, each jealously guarding its laws and traditions. The Low Countries, with their flourishing cities, constituted the state's economic heartland, while the region of Burgundy itself, which gave the state its name, offered rich farmlands and vineyards. Unlike England, whose island geography made it a natural political unit; or France, whose borders were forged in the national experience of repelling English invaders; or Spain, whose national identity came from centuries of warfare against Islam, Burgundy was an artificial creation whose coherence depended entirely on the skillful exercise of statecraft.

At the heart of Burgundian politics was the personal cult of its dukes. Philip the Good (r. 1418–1467) and his son Charles the Bold (r. 1467–1477) were very different kinds of rulers, but both were devoted to enhancing the prestige of their dynasty and the security of their dominion. Philip was a lavish patron of the arts who commissioned numerous illuminated manuscripts, chronicles, tapestries, paintings, and music in his efforts to glorify himself as ruler of Burgundy.

The Burgundians' success depended in large part on their personal relationship with their subjects. Not only did the dukes travel constantly from one part of their dominion to another, but they also staged elaborate ceremonies to enhance their power and promote their legitimacy. Their entries into cities and their presence at weddings, births, and funerals became the centerpieces of a "theater state" in which the dynasty provided the only link among diverse territories. New rituals became propaganda tools. Philip's revival of chivalry at court transformed the semi-independent nobility into courtiers closely tied to the prince. But, as mentioned earlier in this chapter (page 406), when Charles the Bold died in 1477, the duchy was parceled out to France and the Holy Roman Empire.

It was its quick recovery from the Hundred Years' War that allowed France to take a large bite out of Burgundy. Under Louis XI (r. 1461–1483), the French monarchy both expanded its territory and consolidated its power. Soon after Burgundy fell, Louis inherited most of southern France. When he inherited claims to the duchy of Milan and the kingdom of Naples, he was ready to exploit other opportunities in Italy. By the end of

Philip the Good's *History of Alexander the Great Tapestries*
In 1459, Duke Philip of Burgundy bought a series of tapestries that told the story of Alexander the Great's adventures. These had been recounted in popular vernacular romances; now they were illustrated in silk, gold, and silver threads. In this detail, Alexander flies in the sky in a decorated cage held by winged mythical creatures known as griffins. Just to the right of that, he appears on the ground, surrounded by his courtiers. Next, he is inside a glass bell; you can just barely see him behind the white scrim made of sea creatures. (Partial view, from *Episodes in the Life of Alexander: flight of Alexander and Alexander plumbs the depths of the oceans*, Galleria Doria Pamphilij. Rome / photo: akg-images / Pirozzi.)

the century, France had doubled its territory, assuming boundaries close to its modern ones, and was looking to expand even further.

To strengthen royal power at home, Louis promoted industry and commerce, imposed permanent salt and land taxes, maintained western Europe's first standing army (created by his predecessor), and dispensed with the meetings of the Estates General, which included the clergy, the nobility, and representatives from the major towns of France. The French kings had already increased their power with important concessions from the papacy. The Pragmatic Sanction of Bourges (1438) asserted the superiority of a general church council over the pope. Harking back to a long tradition of the high Middle Ages, the Pragmatic Sanction established what would come to be known as Gallicanism (after Gaul, the ancient Roman name for France), in which the French king would effectively control ecclesiastical revenues and the appointment of French bishops.

England, too, recovered quickly from civil wars — called the Wars of the Roses — spawned by the stresses of the Hundred Years' War and concluded with the victory of Henry Tudor, who took the title of Henry VII (r. 1485–1509). Despite the Wars of the Roses, which affected mainly the English nobility, the English economy continued to

- For practice quizzes and other study tools, visit the **Online Study Guide** at bedfordstmartins.com/huntconcise.

- For primary-source material from this period, see *Sources of the Making of the West*, Fourth Edition.

- For Web sites, images, and documents related to topics in this chapter, visit *Make History* at bedfordstmartins.com/huntconcise.

Suggested References

Aberth provides a good overview of the crises. Blumenfeld-Kosinski and Bynum each explore various aspects of late medieval piety. Nauert treats the many ramifications of Renaissance humanism, and Hale gives a useful overview of political developments.

Aberth, John. *From the Brink of the Apocalypse: Confronting Famine, War, Plague, and Death in the Later Middle Ages.* 2001.

*The Black Death. Ed. and trans. Rosemary Horrox. 1994.

Blumenfeld-Kosinski, Renate. *Poets, Saints, and Visionaries of the Great Schism, 1378–1417.* 2006.

Bynum, Caroline. *Wonderful Blood: Theology and Practice in Late Medieval Northern Germany and Beyond.* 2006.

Cohn, Samuel K., Jr. *Lust for Liberty: The Politics of Social Revolt in Medieval Europe, 1200–1425.* 2006.

Grendler, Paul F. *The Universities of the Italian Renaissance.* 2002.

Hale, J. R. *Renaissance Europe, 1480–1520.* 2nd ed. 2000.

Imber, Colin. *The Ottoman Empire, 1300–1650: The Structure of Power.* 2002.

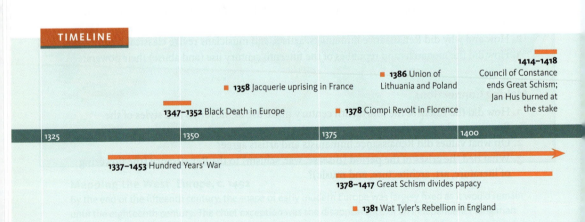

TIMELINE

1347–1352 Black Death in Europe

1358 Jacquerie uprising in France

1386 Union of Lithuania and Poland

1378 Ciompi Revolt in Florence

1414–1418 Council of Constance ends Great Schism; Jan Hus burned at the stake

1325   1350   1375   1400

1337–1453 Hundred Years' War

1378–1417 Great Schism divides papacy

1381 Wat Tyler's Rebellion in England

Conclusion

The years from 1340 to 1492 marked a period of crisis in Europe. The Hundred Years' War broke out in 1337, and ten years later, in 1347, the Black Death hit, taking a heavy toll. In 1378, a crisis shook the church when first two and then three popes claimed universal authority. Revolts and riots plagued the cities and countryside. The Ottoman Turks took Constantinople in 1453, changing the very shape of Europe and the Middle East.

The revival of classical literature, art, architecture, and music helped men and women cope with these crises and gave them new tools for dealing with them. The Renaissance began mainly in the city-states of Italy, but it spread throughout much of Europe via the education and training of humanists, artists, sculptors, architects, and musicians. At the courts of great kings and dukes — even of the sultan — Renaissance music, art, and literature served as a way to celebrate the grandeur of rulers who controlled more of the apparatuses of government (armies, artillery, courts, and taxes) than ever before.

Consolidation was the principle underlying the new states of the Renaissance. Venice absorbed nearby northern Italian cities, and the Peace of Lodi confirmed its new status as a power on land as well as the sea. In eastern Europe, marriage joined together the states of Lithuania and Poland. A similar union took place in Spain when Isabella of Castile and Ferdinand of Aragon married. The Swiss Confederation became a permanent entity. The king of France came to rule over all of the area that we today call France. The consolidated modern states of the fifteenth century would soon look to the Atlantic Ocean and beyond for new lands to explore and conquer.

Review Questions

1. What crises did Europeans confront in the fourteenth and fifteenth centuries, and how did they handle them?

2. How and why did Renaissance humanists, artists, and musicians revive classical traditions?

3. How did the monarchs and republics of the fifteenth century use (and abuse) their powers?

Making Connections

1. How did the rulers of the fourteenth century make use of the forms and styles of the Renaissance?

2. On what values did Renaissance humanists and artists agree?

3. What tied the crises of the period (disease, war, schism) to the Renaissance (the flowering of literature, art, architecture, and music)?

- For practice quizzes and other study tools, visit the **Online Study Guide** at bedfordstmartins.com/huntconcise.

- For primary-source material from this period, see *Sources of the Making of the West*, Fourth Edition.

- For Web sites, images, and documents related to topics in this chapter, visit *Make History* at bedfordstmartins.com/huntconcise.

Suggested References

Aberth provides a good overview of the crises. Blumenfeld-Kosinski and Bynum each explore various aspects of late medieval piety. Nauert treats the many ramifications of Renaissance humanism, and Hale gives a useful overview of political developments.

Aberth, John. *From the Brink of the Apocalypse: Confronting Famine, War, Plague, and Death in the Later Middle Ages*. 2001.

*The Black Death. Ed. and trans. Rosemary Horrox. 1994.

Blumenfeld-Kosinski, Renate. *Poets, Saints, and Visionaries of the Great Schism, 1378–1417*. 2006.

Bynum, Caroline. *Wonderful Blood: Theology and Practice in Late Medieval Northern Germany and Beyond*. 2006.

Cohn, Samuel K., Jr. *Lust for Liberty: The Politics of Social Revolt in Medieval Europe, 1200–1425*. 2006.

Grendler, Paul F. *The Universities of the Italian Renaissance*. 2002.

Hale, J. R. *Renaissance Europe, 1480–1520*. 2nd ed. 2000.

Imber, Colin. *The Ottoman Empire, 1300–1650: The Structure of Power*. 2002.

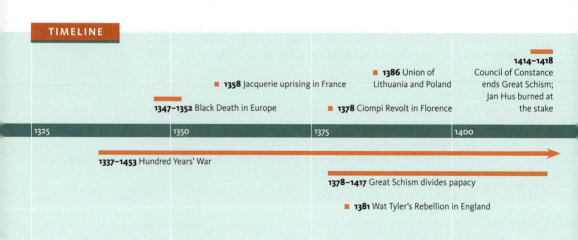

TIMELINE

1414–1418 Council of Constance ends Great Schism; Jan Hus burned at the stake

1386 Union of Lithuania and Poland

1358 Jacquerie uprising in France

1347–1352 Black Death in Europe

1378 Ciompi Revolt in Florence

1325   1350   1375   1400

1337–1453 Hundred Years' War

1378–1417 Great Schism divides papacy

1381 Wat Tyler's Rebellion in England

convert or leave the country. Some did indeed convert, but the experiences of the former conversos soured most on the prospect, and a large number of Jews — perhaps 150,000 — left Spain, scattering around the Mediterranean.

Meanwhile, Ferdinand and Isabella determined to rid Spain of its last Muslim stronghold, Granada. In 1492 — just a few months before they expelled the Jews — Ferdinand and Isabella made their triumphal entry there. In 1502, they demanded that all Muslims adopt Christianity or leave the kingdom.

REVIEW QUESTION How did the monarchs and republics of the fifteenth century use (and abuse) their powers?

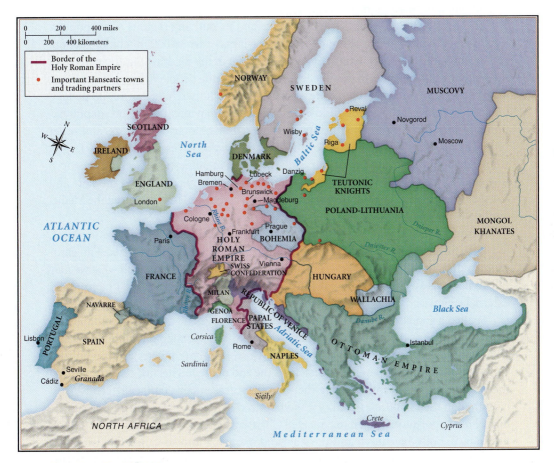

Mapping the West Europe, c. 1492

By the end of the fifteenth century, the shape of early modern Europe was largely fixed as it would remain until the eighteenth century. The chief exception was the disappearance of an independent Hungarian kingdom after 1529.

A good example of the ways in which governments peeked into the lives of their citizens — and picked their pockets — is the Florentine *catasto*. This was an inventory of households within the city and its outlying territory made for the purposes of taxation in 1427. It inquired about names, types of houses, and animals. It asked people to specify their trade, and their answers revealed the levels of Florentine society, ranging from agricultural laborers with no land of their own to soldiers, cooks, grave diggers, scribes, great merchants, doctors, wine dealers, innkeepers, and tanners. The list went on and on. The catasto inquired about private and public investments, real estate holdings, and taxable assets. Finally, it turned to the sex of the head of the family, his or her age and marital status, and the number of mouths to feed in the household. An identification number was assigned to each household.

The catasto showed that in 1427 Florence and its outlying regions had a population of more than 260,000. Although the city itself had only 38,000 inhabitants (about 15 percent of the total population), it held 67 percent of the wealth. Some 60 percent of the Florentine households in the city belonged to the "little people" (a literal translation from the Italian term that referred to artisans and small merchants). The "fat people" (what we would call the upper middle class) made up 30 percent of the urban population and included wealthy merchants, leading artisans, notaries, doctors, and other professionals. At the very bottom of the hierarchy were slaves and servants, largely women from the surrounding countryside employed in domestic service. At the top, a tiny elite of wealthy patricians, bankers, and wool merchants controlled the state and owned more than one-quarter of its wealth. This was the group that produced the Medici family.

European kings had long fought Muslims and expelled Jews from their kingdoms, but in the fifteenth century, their powers became concentrated and centralized. Fifteenth-century kings in western Europe — England, France, Spain — commanded what we may call modern states. They used the full force of their new powers against their internal and external enemies.

Spain is a good example of this new trend. Once Ferdinand and Isabella established their rule over Castile and Aragon, they sought to impose religious uniformity and purity. They began systematically to persecute the *conversos* (converts), Jews who converted to Christianity after vicious attacks at the end of the fourteenth century. During the first half of the fifteenth century, they and their descendants (still called conversos, even though their children were born and baptized in the Christian faith) took advantage of the opportunities open to educated Christians, in many instances rising to high positions in both the church and the state and marrying into so-called Old Christian families. The conversos' success bred resentment, and their commitment to Christianity was questioned as well. Conversos were no longer Jews, so Christians justified their persecution by branding them as heretics who undermined the monarchy. In 1478, Ferdinand and Isabella set up the Inquisition in Spain.

Treating the conversos as heretics, the inquisitors imposed harsh sentences, expelling or burning most of them. That was not enough (in the view of the monarchs) to purify the land. In 1492, Ferdinand and Isabella decreed that all Jews in Spain must

Venetian Art

When he was commissioned in the 1490s to depict the legend of Saint Ursula, Vittore Carpaccio chose Venice as the backdrop. Found in the very popular thirteenth-century *Golden Legend* by Jacobus de Voragine, the tale begins in England, where a pagan king is so inspired by hearing of the virtue of Ursula, daughter of the Christian king of Brittany, that he sends his ambassadors to ask for her hand for his son. In this detail, Carpaccio shows the English ambassadors arriving in a gondola. Note the glass-like colors and the evocation of atmosphere, both characteristic of Venetian style. (Detail from the Ursula Cycle, 1490–96 [oil on canvas], Vittore Carpaccio, Galleria dell' Accademia, Venice, Italy / Cameraphoto Arte Venezia / The Bridgeman Art Library International.)

committees made up of men loyal to him to govern the city. He kept the old forms of the Florentine constitution intact, governing behind the scenes not by force but through a broad consensus among the ruling elite.

Cosimo's grandson Lorenzo "the Magnificent" (1449–1492), who assumed power in 1467, bolstered the regime's legitimacy with his patronage of the humanities and the arts. He himself was a poet and an avid collector of antiquities. Serving on various Florentine committees in charge of building, renovating, and adorning the churches of the city, Lorenzo employed important artists and architects to work on his own palaces. He probably encouraged the young Michelangelo Buonarroti; he certainly patronized the poet Angelo Poliziano, whose verses inspired Botticelli's *Venus*. No wonder humanists and poets sang his praises.

But the Medici family also had enemies. In 1478, Lorenzo narrowly escaped an assassination attempt, and his successor was driven out of Florence in 1494. The Medici returned to power in 1512, only to be driven out again in 1527. In 1530, the republic fell for good as the Medici once again took power, this time declaring themselves dukes of Florence.

The Tools of Power

Whether monarchies, duchies, or republics, the newly consolidated states of the fifteenth century exercised their powers more thoroughly than ever before. Sometimes they reached into the intimate lives of their subjects or citizens; at other times they persecuted undesirables with new efficiency.

longer of small cities, each with its own *contado* (surrounding countryside), but of large territorial city-states.

It is no accident that the Peace of Lodi was signed one year after the Ottoman conquest of Constantinople: Venice wanted to direct its might against the Turks. But the Venetians also knew that peace was good for business; they traded with the Ottomans, and the two powers influenced each other's art and culture: Gentile Bellini's portrait of Mehmed (see the chapter-opening illustration) is a good example of the importance of the Renaissance at the Ottoman court.

Venice was ruled not by a *signore* ("lord") but by the Great Council, which was dominated by the most important families. Far from being a hereditary monarch, the doge — the leading magistrate at Venice — was elected by the Great Council. A major question is why the lower classes at Venice did not rebel and demand their own political power, as happened in so many other Italian cities. The answer may be that Venice's foundation on water demanded so much central planning, so much effort to maintain buildings and services, and such a large amount of public funds to provide the population with necessities that it fostered a greater sense of community than could be found elsewhere.

While Venice was not itself a center of humanism, its conquest of Padua in 1405 transformed its culture. After studying rhetoric at the University of Padua, young Venetian nobles returned home convinced of the values of a humanistic education for administering their empire. Lauro Quirini was one such man; his time at Padua was followed by a long period on Crete, which was under Venetian control.

Like humanism, Renaissance art also became part of the fabric of the city. Because of its trading links with Byzantium, Venice had long been influenced by Byzantine artistic styles. As it acquired a land-based empire in northern Italy, however, its artists adopted the Gothic styles prevalent elsewhere. In the fifteenth century, Renaissance art forms began to make inroads as well. Venice achieved its own unique style, characterized by strong colors, intense lighting, and sensuous use of paint — adapting the work of classical antiquity for its own purposes. Most Venetian artists worked on commission from churches, but lay confraternities — lay religious organizations devoted to charity — also sponsored paintings.

Florence, like Venice, was also a republic. But unlike Venice, its society and political life were turbulent, as social classes and political factions competed for power. The most important of these civil uprisings was the so-called Ciompi Revolt of 1378. Named after the wool workers (*ciompi*), laborers so lowly that they had not been allowed to form a guild, the revolt led to the creation of a guild for them, along with a new distribution of power in the city. But by 1382, the upper classes were once again monopolizing the government, and now with even less sympathy for the commoners.

By 1434, the **Medici** family had become the dominant power in this unruly city. The patriarch of the family, Cosimo de' Medici (1389–1464), founded his political power on the wealth of the Medici bank, which handled papal finances and had numerous branch offices in Italian and northern European cities. Backed by his money, Cosimo took over Florentine politics. He determined who could take public office, and he established new

Philip the Good's *History of Alexander the Great Tapestries*
In 1459, Duke Philip of Burgundy bought a series of tapestries that told the story of Alexander the Great's adventures. These had been recounted in popular vernacular romances; now they were illustrated in silk, gold, and silver threads. In this detail, Alexander flies in the sky in a decorated cage held by winged mythical creatures known as griffins. Just to the right of that, he appears on the ground, surrounded by his courtiers. Next, he is inside a glass bell; you can just barely see him behind the white scrim made of sea creatures. (Partial view, from *Episodes in the Life of Alexander: flight of Alexander and Alexander plumbs the depths of the oceans*, Galleria Doria Pamphilij. Rome / photo: akg-images / Pirozzi.)

the century, France had doubled its territory, assuming boundaries close to its modern ones, and was looking to expand even further.

To strengthen royal power at home, Louis promoted industry and commerce, imposed permanent salt and land taxes, maintained western Europe's first standing army (created by his predecessor), and dispensed with the meetings of the Estates General, which included the clergy, the nobility, and representatives from the major towns of France. The French kings had already increased their power with important concessions from the papacy. The Pragmatic Sanction of Bourges (1438) asserted the superiority of a general church council over the pope. Harking back to a long tradition of the high Middle Ages, the Pragmatic Sanction established what would come to be known as Gallicanism (after Gaul, the ancient Roman name for France), in which the French king would effectively control ecclesiastical revenues and the appointment of French bishops.

England, too, recovered quickly from civil wars — called the Wars of the Roses — spawned by the stresses of the Hundred Years' War and concluded with the victory of Henry Tudor, who took the title of Henry VII (r. 1485–1509). Despite the Wars of the Roses, which affected mainly the English nobility, the English economy continued to

grow during the fifteenth century. The cloth industry expanded considerably, and the English used much of the raw wool that they had been exporting to the Low Countries to manufacture goods at home. London merchants, taking a vigorous role in trade, also assumed greater political prominence, not only in governing London but also in serving as bankers to kings and members of Parliament. In the countryside the landed classes — the nobility, the gentry (the lesser nobility), and the yeomanry (free farmers) — benefited from rising farm and land-rent income as the population increased slowly but steadily. The Tudor monarchs took advantage of the general prosperity to bolster both their treasury and their power.

Power in the Republics

Within the fifteenth-century world of largely monarchical power were three important exceptions: Switzerland, Venice, and Florence. Republics, they prided themselves on traditions of self-rule. At the same time, however, they were in every case dominated by elites — or, in the case of Florence, even by one family.

Of the three, the Swiss Confederation was the most egalitarian. The region's cities had long had alliances with one another. In the fourteenth century, their union became more binding, and they joined with equally well-organized communities in rural and forested areas in the region. Their original purpose was to keep the peace, but soon they also pledged to aid one another against the Holy Roman Emperor. By the end of the fourteenth century, they had become an entity: the Swiss Confederation. While not united by a comprehensive constitution, they were nevertheless an effective political force.

Wealthy merchants and tradesmen dominated the cities of the Swiss Confederation, and in the fifteenth century they managed to supplant the landed nobility. At the same time, the power of the rural communes gave some ordinary folk political importance. No king, duke, or count ever became head of the confederation. In its fiercely independent stance against the Holy Roman Empire, it became a symbol of republican freedom. On the other hand, poor Swiss foot soldiers made their living by hiring themselves out as mercenaries, fueling the wars of kings in the rest of Europe.

Italy at the Peace of Lodi, 1454

Far less open to the lower classes, Venice, a city built on a lagoon, ruled an extensive empire by the fifteenth century. Its merchant ships plied the waters stretching from the Black Sea to the Mediterranean and out to the Atlantic Ocean. Now, for the first time in its career, it turned to conquer land in northern Italy. In the early fifteenth century, Venice took over many surrounding cities, eventually coming up against the equally powerful city-state of Milan to its west. Between 1450 and 1454, two coalitions, one led by Milan, the other by Venice, fought for territorial control of the eastern half of northern Italy. Financial exhaustion and fear of an invasion by France or the Ottoman Turks led to the Peace of Lodi in 1454. Italy was a collection no

Joan of Arc: La Pucelle. Trans. and ed. Craig Taylor. 2006.

Kent, F. W. *Lorenzo de' Medici and the Art of Magnificence*. 2004.

Lambert, Malcolm. *Medieval Heresy: Popular Movements from the Gregorian Reform to the Reformation*. 3rd ed. 2002.

Nauert, Charles G. *Humanism and the Culture of the Renaissance Europe*. 2nd ed. 2006.

The Renaissance in Europe: An Anthology. Eds. Peter Elmer, Nick Webb, and Roberta Wood. 2000.

Rollo-Koster, Joëlle, and Thomas M. Izbicki, eds. *A Companion to the Great Western Schism (1378–1417)*. 2009.

Selections from English Wycliffite Writings. Ed. and trans. Anne Hudson. 1978.

*Primary source.

1454 Peace of Lodi

1453 Conquest of Constantinople by Ottoman Turks; end of Hundred Years' War

1492 Spain conquers Muslim stronghold of Granada, expels Jews

| 1425 | 1450 | 1475 | 1500 |

1477 Dismantling of duchy of Burgundy

1478 Inquisition begins in Spain

14

Global Encounters and the Shock of the Reformation

1492–1560

I N 1539 IN TLAXCALA, NEW SPAIN (present-day Mexico), Indians newly converted to Christianity performed a pageant organized by Catholic missionaries. It featured a combined Spanish and Indian army fighting to protect the pope, defeat the Muslims, and win control of the holy city of Jerusalem. In the play, after a miracle saves the Christian soldiers, the Muslims give up and convert to Christianity. Although it is hard to imagine what the Indians made of this celebration of places and people far away, the event reveals a great deal about the Europeans: the Catholic missionaries hoped that their success in converting Indians in the New World signaled God's favor for Catholicism the world over.

Led first by the Portuguese and then Spanish explorers, Europeans sailed into contact with peoples and cultures previously unknown to them. European voyagers subjugated native peoples, declared their control over vast new lands, and established a new system of slavery linking Africa and the New World. Millions of Indians died of diseases unknowingly imported by the Europeans. The discovery of new crops — corn, potatoes, tobacco, coffee, and cocoa — and of gold and silver mines brought new patterns of consumption, and new objects of conflict, to Europe. Historians now call this momentous spiral of changes in ecology, agriculture, and social patterns the Columbian exchange, after Christopher Columbus, who started the process.

While the Spanish were converting Indians in the New World, a different kind of challenge confronted the Catholic church in central and

Cortés

In this Spanish depiction of the landing of Hernán Cortés in Mexico in 1519, the ships and arms of the Spanish are a commanding presence, especially in comparison to the nakedness of the Indians and the kneeling stance of their leader. A Spanish artist painted this miniature, which measures only 6⅛ inches by 4¼ inches. It probably accompanied an account of the Spanish conquest of Mexico. On the back of the picture is a small map of the west coast of Europe and Africa and the east coast of Central America. Europeans relied on such images, and especially on maps, to help them make sense of all the new information flooding into Europe from faraway places. Many Spaniards viewed Cortés's conquests as a sign of divine favor toward Catholicism in a time of religious division. Some even believed that Cortés was born the same day, or at least the same year, as Martin Luther, the German monk who had initiated the Protestant Reformation just two years before Cortés's landing (in fact, Luther was born two years before Cortés).

(Erich Lessing / Art Resource, NY.)

western Europe. Religious reformers attacked the leadership of the pope in Rome and formed competing groups of Protestants (so-called because they protested against some beliefs of the Catholic church). The movement began when the German Catholic monk Martin Luther criticized the sale of indulgences in 1517. Other reformers raised their voices, too, but did not agree with the Lutherans. Before long, religious division engulfed the German states and reached into Switzerland, France, and England. In response, Catholics undertook their own renewal, which strengthened the Catholic church. Catholic missionaries continued to dominate efforts to convert indigenous peoples for a century or more.

CHAPTER FOCUS How did the conquest of the New World and the Protestant Reformation transform European governments and societies in this era?

These two new factors — the development of overseas colonies and divisions between Catholics and Protestants within Europe — reshaped the long-standing rivalries between princes and determined the course of European history for several generations.

The Discovery of New Worlds

Portugal's and Spain's maritime explorations brought Europe to the attention of the rest of the world. Inspired by a crusading spirit against Islam and by riches to be won through trade in spices and gold, the Portuguese and Spanish sailed across the Atlantic, Indian, and Pacific Oceans. The English, French, and Dutch followed later in the sixteenth century, creating a new global exchange of people, crops, and diseases. As a result of these European expeditions, the people of the Americas for the first time confronted forces that threatened to destroy not only their culture but even their existence.

Portuguese Explorations

The first phase of European overseas expansion began in 1433 with Portuguese exploration of the West African coast. The Portuguese hoped to find a sea route to the spice-producing lands of South and Southeast Asia in order to bypass the Ottoman Turks, who controlled the traditional land routes between Europe and Asia. Success in the voyages of exploration depended on several technological breakthroughs, including the caravel, a small, easily maneuvered three-masted ship that used triangular lateen sails adapted from the Arabs. (The sails permitted a ship to tack against headwinds.) Prince Henry the Navigator of Portugal (1394–1460) personally financed many voyages with revenues from a noble crusading order. The first triumphs of the Portuguese attracted a host of Christian, Jewish, and even Arab sailors, astronomers, and cartographers to the service of Prince Henry and King John II (r. 1481–1495). They compiled better tide calendars and books of sailing directions for pilots that enabled sailors to venture farther into the oceans and reduced — though did not eliminate — the dangers of sea travel.

Searching for gold and then slaves, the Portuguese gradually established forts down the West African coast. In 1487–1488, they reached the Cape of Good Hope at the tip

of Africa; ten years later, Vasco da Gama led a Portuguese fleet around the cape and reached as far as Calicut, India, the center of the spice trade. His return to Lisbon with twelve pieces of Chinese porcelain for the Portuguese king set off two centuries of porcelain mania. Until the early eighteenth century, only the Chinese knew how to produce porcelain. Over the next two hundred years, Western merchants would import no fewer than seventy million pieces of porcelain, still known today as "china." By 1517, a chain of Portuguese forts dotted the Indian Ocean (Map 14.1). In 1519, Ferdinand Magellan, a Portuguese sailor in Spanish service, led the first expedition to circumnavigate the globe.

The Voyages of Columbus

One of many sailors inspired by the Portuguese explorations, **Christopher Columbus** (1451–1506) opened an entirely new direction for discovery. Most likely born in Genoa of Italian parents, Columbus sailed the West African coast in Portuguese service between 1476 and 1485. Fifteenth-century Europeans already knew that the world was round. Columbus wanted to sail west to reach "the lands of the Great Khan," because

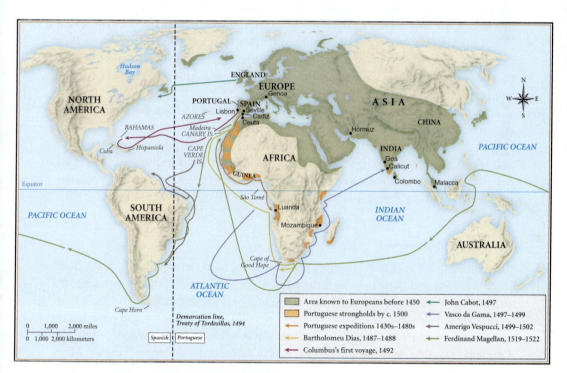

Map 14.1 Early Voyages of World Exploration

Over the course of the fifteenth and early sixteenth centuries, European shipping dominated the Atlantic Ocean after the pioneering voyages of the Portuguese, who also first sailed around the Cape of Good Hope to the Indian Ocean and Cape Horn to the Pacific. The search for spices and the need to circumnavigate the Ottoman Empire inspired these voyages.

he hoped to find a new route to the East's gold and spices. After the Portuguese refused to fund his plan, Columbus turned to the Spanish monarchs Isabella of Castile and Ferdinand of Aragon, who agreed to finance his venture.

On August 3, 1492, with ninety men on board two caravels and one larger merchant ship for carrying supplies, Columbus set sail westward. His contract stipulated that he would claim Castilian sovereignty over any new land and inhabitants, and share any profits with the crown. Reaching what is today the Bahamas on October 12, Columbus mistook the islands to be part of the East Indies, not far from Japan. As the Spaniards explored the Caribbean islands, they encountered communities of peaceful Indians, the Arawaks, who were awed by the Europeans' military technology, not to mention their appearance. Although many positive entries in the ship's log testified to Columbus's personal goodwill toward the Indians, the Europeans' objectives were clear: find gold, subjugate the Indians, and propagate Christianity.

Excited by the prospect of easy riches, many flocked to join Columbus's second voyage. When Columbus departed the Spanish port of Cádiz in September 1493, he commanded a fleet of seventeen ships carrying some fifteen hundred men. Failing to find the imagined gold mines and spices, Columbus and his crew began capturing Caribs, enemies of the Arawaks, with the intention of bringing them back as slaves. The Spaniards exported enslaved Indians to Spain, and slave traders sold them in Seville. When the Spanish monarchs realized the vast potential for material gain from their new dominions, they asserted direct royal authority by sending officials and priests to the Americas, which were named after the Italian navigator Amerigo Vespucci, who led a voyage across the Atlantic in 1499–1502.

To head off looming conflicts between the Spanish and the Portuguese, Pope Alexander VI helped negotiate the Treaty of Tordesillas of 1494. It divided the Atlantic world between the two maritime powers, reserving for Portugal the West African coast and the route to India, and giving Spain the oceans and lands to the west (Map 14.1, page 433). The agreement allowed Portugal to claim Brazil in 1500, when it was accidentally "discovered" by Pedro Alvares Cabral (1467–1520) on a voyage to India.

A New Era in Slavery

The European voyages of discovery initiated a new era in slavery. Slavery had existed since antiquity and flourished in many parts of the world. Some slaves were captured in war or by piracy; others — Africans — were sold by other Africans and Bedouin traders to Christian buyers; in western Asia, parents sold their children out of poverty into servitude; and many in the Balkans became slaves when their land was devastated by Ottoman invasions. Slaves could be Greek, Slav, European, African, or Turkish. Many served as domestics in European cities of the Mediterranean such as Barcelona or Venice. Others sweated as galley slaves in Ottoman and Christian fleets. In the Ottoman army, slaves even formed an important elite contingent.

From the fifteenth century onward, Africans increasingly filled the ranks of slaves. Exploiting warfare between groups within West Africa, the Portuguese traded in gold

and "pieces," as African slaves were called, a practice condemned at home by some con-scientious clergy. Critical voices, however, could not deny the potential for profits that the slave trade brought to Portugal. Most slaves toiled in the sugar plantations that the Portuguese established on the Atlantic islands and in Brazil. African freedmen and slaves — some thirty-five thousand in the early sixteenth century — constituted almost 3 percent of the population of Portugal, a percentage that was much higher than in other European countries.

In the Americas, slavery would expand enormously in the following centuries. Even outspoken critics of colonial brutality toward indigenous peoples defended the develop-ment of African slavery. The Spanish Dominican Bartolomé de Las Casas (1474–1566), for example, argued that Africans were constitutionally more suitable for labor than na-tive Americans and should therefore be imported to the plantations in the Americas to relieve the indigenous peoples, who were being worked to death.

Conquering the New World

The native peoples of the Americas lived in a great diversity of social and political ar-rangements. Some were nomads roaming large, sparsely inhabited territories; others practiced agriculture in complexly organized states. Among the settled peoples, the largest groupings could be found in the Mexican and Peruvian highlands. Combining an elaborate religious culture with a strict social and political hierarchy, the Aztecs in Mexico and the Incas in Peru ruled over subjugated Indian populations in their re-spective empires. From their large urban capitals, the Aztecs and Incas controlled large swaths of land and could be ruthless as conquerors.

The Spanish explorers organized their expeditions to the mainland of the Americas from a base in the Caribbean. Two prominent commanders, **Hernán Cortés** (1485–1547) and Francisco Pizarro (c. 1475–1541), gathered men and arms and set off in search of gold. With them came Catholic priests intending to bring Christianity to suppos-edly uncivilized peoples. When Cortés first landed on the Mexican coast in 1519, the natives greeted him with gifts, thinking that he might be an ancient god returning to reclaim his kingdom. Some natives who resented their subjugation by the Aztecs joined Cortés and his soldiers. With a band of fewer than two hundred men, Cortés captured the Aztec capital, Tenochtitlán (present-day Mexico City), in 1519. Two years later, Mexico, then named New Spain, was added to the empire of the new ruler of Spain, Charles V, grandson of Ferdinand and Isabella. To the south, Pizarro conquered the Pe-ruvian highlands in 1532–1533. The Spanish Empire was now the largest in the world, stretching from Mexico to Chile.

The gold and silver mines in Mexico proved a treasure trove for the Spanish crown, but the real prize was the discovery of vast silver deposits in Potosí (today in Bolivia). When the Spaniards began importing the gold and silver they found in the New World, inflation soared in a fashion never before witnessed in Europe.

Not to be outdone by the Spaniards, other European powers joined the scramble for gold in the New World. In North America, the French went in search of a "northwest

passage" to China. The French wanted to establish settlements in what became Canada, but permanent European settlements in Canada and the present-day United States would succeed only in the seventeenth century. By then the English and Dutch had also entered the contest for world mastery.

The Columbian Exchange

The movement of peoples, animals, plants, manufactured goods, precious metals, and diseases between Europe, the New World, and Africa — the Columbian exchange — was one of the most dramatic transformations of ecology, agriculture, and ways of life in all of human history. Columbus started the process when he brought with him firearms, unknown in the Americas, and on his second voyage, horses, which had become extinct in the Americas, as well as pigs, cows, chickens, goats, sheep, cattle, and various plants including wheat, melons, and sugarcane. Enslaved Africans, first brought to the Caribbean in 1503–1505, worked on sugarcane plantations, foreshadowing the development of a massive slave economy in the seventeenth and eighteenth centuries (see Chapter 17).

The Europeans also brought with them diseases. Amerindians died in catastrophic numbers because they lacked natural immunity from previous exposure. Smallpox first appeared in the New World in 1518; it and other epidemic diseases killed as many as 90 percent of natives in some places (though the precise numbers are unknown). Syphilis, or a genetic predecessor to it, came back with the explorers to Europe.

The Spanish also brought back tobacco, cacao (chocolate), sweet potatoes, maize, and tomato seeds, changing consumption patterns in Europe. (Their native American wives, concubines, and domestics taught them to drink chocolate in the native fashion: frothy, red in color, and flavored with peppers.) At the same time, Spanish and Portuguese slave traders brought these crops and others — such as manioc, capsicum peppers, pineapples, cashew nuts, and peanuts — from the Americas to West Africa, where their cultivation altered local agriculture and diets. The slavers bought African yams, sorghum, millet, and especially rice to feed the slaves in transit, and the slaves then grew those crops in the Americas. Thus the exchange went in every conceivable direction.

REVIEW QUESTION Which European countries led the way in maritime exploration, and what were their motives?

The Protestant Reformation

When Columbus's patrons Ferdinand and Isabella expelled all Jews from Spain in 1492 and chased the last Muslims from Granada in 1502, it appeared as if the triumph of the Catholic church had been assured. Only fifteen years later, however, Martin Luther started a movement for religious reform that would fracture the unity of Western Christianity. Instead of one Catholic church, there would be many different kinds of Christians. The invention of printing with movable type helped spread the Protestant message, which grew in part out of waves of popular piety that washed over Europe in the

closing decades of the 1400s. Reformers had also been influenced by Christian humanists who focused attention on clerical abuses.

The Invention of Printing

Printing with movable type, first developed in Europe in the 1440s by Johannes Gutenberg, a German goldsmith, marked a revolutionary departure from the old practice of copying works by hand or stamping pages with individually carved woodblocks. The Chinese invented movable type in the eleventh century, but they preferred woodblock printing because it was more suitable to the Chinese language, with its thousands of different characters. In Europe, with only twenty-six letters to the alphabet, movable type allowed entire manuscripts to be printed more quickly than ever before. Single letters, made in metal molds, could be emptied out of a frame and new ones inserted to print each new page.

In 1467, two German printers established the first press in Rome; within five years, they had produced twelve thousand volumes, a feat that in the past would have required a thousand scribes working full-time. Printing also depended on the large-scale production of paper. Papermaking came to Europe from China via Arab intermediaries. By the fourteenth century, paper mills in Italy were producing paper that was more fragile but also much cheaper than parchment or vellum, the animal skins that Europeans had previously used for writing.

Early printed books attracted an elite audience. Their expense made them inaccessible to most

Printing Press

This illustration from a French manuscript of 1537 depicts typical printing equipment of the sixteenth century. An artisan is using the screw press to apply the inked type to the paper. Also shown are the composed type secured in a chase, the printed sheet (four pages of text printed on one sheet) held by the seated proofreader, and the bound volume. When two pages of text were printed on one standard-sized sheet, the bound book was called a folio. A bound book with four pages of text on one sheet was called a quarto ("in four"), and a book with eight pages of text on one sheet was called an octavo ("in eight"). The octavo was a pocket-size book, smaller than today's paperback. (The Granger Collection, NYC — All rights reserved.)

literate people, who comprised a minority of the population in any case. Gutenberg's famous two-volume Latin Bible was a luxury item, and only 185 copies were printed. Gutenberg Bibles remain today a treasure that only the greatest libraries possess.

The invention of mechanical printing dramatically increased the speed at which people could transmit knowledge, and it freed individuals from having to memorize everything they learned. Printed books and pamphlets, even one-page flyers, would create a wide community of scholars no longer dependent on personal patronage or church sponsorship for texts. Printing thus encouraged the free expression and exchange of ideas, and its disruptive potential did not go unnoticed by political and religious authorities. Rulers and bishops in the German states, the birthplace of the printing industry, moved quickly to issue censorship regulations, but their efforts could not prevent the outbreak of the Protestant Reformation.

Popular Piety and Christian Humanism

The Christianizing of Europe had taken many centuries to complete, but by 1500 most people in Europe believed devoutly. However, the vast majority of them had little knowledge of Catholic doctrine. More popular forms of piety — such as processions, festivals, and marvelous tales of saints' miracles — captivated ordinary believers.

Urban merchants and artisans, more likely than the general population to be literate and critical of their local priests, yearned for a faith more meaningful to their daily lives and for a clergy more responsive to their needs. They generously donated money to establish new preaching positions for university-trained clerics. The merchants resented the funneling of the Catholic church's rich endowments to the younger children of the nobility who took up religious callings to protect the wealth of their families. The young, educated clerics funded by the merchants often came from cities themselves. They formed the backbone of **Christian humanism** and sometimes became reformers, too.

Humanism had originated during the Renaissance in Italy among highly educated individuals attached to the personal households of prominent rulers. North of the Alps, however, humanists focused more on religious revival and the inculcation of Christian piety, especially through the schools of the Brethren of the Common Life. The Brethren preached religious self-discipline, specialized in the copying of manuscripts, and were among the first to print the ancient classics. Their most influential pupil was the Dutch Christian humanist Desiderius Erasmus (c. 1466–1536). The illegitimate son of a man who became a priest, Erasmus joined the Augustinian Order of monks, but the pope allowed him to leave the monastery and pursue the life of an independent scholar. An intimate friend of kings and popes, he became known across Europe. He devoted years to preparing a critical edition of the New Testament in Greek with a translation into Latin, which was finally published in 1516.

Erasmus strove for a unified, peaceful Christendom in which charity and good works, not empty ceremonies, would mark true religion and in which learning and piety

would dispel the darkness of ignorance. He elaborated many of these ideas in his *Handbook of the Militant Christian* (1503), an eloquent plea for a simple religion devoid of greed and the lust for power. In *The Praise of Folly* (1509), Erasmus used satire to show that modesty, humility, and poverty represented the true Christian virtues in a world that worshipped pomposity, power, and wealth. The wise appeared foolish, he concluded, for their wisdom and values were not of this world.

Erasmus instructed the young future emperor Charles V to rule as a just Christian prince. A man of peace and moderation, Erasmus soon found himself challenged by angry younger men and radical ideas once the Reformation took hold; he eventually chose Christian unity over reform and schism. His dream of Christian pacifism crushed, he lived to see dissenters executed — by Catholics and Protestants alike — for speaking their conscience. Erasmus spent his last years in Freiburg and Basel, isolated from the Protestant community, his writings condemned by many in the Catholic church. After the Protestant Reformation had been secured, the saying arose that "Erasmus laid the egg that Luther hatched." Some blamed the humanists for the emergence of Luther and Protestantism, despite the humanists' decision to remain in the Catholic church.

Albrecht Dürer, *The Knight, Death, and the Devil*

Dürer's 1513 engraving of the knight depicts a grim and determined warrior advancing past death (wearing a crown entwined with a serpent and holding out an hourglass) and the devil (the pig-snouted horned figure wielding a menacing pike). An illustration for Erasmus's *The Handbook of the Militant Christian*, this scene is often interpreted as portraying a Christian clad in the armor of righteousness on a path through life beset by death and demonic temptations. Yet the knight in early-sixteenth-century Germany had become a mercenary, selling his martial skills to princes. Some knights waylaid merchants, robbed rich clerics, and held citizens for ransom. The most notorious of these robber-knights, Franz von Sickingen, was declared an outlaw by the emperor and murdered in 1522. (Bridgeman-Giraudon / Art Resource, NY.)

Martin Luther's Challenge

The crisis of faith of one man, **Martin Luther** (1483–1546), started the international movement known as the Protestant Reformation. The son of a miner and a deeply pious mother, Luther abandoned his studies in the law and, like Erasmus, entered the Augustinian Order. There he experienced his religious crisis: despite fervent prayers, fasting, intense reading of the Bible, a personal pilgrimage to Rome (on foot), and study that led to a doctorate in theology, Luther did not feel saved.

Luther found peace inside himself when he became convinced that sinners were saved only through faith and that faith was a gift freely given by God. Shortly before his death, Luther recalled his crisis:

> Though I lived as a monk without reproach, I felt that I was a sinner before God with an extremely disturbed conscience. Secretly . . . I was angry with God. . . . At last, by the mercy of God, meditating day and night, I gave heed to the context of the words, namely, "In [the gospel] the righteousness of God is revealed, as it is written, 'He who through faith is righteous shall live.'" There I began to understand that the righteousness of God is that by which the righteous live by a gift of God, namely by faith.

No amount of good works, Luther believed, could produce the faith on which salvation depended.

Just as Luther was working out his own personal search for salvation, a priest named Johann Tetzel arrived in Wittenberg, where Luther was a university professor, to sell indulgences. In the sacrament of penance, according to Catholic church doctrine, the sinner confessed his or her sin to a priest, who offered absolution and imposed a penance. Penance normally consisted of spiritual duties (prayers, pilgrimages), but the church also sold the monetary substitutions known as indulgences. A person could even buy indulgences for a deceased relative to reduce that person's time in purgatory and release his or her soul for heaven.

In ninety-five theses that he proposed for academic debate in 1517, Luther denounced the sale of indulgences as a corrupt practice. Printed, the theses became public and unleashed a torrent of pent-up resentment and frustration among the laypeople. What began as a theological debate in a provincial university soon engulfed the Holy Roman Empire. Luther's earliest supporters included younger Christian humanists and clerics who shared his critical attitude toward the church establishment. None of these Evangelicals, as they called themselves, came from the upper echelons of the church; many were from urban middle-class backgrounds, and most were university trained. But illiterate artisans and peasants also rallied to Luther, sometimes with an almost fanatical zeal. They and he believed they were living in the last days of the world, and that Luther and his cause might be a sign of the approaching Last Judgment.

In 1520, Luther burned his bridges with the publication of three fiery treatises. In *Freedom of a Christian,* Luther argued that faith, not good works, saved sinners from damnation, and he sharply distinguished between true Gospel teachings and invented

church doctrines. Luther advocated "the priesthood of all believers," insisting that the Bible provided all the teachings necessary for Christian living and that a professional caste of clerics should not hold sway over laypeople. These principles — "by faith alone," "by Scripture alone," and "the priesthood of all believers" — became central features of the reform movement.

In his second treatise, *To the Nobility of the German Nation,* Luther denounced the corrupt Italians in Rome and called on the German princes to defend their nation and reform the church. Luther's third treatise, *On the Babylonian Captivity of the Church,* condemned the papacy as the embodiment of the Antichrist.

From Rome's perspective, the Luther Affair, as church officials called it, concerned only one unruly monk. When the pope ordered him to obey his superiors and keep quiet, Luther tore up the decree. Spread by the printing press, Luther's ideas circulated throughout the Holy Roman Empire, letting loose forces that neither the church nor Luther could control. Social, nationalist, and religious protests fused with lower-class resentments, much as in the Czech movement that the priest and professor Jan Hus had inspired a century earlier. Like Hus, Luther appeared before an emperor: in 1521, he defended his faith at the Imperial Diet of Worms before **Charles V** (r. 1519–1556), the newly elected Holy Roman Emperor who, at the age of nineteen, ruled over the Low Countries, Spain, Spain's Italian and New World dominions, and the Austrian Habsburg lands. Luther shocked Germans by declaring his admiration for the Czech heretic. But unlike Hus, Luther enjoyed the protection of his lord, Frederick the Wise, the elector of Saxony (called an elector because he was one of seven princes charged with electing the Holy Roman Emperor). Charles V had bribed Frederick to become Holy Roman Emperor, and Charles had to treat him with respect.

Lutheran propaganda flooded German towns and villages. Sometimes only a few pages in length, these broadsheets were often illustrated with crude satirical cartoons. Magistrates began to curtail clerical privileges and subordinate the clergy to municipal authority. From Wittenberg, the reform movement quickly swelled and threatened to swamp all before it. Lutheranism spread northward to Scandinavia when reformers who studied in Germany brought back the faith and converted the kings from Catholic to Protestant beliefs.

Protestantism Spreads and Divides

Other Protestant reformers soon challenged Luther's doctrines even while applauding his break from the Catholic church. In 1520, just three years after Luther's initial rupture with Rome, the chief preacher of Zurich, Huldrych Zwingli (1484–1531), openly declared himself a reformer. Like Luther, Zwingli attacked corruption in the Catholic church hierarchy, and he also questioned fasting and clerical celibacy. Zwingli disagreed with Luther on the question of the Eucharist, the central Christian sacrament that Christians partook of in communion. The Catholic doctrine of transubstantiation held that when the priest consecrated them, the bread and wine of communion actually turned into the body and blood of Christ. Luther insisted that the bread and wine did not change

The Progress of the Reformation	
1517	Martin Luther disseminates ninety-five theses attacking sale of indulgences and other church practices
1520	Reformer Huldrych Zwingli breaks with Rome
1525	Peasants' War in German states divides reform movement
1529	Lutheran German princes protest condemnation of religious reform by Charles V
1534	The Act of Supremacy establishes King Henry VIII as head of the Church of England, severing ties to Rome
1534–1535	Anabaptists take over German city of Münster in failed experiment to create a holy community
1541	John Calvin establishes himself permanently in Geneva, making that city a model of Christian reform and discipline

their nature: they were simultaneously bread and wine and the body and blood of Christ. Zwingli, however, viewed the Eucharistic bread and wine as symbols of Christ's union with believers, not the real blood and body of Christ. This issue aroused such strong feelings because it concerned the role of the priest and the church in shaping the relationship between God and the believer.

In 1529, troubled by these differences and other disagreements, Protestant princes and magistrates assembled the major reformers in the Colloquy of Marburg, in central Germany. After several days of intense discussions, the reformers managed to resolve some differences over doctrine, but Luther and Zwingli failed to agree on the meaning of the Eucharist. The issue of the Eucharist would soon divide Lutherans and Calvinists as well.

Under the leadership of **John Calvin** (1509–1564), another wave of reform challenged Catholic authority. Born in Picardy, in northern France, Calvin studied in Paris and Orléans, where he took a law degree. Experiencing a crisis of faith, like Luther, Calvin sought salvation through intense theological study. Gradually, he, too, came to question fundamental Catholic teachings.

On Sunday, October 18, 1534, Parisians found church doors posted with crude broadsheets denouncing the Catholic Mass. Smuggled into France from the Protestant and French-speaking parts of Switzerland, the broadsheets provoked a wave of royal repression in the capital. In response to this so-called Affair of the Placards, the government arrested hundreds of French Protestants, executed some of them, and forced many more, including Calvin, to flee abroad.

Calvin made his way to Geneva, the French-speaking Swiss city-state where he would find his life's work. Genevans had renounced their allegiance to the Catholic bishop, and local supporters of reform begged Calvin to stay and labor there. Although it took some time for Calvin to solidify his position in the city, his supporters eventually triumphed and he remained in Geneva until his death in 1564.

Under Calvin's leadership, Geneva became a Christian republic on the model set out in his *Institutes of the Christian Religion,* first published in 1536. No reformer prior to Calvin had expounded on the doctrines, organization, history, and practices of Christianity in such a systematic, logical, and coherent manner. Calvin followed Luther's doctrine of salvation to its ultimate logical conclusion: if God is almighty and humans cannot earn their salvation by good works, then no Christian can be certain of salvation. Developing the doctrine of **predestination**, Calvin argued that God had ordained

every man, woman, and child to salvation or damnation — even before the creation of the world. Thus, in Calvin's theology, God saved only the "elect" (a small group).

Predestination could terrify, but it could also embolden. For Calvinists, a righteous life might be a sign of a person's having been chosen for salvation. Thus, Calvinist doctrine demanded rigorous discipline. Fusing church and society into what followers named the Reformed church, Geneva became a theocratic city-state dominated by Calvin and the elders of the Reformed church. Its people were rigorously monitored; detractors said that they were bullied. From its base in Geneva, the Calvinist movement spread to France, the Low Countries, England, Scotland, the German states, Poland, Hungary, and eventually New England.

In Geneva, Calvin tolerated no dissent. While passing through the city in 1553, the Spanish physician Michael Servetus was arrested because he had published books attacking Calvin and questioning the doctrine of the Trinity, the belief that there are three persons in one God — the Father, the Son (Christ), and the Holy Spirit. Upon Calvin's advice, the authorities executed Servetus. Calvin was not alone in persecuting dissenters. Each religious group believed that its doctrine was absolutely true and grounded in the Bible and that therefore violence in its defense was not only justified but required. Catholic and Protestant polemicists alike castigated their critics in the harshest terms, but they often saved their cruelest words for the Jews. Calvin, for example, called the Jews "profane, unholy, sacrilegious dogs," but Luther went even further and advocated burning down their houses and their synagogues. Religious toleration was still far in the future.

The Contested Church of England

England followed yet another path, with reform led by the king rather than by men trained as Catholic clergy. Despite a tradition of religious dissent that went back to the fourteenth-century theologian John Wycliffe, Protestantism gained few English adherents in the 1520s. King **Henry VIII** (r. 1509–1547) changed that when he broke with the Roman Catholic church. The resulting Church of England retained many aspects of Catholic worship but nonetheless aligned itself in the Protestant camp.

At first, Henry opposed the Protestant Reformation, even receiving the title Defender of the Faith from Pope Leo X for a treatise he wrote against Luther. With the aid of his chancellors Cardinal Thomas Wolsey and Thomas More, Henry vigorously suppressed Protestantism and executed its leaders. More had made a reputation as a Christian humanist, publishing a controversial novel about an imaginary island called Utopia (1516), the source of the modern word for an ideal community. Unlike his friend Erasmus, More chose to serve the state directly and became personal secretary to Henry VIII, Speaker of the House of Commons, and finally Lord Chancellor.

By 1527, the king wanted to annul his marriage to Catherine of Aragon (d. 1536), the daughter of Ferdinand and Isabella of Spain and the aunt of Charles V. The eighteen-year marriage had produced a daughter, Mary (known as Mary Tudor), but Henry desperately needed a male heir to consolidate the rule of the still-new Tudor dynasty.

Moreover, he had fallen in love with Anne Boleyn, a lady at court and a supporter of the Reformation. Henry claimed that his marriage to Catherine had never been valid because she was the widow of his older brother, Arthur. Arthur and Catherine's marriage, which apparently was never consummated, had been annulled by Pope Julius II to allow the marriage between Henry and Catherine to take place. Now Henry asked the reigning pope, Clement VII, to declare his marriage to Catherine invalid.

Around "the king's great matter" unfolded a struggle for political and religious control. When Cardinal Wolsey failed to secure papal approval of the annulment, Henry dismissed him and had him arrested. Wolsey died before he could be tried, and More took his place as cardinal. However, More resigned in 1532 because he opposed Henry's new direction; Henry then had him executed as a traitor in 1535. Henry now turned to two Protestants, Thomas Cromwell (1485–1540) as chancellor and Thomas Cranmer (1489–1556) as archbishop of Canterbury. Under their leadership, the English Parliament passed a number of acts that severed ties between the English church and Rome. The most important of these, the Act of Supremacy of 1534, made Henry the head of the Church of England. Other legislation invalidated the claims of Mary Tudor to the throne, recognized Henry's marriage to Anne Boleyn, and allowed the English crown to embark on the dissolution of the monasteries. In an effort to consolidate support behind his version of the Reformation, Henry sold off monastic lands to the local gentry and aristocracy. His actions prompted an uprising in 1536 in the north of the country called the Pilgrimage of Grace. Though suppressed, it revealed that many people remained deeply Catholic in their sympathies.

Henry grew tired of Anne Boleyn, who had given birth to a daughter, the future Queen Elizabeth I, but had produced no sons. He ordered Anne beheaded in 1536 on the charge of adultery. The king would go on to marry four other wives but father only one son, Edward. When Henry died in 1547, the principle of royal supremacy in religious matters was firmly established, but much would now depend on who held the crown.

REVIEW QUESTION How did Luther, Zwingli, Calvin, and Henry VIII each challenge the Roman Catholic church?

Henry himself held ambiguous views on religion: he considered himself Catholic but would not accept the supremacy of the pope; he closed the monasteries and removed shrines but kept the Mass and believed in clerical celibacy.

Reshaping Society through Religion

The religious reformers and their followers challenged political authority and the social order, yet in reaction to any extreme manifestation of disorder, they underlined the need for discipline in worship and social behavior. Some Protestants took the phrase "priesthood of all believers" quite literally and sided with the poor and the downtrodden. Like Catholics, Protestant authorities then became alarmed by the subversive potential of religious reforms. They viewed the Reformation as a way of instilling greater discipline in individual worship and church organization. At the same time, the Roman

Catholic church undertook reforms of its own and launched an offensive against the Protestant Reformation that is sometimes called the Counter-Reformation.

Protestant Challenges to the Social Order

When Luther described the freedom of the Christian, he meant an entirely spiritual freedom. But others interpreted his call for freedom in social and political terms. In the spring of 1525, peasants in southern and central Germany rose in a rebellion known as the Peasants' War and attacked nobles' castles, convents, and monasteries (Map 14.2). Urban workers joined them, and together they looted church properties in the towns. In Thuringia (central/eastern Germany), the rebels followed an ex-priest, Thomas Müntzer (1468?–1525), who promised to chastise the wicked and thus clear the way for the Last Judgment.

The Peasants' War split the reform movement. Princes and city officials, ultimately supported by Luther, turned against the rebels. Catholic and Protestant princes joined forces to crush Müntzer and his supporters. All over the empire, princes trounced peasant armies and hunted down their leaders. By the end of the year, more than 100,000 rebels had been killed. Initially, Luther had tried to mediate the conflict, but he believed that God ordained rulers, who must therefore be obeyed even if they were tyrants. Luther considered Müntzer's mixing of religion and politics the greatest danger to the Reformation, nothing less than "the devil's work." Fundamentally conservative in its political philosophy, the Lutheran church henceforth depended on established political authority for its protection.

Some followers of Zwingli also wanted to pursue their own path to reform. They believed that true faith came only to those with reason and free will. How could a baby knowingly choose Christ? Only adults could believe and accept baptism; hence, the **Anabaptists** ("rebaptizers") rejected the validity of infant baptism and called for adult rebaptism. Many were pacifists who also

German Peasants' War of 1525

This colored woodcut depicts peasants attacking the pope, a monk, and a nobleman during the massive rural uprisings against the church that took place in southern and central Germany in 1525. Even the heavens show signs of trouble: a comet and clouds in the shape of a goat signify bloodshed and sin. (The Granger Collection, NYC — All rights reserved.)

Map 14.2 The Peasants' War of 1525

The centers of uprisings clustered in southern and central Germany, where the density of cities encouraged the spread of discontent and allowed for alliances between urban masses and rural rebels. The proximity to the Swiss Confederation, a stronghold of the Reformation movement, also inspired antiestablishment uprisings.

refused to acknowledge the authority of law courts. The Anabaptist movement drew its leadership primarily from the artisan class and its members from the middle and lower classes—men and women attracted by a simple but radical message of peace and salvation.

Zwingli immediately attacked the Anabaptists for their refusal to bear arms and swear oaths of allegiance, sensing accurately that they were repudiating his theocratic (church-directed) order. When persuasion failed to convince the Anabaptists, Zwingli urged Zurich magistrates to impose the death sentence. Thus, the Evangelical reformers themselves created the Reformation's first martyrs of conscience.

Despite the Holy Roman Emperor's condemnation of the movement in 1529, Anabaptism spread rapidly from Zurich to many cities in southern Germany. In 1534,

one Anabaptist group, believing the end of the world was imminent, seized control of the city of Münster. Proclaiming themselves a community of saints, the Münster Anabaptists abolished private property in imitation of the early Christians and dissolved traditional marriages, allowing men, like Old Testament patriarchs, to have multiple wives, to the consternation of many women. Besieged by a combined Protestant and Catholic army, the city fell in June 1535. The Anabaptist leaders died in battle or were executed, their bodies hung in cages affixed to the church tower. Their punishment was intended as a warning to all who might want to take the Reformation away from the Protestant authorities and hand it to the people. The Anabaptist movement in northwestern Europe nonetheless survived under the determined pacifist leadership of the Dutch reformer Menno Simons (1469–1561), whose followers were eventually named Mennonites.

New Forms of Discipline

Faced with the social firestorms ignited by religious reform, the middle-class urbanites who supported the Protestant Reformation urged greater religious conformity and stricter moral behavior. Protestants did not have monasteries or convents or saints' lives to set examples; they sought moral examples in their own homes, in the sermons of their preachers, and in their own reading of the Bible. Some of these attitudes had medieval roots, yet the Protestant Reformation fostered their spread and Catholics soon began to embrace them.

Although the Bible had been translated into German before, Luther's translations — of the New Testament in 1522 and of the Old Testament in 1534 — quickly became authoritative. A new Bible-centered culture began to take root, as more than 200,000 copies of Luther's New Testament were printed over twelve years, an immense number for the time. Peppered with witty phrases and colloquial expressions, Luther's Bible not only made the sacred writings more accessible to ordinary people but also helped standardize the German language. Bible reading became a common pastime undertaken in solitude or at family and church gatherings. To counter Protestant success, Catholic German Bibles soon appeared, thus sanctioning Bible reading by the Catholic laity, a sharp departure from medieval church practice.

The new emphasis on self-discipline led to growing impatience with the poor. Between 1500 and 1560, rapid economic and population growth created prosperity for some and stress — heightened by increased inflation — for many. Wanderers and urban beggars were by no means novel, but now moralists, both Catholic and Protestant, denounced vagabonds as lazy and potentially criminal.

The Reformation provided an opportunity to restructure relief for the poor. Instead of decentralized, private initiatives often overseen by religious orders, Protestant magistrates appointed officials to head urban agencies that would certify the genuine poor and distribute welfare funds to them. Catholic authorities did the same. In 1531, Henry VIII asked justices of the peace (unpaid local magistrates) to license the poor in England and to differentiate between those who could work and those who could not.

Luther's Bible
This opening page from the Gospel of St. Matthew is taken from Luther's 1522 translation into German of the New Testament. The woodcut illustrations by Lucas Cranach, and Luther's decision to use a style of German that could be widely understood, made the book accessible to a wide audience. Bible reading became a central family activity for Protestants. (Bible Society, London, UK / The Bridgeman Art Library International.)

In 1540, Charles V imposed a welfare tax in Spain to augment that country's inadequate system of private charity.

In their effort to establish order and discipline, Protestant reformers denounced sexual immorality and glorified the family. The early Protestant reformers like Luther championed the end of clerical celibacy and embraced marriage. Luther, once a celibate priest himself, married a former nun. Protestant magistrates closed brothels and established marriage courts to handle disputes over marriage promises, child support, and divorce (allowed by Protestants in some rare situations). The magistrates also levied fines or ordered imprisonment for violent behavior, fornication, and adultery.

Prior to the Reformation, despite the legislation of church councils, marriages had largely been private affairs between families; some couples never even registered with the church. The Catholic church recognized any promise made between two consenting adults (with the legal age of twelve for females, fourteen for males) in the presence of two witnesses as a valid marriage. As the Reformation took hold, Protestants asserted government control over marriage, and Catholic governments followed suit. A marriage was legitimate only if registered by both a government official and a member of the clergy.

Catholic Renewal

The Catholic church decided in the 1540s to undertake drastic action to fend off the Protestant threat. Pope Paul III convened a general council of the church in 1545 at Trent, a town on the border between the Holy Roman Empire and Italy. Meeting spo-

radically over eighteen years (1545–1563), the **Council of Trent** effectively set the course of Catholicism until the 1960s. Catholic leaders sought renewal of religious devotion and reform of clerical morality (some priests had had sexual relationships and fathered children) as well as clarification of church doctrine. New religious orders set out to win converts overseas or to reconvert Catholics who had turned to Protestantism. At the same time, the church did not hesitate to root out dissent by giving greater powers to the Inquisition, including the power to censor books. The papal Index, or list of prohibited books, was established in 1557 and not abolished until 1966.

Italian and Spanish clergy predominated among the 255 bishops, archbishops, and cardinals attending the Council of Trent, which condemned all the central doctrines of Protestantism. According to the council, salvation depended on faith and good works, not faith alone. On the sacrament of the Eucharist, the council reaffirmed that the bread of communion "really, truly" becomes Christ's body. It reasserted the supremacy of clerical authority over the laity; the church's interpretation of the Bible could not be challenged, and the Latin Vulgate was the only authoritative version. The council rejected divorce and reaffirmed the legitimacy of indulgences. It also called for reform from within, however, insisting that bishops henceforth reside in their dioceses and decreeing that seminaries for the training of priests be established in every diocese. Henceforth, the schism between Protestant and Catholic remained permanent, and all hopes of reconciliation faded.

The renewed energy of Catholicism expressed itself most vigorously in the founding of new religious orders such as the Society of Jesus, or **Jesuits**, founded by a Spanish nobleman, Ignatius of Loyola (1491–1556). In 1521, while recovering from an injury suffered as a soldier in the Spanish army, Ignatius read lives (biographies) of the saints; once he recovered, he abandoned his quest for military glory in favor of serving the church. In 1540, the pope recognized his small band of followers.

With Ignatius as its first general, the Jesuits became the most vigorous defenders of papal authority. The society quickly expanded; by the time of Ignatius's death in 1556, Europe had one thousand Jesuits. They established hundreds of colleges throughout the Catholic world, educating future generations of Catholic leaders. Jesuit missionaries played a key role in the Spanish and Portuguese empires and brought Roman Catholicism to Africans, Asians, and native Americans. They saw their effort as proof of the truth of Roman Catholicism and the success of their missions as a sign of divine favor, both particularly important in the face of Protestant challenge.

Catholic missionary zeal brought conflicting messages to indigenous peoples: for some, the message of a repressive and coercive alien religion; for others, a sweet sign of reason and faith. Frustrated in his efforts to convert Brazilian Indians, a Jesuit missionary wrote to his superior in Rome in 1563 that "for this kind of people it is better to be preaching with the sword and rod of iron."

Catholic missionaries focused initially on winning over local elites. They learned the local languages and set up schools for the sons of conquered nobles. After an initial period of relatively little racial discrimination, the Catholic church in the Americas and Africa adopted strict rules based on color. For example, the first Mexican Ecclesiastical

Provincial Council in 1555 declared that holy orders were not to be conferred on Indians, mestizos (people of mixed European-Indian parentage), or mulattoes (people of mixed European-African heritage); along with descendants of Muslims, Jews, and persons who had been sentenced by the Spanish Inquisition, these groups were deemed "inherently unworthy of the sacerdotal [priestly] office."

European missionaries in Asia greatly admired Chinese and Japanese civilization, and thus used the sermon rather than the sword to win converts. The Jesuit Francis Xavier preached in India and Japan, his work greatly assisted by a network of Portuguese trading stations. Overall the efforts of the Catholic missionaries seemed highly successful: vast multitudes of native Americans had become nominal Christians by the second half of the sixteenth century, and thirty years after Francis Xavier's 1549 landing in Japan, the Jesuits could claim more than 100,000 Japanese converts.

> **REVIEW QUESTION** How did the forces for radical change unleashed by the Protestant Reformation interact with the urge for social order and stability?

Striving for Mastery

Although the riches of the New World and the conflicts generated by the Reformation raised the stakes of international politics, life at court did not change all at once. Princes and popes continued to sponsor the arts and literature of the Renaissance. Henry VIII, for example, hired the German artist Hans Holbein as king's painter. While Protestantism was taking root, Catholic monarchs still fought one another and battled the powerful Ottoman Empire. Holy Roman Emperor Charles V dominated the political scene with his central position in Europe and his rising supply of gold and silver from the New World. Yet even his wealth proved insufficient to subdue all his challengers. Religious difference led to violence in every country, even Spain, where there were almost no Protestants but many Muslims who were forced to convert by Charles V in 1526. For the most part, violence failed to settle religious differences. By 1560, an exhausted Europe had achieved a provisional peace, but one sowed with the seeds of future conflict.

Courtiers and Princes

Kings, princes, and popes alike used their courts to keep an eye on their leading courtiers (cardinals in the case of popes) and impress their other subjects. Briefly defined, the court was the ruler's household. Around the prince gathered a community of household servants, noble attendants, councilors, officials, artists, and soldiers. Renaissance culture had been promoted by this political elite, and that culture now entered its "high," or most sophisticated, phase. Its acclaimed representative was Michelangelo Buonarroti (1475–1564), an immensely talented Italian artist who sculpted the gigantic nude *David* for officials in Florence and then painted the ceiling of the Sistine Chapel for the recently elected Pope Julius II.

King Francis I and His Court

In this illustration from a 1534 manuscript, the king of France is shown with his three sons listening to the reading of a translated ancient text. The translator, Antoine Macault, was the king's secretary and is shown wearing the black of officials. Renaissance kings took pride in sponsoring revivals of classical texts (in this case Diodorus of Sicily, a Greek historian from the first century B.C.E.).

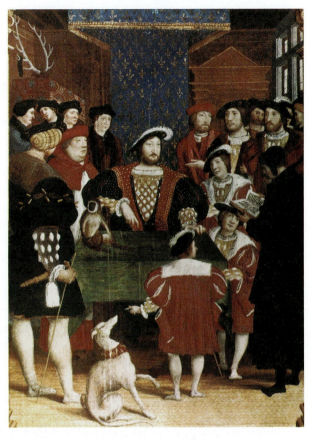

Italian artists also flocked to the French court of Francis I (r. 1515–1547), which swelled to the largest in Europe. In addition to royal officials and guards, physicians, librarians, musicians, dwarfs, animal trainers, and a multitude of hangers-on bloated its size to more than sixteen hundred members. Although Francis built a magnificent Renaissance palace at Fontainebleau, where he hired Italian artists to produce paintings and sculpture, the French court often moved from palace to palace. It took no fewer than eighteen thousand horses to transport the people, furniture, documents, dogs, and falcons for the royal hunt. Hunting represented a form of mock combat, essential in the training of a military elite. Francis almost lost his own life when, storming a house during one mock battle, he was hit on the head by a burning log.

Two Italian writers helped define the new culture of courtesy, or proper court behavior: Ludovico Ariosto (1474–1533), in service at the Este court in Ferrara, and Baldassare Castiglione (1478–1529), a servant of the duke of Urbino and the pope. Ariosto composed an epic poem, *Orlando Furioso*, which represented court culture as the highest synthesis of Christian and classical values. The poem's captivating tales of combat, valor, love, and magic ranged across Europe, Africa, Asia, and even the moon. In *The Courtier*, Castiglione's characters debate the qualities of an ideal courtier in a series of eloquent dialogues. The true courtier, Castiglione asserts, is a gentleman who carries himself with nobility and dignity in the service of his prince and his lady.

Courtesy was recommended to courtiers, but not always to princes. The Italian politician and writer Niccolò Machiavelli (1469–1527) helped found modern political

science by treating the maintenance of power as an end in itself. In his provocative essay *The Prince*, he underlined the need for pragmatic, even cold calculation. Was it better, he asked, for a prince to be feared by his people or loved? "It may be answered that one should wish to be both, but, because it is difficult to unite them in one person, [it] is much safer to be feared than loved." Machiavelli insisted that princes could benefit their subjects only by keeping a firm grip on power, if necessary through deceit and manipulation. *Machiavellian* has remained ever since a term for using cunning and duplicity to achieve one's ends.

Dynastic Wars

Even as the Renaissance developed in the princely courts and the Reformation began in the German states, the Habsburgs (the ruling family in Spain and then the Holy Roman Empire) and the Valois (the ruling family in France) fought each other for domination of Europe. French claims provoked the Italian Wars in 1494, which soon escalated into a general conflict that involved the major Christian monarchs and the Muslim Ottoman sultan as well. From 1494 to 1559, the Valois and Habsburg dynasties, both Catholic, remained implacable enemies. The fighting raged in Italy and the Low Countries. In 1525, the troops of Charles V crushed the French army at Pavia, Italy, counting among their captives the French king himself, Francis I. Forced to renounce all claims to Italian territory to gain his freedom, Francis furiously repudiated the treaty the moment he reached France, reigniting the conflict.

In 1527, Charles's troops captured and sacked Rome because the pope had allied with the French. Many of the imperial troops were German Protestant mercenaries, who pillaged Catholic churches and brutalized the Catholic clergy. Protestants and Catholics alike interpreted the sack of Rome by imperial forces as a punishment of God; even the Catholic church read it as a sign that reform was necessary. Finally, in 1559, the French gave up their claims in Italy and signed the Treaty of Cateau-Cambrésis, ending the conflict. To seal the peace the French king Henry II married his sister to the duke of Savoy, an ally of the Habsburgs, and his daughter to the Habsburg king of Spain, Philip II, who had succeeded his father Charles V in 1556.

The dynastic struggle (Valois versus Habsburg) had drawn in many other belligerents, who fought on one side or the other for their own benefit. Some acted purely out of power considerations, such as England, first siding with the Valois and then with the Habsburgs. Others fought for their independence, such as the papacy and the Italian states, which did not want any one power to dominate Italy. Still others chose sides for religious reasons, such as the Protestant princes in Germany, who exploited the Valois-Habsburg conflict to extract religious concessions from the emperor in 1555. The Ottoman Turks saw in this fight an opportunity to expand their territory.

The Ottoman Empire reached its height of power under Sultan Suleiman I, known as **Suleiman the Magnificent** (r. 1520–1566). In 1526, a Turkish expedition destroyed the Hungarian army at Mohács. Three years later, the Ottomans laid siege to Vienna;

Charles V and Francis I Make Peace
This fresco from the Palazzo Farnese in the town of Caprarola, north of Rome, shows French king Francis I and Holy Roman Emperor Charles V agreeing to the Truce of Nice in 1538, one of many peace agreements made and then broken during the wars between the Habsburgs and the Valois. Pope Paul III, who negotiated the truce, stands behind and between them. Charles is on the right pointing to Francis. The truce is the one celebrated in the Tlaxcala pageant described at the start of this chapter. (Palazzo Farnese Caprarola / Gianni Dagli Orti / The Art Archive — Art Resource, NY.)

though unsuccessful, the attack sent shock waves throughout Christian Europe. (See the illustration on page 454.) In 1535, Charles V led a campaign to capture Tunis, the lair of North African pirates loyal to the Ottomans. Desperate to overcome Charles's superior Habsburg forces, the French king Francis I forged an alliance with the Turkish sultan. The Turkish fleet besieged the Habsburg troops holding Nice, on the southern coast of France. Francis even ordered all inhabitants of nearby Toulon to vacate the town so that he could turn it into a Muslim colony for eight months, complete with a mosque and a slave market.

The French alliance with the Turks reflected the spirit of the times: the age-old idea of the Christian crusade against Islam now had to compete with a new political strategy that considered religion only one factor among many in power politics. Religion could be sacrificed, if need be, on the altar of state building. Constantly distracted by the challenges of the Ottomans to the east and the German Protestants at home, Charles V could not crush the French with one swift blow.

Financing War

The sixteenth century marked the beginning of superior Western military technology. All armies grew in size and their firepower became ever more deadly, increasing the cost of war. Heavier artillery pieces meant that the rectangular walls of medieval cities had to be transformed into fortresses with jutting ramparts and gun emplacements. Royal revenues could not keep up with war expenditures. To pay their bills, governments

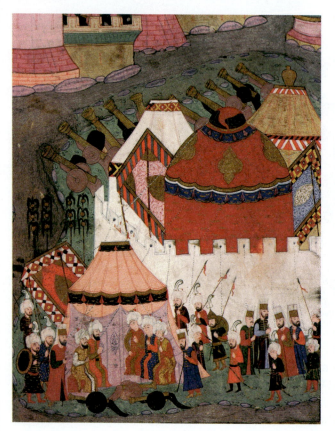

The Siege of Vienna, 1529
This illustration from an Ottoman manuscript of 1588 depicts the Turkish siege of Vienna (the siege guns can be seen toward the top of the picture). Sultan Suleiman I (Suleiman the Magnificent) led an army of more than 100,000 men against Vienna, capital of the Austrian Habsburg lands. Several attacks on the city failed, and the Ottomans withdrew in October 1529. They maintained control over Hungary, but the logistics of moving so many men and horses kept them from advancing farther westward into Europe. (Topkapi Museum Istanbul / Gianni Dagli Orti / The Art Archive — Art Resource, NY.)

routinely devalued their coinage (the sixteenth-century equivalent of printing more paper money), causing prices to rise rapidly.

Charles V boasted the largest army in Europe, supported by the gold and silver coming in from the New World. Immediately after conquest, the Spanish looted gold and silver objects, melted them down, and sent the precious metals to Spain. Mining began with forced Indian labor in the 1520s, and the amount of silver extracted in Mexico and sent to Spain increased twentyfold in the 1530s and 1540s. Nevertheless, Charles could never make ends meet because of his extravagant war costs: the debt of 37 million ducats accumulated during his forty years in power exceeded by 2 million ducats all the gold and silver brought from the Americas. His opponents fared even worse. On his death in 1547, Francis I owed the bankers of Lyon almost 7 million French pounds — approximately the entire royal income for that year. Foremost among the financiers of war debts was the Fugger bank, based in the southern German imperial city of Augsburg. The enterprise began with Jakob Fugger (1459–1525), who became personal banker to Charles V's grandfather Maximilian I. By the end of his life, Maximilian was so deeply in debt to Jakob Fugger that he had to pawn the royal jewels. In 1519, Fugger assembled a consortium of German and Italian bankers to secure the election of Charles V as Holy Roman Emperor. For the next three decades, the alliance between Europe's biggest international bank and its largest empire remained very close. Charles stayed barely one step ahead of his creditors; in 1531, for example, he had to grant to

the Fuggers eight years of mining rights in Spanish lands south of Peru (present-day Bolivia and Chile).

Divided Realms

European rulers viewed religious division as a dangerous challenge to the unity and stability of their rule. Subjects who considered their rulers heretics or blasphemers could only cause trouble, and religious differences encouraged the formation of competing noble factions, which easily led to violence when weak monarchs or children ruled.

In France, King Francis I tolerated Protestants until the Affair of the Placards in 1534. Even then, the government could not stop many French noble families — including some of the most powerful — from converting to Calvinism, especially in southern and western France. Francis and his successor, Henry II (r. 1547–1559), succeeded in maintaining a balance of power between Catholics and Calvinists, but after Henry's death the weakened monarchy could no longer hold together the fragile realm. The real drama of the Reformation in France took place after 1560, when the country plunged into four decades of religious wars, whose savagery was unparalleled elsewhere in Europe (see Chapter 15).

In England and Scotland religious divisions at the very top threatened the control of the rulers. Before his death in 1547, Henry VIII had succeeded in making himself head of the Church of England, but the nature of that church remained ambiguous. The advisers of the boy king Edward VI (r. 1547–1553) furthered the Protestant cause by welcoming prominent religious refugees who had been deeply influenced by Calvinism and wanted to see England move in that austere direction. But Edward died at age fifteen, opening the way to his Catholic half sister, Mary Tudor, who had been restored to the line of succession by an act of Parliament under Henry VIII in 1544.

When Mary (r. 1553–1558) came to the throne, she restored Catholicism and persecuted Protestants. Nearly three hundred Protestants perished at the stake, and more than eight hundred fled to the Protestant German states and Switzerland. Finally, when Anne Boleyn's daughter, Elizabeth, succeeded her half sister Mary, becoming Queen Elizabeth I (r. 1558–1603), the English Protestant cause again gained momentum. Under Elizabeth's leadership, Protestantism came to define the character of the English nation, though the influence of Calvinism within it was still a cause for dispute. Catholics were tolerated only if they kept their opinions on religion and politics to themselves. A tentative but nonetheless real peace returned to England.

Still another pattern of religious politics unfolded in Scotland, where Protestants formed a small minority until the 1550s. At the center of Scotland's conflict over religion stood Mary of Guise, a French native and Catholic married to the king of Scotland, James V. After James died in 1542, Mary surrounded herself and her daughter Mary Stuart, also a Catholic and heir to the throne, with French advisers. When, in 1558, Mary Stuart married Francis, the son of Henry II and the heir to the French throne, many Scottish noblemen, alienated by this pro-French atmosphere, joined the pro-English,

anti-French Protestant cause. They gained control of the Scottish Parliament in 1560 and dethroned the regent, Mary of Guise. Eventually they forced her daughter — by then known as Mary, queen of Scots — to flee to England, and installed Mary's infant son, James, as king. Scotland would turn toward the Calvinist version of the Reformation and thus establish the potential for conflict with England.

In the German states, the Protestant princes and cities formed the Schmalkaldic League in 1531. Headed by the elector of Saxony and Philip of Hesse (the two leading Protestant princes), the league included most of the imperial cities. Opposing the league were Emperor Charles V, the bishops, and the few remaining Catholic princes. Although Charles had to concentrate on fighting the French and the Turks during the 1530s, he eventually secured the western Mediterranean and then turned his attention back home to central Europe to try to resolve the growing religious differences in his lands.

After efforts to mediate between Protestants and Catholics broke down, Charles prepared to fight the Protestant Schmalkaldic League. War broke out in 1547, the year after Martin Luther's death. Using seasoned Spanish veterans and German allies, Charles occupied the German imperial cities in the south, restoring Catholic elites and suppressing the Reformation. When Protestant commanders could not agree on a joint strategy, Charles crushed the Schmalkaldic League's armies at Mühlberg in Saxony and captured the leading Lutheran princes. Jubilant, Charles restored Catholics' right to worship in Protestant lands while permitting Lutherans to keep their own rites. Protestant resistance to the declaration was deep and widespread: many pastors went into exile, and riots broke out in many cities. Charles's success did not last long. The Protestant princes regrouped, declared war in 1552, and chased a surprised, unprepared, and practically bankrupt emperor back to Italy.

Forced to compromise, Charles V agreed to the **Peace of Augsburg** in 1555. The settlement recognized the Lutheran church in the empire; accepted the secularization of church lands but "reserved" the remaining ecclesiastical territories for Catholics; and, most important, established the principle that all princes, whether Catholic or Lutheran, enjoyed the sole right to determine the religion of their lands and subjects. Calvinist, Anabaptist, and other dissenting groups were excluded from the settlement. Ironically, the religious revolt of the common people had culminated in a princes' reformation. The Augsburg settlement preserved a fragile peace in central Europe until 1618, but the exclusion of Calvinists would prompt future conflict.

Exhausted by decades of war and disappointed by the disunity in Christian Europe, Emperor Charles V resigned his many thrones in 1555 and 1556, leaving his Netherlandish-Burgundian and Spanish dominions to his son, Philip II, and his Austrian lands to his brother, Ferdinand (who was also elected Holy Roman Emperor to succeed Charles). Retiring to a monastery in southern Spain, the most powerful of the Christian monarchs spent his last years quietly seeking salvation.

REVIEW QUESTION How did religious divisions complicate the efforts of rulers to maintain political stability and build stronger states?

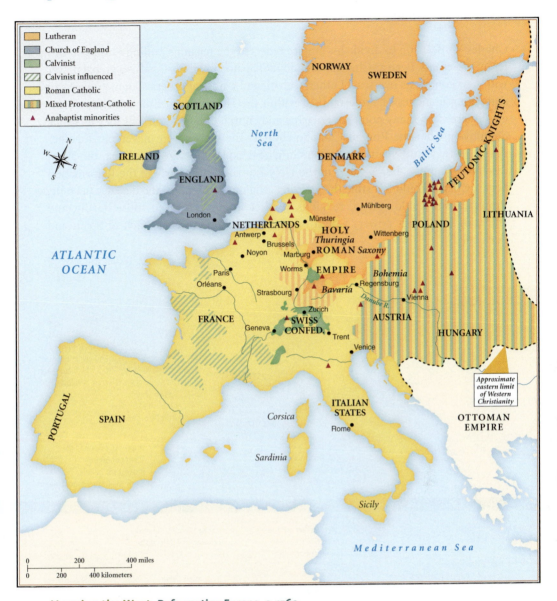

Legend:
- Lutheran
- Church of England
- Calvinist
- Calvinist influenced
- Roman Catholic
- Mixed Protestant-Catholic
- ▲ Anabaptist minorities

NORWAY
SWEDEN
SCOTLAND
North Sea
Baltic Sea
IRELAND
DENMARK
TEUTONIC KNIGHTS
ENGLAND
London
Münster
Mühlberg
LITHUANIA
NETHERLANDS
HOLY
Wittenberg
POLAND
Antwerp
Brussels
Thuringia
ROMAN
Saxony
ATLANTIC
OCEAN
Noyon
Marburg
Paris
Worms
EMPIRE
Bohemia
Orléans
Regensburg
Strasbourg
Bavaria
Vienna
Danube R.
FRANCE
Zurich
SWISS
AUSTRIA
Geneva
CONFED.
HUNGARY
Trent
Venice
Approximate eastern limit of Western Christianity
PORTUGAL
SPAIN
Corsica
ITALIAN
STATES
Rome
OTTOMAN
EMPIRE
Sardinia
Sicily
Mediterranean Sea

0   200   400 miles
0   200   400 kilometers

Mapping the West Reformation Europe, c. 1560

The fortunes of Roman Catholicism were at their lowest point around 1560. Northern Germany and Scandinavia owed allegiance to the Lutheran church; England broke away under a national church headed by its monarchs; and the Calvinist Reformation extended across large areas of western, central, and eastern Europe. Southern Europe remained solidly Catholic.

Conclusion

Charles V's decision to divide his empire reflected the tensions pulling Europe in different directions. Even as Charles's kingdom of Spain joined Portugal as a global power with new conquests overseas, Luther, Calvin, and a host of others sought converts to competing branches of Protestantism within the Holy Roman Empire. The reformers disagreed on many points of doctrine and church organization, but they all broke definitively from the Roman Catholic church. The pieces were never put together again. Portugal and Spain, the leaders in global exploration and conquest, remained resolutely Catholic, but as ruler of the Holy Roman Empire, where the Reformation began, Charles could not stifle the growing religious ferment. In the decades to come, Protestantism would spread, religious conflict would turn even more deadly, and emerging Protestant powers would begin to contest the global reach of Spain and Portugal.

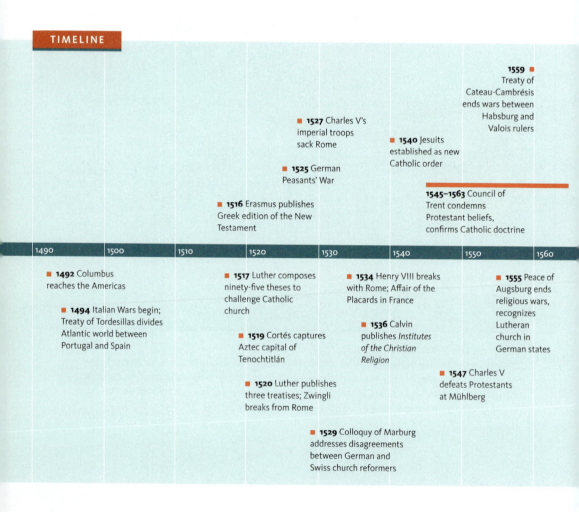

TIMELINE

1559 ■
Treaty of
Cateau-Cambrésis
ends wars between
Habsburg and
Valois rulers

■ **1527** Charles V's
imperial troops
sack Rome

■ **1540** Jesuits
established as new
Catholic order

■ **1525** German
Peasants' War

1545–1563 Council of
Trent condemns
Protestant beliefs,
confirms Catholic doctrine

■ **1516** Erasmus publishes
Greek edition of the New
Testament

| 1490 | 1500 | 1510 | 1520 | 1530 | 1540 | 1550 | 1560 |

■ **1492** Columbus
reaches the Americas

■ **1517** Luther composes
ninety-five theses to
challenge Catholic
church

■ **1534** Henry VIII breaks
with Rome; Affair of the
Placards in France

■ **1555** Peace of
Augsburg ends
religious wars,
recognizes
Lutheran
church in
German states

■ **1494** Italian Wars begin;
Treaty of Tordesillas divides
Atlantic world between
Portugal and Spain

■ **1536** Calvin
publishes *Institutes
of the Christian
Religion*

■ **1519** Cortés captures
Aztec capital of
Tenochtitlán

■ **1547** Charles V
defeats Protestants
at Mühlberg

■ **1520** Luther publishes
three treatises; Zwingli
breaks from Rome

■ **1529** Colloquy of Marburg
addresses disagreements
between German and
Swiss church reformers

Review Questions

1. Which European countries led the way in maritime exploration, and what were their motives?

2. How did Luther, Zwingli, Calvin, and Henry VIII each challenge the Roman Catholic church?

3. How did the forces for radical change unleashed by the Protestant Reformation interact with the urge for social order and stability?

4. How did religious divisions complicate the efforts of rulers to maintain political stability and build stronger states?

Making Connections

1. In what ways did the discovery of the Americas affect Europe?

2. Why was Charles V ultimately unable to prevent religious division in his lands?

3. How did the different religious groups respond to the opportunity presented by the printing press?

4. What motives besides religious differences caused war in this period?

- For practice quizzes and other study tools, visit the **Online Study Guide** at bedfordstmartins.com/huntconcise.

- For primary-source material from this period, see *Sources of the Making of the West*, Fourth Edition.

- For Web sites, images, and documents related to topics in this chapter, visit *Make History* at bedfordstmartins.com/huntconcise.

Suggested References

A more global historical perspective is reshaping the study of both the European voyages of exploration and conquest and the Reformation, especially the Catholic renewal, which included a global missionary effort.

Christopher Columbus: http://www.ibiblio.org/expo/1492.exhibit/Intro.html

Crosby, Alfred W. *The Colombian Exchange: Biological and Cultural Consequences of 1492.* 2003.

Holder, R. Ward. *Crisis and Renewal: The Era of the Reformations.* 2009.

Knecht, Robert Jean. *The French Renaissance Court, 1483–1589.* 2008.

Marshall, Peter. *Religious Identities in Henry VIII's England.* 2006.

McGrath, Alister E. *Luther's Theology of the Cross: Martin Luther's Theological Breakthrough.* 2nd ed. 2011.

*Müntzer, Thomas. *Revelation and Revolution: Basic Writings of Thomas Müntzer.* 1993.

O'Malley, John W. *Trent and All That: Renaming Catholicism in the Early Modern Era.* 2002.

Reston, James. *Defenders of the Faith: Charles V, Suleyman the Magnificent, and the Battle for Europe, 1520–1536.* 2009.

*Schwartz, Stuart B. *Victors and Vanquished: Spanish and Nahua Views of the Conquest of Mexico.* 2000.

Stjerna, Kirsi. *Women and the Reformation.* 2009.

*Symcox, Geoffrey, and Blair Sullivan. *Christopher Columbus and the Enterprise of the Indies: A Brief History with Documents.* 2005.

*Primary source.

ANTORFF.

nier groſſe tyrannej	Der weitter welt gar wolbekant	Vil tauſendt leuth vnſchuldigs bloit	O Gott will dich ein mhal erbarmen
het dieſe wütterej	Verdorben wirt, und gar verbrent,	Vergoſſen wirt, und groſſe noit	Deren ſo ietz ſeind im elend,
Antorff im niderlant	Berauhtt, und jungfrauwen geſchent	Sigit man mitt elendigem karmen	Damitt das morden neem ein endt.

Wars of Religion and the Clash of Worldviews

1560–1648

I N NOVEMBER 1576, SPAIN'S SOLDIERS sacked Antwerp, Europe's wealthiest city. In eleven days of horror known as the Spanish Fury, the troops slaughtered seven to eight thousand people and burned down a thousand buildings, including the city hall. The king of Spain had sent an army of ten thousand men in 1566 to occupy his rebellious northern domains and punish Calvinists, who had smashed stained-glass windows and statues in Catholic churches. By 1575, however, the king had run out of funds, and his men rioted after being unpaid for months. The Spanish Fury was far from an isolated incident in this time of religious upheaval. It showed, moreover, that violence often exploded from a dangerous mixture of religious, political, and economic motives.

Atrocities in Antwerp
The sixteenth-century Netherlandish artist Franz Hogenberg produced this engraving of the Spanish Fury in Antwerp not long after the events took place. It shows the kinds of atrocities — rape, murder, pillage, and burning of houses — that would be committed repeatedly on both sides of the conflict between Catholics and Protestants.
(akg-images.)

The first two generations of battles over the Protestant Reformation had ended with the Peace of Augsburg in 1555. That agreement helped maintain a relative calm in the lands of the Holy Roman Empire, but in western Europe religious strife multiplied after 1560 as Calvinists made inroads in France, the Netherlands, and England. In 1618, fighting broke out again in the Holy Roman Empire — and before it ended in 1648, the Thirty Years' War involved most of the European powers and desolated lands and peoples across central Europe. All in all, nearly constant warfare marked the century between 1560 and 1648. Like the Spanish Fury, these struggles began as religious disputes but soon revealed other motives: political ambitions, long-standing rivalries between the leading powers, and greed — all of which raised the stakes of conflict.

Suffering only increased when a major economic downturn in the early seventeenth century led to food shortages, famine, and disease in much of Europe. These catastrophes hit especially hard in the central European lands devastated by the fighting of the Thirty Years' War. In intellectual life a new understanding of the motion of the planets

in the heavens and of mechanics on earth developed among experimenters in "natural philosophy," that is, what came to be called science. This scientific revolution ultimately reshaped Western attitudes in virtually every field of knowledge, but at its beginnings it still had to compete with traditional religious views and popular beliefs in magic and witchcraft.

CHAPTER FOCUS What were the long-term political, economic, and intellectual consequences of the conflicts over religious belief in this era?

Religious Conflicts Threaten State Power, 1560–1618

The Peace of Augsburg made Lutheranism a legal religion in the predominantly Catholic Holy Roman Empire, but it did not extend recognition to Calvinists. The rapid expansion of Calvinism after 1560 threatened to alter the religious balance of power as Calvinists challenged Catholic dominance in France, the Spanish-ruled Netherlands, Scotland, and Poland-Lithuania. In England, they sought to influence the new Protestant monarch, Elizabeth I. Calvinists were not the only source of religious contention, however. Philip II of Spain fought the Muslim Ottoman Turks in the Mediterranean and expelled the remnants of the Muslim population in Spain. To the east, the Russian tsar Ivan IV fought to establish an empire based on Russian Orthodox Christianity.

French Wars of Religion, 1562–1598

Calvinism spread in France after 1555, when the Genevan Company of Pastors sent missionaries supplied with false passports and often disguised as merchants. By the end of the 1560s, nearly one-third of the nobles had joined the Huguenots (French Calvinists), and they raised their own armies. Conversion to Calvinism in French noble families often began with the noblewomen, who protected pastors, provided money and advice, and helped found schools and establish relief for the poor.

A series of family tragedies prevented the French kings from acting decisively to prevent the spread of Calvinism. King Henry II was accidentally killed during a jousting tournament in 1559, and his fifteen-year-old son, Francis, died soon after. Ten-year-old Charles IX (r. 1560–1574) became king, with his mother, **Catherine de Médicis**, as regent, or acting ruler. The Huguenots followed the lead of the Bourbon family, who stood first in line to inherit the throne if the Valois kings failed to produce a male heir. The most militantly Catholic nobles took their cues from the Guise family. Catherine tried to play the Bourbon and Guise factions against each other, but civil war erupted in 1562. Both sides committed terrible atrocities. Priests and pastors were murdered, and massacres of whole congregations became frighteningly commonplace.

Although a Catholic herself, Catherine feared the rise of Guise influence, so she arranged the marriage of the king's Catholic sister, Marguerite de Valois, to Henry of Navarre, a Huguenot and Bourbon. Just four days after the wedding, in August 1572, an assassin tried but failed to kill one of the Huguenot leaders. Violence against Calvinists

spiraled out of control. On St. Bartholomew's Day, August 24, a bloodbath began, fueled by years of growing animosity between Catholics and Protestants. In three days, Catholic mobs murdered some three thousand Huguenots in Paris. Ten thousand Huguenots died in the provinces over the next six weeks. The pope joyfully ordered the church bells rung throughout Catholic Europe.

Huguenot pamphleteers now proclaimed their right to resist a tyrant who worshipped idols (a practice that Calvinists equated with Catholicism). This right of resistance was linked to a political notion of contract; upholding the true religion was part of the contract binding the ruler to his subjects. Both the right of resistance and the idea of a contract fed into the larger doctrine of constitutionalism — that a government's legitimacy rested on its upholding a constitution, or contract between ruler and ruled.

The religious division in France grew even more dangerous when Charles IX died and his brother Henry III (r. 1574–1589) became king. Like his brothers before him, Henry III failed to produce an heir. Convinced that Henry III lacked the will to root out Protestantism, the Guises formed the Catholic League, which requested help from Spanish king Philip II. Henry III responded in 1588 by having his men kill two Guise leaders. A few months later, a fanatical Catholic monk stabbed Henry III to death, and Henry of Navarre became Henry IV (r. 1589–1610), despite Philip II's military intervention.

With the Catholic League threatening to declare his succession invalid, Henry IV publicly embraced Catholicism, reputedly explaining that "Paris is worth a Mass." Within a few years he defeated the ultra-Catholic opposition and drove out the Spanish. In 1598, he issued the **Edict of Nantes**, in which he granted the Huguenots a large measure of religious toleration. The approximately 1.25 million Huguenots became a legally protected minority within an officially Catholic kingdom of some 20 million people. Protestants were free to worship in specified towns and were allowed their own troops, fortresses, and even courts.

Few believed in religious toleration as an ideal, but Henry IV followed the advice of those moderate Catholics and Calvinists — together called *politiques* — who urged him to give priority to the development of a durable state. The politiques believed that religious disputes could be resolved only in the peace provided by strong government. The French Catholic writer Michel de Montaigne (1533–1592) went even further than this pragmatic position and revived the ancient doctrine of skepticism, which held that total certainty is never attainable. On the beams of his study he painted the statement "All that is certain is that nothing is certain." Like toleration of religious differences, such skepticism was repugnant to Protestants and Catholics alike, both of whom were certain that their religion was the right one.

The Edict of Nantes ended the French Wars of Religion, but Henry still needed to reestablish monarchical authority and hold the fractious nobles in check. He allowed rich merchants and lawyers to buy offices and, in exchange for an annual payment, pass their positions on to their heirs to sell them to someone else. This new social elite was known as the "nobility of the robe" (named after the robes that magistrates wore, much like those judges wear today). Income raised by the increased sale of offices reduced the

state debt and also helped Henry strengthen the monarchy. His efforts did not, however, prevent his enemies from assassinating him in 1610 after nineteen unsuccessful attempts.

Dutch Revolt against Spain

Although he failed to prevent Henry IV from taking the French throne in 1589, Philip II of Spain (r. 1556–1598) was the most powerful ruler in Europe (Map 15.1). In addition to the western Habsburg lands in Spain and the Netherlands, Philip had inherited from his father, Charles V, all the Spanish colonies recently settled in the New World of the

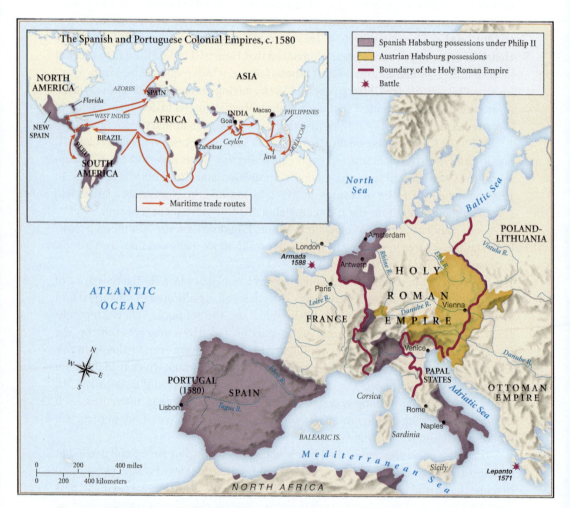

Map 15.1 The Empire of Philip II, r. 1556–1598
Spanish king Philip II drew revenues from a truly worldwide empire. In 1580, he was the richest European ruler, but the demands of governing and defending his control of such far-flung territories eventually drained his resources.

Americas. Gold and silver funneled from the colonies supported his campaigns against the Ottoman Turks and the French and the English Protestants. But all the money of the New World could not prevent Philip's eventual defeat in the Netherlands, where Calvinist rebels established the independent Dutch Republic, which soon vied with Spain, France, and England for commercial supremacy.

A deeply devout Catholic, **Philip II** came to the Spanish throne at age twenty-eight determined to restore Catholic unity in Europe and lead the Christian defense against the Muslims. His brief marriage to Mary Tudor (Mary I of England) did not produce an heir, but it and his subsequent marriage to Elisabeth de Valois, the sister of Charles IX and Henry III of France, gave him reason enough for involvement in English and French affairs. In 1578, the king of Portugal died fighting Muslims in Morocco, and two years later Philip took over this neighboring realm with its rich empire in Africa, India, and the Americas.

Philip insisted on Catholic unity in the lands under his control and worked to forge an international Catholic alliance against the Ottoman Turks. In 1571, he achieved the single greatest military victory of his reign when he joined with Venice and the papacy to defeat the Turks in a great sea battle off the Greek coast at **Lepanto**. Seventy thousand sailors and soldiers fought on the allied side, and eight thousand died. The Turks lost thirty thousand men.

The Battle of Lepanto
The Greek artist Antonio Vassilacchi painted this mural in 1600 to celebrate the Christian victory at the battle of Lepanto. Vassilacchi was working in Venice, which was one of the main Christian allies in the campaign against the Turks. The victory was considered so important that it was celebrated in writings, medals, paintings, and sculptures. The mural captures the violence and confusion of the battle. (Villa Barbarigo, Noventa Vicentina, Italy / Giraudon / The Bridgeman Art Library International.)

Philip II of Spain

The king of Spain is shown here (kneeling in black) with his allies at the battle of Lepanto, the doge of Venice on his left and Pope Pius V on his right. El Greco painted this canvas, sometimes called *The Dream of Philip II*, in 1578 or 1579. The painting is typically mannerist in the way it crowds figures into every available space, uses larger-than-life or elongated bodies, and creates new and often bizarre visual effects. What can we conclude about Philip II's character from the way he is depicted here? (© National Gallery, London / Art Resource, NY.)

Spain now controlled the western Mediterranean but could not pursue its advantage because of threats elsewhere. Between 1568 and 1570, the Moriscos — Muslim converts to Christianity who remained secretly faithful to Islam — had revolted in the south of Spain, killing ninety priests and fifteen hundred Christians. Philip retaliated by forcing fifty thousand Moriscos to leave their villages and resettle in other regions. In 1609, his successor, Philip III, ordered their expulsion from Spanish territory, and by 1614 some 300,000 Moriscos had been forced to relocate to North Africa.

The Calvinists of the Netherlands were less easily intimidated: they were far from Spain and accustomed to being left alone. After the Spanish Fury of 1576 outraged Calvinists and Catholics alike, Prince William of Orange (whose name came from the lands he owned in southern France) led the Netherlands' seven predominantly Protestant northern provinces into a military alliance with the ten mostly Catholic southern provinces and drove out the Spaniards. The Catholic southern provinces returned to the Spanish fold in 1579. Despite the assassination in 1584 of William of Orange, Spanish troops never regained control in the north. Spain would not formally recognize Dutch independence until 1648, but by the end of the sixteenth century the Dutch Republic (sometimes called Holland after the most populous of its seven provinces) was a self-governing state sheltering a variety of religious groups.

Religious toleration in the Dutch Republic developed for pragmatic reasons: the central government did not have the power to enforce religious orthodoxy. Each province governed itself and sent delegates to the one common institution, the States Gen-

eral. Although the princes of Orange resembled a ruling family, their powers paled next to those of local elites, known as regents. One-third of the Dutch population remained Catholic, and local authorities allowed them to worship as they chose in private. The Dutch Republic also had a relatively large Jewish population because many Jews had settled there after being driven out of Spain and Portugal. From 1597, Jews could worship openly in their synagogues. This openness to various religions would help make the Dutch Republic one of Europe's chief intellectual and scientific centers in the seventeenth and eighteenth centuries.

Well situated for maritime commerce, the Dutch Republic developed a thriving economy based on shipping and shipbuilding. Dutch merchants favored free trade in Europe because they could compete at an advantage. After the Dutch gained independence, Amsterdam became the main European money market for two centuries. The Dutch controlled many overseas markets thanks to their preeminence in seaborne commerce: by 1670, the Dutch commercial fleet was larger than the English, French, Spanish, Portuguese, and Austrian fleets combined.

Elizabeth I's Defense of English Protestantism

As the Dutch revolt unfolded, Philip II became increasingly infuriated with **Elizabeth I** (r. 1558–1603), who had succeeded her half sister Mary Tudor as queen of England. Philip had been married to Mary and had enthusiastically seconded Mary's efforts to return England to Catholicism. When Mary died in 1558, Elizabeth rejected Philip's proposal of marriage and promptly brought Protestantism back to England. She had to squash uprisings by Catholics in the north and at least two serious plots against her life. In the long run, however, her greatest challenges came from the Calvinist Puritans and Philip II.

The **Puritans** were strict Calvinists who opposed all vestiges of Catholic ritual in the Church of England. After Elizabeth became queen, many Puritans returned from exile abroad, but

Queen Elizabeth I of England
The Church of England's Prayerbook of 1569 included a hand-colored print of Elizabeth I saying her prayers. As queen, Elizabeth was also "supreme governor" of the Church of England; she named bishops and made final decisions about every aspect of church governance. The scepter or sword at her feet symbolizes her power. (HIP / Art Resource, NY.)

Elizabeth resisted their demands for drastic changes in church ritual and governance. The Church of England's Thirty-Nine Articles of Religion, issued under her authority in 1563, incorporated elements of Catholic ritual along with Calvinist doctrines. Puritans tried to undercut the crown-appointed bishops' authority by placing control of church administration in the hands of a local presbytery, that is, a group made up of the minister and the elders of the congregation. Elizabeth rejected this Calvinist presbyterianism.

The Puritans nonetheless steadily gained influence. Known for their emphasis on strict moral lives, the Puritans tried to close England's theaters and Sunday fairs. Every Puritan father — with the help of his wife — was to "make his house a little church" by teaching the children to read the Bible. Believing themselves God's elect — those whom God has chosen for mercy and salvation — and England an "elect nation," the Puritans also pushed Elizabeth to help Protestants on the continent. After Philip II annexed Portugal and began to interfere in French affairs, Elizabeth dispatched seven thousand soldiers in 1585 to help the Dutch rebels.

Philip II bided his time as long as Elizabeth remained unmarried and her Catholic cousin Mary Stuart, better known as Mary, queen of Scots, stood next in line to inherit the English throne. In 1568, Scottish Calvinists forced Mary to abdicate the throne of Scotland in favor of her one-year-old son James (eventually James I of England), who was then raised as a Protestant. After her abdication, Mary spent nearly twenty years under house arrest in England. In 1587, when a letter from Mary offering her succession rights to Philip was discovered, Elizabeth overcame her reluctance to execute a fellow monarch and ordered Mary's beheading.

Retreat of the Spanish Armada, 1588

Now determined to act, Philip II sent his armada (Spanish for "fleet") of 130 ships from Lisbon toward the English Channel in May 1588. The English scattered the Spanish Armada by sending blazing fire ships into its midst. A great gale then forced the Spanish to flee around Scotland. When the armada limped home in September, half the ships had been lost and thousands of sailors were dead or starving. Protestants throughout Europe rejoiced.

By the time Philip II died in 1598, the costs of fighting the Ottomans, Dutch, English, and French had finally bankrupted the treasury. In his novel *Don Quixote* (1605), the Spanish writer Miguel de Cervantes captured the disappointment of thwarted Spanish ambitions. Cervantes himself had been wounded at Lepanto. His novel's hero, a minor nobleman, reads so many romances and books of chivalry that he loses his sense of proportion and wanders the countryside futilely trying to mimic the heroic deeds he has come across in his reading.

Elizabeth made the most of her limited means and consolidated England's position as a Protestant power. In her early years, she held out the prospect of marriage to many political suitors; but in order to maintain her — and England's — independence, she never married. Her successor, James I (r. 1603–1625), came to the throne as king of both Scotland and England. Shakespeare's tragedies *Hamlet* (1601), *King Lear* (1605), and *Macbeth* (1606), written around the time of James's succession, might all be read as commentaries on the uncertainties faced by Elizabeth and James. But Elizabeth's story, unlike Shakespeare's tragedies, had a happy ending; she left James secure in a kingdom of growing weight in world politics.

The Clash of Faiths and Empires in Eastern Europe

In the east, the most contentious border divided Christian Europe from the Islamic realm of the Ottoman Turks. Even after their defeat at Lepanto in 1571, the Ottomans continued their attacks, seizing Venetian-held Cyprus in 1573. In the Balkans, rather than forcibly converting their Christian subjects to Islam, the Turks allowed them to cling to the Greek Orthodox faith. They also tolerated many prosperous Jewish communities, which grew with the influx of Jews expelled from Spain.

The Muscovite tsars officially protected the Russian Orthodox church, which faced no competition within Russian lands. Building on the base laid by his grandfather Ivan III, Tsar Ivan IV (r. 1533–1584) stopped at nothing in his endeavor to make Muscovy (the grand duchy centered on Moscow) the heart of a mighty Russian empire. Given to unpredictable fits of rage, Ivan murdered his own son with an iron rod during a quarrel. His epithet "the Terrible" reflects not only the terror he unleashed but also the awesome impression he evoked. Cunning and cruel, Ivan came to embody barbarism in the eyes of Westerners.

Russia, Poland-Lithuania, and Sweden in the Late 1500s

Ivan initiated Russian expansion eastward into Siberia, but two formidable foes blocked his plans for expansion westward: Sweden (which then included much of present-day Finland) and Poland-Lithuania. Poland and the grand duchy of Lithuania united into a single commonwealth in 1569 and controlled an extensive territory. After Ivan IV died in 1584, a terrible period of chaos known as the Time of Troubles ensued, during which the king of Poland-Lithuania tried to put his son on the Russian throne. In 1613, an army of nobles, townspeople, and peasants finally expelled the intruders and put on the throne a nobleman, Michael Romanov (r. 1613–1645), who established an enduring new dynasty.

REVIEW QUESTION How did state power depend on religious unity at the end of the sixteenth century and start of the seventeenth?

The Thirty Years' War, 1618–1648

Although the eastern states managed to avoid civil wars over religion in the early seventeenth century, the rest of Europe was drawn into the final and most deadly of the wars of religion, the Thirty Years' War. It began in 1618 with conflicts between Catholics and Protestants within the Holy Roman Empire and eventually involved most European states. By its end in 1648, many central European lands lay in ruins and the balance of power had shifted away from the Habsburg powers — Spain and Austria — toward France, England, and the Dutch Republic. Prolonged warfare created turmoil and suffering, but it also fostered the growth of armies and bureaucracies; out of the carnage would emerge centralized and powerful states that made increasing demands on ordinary people.

Origins and Course of the War

The fighting that devastated central Europe had its origins in a combination of religious disputes, ethnic competition, and political weakness. The Austrian Habsburgs officially ruled over the huge Holy Roman Empire, which comprised eight major ethnic groups. The emperor and four of the seven electors who chose him were Catholic; the other three electors were Protestants. The Peace of Augsburg of 1555 (see page 456) maintained the balance between Catholics and Lutherans, but it had no mechanism for resolving conflicts; tensions rose as Calvinism, unrecognized under the peace, made inroads into Lutheran areas. By 1613, two of the three Protestant electors had become Calvinists.

These conflicts came to a head when the Catholic Habsburg heir Archduke Ferdinand was crowned king of Bohemia (present-day Czech Republic) in 1617. The Austrian Habsburgs held not only the imperial crown of the Holy Roman Empire but also a collection of separately administered royal crowns, of which Bohemia was one. Once crowned, Ferdinand began to curtail the religious freedom previously granted to Czech Protestants. When Ferdinand was elected emperor (as Ferdinand II, r. 1619–1637), the rebellious Czechs deposed him and chose in his place the young Calvinist Frederick V of the Palatinate (r. 1616–1623). A quick series of clashes ended in 1620 when the imperial armies defeated the outmanned Czechs at the battle of White Mountain, near Prague. The Czechs would not gain their independence until 1918.

The battle of White Mountain did not end the war, which soon spread to the German lands of the empire. Private mercenary armies (armies for hire) began to form during the fighting, and the emperor had little control over them. Albrecht von Wallenstein (1583–1634), a Czech Protestant by birth, offered in 1625 to raise an army for Ferdinand II and soon had in his employ 125,000 soldiers, who plundered much of Protestant Germany with the emperor's approval. The Lutheran king of Denmark, Christian IV (r. 1596–1648), responded by invading northern Germany. General Wallenstein's forces defeated him. Emboldened by his general's victories, Emperor Ferdinand issued the Edict of Restitution in 1629, which outlawed Calvinism in the empire and reclaimed Catholic church properties confiscated by the Lutherans.

The Violence of the Thirty Years' War

Toward the end of the Thirty Years' War, the German artist Hans Ulrich Franck began producing a series of twenty-five etchings aimed at capturing the horrors of the conflict. This wood engraving based on one such etching shows how violence was directed at women in particular. Unlike the print that opens this chapter, which shows a whole panorama of atrocities committed in a city, Franck's etchings focused on crimes committed by soldiers against civilians in small rural villages. (akg-images.)

With Protestant interests in serious jeopardy, Gustavus Adolphus (r. 1611–1632) of Sweden marched into Germany in 1630 with a highly trained army of 100,000 soldiers. Hoping to block Spanish intervention in the war, the French monarchy's chief minister, Cardinal Richelieu (1585–1642), offered to subsidize the Lutheran Gustavus. This agreement between the Swedish Lutheran and French Catholic powers to fight the Catholic Habsburgs showed that state interests could outweigh religious considerations.

Gustavus defeated the imperial army and occupied the Catholic parts of southern Germany before he was killed at the battle of Lützen in 1632. Once again the tide turned, but this time it swept Wallenstein with it. Because Wallenstein was rumored to be negotiating with Protestant powers, Ferdinand dismissed his general and had him assassinated.

France openly joined the fray in 1635 by declaring war on Spain. The two Catholic powers pummeled each other. The French king Louis XIII (r. 1610–1643) hoped to profit from the troubles of Spain in the Netherlands and from the conflicts between the

Austrian emperor and his Protestant subjects. A series of internal revolts shook the perennially cash-strapped Spanish crown. In 1640, peasants in the rich northeastern province of Catalonia rebelled, overrunning Barcelona and killing the viceroy of the province. The Portuguese revolted in 1640 and proclaimed independence like the Dutch. In 1643, the Spanish suffered their first major defeat at French hands. Although the Spanish were forced to concede independence to Portugal (annexed to Spain only since 1580), they eventually suppressed the Catalan revolt.

France, too, faced exhaustion after years of rising taxes and recurrent revolts. Richelieu died in 1642. Louis XIII followed him a few months later and was succeeded by his five-year-old son, Louis XIV. With yet another foreign queen mother — she was the daughter of the Spanish king — serving as regent and an Italian cardinal, Mazarin, providing advice, French politics once again moved into a period of instability, rumor, and crisis. All sides were ready for peace.

The Effects of Constant Fighting

When peace negotiations began in the 1640s between the representatives of the various rulers involved in the war, they did not come a moment too soon. Some towns had faced several prolonged sieges during the decades of fighting. Even worse suffering took place in the countryside. Peasants fled their villages, which were often burned down. At times, desperate peasants revolted and attacked nearby castles and monasteries. War and intermittent outbreaks of plague cost some German towns one-third or more of their population. One-third of the inhabitants of Bohemia also perished.

Soldiers did not fare all that much better. An Englishman who fought for the Dutch army in 1633 described how he slept on the wet ground, got his boots full of water, and "at peep of day looked like a drowned ratt." Governments increasingly short of funds often failed to pay the troops, and frequent mutinies, looting, and pillaging resulted. Armies attracted all sorts of displaced people desperately in need of provisions. In the last year of the Thirty Years' War, the Imperial-Bavarian Army had 40,000 men entitled to draw rations — and more than 100,000 wives, prostitutes, servants, children, and other camp followers forced to scrounge for their own food.

The Peace of Westphalia, 1648

The comprehensive settlement provided by the **Peace of Westphalia** — named after the German province where negotiations took place — would serve as a model for resolving future conflicts among warring European states. For the first time, a diplomatic congress convened to address international disputes, and those signing the treaties guaranteed the resulting settlement. A method still in use, the congress was the first to bring *all* parties together, rather than two or three at a time.

France and Sweden gained most from the Peace of Westphalia. France acquired parts of Alsace and replaced Spain as the prevailing power on the continent. Sweden took several northern territories from the Holy Roman Empire (Map 15.2). The Habsburgs lost

Map 15.2 The Thirty Years' War and the Peace of Westphalia, 1648
The Thirty Years' War involved many of the major continental European powers. The arrows marking invasion routes show that most of the fighting took place in central Europe in the lands of the Holy Roman Empire. The German states and Bohemia sustained the greatest damage during the fighting. None of the combatants emerged unscathed because even ultimate winners such as Sweden and France depleted their resources of men and money.

the most. The Spanish Habsburgs recognized Dutch independence after eighty years of war. Each German prince in the Holy Roman Empire gained the right to establish Lutheranism, Catholicism, or Calvinism in his state, a right denied to Calvinist rulers by the Peace of Augsburg in 1555. The independence ceded to German princes sustained political divisions that prepared the way for the emergence of a new power, the Hohenzollern Elector of Brandenburg, who increased his territories and developed a small but effective standing army. After losing considerable territory in the west, the Austrian Habsburgs turned eastward to concentrate on restoring Catholicism to Bohemia and wresting Hungary from the Turks.

The Peace of Westphalia settled the distribution of the main religions in the Holy Roman Empire: Lutheranism would dominate in the north, Calvinism in the area of the Rhine River, and Catholicism in the south. Most of the territorial changes in Europe

remained intact until the nineteenth century. In the future, international warfare would be undertaken for reasons of national security, commercial ambition, or dynastic pride rather than to enforce religious uniformity. As the politiques of the late sixteenth century had hoped, state interests now outweighed motivations of faith in political affairs.

The nearly constant warfare that preceded the peace had one surprising result: despite the death and destruction, warfare had increased state authority. As armies grew to bolster the war effort, governments needed more money and more supervisory officials. The rate of land tax paid by French peasants doubled in the eight years after France joined the war. In addition to raising taxes, governments deliberately depreciated the value of the currency, which often resulted in soaring prices. When all else failed, rulers declared bankruptcy. The Spanish government, for example, did so three times in the first half of the seventeenth century. From Portugal to Muscovy, ordinary people resisted new taxes by forming makeshift armies and battling royal forces. With their col-

The Arts and State Power

In this enigmatic painting from 1656 called *Las Meninas* ("Maids of Honor"), the Spanish artist Diego Velázquez depicts the Spanish king Philip IV's five-year-old daughter, Margarita, with her maids of honor, chaperone, bodyguard, a dwarf, and a large dog. The painter himself is working at a large canvas in the rear of the room. In the background on the left, a mirror reflects the upper bodies of the king and queen, who are presumably watching the scene. Which of these many figures is the real center of the painting? Like most monarchs of the time, Philip employed court painters like Velázquez to paint their portraits and contribute to their prestige. Ten years later Margarita would marry Holy Roman Emperor Leopold I, who was her uncle. (Detail, *Las Meninas*, by Diego Velazquez [1599–1660]. Prado, Madrid, Spain / Giraudon / The Bridgeman Art Library International.)

orful banners, unlikely leaders, strange names (the Nu-Pieds, or "Barefooted," in France, for instance), and crude weapons, the rebels usually proved no match for state armies, but they did keep troops occupied.

To meet these new demands, monarchs relied on advisers who took on the role of modern prime ministers. Louis XIII's chief minister, Cardinal Richelieu, proclaimed the priority of **raison d'état** ("reason of state"), that is, the state's interest above all else. He silenced Protestants within France because they had become too independent, and he crushed noble and popular resistance to Louis's policies. He set up intendants — delegates from the king's council dispatched to the provinces — to oversee police, army, and financial affairs.

To justify the growth of state authority and the expansion of government bureaucracies, rulers carefully cultivated their royal images. James I of England argued that he ruled by divine right and was accountable only to God: "The state of monarchy is the supremest thing on earth; for kings are not only God's lieutenant on earth, but even by God himself they are called gods." He advised his son to maintain a manly appearance even as some courtiers complained of his behavior toward certain male favorites.

Appearance counted for so much that most rulers regulated who could wear which kinds of cloth and decoration, reserving the richest and rarest, such as ermine and gold, for themselves.

> **REVIEW QUESTION** Why did a war fought over religious differences result in stronger states?

Economic Crisis and Realignment

The devastation caused by the Thirty Years' War deepened an economic crisis that was already under way. After a century of rising prices, caused partly by massive transfers of gold and silver from the New World and partly by population growth, in the early 1600s prices began to level off and even to drop, and in most places population growth slowed. International trade fell into recession. Agricultural yields also declined, and peasants and townspeople alike were less able to pay the escalating taxes needed to finance the wars. Famine and disease trailed grimly behind economic crisis and war, in some areas causing large-scale uprisings and revolts. Behind the scenes, the economic balance of power gradually shifted as northwestern Europe began to dominate international trade and broke the stranglehold of Spain and Portugal in the New World.

From Growth to Recession

Population grew and prices rose in the second half of the sixteenth century. England's population grew by 70 percent and in parts of Spain the population grew by 100 percent (that is, it doubled). The supply of precious metals from the New World reached its height in the 1590s (see "Taking Measure," page 476). This flood of precious metals combined with population growth to fuel an astounding inflation in food prices in western Europe — 400 percent in the sixteenth century — and a more moderate rise in

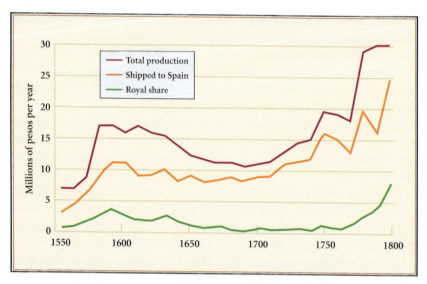

Taking Measure Precious Metals and the Spanish Colonies, 1550–1800
The graph shows that the production of gold and silver spurted upward between 1550 and 1590 and then declined until the beginning of the eighteenth century, paralleling the inflation of the last half of the sixteenth century and the following period of decline and depression. The graph also makes an important distinction between what was produced in the colonies, what was imported into Spain, and what the Spanish crown actually got as its share. (From Timothy R. Walton, *The Spanish Treasure Fleets* [Sarasota, FL: Pineapple Press, 1994], 221.)

the cost of manufactured goods. Wages rose much more slowly, at about half the rate of the increase in food prices.

Recession did not strike everywhere at the same time, but the warning signs were unmistakable. Foreign trade slumped as war and an uncertain money supply made business riskier. Imports of gold and silver declined, in part because so many of the native Americans who worked in Spanish colonial mines died from disease. Textile production fell in many countries, largely because of decreased demand and a shrinking labor force. The trade in African slaves grew steadily between 1580 and 1630 and then it, too, declined by a third, though its growth would resume after 1650 and skyrocket after 1700. African slaves were first transported to the new colony of Virginia in 1619, foreshadowing a major transformation of economic life in the New World colonies.

Demographic slowdown also signaled economic trouble. In the Mediterranean, growth had already stopped in the 1570s. The most sudden reversal occurred in central Europe as a result of the Thirty Years' War: one-fourth of the inhabitants of the Holy Roman Empire perished in the 1630s and 1640s. Population growth continued only in England, the Dutch Republic, the Spanish Netherlands, and Scandinavia.

Where the population stagnated or declined, agricultural prices dropped because of less demand, and farmers who produced for the market suffered. The price of grain fell most precipitously, causing many farmers to convert grain-growing land to pasture or vineyards. The only country that emerged unscathed from this downturn was the

Dutch Republic, thanks to a growing population and a tradition of agricultural innovation. Inhabiting Europe's most densely populated area, the Dutch developed systems of field drainage, crop rotation, and animal husbandry that provided high yields of grain for both people and animals. Their foreign trade, textile industry, crop production, and population all grew. After the Dutch, the English fared best; unlike the Spanish, the English never depended on infusions of New World gold and silver to shore up their economy, and unlike most continental European countries, England escaped the direct impact of the Thirty Years' War.

Historians have long disagreed about the causes of the early-seventeenth-century recession. Some cite the inability of agriculture to support a growing population by the end of the sixteenth century; others blame the Thirty Years' War, the states' demands for more taxes, or the waste caused by middle-class expenditures in the desire to emulate the nobility. To this list of causes, recent researchers have added climatic changes. Cold winters and wet summers meant bad harvests, and these natural disasters ushered in a host of social catastrophes. When the harvest was bad, prices shot back up and many could not afford to feed themselves.

Consequences for Daily Life

The recession of the early 1600s had both short-term and long-term effects. In the short term, it aggravated the threat of food shortages, increased the outbreaks of famine and disease, and caused people to leave their families and homes. In the long term, it deepened the division between prosperous and poor peasants and fostered the development of a new pattern of late marriages and smaller families.

When grain harvests fell short, peasants immediately suffered because, outside of England and the Dutch Republic, grain had replaced more expensive meat as the essential staple of most Europeans' diets. By the end of the sixteenth century, the average adult European ate more than four hundred pounds of grain per year. Peasants lived on bread, soup with a little fat or oil, peas or lentils, garden vegetables in season, and only occasionally a piece of meat or fish.

When faced with famine, most people simply left their huts and hovels and took to the road in search of food and charity. Men left their families to search for better conditions elsewhere. Those left behind might be reduced to eating chestnuts, roots, bark, and grass. In eastern France in 1637, a witness reported, "The roads were paved with people. . . . Finally it came to cannibalism." Compassion sometimes gave way to fear when hungry vagabonds became more aggressive, occasionally threatening to burn a barn if they were not given food.

Successive bad harvests led to malnutrition, which weakened people and made them more susceptible to such epidemic diseases as the plague, typhoid fever, typhus, dysentery, smallpox, and influenza. The plague was feared most: in one year it could cause the death of up to half of a town's or village's population, and it struck with no discernible pattern. Nearly 5 percent of France's entire population died just in the plague of 1628–1632.

The Life of the Poor

This mid-seventeenth-century painting by the Dutch artist Adriaen Pietersz van de Venne depicts the poor peasant weighed down by his wife and child. An empty food bowl signifies their hunger. In reality, many poor men abandoned their homes in search of work, leaving their wives behind to cope with hungry children and what remained of the family farm. What did the artist intend to convey about women? (Allen Memorial Art Museum, Oberlin College, Ohio, Mrs. F. F. Prentiss Fund, 1960.)

Economic crisis widened the gap between rich and poor. Peasants paid rent to their landlords as well as fees for inheriting or selling land and tolls for using mills, wine presses, or ovens. States collected direct taxes on land and sales taxes on consumer goods such as salt, an essential preservative. Protestant and Catholic churches alike exacted a tithe (a tax equivalent to one-tenth of the parishioner's annual income); often the clergy took their tithe in the form of crops and collected it directly during the harvest. Any reversal of fortune could force peasants into the homeless world of vagrants and beggars, who numbered as much as 2 percent of the total population.

In England, the Dutch Republic, northern France, and northwestern Germany, improvements gave some peasants the means to become farmers who rented substantial holdings, produced for the market, and in good times enjoyed relative comfort and higher status. Those who could not afford to plant new crops such as maize (American corn) or to use techniques that ensured higher yields became simple laborers with little or no land of their own. One-half to four-fifths of the peasants did not have enough land to support a family. They descended deeper into debt during difficult times and often lost their land to wealthier farmers or to city officials intent on developing rural estates.

As the recession deepened, women lost some of their economic opportunities. Widows who had been able to take over their late husbands' trade now found themselves excluded by the urban guilds or limited to short tenures. Many women went into domestic service until they married, some for their entire lives. Town governments carefully regulated the work of female servants, requiring women to stay in their positions unless they could prove mistreatment by a master.

European families reacted to economic downturn by postponing marriage and having fewer children. When hard times passed, more people married and had more children. But even in the best of times, one-fifth to one-quarter of all children died in their first year, and half died before age twenty. Childbirth still carried great risks for women, about 10 percent of whom died in the process. Midwives delivered most babies; physicians were scarce, and even those who did attend births were generally less helpful than midwives. The Englishwoman Alice Thornton described in her diary how a doctor bled her to prevent a miscarriage after a fall (bloodletting, often by the application of leeches, was a common medical treatment); her son died anyway in a breech birth that almost killed her, too.

Beginning in the early seventeenth century and continuing until the end of the eighteenth, families in all ranks of society started to limit the number of children. Because methods of contraception were not widely known, they did this for the most part by marrying later; the average age at marriage during the seventeenth century rose from the early twenties to the late twenties. The average family had about four children. Poorer families seem to have had fewer children, wealthier ones more. Because Protestant and Catholic clergy alike stressed sexual fidelity and abstinence before marriage, the number of births out of wedlock was relatively small (2–5 percent of births); premarital intercourse was generally tolerated only after a couple had announced their engagement.

The Economic Balance of Power

Just as the recession of the early seventeenth century produced winners and losers among ordinary people, it also created winners and losers among the competing states of Europe. The economies of southern Europe declined during this period, whereas those of the northwest emerged stronger. Competition in the New World reflected and reinforced this shift as the English, Dutch, and French rushed to establish trading outposts and permanent settlements to compete with the Spanish and Portuguese.

The new powers of northwestern Europe with their growing Atlantic trade gradually displaced the Mediterranean economies, which had dominated European commerce since the time of the Greeks and Romans. England and the Dutch Republic vied with France to become the leading mercantile and slave-trading powers. Northern Italian industries were eclipsed; Spanish commerce with the New World dropped. Even the plague contributed to the new disparity in trading power. Whereas central Europe and the Mediterranean countries took generations to recover from its ravages, northwestern Europe quickly replaced its lost population, no doubt because this area's people had suffered less from the effects of the Thirty Years' War and from the malnutrition related to the economic crisis.

All but the remnants of serfdom had disappeared in western Europe, yet in eastern Europe nobles reinforced their dominance over peasants, and the burden of serfdom increased. The rise in the cost of grain in the sixteenth century prompted Polish and eastern German nobles to increase their holdings and step up their production of grain

for western markets. In the economic downturn of the first half of the seventeenth century, peasants who were already dependent became serfs—completely tied to the land. Although enserfment produced short-term profits for landlords, in the long run it retarded economic development in eastern Europe and kept most of the population in a stranglehold of illiteracy and hardship.

Economic realignment also took place across the Atlantic Ocean. Because Spain and Portugal had divided between themselves the rich spoils of South America, other prospective colonizers had to carve niches in seemingly less hospitable places, especially North America and the Caribbean (Map 15.3). Eventually, the English, French, and Dutch would dominate commerce with these colonies. Many European states, including Sweden and Denmark, chartered private joint-stock companies to enrich investors by importing fish, furs, tobacco, and precious metals (if they could be found), and to develop new markets for European products. British, French, Dutch, and Danish companies also began trading slaves.

In establishing permanent colonies, the Europeans created whole new communities across the Atlantic. Careful plans could not always surmount the hazards of transatlantic shipping, however. In 1620 the *Mayflower,* which had sailed for Virginia with Pilgrim emigrants, landed off-course far to the north in Massachusetts, where the settlers founded New Plymouth Colony. By the 1640s, the British North American colonies had more than fifty thousand people, of whom perhaps a thousand were Africans. The Indians native to the area had been decimated in epidemics and wars.

In contrast, French Canada had only about three thousand European inhabitants by 1640.

Map 15.3 European Colonization of the Americas, c. 1640
Europeans coming to the Americas established themselves first in coastal areas. The English, French, and Dutch set up most of their colonies in the Caribbean and North America because the Spanish and Portuguese had already colonized the easily accessible regions in South America. Vast inland areas still remained unexplored and uncolonized in 1640.

Though thin in numbers, the French rapidly moved into the Great Lakes region. Fur traders sought beaver pelts to make the hats that had taken Paris fashion by storm. Jesuit missionaries lived with native American groups, learning their languages and describing their ways of life.

Both England and France turned some attention as well to the Caribbean in the 1620s and 1630s when they occupied the islands of the West Indies after driving off the native Caribs. These islands would prove ideal for a plantation economy of African slaves tending sugarcane and tobacco crops under the supervision of European settlers.

Even as the British and French moved into North America and the Caribbean, Spanish explorers traveled the Pacific coast up to what is now northern California and pushed into New Mexico. On the other side of the world, in the Philippines, the Spanish competed with local Muslim rulers and indigenous tribal leaders to extend their control. Spanish officials worked closely with Catholic missionaries to rule over a colony composed of indigenous peoples, Spaniards, and some Chinese merchants.

REVIEW QUESTION What were the consequences of economic recession in the early 1600s?

The Rise of Science and a Scientific Worldview

The countries that moved ahead economically in the first half of the seventeenth century — England, the Dutch Republic, and to some extent France — turned out to be the most receptive to the rise of science and a scientific worldview. In the long-term process known as **secularization**, religion gradually became a matter of private conscience rather than public policy. Secularization did not entail a loss of religious faith, but it did prompt a search for nonreligious explanations for political authority and natural phenomena. During the late sixteenth and early seventeenth centuries, science, political theory, and even art began to break their long-standing bonds with religion. Scientists and scholars sought laws in nature to explain politics as well as movements in the heavens and on earth. The visual arts more frequently depicted secular subjects. A scientific revolution was in the making. Yet traditional attitudes did not disappear. Belief in magic and witchcraft pervaded every level of society. People of all classes believed that the laws of nature reflected a divine plan for the universe. They accepted supernatural explanations for natural phenomena, a view only gradually and partially undermined by new ideas.

The Scientific Revolution

Although the Catholic and Protestant churches encouraged the study of science and many prominent scientists were themselves clerics, the search for a secular, scientific method of determining the laws of nature undermined traditional accounts of natural phenomena. Christian doctrine had incorporated the scientific teachings of ancient philosophers, especially Ptolemy and Aristotle; now these came into question. A revolution in astronomy contested the Ptolemaic view, endorsed by the Catholic church, which

held that the sun revolved around the earth. Startling breakthroughs took place in medicine, too. Supporters of these new developments argued for the **scientific method**, which combined experimental observation and mathematical deduction. The use of the scientific method culminated in the astounding breakthroughs of Isaac Newton at the end of the seventeenth century. Newton's ability to explain the motion of the planets, as well as everyday objects on earth, gave science enormous new prestige.

The traditional account of the movement of the heavens derived from the second-century Greek astronomer Ptolemy, who put the earth at the center of the cosmos. Above the earth were fixed the moon, the stars, and the planets in concentric crystalline spheres; beyond these fixed spheres dwelt God and the angels. In this view, the sun revolved around the earth, the heavens were perfect and unchanging, and the earth was "corrupted." Ptolemy insisted that the planets revolved in circular orbits (because circles were more "perfect" than other figures). To account for the actual elliptical paths that could be observed and calculated, he posited orbits within orbits, or epicycles.

In 1543, the Polish clergyman Nicolaus Copernicus (1473–1543) began the revolution in astronomy by publishing his treatise *On the Revolution of the Celestial Spheres*. Copernicus attacked the Ptolemaic account, arguing that the earth and other planets revolved around the sun, a view known as **heliocentrism** (a sun-centered universe). He discovered that by placing the sun instead of the earth at the center of the system of spheres, he could eliminate many epicycles from the calculations and thus simplify the mathematics. Copernicus died soon after publishing his theories, but when the Italian monk Giordano Bruno (1548–1600) taught heliocentrism, the Catholic Inquisition (set up to seek out heretics) arrested him and burned him at the stake.

Copernicus's views began to attract widespread attention in the early 1600s. When the Danish astronomer Tycho Brahe (1546–1601) observed a new star in 1572 and a comet in 1577, the traditional view that the universe was unchanging came into question. Brahe still rejected heliocentrism, but the assistant he employed when he moved to Prague in 1599, Johannes Kepler (1571–1630), was won over to the Copernican view. Kepler developed three laws of planetary motion, published between 1609 and 1619, that provided mathematical backing for heliocentrism and directly challenged the claim long held, even by Copernicus, that planetary motion was circular. Kepler's first law stated that the orbits of the planets are ellipses, with the sun always at one focus of the ellipse.

The Italian astronomer Galileo Galilei (1564–1642) provided more evidence to support the heliocentric view and also challenged the doctrine that the heavens were perfect and unchanging. After learning in 1609 that two Dutch astronomers had built a telescope, Galileo built a better one and observed the earth's moon, four satellites of Jupiter, the phases of Venus (a cycle of changing physical appearances), and sunspots. The moon, the planets, and the sun were no more perfect than the earth, he insisted, and the shadows he could see on the moon could only be the product of hills and valleys like those on earth. Galileo portrayed the earth as a moving part of a larger system, only one of many planets revolving around the sun, not as the fixed center of a single, closed universe.

In 1616, the Catholic church forbade Galileo to teach that the earth moves; then, in 1633, it accused him of not obeying the earlier order. Forced to appear before the

The Trial of Galileo
In this anonymous painting of the trial held in 1633, Galileo appears seated on a chair in the center facing the church officials who accused him of heresy for insisting that the sun, not the earth, was the center of the universe (heliocentrism). Catholic officials forced him to recant or suffer the death penalty. Undated, the painting probably comes from a later time because contemporary paintings rarely included so many different figures each occupied in their own fashion. (Erich Lessing / Art Resource, NY.)

Inquisition, he agreed to publicly recant his assertion about the movement of the earth to save himself from torture and death. Afterward, Galileo lived under house arrest and could publish his work only in the Dutch Republic, which had become a haven for scientists and thinkers who challenged conventional ideas.

In the same year that Copernicus challenged the traditional account in astronomy (1543), the Flemish scientist Andreas Vesalius (1514–1564) did the same for anatomy. Until then, medical knowledge in Europe was based on the writings of the second-century Greek physician Galen, Ptolemy's contemporary. Drawing on public dissections (which had been condemned by the Catholic church since 1300) he performed himself, Vesalius refuted Galen's work in his illustrated anatomical text, *On the Construction of the Human Body*. The English physician William Harvey (1578–1657) used dissection to examine the circulation of blood within the body, demonstrating how the heart worked as a pump. The heart and its valves were "a piece of machinery," Harvey insisted, and they obeyed mechanical laws. Nature, he said, could be understood by experiment and rational deduction, not by following traditional authorities.

In the 1630s, the European intellectual elite began to accept the new scientific views. Ancient learning, the churches and their theologians, and long-standing popular

beliefs all seemed to be undercut by the scientific method. Two men were chiefly responsible for spreading the reputation of the scientific method in the first half of the seventeenth century: the English Protestant politician Sir Francis Bacon (1561–1626) and the French Catholic mathematician and philosopher René Descartes (1596–1650). They represented the two essential halves of the scientific method: inductive reasoning through observation and experimental research, and deductive reasoning from self-evident principles.

In *The Advancement of Learning* (1605), Bacon attacked reliance on ancient writers and optimistically predicted that the scientific method would lead to social progress. The minds of the medieval scholars, he said, had been "shut up in the cells of a few authors (chiefly Aristotle, their dictator) as their persons were shut up in the cells of monasteries and colleges," and they could therefore produce only "cobwebs of learning" that were "of no substance or profit." Knowledge, in Bacon's view, must be empirically based (that is, gained by observation and experiment).

Although Descartes agreed with Bacon's denunciation of traditional learning, he was concerned that the attack on tradition might only replace the dogmatism of the churches with the skepticism of Montaigne — that nothing at all was certain. Descartes aimed to establish the new science on more secure philosophical foundations, those of mathematics and logic. In his *Discourse on Method* (1637), he argued that mathematical and mechanical principles provided the key to understanding all of nature, including the actions of people and states. All prior assumptions must be repudiated in favor of one elementary principle: "I think, therefore I am." Everything else could — and should — be doubted, but even doubt showed the certain existence of someone thinking. Descartes insisted that human reason could not only unravel the secrets of nature but also prove the existence of God. Although he hoped to secure the authority of both church and state, his reliance on human reason rather than faith irritated authorities, and his books were banned in many places. He moved to the Dutch Republic to work in peace. Scientific research, like economic growth, became centered in the northern, Protestant countries, where it was less constrained by church control than in the Catholic south.

The power of the new scientific method was dramatically confirmed in the grand synthesis of the laws of motion developed by the English natural philosopher Isaac Newton (1642–1727). Born five years after the publication of Descartes's *Discourse on Method* and educated at Cambridge University, where he later became a professor, Newton brought his most significant mathematical and mechanical discoveries together in his masterwork, *Principia Mathematica* (1687). In it, he developed his law of universal gravitation, which explained both movement on earth and the motion of the planets. His law held that every body in the universe exerts over every other body an attractive force directly proportional to the product of their masses and inversely proportional to the square of the distance between them. This law of universal gravitation explained Kepler's elliptical planetary orbits just as it accounted for the way an apple fell to the ground.

Newtonian physics combined mass, inertia, force, velocity, and acceleration — all key concepts in modern science — and made them quantifiable. Once set in motion, in Newton's view, the universe operated like a masterpiece made possible by the ingenuity of God. Newton saw no conflict between faith and science. He believed that by demonstrating that the physical universe followed rational principles, natural philosophers could prove the existence of God and so liberate humans from doubt and the fear of chaos. Even while laying the foundation for modern physics, optics, and mechanics, Newton spent long hours trying to calculate the date of the beginning of the world and its end with the second coming of Jesus. Others, less devout than Newton, envisioned a clockwork universe that had no need for God's continuing intervention.

The Natural Laws of Politics

In reaction to the religious wars, writers not only began to defend the primacy of state interests over those of religious conformity but also insisted on secular explanations for politics. The Italian political theorist Machiavelli had pointed in this direction with his advice to Renaissance princes in the early sixteenth century, but this secular intellectual movement gathered steam in the aftermath of the religious violence unleashed by the Reformation.

The French Catholic lawyer and politique Jean Bodin (1530–1596) sought systematic secular answers to the problem of disorder in *The Six Books of the Republic* (1576). Comparing the different forms of government throughout history, he concluded that there were three basic types of sovereignty: monarchy, aristocracy, and democracy. Only strong monarchical power offered hope for maintaining order, he insisted, and so he rejected any doctrine of the right to resist tyrannical authority. While Bodin's ideas helped lay the foundation for absolutism — the idea that the monarch should be the sole and uncontested source of power — his systematic discussion of types of governments implied that they might be subject to choice and undercut the notion that monarchies were ordained by God, as most rulers maintained.

During the Dutch revolt against Spain, the legal scholar Hugo Grotius (1583–1645) furthered secular thinking by attempting to systematize the notion of "natural law" — laws of nature that give legitimacy to government and stand above the actions of any particular ruler or religious group. Grotius argued that natural law stood beyond the reach of either secular or divine authority; natural law would be valid even if God did not exist (though Grotius himself believed in God). By this account, natural law — not scripture, religious authority, or tradition — should govern politics. Such ideas got Grotius into trouble with both Catholics and Protestants. His work *The Laws of War and Peace* (1625) was condemned by the Catholic church, while the Dutch Protestant government arrested him for taking part in religious controversies. Grotius's wife helped him escape prison by hiding him in a chest of books. Grotius was one of the first to argue that international conventions should govern the treatment of prisoners of war and the making of peace treaties.

Grotius's conception of natural law also challenged the widespread use of torture. Most states and the courts of the Catholic church used torture when a serious crime had been committed and the evidence seemed to point to a particular defendant but no definitive proof had been established. The judges ordered torture — hanging the accused by the hands with a rope thrown over a beam or pressing the legs in a leg screw — to extract a confession, which had to be given with a medical expert and notary present and had to be repeated without torture.

To be in accord with natural law, Grotius argued, governments had to defend natural rights, which he defined as life, body, freedom, and honor. Grotius did not encourage rebellion in the name of natural law or rights, but he did hope that someday all governments would adhere to these principles and stop killing their own and one another's subjects in the name of religion. Natural law and natural rights would play an important role in the founding of constitutional governments from the 1640s forward and in the establishment of various charters of human rights in our own time.

The Arts in an Age of Crisis

Two new forms of artistic expression — professional theater and opera — provided an outlet for secular values in an age of conflict over religious beliefs. Religion still played an important role in painting, however, even though many rulers also commissioned paintings on secular subjects.

The first professional acting companies performed before paying audiences in London, Seville, and Madrid in the 1570s. A huge outpouring of playwriting followed upon the formation of permanent professional theater companies. The Spanish playwright Lope de Vega (1562–1635) alone wrote more than fifteen hundred plays. Theaters were extremely popular despite Puritan opposition in England and Catholic objections in Spain. Shopkeepers, apprentices, lawyers, and court nobles crowded into open-air theaters to see everything from bawdy farces to profound tragedies.

The most enduring and influential playwright of the time — in fact, the man considered the greatest playwright of the English language — was William Shakespeare (1564–1616), who wrote three dozen plays (including histories, comedies, and tragedies) and was a member of a chief acting troupe. Although none of Shakespeare's plays were set in contemporary England, they reflected the concerns of his age: the nature of power and the crisis of authority. His tragedies in particular show the uncertainty and even chaos that result when power is misappropriated or misused. In *Hamlet* (1601), for example, the Danish prince Hamlet's mother marries the man who murdered his royal father and usurped the crown. In the end, Hamlet, his mother, and the usurper all die. Like many real-life people, Shakespeare's tragic characters found little peace in the turmoil of their times.

Although painting did not always touch broad popular audiences in the ways that theater could, new styles in art and especially church architecture helped shape ordinary people's experience of religion. In the late sixteenth century, the artistic style known as mannerism emerged in the Italian states and soon spread across Europe. Mannerism

was an almost theatrical style that allowed painters to distort perspective to convey a message or emphasize a theme. The most famous mannerist painter, called El Greco because he was of Greek origin, trained in Venice and Rome before he moved to Spain in the 1570s. The religious intensity of El Greco's pictures found a ready audience in Catholic Spain, which had proved immune to the Protestant suspicion of ritual and religious imagery (see the illustration on page 466).

The most important new style was the **baroque**, which, like mannerism, originated in the Italian states. In place of the Renaissance emphasis on harmonious design, unity, and clarity, the baroque featured curves, exaggerated lighting, intense emotions, release from restraint, and even a kind of artistic sensationalism. Like many other historical designations, the word *baroque* ("irregularly shaped") was not used as a label by people living at the time; art critics in the eighteenth century coined the word to mean shockingly bizarre, confused, and extravagant, and art historians and collectors largely disdained the baroque until the late nineteenth century.

Closely tied to Catholic resurgence after the Reformation, the baroque melodramatically reaffirmed the emotional depths of the Catholic faith and glorified both church and monarchy. The style spread from Rome to other Italian states and then into central Europe. The Spanish built baroque churches in their American colonies as part of their massive conversion campaign.

A new secular musical form, the opera, grew up parallel to the baroque style in the visual arts. First influential in the Italian states, opera combined music, drama, dance, and scenery in a grand sensual display, often with themes chosen to please the ruler and the aristocracy. Composers could base operas on typically baroque sacred subjects or on traditional stories. Like many playwrights, including Shakespeare, opera composers often turned to familiar stories their audiences would recognize and readily follow. One of the most innovative composers of opera was Claudio Monteverdi (1567–1643), whose earliest operatic production, *Orfeo* (1607), was based on Greek mythology.

Magic and Witchcraft

Although artists, political thinkers, and scientific experimenters increasingly pursued secular goals, most remained as devout in their religious beliefs as ordinary people. Many scholars, including Newton, studied alchemy alongside their scientific pursuits. Alchemists aimed to discover techniques for turning lead and copper into gold. The astronomer Tycho Brahe defended his studies of alchemy and astrology as part of "natural magic," as opposed to demonic "black magic."

Learned and ordinary people alike also firmly believed in witchcraft, that is, the exercise of magical powers gained by a pact with the devil. The same Jean Bodin who argued against religious fanaticism insisted on death for witches — and for those magistrates who would not prosecute them. Trials of witches peaked in Europe between 1560 and 1640, the very time of the celebrated breakthroughs of the new science. Montaigne was one of the few to speak out against executing accused witches: "It is taking one's

Witches' Kiss

In this hand-colored print from *The Compendium of Witches* (1608), a witch kisses the backside of the devil himself. The author of the compendium, Francesco Maria Guazzo, was an Italian priest in Milan. His compendium provided detailed descriptions of pacts between witches and the devil. (© Charles Walker / Topham / The Image Works.)

conjectures rather seriously to roast someone alive for them," he wrote in 1580.

Witches had long been blamed for destroying crops and causing personal catastrophes ranging from miscarriage to madness, but never before had they been officially persecuted in such numbers. Denunciation and persecution of witches coincided with the spread of reform, both Protestant and Catholic. Witch trials concentrated especially in the German lands of the Holy Roman Empire, the boiling cauldron of the Thirty Years' War.

The victims of the persecution were overwhelmingly female: women accounted for 80 percent of the accused witches in about 100,000 trials in Europe and North America during the sixteenth and seventeenth centuries. About one-third were sentenced to death. Before 1400, when witchcraft trials were rare, nearly half of those accused had been men. Why did attention now shift to women? Some official descriptions of witchcraft oozed lurid details of sexual orgies, in which women acted as the devil's sexual slaves. Social factors help explain the prominence of women among the accused. Accusers were almost always better off than those they accused. The poorest and most socially marginal people in most communities were elderly spinsters and widows. Because they were thought likely to hanker after revenge on those more fortunate, they were singled out as witches.

The tide turned against witchcraft trials when physicians, lawyers, judges, and even clergy came to suspect that accusations were based on superstition and fear. In 1682, a French royal decree treated witchcraft as fraud and imposture, meaning that the law did not recognize anyone as a witch. In 1693, the jurors who had convicted twenty witches in Salem, Massachusetts, recanted, claiming: "We justly fear that we were sadly deluded and mistaken." The Salem jurors had not stopped believing in witches; they had simply lost confidence in their ability to identify them. When physicians and judges had believed in witches and carried out official persecutions, with torture, those accused of witchcraft had gone to their deaths in record numbers. But when the same groups distanced themselves from popular beliefs, the trials and the executions stopped.

REVIEW QUESTION How could belief in witchcraft and the rising prestige of the scientific method coexist?

Conclusion

The witchcraft persecutions reflected the traumas of these times of religious war, economic decline, and crises of political and intellectual authority. Deep differences over religion came to a head in the Thirty Years' War (1618–1648), which cut a path of destruction through central Europe and involved most of the European powers. Repulsed by the effects of religious violence, European rulers agreed to a peace that effectively removed disputes between Catholics and Protestants from the international arena. Almost everywhere rulers emerged from these decades of war with expanded powers that

Mapping the West The Religious Divisions of Europe, c. 1648
The Peace of Westphalia recognized major religious divisions within Europe that have endured for the most part to the present day. Catholicism dominated in southern Europe, Lutheranism had its stronghold in northern Europe, and Calvinism flourished along the Rhine River. In southeastern Europe, the Islamic Ottoman Turks accommodated the Greek Orthodox Christians under their rule but bitterly fought the Catholic Austrian Habsburgs for control of Hungary.

they would seek to extend further in the second half of the seventeenth century. The constant extension of state power is one of the defining themes of modern history; religious warfare gave it a jump-start.

For all their strength, however, rulers could not control economic, social, or intellectual trends. The economic downturn of the seventeenth century shifted economic power from the Mediterranean world to northwestern Europe because England, France, and the Dutch Republic suffered less from the fighting of the Thirty Years' War and recovered more quickly from bad times. They would become even more powerful in the decades to come.

An underlying shift in cultural attitudes and intellectual expectations accompanied these changes. Secularization encompassed the establishment of the scientific method as the standard of truth, the search for nonreligious foundations of political authority, and the growing popularity of nonreligious forms of art, such as theater and opera. Proponents of these changes did not renounce their religious beliefs, and it would be foolish to claim that everyone's mental universe changed. The significance of secularization would only emerge over the long term.

TIMELINE

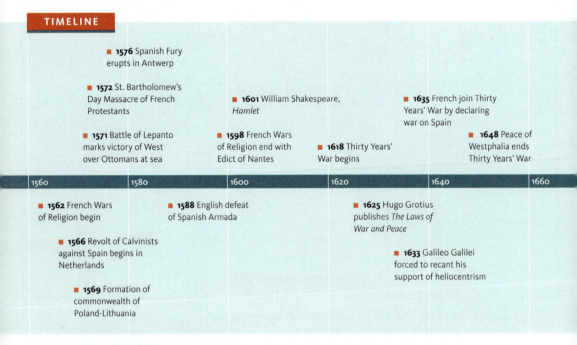

- **1576** Spanish Fury erupts in Antwerp

- **1572** St. Bartholomew's Day Massacre of French Protestants

- **1601** William Shakespeare, *Hamlet*

- **1635** French join Thirty Years' War by declaring war on Spain

- **1571** Battle of Lepanto marks victory of West over Ottomans at sea

- **1598** French Wars of Religion end with Edict of Nantes

- **1618** Thirty Years' War begins

- **1648** Peace of Westphalia ends Thirty Years' War

| 1560 | 1580 | 1600 | 1620 | 1640 | 1660 |

- **1562** French Wars of Religion begin

- **1588** English defeat of Spanish Armada

- **1625** Hugo Grotius publishes *The Laws of War and Peace*

- **1566** Revolt of Calvinists against Spain begins in Netherlands

- **1633** Galileo Galilei forced to recant his support of heliocentrism

- **1569** Formation of commonwealth of Poland-Lithuania

Review Questions

1. How did state power depend on religious unity at the end of the sixteenth century and start of the seventeenth?
2. Why did a war fought over religious differences result in stronger states?
3. What were the consequences of economic recession in the early 1600s?
4. How could belief in witchcraft and the rising prestige of the scientific method coexist?

Making Connections

1. How did the balance of power shift in Europe between 1560 and 1648? What were the main reasons for the shift?
2. What were the limits to the growth of secularization?
3. What was the influence of New World colonies on Europe from 1560 to 1648?
4. How did religious conflict mix with political concerns in this period?

- For practice quizzes and other study tools, visit the **Online Study Guide** at bedfordstmartins.com/huntconcise.

- For primary-source material from this period, see *Sources of the Making of the West*, Fourth Edition.

- For Web sites, images, and documents related to topics in this chapter, visit *Make History* at bedfordstmartins.com/huntconcise.

Suggested References

Religious conflict, the Thirty Years' War, science, witchcraft, and the travails of everyday life have all been the subject of groundbreaking research, yet the personalities of individual rulers still make for great stories, too.

Braudel, Fernand. *The Mediterranean and the Mediterranean World in the Age of Philip the Second.* Trans. Siân Reynolds. 2 vols. 1972, 1973.

*Diefendorf, Barbara B. *The Saint Bartholomew's Day Massacre: A Brief History with Documents.* 2008.

Elliott, John Huxtable. *Empires of the Atlantic World: Britain and Spain in America 1492–1830.* 2007.

Galileo Project: http://galileo.rice.edu

*Jacob, Margaret. *The Scientific Revolution: A Brief History with Documents.* 2010.

Konstam, Angus. *Lepanto 1571: The Greatest Naval Battle of the Renaissance.* 2003.

Levack, Brian P. *The Witch-Hunt in Early Modern Europe.* 2006.

Lynn, John A. *Women, Armies, and Warfare in Early Modern Europe.* 2008.

Madariaga, Isabel De. *Ivan the Terrible.* 2006.

Patterson, Benton Rain. *With the Heart of a King: Elizabeth I of England, Philip II of Spain, and the Fight for a Nation's Soul and Crown.* 2007.

Pitts, Vincent J. *Henri IV of France: His Reign and Age.* 2008.

Tracy, James D. *The Founding of the Dutch Republic: War, Finance, and Politics in Holland, 1572–1588.* 2008.

Wiesner-Hanks, Merry. *Women and Gender in Early Modern Europe.* 2008.

Wilson, Peter H. *The Thirty Years War: Europe's Tragedy.* 2009.

*Primary source.

Absolutism, Constitutionalism, and the Search for Order

I N MAY 1664, KING LOUIS XIV of France organized the first of many spectacular entertainments for his court at Versailles, where he had recently begun construction of a magnificent new palace. More than six hundred members of his court attended the weeklong series of parades, races, ballets, plays, and fireworks. In the opening parade,

Louis XIV and His Bodyguards
One of Louis XIV's court painters, the Flemish artist Adam Frans van der Meulen, depicted the king arriving at the palace of Versailles, still under construction. The painting dates from 1669, when none of the gardens, pools, or statues had yet been installed. Louis is the only figure facing the viewer, and his clothing is much more colorful than that of anyone else in the painting. (Réunion des Musées Nationaux / Art Resource, NY.)

Louis was accompanied by an eighteen-foot-high float in the form of a chariot dedicated to Apollo, Greek god of the sun and Louis's personally chosen emblem. The king's favorite writers and musicians presented works specially prepared for the occasion, and each evening ended with a candlelit banquet served by masked and costumed servants.

Louis XIV designed his pageants to awe those most dangerous to him, the leading nobles of his kingdom. To make his authority and glory concrete, the king relentlessly increased the power of his bureaucracy, expanded his army, and insisted on Catholic orthodoxy. This model of state building was known as **absolutism**, a system of government in which the ruler claims sole and uncontestable power. Other mid-seventeenth-century rulers followed Louis XIV's example or explicitly rejected it, but they could not afford to ignore it.

Although absolutism exerted great influence beginning in the mid-1600s, it faced competition from **constitutionalism**, a system in which the ruler shares power with an assembly of elected representatives. Constitutionalism provided a strong foundation for state power in England, the Dutch Republic, and the British North American colonies, while absolutism dominated in central and eastern Europe. Constitutionalism triumphed in England, however, only after one king had been executed as a traitor and another

493

had been deposed. The English conflicts over the nature of authority found their most enduring expression in the writings of Thomas Hobbes and John Locke, which laid the foundations of modern political science.

The search for order took place not only in government and politics but also in intellectual, cultural, and social life. Artists sought means of glorifying power and expressing order and symmetry in new ways. As states consolidated their power, elites endeavored to distinguish themselves more clearly from the lower orders. Officials, clergy, and laypeople all worked to reform the poor, now seen as a major source of disorder. Whether absolutist or constitutionalist, seventeenth-century states all aimed to extend control over their subjects' lives.

CHAPTER FOCUS What were the most important differences between absolutism and constitutionalism, and how did each system establish order?

Louis XIV: Absolutism and Its Limits

French king **Louis XIV** (r. 1643–1715) personified the absolutist ruler, who in theory shared his power with no one. In 1655, he reputedly told the Paris high court of justice, *"L'état, c'est moi"* ("I am the state"), emphasizing that state authority rested in him personally. Louis cleverly manipulated the affections and ambitions of his courtiers, chose as his ministers middle-class men who owed everything to him, built up Europe's largest army, and snuffed out every hint of religious or political opposition. Yet the absoluteness of his power should not be exaggerated. Like all other rulers of his time, Louis depended on the cooperation of many people: local officials who enforced his decrees, peasants and artisans who joined his armies and paid his taxes, clergy who preached his notion of Catholicism, and nobles who joined court festivities rather than causing trouble.

The Fronde, 1648–1653

Louis XIV's absolutism built on a long French tradition of increasing centralization of state authority, but before he could establish his preeminence he had to weather a series of revolts known as the Fronde. Louis was only five when he came to the throne in 1643 upon the death of his father, Louis XIII, who with his chief minister, Cardinal Richelieu, had steered France through increasing involvement in the Thirty Years' War, rapidly climbing taxes, and innumerable tax revolts. Louis XIV's mother, Anne of Austria, and her Italian-born adviser and rumored lover, Cardinal Mazarin (1602–1661), ruled in the young monarch's name.

To meet the financial pressure of fighting the Thirty Years' War, Mazarin sold new offices, raised taxes, and forced creditors to extend loans to the government. In 1648, a coalition of his opponents presented him with a charter of demands that, if granted, would have given the parlements (high courts) a form of constitutional power with the right to approve new taxes. Mazarin responded by arresting the leaders of the parlements. He soon faced a series of revolts.

Louis XIV, Conqueror of the Fronde

In this painting of 1654, Louis XIV is depicted as the Roman god Jupiter, who crushes the discord of the Fronde (represented on the shield by the Medusa's head, made up of snakes). When the Fronde began, Louis was only ten years old; at the time of this painting, he was sixteen. The propaganda about his divine qualities had already begun. (Réunion des Musées Nationaux / Art Resource, NY.)

Fearing for the young king's safety, his mother took Louis and fled Paris. With civil war threatening, Mazarin and Anne agreed to compromise with the parlements. The nobles saw an opportunity to reassert their claims to power against the weakened monarchy and demanded greater local control. Leading noblewomen often played key roles in the opposition to Mazarin, carrying messages and forging alliances, especially when male family members were in prison. While the nobles sought to regain power and local influence, the middle and lower classes chafed at the repeated tax increases. Conflicts erupted throughout the kingdom as nobles, parlements, and city councils all raised their own armies to fight either the crown or one another. The urban poor, such as those in the southwestern city of Bordeaux, sometimes revolted as well.

Mazarin and Anne eventually got the upper hand because their opponents failed to maintain unity in fighting the king's forces. But Louis XIV never forgot the humiliation and uncertainty that marred his childhood. His own policies as ruler would be designed to prevent the recurrence of any such revolts. Yet, for all his success, peasants would revolt against the introduction of new taxes on at least five more occasions in the 1660s and 1670s, requiring tens of thousands of soldiers to reestablish order.

Court Culture as an Element of Absolutism

When Cardinal Mazarin died in 1661, Louis XIV, then twenty-two years old, decided to rule without a first minister. He described the dangers of his situation in memoirs he wrote later for his son's instruction: "Everywhere was disorder. My Court as a whole was

still very far removed from the sentiments in which I trust you will find it." Louis listed many other problems in the kingdom, but none occupied him more than his attempts to control France's leading nobles, some of whom came from families that had opposed him militarily during the Fronde.

The French nobles had long exercised local authority by maintaining their own fighting forces, meting out justice on their estates, arranging jobs for underlings, and resolving their own conflicts through dueling. Louis set out to domesticate the warrior nobles by replacing violence with court ritual, such as the festivities at Versailles described at the beginning of this chapter. Using a systematic policy of bestowing pensions, offices, honors, gifts, and the threat of disfavor or punishment, Louis induced the nobles to cooperate with him. The aristocracy increasingly vied for his favor and in the process became his clients, dependent on him for advancement. Great nobles competed for the honor of holding his shirt when he dressed, foreign ambassadors squabbled for places near him, and royal mistresses basked in the glow of his personal favor. Far from the court, however, nobles could still make considerable trouble for the king, and royal officials learned to compromise with them.

Those who did come to the king's court were kept on their toes. The preferred styles of behavior changed without notice, and the tiniest lapse in attention to etiquette could lead to ruin. Marie-Madeleine Pioche de La Vergne, known as Madame de Lafayette, described the court in her novel *The Princess of Clèves* (1678): "The Court gravitated around ambition. . . . Everybody was busily trying to better his or her position by pleasing, by helping, or by hindering somebody else."

Louis XIV appreciated the political uses of every form of art. Calling himself the Sun King, after Apollo, Louis stopped at nothing to burnish this radiant image. He played Apollo in ballets performed at court; posed for portraits with the emblems of Apollo (laurel, lyre, and tripod); and adorned his palaces with statues of the god. He also emulated the style and methods of ancient Roman emperors. At a celebration for the birth of his first son in 1662, Louis dressed in Roman attire, and many engravings and paintings showed him as a Roman emperor.

The king gave pensions to artists who worked for him and sometimes protected writers from clerical critics. The most famous of these writers was the playwright Molière (the pen name of Jean-Baptiste Poquelin, 1622–1673), whose comedy *Tartuffe* (1664) made fun of religious hypocrites and was loudly condemned by church leaders. Louis forced Molière to delay public performances of the play after its premiere at the festivities of May 1664 but resisted calls for his dismissal. Louis's ministers set up royal academies of dance, painting, architecture, music, and science. The government regulated the number and locations of theaters and closely censored all forms of publication.

Louis commissioned operas to celebrate royal marriages and military victories. His favorite composer, Jean-Baptiste Lully, wrote sixteen operas for court performances as well as many ballets. Playwrights often presented their new plays first to the court. Pierre Corneille and Jean Racine wrote tragedies set in Greece or Rome that celebrated the

new aristocratic virtues that Louis aimed to inculcate: a reverence for order and self-control. All the characters were regal or noble, all the language lofty, all the behavior aristocratic.

Louis glorified his image as well through massive public works projects. Veterans' hospitals and new fortified towns on the frontiers represented his military might. Urban improvements, such as the reconstruction of the Louvre palace in Paris, proved his wealth. But his most ambitious project was the construction of a new palace at Versailles, twelve miles from the turbulent capital.

Building began in the 1660s. By 1685, the frenzied effort had engaged thirty-six thousand workers, not including the thousands of troops who diverted a local river to supply water for pools and fountains. The gardens designed by landscape architect André Le Nôtre reflected the spirit of Louis XIV's rule: their geometrical arrangements and clear lines showed that art and design could tame nature and that order and control defined the exercise of power. Versailles symbolized Louis's success at reining in the nobility and dominating Europe, and other monarchs eagerly mimicked French fashion and often conducted their business in French.

Yet for all its apparent luxury and frivolity, life at Versailles was often cramped and cold. Fifteen thousand people crowded into the palace's apartments, including all the highest military officers, the ministers of state, and the separate households of each member of the royal family. Refuse collected in the corridors during the incessant building, and thieves and prostitutes overran the grounds. By the time Louis actually moved from the Louvre to Versailles in 1682, he had reigned as monarch for thirty-nine years. After his wife's death in 1683, he secretly married his mistress, Françoise d'Aubigné, marquise de Maintenon, and conducted most state affairs from her apartments at the palace. She inspired Louis XIV to increase his devotion to Catholicism.

Enforcing Religious Orthodoxy

Louis believed that he reigned by divine right. As Bishop Jacques-Bénigne Bossuet (1627–1704) explained, "We have seen that kings take the place of God, who is the true father of the human species. We have also seen that the first idea of power which exists among men is that of the paternal power; and that kings are modeled on fathers." The king, like a father, should instruct his subjects in the true religion, or at least make sure that others did so.

Louis's campaign for religious conformity first focused on the Jansenists, Catholics whose doctrines and practices resembled some aspects of Protestantism. Following the posthumous publication of the book *Augustinus* (1640) by the Flemish theologian Cornelius Jansen (1585–1638), the Jansenists stressed the need for God's grace in achieving salvation. They emphasized the importance of original sin and resembled the English Puritans in their austere religious practice. Prominent among the Jansenists was Blaise Pascal (1623–1662), a mathematician of genius, who wrote his *Provincial Letters* (1656–1657) to defend Jansenism against charges of heresy. Many judges in the

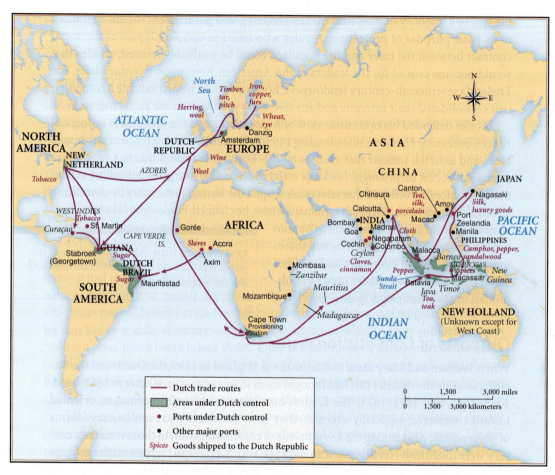

Map 16.2 Dutch Commerce in the Seventeenth Century
Even before gaining formal independence from the Spanish in 1648, the Dutch had begun to compete with the Spanish and Portuguese all over the world. In 1602, a group of merchants established the Dutch East India Company, which soon offered investors an annual rate of return of 35 percent on the trade in spices with countries located on the Indian Ocean. Global commerce gave the Dutch the highest standard of living in Europe and soon attracted the envy of the French and the English.

from eastern Europe. A widely reprinted history of Amsterdam that appeared in 1662 described the city as "risen through the hand of God to the peak of prosperity and greatness. . . . The whole world stands amazed at its riches and from east and west, north and south they come to behold it."

The Dutch rapidly became the most prosperous and best-educated people in Europe. Whereas in other countries kings, nobles, and churches bought art, in the Dutch Republic art buyers were merchants, artisans, and shopkeepers. One foreigner commented that "pictures are very common here, there being scarce an ordinary tradesman whose house is not decorated with them." Relative prosperity decreased the need for married women to work, so Dutch society developed the clear contrast between middle-class male

new aristocratic virtues that Louis aimed to inculcate: a reverence for order and self-control. All the characters were regal or noble, all the language lofty, all the behavior aristocratic.

Louis glorified his image as well through massive public works projects. Veterans' hospitals and new fortified towns on the frontiers represented his military might. Urban improvements, such as the reconstruction of the Louvre palace in Paris, proved his wealth. But his most ambitious project was the construction of a new palace at Versailles, twelve miles from the turbulent capital.

Building began in the 1660s. By 1685, the frenzied effort had engaged thirty-six thousand workers, not including the thousands of troops who diverted a local river to supply water for pools and fountains. The gardens designed by landscape architect André Le Nôtre reflected the spirit of Louis XIV's rule: their geometrical arrangements and clear lines showed that art and design could tame nature and that order and control defined the exercise of power. Versailles symbolized Louis's success at reining in the nobility and dominating Europe, and other monarchs eagerly mimicked French fashion and often conducted their business in French.

Yet for all its apparent luxury and frivolity, life at Versailles was often cramped and cold. Fifteen thousand people crowded into the palace's apartments, including all the highest military officers, the ministers of state, and the separate households of each member of the royal family. Refuse collected in the corridors during the incessant building, and thieves and prostitutes overran the grounds. By the time Louis actually moved from the Louvre to Versailles in 1682, he had reigned as monarch for thirty-nine years. After his wife's death in 1683, he secretly married his mistress, Françoise d'Aubigné, marquise de Maintenon, and conducted most state affairs from her apartments at the palace. She inspired Louis XIV to increase his devotion to Catholicism.

Enforcing Religious Orthodoxy

Louis believed that he reigned by divine right. As Bishop Jacques-Bénigne Bossuet (1627–1704) explained, "We have seen that kings take the place of God, who is the true father of the human species. We have also seen that the first idea of power which exists among men is that of the paternal power; and that kings are modeled on fathers." The king, like a father, should instruct his subjects in the true religion, or at least make sure that others did so.

Louis's campaign for religious conformity first focused on the Jansenists, Catholics whose doctrines and practices resembled some aspects of Protestantism. Following the posthumous publication of the book *Augustinus* (1640) by the Flemish theologian Cornelius Jansen (1585–1638), the Jansenists stressed the need for God's grace in achieving salvation. They emphasized the importance of original sin and resembled the English Puritans in their austere religious practice. Prominent among the Jansenists was Blaise Pascal (1623–1662), a mathematician of genius, who wrote his *Provincial Letters* (1656–1657) to defend Jansenism against charges of heresy. Many judges in the

parlements likewise endorsed Jansenist doctrine. Louis rejected any doctrine that gave priority to considerations of individual conscience over the demands of the official church hierarchy. Therefore, in 1660 he began enforcing various papal bulls (decrees) against Jansenism and closed down Jansenist theological centers.

Protestants posed an even greater obstacle to religious conformity. After many years of escalating pressure on the Calvinist Huguenots, Louis decided to eliminate all of the Calvinists' rights. Louis considered the Edict of Nantes (1598), by which his grandfather Henry IV granted the Protestants religious freedom and a degree of political independence, a temporary measure, and he fervently hoped to reconvert the Huguenots to Catholicism. In 1685, his **revocation of the Edict of Nantes** closed Calvinist churches and schools, forced all pastors to leave the country, and ordered the conversion of all Calvinists. Children of Calvinists could be taken away from their parents and raised Catholic. Tens of thousands of Huguenots responded by illegally fleeing to England, Brandenburg-Prussia, the Dutch Republic, or North America. Protestant European countries were shocked by this crackdown on religious dissent and would cite it in justification of their wars against Louis.

Extending State Authority at Home and Abroad

Louis XIV could not have enforced his religious policies without the services of a nationwide bureaucracy. **Bureaucracy** — a network of state officials carrying out orders according to a regular and routine line of authority — comes from the French word *bureau,* for "desk," which came to mean "office," both in the sense of a physical space and a position of authority. Louis personally supervised the activities of his bureaucrats and worked to ensure his supremacy in all matters. But he always had to negotiate with nobles and local officials who sometimes thwarted his will.

Louis extended the bureaucratic forms his predecessors had developed, especially the use of intendants. He handpicked an intendant for each region to represent his rule against entrenched local interests such as the parlements, provincial estates, and noble governors. The intendants supervised the collection of taxes, the financing of public works, and the provisioning of the army. In 1673, Louis decreed that the parlements could no longer vote against his proposed laws or even speak against them.

To keep tabs on all the issues before him, Louis relied on a series of talented ministers, usually of modest origins, who gained fame, fortune, and even noble status from serving the king. Most important among them was Jean-Baptiste Colbert (1619–1683), a wool merchant's son turned royal official. Colbert had managed Mazarin's personal finances and worked his way up under Louis XIV to become head of royal finances, public works, and the navy.

Colbert used the bureaucracy to establish a new economic doctrine, **mercantilism**. According to mercantilist policy, governments must intervene to increase national wealth by whatever means possible. Such government intervention inevitably increased the number of bureaucrats needed. Under Colbert, the French government established

overseas trading companies and granted manufacturing monopolies. A government inspection system regulated the quality of finished goods and compelled all craftsmen to organize into guilds, in which masters could supervise the work of the journeymen and apprentices. To protect French production, Colbert rescinded many internal customs fees but enacted high foreign tariffs, which cut imports of competing goods. To compete more effectively with England and the Dutch Republic, Colbert also subsidized shipbuilding, a policy that dramatically expanded the number of seaworthy French vessels. Such mercantilist measures aimed to ensure France's prominence in world markets and to provide the resources needed to fight wars against the nation's increasingly long list of enemies. Although later economists questioned the value of mercantilism, virtually every government in Europe embraced it.

Colbert's mercantilist projects shaped life in the French colonies, too. He forbade colonial businesses from manufacturing anything already produced in mainland France. In 1663, he took control of the trading company that had founded New France (Canada). With the goal of establishing permanent settlements like those in the British North American colonies, he transplanted several thousand peasants from western France to the present-day province of Quebec, which France had claimed since 1608. He also tried to limit expansion westward, without success.

Despite the Iroquois' initial interruption of French fur-trading convoys, fur trader Louis Jolliet and Jesuit missionary Jacques Marquette reached the upper Mississippi River in 1672 and traveled downstream as far as Arkansas. In 1684, French explorer Sieur de La Salle went all the way down to the Gulf of Mexico, claiming a vast territory for Louis XIV and calling it Louisiana after him. Colbert's successors embraced the expansion he had resisted, thinking it crucial to competing successfully with the English and the Dutch in the New World.

Colonial settlement occupied only a portion of Louis XIV's attention, however, for his main foreign policy goal was to extend French power in Europe. To expand the army, Louis's minister of war centralized the organization of French troops. Barracks built in major towns received supplies — among which were uniforms to reinforce discipline — from a central distribution system. Louis's wartime army could field a force as large as that of all his enemies combined.

Absolutist governments always tried to increase their territorial holdings, and as Louis extended his reach, he gained new enemies. In 1667–1668, in the War of Devolution (so called because Louis claimed that lands in the Spanish Netherlands should devolve to him since the Spanish king had failed to pay the dowry of Louis's Spanish bride), Louis defeated the Spanish armies but had to make peace when England, Sweden, and the Dutch Republic joined the war. In the Treaty of Aix-la-Chapelle in 1668, he gained control of a few towns on the border of the Spanish Netherlands.

In 1672, Louis XIV opened hostilities against the Dutch because they stood in the way of his acquisition of more territory in the Spanish Netherlands. He declared war again on Spain in 1673. By now the Dutch had allied themselves with their former Spanish masters to hold off the French. Louis also marched his troops into territories of the

Wars of Louis XIV

1667–1668   War of Devolution

Enemies: Spain, Dutch Republic, England, Sweden

Ended by Treaty of Aix-la-Chapelle in 1668, with France gaining towns in Spanish Netherlands (Flanders)

1672–1678   Dutch War

Enemies: Dutch Republic, Spain, Holy Roman Empire

Ended by Treaty of Nijmegen, 1678–1679, which gave several towns in Spanish Netherlands and Franche-Comté to France

1688–1697   War of the League of Augsburg

Enemies: Holy Roman Empire, Sweden, Spain, England, Dutch Republic

Ended by Peace of Rijswijk, 1697, with Louis returning all his conquests made since 1678 except Strasbourg

1701–1713   War of the Spanish Succession

Enemies: Holy Roman Empire, England, Dutch Republic, Prussia

Ended by Peace of Utrecht, 1713–1714, with Louis ceding territories in North America to the British

Holy Roman Empire, provoking many of the German princes to join with the emperor, the Spanish, and the Dutch in an alliance against Louis, whom they now denounced as a "Christian Turk" for his imperialist ambitions. Faced with bloody but inconclusive results on the battlefield, the parties agreed to the Treaty of Nijmegen of 1678–1679, which ceded several Flemish towns and the Franche-Comté region to Louis, linking Alsace to the rest of France. French government deficits soared, and in 1675 increases in taxes touched off the most serious antitax revolt of Louis's reign.

Louis had no intention of standing still. Heartened by the Habsburgs' seeming weakness, he pushed eastward, seizing the city of Strasbourg in 1681 and invading the province of Lorraine in 1684. In 1688, he attacked some of the small German cities of the Holy Roman Empire. So obsessed was Louis with his military standing that he had miniature battle scenes painted on his high heels and commissioned tapestries showing his military processions into conquered cities, even those he did not take by force. It took a large coalition known as the League of Augsburg—made up of England, Spain, Sweden, the Dutch Republic, the Austrian emperor, and various German princes—to hold back the French king. When hostilities between Louis and the League of Augsburg ended in the Peace of Rijswijk in 1697, Louis returned many of his conquests made since 1678, with the exception of Strasbourg (Map 16.1).

Four years later, Louis embarked on his last and most damaging war, the War of the Spanish Succession (1701–1713). It was caused by disagreement over who would inherit the throne of Spain. Before he died, Spanish king Charles II (r. 1665–1700) named Louis XIV's second grandson—Philip, duke of Anjou—as his heir, but the Austrian emperor Leopold I refused to agree and the British and the Dutch supported his refusal. In the ensuing war, the French lost several major battles and had to accept disadvantageous terms in the Peace of Utrecht of 1713–1714. France ceded possessions in North America (Newfoundland, the Hudson Bay area, and most of Nova Scotia) to Britain. Although Philip was recognized as king of Spain, he had to renounce any future claim to the French crown, thus barring unification of the two kingdoms. Spain surrendered its territories in Italy and the Netherlands to the Austrians, and Gibraltar to the

Map 16.1 Louis XIV's Acquisitions, 1668–1697
Every ruler in Europe hoped to extend his or her territorial control, and war was often the result. Louis XIV steadily encroached on the Spanish Netherlands to the north and the lands of the Holy Roman Empire to the east. Although coalitions of European powers reined in Louis's grander ambitions, he nonetheless incorporated many neighboring territories into the French crown.

British. Lying on his deathbed in 1715, the seventy-six-year-old Louis XIV watched helplessly as his accomplishments began to unravel.

Louis XIV's policy of absolutism fomented bitter hostility among his own subjects. Nobles resented his promotions of commoners to high office. The duke of Saint-Simon complained that "falseness, servility, admiring glances, combined with a dependent and cringing attitude, above all, an appearance of being nothing without him, were the only ways of pleasing him." Ordinary people suffered the most for Louis's ambitions. By the end of the Sun King's reign, one in six Frenchmen had served in the military. In addition to the higher taxes paid by everyone, those who lived on the routes leading to the battlefields had to house and feed soldiers; only nobles were exempt from this requirement.

REVIEW QUESTION How "absolute" was the power of Louis XIV?

Constitutionalism in England

Of the two models of state building—absolutism and constitutionalism—the first seemed unquestionably more powerful because Louis XIV could raise such large armies and tax his subjects without much consultation. In the end, however, Louis could not defeat the coalition led by England's constitutional monarch. Constitutionalism had its own distinctive strengths, which came from the ruler sharing power through a representative assembly such as the English houses of Parliament. But the English rulers themselves hoped to follow Louis XIV's lead and install their own absolutist policies. Two revolutions, in 1642–1660 and 1688–1689, overturned two kings and confirmed the constitutional powers of an elected parliament, laying the foundation for the idea that government must guarantee certain rights to the people under the law.

England Turned Upside Down, 1642–1660

Disputes about the right to levy taxes and the nature of authority in the Church of England had long troubled the relationship between the English crown and Parliament. For more than a hundred years, wealthy English landowners had been accustomed to participating in government through Parliament and expected to be consulted on royal policy. Although England had no single constitutional document, it did have a variety of laws, judicial decisions, customary procedures, and charters and petitions granted by the king that all regulated relations between king and Parliament. When Charles I tried to assert his authority over Parliament, a civil war broke out. Some historians view the English civil war of 1642–1646 as the last great war of religion because it pitted Puritans against those trying to push the Church of England toward Catholicism; others see in it the first modern revolution because it gave birth to democratic political and religious movements.

When Charles I (r. 1625–1649) succeeded his father, James I, he faced an increasingly aggressive Parliament that resisted efforts to extend his personal control. In 1628, Parliament forced Charles to agree to the Petition of Right, by which he promised not to levy taxes without Parliament's consent. Charles hoped to avoid further interference with his plans by simply refusing to call Parliament into session between 1629 and 1640. Without it, the king's ministers had to find every loophole possible to raise revenues. They tried to turn "ship money," a levy on seaports in times of emergency, into an annual tax collected everywhere in the country. The crown won the ensuing court case, but many subjects still refused to pay what they considered to be an illegal tax.

Religious tensions brought conflicts over the king's authority to a head. With Charles's encouragement, the archbishop of Canterbury, William Laud (1573–1645), imposed increasingly elaborate ceremonies on the Church of England. Angered by these moves toward "popery," the Puritans responded with pamphlets and sermons filled with fiery denunciations. Laud then hauled them before the feared Court of Star Chamber, which the king personally controlled. The court ordered harsh sentences for Laud's Puritan critics; they were whipped, pilloried, branded, and even had their ears cut off and their

noses split. When Laud tried to apply his policies to Scotland, however, they backfired completely: the stubborn Presbyterian Scots invaded the north of England in 1640. To raise money to fight the war, Charles called Parliament into session and unwittingly opened the door to a constitutional and religious crisis.

The Parliament of 1640 did not intend revolution, but reformers in the House of Commons (the lower house of Parliament) wanted to undo what they saw as the royal tyranny of the 1630s. Parliament removed Laud from office, ordered the execution of an unpopular royal commander, abolished the Court of Star Chamber, repealed recently levied taxes, and provided for a parliamentary assembly at least once every three years, thus establishing a constitutional check on royal authority. Moderate reformers expected to stop there and resisted Puritan pressure to abolish bishops and eliminate the Church of England prayer book. The reformers also faced a rebellion in Ireland by native Catholics against the English and Scottish settlers who had taken over their lands. The reformers in Parliament feared that the Irish Catholics would make common cause with Charles to reestablish Catholicism as the religion of England and Scotland. Their hand was forced in January 1642, when Charles and his soldiers invaded Parliament and tried unsuccessfully to arrest those leaders who had moved to curb his power. Faced with mounting opposition within London, Charles quickly withdrew from the city and organized an army.

The ensuing civil war between king and Parliament lasted four years (1642–1646) and divided the country. The king's army of royalists, known as Cavaliers, enjoyed the most support in northern and western England. The parliamentary forces, called Roundheads because they cut their hair short, had their stronghold in the southeast, including London. Although Puritans dominated on the parliamentary side, they were divided among themselves about the proper form of church government: the Presbyterians wanted a Calvinist church with some central authority, whereas the Independents favored entirely autonomous congregations free from other church government (hence the term *congregationalism,* often associated with the Independents). The Puritans put aside their differences for the sake of military unity and united under an obscure member of the House of Commons, the country gentleman Oliver Cromwell (1599–1658), who sympathized with the Independents. After Cromwell skillfully reorganized the parliamentary troops, his New Model Army defeated the Cavaliers at the battle of Naseby in 1645. Charles surrendered in 1646.

Although the civil war between king and Parliament had ended in victory for Parliament, divisions within the Puritan ranks now came to the fore: the Presbyterians dominated Parliament, but the Independents controlled the army. The disputes between the leaders drew lower-class groups into the debate. When Parliament tried to disband the New Model Army in 1647, disgruntled soldiers protested. Called **Levellers** because of their insistence on leveling social differences, the soldiers took on their officers in a series of debates about the nature of political authority. The Levellers demanded that Parliament meet annually, that members be paid so as to allow common people to participate, and that all male heads of households be allowed to vote. Their ideal of political participation excluded servants, the propertyless, and women but offered access to artisans, shopkeepers, and modest farmers. Cromwell and other army leaders rejected the

Levellers' demands as threatening to property owners. Speaking to his advisers, Cromwell insisted, "You have no other way to deal with these men but to break them in pieces."

While political differences between Presbyterians and Independents helped spark new political movements, their conflicts over church organization fostered the emergence of new religious sects that emphasized the "inner light" of individual religious inspiration and a disdain for hierarchical authority. The Baptists, for example, insisted on adult baptism because they believed that Christians should choose their own church and that children should not automatically become members of the Church of England. The Religious Society of Friends, who came to be called Quakers, demonstrated their beliefs in equality and the inner light by refusing to doff their hats to men in authority. Manifesting their religious experience by trembling, or "quaking," the Quakers believed that anyone — man or woman — inspired by a direct experience of God could preach. In keeping with their notions of equality and individual inspiration, many of the new sects provided opportunities for women to become preachers and prophets.

Parliamentary leaders feared that the new sects would overturn the whole social hierarchy. Some sects did advocate sweeping change. The Diggers promoted rural communism — collective ownership of all property. Seekers and Ranters questioned just about everything. One notorious Ranter, John Robins, even claimed to be God. A few men advocated free love. The political elite decided that tolerating the new sects would lead to skepticism, anarchism, and debauchery, and they therefore took measures to suppress the most radical ones.

The king tried to negotiate with the Presbyterians in Parliament, but Independents in the army purged the Presbyterians from Parliament in late 1648, leaving a "rump" of about seventy members. This Rump Parliament then created a high court to try Charles I. The court found him guilty of attempting to establish "an unlimited and tyrannical power" and pronounced a death sentence. On January 30, 1649, Charles was beheaded before an enormous crowd, which reportedly groaned as one when the ax fell. Although many had objected to Charles's autocratic rule, few had wanted him killed. For royalists, Charles immediately became a martyr, and reports of miracles, such as the curing of blindness by the touch of a handkerchief soaked in his blood, soon circulated.

The Rump Parliament abolished the monarchy and the House of Lords (the upper house of Parliament) and set up a Puritan republic with Oliver Cromwell as chairman of the Council of State. Cromwell did not tolerate dissent from his policies. When his agents discovered plans for mutiny within the army, they executed the perpetrators; new decrees silenced the Levellers. Although under Cromwell the various Puritan sects could worship rather freely and Jews with needed skills were permitted to return to England for the first time since the thirteenth century, Catholics could not worship publicly, nor could adherents of the Church of England use the Book of Common Prayer, thought to be too Catholic. The elites were troubled by Cromwell's religious policies but pleased to see some social order reestablished.

Portrait of Oliver Cromwell (1599–1658)
In this painting by Thomas Wyck, Cromwell's pose on horseback mirrors that of King Charles I in a painting of 1633. Cromwell therefore appears quite literally as Charles's successor. The setting, however, is different. Cromwell is attended by a black servant with a backdrop that suggests North Africa. The artist may be referring to Cromwell's 1655 foray against the pirates who attacked English merchant ships from their headquarters on the Tunisian coast. Cromwell sent twenty ships to bombard the pirates' fortifications and destroy their fleet. (Private Collection / Photo © Philip Mould Ltd., London / The Bridgeman Art Library International.)

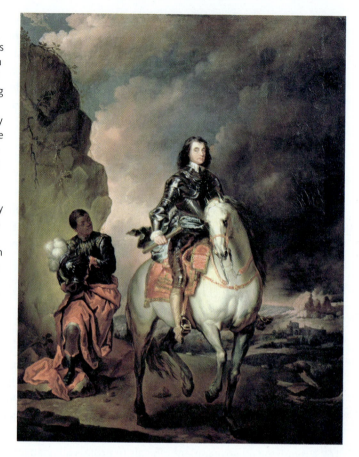

The new regime aimed to extend state power just as Charles I had before. Cromwell laid the foundation for a Great Britain — made up of England, Ireland, and Scotland — by reconquering Scotland and brutally subduing Ireland. When his position was secured in 1649, Cromwell went to Ireland with a large force and easily defeated the rebels, massacring whole garrisons and their priests. He encouraged expropriating more lands of the Irish "barbarous wretches," and Scottish immigrants resettled the northern county of Ulster. This seventeenth-century English conquest left a legacy of bitterness that the Irish even today call "the curse of Cromwell."

In 1651, Parliament turned its attention overseas, putting mercantilist ideas into practice in the first Navigation Act, which allowed imports only if they were carried on English ships or came directly from the producers of goods. The Navigation Act was aimed at the Dutch, who dominated world trade; Cromwell tried to carry the policy further by waging naval war on the Dutch from 1652 to 1654.

At home, however, Cromwell faced growing resistance. His wars required a budget twice the size of Charles I's, and his increases in property taxes and customs duties

alienated landowners and merchants. The conflict reached a crisis in 1653: Parliament considered disbanding the army, whereupon Cromwell abolished the Rump Parliament in a military coup and made himself Lord Protector. He now silenced his critics by banning newspapers and using networks of spies to read mail and keep tabs on his enemies. Cromwell intended that his son should succeed him, but his death in 1658 only revived the prospect of civil war and political chaos. In 1660, a newly elected Parliament invited Charles II, the son of the executed king, to return from exile.

Restoration and Revolution Again

England's traditional monarchical form of government was restored in 1660 under Charles II (r. 1660–1685). More than a thousand Puritan ministers lost their positions, and attending a service other than one conforming with the Book of Common Prayer was illegal after 1664. Two natural disasters in quick succession posed new challenges. The plague struck in 1665, claiming more than thirty thousand victims in just a few months and forcing Charles and Parliament to flee from London. Then in 1666, the Great Fire swept the city. Some saw these disasters as punishment for the sins of the Cromwell era, others as an ill omen for Charles's reign.

Many in Parliament feared that Charles II wanted to emulate Louis XIV. In 1670, Charles made a secret agreement, soon leaked, with Louis in which he promised to announce his conversion to Catholicism in exchange for money for a war against the Dutch. Charles never proclaimed himself a Catholic, but in his Declaration of Indulgence (1673) he did suspend all laws against Catholics and Protestant dissenters. Parliament refused to continue funding the Dutch war unless Charles rescinded his Declaration of Indulgence. Asserting its authority further, Parliament passed the Test Act in 1673, requiring all government officials to profess allegiance to the Church of England and in effect disavow Catholic doctrine. Then in 1678, Parliament precipitated the so-called Exclusion Crisis by explicitly denying the throne to a Roman Catholic. This action was aimed at the king's brother and heir, James, an open convert to Catholicism. Charles refused to allow it to become law.

The dynastic crisis over the succession of a Catholic gave rise to two distinct factions in Parliament: the Tories, who supported a strong, hereditary monarchy and the restored ceremony of the Church of England, and the Whigs, who advocated parliamentary supremacy and toleration of Protestant dissenters such as Presbyterians. Both labels were originally derogatory: *Tory* meant an Irish Catholic bandit; *Whig* was the Irish Catholic designation for a Presbyterian Scot. The Tories favored James's succession despite his Catholicism, whereas the Whigs opposed a Catholic monarch.

When James II (r. 1685–1688) succeeded his brother, he seemed determined to force Catholicism on his subjects. Tories and Whigs joined together when a male heir — who would take precedence over James's two adult Protestant daughters — was born to James's second wife, an Italian Catholic, in 1688. They invited the Dutch ruler **William, prince of Orange**, and his wife, James's older daughter, Mary, to invade England. Mary was brought up as a Protestant and was willing to act with her husband

Great Fire of London, 1666
This view of London shows the three-day fire at its height. The writer John Evelyn described the scene in his diary: "All the sky was of a fiery aspect, like the top of a burning oven, and the light seen above 40 miles round about for many nights. God grant mine eyes may never behold the like, who now saw above 10,000 houses all in one flame; the noise and cracking and thunder of people, the fall of towers, houses, and churches, was like an hideous storm." Everyone in London at the time felt overwhelmed by the catastrophe, and many deemed it God's punishment for the upheavals of the 1640s and 1650s. (Photo © Museum of London, UK / The Bridgeman Art Library International.)

against her father's pro-Catholic policies. James fled to France, and Parliament offered the throne jointly to William (r. 1689–1702) and Mary (r. 1689–1694) on the condition that they accept a bill of rights guaranteeing Parliament's full partnership in a constitutional government.

In the Bill of Rights (1689), William and Mary agreed not to raise a standing army or to levy taxes without Parliament's consent. They also agreed to call meetings of Parliament at least every three years, to guarantee free elections to parliamentary seats, and to abide by Parliament's decisions. The agreement gave England's constitutional government a written, legal basis by formally recognizing Parliament as a self-contained, independent body that shared power with the rulers. Victorious supporters of the coup declared it the **Glorious Revolution** because it was achieved with so little bloodshed (at least in England).

The propertied classes who controlled Parliament prevented any resurgence of the popular turmoil of the 1640s. The Toleration Act of 1689 granted all Protestants freedom of worship, though non-Anglicans (those not in the Church of England) were still excluded from the universities; Catholics got no rights but were more often left alone to

worship privately. When the Catholics in Ireland rose to defend James II, William and Mary's troops savagely suppressed them.

Social Contract Theory: Hobbes and Locke

Out of the turmoil of the English revolutions came a major rethinking of the foundations of all political authority. Although Thomas Hobbes and John Locke wrote in response to the upheavals of their times, they offered opposing arguments that were applicable to any place and any time, not just England of the seventeenth century. Hobbes justified absolute authority; Locke provided the rationale for constitutionalism. Yet both argued that all authority came not from divine right but from a **social contract** among citizens.

Thomas Hobbes (1588–1679) was a royalist who sat out the English civil war of the 1640s in France, where he tutored the future king Charles II. Returning to England in 1651, Hobbes published his masterpiece, *Leviathan,* in which he argued for unlimited authority in a ruler. Absolute authority could be vested in either a king or a parliament; it had to be absolute, Hobbes insisted, in order to overcome the defects of human nature. Believing that people are essentially self-centered and driven by the "right to self-preservation," Hobbes made his case by referring to science, not religion. To Hobbes, human life in a state of nature — that is, any situation without firm authority — was "solitary, poor, nasty, brutish, and short." Only the assurance of social order could make people secure enough to act according to law; consequently, giving up personal liberty, he maintained, was the price of collective security. Rulers derived their power, he concluded, from a contract in which absolute authority protects people's rights.

Hobbes's notion of rule by an absolute authority left no room for political dissent or nonconformity, and it infuriated both royalists and supporters of Parliament. He enraged his fellow royalists by arguing that authority came not from divine right but from the social contract. Parliamentary supporters resisted Hobbes's claim that rulers must possess absolute authority to prevent the greater evil of anarchy. Like Machiavelli before him, Hobbes became associated with a cynical, pessimistic view of human nature, and future political theorists often began their arguments by refuting Hobbes.

Rejecting both Hobbes and the more traditional royalist defenses of absolute authority, John Locke (1632–1704) used the notion of a social contract to provide a foundation for constitutionalism. Locke experienced political life firsthand as physician, secretary, and intellectual companion to the earl of Shaftesbury, a leading English Whig. In 1683, during the Exclusion Crisis, Locke fled with Shaftesbury to the Dutch Republic. There he continued work on his *Two Treatises of Government*, which, when published in 1690, served to justify the revolution of 1688. Locke's position was thoroughly antiabsolutist. He denied the divine right of kings and ridiculed the common royalist idea that political power in the state mirrored the father's authority in the family. Like Hobbes, he posited a state of nature that applied to all people. Unlike Hobbes, however, he thought people were reasonable and the state of nature peaceful.

Locke insisted that government's only purpose was to protect life, liberty, and property, a notion that linked economic and political freedom. Ultimate authority rested in

the will of a majority of men who owned property, and government should be limited to its basic purpose of protection. A ruler who failed to uphold his part of the social contract between the ruler and the populace could be justifiably resisted, an idea that would become crucial for the leaders of the American Revolution a century later. For England's seventeenth-century landowners, however, Locke helped validate a revolution that consolidated their interests and ensured their privileges in the social hierarchy.

Locke defended his optimistic view of human nature in the immensely influential *Essay Concerning Human Understanding* (1690). He denied the existence of any innate ideas and asserted instead that each human is born with a mind that is a tabula rasa (blank slate). Not surprisingly, Locke devoted considerable energy to rethinking educational practices; he believed that education shaped the human personality by channeling all sensory experience. Everything humans know, he claimed, comes from sensory experience, not from anything inherent in human nature. Although Locke himself owned shares in the Royal African Company and justified slavery, his writings were later used by abolitionists in their campaign against slavery.

> **REVIEW QUESTION** What differences over religion and politics caused the conflict between king and Parliament in England?

Outposts of Constitutionalism

When William and Mary came to the throne in England in 1689, the Dutch and the English put aside the rivalries that had brought them to war against each other in 1652–1654, 1665–1667, and 1672–1674. The English and Dutch had much in common: oriented toward commerce, especially overseas, they both had developed representative forms of government. Also among the few outposts of constitutionalism in the seventeenth century were the British North American colonies, which developed representative government while the English were preoccupied with their revolutions at home. Constitutionalism was not the only factor shaping this Atlantic world; as constitutionalism developed in the colonies, so too did the enslavement of black Africans as a new labor force.

The Dutch Republic

When the Dutch Republic gained formal independence from Spain in 1648, it had already established a decentralized, constitutional state. Rich merchants called regents effectively controlled the internal affairs of each province and (through the Estates General) chose the *stadholder,* the executive officer responsible for defense and for representing the state at all ceremonial occasions. They almost always picked one of the princes of the house of Orange, but the stadholder resembled a president more than a king.

The Dutch Republic soon became Europe's financial capital. Praised for their industriousness, thrift, and cleanliness — and maligned as greedy, dull, and fat — the Dutch dominated overseas commerce with their shipping (Map 16.2). They imported products from all over the world: spices, tea, and silk from Asia; sugar and tobacco from the Americas; wool from England and Spain; timber and furs from Scandinavia; grain

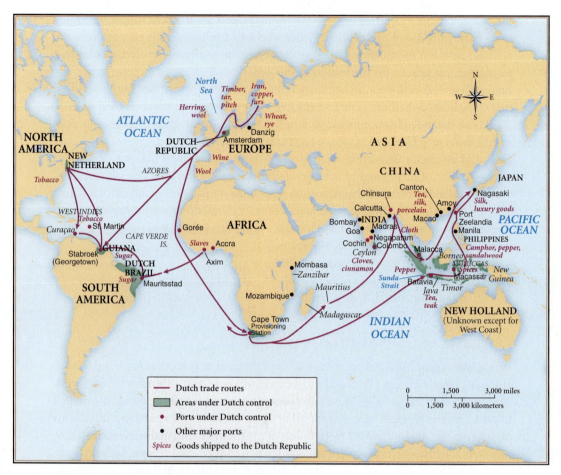

Map 16.2 Dutch Commerce in the Seventeenth Century
Even before gaining formal independence from the Spanish in 1648, the Dutch had begun to compete with the Spanish and Portuguese all over the world. In 1602, a group of merchants established the Dutch East India Company, which soon offered investors an annual rate of return of 35 percent on the trade in spices with countries located on the Indian Ocean. Global commerce gave the Dutch the highest standard of living in Europe and soon attracted the envy of the French and the English.

from eastern Europe. A widely reprinted history of Amsterdam that appeared in 1662 described the city as "risen through the hand of God to the peak of prosperity and greatness. . . . The whole world stands amazed at its riches and from east and west, north and south they come to behold it."

The Dutch rapidly became the most prosperous and best-educated people in Europe. Whereas in other countries kings, nobles, and churches bought art, in the Dutch Republic art buyers were merchants, artisans, and shopkeepers. One foreigner commented that "pictures are very common here, there being scarce an ordinary tradesman whose house is not decorated with them." Relative prosperity decreased the need for married women to work, so Dutch society developed the clear contrast between middle-class male

A Typical Dutch Scene from Daily Life
Dutch artist Jan Steen painted *The Baker Arent Oostward and His Wife* in 1658. Steen ran a brewery and tavern in addition to painting, and he was known for his interest in the details of daily life. Dutch artists popularized this kind of "genre" painting, which showed ordinary people at work and play. (Rijksmuseum, Amsterdam.)

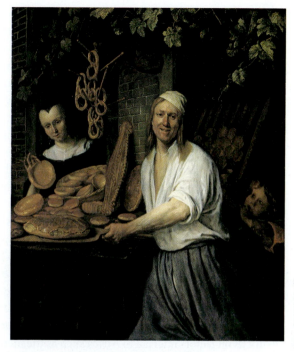

and female roles that would become prevalent elsewhere in Europe and in America more than a century later.

Extraordinarily high levels of urbanization and literacy created a large reading public. Dutch presses printed books censored elsewhere, and the University of Leiden attracted students and professors from all over Europe. Dutch tolerance extended to the works of Benedict Spinoza (1633–1677), a Jewish philosopher and biblical scholar who was expelled by his synagogue for alleged atheism but left alone by the Dutch authorities. Spinoza strove to reconcile religion with science and mathematics, but his work scandalized many Christians and Jews because he seemed to equate God and nature. Like nature, Spinoza's God followed unchangeable laws and could not be influenced by human actions, prayers, or faith.

The Dutch lived, however, in a world of international rivalries in which strong central authority gave their enemies an advantage. The naval wars with England between 1652 and 1674 and the land wars with France, which lasted until 1713, drained the state's revenues. The Dutch survived these direct military challenges but began to lose their position in international trade as both the British and French limited commerce with their own colonies to merchants from their own nations. At the end of the seventeenth century, as the Dutch elites became more preoccupied with ostentation, the Dutch "golden age" came to an end.

Freedom and Slavery in the New World

The Dutch Republic competed with England, France, and other European nations for its share of the burgeoning slave trade, but it lost its only settler colony in North America, New Netherland (present-day New York, New Jersey, Delaware, and Connecticut), to England in 1674. After the Spanish and Portuguese had shown that African slaves could be transported and forced to labor in South and Central America, the English and French endeavored to set up similar labor systems in their new Caribbean island colonies. White

planters with large tracts of land bought African slaves to work fields of sugarcane; and as they gradually built up their holdings, the planters displaced most of the original white settlers.

By the end of the seventeenth century, slavery had become codified as an inherited status that applied only to blacks. In 1661, Barbados instituted a slave code that stripped all Africans of rights under English law. Louis XIV promulgated a "black code" in 1685 to regulate the legal status of slaves in the French colonies and to prevent non-Catholics from owning slaves. The code supposedly set limits on the violence planters could exercise and required them to house, feed, and clothe their slaves. But white planters simply ignored provisions of the code that did not suit them, and in any case, because the code defined slaves as property, slaves could not themselves bring suit in court to demand better treatment.

The highest church and government authorities in Catholic and Protestant countries alike condoned the gradually expanding slave trade. In 1600, seventy-six hundred Africans were exported annually from Africa to the New World; by 1700, this number had increased more than fourfold, to thirty-three thousand. Historians advance several different ideas about which factors increased the slave trade: some claim that improvements in muskets made European slavers more effective; others cite the rising price for slaves, which made their sale more attractive for Africans who sold them; still others focus on factors internal to Africa such as the increasing size of African armies and their use of muskets in fighting and capturing other Africans for sale as slaves. What is clear is that a combination of factors prepared the way for the development of an Atlantic economy based on slavery.

While blacks were being subjected to the most degrading forms of bondage, whites in the colonies enjoyed more freedom than ever before. Virtually left to themselves during the upheavals in England, the fledgling English colonies in North America developed representative government on their own. Almost every colony had a two-house legislature. William and Mary reluctantly allowed emerging colonial elites even more control over local affairs. The social and political elite among the settlers hoped to impose an English social hierarchy dominated by rich landowners. Ordinary immigrants to the colonies, however, took advantage of plentiful land to carve out their own farms using white servants and, later, in some colonies, African slaves.

For native Americans, the expanding European presence meant something else altogether. They faced death through disease, warfare, and the accelerating loss of their homelands. Many native Americans believed that land was a divine gift provided for their collective use and not subject to individual ownership. Europeans' claims that they owned exclusive land rights consequently resulted in frequent skirmishes. In 1675–1676, for instance, three tribes allied under Metacomet (called King Philip by the English) threatened the survival of New England settlers, who savagely repulsed the attacks and sold their captives as slaves. The benefits of constitutionalism were reserved for Europeans.

REVIEW QUESTION Why did constitutionalism thrive in the Dutch Republic and the British North American colonies, even as their participation in the slave trade grew?

Absolutism in Central and Eastern Europe

Constitutionalism had an outpost in central and eastern Europe, too, but there it collapsed in failure. A long crisis in Poland-Lithuania virtually destroyed central state authority and pulled much of eastern Europe into its turbulent wake. Most central and eastern European rulers followed Louis XIV's model of absolutist state building, though they did not blindly emulate him, in part because they confronted conditions peculiar to their regions. Everywhere in eastern Europe, nobles lorded over their serfs but owed almost slavish obedience in turn to their rulers.

Poland-Lithuania Overwhelmed

In the version of constitutionalism adopted in Poland-Lithuania, the great nobles dominated the Sejm (parliament). To maintain an equilibrium among themselves, these nobles each wielded an absolute veto power. This "free veto" constitutional system deadlocked parliamentary government. The monarchy lost its room to maneuver and, with it, much of its remaining power.

In 1648, Ukrainian Cossack warriors revolted against the king of Poland-Lithuania, inaugurating two decades of tumult known as the Deluge. *Cossack* was the name given to runaway serfs and poor nobles who formed outlaw bands in the no-man's-land of southern Russia and Ukraine. In 1654, the Cossacks offered Ukraine to Russian rule, provoking a Russo-Polish war that ended in 1667 when the tsar annexed eastern Ukraine and Kiev.

Poland-Lithuania in the Seventeenth Century

Many towns were destroyed in the fighting, and as much as a third of the Polish population perished. The once prosperous Jewish and Protestant minorities suffered greatly: some fifty-six thousand Jews were killed by either the Cossacks, the Polish peasants, or the Russian troops. Surviving Jews moved from towns to shtetls (Jewish villages), where they took up petty trading, moneylending, tax gathering, and tavern leasing — activities that fanned peasant anti-Semitism. Desperate for protection amid the war, most Polish Protestants backed the violently anti-Catholic Swedes, who tried to intervene militarily, and the victorious Catholic majority branded the Protestants as traitors. In Poland-Lithuania people came to assume that a good Pole was a Catholic. The commonwealth had ceased to be an outpost of toleration.

The commonwealth revived briefly when a man of ability and ambition, Jan Sobieski (r. 1674–1696), was elected king. Sobieski gained a reputation throughout Europe when he led twenty-five thousand Polish cavalrymen into battle in the siege of Vienna in 1683. His cavalry helped rout the Turks and turned the tide against the Ottomans. Despite his efforts to rebuild the monarchy, Sobieski could not halt Poland-Lithuania's decline

into powerlessness. The Polish version of constitutionalism fatally weakened the state and made it prey to neighboring powers.

Brandenburg-Prussia: Militaristic Absolutism

The contrast between Poland-Lithuania and Brandenburg-Prussia could not have been more extreme. The first was huge in territory and constitutional in government but in the end failed as a state. The second was puny and made up of disparate far-flung territories moving toward absolutism but in the nineteenth century would unify the different German states into modern-day Germany.

The ruler of Brandenburg was an elector, one of the seven German princes entitled to select the Holy Roman Emperor. Since the sixteenth century, the ruler of Brandenburg had also controlled the duchy of East Prussia; after 1618, the state was called Brandenburg-Prussia. Despite meager resources, **Frederick William of Hohenzollern**, who was the Great Elector of Brandenburg-Prussia (r. 1640–1688), succeeded in welding his scattered lands into an absolutist state.

Frederick William was determined to force his territories' estates (representative assemblies) to grant him a dependable income. The Great Elector struck a deal with the Junkers (nobles) of each province: in exchange for allowing him to collect taxes, he gave them complete control over their enserfed peasants and exempted them from taxation. By the end of his reign, the estates met only on ceremonial occasions. Frederick William was able to expand his army from eight thousand to thirty thousand

State	Soldiers	Population	Ratio of soldiers/ total population
France	300,000	20 million	1:66
Russia	220,000	14 million	1:64
Austria	100,000	8 million	1:80
Sweden	40,000	1 million	1:25
Brandenburg-Prussia	30,000	2 million	1:66
England	24,000	10 million	1:410

*Figures for the end of the seventeenth century, ranging from 1688 for Prussia to 1710 for France

Taking Measure The Seventeenth-Century Army
The figures in this chart are only approximate, but they tell an important story. Take special note of the relative weight of the military in the different European states. (From André Corvisier, *Armées et sociétés en Europe de 1494 à 1789* [Paris: Presses Universitaires de France, 1976], 126.)

men. (See "Taking Measure," page 514.) Peasants filled the ranks, and Junkers became officers.

As a Calvinist ruler, Frederick William avoided the ostentation of the French court, even while following the absolutist model of centralizing state power. He boldly rebuffed Louis XIV by welcoming twenty thousand French Huguenot refugees after Louis's revocation of the Edict of Nantes. In pursuing foreign and domestic policies that promoted state power and prestige, Frederick William adroitly switched sides in Louis's wars and would stop at almost nothing to crush resistance at home. In 1701, his son Frederick I (r. 1688–1713) persuaded Holy Roman Emperor Leopold I to grant him the title "king in Prussia" in exchange for support in the War of the Spanish Succession. Until then, there was only one kingdom in the Holy Roman Empire, the kingdom of Bohemia. Prussia had arrived as an important power.

An Uneasy Balance: Austrian Habsburgs and Ottoman Turks

Holy Roman Emperor Leopold I (r. 1658–1705) ruled over a variety of territories of different ethnicities, languages, and religions, yet in ways similar to his French and Prussian counterparts, he gradually consolidated his power. Like all other Holy Roman Emperors since 1438, Leopold was an Austrian Habsburg. He was simultaneously duke of Upper and Lower Silesia, count of Tyrol, archduke of Upper and Lower Austria, king of Bohemia, king of Hungary and Croatia, and ruler of Styria and Moravia (Map 16.3). Some of these territories were provinces in the Holy Roman Empire; others were simply ruled from Vienna as Habsburg family holdings.

In response to the weakening of the Holy Roman Empire by the ravages of the Thirty Years' War, the emperor and his closest officials took control over recruiting, provisioning, and strategic planning and worked to replace the mercenaries hired during the war with a permanent standing army that promoted professional discipline. Intent on replacing Bohemian nobles who had supported the 1618 revolt against Austrian authority, the Habsburgs promoted a new nobility made up of Czechs, Germans, Italians, Spaniards, and even Irish who used German as their common tongue, professed Catholicism, and loyally served the Austrian dynasty. Bohemia became a virtual Austrian colony. In addition to holding Louis XIV in check on his western frontiers, Leopold confronted the ever-present challenge of the Ottoman Turks to the east. Austria had fought the Turks for control of Hungary for more than 150 years. In 1682, war broke out again. As they had in 1529, the Turks in 1683 pushed all the way to the gates of Vienna and laid siege to the Austrian capital. With the help of Polish cavalry, the Austrians finally broke the siege and turned the tide in a major counteroffensive. By the Treaty of Karlowitz of 1699, the Ottoman Turks surrendered almost all of Hungary to the Austrians, marking the beginning of the decline of Ottoman power.

Once the Turks had been beaten back, Austrian rule over Hungary tightened. In 1687, the Habsburg dynasty's hereditary right to the Hungarian crown was acknowledged by the Hungarian diet, a parliament revived by Leopold in 1681 to gain the cooperation

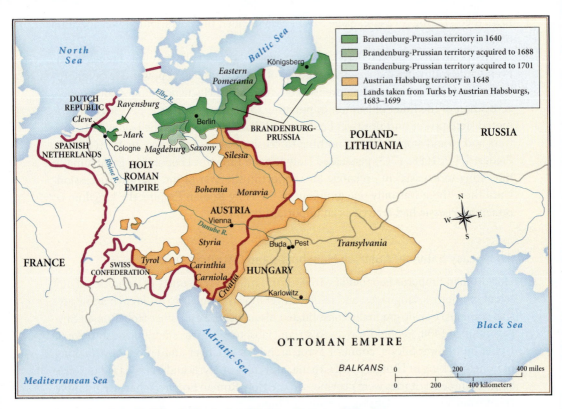

Map 16.3 State Building in Central and Eastern Europe, 1648–1699
The Austrian Habsburgs had long contested the Ottoman Turks for dominance of eastern Europe, and by 1699 they had pushed the Turks out of Hungary. In central Europe, the Austrian Habsburgs confronted the growing power of Brandenburg-Prussia, which had emerged from relative obscurity after the Thirty Years' War to begin an aggressive program of expanding its military and its territorial base. As emperor of the Holy Roman Empire, the Austrian Habsburg ruler governed a huge expanse of territory, but the emperor's control was in fact only partial because of guarantees of local autonomy.

of Hungarian nobles. The diet was dominated by a core of pro-Habsburg Hungarian aristocrats, who would support the dynasty until it fell in 1918. To root out remaining Turkish influence and assert Austrian superiority, Leopold systematically destroyed Turkish buildings and rebuilt Catholic churches, monasteries, roadside shrines, and monuments in the flamboyant Austrian baroque style.

The Ottoman Turks pursued their state consolidation in a different fashion. Hundreds of thousands of Turkish families had moved with Turkish soldiers into the Balkan peninsula in the 1400s and 1500s. As locals converted to Islam, administration passed gradually into their hands. The Ottoman state, ultimately, would last longer than the French absolutist monarchy, even though the Ottoman rulers, the sultans, were often challenged by mutinous army officers. Despite frequent palace coups and assassinations of sultans, the Ottoman state continued to pose a massive military threat on Europe's southeastern borders.

Russia: Setting the Foundations of Bureaucratic Absolutism

Seventeenth-century Russia seemed a world apart from the Europe of Leopold I and Louis XIV. Straddling Europe and Asia, the Russian lands stretched across Siberia to the Pacific Ocean. Western visitors either sneered or shuddered at the "barbarism" of Russian life, and Russians reciprocated by nursing deep suspicions of everything foreign. But under the surface, Russia was evolving as an absolutist state; the tsars wanted to claim unlimited autocratic power, but like their European counterparts they had to surmount internal disorder and come to an accommodation with noble landlords.

In 1649, the Russian tsar Alexei (r. 1645–1676) convened the Assembly of the Land (consisting of noble delegates from the provinces) to consult on a sweeping law code to organize Russian society in a strict social hierarchy. The code of 1649 — which held for nearly two centuries — assigned all subjects to a hereditary class according to their current occupation or state needs. Slaves and free peasants were merged into a serf class. As serfs, they could not change occupations or move; they were tightly tied to the soil and to their noble masters. To prevent tax evasion, the code also forbade townspeople to move from the community where they resided. Nobles owed absolute obedience to the tsar and were required to serve in the army, but in return no other group could own estates worked by serfs. Serfs became the chattel of their lord, who could sell them like horses or land. Their lives differed little from those of the slaves on the plantations in the Americas.

Some peasants resisted enserfment. In 1667, **Stenka Razin**, the head of a powerful band of pirates and outlaws in southern Russia, led a rebellion that promised liberation from the great noble landowners. Captured four years later by the tsar's army, Razin was taken to Moscow, where he was dismembered in front of the public and his body thrown to the dogs. Thousands of his followers also suffered grisly deaths, but Razin's memory lived on in folk songs and legends.

Stenka Razin in Captivity
After leading a revolt of thousands of serfs, peasants, and members of non-Russian tribes of the middle and lower Volga region, Stenka Razin was captured by Russian forces and led off to Moscow, as shown here, where he was executed in 1671. He has been the subject of songs, legends, and poems ever since. (© Imagno / ullstein bild / The Image Works.)

Like his Western rivals, Tsar Alexei wanted a bigger army, exclusive control over state policy, and a greater say in religious matters. The size of the army increased dramatically from 35,000 in the 1630s to 220,000 by the end of the century. The Assembly of the Land, once an important source of consultation for the nobles, never met again after 1653. Alexei also imposed firm control over the Russian Orthodox church. The state-dominated church took action against a religious group called the Old Believers, who rejected church efforts to bring Russian worship in line with Byzantine tradition. Whole communities of Old Believers starved or burned themselves to death rather than submit to the crown.

Nevertheless, modernizing trends prevailed. Tsar Alexei set up the first Western-style theater in the Kremlin, and his daughter Sophia translated French plays. The most adventurous nobles began to wear German-style clothing. Some even argued that service, not just birth, should determine rank. Russia's long struggle over Western influences had begun.

> **REVIEW QUESTION** Why did absolutism flourish everywhere in eastern Europe except Poland-Lithuania?

The Search for Order in Elite and Popular Culture

In the period of state building from 1640 to 1715, questions about obedience, order, and the limits of state power occupied poets, painters, architects, and men of science as much as they did rulers and their ministers. How much freedom of expression could be allowed? How did the individual's needs and aspirations fit with the requirements of state authority? The greatest thinkers and writers wrestled with these issues and helped frame debates for generations to come. At the same time elites worked to distinguish themselves from the lower classes by developing new codes of correct behavior and teaching order and discipline to their social inferiors. Their repeated efforts show, however, that popular culture had its own dynamics that resisted control from above.

Freedom and Constraint in the Arts and Sciences

Most Europeans feared disorder above all else. The French mathematician Blaise Pascal vividly captured their worries in his *Pensées* (Thoughts) of 1660: "I look on all sides, and I see only darkness everywhere." Reason could not determine whether God existed or not, Pascal concluded. Poets, painters, and architects all grappled with similar issues of faith, reason, and authority, but most of them came to more positive conclusions than Pascal about human capacities.

The English Puritan poet John Milton (1608–1674) wrestled with the inevitable limitations on individual liberty. In 1643, in the midst of the civil war between king and Parliament, he published writings in favor of allowing married couples to divorce. When Parliament enacted a censorship law aimed at such literature, Milton responded in 1644 with one of the first defenses of freedom of the press, *Areopagitica*. In it, he argued that even controversial books about religion should be allowed. Forced into retirement

Gian Lorenzo Bernini, *Ecstasy of St. Teresa of Ávila* (c. 1650)
This ultimate statement of baroque sculpture captures all the drama and even sensationalism of a mystical religious faith. Bernini based his figures on a vision reported by St. Teresa in which she saw an angel: "In his hands I saw a great golden spear, and at the iron tip there appeared to be a point of fire. This he plunged into my heart several times so that it penetrated my entrails. When he pulled it out I felt that he took them with it, and left me utterly consumed by the great love of God." (Scala / Art Resource, NY.)

after the restoration of the monarchy, Milton published his epic poem *Paradise Lost* in 1667. He used the biblical Adam and Eve's fall from grace to meditate on human freedom and the tragedies of rebellion. His Satan, the proud angel who challenges God and is cast out of heaven, is so compelling as to be heroic. In the end, Adam and Eve learn the limits to their freedom, yet personal liberty remains essential to their humanity.

The dominant artistic styles of the time — the baroque and the classical — both submerged the ordinary individual in a grander design. The combination of religious and political purposes in baroque art is best exemplified in the architecture and sculpture of Gian Lorenzo Bernini (1598–1680), the papacy's official artist. His architectural masterpiece was the gigantic square facing St. Peter's Basilica in Rome. Bernini's use of freestanding colonnades and a huge open space was meant to impress the individual observer with the power of the popes and the Catholic religion.

Although France was a Catholic country, French artists, like their patron Louis XIV, preferred the standards of **classicism** to those of the baroque. As its name suggests, classicism reflected the ideals of the art of antiquity: geometric shapes, order, and harmony of lines took precedence over the sensuous, exuberant, and emotional forms of the baroque. Rather than being overshadowed by the sheer power of emotional display, in classicism the individual could be found at the intersection of converging, symmetrical, straight lines. These influences were apparent in the work of the leading French painters of the period, Nicolas Poussin (1594–1665) and Claude Lorrain (1600–1682), both of whom tried to re-create classical Roman values in their mythological scenes and Roman landscapes.

French Classicism

This painting by Nicolas Poussin, *Discovery of Achilles on Skyros* (1649–1650), shows the French interest in classical themes and ideals. In the Greek story, Thetis dresses her son Achilles as a young woman and hides him on the island of Skyros so he would not have to fight in the Trojan War. When a chest of treasures is offered to the women, Achilles reveals himself (he is the figure on the far right) because he cannot resist the sword. In telling the story, Poussin emphasizes harmony and almost a sedateness of composition, avoiding the exuberance and emotionalism of the baroque style. (Nicolas Poussin, French [active in Rome], 1594–1665. Oil on canvas, 97.5 x 131.1 cm (38⅜ x 51⅝ in.), William I. Koch Gallery, Museum of Fine Arts, Boston, Juliana Cheney Edwards Collection, 46.463. Photograph © 2012 Museum of Fine Arts, Boston.)

Art could also serve the interests of science. One of the most skilled illustrators of insects and flowers was Maria Sibylla Merian (1646–1717), a German-born painter-scholar whose engravings were widely celebrated for their brilliant realism and microscopic clarity. Merian separated from her husband and accompanied missionaries to the Dutch colony of Surinam, in South America. She painted watercolors of the exotic flowers, birds, and insects she found in the jungle around the cocoa and sugarcane plantations.

Despite the initial religious controversies associated with the scientific revolution, absolutist rulers quickly saw the potential of the new science for enhancing their prestige and glory. Various German princes supported the work of Gottfried Wilhelm Leibniz (1646–1716), who claimed that he, and not Isaac Newton, had invented modern calculus. A lawyer, mathematician, and philosopher who wrote about metaphysics, cosmology, and history, Leibniz also helped establish scientific societies in the German states. Govern-

European Fascination with Products of the New World

In this painting of a banana plant, Maria Sibylla Merian offers a scientific study of one of the many exotic plants and animals found by Europeans who traveled to the colonies overseas. In 1699, Merian traveled to the Dutch South American colony of Surinam with her daughter. (Courtesy of Hunt Institute for Botanical Documentation, Carnegie Mellon University, Pittsburgh, Pennsylvania.)

ment involvement in science was greatest in France. In 1666, Jean-Baptiste Colbert founded the Royal Academy of Sciences, which supplied fifteen scientists with government stipends. The Royal Society of London grew not out of direct government involvement but rather out of informal meetings of scientists at London and Oxford. It received a royal charter in 1662 but maintained complete independence.

Because of their exclusion from most universities, women only rarely participated in the new scientific discoveries. In 1667, nonetheless, the Royal Society of London invited the writer Margaret Cavendish to watch the exhibition of experiments. Labeled "mad" by her critics, she attacked the use of telescopes and microscopes because she detected in the new experimentalism a mechanistic view of the world that exalted masculine prowess and challenged the Christian belief in freedom of the will. Yet she urged the formal education of women, complaining that "we are kept like birds in cages to hop up and down in our houses."

Women and Manners

Although excluded from the universities and the professions, women played important roles not only in the home but also in more formal spheres of social interaction, such as the courts of rulers. Under the tutelage of their mothers and wives, nobles learned manners, or the fine points of social etiquette. In some ways, aristocratic men were expected to act more like women; just as women had long been expected to please men, now aristocratic men had to please their monarch or patron by displaying proper manners and conversing with elegance and wit.

The upper classes began to reject popular festivals and fairs in favor of private theaters, where seats were relatively expensive and behavior was formal. Clowns and buffoons now seemed vulgar; the last king of England to keep a court fool was Charles I. Some tastes spread downward from the upper classes, however. Chivalric romances that had long entranced the nobility, such as Ariosto's *Orlando Furioso,* now appeared in simplified form in cheap booklets printed for lower-class readers.

Molière, the greatest French playwright of the seventeenth century, wrote sparkling comedies of manners that revealed much about the new aristocratic behavior. His play *The Middle-Class Gentleman,* first performed for Louis XIV in 1670, revolves around the yearning of a rich middle-class Frenchman, Monsieur Jourdain, to learn to act like a *gentilhomme* (both "gentleman" and "nobleman"). Monsieur Jourdain buys fancy clothes; hires private instructors in dancing, music, fencing, and philosophy; and lends money to a debt-ridden noble in hopes that the noble will marry his daughter. Only his sensible wife and his daughter's love for a worthier commoner stand in his way. The message for the king's courtiers seemed to be a reassuring one: only born nobles can hope to act like nobles. But the play also showed how the middle classes were learning to emulate the nobility: If one could learn to act nobly through self-discipline, could not anyone with some education and money pass himself off as noble?

As Molière's play demonstrated, new attention to manners trickled down from the court to the middle class. A French treatise on manners written in 1672 explained proper behavior:

> Formerly one was permitted . . . to dip one's bread into the sauce, provided only that one had not already bitten it. Nowadays that would be a kind of rusticity. Formerly one was allowed to take from one's mouth what one could not eat and drop it on the floor, provided it was done skillfully. Now that would be very disgusting.

The key words *rusticity* and *disgusting* reveal the association of unacceptable social behavior with the peasantry, dirt, and repulsion. Similar rules governed spitting and blowing one's nose in public.

Courtly manners often permeated the upper reaches of society by means of the **salon**, an informal gathering held regularly in a private home and presided over by a socially eminent woman. The French government occasionally worried that these gatherings might challenge its authority, but the three main topics of salon conversation were love, literature, and philosophy. Before publishing a manuscript, many authors, including court favorites like Pierre Corneille and Jean Racine, would read their compositions to a salon gathering.

Some women went beyond encouraging male authors and began to write their own works, but they faced many obstacles. Madame de Lafayette wrote several short novels that were published anonymously because it was considered inappropriate for aristocratic women to appear in print. Following the publication of *The Princess of Clèves* in 1678, she denied having written it. Despite these limitations, French women began to

turn out best sellers of a new type of literary form, the novel. Their success prompted the philosopher Pierre Bayle to remark in 1697 that "our best French novels for a long time have been written by women."

The new importance of women in the world of manners and letters did not sit well with everyone. Although the French writer François Poulain de la Barre, in a series of works published in the 1670s, used the new science to assert the equality of women's minds, most men resisted the idea. Clergymen, lawyers, scholars, and playwrights attacked women's growing public influence. Women, they complained, were corrupting forces and needed restraint. Molière wrote plays denouncing women's pretension to judge literary merit. English playwrights derided learned women by creating characters with names such as Lady Knowall, Lady Meanwell, and Mrs. Lovewit.

A real-life target of the English playwrights was Aphra Behn (1640–1689), one of the first professional woman authors. Her short novel *Oroonoko* (1688) told the story of an African prince mistakenly sold into slavery. The story was so successful that it was adapted by playwrights and performed repeatedly in England and France for the next hundred years.

Reforming Popular Culture

Controversies over female influence had little effect on the unschooled peasants who made up most of Europe's population. Peasant culture had three main elements: religion, which shaped every aspect of life and death; knowledge needed to work at farming or in a trade; and popular forms of entertainment such as village fairs and dances. What changed most noticeably in the seventeenth century was the social elites' attitude toward lower-class culture.

In the seventeenth century, Protestant and Catholic churches alike pushed hard to change popular religious practices. Their campaigns against popular "paganism" began during the sixteenth-century Protestant Reformation and Catholic Counter-Reformation but reached much of rural Europe only in the seventeenth century. Puritans in England tried to root out maypole dances, Sunday village fairs, gambling, taverns, and bawdy ballads. In Lutheran Norway, pastors denounced a widespread belief in the miracle-working powers of St. Olaf. The word *superstition* previously meant "false religion" (Protestantism was a superstition for Catholics, Catholicism for Protestants); in the seventeenth century it took on its modern meaning of irrational fears, beliefs, and practices that anyone educated or refined would avoid.

Catholic bishops in the French provinces trained parish priests to reform their flocks by using catechisms in local dialects and insisting that parishioners attend Mass. The church faced a formidable challenge. One bishop in France complained in 1671, "Can you believe that there are in this diocese entire villages where no one has even heard of Jesus Christ?" In some places, believers sacrificed animals to the Virgin; prayed to the new moon; and, as in pre-Christian times, worshipped at the sources of streams.

Like its Protestant counterpart, the Catholic campaign against ignorance and superstition helped extend state power. Clergy, officials, and local police worked together

to limit carnival celebrations, to regulate pilgrimages to shrines, and to replace "indecent" images of saints with more restrained and decorous ones. In Catholicism, the cult of the Virgin Mary and devotions closely connected with Jesus, such as the Holy Sacrament and the Sacred Heart, took precedence over the celebration of popular saints who seemed to have pagan origins or were credited with unverified miracles.

The campaign for more disciplined religious practices helped generate a new attitude toward the poor. In the sixteenth and seventeenth centuries, the upper classes, the church, and the state increasingly regarded the poor as dangerous, deceitful, and lacking in character. The courts had previously expelled beggars from cities; now local leaders, both Catholic and Protestant, tried to reform their character. Municipal magistrates and local notables worked together to transform hospitals into houses of confinement for beggars. In Catholic France, upper-class women's religious associations, known as confraternities, set up asylums that confined prostitutes (by arrest if necessary) and rehabilitated them. Such groups advocated harsh discipline as the cure for poverty.

Even as reformers from church and state tried to regulate popular activities, villagers and townspeople pushed back with reassertions of their own values. For hundreds of years, peasants had maintained their own forms of village justice — called variously "rough music," "charivari," or in North America, "shivaree." If a young man married a much older woman for her money, for example, villagers would serenade the couple by playing crude flutes, banging pots and pans, and shooting muskets. If a man was rumored to have been physically assaulted by his wife, a reversal of the usual sex roles, he (or effigies of him and his wife) might be ridden on a donkey facing backward (to signify the role reversal) and pelted with dung before being ducked in a nearby pond or river. Others directed their mockery at tax officials, gamekeepers on big estates who tried to keep villagers from hunting, or unpopular preachers.

No matter how much care went into controlling religious festivals, such events almost invariably opened the door to popular reinterpretation and sometimes drunken celebration. When the Spanish introduced Corpus Christi processions to their colony in Peru in the seventeenth century, elite Incas dressed in royal costumes to carry the banners of their parishes. Their clothing and ornaments combined Christian symbols with their own indigenous ones. They thus signaled their conversion to Catholicism but also reasserted their own prior identities. The Corpus Christi festival, held in late May or early June, conveniently took place about the same time as Inca festivals from the pre-Spanish era. Carnival, the days preceding Lent on the Christian calendar — of which Mardi Gras ("Fat Tuesday") is the last — offered the occasion for public revelry of all sorts. Although Catholic clergy worked hard to clamp down on the more riotous aspects of Carnival, many towns and villages still held parades, like those of present-day New Orleans or Rio de Janeiro, that included companies of local men dressed in special costumes and gigantic stuffed figures, sometimes with animal skins, animal heads, or elaborate masks.

REVIEW QUESTION How did elite and popular culture become more separate in the seventeenth century?

Conclusion

The search for order took place on various levels, from the reform of the disorderly poor to the establishment of bureaucratic routines in government. The absolutist government of Louis XIV served as a model for all those who aimed to increase the power of the central state. Even Louis's rivals — such as the Holy Roman Emperor Leopold I and Frederick William, the Great Elector of Brandenburg-Prussia — followed his lead in centralizing authority and building up their armies. Whether absolutist or constitutionalist in form,

Mapping the West Europe at the End of the Seventeenth Century

Size was not necessarily an advantage in the late 1600s. Poland-Lithuania, a large country on the map, had been fatally weakened by internal conflicts. In the next century it would disappear entirely. While the Ottoman Empire still controlled an extensive territory, outside of Anatolia its rule depended on intermediaries. The Austrian Habsburgs had pushed the Turks out of Hungary and back into the Balkans. The tiny Dutch Republic, meanwhile, had become very rich through international commerce and was the envy of far larger nations.

seventeenth-century states aimed to penetrate more deeply into the lives of their subjects. They wanted more men for their armed forces; higher taxes to support their projects; and more control over foreign trade, religious dissent, and society's unwanted.

Some tears had begun to appear, however, in the seamless fabric of state power. The civil war between Charles I and Parliament in England in the 1640s opened the way to new demands for political participation. When Parliament overthrew James II in 1688, it also insisted that the new king and queen, William and Mary, agree to the Bill of Rights. In the eighteenth century, new levels of economic growth and the appearance of new social groups would exert pressures on the European state system. The success of seventeenth-century rulers created the political and economic conditions in which their critics would flourish.

Review Questions

1. How "absolute" was the power of Louis XIV?
2. What differences over religion and politics caused the conflict between king and Parliament in England?
3. Why did constitutionalism thrive in the Dutch Republic and the British North American colonies, even as their participation in the slave trade grew?
4. Why did absolutism flourish everywhere in eastern Europe except Poland-Lithuania?
5. How did elite and popular culture become more separate in the seventeenth century?

TIMELINE

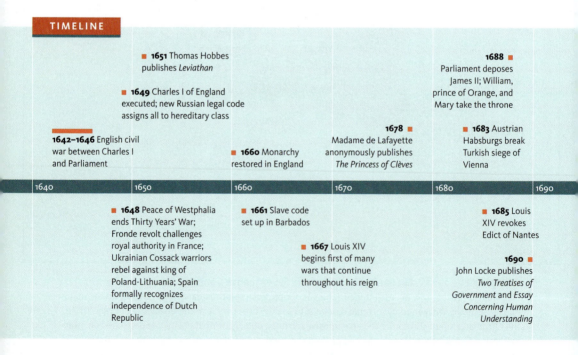

- **1651** Thomas Hobbes publishes *Leviathan*
- **1649** Charles I of England executed; new Russian legal code assigns all to hereditary class
- **1642–1646** English civil war between Charles I and Parliament
- **1660** Monarchy restored in England
- **1678** Madame de Lafayette anonymously publishes *The Princess of Clèves*
- **1683** Austrian Habsburgs break Turkish siege of Vienna
- **1688** Parliament deposes James II; William, prince of Orange, and Mary take the throne

| 1640 | 1650 | 1660 | 1670 | 1680 | 1690 |

- **1648** Peace of Westphalia ends Thirty Years' War; Fronde revolt challenges royal authority in France; Ukrainian Cossack warriors rebel against king of Poland-Lithuania; Spain formally recognizes independence of Dutch Republic
- **1661** Slave code set up in Barbados
- **1667** Louis XIV begins first of many wars that continue throughout his reign
- **1685** Louis XIV revokes Edict of Nantes
- **1690** John Locke publishes *Two Treatises of Government* and *Essay Concerning Human Understanding*

Making Connections

1. What accounts for the success of absolutism in some parts of Europe and its failure in others?

2. How did religious differences in the late seventeenth century still cause political conflict?

3. What were the chief differences between eastern and western Europe in this period?

4. Why was the search for order a major theme in science, politics, and the arts during this period?

- For practice quizzes and other study tools, visit the **Online Study Guide** at bedfordstmartins.com/huntconcise.

- For primary-source material from this period, see *Sources of the Making of the West*, Fourth Edition.

- For Web sites, images, and documents related to topics in this chapter, visit *Make History* at bedfordstmartins.com/huntconcise.

Suggested References

Recent studies have insisted that absolutism could never be entirely absolute because rulers depended on collaboration to enforce their policies. Studies of constitutional governments have emphasized the limitations of freedoms for the lower classes and especially for slaves.

Adamson, J. S. A. *The English Civil War: Conflict and Contexts, 1640–49.* 2009.

Barkey, Karen. *Empire of Difference: The Ottomans in Comparative Perspective.* 2008.

*Beik, William. *Louis XIV and Absolutism: A Brief Study with Documents.* 2000.

Brook, Timothy. *Vermeer's Hat: The Seventeenth Century and the Dawn of the Global World.* 2008.

Cromwell, Oliver: http://www.olivercromwell.org

Davies, Brian L. *Warfare, State and Society on the Black Sea Steppe, 1500–1700.* 2007.

Davis, Natalie Zemon. *Women on the Margins: Three Seventeenth-Century Lives.* 1995.

France in America (site of the Library of Congress on French colonies in North America): http://international.loc.gov/intldl/fiahtml/fiatheme.html#track1

Lepage, Jean-Denis. *Vauban and the French Military Under Louis XIV: An Illustrated History of Fortifications and Strategies.* 2010.

McKay, Derek. *The Great Elector.* 2001.

*Pincus, Steven C. A. *England's Glorious Revolution, 1688–1689: A Brief History with Documents.* 2006.

Stoye, John. *The Siege of Vienna: The Last Great Trial Between Cross & Crescent.* 2006.

Versailles castle: http://en.chateauversailles.fr/homepage

Primary source.

17

The Atlantic System and Its Consequences

1700–1750

N 1699, A FEW COFFEE PLANTS changed the history of the world. European travelers at the end of the sixteenth century noticed Middle Eastern people drinking a "black drink" called *kavah,* but the Arab monopoly on its production kept prices high. This all changed in 1699, when Dutch traders brought a few coffee plants from the east coast of India to their colony of Java (now Indonesia), which proved ideal for growing the beans. Within two decades, the trickle of beans going from Java to Europe became a flood of 200,000 pounds a year. After a shoot from a Dutch plant made its way to the Caribbean island of Martinique in 1721, coffee plants quickly spread throughout the Caribbean, where African slaves provided the plantation labor.

London Coffeehouse

This gouache (a variant on watercolor painting) from about 1725 depicts a scene from a London coffeehouse located in the courtyard of the Royal Exchange (merchants' bank). Middle-class men (wearing wigs) read newspapers, drink coffee, smoke pipes, and discuss the news of the day. The coffeehouse has drawn them out of their homes into a new public space. (The British Museum, London, UK / The Bridgeman Art Library International.)

European consumption of coffee, tea, sugar, and other novelties increased dramatically as European nations forged worldwide economic links. At the center of this new global economy was the **Atlantic system**, the web of trade routes that bound together western Europe, Africa, and the Americas. Europeans bought slaves in western Africa, transported them to be sold in the colonies in North and South America and the Caribbean, bought raw commodities such as coffee and sugar that were produced by the new colonial plantations, and then sold those commodities in European ports for refining and reshipment. This Atlantic system, which first took clear shape in the early eighteenth century, became the hub of European expansion throughout the world.

Coffee drinking is just one example of the many new social and cultural patterns that took root between 1700 and 1750. Improvements in agricultural production at home reinforced the effects of trade overseas; Europeans now had more disposable income for extras, and they spent their money not only in the new coffeehouses and cafés that

sprang up all over Europe but also on newspapers, musical concerts, paintings, and novels. A new middle-class public began to make its presence felt in every domain of culture and social life.

Although the rise of the Atlantic system gave Europe new prominence in the global context, European rulers still focused most of their political, diplomatic, and military energies on their rivalries within Europe. A coalition of countries had succeeded in containing French aggression under Louis XIV, and a more balanced diplomatic system emerged. The more evenly matched competition among the great powers encouraged the development of diplomatic skills and drew attention to public health as a way of encouraging population growth.

In the aftermath of Louis XIV's revocation of the Edict of Nantes in 1685, a new intellectual movement known as the Enlightenment began to germinate. An initial impetus came from French Protestant refugees who published works critical of absolutism in politics and religion. Fed by the popularization of science and the growing interest in travel literature, the early Enlightenment encouraged greater skepticism about religious and state authority. Eventually, the movement would question almost every aspect of social and political life in Europe. The Enlightenment, which began in western Europe in those countries most affected by the new Atlantic system — Britain, France, and the Dutch Republic — can be considered a product of the age of coffee.

CHAPTER FOCUS What were the most important consequences of the growth of the Atlantic system?

The Atlantic System and the World Economy

Although their ships had been circling the globe since the early 1500s, Europeans did not draw most of the world into their economic orbit until the 1700s. Western European nations sent ships loaded with goods to buy slaves from local rulers on the western coast of Africa; the slaves were then transported to the colonies in North and South America and the Caribbean and sold to the owners of plantations producing coffee, sugar, cotton, and tobacco. Money from the slave trade was used to buy the raw commodities produced in the colonies and ship them back to Europe, where they were refined or processed and then sold within Europe and around the world. The Atlantic system and the growth of international trade thus helped create a new consumer society.

Slavery and the Atlantic System

In the eighteenth century, European trade in the Atlantic rapidly expanded and became more systematically interconnected (Map 17.1). By 1650, Portugal had already sent forty thousand African slaves to Brazil to work on the new plantations, which were producing some fifteen thousand tons of sugar a year. A **plantation** was a large tract of land that produced a staple crop such as sugar, coffee, or tobacco; was farmed by slave labor; and was owned by a colonial settler from western Europe.

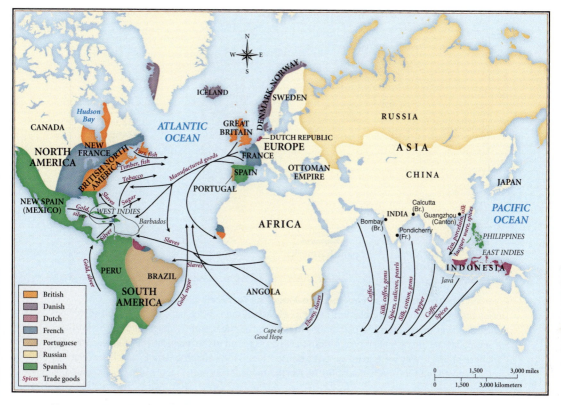

Map 17.1 European Trade Patterns, c. 1740

By 1740, the European powers had colonized much of North and South America and incorporated their colonies there into a worldwide system of commerce centered on the slave trade and plantation production of staple crops. Europeans still sought spices and luxury goods in China and the East Indies, but few Europeans had settled permanently in these areas (with the exception of Java). How did control over colonies determine dominance in international trade in this period?

Realizing that plantations producing staples for Europeans could bring fabulous wealth, the European powers grew less interested in the dwindling trade in precious metals and more eager to colonize. In the 1700s, large-scale planters of sugar, tobacco, and coffee began displacing small farmers who relied on one or two indentured servants (men and women who gained passage to the Americas in exchange for several years of work). Planters and their plantations won out because even cheaper slave labor allowed them to produce mass quantities of commodities at low prices.

State-chartered private companies from Portugal, France, Britain, the Dutch Republic, Prussia, and even Denmark exploited the 3,500-mile coastline of West Africa for slaves. Before 1675, most blacks taken from Africa had been sent to Brazil or Spanish America on Portuguese or Dutch ships, but by 1725 more than 60 percent of African slaves landed in the Caribbean (Figure 17.1), and more and more of them were carried on British or French ships.

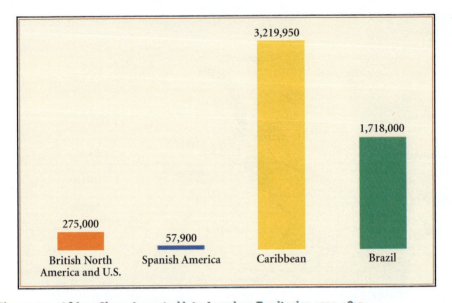

Figure 17.1 African Slaves Imported into American Territories, 1701–1810
During the eighteenth century, planters in the newly established Caribbean colonies imported millions of African slaves to work the new plantations that produced sugar, coffee, indigo, and cotton for the European market. The vast majority of African slaves transported to the Americas ended up in either the Caribbean or Brazil. Why were so many slaves transported to the Caribbean islands, which are relatively small compared to Spanish America or British North America? (Adapted from http://www.slavevoyages.org/.)

After 1700, the plantation economy also began to expand on the North American mainland. The numbers stagger the imagination (Figure 17.2). In all, more than ten million Africans, not counting those who were captured but died before or during the sea voyage, were transported to the Americas before 1850, after which the slave trade finally began to wind down. The lives of those who remained in Africa changed, too. Population declined in West Africa, and because two-thirds of those enslaved were men, husbands were in short supply and men increasingly took two or more wives in a practice known as polygyny. Europeans traded firearms, liquor, and textiles for slaves, altering local power structures and creating political instability.

Enslaved women and men suffered terribly. Most had been sold to European traders by Africans from the west coast who acquired them through warfare or kidnapping. The vast majority were between fourteen and thirty-five years old. Before cramming them onto the ships for the three-month trip, slavers shaved their heads and stripped them naked; they also branded some with red-hot irons. They separated men and women, and shackled men with leg irons. Sailors and officers raped the women at will. In the cramped and appalling conditions of the voyage, as many as one-fourth of the slaves died.

Those who survived the transit were sold and given new names, often only first names. Slaves had no social identities of their own; they were expected to learn their master's language and to do any job assigned. Slaves worked fifteen- to seventeen-hour days and were fed only enough to keep them on their feet. The death rate among slaves

was high, especially on the sugar plantations, where slaves had to cut and haul sugar-cane to the grinders and boilers before it spoiled. During the harvest, grinding and boiling went on around the clock. Because so many slaves died in the sugar-growing regions, more and more slaves, especially strong males, had to be imported. In North America, in contrast, where sugar was a minor crop, the slave population increased tenfold by 1863 through natural growth.

Not surprisingly, despite the threat of torture or death on recapture, slaves sometimes ran away. Outright revolt was uncommon, but slaveholders' fears about conspiracy and revolt lurked beneath the surface of every slave-based society. In 1710, the royal governor of Virginia reminded the colonial legislature of the need for unceasing vigilance: "We are not to Depend on Either Their Stupidity, or that Babel of Languages among 'em; freedom Wears a Cap which Can Without a Tongue, Call Togather all Those who Long to Shake off the fetters of Slavery." Masters defended whipping and other forms of physical punishment as essential to maintaining discipline. Laws called for the castration of a slave who struck a white person.

The balance of white and black populations in the New World colonies varied greatly. Because they did not own plantations, New England merchants and farmers bought few slaves. Blacks — both slave and free — made up only 3 percent of the population in eighteenth-century New England, compared with 60 percent in South Carolina. The imbalance of whites and blacks was even more extreme in the Caribbean, where most

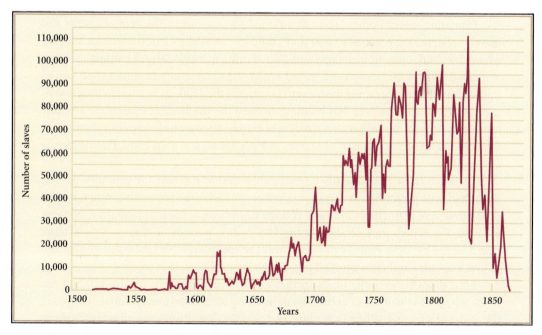

Figure 17.2   Annual Imports in the Atlantic Slave Trade, 1450–1870
The importation of slaves to the American territories increased overall from 1650 until 1800 and did not finally collapse until after 1850. (Adapted from http://www.slavevoyages.org/.)

Conditions on Board a Slave Ship
Visual representations of the horrible conditions on slave ships appeared in the late 1700s as part of the emerging campaign for the abolition of the slave trade. This 1789 wood engraving shows a cross section of an English slave ship built in Liverpool in 1780–1781 for the merchant Joseph Brooks. In 1783, the ship carried more than 600 enslaved Africans across the Atlantic in a space designed for 451 people. Abolitionists showed members of Parliament a model of this ship to convince them of the brutality of the slave trade. (Detail, © The Trustees of the British Museum / Art Resource, NY.)

indigenous people had already died fighting Europeans or the diseases brought by them. By 1713, the French Caribbean colony of St. Domingue (on the western part of Hispaniola, present-day Haiti) had four times as many black slaves as whites; by 1754, slaves there outnumbered whites more than ten to one.

Plantation owners often left their colonial possessions in the care of agents and merely collected the revenue so that they could live as wealthy landowners back home, where they built opulent mansions and gained influence in local and national politics. William Beckford, for example, left his inherited sugar plantations in Jamaica and moved the headquarters of the family business to London in the 1730s to be close to the government and financial markets. His holdings formed the single most powerful economic interest in Jamaica, but he preferred to live in England, where he held political office (he was lord mayor of London and a member of Parliament) and even loaned money to the government.

The slave trade permanently altered consumption patterns for ordinary people. Sugar had been prescribed as a medicine before the end of the sixteenth century, but the development of plantations in Brazil and the Caribbean made it a standard food item. By 1700, the British were sending home fifty million pounds of sugar a year, a figure that doubled by 1730. Equally pervasive was the spread of tobacco; by the 1720s, men of every country and class smoked pipes or took snuff.

Even though the traffic in slaves disturbed some Europeans, in the 1700s slaveholders began to justify their actions by demeaning the mental and spiritual qualities of the enslaved Africans. White Europeans and colonists sometimes described black slaves as animal-like, akin to apes. A leading New England Puritan asserted about the slaves: "Indeed their *Stupidity* is a *Discouragement*. It may seem, unto as little purpose, to *Teach*, as to *wash an Aethiopian* [Ethiopian]." One of the great paradoxes of this time was that

talk of liberty and rights, especially prevalent in Britain and its North American colonies, coexisted with the belief that some people were meant to be slaves. The churches often defended or at least did not oppose the inequities of slavery.

World Trade and Settlement

The Atlantic system helped extend European trade relations across the globe. The textiles that Atlantic shippers exchanged for slaves on the west coast of Africa, for example, were manufactured in India and exported by the British and French East India Companies. As much as one-quarter of the British exports to Africa in the eighteenth century were actually re-exports from India. To expand their trade in the rest of the world, Europeans seized territories and tried to establish permanent settlements. The eighteenth-century extension of European power prepared the way for Western global domination in the nineteenth and twentieth centuries.

In contrast to the sparsely inhabited European trading outposts in Asia and Africa, the colonies in the Americas bulged with settlers. The British North American colonies contained about 1.5 million nonnative (that is, white settler and black slave) residents by 1750. While the Spanish competed with the Portuguese for control of South America, the French competed with the British for control of North America.

Local economies shaped colonial social relations; men in French trapper communities in Canada, for example, had little in common with the men and women of the plantation societies in Barbados or Brazil. Racial attitudes also differed from place to place. Unlike the French and English, the Spanish and Portuguese tolerated intermarriage with the native populations in both America and Asia. By 1800, **mestizos**, people born to a Spanish father and an Indian mother, accounted for more than a quarter of the population in the Spanish colonies. Where intermarriage between colonizers and natives was common, conversion to Christianity proved most successful. However, greater racial diversity seems not to have improved the treatment of slaves.

In the early years of American colonization, many more men than women emigrated from Europe. Although the sex imbalance began to decline at the end of the seventeenth century, it remained substantial; two and a half times more men than women were among the immigrants leaving Liverpool, England, between 1697 and 1707, for example. Women who emigrated as indentured servants ran great risks: many died of disease during the voyage, and at least one in five gave birth to an illegitimate child.

However, the uncertainties of life in the American colonies provided new opportunities for European women and men willing to live outside the law. In the 1500s and 1600s, the English and Dutch governments had routinely authorized pirates to prey on the ships of their rivals, the Spanish and Portuguese. Then, in the late 1600s, English, French, and Dutch bands made up of deserters and crews from wrecked vessels began to form their own associations of pirates, especially in the Caribbean. Called **buccaneers** from their custom of curing strips of beef, called *boucan* by the native Caribs of the islands, the pirates governed themselves and preyed on everyone's shipments without regard to national origin. After 1700, the colonial governments tried to stamp out piracy.

In comparison to those in the Americas, white settlements in Africa and Asia remained small. A handful of Portuguese trading posts in Angola and a few Dutch farms on the Cape of Good Hope provided the only toeholds in Africa for future expansion. In China, the emperors had welcomed Catholic missionaries at court in the seventeenth century, but the priests' credibility diminished as they squabbled among themselves and associated with European merchants, whom the Chinese considered pirates. In 1720, only one thousand Europeans resided in Guangzhou (Canton), the sole place where foreigners could legally trade for spices, tea, and silk (Map 17.1, page 531).

Europeans exercised more influence in Java (in what was then called the East Indies) and in India. Many Dutch settled in Java to oversee coffee production and Asian trade. Dutch, English, French, Portuguese, and Danish companies competed in India for spices, cotton, and silk; by the 1740s, the English and French had become the leading rivals in India, just as they were in North America. Both countries extended their power as India's Muslim rulers lost control to local Hindu princes, rebellious Sikhs, invading Persians, and their own provincial governors. A few thousand Europeans lived

India Cottons and Trade with the East
This colored cotton cloth (now faded with age) was painted and embroidered in Madras, in southern India, sometime in the late 1600s. The male figure with a mustache may be a European, but the female figures are clearly Asian. Europeans — especially the British — discovered that they could make big profits on the export of Indian cotton cloth to Europe. They also traded Indian cottons in Africa for slaves and sold large quantities in the colonies. (Detail, Victoria and Albert Museum, London, UK / The Bridgeman Art Library International.)

in India, though many thousand more soldiers were stationed there to protect them. The staple of trade with India in the early 1700s was calico — lightweight, brightly colored cotton cloth that caught on as a fashion in Europe. (See the illustration on page 536.) English and French slave traders sold calico to the Africans in exchange for slaves.

The Birth of Consumer Society

As worldwide colonization produced new supplies of goods, from coffee to calico, population growth in Europe fueled demand for them. Beginning in Britain, then in France and the Italian states, and finally in eastern Europe, population surged, growing by about 20 percent between 1700 and 1750. The gap between a fast-growing northwest and a more stagnant south and central Europe now diminished as regions that had lost population during the seventeenth-century downturn recovered. Cities, in particular, grew. Between 1600 and 1750, Paris's population more than doubled and London's more than tripled.

Although contemporaries could not have realized it then, this was the start of the modern population explosion. It appears that a decline in the death rate, rather than a rise in the birthrate, explains the turnaround. Three main factors contributed to increased longevity: better weather and hence more bountiful harvests, improved agricultural techniques, and the plague's disappearance after 1720.

By the early eighteenth century, the effects of economic expansion and population growth brought about a **consumer revolution**. For example, at Nantes, the center of the French sugar trade, imports quadrupled between 1698 and 1733. Tea, chocolate, and coffee became virtual necessities. In 1700, England had two thousand coffee-houses; by 1740, every English country town had at least two.

The Exotic as Consumer Item
This painting by the Venetian artist Rosalba Carriera (1675–1757) is titled *Africa*. The young black girl wearing a turban represents the African continent. Carriera was known for her use of pastels. In 1720, she journeyed to Paris, where she became an associate of Antoine Watteau and helped inaugurate the rococo style in painting. Why might the artist have chosen to paint an African girl? (Gemäldegalerie Alte Meister, Staatliche Kunstsammlungen Dresden / Art Resource, NY.)

Paris got its first cafés at the end of the seventeenth century, and Berlin opened its first coffeehouse in 1714.

A new economic dynamic steadily took shape that has influenced all of subsequent history. More and more people escaped the confines of a subsistence economy, in which peasants produced barely enough to support themselves from year to year. As ordinary people gained more disposable income, demand for nonessential consumer goods rose. These included not only the new colonial products such as coffee and tea but also tables, chairs, sheets, chamber pots, lamps, and mirrors — and for the better off still, coffee- and teapots, china, cutlery, chests of drawers, desks, clocks, and pictures for the walls.

Rising demand created more jobs and more income and yet more purchasing power in a mutually reinforcing cycle. In the English economic literature of the 1690s, writers reacted to these developments by expressing a new view of humans as consuming animals with boundless appetites. Change did not occur all at once, however. The consumer revolution spread from the cities to the countryside, from England to the continent, and from western Europe to eastern Europe only over the long run.

Europe was not the only region experiencing such changes. China's population grew even faster — it may have tripled during the 1700s — and there, too, consumption of cloth, furniture, tea, sugar, and tobacco all increased. In China, these goods could be locally produced, and China did not pursue colonization of far-flung lands. Still, foreign trade also increased, especially with lands on China's borders.

REVIEW QUESTION How was consumerism related to slavery in the early eighteenth century?

New Social and Cultural Patterns

The rise of consumption in Europe was fueled in part by a revolution in agricultural techniques that made it possible to produce larger quantities of food with a smaller agricultural workforce. As population increased, more people moved to the cities, where they found themselves caught up in innovative urban customs such as attending musical concerts and reading novels. Along with a general increase in literacy, these activities helped create a public that responded to new writers and artists. As always, people's experiences varied depending on whether they lived in wealth or poverty, in urban or rural areas, or in eastern or western Europe.

Agricultural Revolution

Although Britain, France, and the Dutch Republic shared the enthusiasm for consumer goods, Britain's domestic market grew most quickly. In Britain, as agricultural output increased by 43 percent over the course of the 1700s, the population increased by 70 percent. The British imported grain to feed the growing population, but they also benefited from the development of techniques that together constituted an **agricultural revolution**. It was not new machinery but rather increasingly aggressive attitudes toward investment and management that propelled this revolution. The Dutch and the Flemish

had pioneered many agricultural management techniques in the 1600s, but the British took them further. (See "Taking Measure," below.)

Four major changes occurred in British agriculture that eventually spread to other countries. First, farmers increased the amount of land under cultivation by draining wetlands and by growing crops on previously uncultivated common lands (acreage maintained by the community for grazing). Second, those farmers who could afford it consolidated small, scattered plots into larger, more efficient units. Third, livestock raising became more closely linked to crop growing, and the yields of each increased. For centuries, most farmers had rotated their fields in and out of production to replenish the soil. Now farmers planted carefully chosen fodder crops such as clover and turnips that added nutrients to the soil, thereby eliminating the need to leave a field fallow (unplanted) every two or three years. With more fodder available, farmers could raise more livestock, which in turn produced more manure to fertilize grain fields. Fourth, selective breeding of animals combined with the increase in fodder to improve the quality and size of herds. By the 1730s and 1740s, agricultural output had increased dramatically, and prices for food had fallen because of these interconnected innovations.

Changes in agricultural practices did not benefit all landowners equally. The biggest British landowners consolidated their holdings in the "enclosure movement." They put pressure on small farmers and villagers to sell their land or give up their common lands. The big landlords then fenced off (enclosed) their property. Because enclosure eliminated community grazing rights, it frequently sparked a struggle between the big landlords and villagers, and in Britain it normally required an act of Parliament. Such acts became increasingly common in the second half of the eighteenth century, and by the century's end six million acres

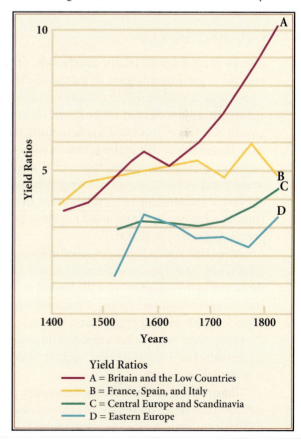

Taking Measure Relationship of Crop Harvested to Seed Used, 1400–1800

The impact and even the timing of the agricultural revolution can be determined by this figure, which shows yield ratios (the number of grains produced for each seed planted) from 1400 to 1800. Britain and the Low Countries (including the Dutch Republic and the Austrian Netherlands) experienced huge increases in crop yields after 1700. Other European regions lagged behind right into the 1800s.

(Peter J. Hugill, *World Trade since 1431: Geography, Technology, and Capitalism* [Johns Hopkins University Press, 1995], 56.)

Yield Ratios
A = Britain and the Low Countries
B = France, Spain, and Italy
C = Central Europe and Scandinavia
D = Eastern Europe

of common lands had been enclosed and developed. In this way the English peasantry largely disappeared, replaced by a more hierarchical society of big landlords, enterprising tenant farmers, and poor agricultural laborers.

The new agricultural techniques spread slowly from Britain and the Low Countries (the Dutch Republic and the Austrian Netherlands) to the rest of western Europe. Outside a few pockets, however, subsistence agriculture (producing just enough to get by rather than surpluses for the market) continued to dominate farming in western Europe and Scandinavia. Unlike the populations of the highly urbanized Low Countries (where half the people lived in towns and cities), most Europeans, western and eastern, eked out their existence in the countryside and could barely participate in the new markets for consumer goods.

In eastern Europe, the condition of peasants worsened in the areas where landlords tried hardest to improve crop yields. To produce more for the Baltic grain market, aristocratic landholders in Prussia, Poland, and parts of Russia drained wetlands, cultivated moors, and built dikes. They also forced peasants off lands that the peasants had worked for themselves, and they increased compulsory labor services (the critical element in serfdom). Some eastern landowners grew fabulously wealthy. The Potocki family in the Polish Ukraine, for example, owned three million acres of land and had 130,000 serfs.

Social Life in the Cities

Because of emigration from the countryside, cities grew in population and consequently exercised a growing influence on culture and social life. Between 1650 and 1750, cities with at least ten thousand inhabitants increased in population by 44 percent. From the eighteenth century onward, urban growth has been continuous. Along with the general growth of cities, an important south-to-north shift occurred in the pattern of urbanization. Around 1500, half of the people in cities of at least ten thousand residents could be found in the Italian states, Spain, or Portugal; by 1700, the urbanization of northwestern and southern Europe was roughly equal. Eastern Europe, despite the huge cities of Istanbul and Moscow, was still less urban than western Europe. With 675,000 inhabitants, London was by far the most populous European city in 1750; Berlin had 90,000 people, Warsaw only 23,000.

Many landowners kept a residence in town, so the separation between rural and city life was not as extreme as might be imagined, at least not for the very rich. At the top of the ladder in the big cities were the landed nobles. Some of them filled their lives only with conspicuous consumption of fine food, extravagant clothing, carriages, books, and opera; others held key political, administrative, or judicial offices. However they spent their time, these rich families employed thousands of artisans, shopkeepers, and domestic servants. Many English peers (highest-ranking nobles) had thirty or forty servants at each of their homes.

The middle classes of officials, merchants, professionals, and landowners occupied the next rung down on the social ladder. London's population, for example, included about twenty thousand middle-class families (constituting, at most, one-sixth of the city's

Vauxhall Gardens, London
This hand-colored print from the mid-eighteenth century shows the newly refurbished gardens near the Thames River. Prosperous families show off their brightly colored clothes and listen to a public concert by the orchestra seated just above them. These activities helped form a more self-conscious public. (Bibliothèque des Arts Décoratifs, Paris, France / Archives Charmet / The Bridgeman Art Library.)

population). In this period the middle classes began to develop distinctive ways of life that set them apart from both the rich noble landowners and the lower classes. Unlike the rich nobles, the middle classes lived primarily in the cities and towns, even if they owned small country estates.

Below the middle classes came the artisans and shopkeepers (most of whom were organized in professional guilds), then the journeymen, apprentices, servants, and laborers. At the bottom of the social scale were the unemployed poor, who survived by intermittent work and charity. Women married to artisans and shopkeepers often kept the accounts, supervised employees, and ran the household as well. Every middle-class and upper-class family employed servants; artisans and shopkeepers frequently hired them, too. Women from poorer families usually worked as domestic servants until they married. Four out of five domestic servants in the city were female. In large cities such as London, the servant population grew faster than the population of the city as a whole.

Social status in the cities was readily visible. Wide, spacious streets graced rich districts; the houses had gardens, and the air was relatively fresh. In poor districts, the streets were narrow, dirty, dark, humid, and smelly, and the houses were damp and crowded. The poorest people were homeless, sleeping under bridges or in abandoned buildings. A Neapolitan prince described his homeless neighbors as "lying like filthy animals, with no distinction of age or sex."

Like shelter, clothing was a reliable social indicator. The poorest workingwomen in Paris wore woolen skirts and blouses of dark colors over petticoats, a bodice, and a corset. They also donned caps of various sorts, cotton stockings, and shoes (probably their only pair). Workingmen dressed even more drably. Many occupations could be recognized by their dress: no one could confuse lawyers in their dark robes with masons or butchers in their special aprons, for example. People higher on the social ladder were more likely to sport a variety of fabrics, colors, and unusual designs in their clothing and to own many different outfits. Social status was not an abstract idea; it permeated every detail of daily life.

The ability to read and write also reflected social differences. People in the upper classes were more literate than those in the lower classes; city people were more literate than peasants. Protestant countries appear to have been more successful at promoting education and literacy than Catholic countries, perhaps because of the Protestant emphasis on Bible reading. Widespread literacy among the lower classes was first achieved in the Protestant areas of Switzerland and in Presbyterian Scotland. In France, literacy doubled in the eighteenth century thanks to the spread of parish schools, but still only one in two men and one in four women could read and write. Most peasants remained illiterate. Few schools existed, teachers received low wages, and no country had yet established a national system of education.

A new literate public nonetheless arose among the middle classes of the cities. More books and periodicals were published than ever before, another aspect of the consumer revolution. The trend began in the 1690s in Britain and the Dutch Republic and gradually accelerated. In 1695, new newspapers and magazines proliferated when the British government stopped demanding that each publication have a government-approved license. The first London daily newspaper came out in 1702, and in 1709 Joseph Addison and Richard Steele published the first literary magazine, *The Spectator*. They devoted their magazine to the cultural improvement of the increasingly influential middle class. By the 1720s, twenty-four provincial newspapers were published in England. In the London coffeehouses, an edition of a single newspaper might reach ten thousand male readers. Women did their reading at home. Except in the Dutch Republic, newspapers on the continent lagged behind and often consisted mainly of advertising with little critical commentary. France, for example, had no daily paper until 1777.

New Tastes in the Arts

The new literate public did not just read newspapers; its members now pursued an interest in painting, attended concerts, and besieged booksellers in search of popular novels. Because increased trade and prosperity put money into the hands of the growing middle classes, a new urban audience began to compete with the churches, rulers, and courtiers as chief patrons for new work.

Developments in painting reflected the tastes of the new public, as the **rococo** style challenged the hold of the baroque and classical schools, especially in France. *Rococo,* like *baroque,* was an invented word (from the French word *rocaille,* "shell-

Rococo Painting

The rococo emphasis on interiors, on decoration, and on intimacy rather than monumental grandeur are evident in François Boucher's painting *The Luncheon* (1739). The painting also draws attention to new consumer items, from the mirror and the clock to chocolate, children's toys, a small Buddha statue, and the intricately designed furniture. (Musée du Louvre, Paris / Collection Dagli Orti / The Art Archive at Art Resource, NY.)

work") and originally a derogatory label, meaning "frivolous decoration." Many rococo paintings depicted scenes of intimate sensuality rather than the monumental, emotional grandeur favored by classical and baroque painters. Personal portraits and pastoral paintings took the place of heroic landscapes and grand, ceremonial canvases. Rococo paintings adorned homes as well as palaces and served as a form of interior decoration rather than as a statement of piety. Its decorative quality made rococo art an ideal complement to newly discovered materials such as stucco and porcelain, especially the porcelain vases now imported from China.

Public music concerts were first performed in England in the 1670s and became much more regular and frequent in the 1690s. On the continent, Frankfurt organized the first regular public concerts in 1712; Hamburg and Paris began holding them within a few years. Opera continued to spread in the eighteenth century; Venice had sixteen public opera houses by 1700, and the Covent Garden opera house opened in London in 1732.

The growth of a public that appreciated and supported music had much the same effect as the extension of the reading public: like authors, composers could now begin to liberate themselves from court patronage and work for a paying audience. The composer George Frideric Handel (1685–1759) was among the first to grasp the new directions in music. A German by birth, Handel wrote operas in Italy and then moved in 1710 to Britain, where he wrote music for the court and began composing oratorios. The oratorio, a form Handel introduced in Britain, combined the drama of opera with the majesty of religious and ceremonial music and featured the chorus over the soloists. The "Hallelujah Chorus" from Handel's oratorio *Messiah* (1741) is perhaps the single best-known piece of Western classical music. It reflected the composer's personal, deeply felt piety but also his willingness to combine musical materials into a dramatic form that captured the enthusiasm of the new public.

Nothing captured the imagination of the new public more than the novel, the literary genre whose very name underscored the eighteenth-century taste for novelty. More than three hundred French novels appeared between 1700 and 1730. During this unprecedented explosion, the novel took on its modern form and became more concerned with individual psychology and social description than with the adventure tales popular earlier (such as Miguel de Cervantes's *Don Quixote*). The novel's popularity was closely tied to the expansion of the reading public, and novels were available in serial form in periodicals or from the many booksellers who served the new market.

Women figured prominently in novels as characters, and women writers abounded. The English author Eliza Haywood (1693?–1756) earned her living turning out a stream of novels with titles such as *Persecuted Virtue, Constancy Rewarded,* and *The History of Betsy Thoughtless*— all showing a concern for the proper place of women as models of virtue in a changing world. Haywood's male counterpart was Daniel Defoe (1660–1731), a merchant's son who had a diverse and colorful career as a manufacturer, political spy, novelist, and social commentator. Defoe is best known for his novel *Robinson Crusoe* (1719). The story of the adventures of a shipwrecked sailor, *Robinson Crusoe* portrayed the new values of the time: to survive, Crusoe had to employ fearless entrepreneurial ingenuity. He had to be ready for the unexpected and be able to improvise in every situation. He was, in short, the model for the new man in an expanding economy. Crusoe's patronizing attitude toward the black man Friday now draws much critical attention, but his discovery of Friday shows how the fate of blacks and whites had become intertwined in the new colonial environment.

Religious Revivals

Despite the novel's growing popularity, religious books and pamphlets still sold in huge numbers, and most Europeans remained devout, even as their religions were changing. In this period, a Protestant revivalist movement known as **Pietism** rocked the complacency of the established churches in northern Europe. Pietists believed in a mystical religion of the heart; they wanted a deeply emotional, even ecstatic religion. They urged intense Bible study, which in turn promoted popular education and contributed to the increase in literacy. Many Pietists attended catechism instruction every day and also went to morning and evening prayer meetings in addition to regular Sunday services. Although Pietism appealed to both Lutherans and Calvinists, it had the greatest impact in Lutheran Prussia, where it taught the virtues of hard work, obedience, and devotion to duty.

Catholicism also had its versions of religious revival, especially in France. A Frenchwoman, Jeanne Marie Guyon (1648–1717), attracted many noblewomen and a few leading clergymen to her own Catholic brand of Pietism, known as Quietism. Claiming miraculous visions and astounding prophecies, she urged a mystical union with God through prayer and simple devotion. Despite papal condemnation and intense controversy within Catholic circles in France, Guyon had followers all over Europe.

Even more influential were the Jansenists, who gained many new adherents to their austere form of Catholicism despite Louis XIV's harassment and repeated condemna-

tion by the papacy. Under the pressure of religious and political persecution, Jansenism took a revivalist turn in the 1720s. At the funeral of a Jansenist priest in Paris in 1727, the crowd who flocked to the grave claimed to witness a series of miraculous healings. Some believers fell into frenzied convulsions, claiming to be inspired by the Holy Spirit through the intercession of the dead priest. After midcentury, Jansenism became even more politically active as its adherents joined in opposition to the crown's policies on religion.

REVIEW QUESTION How were new social trends reflected in cultural life in the early 1700s?

Consolidation of the European State System

The spread of Pietism and Jansenism reflected the emergence of a middle-class public that now participated in every new development, including religion. The middle classes could pursue these interests because the European state system gradually stabilized despite the increasing competition for wealth in the Atlantic system. Warfare settled three main issues between 1700 and 1750: a coalition of powers held France in check on the continent, Great Britain emerged from the wars against France as the preeminent maritime power, and Russia defeated Sweden in the contest for supremacy in the Baltic. After Louis XIV's death in 1715, Europe enjoyed the fruits of a more balanced diplomatic system, in which warfare became less frequent and less widespread. States could then spend their resources establishing and expanding control over their own populations, both at home and in their colonies.

A New Power Alignment

The peace treaties that ended the War of the Spanish Succession (1701–1713) signaled a new alignment of power in western Europe (see Chapter 16). Spain began a long decline, French ambitions for dominance were thwarted, and Great Britain emerged as the new center in the balance of power. A coalition led by Britain and joined by most of the European powers had confronted Louis XIV's French forces across Europe. The conflict extended to the Caribbean and North and South America as well. The casualties mounted inexorably: in the battle of Blenheim in southern Germany in 1704, 108,000 soldiers fought and 33,000 were killed or wounded — in just one day. At Malplaquet, near the northern French border, a great battle in 1709 engaged 166,000 soldiers and cavalrymen, and 36,000 of them were killed or wounded. Those allied against Louis won at Malplaquet, but they lost twice as many men as the French did and could not pursue their advantage. Everyone rejoiced when peace came (Map 17.2).

By the terms of the peace, Louis XIV's grandson was confirmed as King Philip V of Spain (r. 1700–1746) but only on the condition that he renounce any claim to the French throne. None of the other powers could countenance a joint French-Spanish monarchy. Philip opened Spain further to the rest of Europe and stabilized the currency, but he could not revive Spain's military prestige or commercial position. Spain

British and French Claims after the Peace of Utrecht, 1714

Hudson Bay

Newfoundland

British claim

French claim

Nova Scotia

British claim

0   500   1000 miles
0   500   1000 kilometers

0   200   400 miles
0   200   400 kilometers

SWEDEN

St. Petersburg

DENMARK–NORWAY

North Sea

Baltic Sea

Moscow

RUSSIA

SCOTLAND

Edinburgh

IRELAND

Dublin

GREAT BRITAIN

ENGLAND

London

DUTCH REPUBLIC

Utrecht

Hanover

POLAND-LITHUANIA

BRANDENBURG-PRUSSIA

Berlin

Warsaw

Kiev

ATLANTIC OCEAN

English Channel

Malplaquet

Paris

Loire R.

FRANCE

Austrian Neth.

Cologne

Rhine R.

HOLY ROMAN EMPIRE

Blenheim

Oder R.

Elbe R.

Vistula R.

AUSTRIA

Vienna

HUNGARY

Buda   Pest

Danube R.

Black Sea

SWISS CONFED.

SAVOY

MILAN VENICE

GENOA

Marseille

TUSCANY

PAPAL STATES

Rome

KINGDOM OF NAPLES

OTTOMAN EMPIRE

Constantinople

PORTUGAL

Madrid

Lisbon

SPAIN

Corsica

Minorca (Gr. Br.)

BALEARIC IS.

Sardinia

Sicily

Gibraltar (Gr. Br.)

Mediterranean Sea

Territories gained after the Peace of Utrecht, 1714

- French Bourbon lands
- Spanish Bourbon lands
- Austrian Habsburg lands
- Prussian lands
- Great Britain
- To Great Britain
- To the Austrian Empire
- The Jacobite rising of 1715
- Main areas of fighting during the War of the Spanish Succession, 1701–1713
- Boundary of the Holy Roman Empire

Map 17.2 Europe, c. 1715

Although Louis XIV succeeded in putting his grandson Philip on the Spanish throne, France emerged considerably weakened from the War of the Spanish Succession. France ceded large territories in Canada to Britain, which also gained key Mediterranean outposts from Spain as well as a monopoly on providing slaves to the Spanish colonies. Spanish losses were catastrophic. Philip had to renounce any future claim to the French crown and give up considerable territories in the Netherlands and Italy to the Austrians. How did the competing English and French claims in North America around 1715 create potential conflicts for the future?

consistently imported more from Britain and France than it exported to them. As a country that had been created by a campaign against Muslims within its boundaries, Spain remained firmly in the grip of the Catholic clergy, which insisted on the censorship of dissident or heretical ideas. Although the capital city, Madrid, had 200,000 inhabitants, laws prohibited people from smoking, reading newspapers, or talking politics in the cafés and inns of the city—precisely the activities flourishing in England, France, and the Dutch Republic.

When French king Louis XIV died in 1715, his five-year-old great-grandson succeeded him as Louis XV (r. 1715–1774), with the duke of Orléans (1674–1723), nephew of the dead king, serving as regent for the young boy. To raise much-needed funds, in 1719 the regent encouraged the Scottish financier John Law to set up an official trading company for North America and a state bank that issued paper money and stock (without which trade depended on the available supply of gold and silver). The bank was supposed to offer lower interest rates to the state, thus cutting the cost of financing the government's debts. The value of the stock rose rapidly in a frenzy of speculation, only to crash a few months later. France finally achieved a measure of financial stability under the leadership of Cardinal Hercule de Fleury (1653–1743), the most powerful member of the government after the death of the regent. Colonial trade boomed. Peace and the acceptance of limits on territorial expansion inaugurated a century of French prosperity.

British Rise and Dutch Decline

The British and the Dutch had formed a coalition against Louis XIV under their joint ruler, William III, who was simultaneously *stadholder* (elected head) of the Dutch Republic and, with his English wife, Mary (d. 1694), ruler of England, Wales, and Scotland. After William's death in 1702, the British and Dutch went their separate ways. Over the next decades, England incorporated Scotland and subjugated Ireland, becoming "Great Britain" in 1707. At the same time, Dutch imperial power declined; by 1700, the British dominated the seas, and the Dutch, with their small population of less than two million, came to depend on alliances with bigger powers.

English relations with Scotland and Ireland were complicated by the problem of succession: William and Mary had no children. To ensure a Protestant succession, Parliament ruled that Mary's sister, Anne, would succeed William and Mary and that the Protestant House of Hanover in Germany would succeed Anne if she had no surviving heirs. Catholics were excluded. When Queen Anne (r. 1702–1714) died leaving no children, the elector of Hanover, a Protestant great-grandson of James I, consequently became King George I (r. 1714–1727). The house of Hanover—renamed the house of Windsor during World War I—still occupies the British throne today.

Support from the Scots and Irish for this solution did not come easily, because many in Scotland and Ireland supported the claims to the throne of the deposed Catholic king, James II, and, after his death in 1701, his son James Edward. Out of fear of this Jacobitism (from the Latin *Jacobus,* for "James"), Scottish Protestant leaders agreed to the Act of Union of 1707, which abolished the Scottish Parliament and affirmed the Scots'

recognition of the Protestant Hanoverian succession. The Scots agreed to obey the Parliament of Great Britain, which would include Scottish members in the House of Commons and the House of Lords. A Jacobite rebellion in Scotland in 1715, aiming to restore the Stuart line, was suppressed (Map 17.2, page 546). The threat of Jacobitism nonetheless continued into the 1740s.

The Irish — 90 percent of whom were Catholic — proved even more difficult to subdue. William III had to take command of the joint English and Dutch forces to defeat the Irish supporters of James II, and after that defeat Catholics in Ireland faced yet more confiscation and legal restrictions. By 1700, Irish Catholics, who in 1640 had owned 60 percent of the land in Ireland, owned just 14 percent. The Protestant-controlled Irish Parliament passed a series of laws limiting the rights of the Catholic majority: Catholics could not marry Protestants, send children abroad for education, or establish Catholic schools at home. Moreover, Catholics could not sit in Parliament, nor could they vote for its members unless they took an oath renouncing Catholic doctrine. These and a host of other laws reduced Catholic Ireland to the status of a colony.

In Britain's constitutional system, the monarch ruled with Parliament. The crown chose ministers, directed policy, and supervised administration, while Parliament raised revenue, passed laws, and represented the interests of the people to the crown. The powers of Parliament were reaffirmed by the Triennial Act in 1694, which provided that Parliaments meet at least once every three years (this was extended to seven years in 1716, after the Whigs had established their ascendancy). Only 200,000 propertied men could vote, out of a population of more than 5 million, and a few hundred families controlled all the important political offices.

George I and George II (r. 1727–1760) relied on one man, Sir **Robert Walpole** (1676–1745), to help them manage their relations with Parliament. From his position as First Lord of the Treasury, Walpole made himself into the first, or "prime," minister, leading the House of Commons from 1721 to 1742. Although appointed initially by the king, Walpole established an enduring pattern of parliamentary government in which a prime minister from the leading party guided legislation through the House of Commons. Walpole also built a vast patronage machine that dispensed government jobs to win support for the crown's policies.

The partisan division between the Whigs, who supported the Hanoverian succession and the rights of dissenting Protestants, and the Tories, who had backed the Stuart line and the Church of England, did not hamper Great Britain's pursuit of economic, military, and colonial power. In this period, Great Britain became a great power on the world stage by virtue of its navy and its ability to finance major military involvement in wars. The founding in 1694 of the Bank of England — which, unlike the French bank, endured — enabled the government to raise money at low interest for foreign wars. By the 1740s, the government could borrow more than four times what it could in the 1690s.

When William of Orange (William III of England) died in 1702, he left no heirs, and for forty-five years the Dutch lived without a stadholder. The merchant ruling class of some two thousand families dominated the Dutch Republic more than ever, but they presided over a country that counted for less in international power politics. The Dutch

population was not growing as fast as others, and the Dutch share of the Baltic trade decreased from 50 percent in 1720 to less than 30 percent by the 1770s. The output of Leiden textiles dropped to one-third of its 1700 level by 1740. Shipbuilding, paper manufacturing, tobacco processing, salt refining, and pottery production all dwindled as well. The biggest exception to the downward trend was trade with the New World, which increased with escalating demands for sugar and tobacco. The Dutch shifted their interest away from great-power rivalries and toward those areas of international trade and finance where they could establish an enduring presence.

Russia's Emergence as a European Power

The commerce and shipbuilding of the Dutch and British so impressed Russian tsar Peter I (r. 1689–1725) that he traveled incognito to their shipyards in 1697 to learn their methods firsthand. Known to history as **Peter the Great**, he dragged Russia kicking and screaming all the way to great-power status. Although he came to the throne while still a minor (on the eve of his tenth birthday), grew up under the threat of a palace coup, and enjoyed little formal education, his accomplishments soon matched his seven-foot-tall stature. Peter transformed public life in Russia and established an absolutist state based on the Western model. His attempts to create a society patterned after western Europe, known as **Westernization**, ignited an enduring controversy: Did Peter set Russia on a course of inevitable Westernization required to compete with the West? Or did he forever and fatally disrupt Russia's natural evolution into a distinctive Slavic society?

To pursue his goal of Westernizing Russian culture, Peter set up the first laboratories and technical schools and founded the Russian Academy of Sciences. He ordered translations of Western classics and hired a German theater company to perform the French plays of Molière. He replaced the traditional Russian calendar with the Western one,* introduced Arabic numerals, and brought out the first public newspaper. He ordered his officials and the nobles to shave their beards (see the illustration on page 550) and dress in Western fashion.

Peter encouraged foreigners to move to Russia to offer their advice and skills, especially for building the capital city. Named St. Petersburg after the tsar, the new capital symbolized Russia's opening to the West. Construction began in 1703 in a Baltic province that had been recently conquered from Sweden. By the end of 1709, thirty thousand laborers had been enlisted in the construction. Peter ordered skilled workers to move to the new city and commanded all landowners possessing more than forty serf households to build houses there. In the 1720s, a German minister described St. Petersburg "as a wonder of the world, considering its magnificent palaces, . . . and the short time that

---

*Peter introduced the Julian calendar, then still used in Protestant but not Catholic countries. Later in the eighteenth century, Protestant Europe abandoned the Julian for the Gregorian calendar. Not until 1918 was the Gregorian calendar adopted in Russia, at which point Russia's calendar had fallen thirteen days behind Europe's.

Peter the Great Modernizes Russia

In this popular print, a barber forces a protesting noble to conform to Western fashions. Peter the Great ordered all nobles, merchants, and middle-class professionals to cut off their beards or pay a huge tax to keep them. An early biographer of Peter claimed that those who lost their beards saved them to put in their coffins, in fear that they would not enter heaven without them. Most western Europeans applauded these attempts to modernize Russia, but many Russians deeply resented the attack on traditional ways. Why was everyday appearance such a contested issue in Russia? (Visual Connection Archive.)

was employed in the building of it." At Peter's death in 1725, the new city had forty thousand residents.

Peter aimed to set Russia on a new course. At his new capital he tried to improve the traditionally denigrated, secluded status of women by ordering them to dress in European styles and appear publicly at his dinners for diplomatic representatives. A foreigner headed every one of Peter's new technical and vocational schools, and for its first eight years the new Academy of Sciences included no Russians. Every ministry was assigned a foreign adviser. Upper-class Russians learned French or German, which they spoke even at home. Such changes affected only the very top of Russian society, however; the mass of the population had no contact with the new ideas and ended up paying for the innovations either in ruinous new taxation or by building St. Petersburg, a project that cost the lives of thousands of workers. Serfs remained tied to the land, completely dominated by their noble lords.

Peter also reorganized government and finance on Western models and, like other absolute rulers, strengthened his army. With ruthless recruiting methods, which included branding a cross on every recruit's left hand to prevent desertion, he forged an army of 200,000 men and equipped it with modern weapons. He not only built the first navy in Russian history but also created schools for artillery, engineering, and military medicine. Not surprisingly, taxes tripled.

The tsar allowed nothing to stand in his way. He did not hesitate to use torture, and he executed thousands. He gave a special guard regiment unprecedented power to expedite cases against those suspected of rebellion, espionage, pretensions to the throne, or just "unseemly utterances" against him. Because his only son, Alexei, had allied himself with Peter's critics, the tsar threw him into prison, where the young man mysteriously died.

To control the often restive nobility, Peter insisted that all noblemen engage in state service. The Table of Ranks (1722) classified them into military, administrative, and court categories, a codification of social and legal relationships in Russia that would last for

nearly two centuries. Because the nobles lacked a secure independent status, Peter could command them to a degree that was unimaginable in western Europe. State service was not only compulsory but also permanent. Moreover, the male children of those in service had to be registered by the age of ten and begin serving at fifteen. To increase his authority over the Russian Orthodox church, Peter allowed the office of patriarch (supreme head) to remain vacant, and in 1721 he replaced it with the Holy Synod, a bureaucracy of laymen under his supervision.

Peter the Great's success in building up state authority changed the balance of power in eastern Europe. First he took on Sweden, which had dominated the Baltic region since the Thirty Years' War (1618–1648). Peter joined an anti-Swedish coalition in 1700 with Denmark, Saxony, and Poland, but the ensuing Great Northern War (1700–1721) went badly for the allies at first. The Swedes defeated Denmark, and the new Russian army quickly marched into Poland and Saxony, and then invaded Russia. Peter's rebuilt army finally defeated the Swedes at the battle of Poltava (1709), taking twenty-three thousand Swedish soldiers prisoner and marking the end of Swedish imperial ambitions in the Baltic (Map 17.3). Russia could then begin to compete with the great powers Prussia, Austria, and France.

When the tide turned in the Great Northern War, King Frederick William I of Prussia (r. 1713–1740) joined the Russian side and gained new territories. Prussia had to

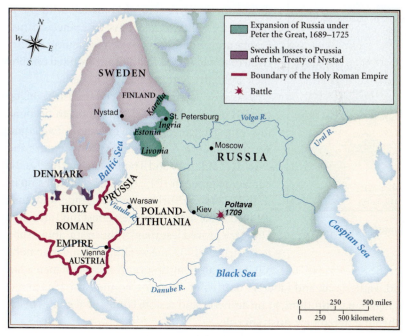

Map 17.3 Russia and Sweden after the Great Northern War, 1721
After the Great Northern War, Russia supplanted Sweden as the major power in the north. Although Russia had a much larger population from which to draw its armies, Sweden made the most of its advantages and gave way only after a great military struggle.

make the most of every military opportunity because it was much smaller in size and population than the other powers. Frederick William doubled the size of the Prussian army; though still smaller than those of his rivals, it was the best-trained and most up-to-date force in Europe. The army so dominated life in Prussia that the country earned the label "a large army with a small state attached." One of the first rulers to wear a military uniform as his everyday dress, Frederick William subordinated the entire domestic administration to the army's needs. He financed the army's growth by subjecting all the provinces to an excise tax on food, drink, and manufactured goods and by increasing rents on crown lands.

Continuing Dynastic Struggles

War broke out again in 1733 when the king of Poland-Lithuania died. France, Spain, and Sardinia joined in the War of the Polish Succession (1733–1735) against Austria and Russia, each side supporting rival claimants to the Polish throne. Prussia chose to sit on the sidelines. Although Peter the Great had been followed by a series of weak rulers, Russian forces were still strong enough to drive the French candidate out of Poland-Lithuania, prompting France to accept the Austrian candidate. In exchange, Austria gave the province of Lorraine to the French candidate, the father-in-law of Louis XV, with the promise that the province would pass to France on his death. France and Britain went back to pursuing their colonial rivalries. Prussia and Russia concentrated on shoring up their influence within Poland-Lithuania.

Because its armies still faced the Turks on its southeastern border, Austria did not want to become mired in a long struggle in Poland-Lithuania. Even though the Austrians had forced the Turks to recognize their rule over all of Hungary and Transylvania in 1699 and had occupied Belgrade in 1717, the Turks did not stop fighting. In the 1730s, the Turks retook Belgrade, and Russia now claimed a role in the struggle against the Turks. Moreover, Hungary proved less than enthusiastic about submitting to Austria. In 1703, the wealthiest Hungarian noble landlord, Ferenc Rákóczi (1676–1735), raised an army of seventy thousand men who fought for "God, Fatherland, and Liberty" until 1711. They forced the Austrians to recognize local Hungarian institutions, grant amnesty, and restore confiscated estates in exchange for confirming hereditary Austrian rule.

Austrian Conquest of Hungary, 1657–1730

When Holy Roman Emperor Charles VI died without a male heir in 1740, another war of succession, the **War of the Austrian Succession** (1740–1748), began. Most European rulers recognized the emperor's chosen heiress, his daughter Maria Theresa, because Charles's Pragmatic Sanction of 1713 had given a woman the right to inherit the

Habsburg crown lands. The new king of Prussia, Frederick II, who had just succeeded his father a few months earlier in 1740, saw his chance to grab territory and immediately invaded the rich Austrian province of Silesia. France joined Prussia in an attempt to further humiliate its traditional enemy Austria, and Great Britain allied with Austria to prevent the French from taking the Austrian Netherlands. The war soon expanded to the overseas colonies of Great Britain and France. French and British colonials in North America fought each other all along their boundaries, enlisting native American auxiliaries. Hostilities broke out in India, too.

Maria Theresa (r. 1740–1780) survived only by conceding Silesia to Prussia in order to split the Prussians off from France. The Peace of Aix-la-Chapelle (1748) recognized Maria Theresa as the heiress to the Austrian lands; her husband, Francis I, became Holy Roman Emperor, thus reasserting the integrity of the Austrian Empire. The peace of 1748 failed to resolve the colonial conflicts between Britain and France, however, and fighting for domination continued unofficially.

The Power of Diplomacy and the Importance of Population

No single power emerged from the wars of the first half of the eighteenth century clearly superior to the others, and the Peace of Utrecht explicitly declared that maintaining a balance of power was crucial to keeping peace in Europe. Diplomacy helped preserve that balance, and to meet the new demands placed on it, the diplomatic service, like the military and financial bureaucracies before it, had to develop regular procedures. The French set a pattern that the other European states soon imitated. By 1685, France had embassies in all the important capitals. Nobles of ancient families served as ambassadors to Rome, Madrid, Vienna, and London, whereas royal officials were chosen for Switzerland, the Dutch Republic, and Venice. The ambassador selected and paid for his own staff, which might be as large as eighty people. The diplomatic system ensured a continuation of the principles of the Peace of Westphalia (1648); in the midst of every crisis and war, the great powers would convene and hammer out a written agreement detailing the requirements for peace.

Adroit diplomacy could smooth the road toward peace, but success in war still depended on sheer numbers — of men and of muskets. Because each state's strength depended largely on the size of its army, the growth and health of the population increasingly entered into government calculations. William Petty's *Political Arithmetick* (1690) offered statistical estimates of human capital — that is, of population and wages — to determine Britain's national wealth. Government officials devoted increased effort to the statistical estimation of total population and rates of births, deaths, and marriages.

Physicians used the new population statistics to explain the environmental causes of disease, another new preoccupation in this period. Petty, trained as a physician himself, devised a quantitative scale that distinguished healthy from unhealthy places largely on the basis of air quality, an early precursor of modern environmental studies. Cities were the unhealthiest places because garbage and excrement (animal and human) accumulated where people lived densely packed together. The Irish writer Jonathan

Swift described what happened in London after a big rainstorm: "Filths of all hues and colors . . . sweepings from butchers' stalls, dung, guts and blood . . . dead cats and turniptops come tumbling down the flood." Reacting to newly collected data on climate, disease, and population, local governments undertook such measures as draining low-lying areas, burying refuse, and cleaning wells.

Not all changes came from direct government intervention. Hospitals, founded originally as charities concerned foremost with the moral worthiness of the poor, gradually evolved into medical institutions that defined patients by their diseases. Physicians began to rely on postmortem dissections in the hospital to gain better knowledge, a practice most patients' families resented. Press reports of body snatching and grave robbing by surgeons and their apprentices outraged the public well into the 1800s.

Despite the change in hospitals, a medical profession with nationwide organizations and licensing had not yet emerged, and no clear line separated trained physicians from quacks. Even patients in a hospital were as likely to catch a deadly disease as to be cured there. Antiseptics were virtually unknown. Because doctors believed that most insanity was caused by disorders in the system of bodily "humors," their prescribed treatments included blood transfusions; ingestion of bitter substances such as coffee, quinine, and soap; immersion in water; various forms of exercise; and burning or cauterizing the body to allow "black vapors" to escape.

Hardly any infectious diseases could be cured, though inoculation against smallpox spread from the Middle East to Europe in the early eighteenth century, thanks largely to the efforts of Lady Mary Wortley Montagu (1689–1762). Wife of the British ambassador to the Ottoman Empire, Montagu witnessed firsthand the Turkish use of inoculation. When a new smallpox epidemic threatened England in 1721, she called on her physician to inoculate her daughter. Inoculation against smallpox spread more widely only after 1796, when the English physician Edward Jenner developed a serum based on cowpox, a milder disease.

Public bathhouses had disappeared from cities in the sixteenth and seventeenth centuries because they seemed to be a source of disorderly behavior and epidemic illness. In the eighteenth century, even private bathing came into disfavor because people feared the effects of contact with water. Bathing was hazardous, physicians insisted, because it opened the body to disease. The upper classes associated cleanliness not with baths but with frequently changed linens, powdered hair, and perfume, which was thought to strengthen the body and refresh the brain by counteracting corrupt and foul air.

REVIEW QUESTION What events and developments led to greater stability and more limited warfare within Europe?

The Birth of the Enlightenment

Economic expansion, the emergence of a new consumer society, and the stabilization of the European state system all generated optimism about the future. The intellectual corollary was the **Enlightenment**, a term used later in the eighteenth century to describe

the movement begun by a loosely knit group of writers and scholars who believed that human beings could apply a critical, reasoning spirit to every problem they encountered in this world. The new secular, scientific, and critical attitude first emerged in the 1690s, scrutinizing everything from the absolutism of Louis XIV to the traditional role of women in society. After 1750, criticism took a more systematic turn as writers provided new theories for the organization of society and politics; but as early as the 1720s, established authorities realized they faced a new set of challenges. Even while slavery expanded in the Atlantic system, Enlightenment writers began to insist on the need for new freedoms in Europe.

Popularization of Science and Challenges to Religion

The writers of the Enlightenment glorified the geniuses of the new science and championed the scientific method as the solution for all social problems. By 1700, mathematics and science had become fashionable topics in high society, and the public flocked to lectures explaining scientific discoveries.

As the prestige of science increased, some developed a skeptical attitude toward attempts to enforce religious conformity. A French Huguenot refugee from Louis XIV's persecutions, Pierre Bayle (1647–1706), launched an internationally influential campaign against religious intolerance from his safe haven in the Dutch Republic. His *News from the Republic of Letters* (first published in 1684) bitterly criticized the policies of Louis XIV and was quickly banned in Paris and condemned in Rome. After attacking Louis XIV's anti-Protestant policies, Bayle took a more general stand in favor of religious toleration. No state in Europe officially

A Budding Scientist
In this engraving, *Astrologia*, by the Dutch artist Jacob Gole (c. 1660–1723), an upper-class woman looks through a telescope to do her own astronomical investigations. Women with intellectual interests were often disparaged by men, and women were not allowed to attend university classes in any European country. Yet because many astronomical observatories were set up in private homes rather than public buildings or universities, wives and daughters of scientists could make observations and even publish their own findings. (Bibliothèque nationale de France.)

offered complete tolerance, though the Dutch Republic came closest with its tacit acceptance of Catholics, dissident Protestant groups, and open Jewish communities. In 1697, Bayle published his *Historical and Critical Dictionary,* which cited all the errors and delusions that he could find in past and present writers of all religions. Even religion must meet the test of reasonableness: "Any particular dogma, whatever it may be, whether it is advanced on the authority of the Scriptures, or whatever else may be its origins, is to be regarded as false if it clashes with the clear and definite conclusions of the natural understanding [reason]."

Bayle's insistence on rational investigation seemed to challenge the authority of faith. Other scholars challenged the authority of the Bible by subjecting it to historical criticism. Discoveries in geology in the early eighteenth century showed that marine fossils dated immensely further back than the biblical flood story suggested. Investigations of miracles, comets, and oracles — like the growing literature against belief in witchcraft — urged the use of reason to combat superstition and prejudice. Defenders of church and state published books warning of the new skepticism's dangers. The spokesman for Louis XIV's absolutism, the bishop Jacques-Bénigne Bossuet, warned that "reason is the guide of their choice, but reason only brings them face to face with vague conjectures and baffling perplexities." Human beings, the traditionalists held, were simply incapable of subjecting everything to reason, especially in the realm of religion.

State authorities found religious skepticism equally unsettling because it threatened to undermine state power, too. The extensive literature of criticism was not limited to France, but much of it was published in French, and the French government took the lead in suppressing the more outspoken works. Forbidden books were then often published in the Dutch Republic, Britain, or Switzerland and smuggled back across the border to a public whose appetite was only whetted by censorship.

The most influential writer of the early Enlightenment was a Frenchman born into the upper middle class, François-Marie Arouet, known by his pen name, **Voltaire** (1694–1778). Voltaire took inspiration from Bayle, once giving him the following tongue-in-cheek description: "He gives facts with such odious fidelity, he exposes the arguments for and against with such dastardly impartiality, he is so intolerably intelligible, that he leads people of only ordinary common sense to judge and even to doubt." Voltaire's tangles with church and state began in the early 1730s, when he published his *Letters Concerning the English Nation* (the English version appeared in 1733), in which he devoted several chapters to scientist Isaac Newton and philosopher John Locke and used the virtues of the British as a way to attack Catholic bigotry and government rigidity in France. He spent two years in exile in Britain when the French state responded to his book with an order for his arrest.

Voltaire also popularized Newton's scientific discoveries in his *Elements of the Philosophy of Newton* (1738). The French state and many European theologians considered Newtonianism threatening because it glorified the human mind and seemed to reduce God to an abstract, external, rationalistic force. So sensational was the success of Voltaire's book on Newton that a hostile Jesuit reported that "all Paris resounds with Newton, all Paris stammers Newton, all Paris studies and learns Newton." Before long, Voltaire was

elected a fellow of the Royal Society in London and in Edinburgh as well as being admitted to twenty other scientific academies. Voltaire's fame continued to grow, reaching truly astounding proportions in the 1750s and 1760s.

Travel Literature and the Challenge to Custom and Tradition

Just as scientific method could be used to question religious and even state authority, a more general skepticism also emerged from the expanding knowledge about the world outside of Europe. During the seventeenth and eighteenth centuries, the number of travel accounts dramatically increased as travel writers used the contrast between their home societies and other cultures to criticize the customs of European society.

Travelers to the Americas found "noble savages" (native peoples) who appeared to live in conditions of great freedom and equality; they were "naturally good" and "happy" without taxes, lawsuits, or much organized government. In China, in contrast, travelers found a people who enjoyed prosperity and an ancient civilization. Christian missionaries made little headway in China, and visitors had to admit that China's religious systems had flourished for four or five thousand years with no input from Europe or from Christianity. The basic lesson of travel literature in the 1700s, then, was that customs varied: justice, freedom, property, good government, religion, and morality all were relative

A Jesuit Missionary in China
Father Ferdinand Verbiest (1623–1688), shown here in a colored German engraving from the late 1600s, was a Flemish (Belgian) Jesuit who worked in China as a missionary and astronomer from 1660 until his death in Beijing in 1688. After winning an astronomy contest with the leading Chinese astronomer in 1669, he became a close friend of the new Chinese emperor, helped correct the Chinese calendar, and directed the astronomical observatory in Beijing. Relations were not always so friendly, however. The Jesuits lost an earlier contest in 1664 and were nearly executed. In the eighteenth century the Catholic church authorities worried that collaboration with the Chinese had become too close, and they insisted that converts refuse to participate in traditional Chinese ceremonies. (Bibliothèque Les Fontaines, Chantilly, France / Archives Charmet / The Bridgeman Art Library International.)

P. Ferdinandus Verbiest, S. J. ein Niderländer/ kommete 1659. da die Tartarische Regierung völligen Besitz in China genommen/ nacher Pequin, wurde aber/ ungeachtet er zuvor herrlich empfangen/ also bald vor Gericht beruffen/ verantwortete sich aber tapffer zu Schutz des Glaubens/ und wird wegen seinen mathematischen Wissenschafften zu grossen Ehren-Würden erhebt. Stirbt umb das Jahr 1670.

to the place. One critic complained that travel encouraged the destruction of religion: "Some complete their demoralization by extensive travel, and lose whatever shreds of religion remained to them. Every day they see a new religion, new customs, new rites."

Travel literature turned explicitly political in Montesquieu's *Persian Letters* (1721). Charles-Louis de Secondat, baron of Montesquieu (1689–1755), the son of an eminent judicial family, was a high-ranking judge in a French court. He published *Persian Letters* anonymously in the Dutch Republic, and the book went into ten printings in just one year—a best seller for the times. Montesquieu tells the fictional story of two Persians, Rica and Usbek, who visit France in the last years of Louis XIV's reign and write home with their impressions. By imagining an outsider's perspective, Montesquieu could satirize French customs and politics without taking them on directly. Montesquieu chose Persians for his travelers because they came from what was widely considered the most despotic of all governments, in which rulers had life-and-death powers over their subjects. In the book, the Persians constantly compare France to Persia, suggesting that the French monarchy might verge on despotism.

Montesquieu's anonymity did not last long, and in the late 1720s, he sold his judgeship and traveled extensively in Europe, staying eighteen months in Britain. In 1748, he published a widely influential work on comparative government, *The Spirit of Laws.* Like the politique Jean Bodin before him (see Chapter 15), Montesquieu examined the various types of government, but unlike Bodin he did not favor absolute power in a monarchy. His time in Britain made him much more favorable to constitutional forms of government. The Vatican soon listed both *Persian Letters* and *The Spirit of Laws* on its Index (its list of forbidden books).

Raising the Woman Question

Many of the letters exchanged in *Persian Letters* focused on women because Montesquieu considered the position of women a sure indicator of the nature of government and morality. Although Montesquieu was not a feminist, his depiction of Roxana, the favorite wife in Usbek's harem, struck a chord with many women. Roxana revolts against the authority of Usbek's eunuchs and writes a final letter to her husband announcing her impending suicide: "I may have lived in servitude, but I have always been free, I have amended your laws according to the laws of nature, and my mind has always remained independent." Women writers used the same language of tyranny and freedom to argue for concrete changes in their status. Feminist ideas were not entirely new, but they were presented systematically for the first time during the Enlightenment and represented a fundamental challenge to the ways of traditional societies.

The most systematic and successful of these women writers was the English author Mary Astell (1666–1731). In 1694, she published *A Serious Proposal to the Ladies,* in which she advocated founding a private women's college to remedy women's lack of education. Addressing women, she asked, "How can you be content to be in the World like Tulips in a Garden, to make a fine *shew* [show] and be good for nothing?" In later works such as *Reflections upon Marriage* (1706), Astell criticized the relationship between the

sexes within marriage: "If absolute sovereignty be not necessary in a state, how comes it to be so in a family? . . . *If all men are born free,* how is it that all women are born slaves?"

Most male writers held that women were less capable of reasoning than men and therefore did not need systematic education. Such opinions often rested on biological suppositions. The long-dominant Aristotelian view of reproduction held that only the male seed carried spirit and individuality. At the beginning of the eighteenth century, however, scientists began to undermine this belief. Physicians and surgeons began to champion the doctrine of *ovism* — that the female egg was essential in making new humans. During the decades that followed, male Enlightenment writers would continue to debate women's nature and appropriate social roles.

> **REVIEW QUESTION** What were the major issues in the early decades of the Enlightenment?

Conclusion

Expansion of colonies overseas and economic development at home created greater wealth, longer life spans, and higher expectations for Europeans in the first half of the eighteenth century. In these better times for many, a spirit of optimism prevailed. People could now spend money on newspapers, novels, travel literature, and music as well as on coffee, tea, and cotton cloth. Not everyone shared equally in the benefits, however: slaves toiled in misery for their masters in the Americas, eastern European serfs found themselves ever more closely bound to their noble lords, and rural folk almost everywhere tasted few fruits of consumer society.

Politics changed, too, as experts urged government intervention to improve public health, and states found it in their interest to settle many international disputes by diplomacy, which itself became more regular and routine. The consolidation of the European state system allowed a tide of criticism and new thinking about society to swell in Great Britain and France and begin to spill throughout Europe. Ultimately, the combination of the Atlantic system and the Enlightenment would give rise to a series of Atlantic revolutions.

Review Questions

1. How was consumerism related to slavery in the early eighteenth century?
2. How were new social trends reflected in cultural life in the early 1700s?
3. What events and developments led to greater stability and more limited warfare within Europe?
4. What were the major issues in the early decades of the Enlightenment?

Making Connections

1. How did the rise of slavery and the plantation system change European politics and society?
2. Why was the Enlightenment born just at the moment that the Atlantic system took shape?
3. What were the major differences between the wars of the first half of the eighteenth century and those of the seventeenth century? (Refer to Chapters 15 and 16.)
4. During the first half of the eighteenth century, what were the major issues affecting peasants in France and serfs in Poland and Russia?

Suggested References

The slave trade Web site listed here offers the most up-to-date information about the workings of the Atlantic system, and another allows the viewer to trace the growth of certain cities over time. The definitive study of the early Enlightenment is the book by Hazard, but many others have contributed biographies of individual figures or studies of women writers.

Black, Jeremy. *European Warfare in a Global Context, 1660–1815.* 2007.

Blackburn, Robin. *The Making of New World Slavery: From the Baroque to the Modern, 1492–1800.* 1997.

Dickson, Peter, George Muir, and Christopher Storrs, eds. *The Fiscal-Military State in Eighteenth-Century Europe.* 2009.

Englund, Peter. *The Battle That Shook Europe: Poltava and the Birth of the Russian Empire.* 2003.

Handel's Messiah: The New Interactive Edition (CD-ROM). 1997.

Hazard, Paul. *The European Mind: The Critical Years, 1680–1715.* 1990.

*Hill, Bridget. *The First English Feminist: Reflections upon Marriage and Other Writings by Mary Astell.* 1986.

Hunt, Margaret R. *Women in Eighteenth-Century Europe.* 2010.

Hypercities project (includes Berlin): http://hypercities.ats.ucla.edu

*Jacob, Margaret C. *The Enlightenment: A Brief History with Selected Readings.* 2000.

Norton, Marcy. *Sacred Gifts, Profane Pleasures: A History of Tobacco and Chocolate in the Atlantic World.* 2010.

Pearson, Roger. *Voltaire Almighty: A Life in Pursuit of Freedom.* 2005.

Sarti, Raffaella, *Europe at Home: Family and Material Culture, 1500–1800.* Trans. Allan Cameron. 2004.

Slave trade: http://www.slavevoyages.org/tast/index.faces

Primary source.

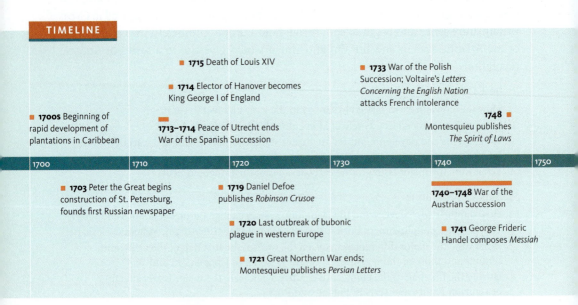

TIMELINE

- **1715** Death of Louis XIV

- **1714** Elector of Hanover becomes King George I of England

- **1733** War of the Polish Succession; Voltaire's *Letters Concerning the English Nation* attacks French intolerance

- **1700s** Beginning of rapid development of plantations in Caribbean

- **1713–1714** Peace of Utrecht ends War of the Spanish Succession

- **1748** Montesquieu publishes *The Spirit of Laws*

| 1700 | 1710 | 1720 | 1730 | 1740 | 1750 |

- **1703** Peter the Great begins construction of St. Petersburg, founds first Russian newspaper

- **1719** Daniel Defoe publishes *Robinson Crusoe*

- **1740–1748** War of the Austrian Succession

- **1720** Last outbreak of bubonic plague in western Europe

- **1741** George Frideric Handel composes *Messiah*

- **1721** Great Northern War ends; Montesquieu publishes *Persian Letters*

Mapping the West Europe in 1750

By 1750, Europe had achieved a kind of diplomatic equilibrium in which no one power predominated despite repeated wars over dynastic succession. Spain, the Dutch Republic, Poland-Lithuania, and Sweden had all declined in power and influence while Great Britain, Russia, and Prussia gained prominence. France's ambitions to dominate had been thwarted, but its combination of a big army and rich overseas possessions made it a major player for a long time to come. In the War of the Austrian Succession, Austria lost its rich province of Silesia to Prussia.

- For practice quizzes and other study tools, visit the **Online Study Guide** at bedfordstmartins.com/huntconcise.

- For primary-source material from this period, see *Sources of the Making of the West*, Fourth Edition.

- For Web sites, images, and documents related to topics in this chapter, visit *Make History* at bedfordstmartins.com/huntconcise.

The Promise of Enlightenment

I N THE SUMMER OF 1766, Empress Catherine II of Russia (known as Catherine the Great) wrote to Voltaire, one of the leaders of the Enlightenment, praising him for entering "into combat against the enemies of mankind" and for fighting superstition, fanaticism, ignorance, and "evil judges." Catherine corresponded regularly with Voltaire, a writer who, at home in France, found himself in constant conflict with authorities of church and state. Her admiring letter shows how influential Enlightenment ideals had become by the middle of the eighteenth century. Even an absolutist ruler such as Catherine endorsed many aspects of the Enlightenment call for reform.

Enlightenment writers such as Voltaire used every means at their disposal — including personal interaction with rulers — to argue for reform. Everything had to be examined in the cold light of reason, and anything that did not promote the improvement of humanity was to be jettisoned. As a result, Enlightenment writers supported religious toleration, attacked the legal use of torture to extract confessions, and criticized censorship by state or church. The book trade and new places for urban socializing, such as coffeehouses and learned societies, spread these ideas within a new elite of middle- and upper-class men and women. In contrast, the lower classes had little contact with Enlightenment ideas. Their lives were shaped more profoundly by an increasing population, rising food prices, and ongoing wars among the great powers.

Catherine the Great
In this portrait (c. 1762) by the Danish painter Vigilius Eriksen, the Russian empress Catherine the Great is shown on horseback, much like any male ruler of the time. Born Sophia Augusta Frederika of Anhalt-Zerbst in 1729, Catherine was the daughter of a minor German prince. When she married the future tsar Peter III in 1745, she promptly learned Russian and adopted Russian Orthodoxy. Peter, physically and mentally frail, proved no match for her; in 1762 she staged a coup against him and took his place when he was killed. (Erich Lessing / Art Resource, NY.)

Rulers pursued Enlightenment reforms that they believed might enhance state power, but they feared changes that might unleash popular discontent. All reform-minded rulers

faced potential challenges to their authority. They were right to be concerned, for Enlightenment ideas paved the way for something much more radical and unexpected.

The American Declaration of Independence in 1776 showed how Enlightenment ideals could be translated into democratic political practice. After 1789, democracy would come to Europe as well.

CHAPTER FOCUS How did the Enlightenment influence Western politics, culture, and society?

The Enlightenment at Its Height

The Enlightenment emerged as an intellectual movement before 1750 but reached its peak in the second half of the eighteenth century. The writers of the Enlightenment called themselves **philosophes**; the word is French for "philosophers," but that definition is somewhat misleading. Whereas philosophers concern themselves with abstract theories, the philosophes were public intellectuals dedicated to solving the real problems of the world. They wrote on subjects ranging from current affairs to art criticism, and they wrote in every conceivable format. Between 1750 and 1789, the Enlightenment acquired its name and, despite heated conflicts between the philosophes and state and religious authorities, gained support in the highest reaches of government.

Men and Women of the Republic of Letters

Although *philosophe* is a French word, the Enlightenment was distinctly cosmopolitan; philosophes could be found from Philadelphia to St. Petersburg. The philosophes considered themselves part of a grand "republic of letters" that transcended national political boundaries. They were not republicans in the usual sense, that is, people who supported representative government and opposed monarchy. What united them were the ideals of reason, reform, and freedom. In 1784, the German philosopher Immanuel Kant summed up the program of the Enlightenment in two Latin words: *sapere aude* ("dare to know") — have the courage to think for yourself.

The philosophes used reason to attack superstition, bigotry, and religious fanaticism, which they considered the chief obstacles to free thought and social reform. Voltaire took religious fanaticism as his chief target: "Once fanaticism has corrupted a mind, the malady is almost incurable. . . . The only remedy for this epidemic malady is the philosophical spirit." Enlightenment writers did not necessarily oppose organized religion, but they strenuously objected to religious intolerance. They believed that the systematic application of reason could do what religious belief could not: improve the human condition by pointing to needed reforms. Reason meant critical, informed, scientific thinking about social issues and problems.

Many Enlightenment writers collaborated on the multivolume *Encyclopedia* (published 1751–1772), which aimed to gather together knowledge about science, religion, industry, and society. The ancestor of all modern encyclopedias from the *Encyclopædia Britannica* to Wikipedia online, the Enlightenment version differed by using knowledge to criticize defects in society. The chief editor of the *Encyclopedia,* Denis Diderot (1713–

Science in Action

In September 1783, the Montgolfier brothers demonstrated their newly invented hot air balloon at Versailles with the royal family in attendance. The flight reached an altitude of 1,500 feet, covered two miles, and lasted eight minutes. The passengers — a sheep, a duck, and a rooster — landed safely. Hydrogen balloons were developed at the same time and quickly replaced the hot air versions because they could fly higher and longer. Thousands of people flocked to see the launches. Colored etchings such as the one shown here helped increase public interest. (Private Collection / The Bridgeman Art Library International.)

1784), explained the goal: "All things must be examined, debated, investigated without exception and without regard for anyone's feelings."

The philosophes believed that the spread of knowledge would encourage reform in every aspect of life, from the grain trade to the penal system. Chief among their desired reforms was intellectual freedom — the freedom to use one's own reason to conduct studies and to publish the results. The philosophes wanted freedom of the press and freedom of religion, which they considered "natural rights" guaranteed by "natural law." In their view, progress depended on these freedoms.

Most philosophes, like Voltaire, came from the upper classes, yet the Swiss philosophe Jean-Jacques Rousseau had been born to a modest watchmaker in Geneva, and Diderot was the son of a cutlery maker. Rarely were women philosophes; one, however, was the French noblewoman Émilie du Châtelet (1706–1749), who wrote extensively about the mathematics and physics of Gottfried Wilhelm Leibniz and Isaac Newton. (Châtelet's lover Voltaire learned much of his science from her.)

Few of the leading writers held university positions. Enlightenment ideas developed instead through printed books and pamphlets, through hand-copied letters that were circulated and sometimes published, and through informal readings of manuscripts. Salons — informal gatherings, usually sponsored by middle-class or aristocratic women — gave intellectual life an anchor outside the royal court and the church-controlled universities (see page 522). In the Parisian salons of the eighteenth century, the philosophes could discuss ideas they might hesitate to put into print. Best known was the salon of Madame Marie-Thérèse Geoffrin (1699–1777), a wealthy middle-class widow. She

Madame Geoffrin's Salon in 1755
This 1812 painting by Anicet Charles Lemonnier claims to depict the best-known Parisian salon of the 1750s. Lemonnier was only twelve years old in 1755 and so could not have based his rendition on first-hand knowledge. Madame Geoffrin is the figure in blue on the right facing the viewer. The bust is of Voltaire. Rousseau is the fifth person to the left of the bust (facing right), and behind him (facing left) is Raynal. (Réunion des Musées Nationaux / Art Resource, NY.)

corresponded extensively with influential people across Europe, including Catherine the Great. Women's salons helped galvanize intellectual life and reform movements all over Europe. Wealthy Jewish women created nine of the fourteen salons in Berlin at the end of the eighteenth century, and Princess Zofia Czartoryska gathered around her in Warsaw the reform leaders of Poland-Lithuania.

Conflicts with Church and State

Madame Geoffrin did not approve of discussions that attacked the Catholic church, but elsewhere voices against organized religion could be heard. Criticisms of religion required daring because the church, whatever its denomination, wielded enormous power in society, and most influential people considered religion an essential foundation of good society and government. Defying such opinion, the Scottish philosopher David Hume (1711–1776) boldly argued in *The Natural History of Religion* (1755) that belief in God rested on superstition and fear rather than on reason.

At the time, most Europeans believed in God. After Newton, however, and despite Newton's own deep religiosity, people could conceive of the universe as an eternally existing, self-perpetuating machine, in which God's intervention was unnecessary. In short, such people could become either atheists (people who do not believe in God) or **deists** (people who believe in God but give him no active role in earthly affairs). For the first time, writers claimed the label *atheist* and disputed the common view that atheism led inevitably to immorality.

Deists continued to believe in a benevolent, all-knowing God who had designed the universe and set it in motion. But they usually rejected the idea that God directly

intercedes in the functioning of the universe, and they often criticized the churches for their dogmatic intolerance of dissenters. Voltaire was a deist, and in his influential *Philosophical Dictionary* (1764) he attacked most of the claims of organized Christianity, both Catholic and Protestant. Christianity, he argued, had been the prime source of fanaticism and brutality among humans. Throughout his life, Voltaire's motto was *Écrasez l'infâme* — "Crush the infamous thing" (the "thing" being bigotry and intolerance). French authorities publicly burned his *Philosophical Dictionary*.

Criticism of religious intolerance involved more than simply attacking the church. Critics also had to confront the states to which churches were closely tied. In 1762, a judicial case in Toulouse provoked an outcry throughout France that Voltaire soon joined. When the son of a local Calvinist was found hanged (he had probably committed suicide), magistrates accused the father, Jean Calas, of murdering him to prevent his conversion to Catholicism. (Since Louis XIV's revocation of the Edict of Nantes in 1685, it had been illegal to practice Calvinism publicly in France.) The all-Catholic parlement of Toulouse tried to extract the names of accomplices through torture — using a rope to pull up Calas's arm while weighing down his feet and then pouring water down his throat — but Calas refused to confess. The torturers then executed him by breaking every bone in his body with an iron rod. Voltaire launched a successful crusade to rehabilitate Calas's good name and to restore the family's properties, which had been confiscated after his death. Voltaire's efforts eventually helped bring about the extension of civil rights to French Protestants and encouraged campaigns to abolish the judicial use of torture.

Critics also assailed state and church support for European colonization and slavery. One of the most popular books of the time was the *Philosophical and Political History of European Colonies and Commerce in the Two Indies,* published in 1770 by the abbé Guillaume Raynal (1713–1796), a French Catholic clergyman. Raynal and his collaborators described in excruciating detail the destruction of native populations by Europeans and denounced the slave trade. Despite the criticism, the slave trade continued. So did European exploration. British explorer James Cook (1728–1779) charted the coasts of New Zealand and Australia, discovered New Caledonia, and visited the ice fields of Antarctica.

The Enlightenment belief in natural rights helped fuel the antislavery movement, which began to organize political campaigns against slavery in Britain, France, and the new United States in the 1780s. Advocates of the abolition of slavery encouraged freed slaves to write the story of their enslavement. One such freed slave, Olaudah Equiano, wrote of his kidnapping and enslavement in Africa and his long effort to free himself. *The Interesting Narrative of the Life of Olaudah Equiano,* published in 1788, became an international best seller. Armed with such firsthand accounts of slavery, **abolitionists** began to petition their governments for the abolition of the slave trade and then of slavery itself.

Enlightenment critics of church and state usually advocated reform, not revolution. For example, though he resided near the French-Swiss border in case he had to flee, Voltaire made a fortune in financial speculations and ended up being celebrated in his last years as a national hero even by many former foes. Other philosophes also believed

that published criticism, rather than violent action, would bring about necessary reforms. The philosophes generally regarded the lower classes — "the people" — as ignorant, violent, and prone to superstition; as a result, they pinned their hopes on educated elites and enlightened rulers.

The Individual and Society

The controversy created by the conflicts between the philosophes and the various churches and states of Europe drew attention away from a subtle but profound transformation in worldviews. In previous centuries, questions of theological doctrine and church organization had been the main focus of intellectual and even political interest. The Enlightenment writers shifted attention away from religious questions and toward the secular (nonreligious) study of society and the individual's role in it. Religion did not drop out of sight, but the philosophes tended to make religion a private affair of individual conscience, even while rulers and churches still considered religion very much a public concern.

The Enlightenment interest in secular society produced two major results: it advanced the secularization of European political life that had begun after the French Wars of Religion of the sixteenth and seventeenth centuries, and it laid the foundations for the social sciences of the modern era. Not surprisingly, then, many historians and philosophers consider the Enlightenment to be the origin of modernity, which they define as the belief that human reason, rather than theological doctrine, should set the patterns of social and political life. This belief in reason as the sole foundation for secular authority has often been contested, but it has also proved to be a powerful force for change.

Although most of the philosophes believed that humans could use reason to understand and even remake society and politics, they disagreed about what reason revealed. Among the many different approaches were two that proved enduringly influential, those of the Scottish philosopher Adam Smith and the Swiss writer Jean-Jacques Rousseau. Smith provided a theory of modern capitalist society and devoted much of his energy to defending free markets as the best way to make the most of individual efforts. The modern discipline of economics took shape around the questions raised by Smith. Rousseau, by contrast, emphasized the needs of the community over those of the individual. His work, which led both toward democracy and toward communism, continues to inspire heated debate in political science and sociology.

Adam Smith (1723–1790) optimistically believed that individual interests naturally harmonized with those of the whole society. To explain how this natural harmonization worked, he published *An Inquiry into the Nature and Causes of the Wealth of Nations* in 1776. In this work, commonly known as *The Wealth of Nations,* Smith insisted that individual self-interest, even greed, was quite compatible with society's best interest: the laws of supply and demand served as an "invisible hand" ensuring that individual interests would be synchronized with those of the whole society. Market forces naturally brought individual and social interests in line.

Smith rejected the prevailing mercantilist views that the general welfare would be served by accumulating national wealth through agriculture or the hoarding of gold and silver. Instead, he argued that the division of labor in manufacturing increased productivity and generated more wealth for society and well-being for the individual. Using the example of the ordinary pin, Smith showed that when the manufacturing process was broken down into separate operations — one man to draw out the wire, another to straighten it, a third to cut it, a fourth to point it, and so on — workers who could make only one pin a day on their own could make thousands by pooling their labor.

To maximize the effects of market forces and the division of labor, Smith endorsed a concept called **laissez-faire** ("to leave alone"), in which the government neither controls nor intervenes in the economy. He insisted that governments eliminate all restrictions on the sale of land, remove restraints on the grain trade, and abandon duties on imports. Free international trade, he argued, would stimulate production everywhere and thus ensure the growth of national wealth. Governments, he insisted, should restrict themselves to providing "security," that is, national defense, internal order, and public works.

Much more pessimistic about the relation between individual self-interest and the good of society was **Jean-Jacques Rousseau** (1712–1778). In Rousseau's view, society itself threatened natural rights or freedoms: "Man is born free, and everywhere he is in chains." Rousseau first gained fame by writing a prize-winning essay in 1749 in which he argued that the revival of science and the arts had corrupted social morals, not improved them. This startling conclusion seemed to oppose some of the Enlightenment's most cherished beliefs. Rather than improving society, he claimed, science and art raised artificial barriers between people and their natural state. Rousseau's works extolled the simplicity of rural life over urban society.

Whereas earlier Rousseau had argued that society corrupted the individual by taking him out of nature, in *The Social Contract* (1762) he aimed to show that the right kind of political order could make people truly moral and free. Individual moral freedom could be achieved only by learning to subject one's individual interests to "the general will," that is, the good of the community. Individuals did this by entering into a social contract not with their rulers, but with one another. If everyone followed the general will, then all would be equally free and equally moral because they lived under a law to which they had all consented.

Like Thomas Hobbes and John Locke before him, Rousseau derived his social contract from human nature, not from history, tradition, or the Bible. He went much further than Hobbes or Locke, however, when he implied that people would be most free and moral under a republican form of government with direct democracy. Neither Hobbes nor Locke favored republics. Moreover, Rousseau roundly condemned slavery. Authorities in both Geneva and Paris banned *The Social Contract* for undermining political authority. Rousseau's works would become a kind of political bible for the French revolutionaries of 1789, and his attacks on private property inspired the communists of the nineteenth century such as Karl Marx. Rousseau's rather mystical concept of the general will remains controversial because he insisted that the individual could be "forced

to be free." Rousseau's version of democracy did not preserve the individual freedoms so important to Adam Smith.

Spreading the Enlightenment

The Enlightenment flourished in places where an educated middle class provided an eager audience for ideas of constitutionalism and reform. It therefore found its epicenter in the triangle formed by London, Amsterdam, and Paris and diffused outward to eastern and southern Europe and North America. Where constitutionalism and guarantees of individual freedoms were most advanced, as in Great Britain and the Dutch Republic, the movement had less of an edge because there was, in a sense, less need for it. As a result, Scottish and English writers concentrated on economics, philosophy, and history rather than on politics or social relations. The English historian Edward Gibbon, for example, portrayed Christianity in a negative light in his immensely influential work *The History of the Decline and Fall of the Roman Empire* (1776–1788), but when he served as a member of Parliament he never even gave a speech. At the other extreme, in places with small middle classes, such as Spain and Russia, Enlightenment ideas did not get much traction because governments successfully suppressed writings they did not like. France was the Enlightenment hot spot because the French monarchy alternated between encouraging ideas for reform and harshly censuring criticisms it found too threatening.

French writers published the most daring critiques of church and state, and they often suffered harassment and persecution as a result. Voltaire, Diderot, and Rousseau all faced arrest, exile, or even imprisonment. The Catholic church and royal authorities routinely forbade the publication of their books, and the police arrested booksellers who ignored the warnings. Yet the French monarchy was far from the most autocratic in Europe, and Voltaire, Diderot, and Rousseau all ended their lives as cultural heroes. France seems to have been curiously caught in the middle during the Enlightenment: with fewer constitutional guarantees of individual freedom than Great Britain, it still enjoyed much higher levels of prosperity and cultural development than most other European countries. In short, French elites had reason to complain, the means to make their complaints known, and a government torn between the desire to censor dissident ideas and the desire to appear open to modernity and progress.

By the 1760s, the French government regularly ignored the publication of many works once thought offensive or subversive. In addition, a growing flood of works printed abroad poured into France and circulated underground. Private companies in Dutch and Swiss cities made fortunes smuggling illegal books into France over mountain passes and back roads. Foreign printers provided secret catalogs of their offerings and sold their products through booksellers who were willing to market forbidden books for a high price — among them not only philosophical treatises of the Enlightenment but also pornographic books and pamphlets (some by Diderot) lampooning the Catholic clergy and leading members of the royal court. In the 1770s and 1780s, lurid descrip-

tions of sexual promiscuity at the French court helped undermine the popularity of the throne.

Whereas the French philosophes often took a violently anticlerical and combative tone, their German counterparts avoided direct political confrontations with authorities. Gotthold Lessing (1729–1781) complained in 1769 that Prussia was still "the most slavish society in Europe" in its lack of freedom to criticize government policies. Lessing promoted religious toleration for the Jews and spiritual emancipation of Germans from foreign, especially French, models of culture,

Major Works of the Enlightenment	
1751	Beginning of publication of the French *Encyclopedia*
1755	David Hume, *The Natural History of Religion*
1762	Jean-Jacques Rousseau, *The Social Contract*
1764	Voltaire, *Philosophical Dictionary*
1770	Abbé Guillaume Raynal, *Philosophical and Political History of European Colonies and Commerce in the Two Indies*
1776	Adam Smith, *An Inquiry into the Nature and Causes of the Wealth of Nations*
1781	Immanuel Kant, *The Critique of Pure Reason*

which still dominated. Lessing also introduced the German Jewish writer Moses Mendelssohn (1729–1786) into Berlin salon society. Mendelssohn labored to build bridges between German and Jewish culture by arguing that Judaism was a rational and undogmatic religion. He believed that persecution and discrimination against the Jews would end as reason triumphed.

Reason was also the chief focus of the most influential German thinker of the Enlightenment, Immanuel Kant (1724–1804). A university professor who lectured on everything from economics to astronomy, Kant wrote one of the most important works in the history of Western philosophy, *The Critique of Pure Reason* (1781). Kant admired Smith and especially Rousseau, whose portrait he displayed proudly in his study. Kant established the doctrine of idealism, the belief that true understanding can come only from examining the ways in which ideas are formed in the mind. Ideas are shaped, Kant argued, not just by sensory information (a position central to empiricism, a philosophy based on John Locke's writings) but also by the operation on that information of mental categories such as space and time. In Kant's philosophy, these "categories of understanding" were neither sensory nor supernatural; they were entirely ideal and abstract and located in the human mind.

The Limits of Reason: Roots of Romanticism and Religious Revival

In reaction to what some saw as the Enlightenment's excessive reliance on the authority of human reason, a new artistic movement called **romanticism** took root. Although it would not fully flower until the early nineteenth century, romanticism traced its emphasis on individual genius, deep emotion, and the joys of nature to thinkers like Rousseau who had scolded the philosophes for ignoring those aspects of life that escaped and even conflicted with the power of reason.

A novel by the young German writer Johann Wolfgang von Goethe (1749–1832) captured the early romantic spirit with its glorification of emotion. *The Sorrows of Young*

George Whitefield
This colored etching depicts one of the most prominent preachers of the Great Awakening, the English Methodist George Whitefield, preaching in the British North American colonies. Whitefield visited the colonies seven times, sometimes for long periods, and drew tens of thousands of people to his dramatic and emotional open-air sermons, which moved many listeners to tears of repentance. Whitefield was a celebrity in his time and is considered by many to be the founder of the Evangelical movement. (The Granger Collection, NYC — All rights reserved.)

Werther (1774) told of a young man who loves nature and rural life and is unhappy in love. When the woman he loves marries someone else, he falls into deep melancholy and eventually kills himself. Reason cannot save him. The book spurred a veritable Werther craze: in addition to Werther costumes, engravings, embroidery, and medallions, there was even a perfume called Eau de Werther. The young Napoleon Bonaparte, who was to build an empire for France, claimed to have read Goethe's novel seven times.

Religious revivals sought to underline the limits of reason by emphasizing a direct emotional connection with God. Much of the Protestant world experienced an "awakening" in the 1740s. In the German states, Pietist groups founded new communities; and in the British North American colonies, revivalist Protestant preachers drew thousands of fervent believers in a movement called the Great Awakening. In North America, bitter conflicts between revivalists and their opponents in the established churches prompted the leaders on both sides to set up new colleges to support their beliefs. These included Princeton, Columbia, Brown, and Dartmouth, all founded between 1746 and 1769 by either revivalists or antirevivalists.

Revivalism also stirred eastern European Jews at about the same time. Israel ben Eliezer (1698–1760) laid the foundation for Hasidism in the 1740s and 1750s. He traveled the Polish countryside offering miraculous cures and became known as the Ba'al

Shem Tov ("Master of the Good Name") because he used divine names to effect healing and bring believers into closer personal contact with God. He emphasized mystical contemplation of the divine, rather than study of Jewish law, and his followers, the Hasidim (Hebrew for "most pious" Jews), often expressed their devotion through music, dance, and fervent prayer. Their practices soon spread all over Poland-Lithuania.

Most of the waves of Protestant revivalism ebbed after the 1750s, but in Great Britain one movement continued to grow through the end of the century. John Wesley (1703–1791), the Oxford-educated son of a cleric in the Church of England, founded **Methodism**, a term evoked by Wesley's insistence on strict self-discipline and a methodical approach to religious study and observance. In 1738, Wesley began preaching his new brand of Protestantism, which emphasized an intense personal experience of salvation and a life of thrift, abstinence, and hard work. Traveling all over the British Isles, Wesley preached forty thousand sermons in fifty years, an average of fifteen a week. The Church of England refused to let him preach in the churches. In response, Wesley began to ordain his own clergy. While considered radical in religious views, the Methodist leadership remained politically conservative during Wesley's lifetime; Wesley himself wrote many pamphlets urging order, loyalty, and submission to higher authorities.

> **REVIEW QUESTION** What were the major differences between the Enlightenment in France, Great Britain, and the German states?

Society and Culture in an Age of Enlightenment

Religious revivals and the first stirrings of romanticism show that not all intellectual currents of the eighteenth century were flowing in the same channel. Some social and cultural developments manifested the influence of Enlightenment ideas, but others did not. The traditional leaders of European societies — the nobles — responded to Enlightenment ideals in contradictory fashion: many simply reasserted their privileges and resisted the influence of the Enlightenment, but an important minority embraced change and actively participated in reform efforts. The expanding middle classes saw in the Enlightenment a chance to make their claim for joining society's governing elite. They bought Enlightenment books, joined Masonic lodges, and patronized new styles in art, music, and literature. The lower classes were more affected by economic growth than by ideas. Trade boomed and the population grew, but people did not benefit equally. The ranks of the poor swelled, too, and with greater mobility, births to unmarried mothers also increased.

The Nobility's Reassertion of Privilege

Nobles made up about 3 percent of the European population, but their numbers and ways of life varied greatly from country to country. At least 10 percent of the population in Poland and 7 to 8 percent in Spain was noble, in contrast to only 2 percent in

Russia and between 1 and 2 percent in the rest of western Europe. Many Polish and Span-ish nobles lived in poverty, but the wealthiest European nobles luxuriated in almost unimaginable opulence. Many of the English peers, for example, owned more than ten thousand acres of land; invested widely in government bonds and trading companies; kept several country residences with scores of servants as well as houses in London; and occasionally even had their own private orchestras to complement libraries of expensive books, greenhouses for exotic plants, kennels of pedigreed dogs, and collections of an-tiques, firearms, and scientific instruments.

To support an increasingly expensive lifestyle in a period of inflation, European aris-tocrats sought to cash in on their remaining legal rights, called seigneurial dues (from the French *seigneur*, "lord"). Peasants felt the squeeze as a result. French landlords re-quired their peasants to pay dues to grind grain at the lord's mill, bake bread in his oven, press grapes at his winepress, or even pass on their own land as inheritance. In addi-tion, peasants had to work without compensation for a specified number of days every year on the public roads. They also paid taxes to the government on salt, an essential preservative, and on the value of their land; customs duties if they sold produce or wine in town; and the tithe on their grain (one-tenth of the crop) to the church.

In Britain, the landed gentry could not claim these same onerous dues from their tenants, but they tenaciously defended their exclusive right to hunt game. The game laws kept the poor from eating meat and helped protect the social status of the rich. The gen-try enforced the game laws themselves by hiring gamekeepers who hunted down poach-ers and even set traps for them in the forests. According to the law, anyone who poached deer or rabbits while armed or disguised could be sentenced to death. In most other countries, too, hunting was the special right of the nobility, a cause of deep popular resentment.

Even though Enlightenment writers sharply criticized nobles' insistence on special privileges, most aristocrats maintained their marks of distinction. The male court no-bility continued to sport swords, plumed hats, makeup, and elaborate wigs, while middle-class men wore simpler and more somber clothing. Aristocrats had their own seats in church and their own quarters in the universities. Frederick II of Prussia (r. 1740–1786), who came to be known as Frederick the Great, made sure that nobles dominated both the army officer corps and the civil bureaucracy. Russia's Catherine the Great (r. 1762–1796) granted the nobility vast tracts of land, the exclusive right to own serfs, and ex-emption from personal taxes and corporal punishment. Her Charter of the Nobility of 1785 codified these privileges in exchange for the nobles' political subservience to the state. In Austria, Spain, the Italian states, Poland-Lithuania, and Russia, most nobles con-sequently cared little about Enlightenment ideas; they did not read the books of the phi-losophes and feared reforms that might challenge their dominance of rural society.

In France, Britain, and the western German states, however, the nobility proved more open to the new ideas. Half of Rousseau's correspondents, for example, were nobles. The nobles of western Europe sometimes married into middle-class families and formed with them a new mixed elite, united by common interests in reform and new cultural tastes.

The Middle Class and the Making of a New Elite

The Enlightenment offered middle-class people an intellectual and cultural route to social improvement. The term *middle class* referred to the middle position on the social ladder; middle-class families did not have legal titles like the nobility above them, but neither did they work with their hands like the peasants, artisans, or laborers below them. Most middle-class people lived in towns or cities and earned their living in the professions — as doctors, lawyers, or lower-level officials — or through investment in land, trade, or manufacturing. In the eighteenth century, the ranks of the middle class — also known as the bourgeoisie (from *bourgeois,* French for "city dweller") — grew steadily in western Europe as a result of economic expansion. In France, for example, the overall population grew by about one-third in the 1700s, but the bourgeoisie nearly tripled in size. (See "Taking Measure," below.)

Nobles and middle-class professionals mingled in Enlightenment salons and joined the new Masonic lodges and local learned societies. The Masonic lodges began as social clubs organized around elaborate secret rituals of stonemasons' guilds. They called their members **Freemasons** because that was the term given to apprentice masons when they were deemed "free" to practice as masters of their guild. Although the Freemasons were not explicitly political in aim, their members wrote constitutions for their lodges and elected their own officers, thus promoting a direct experience of constitutional government.

Freemasonry arose in Great Britain and spread eastward: the first French and Italian lodges opened in 1726; Prussia's Frederick the Great founded a lodge in 1740; and after 1750, Freemasonry spread in Poland, Russia, and British North America. In France, women set up their own Masonic lodges. Despite the papacy's condemnation

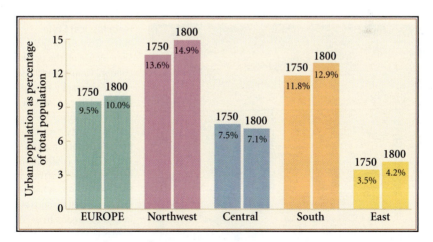

Taking Measure European Urbanization, 1750–1800

The bar graph shows that northwestern Europe was the most urbanized region, followed by the Mediterranean countries. Central and eastern Europe were much less urbanized, which meant that they had much smaller middle classes. (Adapted from Andrew Lees and Lynn Hollen Lees, *Cities and the Making of Modern Europe, 1750–1914* [Cambridge: Cambridge University Press], 2008.)

of Freemasonry in 1738 as subversive of religious and civil authority, lodges continued to multiply throughout the eighteenth century. After 1789 and the outbreak of the French Revolution, conservatives would blame the lodges for every kind of political upheaval, but in the 1700s many high-ranking nobles became active members and saw no conflict with their privileged status.

Nobles and middle-class professionals also met in local learned societies, whose numbers greatly increased in this period. The societies, sometimes called academies, brought the Enlightenment down from the realm of books and ideas to the level of concrete reforms. They sponsored essay contests, such as the one won by Rousseau in 1749 and the one set by the society in Metz in 1785 on the question "Are there means for making the Jews happier and more useful in France?" The Metz society approved essays that argued for granting civil rights to Jews.

Shared tastes in travel, architecture, the arts, and even reading helped strengthen the links between nobles and members of the middle class. "Grand tours" of Europe often led upper-class youths to recently discovered Greek and Roman ruins at Pompeii, Herculaneum, and Paestum in Italy. These excavations aroused enthusiasm for the neoclassical style in architecture and painting, which began pushing aside the rococo and the long-dominant baroque. Urban residences, government buildings, furniture, fabrics, wallpaper, and even pottery soon reflected the neoclassical emphasis on purity and clarity of forms. Employing neoclassical motifs, the English potter Josiah Wedgwood (1730–1795) almost single-handedly created a mass market for domestic crockery and appealed to middle-class desires to emulate the rich and royal. His designs of special tea sets for the British queen, for Catherine the Great of Russia, and for leading aristocrats allowed him to advertise his wares as fashionable. His pottery was marketed in France, Russia, Venice, the Ottoman Empire, and British North America.

Neoclassical Style
In this Georgian interior of Syon House on the outskirts of London, various neoclassical motifs are readily apparent: Greek columns, Greek-style statuary on top of the columns, and Roman-style mosaics in the floor. The Scottish architect Robert Adam created this room for the duke of Northumberland in the 1760s. Adam had spent four years in Italy and returned in 1758 to London to decorate homes in the "Adam style," meaning the neoclassical manner. (Syon House, Middlesex, UK / The Bridgeman Art Library International.)

This period also supported artistic styles other than neoclassicism. Frederick the Great built himself a palace outside of Berlin in the earlier rococo style, gave it the French name of Sanssouci ("worry-free"), and filled it with the works of French masters of the rococo. A growing taste for moralistic family scenes in painting reflected the same middle-class preoccupation with the emotions of ordinary private life that could be seen in novels. The middle-class public now attended the official painting exhibitions in France that were held regularly every other year after 1737. Court painting (works commissioned by rulers and nobles) nonetheless remained much in demand.

Although wealthy nobles still patronized Europe's leading musicians, music, too, began to reflect the broadening of the elite and the spread of Enlightenment ideals as classical forms replaced the baroque style. Large sections of string instruments became the backbone of professional orchestras, which now played to large audiences of well-to-do listeners in sizable concert halls. A new attitude toward "the classics" developed: for the first time in the 1770s and 1780s, concert groups began to play older music rather than simply playing the latest commissioned works.

The two supreme masters of the new musical style of the eighteenth century show that the transition from noble patronage to classical concerts was far from complete. Franz Joseph Haydn (1732–1809) and his fellow Austrian Wolfgang Amadeus Mozart (1756–1791) both wrote for noble patrons, but by the early 1800s their compositions had been incorporated into the canon of concert classics all over Europe. Incredibly prolific, both excelled in combining lightness, clarity, and profound emotion. Both also wrote numerous Italian operas, a genre whose popularity continued to grow: in the 1780s, the Papal States alone boasted forty opera houses. Haydn spent most of his career working for a Hungarian noble family, the Eszterházys. Asked once why he had written no string quintets (at which Mozart excelled), he responded simply: "No one has ordered any."

Interest in reading, like attending public concerts, took hold of the middle classes and fed a frenzied increase in publication. By the end of the eighteenth century, six times as many books were being published in the German states, for instance, as at the beginning. Local newspapers, lending libraries, and book clubs multiplied. Despite the limits of women's education, women benefited as much as men from the spread of print. As one Englishman observed, "By far the greatest part of ladies now have a taste for books." Women also wrote them. Catherine Macaulay (1731–1791) published best-selling histories of Britain, and in France Stéphanie de Genlis (1746–1830) wrote children's books — a genre that was growing in importance as middle-class parents became more interested in education.

Life on the Margins

Booming foreign trade fueled a dramatic economic expansion — French colonial trade increased tenfold in the 1700s — but the results did not necessarily trickle all the way down the social scale. The population of Europe grew by nearly 30 percent. Even though food production increased, shortages and crises still occurred periodically. Prices went up in many countries after the 1730s and continued to rise gradually until the early

nineteenth century; wages in many trades rose as well, but less quickly than prices. Some people prospered, but those at the bottom of the social ladder — day laborers in the cities and peasants with small holdings — lived on the edge of dire poverty, and when they lost their land or work, they either migrated to the cities or wandered the roads in search of food and work. In France alone, 200,000 workers left their homes every year in search of seasonal employment elsewhere. At least 10 percent of Europe's urban population depended on some form of charity.

The growing numbers of poor people overwhelmed local governments. In some countries, beggars and vagabonds had been locked up in workhouses since the mid-1600s. The expenses for running these overcrowded institutions increased by 60 percent in England between 1760 and 1785. After 1740, most German towns created workhouses that were part workshop, part hospital, and part prison. Such institutions also appeared for the first time in Boston, New York, and Philadelphia. The French government created *dépôts de mendicité* ("beggar houses") in 1767. The government sent people to these new workhouses to labor in manufacturing, but most were too weak or sick to work, and 20 percent of them died within a few months of incarceration.

Those who were able to work or keep their land fared better: an increase in literacy, especially in the cities, allowed some lower-class people to participate in new tastes and ideas. One French observer insisted, "These days, you see a waiting-maid in her backroom, a lackey in an ante-room reading pamphlets. People can read in almost all classes of society." In France, only 50 percent of men and 27 percent of women could read and write in the 1780s, but that was twice the rate of a century earlier. Literacy rates were higher in England and the Dutch Republic, much lower in eastern Europe.

Whereas the new elite might attend salons, concerts, or art exhibitions, peasants enjoyed their traditional forms of popular entertainment, such as fairs and festivals, and the urban lower classes relaxed in cabarets and taverns. Sometimes pleasures were cruel to animals. In Britain, bullbaiting, bearbaiting, dogfighting, and cockfighting were all common forms of entertainment that provided opportunities for organized gambling.

As population increased and villagers began to move to cities to better their prospects, the rates of births out of wedlock soared, from less than 5 percent of all births in the seventeenth century to nearly 20 percent at the end of the eighteenth. Some detect in this change a sign of sexual liberation and the beginnings of a modern sexual revolution: as women moved out of the control of their families, they began to seek their own sexual fulfillment. Others view this change more bleakly, as a story of seduction and betrayal: family and community pressure had once forced a man to marry a woman pregnant with his child, but now a man could abandon a pregnant lover by simply moving away.

Women who came to the city as domestic servants had little recourse against masters or fellow servants who seduced or raped them. The result was a startling rise in abandoned babies. Most European cities established foundling hospitals in the 1700s, but infant and child mortality was 50 percent higher in such institutions than for children brought up at home.

Jean-Baptiste Greuze, *Broken Eggs* (1756)
Greuze made his reputation as a painter of moralistic family scenes. In this one, an old woman (perhaps the mother) confronts the lover of a young girl and points to the eggs that have fallen out of a basket, a symbol of lost virginity. Denis Diderot praised Greuze's work as "morality in paint," but the paintings often had an erotic subtext. (© Francis G. Mayer / Corbis.)

European states had long tried to regulate sexual behavior; every country had laws against prostitution, adultery, fornication, sodomy, and infanticide. Reformers criticized the harshness of laws against infanticide, but they showed no mercy for "sodomites" (as male homosexuals were called), who in some places, in particular the Dutch Republic, were systematically persecuted and imprisoned or even executed. Male homosexuals attracted the attention of authorities because they had begun to develop networks and special meeting places. The stereotype of the effeminate, exclusively homosexual male seems to have appeared for the first time in the eighteenth century, perhaps as part of a growing emphasis on separate roles for men and women.

The Enlightenment's emphasis on reason, self-control, and childhood innocence made parents increasingly anxious about their children's sexuality. Moralists and physicians wrote books about the evils of masturbation, "proving" that it led to physical and mental degeneration and even madness.

While the Enlightenment thus encouraged excessive concern about children being left to their own devices, it nevertheless taught the middle and upper classes to value their children and to expect their improvement through education. Writers such as de Genlis and Rousseau drew attention to children, who were no longer viewed only as little sinners in need of harsh discipline. Toys, jigsaw puzzles, and clothing designed for children all appeared for the first time in the 1700s. Children were no longer considered miniature adults.

> **REVIEW QUESTION** What were the major differences in the impact of the Enlightenment on the nobility, the middle classes, and the lower classes?

State Power in an Era of Reform

Rulers turned to Enlightenment-inspired reforms to improve life for their subjects and to gain commercial or military advantage over rival states. Historians label many of the sovereigns of this time **enlightened despots** or enlightened absolutists, for they aimed to promote Enlightenment reforms without giving up their absolutist powers. Catherine the Great's admiring relationship with Voltaire showed how even the most absolutist rulers championed reform when it suited their own goals. Foremost among those goals was the expansion of a ruler's territory.

War and Diplomacy

Europeans no longer fought devastating wars over religion that killed hundreds of thousands of civilians; instead, professional armies and navies battled for control of overseas empires and for dominance on the European continent. Rulers continued to expand their armies: the Prussian army, for example, nearly tripled in size between 1740 and 1789. Widespread use of flintlock muskets required deployment in long lines, usually three men deep, with each line in turn loading and firing on command. Military strategy became cautious and calculating, but this did not prevent the outbreak of hostilities. Between 1750 and 1775, the instability of the European balance of power resulted in a diplomatic reversal of alliances, a major international conflict, and the partition of Poland-Lithuania among Russia, Austria, and Prussia.

In 1756, a set of events that historians call the Diplomatic Revolution reshaped relations among the great powers. Prussia and Great Britain signed a defensive alliance, prompting Austria to overlook two centuries of hostility and ally with France. Russia and Sweden soon joined the Franco-Austrian alliance. When Frederick the Great invaded Austria's ally Saxony with his large, well-disciplined army, the long-simmering hostilities between Great Britain and France over colonial boundaries flared into a general war that became known as the **Seven Years' War** (1756–1763).

Fighting soon raged around the world (Map 18.1). The French and British battled on land and sea in North America (where the conflict was called the French and Indian War), the West Indies, and India. The two coalitions also fought each other in central Europe. At first, in 1757, Frederick the Great surprised Europe with a spectacular vic-

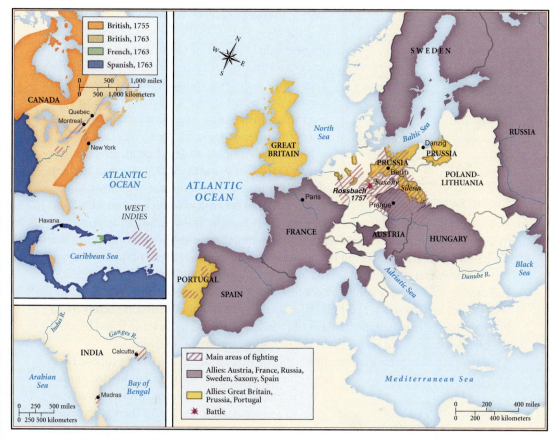

Map 18.1 The Seven Years' War, 1756–1763

In what might justly be called the first worldwide war, the French and British fought each other in Europe, the West Indies, North America, and India. Skirmishing in North America helped precipitate the war, which became more general when Austria, France, and Russia allied to check Prussian influence in central Europe. The treaty between Austria and Prussia simply restored the status quo in Europe, but the changes overseas were much more dramatic. Britain gained control over Canada and India but gave back to France the West Indian islands of Guadeloupe and Martinique. Britain was now the dominant power of the seas.

tory at Rossbach in Saxony over a much larger Franco-Austrian army. But in time, Russian and Austrian armies encircled his troops. A fluke of history saved him. Empress Elizabeth of Russia (r. 1741–1762) died and was succeeded by the mentally unstable Peter III, a fanatical admirer of Frederick and all things Prussian. Peter withdrew Russia from the war. (This was practically his only accomplishment as tsar. He was soon mysteriously murdered, probably at the instigation of his wife, Catherine the Great.) A separate peace treaty allowed Frederick to keep all his territory, including Silesia, that had been conquered in the War of the Austrian Succession (1740–1748).

The Anglo-French overseas conflicts ended more decisively than the continental land wars. British naval superiority, fully achieved only in the 1750s, enabled Great

The First Partition of Poland, 1772

Britain to rout the French in North America, India, and the West Indies. In the Treaty of Paris of 1763, France ceded Canada to Great Britain and agreed to remove its armies from India, in exchange for keeping its rich West Indian islands. Eagerness to avenge this defeat would motivate France to support the British North American colonists in their War of Independence just fifteen years later.

Although Prussia suffered great losses in the Seven Years' War — some 160,000 Prussian soldiers died either in action or of disease — its army helped vault Prussia to the rank of leading powers. By 1740, the Prussians had the third or fourth largest army in Europe even though Prussia was tenth in population and thirteenth in land area. Under Frederick II, Prussia's military expenditures rose to two-thirds of the state's revenue. Virtually every nobleman served in the army, paying for his own support as officer and buying a position as company commander. Once retired, the officers returned to their estates and served as local officials. This militarization of Prussian society had a profoundly conservative effect: it kept the peasants enserfed to their lords and blocked the middle classes from access to estates or high government positions.

Prussia's power grew so dramatically that in 1772 Frederick the Great proposed that large chunks of Poland-Lithuania be divided among Austria, Prussia, and Russia. Although the Austrian empress Maria Theresa protested that the partition would spread "a stain over my whole reign," she agreed to the first **partition of Poland**, splitting one-third of Poland-Lithuania's territory and

Dividing Poland, 1772

In this contemporary depiction, Catherine the Great, Joseph II, and Frederick the Great point on the map to the portion of Poland-Lithuania each plans to take. The artist makes it clear that Poland's fate rested in the hands of neighboring rulers, not its own people. Can you infer the sentiments of the artist from the content of this engraving? (Hulton Archive / Getty Images.)

half of its people among the three powers. Russia took over most of Lithuania, effectively ending the large but weak Polish-Lithuanian commonwealth.

State-Sponsored Reform

In the aftermath of the Seven Years' War, all the belligerents faced pressing needs for more money. To make tax increases more palatable to public opinion, rulers appointed reform-minded ministers and gave them a mandate to modernize government. Such reforms always threatened the interests of traditional groups, however, and the spread of Enlightenment ideas aroused sometimes unpredictable desires for more change.

Monarchs dedicated to reform insisted on greater attention to merit, hard work, and professionalism. In this view, the ruler should be a benevolent, enlightened administrator who worked for the general well-being of his or her people. Frederick the Great, who drove himself as hard as he drove his officials, boasted, "I am the first servant of the state." A Freemason and supporter of religious toleration, Frederick abolished torture, reorganized taxation, and hosted leading French philosophes at his court. The Prussian king also composed more than a hundred original pieces of music.

Legal reform, both of the judicial system and of the often disorganized and irregular law codes, was central to the work of many reform-minded monarchs. Like Frederick the Great, Joseph II of Austria (r. 1780–1790) ordered the compilation of a unified law code, a project that required many years for completion. Catherine the Great began such an undertaking even more ambitiously. In 1767, she called together a legislative commission of 564 deputies and asked them to consider a long document called the *Instruction,* which represented her hopes for legal reform based on the ideas of Montesquieu and the Italian jurist Cesare Beccaria. Montesquieu had insisted that punishment should fit the crime; he criticized the use of torture and brutal corporal punishment. In his influential book *On Crimes and Punishments* (1764), Beccaria argued that justice should be administered in public, that judicial torture should be abolished as inhumane, and that the accused should be presumed innocent until proven guilty. Despite much discussion and hundreds of petitions and documents about local problems, little came of Catherine's commission.

Rulers everywhere wanted more control over church affairs, and they used Enlightenment criticisms of the organized churches to get their way. In Catholic countries, many government officials resented the influence of the Jesuits, the major Catholic teaching order. Critics mounted campaigns against the Jesuits in many countries, and in 1773, Pope Clement XIV (r. 1769–1774) agreed under pressure to disband the order, an edict that held until a reinvigorated papacy restored the society in 1814. Joseph II of Austria not only applauded the suppression of the Jesuits but also required Austrian bishops to swear fidelity and submission to him. Joseph had become Holy Roman Emperor and co-regent with his mother, Maria Theresa, in 1765. After her death in 1780, he initiated a wide-ranging program of reform. Under him, the Austrian state supervised Catholic seminaries, abolished contemplative monastic orders, and confiscated monastic property to pay for education and poor relief.

Maria Theresa
Like Catherine the Great, Maria Theresa had herself painted on horseback to emphasize her sovereign position, which the crown over her head makes apparent. This portrait from 1757 does not make her seem warlike, however, as she carries no sword. She had sixteen children, two of whom became Holy Roman Emperor (Joseph II and Leopold II) and two of whom became queens (Marie-Antoinette of France and Maria Carolina of Naples). (Scala / White Images / Art Resource, NY.)

Joseph II launched the most ambitious educational reforms of the period. In 1774, once the Jesuits had been disbanded, the General School Ordinance in Austria ordered state subsidies for local schools, which the state would regulate. By 1789, one-quarter of the school-age children attended school. In Prussia, the school code of 1763 required all children between the ages of five and thirteen to attend school. Although not enforced uniformly, the Prussian law demonstrated Frederick the Great's belief that modernization depended on education.

No ruler pushed the principle of religious toleration as far as Joseph II of Austria, who in 1781 granted freedom of religious worship to Protestants, Orthodox Christians, and Jews. For the first time, these groups were allowed to own property, build schools, enter the professions, and hold political and military offices. Louis XVI signed an edict in 1787 restoring French Protestants' civil rights — but still, Protestants could not hold political office. Great Britain continued to deny Catholics freedom of open worship and the right to sit in Parliament. Most European states limited the rights and opportunities available to Jews. Even in Austria, where Joseph encouraged toleration, the laws forced Jews to take German-sounding names. The leading philosophes in theory opposed persecution of the Jews but often in practice treated them with undisguised contempt.

Diderot's comment was all too typical: the Jews, he said, bore "all the defects peculiar to an ignorant and superstitious nation."

Limits of Reform

When enlightened absolutist leaders introduced reforms, they often ran into resistance from groups threatened by the proposed changes. Joseph II tried to remove the burdens of serfdom in the Habsburg lands. After 1781, serfs could move freely, enter trades, or marry without their lords' permission. Joseph also abolished the tithe to the church, shifted more of the tax burden to the nobility, and converted peasants' labor services into cash payments.

The Austrian nobility furiously resisted these far-reaching reforms. When Joseph died in 1790, his brother Leopold II had to revoke most reforms to appease the nobles. Prussia's Frederick the Great, like Joseph, encouraged such agricultural innovations as planting potatoes and turnips (new crops that could help feed a growing population), but Prussia's noble landlords, called Junkers, continued to expand their estates at the expense of poorer peasants and thwarted Frederick's attempts to improve the status of serfs.

In France, a group of economists called the physiocrats urged the government to deregulate the grain trade and make the tax system more equitable to encourage agricultural productivity. In the interest of establishing a free market, they also insisted that urban guilds be abolished because the guilds prevented free entry into the trades. The French government heeded some of this advice and gave up its system of price controls on grain in 1763, but it had to reverse the decision in 1770 when grain shortages caused a famine.

A conflict with the parlements (the thirteen high courts of law) prompted Louis XV to go even further in 1771. He replaced the parlements with courts in which the judges no longer owned their offices and thus could not sell them or pass them on as an inheritance. Justice, he hoped, would then be more impartial. The displaced judges of the parlements succeeded in arousing widespread opposition to what they portrayed as tyrannical royal policy. The furor calmed down only when Louis XV died in 1774 and his successor, Louis XVI (r. 1774–1792), yielded to aristocratic demands and restored the old parlements.

Louis XVI tried to carry out part of the program suggested by the physiocrats, and he chose one of their disciples, Jacques Turgot (1727–1781), as his chief minister. A contributor to the *Encyclopedia,* Turgot pushed through several edicts that again freed the grain trade, suppressed guilds, converted the peasants' forced labor on roads into a money tax payable by all landowners, and reduced court expenses. He also began making plans to introduce a system of elected local assemblies, which would have increased representation in the government. Faced with broad-based resistance led by the parlements and his own courtiers as well as with riots against rising grain prices, Louis XVI dismissed Turgot, and one of the last possibilities to overhaul France's government collapsed.

The failure of reform in France paradoxically reflected the power of Enlightenment thinkers; everyone now endorsed Enlightenment ideas but used them for different

ends. The nobles in the parlements blocked the French monarchy's reform efforts using the very same Enlightenment language spoken by the crown's ministers. Where Frederick the Great, Catherine the Great, and even Joseph II used reform to bolster the efficiency of absolutist government, attempts at change in France backfired. French kings found that their ambitious programs for reform succeeded only in arousing unrealistic hopes.

> **REVIEW QUESTION** What prompted enlightened absolutists to undertake reforms in the second half of the eighteenth century?

Rebellions against State Power

Although traditional forms of popular discontent had not disappeared, Enlightenment ideals and reforms changed the rules of the game in politics. Governments had become accountable for their actions to a much wider range of people than ever before. In Britain and France, ordinary people rioted when they perceived government as failing to protect them against food shortages. The growth of informed public opinion had its most dramatic consequences in the North American colonies, where a struggle over the British Parliament's right to tax turned into a full-scale war for independence. The American War of Independence showed that, once put into practice, Enlightenment ideals could have revolutionary implications.

Food Riots and Peasant Uprisings

Population growth, inflation, and the extension of the market system put added pressure on the already beleaguered poor. In the last half of the eighteenth century, the food supply became the focus of political and social conflict. Poor people in Europe's villages and towns believed that it was the government's responsibility to ensure they had enough food, and many governments did stockpile grain to make up for the occasional bad harvest. At the same time, in keeping with Adam Smith's and the French physiocrats' free-market proposals, governments wanted to allow grain prices to rise with market demand, because higher profits would motivate producers to increase the overall supply of food.

Free trade in grain meant selling to the highest bidder, even if that bidder was a foreign merchant. In the short run, in times of scarcity, big landowners and farmers could make huge profits by selling grain outside their hometowns. This practice enraged poor farmers, agricultural workers, and urban wageworkers, who could not afford the higher prices. Lacking the political means to affect policy, the poor could enforce their desire for old-fashioned price regulation only by rioting. Most did not pillage or steal grain but rather forced the sale of grain or flour at a "just" price and blocked the shipment of grain out of their villages to other markets. Women often led these "popular price fixings," as they were called in France, in desperate attempts to protect the food supply for their children.

Such food riots occurred regularly in Britain and France in the last half of the eighteenth century. One of the most turbulent was the so-called Flour War in France in

1775. Turgot's deregulation of the grain trade in 1774 caused prices to rise in several provincial cities. Rioting spread from there to the Paris region, where villagers attacked grain convoys heading to the capital city. Local officials often ordered merchants and bakers to sell at the price the rioters demanded, only to find themselves arrested by the central government for overriding free trade. The government brought in troops to restore order and introduced the death penalty for rioting.

Frustrations with serfdom and hopes for a miraculous transformation provoked the **Pugachev rebellion** in Russia beginning in 1773. An army deserter from the southeast frontier region, Emelian Pugachev (1742–1775) claimed to be Tsar Peter III, the dead husband of Catherine the Great. Pugachev's appearance seemed to confirm peasant hopes for a "redeemer tsar" who would save the people from oppression. He rallied around him Cossacks like himself who resented the loss of their old tribal independence. Nearly three million people eventually participated, making this the largest single rebellion in the history of tsarist Russia. When Pugachev urged the peasants to attack the nobility and seize their estates, hundreds of noble families perished. Finally, the army captured the rebel leader and brought him in an iron cage to Moscow, where he was tortured and executed. In the aftermath, Catherine tightened the nobles' control over their serfs with the Charter of the Nobility and harshly punished those who dared to criticize serfdom.

The Pugachev Rebellion, 1773

Public Opinion and Political Opposition

Peasant uprisings might have briefly shaken even a powerful monarchy, but the rise of public opinion as a force independent of court society caused more enduring changes in European politics. Across much of Europe and in the North American colonies, demands for broader political participation reflected Enlightenment notions about individual rights. Aristocratic bodies such as the French parlements, which had no legislative role like that of the British Parliament, insisted that the monarch consult them on the nation's affairs, and the new educated elite wanted more influence, too. Newspapers began to cover daily political affairs, and the public learned the basics of political life, despite the strict limits on political participation in most countries.

The Wilkes affair in Great Britain showed that public opinion could be mobilized to challenge a government. In 1763, during the reign of George III (r. 1760–1820), John Wilkes, a member of Parliament, attacked the government in his newspaper, *North Briton,* and sued the crown when he was arrested. He won his release as well as damages. When he was reelected, Parliament denied him his seat, not once but three times.

The Wilkes episode soon escalated into a major campaign against the corruption and social exclusiveness of Parliament, complaints the Levellers had first raised during the English Revolution of the late 1640s. In one incident eleven people died when soldiers broke up a huge gathering of Wilkes's supporters. The slogan "Wilkes and Liberty" appeared on walls all over London. Middle-class voters formed the Society of Supporters of the Bill of Rights, which circulated petitions for Wilkes; they gained the support of about one-fourth of all the voters. The more determined Wilkesites proposed sweeping reforms of Parliament, including more frequent elections, more representation for the counties, elimination of "rotten boroughs" (election districts so small that they could be controlled by one big patron), and restrictions of pensions used by the crown to gain support. These demands would be at the heart of agitation for parliamentary reform in Britain for decades to come.

Popular demonstrations did not always support reforms. In 1780, the Gordon riots devastated London. They were named after the fanatical anti-Catholic crusader Lord George Gordon, who helped organize huge marches and petition campaigns against a bill the House of Commons passed to grant limited toleration to Catholics. The demonstrations culminated in a seven-day riot that left fifty buildings destroyed and three hundred people dead. Despite the continuing limitation on voting rights in Great Britain, British politicians were learning that they could ignore public opinion only at their peril.

Political opposition also took artistic forms, particularly in countries where governments restricted organized political activity. A striking example of a play with a political message was *The Marriage of Figaro* (1784) by Pierre-Augustin Caron de Beaumarchais (1732–1799). When finally performed publicly, the play caused a sensation. The chief character, Figaro, is a clever servant who gets the better of his noble employer, a count. When speaking of the count, Figaro cries, "What have you done to deserve so many rewards? You went to the trouble of being born, and nothing more." Looking back, Napoleon would say that the play was the "revolution in action."

Revolution in North America

Oppositional forms of public opinion came to a head in Great Britain's North American colonies, where the result was American independence and the establishment of a republican constitution that stood in stark contrast to most European regimes. Many Europeans saw the American War of Independence, or the American Revolution, as a triumph for Enlightenment ideas. As one German writer exclaimed in 1777, American victory would give "greater scope to the Enlightenment, new keenness to the thinking of peoples and new life to the spirit of liberty."

The American revolutionary leaders had participated in the Enlightenment and shared political ideas with the opposition Whigs in Britain. In the 1760s and 1770s, American opposition leaders became convinced that the British government was growing increasingly corrupt and despotic. The colonies had no representatives in Parliament, and colonists claimed that "no taxation without representation" should be allowed. Indeed, they denied that Parliament had any jurisdiction over the colonies, insisting that

Resistance to British Rule
To demonstrate their resistance to the 1765 Stamp Act, Boston citizens tar and feather a tax collector. The Stamp Act is nailed upside down to a tree. (Private Collection / Peter Newark Pictures / The Bridgeman Art Library International.)

the king govern them through colonial legislatures and recognize their traditional British liberties. The failure of the "Wilkes and Liberty" campaign to produce concrete results convinced many Americans that Parliament was hopelessly tainted.

Parliament's encroachment on the autonomy of the colonies transformed colonial attitudes. With the British clamoring for lower taxes at the end of the Seven Years' War and the colonists paying only a fraction of the tax rate paid by the Britons at home, Parliament passed new taxes on the colonies, including the Stamp Act in 1765, which required a special tax stamp on all legal documents and publications. After violent rioting in the colonies, the British repealed the tax, but in 1773 the new Tea Act revived colonial resistance, which culminated in the so-called Boston Tea Party of 1773. Colonists dressed as Indians boarded British ships and dumped the imported tea (by this time an enormously popular beverage) into Boston's harbor.

Political opposition in the American colonies turned belligerent when Britain threatened to use force to maintain control. After actual fighting had begun, in 1776, the Second Continental Congress issued the Declaration of Independence. An eloquent statement of the American cause written by the Virginia planter and lawyer Thomas Jefferson, the Declaration of Independence was couched in the language of universal human rights, which enlightened Europeans could be expected to understand. In 1778, France boosted the American cause by entering on the colonists' side. Spain declared war on Britain in 1779; in 1780, Great Britain declared war on the Dutch Republic in retaliation for Dutch support of the rebels. The worldwide conflict that resulted was more

than Britain could handle. The American colonies achieved their independence in the peace treaty of 1783.

The newly independent states still faced the challenge of republican self-government. The Articles of Confederation, drawn up in 1777 as a provisional constitution, proved weak because they gave the central government few powers. In 1787, a constitutional convention met in Philadelphia to draft a new constitution, which was ratified the following year. It established a two-house legislature, an indirectly elected president, and an independent judiciary. The U.S. Constitution's preamble insisted explicitly, for the first time in history, that government derived its power solely from the people and did not depend on divine right or on the tradition of royalty or aristocracy. The new educated elite of the eighteenth century had now created government based on a "social contract" among male, property-owning, white citizens. It was by no means a complete democracy (women and slaves were excluded from political participation), but the new government represented a radical departure from European models. Appended to the Constitution in 1791, the Bill of Rights outlined the essential rights (such as freedom of speech) that the government could never overturn. Although slavery continued in the American republic, the new emphasis on rights helped fuel the movement for its abolition in both Britain and the United States.

Interest in the new republic was greatest in France. The U.S. Constitution and various state constitutions were published in French with commentary by leading thinkers. Even more important in the long run were the effects of the American war. Dutch losses to Great Britain aroused a widespread movement for political reform in the Dutch Republic, and debts incurred by France in supporting the American colonies would soon force the French monarchy to the edge of bankruptcy and then to revolution. Ultimately, the entire European system of royal rule would be challenged.

REVIEW QUESTION Why did public opinion become a new factor in politics in the second half of the eighteenth century?

Conclusion

What began as a cosmopolitan movement of a few intellectuals in the first half of the eighteenth century had reached a relatively wide audience among the educated elite of men and women by the 1770s and 1780s. The spirit of Enlightenment swept from the salons, coffeehouses, and Masonic lodges into the halls of government from Philadelphia to Vienna. Scientific inquiry into the causes of social misery and laws defending individual rights and freedoms gained adherents even among the rulers and ministers responsible for censoring Enlightenment works.

For most Europeans, however, the promise of the Enlightenment did not become a reality. Rulers such as Catherine the Great had every intention of retaining their full, often unchecked powers even as they corresponded with leading philosophes and entertained them at their courts. Yet even the failure of reform contributed to the ferment in Europe after 1770. Peasant rebellions in eastern Europe, the "Wilkes and Liberty" cam-

Mapping the West Europe and the World, c. 1780

Although Great Britain lost control over part of its North American colonies, which became the new United States, European influence on the rest of the world grew dramatically in the eighteenth century. The slave trade linked European ports to African slave-trading outposts and to plantations in the Caribbean, South America, and North America. The European countries on the Atlantic Ocean benefited most from this trade. Yet almost all of Africa, China, Japan — as well as large parts of India — still resisted European incursion, and the Ottoman Empire, with its massive territories, still presented Europe with a formidable military challenge.

paign in Great Britain, the struggle over reform in France, and the revolution in America all occurred around the same time, and their conjunction convinced many Europeans that change was brewing. Just how much could change, and whether change made life better or worse, would come into question in the next ten years.

Review Questions

1. What were the major differences between the Enlightenment in France, Great Britain, and the German states?

2. What were the major differences in the impact of the Enlightenment on the nobility, the middle classes, and the lower classes?

3. What prompted enlightened absolutists to undertake reforms in the second half of the eighteenth century?

4. Why did public opinion become a new factor in politics in the second half of the eighteenth century?

Making Connections

1. Why might rulers have felt ambivalent about the Enlightenment, supporting reform on the one hand while clamping down on political dissidents on the other hand?

2. Which major developments in this period ran counter to the influence of the Enlightenment?

3. In what ways had politics changed, and in what ways did they remain the same during the Enlightenment?

4. Explain how Catherine the Great of Russia could be taken as a symbol of both the promise and the limits of the Enlightenment.

- For practice quizzes and other study tools, visit the **Online Study Guide** at bedfordstmartins.com/huntconcise.

- For primary-source material from this period, see *Sources of the Making of the West*, Fourth Edition.

- For Web sites, images, and documents related to topics in this chapter, visit *Make History* at bedfordstmartins.com/huntconcise.

TIMELINE

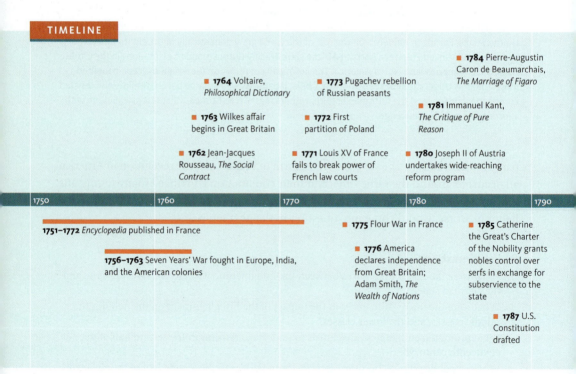

- **1764** Voltaire, *Philosophical Dictionary*
- **1763** Wilkes affair begins in Great Britain
- **1762** Jean-Jacques Rousseau, *The Social Contract*

- **1773** Pugachev rebellion of Russian peasants
- **1772** First partition of Poland
- **1771** Louis XV of France fails to break power of French law courts

- **1784** Pierre-Augustin Caron de Beaumarchais, *The Marriage of Figaro*
- **1781** Immanuel Kant, *The Critique of Pure Reason*
- **1780** Joseph II of Austria undertakes wide-reaching reform program

| 1750 | 1760 | 1770 | 1780 | 1790 |

1751–1772 *Encyclopedia* published in France

1756–1763 Seven Years' War fought in Europe, India, and the American colonies

- **1775** Flour War in France
- **1776** America declares independence from Great Britain; Adam Smith, *The Wealth of Nations*

- **1785** Catherine the Great's Charter of the Nobility grants nobles control over serfs in exchange for subservience to the state
- **1787** U.S. Constitution drafted

Suggested References

Gay's interpretive study of the Enlightenment remains useful, but the Kors volumes offer the most up-to-date views on the Enlightenment. Readers can find different perspectives in studies of individual rulers, their routes to power, and their reactions to the Enlightenment.

Beales, Derek. *Joseph II: In the Shadow of Maria Theresa: 1741–1780.* 2008.

Cash, Arthur H. *John Wilkes: The Scandalous Father of Civil Liberty.* 2006.

Catherine the Great: http://russia.nypl.org/home.html

Gay, Peter. *The Enlightenment: An Interpretation.* 2 vols. 1966, 1969.

Kors, Alan Charles, ed. *Encyclopedia of the Enlightenment.* 4 vols. 2003.

Mozart Project: http://www.mozartproject.org

*Rousseau, Jean-Jacques. *Discourse on the Origin and Foundations of Inequality among Men.* Ed. Helena Rosenblatt. 2011.

Schumann, Matt, and Karl W. Schweizer. *The Seven Years War: A Transatlantic History.* 2008.

Seven Years' War: http://www.historyworld.net/wrldhis/PlainTextHistories.asp?historyid=aa66

Venturi, Franco. *The End of the Old Regime in Europe, 1768–1776: The First Crisis.* Trans. R. Burr Litchfield. 1989.

Wilson, Peter H. *A Companion to Eighteenth-Century Europe.* 2008.

*Primary source.

Republicanism, democracy, terrorism, nationalism, and military dictatorship all took their modern forms during the French Revolution.

The Revolution might have remained a strictly French affair if war had not involved the rest of Europe. After 1792, huge French republican armies, fueled by patriotic nationalism, marched across Europe, promising liberation from traditional monarchies but often delivering old-fashioned conquest and annexation. French victories spread revolutionary ideas far and wide, from Poland to the colonies in the Caribbean, where the first successful slave revolt established the republic of Haiti.

CHAPTER FOCUS What was so revolutionary about the French Revolution?

The Revolutionary Wave, 1787–1789

Between 1787 and 1789, revolts in the name of liberty broke out in the Dutch Republic, the Austrian Netherlands (present-day Belgium and Luxembourg), and Poland as well as in France. At the same time, the newly independent United States of America was preparing a new federal constitution. Historians have sometimes referred to these revolts as the Atlantic revolutions because so many protest movements arose in countries on both shores of the North Atlantic. The French Revolution nonetheless differed greatly from the others. Not only was France the richest, most powerful, and most populous state in western Europe, but its revolution was also more violent, more long-lasting, and ultimately more influential.

Protesters in the Low Countries and Poland

Political protests in the Dutch Republic attracted European attention because Dutch banks still controlled a hefty portion of the world's capital at the end of the eighteenth century. The Dutch Patriots, as they chose to call themselves, wanted to reduce the powers of the prince of Orange, the kinglike stadholder who favored close ties with Great Britain. Government-sponsored Dutch banks owned 40 percent of the British national debt, and by 1796 they held the entire foreign debt of the United States. Relations with the British deteriorated during the American War of Independence, however, and by the middle of the 1780s, agitation in favor of the Americans had boiled over into an attack on the stadholder.

Building on support among middle-class bankers and merchants, the Dutch Patriots soon gained a more popular audience by demanding political reforms and organizing armed citizen militias of men, called Free Corps. Before long, the Free Corps took on the troops of the prince of Orange and got the upper hand. In response, Frederick William II of Prussia, whose sister had married the stadholder, intervened in 1787 with tacit British support. Thousands of Prussian troops soon occupied Utrecht and Amsterdam, and the house of Orange regained its former position. The Orangists got their revenge: lower-class mobs pillaged the houses of prosperous Dutch Patriot leaders, forcing many to flee

The Cataclysm
of Revolution

O N OCTOBER 5, 1789, a crowd of several thousand women marched in a drenching rain from the center of Paris to Versailles, a distance of twelve miles. They demanded the king's help in securing more grain for the hungry and his reassurance that he did not intend to resist the emerging revolutionary movement. Joined the next morning by thousands of men who came from Paris to reinforce them, they broke into the royal family's private apartments, killing two of the royal bodyguards.

Women's March to Versailles
Thousands of prints broadcast the events of the French Revolution to the public in France and elsewhere. This colored engraving shows a crowd of armed women marching to Versailles on October 5, 1789, to confront the king. The sight of armed women frightened many observers and demonstrated that the Revolution was not only a men's affair. Note the middle-class woman on the left being forced to join with the others. (The Granger Collection, NYC — All rights reserved.)

To prevent further bloodshed, the king agreed to move his family and his government to Paris. A dramatic procession of the royal family guarded by throngs of ordinary men and women made its slow way back to the capital. The people's proud display of cannons and pikes underlined the fundamental transformation that was occurring. Ordinary people had forced the king of France to respond to their grievances. The French monarchy was in danger, and if such a powerful and long-lasting institution could come under fire, then could any monarch of Europe rest easy?

The French Revolution first grabbed the attention of the entire world because it seemed to promise human rights and broad-based political participation. Its most famous slogan pledged "Liberty, Equality, and Fraternity" for all. Even as the Revolution promised democracy, however, it also inaugurated a cycle of violence and intimidation, seen already in October 1789. When the revolutionaries encountered resistance to their programs, they tried to compel obedience. Some historians therefore see in the French Revolution the origins of modern totalitarianism — that is, a government that tries to control every aspect of life, including daily activities, while limiting all forms of political dissent. As events unfolded after 1789, the French Revolution became the model of modern revolution.

595

Republicanism, democracy, terrorism, nationalism, and military dictatorship all took their modern forms during the French Revolution.

The Revolution might have remained a strictly French affair if war had not involved the rest of Europe. After 1792, huge French republican armies, fueled by patriotic nationalism, marched across Europe, promising liberation from traditional monarchies but often delivering old-fashioned conquest and annexation. French victories spread revolutionary ideas far and wide, from Poland to the colonies in the Caribbean, where the first successful slave revolt established the republic of Haiti.

CHAPTER FOCUS What was so revolutionary about the French Revolution?

The Revolutionary Wave, 1787–1789

Between 1787 and 1789, revolts in the name of liberty broke out in the Dutch Republic, the Austrian Netherlands (present-day Belgium and Luxembourg), and Poland as well as in France. At the same time, the newly independent United States of America was preparing a new federal constitution. Historians have sometimes referred to these revolts as the Atlantic revolutions because so many protest movements arose in countries on both shores of the North Atlantic. The French Revolution nonetheless differed greatly from the others. Not only was France the richest, most powerful, and most populous state in western Europe, but its revolution was also more violent, more long-lasting, and ultimately more influential.

Protesters in the Low Countries and Poland

Political protests in the Dutch Republic attracted European attention because Dutch banks still controlled a hefty portion of the world's capital at the end of the eighteenth century. The Dutch Patriots, as they chose to call themselves, wanted to reduce the powers of the prince of Orange, the kinglike stadholder who favored close ties with Great Britain. Government-sponsored Dutch banks owned 40 percent of the British national debt, and by 1796 they held the entire foreign debt of the United States. Relations with the British deteriorated during the American War of Independence, however, and by the middle of the 1780s, agitation in favor of the Americans had boiled over into an attack on the stadholder.

Building on support among middle-class bankers and merchants, the Dutch Patriots soon gained a more popular audience by demanding political reforms and organizing armed citizen militias of men, called Free Corps. Before long, the Free Corps took on the troops of the prince of Orange and got the upper hand. In response, Frederick William II of Prussia, whose sister had married the stadholder, intervened in 1787 with tacit British support. Thousands of Prussian troops soon occupied Utrecht and Amsterdam, and the house of Orange regained its former position. The Orangists got their revenge: lower-class mobs pillaged the houses of prosperous Dutch Patriot leaders, forcing many to flee

Suggested References

Gay's interpretive study of the Enlightenment remains useful, but the Kors volumes offer the most up-to-date views on the Enlightenment. Readers can find different perspectives in studies of individual rulers, their routes to power, and their reactions to the Enlightenment.

Beales, Derek. *Joseph II: In the Shadow of Maria Theresa: 1741–1780*. 2008.

Cash, Arthur H. *John Wilkes: The Scandalous Father of Civil Liberty*. 2006.

Catherine the Great: http://russia.nypl.org/home.html

Gay, Peter. *The Enlightenment: An Interpretation*. 2 vols. 1966, 1969.

Kors, Alan Charles, ed. *Encyclopedia of the Enlightenment*. 4 vols. 2003.

Mozart Project: http://www.mozartproject.org

*Rousseau, Jean-Jacques. *Discourse on the Origin and Foundations of Inequality among Men*. Ed. Helena Rosenblatt. 2011.

Schumann, Matt, and Karl W. Schweizer. *The Seven Years War: A Transatlantic History*. 2008.

Seven Years' War: http://www.historyworld.net/wrldhis/PlainTextHistories.asp?historyid=aa66

Venturi, Franco. *The End of the Old Regime in Europe, 1768–1776: The First Crisis*. Trans. R. Burr Litchfield. 1989.

Wilson, Peter H. *A Companion to Eighteenth-Century Europe*. 2008.

*Primary source.

to the United States, France, or the Austrian Netherlands. Those Patriots who remained nursed their grievances until the French republican armies invaded in 1795.

If Austrian emperor Joseph II had not tried to introduce Enlightenment-inspired reforms, the Belgians of the ten provinces of the Austrian Netherlands might have remained tranquil. Just as he had done previously in his own crown lands (see Chapter 18, page 584), Joseph abolished torture, decreed toleration for Jews and Protestants (in this resolutely Catholic area), and suppressed monasteries. His reorganization of the administrative and judicial systems eliminated many offices that belonged to nobles and lawyers, sparking resistance among the upper classes in 1788.

Upper-class protesters intended only to defend historic local liberties against an overbearing government. Nonetheless, their resistance galvanized democrats, who wanted a more representative government and organized clubs to give voice to their demands. At the end of 1788, a secret society formed armed companies to prepare an uprising. By late 1789, each province had separately declared its independence, and the Austrian administration had collapsed. Delegates from the various provinces declared themselves the United States of Belgium, a clear reference to the American precedent.

Once again, however, social divisions doomed the rebels. When the democrats began to challenge noble authority, aristocratic leaders drew to their side the Catholic clergy and peasants, who had little sympathy for the democrats of the cities. Every Sunday in May and June 1790, thousands of peasant men and women, led by their priests, streamed into Brussels carrying crucifixes, nooses, and pitchforks to intimidate the democrats and defend the church. Faced with the choice between the Austrian emperor and "our current tyrants," the democrats chose to support the return of the Austrians under Emperor Leopold II (r. 1790–1792), who had succeeded his brother.

A reform party calling itself the Patriots also emerged in Poland, which had been shocked by the loss of a third of its territory in the first partition of 1772. The Patriots sought to overhaul the weak commonwealth along modern western European lines and looked to King Stanislaw August Poniatowski (r. 1764–1795) to lead them.

In 1788, the Patriots got their golden chance. Bogged down in war with the Ottoman Turks, Catherine the Great of Russia could not block the summoning of a reform-minded parliament, which eventually enacted the constitution of May 3, 1791. It ended the veto power that each aristocrat had over legislation, granted townspeople limited political rights, and vaguely promised future Jewish emancipation. Abolishing serfdom was hardly mentioned. Within a year, however, Catherine had turned her attention to Poland and engineered the downfall of the Patriots.

Origins of the French Revolution, 1787–1789

Many French enthusiastically greeted the American experiment in republican government and supported the Dutch, Belgian, and Polish Patriots. After suffering humiliation at the hands of the British in the Seven Years' War (1756–1763), the French had regained international prestige by supporting the victorious Americans. Yet by the late

1780s, the French monarchy was facing a serious fiscal crisis caused by a mounting deficit. The fiscal crisis soon provoked a constitutional crisis of epic proportions.

About half of the French national budget went to paying interest on the debt that had ballooned because of the American war. In contrast to the British government, which had a national bank to help raise loans, the French government lived off relatively short-term, high-interest loans from private sources, including Swiss banks, government annuities, and advances from tax collectors.

For years the French government had been trying unsuccessfully to modernize the tax system to make it more equitable. The peasants bore the greatest tax burden, whereas the nobles and clergy were largely exempt. Tax collection was also far from systematic: private contractors collected many taxes and pocketed a large share of the proceeds. With the growing support of public opinion, the bond and annuity holders from the middle and upper classes now demanded a clearer system of fiscal accountability.

In a monarchy, the ruler's character is always crucial. Many complained that **Louis XVI** (r. 1774–1792) showed more interest in hunting and in his hobby of making locks than in the problems of government. His wife, **Marie-Antoinette**, was blond, beautiful, and much criticized for her extravagant taste in clothes, elaborate hairdos, and supposed indifference to popular misery. It was reported that, when told the poor had no bread, the queen gave a reply that has come to epitomize oblivious cold-heartedness:

"Let them eat cake." The queen, whom underground writers called the "Austrian bitch," had been the target of an increasingly nasty pamphlet campaign in the 1780s. By 1789, Marie-Antoinette had become an object of popular hatred. The king's ineffectiveness and the queen's growing unpopularity helped undermine the monarchy as an institution.

Queen Marie-Antoinette (detail)

Marie-Louise-Élizabeth Vigée-Lebrun painted this portrait of the French queen Marie-Antoinette and her children in 1788. The queen appears in the most stylish and lavish fashions of the day. When her eldest son (not shown in this detail) died in 1789, her second son (on her lap here) became heir to the throne. Known to supporters of the monarch as Louis XVII, the child died in prison in 1795 and never ruled. Vigée-Lebrun fled France in 1789 and returned only in 1805. (Chateau de Versailles, France / Giraudon / The Bridgeman Art Library International.)

Faced with a mounting deficit, in 1787 Louis submitted a package of reforms first to the Assembly of Notables and then to his old rival the parlement of Paris. Both refused to consider the reforms. Louis finally gave in to demands that he call a meeting of the Estates General, which had last met 175 years before.

The calling of the Estates General electrified public opinion. The **Estates General** was a body of deputies from the three estates, or orders, of France. The deputies in the First Estate represented some 100,000 clergy of the Catholic church, which owned about 10 percent of the land in France and collected a 10 percent tax (the tithe) on peasants. The deputies of the Second Estate represented the nobility, about 400,000 men and women who owned about 25 percent of the land, enjoyed many tax exemptions, and collected seigneurial dues and rents from their peasant tenants. The deputies of the Third Estate represented everyone else, at least 95 percent of the nation. Included in the Third Estate were the vast mass of peasants, some 75 percent of the population, and the *sans-culottes* ("without breeches") and middle classes of the cities. The sans-culottes were those who worked with their hands and wore long trousers rather than the knee breeches of the upper classes.

Before the elections to the Estates General in 1789, the king agreed to double the number of deputies from the Third Estate (making those deputies equal in number to the other two orders combined), but he refused to mandate voting by individual head rather than by order. Voting by order, allowing each order to have one vote, would conserve the traditional powers of the clergy and nobility; voting by head, allowing each deputy one vote, would give the Third Estate an advantage since many clergymen and even some nobles sympathized with the Third Estate.

As the state's censorship apparatus broke down, pamphleteers by the hundreds denounced the traditional privileges of the nobility and clergy and called for voting by head rather than by order. In the most vitriolic of all the pamphlets, *What Is the Third Estate?*, the middle-class abbé ("abbot") Emmanuel-Joseph Sieyès charged that the nobility contributed nothing at all to the nation's well-being; they were, he said, "a malignant disease which preys upon and tortures the body of a sick man." In the winter and spring of 1789, villagers and townspeople alike held meetings to elect deputies and write down their grievances. The effect was immediate. Although lawyers dominated the meetings at the regional level, the humblest peasants voted in their villages and burst forth with complaints, especially about taxes. As one villager lamented, "The last crust of bread has been taken from us." The long series of meetings raised expectations that the Estates General would help the king solve all the nation's ills.

These new hopes soared just at the moment France experienced a food shortage, an increasingly rare but always dangerous situation. Bad weather had damaged the harvest of 1788, causing bread prices to rise dramatically in many places in the spring and summer of 1789 and threatening starvation for the poorest people. In addition, a serious slump in textile production had been causing massive unemployment since 1786. Hundreds of thousands of textile workers were out of work and hungry, adding another volatile element to an already tense situation.

When some twelve hundred deputies journeyed to the king's palace of Versailles for the opening of the Estates General in May 1789, many readers avidly followed the developments in newspapers that sprouted overnight. Although most nobles insisted on voting by order, the deputies of the Third Estate refused to proceed on that basis. After six weeks of stalemate, the deputies of the Third Estate took unilateral action on June 17 and declared themselves and whoever would join them the National Assembly, in which each deputy would vote as an individual. Two days later, the clergy voted by a narrow margin to join them. Suddenly denied access to their meeting hall on June 20, the deputies met on a nearby tennis court and swore an oath not to disband until they had given France a constitution that reflected their newly declared authority. This "tennis court oath" expressed the determination of the Third Estate to carry through a constitutional revolution.

At first, Louis XVI appeared to agree to the new National Assembly, but he also ordered thousands of soldiers to march to Paris. The deputies who supported the Assem-

Fall of the Bastille

A central moment from the storming of the Bastille prison on July 14, 1789, is depicted in this colored print of a 1793 painting by Charles Thévenin. The insurgents have won the battle and are arresting the governor of the prison; in the next moments, they will cut off his head and parade it on a pike. The artist expresses his ambivalence about the violence by showing an insurgent in the right foreground brutally killing one of the defenders even though the battle is over. (Réunion des Musées Nationaux / Art Resource, NY.)

bly feared a plot to arrest them and disperse the Assembly. Their fears were confirmed when, on July 11, the king fired Jacques Necker, the Swiss Protestant finance minister and the one high official regarded as sympathetic to the deputies' cause.

The popular reaction in Paris changed the course of the French Revolution. When the news spread, the sans-culottes in Paris began to arm themselves and attack places where either grain or arms were thought to be stored. A deputy in Versailles reported home: "Today all of the evils overwhelm France, and we are between despotism, carnage, and famine." On July 14, an armed crowd marched on the Bastille, a huge fortified prison that symbolized royal authority (even though only a few prisoners were actually incarcerated there). After a chaotic battle in which a hundred armed citizens died, the prison officials surrendered.

The fall of the Bastille (an event now commemorated each July 14 as the French national holiday) set an important precedent. The common people showed themselves

REVEIL DU TIERS ETAT.

The Third Estate Awakens

This colored etching, produced after the fall of the Bastille (note the heads on pikes outside the prison), shows a clergyman (First Estate) and a noble (Second Estate) alarmed by the awakening of the commoners (Third Estate). The Third Estate breaks the chains of oppression and arms itself. In what ways does this print draw attention to the social conflicts that lay behind the political struggles in the Estates General? (Réunion des Musées Nationaux / Art Resource, NY.)

willing to intervene violently at a crucial political moment. All over France, local governments were forced out of power and replaced by committees of "patriots." To restore order, the patriots relied on newly formed National Guard units composed of civilians. In Paris, the Marquis de Lafayette, a hero of the American War of Independence and a noble deputy in the National Assembly, became commander of the new National Guard. One of Louis XVI's brothers and many other leading aristocrats fled into exile. The Revolution thus had its first heroes, its first victims, and its first enemies.

REVIEW QUESTION How did the beginning of the French Revolution resemble the other revolutions of 1787–1789?

From Monarchy to Republic, 1789–1793

Until July 1789, the French Revolution had followed a course much like that of the protest movements in the Low Countries. After that point, however, events in France escalated at a pace never before seen in history, leaving witnesses breathless with anticipation, anxiety, even shock. The French revolutionaries first tried to establish a constitutional monarchy based on the Enlightenment principles of human rights and rational government. This effort failed when the king attempted to flee and raise a counterrevolutionary army. When war broke out in 1792 and foreign soldiers invaded, a popular uprising on August 10 led to the arrest of the king and, for the first time in French history, the establishment of a republic.

The Revolution of Rights and Reason

Before drafting a constitution in 1789, the deputies of the National Assembly had to confront growing violence in the countryside. As food shortages spread, peasants feared that the beggars and vagrants crowding the roads might be part of an aristocratic plot to starve the French people by burning crops or barns. In many places, the **Great Fear** (the term used by historians to describe this rural panic) turned into peasant attacks on aristocrats or on the records of peasants' seigneurial dues kept in lords' châteaus.

Alarmed by peasant unrest, the National Assembly decided to make sweeping changes. On the night of August 4, 1789, noble deputies announced their willingness to give up their tax exemptions and seigneurial dues. The National Assembly decreed the abolition of what it called the feudal regime — that is, it freed the few remaining serfs and eliminated all special privileges in matters of taxation, including all seigneurial dues on land. (A few days later the deputies insisted on financial compensation for some of these dues, but most peasants refused to pay.) The Assembly also mandated equality of opportunity in access to government positions. Talent, rather than birth, was to be the key to success. Enlightenment principles were beginning to become law.

Three weeks later, the deputies drew up the **Declaration of the Rights of Man and Citizen** as the preamble to a new constitution. In words reminiscent of the American Declaration of Independence, whose author, Thomas Jefferson, was in Paris at the time,

it proclaimed, "Men are born and remain free and equal in rights." The Declaration granted freedom of religion, freedom of the press, equality of taxation, and equality before the law. It established the principle of national sovereignty: the king derived his authority henceforth from the nation rather than from tradition or divine right.

By pronouncing all *men* free and equal, the Declaration immediately created new dilemmas. Did women have equal rights with men? What about free blacks in the colonies? How could slavery be justified if all men were born free? Did religious toleration of Protestants and Jews include equal political rights? Women never received the right to vote during the French Revolution, though Protestant and Jewish men did.

Some women did not accept their exclusion. In addition to joining demonstrations, such as the march to Versailles in October 1789 (see chapter opener), women wrote petitions, published tracts, and organized political clubs to demand more participation. In her Declaration of the Rights of Woman of 1791, writer and political activist Olympe de Gouges (1748–1793) played on the language of the official Declaration to make the point that women should also be included: "Woman is born free and lives equal to man in her rights." De Gouges linked her complaints to a program of social reform in which women would have equal rights to property and public office and equal responsibilities in taxes and criminal punishment.

Unresponsive to calls for women's equality, the National Assembly turned to preparing France's first written constitution. The deputies gave voting rights only to white men who passed a test of wealth. Despite these limitations, France became a constitutional monarchy in which the king served as the leading state functionary. A one-house legislature was responsible for making laws. The king could postpone enactment of laws but not veto them. The deputies abolished all the old administrative divisions of the provinces and replaced them with a national system of eighty-three departments with identical administrative and legal structures (Map 19.1). All officials were elected; no offices could be bought or sold. The deputies also abolished the old taxes and replaced them with new ones that were supposed to be uniformly levied. The National Assembly had difficulty collecting taxes, however, because many people had expected a substantial cut in the tax rate. The new administrative system survived nonetheless, and the departments are still the basic units of the French state today.

When the deputies to the National Assembly turned to reforming the Catholic church, however, they created enduring conflicts. Convinced that monastic life encouraged idleness and a decline in the nation's population, the deputies outlawed any future monastic vows and encouraged monks and nuns to return to private life by offering state pensions. Motivated partly by the ongoing financial crisis, the National Assembly confiscated all the church's property and promised to pay clerical salaries in return. The Civil Constitution of the Clergy, passed in July 1790, provided that the voters elect their own parish priests and bishops just as they elected other officials. The impounded property served as a guarantee for the new paper money, called assignats, issued by the government. The assignats soon became subject to inflation because the government began to sell the church lands to the highest bidders in state auctions.

Map 19.1 Redrawing the Map of France, 1789–1791

Before 1789, France had been divided into provinces named after the territories owned by dukes and counts in the Middle Ages. Many provinces had their own law codes and separate systems of taxation. As it began its deliberations, the new National Assembly determined to install uniform administrations and laws for the entire country. Discussion of the administrative reforms began in October 1789 and became law on February 15, 1790, when the Assembly voted to divide the provinces into eighty-three departments, with names based on their geographical characteristics: Basses-Pyrénées, Haute-Pyrénées, and Pyrénées-Orientales for regions containing the Pyrénées Mountains; Marne and Haute-Marne for areas containing the Marne River; and so on. How did this redrawing of the administrative map reflect the deputies' emphasis on reason over history?

Faced with resistance to these changes, the National Assembly in November 1790 required all clergy to swear an oath of loyalty to the Civil Constitution of the Clergy. Pope Pius VI in Rome condemned the constitution, and half of the French clergy refused to take the oath. The oath of allegiance permanently divided the Catholic population. The revolutionary government lost many supporters by passing laws against the clergy who refused the oath and by sending them into exile, deporting them forcibly, or executing them as traitors.

The End of Monarchy

The reorganization of the Catholic church offended Louis XVI and gave added weight to those pushing him to organize resistance. On June 20, 1791, the royal family escaped in disguise from Paris and fled toward the eastern border of France, where they hoped

to gather support from Austrian emperor Leopold II, the brother of Marie-Antoinette. The plans went awry when a postmaster recognized the king from his portrait on the new French money, and the royal family was arrested at Varennes, forty miles from the Austrian Netherlands border. The "flight to Varennes" touched off demonstrations in Paris against the royal family. Cartoons circulated depicting the royal family as animals being returned "to the stable."

The constitution, finally completed in 1791, provided for the immediate election of a new legislature. The status of the king might have remained uncertain if war had not intervened, but by early 1792 everyone seemed intent on war with Austria. Louis and Marie-Antoinette hoped that such a war would lead to the defeat of the Revolution, whereas the deputies who favored a republic believed that war would lead to the king's downfall. On April 21, 1792, Louis declared war on Austria. Prussia immediately entered on the Austrian side. Thousands of French aristocrats, including both of the king's brothers and two-thirds of the army officer corps, had already emigrated and were gathering along France's eastern border in expectation of joining a counterrevolutionary army.

When the fighting broke out, all the powers expected a short, relatively contained war. Instead, it would continue despite brief interruptions for the next twenty-three years. War had an immediate radicalizing effect on French politics. When the French armies proved woefully unprepared for battle, the authority of the new legislature came under fire. In June 1792, an angry crowd invaded the hall of the legislature in Paris and

The King as a Farmyard Animal
This simple print makes a powerful point: King Louis XVI has lost not only his authority but also the respect of his subjects. Engravings and etchings like this one appeared in reaction to the attempted flight of the king and queen in June 1791.

threatened the royal family. The Prussian commander, the duke of Brunswick, issued a manifesto announcing that Paris would be totally destroyed if the royal family suffered any violence.

The sans-culottes of Paris did not passively await their fate. Faced with the threat of military retaliation and frustrated with the inaction of the deputies, on August 10 the sans-culottes organized an insurrection and attacked the Tuileries palace, the residence of the king. The king and his family had to seek refuge in the meeting room of the legislature, where the frightened deputies ordered elections for a constitutional convention. By abolishing the property qualifications for voting, the deputies instituted universal male suffrage for the first time.

Violence soon exploded again when early in September 1792 the Prussians approached Paris. Hastily gathered mobs stormed the overflowing prisons to seek out traitors, and eleven hundred inmates were killed, including many ordinary and completely innocent people. The princess of Lamballe, one of the queen's favorites, was hacked to pieces and her mutilated body displayed beneath the windows where the royal family was kept under guard. These "September massacres" showed the dark side of popular revolution, in which the common people demanded instant revenge on supposed enemies and conspirators.

When it met, the National Convention abolished the monarchy and on September 22 established the first republic in French history. The republic would answer only to the people, not to any royal authority. Many of the deputies in the Convention belonged to the devotedly republican (and therefore left-wing) **Jacobin Club**, named after the former monastery in Paris where the club had first met in 1789. The Jacobin Club in Paris headed a national political network of clubs that linked all the major towns and cities. Lafayette and other liberal aristocrats who had supported the constitutional monarchy fled into exile.

The National Convention faced a dire situation. It needed to write a new constitution for the republic while fighting a war with external enemies and confronting increasing resistance at home. The French people had never known any government other than monarchy. Only half the population could read and write at even a basic level. In this situation, symbolic actions became very important. Revolutionaries soon pulled down statues of kings and burned reminders of the former regime.

The fate of Louis XVI and the direction of the republic divided the deputies elected to the National Convention. Most of the deputies were middle-class lawyers and professionals who had developed their ardent republican beliefs in the network of Jacobin Clubs. After the fall of the monarchy in August 1792, however, the Jacobins had divided into two factions. The Girondins (named after a department in southwestern France, the Gironde, which provided some of its leading orators) met regularly at the salon of Jeanne Roland, the wife of a minister. They resented the growing power of Parisian militants and tried to appeal to the departments outside of Paris. The Mountain (so called because its deputies sat in the highest seats of the National Convention), in contrast, was closely allied with the Paris militants.

The first showdown between the Girondins and the Mountain occurred during the trial of the king in December 1792. Although the Girondins agreed that the king was guilty of treason, many of them argued for clemency, exile, or a popular referendum on his fate. After a long and difficult debate, the National Convention supported the Mountain and voted by a very narrow majority to execute the king. Louis XVI went to the guillotine on January 21, 1793, sharing the fate of Charles I of England in 1649.

REVIEW QUESTION Why did the French Revolution turn in an increasingly radical direction after 1789?

Terror and Resistance

The execution of the king did not solve the new regime's problems. The continuing war required even more men and money, and the introduction of a national draft provoked massive resistance. In response to growing pressures, the National Convention named the Committee of Public Safety to supervise food distribution, direct the war effort, and root out counterrevolutionaries. The leader of the committee, **Maximilien Robespierre** (1758–1794), wanted to go beyond these stopgap measures and create a "republic of virtue," in which the government would teach, or force, citizens to become virtuous republicans through a massive program of political reeducation. Thus began the **Terror**, in which the guillotine became the most terrifying instrument of a government that suppressed almost every form of dissent.

The Guillotine

Before 1789, only nobles were decapitated if condemned to death; commoners were usually hanged. Equalization of the death penalty was first proposed by J. I. Guillotin, a professor of anatomy and a deputy in the National Assembly. He also suggested that a mechanical device be constructed for decapitation, leading to the instrument's association with his name. The Assembly decreed decapitation as the death penalty in June 1791 and another physician, A. Louis, actually invented the guillotine. The executioner pulled up the blade by a cord and then released it. Use of the guillotine began in April 1792 and did not end until 1981, when the French government abolished the death penalty. The guillotine fascinated as much as it repelled. Reproduced in miniature, painted onto snuffboxes and china, worn as jewelry, and even serving as a toy, the guillotine became a part of popular culture. How could the guillotine be simultaneously celebrated as the people's avenger by supporters of the Revolution and vilified as the preeminent symbol of the Terror by opponents? (Réunion des Musées Nationaux / Art Resource, NY.)

Robespierre and the Committee of Public Safety

The conflict between the more moderate Girondins and the more radical Mountain came to a head in spring 1793. Militants in Paris agitated for the removal of the deputies who had proposed a referendum on the king, and in retaliation the Girondins engineered the arrest of Jean-Paul Marat, a deputy allied with the Mountain who in his newspaper had been calling for more and more executions. Marat was acquitted, and Parisian militants marched into the National Convention on June 2, forcing the deputies to decree the arrest of their twenty-nine Girondin colleagues. The Convention consented to the establishment of paramilitary bands called revolutionary armies to hunt down political suspects and hoarders of grain. The deputies also agreed to speed up the operation of special revolutionary courts.

Setting the course for government and the war increasingly fell to the twelve-member Committee of Public Safety. When Robespierre was elected to the committee in July 1793, he became the chief spokesman of the Revolution. A lawyer from northern France known as "the incorruptible" for his stern honesty and fierce dedication to democratic ideals, Robespierre remains one of the most controversial figures in world history because of his association with the Terror. Although he originally opposed the death penalty and the war, he was convinced that the emergency situation of 1793 required severe measures, including death for those, such as the Girondins, who opposed the committee's policies.

Robespierre defended the people's right to democratic government, while in practice he supported many emergency measures that restricted their liberties. He personally favored a free-market economy, as did almost all middle-class deputies, but in this time of crisis he was willing to enact price controls and requisitioning. In an effort to stabilize prices, the National Convention established the General Maximum on September 29, 1793, which set limits on the prices of thirty-nine essential commodities and on wages. In a speech to the Convention, Robespierre explained the necessity of government by terror: "The first maxim of your policies must be to lead the people by reason and the people's enemies by terror. . . . Without virtue, terror is deadly; without terror, virtue is impotent." *Terror* was not an idle term; it seemed to imply that the goal of democracy justified what we now call totalitarian means, that is, the suppression of all dissent.

Through a series of desperate measures, the Committee of Public Safety set the machinery of the Terror in motion. It sent deputies out "on mission" to purge unreliable officials and organize the war effort. Revolutionary tribunals tried political suspects. In October 1793, the Revolutionary Tribunal in Paris convicted Marie-Antoinette of treason and sent her to the guillotine. The Girondin leaders and Jeanne Roland were also guillotined, as was Olympe de Gouges.

The new republic won its greatest success on the battlefield. As of April 1793, France faced war with Austria, Prussia, Great Britain, Spain, Sardinia, and the Dutch Republic — all fearful of the impact of revolutionary ideals on their own populations. The execution of Louis XVI, in particular, galvanized European governments; according to William Pitt, the British prime minister, it was "the foulest and most atrocious act the

world has ever seen." To face this daunting coalition of forces, the French republic ordered the first universal draft of men in history. Every unmarried man and childless widower between the ages of eighteen and twenty-five was declared eligible for conscription. The government also tapped a new and potent source of power — nationalist pride.

Forges were set up in the parks and gardens of Paris to produce thousands of guns, and citizens everywhere helped collect saltpeter to make gunpowder. By the end of 1793, the French nation in arms had stopped the advance of the allied powers, and in the summer of 1794 it invaded the Austrian Netherlands and crossed the Rhine River. The army was ready to carry the gospel of revolution and republicanism to the rest of Europe.

The Republic of Virtue, 1793–1794

The program of the Terror went beyond pragmatic measures to fight the war and internal enemies to include efforts to "republicanize everything" — in other words, to effect a cultural revolution. The republic left no stone unturned in its endeavor to get its message across. Songs — especially the new national anthem, "La Marseillaise" — and placards, posters, pamphlets, books, engravings, paintings, sculpture, even everyday crockery, chamber pots, and playing cards conveyed revolutionary slogans and symbols. Foremost among the symbols was the figure of Liberty, which appeared on coins and bills, on

Representing Liberty
Liberty was represented by a female figure because in French the noun is feminine (*la liberté*). This painting from 1793–1794, by Jeanne-Louise Vallain, captures the usual attributes of Liberty: she is soberly seated, wearing a Roman-style toga and holding a pike with a Roman liberty cap on top. Her Roman appearance signals that she represents an abstract quality. The fact that she holds an instrument of battle suggests that women might be active participants. The Statue of Liberty in New York harbor, given by the French to the United States, is a late-nineteenth-century version of the same figure, but without any suggestion of battle. (Nanine Vallain, La Liberté, Huile sur toile, 1794, © Coll. Musée de la Révolution française / Domaine de Vizille.)

letterheads and seals, and as statues in festivals. Hundreds of new plays were produced and old classics revised. To encourage the production of patriotic and republican works, the government sponsored state competitions for artists.

At the center of this elaborate cultural campaign were the revolutionary festivals modeled on Rousseau's plans for a civic religion. The Festival of Federation on July 14, 1790, marked the first anniversary of the fall of the Bastille. Under the National Convention, the well-known painter Jacques-Louis David (1748–1825), who was a deputy and an associate of Robespierre, took over festival planning. David aimed to destroy the mystique of monarchy and to make the republic sacred. His Festival of Unity on August 10, 1793, for example, celebrated the first anniversary of the overthrow of the monarchy. In front of the statue of Liberty built for the occasion, a bonfire consumed crowns and scepters symbolizing royalty while a cloud of three thousand white doves rose into the sky. This was all part of preaching the "moral order of the Republic . . . that will make us a people of brothers, a people of philosophers."

Some revolutionaries hoped the festival system would replace the Catholic church altogether. They initiated a campaign of **de-Christianization** that included closing churches (Protestant as well as Catholic), selling many church buildings to the highest bidder, and trying to force even those clergy who had taken the oath of loyalty to abandon their clerical vocations and marry. Great churches became storehouses for arms or grain, or their stones were sold off to contractors. The medieval statues of kings on the facade of Notre Dame cathedral were beheaded. Church bells were dismantled and church treasures melted down for government use.

In the ultimate step in de-Christianization, extremists tried to establish what they called the Cult of Reason to supplant Christianity. In Paris in the fall of 1793, a goddess of Liberty, played by an actress, presided over the Festival of Reason in Notre Dame cathedral. Robespierre objected to the de-Christianization campaign's atheism; he favored a Rousseau-inspired deistic religion without the supposedly superstitious trappings of Catholicism. The Committee of Public Safety halted the de-Christianization campaign, and Robespierre, with David's help, tried to institute an alternative, the Cult of the Supreme Being, in June 1794. Neither the Cult of Reason nor the Cult of the Supreme Being attracted many followers, but both show the depth of the commitment to overturning the old order and all its traditional institutions.

In principle, the best way to ensure the future of the republic was through the education of the young. The deputy Georges-Jacques Danton (1759–1794), Robespierre's main competitor, maintained that "after bread, the first need of the people is education." The National Convention voted to make primary schooling free and compulsory for both boys and girls. It took control of education away from the Catholic church and tried to set up a system of state schools at both the primary and secondary levels, but it lacked trained teachers to replace those the Catholic religious orders had provided. As a result, opportunities for learning how to read and write may have diminished. In 1799, only one-fifth as many boys were enrolled in the state secondary schools as had studied in church schools ten years earlier.

Although many of the ambitious republican programs failed, colors, clothing, and daily speech were all politicized. The tricolor — the combination of red, white, and blue that was to become the flag of France — was devised in July 1789, and by 1793 everyone had to wear a tricolor cockade (a badge made of ribbons). Using the formal forms of speech — *vous* for "you" or the title *monsieur* or *madame* — might identify someone as an aristocrat; true patriots used the informal *tu* and *citoyen* or *citoyenne* ("citizen") instead. Some people changed their names or gave their children new kinds of names. Biblical and saints' names such as John, Peter, Joseph, and Mary gave way to names recalling heroes of the ancient Roman republic (Brutus, Gracchus, Cornelia), revolutionary heroes, or flowers and plants. Such changes symbolized adherence to the republic and to Enlightenment ideals rather than to Catholicism.

Even the measures of time and space were revolutionized. In October 1793, the National Convention introduced a new calendar to replace the Christian one. Its bases were reason and republican principles. Year I dated from the beginning of the republic on September 22, 1792. Twelve months of exactly thirty days each received new names derived from nature — for example, Pluviôse (roughly equivalent to February) recalled the rain (*la pluie*) of late winter. Instead of seven-day weeks, ten-day *décades* provided only one day of rest every ten days and pointedly eliminated the Sunday of the Christian calendar. The calendar remained in force for twelve years despite continuing resistance to it. More enduring was the new metric system based on units of ten that was invented to replace the hundreds of local variations in weights and measures. Other countries in Europe and throughout the world eventually adopted the metric system.

Revolutionary laws also changed the rules of family life. The state took responsibility for all family matters away from the Catholic church: people now registered births, deaths, and marriages at city hall, not the parish church. Marriage became a civil contract and as such could be broken and thereby nullified. The new divorce law of September 1792 was the most far-reaching in Europe: a couple could divorce by mutual consent or for reasons such as insanity, abandonment, battering, or criminal conviction. Thousands of men and women took advantage of the law to dissolve unhappy marriages, even though the pope had condemned the measure. (In 1816, the government revoked the right to divorce, and not until the 1970s did French divorce laws return to the principles of the 1792 legislation.) In one of its most influential actions, the National Convention passed a series of laws that created equal inheritance among all children in the family, including girls. The father's right to favor one child, especially the oldest male, was considered aristocratic and hence antirepublican.

Resisting the Revolution

By intruding into religion, culture, and daily life, the republic inevitably provoked resistance. Shouting curses against the republic, uprooting liberty trees, carrying statues of the Virgin Mary in procession, hiding a priest who would not take the oath, singing a royalist song — all these expressed dissent with the new symbols, rituals, and policies.

Long bread lines in the cities exhausted the patience of women, and their constant grumbling occasionally turned into spontaneous demonstrations or riots over high prices or food shortages.

Other forms of resistance were more individual. One young woman, Charlotte Corday, assassinated the outspoken deputy Jean-Paul Marat in July 1793. Corday fervently supported the Girondins, and she considered it her patriotic duty to kill the deputy who, in the columns of his paper, had constantly demanded more heads and more blood. Marat was immediately eulogized as a great martyr, and Corday went to the guillotine vilified as a monster but confident that she had "avenged many innocent victims."

Organized resistance against the republic broke out in many parts of France. The arrest of the Girondin deputies in June 1793 sparked insurrections in several departments. After the government retook the city of Lyon, one of the centers of the revolt, the deputy on mission ordered sixteen hundred houses demolished and the name of the city changed to Liberated City. Special courts sentenced almost two thousand people to death.

In the Vendée region of western France, resistance turned into a bloody and prolonged civil war. Between March and December 1793, peasants, artisans, and weavers joined under noble leadership to form a "Catholic and Royal Army." One rebel group explained its motives: "They [the republicans] have killed our king, chased away our priests, sold the goods of our church, eaten everything we have and now they want to take our bodies [in the draft]." The rebels stormed the largest towns in the region. Both sides committed horrible atrocities. At the small town of Machecoul, for example, the rebels massacred five hundred republicans, including administrators and National Guard members; many were tied together, shoved into freshly dug graves, and shot. By the fall, however, republican soldiers had turned back the rebels. Military courts ordered thousands executed, and republican soldiers massacred thousands of others. In one especially gruesome incident, the deputy Jean-Baptiste Carrier supervised the drowning of some two thousand Vendée rebels, including a number of priests. Barges loaded with prisoners were floated into the Loire River near Nantes and then sunk. Controversy still rages about the rebellion's death toll because no accurate count could be taken. Estimates of rebel deaths alone range from about 20,000 to higher than 250,000. Many thousands of republican soldiers and civilians also lost their lives in fighting that continued on and off for years. Even the low estimates reveal the carnage of this catastrophic confrontation between the republic and its opponents.

The Fall of Robespierre and the End of the Terror

In the atmosphere of fear of conspiracy that the outbreaks of rebellion fueled, Robespierre tried simultaneously to exert the National Convention's control over popular political activities and to weed out opposition among the deputies. As a result, the Terror intensified until July 1794, when a group of deputies joined within the Convention to order the arrest and execution of Robespierre and his followers. The Convention then ordered elections and drew up a new republican constitution that gave executive power to five

Major Events of the French Revolution

May 5, 1789	The Estates General opens at Versailles
June 17, 1789	Third Estate decides to call itself the National Assembly
June 20, 1789	Tennis court oath demonstrates resolve of deputies to carry out constitutional revolution
July 14, 1789	Fall of the Bastille
August 4, 1789	National Assembly abolishes feudalism
August 26, 1789	National Assembly passes Declaration of the Rights of Man and Citizen
October 5–6, 1789	Women march to Versailles, joined by men in bringing royal family back to Paris
July 12, 1790	Civil Constitution of the Clergy
June 20, 1791	Louis XVI and Marie-Antoinette attempt to flee in disguise, are captured at Varennes
April 20, 1792	Declaration of war on Austria
August 10, 1792	Insurrection in Paris and attack on Tuileries palace lead to removal of king's authority
September 2–6, 1792	Prisoners murdered in September massacres in Paris
September 22, 1792	Establishment of republic
January 21, 1793	Execution of Louis XVI
March 11, 1793	Beginning of uprising in Vendée
May 31–June 2, 1793	Insurrection leading to arrest of Girondins
July 27, 1793	Robespierre named to Committee of Public Safety
September 29, 1793	Convention establishes General Maximum on prices and wages
October 16, 1793	Execution of Marie-Antoinette
February 4, 1794	Slavery abolished in French colonies
March 13–24, 1794	Arrest, trial, and executions of so-called ultrarevolutionaries
March 30–April 5, 1794	Arrest, trial, and executions of Danton and his followers
July 27, 1794	Arrest of Robespierre and his supporters (executed July 28–29); beginning of end of the Terror
October 26, 1795	Directory government takes office
April 1796–October 1797	Succession of Italian victories by Bonaparte

directors. This "Directory government" maintained power during four years of seesaw battles between royalists and former Jacobins.

In the fall of 1793, the National Convention cracked down on popular clubs and societies. First to be suppressed were women's political clubs. Founded in early 1793, the Society of Revolutionary Republican Women urged harsher measures against the republic's enemies and insisted that women have a voice in politics even if they did not have the vote. Women had set up their own clubs in many provincial towns and also attended the meetings of local men's organizations. Using traditional arguments about women's inherent unsuitability for politics, the deputies abolished women's political

clubs. The closing of women's clubs marked an important turning point in the Revolution. From then on, the sans-culottes and their political organizations came increasingly under the thumb of the Jacobin deputies in the National Convention.

In the spring of 1794, the Committee of Public Safety moved against its critics among leaders in Paris and deputies in the National Convention itself. First, a handful of "ultrarevolutionaries" — a collection of local Parisian politicians — were arrested and executed. Next came the other side, the "indulgents," so called because they favored a moderation of the Terror. Included among them was the deputy Danton, himself once a member of the Committee of Public Safety and a friend of Robespierre. Danton was the Revolution's most flamboyant orator and, unlike Robespierre, a high-living, high-spending politician. At every critical turning point in national politics, his booming voice had swayed opinion. Now, under pressure from the Committee of Public Safety, the Revolutionary Tribunal convicted him and his friends of treason and sentenced them to death.

"The Revolution," as one of the Girondin victims of 1793 had remarked, "was devouring its own children." Even after the major threats to the Committee of Public Safety's power had been eliminated, the Terror not only continued but worsened. A law passed in June 1794 denied the accused the right of legal counsel, reduced the number of jurors necessary for conviction, and allowed only two judgments: acquittal or death. The category of political crimes expanded to include "slandering patriotism" and "seeking to inspire discouragement." Ordinary people risked the guillotine if they expressed any discontent. The rate of executions in Paris rose from five a day in the spring of 1794 to twenty-six a day in the summer. The political atmosphere darkened even though the military situation improved. At the end of June, the French armies decisively defeated the main Austrian army and advanced through the Austrian Netherlands to Brussels and Antwerp. The emergency measures for fighting the war were working, yet Robespierre and his inner circle had made so many enemies that they could not afford to loosen the grip of the Terror.

The Terror hardly touched many parts of France, but overall the experience was undeniably traumatic. Across the country, the official Terror cost the lives of at least 40,000 French people, most of them living in the regions of major insurrections or near the borders with foreign enemies, where suspicion of collaboration ran high. As many as 300,000 French people — 1 out of every 50 — went to prison as suspects between March 1793 and August 1794. The toll for the aristocracy and the clergy was especially high. Many leading nobles perished under the guillotine, and thousands emigrated. Thirty thousand to forty thousand clergy who refused the oath left the country, at least two thousand (including many nuns) were executed, and thousands were imprisoned. The clergy were singled out in particular in the civil war zones: 135 priests were massacred at Lyon in November 1793, and 83 were shot in one day during the Vendée revolt. Yet many victims of the Terror were peasants or sans-culottes.

The final crisis of the Terror came as conflicts within the Committee of Public Safety and the National Convention left Robespierre isolated. On July 27, 1794 (the ninth of Thermidor, Year II, according to the revolutionary calendar), Robespierre appeared

before the Convention with yet another list of deputies to be arrested. Many feared they would be named, and they shouted him down and ordered him arrested along with the president of the Revolutionary Tribunal in Paris and the commander of the Parisian National Guard. An armed uprising led by the Paris city government failed to save Robespierre when most of the National Guard took the side of the Convention. Robespierre tried to kill himself with a pistol but only broke his jaw. The next day he and scores of followers went to the guillotine.

The men who led the July 27 attack on Robespierre did not intend to reverse all his policies, but that happened nonetheless because of a violent backlash known as the **Thermidorian Reaction**. The new government released hundreds of suspects and arranged a temporary truce in the Vendée. It purged Jacobins from local bodies and replaced them with their opponents. It arrested some of the most notorious "terrorists" in the National Convention, such as Carrier, and put them to death. Within the year, the new leaders abolished the Revolutionary Tribunal and closed the Jacobin Club in Paris. Popular demonstrations met severe repression. In southeastern France, in particular, the "White Terror" replaced the Jacobins' "Red Terror." Former officials and local Jacobin leaders were harassed, beaten, and often murdered by paramilitary bands who had tacit support from the new authorities. Those who remained in the National Convention prepared yet another constitution in 1795, setting up a two-house legislature and an executive body — the Directory, headed by five directors.

The Directory regime tenuously held on to power for four years, all the while trying to fend off challenges from the remaining Jacobins and the resurgent royalists. The puritanical atmosphere of the Terror gave way to the pursuit of pleasure — low-cut dresses of transparent materials, the reappearance of prostitutes in the streets, and "victims' balls" where guests wore red ribbons around their necks as reminders of the guillotine. Bands of young men dressed in knee breeches and rich fabrics picked fights with known Jacobins and disrupted theater performances with loud antirevolutionary songs. All over France, people petitioned to reopen churches closed during the Terror. If necessary, they broke into a church to hold services with a priest who had been in hiding or a lay schoolteacher who was willing to say Mass.

Although the Terror had ended, the revolution had not. Both the most democratic and the most repressive phases of the Revolution had ended at once in July 1794. Between 1795 and 1799, the republic endured in France, but it directed a war effort abroad that would ultimately bring to power the man who would dismantle the republic itself.

> **REVIEW QUESTION** What factors can explain the Terror? To what extent was it simply a response to a national emergency or a reflection of deeper problems within the French Revolution?

Revolution on the March

War raged almost constantly from 1792 to 1815. At one time or another, and sometimes all at once, France faced every principal power in Europe. The French republic — and later the French Empire under its supreme commander, Emperor Napoleon

Bonaparte — proved an even more formidable opponent than the France of Louis XIV. New means of mobilizing and organizing soldiers enabled the French to dominate Europe for a generation. The influence of the French Revolution as a political model and the threat of French military conquest combined to challenge the traditional order in Europe and offer new prospects to the rest of the world as well.

Arms and Conquests

The powers allied against France squandered their best chance to triumph in early 1793, when the French armies verged on chaos because of the emigration of noble army officers and the problems of integrating new draftees. By the end of 1793, the French had a huge and powerful fighting force of 700,000 men. But the army still faced many problems in the field. As many as a third of the recent draftees deserted before or during battle. Generals might pay with their lives if they lost a key battle and their loyalty to the Revolution came under suspicion.

France nevertheless had one overwhelming advantage: those soldiers who agreed to serve fought for a revolution that they and their brothers and sisters had helped make. The republic was their government, and the army was in large measure theirs, too; many officers had risen through the ranks by skill and talent rather than by inheriting or purchasing their positions. One young peasant boy wrote to his parents, "Either you will see me return bathed in glory, or you will have a son who is a worthy citizen of France who knows how to die for the defense of his country."

When the French armies invaded the Austrian Netherlands and crossed the Rhine in the summer of 1794, they proclaimed a war of liberation (Map 19.2). In the Austrian Netherlands, Mainz, Savoy, and Nice, French officers organized Jacobin Clubs that attracted locals. The clubs petitioned for annexation to France, and French legislation was then introduced, including the abolition of seigneurial dues. As the French annexed more and more territory, however, "liberated" people in many places began to view them as an army of occupation. Despite resistance, especially in the Austrian Netherlands, these areas remained part of France until 1815, and the legal changes were permanent.

The Directory government that came to power in 1795 launched an even more aggressive policy of creating semi-independent "sister republics" wherever the armies succeeded. When Prussia declared neutrality in 1795, the French armies swarmed into the Dutch Republic, abolished the stadholderate, and — with the revolutionary penchant for renaming — created the new Batavian Republic, a satellite of France. The brilliant young general Napoleon Bonaparte gained a reputation by defeating the Austrian armies in northern Italy in 1797 and then created the Cisalpine Republic. Next he overwhelmed Venice and then handed it over to the Austrians in exchange for a peace agreement that lasted less than two years. After the French attacked the Swiss cantons in 1798, they set up the Helvetic Republic and curtailed many of the Catholic church's privileges. They conquered the Papal States in 1798 and installed a Roman Republic, forcing the pope to flee to Siena.

Map 19.2 French Expansion, 1791–1799

The influence of the French Revolution on neighboring territories is dramatically evident in this map. The French directly annexed the papal territories in southern France in 1791, Nice and Savoy in 1792, and the Austrian Netherlands in 1795. They set up a series of sister republics in the former Dutch Republic and in various Italian states. Local people did not always welcome these changes. For example, the French made the Dutch pay a huge war indemnity, support a French occupying army of 25,000 soldiers, and give up some southern territories. The sister republics faced a future of subordination to French national interests.

The revolutionary wars had an immediate impact on European life at all levels of society. Thousands of men died in every country involved, with perhaps as many as 200,000 casualties in the French armies alone in 1794 and 1795. More soldiers died in hospitals as a result of their wounds than on the battlefields. Constant warfare hampered world commerce and especially disrupted French overseas shipping. Times were now

Map 19.3 The Second and Third Partitions of Poland, 1793 and 1795
In 1793, Prussia took over territory that included 1.1 million Poles while Russia gained 3 million new inhabitants. Austria gave up any claims to Poland in exchange for help from Russia and Prussia in acquiring Bavaria. In the final division of 1795, Prussia absorbed an additional 900,000 Polish subjects, including those in Warsaw; Austria incorporated 1 million Poles and the city of Cracow; Russia gained another 2 million Poles. The three powers determined never to use the term *Kingdom of Poland* again. How had Poland become such a prey to the other powers?

hard almost everywhere, because the dislocations of internal and external commerce provoked constant shortages.

Poland Extinguished, 1793–1795

France had survived in 1793 in part because its enemies were busy elsewhere. Fearing French influence, Prussia joined Russia in dividing up generous new slices of territory in the second partition of Poland (Map 19.3). As might be expected, Poland's reform movement became even more pro-French. Some leaders fled abroad, including Tadeusz Kościuszko (1746–1817), an officer who had been a foreign volunteer in the War of American Independence and who now escaped to Paris. In the spring of 1794, Kościuszko returned from France to lead a nationalist revolt.

The uprising failed. Kościuszko won a few victories, but when the Russian empress Catherine the Great's forces regrouped, they routed the Poles and Lithuanians. Kościuszko and other Polish Patriot leaders languished for years in Russian and Austrian prisons. Taking no further chances, Russia, Prussia, and Austria wiped Poland completely from the map in the third partition (1795). "The Polish question" would plague international relations for more than a century as Polish rebels flocked to any international upheaval that might undo the partitions. Beyond all this maneuvering lay the unsolved problem of Polish serfdom, which isolated the nation's gentry and townspeople from the rural masses.

Revolution in the Colonies

The revolution that produced so much upheaval in continental Europe transformed life in France's Caribbean colonies, too. These colonies were crucial to the French economy. Twice the size in land area of the neighboring British colonies, they also produced nearly

twice as much revenue in exports. The slave population had doubled in the French colonies in the twenty
years before 1789. St. Domingue (present-day Haiti)
was the most important French colony. Occupying
the western half of the island of Hispaniola, it was
inhabited not only by 465,000 slaves and 30,000
whites but also by 28,000 free people of color, whose
primary job was to apprehend runaway slaves and
ensure plantation security.

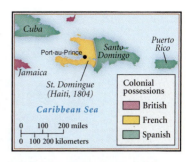

St. Domingue on the Eve of the Revolt, 1791

Despite the efforts of a Paris club called the
Friends of Blacks, most French revolutionaries did
not consider slavery a pressing problem. In August
1791, however, the slaves in northern St. Domingue organized a large-scale revolt. To
restore authority over the slaves, the deputies in Paris granted civil and political rights to
the free blacks. This action infuriated white planters and merchants, who in 1793 signed
an agreement with Great Britain, now France's enemy in war, declaring British sovereignty over St. Domingue. To complicate matters further, Spain, which controlled the
rest of the island and had entered on Great Britain's side in the war with France, offered
freedom to individual slave rebels who joined the Spanish armies as long as they agreed
to maintain the slave regime for the other blacks.

The few thousand French republican troops on St. Domingue were outnumbered,
and to prevent complete military disaster, the French commissioner freed all the slaves
in his jurisdiction in August 1793 without permission from the government in Paris.
In February 1794, the National Convention formally abolished slavery and granted full
rights to all black men in the colonies. These actions had the desired effect. One of the
ablest black generals allied with the Spanish, the ex-slave François Dominique Toussaint
L'Ouverture (1743–1803), changed sides and committed his troops to the French.
Toussaint remained in charge until 1802, when Napoleon sent French armies to regain
control of the island. They arrested Toussaint and transported him to France, where he
died in prison. Toussaint became a hero to abolitionists everywhere, a potent symbol of
black struggles to win freedom. Napoleon attempted to restore slavery, as he had in the
other French Caribbean colonies of Guadeloupe and Martinique, but the remaining
black generals defeated his armies and in 1804 proclaimed the Republic of Haiti.

Worldwide Reactions to Revolutionary Change

As the example of the colonies shows, the French Revolution inflamed politics and social relations far beyond Europe. It soon became one of the most divisive political issues
in the United States. Thomas Jefferson wrote in January 1793 that "the liberty of the
whole earth" depended on the Revolution's success; John Adams, in contrast, believed
that the French Revolution had set back human progress hundreds of years. In India, the
ruler of the southern kingdom of Mysore, Tipu Sultan, planted a liberty tree and set up
a Jacobin Club in the futile hope of gaining French allies against the British.

Toussaint L'Ouverture
The leader of the St. Domingue slave uprising appears on horseback, in his general's uniform, sword in hand. His depiction in this colored print from the early nineteenth century makes him seem much like other military heroes from the time, including Napoleon Bonaparte. (Bibliothèque nationale, Paris, France / Archives Charmet / The Bridgeman Art Library International.)

Many had greeted the events of 1789 with unabashed enthusiasm. The English Unitarian minister Richard Price had exulted, "Behold, the light . . . after setting AMERICA free, reflected to FRANCE, and there kindled into a blaze that lays despotism in ashes, and warms and illuminates EUROPE." Democrats and reformers from many countries flooded to Paris to witness events firsthand. Supporters of the French Revolution in Great Britain joined constitutional and reform societies that sprang up in many cities. Pro-French feeling ran even stronger in Ireland. Catholics and Presbyterians, both excluded from the vote, came together in 1791 in the Society of United Irishmen, which eventually pressed for secession from England.

European elites became alarmed when the French abolished monarchy and nobility and encouraged popular participation in politics. The British government, for example, quickly suppressed the corresponding societies, charging that their contacts with the French were seditious. When the Society of United Irishmen timed a rebellion to coincide with an attempted French invasion in 1798, the British mercilessly repressed them, killing thirty thousand rebels.

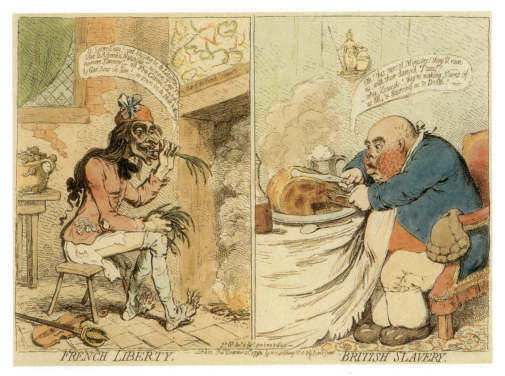

FRENCH LIBERTY.   BRITISH SLAVERY.

The English Rebuttal
In this caricature, James Gillray satirizes the French version of liberty. Gillray produced thousands of political caricatures. How would you interpret the message of this print? (© The Trustees of the British Museum / Art Resource, NY.)

Many leading intellectuals in the German states, including the philosopher Immanuel Kant, initially supported the revolutionary cause, but after 1793 most of them turned against the popular violence and military aggressiveness of the Revolution. The German states, still run by many separate rulers, experienced a profound artistic and intellectual revival, which eventually stimulated anti-French nationalism. This renaissance included a resurgence of intellectual life in the universities, a thriving press (1,225 journals were launched in the 1780s alone), and the multiplication of Masonic lodges and literary clubs.

Despite the turn in opinion, European rulers still dreaded the mere mention of revolution. Spain's royal government simply suppressed all news from France, fearing that it might ignite the spirit of revolt. Despite similar government controls on news in Russia, 278 outbreaks of peasant unrest occurred there between 1796 and 1798. When Naples revolted under French influence in 1799, 100 republicans, including leading intellectuals, were executed when the royalists returned to power.

REVIEW QUESTION Why did some groups outside of France embrace the French Revolution while others resisted it?

Mapping the West Europe in 1799

France's expansion during the revolutionary wars threatened to upset the balance of power in Europe. A century earlier, the English and Dutch had allied and formed a Europe-wide coalition to check the territorial ambitions of Louis XIV. Thwarting French ambitions after 1799 would prove to be even more of a challenge to the other European powers. The Dutch had been reduced to satellite status, as had most of the Italian states. Even Austria and Prussia would suffer devastating losses to the French on the battlefield. Only a new coalition of European powers could stop France in the future.

Conclusion

Growing out of aspirations for freedom that also inspired the Dutch, Belgians, and Poles, the revolution that shook France permanently altered the political landscape of the Western world. Between 1789 and 1799, monarchy as a form of government gave way in France to a republic whose leaders were elected. Aristocracy based on rank and birth was undermined in favor of civil equality and the promotion of merit. Thousands of men held elective office for the first time. A revolutionary government tried to teach new values with a refashioned calendar, state festivals, and a civic religion. Its example inspired would-be revolutionaries everywhere.

But the French Revolution also had its darker side. The divisions created by the Revolution within France endured in many cases until after World War II. Even now, when asked by public-opinion surveys if it was right to execute the king in 1793, most French respondents say they believe that Louis XVI was guilty of treason but should not have been executed. The revolutionaries proclaimed human rights and democratic government as universal goals, but they also explicitly excluded women, even though they admitted Protestant, Jewish, and eventually black men. They used the new spirit of national pride to inspire armies and then used those armies to conquer other peoples. Their ideals of universal education, religious toleration, and democratic participation could not prevent the institution of new forms of government terror to persecute, imprison, and kill dissidents. These paradoxes created an opening for Napoleon Bonaparte, who rushed in with his remarkable military and political skills to push France — and with it all of Europe — in new directions.

Review Questions

1. How did the beginning of the French Revolution resemble the other revolutions of 1787–1789?
2. Why did the French Revolution turn in an increasingly radical direction after 1789?
3. What factors can explain the Terror? To what extent was it simply a response to a national emergency or a reflection of deeper problems within the French Revolution?
4. Why did some groups outside of France embrace the French Revolution while others resisted it?

Making Connections

1. Should the French Revolution be viewed as the origin of democracy or the origin of totalitarianism (a government in which no dissent is allowed)? Explain.
2. Why did other European rulers find the French Revolution so threatening?
3. What made the French revolutionary armies so powerful in this period?
4. How was the French Revolution related to the Enlightenment that preceded it?

- For practice quizzes and other study tools, visit the **Online Study Guide** at bedfordstmartins.com/huntconcise.

- For primary-source material from this period, see *Sources of the Making of the West*, Fourth Edition.

- For Web sites, images, and documents related to topics in this chapter, visit *Make History* at bedfordstmartins.com/huntconcise.

Suggested References

The most influential book on the meaning of the French Revolution is still the classic study by Tocqueville, who insisted that the Revolution continued the process of state centralization undertaken by the monarchy. The revolutions in the colonies are now the subject of many new and important studies.

Andress, David. *The Terror: The Merciless War for Freedom in Revolutionary France.* 2006.

Armitage, David, and Sanjay Subrahmanyam, eds. *The Age of Revolutions in Global Context, c. 1760–1840.* 2010.

Censer, Jack R., and Lynn Hunt. *Liberty, Equality, Fraternity: Exploring the French Revolution* (includes CD-ROM of images and music). 2001. See also the accompanying Web site: http://www.chnm.gmu .edu/revolution

TIMELINE

- **1790** Internal divisions lead to collapse of resistance in Austrian Netherlands

- **1795** Third (final) partition of Poland; France annexes Austrian Netherlands

- **1793** Second partition of Poland by Austria and Russia; Louis XVI executed for treason

- **1789** French Revolution begins

- **1797–1798** Creation of sister republics in Italian states and Switzerland

1787   1789   1791   1793   1795   1797   1799

- **1787** Dutch Patriot revolt stifled by Prussian invasion

- **1788** Beginning of Austrian Netherlands resistance against reforms of Joseph II; opening of reform parliament in Poland

- **1791** Beginning of slave revolt in St. Domingue (Haiti)

- **1792** Beginning of war between France and rest of Europe; second revolution of August 10 overthrows monarchy

- **1794** Abolition of slavery in French colonies; Robespierre's government by terror falls

Chickering, Roger, and Stig Förster, eds. *War in an Age of Revolution, 1775–1815.* 2010.

Desan, Suzanne. *The Family on Trial in Revolutionary France.* 2006.

*Dubois, Laurent, and John D. Garrigus, eds. *Slave Revolution in the Caribbean, 1789–1804: A Brief History with Documents.* 2006.

*Hunt, Lynn, ed. *The French Revolution and Human Rights: A Brief Documentary History.* 1996.

*Levy, Darline Gay, Harriet Branson Applewhite, and Mary Durham Johnson, eds. *Women in Revolutionary Paris, 1789–1795.* 1979.

Palmer, R. R. *The Age of the Democratic Revolution: A Political History of Europe and America, 1760–1800.* Vol. 2, *The Struggle.* 1964.

*Popkin, Jeremy D. *You Are All Free: The Haitian Revolution and the Abolition of Slavery.* 2010.

Schechter, Ronald, ed. *The French Revolution: The Essential Readings.* 2001.

Tocqueville, Alexis de. *The Old Regime and the French Revolution.* Trans. Stuart Gilbert. 1856; repr. 1955.

Primary source.

Napoleon and the Revolutionary Legacy

I N HER NOVEL *FRANKENSTEIN* (1818), the prototype for modern thrillers, Mary Shelley tells the story of a Swiss inventor, Dr. Frankenstein, who creates a human-like monster. The monster terrifies all who encounter him and ends by destroying Frankenstein's own loved ones. Despite desperate chases across deserts and frozen landscapes, Frankenstein never manages to trap the monster, who is last seen hunched over his creator's deathbed.

Napoleon as Military Hero
In this painting from 1800–1801, *Napoleon Crossing the Alps at St. Bernard,* Jacques-Louis David reminds the French of Napoleon's heroic military exploits. Napoleon is a picture of calm and composure while his horse shows the fright and energy of the moment. David painted this propagandistic image shortly after one of his former students went to the guillotine on a trumped-up charge of plotting to assassinate the new French leader. The former organizer of republican festivals during the Terror had become a kind of court painter for the new regime. (Réunion des Musées Nationaux / Art Resource, NY.)

Those who witnessed Napoleon Bonaparte's stunning rise to European dominance might have cast him as either Frankenstein or his monster. Like the scientist Frankenstein, Bonaparte created something dramatically new: the French Empire with himself as emperor. Like the former kings of France, he ruled under his first name. This Corsican artillery officer who spoke French with an Italian accent ended the French Revolution even while maintaining some of its most important innovations.

Bonaparte continued the revolutionary policy of conquest and annexation until it reached grotesque dimensions. His foreign policies made many see him as a monster hungry for dominion; he turned the sister republics of the revolutionary era into kingdoms personally ruled by his relatives, and he exacted tribute wherever he triumphed. Eventually, resistance to the French armies and the ever-mounting costs of military glory toppled Napoleon. The powers allied against him met and agreed to restore the monarchical governments that had been overthrown by the French, shrink France back to its prerevolutionary boundaries, and maintain this settlement against future demands for change.

627

Although the people of Europe longed for peace and stability in the aftermath of the Napoleonic whirlwind, they lived in a deeply unsettled world. Profoundly affected by French military occupation, many groups of people organized to demand ethnic and cultural autonomy, first from Napoleon and then from the restored governments after 1815. In 1830, a new round of revolutions broke out in France, Belgium, Poland, and some of the Italian states. The revolutionary legacy was far from exhausted.

CHAPTER FOCUS How did Napoleon Bonaparte's actions force other European rulers to change their policies?

The Rise of Napoleon Bonaparte

In 1799, a charismatic young general took over the French republic and set France on a new course. Within a year, **Napoleon Bonaparte** (1769–1821) had effectively ended the French Revolution and steered France toward an authoritarian state. As emperor after 1804, Bonaparte dreamed of European integration in the tradition of Augustus and Charlemagne. To achieve his goals, he compromised with the Catholic church and with exiled aristocrats willing to return to France. His most enduring accomplishment, the new Civil Code, tempered the principles of the Enlightenment and the Revolution with an insistence on the powers of fathers over children, husbands over wives, and employers over workers. His influence spread into many spheres as he personally patronized scientific inquiry and encouraged artistic styles in line with his vision of imperial greatness.

A General Takes Over

It would have seemed astonishing in 1795 that the twenty-six-year-old son of a noble family from the island of Corsica off the Italian coast would within four years become the supreme ruler of France and one of the greatest military leaders in world history. That year, Bonaparte was a penniless artillery officer, only recently released from prison as a presumed Robespierrist. Thanks to some early military successes and links to Parisian politicians, however, he was named commander of the French army in Italy in 1796.

Bonaparte's astounding success in the Italian campaigns of 1796–1797 launched his meteoric career. With an army of fewer than fifty thousand men, he defeated the Piedmontese and the Austrians. In quick order, he established client republics dependent on his own authority, negotiated with the Austrians himself, and molded the army into his personal force by paying the soldiers in cash taken as tribute from the newly conquered territories. He pleased the Directory government by sending home wagonloads of Italian masterpieces of art, which were added to Parisian museum collections (most are still there) after being paraded in victory festivals.

In 1798, the Directory set aside its plans to invade England, gave Bonaparte command of the army raised for that purpose, and sent him across the Mediterranean Sea to Egypt. The Directory government hoped that French occupation of Egypt would

strike a blow at British trade by cutting the route to India. Although the French imme-diately defeated a much larger Egyptian army, the British admiral Lord Horatio Nelson destroyed the French fleet while it was anchored in Aboukir Bay, cutting the French off from home. In the face of determined resistance and an outbreak of the bubonic plague, Bonaparte's armies retreated from a further expedition in Syria. But the French occupation of Egypt lasted long enough for that largely Muslim country to experience Enlightenment-inspired legal reforms: the French abolished torture, introduced equality before the law, and proclaimed religious toleration.

Even the failures of the Egyptian campaign did not dull Bonaparte's luster. Bonaparte had taken France's leading scientists with him on the expedition, and his soldiers had discovered a slab of black basalt dating from 196 B.C.E. written in both hieroglyphic and Greek. Called the Rosetta stone after a nearby town, it enabled scholars to finally deci-pher the hieroglyphs used by the ancient Egyptians.

With his army pinned down by Nelson's victory at sea, Bonaparte slipped out of Egypt and made his way secretly to southern France in October 1799. He arrived home at just the right moment: the war in Europe was going badly. The territories of the former Austrian Netherlands had revolted against French conscription laws, and desert-ers swelled the ranks of rebels in western France. Disillusioned members of the gov-ernment saw in Bonaparte's return an occasion to overturn the constitution of 1795. They got their wish on November 9, 1799, when troops guarding the legislature ejected those who opposed Bonaparte and left the remaining ones to vote to abolish the Direc-tory and establish a new three-man executive called the consulate.

Bonaparte became **First Consul**, a title revived from the ancient Roman republic. A new constitution — with no declaration of rights — was submitted to the voters. Mil-lions abstained from voting, and the government falsified the results to give an appear-ance of even greater support to the new regime.

From Republic to Empire

When the constitution of 1799 made Napoleon the First Consul (of three), it gave him the right to pick the Council of State, which drew up all laws. The French government was no longer representative in any real sense: the new constitution eliminated direct elections for deputies and granted no independent powers to the three houses of the legislature. Napoleon and his advisers chose the legislature's members out of a small pool of "notables." Almost all men over twenty-one could vote in the plebiscite (referen-dum) to approve the constitution, but their only option was to choose *yes* or *no*.

Napoleon's most urgent task was to reconcile to his regime Catholics who had been alienated by revolutionary policies. Although nominally Catholic, Napoleon held no deep religious convictions. "How can there be order in the state without religion?" he asked cynically. "When a man is dying of hunger beside another who is stuffing him-self, he cannot accept this difference if there is not an authority who tells him: 'God wishes it so.'" In 1801, a concordat with Pope Pius VII (r. 1800–1823) ended a decade of

church-state conflict in France. The pope validated all sales of church lands, and the government agreed to pay the salaries of bishops and priests who would swear loyalty to the state. Catholicism was officially recognized as the religion of "the great majority of French citizens." (The state also paid Protestant pastors' salaries.)

Napoleon continued the centralization of state power that had begun under the absolutist monarchy of Louis XIV. As First Consul, he appointed prefects who directly supervised local affairs in every department in the country. He created the Bank of France to facilitate government borrowing and relied on gold and silver coinage rather than paper money. He improved tax collection but balanced the budget only by exacting tribute from the territories he conquered.

Napoleon never relied on mass executions to maintain control, but he refused to allow those who opposed him to meet in clubs, influence elections, or publish newspapers. A decree reduced the number of newspapers in Paris from seventy-three to thirteen (and then finally to four). Government censors had to approve all operas and plays, and they banned "offensive" artistic works even more frequently than their royal predecessors had. The minister of police, Joseph Fouché, once a leading figure in the Terror of 1793–1794, imposed house arrest, arbitrary imprisonment, and surveillance of political dissidents. Political contest and debate shriveled to almost nothing. When a bomb attack on Napoleon's carriage failed in 1800, Fouché suppressed the evidence of a royalist plot and instead arrested hundreds of former Jacobins.

When it suited him, Napoleon also struck against royalist conspirators. In 1804, he ordered his police to kidnap the duke d'Enghien from his residence in Germany. Napoleon had intelligence, which proved to be false, that d'Enghien had joined a plot in Paris against him. Even when he learned the truth, he insisted that a military tribunal try d'Enghien, a close relative of the dead king Louis XVI. After a summary trial, d'Enghien was shot on the spot.

By then, Napoleon's political intentions had become clear. He had named himself First Consul for life in 1802, and in 1804, with the pope's blessing, he crowned himself emperor. Once again, plebiscites approved his decisions but only yes/no alternatives were offered.

Napoleon's face and name soon adorned coins, engravings, histories, paintings, and public monuments. His favorite painters embellished his legend by depicting him as a warrior-hero of mythic proportions even though he was short and physically unimpressive in person. He embarked on ostentatious building projects including the Arc de Triomphe and the Stock Exchange.

Napoleon worked hard at establishing his reputation as an efficient administrator with broad intellectual interests. When not on military campaigns, he worked on state affairs, usually until 10:00 p.m., taking only a few minutes for each meal. To establish his authority, Napoleon relied on men who had served with him in the army. His bureaucracy was based on a patron-client relationship, with Napoleon as the ultimate patron.

Combining aristocratic and revolutionary values in a new social hierarchy that rewarded merit and talent, Napoleon personally chose as senators the nation's most illus-

Napoleon's Coronation as Emperor
In this detail from *The Coronation of Napoleon and Josephine* (1805–1807), Jacques-Louis David shows Napoleon crowning his wife at the ceremony of 1804. Napoleon orchestrated the entire event and took the only active role in it: Pope Pius VII gave his blessing to the ceremony (he can be seen seated behind Napoleon), but Napoleon crowned himself. What is the significance of Napoleon crowning himself? (Erich Lessing / Art Resource, NY.)

trious men, among them former nobles. Intending to replace both the old nobility of birth and the republic's strict emphasis on equality, in 1802 he took the first step toward creating a new nobility by founding the Legion of Honor. (Members of the legion received lifetime pensions along with their titles.) In 1808, Napoleon introduced a complete hierarchy of noble titles, ranging from princes down to barons and chevaliers. To go along with their new titles, Napoleon gave his favorite generals huge fortunes, often in the form of estates in the conquered territories.

Napoleon's own family reaped the greatest benefits. He made his older brother, Joseph, ruler of the newly established kingdom of Naples in 1806, the same year he installed his younger brother Louis as king of Holland. He proclaimed his twenty-three-year-old stepson, Eugène de Beauharnais, viceroy of Italy in 1805 and established his sister Caroline and brother-in-law General Joachim Murat as king and queen of Naples in 1808 when he moved Joseph to the throne of Spain. Napoleon wanted to establish an imperial succession, but he lacked an heir. In thirteen years of marriage, his wife, Josephine, had borne no children, so in 1809 he divorced her and in 1810 married the eighteen-year-old princess Marie-Louise of Austria. The next year Marie-Louise gave birth to a son, to whom Napoleon immediately gave the title king of Rome.

The New Paternalism: The Civil Code

As part of his restoration of order, Napoleon brought a paternalistic model of power to his state. He successfully established a new **Civil Code**, completed in 1804. Called the Napoleonic Code as a way of further exalting the emperor's image, it reasserted the Old Regime's patriarchal system of male domination over women and insisted on a father's control over his children, which revolutionary legislation had limited. For example, a child under age sixteen who refused to follow his or her father's commands could be sent to prison for up to a month with no hearing of any sort. Still, the Civil Code protected many of the gains of the French Revolution by defining and ensuring property rights, guaranteeing religious liberty, and establishing a uniform system of law that provided equal treatment for all adult males and affirmed the right of men to choose their professions.

Although the code maintained the equal division of family property between all children, both male and female, it sharply curtailed women's rights in other respects. Napoleon wanted to restrict women to the private sphere of the home. The law obligated a husband to support his wife, but the husband alone controlled any property held in common; a wife could not sue in court, sell or mortgage her own property, or contract a debt without her husband's consent. Divorce was severely restricted. A wife could petition for divorce only if her husband brought his mistress to live in the family home. In contrast, a wife convicted of adultery could be imprisoned for up to two years. The code's framers saw these discrepancies as a way to reinforce the family and make women responsible for private virtue, while leaving public decisions to men. Not until 1965 did French wives gain legal status equal to that of their husbands.

Napoleon took little interest in girls' education, believing that girls should spend most of their time at home learning religion, manners, and such "female occupations" as sewing and music. For boys, by contrast, the government set up a new system of lycées, state-run secondary schools in which students wore military uniforms and drumrolls signaled the beginning and end of classes. The lycées offered wider access to education and thus helped achieve Napoleon's goal of opening careers to those with talent, regardless of their social origins. (The lycées have dropped the military trappings and are now coeducational, but they are still the heart of the French educational system.)

The new paternalism extended to relations between employers and employees. The state required all workers to carry a work card attesting to their good conduct, and it prohibited all workers' organizations. After 1806, arbitration boards settled labor disputes, but they took employers at their word while treating workers as minors, demanding that foremen and shop superintendents represent them. The limitations on workers' rights won Napoleon the support of French business.

Patronage of Science and Intellectual Life

An impressive outpouring of new theoretical and practical scientific work rewarded Napoleon's efforts to promote science. Experiments with balloons led to the discovery of laws about the expansion of gases, and research on fossil shells prepared the way for

Germaine de Staël

One of the most fascinating intellectuals of her time, Anne-Louise-Germaine de Staël seemed to irritate Napoleon more than any other person did. Daughter of Louis XVI's Swiss Protestant finance minister, Jacques Necker, and wife of a Swedish diplomat, Madame de Staël frequently criticized Napoleon's policies. She published best-selling novels and influential literary criticism, and whenever allowed to reside in Paris she encouraged the intellectual and political dissidents from Napoleon's regime. In this painting from 1809, Élisabeth Vigée-Lebrun depicts her as Corinne, the heroine of one of her novels. (Musée d'Art et d'Histoire, Geneva, Switzerland / The Bridgeman Art Library International.)

new theories of evolutionary change later in the nineteenth century. The surgeon Dominique-Jean Larrey developed new techniques of battlefield amputation and medical care during Napoleon's wars, winning an appointment as an officer in the Legion of Honor and becoming a baron with a pension.

Napoleon aimed to modernize French society through science, but he could not tolerate criticism. Napoleon considered most writers useless or dangerous. Among those forced into exile was Anne-Louise-Germaine de Staël (1766–1817), the daughter of Louis XVI's finance minister, Jacques Necker. When explaining his desire to banish her, Napoleon exclaimed, "She is a machine in motion who stirs up the salons." While exiled in the German states, de Staël wrote *Corinne* (1807), a novel whose heroine is a brilliant woman thwarted by a patriarchal system, and *On Germany* (1810), an account of the important new literary currents east of the Rhine. Her books were banned in France.

Although Napoleon restored the strong authority of state and religion in France, many royalists and Catholics still criticized him as an impious usurper. François-René de Chateaubriand (1768–1848) admired Napoleon as "the strong man who has saved us from the abyss," but he preferred a restored Bourbon monarchy. In his view, Napoleon had not properly understood the need to defend Christian values against the Enlightenment's excessive reliance on reason. Chateaubriand wrote his *Genius of Christianity* (1802) to draw attention to the power and mystery of faith. His book appeared during a rare lull in wars that soon engulfed much of Europe.

REVIEW QUESTION In what ways did Napoleon continue the French Revolution, and in what ways did he break with it?

"Europe Was at My Feet": Napoleon's Conquests

Napoleon revolutionized the art of war with tactics and strategies based on a highly mobile army. By 1812, he was ruling a European empire more extensive than any since ancient Rome (Map 20.1). Yet that empire had already begun to crumble, and with it went Napoleon's power at home. Napoleon's empire failed because it was based on a contradiction: Napoleon tried to reduce virtually all nations of Europe to the status of co-

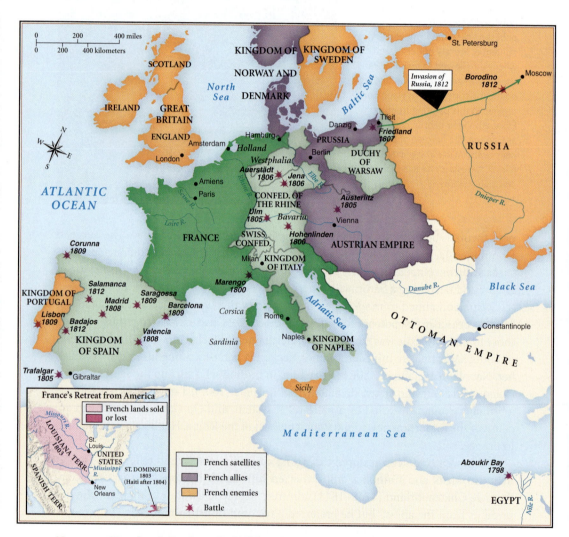

Map 20.1 Napoleon's Empire at Its Height, 1812

In 1812, Napoleon had at least nominal control of almost all of western Europe. Even before he made his fatal mistake of invading Russia, however, his authority had been undermined in Spain and seriously weakened in the Italian and German states. Still earlier, he had given up his dreams of a worldwide empire. French armies withdrew from Egypt in 1801 and from St. Domingue (Haiti) in 1802. In 1803, Napoleon sold the Louisiana Territory to the United States.

lonial dependents when Europe had long consisted of independent states. The result, inevitably, was a great upsurge in nationalist feeling that has dominated European politics to the present.

The Grand Army and Its Victories, 1800–1807

Napoleon attributed his military success "three-quarters to morale" and the rest to leadership and superiority of numbers at the point of attack. Conscription provided the large numbers: 1.3 million men ages twenty to twenty-four were drafted between 1800 and 1812, another 1 million in 1813–1814. Military service was a means of social mobility. The men who rose through the ranks to become officers were young, ambitious, and accustomed to the new ways of war. Consequently, the French army had higher morale than the armies of other powers, most of which rejected conscription as too democratic and continued to restrict their officer corps to the nobility.

To end squabbling among his generals, Napoleon united all the French armies into one — the Grand Army — under his personal command. By 1812, he was commanding 700,000 troops; while 250,000 soldiers fought in Spain, others remained garrisoned in France. In any given battle, between 70,000 and 180,000 men, not all of them French, fought for France. Napoleon inspired almost fanatical loyalty. He fought alongside his soldiers in some sixty battles and had nineteen horses shot from under him. One opponent said that Napoleon's presence alone was worth fifty thousand men.

A brilliant strategist who carefully studied the demands of war, Napoleon outmaneuvered virtually all his opponents. He went directly for the main body of the opposing army and tried to crush it in a lightning campaign. He gathered the largest possible army for one great and decisive battle and then followed with a relentless pursuit to break enemy morale altogether. His military command, like his rule within France, was personal and highly centralized. He essentially served as his own operations officer. This style worked as long as Napoleon could be on the battlefield, but he failed to train independent subordinates to take over in his absence. He also faced constant difficulties in supplying a rapidly moving army, which, because of its size, could not always live off the land.

One of Napoleon's greatest advantages was the lack of coordination among his enemies. Britain dominated the seas but did not want to field huge land armies. On the continent, the French republic had already set up satellites in the Netherlands and Italy, which served as a buffer against the big powers to the east — Austria, Prussia, and Russia. By maneuvering diplomatically and militarily, Napoleon could usually take these on one by one. He won striking victories against the Austrians at Marengo and Hohenlinden in 1800, forcing them to agree to peace terms. Once the Austrians had withdrawn, Britain agreed to the Treaty of Amiens in 1802, effectively ending hostilities on the continent. Napoleon considered the peace with Great Britain merely a truce, however, and it lasted only until 1803.

Napoleon used the breathing space not only to consolidate his position before taking up arms again but also to send an expeditionary force to the Caribbean colony

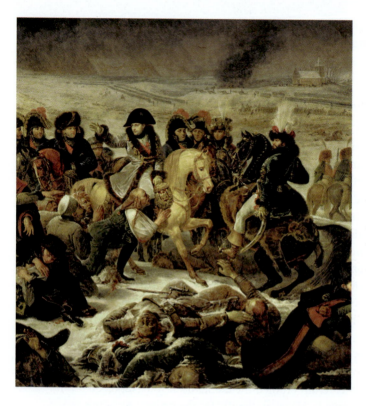

Napoleon Visiting the Battlefield

Antoine-Jean Gros painted this scene of the battle of Eylau (now in northwestern Russia, then in East Prussia) shortly after Napoleon's victory against the Russian army in 1807. The painter aims to show the compassion of Napoleon for his men, but he also draws attention to the sheer carnage of war. Each side lost 25,000 men, killed or wounded, in this battle. What would you conclude from the way the ordinary soldiers are depicted here? (Louvre, Paris, France / The Bridgeman Art Library International.)

of St. Domingue to regain control of the island. Continuing resistance among the black population and an epidemic of yellow fever forced Napoleon to withdraw his troops from St. Domingue and abandon his plans to extend his empire to the Western Hemisphere. As part of his retreat, he sold the Louisiana Territory to the United States in 1803.

When war resumed in Europe, the British navy once more proved its superiority by blocking an attempted French invasion and by defeating the French and their Spanish allies in a huge naval battle at Trafalgar in 1805. France lost many ships; the British lost no vessels, but their renowned admiral Lord Horatio Nelson died in the battle.

On land, Napoleon remained invincible. In 1805, Austria took up arms again when Napoleon demanded that it declare neutrality in the conflict with Britain. Napoleon promptly captured twenty-five thousand Austrian soldiers at Ulm, in Bavaria, in 1805. After marching on to Vienna, he again trounced the Austrians, who had been joined by their new ally, Russia. The battle of Austerlitz, often considered Napoleon's greatest victory, was fought on December 2, 1805, the first anniversary of his coronation.

After maintaining neutrality for a decade, Prussia now declared war on France. In 1806, the French routed the Prussian army at Jena and Auerstädt. In 1807, Napoleon defeated the Russians at Friedland. Personal negotiations between Napoleon and the young tsar Alexander I (r. 1801–1825) resulted in a humiliating settlement imposed on

Prussia, which paid the price for temporary reconciliation between France and Russia; the Treaties of Tilsit turned Prussian lands west of the Elbe River into the kingdom of Westphalia under Napoleon's brother Jerome, and Prussia's Polish provinces became the duchy of Warsaw.

The Impact of French Victories

By annexing some territories and setting up others as satellite kingdoms with much-reduced autonomy, Napoleon attempted to colonize large parts of Europe (Map 20.1, page 634). He brought the disparate German and Italian states together so that he could rule them more effectively and exploit their resources for his own ends. In July 1806, he established the Confederation of the Rhine, which soon included almost all the German states except Austria and Prussia. The Holy Roman Emperor gave up his title, held since the thirteenth century, and became simply the emperor of Austria. Napoleon established three units in Italy: the territories directly annexed to France and the satellite kingdoms of Italy and Naples. Italy had not been so unified since the Roman Empire.

Napoleon forced French-style reforms on both the annexed territories, which were ruled directly from France, and the satellite kingdoms, which were usually ruled by one or another of Napoleon's relatives but with a certain autonomy. French-style reforms included abolishing serfdom, eliminating seigneurial dues, introducing the Napoleonic Code, suppressing monasteries, and subordinating church to state, as well as extending civil rights to Jews and other religious minorities. Yet almost everyone had some cause for complaint. Republicans regretted Napoleon's conversion of the sister republics into kingdoms. Tax increases and ever-rising conscription quotas fomented discontent as well. The annexed territories and satellite kingdoms paid half the cost of Napoleon's wars.

Almost everywhere, conflicts arose between Napoleon's desire for a standardized, centralized government and local insistence on maintaining customs and traditions. Sometimes his own relatives sided with the countries they ruled. Napoleon's brother Louis, for instance, would not allow conscription in the Netherlands because the Dutch had never had compulsory military service. When Napoleon tried to introduce an economic policy banning trade with Great Britain, Louis's lax enforcement infuriated the emperor, and Napoleon annexed the satellite kingdom in 1810.

Napoleon's victories forced defeated rulers to rethink their political and cultural assumptions. After the crushing defeat of Prussia in 1806 left his country greatly reduced in territory, Frederick William III (r. 1797–1840) abolished serfdom and allowed non-nobles to buy and enclose land. Peasants gained their personal independence from their noble landlords, who could no longer sell them to pay gambling debts, for example, or refuse them permission to marry. Yet the lives of the former serfs remained bleak; they were left without land, and their landlords no longer had to care for them in hard times. The king's advisers also overhauled the army to make the high command

more efficient and to open the way to the appointment of middle-class officers. Prussia instituted these reforms to try to compete with the French, not to promote democracy. As one reformer wrote to Frederick William, "We must do from above what the French have done from below."

Reform received lip service in Russia. Tsar Alexander I had gained his throne after an aristocratic coup deposed and killed his autocratic and capricious father, Paul (r. 1796–1801), and in the early years of his reign the remorseful young ruler created Western-style ministries, lifted restrictions on importing foreign books, and founded six new universities. In addition, reform commissions studied abuses, nobles were encouraged to free their serfs voluntarily (a few actually did so), and there was even talk of drafting a constitution. But none of these efforts reached beneath the surface of Russian life, and by the second decade of his reign Alexander began to reject the Enlightenment spirit that his grandmother Catherine the Great had instilled in him.

The one power always standing between Napoleon and total dominance of Europe was Great Britain. The British ruled the seas and financed anyone who would oppose Napoleon. In an effort to bankrupt this "nation of shopkeepers" by choking its trade, Napoleon inaugurated the **Continental System** in 1806. It prohibited all commerce between Great Britain and France or France's dependent states and allies. At first, the system worked: in 1807–1808, British exports dropped by 20 percent and manufacturing by 10 percent. The British retaliated by confiscating merchandise from ships that sailed into or out of the prohibited ports — they even took merchandise from powers who were neutral in the wars.

In the midst of continuing wars, moreover, the Continental System proved impossible to enforce, and widespread smuggling brought British goods into the European market. British growth continued, despite some setbacks; calico-printing works, for example, quadrupled their production, and imports of raw cotton increased by 40 percent. At the same time, French and other continental industries benefited from the temporary protection from British competition.

Smuggling British goods was only one way of opposing the French. Almost everywhere in Europe, resistance began as local opposition to French demands for money or draftees but eventually prompted a more nationalistic patriotic defense. Italians formed a network of secret societies called the *carbonari* ("charcoal burners"), which got its name from the practice of marking each new member's forehead with a charcoal mark. Throughout the nineteenth century, the carbonari played a leading role in Italian nationalism. In the German states, intellectuals wrote passionate defenses of the virtues of the German nation and of the superiority of German literature.

No nations bucked under Napoleon's reins more than Spain and Portugal. In 1807, Napoleon sent 100,000 troops through Spain to invade Portugal, Great Britain's ally. The royal family fled to the Portuguese colony of Brazil, but fighting continued, aided by a British army. When Napoleon got his brother Joseph named king of Spain in place of the senile Charles IV (r. 1788–1808), the Spanish clergy and nobles raised bands of peasants to fight the French occupiers. Even Napoleon's taking personal command of

French Atrocities in Spain

In 1814, the Spanish painter Francisco Jose de Goya y Lucientes was inspired to depict a popular rebellion that took place in Madrid in 1808. The Spanish rebelled against the invading French when they learned that the French armies were forcing members of the Spanish royal family to leave Madrid. In this detail of the painting *The Second of May, 1808*, Mamelukes of the French army charge the rioting Spanish. (Mamelukes were Muslim soldiers who had originally been slaves.) (Image © Francis G. Meyer / Corbis.)

the French forces failed to quell the Spanish, who for six years fought a war of national independence that pinned down thousands of French soldiers. Germaine de Staël commented that Napoleon "never understood that a war might be a crusade. . . . He never reckoned with the one power that no arms could overcome — the enthusiasm of a whole people."

Spanish peasants hated French requisitioning of their food supplies and sought to defend their priests against French anticlericalism. Spanish nobles feared revolutionary reforms and were willing to defend the old monarchy in the person of the young Ferdinand VII, heir to Charles IV, even while Ferdinand himself was congratulating Napoleon on his victories. The Spanish Catholic church spread anti-French propaganda that equated Napoleon with heresy. As the former archbishop of Seville wrote to the archbishop of Granada in 1808, "You realize that we must not recognize as king a Freemason, heretic, Lutheran, as are all the Bonapartes and the French nation." The Spanish peasant rebels, assisted by the British, countered every French massacre with atrocities

of their own. They tortured their French prisoners (boiling one general alive) and lynched collaborators.

From Russian Winter to Final Defeat, 1812–1815

Despite opposition, Napoleon ruled over an extensive empire by 1812. Only two major European states remained fully independent — Great Britain and Russia — but once allied they would successfully challenge his dominion and draw many other states to their side. Britain sent aid to the Portuguese and Spanish rebels, while Russia once again prepared for war. Tsar Alexander I made peace with Turkey and allied himself with Great Britain and Sweden. In 1812, Napoleon invaded Russia with 250,000 horses and 600,000 men, including contingents of Italians, Poles, Swiss, Dutch, and Germans. This daring move proved to be his undoing.

Napoleon followed his usual strategy of trying to strike quickly, but the Russian generals avoided confrontation and retreated eastward, destroying anything that might be useful to the invaders. In September, on the road to Moscow, Napoleon finally engaged the main Russian force in the gigantic battle of Borodino (Map 20.1, page 634). French casualties numbered 30,000 men; the Russians lost 45,000. Once again the Russians retreated, leaving Moscow undefended. When Napoleon approached, the departing Russians set the wooden city on fire. Within a week, three-fourths of it had burned to the ground. Still Alexander refused to negotiate, and French morale plunged with worsening problems of supply. Weeks of constant marching in the dirt and heat had worn down the foot soldiers, who were dying of disease or deserting in large numbers.

In October, Napoleon began his retreat; in November came the cold. A German soldier in the Grand Army described trying to cook fistfuls of raw bran with snow to make something like bread. Within a week the Grand Army lost 30,000 horses and had to abandon most of its artillery and food supplies. Russian forces harassed the retreating army, now more pathetic than grand. By December only 100,000 troops remained, one-sixth the original number, and the retreat had turned into a rout: the Russians had captured 200,000 soldiers, including 3,000 officers.

Napoleon had made a classic military mistake that would be repeated by Adolf Hitler in World War II: fighting a war on two distant fronts simultaneously. The Spanish war tied down 250,000 French troops and forced Napoleon to bully Prussia and Austria into supplying soldiers of dubious loyalty for the Moscow campaign; those soldiers deserted at the first opportunity. The fighting in Spain and Portugal also exacerbated the already substantial logistical and communications problems involved in marching to Moscow.

Napoleon's humiliation might have been temporary if the British and Russians had not successfully organized a coalition to complete the job. By the spring of 1813, Napoleon had replenished his army with another 250,000 men. With British financial support, Russian, Austrian, Prussian, and Swedish armies met the French outside Leipzig in October 1813 and defeated Napoleon in the Battle of the Nations. One by one, Napoleon's German allies deserted him to join the German nationalist "war of libera-

tion." The Confederation of the Rhine dissolved, and the Dutch revolted and restored the prince of Orange. Joseph Bonaparte fled Spain, and a combined Spanish-Portuguese army under British command invaded France. In only a few months, the allied powers crossed the Rhine and marched toward Paris. In March 1814, the French Senate deposed Napoleon, who abdicated when his remaining generals refused to fight. Napoleon went into exile on the island of Elba off the Italian coast. His wife, Marie-Louise, refused to accompany him. The allies restored to the throne Louis XVIII (r. 1814–1824), the brother of Louis XVI, beheaded during the Revolution. (Louis XVI's son was known as Louis XVII even though he died in prison in 1795 without ever ruling.)

Napoleon had one last chance to regain power. Louis XVIII was caught between nobles returning from exile, who demanded a complete restoration of their lands and powers, and the vast majority of ordinary people, who had supported either the republic or Napoleon during the previous twenty-five years. Sensing an opportunity, Napoleon escaped from Elba in early 1815 and, landing in southern France, made swift progress to Paris. Although he had left in ignominy, now crowds cheered him and former soldiers volunteered to serve him. The period eventually known as the Hundred Days (the length of time between Napoleon's escape and his final defeat) had begun. Louis XVIII fled across the border, waiting for help from the powers allied against Napoleon.

Napoleon quickly moved his reconstituted army of 74,000 men into present-day Belgium. At first, it seemed that he might succeed in separately fighting the two armies arrayed against him — a Prussian army of some 60,000 men and a joint force of 68,000 Belgian, Dutch, German, and British troops led by British general Sir Arthur Wellesley (1769–1852), duke of Wellington. The decisive **battle of Waterloo** took place on June 18, 1815, less than ten miles from Brussels. Napoleon's forces attacked but failed to dislodge their opponents. Late in the afternoon, the Prussians arrived and completed the rout. Napoleon had no choice but to abdicate again. This time the victorious allies banished him permanently to the remote island of St. Helena, far off the coast of West Africa, where he died in 1821 at the age of fifty-two.

The cost of Napoleon's rule was high: 750,000 French soldiers and 400,000 others from annexed and satellite states died between 1800 and 1815. Yet his impact on world history was undeniable. Napoleon's plans for a united Europe, his insistence on spreading the legal reforms of the French Revolution, his social welfare programs, and even his inadvertent awakening of national sentiment set the agenda for European history in the modern era.

> **REVIEW QUESTION** Why was Napoleon able to gain control over so much of Europe's territory?

The "Restoration" of Europe

Even while Napoleon was making his last desperate bid for power, his enemies were meeting in the Congress of Vienna (1814–1815) to decide the fate of postrevolutionary, post-Napoleonic Europe. Although interrupted by the Hundred Days, the **Congress of Vienna** settled the boundaries of European states, determined who would rule each

nation, and established a new framework for international relations based on periodic meetings, or congresses, between the major powers. The doctrine of conservatism that emerged in reaction to the events of the French Revolution bolstered this post-Napoleonic order and in some places went hand in hand with a revival of religion.

The Congress of Vienna, 1814–1815

In addition to determining the boundaries of France, the congress had to decide the fate of Napoleon's duchy of Warsaw, the German province of Saxony, the Netherlands, the states once part of the Confederation of the Rhine, and various Italian territories. All had either changed hands or been created during the wars. These issues were resolved by face-to-face negotiations among representatives of the five major powers: Austria, Russia, Prussia, Britain, and France. With its aim to establish a long-lasting, negotiated peace endorsed by all parties, both winners and losers, the Congress of Vienna provided a model for the twentieth-century League of Nations and United Nations. The congress system, or "concert of Europe," helped prevent another major war

Congress of Vienna
An unknown French engraver caricatured the efforts of the diplomats at the Congress of Vienna, complaining that they used the occasion to divide the spoils of European territory. What elements in this engraving make it a caricature? (Photo: akg-images)

until the 1850s, and no conflict comparable to the Napoleonic wars would occur again until 1914.

Austria's chief negotiator, Prince **Klemens von Metternich** (1773–1859), took the lead in devising the settlement and shaping the post-Napoleonic order. A well-educated nobleman who spoke five languages, Metternich served as a minister in the Austrian cabinet from 1809 to 1848. He aimed to return as much as possible to the pre-1789 political order, but to do so he also needed to maintain France's great-power status as a counter to Russia and Prussia. He therefore worked with the British prime minister Robert Castlereagh (1769–1822) to ensure a moderate agreement. Metternich and Castlereagh believed that French aggression must be contained, because it had threatened the European peace since the days of Louis XIV, but at the same time that France must remain a major player to prevent any one European power from dominating the others. Castlereagh hoped to make Britain the arbiter of European affairs, but he knew this could be accomplished only through adroit diplomacy because the British constitutional monarchy had little in common with most of its more absolutist continental counterparts.

The task of ensuring France's status at the Congress of Vienna fell to Prince Charles Maurice de Talleyrand (1754–1838), an aristocrat and former bishop who had embraced the French Revolution, served as Napoleon's foreign minister, and ended as foreign minister to Louis XVIII after helping arrange the emperor's overthrow. When the French army failed to oppose Napoleon's return to power in the Hundred Days, the allies took away all territory conquered since 1790, levied an indemnity against France, and required it to support an army of occupation until it had paid.

The goal of the Congress of Vienna was to achieve postwar stability by establishing secure states with guaranteed borders (Map 20.2). Because the congress aimed to "restore" as many regimes as possible to their former rulers, this epoch is sometimes labeled the **restoration**. But simple restoration was not always feasible. The congress turned the duchy of Warsaw, for example, into a new Polish kingdom but made the tsar of Russia its king. (Poland would not regain its independence until 1918.) The former Dutch Republic and the Austrian Netherlands, both annexed to France, were now united as the new kingdom of the Netherlands under the restored stadholder. Austria took charge of the German Confederation, which replaced the defunct Holy Roman Empire and also included Prussia.

The Congress of Vienna also resolved various international trade issues. Great Britain, which had abolished its slave trade in 1807, urged the congress to condemn that trade for other nations. The congress agreed in principle; in reality, however, the slave trade continued in many places until 1850. Nearly three million Africans were sold into slavery between 1800 and 1850, and most were transported on either Portuguese or Brazilian slave ships.

To impart spiritual substance to this very calculated settlement of political affairs, Tsar Alexander proposed the Holy Alliance, which called on divine assistance in upholding religion, peace, and justice. Prussia and Austria signed the agreement, but Great

Map 20.2 **Europe after the Congress of Vienna, 1815**
The Congress of Vienna forced France to return to its 1789 borders. The Austrian Netherlands and the Dutch Republic were united in a new kingdom of the Netherlands, the German states were joined in a German Confederation that built on Napoleon's Confederation of the Rhine, and Napoleon's duchy of Warsaw became the kingdom of Poland with the tsar of Russia as king. To compensate for its losses in Poland, Prussia gained territory in Saxony and on the left bank of the Rhine. Austria reclaimed the Italian provinces of Lombardy and Venetia and the Dalmatian coast.

Britain refused to accede to what Castlereagh called "a piece of sublime mysticism and nonsense." Despite the reassertion of traditional religious principles, the congress had in fact given birth to a new diplomatic order: in the future, the legitimacy of states depended on the treaty system, not on "divine right."

The Emergence of Conservatism

The French Revolution and Napoleonic domination of Europe had shown contemporaries that government could be changed overnight, that the old hierarchies could be overthrown in the name of reason, and that even Christianity could be written off or

at least profoundly altered with the stroke of a pen. After the French Revolution and the Napoleonic domination of Europe, the old order no longer commanded automatic obedience. It was now merely *old,* no longer "natural" and "timeless." It had been ousted once and therefore might fall again. People needed reasons to believe in their restored governments. The political doctrine that justified the restoration was **conservatism**.

Conservatives benefited from the disillusionment that permeated Europe after 1815. They saw a logical progression in recent history: the Enlightenment, based on reason, led to the French Revolution, with its bloody guillotine and horrifying Terror, which in turn spawned the authoritarian and militaristic Napoleon. Therefore, those who espoused conservatism rejected both the Enlightenment and the French Revolution. They favored monarchies over republics, tradition over revolution, and established religion over Enlightenment skepticism.

The original British critic of the French Revolution, Edmund Burke (1729–1799), inspired many of the conservatives who followed. He had argued that the revolutionaries erred in thinking they could construct an entirely new government based on reason. Government, Burke said, had to be rooted in long experience, which evolved over generations. All change must be gradual and must respect national and historical traditions. Like Burke, later conservatives believed that religious and other major traditions were an essential foundation for any society. Most of them took their resistance to change even further, however, and tried to restore the pre-1789 social order.

Conservatives blamed the French Revolution's attack on religion on the skepticism and anticlericalism of such Enlightenment thinkers as Voltaire, and they defended both hereditary monarchy and the authority of the church, whether Catholic or Protestant. Louis de Bonald, an official under the restored French monarchy, insisted that "the revolution began with the declaration of the rights of man and will only finish when the rights of God are declared." In this view, an enduring social order could be constructed only on the foundations provided by the church, the state, and the patriarchal family. Faith, sentiment, history, and tradition must fill the vacuum left by the failures of reason and excessive belief in individual rights. Across Europe, these views were taken up and elaborated by government advisers, professors, and writers.

The restored French monarchy provided a major test for conservatism because the returning Bourbons had to confront the legacy of twenty-five years of upheaval. Louis XVIII tried to ensure a measure of continuity by maintaining Napoleon's Civil Code. He also guaranteed the rights of ownership to church lands sold during the revolutionary period and created a parliament composed of the Chamber of Peers, nominated by the king, and the Chamber of Deputies, elected by very restricted suffrage (fewer than 100,000 voters in a population of 30 million). In making these concessions, the king tried to follow a moderate course of compromise, but the Ultras (ultraroyalists) pushed for complete repudiation of the revolutionary past. When Louis returned to power after Napoleon's final defeat, armed royalist bands attacked and murdered hundreds of Bonapartists and former revolutionaries. In 1816, the Ultras insisted on abolishing divorce and set up special courts to punish opponents of the regime. When an assassin killed Louis XVIII's nephew in 1820, the Ultras successfully demanded even more extreme measures.

The Revival of Religion

The experience of revolutionary upheaval and nearly constant warfare prompted many to renew their religious faith once peace returned. In France, the Catholic church sent missionaries to hold open-air "ceremonies of reparation" to express repentance for the outrages of revolution. In Rome, the papacy reestablished the Jesuit order, which had been disbanded during the Enlightenment.

In parts of Protestant Germany and Britain, religious revival had begun in the eighteenth century with the rise of Pietism and Methodism, movements that stressed individual religious experience. The English Methodists followed John Wesley (1703–1791), who had preached an emotional, morally austere, and very personal "method" of gaining salvation. The Methodists, or Wesleyans, gradually separated from the Church of England and in the early decades of the nineteenth century attracted thousands of members in huge revival meetings that lasted for days. Shopkeepers, artisans, agricultural laborers, miners, and workers in cottage industries, both male and female, flocked to the new denomination. In their hostility to elaborate ritual and their encouragement of popular preaching, the Methodists in England fostered a sense of democratic community and even a rudimentary sexual equality. From the beginning, women preachers traveled on horseback to preach in barns, town halls, and textile dye houses. The Methodist Sunday schools that taught thousands of poor children to read and write eventually helped create greater demands for working-class political participation.

The religious revival was not limited to Europe. In the United States, the second Great Awakening began around 1790 with huge camp meetings that brought together thousands of worshippers and scores of evangelical preachers, many of them Methodist. (The original Great Awakening had taken place in the 1730s and 1740s, sparked by the preaching of George Whitefield, a young English evangelist and follower of John Wesley — see Chapter 18, page 572.) Men and women danced to exhaustion, fell into trances, and spoke in tongues. During this period, Protestant sects began systematic missionary activity in other parts of the world. In the British colony of India, for example, Protestant missionaries pushed the British administration to abolish the Hindu custom of *sati* — the burning of widows on the funeral pyres of their husbands — in 1829. The missionaries hoped such actions would make Indians more likely to embrace Christianity. Missionary activity by Protestants and Catholics would become one of the arms of European imperialism and cultural influence in the nineteenth century.

> **REVIEW QUESTION** To what extent did the Congress of Vienna restore the old order?

Challenges to the Conservative Order

Conservatives hoped to clamp a lid on European affairs, but the lid kept threatening to fly off. Drawing on the turmoil in society and politics was romanticism, the burgeoning international movement in the arts and literature that dominated artistic expression in the first half of the nineteenth century. Although romantics shared with conserva-

tives a distrust of the Enlightenment's emphasis on reason, romanticism did not translate into a unified political position. Isolated revolts threatened the hold of some conservative governments in the 1820s, but most of these rebellions were quickly bottled up. Then, in 1830, successive uprisings briefly overwhelmed the established order. Across Europe, angry protesters sought constitutional guarantees of individual liberties and national unity and autonomy. The revolutionary legacy came back to life again.

Romanticism

As an artistic movement, romanticism encompassed poetry, music, painting, history, and literature. (See Chapter 18, page 571, on the origins of romanticism.) It glorified nature, emotion, genius, and imagination as antidotes to the Enlightenment and to classicism in the arts, challenging the reliance on reason, symmetry, and cool geometric spaces. Classicism idealized models from Roman history; romanticism turned to folklore and medieval legends. Classicism celebrated orderly, crisp lines; romantics sought out all that was wild, fevered, and disorderly. Romantics might take any political position, but they exerted the most political influence when they expressed nationalist feelings.

Romantic poetry celebrated overwhelming emotion and creative imagination. George Gordon, Lord Byron (1788–1824), explained his aims in writing poetry:

> For what is Poesy but to create
> From overfeeling, Good and Ill, and aim
> At an external life beyond our fate,
> And be the new Prometheus of new man.

Prometheus was the mythological figure who brought fire from the Greek gods to human beings. Byron did not seek the new Prometheus among political leaders or military men; he sought him within his own "overfeeling," his own intense emotions. Byron became a romantic hero himself when he rushed off to act on his emotions by fighting and dying in the Greek war for independence from the Turks.

Romantic poetry elevated the wonders of nature almost to the supernatural. In a poem that became one of the most beloved exemplars of romanticism, "Tintern Abbey" (1798), the English poet William Wordsworth (1770–1850) compared himself to a deer even while making nature seem filled with human emotions. Wordsworth had greeted the French Revolution with joy but had gradually become disenchanted and celebrated British nationalism instead.

Their emphasis on authentic self-expression at times drew romantics to exotic, mystical, or even reckless experiences. Some romantics depicted the artist as possessed by demons and obsessed with hallucinations. This more nightmarish side was captured, and perhaps criticized, by Mary Shelley in *Frankenstein*. In his old age, German poet Johann Wolfgang von Goethe (1749–1832) likewise denounced the extremes of romanticism, calling it "everything that is sick."

Romanticism in painting similarly idealized nature and the individual of deep feelings. The German romantic painter Caspar David Friedrich (1774–1840) depicted

Romantic Painting

Johann Heinrich Fuseli painted *The Nightmare* in 1781, and it instantly became controversial because of the pose of the woman and the accompanying nightmarish figures. Are they actually present in the room, or are they only in the mind of the sleeper? Mary Shelley based a scene in *Frankenstein* on the painting; her parents were close friends of Fuseli. In what ways does this painting capture the themes of romanticism? (Oil on canvas, 1781, Johann Heinrich Fuseli [1741–1825]. Detroit Institute of Arts, USA / Founders Society purchase with Mr. and Mrs. Bert L. Smokler and Mr. and Mrs. Lawrence A. Fleischman funds / The Bridgeman Art Library International.)

scenes — often far away in the mountains — that captured the romantic fascination with the sublime power of nature. His melancholy individual figures looked lost in the vastness of an overpowering nature. Friedrich hated the modern world. His landscapes often had religious meaning as well, as in his controversial painting *The Cross in the Mountains* (1808), which showed a Christian cross standing alone in a mountain scene. It symbolized the steadfastness of faith but seemed to separate religion from the churches and attach it to mystical experience.

The English painter Joseph M. W. Turner (1775–1851) depicted his vision of nature in mysterious, misty seascapes, anticipating later artists by blurring the outlines of objects. The French painter Eugène Delacroix (1798–1863) chose contemporary as well as medieval scenes of great turbulence to emphasize light and color and break away from what he saw as "the servile copies repeated *ad nauseum* in academies of art." Critics denounced his techniques as "painting with a drunken broom." To broaden his experience of light and color, Delacroix traveled in the 1830s to North Africa and painted many exotic scenes in Morocco and Algeria.

Eugène Delacroix, *Massacre at Chios* (1824)

More than any other painter associated with romanticism, Delacroix focused on dramatic events of his time. Here he shows sick and dying Greek civilians about to be massacred by the Turks. He aims to elicit sympathy for the Greek campaign for independence, a cause that had many followers in France and the rest of Europe. (Oil on canvas, 1824 / The Granger Collection, NYC — All rights reserved.)

The towering presence of the German composer **Ludwig van Beethoven** (1770–1827) in early-nineteenth-century music helped establish the direction for musical romanticism. His music, according to one leading German romantic, "sets in motion the lever of fear, of awe, of horror, of suffering, and awakens just that infinite longing which is the essence of Romanticism." Beethoven transformed the symphony into a connected work with recurring and evolving musical themes. Some of his work was explicitly political; his Ninth Symphony (1824) employed a chorus to sing the German poet Friedrich Schiller's verses in praise of universal human solidarity. Beethoven had admired Napoleon and even dedicated his Third Symphony, the *Eroica* (1804), to him, but when he learned of Napoleon's decision to name himself emperor, the composer tore up the dedication in disgust.

If romantics had any common political thread, it was the support of nationalist aspirations, especially through the search for the historical origins of national identity. Romantic poets and writers collected old legends and folktales that expressed a shared cultural and linguistic heritage stretching back to the Middle Ages. These collections showed that Germany, for example, had always existed even if it did not currently take the form of a single unified state. Italian nationalists took *The Betrothed* (1825–1827), a novel by Alessandro Manzoni (1785–1873), as a kind of bible. Manzoni, the grandson of the Italian Enlightenment hero Cesare Beccaria, set his novel in the seventeenth century, when Spain controlled Italy's destiny, but his readers understood that he intended to attack the Austrians who controlled northern Italy in his own day.

Manzoni had been inspired to write his novel by the most influential of all historical novelists, **Sir Walter Scott** (1771–1832). While working as a lawyer and then judge in Scotland, Scott first collected and published traditional Scottish ballads that

he had heard as a child. After achieving immediate success with his own poetry, especially *The Lady of the Lake* (1810), he switched to historical novels. His novels are almost all renditions of historical events, from *Rob Roy* (1817), with its account of Scottish resistance to the English in the early eighteenth century, to *Ivanhoe* (1819), with its tales of medieval England. One contemporary critic claimed, "There is more history in the novels of Walter Scott than in half of the historians." Scott captured the truths of human nature rather than sticking to the bare facts recorded by historians.

Political Revolts in the 1820s

The restoration of regimes after Napoleon's fall disappointed those who dreamed of constitutional freedoms and national independence. Membership grew in secret societies such as the carbonari, attracting tens of thousands of members. Revolts broke out in the 1820s in Spain, Italy, Russia, and Greece (Map 20.3), as well as across the Atlantic in the Spanish and Portuguese colonies of Latin America (Map 20.4, page 653).

When Ferdinand VII regained the Spanish crown in 1814, he ordered foreign books and newspapers to be confiscated at the frontier and allowed the publication of only two newspapers. Many army officers who had encountered French ideas responded by joining secret societies. In 1820, disgruntled soldiers demanded that Ferdinand proclaim his adherence to the constitution of 1812, which he had abolished in 1814. Ferdinand bided his time, and in 1823 a French army invaded and restored him to absolute power. The French acted with the consent of the other great powers. The restored Spanish government tortured and executed hundreds of rebels; thousands were imprisoned or forced into exile.

Hearing of the Spanish uprising, rebellious soldiers in the kingdom of Naples joined forces with the carbonari and demanded a constitution. The promise of reform sparked rebellion in the northern Italian kingdom of Piedmont-Sardinia, where rebels urged Charles Albert, the young heir to the Piedmont throne, to fight the Austrians for Italian unification. After the rulers of Austria, Prussia, and Russia met and agreed on intervention in

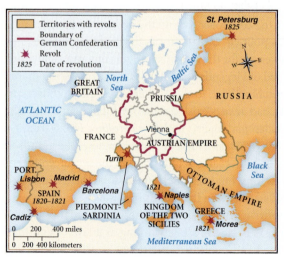

Map 20.3 Revolutionary Movements of the 1820s

The revolts of the 1820s took place on the periphery of Europe, in Spain, Italy, Greece, Russia, and in the Spanish and Portuguese colonies of Latin America. Rebels in Spain and Russia wanted constitutional reforms. Although the Italian revolts failed, as did the uprisings in Spain and Russia, the Greek and Latin American independence movements eventually succeeded.

1821, the Austrians defeated the rebels in Naples and Piedmont. Although Great Britain condemned the indiscriminate suppression of revolutionary movements, Metternich convinced the other powers to agree to his silencing the Italian opposition to Austrian rule.

Metternich acted quickly to suppress any sign of dissent closer to home. University students had formed nationalist student societies called *Burschenschaften,* and in 1817 they held a mass rally at which they burned books they did not like, including Napoleon's Civil Code. Metternich was convinced — incorrectly — that the Burschenschaften in the German states and the carbonari in Italy were linked in an international conspiracy. In 1819, when a student assassinated the playwright August Kotzebue because he had ridiculed the student movement, Metternich convinced the leaders of the biggest German states to pass the Carlsbad Decrees, dissolving the student societies and more strictly censoring the press. Professors who criticized their rulers were immediately fired.

Aspirations for constitutional government surfaced in Russia when Alexander I died suddenly in 1825. On a day in December when the troops assembled in St. Petersburg to take an oath of loyalty to Alexander's brother Nicholas as the new tsar, rebel officers insisted that the crown belonged to another brother, Constantine, whom they hoped would be more favorable to constitutional reform. Constantine, though next in the line of succession after Alexander, had refused the crown. Soldiers loyal to Nicholas easily suppressed the Decembrist Revolt (so called after the month of the uprising). The subsequent trial, however, made the rebels into legendary heroes. For the next thirty years, Nicholas I (r. 1825–1855) used a new political police, the Third Section, to spy on potential opponents and stamp out rebelliousness.

The Ottoman Turks faced growing nationalist challenges in the Balkans. The Serbs revolted against Turkish rule and won virtual independence by 1817. A Greek general in the Russian army, Prince Alexander Ypsilanti, tried to lead a revolt against the Turks in 1820 but failed when the tsar, urged on by Metternich, disavowed him. Metternich feared rebellion even by Christians against their Turkish rulers. A second revolt, this time by Greek peasants, sparked a wave of atrocities in 1821 and 1822. The Greeks killed every Turk who did not escape; in retaliation, the Turks hanged the Greek patriarch of Constantinople and, in the areas they still controlled, pillaged churches, massacred thousands of men, and sold the women into slavery.

Western opinion turned against the Turks; Greece, after all, was the birthplace of Western civilization. While the great powers negotiated, Greeks and pro-Greece committees around the world sent

Nationalistic Movements in the Balkans, 1815–1830

food and military supplies; like the English poet Byron, a few enthusiastic European and American volunteers joined the Greeks. The Greeks held on until the great powers were willing to intervene. In 1827, a combined force of British, French, and Russian ships destroyed the Turkish fleet at Navarino Bay; and in 1828, Russia declared war on Turkey and advanced close to Constantinople. The Treaty of Adrianople of 1829 gave Russia a protectorate over the Danubian principalities in the Balkans and provided for a conference among representatives of Britain, Russia, and France, all of whom had broken with Austria in support of the Greeks. In 1830, Greece was declared an independent kingdom under the guarantee of the three powers; in 1833, the second son of King Ludwig of Bavaria became Otto I of Greece. Greek independence, supported by European public opinion, showed that Metternich's systematic suppression of nationalism was reaching its limits.

Across the Atlantic, national revolts also succeeded after a series of bloody wars of independence. Taking advantage of the upheavals in Spain and Portugal that began under Napoleon, restive colonists from Mexico to Argentina rebelled. One leader who stood out was **Simón Bolívar** (1783–1830), born in Caracas (present-day Venezuela), to an aristocratic slave-owning family of Spanish descent. He was educated in Europe on the works of Voltaire and Rousseau. Although Bolívar fancied himself a Latin

Simón Bolívar

This watercolor by Fernandez Luis Cancino celebrates Bolívar's promise to abolish slavery in territories he freed from Spanish rule. Although Bolívar liberated his own slaves in 1820, he was unable to persuade the legislators of the newly independent countries to act immediately. They insisted on gradual emancipation. (Watercolor on paper by Luis Fernandez Cancino [19th century], Casa-Museo 20 de Julio de 1810, Bogotá, Colombia / Giraudon / The Bridgeman Art Library International.)

Map 20.4 Latin American Independence, 1804–1830
Napoleon's occupation of Spain and Portugal seriously weakened those countries' hold on their Latin American colonies. Despite the restoration of the Spanish and Portuguese rulers in 1814, most of their colonies successfully broke away in a wave of rebellions between 1811 and 1830.

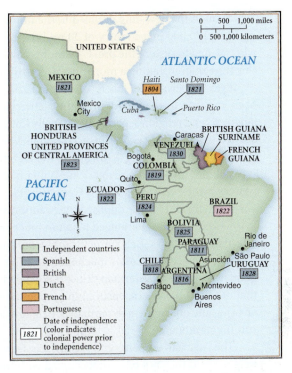

American Napoleon, he had to acquiesce to the formation of a series of independent republics between 1821 and 1823, even in Bolivia, which is named after him.

By 1825, Portugal had lost all its American colonies, including Brazil, and Spain was left with only Cuba and Puerto Rico (Map 20.4). Brazil declared its independence under the banner of the Portuguese king's own son and therefore maintained a monarchical form of government along with slavery. In contrast, the new republics freed those slaves who fought on their side, abolished the slave trade, and gradually eliminated slavery. The United States and Great Britain recognized the new states, and in 1823 U.S. president James Monroe announced his Monroe Doctrine, closing the Americas to European intervention—a prohibition that depended on British naval power and British willingness to declare neutrality.

Revolution and Reform, 1830–1832

In 1830, a new wave of liberal and nationalist revolts broke out. The revolts of the 1820s had served as warning shots but had been largely confined to the peripheries of Europe. Now revolution once again threatened the established order in western Europe.

French king Louis XVIII's younger brother and successor, Charles X (r. 1824–1830), brought about his own downfall by steering the monarchy in an increasingly repressive direction. In 1825, he agreed to compensate nobles who had emigrated during the French Revolution for the loss of their estates and imposed the death penalty for such offenses as stealing religious objects from churches. He further enraged liberals when he dissolved the legislature and imposed strict censorship. On July 26, 1830, spontaneous demonstrations in Paris turned into street battles that, over three days, left 500 citizens and 150 soldiers dead. A group of moderate liberal leaders, fearing the reestablishment of a republic, offered the crown to Charles X's cousin Louis-Philippe, duke of Orléans, and sent Charles into exile in England.

Though the new king doubled it, the number of men eligible to vote was still minuscule: 170,000 in a country of 30 million. Revolution had broken the hold of those who wanted to restore the pre-1789 monarchy and nobility, but it had gone no further this time than installing a more liberal, constitutional monarchy.

Even so, news of the July revolution in Paris ignited the Belgians, whose country had been annexed to the kingdom of the Netherlands in 1815. Differences in traditions, language, and religion separated the largely Catholic Belgians from the Dutch. An opera about a seventeenth-century insurrection in Naples provided the spark, and students in Brussels rioted, shouting "Down with the Dutch!"

The riot turned into revolt. King William of the Netherlands appealed to the great powers to intervene; after all, the Congress of Vienna had established his kingdom. But Great Britain and France opposed intervention and invited Russia, Austria, and Prussia to a conference that guaranteed Belgium independence in exchange for its neutrality in international affairs. Belgian neutrality would remain a cornerstone of European diplomacy for a century. After much maneuvering, the crown of the new kingdom of Belgium was offered to a German prince, Leopold of Saxe-Coburg, in 1831. The choice, like that of Otto I of Greece, ensured the influence of the great European powers without favoring any one of them in particular. Belgium, like France and Britain, now had a constitutional monarchy.

The Austrian emperor and the Russian tsar would have supported intervention in Belgium had they not been preoccupied with their own revolts. In the south, rebels in Naples and Palermo demanded constitutional government; in the north, rebels in Piedmont fought for an Italy independent of Austria. Metternich sent Austrian armies to quell the unrest.

The Polish revolt was more serious. In 1830, in response to news of revolution in France, students raised the banner of rebellion. Polish aristocrats formed a provisional government, but it was defeated by the Russian army. In reprisal, Tsar Nicholas abolished the Polish constitution that his brother Alexander had granted in 1815 and ordered thousands of Poles executed or banished. The independence movements in Poland and Italy went underground only to reemerge later.

Reform of Parliament rather than revolution preoccupied the British. In August 1819, sixty thousand people attended an illegal political meeting held in St. Peter's Fields in Manchester to demand reform of parliamentary elections, which had long been controlled by aristocratic landowners. When the local authorities sent the cavalry to arrest the speaker, panic resulted; eleven people were killed and many hundreds injured. Punsters called it the battle of Peterloo or the Peterloo massacre. An alarmed government passed the Six Acts, which forbade large political meetings and restricted press criticism.

In the 1820s, however, new men came into government. Sir Robert Peel (1788–1850), the secretary for home affairs, revised the criminal code to reduce the number of crimes punishable by death and introduced a municipal police force in London, called the Bobbies after him. In 1824, the laws prohibiting labor unions were repealed, and though restrictions on strikes remained, workers could now organize themselves legally to confront their employers collectively. In 1828, the appointment of the duke of Wel-

lington, the hero of Waterloo, as prime minister kept the Tories in power. Wellington's government pushed through a bill in 1829 allowing Catholics to sit in Parliament and hold most public offices.

When in 1830, and again in 1831, the Whigs in Parliament proposed an extension of the right to vote, Tory diehards, principally in the House of Lords, dug in their heels and predicted that even the most modest proposals would doom civilization itself. Even though the proposed law would grant only limited, not universal, male suffrage, mass demonstrations in favor of it took place in many cities. In this "state of diseased and feverish excitement" (according to its opponents), the **Reform Bill of 1832** passed, after the king threatened to create enough new peers to obtain its passage in the House of Lords.

Although the Reform Bill altered Britain's political structure in significant ways, the gains were not revolutionary. One of the bill's foremost backers, historian and member of Parliament Thomas Macaulay, explained, "I am opposed to Universal Suffrage, because I think that it would produce a destructive revolution. I support this plan, because I am sure that it is our best security against a revolution." Although the number of male voters increased by about 50 percent, only one in five Britons could now vote. Nevertheless, the bill set a precedent for widening suffrage further. Those disappointed with the outcome would organize with renewed vigor in the 1830s and 1840s.

> **REVIEW QUESTION** Why were independence movements thwarted in Italy and Poland in this era, but not in Greece, Belgium, and Latin America?

Conclusion

The agitations and uprisings of the 1820s and early 1830s showed that the revolutionary legacy still smoldered and might erupt into flames again at any moment. Napoleon Bonaparte transformed the legacy but also kept it alive. He reshaped French institutions and left a lasting imprint in many European countries. Moreover, like Frankenstein's monster, he bounced back from numerous reversals; between the French retreat from Moscow in 1812 and his final defeat at Waterloo in 1815, Napoleon lost many battles yet managed to raise an army again and again.

The powers who eventually defeated Napoleon tried to maintain the European peace by shoring up monarchical governments and damping down aspirations for constitutional freedoms and national autonomy. Nevertheless, Belgium separated from the Netherlands, Greece achieved independence from the Turks, Latin American countries shook off the rule of Spain and Portugal, and the French installed a more liberal monarchy than the one envisioned by the Congress of Vienna. Metternich's vision of a conservative Europe still held, but in the next two decades dramatic social changes would prompt a new and much more deadly round of revolutions.

Review Questions

1. In what ways did Napoleon continue the French Revolution, and in what ways did he break with it?

2. Why was Napoleon able to gain control over so much of Europe's territory?

3. To what extent did the Congress of Vienna restore the old order?

4. Why were independence movements thwarted in Italy and Poland in this era, but not in Greece, Belgium, and Latin America?

Making Connections

1. What was the long-term significance of Napoleon for Europe?

2. What best explains Napoleon's fall from power: apathy at home, resistance to his rule, or military defeat?

3. In what ways did Metternich succeed in holding back the revolutionary legacy? In what ways did he fail?

4. How did the revolts and rebellions of the 1820s reflect the revolutionary legacy? In what ways did they move in new directions?

- For practice quizzes and other study tools, visit the **Online Study Guide** at bedfordstmartins.com/huntconcise.

- For primary-source material from this period, see *Sources of the Making of the West*, Fourth Edition.

- For Web sites, images, and documents related to topics in this chapter, visit *Make History* at bedfordstmartins.com/huntconcise.

Suggested References

Napoleon and his wars have always been the subject of great interest, but recent scholars have devoted more attention to the long-term influence of the wars. The years between 1815 and 1830 have not attracted as much scholarship, even though those years are arguably even more significant than the Napoleonic era for their long-term cultural and political effects.

TIMELINE

- **1804** Napoleon crowned emperor of France, issues new Civil Code
- **1801** Napoleon signs concordat with pope
- **1807–1814** French invade and occupy Spain and Portugal
- **1815** Napoleon defeated at Waterloo and exiled to island of St. Helena
- **1820** Revolt of liberal army officers against Spanish crown
- **1825** Russian army officers demand constitutional reform in Decembrist Revolt
- **1832** English Parliament passes Reform Bill

1800   1805   1810   1815   1820   1825   1830   1835

- **1799** Coup against Directory government in France; Napoleon Bonaparte named First Consul
- **1812** Napoleon invades Russia
- **1814–1815** Congress of Vienna
- **1818** Mary Shelley, *Frankenstein*
- **1824** Ludwig van Beethoven, Ninth Symphony
- **1830** Greece gains independence from Ottoman Turks; rebels overthrow Charles X of France, install Louis-Philippe; rebellion in Poland against Russia fails
- **1805** British naval forces defeat French at battle of Trafalgar; Napoleon wins his greatest victory at battle of Austerlitz

Mapping the West   Europe in 1830

By 1830, the fragilities of the Congress of Vienna settlement had become apparent. Rebellion in Poland failed, but Belgium won its independence from the kingdom of the Netherlands, and a French revolution in July chased out the Bourbon ruler and installed Louis-Philippe, who promised constitutional reform. Most European rulers held on to their positions in this period of ferment, but they had to accommodate new desires for constitutional guarantees of rights and growing nationalist sentiment.

Bell, David A. *The First Total War: Napoleon's Europe and the Birth of Warfare as We Know It.* 2007.

Black, Jeremy. *The Battle of Waterloo.* 2010.

*Blaufarb, Rafe. *Napoleon: A Symbol for an Age. A Brief Biography with Documents.* 2008.

*Breckman, Warren. *European Romanticism: A Brief History with Documents.* 2007.

Cole, Juan. *Napoléon's Egypt: Invading the Middle East.* 2007.

Englund, Steven. *Napoleon: A Political Life.* 2004.

Hobsbawm, E. J. *The Age of Revolution, 1789–1848.* 1996.

Johnson, Paul. *The Birth of the Modern: World Society, 1815–1830.* 1991.

Napoleon Foundation: http://www.napoleon.org

Romantic Chronology: http://english.ucsb.edu:591/rchrono

Sandeman, G. A. C. *Metternich.* 2006.

Schroeder, Paul W. *The Transformation of European Politics 1763–1848.* 1996.

*Primary source.

Industrialization and Social Ferment

IN 1830, THE LIVERPOOL AND MANCHESTER Railway Line opened to the cheers of crowds and the congratulations of government officials, including the duke of Wellington, the hero of Waterloo who had been named British prime minister. In the excitement, some of the dignitaries gathered on a parallel track. Another engine, George Stephenson's *Rocket*, approached at high speed — the engine could go as fast as twenty-seven miles per hour. Most of the gentlemen scattered to safety, but former cabinet minister William Huskisson fell and was hit. A few hours later he died, the first official casualty of the newfangled railroad.

Dramatic and expensive, railroads were the most striking symbol of the new industrial age. Industrialization and its by-product of rapid urban growth fundamentally changed political conflicts, social relations, cultural concerns, and even the landscape. So great were the changes that they are collectively labeled the Industrial Revolution. Although this revolution did not take place in a single decade like the French Revolution, the introduction of steam-driven machinery, large factories, and a new working class transformed life in the Western world.

Inauguration of the Railway Line from Naples to Portici, Italy, 1839
People of all classes flocked to the inauguration of new railway lines. This lithograph by the Italian artist Salvatore Fergola depicts the opening of the first railway line in Italy, which ran from Naples to Portici, a town five miles south of Naples. Portici housed a royal palace and offered access to Herculaneum, an important classical ruin visited by many foreigners. (By Salvatore Fergola, Museum San Martino, Naples, photo © Roger Viollet / The Image Works.)

The shock of industrial and urban growth generated an outpouring of commentary on the need for social reforms. Many who wrote on social issues expected middle-class women to organize their homes as a domestic haven from the heartless process of upheaval. Yet despite the emphasis on domesticity, middle-class women participated in public issues, too: they set up reform societies that fought prostitution and helped poor mothers, they agitated for temperance (abstention from alcohol), and they joined the campaigns to abolish slavery.

Social ferment set the ideological pots to a boil. A word coined during the French Revolution, **ideology** refers to a coherent set of beliefs about the way the social and political order should be organized. The dual impact of the French Revolution and the Industrial Revolution prompted the development of a whole spectrum of ideologies to explain the meaning of the changes taking place. Nationalists, liberals, socialists, and communists offered competing visions of the social order they desired: they all agreed that change was necessary, but they disagreed about both the means and the ends of change. Their contest came to a head in 1848 when the rapid transformation of European society led to a new set of revolutionary outbreaks, more consuming than any since 1789.

CHAPTER FOCUS How did the Industrial Revolution create new social and political conflicts?

The Industrial Revolution

French and English writers of the 1820s invented the term **Industrial Revolution** to capture the drama of contemporary change and to draw a parallel with the French Revolution. The chief components of the Industrial Revolution, industrialization and urbanization, are long-term processes that have continued to the present. The Industrial Revolution began in England in the 1770s and 1780s in textile manufacturing and spread from there across the continent. In the 1830s and 1840s, industrialization and urbanization both accelerated quite suddenly, as governments across Europe encouraged railroad construction and the mechanization of manufacturing. Many officials, preachers, and intellectuals worried that unchecked growth would destroy traditional social relationships and create disorder.

Roots of Industrialization

British inventors had been steadily perfecting steam engines for five decades before George Stephenson built his *Rocket*. A key breakthrough took place in 1776 when Scottish engineer James Watt developed an efficient steam engine that could be used to pump water from coal mines or drive machinery in textile factories. Since coal fired the steam engines that drove new textile machinery, innovations tended to reinforce one another. This kind of synergy built on previous changes in the textile industry. In 1733, the Englishman John Kay had patented the flying shuttle, which enabled weavers to "throw" yarn across the loom rather than draw it back and forth by hand. Weavers began producing cloth more quickly than spinners could produce the thread. The resulting shortage of spun thread propelled the invention of the spinning jenny, a spinning wheel that enabled one worker to run eight spools at once. The increased output of yarn then stimulated the mechanization of weaving. Using the engines produced by James Watt and his partner Matthew Boulton, Edmund Cartwright designed a mechanized loom in the 1780s that, when perfected, could be run by a small boy and yet yield fifteen times the output of a skilled adult working a handloom. By the end of the century, manufacturers

were assembling new power machinery in large factories that hired semiskilled men, women, and children to replace skilled weavers.

Several factors interacted to make England the first site of the Industrial Revolution. England had a good supply of private investment capital from overseas trade and commercial profits, ready access to raw cotton from the plantations of its Caribbean colonies and the southern United States, and the necessary natural resources at home such as coal and iron. Good opportunities for social mobility provided an environment that fostered the pragmatism of the English and Scottish inventors who designed the machinery. The agricultural revolution of the eighteenth century had enabled England to produce food more efficiently, freeing some agricultural workers to move to the new sites of manufacturing. Cotton textile production skyrocketed.

Elsewhere in Europe, textile manufacturing — long a linchpin in the European economy — expanded even without the introduction of new machines and factories because of the spread of the "putting-out," or "domestic," system. Under the putting-out system, manufacturers supplied the raw materials, such as woolen or cotton fibers, to families working at home. The mother and her children washed, carded, and combed the fibers. Then the mother and oldest daughters spun them into thread. The father, assisted by the children, wove the cloth. The cloth was then finished (bleached, dyed, smoothed, and so on) under the supervision of the manufacturer in a large workshop, located either in town or in the countryside. This system had existed in the textile industry for hundreds of years, but it grew dramatically in the eighteenth century, and the manufacture of other products — such as glassware, baskets, nails, and guns — followed suit. The spread of the putting-out system of manufacturing is sometimes called proto-industrialization to signify that the process helped pave the way for the full-scale Industrial Revolution. Because of the increase in textile production, ordinary people began to wear underclothes and nightclothes, both rare in the past. White, red, blue, yellow, green, and even pastel shades of cotton now replaced the black, gray, or brown of traditional wool.

Workers in the textile industry enjoyed few protections against fluctuations in the market. Hundreds of thousands of families might be reduced to bankruptcy in periods of overproduction. Handloom weavers sometimes violently resisted the establishment of the factory power looms that would force them out of work. In England in 1811 and 1812, for example, bands of handloom weavers wrecked factory machinery and burned mills in the Midlands, Yorkshire, and Lancashire. To restore order and protect industry, the government sent in an army of twelve thousand regular soldiers and made machine wrecking punishable by death. The rioters were called Luddites after the fictitious figure Ned Ludd, whose signature appeared on their manifestos. (The term is still used to describe those who resist new technology.)

Engines of Change

Steam-driven engines took on a dramatic new form in the 1820s when the English engineer George Stephenson perfected an engine to pull wagons along rail tracks. The idea of a railroad was not new: iron tracks had been used since the seventeenth century to

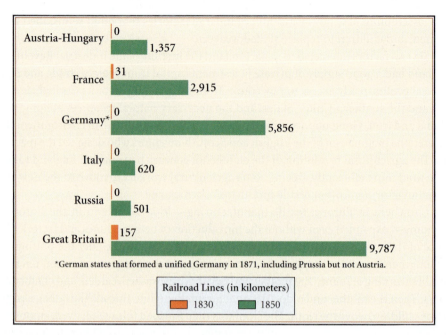

Taking Measure **Railroad Lines, 1830–1850**
Great Britain quickly extended its lead in the building of railroads. The extension of commerce and, before long, the ability to wage war would depend on the development of effective railroad networks. These statistics might be taken as predicting a realignment of power within Europe after 1850. (B. R. Mitchell, *European Historical Statistics 1750–1970* [New York: Columbia University Press, 1975], F1.)

haul coal from mines in wagons pulled by horses. A railroad system as a mode of human transport, however, developed only after Stephenson's invention of a steam-powered locomotive. Placed on the new tracks, steam-driven carriages could transport people and goods to the cities and link coal and iron deposits to the new factories. In the 1840s alone, railroad track mileage more than doubled in Great Britain, and British investment in railways jumped tenfold. The British also began to build railroads in India. Private investment that had been going into the building of thousands of miles of canals now went into railroads. Britain's success with rail transportation led other countries to develop their own projects. Railroads grew spectacularly in the United States in the 1830s and 1840s, reaching 9,000 miles of track by midcentury. In 1835, Belgium (newly independent in 1830) opened the first continental European railroad with state bonds backed by British capital. By 1850, the world had 23,500 miles of track, most of it in western Europe. (See "Taking Measure," above.)

Railroad building spurred both industrial development and state power (Map 21.1). Governments everywhere participated in the construction of railroads, which depended on both private and state funds to pay for the massive amounts of iron, coal, heavy machinery, and human labor required to build and run them. Demand for iron products accelerated industrial development. Until the 1840s, cotton had led industrial pro-

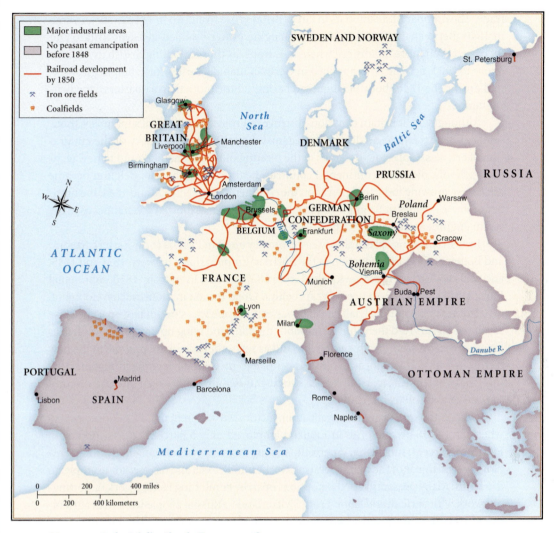

Map 21.1 Industrialization in Europe, c. 1850
Industrialization (mainly mechanized textile production) first spread in a band across northern Europe
that included Great Britain, northern France, Belgium, the northern German states, the region around
Milan in northern Italy, and Bohemia. Although railroads were not the only factor in promoting industrialization, the map makes clear the interrelationship between railroad building and the development of
new industrial sites of coal mining and textile production.

duction; between 1816 and 1840, cotton output more than quadrupled in Great Britain.
But from 1830 to 1850, Britain's output of iron and coal doubled. Similarly, Austrian
output of iron doubled between the 1820s and the 1840s. One-third of all investment
in the German states in the 1840s went into railroads.

Steam-powered engines made Britain the world leader in manufacturing. By midcentury, more than half of Britain's national income came from manufacturing and

trade. The number of steamboats in Great Britain rose from two in 1812 to six hundred in 1840. Between 1840 and 1850, steam-engine power doubled in Great Britain and increased even more rapidly elsewhere in Europe, as those adopting British inventions strove to catch up. The power applied in German manufacturing, for example, grew six-fold during the 1840s but still amounted to only a little more than a quarter of the British figure.

Although Great Britain consciously strove to protect its industrial supremacy, thousands of British engineers defied laws against the export of machinery or the emigration of artisans. Only slowly, thanks to the pirating of British methods and to new technical schools, did most continental countries begin closing the gap. Belgium became the fastest-growing industrial power on the continent: between 1830 and 1844, the number of steam engines in Belgium quadrupled, and Belgians exported seven times as many steam engines as they imported.

Industrialization spread slowly east from key areas in Prussia (near Berlin), Saxony, and Bohemia. Cotton production in the Austrian Empire tripled between 1831 and 1845, and coal production increased fourfold from 1827 to 1847. Even so, by 1850, continental Europe still lagged almost twenty years behind Great Britain in industrial development.

The advance of industrialization in eastern Europe was slow, in large part because serfdom still survived there, hindering labor mobility and tying up investment capital: as long as peasants were legally tied to the land as serfs, they could not migrate to the new factory towns and landlords felt little incentive to invest their income in manufacturing. The problem was worst in Russia, where industrialization would not take off until the end of the nineteenth century.

Despite the spread of industrialization, factory workers remained a minority everywhere. In the 1840s, factories in England employed only 5 percent of the workers; in France, 3 percent; in Prussia, 2 percent. The putting-out system remained strong, employing two-thirds of the manufacturing workers in Prussia and Saxony, for example, in the 1840s. Many peasants kept their options open by combining factory work or putting-out work with agricultural labor. From Switzerland to Russia, people worked in agriculture during the spring and summer and in manufacturing in the fall and winter.

Even though factories employed only a small percentage of the population, they attracted much attention. Already by 1830, more than a million people in Britain depended on the cotton industry for employment, and cotton cloth constituted 50 percent of the country's exports. Factories sprang up in urban areas, where the growing population provided a ready source of labor. The rapid expansion of the British textile industry had a colonial corollary: the destruction of the hand manufacture of textiles in India. The British put high import duties on Indian cloth entering Britain and kept such duties very low for British cloth entering India. The effects were catastrophic for Indian manufacturing: in 1813, the Indian city of Calcutta exported to England £2 million worth of cotton cloth; by 1830, Calcutta was importing from England £2 million worth of the product. When Britain abolished slavery in its Caribbean colonies in 1833, British manufacturers began to buy raw cotton in the southern United States, where slavery still flourished.

Factories drew workers from the urban population surge, which had begun in the eighteenth century and now accelerated. The number of agricultural laborers also increased during industrialization in Britain, suggesting that a growing birthrate created a larger population and fed workers into the new factory system. Factory employment resembled labor on family farms or in the putting-out system: entire families came to toil for a single wage, although family members performed different tasks. Workdays of twelve to seventeen hours were typical, even for children, and the work was grueling.

As urban factories grew, their workers gradually came to constitute a new socioeconomic class with a distinctive culture and traditions. The term *working class,* like *middle class,* came into use for the first time in the early nineteenth century. It referred to the laborers in the new factories. In the past, urban workers had labored in isolated trades: water and wood carrying, gardening, laundry, and building. In contrast, factories brought working people together with machines, under close supervision by their employers. Soon developing a sense of common interests, they organized societies for mutual help and political reform. From these would come the first labor unions.

Industry returned unheard-of riches to factory owners and managers even as it caused pollution and created new forms of poverty for exhausted workers. "From this foul drain the greatest stream of human industry flows out to fertilize the whole world," wrote the French aristocrat Alexis de Tocqueville after visiting the new English industrial city of Manchester in the 1830s. "From this filthy sewer pure gold flows." Studies by physicians set the life expectancy of workers in Manchester at just seventeen years (partly because of high rates of infant mortality), whereas the average life expectancy in England was forty years in 1840. In some parts of Europe, city leaders banned factories, hoping to insulate their towns from the effects of industrial growth.

Investigators detailed the pitiful condition of workers. A physician in the town of Mulhouse, in eastern France, described the "pale, emaciated women who walk barefooted through the dirt" to reach the factory. The young children who worked in the factory appeared "clothed in rags which are greasy with the oil from the looms and frames." A report to the city government in Lille, France, in 1832 described the "dark cellars" where the cotton workers lived: "The air is never renewed, it is infected; the walls are plastered with garbage."

Government inquiries often focused on women and children. In Great Britain, the Factory Act of 1833 outlawed the employment of children under the age of nine in textile mills (except in the lace and silk industries); it also limited the workdays for those ages nine to thirteen to nine hours a day, and those ages thirteen to eighteen to twelve hours. Adults worked even longer hours. Women and young children, sometimes under age six, hauled coal trucks through low, cramped passageways in coal mines. One nine-year-old girl, Margaret Gomley, described her typical day in the mines as beginning at 7:00 a.m. and ending at 6:00 p.m.: "I get my dinner at 12 o'clock, which is a dry muffin, and sometimes butter on, but have no time allowed to stop to eat it, I eat it while I am thrusting the load."

In 1842, the British Parliament prohibited the employment of women and girls underground. In 1847, the Central Short Time Committee, one of Britain's many social

Child Labor in Coal Mines
The passage of legislation in 1842 against women and girls working underground did nothing to prevent boys from continuing to perform essential tasks in cramped spaces in British coal mines. Lithographs such as this one from 1844 accompanied campaigns against these practices. (akg-images.)

reform organizations, successfully pressured Parliament to limit the workday of women and children to ten hours. The continental countries followed the British lead, but since most did not insist on government inspection, enforcement was lax.

Urbanization and Its Consequences

Industrial development spurred urban growth, yet cities with little industry grew as well. **Urbanization** is the growth of towns and cities due to the movement of people from rural to urban areas. Here, too, Great Britain led the way: half the population of England and Wales was living in towns by 1850, while in France and the German states only about a quarter of the total population was urban. Both old and new cities teemed with rising numbers in the 1830s and 1840s; the population of Vienna ballooned by 125,000 between 1827 and 1847, and the new industrial city of Manchester grew by 70,000 just in the 1830s.

Massive emigration from rural areas, rather than births to women already living in cities, accounted for this remarkable increase. City life and new factories beckoned those faced with hunger and poverty, including immigrants from other lands: thousands of Irish emigrated to English cities, Italians went to French cities, and Poles flocked to German cities. Settlements sprang up outside the old city limits but gradually became part of the urban area. Cities incorporated parks, cemeteries, zoos, and greenways — all imitations of the countryside, which itself was being industrialized by railroads and factories.

The rapid influx of people caused serious overcrowding in the cities because the housing stock expanded much more slowly than the population did. In Paris, thirty thousand workers lived in lodging houses, eight or nine to a room, with no separation of the sexes. In 1847, in St. Giles, the Irish quarter of London, 461 people lived in just twelve houses. Men, women, and children with no money for fuel huddled together for warmth on piles of filthy rotting straw or potato peels.

Severe crowding worsened already dire sanitation conditions. Residents dumped refuse into streets or courtyards, and human excrement collected in cesspools under apartment houses. At midcentury, London's approximately 250,000 cesspools were emptied only once or twice a year. Water was scarce and had to be fetched daily from nearby fountains. Parisians, on average, had enough water for only two baths annually per person (the upper classes enjoyed more baths, of course; the lower classes, fewer). In London, private companies that supplied water turned on pumps in the poorer sections for only a few hours three days a week. In rapidly growing British industrial cities such as Manchester, one-third of the houses contained no latrines. Human waste ended up in the rivers that supplied drinking water. The horses that provided transportation inside the cities left droppings everywhere, and city dwellers often kept chickens, ducks, goats, pigs, geese, and even cattle, as well as dogs and cats, in their houses. The result was a "universal atmosphere of filth and stink," as one observer recounted.

Such conditions made cities prime breeding grounds for disease. In 1830–1832 and again in 1847–1851, devastating outbreaks of cholera swept across Asia and Europe, touching the United States as well in 1849–1850 (Map 21.2). Today we know that a waterborne bacterium causes cholera, but at the time no one understood the disease and everyone feared it. The usually fatal illness induced violent vomiting and diarrhea and left the skin blue, eyes sunken and dull, and hands and feet ice cold. While cholera particularly ravaged the crowded, filthy neighborhoods of rapidly growing cities, it also claimed many rural and some well-to-do victims. In Paris, 18,000 people died in the 1832 epidemic and 20,000 in that of 1849; in London, 7,000 died in each epidemic; and in Russia, the epidemic was catastrophic, claiming 250,000 victims in 1831–1832 and 1 million in 1847–1851.

Epidemics revealed the social tensions lying just beneath the surface of urban life. Middle-class reformers often considered the poor to be morally degenerate. In their view, overcrowding led to sexual promiscuity and illegitimacy. They depicted the lower classes as dangerously lacking in sexual self-control. Officials collected statistics on illegitimacy that seemed to bear out these fears: one-quarter to one-half of the babies born in the big European cities in the 1830s and 1840s were illegitimate, and alarmed

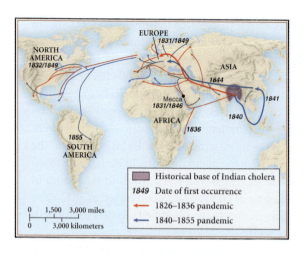

Map 21.2 The Spread of Cholera, 1826–1855

Contemporaries did not understand the causes of the cholera epidemics in the 1830s and the 1840s in Europe. Western Europeans knew only that the disease marched progressively from east to west across Europe. Nothing seemed able to stop it. It appeared and died out for reasons that could not be grasped at the time. Nevertheless, the cholera epidemics prompted authorities in most European countries to set up public health agencies to coordinate the response and study sanitation conditions in the cities.

medical men wrote about thousands of infanticides. In contrast, only a tiny fraction of rural births were illegitimate. The rising rate of births outside of marriage seemed to go hand in hand with drinking and crime. Beer halls and pubs dotted the urban landscape. By the 1830s, Hungary's twin cities of Buda and Pest had eight hundred beer and wine houses for the working classes. Police officials estimated that London had seventy thousand thieves and eighty thousand prostitutes. In many cities, nearly half the population lived at the level of bare subsistence, and increasing numbers depended on public welfare, charity, or criminality to make ends meet.

Everywhere reformers warned of a widening separation between rich and poor and a growing sense of hostility between the classes. A Swiss pastor noted: "A new spirit has arisen among the workers. Their hearts seethe with hatred of the well-to-do; their eyes lust for a share of the wealth about them; their mouths speak unblushingly of a coming day of retribution." In 1848, as we will see, it would seem that day of retribution had arrived.

Agricultural Perils and Prosperity

Rising populations created increased demand for food and spurred changes in the countryside, too. Although agricultural yields increased by 30 to 50 percent in the first half of the nineteenth century, population grew by nearly 100 percent. Railroads and canals improved food distribution, but much of Europe — particularly in the east — remained isolated from markets and vulnerable to famines.

Most people still lived on the land, and the upper classes still dominated rural society. In France at midcentury, almost two million economically independent peasants tended their own small properties. But in England, southern Italy, Prussia, and eastern Europe, large landowners, usually noblemen, consolidated and expanded their estates by buying up the land of less successful nobles or peasants. As agricultural prices rose, the big landowners pushed for legislation to allow them to continue converting common land to private property.

Class Differences

In 1841, a new satirical weekly in London called *Punch* began publishing "cartoons" (humorous drawings). This one from 1843 depicts the dramatic differences between the life experiences of those with money ("Capital") and those who worked with their hands ("Labour"). (From *Punch*, vol. 5, London, 1843, cartoon number 5 / akg-images.)

Wringing a living from the soil under such conditions put pressure on traditional family life. Men often migrated seasonally to earn cash in factories or as village artisans, while their wives, sisters, and daughters did the traditional "men's work" of tending crops. In the past, population growth had been contained by postponing marriage (leaving fewer years for childbearing) and by high rates of death in childbirth as well as infant mortality. Now, as child mortality declined outside the industrial cities and people without property began marrying earlier, Europeans became more aware of birth control methods. The vulcanization of rubber in the 1840s improved the reliability of condoms. When such methods failed and population increase left no options open at home, people emigrated, often to the United States. Between 1816 and 1850, five million Europeans left their home countries for new lives overseas. When France colonized Algeria in the 1830s and 1840s, officials tried to attract settlers by emphasizing the fertility of the land; they offered the prospect of agricultural prosperity in the colony as an alternative to the rigors of industrialization and urbanization at home.

Rural political power remained in the hands of traditional elites. The biggest property owners controlled the political assemblies and often personally selected local officials. Nowhere did the old rural social order seem more impregnable than in Russia. Most Russian serfs remained tied to the land, and troops easily suppressed serfs' uprisings

in 1831 and 1842. Yet in the 1850s railroad construction would begin to transform life in Russia, too, and the railroads would bring with them the same social problems — urbanization, the beginning of industrialization, and a growing awareness of social disparities — that threatened the social and political order in western Europe in the 1830s and 1840s. These new social problems demanded a response. But would that response be reform or revolution?

REVIEW QUESTION What dangers did the Industrial Revolution pose to both urban and rural life?

Reforming the Social Order

The experience of dramatic economic and social changes prompted artists and writers to focus on emerging social problems and inspired the creation of new organizations for social reform. Middle-class women often took the lead in establishing charitable organizations that tried to bring religious faith, educational uplift, and the reform of manners to the lower classes. The middle class, both men and women, expected women to soften the rigors of a rapidly changing society, but this expectation led to some confusion about women's proper role: Should they devote themselves to social reform in the world or to their own domestic spaces? Many hoped to apply the same zeal for reform to the colonial peoples living in places administered by Europeans.

Cultural Responses to the Social Question

The *social question,* an expression reflecting the widely shared concern about social changes arising from industrialization and urbanization, pervaded all forms of art and literature. The dominant artistic movement of the time, romanticism, generally took a dim view of industrialization. The English-born American painter Thomas Cole (1801–1848) complained in 1836: "In this age . . . a meager utilitarianism seems ready to absorb every feeling and sentiment, and what is sometimes called improvement in its march makes us fear that the bright and tender flowers of the imagination shall all be crushed beneath its iron tramp." Yet culture itself underwent important changes as the growing capitals of Europe attracted flocks of aspiring painters and playwrights; the 1830s and 1840s witnessed an explosion in culture as the number of would-be artists increased dramatically and new technologies such as photography and lithography (see the illustration on page 672) brought art to the masses. Many of these new intellectuals would support the revolutions of 1848.

Because romanticism tended to glorify nature and reject industrial and urban growth, romantics often gave vivid expression to the problems created by rapid economic and social transformation. The English poet Elizabeth Barrett Browning, best known for her love poems, denounced child labor in "The Cry of the Children" (1843). In *Rain, Steam, and Speed: The Great Western Railway* (1844), the leading English romantic painter, Joseph M. W. Turner (1775–1851), portrayed the struggle between the forces of nature and the means of economic growth. Turner was fascinated by steamboats: in

Joseph M. W. Turner, *The Fighting "Téméraire" Tugged to Her Last Berth to Be Broken Up* (1838)
In this painting a steamer belching smoke tows a wooden sailing ship to its last berth, where it will be destroyed. Turner muses about the passing of old ways but also displays his mastery of color in the final blaze of sunset, itself another sign of the passing of time. Turner was an avid reader of the romantic poets, especially Byron. British opinion polls have rated this painting the best of all British paintings. How does the painting capture the clash of old and new? (© National Gallery, London, UK / Art Resource, NY.)

The Fighting "Téméraire" Tugged to Her Last Berth to Be Broken Up (1838), he featured the victory of steam power over more conventional sailing ships.

Increased literacy, the spread of reading rooms and lending libraries, and serialization in newspapers and journals gave novels a large reading public. Unlike the fiction of the eighteenth century, which had focused on individual personalities, the great novels of the 1830s and 1840s specialized in the portrayal of social life in all its varieties. Manufacturers, financiers, starving students, workers, bureaucrats, prostitutes, underworld figures, thieves, and aristocratic men and women filled the pages of works by popular writers. Hoping to get out of debt, the French writer Honoré de Balzac (1799–1850) pushed himself to exhaustion and a premature death by cranking out ninety-five novels and many short stories. He aimed to catalog the social types that could be found in French society. Many of his characters, like himself, were driven by the desire to climb higher in the social order.

The English fiction writer Charles Dickens (1812–1870) worked with a similar frenetic energy and for much the same reason. When his father was imprisoned for debt in 1824, the young Dickens took a job in a shoe-polish factory. He eventually became a journalist and managed to produce a series of novels that attracted thousands of readers. In them, he paid close attention to the distressing effects of industrialization and urbanization. In *The Old Curiosity Shop* (1841), for example, he depicts the Black Country, the manufacturing region west and northwest of Birmingham, as a "cheerless region," a "mournful place," in which tall chimneys "made foul the melancholy air."

Novels by women often revealed the bleaker side of women's situations. Charlotte Brontë's *Jane Eyre* (1847) describes the difficult life of an orphaned girl who becomes a governess, the only occupation open to most single middle-class women. The French novelist Amandine-Aurore-Lucile Dupin Dudevant (1804–1876), writing under the pen name **George Sand**, took her social criticism a step further. She announced her independence in the 1830s by dressing like a man and smoking cigars. Though she published her work under a male pseudonym, as did many other women writers of the time, she created female characters who prevail in difficult circumstances through romantic love and moral idealism. Her notoriety — she became the lover of the Polish pianist and composer Frédéric Chopin, among others, and threw herself into socialist politics — made the term *George-Sandism* a common expression of disdain toward independent women.

As artists became more interested in society and social relations, ordinary citizens crowded cultural events. Museums opened to the public across Europe. Popular theaters in big cities drew thousands from the lower and middle classes every night; in London, for example, some twenty-four thousand people attended eighty "penny theaters" nightly. The audience for print culture also multiplied. In the German states, for example, the production of new literary works doubled between 1830 and 1843, as did the number of periodi-

George Sand

In this lithograph by Alcide Lorentz of 1842, George Sand is shown in one of her notorious male costumes standing on a cloud created by the cigar in her left hand. Sand published numerous works, including novels (*Indiana* is shown at her feet), plays, essays, travel writing, and an autobiography. She advocated setting up a Chamber of Mothers to go alongside the Chamber of Deputies (her right arm rests on sheets with those words on them), and she actively participated in the revolution of 1848 in France, writing pamphlets in support of the new republic. Disillusioned by the rise to power of Louis-Napoleon Bonaparte, she withdrew to her country estate and devoted herself exclusively to her writing. (The Granger Collection, NYC — All rights reserved.)

The First Daguerreotype

Jacques Daguerre experimented extensively with producing an image on a metal plate before he came up with a viable photographic process in 1837. He called this first daguerreotype *Still Life*, a common title for paintings. In 1839, the French government bought the rights and made the process freely available. (Louis Daguerre / Time & Life Pictures / Getty Images.)

cals and newspapers and the number of booksellers. Young children and ragpickers sold cheap prints and books door-to-door or in taverns.

The advent of photography in 1839 provided an amazing new medium for artists. The daguerreotype, named after its inventor, French painter Jacques Daguerre (1787–1851), prompted one artist to claim that "from today, painting is dead." Although this prediction was highly exaggerated, photography did open up new ways of portraying reality. It did so only gradually, however, as early photographs required exposure times of twenty to thirty minutes, making it impossible to capture anything or anyone in movement.

Culture expanded its reach in part because the ranks of artists and writers swelled. Estimates suggest that the number of painters and sculptors in France, the undisputed center of European art at the time, grew sixfold between 1789 and 1838. Not everyone could succeed in this hothouse atmosphere, in which writers and artists furiously competed for public attention. Their own troubles made some of them more keenly aware of the hardships faced by the poor. A satirical article in one of the many bitingly critical journals and booklets published in Berlin proclaimed: "In Ipswich in England a mechanical genius has invented a stomach, whose extraordinary efficient construction is remarkable. This artificial stomach is intended for factory workers there and is adjusted so that it is fully satisfied with three lentils or peas; one potato is enough for an entire week."

The Varieties of Social Reform

Lithographs, novels, and even joke booklets helped drive home the need for social reform, but religious conviction also inspired efforts to help the poor. Moral reform societies, Bible groups, Sunday schools, and temperance groups aimed to turn the poor into respectable people. In 1844, for example, 450 different relief organizations operated in London alone.

Religiously motivated reformers first had to overcome the perceived indifference of the working classes. Protestant and Catholic clergy complained that workers had no interest in religion; less than 10 percent of the workers in the cities attended religious

services. To combat indifference, British religious groups launched the Sunday school movement, which reached its zenith in the 1840s. By 1851, more than half of all working-class children ages five to fifteen were attending Sunday school, even though very few of their parents regularly went to religious services. The Sunday schools taught children how to read at a time when few working-class children could go to school during the week.

Women took a more prominent role than ever before in charitable work. Catholic religious orders, which by 1850 enrolled many more women than men, ran schools, hospitals, leper colonies, insane asylums, and old-age homes. The Catholic church established new orders, especially for women, and increased missionary activity overseas. Protestant women in Great Britain and the United States established Bible, missionary, and female reform societies by the hundreds. Chief among their concerns was prostitution, and many societies dedicated themselves to reforming "fallen women" and castigating men who visited prostitutes.

Catholics and Protestants alike promoted the temperance movement. The first societies had appeared in the United States as early as 1813, and by 1835 the American Temperance Society claimed 1.5 million members. Temperance advocates viewed drunkenness as a sign of moral weakness and a threat to social order. Yet temperance societies also attracted working-class people who shared the desire for respectability.

Social reformers saw education as one of the main prospects for uplifting the poor and the working class. In 1833, the French government passed an education law that required every town to maintain a primary school, pay a teacher, and provide free education to poor boys. As the law's author, François Guizot, argued, "Ignorance renders the masses turbulent and ferocious." Girls' schools were optional, although hundreds of women taught at the primary level, most of them in private, often religious schools. Despite these efforts, only one out of every thirty children went to school in France, many fewer than in Protestant states such as Prussia, where 75 percent of children were in primary school by 1835. Popular education remained woefully undeveloped in most of eastern Europe. Peasants were specifically excluded from the few primary schools in Russia, where Tsar Nicholas I blamed the Decembrist Revolt of 1825 on education.

Above all else, the elite sought to impose discipline and order on working people. Popular sports, especially blood sports such as cockfighting and bearbaiting, suggested a lack of control, and long-standing efforts in Great Britain to eliminate these recreations now gained momentum through organizations such as the Society for the Prevention of Cruelty to Animals. By the end of the 1830s, bullbaiting had been abandoned in Great Britain. The other blood sports died out more slowly, and efforts in other countries generally lagged behind those of the British.

When private charities failed to meet the needs of the poor, governments often intervened. Great Britain sought to control the costs of public welfare by passing a new poor law in 1834, called by its critics the Starvation Act. The law required that all able-bodied persons receiving relief be housed together in workhouses, with husbands separated from wives and parents from children. Workhouse life was designed to be as unpleasant as possible so that poor people would move on to regions that had better

employment prospects. British women from all social classes organized anti–poor law societies to protest the separation of mothers from their children in the workhouses.

Many women viewed charitable work as the extension of their domestic roles: they promoted virtuous behavior and morality in their efforts to improve society. But women's social reform activities concealed a paradox. According to the ideology that historians call **domesticity**, women were to live their lives entirely within the domestic sphere, devoting themselves to their families and the home. The English poet Alfred, Lord Tennyson, captured this view in a popular poem published in 1847: "Man for the field and woman for the hearth; / Man for the sword and for the needle she. / . . . All else confusion."

Most women had little hope of economic independence. The notion that they belonged in a separate, domestic sphere prevented women from pursuing higher education, work in professional careers, or participation in politics through voting or holding office — all activities deemed appropriate only to men. Laws everywhere codified the subordination of women. Many countries followed the model of Napoleon's Civil Code, which classified married women as legal incompetents along with children, the insane, and criminals. In some countries, such as France and Austria, unmarried women enjoyed some rights over property, but elsewhere laws explicitly defined them as perpetual minors under paternal control.

Distinctions between men and women were most noticeable in the privileged classes. Whereas boys attended secondary schools, most middle- and upper-class girls still received their education at home or in church schools, where they were taught to be religious, obedient, and accomplished in music and languages. As men's fashions turned practical — long trousers and short jackets of solid, often dark colors; no makeup (previously common for aristocratic men), and simply cut hair — women continued to dress for decorative effect, now with tightly corseted waists that emphasized the differences between female and male bodies. Middle- and upper-class women favored long hair that required hours of brushing and pinning up, and they wore long, cumbersome skirts.

Scientists reinforced stereotypes. Once considered sexually insatiable, women were now described as incapacitated by menstruation and largely uninterested in sex, an attitude that many equated with moral superiority. Thus was born the "Victorian" woman (the epoch gets its name from England's Queen Victoria — see page 689), a figment of the largely male medical imagination. Physicians and scholars considered women mentally inferior. In 1839, Auguste Comte, an influential early French sociologist, wrote, "As for any functions of government, the radical inaptitude of the female sex is there yet more marked . . . and limited to the guidance of the mere family."

Some women denounced the ideology of domesticity and separate spheres; the English writer Ann Lamb, for example, proclaimed that "the duty of a wife *means* the obedience of a Turkish slave." Middle-class women who did not marry, however, had few options for earning a living; they often worked as governesses or ladies' companions for the well-to-do. Most lower-class women worked because of financial necessity; as the wives of peasants, laborers, or shopkeepers, they had to supplement the family's meager

income by working on the farm, in a factory, or in a shop. Domesticity might have been an ideal for them, but rarely was it a reality.

Abuses and Reforms Overseas

Like the ideal of domesticity, the ideal of colonialism often conflicted with the reality of economic interests. In the first half of the nineteenth century, those economic interests changed as European colonialism underwent a subtle but momentous transformation. Colonialism became **imperialism** — a word coined only in the mid-nineteenth century — as Europeans turned their interest away from the plantation colonies of the Caribbean and toward new colonies in Asia and Africa. Colonialism had most often led to the establishment of settler colonies, direct rule by Europeans, the introduction of slave labor from Africa, and the wholesale destruction of indigenous peoples. In contrast, imperialism usually meant more indirect forms of economic exploitation and political rule. Europeans still profited from their colonies, but now they also aimed to re-form colonial peoples in their own image — when it did not conflict too much with their economic interests to do so.

Colonialism — as opposed to imperialism — rose and fell with the enslavement of black Africans. British religious groups, especially the Quakers, had taken the lead in forming antislavery societies. They gained a first victory in 1807 when the British House of Lords voted to abolish the slave trade (though not the institution of slavery itself). British reformers finally obtained the abolition of slavery in the British Empire in 1833. Antislavery petitions to Parliament bore 1.5 million signatures, including those of 350,000 women on one petition alone. In France, the new government of Louis-Philippe took strong measures against clandestine slave traffic, virtually ending French participation during the 1830s. Slavery was abolished in the remaining French Caribbean colonies in 1848.

Neither slavery nor the slave trade disappeared immediately just because the British and French had given it up. Because of increased participation by Spanish and Portuguese traders, almost as many slaves were traded in the 1820s as in the 1780s and the overall traffic did not dwindle until the 1850s. Human bondage continued unabated in Brazil, Cuba (still a Spanish colony), and the United States. Some American reformers supported abolition, but they remained a minority. Like serfdom in Russia, slavery in the Americas involved a quagmire of economic, political, and moral problems that worsened as the nineteenth century wore on.

Despite the abolition of slavery, Britain and France had not lost interest in overseas colonies. Using the pretext of an insult to its envoy, France invaded Algeria in 1830 and, after a long military campaign, established political control over most of the country in the next two decades. By 1848, more than seventy thousand French, Italian, and Maltese colonists had settled there with government encouragement, often confiscating the lands of native peoples. In that year, the French government officially incorporated Algeria as part of France. France also imposed a protectorate government over the South Pacific island of Tahiti.

Although the British granted Canada greater self-determination in 1839, they extended their dominion elsewhere by annexing Singapore (1819), an island off the Malay peninsula, and New Zealand (1840). They also increased their control in India through the administration of the East India Company, a private group of merchants chartered by the British crown. The British educated a native elite to take over much of the day-to-day business of administering the country, and they used native soldiers to augment their military control. By 1850, only one in six soldiers serving Britain in India was European.

The East India Company also tried to establish a regular trade with China in opium, long known for its medicinal uses but increasingly bought in China as a recreational drug. The Chinese government forbade Western merchants to venture outside the southern city of Guangzhou (Canton) and banned the import of opium, but these measures failed. By smuggling Indian opium into China and bribing local officials, British traders built up a flourishing market, and by the mid-1830s they were pressuring the British government to force an expanded opium trade on the Chinese. When the Chinese authorities expelled British merchants from southern China in 1839, Britain retaliated by bombarding Chinese coastal cities. The **Opium War** ended in 1842, when Britain dictated to a defeated China the Treaty of Nanking, by which four more Chinese ports were opened to Europeans and the British took sovereignty over the island of Hong Kong, received a substantial war indemnity, and were assured of a continuation of the opium trade. In this case, reform took a backseat to economic interest, despite the complaints of religious groups in Britain.

The Opium War, 1839–1842

REVIEW QUESTION In which areas did reformers trying to address the social problems created by industrialization and urbanization succeed, and in which did they fail?

Ideologies and Political Movements

Although reform organizations grew rapidly in the 1830s and 1840s, many Europeans found them insufficient to answer the questions raised by industrialization and urbanization. How did the new social order differ from the earlier one, which was less urban and less driven by commercial concerns? Who should control this new order? Should governments try to moderate or accelerate the pace of change? New ideologies such as liberalism and socialism offered competing answers to these questions and provided the platform for new political movements. Established governments faced challenges not only from liberals and socialists but also from the most potent of the new doctrines, nationalism. Nationalists looked past social problems to concentrate on achieving political autonomy and self-determination for groups identified by ethnicity rather than by class.

The Spell of Nationalism

According to the doctrine of **nationalism**, all peoples derive their identities from their nations, which are defined by common language, shared cultural traditions, and sometimes religion. When such nations do not coincide with state boundaries, nationalism can produce violence and warfare as different national groups compete for control over territory (Map 21.3).

Nationalist aspirations were especially explosive for the Austrian Empire, which included a variety of peoples united only by their enforced allegiance to the Habsburg emperor. The empire included three main national groups: the Germans, who made up

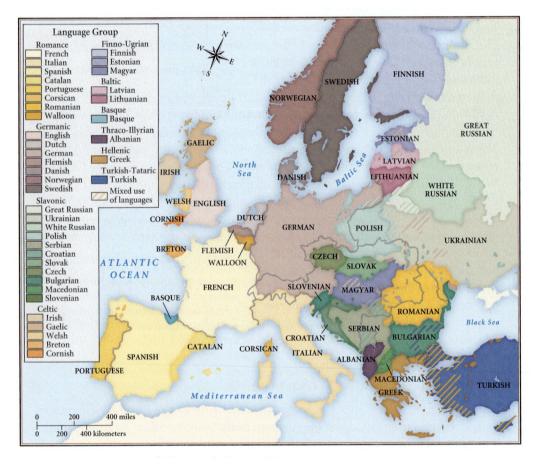

Map 21.3 Languages of Nineteenth-Century Europe

Even this detailed map of linguistic diversity understates the number of different languages and dialects spoken in Europe. In Italy, for example, few people spoke Italian as their first language. Instead, they spoke local dialects such as Piedmontese or Ligurian, and some who came from the regions bordering France spoke better French than Italian. How does the map underline the inherent contradictions of nationalism in Europe? What were the consequences of linguistic diversity within national borders? Keep in mind that even in Spain, France, and Great Britain, linguistic diversity continued right up to the beginning of the 1900s.

one-fourth of the population; the Magyars of Hungary (which included Transylvania and Croatia); and the Slavs, who together formed the largest group in the population but were divided into different ethnic groups such as Poles, Czechs, Croats, and Serbs. The Austrian Empire also included Italians in Lombardy and Venetia, and Romanians in Transylvania. Efforts to govern such diverse peoples preoccupied Prince Klemens von Metternich, chief minister to the weak Habsburg emperor Francis I (r. 1792–1835). Metternich's domestic policy aimed to restrain nationalist impulses, and it largely succeeded until the 1840s. He set up a secret police organization on the Napoleonic model that opened letters of even the highest officials. Metternich's policies forced the leading Italian nationalist, **Giuseppe Mazzini** (1805–1872), into exile in France in 1831. There Mazzini founded Young Italy, a secret society that attracted thousands with its message that Italy would touch off a European-wide revolutionary movement. The conservative order throughout Europe felt threatened by Mazzini's charismatic leadership and conspiratorial scheming, but he lacked both European allies against Austria and widespread support among the Italian masses.

Austria was deliberately excluded when the German states formed a *Zollverein* ("customs union") in 1834, under Prussian leadership. German nationalists sought a government uniting German-speaking peoples, but they could not agree on its boundaries: Would the unified German state include both Prussia and the Austrian Empire? If it included Austria, what about the non-German territories of the Austrian Empire? And could the powerful, conservative kingdom of Prussia coexist in a unified German state with other, more liberal but smaller states? These questions would vex German history for decades to come.

Polish nationalism revived after the collapse of the revolt in 1830 against Russian domination. It found its most ringing voice in the poet Adam Mickiewicz (1798–1855), whose mystical writings portrayed the Polish exiles as martyrs of a crucified nation with an international Christian mission. Mickiewicz formed the Polish Legion to fight for national restoration, but rivalries and divisions prevented united action until 1846, when Polish exiles in Paris tried to launch a coordinated insurrection for Polish independence. Plans for an uprising in the Polish province of Galicia in the Austrian Empire collapsed when peasants instead revolted against their noble Polish masters.

In Russia, nationalism took the form of opposition to Western ideas. Russian nationalists, or Slavophiles (lovers of the Slavs), opposed the Westernizers, who wanted Russia to follow Western models of industrial development and constitutional government. The Slavophiles favored maintaining rural traditions infused by the values of the Russian Orthodox church. Only a return to Russia's basic historical principles, they argued, could protect the country against the corrosion of rationalism and materialism. The conflict between Slavophiles and Westernizers has continued to shape Russian cultural and intellectual life to the present day.

The most significant nationalist movement in western Europe could be found in Ireland. The Irish had struggled for centuries against English occupation, but Irish nationalists developed strong organizations only in the 1840s. In 1842, a group of writers founded the Young Ireland movement, which aimed to recover Irish traditions and

preserve the Gaelic language (spoken by at least one-third of the peasantry). Daniel O'Connell (1775–1847), a Catholic lawyer and landowner who sat in the British House of Commons, hoped to force the British Parliament to repeal the Act of Union of 1801, which had made Ireland part of Great Britain. In 1843, London newspapers reported "monster meetings" that drew crowds of as many as 300,000 people in support of repeal of the union. In response, the British government arrested O'Connell and convicted him of conspiracy.

Liberalism in Economics and Politics

As an ideology, **liberalism** had a longer lineage than nationalism but enjoyed less influence among the common people. Liberalism traced its origins to the writings of John Locke in the seventeenth century and the Enlightenment philosophy in the eighteenth. The adherents of liberalism defined themselves in opposition to conservatives on one end of the political spectrum and revolutionaries on the other. Unlike conservatives, liberals supported the Enlightenment ideals of constitutional guarantees of personal liberty and free trade in economics, believing that they would promote social improvement and economic growth. Liberals generally applauded the social and economic changes produced by the Industrial Revolution, while opposing the violence and excessive state power promoted by the French Revolution. The leaders of the expanding middle class composed of manufacturers, merchants, and professionals favored liberalism.

The rapid industrialization and urbanization of Great Britain created a receptive environment for liberalism. Its foremost proponent in the early nineteenth century was the philosopher and jurist Jeremy Bentham (1748–1832). He called his brand of liberalism utilitarianism because he held that the best policy is the one that produces "the greatest good for the greatest number" and is thus the most useful, or utilitarian. Bentham criticized the injustices of the British parliamentary process, the abuses of the prisons and the penal code, and the educational system. In his zeal for social engineering, Bentham proposed model prisons that would emphasize rehabilitation through close supervision rather than corporal punishment.

British liberals wanted government to limit its economic role to maintaining the currency, enforcing contracts, and financing major enterprises like the military and the railroads. They therefore sought to lower or eliminate British tariffs, especially through repeal of the **Corn Laws**, which benefited landowners by preventing the import of cheap foreign grain while keeping the price of food artificially high for the workers. When landholders in the House of Commons thwarted efforts to lower grain tariffs, two Manchester cotton manufacturers set up the Anti–Corn Law League. The league appealed to the middle class against the landlords, who were labeled "a bread-taxing oligarchy" and "blood-sucking vampires," and attracted thousands of workers to its meetings. League members established local branches, published newspapers and the journal *The Economist* (founded in 1843 and now one of the world's most influential periodicals), and campaigned in elections. They finally won the support of the Tory prime minister Sir Robert Peel, whose government repealed the Corn Laws in 1846.

Free trade had less appeal in continental Europe than in England because continental industries needed protection against British industrial dominance. As a consequence, liberals on the continent focused on constitutional reform. French liberals, for example, agitated for greater press freedoms and a broadening of the vote. Louis-Philippe's government thwarted liberals' hopes for reforms by suppressing many political organizations and reestablishing censorship. Repression muted criticism in most other European states as well. Nevertheless, some state bureaucrats, especially university-trained middle-class officials, favored economic liberalism. Hungarian count Stephen Széchenyi (1791–1860) personally campaigned for the introduction of British-style changes. He helped start up steamboat traffic on the Danube, encouraged the importation of machinery and technicians for steam-driven textile factories, and pushed the construction of Hungary's first railway line, from Budapest to Vienna.

In the 1840s, however, Széchenyi's efforts paled before those of the flamboyant Magyar nationalist Lajos Kossuth (1802–1894). After spending four years in prison for sedition, Kossuth grabbed every opportunity to publicize American democracy and British political liberalism, all in a fervent nationalist spirit. In 1844, he founded the Protective Association, whose members bought only Hungarian products; to Kossuth, boycotting Austrian goods was crucial to ending "colonial dependence" on Austria.

Even in Russia, signs of liberal opposition appeared in the 1830s and 1840s. Small circles of young noblemen serving in the army or bureaucracy met in cities, especially Moscow, to discuss the latest Western ideas. Out of these groups came such future revolutionaries as Alexander Herzen (1812–1870), described by the police as "a daring free-thinker, extremely dangerous to society." Tsar Nicholas I (r. 1825–1855) banned Western liberal writings as well as all books about the United States. He sent nearly ten thousand people a year into exile in Siberia as punishment for their political activities.

Socialism and the Early Labor Movement

The newest ideology, **socialism**, took up where liberalism left off: socialists believed that the liberties advocated by liberals benefited only the middle class — the owners of factories and businesses — not the workers. They sought to reorganize society totally rather than to reform it piecemeal through political measures. They envisioned a future society in which workers would share a harmonious, cooperative, and prosperous life.

Early socialists criticized the emerging Industrial Revolution for dividing society into two classes: the new middle class, or capitalists (who owned the wealth), and the working class, their downtrodden and impoverished employees. As their name suggests, the socialists aimed to restore harmony and cooperation through social reorganization. Robert Owen (1771–1858), a successful Welsh-born manufacturer, founded British socialism. In 1800, he bought a cotton mill in New Lanark, Scotland, and began to set up a model factory town, where workers labored only ten hours a day (instead of seventeen, as was common) and children between the ages of five and ten attended school rather than working. Owen moved to the United States in the 1820s and founded a community named New Harmony in Indiana. The experiment collapsed after three years, a victim

of internal squabbling. But out of Owen's experiments and writings, such as *The Book of the New Moral World* (1820), would come the movement for producer cooperatives (businesses owned and controlled by their workers), consumers' cooperatives (stores in which consumers owned shares), and a national trade union.

The French socialists Claude Henri de Saint-Simon (1760–1825) and Charles Fourier (1772–1837) shared Owen's alarm about the effects of industrialization on social relations. Saint-Simon — who coined the terms *industrialism* and *industrialist* to define the new economic order and its chief animators — believed that work was the central element in the new society and that it should be controlled not by politicians but by scientists, engineers, artists, and industrialists themselves. To correct the abuses of the new industrial order, Fourier urged the establishment of communities that were part garden city and part agricultural commune; all jobs would be rotated to maximize happiness. Fourier hoped that a network of small, decentralized communities would replace the state.

Women often played key roles in early socialism. In 1832, Saint-Simonian women founded a feminist newspaper, *The Free Woman,* asserting that "with the emancipation of woman will come the emancipation of the worker." In Great Britain, many women joined the Owenites and helped form cooperative societies and unions. They defended women's working-class organizations against the complaints of men in the new societies and trade unions. The French activist Flora Tristan (1801–1844) devoted herself to reconciling the interests of male and female workers. She published a stream of books and pamphlets urging male workers to address women's unequal status, arguing that "the emancipation of male workers is *impossible* so long as women remain in a degraded state."

Even though most male socialists ignored Tristan's plea for women's participation, they did strive to create working-class associations. The French socialist Louis Blanc (1811–1882) explained the importance of working-class associations in his book *Organization of Labor* (1840), which deeply influenced the French labor movement. Similarly, the printer turned journalist Pierre-Joseph Proudhon (1809–1865) urged workers to form producers' associations so that the workers could control the work process and eliminate profits made by capitalists. His 1840 book *What Is Property?* argues that property is theft: labor alone is productive, and rent, interest, and profit unjust.

After 1840, some socialists began to call themselves **communists**, emphasizing their desire to replace private property by communal, collective ownership. The Frenchman Étienne Cabet (1788–1856) was the first to use the word *communist*. In 1840, he published *Travels in Icaria,* a novel describing a communist utopia in which a popularly elected dictatorship efficiently organized work and reduced the workday to seven hours.

Out of the churning of socialist ideas of the 1840s emerged two men whose collaboration would change the definition of socialism and remake it into an ideology that would shake the world for the next 150 years. Karl Marx (1818–1883) had studied philosophy at the University of Berlin, edited a liberal newspaper until the Prussian government suppressed it, and then left for Paris, where he met Friedrich Engels (1820–1895). While working in the offices of his wealthy family's cotton manufacturing interests in

Manchester, England, Engels had been shocked into writing *The Condition of the Working Class in England in 1844* (1845), a sympathetic depiction of industrial workers' dismal lives. In Paris, where German and eastern European intellectuals could pursue their political interests more freely than at home, Marx and Engels organized the Communist League, in whose name they published *The Communist Manifesto* in 1848.

It eventually became the touchstone of Marxist and communist revolutions all over the world. Communists, the *Manifesto* declared, must aim for "the downfall of the bourgeoisie [capitalist class] and the ascendancy of the proletariat [working class], the abolition of the old society based on class conflicts and the foundation of a new society without classes and without private property." Marx and Engels embraced industrialization because they believed it would eventually bring on the proletarian revolution and thus lead inevitably to the abolition of exploitation, private property, and class society.

Even when not overtly revolutionary, the upsurge in working-class organizations frightened the middle classes. A newspaper exclaimed in 1834, "The trade unions are, we have no doubt, the most dangerous institutions that were ever permitted to take root." Many British workers joined in **Chartism**, which aimed to transform Britain into a democracy. In 1838, political radicals drew up the People's Charter, which demanded universal manhood suffrage, vote by secret ballot, equal electoral districts, annual elections, and the elimination of property qualifications for and the payment of stipends to members of Parliament. Women took part by founding female political unions, setting up Chartist Sunday schools, organizing boycotts of unsympathetic shopkeepers, and joining Chartist temperance associations. Nevertheless, the People's Charter refrained from calling for woman suffrage because the movement's leaders feared that doing so would alienate potential supporters.

The Chartists organized a massive campaign during 1838 and 1839, with large public meetings, fiery speeches, and torchlight parades. Presented with petitions for the People's Charter signed by more than a million people, the House of Commons refused to act. In response to this rebuff from middle-class liberals, the Chartists allied themselves in the 1840s with working-class strike movements in the manufacturing districts and associated with various European revolutionary movements.

Continental European workers were less well organized because trade unions and strikes were illegal everywhere except Great Britain. Nevertheless, artisans and skilled workers in France formed mutual aid societies that provided insurance, death benefits, and education. In eastern and central Europe, socialism and labor organization — like liberalism — had less impact than in western Europe. Cooperative societies and workers' newspapers did not appear in the German states until 1848. In general, labor organization tended to flourish where urbanization and industrialization were most advanced; even though factory workers rarely organized, skilled artisans did so in order to resist mechanization and wage cuts. When revolutions broke out in 1848, artisans and workers played a prominent — and controversial — role.

REVIEW QUESTION Why did ideologies have such a powerful appeal in the 1830s and 1840s?

The Revolutions of 1848

Food shortages, overpopulation, and unemployment helped turn ideological turmoil into revolution. In 1848, demonstrations and uprisings toppled governments, forced rulers and ministers to flee, and offered revolutionaries an opportunity to put liberal, socialist, and nationalist ideals into practice. In the end, the revolutions failed because the various ideological movements quarreled, leaving an opening for rulers and their armies to return to power. Rulers returned, but they now faced populations with greater expectations for political participation, national unification, and government responsiveness to social problems.

The Hungry Forties

Beginning in 1845, crop failures across Europe caused food prices to shoot skyward. In the best of times, urban workers paid 50 to 80 percent of their income for a diet consisting largely of bread; now even bread was beyond their means. Overpopulation hastened famine in some places, especially Ireland, where blight destroyed the staple crop, potatoes, first in 1846 and again in 1848 and 1851. Irish peasants had planted potatoes because a family of four might live off one acre of potatoes but would require at least two acres of grain. By the 1840s, Ireland was especially vulnerable to the potato blight. Out of a population of eight million, as many as one million people died of starvation or disease. Corpses lay unburied on the sides of roads, and whole families were found dead in their cottages, half-eaten by dogs. Hundreds of thousands emigrated to England, the United States, and Canada.

Throughout Europe, famine jeopardized social peace. In age-old fashion, rumors circulated about farmers hoarding grain to drive up prices. Believing that governments should ensure fair prices, crowds took to the streets to protest, often attacking markets or bakeries. Although harvests improved in 1848, by then many people had lost their land or become hopelessly indebted. High food prices also drove down the demand for manufactured goods, resulting in increased unemployment. Industrial workers' wages had been rising, but the cost of living rose even faster.

Another French Revolution

The specter of hunger amplified the voices criticizing established rulers. A Parisian demonstration in favor of reform turned violent on February 23, 1848, when panicky soldiers opened fire on the crowd, killing forty or fifty demonstrators. The next day, faced with fifteen hundred barricades and a furious populace, King Louis-Philippe abdicated and fled to England. A hastily formed provisional government declared France a republic once again.

The new French republican government issued liberal reforms — an end to the death penalty for political crimes, the abolition of slavery in the colonies, and freedom of the press — and agreed to introduce universal adult male suffrage despite misgivings about

The Violence of Revolution

Their red flag of revolt is all that is left to these victims at a barricade thrown up in Paris during the uprising of June 1848. What was the intention of artist Louis Adolphe Hervier when he chose to paint this scene? (Oil on panel by Louis Adolphe Hervier, Private Collection / Archives Charmet / The Bridgeman Art Library International.)

political participation by peasants and unemployed workers. The government allowed Paris officials to organize a system of "national workshops" to provide the unemployed with construction work. To meet a mounting deficit, the provisional government then levied a 45 percent surtax on property taxes, alienating peasants and landowners.

While peasants grumbled, scores of newspapers and political clubs inspired grassroots democratic fervor in Paris and other cities. Meeting in concert halls, theaters, and government auditoriums, the clubs became a regular evening attraction for the citizenry. Women also formed clubs, published women's newspapers, and demanded representation in national politics.

This street-corner activism alarmed middle-class liberals and conservatives. Tension between the government and the workers in the national workshops rose. Faced with rising radicalism in Paris and other big cities, the voters elected a largely conservative National Assembly in April 1848; most of the deputies chosen were middle-class professionals or landowners who favored either a restoration of the monarchy or a moderate republic. The Assembly immediately appointed a five-man executive committee to run the government and pointedly excluded known supporters of workers' rights. Suspicious of all demands for rapid change, the deputies dismissed a petition to restore divorce and voted down woman suffrage by 899 to 1. When the numbers enrolled in the national workshops in Paris rocketed from a predicted 10,000 to 110,000, the government ordered the workshops closed to new workers, and on June 21 it directed that those already enrolled move to the provinces or join the army.

The workers exploded in anger. In the June Days, as the following week came to be called, the government forces crushed the workers: more than 10,000 people, most of them workers, were killed or injured; 12,000 were arrested; and 4,000 eventually were convicted and deported.

After the National Assembly adopted a new constitution calling for a presidential election in which all adult men could vote, the electorate chose **Louis-Napoleon**

Bonaparte (1808–1873), nephew of the dead emperor. Bonaparte got more than 5.5 million votes out of some 7.4 million cast. His election spelled the end of the Second Republic, just as his uncle had dismantled the first one established in 1792. In 1852, on the forty-eighth anniversary of Napoleon I's coronation as emperor, Louis-Napoleon declared himself Emperor Napoleon III, thus inaugurating the Second Empire. (Napoleon I's son died and never became Napoleon II, but Napoleon III wanted to create a sense of legitimacy and so used the Roman numeral III.) Although the revolution of 1848 never had a period of terror like that in 1793–1794, it nonetheless ended in similar fashion, with an authoritarian government that tried to play monarchists and republicans off against each other.

Nationalist Revolution in Italy

In January 1848, a revolt broke out in Palermo, Sicily, against the Bourbon ruler. Then came the electrifying news of the February revolution in Paris. In Milan, a huge nationalist demonstration quickly degenerated into battles between Austrian forces and armed demonstrators. In Venice, an uprising drove out the Austrians. Peasants in the south occupied large landowners' estates. Artisans and workers called for higher wages, restrictions on the use of machinery, and unemployment relief.

But class divisions and regional differences stood in the way of national unity. Property owners, businessmen, and professionals wanted liberal reforms and national unification under a conservative regime; intellectuals, workers, and artisans dreamed of democracy and social reforms. Some nationalists favored a loose federation; others wanted a monarchy under Charles Albert of Piedmont-Sardinia; still others urged rule by the pope; a few shared Giuseppe Mazzini's vision of a republic with a strong central government. Many leaders of national unification spoke standard Italian only as a second language; most Italians spoke regional dialects.

As king of the most powerful Italian state, Charles Albert (r. 1831–1849) inevitably played a central role. After some hesitation caused by fears of French intervention, he led a military campaign against Austria. Although Austrian troops defeated Charles Albert in the north, democratic and nationalist forces prevailed at first in the south. In the fall, the Romans drove the pope from the city and declared Rome a republic. For the next few months, republican leaders, such as Giuseppe Mazzini and Giuseppe Garibaldi (1807–1882), congregated in Rome to organize the new republic. These efforts faltered when foreign powers intervened. The new president of France, Louis-Napoleon Bonaparte, sent an expeditionary force to secure the papal throne for Pius IX. Mazzini and Garibaldi fled. Revolution had been defeated in Italy, but the memory of the Roman republic and the commitment to unification remained, and they would soon emerge again with new force.

The Divisions of Italy, 1848

Revolt and Reaction in Central Europe

News of the revolution in Paris also provoked popular demonstrations in central and eastern Europe. When the Prussian army tried to push back a crowd gathered in front of Berlin's royal palace on March 18, 1848, their actions provoked panic and street fighting. The next day the crowd paraded wagons loaded with the dead bodies of demonstrators under the window of the Prussian king Frederick William IV (r. 1840–1860), forcing him to salute the victims killed by his own army. In a state of near collapse, the king promised to call an assembly to draft a constitution.

The goal of German unification soon took precedence over social reform or constitutional changes within the separate states. In March and April, most of the German states agreed to elect delegates to a federal parliament at Frankfurt that would attempt to unite Germany. Local princes and even the more powerful kings of Prussia and Bavaria seemed to totter. Yet the revolutionaries' weaknesses soon became apparent. The eight hundred delegates to the Frankfurt parliament had little practical political experience and no access to an army. Unemployed artisans and workers smashed machines; peasants burned landlords' records and occasionally attacked Jewish moneylenders; women set up clubs and newspapers to demand their emancipation from "perfumed slavery."

The advantage lay with the princes, who bided their time. While the Frankfurt parliament laboriously prepared a liberal constitution for a united Germany — one that denied self-determination to Czechs, Poles, and Danes within its proposed German borders — Frederick William recovered his confidence. First, his army crushed the revolution in Berlin in the fall of 1848. Prussian troops then intervened to help other local rulers put down the last wave of democratic and nationalist insurrections in the spring of 1849. When the Frankfurt parliament finally concluded its work, offering the emperorship of a constitutional, federal Germany to the king of Prussia, Frederick William contemptuously refused this "crown from the gutter."

Events followed a similar course in the Austrian Empire. Just as Italians were driving the Austrians out of their lands in northern Italy and Magyar nationalists were demanding political autonomy for Hungary, a student-led demonstration for political reform on March 13, 1848, in Vienna turned into rioting, looting, and machine breaking. Metternich resigned, escaping to England in disguise. Emperor Ferdinand promised a constitution, an elected parliament, and the end of censorship. The beleaguered authorities in Vienna could not refuse Magyar demands for home rule, and Széchenyi and Kossuth both became ministers in the new Hungarian government. The Magyars were the largest ethnic group in Hungary but still did not make up 50 percent of the population, which included Croats, Romanians, Slovaks, and Slovenes, all of whom preferred Austrian rule to domination by local Magyars.

The ethnic divisions in Hungary foreshadowed the many political and social divisions that would doom the revolutionaries. Fears of peasant insurrection prompted the Magyar nationalists around Kossuth to abolish serfdom, thereby alienating the largest noble landowners. The new government infuriated the other nationalities when it imposed the Magyar language on them. In Prague, Czech nationalists convened a Slav

Revolutions of 1848

1848

January	Uprising in Palermo, Sicily
February	Revolution in Paris; proclamation of republic
March	Insurrections in Vienna, German cities, Milan, and Venice; autonomy movement in Hungary; Charles Albert of Piedmont-Sardinia declares war on Austrian Empire
May	Frankfurt parliament opens
June	Austrian army crushes revolutionary movement in Prague; June Days end in defeat of workers in Paris
July	Austrians defeat Charles Albert and Italian forces
November	Insurrection in Rome
December	Francis Joseph becomes Austrian emperor; Louis-Napoleon elected president in France

1849

February	Rome declared a republic
April	Frederick William of Prussia rejects crown of united Germany offered by Frankfurt parliament
July	Roman republic overthrown by French intervention
August	Russian and Austrian armies combine to defeat Hungarian forces

congress as a counter to the Germans' Frankfurt parliament and called for a reorganization of the Austrian Empire that would recognize the rights of ethnic minorities.

The Austrian government took advantage of these divisions. To quell peasant discontent, it abolished all remaining peasant obligations to the nobility in March 1848. Rejoicing country folk soon lost interest in the revolution. Military force finally broke up the revolutionary movements. The first blow fell in Prague in June 1848; General Prince Alfred von Windischgrätz, the military governor, bombarded the city into submission when a demonstration led to violence (including the shooting death of his wife, watching from a window). After another uprising in Vienna a few months later, Windischgrätz marched seventy thousand soldiers into the capital and set up direct military rule. In December, the Austrian monarchy came back to life when the eighteen-year-old Francis Joseph (r. 1848–1916), unencumbered by promises extracted by the revolutionaries from his now feeble uncle Ferdinand, assumed the imperial crown after intervention by leading court officials. In the spring of 1849, the Austrian army teamed up with Tsar Nicholas I, who marched into Hungary with more than 300,000 Russian troops. Hungary was put under brutal martial law. Széchenyi went mad, and Kossuth found refuge in the United States.

Aftermath to 1848: Reimposing Authority

Although the revolutionaries of 1848 failed to achieve their goals, their efforts left a profound mark on the political and social landscape. Between 1848 and 1851, the French served a kind of republican apprenticeship that prepared the population for another, more lasting republic after 1870. In Italy, the failure of unification did not stop the spread of nationalist ideas and the rooting of demands for democratic participation. In the German states, the revolutionaries of 1848 turned nationalism from an idea devised by professors and writers into a popular enthusiasm and even a practical reality. The initiation of artisans, workers, and journeymen into democratic clubs increased political awareness in the lower classes and helped prepare them for broader

political participation. Almost all the German states had a constitution and a parliament after 1850. The spectacular failures of 1848 thus hid some important underlying successes.

The absence of revolution in 1848 in some regions of the West was just as significant as its presence. No revolution occurred in Great Britain, the Netherlands, or Belgium, the three places where industrialization and urbanization had developed most rapidly. In Great Britain, the Chartist movement mounted several gigantic demonstrations to force Parliament into granting all adult males the vote. But even though Parliament refused, no uprising occurred — in part because the government had already proved its responsiveness: the middle classes in Britain had been co-opted into the established order by the Reform Bill of 1832, and the working classes had won parliamentary regulation of children's and women's work.

The other notable exception to revolution among the great powers was Russia, where Tsar Nicholas I maintained a tight grip through police surveillance and censorship. The Russian schools, limited to the upper classes, taught Nicholas's three most cherished principles: autocracy (the unlimited power of the tsar), orthodoxy (obedience to the church in religion and morality), and nationality (devotion to Russian traditions). These provided no space for political dissent.

Although much had changed, the aristocracy remained the dominant power almost everywhere. As army officers, aristocrats put down revolutionary forces. As landlords, they continued to dominate the rural scene and control parliamentary bodies. They also held many official positions in the state bureaucracies. As conservatives returned to power, all signs of women's political activism disappeared. The French feminist movement, the most advanced in Europe, fell apart when, after the June Days, the increasingly conservative republican government forbade women to form political clubs and arrested and imprisoned two of the most outspoken women leaders for their socialist activities. As rulers reimposed their authority in the years after 1848, many socialists, communists, and nationalists suffered a similar fate: if they did not fall in battle or go to prison, they fled into exile, waiting for another opportunity to voice their demands.

REVIEW QUESTION   Why did the revolutions of 1848 fail?

Conclusion

In 1851, Europe's most important female monarch presided over a midcentury celebration of peace and industrial growth that helped dampen the still-smoldering fires of revolutionary passion. In the place of revolutionary fervor was a government-sponsored spectacle of what industry, hard work, and technological imagination could produce. Queen Victoria (r. 1837–1901), who herself promoted the notion of domesticity as women's sphere, opened the Great Exhibition of the Works of Industry of All Nations in London on May 1. A huge iron-and-glass building housed the display. Soon people referred to it as the Crystal Palace; its nine hundred tons of glass created an aura of fantasy, and the abundant goods from around the world inspired satisfaction and pride.

The Crystal Palace, 1851

George Baxter's lithograph (above) shows the exterior of the main building for the Great Exhibition of the Works of Industry of All Nations in London. It was designed by Sir Joseph Paxton to gigantic dimensions: 1,848 feet long by 456 feet wide; 135 feet high; 772,784 square feet of ground-floor area covering no less than 18 acres. The lithograph by Peter Mabuse (left) offers a view of one of the colonial displays at the Great Exhibition. The tented room and carved ivory throne are meant to recall India, Britain's premier colony.

(Top: © Maidstone Museum and Art Gallery, Kent, UK / The Bridgeman Art Library. Left: Private Collection / The Stapleton Collection / The Bridgeman Art Library International.)

Many of the six million people who visited the Crystal Palace display traveled on the new railroads, the foremost symbol of the age of industrial transformation. Along with the railroads, the application of steam engines to textile manufacturing set in motion a host of economic and social changes: cities burgeoned with rapidly growing populations; factories concentrated laborers who formed a new working class; manufacturers now

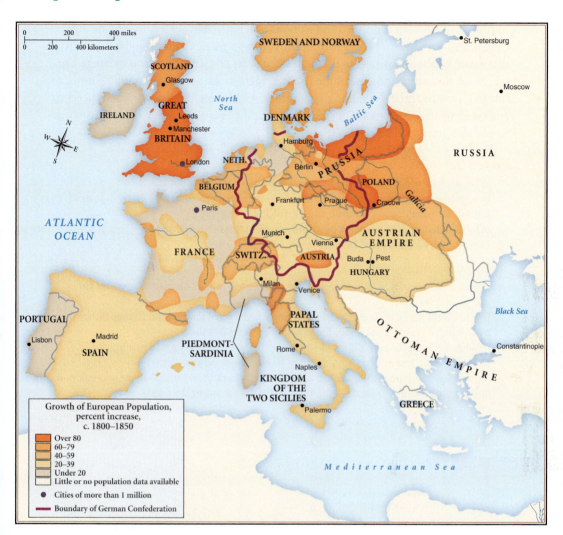

Mapping the West Europe in 1850

This map of population growth between 1800 and 1850 reveals important trends that would not otherwise be evident. Although population growth correlated for the most part with industrialization, population also grew in more agricultural regions such as East Prussia, Poland, and Ireland. Ireland's rapid population growth in the early nineteenth century does not appear on this map because the famine of 1846–1851 killed more than 10 percent of the population and forced many others to emigrate. Compare this map to Map 21.1 (page 663): Which areas experienced both industrialization and population increase?

challenged landed elites for political leadership; and social problems galvanized reform organizations and governments alike. The Crystal Palace presented the rosy view of modern, industrial, urban life, but the housing shortages, inadequacy of water supplies, and recurrent epidemic diseases had not disappeared.

The revolutions of 1848 brought to the surface the profound tensions within a European society in transition toward industrialization and urbanization. After them, the

Industrial Revolution continued and workers developed more extensive organizations. Confronted with the menace of revolution, conservative elites now sought alternatives that would be less threatening to the established order and still permit some change. This search for alternatives became immediately evident in the question of national unification in Germany and Italy. National unification would hereafter depend not on speeches and parliamentary resolutions, but rather on what the Prussian leader Otto von Bismarck would call "iron and blood."

Review Questions

1. What dangers did the Industrial Revolution pose to both urban and rural life?
2. In which areas did reformers trying to address the social problems created by industrialization and urbanization succeed, and in which did they fail?
3. Why did ideologies have such a powerful appeal in the 1830s and 1840s?
4. Why did the revolutions of 1848 fail?

Making Connections

1. Which of the ideologies of this period had the greatest impact on political events? How can you explain this?
2. In what ways might industrialization be considered a force for peaceful change rather than a revolution? (*Hint:* Think about the situation in Great Britain.)
3. In what ways did the revolutions of 1848 repeat elements of the French revolutions in 1789 and 1830, and in what ways did they break with those precedents?
4. Neither Great Britain nor Russia had a revolution in 1848. How is the absence of revolution in those two countries related to their history in the preceding decades?

TIMELINE

- **1835** Belgium opens first continental railway built with state funds
- **1834** German *Zollverein* established under Prussian leadership
- **1846** Famine strikes Ireland; Corn Laws repealed in England; peasant insurrection in Austrian province of Galicia
- **1830–1832** Cholera epidemic sweeps across Europe
- **1841** Charles Dickens, *The Old Curiosity Shop*
- **1851** Crystal Palace exhibition in London

| 1830 | 1835 | 1840 | 1845 | 1850 | 1855 |

- **1830** France invades and begins conquest of Algeria
- **1839** Beginning of Opium War; invention of photography
- **1848** Revolutions of 1848 throughout Europe; last great wave of Chartist demonstrations in Britain; Karl Marx and Friedrich Engels, *The Communist Manifesto*; abolition of slavery in French colonies; end of serfdom in Austrian Empire
- **1832** George Sand, *Indiana*
- **1833** Factory Act regulates work of children in Great Britain; abolition of slavery in British Empire

- For practice quizzes and other study tools, visit the **Online Study Guide** at bedfordstmartins.com/huntconcise.

- For primary-source material from this period, see *Sources of the Making of the West*, Fourth Edition.

- For Web sites, images, and documents related to topics in this chapter, visit *Make History* at bedfordstmartins.com/huntconcise.

Suggested References

The spread of industrialization has elicited much more historical interest than the process of urbanization because the analysis of industrialization occupied a central role in Marxism. The Web site Gallica, produced by the National Library of France, offers a wealth of imagery and information on French cultural history.

Davidoff, Leonore, and Catherine Hall. *Family Fortunes: Men and Women of the English Middle Class, 1780–1850.* 2002.

Gallica: Images and Texts from Nineteenth-Century French-Speaking Culture: http://gallica.bnf.fr

Hanes, W. Travis, and Frank Sanello. *The Opium Wars: The Addiction of One Empire and the Corruption of Another.* 2004.

Hobsbawm, E. J. *The Age of Revolution, 1789–1848.* 1996.

Kinealy, Christine. *Repeal and Revolution: 1848 in Ireland.* 2009.

Kostantaras, Dean J. *Nationalism and Revolution in Europe, 1815–1848.* 2010.

Lees, Andrew, and Lynn Hollen Lees. *Cities and the Making of Modern Europe, 1750–1914.* 2007.

*Marx, Karl, and Frederick Engels. *The Communist Manifesto: With Related Documents.* Ed. John E. Toews. 1848; repr. 1999.

Mokyr, Joel. *The Enlightened Economy: An Economic History of Britain, 1700–1850.* 2009.

*Pollard, S., and C. Holmes. *Documents of European Economic History.* Vol. 1, *The Process of Industrialization, 1750–1870.* 1968.

Rapport, Michael. *1848, Year of Revolution.* 2009.

Sked, Alan. *Metternich and Austria: An Evaluation.* 2008.

Thompson, E. P. *The Making of the English Working Class.* 1964.

Primary source.

investment banks. Railway mileage increased fivefold during Napoleon III's reign. During the economic downturn of the late 1850s, he wooed support by allowing working-class organizations to form and introducing features of democratic government that offered practical responses to economic change.

On the international scene, Napoleon III's main goals were to overcome the containment of France imposed by the Congress of Vienna and to acquire international glory like a true Bonaparte. To reshape European politics in France's favor, Napoleon pitted France first against Russia in the Crimean War and then against Austria in the War of Italian Unification (1860–1861). Napoleon also looked beyond Europe. In Algeria and Southeast Asia, his army continued to enforce French rule. In Mexico, he attempted to install Maximilian, the brother of Habsburg emperor Francis Joseph, as emperor. In Egypt, he successfully encouraged the construction of the Suez Canal to connect the Mediterranean and the Red Sea. Overall, his foreign policy broke down the international order established at the Congress of Vienna.

The Crimean War, 1853–1856: Turning Point in European Affairs

Napoleon III first flexed his diplomatic muscle in the Crimean War (1853–1856), which began as a conflict between the Russian and Ottoman Empires but ended as a war with long-lasting consequences for much of Europe. While professing to uphold the status quo, Russia had been expanding into Asia and the Middle East. In particular, Tsar Nicholas I wanted territory in the Ottoman Empire, and Napoleon encouraged Nicholas to be even more aggressive in his expansionism — a maneuver that provoked war in October 1853 between the two eastern empires (Map 22.1).

The war drew in other states and upset Europe's balance of power as set in the Congress of Vienna. Napoleon III convinced Austria to remain neutral during the war, thus splitting the conservative Russian-Austrian coalition that had checked French ambitions since 1815. The Austrian government was concerned that the defeat of the Ottomans would bring Russian expansion into the Balkans. To protect its Mediterranean routes to East Asia, Britain prodded the Ottomans to stand up to Russia, but in the fall of 1853, the Russians blasted the Turkish wooden

Map 22.1 The Crimean War, 1853–1856
The most destructive war in Europe between the Napoleonic Wars and World War I, the Crimean War drew attention to the conflicting ambitions around territories of the declining Ottoman Empire. The war fractured the alliance of conservative forces from the Congress of Vienna, allowing Italy and Germany to come into being as unified states.

European power but also resulted in the end of serfdom in Russia and the birth of new European nations.

Napoleon III and the Quest for French Glory

Louis-Napoleon Bonaparte, who declared himself Napoleon III in 1852, encouraged the cult of his famous uncle as part of nation building, showing Europe's leaders how to combine economic liberalism and nationalism with authoritarian rule. He claimed to represent people's "families, your property — rich and poor alike," but he closed cafés where men might discuss politics and established a rubber-stamp legislature, the Corps législatif, that made representative government a charade. Napoleon's opulent court dazzled the public, while his wife, Empress Eugénie, followed middle-class norms by playing up her domestic role as devoted mother to her only son and supporting many charities. The authoritarian, apparently old-fashioned order imposed by Napoleon showed that the radicalism of 1848 was under control.

Napoleon III was nonetheless a modernizer. He promoted a strong economy and public works programs that provided jobs. The magnificent rebuilding of Paris made France prosper as Europe recovered from the hard times of the late 1840s. Empress Eugénie wore lavish gowns, encouraging French silk production. The regime also reached a free-trade agreement with Britain and backed the establishment of innovative

Napoleon III and Eugénie Receive the Siamese Ambassadors, 1864
At a splendid gathering of their court, the emperor Napoleon III, his consort Eugénie, and their son and heir greet ambassadors from Siam, whose exoticism and servility before the imperial family are the centerpiece of this depiction by Jean-Léon Gerome. How might a middle-class French citizen have reacted to this scene? (Bridgeman-Giraudon / Art Resource, NY.)

investment banks. Railway mileage increased fivefold during Napoleon III's reign. During the economic downturn of the late 1850s, he wooed support by allowing working-class organizations to form and introducing features of democratic government that offered practical responses to economic change.

On the international scene, Napoleon III's main goals were to overcome the containment of France imposed by the Congress of Vienna and to acquire international glory like a true Bonaparte. To reshape European politics in France's favor, Napoleon pitted France first against Russia in the Crimean War and then against Austria in the War of Italian Unification (1860–1861). Napoleon also looked beyond Europe. In Algeria and Southeast Asia, his army continued to enforce French rule. In Mexico, he attempted to install Maximilian, the brother of Habsburg emperor Francis Joseph, as emperor. In Egypt, he successfully encouraged the construction of the Suez Canal to connect the Mediterranean and the Red Sea. Overall, his foreign policy broke down the international order established at the Congress of Vienna.

The Crimean War, 1853–1856: Turning Point in European Affairs

Napoleon III first flexed his diplomatic muscle in the Crimean War (1853–1856), which began as a conflict between the Russian and Ottoman Empires but ended as a war with long-lasting consequences for much of Europe. While professing to uphold the status quo, Russia had been expanding into Asia and the Middle East. In particular, Tsar Nicholas I wanted territory in the Ottoman Empire, and Napoleon encouraged Nicholas to be even more aggressive in his expansionism — a maneuver that provoked war in October 1853 between the two eastern empires (Map 22.1).

The war drew in other states and upset Europe's balance of power as set in the Congress of Vienna. Napoleon III convinced Austria to remain neutral during the war, thus splitting the conservative Russian-Austrian coalition that had checked French ambitions since 1815. The Austrian government was concerned that the defeat of the Ottomans would bring Russian expansion into the Balkans. To protect its Mediterranean routes to East Asia, Britain prodded the Ottomans to stand up to Russia, but in the fall of 1853, the Russians blasted the Turkish wooden

Map 22.1 The Crimean War, 1853–1856
The most destructive war in Europe between the Napoleonic Wars and World War I, the Crimean War drew attention to the conflicting ambitions around territories of the declining Ottoman Empire. The war fractured the alliance of conservative forces from the Congress of Vienna, allowing Italy and Germany to come into being as unified states.

liberalism that had led to earlier romantic revolts. Their achievements changed the face of Europe.

Making a modern nation-state was a complicated task. Economic development was also crucial, as was using government policy and culture to create a sense of national identity and common purpose. Governments took vigorous steps to improve rapidly growing cities, promote public health, and boost national loyalty. State institutions such as public schools helped establish a common fund of knowledge and political beliefs. Authoritarian leaders like Bismarck and the new French emperor Napoleon III believed that a better quality of life would not only make the state more stable by calming revolutionary impulses of years past but also silence liberal critics.

Culture built a sense of belonging. Reading novels, attending operas and art exhibitions, and visiting the newly fashionable world's fairs gave ordinary people a stronger sense of being French or German or British. Like politicians, artists and writers also came to reject romanticism, featuring instead harsher, more realistic aspects of everyday life. Artists painted nudes in shockingly blunt ways, eliminating romantic hues and dreamy poses. Authors wrote about the bleak life of soldiers in wartime or about ordinary people suffering poverty or turning to crime. Alongside the tough-minded nation-building policies there arose tough-minded art, not just mirroring Realpolitik but encouraging it.

In their quest to build strong nations, Western politicians did not shy away from using violence or causing harm. They sent armies to distant areas to stamp out resistance to their continuing global expansion. At home, governments uprooted neighborhoods to construct public buildings, roads, and parks. The process of nation building was often brutal, bringing foreign wars, arrests, and even civil war — all the centerpieces of many Verdi operas. In 1871, an uprising of Parisians challenged the central government's intrusion into everyday life and its failure to count the costs. Thus, for the most part, the powerful Western nation-state did not arise spontaneously. Instead, its growth and the tighter unification of peoples depended on shrewd policy, deliberate warfare, and new inroads into societies around the world — which together formed the basis of Realpolitik.

CHAPTER FOCUS How did the creation and strengthening of nation-states change European politics, society, and culture in the mid-nineteenth century?

The End of the Concert of Europe

The revolutions of 1848 had weakened the concert of Europe and thus allowed the forces of nationalism to flourish. It became more difficult for countries to control their competing ambitions and act together. In addition, the dreaded revival of Bonapartism in the person of Louis-Napoleon Bonaparte, the nephew of Napoleon I, added to European instability as France reasserted itself. One of Louis-Napoleon's targets was Russia, formerly a mainstay of the concert of Europe. To limit Russia's and Austria's grip on power, France helped engineer the Crimean War, which not only changed the distribution of

22

Politics and Culture of the Nation-State

1850–1870

I N 1859, THE NAME *VERDI* suddenly appeared scrawled on walls across the cities of the Italian peninsula. The graffiti seemed to celebrate the composer Giuseppe Verdi, whose operas thrilled crowds of Europeans. Among Italians, Verdi was a particular hero; his stories of downtrodden groups struggling against tyrannical government seemed to refer specifically to them. As his operatic choruses thundered out calls to rebellion in the name of the nation, Italian audiences were sure that Verdi was telling them to throw off Austrian and papal rule and unite in a newborn Roman Empire. *VERDI* also formed an acronym for *Vittorio Emmanuele Re d'Italia* ("Victor Emmanuel, King of Italy"), and in 1859 it summoned Italians to unite under Victor Emmanuel II, king of Sardinia and Piedmont — the one Italian leader with a nationalist, modernizing profile. The graffiti was good publicity, for the very next year Italy united as a result of warfare and hard bargaining by political realists.

After the failed revolutions of 1848, European statesmen and the politically aware public increasingly rejected idealism in favor of **Realpolitik** — a politics of tough-minded realism aimed at strengthening the state and tightening social order. Realpolitikers disliked the romanticism of the revolutionaries. Instead, they put their faith in power politics and even the use of violence to attain their goals. Two particularly skilled practitioners of Realpolitik, the Italian Camillo di Cavour and the Prussian Otto von Bismarck, succeeded in unifying Italy and Germany not by romantic slogans but by war and diplomacy. Most leading figures of the decades 1850–1870, enmeshed like Verdi's operatic heroes in power politics, strengthened their states by harnessing the forces of nationalism and

Aïda Poster
Aïda (1871), Giuseppe Verdi's opera of human passion and state power among people of different nations, became a staple of Western culture, bringing people across Europe into a common cultural orbit. Written to celebrate the opening of the Suez Canal, *Aïda* also celebrated the improvement of Europe's access to Asian resources provided by the new waterway. The opera was a prime example of the surge of interest in Egyptian styles and objects that followed the opening of the canal. (Madeline Grimoldi.)

- For practice quizzes and other study tools, visit the **Online Study Guide** at bedfordstmartins.com/huntconcise.

- For primary-source material from this period, see *Sources of the Making of the West*, Fourth Edition.

- For Web sites, images, and documents related to topics in this chapter, visit *Make History* at bedfordstmartins.com/huntconcise.

Suggested References

The spread of industrialization has elicited much more historical interest than the process of urbanization because the analysis of industrialization occupied a central role in Marxism. The Web site Gallica, produced by the National Library of France, offers a wealth of imagery and information on French cultural history.

Davidoff, Leonore, and Catherine Hall. *Family Fortunes: Men and Women of the English Middle Class, 1780–1850.* 2002.

Gallica: Images and Texts from Nineteenth-Century French-Speaking Culture: http://gallica.bnf.fr

Hanes, W. Travis, and Frank Sanello. *The Opium Wars: The Addiction of One Empire and the Corruption of Another.* 2004.

Hobsbawm, E. J. *The Age of Revolution, 1789–1848.* 1996.

Kinealy, Christine. *Repeal and Revolution: 1848 in Ireland.* 2009.

Kostantaras, Dean J. *Nationalism and Revolution in Europe, 1815–1848.* 2010.

Lees, Andrew, and Lynn Hollen Lees. *Cities and the Making of Modern Europe, 1750–1914.* 2007.

*Marx, Karl, and Frederick Engels. *The Communist Manifesto: With Related Documents.* Ed. John E. Toews. 1848; repr. 1999.

Mokyr, Joel. *The Enlightened Economy: An Economic History of Britain, 1700–1850.* 2009.

*Pollard, S., and C. Holmes. *Documents of European Economic History.* Vol. 1, *The Process of Industrialization, 1750–1870.* 1968.

Rapport, Michael. *1848, Year of Revolution.* 2009.

Sked, Alan. *Metternich and Austria: An Evaluation.* 2008.

Thompson, E. P. *The Making of the English Working Class.* 1964.

Primary source.

ships to bits at the Ottoman port of Sinope on the Black Sea. The Russians justified their actions as a necessary defense of Christians in the Ottoman Empire. In 1854, France and Great Britain, though enemies in war for more than a century, allied to declare war on Russia and defend the Ottoman Empire.

The Crimean War was spectacularly bloody. British and French troops landed in the Crimea in September 1854 and waged a long siege of the Russian naval base at Sevastopol, which fell only after a year of savage and costly combat. Generals on both sides demonstrated their incompetence, and governments failed to provide combatants with even minimal supplies, sanitation, or medical care. Hospitals had no beds, no dishes, and no water. A million men died, more than two-thirds from disease or starvation.

In the midst of this unfolding catastrophe, **Alexander II** (r. 1855–1881) ascended the Russian throne after the death of Nicholas I, his father. With casualties mounting, the new tsar asked for peace. As a result of the Peace of Paris, signed in March 1856, Russia lost the right to base its navy in the Strait of Dardanelles and the Black Sea, which were declared neutral waters. Moldavia and Wallachia (which soon merged to form Romania) became autonomous Turkish provinces under the victors' protection, drastically reducing Russian influence in that region, too.

The Crimean War was full of consequence. New technologies were introduced into warfare: the railroad, shell-firing cannons, breech-loading rifles, and steam-powered ships. The telegraph and increased press coverage brought news from the Crimean front lines to home audiences more rapidly and in more detail than ever before. Reports of incompetent leadership, poor sanitation, and the huge death toll outraged the public, inspiring some civilians, such as the British nurse **Florence Nightingale**, to head for the front lines to help. Nightingale seized the moment to escape the confines of middle-class domesticity by organizing a battlefield nursing service to care for the British sick and wounded. (See the illustration on page 700.) Through her tough-minded organization of nursing units, she pioneered nursing as a profession and made sanitary conditions for soldiers a new and enduring priority.

More immediately, the war accomplished Napoleon III's goal of severing the alliance between Austria and Russia, the two conservative powers on which the Congress of Vienna peace settlement had rested since 1815. It thus ended Austria's and Russia's grip on European affairs and undermined their ability to contain the forces of liberalism and nationalism.

Reform in Russia

Russia's defeat in the Crimean War also made clear the need for meaningful reform. Hundreds of peasant insurrections had erupted in the decade before the war. "Our own and neighboring households were gripped with fear," one aristocrat reported. The Russian economy stagnated compared with that of western Europe. Old-fashioned farming techniques depleted soil and led to food shortages, and the nobility was often contemptuous of the suffering caused by malnutrition and hard labor. When Russia lost the Crimean War, the educated public, including some government officials, found

Nurse Tending Wounded Man
The Crimean War exposed the backward, and lethal, sanitary conditions of warfare — conditions that became intolerable to nation-states concerned with the well-being of their citizen soldiers. Women's contribution as nurses during both the Crimean War (shown in this photograph) and the U.S. Civil War helped rectify the situation, but voluntary assistance was not enough to prevent horrific death rates from disease and lack of coordinated medical attention. (Private Collection / The Bridgeman Art Library International.)

the poor performance of serf armies a disgrace and the system of serf labor a glaring liability.

Confronted with the need for change, Tsar Alexander II acted. Well educated and more widely traveled than his father, Alexander ushered in what came to be known as the Great Reforms, granting Russians new rights from above as a way of preventing violent action from below. The most dramatic reform was the emancipation of almost fifty million serfs beginning in 1861. By the terms of emancipation, communities of newly freed serfs, headed by male village elders, received grants of land. The community itself, traditionally called a **mir**, had full power to allocate this land among individuals and to direct their economic activity. Communal landowning and decision making meant that individual peasants could not simply sell their parcel of land and leave their rural communities to work in factories, as laborers had been doing elsewhere in Europe.

In Russia peasants were not *given* land along with their personal freedom: they were forced to "redeem" the land they farmed by paying off long-term loans from the government, which in turn compensated the original landowners. The best land remained in the hands of the nobility, and the huge burden of debt and communal regulations

VÉRITABLE EXTRAIT DE VIANDE LIEBIG.

Episodes de l'histoire de la Russie.
Abolition du servage par Alexandre II, le 3 Mars 1861.   6.

Voir l'explication au verso.

Emancipation of the Russian Serfs

This trading card was used as a marketing gimmick to promote canned meat. Cards like these were given away by the thousands and traded just as baseball cards are today. Historical scenes were popular subjects for the cards — this one shows the 1861 emancipation of the serfs in Russia. Note that the caption is in French, the language of the European upper classes, including those in Russia, who would have consumed this product. The emancipation is presented as a wholly beneficial act with no strings attached. (Mary Evans Picture Library.)

slowed Russian agricultural development for decades. Even so, idealistic reformers believed that the emancipation of the serfs, once treated by the nobility virtually as livestock, had produced miraculous results. As one of them put it, "The people are without any exaggeration transfigured from head to foot. . . . The look, the walk, the speech, everything is changed."

The Russian state also reformed local administration, the judiciary, and the military. The government set up zemstvos — regional councils — through which aristocrats could control local affairs such as education, public health, and welfare. Zemstvos became a new political force with the potential for challenging the authoritarian central government. Some aristocrats took advantage of newly relaxed rules on travel to see how the rest of Europe was governed. Their vision broadened as they observed different ways of solving social and economic problems. The principle of equality of all persons before the law, regardless of social rank, was introduced in Russia for the first time as judicial reform gave all Russians access to modern civil courts. Military reform followed in 1874 when the government reduced the twenty-five-year period of service to a six-year term and began focusing on educating troops in an effort to match the efficiency and fitness of soldiers in western Europe.

Alexander's reforms helped landowners be more effective in the market even as they reduced the privileges of the nobility, weakening their authority and sparking family conflict. "An epidemic seemed to seize upon [noble] children . . . an epidemic of fleeing from the parental roof," one observer noted. Rejecting aristocratic leisure, youthful

rebels from the upper class valued practical activity and sometimes identified with peasants and workers instead of their own class. Some formed communes in which they hoped to do humble manual labor; others turned to higher education, especially the sciences. Daughters of the nobility opposed their parents, escaping from home through phony marriages so they could study in western European universities. This rejection of traditional society led some to label these young people as nihilists (from the Latin for "nothing") — implying a lack of belief in any values whatsoever. In fact, however, the so-called nihilists represented a defiant spirit percolating not just at the bottom but also at the top of Russian society.

The atmosphere of change also inspired resistance among the more than one hundred Russian-dominated ethnic groups in the Russian Empire. Aristocratic and upper-class nationalist Poles staged an uprising in 1863, demanding full national independence for their country. By 1864, however, Alexander II's army had crushed them. The government then swiftly clamped down on other nationalist uprisings and enforced **Russification** — a tactic meant to reduce the threat of future rebellion by insisting that ethnic minorities within the empire adopt Russian language and culture. Despite these measures, the tsarist regime only partially succeeded in developing the administrative, economic, and civic institutions that made the nation-state strong elsewhere in Europe, allowing few to share in power. In imperial Russia, autocracy and continued abuse of many in the population slowed the development of the sense of common citizenship forming elsewhere in the West, while the urge to revolt grew.

REVIEW QUESTION What were the main results of the Crimean War?

War and Nation Building

Dynamic leaders in the German and Italian states used the opportunity provided by the weakened concert of Europe to unify their fragmented countries through warfare. When national disunity threatened, the United States waged a bloody civil war, which opened the way for further expansion and vigorous economic growth. The rise of powerful **nation-states** such as Italy, Germany, and the United States was accompanied by a sense of pride in national identity — or nationalism — among their peoples. This was not an inevitable or universal trend in the West, however. Millions of individuals in the Austrian Empire, Ireland, and elsewhere maintained a regional, local, or distinct ethnic identity even as the nation-state was strengthening and national sentiment was on the rise.

Cavour, Garibaldi, and the Process of Italian Unification

Despite the failure of the revolutions of 1848, hope for national unification remained strong in the Italian states, aided by diplomatic instability across Europe. The pragmatic **Camillo di Cavour** (1810–1861), prime minister of the kingdom of Piedmont-Sardinia from 1852 until his death, had a Realpolitiker's vision of how to unify the Italian states. A rebel in his youth, Cavour in his maturity organized steamship companies, played the

stock market, and inhaled the heady air of modernization during his travels to Paris and London. He promoted economic development rather than idealistic uprisings as the means to achieve a united Italy. As a skilled prime minister, Cavour helped King Victor Emmanuel II (r. Piedmont-Sardinia 1849–1861, r. Italy 1861–1878) achieve a strong Piedmontese economy and a modern army as the foundation for Piedmont's claim to lead the unification process (Map 22.2).

To unify Italy, however, Piedmont would have to confront Austria, which governed the provinces of Lombardy and Venetia and exerted strong influence over most of the

Map 22.2 Unification of Italy, 1859–1870
The many states of the Italian peninsula had different languages, ways of life, and economic interests. The northern kingdom of Sardinia, which included the commercially advanced state of Piedmont, had much to gain from a unified market and a more extensive pool of labor. Although the armies of King Victor Emmanuel II and Giuseppe Garibaldi brought the Italian states together as a single country, it would take decades to construct a culturally, socially, and economically unified nation.

peninsula. Cavour turned for help to Napoleon III, who promised French assistance in exchange for the city of Nice and the region of Savoy. Napoleon III expected that France rather than Austria would then influence the peninsula thereafter. Sure of French help, Cavour provoked the Austrians to invade northern Italy in April 1859. The cause of Piedmont-Sardinia's monarchy now became the cause of nationalist Italians everywhere, even those who had supported romantic republicanism in 1848. The French and Piedmontese armies used the newly built Piedmontese railroad to move troops, thereby achieving rapid victories. Napoleon, suddenly fearing the growth of Piedmont as a potential competing force, independently signed a peace treaty with Austria that gave Lombardy, but not Venetia, to Piedmont. The rest of Italy remained disunited, leaving Cavour's nationalist ambitions not yet realized.

Napoleon III's plan to keep Italy disunited was soon derailed. Support for Piedmont continued to swell among Italians. Giuseppe Garibaldi (1807–1882), a committed republican and veteran of the revolutions of 1848, set sail from Genoa in May 1860 with a thousand red-shirted volunteers (many of them teenage boys) to liberate Sicily. In the autumn of that year, King Victor Emmanuel II's victorious forces descending from the north and Garibaldi's moving up from the south met in Naples. Garibaldi threw his support to the king, and in 1861, the kingdom of Italy was proclaimed with Victor Emmanuel as its ruler.

Exhausted by a decade of overwork, Cavour died within months of leading the unification, leaving lesser men to organize the new Italy. The task ahead was enormous and complex: there was still no common Italian language; 90 percent of the peninsula's inhabitants spoke local dialects. Moreover, consensus among Italy's elected political leaders was often difficult to reach after the war, and admirers of Cavour, such as Verdi (who had been made a senator), quit the quarrelsome politi-

Seamstresses of the Red Shirts
Sewing uniforms and making battle flags, European women like these Italian volunteers saw themselves as contributors to the nation. Many nineteenth-century women participated in nation building as "republican mothers" by donating their domestic skills and raising the next generation of citizens to be patriotic. (Oil on canvas, Florence / Private Collection / © Electa / akg-images / The Image Works.)

cal stage. Politicians from the wealthy commercial north and the impoverished agricultural south disagreed over issues like taxation and development, as they do even today. Finally, Italian borders did not yet seem complete because Venetia and Rome remained outside them, under Austrian and French control, respectively. Holding the new nation together amid these difficulties was the romanticized retelling of the Italian struggle for freedom from foreign and domestic tyrants, under the daring leadership of Garibaldi and his Red Shirts — a legend that papered over Cavour's economic and military Realpolitik.

Bismarck and the Realpolitik of German Unification

The most momentous act of nation building for Europe and the world was the creation of a united Germany in 1871 under Prussian leadership. The architect of the unified Germany was **Otto von Bismarck** (1815–1898). Bismarck came from a traditional Junker (Prussian landed nobility) family on his father's side; his mother's family included high-ranking bureaucrats. At university, the young Bismarck had gambled and womanized. After failing in the civil service, he worked to modernize operations on his landholdings while leading an otherwise decadent life. His marriage to a pious Lutheran woman gave him new seriousness. In the 1850s, his diplomatic service to the Prussian state made him increasingly angry at the Habsburg grip on German affairs. Establishing Prussia as the dominant German power became Bismarck's cause.

In 1862, William I (king of Prussia, r. 1861–1888; German emperor, r. 1871–1888) appointed Bismarck prime minister in hopes that he would crush the growing power of the liberals in the Prussian parliament. The liberals, representing the prosperous professional and business classes, had gained parliamentary strength at the expense of conservative landowners during the decades of industrial expansion. Indeed, the liberals' wealth was crucial to the Prussian state's power, but liberals wanted Prussia to be like other parts of western Europe, with political rights for citizens and increased civilian control of the military. William I, along with members of the traditional Prussian elite such as Bismarck, rejected the western European model. Acting on his conservative beliefs, Bismarck simply rammed through programs to build the army and prevent civilian control. "Germany looks not to Prussia's liberalism, but to its power," he proclaimed. "The great questions of the day will not be settled by speeches and majority decisions — that was the great mistake of 1848 and 1849 — but by iron and blood."

After his triumph over the parliament, Bismarck led Prussia into a series of wars: against Denmark in 1864, Austria in 1866, and France in 1870. Using war as a political tactic, he kept the disunited German states from choosing Austrian leadership and instead united them around Prussia. Bismarck drew Austria into the 1864 war over Denmark's proposed incorporation of the provinces of Schleswig and Holstein, with their partially German population. The Prussian-Austrian victory resulted in an agreement that Prussia would administer Schleswig, and Austria, Holstein. That arrangement stretched Austria's geographic interests far from its central European base: "We were

King William I of Prussia and His Generals
Realpolitik politicians used warfare to create new nations like the unified Germany, which led other states in using up-to-date weaponry and transportation. Nonetheless, horses, swords, and flashing helmets such as those worn by King William I and the generals of Prussia were still a major feature of developing modern warfare. (Reproduction of a painting by G. Koch / Mary Evans Picture Library / Everett Collection.)

very honorable, but very dumb," Emperor Francis Joseph later said of being drawn into the Schleswig-Holstein debacle.

Austria proved weaker than Prussia, because the Austrian empire lagged in economic development. Bismarck, however, so encouraged Austria's pretensions to grandeur that it disputed the administration of Schleswig and Holstein and in the summer of 1866 confidently declared war on Prussia itself. Within seven weeks, the modernized Prussian army won a decisive victory that allowed Bismarck to drive Austria from the German Confederation and create the North German Confederation, led by Prussia (Map 22.3).

To bring the remaining German states into Prussia's expanding orbit, Bismarck next provoked France into war. The atmosphere became charged when Spain proposed a Prussian prince to fill its vacant royal throne. This candidacy at once threatened France with Prussian rulers on two of its borders and inflated Prussian pride at the possibility of its own princes ruling grand states. To get nationalist sentiments onto the news pages in both countries, Bismarck edited a diplomatic communication to make it look as if

Map 22.3 Unification of Germany, 1862–1871
In a complex series of diplomatic maneuvers, Prussian leader Otto von Bismarck welded disunited
kingdoms and small states into a major continental power independent of the other dominant German
dynasty, the Habsburg monarchy. That unity almost immediately unleashed the new nation's economic
and industrial potential, but an aristocratic and agrarian elite remained firmly in power.

the king of Prussia had insulted France over the issue of the vacant throne. Publication of
the revised telegram inflamed the French into demanding war. The parliament gladly
declared it on July 19, 1870, launching the Franco-Prussian War. The Prussians captured
Napoleon III with his army on September 2, 1870, and France's Second Empire fell two
days later.

A new French government struggled to carry on, and as Prussian forces besieged
Paris, in January 1871 in the Hall of Mirrors at Versailles, King William of Prussia was
proclaimed kaiser ("emperor") of the new German Reich ("empire"). The peace terms
ending the Franco-Prussian War, signed in May, required France to cede the rich industrial provinces of Alsace and Lorraine to Germany and to pay a multibillion-franc

indemnity. Without French protection for the papacy, Rome became part of Italy. Germany was now poised to dominate continental politics.

Prussian military might served as the foundation for German nation building, and a complex constitution for the German Empire ensured the continued political dominance of the aristocracy and monarchy — despite the growing wealth and influence of the liberal business classes. Kaiser William, who remained Prussia's king, controlled the military and appointed Bismarck to the powerful position of chancellor for the Reich. Individual German states were represented in a council called the Bundesrat, while the Reichstag was an assembly elected by universal male suffrage. The Reichstag ratified all budgets but had little power to initiate programs. In framing this political settlement, Bismarck accorded rights such as suffrage in the belief that the masses would uphold conservatism and the monarchy out of their fear of modernizing businessmen. Taking no chances, he balanced this move with an electoral system in Prussia in which the votes from the upper classes counted more than those from the lower. He had little to fear from liberals, however. Dizzy with German military success, liberals came to support the blend of economic progress, constitutional government, and militaristic nationalism that Bismarck represented.

Francis Joseph and the Creation of the Austro-Hungarian Monarchy

The Austrian monarchy took a different approach to nation building, proving that there was no one blueprint for the modern nation-state. The confrontations with Cavour and Bismarck left the Habsburg Empire struggling to keep its standing in a rapidly changing Europe. The young monarch Francis Joseph (r. 1848–1916) favored absolutist rule and enhanced his authority through stiff court ceremonies, playing to the popular fascination with celebrity and power. Though the emperor resisted reform, official standards of honesty and efficiency improved, and the government promoted local education. The administration used the German language and the schools taught it, but the government respected the rights of national minorities — Czechs and Poles, for instance — to receive education and communicate with officials in their native tongue. Above all, the government abolished most internal customs barriers, boosted railway construction, and attracted foreign capital. Like Paris, the capital city of Vienna underwent extensive rebuilding, and industrialization progressed, if unevenly.

In the fast-moving nineteenth century, the absolutist Austrian emperor Francis Joseph could not match Bismarck in nation building. Too much of the old regime remained as a roadblock: the Catholic church controlled education and civil institutions such as marriage, prosperous liberals lacked representation in such important policy matters as taxation and finance, and police informers swarmed around them. Wanting truly representative government and free speech, the liberals prevented measures — such as providing funds for modernizing the military — that would have strengthened the reactionary government in Austria. Unlike Bismarck in Prussia, there was no one to override the liberals to bring about change.

After Prussia's 1866 victory over Austria, the vast, wealthy kingdom of Hungary became the key to the Habsburg Empire's existence. The leaders of the Hungarian agrarian elites forced the Austrian emperor to accept a **dual monarchy** — that is, one in which the Magyars had home rule over the Hungarian kingdom within the Habsburg lands. This agreement restored the Hungarian parliament and gave it control of internal policy (including the right to decide how to treat Hungary's national minorities). Although the Habsburg emperor Francis Joseph was

The Austro-Hungarian Monarchy, 1867

king of Hungary and Austro-Hungarian foreign policy was coordinated from Vienna, the Hungarians mostly ruled themselves after 1867, weakening the process of nation building in the empire.

Although designed specifically to address the Hungarian demands, the dual monarchy led to claims by Czechs, Slovaks, and other national groups in the Habsburg Empire for a similar kind of self-rule. Czechs who had helped the empire advance industrially, for example, wanted Hungarian-style liberties. Other leaders of dissatisfied ethnic groups turned to **Pan-Slavism** — that is, the transnational loyalty of all ethnic Slavs. Instead of looking toward Vienna, they turned to the largest Slavic country — Russia — as key to achieving the unity of all Slavs outside the Habsburg Empire. With so many competing ethnicities, the Austro-Hungarian monarchy remained a dynastic state in which people could show loyalty to the Habsburg dynasty but had difficulty relating to one another as members of a single nation.

Political Stability through Gradual Reform in Great Britain

In contrast to the turmoil on the continent, Great Britain appeared the ideal of liberal progress. By the 1850s, the monarchy symbolized domestic tranquillity and propriety. Queen Victoria (r. 1837–1901) and her husband, Prince Albert, portrayed themselves as models of morality, British stability, and middle-class virtues. Britain's parliamentary system steadily brought more men into the political process. Economic prosperity supported peaceful political reform, except that politicians did little to relieve Ireland's continued suffering. A flexible party system helped smooth governmental decision making: the Tories evolved into the Conservatives, who favored a more status-oriented politics but still went along with the emerging liberal consensus around economic development and representative government. The Whigs became the Liberals, so named for their commitment to progress, free trade, and an active role for industrialists as well as the aristocracy. In 1867, the Conservatives, led by Benjamin Disraeli (1804–1881), passed the Second Reform Bill, which extended voting rights to a million more men. Disraeli proposed, like Bismarck somewhat later, that the working classes would choose "the most conservative interests in the country" — not the business ones.

Both political parties supported reforms because citizens had formed pressure groups to influence national policies. Women's groups advocated the Matrimonial Causes Act of 1857, which facilitated divorce, and the Married Women's Property Act of 1870, which allowed married women to own property and keep the wages they earned. The Reform League, another pressure organization, had held mass demonstrations in London to bring about passage of the Second Reform Bill. Plush royal ceremonies united critics and activists and masked political conflict but, more important, involved all social classes. Queen Victoria and Prince Albert, with their newly devised celebrations of royal marriages, anniversaries, and births, promoted the monarchy so successfully that the term *Victorian* came to symbolize almost the entire nineteenth century. Yet Britain's politicians were as devoted to Realpolitik as those in Germany, Italy, or France. Their policies included the use of violence to expand their overseas empire and, increasingly, to control Ireland, where reform stopped short. This violence occurred beyond the view of most British people, however, allowing them to imagine their nation as peaceful, advanced, and united.

Nation Building in North America

Nation building in the United States involved unprecedented and destructive upheaval at midcentury. The young nation had a more democratic political culture than that of Europe, and nationalism was on the rise. Virtually universal white male suffrage, a rambunctiously independent press, and mass political parties promoted the belief that sovereignty derived from the people. From the beginning, a combative public politics shaped America.

The United States continued to expand westward (Map 22.4). In 1848, victory in the Mexican-American War almost doubled the size of the country: the United States officially annexed Texas, and large portions of California and the Southwest extended U.S. borders into formerly Mexican land. Politicians and citizens alike favored banning native Americans from these western lands and confining them to reservations. There was no agreement, however, on whether slavery would be allowed in the new western territories. The issue polarized the country. In the North, politicians in the new Republican Party ran on a platform of "free soil, free labor, free men."

After Republican Abraham Lincoln was elected president in 1860, most of the slaveholding states seceded to form the Confederate States of America. Civil war broke out in 1861 when, under Lincoln's leadership, the North fought to preserve the Union. The future of nation building in the United States hung in the balance. Lincoln did not initially aim to abolish slavery, but his Emancipation Proclamation of January 1863 officially freed all slaves in the Confederacy and turned the war into a fight not only for union but also for an end to human bondage. After the summer of 1863, the North's superior industrial strength and military might overpowered and physically destroyed much of the South. By April 1865, the North had prevailed, though a Confederate sympathizer assassinated Lincoln. Constitutional amendments ended slavery and promised full political rights to African American men.

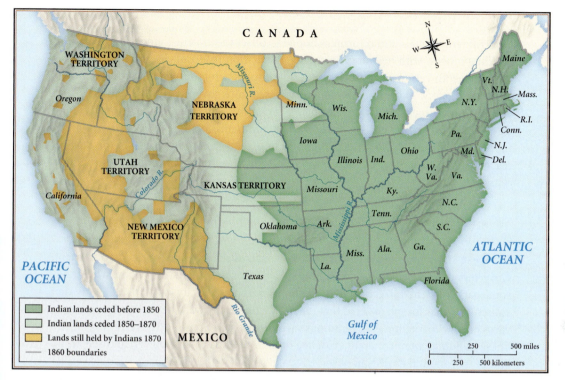

Map 22.4 U.S. Expansion, 1850–1870
Like Russia, the United States expanded into adjacent regions to create a continental nation-state. In taking over territories, however, the United States differed from Russia by herding native peoples into small confined spaces called reservations so that settlers could acquire thousands of square miles for farming and other enterprises. The U.S. government granted full citizenship for all native Americans only in 1925.

By 1871, northern interest in promoting African American political rights was waning, and whites began regaining control of state politics in the South, often by organized violence and intimidation. The end of northern occupation of the South in 1877 was a setback in obtaining rights for blacks. Nonetheless, in ending slavery, the Union victory opened the way to stronger national government and to economic advancement no longer tied to the old Atlantic plantation system.

The North's triumph had profound effects elsewhere in North America. The United States also threatened the annexation of Canada to punish Great Britain, whose dependence on cotton had led it to support the Confederacy. To prevent the loss of Britain's largest territory, the British government allowed Canadians to form a united dominion — that is, a self-governing unit of the empire — in 1867. Dominion status answered Canadians' appeal for home rule, weakened the cause of those opposing Britain's control of Canada, and strengthened Canadian national unity.

REVIEW QUESTION What role did warfare play in the various nineteenth-century nation-building efforts?

Nation Building through Social Order

Government officials and reformers hoped to offset the violent changes of the nation-building process with new improvements. Population rose and cities grew crowded as the nineteenth century progressed, leading officials across Europe to promote public health and safety. Many liberals wanted a laissez-faire government that left social and economic life largely to private enterprise. In contrast, bureaucrats and reformers took direct action to improve citizens' lives and, along with missionaries and explorers, worked more actively to establish social order and to extend European power to the farthest reaches of the globe. Some of these efforts met violent resistance both within Europe and outside it.

Bringing Order to the Cities

European cities became the backdrop for displays of state power and accomplishment. Governments focused on improving capital cities such as Vienna and Rome with handsome parks, widened streets, stately museums, and massive city halls. In 1857, Austrian emperor Francis Joseph ordered that the old Viennese city walls be replaced with boulevards lined with major public buildings such as the opera house and government offices. These buildings were concrete evidence of national wealth and power, and the broad boulevards allowed crowds to observe royal pageantry. The wide roads were also easier for troops to navigate than the twisted, narrow medieval streets that in 1848 had concealed insurrectionists in cities like Paris and Vienna. Impressive parks and public gardens showed the state's control of nature, ordered people's leisure time, and inspired respect for the nation-state's achievements.

Construction first required destruction; buildings and entire neighborhoods that had intermingled rich and poor disappeared, and thousands of city dwellers were dislocated. Newly built rich quarters were separated from the poor sections of the city. In Paris, the process of urban change was called Haussmannization, named for the prefect Georges-Eugène Haussmann, who implemented a grand design that included eighty-five miles of new streets, many lined with showy dwellings for the wealthy. In London, the many new banks and insurance companies, one architect believed, "help[ed] the impression of stability." There was an expectation that the civic pride resulting from urban rebuilding would replace rebelliousness and disunity.

Amid redevelopment, serious problems menaced the urban population. Repeated epidemics of diseases such as cholera killed alarming numbers of city dwellers and gave the strong impression of social decay, not national power. Poor sanitation allowed typhoid bacteria to spread through sewage and into water supplies, infecting rich and poor alike. In 1861, Britain's Prince Albert — the beloved husband of Queen Victoria — reputedly died of typhoid fever, commonly known as a "filth disease." Heaps of animal excrement in chicken coops, pigsties, and stables; unregulated urban slaughterhouses; and piles of human waste were breeding grounds for disease, making sanitation a top priority.

Scientific research, increasingly undertaken in publicly financed laboratories and hospitals, provided the means to promote public health and control disease. France's Louis Pasteur, three of whose young daughters had also died of typhoid, advanced the germ theory of disease. He suggested that bacteria and parasites might be responsible for human and animal diseases. Pasteur demonstrated that heating foods such as wine and milk to a certain temperature, a process that soon became known as pasteurization, killed these organisms and made food safe. English surgeon Joseph Lister applied Pasteur's germ theory of disease to infection and developed antiseptics for treating wounds and preventing puerperal fever, a condition, caused by the dirty hands of physicians and midwives, that killed innumerable women after childbirth.

Governments undertook projects to modernize sewer and other sanitary systems and to straighten rivers. Citizens often prized such improvements as signs of national superiority. In Paris, sewage flowed into newly built, watertight underground collectors. In addition, Haussmann piped in water from uncontaminated sources in the countryside to provide each household with a secure supply. To prevent devastating floods and to eliminate disease-ridden marshlands, governments rerouted and straightened rivers such as the Rhine and built canals. Improved sanitation testified to the activist state's ability to bring about progress.

Citizens responded positively to improvements in everyday life. When sanitary public toilets for men became a feature of modern cities, women petitioned governments for similar facilities. More aware of dirt, disease, and smells, the middle classes bathed more regularly, sometimes even once a week. People's concerns for refinement and health mirrored governments' pursuit of order.

Expanding Government Bureaucracy

To build an orderly national community required a more active role for the state, and bureaucracies expanded in these years as government authority reached further into everyday life. Censuses became routine and provided the state with personal details of citizens' lives such as age, occupation, residence, marital status, and number of children. Governments then used these data for everything from setting quotas for military conscription to predicting the need for new prisons. Reformers like Florence Nightingale, who gathered medical, public health, and other statistics to support sanitary reform, believed that such quantitative information would help a government base decisions on facts rather than on influence peddling or ill-informed hunches, and thus make it less susceptible to corruption and inefficiency.

To bring about their vision of social order, many governments also expanded the regulation of prostitution. Venereal disease, especially syphilis, was common, and like typhoid fever, it infected individuals and whole families. Officials blamed prostitutes, not their clients, for its spread. The police picked up suspect women, examined them for syphilis, and confined infected ones for treatment. As states began monitoring prostitution and other social matters like public health and housing, they had to add departments and agencies. In 1867, Hungary's bureaucracy handled fewer than 250,000 individual

cases ranging from health to poverty issues; twenty years later, it handled more than 1 million.

Schooling and Professionalizing Society

Emphasis on empirical knowledge and objective standards changed the professions and raised their status. Growing numbers of middle-class doctors, lawyers, professors, and journalists employed solid information in their work. The middle classes argued that jobs in government should be awarded according to expertise rather than aristocratic birth or political connections. In Britain, a civil service law passed in 1870 required competitive examinations to ensure competency in government posts — a system long used in China. Governments began to allow professionals to determine rules for admission to their fields. Such legislation had both positive and negative effects: groups could set high standards, but otherwise qualified people were sometimes prohibited from working because they lacked the credentials. The medical profession, for example, gained the authority to license physicians, but it tried to block experienced midwives from attending childbirths.

Nation building required the education of all citizens, professional or not. "We have made Italy," one Italian official announced. "Now we have to make Italians." Education was one way of bringing citizens to hold common beliefs and values. Expansion of the electorate and lower-class activism prompted one British aristocrat to say of the common people, whom he feared as they gained influence, "We must now educate our masters!" Governments introduced compulsory schooling to reduce illiteracy rates, which were more than 65 percent in Italy and Spain in the 1870s and even higher in eastern Europe. As ordinary people were allowed to vote, books taught them about the responsibilities of citizenship and provided the practical knowledge necessary for contributing to industrial society.

Educational reform was not easy. At midcentury, religious authorities supervised schools and charged tuition, making primary education an option only for prosperous or religious parents. After the 1850s, critics questioned the relevance of religion in the curricula of modern schools. In 1861, an English commission on education concluded that instead of knowledge of the Bible, "the knowledge most important to a labouring man is that of the causes which regulate the amount of his wages, the hours of his work, the regularity of his employment, and the prices of what he consumes." To feel part of a nation, the young had to learn its language, literature, and history. Replacing religion was a challenge for the secular and increasingly knowledge-based state.

Enforcing school attendance was another challenge. Although the Netherlands, Sweden, and Switzerland had functioning primary-school systems before midcentury, rural parents in these and other countries resisted sending their children to school. Farm families depended on children to perform chores and believed that work in the fields or the household provided the best and most useful education. Urban homemakers from the lower classes needed their children to fetch water, tend younger children, and scavenge for household necessities such as stale bread from bakers or soup from local mis-

sions. Yet some of the working poor developed a craze for learning, which made traveling lecturers, reading groups, and debating societies popular.

Secondary education also expanded through the creation of more lycées (high schools) and technical schools, yet it remained even more of a luxury. In authoritarian countries such as Russia, advanced knowledge, including education in science and technology, was considered suspect because it empowered the young with information and taught them to think for themselves. Reformers pushed for advanced courses for young women to make them more interesting wives and better mothers of future citizens. In Britain, the founders of two women's colleges — Girton (1869) and Newnham (1871) — at Cambridge University believed, and were later proved right, that exacting standards and a modern curriculum in women's higher education would inspire improvements in the men's colleges of Cambridge and Oxford.

Education also opened professional doors to women, who came to attend universities — in particular, medical schools — in Zurich and Paris in the 1860s. Women doctors argued that they could not only bring feminine values to health care but also get better results because women patients would be more open with them than with male doctors. The need for educated citizens also offered opportunities for large numbers of women to enter teaching, a field once dominated by men. Thousands of women founded nursery schools and kindergartens based on the Enlightenment idea that developmental processes start at an early age. Yet many men opposed the idea of women studying or teaching. "I shudder at philosophic women," wrote one critic of female education.

Spreading National Power and Order beyond the West

In an age of nation building, colonies took on new importance because they seemed to add to the power of the nation-state. This benefit led Great Britain, France, and Russia to expand their political control of colonies. Sometimes the imperial powers offered social and cultural services, such as schools. For instance, in the 1850s and 1860s provincial governors and local officials promoted the extension of Russian borders to gain control over nomadic tribes in central and eastern Asia. Russian officials then instituted common educational and religious policies, such as instruction in the Russian language and in the principles of the Russian Orthodox church, as a means to social order.

Great Britain, the era's mightiest imperial power, imposed direct political rule abroad as part of nation building. Before the 1850s, British liberals desired commercial profits from colonies, but, believing in laissez-faire, they kept political involvement in colonial affairs minimal. Since the eighteenth century, the East India Company had been gaining control over various kingdoms' trading and tax collection rights and then began building railroads throughout the Indian countryside. As commerce with Britain grew, many Indian businessmen became wealthy. Other local men served in the colonial army, which became one of the largest standing armies in the world.

In 1857, a contingent of Indian troops, both Muslim and Hindu, violently rebelled when a rumor spread that Britain would force them to use cartridges of ammunition greased with cow and pig fat, which violated the Hindu ban on beef and the Muslim

prohibition of pork. This was not their main grievance, however. The soldiers, more generally angered at widening British control, overran the old Moghul capital at Delhi and declared the independence of the Indian nation — an uprising that became known as the Indian Rebellion of 1857.

Simultaneously, local rulers rebelled, condemning "the tyranny and oppression of the infidel and treacherous English." Lakshmibai, the *rani* ("queen") of the state of Jhansi in central India, led a separate military revolt when the East India Company tried to take over her lands after her husband died. Even as the British brutally crushed the rebels, Indian nationalism was born. Victorious, the British government took direct control of India in 1858, and the British Parliament declared Queen Victoria the empress of India in 1876.

A system of rule took shape in which close to half a million South Asians, supervised by a few thousand British men, governed a region that they now called India. Colonial rule meant both outright domination and subtle intervention in everyday life. For example, British taxes on high-quality Indian textiles led many to buy cheaper British cottons. Artisans were directed instead to farm raw materials such as wheat, cotton, and jute to supply Britain's industry and feed its workers. Nevertheless, some of the Indians who benefited from improved sanitation and medicine chose to accept British arguments against Indian customs such as child marriage and *sati* — the self-immolation of a widow on her husband's funeral pyre. Others found Europe's scientific values attractive and came to appreciate that British rule, ironically, brought a kind of unity to India's many separate princedoms, thus laying the foundation for an Indian nation.

French political expansion was similarly complex. The French government pushed to establish its dominion over Cochin China (modern southern Vietnam) in the 1860s. Missionaries in the area, ambitious French naval officers, and even some local peoples — much like Indian merchants and financiers — pulled the French government farther into the region. Like the British, the French brought improvements, but sanitation and public health programs led to a rise in population that strained resources. Furthermore, landowners and French imperialists siphoned off most of the profits from economic improvement. The French also undertook a cultural mission to transform cities like Saigon with tree-lined boulevards similar to those of Paris. French literature, theater, and art were popular with both colonial officials and upper-class local people.

In this age of Realpolitik, the Crimean War had shown the great powers the importance of the Mediterranean basin. Napoleon III, remembering his uncle's campaign in Egypt, took an interest in building the Suez Canal, which would connect the Mediterranean with the Red Sea and the Indian Ocean and thus dramatically shorten the route from Europe to Asia. Following the canal's completion in 1869, "canal fever" spread: Verdi composed the opera *Aïda* (set in ancient Egypt), and people across the West applied Egyptian designs to textiles, furniture, art, and even public monuments in cities. The French army had occupied all of Algeria by 1870, when the number of European immigrants to the region reached one-quarter million. French rule in Algeria, as elsewhere, was aided by local people's attraction to European goods and technology and by the opportunity to make money.

Its vastness allowed China to escape complete takeover, but traders and Christian missionaries from Europe made inroads for the Western powers. Defeat in the Opium War caused an economic slump and helped generate the mass movement known as the Taiping ("Heavenly Kingdom"). Headed by a leader who claimed to be the brother of Jesus, the Taiping's millions of adherents wanted an end to the ruling Qing dynasty, the expulsion of foreigners, more equal treatment of women, and land reform. By the mid-1850s, the Taiping controlled half of China. The threatened Qing regime promised the British and French greater influence in exchange for aid in defeating the Taiping. More than 20 million Chinese died in the resulting civil war. When peace finally came in 1864, Western governments controlled much of the Chinese customs service and had virtually unlimited access to the country.

Japan alone in East Asia was able to escape Western domination, because it was keenly aware of the innovations taking place in the West. In 1854, the Japanese agreed to open the country to foreign trade in part to gain Western goods, including the West's superior weaponry. Japanese reformers in 1867 overthrew a government that resisted such change and in 1868 enacted the Meiji Restoration. The word *Meiji* pointed to the "enlightened rule" of the new emperor, whose power reformers had restored. The goal was to combine "Western science and Eastern values" as a way of "making new" — hence, a combination of restoration and innovation. The new regime pushed Japan to become a modern, technologically powerful state free from Western control.

Contesting the Nation-State's Order at Home

Europeans did not simply sit by as the growing nation-state changed and often disrupted their lives. A better-informed urban working class protested the upheavals in everyday life caused when cities were ripped apart for improvements and when the growth of factories destroyed artisans' livelihoods. Increasingly educated by public schools, urban workers frequented cafés and pubs to hear news and discuss economic and political events. After the post-1848 repression of worker organizations, unions gradually started to take shape, sometimes in secret because of continuing opposition from governments.

Many of the most outspoken labor activists were artisans struggling to survive in the new industrializing climate. They were attracted at first by the ideas of former printer Pierre-Joseph Proudhon (1809–1865). In the 1840s, Proudhon proclaimed, "Property is theft," suggesting that property ownership robbed people of their rightful share of the earth's benefits (see page 682). He opposed the centralized state and proposed that society be organized instead around natural groupings of men in artisans' workshops. (Women, he believed, should work in seclusion at home for their husbands' comfort.) These workshops and a central bank crediting each worker for his labor would replace government.

As the nation-state expanded its power, workers were also drawn to **anarchism**, which maintained that the existence of the state was the root of social injustice. According to Russian nobleman and anarchist leader Mikhail Bakunin (1814–1876), the slightest infringement on freedom, especially by the central state and its laws, was unacceptable.

Anarchism thus advocated the destruction of all state power. Its appeal grew as government grew in the second half of the nineteenth century.

Political theorist and labor organizer Karl Marx (1818–1883) opposed both doctrines as lacking the sound, scientific basis of his own theory, subsequently called **Marxism**. Marx's analysis, appearing most notably in *Das Kapital* (*Capital*), adopted the liberal idea, dating back to John Locke in the seventeenth century, that human existence was defined by the necessity to work to fulfill basic needs such as food, clothing, and shelter. Using mathematical calculations of production and profit that would justify Realpolitik for the working classes, Marx held that the fundamental organization of any society derived from the relationships arising from work or production. This idea, known as *materialism,* meant that society rested on class relationships — such as those between serf and medieval lord, slave and master, or worker and capitalist. Marx called the class relationships that developed around work the *mode of production* — for instance, feudalism, slavery, or capitalism. He rejected the liberal focus on individual rights and emphasized instead the unequal class relations caused by those who had taken from workers control of the means of production — that is, the capital, land, tools, or factories that allowed basic human needs to be met.

Marx, like the politicians around him, took a tough-minded and realistic look at the economy, discarding the romantic views of the utopian socialists. He saw struggle, not warmhearted cooperation, as the means for bringing about change. Workers' awareness of their oppression would produce class consciousness, he argued, leading them to overthrow their exploiters. Society was not basically harmonious; instead social progress could occur only through conflict.

As the Franco-Prussian War ended, revolution and civil war erupted not only in Paris but also in other French cities — catching the attention of Marx as a sign that his predictions were coming true. As the Prussians laid siege to Paris in the winter of 1870–1871, causing many deaths from starvation and bitter cold, Parisians rose up and demanded new republican liberties, new systems of work, and a more balanced distribution of power between the central government and localities. On March 28, 1871, to counter what they saw as the despotism of the centralized government, they declared themselves a self-governing commune. One issue behind the unrest was the nation-state's destruction of city life through urban renovation.

In the Paris Commune's two months of existence, and while trying to maintain "communal" instead of "national" values, Parisians quickly developed a wide array of political clubs, local ceremonies, and self-managed workshops. Women workers, for example, banded together to make National Guard uniforms on a cooperative rather than a for-profit basis. The Commune proposed to liberate the worker and ensure "the absolute equality of women laborers." Thus, a *commune* — in contrast to a *republic* — was meant to bring about social revolution. Communards, however, often disagreed on how to change society. Anticlericalism, feminism, socialism, and anarchism were but a few of the proposed routes to social justice.

In the meantime, the provisional government that succeeded the defeated Napoleon III stamped out similar uprisings in other French cities. In late May, the well-

supplied national army crushed the Commune and shot tens of thousands of citizens on the streets. Parisian rebels, one citizen commented, "deserved no better judge than a soldier's bullet." The Communards had promoted a kind of antistate in an age of rising state power. Others saw the Commune was the work of the *pétroleuse* ("woman incendiary") — a case of frenzied women running amok through the streets. While revolutionary men became heroes in the history books, writers were soon blaming the burning of Paris on women — "shameless slatterns, half-naked women, who kindled courage and breathed life into arson."

Defeat in the Franco-Prussian War, the rise of the Paris Commune, and the civil war were all horrendous blows to the French state. Yet in the struggle against the Commune, the nation-state once again showed its strengthening muscle. Executions and deportations by the thousands followed, and fear of workers spread across Europe.

> **REVIEW QUESTION** How did Europe's expanding nation-states attempt to impose social order within and beyond Europe, and what resistance did they face?

The Culture of Social Order

Artists and writers of the mid-nineteenth century had complex reactions to the state's expanding reach and the economic growth that sustained it. They saw daily life as filled with commercial values and organized by mindless officials. Ordinary people no longer appeared heroic, as they had during the revolutionary years. "How tired I am of the ignoble workman, the inept bourgeois, the stupid peasant, and the odious priest," wrote the French novelist Gustave Flaubert. Rejecting romanticism, he described ordinary people in a harsh new style called **realism**. Intellectuals of the time proposed scientific theories that also took a cold, hard look at human life in society and challenged fervent religious belief. Theirs was a detached point of view similar to that applied by statesmen to politics.

The Arts Confront Social Reality

Culture helped the cause of national unity. A hungry reading public devoured biographies of political leaders, past and present, and credited daring heroes with creating the triumphant nation-state. As schooling spread literacy and a craving for realism — that is, true-to-life portrayals of society without romantic or idealistic overtones — commercially minded publishers produced an age of best sellers. Newspapers published the novels of Charles Dickens in serial form, and each installment attracted buyers eager for the latest plot twist. Drawn from English society, Dickens's characters included starving orphans, grasping lawyers, greedy bankers, and ruthless opportunists. *Hard Times* (1854) depicts the grinding poverty and ill health of workers alongside the heartlessness of businessmen. Novelist **George Eliot** (the pen name of Mary Ann Evans) probed real-life dilemmas in *The Mill on the Floss* (1860) and *Middlemarch* (1871–1872). Describing rural society, Eliot allowed her readers to see one another's predicaments, wherever they lived.

She knew the pain of ordinary life from her own experience: despite her fame, she was a social outcast because she lived with a married man. Popular novels that showed a hard reality helped form a shared culture much as state institutions did.

French writers also scorned dreams of utopian, trouble-free societies and ideal beauty. Gustave Flaubert's novel *Madame Bovary* (1857) tells the story of a doctor's wife who longs to escape her provincial surroundings. Filled with romantic fantasies, she has two love affairs to escape her boredom, becomes hopelessly indebted buying gifts for her lovers, and commits suicide by swallowing arsenic. *Madame Bovary* scandalized French society with its frank picture of women's sexuality, but it attracted a wide readership. Poet Charles-Pierre Baudelaire wrote explicitly about sex; in his 1857 collection, *Les Fleurs du mal* (*Flowers of Evil*), he expressed drug- and alcohol-induced passions — some focused on the brown body of his African mistress — and spun out visions that critics condemned as perverse. French authorities brought charges of obscenity against both Flaubert and Baudelaire. At issue was social and artistic order: "Art without rules is no longer art," maintained the prosecutor.

During the era of Alexander II's Great Reforms, Russian writers debated whether western European values were harming Russian culture. Adopting one viewpoint, Ivan Turgenev created a powerful novel of Russian life, *Fathers and Sons* (1862), a story of nihilistic children rejecting both parental authority and their parents' spiritual values in favor of science and facts. Fyodor Dostoevsky, in contrast, portrayed nihilists as dark, ridiculous, and neurotic. The highly intelligent characters in Dostoevsky's *Crime and Punishment* (1866) are personally tormented and condemned to lead absurd, even criminal lives. Dostoevsky used antiheroes to emphasize spirituality and traditional Russian values but added a realistic spin by planting such values in ordinary, often seedy people. The Russian public was drawn together by these debates about Russian identity.

While writers of realism depended on sales to thousands of readers, painters usually depended on government support. Leaders such as Prince Albert of Great Britain actively patronized the arts and purchased works for official collections and for themselves. Having their artwork chosen for display at government-sponsored exhibitions was another way for artists to earn a living. Hundreds of thousands from all social classes attended these exhibitions, though not all could afford to buy the art.

After the revolutions of 1848, artists began rejecting the romantic idealizing of ordinary folk or grand historic events. Instead, painters like Gustave Courbet portrayed groaning laborers at backbreaking work because, as he stated, an artist should "never permit sentiment to overthrow logic." The renovated city, artists found, had become a visual spectacle; its wide new boulevards served as a stage on which urban residents performed. *Universal Exhibition* (1867) by Édouard Manet shows figures from all social classes gazing at the Paris scene and observing one another to learn correct modern behavior. Manet also broke with romantic conventions of the nude. His *Olympia* (1865) depicts a white courtesan lying on her bed, attended by a black woman (see the illustration on page 721). This disregard for women in mythical or idealized settings was too much for the critics: "A sort of female gorilla," one wrote of *Olympia,* as debate raged over realism.

Daumier, *The Burden*

Artists painted stark images of ordinary people as they struggled to survive in an industrializing age. Despite romantic views of a secluded separate sphere for women that was protected from life's realities, the majority of women hardly enjoyed such an existence, as shown by this depiction of a weighted-down working woman and her child. Daumier was one of the artists who captured that reality. (National Gallery, Prague, Czech Republic / photo by Erich Lessing / Art Resource, NY.)

A Realist View of the Nude

Manet's *Olympia* (1865) was one of the most shocking works of art of its day. The central woman is not glamorously dressed or posed erotically; rather, she stares candidly and boldly at the viewer. The black maid offers the woman — obviously a courtesan — flowers from an admirer. This scene was far too modern in its style and subject matter for most critics. (Musée d'Orsay, Paris, France / Giraudon / The Bridgeman Art Library International.)

Unlike most of the visual arts, opera was commercially profitable and an effective means of reaching the nineteenth-century public. Verdi used musical theater to contrast noble ideals with the deadly effects of power and the lure of passion with the need for social order. The German composer Richard Wagner hoped to revolutionize opera by fusing music and drama to arouse the audience's fear and awe. A gigantic cycle of four operas, *The Ring of the Nibelungen* reshaped ancient German myths into a modern, nightmarish story of a world doomed by its obsessive pursuit of money and power and saved only through unselfish love. His opera *The Mastersingers of Nuremberg* was said to be implicitly anti-Semitic because of its rejection of influences other than German ones in the arts. Wagner's musical innovation made him a major force in philosophy, politics, and the arts across Europe. To his fellow citizens, however, his operas stood for Germany. Artists both implicitly (like George Eliot) and more explicitly (like Richard Wagner) promoted nation building even as they experimented with new forms.

Religion and National Order

The expansion of state power set the stage for clashes over the role of organized religion in the nation-state. In the 1850s, many politicians supported religious institutions and attended public church rituals because they were another source of order. Simultaneously, some nation builders, intellectuals, and economic liberals came to reject the religious worldview of established churches, particularly Roman Catholicism, because it was based in faith, not reason, and slowed the growth of nationalist sentiment.

Bismarck mounted a full-blown **Kulturkampf** ("culture war") against religion. The German government expelled the Jesuits from Germany in 1872, increased state power over the clergy in Prussia in 1873, and introduced a civil ceremony as an obligatory part of marriage in 1875. Bismarck had bragged, "I am the master of Germany in all but name," but he miscalculated his ability to manipulate politics. The pope fought back: "One must obey God more than men," he ordered. German Catholics rebelled, and even conservative Protestants thought Bismarck wrongheaded in attacking religion. Competition between church and state for power and influence heated up in the age of Realpolitik.

The Catholic church felt assaulted. Nation builders had also extended liberal rights to Jews, whom many Christians considered enemies. Attacking changing values, Pope Pius IX issued *The Syllabus of Errors* (1864), which found fault "with progress, with liberalism, and with modern civilization." Becoming pope in 1878, Leo XIII began reconciling the church to modern politics by encouraging up-to-date scholarship in Catholic institutes and universities and by accepting aspects of representative democracy. The Kulturkampf between church and state ended, making it easier for the faithful to be both Catholic and patriotic.

The place of organized religion in society was changing. While many in the upper and middle classes and most of the peasantry remained faithful, church attendance declined among workers and artisans. There was a religious gender gap, too. Women's spiritual beliefs became more intense, with both Roman Catholic and Russian Orthodox

women's religious orders increasing in size and number; men, by contrast, were falling away from religious devotion. Many urban Jews abandoned religious practices and assimilated instead to secular, national cultures. Religion no longer included everyone.

In 1854, the pope's announcement of the doctrine of the Immaculate Conception (stating that Mary, alone among all humans, had been born without original sin) was followed by an outburst of popular religious fervor, especially among women. In 1858, a young peasant girl, Bernadette Soubirous, began having visions of the Virgin Mary at Lourdes in southern France. Crowds, mostly of women, flocked to Lourdes, believing that its waters could cure their ailments. In 1867, less than ten years later, a new railroad line to Lourdes enabled millions of pilgrims to visit the shrine on church-organized trips. The Catholic church thus showed that it, too, could use such modern means as railroads, shopping centers, and medical verifications of miraculous cures to make the religious experience more up-to-date. Traditional institutions began making themselves as effective as the nation-state.

At about the time of Soubirous's vision, the English naturalist **Charles Darwin** (1809–1882) published *On the Origin of Species* (1859). In his writings, Darwin argued that life on earth had taken shape over countless millions of years before humans existed and that human life was the result of this slow development, called evolution. This

"Gentlemen, We Are Descended from Monkeys," Spain, Late Nineteenth Century

Darwin's scientific ideas aroused anger, admiration, and even mirth, as shown in this engraving some decades after the publication of his major works. As you consider this image, what message would you say the artist is trying to convey about evolution? (Bibliothèque des Arts Décoratifs Paris / Alfredo Dagli Orti / The Art Archive at Art Resource, NY.)

theory directly challenged the Judeo-Christian dogma that God miraculously brought the universe and all life into being in six days as described in the Bible. Instead Darwin held that life developed from lower forms through a primal battle for survival and through the sexual selection of mates — a process he called natural selection. For Darwin the Bible gave a "manifestly false history of the world." Darwin's theories also undermined Enlightenment principles that glorified nature as tranquil and noble, and human beings as essentially rational. The theory of natural selection, in which the fittest survive, suggested a different kind of human society, one composed of warlike individuals and groups constantly fighting one another to triumph over hostile surroundings.

Other innovative biological research placed religious views of reproduction under attack. Working with pea plants in his monastery garden in the 1860s, the Austrian monk Gregor Mendel (1822–1884) discovered the principles of heredity, from which the science of genetics later developed. Investigation into the female reproductive cycle led German scientists to discover the principle of spontaneous ovulation — the automatic release of the egg by the ovary independent of sexual intercourse. Theorists concluded that men had strong sexual drives because reproduction depended on their sexual arousal. In contrast, the automatic release of the egg each month indicated to them that women were passive and lacked sexual feeling.

Many other ideas disturbed the status quo. Even before Darwin, the writer Herbert Spencer (1820–1903) had written that the "unfit" should be allowed to perish in the name of progress. On these grounds Spencer opposed public education and any other attempt to soften the struggle for existence. Darwin continued this line of argument when he claimed that white European men in the nineteenth century were wealthier and better because they were more highly evolved than white women or people of color. A school of thought known as Social Darwinism grew out of Darwin's and Spencer's ideas; it promoted racist, sexist, and other discriminatory policies as a way of strengthening the nation-state.

From the Natural Sciences to Social Science

In an age influenced by Realpolitik, Darwin's revolutionary thought was part of a quest to find alternatives to the idea that the social order was created by God. French thinker Auguste Comte (1798–1857) developed **positivism** — a theory claiming that careful study of facts would generate accurate and useful, or "positive," laws of society. Comte's "sociology" inspired people to believe they could solve the problems resulting from economic and social changes. To accomplish this goal, tough-minded reformers founded study groups and scientifically oriented associations to dig up social facts such as statistics on poverty or the conditions of working-class life. Comte encouraged women's participation in reform because he deemed "womanly" compassion and love as fundamental to social harmony as scientific public policy was. Positivism led not only to women's increased public activism but also to the development of the social sciences in this period. Among them, sociology brought a new realism to the study of human society.

The celebrated English philosopher John Stuart Mill (1806–1873) used Comte's theories to advocate widespread reform and mass education. In his political treatise *On Liberty* (1859), Mill advocated the improvement of society generally, but he also worried that superior people would be brought down by the will of the masses. Influenced by his wife, Harriet Taylor Mill, as well as by Comte, he argued for women's rights and introduced a woman suffrage bill into the House of Commons. The bill's defeat led Mill to publish *The Subjection of Women* (1869), an influential work around the world. *The Subjection of Women* showed the family as a despotic institution, lacking modern values such as rights and freedom. To make a woman appear "not a forced slave, but a willing one," he said, she was trained from childhood not to value her own talent and independence but to welcome her "submission" to men. Mill's progressive thought was soon lost in a flood of Social Darwinist theories. Still, inspired by the social sciences, policymaking came to rely on statistics and fact-gathering for building strong, unified nations.

REVIEW QUESTION How did cultural expression and scientific and social thought help produce the hardheaded and realistic values of the mid-nineteenth century?

Conclusion

Throughout modern history, the development of nation-states has been neither inevitable nor uniform nor peaceful. In the nineteenth century, ambitious politicians, shrewd monarchs, and determined bureaucrats used a variety of methods and policies to transform very different countries into effective nation-states. Nation building was most dramatic in Germany and Italy, where states unified through military force and where people of opposing political opinions ultimately agreed that national unity should be the primary goal. Compelled by military defeat to shake off centuries of tradition, the Austrian and Russian monarchs instituted reforms as a way of keeping their systems in place. The Habsburg Empire became a dual monarchy, an arrangement that gave the Hungarians virtual home rule and raised the level of disunity. Reforms in Russia left the authoritarian monarchy intact and only partially transformed the social order.

After decades of romantic fervor, no-nonsense realism in politics — Realpolitik — became a much touted principle. Realist thinkers such as Darwin and Marx developed theories disturbing to those who maintained an Enlightenment faith in social and political harmony. Realist novels and artworks jarred polite society, and, like the operas of Verdi, portrayed dilemmas of the times. Growing government administrations set policies that were meant to bring order but often brought disorder, including the destruction of entire neighborhoods and violence toward people in far-off lands. In the long term, schooling taught the lower classes to be orderly citizens, and urban renewal ultimately improved cities and public health to complement nation building.

Objections arose to the expanding power of the nation-state. The Indian Rebellion of 1857 against Britain and the Paris Commune of 1871 against the French state were but two examples where violent actions raised difficult questions about nation-building

methods. How far should the power of the state extend in both domestic and international affairs? Would nationalism be a force for war or for peace? In the face of state power, would ordinary people have any say in their destiny? As these issues ripened, the next decades saw extraordinary economic advances and an unprecedented surge in Europe's global power — much of it the result of successes in nation building.

Review Questions

1. What were the main results of the Crimean War?

2. What role did warfare play in the various nineteenth-century nation-building efforts?

3. How did Europe's expanding nation-states attempt to impose social order within and beyond Europe, and what resistance did they face?

4. How did cultural expression and scientific and social thought help produce the hardheaded and realistic values of the mid-nineteenth century?

Making Connections

1. What were the main methods of nation building in the mid-nineteenth century, and how did they differ from those of state building in the early modern period?

2. How did realism in social thought break with Enlightenment values?

3. In what ways did religion emerge as an issue (both within and outside Europe) during the course of nation building?

4. How was the Paris Commune related to earlier revolutions in France? How did it differ from them? How was it related to nation building?

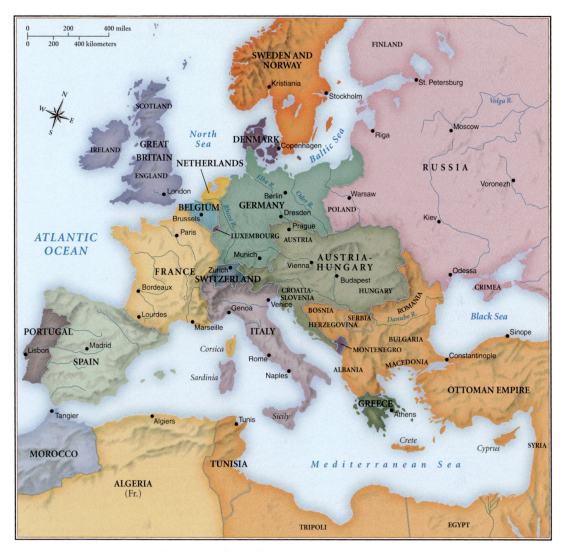

Mapping the West **Europe and the Mediterranean, 1871**

European nation-states consolidated their power by building unified state structures and by developing the means for the diverse peoples within their borders to become socially and culturally integrated. Nation-states were also rapidly expanding outside their boundaries, extending their economic and political reach. North Africa and the Middle East — parts of the declining Ottoman Empire — particularly appealed to European governments because of their resources and their potential for further European settlement. They offered a gateway to the rest of the world.

- For practice quizzes and other study tools, visit the **Online Study Guide** at bedfordstmartins.com/huntconcise.

- For primary-source material from this period, see *Sources of the Making of the West*, Fourth Edition.

- For Web sites, images, and documents related to topics in this chapter, visit *Make History* at bedfordstmartins.com/huntconcise.

Suggested References

Nation building took many forms in the nineteenth century, including wars, urban improvement, mythmaking, and the development of scientific and realistic attitudes — all of these themes are found in the following books.

Barnes, David S. *The Great Stink of Paris and the Nineteenth-Century Struggle against Filth and Germs.* 2006.

Berra, Tim M. *Charles Darwin: The Concise Story of an Extraordinary Man.* 2009.

Blackbourn, David. *The Conquest of Nature: Water, Landscape, and the Making of Modern Germany.* 2006.

Gross, Michael B. *The War against Catholicism: Liberalism and the Anti-Catholic Imagination in Nineteenth-Century Germany.* 2005.

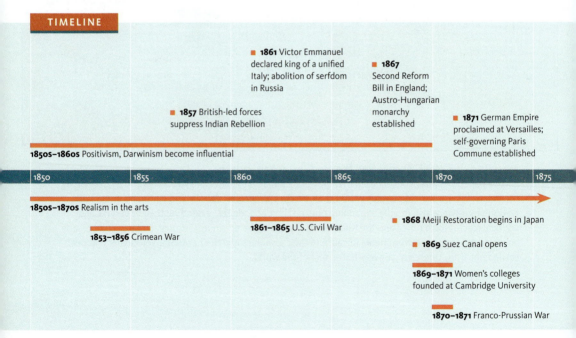

TIMELINE

1861 Victor Emmanuel declared king of a unified Italy; abolition of serfdom in Russia

1867 Second Reform Bill in England; Austro-Hungarian monarchy established

1857 British-led forces suppress Indian Rebellion

1871 German Empire proclaimed at Versailles; self-governing Paris Commune established

1850s–1860s Positivism, Darwinism become influential

| 1850 | 1855 | 1860 | 1865 | 1870 | 1875 |

1850s–1870s Realism in the arts

1853–1856 Crimean War

1861–1865 U.S. Civil War

1868 Meiji Restoration begins in Japan

1869 Suez Canal opens

1869–1871 Women's colleges founded at Cambridge University

1870–1871 Franco-Prussian War

Heretz, Leonid. *Russia on the Eve of Modernity: Popular Religion and Traditional Culture under the Last Tsars*. 2008.

Kaufman, Suzanne. *Consuming Visions: Mass Culture and the Lourdes Shrine*. 2005.

Parker, Kate, and Julia Shone, eds. *The Austro-Hungarian Dual Monarchy, 1867–1918*. 2008.

Riall, Lucy. *Garibaldi: The Invention of a Hero*. 2007.

Roy, Tapti. *The Raj of the Rani*. 2007.

*Seacole, Mary. *Wonderful Adventures of Mrs. Seacole in Many Lands*. 1857.

Steinberg, Jonathan. *Bismarck: A Life*. 2011.

Unowsky, Daniel L. *The Pomp and Politics of Patriotism: Imperial Celebrations in Habsburg Austria, 1848–1916*. 2005.

The Victorian Web: http://www.victorianweb.org

Wetzel, David. *A Duel of Giants: Bismarck, Napoleon III, and the Origins of the Franco-Prussian War*. 2001.

Wirtschafter, Elise Kimerling. *Russia's Age of Serfdom, 1649–1861*. 2008.

*Primary source.

23

Empire, Industry, and Everyday Life

1870–1890

N THE MID-1880s, Frieda von Bülow, a young German woman of aristocratic birth, joined several activist groups interested in promoting German colonial expansion in Africa. Like other women in these pro-imperial organizations, von Bülow was eager to help German settlers — and even some Africans — in East Africa, which Germany was in the process of colonizing. She also met adventurous men such as Carl Peters, a fanatical nationalist and leading figure in imperialist circles. As Europeans competed to take over the African continent, von Bülow and Peters headed for Zanzibar and other distant cities not only to conquer them but also to carry on a passionate romance. Once in Africa, von Bülow basked in the freedom from her society's restrictions on women and in German superiority over local African peoples. For his part, Peters followed his usual pattern of tricking Africans into giving up their lands and using guns, rape, and other violence to get his way. Peters seduced one African woman and then had her executed because of her relationship with another man. Though Peters's womanizing caused von Bülow to break up with him, she maintained both her racism and her German nationalism, learning to shoot a gun on behalf of colonial conquest, writing popular novels about empire and white superiority, and setting up a plantation in Southeast Africa.

European Immigrants Arriving in New York

This calm image of an immigrant ship arriving in New York harbor hardly captures the emotions the immigrants had (as we know from their letters and diaries) on leaving their communities and facing an unknown life in the United States or other parts of the Western Hemisphere. Many came from agricultural regions and would soon be the labor behind the advance of industry; others would become settlers, driving out native Americans and thus becoming agents of empire. (The Granger Collection, NYC — All rights reserved.)

Von Bülow and Peters were just two of the tens of thousands of Europeans pursuing imperial adventure, as the search for lands to colonize reached a feverish pitch after the 1870s. Those involved in imperialism had a variety of motives and, like Peters, were often swaggering and violent. The rapid expansion of Western takeovers was called the

731

"new imperialism" because the race for empire now aimed at political rather than mere economic power.

Europeans had been acquiring global territory since the late fifteenth century; the new imperialism intensified this process. In their rush for empire, Europeans like Frieda von Bülow and Carl Peters worked to control whole societies instead of dominating coastal trade until, by the beginning of the twentieth century, Western nations claimed jurisdiction over vast stretches of the world's surface. Beyond political control, Europeans tried to stamp other continents with European-style place names, architecture, clothing, languages, and domestic customs. They used culture to secure their empires just as they used it to forge the nation-state.

Millions of people traveled vast distances in the nineteenth century—a time of greatly increased mobility and migration, much of which was made possible by an expansion of industry and colonization. Some migrated temporarily to serve in colonial governments or to find business opportunities. Others relocated permanently within Europe or outside it. Such migration uprooted tens of millions of people, disrupted social and family networks, and often inflicted terrible violence on native peoples dislocated by European migrants.

The decades from 1870 to 1890 were also an era of expanding industry in the West. Empire and industry fed on each other as raw materials from conquered areas supplied Western factories and as innovations in weaponry, transportation, medicine, and communication allowed imperialism to thrive. Industrialization spread from Britain to central and eastern Europe and brought a continuous new supply of products to the market. A growing appetite for these products, many of them for household consumption, changed the fabric of everyday life and built pride in a nation's conquests. Urban workers began demanding greater participation in the political process. Proud Europeans brimmed with confidence and hope, while the grimmer aspects of empire and industrialization played themselves out in distant colonies, urban slums, and declining rural areas of Europe.

CHAPTER FOCUS How were imperial conquest and industrial advances related, and how did they affect Western society, culture, and politics in the late nineteenth century?

The New Imperialism

Imperialism surged in the last third of the nineteenth century. Industrial demand for raw materials and business rivalry for new markets fueled competition for territory in Africa and Asia, and European nations, the United States, and Japan now aimed to rule sizable portions of the world directly. "Nations are not great except for the activities they undertake," declared a French advocate of imperialism in 1885. Conquering foreign territory and developing wealth through industry appeared to heap glory on the nation-state. Although some missionaries and reformers aimed to spread Western religions and culture as a benefit to colonized peoples, the expansion of the West increased the subjugation of those peoples, inflicted violence on them, and radically altered their lives.

The Scramble for Africa — North and South

European countries had long viewed Africa — North and South — as a vast region for profit through trade and investment. In the late nineteenth century, they aimed for political control as well. Egypt, a convenient and profitable stop on the way to Asia, was an early target. Modernizing rulers had made Cairo into a bustling metropolis with lively commercial and manufacturing enterprises. Production of raw materials, such as cotton for European textile mills, was booming. Europeans invested heavily in the region, first in ventures such as building the Suez Canal in the 1860s, then in laying thousands of miles of railroad track, improving harbors, creating telegraph systems, and finally and most important, loaning money at exorbitant rates of interest.

In 1879, the British and the French took over the Egyptian treasury, allegedly to secure their investments and guarantee the repayment of loans. In 1882, they invaded the country with the excuse of squashing Egyptian nationalists who protested the take-over of the treasury. The British next seized control of the government as a whole and forcibly reshaped the Egyptian economy from a system based on multiple crops that maintained the country's self-sufficiency to one that emphasized the production of a few crops — mainly cotton, raw silk, wheat, and rice — that cheaply fed both European manufacturing and the European working classes. Businessmen from the colonial powers, Egyptian landowners, and local merchants profited from these agricultural changes, while the bulk of the rural population barely eked out an existence.

Alongside the takeover of the Egyptian government, France occupied neighboring Tunisia in 1881. Europeans also turned their attention to sub-Saharan Africa. In the past, contact between Europe and Africa had principally involved the trade of African slaves for a variety of goods, but by this time Europeans had begun to want Africa's raw materials, such as palm oil, cotton, metals, diamonds, cocoa, and rubber. Additionally, Britain needed the southern and eastern coasts of Africa for stopover ports on the route to Asia and its empire in India.

In the 1880s, European military forces conquered one sub-Saharan African territory after another (Map 23.1) to dominate peoples, land, and resources — "the magnificent cake of Africa," as King **Leopold II** of Belgium (r. 1865–1909) put it. Insatiable greed drove Leopold to claim the Congo region of central Africa, inflicting on its peoples unparalleled acts of cruelty (see the illustration on page 735). German chancellor Otto von Bismarck, who saw colonies mostly as political bargaining chips, established German control over Cameroon and a section of East Africa, to which Frieda von Bülow and Carl Peters headed. Faced with competition, the British poured millions of pounds into conquering the continent "from Cairo to Cape Town," as the slogan went, and the French cemented their hold on large portions of western Africa.

The scramble for Africa escalated tensions in Europe and prompted Bismarck to call a conference at Berlin. The European nations represented at the conference, held in a series of meetings in 1884 and 1885, decided that control of settlements along the African coast guaranteed rights to interior territory. This agreement led to the strictly linear dissection of the continent — a dissection that cut across boundaries of African

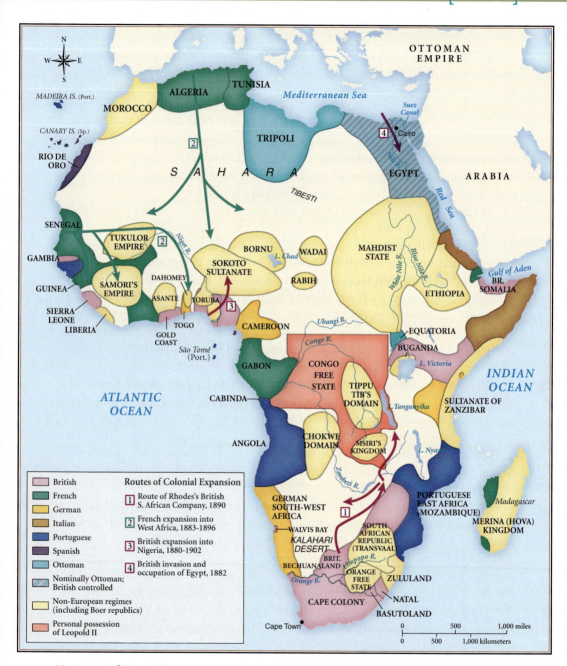

Map 23.1 Africa, c. 1890

The scramble for Africa entailed a change in European trading practices, which generally had been limited to the coastline. Trying to penetrate economically and rule the interior ultimately resulted in a map of the continent that made sense only to the imperial powers, for it divided ethnic groups and made territorial unities that had nothing to do with Africans' sense of geography or patterns of settlement. This map shows the unfolding of that process and the political and ethnic groupings to be conquered.

The Violence of Colonization

King Leopold II, ruler of the Belgian Congo, was so greedy and ruthless that his agents squeezed the last drop of rubber and other resources from local peoples. Missionaries reported and photographed atrocities such as the killing of workers whose quotas were even slightly short or the amputation of hands for the same offense. Belgian agents collected amputated hands and sent them to government officials to show Leopold that they were enforcing his kind of discipline. (Anti-Slavery International.)

culture and ethnic life. The Berlin conference also banned the sale of alcohol and controlled the flow of arms to African peoples. In theory, the meeting was supposed to reduce bloodshed and ambitions for territory in Africa. In reality, the agreement accelerated conquest of the continent and left everyone on edge over the threat of more violence. Newspaper accounts whetted the popular appetite for more takeovers. Music hall audiences rose to their feet and cheered at the sound of popular songs about imperial heroes of the day.

The lust for conquest had perhaps its greatest effect in southern Africa. The Dutch had moved into the area in the seventeenth century, but by 1815 the British had gained control. Thereafter, descendants of the Dutch, called Boers (Dutch for "farmers"), and British immigrants joined together in their fight to wrest farmland and mineral resources from the Xhosa, Zulu, and other African peoples. British businessman and politician Cecil Rhodes, sent to South Africa for his health just as diamonds were being discovered in 1870, cornered the diamond market and claimed a huge amount of African territory hundreds of miles into the interior. His ambition for Britain and for himself was boundless: "I contend that we are the finest race in the world," he explained, "and that the more of the world we inhabit the better it is." Although notions of European racial superiority had been advanced before, Social Darwinism strengthened racism to justify the conquest of African lands.

Wherever necessary to ensure domination, Europeans either destroyed African economic and political systems or transformed them into instruments of their rule. A British governor of the West African region known as the Gold Coast put the matter succinctly in 1886: the British would "rule the country as if there were no inhabitants."

Indeed, most Europeans considered Africans barely civilized, despite the wealth local rulers and merchants accumulated in their international trade and despite individual Africans' accomplishments in everything from fabric dyeing to road building and architecture. They felt this justified the confiscation of land from Africans, who were then forced to work for them to pay European-imposed taxes. Agriculture to support families, often performed by women and slaves, declined in favor of mining and farming cash crops. Men were made to leave their homes to work in mines or to build railroads. Family and community networks, though upset by the new arrangements, helped support Africans during this upheaval in everyday life.

Acquiring Territory in Asia

The expansion of imperial power from the 1870s on was occurring around the world, not just in Africa. Much of Asia, with India as the centerpiece, was integrated into Western empires. At the same time, resistance to outside domination was also growing: the educated Indian elite in 1885 founded the Indian National Congress. Some of its members welcomed opportunities for trade, education, and social advancement. Others, however, challenged Britain's right to rule India at all. In the next century, the Indian National Congress would develop into a mass movement.

To the east, British military forces took control of the Malay peninsula in 1874 and of the interior of Burma in 1885. In both areas, political instability often threatened secure trade. The British depended on the region's tin, oil, rice, teak, and rubber as well as on its access to the numerous interior trade routes of China. British troops guaranteed the order necessary to expand railroads for more efficient export of raw materials and the development of Western systems of communication.

The British added to their holdings in Asia partly to counter Russian and French annexations. Since 1865, Russia had been absorbing the small Muslim states of central Asia, including provinces of Afghanistan (Map 23.2). Besides extending into the Ottoman Empire, Russian tentacles reached Persia, India, and China, often encountering British competition. The Trans-Siberian Railroad allowed Russia to begin integrating Siberia as hundreds of thousands of hungry peasants moved to the region. France meanwhile

British Colonialism in the Malay Peninsula and Burma, 1826–1890

used the threat of military action to negotiate favorable treaties with Indochinese rulers, creating the Union of Indochina from the ancient states of Cambodia, Tonkin, Annam,

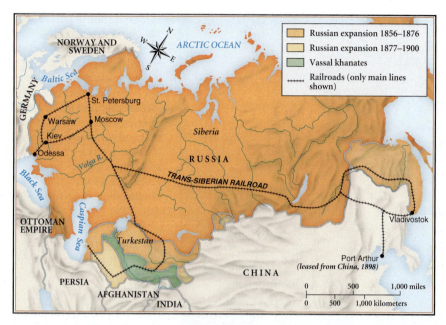

Map 23.2 Expansion of Russia in Asia, 1865–1895
Russian administrators and military men continued enlarging Russia, bringing in Asians of many different ethnicities, ways of life, and religions. Land-hungry peasants in western Russia followed the path of expansion into Siberia and Muslim territories to the south. In some cases they drove native peoples from their lands, but in others they settled unpopulated frontier areas. As in all cases of imperial expansion, local peoples resisted any expropriation of their livelihood, while the central government tried various policies for integration.

and Cochin China in 1887 (the last three now constitute Vietnam). Laos was added to Indochina in 1893.

Japan's Imperial Agenda

Japan escaped European rule by rapidly transforming itself into a modern industrial nation with its own imperial agenda. The Japanese embraced foreign trade and industry. "All classes high and low shall unite in vigorously promoting the economy and welfare of the nation," ran one of the first pronouncements of the Meiji regime that had come to power in 1868. Unlike China, the Japanese government directed the country's turn toward modern industry, and state support led daring innovators like Iwasaki Yataro, founder of the Mitsubishi firm, to develop heavy industries such as mining and shipping. The Japanese sent students, entrepreneurs, and government officials to the West to bring back as much new knowledge as they could.

Change was the order of the day in Japan. Japanese legal scholars, following German models, helped draft a constitution in 1889 that emphasized state power rather than

Modernization in Japan

Like the West, Japan bustled with commerce and industry thanks to improved and expanding transportation. Railroads, ships, and a range of new inventions such as the rickshaw speeded goods and individuals within cities, across the country, and ultimately to new, foreign destinations. The Japanese traveled widely to learn about ongoing technological innovation. (Rue des Archives / The Granger Collection, NYC — All rights reserved.)

individual rights. Western dress became the rule at the imperial court, and when fire destroyed Tokyo in 1872, a European planner directed the rebuilding in Western architectural style. The Japanese adapted samurai traditions such as spiritual discipline to create a large and technologically modern military. In the 1870s, Japan purchased naval ships from Britain and began conquering adjacent islands, including Okinawa.

The Paradoxes of Imperialism

Imperialism ignited constant, sometimes heated debate because of its many paradoxes. Although it was meant to make European nations more economically secure, imperialism intensified distrust in international politics as countries vied with one another for a share of world influence. In securing India's borders, for example, the British faced Russian expansion in Afghanistan and along the borders of China, and the costs of empire were high. Britain spent enormous amounts of tax revenue to maintain its empire even as its industrial lead began to slip. Yet for certain businesses, colonies provided crucial markets and large profits: late in the century, French colonies bought 65 percent of France's exports of soap and 41 percent of its metallurgical exports. Imperialism provided huge numbers of jobs to people in European port cities, but taxpayers in all parts of a nation — whether they benefited or not — paid for colonial armies, increasingly costly weaponry, and administrators.

Advocates of imperialism pointed out that whites had a "civilizing mission." The French thus taught some of their colonial subjects French language, literature, and history. In Germany's African colonies, an exam for students in a school run by missionaries asked them to write on "Germany's most important mountains" and "the reign of William I and the wars he waged." The deeds of Africa's great rulers and the accomplishments of its kingdoms disappeared from the curriculum. While Europeans believed in instructing colonial subjects, they did not believe that Africans and Asians were as capable as Europeans of great achievements.

Imperialism's goal of "civilizing" was also in conflict. French advocates argued that their nation "must keep its role as the soldier of civilization." But it was unclear whether imperialism should emphasize soldiering (that is, the conquest and murder of local peoples) or civilizing (the education of local peoples in the European tradition). Western scholars and travelers had long studied Asian and African languages, art, and literature, and had gathered and used botanical and other scientific knowledge. Yet appreciation of foreign cultures was tinged with bias and error. European scholars of Islam characterized Muhammad as an inferior imitation of Jesus, for example, and many Europeans stereotyped Asians and Africans as lying, lazy, self-indulgent, or irrational. One English official pontificated that "accuracy is abhorrent to the Oriental mind." Such beliefs offered still another justification for conquest: that inferior colonized peoples would ultimately be grateful for what Europe had brought them.

European missionaries ventured to newly secured areas of Africa and Asia with attitudes similarly full of contradictions. A woman missionary reflected a common view when she remarked that the Tibetans with whom she worked were "going down, down into hell, and there is no one but me . . . to witness for Jesus amongst them." Many people under colonial rule did accept Christianity, often blending their local religious

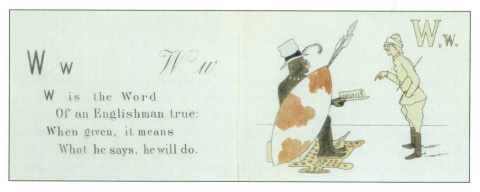

An ABC for Baby Patriots (1899)
Pride in empire began at an early age, when learning the alphabet from this kind of book helped develop an imperial sensibility. The subject of geography became important in schools during the decades between 1870 and 1890 and helped young people know what possessions they could claim as citizens. In British schools, the young celebrated the holiday Empire Day with ceremonies and festivities emphasizing imperial power. (Bodleian Library, University of Oxford. Mary F. Ames, shelfmark 2523 c. 24 [1899].)

practices with Christian ones. Christianizing entire populations proved impossible, however, and when native people resisted, missionaries often supported brutal military measures against them in the name of upholding Christian values and Western order.

The paradoxes of imperialism are clear in hindsight, but at the time European self-confidence hid many of them. There was the belief that through imperialist ventures "a country exhibits before the world its strength or weakness as a nation," as one French politician announced. Some in government, however, worried that imperialism — because of its expense and the constant possibility of war — might weaken rather than strengthen the nation-state. The most glaring paradox of all was that Western peoples who believed in nation building and national independence invaded the territory of others thousands of miles away and refused them the right to rule themselves.

> **REVIEW QUESTION** What were the goals of the new imperialism, and how did Europeans accomplish those goals?

The Industry of Empire

Behind the expansion of Western empires lay dramatic developments in economic and technological power. Fed by raw materials from around the world, industry turned out a flood of new products, including the increasingly powerful guns that served imperial conquest, and many workers' wages increased. Beginning in 1873, however, downturns in business threatened both entrepreneurs and the working class. Businesspeople sought remedies in new technology, managerial techniques, and a revolutionary marketing institution — the department store. Governments played their part by changing business law and supporting the drive for raw materials and global profits. The steady advance of industry, global trade, and the consumer economy further transformed people's daily lives.

Industrial Innovation

An abundance of industrial, technological, and commercial innovation backed the ambitions of the nation-state and the drive for empire. The last third of the nineteenth century saw new products ranging from the bicycle to the typewriter to the telephone. In 1885, sophisticated German engineer Karl Benz devised a workable gasoline engine; six years later, France's Armand Peugeot constructed a functioning automobile. Electricity became more widely used after 1880, providing power to light everything from private drawing rooms to government office buildings. The Eiffel Tower, constructed in Paris for the Universal Exposition of 1889, stood as a monument to the age's engineering wizardry. Visitors rode to the Eiffel Tower's summit in electric elevators, while to fuel the West's explosive industrial growth, the leading industrial nations mined and produced massive quantities of coal, iron, and steel in the 1870s and 1880s. Manufacturers used the metal to build the more than 100,000 locomotives that pulled trains — trains that transported two billion people a year.

The Invention of Electric Lighting
By the 1890s, residents of major European cities could see many fresh inventions in a single walk down the newly widened boulevards. In this illustration of Piccadilly in London, electric lighting illuminates the way for modern bicycles and automobiles as well as horse-drawn carriages. By the turn of the century, streets had also become crowded with electric trams. (Mary Evans Picture Library.)

The factory system spread across Europe and around the world, while agriculture continued to be modernized. Historians used to contrast a "second" Industrial Revolution of the late nineteenth century, in which manufacturers concentrated on heavy industrial products like iron and steel, to the "first" one of the eighteenth and early nineteenth centuries, in which innovations in the manufacture of textiles and the use of steam energy predominated. Many historians now believe this distinction mainly applies to Britain, where industrialization did rise in two stages. In countries where industrialization came later, the two developments occurred simultaneously. Numerous and increasingly advanced textile mills were installed on the European continent later than in Britain, for instance, at the same time that blast furnaces were being constructed. Although industrialization led to the decline of traditional crafts like weaving, home industry — or **outwork**, the process of having some aspects of industrial work done outside factories in individual homes (similar to the putting-out system described on page 661) — persisted in garment making, metalwork, and porcelain painting. Industrial production occurring simultaneously in homes, small workshops, and factories has continued down to the present day.

Industrial innovations also changed agriculture. Chemical fertilizers boosted crop yields, and reapers and threshers mechanized harvesting. In the 1870s, Sweden produced a cream separator, a first step toward mechanizing dairy farming, while wire fencing and barbed wire replaced wooden fencing and stone walls. Refrigeration, developed during this period, allowed fruits, vegetables, and meat to be transported without spoiling, thus diversifying and increasing the urban food supply. Tin from colonies facilitated large-scale commercial canning, which made many foods available year-round to people in the cities and thus improved their health.

New, more powerful guns, railroads, steamships, and medicines accelerated Western penetration of Asia and Africa. Improvements in steamboat technology helped in the conquest of the African interior, but the scientific development of quinine was also crucial. Before the development of medicinal quinine in the 1840s and 1850s, the deadly tropical disease malaria decimated many a European party embarking on exploration or military conquest, giving Africa the nickname "White Man's Grave." The use of quinine, extracted from cinchona bark from the Andes, radically cut deaths from malaria among soldiers, missionaries, adventurers, traders, and bureaucrats.

Drought and famine plagued large stretches of both Africa and Asia in these decades, thus weakening local peoples' ability to resist European attacks. Europeans kept their health, thanks to quinine and abundant food; then their weapons did the work of conquest. Improvements to the breech-loading rifle and the development of the machine gun, or "repeater," between 1862 and the 1880s dramatically increased firepower. Europeans sold outmoded guns to peoples needing protection both from their internal enemies and from the Europeans themselves. In contrast, Europeans crushed African resistance with rapid, accurate, and blazing gunfire: "The whites did not seize their enemy as we do by the body, but thundered from afar," claimed one local African resister. "Death raged everywhere — like the death vomited forth from the tempest."

Despite global expansion, Britain's rate of industrial growth slowed as its entrepreneurs remained wedded to older technologies. Neglecting innovation, Great Britain profited from its investments worldwide and consolidated its global power in the latter nineteenth century. Meanwhile, Germany and the United States began surpassing Britain in research, technical education, and innovation — and ultimately in overall rates of economic growth.

Following the Franco-Prussian War, Germany annexed Alsace and Lorraine, territories with both textile industries and rich iron deposits. Investing heavily in research, German businesses devised new industrial processes and began to mass-produce goods. Germany also spent as much money on education as on its military in the 1870s and 1880s, sending German industrial productivity soaring. The United States began intensive exploitation of its vast natural resources, including coal, metal ores, gold, and oil. Whereas German productivity rested more on state promotion of industrial efforts, U.S. growth often involved innovative entrepreneurs, such as Andrew Carnegie in iron and steel and John D. Rockefeller in oil. Most other countries trailed the three leaders in economic development.

French industry grew steadily, but French businesses remained smaller than those in Germany and the United States. In Spain, Austria-Hungary, and Italy, industrial development was primarily a local phenomenon. Austria-Hungary, for example, had densely industrialized areas around Vienna and in Styria and Bohemia, but the rest of the country remained tied to traditional, nonmechanized agriculture. The Italian government spent more on building Rome into a grand capital than it invested in economic growth. A mere 1.4 percent of Italy's 1872 budget went to education and science, compared with 10.8 percent in Germany. Scandinavian countries eventually made commercial use of electricity to industrialize in the last third of the nineteenth century and become leaders in the use of hydroelectric power.

Russia's road to industrialization was tortuous. The terms of serf emancipation bound many Russian peasants to the mir, or landed community. Some villages sent men and women to industrializing cities, but on the condition that they return for plowing and harvesting. Nevertheless, by the 1890s, Moscow, St. Petersburg, and a few other cities had substantial working-class populations, and the Russian government constructed railroads, including the Trans-Siberian Railroad (1891–1916), which upon completion stretched 5,787 miles from Moscow to Vladivostok. Even as Russia's industrial and military power increased, it exemplified the uneven benefits of industrialization: neither Russian peasants nor underpaid urban workers could afford to buy the goods their country produced.

Facing Economic Crisis

Economic conditions were far from rosy throughout the 1870s and 1880s despite industrial innovation. In 1873, prosperity abruptly gave way to a severe economic depression, followed by almost three decades of economic downturns. People of all classes lost their jobs or businesses and faced long stretches of unemployment or bankruptcy. Because economic ties bound industrialized western Europe to international markets, the downturns affected economies around the world: Australia, South Africa, California, Newfoundland, and the West Indies.

By the 1870s, as industry gained in influence, industrial and financial setbacks — not agricultural ones as in the past — were capable of sending the economy into a long tailspin. Innovation created new or modernized industries on an unprecedented scale, but economic uncertainty accompanied the forward march of Western industrial development, and businesspeople faced real problems. First, the start-up costs of new enterprises skyrocketed. The early textile mills had required relatively small amounts of capital in comparison to the new factories producing steel and iron. **Capital-intensive industry**, which required huge financial investment for the purchase of expensive machinery, replaced labor-intensive production, which relied on the hiring of more workers. Second, the distribution and consumption of goods failed to keep pace with industrial growth, in part because businessmen kept wages so low that workers could afford little besides food. For them, purchasing the new industrial goods was impossible. The

series of slumps turned industrialists' attention to finding ways to enhance sales and distribution and to control markets and prices.

Governments took steps to address the economic crisis. New laws spurred the development of the **limited liability corporation**, which protected investors from personal responsibility for a firm's debt and thus encouraged investment. Before limited liability, owners or investors were personally responsible for the debts of a bankrupt business. In one case in England, a former partner who had failed to have his name removed from a legal document after leaving the business remained responsible to creditors when the company went bankrupt. He lost everything he owned except a watch and the equivalent of one hundred dollars. By reducing personal risk, limited liability made investors more confident about financing business ventures, which led to the growth of stock markets. These stock markets raised money from a larger pool of private capital than before and gave businesses the funds to innovate.

Businesses also met the crisis that began in 1873 by banding together in cartels and trusts. Cartels were combinations of industries formed to control prices and competition. A single German coal cartel, founded in the 1880s, eventually dominated more than 95 percent of coal production in Germany and could therefore restrict output and set prices. Trusts — similar to cartels in their power to control prices but different in structure — appeared first in the United States in 1882, when John D. Rockefeller created the Standard Oil Trust by acquiring stock from many different oil companies and placing it under the direction of trustees. The trustees then controlled so much of the companies' stock that they could set prices for the entire industry and even dictate to the railroads the rates for transporting the oil. While expressing their belief in free trade, those who set up cartels and trusts actually restricted the free market.

Much of Europe had adopted free trade after midcentury, but during the downturn of the 1870s and 1880s the resulting huge trade deficits — caused when imports exceeded exports — soured many Europeans on the concept. Countries with trade deficits had less capital available to invest internally, slowing job growth. Farmers in many European countries suffered when improvements in transportation brought in cheap grain from the United States and Ukraine. With broad popular support, governments approved tariffs to make foreign goods including grain more expensive.

Revolution in Business Practices

Industrialists also tried to minimize the damage of economic downturns by revolutionizing the everyday conduct of their businesses. Instead of running their firms on their own in the late 1800s, industrialists began to hire managers specializing in a particular aspect of a business — such as sales and distribution, finance, or the purchase of raw materials. A white-collar service sector, composed of workers with mathematical skills and literacy acquired in the new public primary schools, emerged as part of the development of management. Businesses employed armies of secretaries, file clerks, and typists to guide the flow of business information.

Berlin Telephone Operators
Middle-class women needing jobs embraced the opportunities offered by the growing service sector in telephone, telegraph, and office work and other respectable employment. These Berlin telephone operators probably earned less than women factory workers, as service sector employers took advantage of an untapped educated pool of labor to advance industrial development. (akg-images.)

　　Women, responding to the availability of clean, respectable work, formed the bulk of service employees. At the beginning of the nineteenth century, middle-class women still tended businesses with their husbands, but the new ideology of domesticity became so strong that male employers were unwilling to hire married women, and women in the lower-middle and middle classes were themselves ashamed to work outside the home. By the late nineteenth century, the costs of middle-class family life had increased, especially because school-attendance laws meant that children were no longer contributing to family resources by working. Whether to help pay family expenses or to support themselves, both unmarried and married women of the respectable middle class increasingly took jobs despite the ideal of domesticity. Since society had come to believe that women were not meant to work or even not fit to work, businesses made greater profits by consistently paying women in the service sector much less than they would have paid men for doing the same tasks.

　　The drive to boost consumption led to the development of the department store. Founded after midcentury in the largest cities, department stores such as the Bon Marché in Paris and Wanamaker's in Philadelphia gathered an impressive variety of goods in

one place in imitation of the Middle Eastern bazaar. Unlike stores that sold single lines of goods such as dishware or fabrics, department stores were modern shopping palaces built of marble and filled with lights and mirrors. In the department store, luxurious silks and embellished tapestries spilled over railings and counters to stimulate consumer desire. Frenzied shoppers no longer limited their purchases to necessities. Department stores became the domain of women, who came out of their domestic sphere into a new public role. Stores hired attractive salesgirls, another variety of service workers, to inspire customers to buy. Department-store shopping also took place outside of cities: glossy mail order catalogs from the Bon Marché or Sears, Roebuck in Chicago arrived regularly in rural areas, with both necessities and exotic items from the faraway dream world of the city.

Consumerism was shaped by empire. Travelers like Frieda von Bülow and Carl Peters journeyed on speedier ocean liners, carrying quinine, antiseptics, and other medicines as well as cameras, revolvers, and the latest in rubber goods and apparel. Colonial products such as coffee, tea, sugar, tobacco, and cocoa became more widespread for the stimulation they offered hardworking Westerners. Tons of palm oil from Africa were turned into both margarine and soap, allowing even ordinary people in the West to see themselves as cleaner and more civilized than those in other parts of the world, including areas from which those raw materials came. Empire and industry jointly shaped everyday life by exciting the desire for things — whether industrial goods or products from the colonies.

REVIEW QUESTION What were the major changes in Western industry and business by the end of the nineteenth century?

Imperial Society and Culture

The spread of empire not only made the world an interconnected marketplace but also transformed everyday culture and society. Success in manufacturing and foreign ventures not only created millionaires but also expanded the professional middle class and the service sector. Many Europeans grew healthier, partly because of improved diet and partly because of government-sponsored programs aimed at promoting the fitness necessary for citizens of imperial powers. At the same time, millions of poor Europeans migrated in search of opportunities around the world — even in the colonies — while artists found new subject matter in the industrial and imperial changes around them.

The "Best Circles" and the Expanding Middle Class

Profits from empire and industrial growth added new members to the upper class, or "best circles," so called at the time because of their members' wealth, education, and social status. People in the best circles often came from the aristocracy, which remained powerful even as they had to share their social position with new millionaires from the ranks of the upper middle class, or bourgeoisie. Monarchs gratefully bestowed aristocratic titles on wealthy businesspeople, and poorer aristocrats approved marriages be-

tween their children and those of the newly rich. Such arrangements brought much-needed money to old, established families and the glamour of an aristocratic title to newly wealthy families. Thus, Jeanette Jerome, daughter of a wealthy New York financier, married England's Lord Randolph Churchill (their son Winston later became England's prime minister). To justify their success, the wealthy often quoted Social Darwinist principles, maintaining that their prosperity resulted from their natural superiority over the poor.

Empire reshaped leisure time. Upper-class men bonded over big-game hunting in Asia and Africa, which replaced age-old traditions of fox and bird hunting. European hunters forced native Africans, who had depended on hunting for income, food, and group unity, to work as guides, porters, and domestics on hunts. Collectors brought exotic specimens back to Europe for natural history museums, and wealthy Europeans added empire to their homes with displays of stags' heads, elephant tusks, and animal skins.

People in the best circles saw themselves as an imperial elite, and upper-class women devoted themselves to maintaining its standards of social conduct. Members of the upper class did their best to exclude inferiors by controlling their children's social lives, especially by arranging marriages themselves. Instead of working for pay, upper-class women devoted themselves to raising children and directing staffs of servants. They took their role seriously, keeping detailed accounts of their expenditures and monitoring their children's religious and intellectual development. Being active consumers of Oriental carpets, bamboo furniture, Chinese porcelains, and fashionable clothing was also time-consuming for women. In contrast to men's plain garments, upper-class women wore elaborate costumes — featuring constricting corsets, voluminous skirts, bustles, and low-cut necklines for evening wear — that made them symbols of elite leisure. Women offset the grim side of imperial and industrial society with the rigorous practice of art and music. With keys made of ivory from Africa, the piano symbolized the imperial elite's accomplishments and superiority.

Below the best circles, or upper crust, the solid middle class of businesspeople and professionals such as lawyers was expanding, most notably in western and central Europe. In eastern Europe, this expansion did not happen naturally, and the Russian government often sought out foreigners to build its professional and business classes. Although middle-ranked businessmen and professionals occasionally mingled with those at the apex of society, their lives remained more modest. They did, however, employ at least one servant, which might give the appearance of leisure to the middle-class woman in the home even though she did many household chores herself. Professional men working at home did so from a well-appointed, if not lavish, room. Overall, middle-class domesticity celebrated the imperial value of cleanliness.

Working People's Strategies

For centuries, working people had migrated from countryside to city and from country to country to make a living. After the middle of the nineteenth century, empire and industry were powerful factors in migration for a variety of reasons. In parts of Europe,

the land simply could not produce enough to support a rapidly expanding population. Because of eroded soil, hundreds of thousands of Sicilians left, often temporarily, to find work in the industrial cities of North and South America. One-third of all European immigrants came from the British Isles, especially Ireland between 1840 and 1920, first because of the potato famine and then because English landlords drove them from their farms to get higher rents by simply changing tenants. Between 1886 and 1900, half a million Swedes out of a population of 4.75 million quit their country. Millions of rural Jews from eastern Europe also fled vicious anti-Semitism. Russian mobs brutally attacked Jewish communities, destroying homes and businesses and even murdering some Jews. These ritualized attacks, called pogroms, were scenes of horror. "People who saw such things never smiled anymore, no matter how long they lived," recalled one Russian Jewish woman who migrated to the United States in the early 1890s.

Commercial and imperial development determined destinations for international migration. (See "Taking Measure," page 749.) Most migrants who left Europe went to North and South America, Australia, and New Zealand, as news of opportunity reached Europe. The railroad and steamship made journeys across and out of Europe faster, though most workers traveled in steerage with few comforts. Once established elsewhere, migrants frequently sent money back home; European farm families often received a good deal of their income from husbands or grown sons and daughters who had left. Cash-starved peasants in eastern and central Europe welcomed the arrival of "magic dollars" from their kin. Even though they formed the cheapest pool of labor, often in factories or sweatshops, migrants themselves appreciated the chance to begin anew. One settler in the United States was relieved to escape the meager peasant fare of rye bread and herring: "God save us from . . . all that is Swedish," he wrote home sourly.

More common than international migration was internal migration from rural areas to European cities, accelerating the urbanization of Europe. The most urbanized countries were Great Britain and Belgium, followed by Germany, France, and the Netherlands; established port cities like Riga, Marseille, and Hamburg offered opportunities for work in global trade. Many who moved to the cities were seasonal migrants who worked as masons, cabdrivers, or factory hands to supplement declining income from agriculture. When they returned to the countryside, they provided hands for the harvest. In villages across Europe, independent artisans such as handloom weavers often supported their unprofitable livelihoods by sending their wives and daughters to work in industrial cities.

Changes in technology and management practices often made factory work more stressful. Workers complained that new machinery speeded up the pace of work to an unrealistic level. For example, employers at a foundry in suburban Paris required workers using new furnaces to turn out 50 percent more metal per day than they had produced using the old furnaces. Despite more physical exertion, workers received no additional pay for their extra efforts. Workers also grumbled about the increased number of managers; many believed that foremen, engineers, and other supervisors interfered with their work. Some women kept their jobs only in return for granting sexual favors to the male manager.

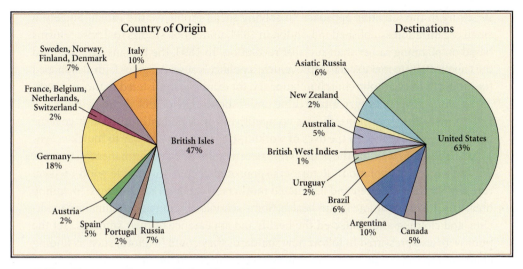

Taking Measure European Emigration, 1870–1890
The suffering caused by economic change and by political persecution motivated people from almost every European country to leave their homes for greater security elsewhere. North America attracted more than two-thirds of these migrants, many of whom followed reports of vast quantities of available land in both Canada and the United States. Both countries were known for following the rule of law and for providing economic opportunity in urban as well as rural areas. (Theodore Hamerow, *The Birth of New Europe: State and Society in the Nineteenth Century* [Chapel Hill: University of North Carolina Press, 1983], 169.)

Many in the urban and rural labor force continued to do outwork at home. In Russia, workers made bricks, sieves, shawls, lace, and locks during the slow winter season. Every branch of industry, from metallurgy to toy manufacturing to food processing, also employed urban women at home — and their work was essential to the family economy. Women painted tin soldiers, wrapped chocolate, made cheese boxes, and polished metal. Factory owners liked the system because low piece rates made outworkers willing to work extremely long days. A German seamstress at her new sewing machine reported that she "pedaled at a stretch from six o'clock in the morning until midnight. . . . At four o'clock I got up and did the housework and prepared meals." Owners could lay off women at home during slack times and rehire them whenever needed with little fear of organized protest, as joblessness and destitution constantly threatened. By and large, however, urban workers were better informed and more connected to the progress of industry and empire than their rural counterparts were.

National Fitness: Reform, Sports, and Leisure

In an age of Social Darwinist concerns about national fitness in the international struggle to survive, middle- and upper-class reformers founded organizations for social improvement. Settlement houses, clinics, and maternal and child health centers sprang up overnight in cities. Young middle- and upper-class men and women, often from universities, eagerly took up residence in poor neighborhoods to study and help the people there.

Believing in the scientific approach to solving social problems, the Fabian Society, a small organization established in London in 1884, undertook studies to devise reforms based on planning rather than socialist revolution. In 1893, the Fabians helped found the Labour Party to make social improvement a political cause. Religious faith also shaped these efforts: the Catholic church in Hungary, for example, ministered to those experiencing rural poverty as agriculture came under the stresses of global competition.

To make the poor more fit in a competitive world, philanthropists and government officials intervened in the lives of working-class families as a way to "quicken evolution." The worry was that the poor, as one reformer put it, "were permanently stranded on lower levels of evolution." Reformers sponsored centers to provide good medical care and food for children and instructed mothers in child-care techniques, including breast-feeding to promote infant health. Some schools distributed free lunches, medicine, and clothing and inspected the health and appearance of their students. Yet the poor were also pressured to follow new standards they could ill afford, such as finding children respectable shoes, and reformers believed they had the right to enter working-class apartments whenever they chose to inspect them.

A few professionals began to distribute birth-control information in the belief that smaller families could better survive the challenges of urban life. In the 1880s, Aletta Jacobs (1851–1929), a Dutch physician, opened the first birth-control clinic, which specialized in promoting the new, German-invented diaphragm. Jacobs wanted to help women in Amsterdam slums who were worn out by numerous pregnancies. Working-class women used these clinics, and knowledge of birth-control techniques spread by word of mouth among workers. The churches adamantly opposed this trend, and even reformers wondered whether birth control would increase sexual exploitation.

Another government reform effort consisted of legislation barring women from night work and from "dangerous" professions such as florist and bartender — allegedly for health reasons. Even though medical statistics demonstrated that women in even the most strenuous jobs became sick less often than men, lawmakers and workingmen claimed that women were not producing healthy enough children and were stealing jobs from men. Women who had worked in trades newly defined as dangerous were forced to find other, lower-paying jobs or work at home. The new laws did not prevent women from holding jobs, but they made earning a living harder.

As nations competed for territory and global trade, male athletes created sports teams. Soccer, rugby, and cricket matches drew mass audiences that welded the lower and higher classes into an imperial culture. Competitive sports began to be seen as signs of national strength and spirit, as newspapers reported all sorts of new contests, whether they concerned nations vying for colonies or bicyclists participating in cross-country races such as the Tour de France. "The Battle of Waterloo was won on the playing fields of Eton," ran the wisdom of the day, suggesting that the games played in school could mold the strength of an army — an army that competed with those of other nations in pursuit of empire.

Team sports for men — like civilian military service — helped differentiate male and female spheres and thus promoted a social order based on distinction between the sexes.

Anglo-Indian Polo Team
Team sports underwent rapid development during the imperial years as spectators rooted for the success of their football team in the same spirit they rooted for their armies abroad. Some educators believed that team sports molded the male character so that men could be more effective soldiers against peoples of other races. In the case of polo, as illustrated by the team photo here, the English learned from the Indians what would soon be seen as a typically English sport. (Hulton Archive / Getty Images.)

Reformers introduced exercise classes and gymnastics into schools for girls, often with the idea that these would strengthen them for motherhood and thus help build the nation-state. As knowledge of the world developed, some women began to practice yoga, while wealthy men crossed the empire to challenge themselves with mountain climbing.

Working-class people adopted middle-class habits by joining clubs for such pursuits as bicycling, touring, and hiking. Clubs that sponsored trips often had names like the Patriots or the Nationals, making a clear association between physical fitness and national strength. The emphasis on healthy recreation gave people a greater sense of individual might and promoted an imperial citizenship based less on constitutions and rights than on an individual nation's exercise of raw power. A farmer's son in the 1890s boasted that with a bicycle, "I was king of the road, since I was faster than a horse."

Artistic Responses to Empire and Industry

In the 1870s and 1880s, the arts explored the process of global expansion and economic innovation, often in the same gloomy Darwinistic terms that made reformers anxious. Darwin's theory held out the possibility that strong civilizations, if they failed to adapt

to changing conditions, could weaken and collapse. French writer Émile Zola, influenced by fears of social decay, had a dark vision of how industrial society affected individuals. He produced a series of novels set in industrializing France about a family plagued by alcoholism and madness. His characters led violent strikes and in one case even castrated an oppressive grocer. Zola's novel *Women's Paradise* (1883) depicts the upper-class shopper who abandons rational decision making as a consumer for the frenzy of the new department stores. Other fictional heroines were equally upsetting because they violated other long-standing rules. The character Nora in the drama *A Doll's House* (1879), by Norwegian playwright Henrik Ibsen, undermines accepted values and the health of society by leaving an oppressive marriage.

Some decorative arts of this period featured a countertrend that celebrated a healthy and heroic rural life away from stark realism. Country people used mass-produced textiles to create traditional-looking costumes and developed ceremonies based on a mythical past. Such invented customs, romanticized as old and authentic, brought tourists from the cities to villages. Urban architects and industrial designers copied rustic styles when creating household goods and decorative objects. The influence of empire is apparent in the traditional Persian and Indian motifs used by English designers William Morris (1834–1896) and his daughter May Morris (1862–1938) in their designs of fabrics, wallpaper, and household items based on such natural imagery as the silhouettes of plants. They, too, wanted to replace "dead" and "ornate" styles of the early industrial years with the simple crafts of the past. Their work gave birth to the arts and crafts style, which paradoxically attracted consumers living in the industrial age.

Industrial developments directly influenced the work of painters, who by the 1870s felt intense competition from a popular industrial invention — the camera. Photographers could produce cheap copies of paintings and create more realistic portraits than painters could, at affordable prices. In response, painters altered their style, employing new and varying techniques to distinguish their art from the photographic realism of the camera. Claude Monet, for example, was fascinated by the way light transformed an object, and he often portrayed the same place — a bridge or a railroad station — at different times of day.

This daring style of art generally came to be called **impressionism**. It emphasizes the artist's attempt to capture a single moment by focusing on the ever-changing light and color found in ordinary scenes. Using splotches and dots, impressionists moved away from the precise realism of earlier painters. Vincent Van Gogh used vibrant colors in great swirls to capture sunflowers, haystacks, and the starry evening sky. Closely following the impressionists, French painter Georges Seurat depicted with thousands of dots and dabs the Parisian suburbs' newly created parks with their Sunday bicyclists and office workers in their store-bought clothing, carrying books or newspapers. Industry contributed to the new styles of painting, as factories produced a range of pigments that allowed artists to use a wider and more intense spectrum of colors than ever before.

An increasingly global vision also influenced painting in the age of empire. In both composition and style, impressionists borrowed heavily from Asian art and architecture. The impressionist goal of portraying the fleetingness of light or human situa-

Mary Cassatt, *The Letter* (c. 1890)
Mary Cassatt, an American artist who spent much of her time in Europe, was one of the many Western artists smitten by Japanese prints. Like many other Western artists of her day, she learned Japanese techniques for printmaking, but she also reshaped her painting style to follow Japanese conventions in composition, perspective, and the use of color. Cassatt is known for her many depictions of Western mothers and children and of individual women. In this painting, the woman herself even looks Japanese. (Worcester Art Museum, Worcester, Massachusetts, USA / The Bridgeman Art Library International.)

tions came from an ancient Japanese concept — *mono no aware* ("sensitivity to the fleetingness of life"). The color, line, and delicacy of Japanese art (which many impressionists collected) is evident, for example, in Monet's later paintings of water lilies and even his re-creation of a Japanese garden at his home in France as the subject for artistic study. Similarly, the American expatriate Mary Cassatt used the two-dimensionality of Japanese art in *The Letter* (1890–1891) and other paintings. Van Gogh sometimes filled the background of portraits with copies of intensely colored Japanese prints, and in some paintings he imitated classic Japanese woodcuts.

The graphic arts advanced the West's ongoing borrowing from around the globe while responding to the changes brought about by industry.

REVIEW QUESTION How did empire and industry influence art and everyday life?

The Birth of Mass Politics

Ordinary people struggled for political voice, especially through the vote, as they watched the wealth and influence of industry and empire increase. By bringing more people into closer contact with one another in cities, the growth of industries helped develop networks of political communication and awareness, leading western European

governments to allow more men to vote. Although only men profited from electoral reform in these nations, the era's expanding franchise marked the beginning of mass politics. Women could not vote, but they participated in public life by forming auxiliary groups to support political parties. Among the authoritarian monarchies, Germany had male suffrage, but in more autocratic states to the east — for instance, Russia — violence and ethnic conflict shaped political systems. In such places, the harsh rule from above often resembled the control imposed on colonized peoples.

Workers, Politics, and Protest

As the nineteenth century entered its final decades, workers organized formal unions, which attracted the allegiance of millions. Unions reacted to workplace hardships, demanding a say in working conditions and aiming, as one union's rule book put it, "to ensure that wages never suffer illegitimate reductions and that they always follow the rises in the price of basic commodities." Businessmen and governments viewed striking workers as insubordinate, threatening political unrest and destructive violence. Even so, strong unions appealed to some industrialists because a union could make strikes more predictable (or even prevent them) and present worker demands coherently instead of piecemeal by groups of angry workers.

From the 1880s on, the pace of collective action for better pay, lower prices, and better working conditions accelerated. In 1888, for example, hundreds of young women who made matches, the so-called London matchgirls, went on strike to end the fining system, under which they could be penalized an entire day's wage for being a minute or two late to work. The fines, the matchgirls maintained, helped companies reap profits of more than 20 percent. In 1890, sixty thousand workers took to the streets of Budapest to agitate for safer working conditions and the vote; the next year, day laborers on Hungarian farms struck, too. Across Europe between 1888 and 1890, the number of strikes and major demonstrations rose by more than 50 percent, from 188 to 289.

Housewives, who often acted in support of strikers, carried out their own protests against high food prices. They confiscated merchants' goods and sold them at what they considered a fair price. "There should no longer be either rich or poor," argued Italian peasant women. "All should have bread for themselves and for their children." Housewives often hid neighbors' truant children from school officials so that the children could continue to help with work at home. When landlords evicted tenants, women gathered in the streets to return the ousted families' household goods as fast as they were removed. Meeting on doorsteps or at markets, women initiated rural newcomers into urban ways. In doing so, they helped cement the working-class unity created by workers in the factory.

Governments increasingly responded to strikes by calling out troops or armed police, even though most strikes were about working conditions and not about political revolution. Despite government force, unions did not back down or lose their commitment to solidarity. Craft-based unions of skilled artisans, such as carpenters and printers, were the most active and cohesive, but from the mid-1880s on, a movement known

as **new unionism** attracted transport workers, miners, matchgirls, and dockworkers. These new unions were nationwide groups with salaried managers who could plan a widespread general strike across the trades, focusing on such common goals as achieving the eight-hour workday but also paralyzing an entire nation through work stoppages. Large unions had the potential for challenging large industries, cartels, and trusts.

Working-class political parties developed from unions. Workingmen helped create the Labour Party in England, the Socialist Party in France, and the Social Democratic Parties of Sweden, Hungary, Austria, and Germany — most of them inspired by Marxist theories. Germany was home to the largest socialist party in Europe after 1890. Socialist parties held out hope that newly enfranchised male working-class voters could become a collective force in national elections, even triumphing over the power of the upper class.

Those who accepted Marx's assertion that "workingmen have no country" also founded an international movement to address workers' common interests across national boundaries. In 1889, some four hundred socialists from across Europe met to form the **Second International**, a federation of working-class organizations and political parties that replaced the First International, founded by Marx before the Paris Commune. The Second International adopted a Marxist revolutionary program, but it also advocated suffrage (in countries where it still did not exist) and better working conditions.

Members of the Second International determined to rid the organization of anarchists, who flourished in the less industrial parts of Europe — Russia, Italy, and Spain — where Marxist theories of worker-controlled factories had less appeal. In an age of tough international competition in agriculture, many rural workers sought a life free from governments that backed the landowners' interests. Thus, many advocated extreme tactics, including physical violence. "We want to overthrow the government . . . with violence since it is by the use of violence that they force us to obey," wrote one Italian anarchist. In the 1880s, anarchists bombed stock exchanges, parliaments, and businesses. Members of the Second International felt that such random violence was counterproductive.

Workingwomen joined unions and workers' political parties, but in much smaller numbers than men. Unable to vote in national elections and usually responsible for housework in addition to their paying jobs, women had little time for party meetings. In addition, their lower wages hardly allowed them to survive, much less pay party or union dues. Many workingmen also opposed women's presence in unions. Contact with women would mean "suffocation," one Russian workingman believed, and end male union members' sense of being "comrades in the revolutionary cause." Unions glorified the heroic struggles of a male proletariat against capitalism. Marxist leaders maintained that capitalism alone caused injustice to women and thus that the creation of a socialist society would automatically end gender inequality. As a result, although the new political organizations wanted women's support, they dismissed women's concerns about lower wages and sexual harassment.

Popular community activities further strengthened worker solidarity. The gymnastics and musical societies that had once united Europeans in nationalistic fervor now

served working-class goals. Socialist gymnastics, bicycling, and marching societies promoted physical fitness because it could help workers in the "struggle for existence" — a reflection of the spread of Darwinian thinking to all levels of society. Workers also held festivals and cheerful parades, most notably on May 1 — a centuries-old holiday that the Second International now claimed as a labor holiday. Like religious processions of an earlier time, parades fostered unity. As a result, governments frequently banned such public gatherings, calling them a public danger.

Expanding Political Participation in Western Europe

Ordinary people everywhere in the West were becoming aware of politics through newspapers, which, combined with industrial and imperial progress, were important in developing a sense of citizenship in a nation. After 1880, western European countries moved toward mass politics more rapidly than did countries to the east, thanks in part to the rise of mass journalism — itself the product of imperial and industrial development. The invention of automatic typesetting and the production of newsprint from wood pulp lowered the costs of printing, and the telephone allowed reporters to communicate news to their papers almost instantly. Once literary in content, many daily newspapers now emphasized sensational news, using banner headlines, dramatic pictures, and gruesome or lurid details — particularly about murders and sexual scandals — to sell papers. In the hustle and bustle of industrial society, one editor wrote that "you must strike your reader right between the eyes." Stories of imperial adventurers and exaggerated accounts of exploited women workers, some in the white slave trade, drew ordinary people to the mass press.

Journalism created a national community of up-to-date citizens, whether or not they could vote. Unlike the book, the newspaper was meant not for quiet reflection at home or in the upper-class club but for quick reading of attention-grabbing stories on mass transportation and on the streets. Elites complained that the sensationalist press was a sign of social decay, but in western Europe increasing political literacy opened the political process to wider participation.

A change in political campaigning was one example of this widening participation. In the fall of 1879, **William Gladstone** (1809–1898), leader of the British Liberals, whose party was then out of power, took a train trip across Britain to campaign for a seat in the House of Commons. During his campaign, Gladstone addressed thousands of workers, arguing for the people of India and Africa to have more rights and summoning his audiences to "honest, manful, humble effort" in the middle-class tradition of "hard work." Newspapers around the country reported on his trip, and these accounts, along with mass meetings, fueled public interest in politics. Gladstone's campaign was successful, and he took the post of prime minister for the second of the four nonconsecutive terms he served between 1868 and 1894.

Other changes fostered the growth of political participation in Britain. The Ballot Act of 1872 made voting secret, a reform that reduced the ability of landlords and employers to control how their workers voted. The **Reform Act of 1884** doubled the elec-

torate to around 4.5 million men, enfranchising many urban workers and artisans and thus further diminishing traditional aristocratic influence in the countryside. To win the votes of the newly enfranchised, Liberal and Conservative parties alike established national political clubs that competed with small cliques of parliamentary elites for control of party politics. Broadly based interest groups such as unions and national political clubs opened up politics by appealing to many more voters.

British political reforms immediately affected Irish politics by arming poor tenant farmers with the secret ballot. The political climate in Ireland was explosive mainly because of the repressive tactics of absentee landlords, many of them English and Protestant, who drove Irish tenants from their land in order to charge higher rents to newcomers. In 1879, opponents of these landlords formed the Irish National Land League and launched fiery protests. Irish tenants elected a solid bloc of nationalist representatives to the British Parliament, who, voting as a group, had sufficient strength to defeat either the Conservatives or the Liberals. Irish leader **Charles Stewart Parnell** (1846–1891) demanded British support for **home rule** — a system giving Ireland its own parliament — in return for Irish votes. Conservatives called home rule "a conspiracy against the honor of Britain," and when they were in power (1885–1886 and 1886–1892), they cracked down on Irish activism. Scandals reported in the press, some of them totally invented, weakened Parnell's influence. In 1890, the news broke of his affair with a married woman, and he died in disgrace soon after, as the media determined politics. Still, Irish home rule remained a heated political issue, as did the determination to end Ireland's colonial status.

France's **Third Republic** replaced the Second Empire. The republic was shaky at the start because the monarchist political factions — Bonapartist, Orléanist, and Bourbon — all struggled to destroy it. Their failure to do so led in 1875 to the adoption of a new constitution, which created a ceremonial presidency and a premier (prime minister) dependent on support from the elected Chamber of Deputies. An alliance of businessmen, shopkeepers, professionals, and rural property owners hoped the new system would prevent the kind of strongman politics that had seen previous republics give way to the rule of emperors and the return of monarchs.

Fragile at birth, the Third Republic would remain so until World War II. Economic downturns, widespread corruption, and growing anti-Semitism fueled by a highly partisan and monarchist press kept the Third Republic on shaky ground. Newspaper stories about members of the Chamber of Deputies selling their votes to business interests and about the alleged trickery of Jewish businessmen manipulating the economy added to the instability. As a result, the public also blamed Jews for problems in the republican government and the economy.

In 1889, those disgusted by the messiness of parliamentary politics backed Georges Boulanger, a dashing and highly popular general, in his attempt to take over the government. Boulanger soon lost his nerve, however, thereby saving the French from rule by another strongman. Still, Boulanger's popularity showed that in hard economic times, liberal values based on constitutions, elections, and the rights of citizens could be called into question by someone promising easy solutions.

middle class was gaining power and influence. Working-class people often suffered from the effects of rapid industrial change when their labor was replaced by machinery. Millions relocated to escape poor conditions in the countryside and to find new opportunities. Political reform, especially the expansion of suffrage, helped working-class men gain a political voice. Workers formed unions and political parties to protect their interests, but governments often responded to workers' activism with repression.

As workers struck for improved wages and conditions and the impoverished migrated to find a better life, the advance of empire and industry was bringing unprecedented tensions to national politics, the international scene, and everyday life. By the 1890s, racism and anti-Semitism were spreading, and many were questioning the costs of empire both to their own nation and conquered peoples. Politics in the authoritarian countries of central and eastern Europe was taking a more conservative turn, resisting participation and reform. The rising tensions of modern life would soon have grave consequences for the West as a whole.

Review Questions

1. What were the goals of the new imperialism, and how did Europeans accomplish those goals?
2. What were the major changes in Western industry and business by the end of the nineteenth century?

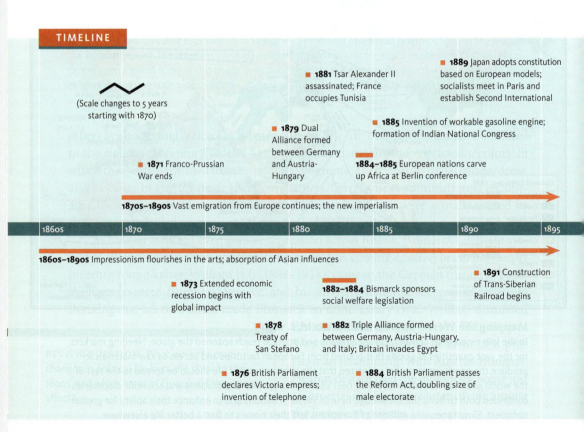

TIMELINE

(Scale changes to 5 years starting with 1870)

- **1881** Tsar Alexander II assassinated; France occupies Tunisia

- **1889** Japan adopts constitution based on European models; socialists meet in Paris and establish Second International

- **1879** Dual Alliance formed between Germany and Austria-Hungary

- **1885** Invention of workable gasoline engine; formation of Indian National Congress

- **1871** Franco-Prussian War ends

- **1884–1885** European nations carve up Africa at Berlin conference

1870s–1890s Vast emigration from Europe continues; the new imperialism

| 1860s | 1870 | 1875 | 1880 | 1885 | 1890 | 1895 |

1860s–1890s Impressionism flourishes in the arts; absorption of Asian influences

- **1873** Extended economic recession begins with global impact

- **1882–1884** Bismarck sponsors social welfare legislation

- **1891** Construction of Trans-Siberian Railroad begins

- **1878** Treaty of San Stefano

- **1882** Triple Alliance formed between Germany, Austria-Hungary, and Italy; Britain invades Egypt

- **1876** British Parliament declares Victoria empress; invention of telephone

- **1884** British Parliament passes the Reform Act, doubling size of male electorate

Conclusion

The period from the 1870s to the 1890s has been called the age of empire and industry because Western society pursued both these ends in a way that rapidly transformed Europe and the world. Much of Europe thrived due to industrial innovation, becoming more populous and more urbanized. Using the innovative weapons streaming from Europe's factories, the great powers undertook a new imperialism that established political rule over foreign peoples. As they tightened connections with the rest of the globe, Europeans proudly spread their supposedly superior culture throughout the world and, like Frieda von Bülow and Carl Peters, sought out more power and wealth.

Imperial expansion and industrial change affected all social classes. The upper class attempted to maintain its position of social and political dominance, while an expanding

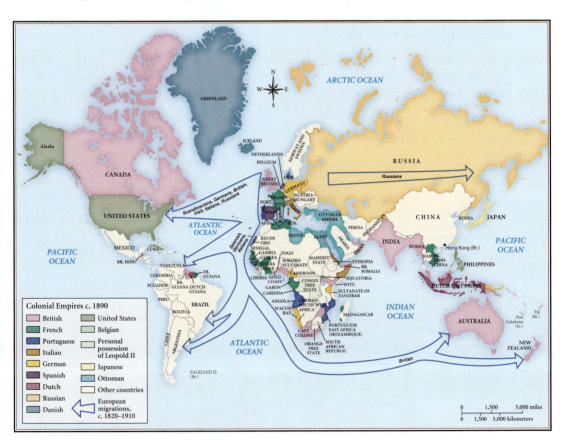

Mapping the West The West and the World, c. 1890
In the late nineteenth century, European trade and political reach spanned the globe. Needing markets for the vast quantities of goods that poured from European factories and access to raw materials to produce the goods, governments asserted that the Western way of life should be spread to the rest of the world and that resources would be best used by Europeans. Explorations and scientific discoveries continued both to build the knowledge base of Western nations and to enhance their ability for greater conquest. Simultaneously, millions of Europeans left their homes to find a better life elsewhere.

middle class was gaining power and influence. Working-class people often suffered from the effects of rapid industrial change when their labor was replaced by machinery. Millions relocated to escape poor conditions in the countryside and to find new opportunities. Political reform, especially the expansion of suffrage, helped working-class men gain a political voice. Workers formed unions and political parties to protect their interests, but governments often responded to workers' activism with repression.

As workers struck for improved wages and conditions and the impoverished migrated to find a better life, the advance of empire and industry was bringing unprecedented tensions to national politics, the international scene, and everyday life. By the 1890s, racism and anti-Semitism were spreading, and many were questioning the costs of empire both to their own nation and conquered peoples. Politics in the authoritarian countries of central and eastern Europe was taking a more conservative turn, resisting participation and reform. The rising tensions of modern life would soon have grave consequences for the West as a whole.

Review Questions

1. What were the goals of the new imperialism, and how did Europeans accomplish those goals?
2. What were the major changes in Western industry and business by the end of the nineteenth century?

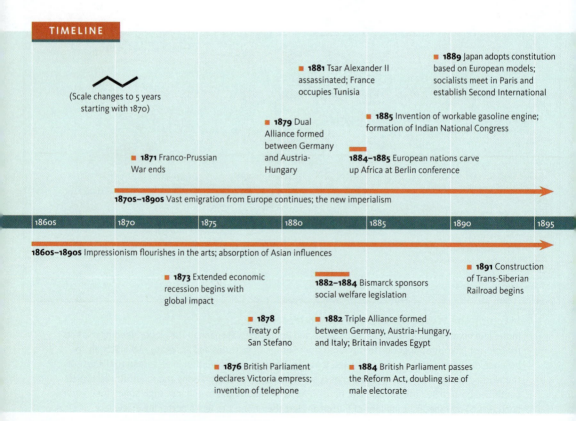

TIMELINE

(Scale changes to 5 years starting with 1870)

■ **1881** Tsar Alexander II assassinated; France occupies Tunisia

■ **1889** Japan adopts constitution based on European models; socialists meet in Paris and establish Second International

■ **1879** Dual Alliance formed between Germany and Austria-Hungary

■ **1885** Invention of workable gasoline engine; formation of Indian National Congress

■ **1871** Franco-Prussian War ends

1884–1885 European nations carve up Africa at Berlin conference

1870s–1890s Vast emigration from Europe continues; the new imperialism

| 1860s | 1870 | 1875 | 1880 | 1885 | 1890 | 1895 |

1860s–1890s Impressionism flourishes in the arts; absorption of Asian influences

■ **1873** Extended economic recession begins with global impact

1882–1884 Bismarck sponsors social welfare legislation

■ **1891** Construction of Trans-Siberian Railroad begins

■ **1878** Treaty of San Stefano

■ **1882** Triple Alliance formed between Germany, Austria-Hungary, and Italy; Britain invades Egypt

■ **1876** British Parliament declares Victoria empress; invention of telephone

■ **1884** British Parliament passes the Reform Act, doubling size of male electorate

Torah Scrolls
After the assassination of Alexander II in 1881, the government unleashed pogroms against the Jews of the Russian Empire. The pogroms involved violent acts such as murder, beatings, and the destruction of property on a grand scale. In this image, Jewish men survey the damage done to the sacred texts of their religion during one such vicious attack. (© From the Jewish Chronicle Archive / Heritage Images / The Image Works.)

others as a horrifying menace to Russian culture. The five million Russian Jews, confined to the eighteenth-century Pale of Settlement (the name for the restricted territory in which they were permitted to live), endured pogroms. Their distinctive language, dress, and isolation in ghettos made them easy targets. Government administrators encouraged these pogroms, blaming Jews for rising living costs that were actually caused by the high taxes levied on peasants to pay for industrialization.

As the tsar inflicted even greater repression across Russia, Bismarck's delicate system of alliances of the three conservative powers was coming apart. A brash but deeply insecure young kaiser, William II (r. 1888–1918), came to the German throne in 1888. William resented Bismarck's power, and his advisers flattered the young man into thinking that his own talent made Bismarck an unnecessary rival. William dismissed Bismarck in 1890 and let the Reinsurance Treaty with Russia lapse in favor of a pro-German relationship with Austria-Hungary. He thus destabilized the diplomatic scene just as imperial rivalries were intensifying among the European powers.

REVIEW QUESTION What were the major changes in political life from the 1870s to the 1890s, and which areas of Europe did they most affect?

Map 23.4 The Balkans, c. 1878
After midcentury, the map of the Balkans was almost constantly redrawn. This resulted in part from
the weakness of the dominant Ottoman Empire but also from the ambitions of inhabitants themselves
and from great-power rivalry. In tune with the growing sense of national identities based on shared
culture, history, and ethnicity, various Balkan peoples sought to emphasize local, small-group identities
rather than merging around a single dominant group such as the Serbs. Yet there was also a move by
some intellectuals to transcend borders and create a southern Slav culture.

like Tolstoy, idealizes the peasantry's stoic endurance. Dostoevsky satirized Russia's radicals in *The Possessed* (1871), a novel in which a group of revolutionaries murders one of
its own members. In Dostoevsky's view, the radicals were simply destructive, offering no
solutions whatsoever to Russia's ills.

Despite the influential critiques published by Tolstoy and Dostoevsky, violent action
rather than spiritual uplift remained the foundation of radicalism. In 1881, the People's
Will, a splinter group of Land and Liberty, killed Tsar Alexander II in a bomb attack.
The tsar's death, however, failed to provoke the general uprising the terrorists expected.
Alexander III (r. 1881–1894) unleashed a new wave of oppression against religious and
ethnic minorities. Popular books and drawings depicted Tatars, Poles, Ukrainians, and

sent aid to the Balkan rebels and so pressured the tsar's government that Russia declared war on Turkey in 1877 in the name of protecting Orthodox Christians. With help from Romania and Greece, Russia defeated the Ottomans and by the Treaty of San Stefano (1878) created a large, pro-Russian Bulgaria.

The Treaty of San Stefano sparked an international uproar. Austria-Hungary and Britain feared that an enlarged Bulgaria would become a Russian satellite that would enable the tsar to dominate the Balkans. Austrian officials worried about an uprising of their own restless Slavs. British prime minister Benjamin Disraeli moved warships into position against Russia in order to halt the advance of Russian influence in the eastern Mediterranean, so close to Britain's routes through the Suez Canal. The public was drawn into foreign policy: the music halls and newspapers of England echoed a new jingoism, or political sloganeering, that throbbed with militarism: "We don't want to fight, but by jingo if we do, / We've got the ships, we've got the men, we've got the money too!"

The other great powers, however, did not want a Europe-wide war, and in 1878 they attempted to revive the concert of Europe by meeting at Berlin under the auspices of Bismarck — now a calming presence on the diplomatic scene. The Congress of Berlin rolled back the Russian victory by partitioning the large Bulgarian state carved out of Ottoman territory and denying any part of Bulgaria full independence from the Ottomans (Map 23.4). Austria occupied (but did not annex) Bosnia and Herzegovina as a way of gaining clout in the Balkans; Serbia and Montenegro became fully independent. The Balkans remained a site of ambition for independence and great-power rivalries.

Following the Congress of Berlin, the European powers attempted to guarantee stability through a complex series of alliances and treaties. Anxious about the Balkans, Austria-Hungary forged a defensive alliance with Germany in 1879. The **Dual Alliance**, as it was called, offered protection against Russia and its potential for inciting Slav rebellions. In 1882, Italy joined this partnership (henceforth called the Triple Alliance), largely because of Italy's imperial rivalries with France. Bismarck negotiated the Reinsurance Treaty (1887) with Russia to keep the Habsburgs from recklessly starting a war over Pan-Slavism.

Russia itself was beset by domestic problems in the 1870s and 1880s. Young Russians were turning to revolution for solutions to political and social problems. One such group, the Populists, wanted to rouse debt-ridden peasants to revolt. Other people formed terrorist bands to assassinate public officials. The secret police rounded up hundreds of members of one of the largest groups, Land and Liberty, and subjected them to brutal torture and show trials. When in 1877 a young radical, Vera Zasulich, tried unsuccessfully to assassinate the chief of the St. Petersburg police, the people of the capital city applauded her act and acquittal, so great was their outrage at government treatment of young radicals from respectable families.

Writers debated Russia's future, mobilizing public opinion over these issues. Novelists Leo Tolstoy, author of the epic *War and Peace* (1869), and Fyodor Dostoevsky, a former radical, believed that Russia above all required spiritual regeneration — not revolution. Tolstoy's novel *Anna Karenina* (1877) tells the story of an impassioned love affair, but it also weaves in the spiritual quest of Levin, a former "progressive" landowner who,

Map 23.3 Expansion of Berlin to 1914
"A capital city is essential for the state to act as a pivot for its culture," the German historian Heinrich von Treitschke asserted. No other capital city grew as dramatically as Berlin after German unification in 1871. Industrialists and bankers set themselves up in the new capital, while workers migrated there for jobs, swelling the population. The city was newly dotted with military monuments and with museums to show off its culture.

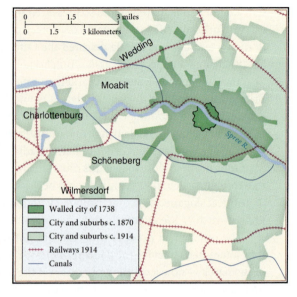

Party in 1878, and, hoping to lure the working class away from socialism, between 1882 and 1884 he sponsored an accident and disability insurance program — the first of its kind in Europe. In 1879, he put through tariffs protecting German agriculture and industry from foreign competition but also raising the prices of consumer goods, including food for ordinary people. Ending his support for laissez-faire economics, Bismarck broke with political liberals while simultaneously increasing the power of the agrarian conservatives by attacking the interests of Germany's industrial sector.

Like Germany, Austria-Hungary frequently employed liberal economic policies and practices. From the 1860s, liberal businessmen succeeded in industrializing parts of the empire, and the prosperous middle classes erected conspicuously large homes, giving themselves a prominence in urban life that rivaled the aristocracy's. They persuaded the government to enact free-trade provisions in the 1870s and to search out foreign investment to build up infrastructure, such as railroads.

Despite these measures, Austria-Hungary remained monarchist and authoritarian. Liberals in Austria — most of them ethnic Germans — saw their influence weaken under the leadership of Count Edouard von Taaffe, Austrian prime minister from 1879 to 1893. Building a coalition of clergy, conservatives, and Slavic parties, Taaffe used its power to weaken the liberals. In Bohemia, for example, he designated Czech as an official language of the bureaucracy and school system, thus breaking the German speakers' monopoly on officeholding. Reforms outraged individuals at whose expense other ethnic groups received benefits, yet those who won concessions, such as the Czechs, clamored for even greater autonomy. By playing nationalities off one another, the government ensured the monarchy's central role in holding together competing interest groups.

Nationalists in the Balkans demanded independence from the declining Ottoman Empire, raising Austro-Hungarian fears and ambitions. In 1876, Slavs in Bulgaria and Bosnia-Herzegovina revolted against Turkish rule, killing Ottoman officials. As the Ottomans slaughtered thousands of Bulgarians in turn, two other small Balkan states, Serbia and Montenegro, rebelled against the sultan, too. Russian Pan-Slavic organizations

torate to around 4.5 million men, enfranchising many urban workers and artisans and thus further diminishing traditional aristocratic influence in the countryside. To win the votes of the newly enfranchised, Liberal and Conservative parties alike established national political clubs that competed with small cliques of parliamentary elites for control of party politics. Broadly based interest groups such as unions and national political clubs opened up politics by appealing to many more voters.

British political reforms immediately affected Irish politics by arming poor tenant farmers with the secret ballot. The political climate in Ireland was explosive mainly because of the repressive tactics of absentee landlords, many of them English and Protestant, who drove Irish tenants from their land in order to charge higher rents to newcomers. In 1879, opponents of these landlords formed the Irish National Land League and launched fiery protests. Irish tenants elected a solid bloc of nationalist representatives to the British Parliament, who, voting as a group, had sufficient strength to defeat either the Conservatives or the Liberals. Irish leader **Charles Stewart Parnell** (1846–1891) demanded British support for **home rule** — a system giving Ireland its own parliament — in return for Irish votes. Conservatives called home rule "a conspiracy against the honor of Britain," and when they were in power (1885–1886 and 1886–1892), they cracked down on Irish activism. Scandals reported in the press, some of them totally invented, weakened Parnell's influence. In 1890, the news broke of his affair with a married woman, and he died in disgrace soon after, as the media determined politics. Still, Irish home rule remained a heated political issue, as did the determination to end Ireland's colonial status.

France's **Third Republic** replaced the Second Empire. The republic was shaky at the start because the monarchist political factions — Bonapartist, Orléanist, and Bourbon — all struggled to destroy it. Their failure to do so led in 1875 to the adoption of a new constitution, which created a ceremonial presidency and a premier (prime minister) dependent on support from the elected Chamber of Deputies. An alliance of businessmen, shopkeepers, professionals, and rural property owners hoped the new system would prevent the kind of strongman politics that had seen previous republics give way to the rule of emperors and the return of monarchs.

Fragile at birth, the Third Republic would remain so until World War II. Economic downturns, widespread corruption, and growing anti-Semitism fueled by a highly partisan and monarchist press kept the Third Republic on shaky ground. Newspaper stories about members of the Chamber of Deputies selling their votes to business interests and about the alleged trickery of Jewish businessmen manipulating the economy added to the instability. As a result, the public also blamed Jews for problems in the republican government and the economy.

In 1889, those disgusted by the messiness of parliamentary politics backed Georges Boulanger, a dashing and highly popular general, in his attempt to take over the government. Boulanger soon lost his nerve, however, thereby saving the French from rule by another strongman. Still, Boulanger's popularity showed that in hard economic times, liberal values based on constitutions, elections, and the rights of citizens could be called into question by someone promising easy solutions.

Republican leaders attempted to strengthen citizen loyalty by instituting compulsory and free public education in the 1880s. In public schools, secular teachers who supported republicanism replaced the Catholic clergy, who usually favored a return to monarchy. A common curriculum — identical in every schoolhouse in the country — featured patriotic reading books and courses in French geography, literature, and history. The government established secular public high schools for young women, seen as the educators of future citizens, while mandatory military service for men inculcated pride in the republic rather than in the monarchy or the church.

Although many western European leaders believed in economic liberalism, constitutions, and efficient government, these ideals did not always translate into universal male suffrage and citizens' rights in the less powerful western European countries. Spain and Belgium abruptly awarded suffrage to all men in 1890 and 1893, respectively, while remaining monarchies. An alliance of conservative landowners and the Catholic church dominated Spain, although there was increasingly lively urban activism in the industrial centers of Barcelona and Bilbao. Reform in the Netherlands increased male suffrage to only 14 percent by the mid-1890s, and an 1887 law in Italy gave the vote to all men who had a primary school education, also 14 percent of the male population. Without receiving the benefits of nation building — education, urban improvements, industrial progress, and the vote — the average Italian in the south felt less loyalty to the new nation than fear of the devastating effects of national taxes and the draft on the family economy.

Power Politics in Central and Eastern Europe

Germany, Austria-Hungary, and Russia diverged from the political paths taken by western European countries in the decades 1870–1890. In all three countries, conservative large landowners remained powerful, often blocking improvements in transport, sanitation, and tariff policy that would support a growing urban population. But Bismarck, who had upset the European balance of power by humiliating France in the Franco-Prussian War, created a powerful, unified Germany, with explosive economic growth and rapid development of every aspect of the nation-state, from transport to the thriving capital city of Berlin (Map 23.3).

His goals achieved, Bismarck now desired stability built on diplomacy instead of war. Needing peace to consolidate the new nation, he pronounced Germany "satisfied," meaning that it sought no new territory in Europe. To ensure Germany's long-term security, in 1873 Bismarck forged the Three Emperors' League — an alliance of Germany, Austria-Hungary, and Russia. The three conservative powers shared a commitment to maintaining the political status quo.

At home, Bismarck, who owned land and invested personally in industry, joined with the liberals to create a variety of financial institutions, including a central bank to advance German commerce and industry. After religious leaders defeated his Kulturkampf against Catholicism, Bismarck turned to attacking socialists and liberals instead of Catholics as enemies of the regime. He outlawed the workers' Social Democratic

3. How did empire and industry influence art and everyday life?

4. What were the major changes in political life from the 1870s to the 1890s, and which areas of Europe did they most affect?

Making Connections

1. How did the new imperialism differ from European expansion of two centuries earlier? Of four centuries earlier?

2. Describe the effects of imperialism on European politics and society as a whole in 1870–1890.

3. Compare the political and social goals of the newly enfranchised male electorate with those of people from the "best circles."

- For practice quizzes and other study tools, visit the **Online Study Guide** at bedfordstmartins.com/huntconcise.

- For primary-source material from this period, see *Sources of the Making of the West*, Fourth Edition.

- For Web sites, images, and documents related to topics in this chapter, visit *Make History* at bedfordstmartins.com/huntconcise.

Suggested References

The literature on imperialism is becoming increasingly exciting, especially as authors such as Burbank and Cooper show imperialism's relationship with the nation-state. Others show its confusions and chaotic nature.

Burbank, Jane, and Frederick Cooper. *Empires in World History: Power and the Politics of Difference*. 2010.

Cain, P. J., and A. G. Hopkins. *British Imperialism, 1688–2000*. 2002.

Davis, Mike. *Late Victorian Holocausts: El Niño Famines and the Making of the Third World*. 2001.

Eley, Geoff. *Forging Democracy: A History of the Left in Europe, 1850–2000*. 2002.

Headrick, Daniel R. *Power over Peoples: Technology, Environments, and Western Imperialism 1400 to the Present*. 2010.

Lorcin, Patricia M. E., ed. *Algeria and France 1800–2000: Identity, Memory, Nostalgia*. 2006.

Manning, Patrick. *Migration in World History*. 2005.

Maynes, Mary Jo, et al. *Secret Gardens, Satanic Mills: Placing Girls in European History, 1750–1960*. 2005.

Rappaport, Erika. *Shopping for Pleasure: Women in the Making of London's West End*. 2000.

Reeder, Linda. *Widows in White: Migration and the Transformation of Rural Italian Women, Sicily, 1880–1920*. 2003.

Reid, Richard J. *A History of Modern Africa*. 2009.

Smith, Michael S. *The Emergence of Modern Business Enterprise in France, 1800–1930*. 2005.

Streets, Heather. *Martial Races: The Military, Race, and Masculinity in British Imperial Culture, 1857–1918*. 2004.

Weaver, Stewart, and Maurice Isserman. *Fallen Giants: A History of Himalayan Mountaineering from the Age of Empire to the Age of Extremes*. 2008.

Wildenthal, Lora. *German Women for Empire, 1884–1945*. 2001.

Modernity and the Road to War

I N THE FIRST DECADE of the twentieth century, a wealthy young Russian man traveled from one country to another to find relief from a common malady of the time called neurasthenia. Its symptoms included fatigue, lack of interest in life, depression, and sometimes physical illness. In 1910, the young man consulted Sigmund Freud, a Viennese physician whose unconventional treatment — eventually called psychoanalysis — took the form of a conversation about the patient's dreams, sexual experiences, and everyday life. Over the course of four years, Freud uncovered his patient's deeply hidden fear of castration, which was disguised as a fear of wolves — thus the name Wolf-Man, by which he is known to us. Freud worked his cure, as the Wolf-Man himself put it, "by bringing repressed ideas into consciousness" through extensive talking.

In many ways, the Wolf-Man could be said to represent his time. Born into a family that owned vast estates, he reflected Europe's growing prosperity, though on a grander scale than most. Countless individuals were troubled, even mentally disturbed like the Wolf-Man, and suicides were not uncommon. The Wolf-Man's own sister and father died from intentional drug overdoses. As the twentieth century opened, Europeans raised questions about family, gender relationships, empire, religion, and the consequences of technology. Every sign of imperial wealth brought on an apparently irrational sense of Europe's decline. British writer H. G. Wells saw in this prosperous era "the sunset of mankind." Gloom filled the pages of many a book and upset the lives of individuals like the Wolf-Man.

Edvard Munch, *The Scream* (1893)
In some of his paintings, Norwegian artist Edvard Munch captured a certain spirit of the turn of the century, depicting in soft pastel colors the newly leisured life of people strolling in the countryside. But modern life also had a tortured side, which Munch was equally capable of portraying. *The Scream* is taken as emblematic of the torments of modernity as the individual turns inward, beset by neuroses, self-destructive impulses, and even madness. It can also be suggested that the screamer, like Europe, travels the road to World War I. (Scala / Art Resource, NY / © 2012 The Munch Museum / The Munch-Ellingsen Group / Artists Rights Society [ARS], New York.)

Conflict rattled the world as a growing number of powers, including Japan and the United States, fought their way into even more territories. The nations of Europe had lurched from one diplomatic crisis to another over access to global resources and control of territory — both within Europe and outside it. Competition for empire fueled an arms race that threatened to turn Europe — the most civilized region of the world, according to its leaders — into a savage battleground. In domestic politics, militant nationalism stirred ethnic hatreds and furthered anti-Semitic violence. Women suffragists along with other politically disadvantaged groups such as the Slavs and Irish demanded full rights, even as political assassinations and public brutality swept away the liberal values of tolerance and human rights.

These were just some of the conflicts associated with the term *modernity*, often used to describe the rise of mass politics, the spread of technology, and the faster pace of life — all of which were visible in the West from the late nineteenth century on. The word *modern* was also applied to art, music, science, and philosophy of this period. Although many people today admire the brilliant, innovative qualities of modern art, music, and dance, people of the time were offended, even outraged, by the new styles and sounds. Freud's theory that sexual drives exist in even the youngest children shocked people. Every advance in science and the arts simultaneously undermined middle-class faith in the stability of Western civilization.

That faith was further tested when the heir to the Austro-Hungarian throne was assassinated in June 1914. Few gave much thought to the global significance of the event, least of all the Wolf-Man, whose treatment with Freud was just ending. He viewed the fateful day of June 28 simply as the day he "could now leave Vienna a healthy man." Yet the assassination put the spark to the powder keg of international discord that had been building for several decades. The resulting disastrous war, World War I, like the insights of Freud, would transform life in the West.

CHAPTER FOCUS How did developments in social life, art, intellectual life, and politics at the turn of the twentieth century produce instability and set the backdrop for war?

Public Debate over Private Life

At the beginning of the twentieth century, an increasing number of people could aspire to a comfortable family life because of Europe's improved standard of living. Yet as the twentieth century opened, traditional social norms such as heterosexual marriage and woman's domestic role as wife and mother came under attack by what were seen as the forces of modernity. The falling birthrate, rising divorce rate, and growing activism for marriage reform provoked heated accusations that changes in private life were endangering national health. Discussions about sexual identity became a political issue, and some feared the disappearance of distinct gender roles. Women's visibility in public life prompted one British songster in the late 1890s to write:

> Rock-a-bye baby, for father is near
> Mother is "biking" she never is here!

> Out in the park she's scorching all day
> Or at some meeting is talking away!

Discussions of gender roles and private life contributed to rising social tensions because they challenged so many traditional ideals. Freud and other scientists tried to be dispassionate in their study of such phenomena — sexuality, for example — and to formulate treatments for so-called modern ailments such as those afflicting the Wolf-Man.

Population Pressure

From the 1890s on, European politicians and the public hotly discussed urgent concerns over trends in population, marriage, and sexuality. The European population continued to grow as the twentieth century opened. Germany's population increased from 41 million in 1871 to 64 million in 1910, and tiny Denmark's grew from 1.7 million in 1870 to 2.7 million in 1911. Contributing to the increase were improvements in sanitation and public health, which reduced infant mortality and extended the average human life span. Following the earlier examples of Vienna and Paris, planners tore apart and rebuilt Budapest, Moscow, and Berlin (whose population grew to over 4 million). Less-powerful states also rebuilt cities to absorb population growth: the Balkan capitals of Sofia, Belgrade, and Bucharest gained tree-lined boulevards and improved sanitation facilities.

While the absolute size of the population was rising in the West, the birthrate (measured in births per thousand people) was falling. The birthrate had been decreasing in France since the eighteenth century; other European countries began experiencing the decline late in the nineteenth century. The Swedish birthrate dropped from thirty-five births per thousand people in 1859 to twenty-four per thousand in 1911; Germany went from forty births per thousand in 1875 to twenty-seven per thousand in 1913.

Industrialization and urbanization helped bring about this change. Farm families needed fewer hands because new agricultural machinery was taking the place of human laborers. In cities, individual couples were free to make their own decisions about limiting family size, learning from neighbors or, for those with enough money and education, from pamphlets and advice books about birth-control practices, including coitus interruptus (the withdrawal method of preventing pregnancy). Industrial technology played a further role in curtailing reproduction: condoms, improved after the vulcanization of rubber in the 1840s, proved fairly reliable in preventing conception, as did the diaphragm. Abortions were also common.

The wider use of birth control roused critics who accused middle-class women of holding a "birth strike." Bishops in the Church of England condemned family limitation as "demoralizing to character and hostile to national welfare." Politicians worried that the drop in the birthrate was due to a crisis in masculinity, which would put military strength at risk. The "quality" of those being born worried activists: If the "best" classes had fewer children, politicians asked, what would society look like if only the "worst" classes grew in number? The decline in fertility, one German nationalist warned, would fill the country with "alien peoples, above all Slavs and probably East European

Large Czech Family
This photograph of a rural family in Czechoslovakia shows the differences that were coming to distinguish urban from rural people. Although even members of a farm family, especially in eastern Europe, might proudly display technology such as a new phonograph, they might not practice family limitation, which was gradually reducing the size of urban households. In eastern Europe, several generations lived together more commonly in rural areas than in cities. How many generations do you see in this image? (© Scheufler Collection / Corbis.)

Jews as well." Nationalist groups inflamed the political climate with such racial hatreds. Instead of building consensus to create an inclusive political community, politicians won votes by demonizing ethnic minorities, the poor, and women who limited family size.

Reforming Marriage

Reformers thought that improving conditions within marriage would raise both the quality and quantity of children born. Many educated Europeans believed in eugenics — a set of ideas about producing "superior" people through selective breeding. A famed Italian criminologist declared that "lower" types of people were not humans but "orangutans." Eugenicists wanted increased childbearing for "the fittest" and decreased childbearing — even sterilization — for "degenerates," that is, those deemed inferior. Women of the "better" classes, reformers also believed, would have more children if marriage were made more equal. One step would be to allow married women to keep their wages and to own property, both of which in most legal systems belonged to their husbands. Another step would be to allow women guardianship of their own children.

Reformers worked to improve marriage laws in order to boost the birthrate, while feminists sought to improve the lot of mothers and their children. Sweden made men's and women's control over property equal in marriage and allowed married women to

work without their husband's permission. Other countries, among them France (1884), legalized divorce and made it less complicated to obtain. Reformers reasoned that divorce would allow unhappy couples to separate and undertake more loving and thus more fertile marriages. By the early twentieth century, several countries had passed legislation that provided government subsidies for medical care and child support as concerns about population partially laid the foundations for the welfare state—that is, a nation-state whose policies addressed not just military defense, foreign policy, and political processes but also the social and economic well-being of its people.

The conditions of women's lives varied across Europe. For example, a greater number of legal reforms occurred in western versus eastern Europe, but women could get university degrees in Austria-Hungary long before they could at Oxford or Cambridge in England. However, in much of rural eastern Europe, the father's power over the extended family remained almost dictatorial. According to a survey of family life in eastern Europe in the early 1900s, fathers married off their children so young that 25 percent of women in their early forties had been pregnant more than ten times. Yet reform of everyday customs did occur: for instance, among the middle and upper classes of Europe, many grown children were coming to believe that they had a right to select a marriage partner instead of accepting the spouse their parents chose for them.

New Women, New Men, and the Politics of Sexual Identity

Rapid social change set the stage for even bolder behaviors among some middle-class women. Adventurous women traveled the globe on their own to promote Christianity, make money, or learn about other cultures. The increasing availability of white-collar jobs for educated women meant that more of them could adopt an independent way of life. The so-called **new woman** dressed more practically, with fewer petticoats and looser corsets, biked down city streets and country lanes, lived apart from her family, and supported herself. Italian educator Maria Montessori (1870–1952), the first woman in Italy

Maria Montessori

Maria Montessori, famous today for the global network of schools that bear her name, was the perfect example of a "new woman." Her work outside the home with children was controversial; she was also a highly skilled medical doctor and, secretly, an unwed mother. While she developed a set of sophisticated theories for the advancement of young children generally, others cared for her own son. (akg-images / ullstein bild.)

to earn a medical degree and the founder of an educational system that still bears her name, secretly gave birth to an illegitimate child. Other new women lived openly with their lovers. Not surprisingly, there was loud criticism: the new woman, German philosopher Friedrich Nietzsche wrote, had led to the "uglification of Europe."

Sexual identity also fueled debate. A popular book in the new field of "sexology," which studied sex scientifically, was *Sexual Inversion* (1896) by Havelock Ellis. Ellis, a British medical doctor, claimed that there was a new personality type — the homosexual — identifiable by physical affection for members of their own sex. Homosexuals joined the discussion, calling for recognition that they composed a natural "third sex" and were not just people behaving sinfully. Some maintained that, possessing both male and female traits, they marked "a higher order" on the scale of human evolution. The discussion of homosexuality started the trend toward seeing sexuality in general as a basic part of human identity.

The issue became explosive in the spring of 1895, when Irish playwright Oscar Wilde (1854–1900) was convicted of indecency — a charge that referred to his sexual

affairs with younger men — and sentenced to two years in prison. "Open the windows! Let in the fresh air!" one newspaper rejoiced at the conviction. Between 1907 and 1909, German newspapers broadcast the courts-martial of military men in Kaiser William II's closest circle who were condemned for homosexuality and transvestitism. The government had to assure the public that William's own family life was "a fine model" for the German nation, as heterosexuality took on patriotic overtones. Despite the harsh judgments against homosexuals, these cases paved the way for growing sexual openness. Yet they also made sexual issues regular weapons in politics.

Oscar Wilde

The Irish-born writer Oscar Wilde symbolized the persecution experienced by homosexuals in the late nineteenth century. Convicted of indecency for having sexual relations with another man, Wilde served time in prison — a humiliation for the husband, father, acclaimed author, and witty playwright. (Library of Congress, Prints and Photographs Division, LC-USZ62 914833.)

Sciences of the Modern Self

Scientists and Social Darwinists found cause for alarm not only in the poor condition of the working class but also in modern society's mental complaints such as those of the Wolf-Man. New sciences of the mind such as psychology and psychoanalysis aimed to treat everyone, not just the insane. A number of books in the 1890s presented arguments on causes and cures for modern nervous ailments. *Degeneration* (1892–1893), by Hungarian-born physician Max Nordau, blamed overstimulation for both individual and national deterioration. According to Nordau, nervous complaints and the increasingly bizarre art world reflected a general downturn in the human species. The Social Darwinist remedy for such mental decline was imperial adventure for men and increased childbearing for both sexes because it would restore men's virility and women's femininity.

Sigmund Freud (1856–1939) devised a different approach to treating mental problems — one that challenged the widespread liberal belief in a rational self that consistently acts in its own best interest. Dreams, he explained in *The Interpretation of Dreams* (1900), reveal an unseen and powerful part of one's personality — the "unconscious" — where all sorts of desires are more or less hidden from one's rational understanding.

Freud's Office and Collection

Sigmund Freud surrounded himself with imperial trophies such as Oriental rugs and African art objects in his study and therapy room in Vienna. Freud was fascinated by cures brought about through shamanism, trances, and other practices of non-Western medicine. Despite his successes, Freud, like other Jews, was a target of anti-Semitism from Nazis and others; he eventually escaped Vienna for exile in London in 1938. (ullstein bild / The Granger Collection, NYC — All rights reserved.)

Freud also believed that the human psyche is made up of three competing parts: the ego, the part that is most in touch with the need to work and survive — that is, reality; the id (or libido), the part that contains instincts and sexual energies; and the superego, the part that serves as the conscience. Freud's theory of human mental processes and his method for treating their malfunctioning came to be called psychoanalysis.

Freud believed that sexual life should be understood objectively, free from religious or moral judgments. Children, he insisted, have sexual drives from the moment of birth; for the individual to attain maturity and for society to remain civilized, sexual desires — such as impulses toward incest — had to be repressed. Gender identity is more complicated than biology alone, he claimed, adding that girls and women have powerful sexual feelings, an idea that broke sharply with existing beliefs that women were passionless.

The influence of psychoanalysis became pervasive in the twentieth century. For example, Freud's "talking cure," as his method of treatment was quickly labeled, gave rise to a general acceptance of talking out one's problems to a therapist. Terms such as *neurotic* and *unconscious* came into widespread use. Freud attributed girls' complaints about sexual harassment or abuse to fantasy caused by "penis envy," an idea that led members of the new profession of social work to believe that most instances of such abuse had not actually occurred. Like Darwin, Freud rejected optimistic views of the world, believing instead that humans individually and collectively were motivated by irrational drives toward death and destruction.

REVIEW QUESTION How did ideas about the self and about personal life change at the beginning of the twentieth century?

Modernity and the Revolt in Ideas

Toward the beginning of the twentieth century, intellectuals and artists so completely rejected long-standing beliefs and traditional artistic forms that they ushered in a new era. In science, the theories of Albert Einstein and other researchers established new truths in physics. Artists and musicians produced shocking works but, like Freud, they were influenced by advances in science and the progress of empire. Their blending of the scientific and the irrational, and of Western and non-Western styles, helped launch the revolution in ideas and creative expression called **modernism**.

The Opposition to Positivism

Late in the nineteenth century, many philosophers and social thinkers rejected the century-old belief that using scientific methods would uncover enduring social laws. This belief, called positivism, had emphasized the verifiable nature of fundamental laws and had motivated attempts to enact legislation based on studies of society. Challenging positivism, some critics declared that because human experience is ever changing, there are no constant social laws. German political theorist Max Weber (1864–1920) maintained that the sheer number of facts involved in policymaking could make deci-

sive action by bureaucrats impossible. In times of crisis, a charismatic leader might usurp power because of his ability to act simply on intuition. These turn-of-the-century thinkers, called relativists and pragmatists, influenced thinking throughout the twentieth century.

The most radical among the scholars was the German philosopher **Friedrich Nietzsche** (1844–1900), who asserted that "truth" is not certain but rather a human representation of reality. Neither scientists nor other careful observers, he said, can have knowledge of nature that is not filtered through human perception. Nietzsche was convinced that late-nineteenth-century Europe was witnessing the decline of absolute truths such as those found in religion. Thus, he announced, "God is dead, we have killed him." Far from arousing dread, however, the death of God, according to Nietzsche, would give birth to a joyful quest for new "poetries of life" to replace worn-out religious and middle-class rules. Nietzsche believed that an uninhibited, dynamic "superman," free from traditional religious and moral values, would replace the rule-bound middle-class person.

Nietzsche thought that each individual had a vital life energy that he called "the will to power." The idea inspired many people, including his students. As a teacher, Nietzsche was so vibrant — like his superman — that his first students thought they were hearing another Socrates. However, Nietzsche contracted syphilis and was insane in the last eleven years of his life, cared for by his sister. She edited his attacks on middle-class values into attacks on Jews and revised his complicated concepts of the will to power and of superman to appeal to nationalists, anti-Semites, and militarists, all of whom he actually hated.

The Revolution in Science

While Nietzsche and other philosophers questioned the ability of traditional science to provide timeless truths, scientific inquiry itself gained in prestige. Around the turn of the century, however, discoveries by pioneering researchers shook the foundations of scientific certainty. In 1896, French physicist Antoine Becquerel discovered radioactivity. He also suggested the mutability of elements by the rearrangement of their atoms. French chemist Marie Curie and her husband, Pierre Curie, isolated the elements polonium and radium, which are more radioactive than the uranium Becquerel used. From these and other discoveries, scientists concluded that atoms are not solid, as had long been believed, but are composed of subatomic particles moving about a core. In 1900, German physicist Max Planck announced his quantum theory, stating that energy is delivered not in a steady stream but in discrete packets, which he later called quanta.

In this atmosphere of discovery, physicist **Albert Einstein** (1879–1955) proclaimed his special theory of relativity in 1905. According to this theory, space and time are not absolute categories but instead vary according to the vantage point of the observer. Only the speed of light is constant. That same year, Einstein suggested that the solution to problems in Planck's theory lay in considering light both as little packets *and* as waves. Einstein later proposed yet another blurring of two distinct physical properties,

mass and energy. He expressed this equivalence in the equation $E = mc^2$, or energy equals mass times the square of the speed of light. In 1916, Einstein published his general theory of relativity, which connected the force, or gravity, of an object with its mass and proposed a fourth mathematical dimension to the universe. Much more lay ahead once Einstein's theories of energy were applied to technology: television, nuclear power, and, within forty years, nuclear bombs.

The findings of Planck, Einstein, and others were not readily accepted, because long-standing scientific truths were at stake. Additionally, Marie Curie faced such sexism from the scientific establishment that even after she became the first person ever to receive a second Nobel Prize (1911), the prestigious French Academy of Science turned down her candidacy for membership. The academy claimed that a woman simply could not have done such outstanding work. Acceptance of these scientists' discoveries gradually came, and Einstein's name became synonymous with *genius*. Scientists of the modern era achieved what historians call a paradigm shift — that is, despite resistance, they transformed the foundations of science as their theories came to replace those of earlier pioneers.

Modern Art

Conflicts between traditional values and new ideas also raged in the arts as artists distanced themselves further from classical Western styles. French painter Paul Cézanne initiated one of the most powerful trends in modern art by using rectangular daubs of paint to portray his geometric vision of dishes, fruit, drapery, and the human body. Cézanne's art accentuated structure — the lines and planes found in nature — instead of presenting nature as it appeared in everyday life. Following in Cézanne's footsteps, Spanish artist Pablo Picasso (1881–1973) developed a style called cubism. Its radical emphasis on planes and surfaces converted his models into bizarre, almost unrecognizable forms. Picasso's painting *Les Demoiselles d'Avignon* (1907), for example, depicted the bodies of the *demoiselles* ("young ladies" or in this case "prostitutes") as fragmented and angular, with their heads modeled on African masks. Picasso's work showed the profound influences of African, Asian, and South American arts, but his use of these features was less decorative and more brutal than that of many other modern artists. Like imperialists who recounted their brutal exploits in speeches and memoirs, Picasso brought knowledge of the empire home in a disturbing style that captured the jarring uncertainties of society and politics in these decades.

Across Europe, artists made stylistic changes in their work that incorporated political criticism and even outrage. "Show the people how hideous is their actual life," anarchists challenged. Picasso, who had spent his youth in working-class Barcelona, a hotbed of anarchist thought, aimed to present the plain truth about industrial society in his art. In 1912, Picasso and French painter Georges Braque devised a new kind of collage that incorporated bits of newspaper stories, string, and various useless objects. The effect was a work of art that appeared to be made of trash. The newspaper clippings Picasso included described battles and murders, suggesting that Western civilization was not as

refined as it claimed to be. In eastern and central Europe, artists criticized the boastful nationalism that determined royal purchases of sculpture and painting: "The whole empire is littered with monuments to soldiers and monuments to Kaiser William," one German artist complained.

Scandinavian and eastern European artists produced works expressing the torment many felt at the time. Like the ideas of Freud, their style of portraying inner feelings — called expressionism — broke with middle-class optimism. Norwegian painter Edvard Munch aimed "to make the emotional mood ring out again as happens on a gramophone." His painting *The Scream* (1893), shown in the chapter-opening illustration, used twisting lines and a tortured skeletal human form to convey the horror of modern life that many artists perceived. The Blue Rider group of artists, led by German painter Gabriele Münter and Russian painter Wassily Kandinsky, used geometric forms and striking colors to express an inner, spiritual truth. Kandinsky is often credited with producing the first fully abstract paintings around 1909; shapes in these paintings no longer bear any resemblance whatsoever to physical objects or reality but are meant to express deep feelings. The work of expressionists and cubists before World War I was a commercial failure in a marketplace run not only by museum curators but by professional dealers — "experts" — like the professionals in medicine and law.

Only one style of this period, **art nouveau** ("new art"), was an immediate, commercial success. Designers manufactured everything from dishes, calendars, and advertising posters to streetlamps and even entire buildings in this new style. As one French official said about the first art nouveau coins issued in 1895, "Soon even the most humble among us will be able to have a masterpiece in his pocket." Adapting elements from Asian design, art nouveau replaced the impersonality of machines with vines and flowers and the softly curving bodies of female nudes intended to soothe the individual viewer. This idea directly contrasted with Picasso's artistic vision. Art nouveau was the notable exception to the public outcries over innovations in the visual arts.

The Revolt in Music and Dance

"Astonish me!" was the motto of modern dance and music, both of which shocked audiences in the concert halls of Europe. American dancer Isadora Duncan took Europe by storm at the turn of the twentieth century when, draped in a flowing garment, she appeared barefoot in one of the first performances of modern dance. Her sophisticated style was called "primitive" because it no longer followed the steps of classical ballet. Experimentation with forms of bodily expression animated the Russian Ballet's 1913 performance of *The Rite of Spring*, by Igor Stravinsky, the tale of an orgiastic dance to the death performed to ensure a plentiful harvest. The dance troupe struck awkward poses and danced to rhythms intended to sound primitive. At the work's premiere in Paris, one journalist reported that "the audience began shouting its indignation. . . . Fighting actually broke out among some of the spectators."

Composers had been rebelling against Western traditions for several decades, producing music that was disturbing rather than pretty. Having heard Asian musicians

at international expositions, French composer Claude Debussy transformed his style to reflect non-European musical patterns and wrote articles in praise of Asian harmonies. Italian composer Giacomo Puccini used non-Western subject matter for his opera *Madame Butterfly,* which debuted in 1904. Listeners were jarred when they heard non-Western tonalities. Like the bizarre representation of reality in cubism, the works of Austrian composer Richard Strauss added to the revolution in music by using several musical keys simultaneously, thus distorting familiar musical patterns. The early orchestral work of Austrian composer Arnold Schoenberg, who also wrote cabaret music to earn a living, shocked even Strauss. Schoenberg proposed eliminating tonality altogether; a decade later, he devised a new twelve-tone scale. "I am aware of having broken through all the barriers of a dated aesthetic ideal," Schoenberg wrote of his music. Audiences, however, found this music unpleasant and incomprehensible. "Anarchist! Nihilist!" they shouted, using political terms to show their distaste for modernist music.

REVIEW QUESTION How did modernism transform the arts and the world of ideas?

Growing Tensions in Mass Politics

Alongside disturbances in artistic life, the political atmosphere grew charged. On the one hand, liberal opinions led to political representation for workingmen. Networks of communication, especially the development of journalism, created a common fund of political knowledge that made mass politics possible. On the other hand, many political activists were no longer satisfied with the liberal rights such as the vote sought by earlier reformers. Some militant nationalists, anti-Semites, socialists, suffragists, and others demanded changes that challenged liberal values and individual rights. Traditional elites, resentful of the rising middle classes and urban peoples, aimed to overturn constitutional processes and crush city life. Politics soon threatened national unity.

The Expanding Power of Labor

European leaders worried about the rise of working-class political power late in the nineteenth century. Laboring people's growing confidence came in part from expanding educational opportunities. Workers in England, for example, avidly read works by Shakespeare and took literally his calls for political action in the cause of justice that rang out in plays such as *Julius Caesar.* Unions gained members among factory workers, while the labor and socialist parties won seats in parliaments as men in the lower classes received the vote. In Germany, Kaiser William II had allowed antisocialist laws to lapse after dismissing Bismarck as chancellor in 1890. Through grassroots organizing at the local level, the German Social Democratic Party became the largest group in the Reichstag by 1912.

Winning elections actually raised problems among socialists. Some felt uncomfortable sitting in parliaments alongside the upper classes — in Marxism, the enemies

of working people. Others worried that accepting high public offices would weaken socialists' commitment to the goal of revolution. These issues divided socialist organizations. Between 1900 and 1904, the Second International wrestled with the question of revisionism — that is, whether socialists should work from within governments to improve the daily lives of laborers or push for a violent revolution to overthrow governments. Powerful German Marxists argued that settling for reform would leave the wealthy unchallenged while throwing small crumbs to a few working-class politicians. Police persecution forced some working-class parties to operate in exile. The Russian government, for instance, outlawed political parties, imprisoned activists, and gave the vote to only a limited number of men when it finally introduced a parliament in 1905. Thus, Russian Marxist V. I. Lenin (1870–1924), who would take power during the Russian Revolution of 1917, operated outside the country. Lenin advanced the theory that a highly disciplined socialist elite — rather than the working class as a whole — would lead a lightly industrialized Russia into socialism. At a 1903 party meeting of Russian Marxists, he maneuvered his opponents into walking out of the proceedings so that his supporters gained control of the party. Thereafter, his faction was known as the Bolsheviks, so named after the Russian word for "majority," which they had temporarily formed. They struggled to suppress the Mensheviks ("minority"), who had been the dominant voice in Russian Marxism until Lenin outmaneuvered them. Neither of these factions, however, had as large a constituency within Russia as the Socialist Revolutionaries, whose objective was to politicize peasants, rather than industrial workers, to bring about revolution. All of these groups organized in secret instead of using electoral politics.

During this same period, anarchists, along with some trade union members known as syndicalists, kept Europe in a panic with their terrorist acts. In the 1880s, anarchists had bombed stock exchanges, parliaments, and businesses; by the 1890s, they were assassinating heads of state: the Spanish premier in 1897, the empress of Austria-Hungary in 1898, the king of Italy in 1900, and the president of the United States in 1901, to name a few famous victims. Syndicalists advocated the use of direct action, such as general strikes and sabotage, to paralyze the economy and give labor unions more power. In response, politicians from the old landowning and military elites of eastern and central Europe worked to reverse the trend toward constitutionalism and mass political participation.

Rights for Women and the Battle for Suffrage

Women continued to agitate for the benefits of liberalism such as the right to vote and to own their wages if married. German women focused on widening opportunities for female education. Their activism aimed to achieve the German cultural ideal of *Bildung* — the belief that education can build character and that individual development has public importance. In several countries, women worked to prevent prostitutes from being imprisoned on suspicion of having syphilis when men with syphilis faced no such penalty. Other women took up pacifism — among them Bertha von Suttner, whose popular

writing emphasized how war inflicted terror on women and families. (Von Suttner influenced Alfred Nobel to institute a peace prize and then won the prize herself in 1903.)

By the 1890s, many women activists decided to focus their efforts on a single issue — suffrage (the right to vote) — as the most effective way to correct the many problems caused by male privilege. Thereafter, suffragists created major organizations involving millions of activists. British suffrage leader Millicent Garrett Fawcett (1847–1929) pressured members of Parliament for women's right to vote. Across the Atlantic, American Susan B. Anthony (1820–1906) traveled the country to speak at mass suffrage rallies, edited a suffragist newspaper, and founded the International Woman Suffrage Alliance in 1904. Its leadership argued that despite men's promises to protect women in exchange for their inequality, the system of male chivalry had led to exploitation and abuse. "So long as the subjection of women endures, and is confirmed by law and custom, . . . women will be victimized," a leading British suffragist claimed. Other activists believed that the characteristics associated with mothering were necessary in shaping a country's policies.

Women's rights activists were predominantly, though not exclusively, from the middle class. Free from the need to earn a living, they simply had more time to be activists and to read the works of feminists such as Harriet Taylor and John Stuart Mill. Working-class women also participated in the suffrage movement, though many distrusted the middle class and believed suffrage to be less crucial than women's pressing economic concerns. Textile workers of Manchester, England, for example, put together a vigorous movement for the vote, seeing it as essential to improved working conditions.

In 1906 in Finland, suffragists achieved their first major victory when the Finnish parliament granted women the vote. The failure of parliaments elsewhere in Europe to enact similar legislation provoked British suffragist **Emmeline Pankhurst** (1858–1928)

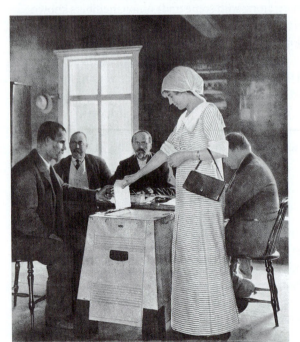

Woman Suffrage in Finland
In 1906, Finnish women became the first in Europe to receive the vote in national elections when the socialist party there — usually opposed to feminism as a middle-class rather than a working-class project — supported woman suffrage. The Finnish vote encouraged activists in the West, now linked together by many international organizations and ties, because it showed that more than a century of lobbying for reform could lead to gains. (Mary Evans Picture Library.)

and her daughters to found the Women's Social and Political Union (WSPU) in 1903. Starting in 1907, members of the WSPU held parades in English cities, and in 1909 they began a campaign of violence, blowing up railroad stations, slashing works of art, and chaining themselves to the gates of Parliament. Disguising themselves as ordinary shoppers, they carried little hammers to smash the plate-glass windows of department stores and shops. Parades and demonstrations made suffrage a public spectacle; some outraged men responded by attacking the marchers. Arrested for disturbing the peace, the marchers went on hunger strikes in prison. Like striking workers, these women were willing to use confrontational tactics to obtain rights.

Liberalism Tested

Governments in western Europe, where liberal institutions were seemingly well entrenched, sought to control turn-of-the-century conflicts with pragmatic policies that often struck at liberalism's very foundations. Political parties in Britain discovered that the recently enfranchised voter wanted solid benefits in exchange for his support. In 1905, the British Liberal Party won a majority in the House of Commons and pushed for social legislation aimed at the working class. "We are keenly in sympathy with the representatives of Labour," one Liberal politician announced. "We have too few of them in the House of Commons." The National Insurance Act of 1911 instituted a program of unemployment assistance funded by new taxes on the wealthy.

The Irish question, however, tested Britain's commitment to such liberal values as autonomy, opportunity, and individual rights. In the 1890s, new groups formed to foster Irish culture as a way of heightening the political challenge to what they saw as Britain's continuing colonization of the country. In 1901, the circle around poet William Butler Yeats and actress Maud Gonne founded the Irish National Theater to present Irish rather than English plays. Gonne took Irish politics into everyday life by opposing British efforts to gain the loyalty of the young. Every time an English monarch visited Ireland, he or she held special receptions for children. Gonne and other Irish volunteers sponsored competing events, handing out candies and other treats for patriotic youngsters. One home rule supporter marveled at "the procession . . . of thirty thousand school children who refused to be bribed into parading before the Queen of England." Promoters of an "Irish way of life" encouraged speaking Irish Gaelic instead of English and supporting Catholicism instead of the Church of England. This cultural agenda gained political force with the founding in 1905 of Sinn Féin ("We Ourselves"), a group that strove for complete Irish independence.

Once committed to economic growth and the rule of law, Italian leaders, now saddled with debt from unification, began to drift away from these liberal values. Instead, corruption plagued Italy's constitutional monarchy, which had not yet developed either the secure parliamentary system of England or the authoritarian monarchy of Germany to guide its growth. To forge national unity in the 1890s, prime ministers used patriotic rhetoric and imperial adventure, notably a second unsuccessful attempt to conquer Ethiopia in 1896. Giovanni Giolitti, who served as prime minister for three

terms between 1903 and 1914, adopted a policy known as *trasformismo* (from the word for "transform"), using bribes and public works programs to gain support from deputies in parliament. Political opponents called Giolitti the "Minister of the Underworld" and accused him of preferring to buy the votes of local bosses rather than spending money to develop the Italian economy. In a wave of protest, urban workers in the industrial cities of Turin and Milan and rural laborers in the depressed agrarian south demanded change. Giolitti appeased the protesters by instituting social welfare programs and, in 1912, virtually complete manhood suffrage.

Anti-Semitism, Nationalism, and Zionism in Mass Politics

The real crisis for liberal political values of equal citizenship and tolerance came in the two decades leading up to World War I when politicians used anti-Semitism and militant nationalism to win elections. They told voters that Jews were responsible for the difficulties of everyday life and that anti-Semitism and increased patriotism would fix all problems. Voters from many levels of society responded enthusiastically, agreeing that Jews were villains and the nation-state was the hero in the struggle to survive. In both republics and monarchies, anti-Semitism and militant nationalism provided those on the radical right with a platform to gain working-class votes and thus combat the radical left of social democracy. This new radical right included representatives of the agrarian nobility, aristocrats who controlled the military, and highly placed clergy, and it broke with liberal ideas of the rule of law and the equality of all citizens. Liberals had hoped that voting by the masses would make politics more harmonious as parliamentary debate and compromise smoothed out class and other differences. Instead politics became loud and hateful, a distinct departure from consensus building and rational debate.

A strong tradition of anti-Semitism already existed in Russian politics. Russian tsar **Nicholas II** (r. 1894–1917) believed firmly in Russian orthodox religion, autocratic politics, and anti-Semitic social values. Taught as a child to hate Jews, Nicholas blamed them for any failure in Russian policy. Pogroms became a regular threat to Russian Jews, as Nicholas increasingly limited where Jews could live and how they could earn a living.

Principles of equal citizenship and tolerance were also tested in France. Powerful forces in the aristocracy, the military, and the Catholic church hoped that the Third Republic, like earlier ones, could be overthrown. Economic downturns, widespread corruption, and attempted coups made the republic more vulnerable, and the press attributed failures of almost any kind to Jews. Despite an excellent system of primary education promoting literacy and rational thinking, the public tended to agree, while the clergy and monarchists kept hammering the message that the republic was nothing but a conspiracy of Jews.

Amid rising anti-Semitism, a Jewish captain in the French army, Alfred Dreyfus, was charged with spying for Germany in 1894. The military, whose upper echelons were traditionally aristocratic, Catholic, and monarchist, produced manufactured "evi-

The Humiliation of Alfred Dreyfus

French captain Alfred Dreyfus was sent to a harsh exile after being convicted of spying for Germany. Before he was taken to Devil's Island, he was subjected to the extreme humiliation of having his officer's insignia and ribbons stripped from his uniform and his sword broken before hundreds of troops and a mob of screaming anti-Semites. We can only imagine what this meant to a man in his mid-thirties who, despite being Jewish, had worked his way through an elite military school and up the ranks of the army. What do you see in his bearing? (The Granger Collection, NYC — All rights reserved.)

dence" to gain Dreyfus's conviction even though the espionage continued. Then several newspapers received proof that the army had fabricated documents to convict Dreyfus. In 1898, the celebrated French novelist Émile Zola published an article titled "*J'accuse*" (I accuse) on the front page of a Paris daily, exposing the web of perjury that had created the impression of Dreyfus's guilt.

The article, which named the truly guilty parties, led to public riots, quarrels among families and friends, and denunciations of the army. The government finally pardoned Dreyfus in 1899, dismissed the aristocratic and Catholic officers responsible for the false accusations, and ended religious teaching orders to ensure a secular public school system that honored toleration and the rule of law. Still, the Dreyfus Affair made anti-Semitism and official lies a standard tool of politics by showing their effectiveness with the public.

The ruling elites in Germany also used anti-Semitism to win support from those who feared the consequences of Germany's sudden and overwhelming industrialization. The agrarian elites, who still controlled the highest reaches of government, lost ground to industry as agriculture (from which they drew their fortunes) declined as a force in Germany's economy. As industrialists grew wealthier and new opportunities drew rural workers to the cities, the agrarian elites came to loathe industry for challenging their traditional authority. A Berlin newspaper noted, "The agrarians' hate for cities . . . blinds them to the simplest needs and the most natural demands of the urban population." To woo the masses, conservatives and a growing radical right claimed that Jews, who made up less than 1 percent of the German population, were responsible for destroying traditional society. They hurled diatribes against Jews, new women, and Social Democrats, whom they branded as internationalist and unpatriotic. This new right invented a modern politics that rejected the liberal value of parliamentary consensus,

relying instead on inventing enemies and thus dividing what was supposed to be a unified nation-state.

Politicians in the dual monarchy of Austria-Hungary also used militant nationalism and anti-Semitism to win votes, but here the presence of many ethnic groups meant greater complexity in the politics of hate. Foremost among the nationalists were the Hungarians, who wanted autonomy for themselves while forcibly imposing Hungarian language and culture on all other, supposedly inferior, ethnic groups in Hungary. Their nationalist claims rested on two pieces of evidence: Budapest was a thriving industrial city, and the export of Hungarian grain from the vast estates of the Magyar nobility saved the monarchy's finances. The nationalists disrupted the Hungarian parliament so regularly that it weakened the orderly functioning of the government.

Although capable of causing trouble for the empire, Hungarian nationalists, who mostly represented agrarian wealth, were themselves vulnerable. Hungary's exploited ethnic groups — Slovaks, Romanians, and Ruthenians — resisted Magyarization. Industrial workers struck to protest horrendous labor conditions, and 100,000 activists gathered in the fall of 1905 in front of the Hungarian parliament to demonstrate for the vote. Other nationalities across the Dual Monarchy intensified their demands for rights. Croats, Serbs, and other Slavic groups in the south called for equality with the Hungarians. The central government allowed the Czechs a greater number of Czech officials in the government because of the growing industrial prosperity of their region. But every step favoring the Czechs provoked outrage from the traditionally dominant ethnic Germans. When Austria-Hungary decreed in 1897 that government officials in the Czech region of the empire would have to speak Czech as well as German, the Germans rioted. Discriminatory policies toward these groups and scorn for the imperial government in Vienna made for instability throughout Austria-Hungary.

Tensions mounted as German politicians in Vienna linked the growing power of Hungarians and Czechs to Jews. Karl Lueger's newly formed Christian Social Party attracted members from among the aristocracy, Catholics, artisans, shopkeepers, and white-collar workers. Lueger appealed to those for whom modern life meant a loss of privilege and security. His hate-filled speeches helped elect him mayor of Vienna in 1895, but his ethnic nationalism and anti-Semitism threatened the multinationalism on which Austria-Hungary was based. Thereafter a widening group of politicians made anti-Semitism an integral part of their election campaigns, calling Jews the "sucking vampire" of modernity and blaming them for the tumult of migration, the economy, and just about anything else people found disturbing. Politics became a thing not of debate in parliaments but of violent racism in the streets.

Anti-Semites lumped Jewish people into one hated group, but like members of any other religion, Jews were divided by social class and education. Many Jews in western Europe moved out of Jewish neighborhoods, intermarried with Christians, and in some cases converted to Christianity — practices known as assimilation. Many well-educated Jews favored the classical culture of the German Empire because it seemed more rational and liberal than the ritualistic Catholicism of Austria-Hungary. By contrast, less prosperous Jews, such as those in Russia and Romania, were increasingly

Map 24.1 Jewish Migrations in the Late Nineteenth Century
Pogroms in eastern Europe, increasingly violent anti-Semitism across the continent, and the search for opportunity motivated Jews to migrate to many parts of the world. Between 1890 and 1914, some five million Jews left Russia alone. They moved to European cities, to North and South America, and, as Zionism progressed, to Palestine.

singled out for persecution, legally disadvantaged, and forced to live in ghettos. Jews from these countries might seek refuge in the nearby cities of central and eastern Europe where they could eke out a living as day laborers or artisans. Jewish migration to the United States and other countries also swelled (Map 24.1). By 1900, some Jews such as Freud were prominent in cultural and economic affairs in cities across the European continent even as far more were discriminated against and victimized elsewhere.

Amid vast migration and continued persecution, a spirit of Jewish nationalism arose. "Why should we be any less worthy than any other . . . people?" one Jewish leader asked. "What about our nation, our language, our land?" In the 1880s, the Ukrainian physician Leon Pinsker, seeing the Jews' lack of national territory as fundamental to their

persecution, advocated the migration of Jews to Palestine. In 1896, Theodor Herzl, strongly influenced by Pinsker, called not simply for migration but for the creation of a Jewish nation-state, the goal of a movement known as **Zionism**. A Hungarian-born Jew, Herzl experienced anti-Semitism firsthand as a Viennese journalist and a writer in Paris during the Dreyfus Affair. Backed by eastern European Jews, he organized the first International Zionist Congress (1897). By 1914, some eighty-five thousand Jews had moved into Palestine.

REVIEW QUESTION What were the points of tension in European political life at the beginning of the twentieth century?

European Imperialism Challenged

Anti-Semitism was only one sign that the conditions of modern life were deeply troubling and that the rule of law and other liberal values like tolerance were threatened. Militant nationalism across the West made it difficult for nations to calm international tensions.

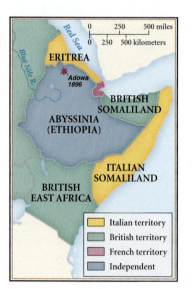

The Struggle for Ethiopia, 1896

This nationalist atmosphere heated up, and newcomers Italy and Germany now fought for a place at the imperial table, making imperial rivalries among the European powers alarmingly worse. As colonized peoples challenged European control, Japan's growth as an Asian power also threatened stability: in 1904–1905, Japanese expansionism came close to toppling the mighty Russian Empire.

The Trials of Empire

Everyone was quick to violence when it came to empire, and Britain in its pursuit of the **South African War** (or Boer War) of 1899–1902 was no exception. In 1896, Cecil Rhodes, then prime minister of the Cape Colony in southern Africa, directed a raid into the neighboring territory of the Transvaal in hopes of stirring up trouble between the Boers, descendants of early Dutch settlers, and the more recent immigrants from Britain who had come to southern Africa in search of gold and other riches. Rhodes aimed for a British takeover of the Transvaal and the Orange Free State, which the Boers independently controlled. The Boers, however, dealt Britain a bloody defeat.

In 1899, Britain began full-scale operations against the Boers. Foreign correspondents covering the South African War reported on appalling bloodshed, the unfit condition of the average British soldier, and the inhumane treatment of South Africans herded into an unfamiliar institution — the concentration camp, which became the graveyard of tens of thousands, mostly women and children. Britain finally annexed the area after defeating the Boers in 1902, but prominent Britons began to call imperialism not the work of civilization but an act of barbarism (Map 24.2).

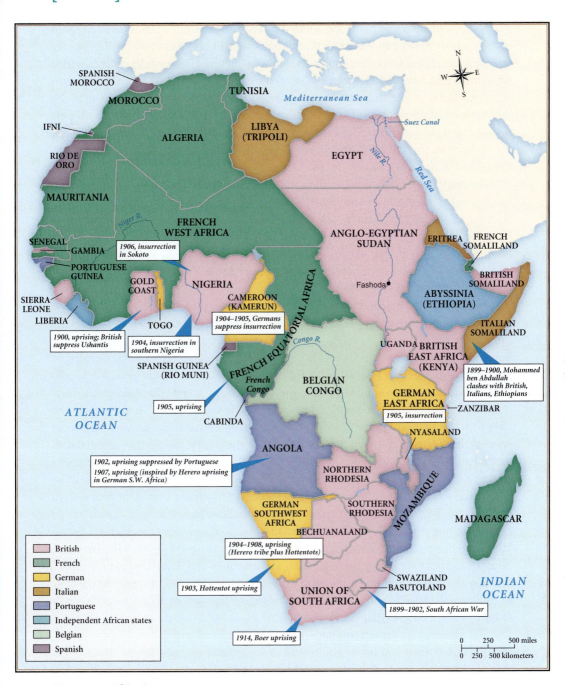

Map 24.2 Africa in 1914

Uprisings intensified in Africa in the early twentieth century as Europeans tried both to consolidate their rule and to extract more wealth from the Africans. As Europeans were putting down rebellions against their rule, a pan-African movement arose, attempting to unite Africans as one people.

Nearly simultaneously with the South African War, the United States defeated Spain in the Spanish-American War in 1898 and took Cuba, Puerto Rico, and the Philippines as its trophies. Experienced in empire, the United States had successfully crushed native Americans and annexed Hawaii in 1898. Both Cuba and the Philippines had begun vigorous efforts to free themselves from Spanish rule before the war. Urged on by the inflammatory daily press, the United States went to war against Spain, but instead of allowing independence the U.S. government annexed Puerto Rico and Guam and bought the Philippines from Spain. Cuba was theoretically independent, but the United States monitored its activities.

The triumphant United States then waged a bloody war against the Filipinos, who wanted independence, not another imperial ruler. British poet Rudyard Kipling had encouraged the United States to "take up the white man's burden" by bringing the benefits of Western civilization to those liberated from Spain. However, reports of American brutality in the Philippines, where some 200,000 local people were slaughtered, disillusioned some in the Western public, who liked to imagine native peoples joyously welcoming the bearers of civilization.

Almost simultaneously, Italy won a costly victory over the Ottoman Empire in Libya, and Italian hopes rose for imperial grandeur in the future. Germany likewise joined the imperial contest, demanding an end to Britain's and France's domination among the colonial powers. German bankers and businessmen were active across Asia, the Middle East, and Latin America, and by the turn of the century, Germany had colonies in Southwest Africa, the Cameroons, Togoland, and East Africa. Despite these successes, Germany, too, met humiliation and faced constant problems, especially in its dealings not only with Britain and France but also with local peoples in Africa and elsewhere who resisted the German takeover. As Italy and Germany joined the aggressive pursuit of new territory, the confident rule-setting for imperialism at the Berlin Conference a generation earlier was diluted by general anxiety, heated rivalry, and nationalist passion.

Japan's rise as an imperial power further ate into Europeans' confident approach to imperialism. Japan defeated China in 1894 in the Sino-Japanese War, which ended China's domination of Korea. The European powers, alarmed by this victory, forced Japan to relinquish most of its gains, a move that outraged and affronted the Japanese. Japan's insecurity had risen with Russian expansion of the Trans-Siberian Railroad through Manchuria, sending millions of Russian settlers eastward. Angered by the continuing presence of Russian troops in Manchuria, the Japanese attacked the tsar's forces at Port Arthur in 1904 (Map 24.3).

The conservative Russian military proved inept in the ensuing Russo-Japanese War, even though it often had better equipment or strategic advantage. Russia's Baltic Fleet sailed halfway around the globe only to be completely destroyed by Japan in the battle of Tsushima Strait (1905). The Russian defeat opened an era of Japanese domination in East Asian politics. As one English general observed: "I have today seen the most stupendous spectacle it is possible for the mortal brain to conceive — Asia advancing, Europe falling back." Japan annexed Korea in 1910 and began to target other areas for colonization.

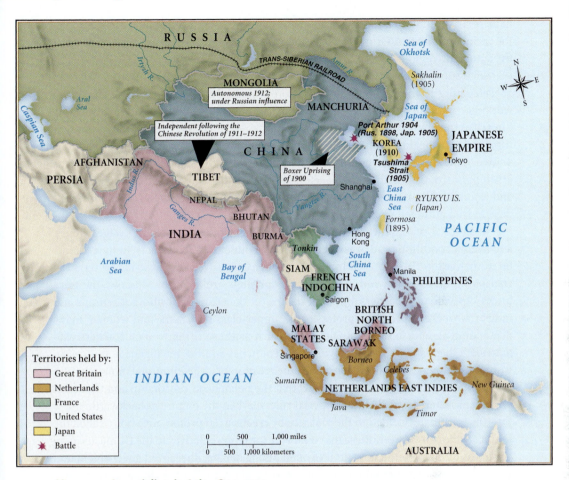

Map 24.3 Imperialism in Asia, 1894–1914
The established imperialists came to blows in East Asia as they struggled for influence in China and as they met a formidable new rival — Japan. Simultaneously, liberation groups like the Boxers were taking shape, committed to throwing off restraints imposed by foreign powers and eliminating these interlopers altogether. In 1911, revolutionary Sun Yat-sen overthrew the Qing dynasty, which had left China unprepared to resist foreign takeover, and started the country on a different course.

The Russian Empire Threatened

Alongside the humiliating loss to Japan, revolution erupted in Russia in 1905, and the empire tottered on the brink of chaos. The mighty Russian Empire had concealed its weaknesses well: state-sponsored industrialization in the 1890s had made the country appear modern to outside observers, and Russification attempted to impose a unified national culture on Russia's diverse population. Burdened by heavy taxes to pay for industrialization and by debts owed for the land they acquired during emancipation, peasants revolted in isolated uprisings at the turn of the century. Unrest occurred in the cities, too: in 1903, skilled workers led strikes in Baku; the unity of Armenians and Tatars

in these strikes showed how Russification had made political cooperation possible among the various ethnicities. Growing worker activism, along with Japan's victory, challenged the autocratic regime.

On a Sunday in January 1905, a crowd gathered outside the tsar's Winter Palace in St. Petersburg to march in a demonstration to make Nicholas II aware of the brutal working conditions they suffered. Nicholas had often traveled the empire, displaying himself as the divinely ordained "father" of his people; therefore, his "children" thought it natural to appeal to him for aid. Leading the demonstration was a priest who, unknown to the crowd, was a police informant and agitator. Instead of allowing the marchers to pass, troops guarding the palace shot into the trusting crowd, killing hundreds and wounding thousands. Thus began the Revolution of 1905, as news of "Bloody Sunday" moved outraged workers elsewhere to rebel.

In almost a year of turmoil across Russia, urban workers struck over wages, hours, and factory conditions and organized their own councils, called soviets. In June, sailors on the battleship *Potemkin* mutinied; in October, a massive railroad strike brought rail transportation to a halt; and in November, uprisings broke out in Moscow. The tsar's forces kept killing protesters, but their deaths produced an opposition of artisans and industrial workers, peasants, professionals, upper-class reformers, and women, many demanding an end to discriminatory laws such as those firing women teachers who married. Liberals from the zemstvos (local councils) and the intelligentsia (a Russian word for well-educated elites) demanded the creation of a constitutional monarchy and representative legislature. They believed that the reliance on censorship and the secret police, characteristic of Russian imperial rule, marked the empire as backward.

The tsar finally yielded to the violence by creating a representative body called the **Duma**. Although very few Russians could vote for representatives to the Duma, its mere existence, along with the new right of open public debate, liberalized government and allowed people to present their grievances to a responsive body. Political parties committed to parliamentary rather than revolutionary programs also took shape. From 1907 to 1917, the Duma convened, but twice when the tsar disliked its recommendations he simply sent the delegates home. Nicholas had an able administrator in Prime Minister Pyotr Stolypin (1863–1911), who ended the mir system of communal farming and canceled the land redemption payments that had burdened the peasants since their emancipation in 1861. His reforms allowed people to move to the cities in search of jobs and created a larger group of independent peasants.

Stolypin was determined to restore law and order. He clamped down on revolutionary organizations, sentencing so many of their members to death by hanging that nooses were nicknamed "Stolypin neckties." But rebels continued to assassinate government officials, and Stolypin himself was assassinated in 1911. Stolypin's reforms promoted peasant well-being, which encouraged what one historian has called a "new peasant assertiveness." The industrial workforce also grew, but more strikes broke out, culminating in a general strike in St. Petersburg in 1914. The imperial government's refusal to share power through the Duma left the way open to an even greater upheaval in 1917.

Growing Resistance to Colonial Domination

Japanese military victories over the Qing in China and the Romanovs in Russia upset the status quo in both countries and encouraged nationalist protests throughout the globe, further setting the West on edge. Uprisings began in China after the 1895 defeat by Japan. Nonhuman factors also affected the Chinese people as drought and famine came to plague the empire. Despairing peasants organized into secret societies to expel the foreigners and restore Chinese dignity and power. One organization was the Society of the Righteous and Harmonious Fists, commonly called the Boxers, whose members maintained that ritual boxing would protect them from a variety of evils, including bullets. Encouraged by the Qing ruler, the dowager empress Tz'u-hsi (Cixi; 1835–1908), the Boxers rebelled in 1900, massacring the missionaries and Chinese Christians to whom they attributed China's troubles. Seven of the colonial powers united to put down the Boxer Uprising and to devastate the areas in which the Boxers operated. Defeated once more, the Chinese had to pay a huge indemnity and allow even greater foreign military occupation.

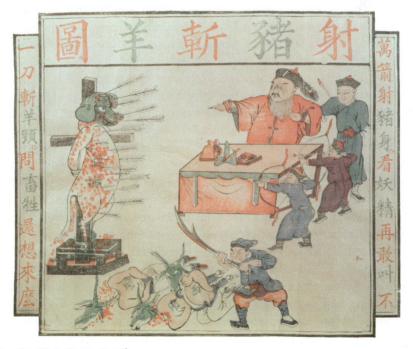

The Foreign Pig Is Put to Death
The Boxers used brightly colored placards to spread information about their movement in order to build wide support among the Chinese population. They felt that the presence of foreigners had caused a series of disasters, including the defection of the Chinese from traditional religion, the flow of wealth from the country, and a string of natural disasters such as famine. This depiction shows the harsh judgment of the Boxers toward foreigners and their Chinese allies — they are pigs to be killed. (Private Collection / The Bridgeman Art Library International.)

The Boxer Uprising thoroughly discredited the Qing dynasty, leading a group of revolutionaries to overthrow the dynasty in 1911 and to declare China a republic the next year. Their leader, Sun Yat-sen (1866–1925), who had been educated in Hawaii and Japan, combined Western ideas and Chinese values in his Three Principles of the People: "nationalism, democracy, and socialism." For example, Sun's socialism included the Chinese belief that all people should have enough food, and his Nationalist Party called for revival of the Chinese tradition of correctness in behavior between governors and the governed, modern economic reform, and an end to Western domination of trade. Sun's stirring leadership and the changes brought about by the 1911 revolution helped weaken Western imperialism.

In India, the Japanese victory over Russia and the Revolution of 1905 stimulated politicians to take a more radical course than that offered by the Indian National Congress. The anti-British Hindu leader B. G. Tilak, less moderate than Congress reformers, urged noncooperation: "We shall not give them assistance to collect revenue and keep peace. We shall not assist them in fighting beyond the frontiers or outside India with Indian blood and money." Tilak asserted the distinctiveness of Hindu values from British ways and urged outright rebellion against the British. This brand of nationalism contrasted with that based on assimilating to British culture and promoting gradual change. Trying to stop Tilak, the British sponsored a rival nationalist group, the Muslim League, in a blatant attempt to divide Muslims from Hindus in the Congress. Faced with political activism, Britain conceded to Indians' representation in ruling councils and their right to vote based on property ownership. But discontent also mounted, sometimes silently, as did worries among the most clear-sighted imperialists about the future.

Revolutionary nationalism was simultaneously weakening the Ottoman Empire, which for centuries had controlled much of the Mediterranean. Rebellions plagued Ottoman rule, and this resistance allowed European influence to grow even as Ottoman reformers aimed to strengthen the government. Sultan Abdul Hamid II (r. 1876–1909) tried to revitalize the multiethnic empire by using Islam to counteract the rising nationalism of the Serbs, Bulgarians, and Macedonians. Instead, he unintentionally provoked Turkish nationalism, which built on the uniqueness of their culture, history, and language, as many European ethnic groups were also doing. The Japanese defeat of Russia in 1904–1905 electrified these nationalists with the vision of a modern Turkey becoming "the Japan of the Middle East," as they called it. In 1908, a group of nationalists called the Young Turks took control of the government in Constantinople. The Young Turks' triumph motivated other ethnic groups in the Middle East and the Balkans to demand an end to Ottoman domination in their regions. Strong contingents of feminist-nationalists mobilized women to work for independence. However, the Young Turks, often aided by European powers with financial interests in the region, brutally repressed nationalist uprisings in Egypt, Syria, and the Balkans that their own success had encouraged.

The rebellions were part of the turmoil in global relations during the years just before World War I, as empires became the scene of growing opposition in the wake of Japanese, Russian, and Turkish events. In German East Africa, colonial forces responded to native resistance in 1905 with a scorched-earth policy, eventually killing more than

100,000 Africans there. To maintain their grip on Indochina, the French closed the University of Hanoi, executed Indochinese intellectuals, and deported thousands of suspected nationalists. A French general stationed there summed up the fears of many co-lonial rulers: "The gravest fact of our actual political situation in Indochina is not the re-cent trouble in Tonkin [or] the plots under-taken against us but in the muted but grow-ing hatred that our subjects show toward us."

REVIEW QUESTION How and why did events in overseas empires from the 1890s on challenge Western faith in imperialism?

Roads to War

Internationally, competition intensified among the great powers and drove Western nationalists to become more aggressive. In the spring of 1914, U.S. president Woodrow Wilson (1856–1924) sent his trusted adviser Colonel Edward House to Europe to observe the rising tensions there. "It is militarism run stark mad," House reported, adding that he foresaw an "awful cataclysm" ahead. Government spending on what people called the arms race had promoted economic growth while it menaced the future. As early as the mid-1890s, one socialist had called the situation a "cold war" because the hostile atmo-sphere made war seem a certainty. By 1914, the air was even more charged, with militant nationalism in the Balkan states and politics — both at home and worldwide — propelling Europeans toward mass destruction.

Competing Alliances and Clashing Ambitions

As the twentieth century opened, the Triple Alliance that Bismarck had negotiated among Germany, Austria-Hungary, and Italy confronted an opposing alliance between France and Russia, created in the 1890s. The wild card in the diplomatic scenario was Great Brit-ain, traditional enemy of France, especially in the contest for global power. Britain and France — constant rivals in Africa — edged to the brink of war in 1898 over competing claims to Fashoda, a town in the Sudan. The threat of conflict led France to withdraw, showing both nations as embracing a truce out of mutual self-interest. To prevent another Fashoda, they entered into secret agreements, the first of which (1904) recognized Brit-ish claims in Egypt and French claims in Morocco. This agreement marked the begin-ning of the British-French alliance called the **Entente Cordiale**. Still, French statesmen feared that, should war break out, their ally might decide to remain neutral.

Kaiser William II inflamed the diplomatic atmosphere just as France and Britain were developing the Entente Cordiale. After victory in the Franco-Prussian War, Bismarck had proclaimed Germany a "satisfied" nation and worked to avoid further wars. William II, in contrast, was emboldened by Germany's growing industrial might and announced in 1901 that Germany needed greater global power to be achieved by "friendly conquests." His actions, however, were far from friendly, and he used the op-portunity presented by the defeat of France's ally Russia in 1904–1905 to contest French advances in Morocco. A boastful, blustery man who was easily prodded to rash actions

by his advisers, William landed in Morocco in 1905 to block the French. To resolve what became known as the First Moroccan Crisis, an international conference met in Spain in 1906. There the powers upheld French claims in North Africa. France and Britain, seeing German interference in Morocco, drew closer together.

When the French took over Morocco completely in 1911, Germany triggered the Second Moroccan Crisis by sending a gunboat to the port of Agadir and again demanding concessions from the French. This time no power — not even Austria-Hungary — backed Germany. The British and French now strengthened the Entente Cordiale, and Germany, smarting from its setbacks on the world stage, refocused on its own alliances.

Germany's bold territorial claims unsettled the rest of Europe, particularly the Balkans. German statesmen began envisioning the creation of a **Mitteleuropa** — a term that literally meant "central Europe" but in their minds also included the Balkans and Turkey. The Habsburgs, firmly backed by Germany, judged that their own expansion into the Balkans and the resulting addition of even more ethnic groups would weaken the claims of any single ethnic minority in the Dual Monarchy. Russia, however, saw *itself* as the protector of Slavs in the region and wanted to replace the Ottomans as the dominant Balkan power, especially since Japan had crushed Russian hopes for expansion to the east. Austria's swift annexation of Bosnia-Herzegovina during the Young Turks' revolt in 1908 enraged not only the Russians but the Serbs as well, who wanted Bosnia as part of an enlarged Serbia (Map 24.4).

Even without the greedy eyes cast on the Balkans, the situation would have been extremely volatile. The nineteenth century had seen the rise of nationalism and ethnicity as the basis for the unity of the nation-state, and by late in the century, ethnic loyalty challenged the dynastic rule of the Habsburgs and Ottomans in the Balkans. Greece, Serbia, Bulgaria, Romania, and Montenegro emerged as autonomous states. All of them sought more Ottoman and Habsburg territory to cement a common ethnicity — an impossible desire given the intermingling of ethnicities throughout the region. Nonetheless, war for territory was on these nationalists' agenda.

In the First Balkan War, in 1912, Serbia, Bulgaria, Greece, and Montenegro joined forces to gain Macedonia and Albania from the Ottomans. The victors divided up their booty, with Bulgaria gaining the most territory, but in the Second Balkan War, in 1913, Serbia, Greece, and Montenegro contested Bulgarian gains. The quick victory of these allies increased Austria's concern at Serbia's rising power. The region had become perilous: both Austria-Hungary (as ruler of many Slavs) and Russia (as their would-be protector) stationed increasing numbers of troops along the borders. The situation led strategists to think hopefully that a quick war there — something like Bismarck's wars — could resolve tension and uncertainty.

The Race to Arms

In the nineteenth century, global rivalries and aspirations for national greatness made constant readiness for war seem increasingly necessary. On the seas and in foreign lands, violence became an everyday occurrence in the drive for empire. Governments

Map 24.4　The Balkans, 1908–1914

Balkan peoples — mixed in religion, ethnicity, and political views — were successful in asserting their desire for independence, especially in the First Balkan War, which claimed territory from the Ottoman Empire. Their increased autonomy sparked rivalries among them and continued to attract attention from the great powers. Three empires in particular — the Russian, Ottoman, and Austro-Hungarian — simultaneously wanted influence for themselves in the region, which became a powder keg of competing ambitions.

began to draft ordinary citizens for periods of two to six years into large standing armies, in contrast to the smaller forces that had served the more limited military goals of the eighteenth century. The per capita expenditure on the military rose in all the major powers between 1890 and 1914; the proportion of national budgets devoted to defense in 1910 was lowest in Austria-Hungary (at 10 percent) and highest in Germany (at 45 percent).

The modernization of weaponry also transformed warfare. Swedish arms manufacturer Alfred Nobel patented dynamite and developed a kind of gunpowder that improved the accuracy of guns and produced a clearer battlefield environment by reducing firearm smoke. By 1914, long-range artillery could fire on targets as far as six miles away. Munitions factories across Europe manufactured ever-growing stockpiles of howitzers, Mauser rifles, and Hotchkiss machine guns. In the Russo-Japanese and South African wars, military leaders had devised new strategies to protect their armies from the heavy firepower and deadly accuracy of the new weapons: in the Russo-Japanese War, trenches and barbed wire blanketed the front around Port Arthur.

Naval construction figured in both the arms race and the rising nationalism in politics. To defend against powerful weaponry, ships built after the mid-nineteenth century were made of metal rather than wood. Launched in 1905, HMS *Dreadnought,* a warship with unprecedented firepower, was the centerpiece of the British navy's plan to construct at least seven battleships per year. Germany also built up its navy and made itself a great land and sea power and planned naval bases as far away as the Pacific. The Germans described their fleet buildup as "a peaceful policy," but, like British naval expansion, it only fed the hostile international climate and intense competition in weapons manufacture. (See "Taking Measure," page 797.)

Public relations campaigns encouraged military buildup. When critics of the arms race suggested a temporary "naval holiday" to stop British and German building, British officials sent out news releases warning that such a cutback "would throw innumerable men on the pavement." Advocates of imperial expansion and nationalist groups lobbied for military spending as boosting national pride, while businessmen promoted large navies as beneficial to international trade and domestic industry. When Germany's Social Democrats questioned the use of taxes and their heavy burden on workers, the press criticized the party for lack of patriotism. The Conservative Party in Great Britain, eager for more battleships, made popular the slogan "We want eight and we won't wait." Public enthusiasm for arms buildups, militant nationalism, and growing international competition set the stage for war. When asked in 1912 about his predictions for war and peace, a French military leader responded enthusiastically, "We shall have war. I will make it. I will win it."

1914: War Erupts

June 28, 1914, began as an ordinary, even happy day not only for Freud's patient the Wolf-Man but also for the Austrian archduke and heir to the Habsburg throne, Francis Ferdinand, and his wife, Sophie, as they ended a state visit to Sarajevo in Bosnia riding in a motorcade. In the crowd was a Serb nationalist, Gavrilo Princip, who had traveled in secret for several weeks to reach this destination, dreaming of reuniting his homeland of Bosnia-Herzegovina with Serbia and smuggling weapons with him to accomplish his end. Princip shot dead the unprotected and unsuspecting Austrian couple.

Some in the Habsburg government saw the assassination as an opportunity to put down the Serbians once and for all. Evidence showed that Princip had received arms

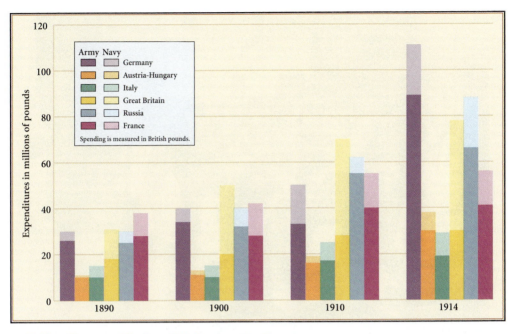

Taking Measure **The Growth in Armaments, 1890–1914**

At the beginning of the twentieth century, the European powers engaged in a massive arms race that was part of industrial innovation. Even as sophisticated weaponry was one key to advancing global conquest, it also became part of national rivalries including economic, military, and imperial ones. Several comparisons offer themselves, not only in terms of the rates of increase but in terms of the military sectors that saw those increases. There is no doubt that the arms race stoked the fires of war, but historians often ask whether better diplomacy could have prevented the outbreak of the global conflict in 1914. The enormous military buildup, however, made some people living in the early twentieth century, as well as some later historians, see war as inevitable. (*The Hammond Atlas of the Twentieth Century* [London: Times Books, 1996], 29.)

and information from Serbian officials, who directed a terrorist organization from within the government. Endorsing a quick defeat of Serbia, German statesmen and military leaders urged the Austrians to be unyielding and promised support in case of war. The Austrians sent an ultimatum to the Serbian government, demanding suppression of terrorist groups and the participation of Austrian officials in an investigation of the crime, among other things. "You are setting Europe ablaze," the Russian foreign minister remarked of the Austrians' humiliating demands made on a sovereign state. Yet the Serbs were conciliatory, accepting all the terms except the presence of Austrian officials in the investigation. Kaiser William was pleased: "All reason for war is gone." His relief proved unfounded. Austria-Hungary, confident of German backing, used the Serbs' resistance to one demand as the pretext for declaring war against them on July 28.

Some statesmen tried desperately to avoid war. Even the tsar and the kaiser sent pleading letters to one another not to start a European war. Still, Germany displayed firm support for Austria in hopes of convincing the French and British to stay out of the

Arrest of the Assassin

Gavrilo Princip belonged to the Young Bosnians, a group devoted to killing Habsburgs in revenge for the Austro-Hungarian monarchy's having sent workers to colonize their homeland. In June 1914, at the age of nineteen, Princip lived out his dream, killing the heir to the Habsburg throne and his wife. Here Princip is shown being apprehended. He spent the rest of his life in prison and was appalled at the carnage of World War I. (© Bettmann / Corbis.)

war and thus keep Russia from mobilizing. Additionally, German military leaders had become fixed on fighting a short, preemptive war that would provide territorial gains leading toward the goal of a Mitteleuropa. As conservatives, they planned to impose martial law the minute war began, using it as an excuse for arresting the leadership of the German Social Democratic Party, which threatened their rule.

The European press caught the war fever of nationalist and pro-war organizations, and military leaders, especially in Germany and Austria-Hungary, promoted mobilization rather than diplomacy in the last days of July. The Austrians declared war and then ordered mobilization on July 31 in full confidence of German military aid, because as early as 1909 Germany had promised to defend Austria-Hungary, even if that country took the offensive. Nicholas II ordered the mobilization in defense of the Serbs — Russia's Slavic allies. Encouraging the Austrians to attack Serbia, the German general staff mobilized on August 1. France declared war by virtue of its agreement to aid its ally Russia, and when Germany violated Belgian neutrality on its way to invade France, Britain entered the war on the side of France and Russia.

REVIEW QUESTION What were the major factors leading to the outbreak of World War I?

Mapping the West Europe at the Outbreak of World War I, August 1914
All the powers expected a great, swift victory when war broke out. Many saw war as a chance to increase their territories; as rivals for trade and empire, almost all believed that war would bring them many advantages. But if European nations appeared well prepared and invincible at the start of the war, relatively few would survive the conflict intact.

Conclusion

Rulers soon forgot their last-minute hesitations when in some capitals celebration erupted with the declaration of war. "A mighty wonder has taken place," wrote a Viennese actor after watching the troops march off amid public enthusiasm. "We have become *young*." Both sides exulted, as militant nationalism led many Europeans to favor war over peace.

There were advantages to war: disturbances in private life and challenges to established truths would disappear, it was believed, in the crucible of war. A short conflict, people maintained, would resolve tensions ranging from the rise of the working class to political problems caused by global imperial competition. German military men saw war as an opportune moment to round up social democrats and reestablish the traditional power of an agrarian aristocracy. Liberal government based on rights and constitutions, some believed, had simply gone too far in allowing new groups full citizenship and political influence.

Modernity helped blaze the path to war. New technology, mass armies, and new techniques of persuasion supported the military buildup. With continuing violence in politics, chaos in the arts, and problems in the industrial order, there was a belief that war would save nations from the modern perils they faced and replace nervous pessimism with patriotism. "Like men longing for a thunderstorm to relieve them of the summer's sultriness," wrote an Austrian official, "so the generation of 1914 believed in the relief that war might bring." Tragically, any hope of relief soon faded. Instead of bringing the refreshment of summer rain, war opened an era of political turmoil, widespread suffering, massive human slaughter, and even greater doses of modernity.

Review Questions

1. How did ideas about the self and about personal life change at the beginning of the twentieth century?
2. How did modernism transform the arts and the world of ideas?

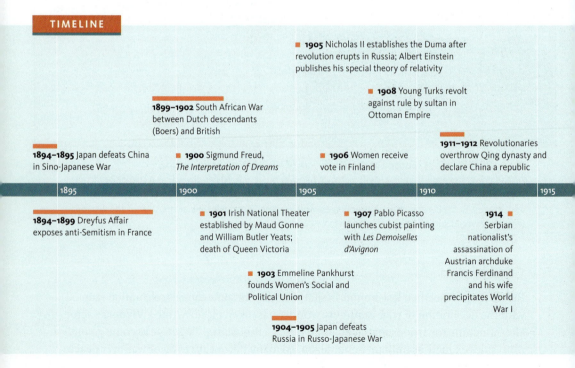

TIMELINE

1905 Nicholas II establishes the Duma after revolution erupts in Russia; Albert Einstein publishes his special theory of relativity

1908 Young Turks revolt against rule by sultan in Ottoman Empire

1899–1902 South African War between Dutch descendants (Boers) and British

1894–1895 Japan defeats China in Sino-Japanese War

1900 Sigmund Freud, *The Interpretation of Dreams*

1906 Women receive vote in Finland

1911–1912 Revolutionaries overthrow Qing dynasty and declare China a republic

| 1895 | 1900 | 1905 | 1910 | 1915 |

1894–1899 Dreyfus Affair exposes anti-Semitism in France

1901 Irish National Theater established by Maud Gonne and William Butler Yeats; death of Queen Victoria

1907 Pablo Picasso launches cubist painting with *Les Demoiselles d'Avignon*

1914 Serbian nationalist's assassination of Austrian archduke Francis Ferdinand and his wife precipitates World War I

1903 Emmeline Pankhurst founds Women's Social and Political Union

1904–1905 Japan defeats Russia in Russo-Japanese War

3. What were the points of tension in European political life at the beginning of the twentieth century?
4. How and why did events in overseas empires from the 1890s on challenge Western faith in imperialism?
5. What were the major factors leading to the outbreak of World War I?

Making Connections

1. How did changes in society at the turn of the twentieth century affect the development of mass politics?
2. How was culture connected to the world of politics in the years 1890–1914?
3. How had nationalism changed since the French Revolution?
4. In what ways were imperial wars from the 1890s to 1914 relevant to the outbreak of World War I?

- For practice quizzes and other study tools, visit the **Online Study Guide** at bedfordstmartins.com/huntconcise.

- For primary-source material from this period, see *Sources of the Making of the West*, Fourth Edition.

- For Web sites, images, and documents related to topics in this chapter, visit *Make History* at bedfordstmartins.com/huntconcise.

Suggested References

The cultural ferment, social turmoil, and actual violence of the pre–World War I years come alive in the works listed here.

Adamson, Walter L. *Embattled Avant-Gardes: Modernism's Resistance to Commodity Culture in Europe.* 2007.

Forth, Christopher E. *The Dreyfus Affair and the Crisis of French Manhood.* 2005.

Frevert, Ute. *A Nation of Barracks: Modern Germany, Military Conscription and Civil Society.* 2004.

Gingeras, Ryan. *Sorrowful Shores: Violence, Ethnicity, and the End of the Ottoman Empire 1912–1923.* 2011.

Hull, Isabel. *Absolute Destruction: Military Culture and the Practices of War in Imperial Germany.* 2005.

Hunt, Nancy Rose. *A Nervous State: Violence, Sterility, and Healing Movements in Colonial Congo.* 2012.

Kaplan, Morris B. *Sodom on the Thames: Sex, Love, and Scandal in Wilde Times.* 2005.

Marchand, Suzanne, and David Lindenfeld, eds. *Germany at the Fin-de-Siècle.* 2004.

Meir, Natan M. *Kiev, Jewish Metropolis: A History, 1859–1914.* 2010.

Nolan, Michael E. *The Inverted Mirror: Mythologizing the Enemy in France and Germany, 1898–1914.* 2005.

Reagin, Nancy R. *Sweeping the German Nation: Domesticity and National Identity in Germany 1870–1945.* 2006.

Stanford Encyclopedia of Philosophy: http://plato.stanford.edu

Stanislawski, Michael. *Zionism and the Fin-de-Siècle: Cosmopolitanism and Nationalism from Nordau to Jabotinsky.* 2001.

Thompson, J. Lee. *Theodore Roosevelt Abroad: Nature, Empire and the Journey of an American President.* 2010.

Willmott, H. P. *The Last Century of Sea Power: From Port Arthur to Chanak, 1894–1922.* 2009.

World War I and Its Aftermath

1914–1929

J ules Amar, a French expert on improving the efficiency of industrial work, changed his career as a result of war. After 1914, as hundreds of thousands of soldiers returned from the battlefront missing body parts, plastic surgery and the construction of masks and other devices to hide deformities developed rapidly. Amar devised artificial limbs that would allow the wounded soldier to return to normal life by "making up for a function lost, or greatly reduced." The artificial arms featured hooks, magnets, and other mechanisms with which veterans could hold a cigarette, play a violin, and, most important, work with tools such as typewriters. Those who had been mangled by the weapons of modern technological warfare would be made whole, it was thought, by technology such as Amar's.

Jules Amar did his part to confront the tragedy of the Great War, so named by contemporaries because of its staggering human toll — forty million wounded or killed in battle. The Great War did not settle problems or restore social order as the European powers hoped it would. Instead, the war produced political chaos, overturning the Russian, German, Ottoman, and Austro-Hungarian Empires. The burden of war crushed the European powers and accelerated the rise of the United States, while colonized peoples who served in the war intensified their demands for independence. In fact, the armistice in 1918 did not truly end conflict: many soldiers remained actively fighting long into what was supposed to be peacetime, and others had been so militarized that they longed for a life that was more like wartime.

Grieving Parents

Before World War I, the German artist Käthe Kollwitz gained her artistic reputation with woodcuts of handloom weavers whose livelihoods were threatened by industrialization. From 1914 on, she depicted the suffering and death that swirled around her — and never with more sober force than in these two monuments to her son Peter, who died on the western front in the first months of battle. Today one can still travel to Peter's burial place in Vladslo, Belgium, to see this father and mother mourning their loss, like millions across Europe in those heartbreaking days. (photo © Paul Maeyaert / The Bridgeman Art Library International. © 2012 Artists Rights Society [ARS], New York / VG Bild-Kunst, Bonn.)

World War I transformed society, too. A prewar feeling of doom and decline gave way to postwar cynicism. Many Westerners turned their backs on politics and in the Roaring Twenties embraced life with wild gaiety, shopping for new consumer goods, enjoying once forbidden personal freedoms, and taking pleasure in the entertainment provided by films and radio. Others found reason for hope in the new political systems the war made possible: Soviet communism and Italian fascism. Modern communication technologies such as radio gave politicians the means to promote a utopian mass politics that, ironically, was antidemocratic, militaristic, and violent —

CHAPTER FOCUS What political, social, and economic impact did World War I have during the conflict, immediately after it, and through the 1920s?

like the war itself. A war that was welcomed in some quarters as a remedy for modernity destabilized Europe far into the following decades leaving Europeans, including Jules Amar and those he helped, to deal with its violent aftermath.

The Great War, 1914–1918

When war erupted in August 1914, two months after the assassination of the Austrian archduke and his wife at Sarajevo, there already existed long-standing alliances, well-defined strategies, and a stockpile of military technologies such as heavy artillery, machine guns, and airplanes. Most people felt that this would be a short, decisive conflict similar to Prussia's rapid victories in the 1860s and 1870–1871. In fact, the war lasted for more than four long years. It was what historians call a **total war**, meaning one built on the full mobilization of entire societies — soldiers and civilians — and the industrial capacities of the nations involved. It was the war's unexpected and unprecedented horror that made World War I "great."

Blueprints for War

World War I's two sets of opponents were formed roughly out of the alliances developed during the previous fifty years. On one side stood the Central Powers (Austria-Hungary and Germany), which had evolved from Bismarck's Triple Alliance. On the other side were the Allies (France, Great Britain, and Russia), which had emerged as a bloc from the Entente Cordiale between France and Great Britain and the 1890s treaties between France and Russia. In 1915, Italy, originally part of the Triple Alliance, joined the Allies in hopes of postwar gain. The war soon exploded globally: in late August 1914, Japan, eager to extend its empire into China, went over to the Allies, while in the fall the Ottoman Empire united with the Central Powers against its traditional enemy, Russia (Map 25.1).

Of the Central Powers, Germany wanted a bigger empire, to be gained by annexing Russian territory and incorporating parts of Belgium, France, and Luxembourg. Some German leaders wanted to annex Austria-Hungary as well. Austria-Hungary hoped to keep its great-power status despite the competing nationalisms of ethnic groups within

Map 25.1 The Fronts of World War I, 1914–1918
Because the western front remained relatively stationary, devastation of land and resources was intense. All fronts, however, destroyed segments of Europe's hard-won industrial and agricultural capacity, while the immobile trenches increased military casualties whenever heavy artillery fire pounded them. Men long engaged in trench warfare developed an intense camaraderie based on their mutual suffering and deprivation.

its borders. Among the Allies, Russia wished to reassert its status as a great power and as the protector of the Slavs by adding a reunified Poland to the Russian Empire and by taking formal leadership of other Slavic peoples. The French, too, craved territory, especially the return of Alsace and Lorraine, ceded to Germany after the Franco-Prussian

War of 1870–1871. The British wanted to cement their hold on Egypt and the Suez Canal and keep the rest of their world empire secure. By the Treaty of London (1915), France and Britain promised Italy territory in Africa, Asia Minor, the Balkans, and elsewhere in return for joining the Allies.

The colonies participated in the war too, providing massive assistance and serving as battlegrounds. Some one million Africans, one million Indians, and more than a million men from the British commonwealth countries fought on the battlefronts. The imperial powers also conscripted uncounted numbers of colonists as forced laborers: a million Kenyans and Tanzanians alone are estimated to have been conscripted for menial labor in the battle for East Africa. Using Arab, African, and Indian troops, the British waged successful war in the Ottoman lands of the Middle East. In sub-Saharan Africa, the vicious campaign for East Africa cost many lives, including many civilians whose resources were confiscated and whose villages were burned.

Unprecedented use of new machinery determined the course of war. In August 1914, machine guns, fast breech-loading rifles, and military vehicles such as airplanes, battleships, submarines, and motorized transport (cars and trains) were all at the armies' disposal. New technologies such as chlorine gas, tanks, and bombs were developed between 1914 and 1918. The war itself became a lethal testing ground, as both new and old weapons were used, often ineffectively. Many officers on both sides believed in a **cult of the offensive**, which called for spirited attacks against the enemy and high troop morale. Despite the availability of powerful war technology, an old-fashioned, heroic vision of war made many officers unwilling to abandon the more familiar sabers, lances, and bayonets. In the face of massive firepower, the cult of the offensive would cost millions of lives.

The Battlefronts

The first months of the war crushed any hope of a quick victory. The Germans were guided by the **Schlieffen Plan**, named after a former chief of the general staff. The plan outlined a way to combat enemies on two fronts by concentrating on one foe at a time. It called for a concentrated blow to the west against France, which would lead to that nation's defeat in six weeks, accompanied by a light holding action against Russia to the east. The attack on France was to proceed without resistance through neutral Belgium. Once France had fallen, Germany's western armies would move against Russia, which, it was believed, would mobilize far more slowly. None of the great powers expected that war would turn into the prolonged massacre of their nations' youth.

When German troops reached Belgium and Luxembourg at the beginning of August 1914, the Belgians surprisingly mounted a vigorous defense, which slowed the German advance. In September, the British and French armies engaged the Germans along the Marne River in France. Neither side could defeat the other, and in the first three months of war, more than 1.5 million men fell on the western front alone. Guns like the 75-millimeter howitzer, accurate at long range, turned what was supposed to be

an offensive war of movement into a stationary standoff along a line that stretched from the North Sea through Belgium and northern France to Switzerland.

On the eastern front, the Russians drove far more quickly than expected into East Prussia in mid-August. The Russians believed that no army could stand up to the massive number of their soldiers, regardless of how badly equipped and poorly trained those soldiers were. Their success was short-lived. The Germans overwhelmed the tsar's army in East Prussia. Victory made heroes of the German military leaders Paul von Hindenburg (1847–1934) and Erich Ludendorff (1865–1937), who demanded more troops for the eastern front, undermining the Schlieffen Plan by removing forces from the west before the western front had been won.

War at sea proved equally indecisive. The Allies blockaded ports to prevent supplies from reaching Germany and Austria-Hungary. Kaiser William and his advisers planned a massive U-boat (*Unterseeboot*, "underwater boat," or submarine) campaign against Allied and neutral shipping. In May 1915, U-boats sank the British passenger ship *Lusitania* and killed 1,198 people, including 124 Americans. Despite U.S. outrage, President Woodrow Wilson (1856–1924) maintained a policy of neutrality; Germany, unwilling to provoke Wilson further, called off unrestricted submarine warfare. In May 1916, the navies of Germany and Britain finally clashed in the North Sea at Jutland. This inconclusive battle demonstrated that the German fleet could not master British seapower.

Ideas of a negotiated peace were discarded: "No peace before England is defeated and destroyed," William II stormed against his cousin King George V. French leaders called for a "war to the death." General staffs on both sides continued to prepare fierce attacks several times a year. Campaigns opened with heavy artillery pounding enemy trenches and gun emplacements. Troops then responded to the order to go "over the top" by scrambling out of their trenches and into battle, usually to be mowed down by machine-gun fire from defenders secure in their own trenches. On the western front, the French assaulted the Germans throughout 1915 but accomplished little. On the eastern front, Russian armies captured parts of Galicia in the spring of 1915 and lumbered toward Hungary.

The next year's battles were even more disastrous and futile. To cripple French morale, the Germans launched massive assaults on the fortress at Verdun, firing as many as a million shells in a single day. Combined French and German losses totaled close to a million men. Nonetheless, the French held. The British unleashed an artillery pounding of German trenches in the Somme region in June 1916; 1.25 million men were killed or wounded, but the final result was stalemate. By the end of 1916, the French had suffered more than 3.5 million casualties. To help the Allies engaged at Verdun and the Somme, the Russians struck again, driving into the Carpathian Mountains, recouping territory, and menacing Austria-Hungary. The German army stopped the advance, as the German general staff decided it would take over Austrian military operations.

Had military leaders thoroughly dominated the scene, historians judge, all armies would have been utterly demolished by the end of 1915. Yet ordinary soldiers in this

War in the Skies (1914)

As the war started, aviators and the machines they piloted became symbols of the human potential to transcend time and space. The Great War, however, featured the airplane as the new weapon in what British writer H. G. Wells called the "headlong sweep to death." Daring pilots, or "aces," took the planes on reconnaissance flights and guided them in the totally new practice of aerial combat, as shown in this engraving from an Italian newspaper of a French airplane shooting down a German one. (Domenica del Corriere / Gianni Dagli Orti / The Art Archive at Art Resource, NY.)

war were not automatons in the face of what seemed to them suicidal orders from their commanders. Informal agreements to avoid battles against each other allowed some battalions to go for long stretches with hardly a casualty. Enemies facing each other across the trenches frequently ate their meals in peace, even though the trenches were within hand-grenade reach. Throughout the war, soldiers on both fronts played an occasional game of soccer or made gestures of agreement not to fight. A British veteran of the trenches explained to a new recruit that the Germans "don't want to fight any more than we do, so there's a kind of understanding between us. Don't fire at us and we'll not fire at you." Many ordinary soldiers came to feel more warmly toward enemies who shared the trench experience than toward civilians back home. This camaraderie relieved some of the misery of trench life and aided survival. In some cases, upper-class officers and working-class recruits became friends in that "wholly masculine way of life uncomplicated by women," as another soldier put it. Soldiers tended one another's blistered feet and came to love one another, sometimes even passionately. This sense of frontline community survived the war and influenced postwar politics.

Troops of colonized soldiers from Asia and Africa often were put in the very front ranks, where the risks were greatest. Yet, like class divisions, racial barriers sometimes fell: a European might give extra blankets and clothing to soldiers from warmer regions. These troops saw their "masters" completely undone and "uncivilized," for when fighting did break out, trenches became a veritable hell of shelling and sniping, flying body parts, blinding gas, and rotting cadavers. Some soldiers became hysterical or shell-shocked through the stress and violence of battle. Those who had gone to war to escape

War in the Trenches

Men at the front developed close friend-ships while they lived with daily discomfort, death, and the horrors of modern techno-logical warfare. Some of the complexities of trench warfare appear in this image show-ing soldiers rescuing their fallen comrades after fighting at Bagatelle in northern France. (Hulton Archive / Getty Images.)

ordinary life in industrial society learned, as one German put it, "that in the modern war . . . the triumph of the machine over the individual is carried to its most extreme form."

The Home Front

Total war demanded the involvement of civilians in manufacturing shells, machine guns, poisonous gases, bombs, airplanes, and eventually tanks — which together formed the backbone of technological warfare. Increased production of coffins, canes, wheelchairs, and artificial limbs (devised by the likes of Jules Amar) was also required. Because their armies would have utterly failed without them, civilians had to believe in the war and to work overtime and sacrifice for victory. To keep the war machine operating smoothly, governments oversaw factories, trans-portation systems, and the use of resources. People accepted tight government control as necessary to win the war.

At first, most political parties put aside their differences. Many socialists and working-class people who had formerly criticized the military buildup announced their support for the war. For decades, socialist parties had preached that "the worker has no country" and that nationalism was an ideology meant to keep workers disunited and subjected to the will of their employers. In August 1914, however, most socialists be-came as patriotic as the rest of society. Although many feminists actively opposed the conflict, the British suffrage leader Emmeline Pankhurst and her daughter Christabel were among those who became militant nationalists. In the name of victory, national leaders wanted to end political division of all kinds: "I no longer recognize [political] parties," William II declared on August 4, 1914. "I recognize only Germans." Those who had been at the receiving end of discrimination promoted unity. One rabbi proudly echoed the kaiser: "In the German fatherland there are no longer any Christians and Jews, any believers and disbelievers, there are only Germans."

Governments mobilized the home front with varying degrees of success. War ministries set up boards to allocate labor on both the home front and the battlefront and to give industrialists financial incentives to encourage productivity. The Russian bureaucracy, however, only cooperated halfheartedly with industrialists and other groups that could aid the war effort. In several countries, emergency measures allowed the drafting of both men and women for military or industrial service. Municipal governments set up canteens and day-care centers, but rural Russia, Austria-Hungary, Bulgaria, and Serbia, where youths, women, and old men struggled to sustain farms, had no such relief programs.

Governments throughout Europe passed sedition laws that made it a crime to criticize war-related policies and created propaganda agencies, sometimes fabricating atrocities, to advertise the war as a patriotic mission to resist villainous enemies. In Russia, Tsar Nicholas II had changed the German-sounding name of the capital St. Petersburg to the Russian Petrograd as a patriotic move. Maintaining that Armenians in the Ottoman Empire were plotting against the Central Powers, the Ottomans drove those Armenians living in Turkey from their homes, forcing them onto long marches or into concentration camps where they were murdered or simply died. The Allies also caused the deaths of civilians en masse by creating famines, blockading the Syrian provinces of the Ottoman Empire in hopes that the people there would rebel or die of starvation.

Despite widespread popular support for the war, some individuals worked to bring about a negotiated peace. In 1915, activists in the international women's movement met in The Hague to call for an end to the war. "We can no longer endure . . . brute force as the only solution of international disputes," declared Dutch physician Aletta Jacobs. The women had no success, though many brought their cause to individual heads of state. In Austria-Hungary, agitating for ethnic self-determination, the Czechs undertook a vigorous anti-Habsburg campaign, while Croats, Slovenes, and Serbs in the Balkans formed a committee to plan a southern Slavic state independent of Austria-Hungary. The Allies encouraged such independence movements as part of their strategy to defeat Austria-Hungary.

The war upset the social order as well as the political one. In the war's early days, many women lost their jobs when luxury shops, textile factories, and other nonessential businesses closed. As more and more men left for the trenches, women who had lost employment elsewhere joined with low-paid domestic workers to take over higher-paying jobs in munitions and metallurgical industries. In Warsaw women drove trucks, and in London they conducted streetcars. Some young women drove ambulances and nursed the wounded near the front lines.

Women's assumption of men's jobs looked to many like a sign of social disorder. In the words of one metalworker, women were "sending men to the slaughter." Men feared that women would remain in the workforce after the war, robbing men of the breadwinner role. Others criticized young female munitions workers for squandering their pay on ribbons and jewelry. The heated prewar debates over the "new woman" and gender roles returned.

A New Workforce in Wartime

With men at the front, women (at right in this French photograph) moved into factory work at jobs from which they had been unofficially barred before the war. In addition, tens of thousands of forced laborers from the colonies were moved to Europe also to replace men sent to the front. The European experience of forced labor and service at the front politicized colonial subjects, fortifying independence movements in the postwar period. (Roger Viollet / Getty Images.)

Although soldiers from different backgrounds often felt bonds of solidarity in the trenches, difficult wartime conditions increasingly pitted civilians against one another on the home front. Workers toiled long hours with less to eat, while many in the upper classes bought fancy food and fashionable clothing on the black market (outside the official system of rationing). The cost of living surged and thus contributed to social tensions as shortages of staples like bread, sugar, and meat occurred across Europe and people went hungry. Reviving prewar anti-Semitism, some blamed Jews for the shortages. Colonial populations suffered oppressive conditions as well. The French forcibly transported some 100,000 Vietnamese to work in France for the war effort. Africans also faced grueling forced labor along with skyrocketing taxes and prices. Civilian suffering during the war, whether in the colonies or in Europe, laid the groundwork for ordinary people to take political action.

REVIEW QUESTION In what ways was World War I a total war?

Protest, Revolution, and War's End, 1917–1918

By 1917, the situation was becoming desperate for everyone — politicians, the military, and civilians. Discontent on the home front started shaping the course of the war. Neither patriotic slogans before the war nor propaganda during it had prepared people for wartime devastation. Civilians rebelled in cities across Europe. While soldiers in some armies mutinied, nationalist struggles continued to plague Britain and Austria-Hungary. Soon full-fledged revolution was sweeping Europe, toppling the Russian dynasty, and threatening not just war but civil war as well.

War Protest

On February 1, 1917, the German government, hard-pressed by the public clamor over mounting casualties and by the military's growing control, resumed full-scale submarine warfare. The British responded by mining their harbors and the surrounding seas and by developing the convoy system of shipping to drive off German submarines. The Germans' submarine gamble not only failed to defeat the British but also brought the United States into the war in April 1917, after German U-boats sank several American ships.

Political opposition increased in Europe. Irish republicans attacked government buildings in Dublin on Easter Monday 1916 in an effort to gain Ireland's independence from Britain during the crisis. The ill-prepared rebels were easily defeated, and many of them were executed. In the cities of Italy, Russia, Germany, and Austria, women rioted to get food for their families, and factory hands and white-collar workers alike walked off the job. Amid these protests, Austria-Hungary secretly asked the Allies for a negotiated peace; the German Reichstag also made overtures for a "peace of understanding and permanent reconciliation of peoples." In January 1918, President Woodrow Wilson issued his **Fourteen Points**, a blueprint for a nonvindictive peace settlement held out to the war-weary citizens of the Central Powers.

Revolution in Russia

Of all the warring nations, Russia sustained the greatest number of casualties — 7.5 million by 1917. In March,* crowds of workingwomen swarmed the streets of Petrograd demanding relief from the harsh conditions. They soon fell in with other protesters commemorating International Women's Day and were then joined by factory workers and other civilians. Instead of remaining loyal to the tsar, many soldiers were embittered by the massive casualties and their leaders' foolhardy tactics. The government's incompetence and Nicholas II's stubborn resistance to change had made the war even worse in

---

*Until February 1918, Russia observed the Julian calendar, which was thirteen days behind the Gregorian calendar used by the rest of Europe. Hence, the first phase of the revolution occurred in March according to the Gregorian calendar (but February in the Julian calendar), the later phase in November on the Gregorian calendar (October according to the Julian). All dates used in this book follow the Gregorian calendar.

Russia than elsewhere. When the riots erupted in March 1917, Nicholas finally realized the situation was hopeless. He abdicated, bringing the three-hundred-year-old Romanov dynasty to a sudden end.

Aristocratic and middle-class politicians from the old Duma formed a new administration called the Provisional Government. At first, hopes were high that under the Provisional Government, as one revolutionary poet put it, "our false, filthy, boring, hideous life should become a just, pure, merry, and beautiful life." To survive, the Provisional Government had to pursue the war successfully, manage internal affairs better, and set the government on a firm constitutional footing, but other political forces had also strengthened during the revolution. Among them, the **soviets**—councils elected from workers and soldiers—competed with the government for political support. Born during the Revolution of 1905, the soviets in 1917 campaigned to end the deference usually given to the wealthy and to military officers, urged respect for workers and the poor, and temporarily gave an air of celebration and carnival to the political upheaval. The peasants, also competing for power, began to confiscate landed estates and withhold produce from the market, threatening the Provisional Government.

In hopes of adding to the turmoil in Russia, the Germans in April 1917 provided safe rail transportation for **V. I. Lenin** (1870–1924) and other prominent Bolsheviks to return to Russia through German territory. Lenin had devoted his entire existence to bringing about socialism through the force of his small band of Bolsheviks. Upon his return to Petrograd, he issued the April Theses, a radical document that called for Russia to withdraw from the war, for the soviets to seize power on behalf of workers and poor peasants, and for all private land to be nationalized. As the Bolsheviks aimed to supplant the Provisional Government, they employed such slogans as "All power to the soviets" and "Peace, land, and bread."

New prime minister Aleksandr Kerensky used his commanding oratory to arouse patriotism, but he lacked the political skills needed to create an effective wartime government. The Bolshevik leadership, urged on by Lenin, overthrew the weakened Provisional Government in November 1917, an event called the **Bolshevik Revolution**. In January 1918, elections for a constituent assembly failed to give the Bolsheviks a plurality, so the party used troops to take over the new government completely. The Bolsheviks, observing Marxist doctrine, abolished private property and nationalized factories in order to stimulate production. The Provisional Government had allowed both men and women to vote in 1917, making Russia the first great power to legalize universal suffrage. This soon became a hollow privilege once the Bolsheviks limited the candidates to chosen members of the Communist Party.

The Bolsheviks asked Germany for peace and agreed to the Treaty of Brest-Litovsk (March 1918), which placed vast regions of the old Russian Empire under German occupation. Because the loss of millions of square miles to the Germans put Petrograd at risk, the Bolsheviks relocated the capital to Moscow and formally adopted the name Communists (taken from Karl Marx's writings) to distinguish themselves from the socialists/social democrats who had voted for the disastrous war in the first place. Lenin called the catastrophic terms of the treaty "obscene." However, he accepted them—not

Lenin Addressing Soldiers
Lenin mobilized the masses with his oratory, but he also used traditional weapons of the Russian Empire such as secret police, imprisonment and torture, and executions. At the time of the civil war it was more than ever important to keep soldiers loyal. Understanding this, Lenin, with the crucial aid of Leon Trotsky, began building the Red Army into a formidable fighting force. (Rue des Archives / The Granger Collection, NYC — All rights reserved.)

only because he had promised to bring peace to Russia but also because he believed that the rest of Europe would soon rebel against the war and overthrow the capitalist order.

A full-blown civil war now broke out in Russia, with the pro-Bolsheviks (or "Reds") pitted against an array of forces (the "Whites") who wanted to turn back the revolution (Map 25.2). Among the Whites were three distinct groups: the tsarist military leadership, composed mainly of landlords and supporters of aristocratic rule; the liberal educated class, including businessmen whose property had been nationalized; and non-Russian nationalities who saw their chance for independence. In addition, before World War I ended, Russia's former allies — notably the United States, Britain, France, and Japan — landed troops in the country to fight the Bolsheviks. The counterrevolutionary groups lacked a strong leader and unified goals, however. Pro-tsarist forces, for example, alienated groups seeking independent nation-state status, such as the Ukrainians, Estonians, and Lithuanians, by stressing the goal of restoring the Russian Empire. Even with the presence of Allied troops, the opponents of revolution could not defeat the Bolsheviks without a common purpose.

The civil war shaped Russian communism. Leon Trotsky (1879–1940), Bolshevik commissar of war, built the highly disciplined army by ending democratic procedures,

Map 25.2 The Russian Civil War, 1917–1922

Nationalists, aristocrats, middle-class citizens, and property-owning peasants tried to combine their interests to defeat the Bolsheviks, but they failed to create an effective political consensus. As fighting covered the countryside, ordinary people suffered, especially when their grain was confiscated by armies on both sides. The Western powers and Japan also sent in troops to put down this threatening revolution.

such as the election of officers, that had originally attracted soldiers to Bolshevism. Lenin and Trotsky introduced the policy of war communism — seizing grain from the peasantry to feed the civil war army and workforce. The Cheka (secret police) imprisoned political opponents and black marketers and often shot them without trial. The result was a more authoritarian government — a development that broke Marx's promise that revolution would bring a "withering away" of the state.

As the Bolsheviks clamped down on their opponents during the bloody civil war, they organized their supporters to foster revolutionary Marxism across Europe. In March 1919, they founded the Third International, also known as the Communist International (Comintern), to replace the Second International with a centralized organization dedicated to preaching communism. By mid-1921, the Red Army had defeated the Whites in the Crimea, the Caucasus, and the Muslim borderlands in central Asia. After ousting

the Japanese from Siberia in 1922, the Bolsheviks governed a state as multinational as the old Russian Empire had been, and one at odds with socialist promises for a humane and flourishing society.

Ending the War, 1918

In the spring of 1918, the Central Powers made one final attempt to smash through the Allied lines using a new offensive strategy. It consisted of concentrated forces piercing single points of the enemy's defense lines and then wreaking havoc from the rear. Using these tactics, the Central Powers overwhelmed the Italian army at Caporetto in the fall of 1917, but a similar offensive on the western front in the spring of 1918 ground to a bloody halt within weeks. By then, the British and French had started making limited but effective use of tanks supported by airplanes. The German armies, suffering more than two million casualties between spring and summer, rapidly disintegrated.

By October 1918, the desperate German command helped create a civilian government to take over rule of the home front. As these inexperienced politicians took power,

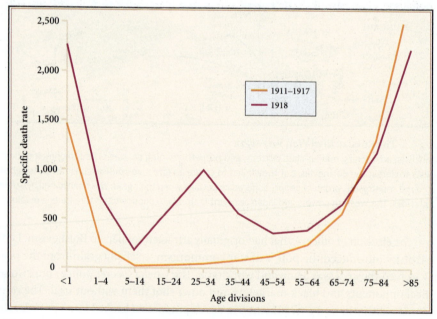

Taking Measure The Victims of Influenza, 1918–1919
The influenza pandemic that broke out among soldiers and civilians during World War I was devastating, claiming between 50 and 100 million lives worldwide. Not only was the death toll unprecedented but the victims of the flu differed significantly from those in the general population who had normally died from influenza and pneumonia. The graph above, showing the "terrible W" shape of flu deaths, illustrates that difference. (*Specific death rate* refers to a method of calculating mortality rates from a specified cause.) (Jeffrey K. Taubenberger and David Morens, "1918 Influenza: The Mother of All Pandemics," *Emerging Infectious Diseases* 12, no. 1 [2006]: 15–22.)

they were also taking blame for the defeat. Shifting the blame from the military, the generals proclaimed themselves fully capable of winning the war. Weak-willed civilians, they announced, had dealt the military a "stab in the back" by forcing a surrender. A sailors' revolt and workers' uprisings led the Social Democratic Party to declare a German republic in an effort to prevent revolution. At the end of October, Czechs and Slovaks declared an independent state, while the Croatian parliament simultaneously announced Croatia's independence. On November 9, 1918, Kaiser William II fled as the Central Powers collapsed on all fronts. Finally, on the morning of November 11, 1918, an armistice was signed and the guns fell silent.

In the course of four years, European civilization had been sorely tested, if not shattered. Conservative figures put the battlefield toll at a minimum of ten million dead and thirty million wounded, incapacitated, or doomed eventually to die of their wounds. In every European combatant country, industrial and agricultural production had plummeted. From 1918 to 1919, a worldwide influenza epidemic left as many as one hundred million more dead (see "Taking Measure," page 816). Soldiers returning home in 1918 and 1919 flooded the book market with their memoirs; whereas many had begun by emphasizing heroism and glory, others cynically insisted that the fighting had been absolutely meaningless. Total war had not only drained society of resources and population but also sown the seeds of further catastrophe.

> **REVIEW QUESTION** Why did people rebel during World War I, and what turned rebellion into outright revolution in Russia?

The Search for Peace in an Era of Revolution

World War I had unforeseen and dramatic consequences. Revolutionary fervor now swept the continent, especially in the former empires of Germany and Austria-Hungary. Many of the newly independent peoples of eastern and central Europe supported socialist principles, and activists on both the left and the right hoped for a political order based on military authority of the kind they had relied on during the war. Diplomats from around the world arrived in Paris in January 1919 to negotiate the terms of peace, though without fully recognizing the fact that the war was still going on not only in city streets, where soldiers were bringing the war home, but also in people's hearts.

Europe in Turmoil

Urban citizens and returning soldiers ignited the protests that swept Europe in 1918 and 1919. In January 1919, the red flag of socialist revolution flew from the city hall in Glasgow, Scotland, while in cities of the collapsing Austro-Hungarian monarchy, workers set up councils to take over factory production and direct politics. Many soldiers did not disband at the armistice but formed volunteer armies, preventing the return to peacetime politics. Germany was especially unstable, partly because of the shock of defeat; German workers and veterans filled the streets, demanding food and back pay. Whereas in 1848, revolutionaries had marched to city hall or the king's residence, the protesters

in 1919 took over newspapers and telegraph offices to control the flow of information. One of the most radical socialist factions was the Spartacists, led by cofounders Karl Liebknecht (1871–1919) and Rosa Luxemburg (1870–1919). Unlike Lenin, the two leading Spartacists wanted workers to gain political experience from any uprisings instead of simply following an all-knowing party leadership on a set course.

German conservatives had believed that the war would put an end to Social Democratic influence; instead, it brought German socialists to power. Social Democratic leader Friedrich Ebert, who headed the new German government, rejected revolution and supported the creation of a parliamentary republic to replace the monarchy. He called on the German army and the Freikorps — a roving paramilitary band of students, demobilized soldiers, and others — to suppress the workers' councils and demonstrators. "The enthusiasm is marvelous," wrote one young soldier. "No mercy's shown. We shoot even the wounded." Members of the Freikorps hunted down Luxemburg and Liebknecht, among others, and murdered them.

Violence continued in Europe even as an assembly meeting in the city of Weimar in February 1919 approved a constitution and founded a parliamentary republic called the **Weimar Republic**. This time the right rebelled, for the military leadership dreamed of a restored monarchy: "As I love Germany, so I hate the Republic," wrote one officer. To defeat a military coup by Freikorps officers, Ebert called for a general strike. This action showed the lack of popular support for a military regime. Late in the winter of 1919, leftists proclaimed "soviet republics" — governments led by workers' councils — in Bavaria and Hungary. Volunteer armies and troops soon put the soviets down. The Bolsheviks tried to establish a Marxist regime in Poland, but the Poles resisted and drove the Red Army back in 1920, while the Allied powers rushed supplies and advisers to Warsaw. Though they failed, the various revolts provided further proof that total war had let loose the forces of political chaos. War, it seemed, continued.

The Paris Peace Conference, 1919–1920

As political turmoil engulfed peoples from Berlin to Moscow, the Paris Peace Conference opened in January 1919. Visions of communism spreading westward haunted the deliberations, but the assembled statesmen were also focused on the reconstruction of a secure Europe and the status of Germany. Leaders such as French premier Georges Clemenceau had to satisfy angry citizens: France had lost 1.3 million people — almost an entire generation of young men — and more than a million buildings, six thousand bridges, and thousands of miles of railroad lines and roads. Great Britain's representative, Prime Minister David Lloyd George, caught the mood of the British public by campaigning in 1918 with such slogans as "Hang the kaiser." The Italians arrived on the scene demanding the territory promised to them in the 1915 Treaty of London. Meanwhile, U.S. president Woodrow Wilson, head of the new world power that had helped achieve the Allied victory, had his own agenda. His Fourteen Points, on which the truce had been based, were steeped in the language of freedom and called for open

diplomacy, arms reduction, and the right of nationality groups to determine their own government.

The Fourteen Points did not represent the mood of the victors. Allied propaganda had made the Germans seem like inhuman monsters, and some military experts feared that Germany was using the armistice only to regroup for more warfare. Indeed, Germans widely refused to admit that their army had lost the war. Eager for army support, Ebert had given returning soldiers a rousing welcome: "As you return unconquered from the field of battle, I salute you." Wilson's plan, based on *settlement* as opposed to *surrender*, however, recognized that Germany was still the strongest state on the continent. Economists and other specialists agreed that, harshly dealt with and humiliated, Germany might soon become vengeful and chaotic — a lethal combination.

After six months, the statesmen and their teams of experts produced the **Peace of Paris** (1919–1920), a cluster of individual treaties that shocked the citizens of the countries that had to accept them. The treaties separated Austria from Hungary, reduced Hungary by almost two-thirds of its inhabitants and three-quarters of its territory, broke up the Ottoman Empire, and treated Germany severely. They replaced the Habsburg Empire with a group of small, internally divided, and economically weak states: Czechoslovakia; Poland; and the Kingdom of the Serbs, Croats, and Slovenes (soon renamed Yugoslavia). After a century and a half of partition, Poland was reconstructed from parts of Russia, Germany, and Austria-Hungary — leaving one-third of its population ethnically non-Polish. The statesmen in Paris also created the Polish Corridor, which connected Poland to the Baltic Sea and separated East Prussia from the rest of Germany (Map 25.3). Austria and Hungary were both left reeling at their drastic loss of territory and resources.

The Treaty of Versailles, the centerpiece of the Peace of Paris, specifically dealt with Germany. In it, France recovered Alsace and Lorraine, and the Allies would temporarily occupy the left, or western, bank of the Rhine and the coal-bearing Saar basin. Germany would pay substantial reparations for civilian damage during the war, set in 1921 at the crushing sum of 132 billion gold marks. Germany also had to reduce its army, almost eliminate its navy, stop manufacturing offensive weapons, and deliver a large amount of free coal each year to Belgium and France. Furthermore, it was forbidden to have an air force and had to give up its colonies. Article 231 of the treaty described Germany's "responsibility" for damage caused "by the aggression of Germany and her allies." Outraged Germans interpreted this as a **war guilt clause**, which blamed Germany for the war and allowed the victors to collect reparations from their economically developed country rather than from ruined Austria. War guilt made Germans feel like outcasts in the community of nations.

Besides redrawing the map of Europe, the Peace of Paris set up an organization called the **League of Nations**, whose members had a joint responsibility for maintaining peace — a principle called collective security. It was supposed to replace the divisive secrecy of prewar power politics and arbitrate its members' disputes. The U.S. Senate failed to ratify the peace settlement and refused to join the league. Moreover, Germany

Map 25.3 Europe and the Middle East after the Peace Settlements of 1919–1920
The political landscape of central, east, and east-central Europe changed dramatically as a result of the Russian Revolution and the Peace of Paris. The Ottoman, German, Russian, and Austro-Hungarian Empires were either broken up into multiple small states or territorially reduced. The settlement left resentments among Germans and Hungarians and created a group of weak, struggling nations in the heartland of Europe. The victorious powers took over much of the oil-rich Middle East. Why is it significant that the postwar geopolitical changes were so concentrated in one section of Europe?

and Russia initially were excluded from the league and were thus blocked from working cooperatively with it. The absence of these three important powers weakened the league as a global peacekeeper.

The League of Nations also organized the administration of the former colonies and territories of Germany and the Ottoman Empire — such as Togo, Cameroon, Syria, and

Palestine — through systems of political control called mandates. While the victorious powers exercised their mandates, local leaders retained limited authority. The league justified the **mandate system** as providing governance by "advanced nations" over territories "not yet able to stand by themselves under the strenuous conditions of the modern world." The mandate system not only kept imperialism alive at a time when the powers were bankrupt and weak but also, like the Peace of Paris, aroused anger and resistance.

Economic and Diplomatic Consequences of the Peace

The Peace of Paris extended at least two problems into the 1920s and beyond. The first was economic recovery and its relationship to war debts and German reparation payments. The second was ensuring that peace actually came about and lasted. France, hardest hit by wartime destruction and billions of dollars in debt to the United States, estimated that Germany owed it at least $200 billion. Britain, by contrast, had not been physically devastated and was worried instead about maintaining its empire and restoring trade with Germany, not exacting huge reparations to rebuild. Nevertheless, both France and Britain were dependent on some German payments to settle their war debts to the United States.

Germany claimed that the demand for reparations strained its government, already facing political upheaval. In fact, Germany's economic problems had begun long before the Peace of Paris; they had started with the kaiser's policy of not raising taxes — especially on the rich — to pay for the war, leaving the new republic with a staggering debt. Now this republic, an experiment in democracy, needed to win over its citizens, and hiking taxes to pay Germany's debt would only anger them. In 1921, when Germans refused to present a realistic plan for paying reparations, the French occupied several cities in the Ruhr basin until a settlement was reached.

Germany's relations with powers to the west continued to deteriorate. In 1923, after Germany defaulted on coal deliveries, the French (this time joined by the Belgians) again sent troops into the Ruhr basin, planning to seize its output to pay the wartime debt. Urged on by the government, Ruhr citizens shut down industry by staying home from work. The German government printed trillions of marks to support the workers and to pay its own war debts with practically worthless currency. The result was a staggering inflation in Germany: at one point, a single U.S. dollar cost 4.42 trillion marks, and wheelbarrows of money were required to buy a turnip. Negotiations to resolve this economic chaos resulted in the Dawes Plan (1924) and the Young Plan (1929), which reduced reparations and restored the value of German currency. Before that happened, however, the inflation had wiped out people's savings and turned many more Germans against their democratic government. (See the illustration on page 822.)

The second burning issue unresolved by the Peace of Paris involved making the peace take hold and last. Statesmen determined that peace needed disarmament, a return of Germany to the community of nations, and security for the new countries of eastern Europe. Hard diplomatic bargaining produced two plans in Germany's favor.

Gegen eine neue
Jnflation
**Für Reichseinheit
und Republik
Für Loslösung von
unseren Feinden**

*Rettung
bringt die O.D.P.*

**Wählt
Deutsch-Demokratisch**

Inflation and the German Elections

The extraordinary inflation that struck the German economy in 1923 haunted those who lived through it and lost their life savings as money became worthless. The disaster gravely affected both the social and political order, leaving a legacy of fear and outrage. In this poster, the German Democratic Party rouses terror with its highly charged image of inflation as a monstrous enemy of the nation in the election campaign of 1924.
(© Photo 12 / The Image Works.)

At the Washington Conference in 1921, the United States, Great Britain, Japan, France, and Italy agreed to reduce their number of battleships and to stop constructing new ones for ten years. Four years later, in 1925, the League of Nations sponsored a meeting of the great powers, including Germany, at Locarno, Switzerland. The Treaty of Locarno provided Germany with a seat in the league as of 1926. In return, Germany agreed not to violate the borders of France and Belgium and to keep the nearby Rhineland demilitarized — that is, unfortified by troops.

To the east, statesmen feared a German attempt to regain territory lost to Poland, to merge with Austria, or to launch any attack on states spun off from Austria-Hungary. To meet this threat, Czechoslovakia, Yugoslavia, and Romania formed the Little Entente in 1920–1921, a collective security agreement intended to protect them from Germany and Russia. Between 1924 and 1927, France allied itself with the Little Entente and with Poland. In 1928, sixty nations, including the major European powers, Japan, and the United States, signed the Kellogg-Briand Pact, which formally rejected international violence. The pact lacked any mechanism for enforcement and thus resembled, as one critic put it, "an international kiss."

The publicity surrounding the international agreements of the 1920s sharply contrasted with old-style diplomacy, which had been conducted in secret and subject to little public scrutiny. The development of a system of open, collective security suggested a diplomatic revolution that would promote international peace. Yet openness allowed diplomats to feed the press information designed to provoke the masses. For example, the press

and opposition parties whipped the German populace into a nationalist fury whenever Germany's diplomats appeared to compromise, even though these compromises worked to undo the Treaty of Versailles. Journalists who hated republican government used international meetings such as the one at Locarno to fire up political hatreds rather than promote peace or rational public discussion.

> **REVIEW QUESTION** What were the major outcomes of the postwar peacemaking process?

A Decade of Recovery: Europe in the 1920s

Even after the armistice and the peace treaties, the wartime spirit endured. Towns and villages built their monuments to the fallen, and battlefield tourism sprang up for veterans and their families in search of a relative's final resting place. Words and phrases from the battlefield became part of everyday speech. Before the war the word *lousy* had meant "lice-infested," but English-speaking soldiers returning from the trenches now applied it to anything bad. Raincoats became *trenchcoats*. Maimed, disfigured veterans were present everywhere. While some received prostheses designed by Jules Amar, others without limbs were sometimes carried in baskets — hence the expression *basket case*. Four autocratic governments had collapsed as a result of the war, but whether these states would become workable democracies remained an open question. The Roaring Twenties masked the serious problem of restoring stability and implementing democracy amid the grim legacy of war.

Changes in the Political Landscape

The collapse of autocratic governments and the widespread extension of suffrage to women brought political turmoil as well as the expansion of democracy. Woman suffrage resulted in part from decades of activism, but many men in government claimed that suffrage was a "reward" for women's war efforts. Women were voted into parliaments in the first postwar elections, but French men pointedly denied women the vote, threatening that women voters would bring back the rule of kings and priests. (Only at the end of World War II would France and Italy extend suffrage to women.) The welfare state also expanded, with payments being made to veterans and victims of workplace accidents. These benefits stemmed from the belief that more evenly distributed wealth — sometimes called economic democracy — would prevent the outbreak of revolution.

Women Gain Suffrage in the West	
1906	Finland
1913	Norway
1915	Denmark, Iceland
1917	Netherlands, Russia
1918	Czechoslovakia, Great Britain (limited suffrage)
1919	Germany
1920	Austria, United States
1921	Poland
1925	Hungary (limited suffrage)
1945	Italy, France
1971	Switzerland

The trend toward economic democracy was not easy to maintain, however, because the cycles of boom and bust that had characterized the late nineteenth century reemerged. A short postwar economic boom prompted by reconstruction and consumer spending was followed by an economic downturn that was most severe between 1920 and 1922. By the mid-1920s, women made up a smaller percentage of the workforce than in 1913, and skyrocketing unemployment produced more discontent with governments. Veterans were especially angered by economic insecurity after years of enduring the war's horrors.

The new republics of eastern Europe were especially unprepared for hard economic times and poorly equipped to compete in the world market. None but Czechoslovakia had a mature industrial sector, and agricultural techniques were often primitive. Still more pressing problems hampered them. Vast migrations occurred as some 1 million citizens escaped the civil war in Russia and 800,000 soldiers from the defeated Whites searched for safety. Two million people fled Turkey, Greece, and Bulgaria because the postwar settlement called for the new nations to be built along "nationality" lines. Hundreds of thousands landed in new nations: Hungary, for example, had to receive 300,000 people of Magyar ethnicity who were no longer welcome in Romania, Czechoslovakia, or Yugoslavia. Most of these millions of refugees lacked land or jobs. They had nothing to do "but loaf and starve," one English journalist observed of refugees in Bulgaria. The influx of people brought more conflict in various parts of eastern Europe.

Poland exemplified how postwar turmoil could destroy a new nation's parliamentary democracy. One-third of the reunified Poland consisted of Ukrainians, Belorussians, Germans, and other ethnic minorities — many of whom had grievances against the dominant Poles. Varying religious and cultural traditions also divided the Poles, who for 150 years had been split among Austria, Germany, and Russia. Polish reunification occurred without a common currency or political heritage — even the railroad tracks were not a standard size. Despite a new constitution that professed equal rights for all ethnicities and religions, declining crop prices and overpopulation made life in the countryside difficult. The economic downturn brought strikes and violence in 1922–1923. Ultimately, former military leader Jozef Pilsudski took power via a coup in 1926 because of the government's inability to bring about prosperity. In postwar east-central Europe, military solutions to economic hardship demonstrated the endurance of war long after the peace had officially begun.

National Minorities in Postwar Poland

Germany was a different case. Although its economy picked up and the nation became a center of experimentation in the arts, political life remained

unstable because so many people, nostalgic for imperial glory, associated defeat with the new Weimar Republic. Extremist politicians heaped daily abuse on Weimar's democracy. A wealthy newspaper and film tycoon called anyone cooperating with the parliamentary system "a moral cripple." Right-wing parties favored violence rather than consensus building, and nationalist thugs murdered democratic leaders and Jews. Communists were not shy about jumping into street brawls, either.

Support for the far right came from wealthy landowners and businessmen, white-collar workers whose standard of living had dropped during the war, and members of the lower-middle and middle classes hurt by inflation. Bands of disaffected youth and veterans multiplied, among them a group called the Brown Shirts. Their leader was an ex-soldier named Adolf Hitler (1889–1945) — a favorite speaker among antigovernment crowds. In the wake of the Ruhr occupation of 1923, Hitler and German military hero Erich Ludendorff launched a coup d'état — or *putsch* in German — from a beer hall in Munich. Government troops suppressed the Beer Hall Putsch and arrested its leaders, but Ludendorff was acquitted and Hitler spent less than a year in jail. To conservative judges, former aristocrats, and most of the prewar bureaucrats who still staffed the government, such men were national heroes.

In France and Britain, parties on the right were less effective than in Germany because representative institutions were better established and the upper classes were not plotting to restore an authoritarian monarchy. In France, politicians from the conservative right and moderate left successively formed coalitions and rallied general support to rebuild war-torn regions and to force Germany to pay for the reconstruction. Hoping to stimulate population growth after the devastating loss of life, the French parliament made distributing birth-control information illegal and abortion a severely punished crime.

Britain encountered postwar boom-and-bust cycles and continuing conflict in Ireland. Ramsay MacDonald (1866–1937), elected the first Labour prime minister in 1924, represented the political strength of workers. He had to face the unpleasant truth that although Britain had the largest world empire, many of its industries were obsolete or in poor condition. A showdown came in the ailing coal industry. On May 3, 1926, workers launched a nine-day general strike against wage cuts and dangerous conditions in the mines. The strike provoked unprecedented middle-class resistance. University students, homemakers, and businessmen shut down the strike by driving trains, working on docks, and replacing workers in other jobs. Citizens from many walks of life revived the wartime spirit to defeat those who appeared to them to be attacking the national economy.

In January 1919, Ireland's republican leaders declared their nation's independence and created a separate parliament. The British government refused to recognize the parliament and sent in the Black and Tans, a volunteer army of demobilized soldiers named for the color of their uniforms. Terror reigned in Ireland, and by 1921, public outrage had forced the British to negotiate a treaty, one that reversed the Irish declaration of independence and made the Irish Free State a self-governing dominion. Northern Ireland,

The Irish Free State and Ulster, 1921

a group of six northern counties containing a majority of Protestants, gained a separate status: it was self-governing but still had representation in the British Parliament. This settlement left bitter discontent.

War had also changed everything in the colonies. European politicians and military recruiters had promised colonized peoples reforms, even independence, in exchange for their support during the war. However, these peoples' political activism — now enhanced by increasing education, trade, and experience with the West — mostly met with a brutal response. British forces massacred protesters at Amritsar, India, in 1919 and put down revolts against the mandate system in Egypt and Iran in the early 1920s. The Dutch jailed political leaders in Indonesia; the French punished Indochinese nationalists. For many Western governments, maintaining empires abroad was crucial to ensuring democracy at home, for any hint of declining national prestige fed antidemocratic forces.

Despite resistance, the 1920s marked the high tide of imperialism. Britain and France, enjoying new access to Germany's colonies in Africa and the territories of the fallen Ottoman Empire in the Middle East, were at the height of their global power because of the growing profitability that enterprise around the world could bring. Middle Eastern and Indonesian oil, for instance, fueled the West's growing number of automobiles, airplanes, trucks, ships, and buses. Products like chocolate and tropical fruit became regular items in Westerners' diets.

The balance of power among the imperial nations was shifting, however. The most important change was Japan's surging competition for markets, resources, and ultimately colonies. During the war, Japanese output of industrial goods such as metal and ships grew dramatically because the Western powers outsourced their wartime needs for such products. Japan's prosperity skyrocketed, allowing the country to become the dominant power in China. The Japanese government advertised its success as a sign of hope for non-Westerners. Japan's prosperity, the country's politicians claimed, would end the West's domination. Ardently nationalist, the Japanese government was not yet strong enough to challenge the Western powers militarily. Thus, although outraged when the Western powers at Paris refused a nondiscrimination clause in the charter of the League of Nations, Japan cooperated in the Anglo-American–dominated peace.

Reconstructing the Economy

The war had weakened European economies and allowed rivals — Japan, India, the United States, Australia, and Canada — to flourish. At the same time, the war had forced European manufacturing to become more efficient and had expanded the demand for automotive and air transport, electrical products, and synthetic goods. The prewar pattern

of mergers and cartels continued after 1918, giving rise to gigantic food-processing firms such as Nestlé in Switzerland and petroleum enterprises such as Royal Dutch Shell. By the late 1920s, Europe was enjoying renewed economic prosperity.

The United States had become the trendsetter in economic modernization: by 1929, Ford Motor Company's Detroit assembly line was producing a Ford automobile every ten seconds. Increased productivity, founder Henry Ford pointed out, resulted in a lower cost of living and thus increased workers' purchasing power. American efficiency expert Frederick Taylor (1856–1915) had developed methods to streamline workers' tasks for maximum productivity. Industrialists who adopted Taylor's methods were also influenced by European psychologists who emphasized the mental aspects of productivity and thus the need to balance work and leisure activities. In theory, increased productivity not only produced prosperity for all but also united workers and management, avoiding Russian-style worker revolution. For many workers, however, the emphasis on efficiency seemed inhumane; in some businesses restrictions were so severe that workers were allowed to use the bathroom only on a fixed schedule.

The managerial sector in industry had expanded during the war and continued to do so thereafter. Workers' experience became devalued, with managers alone seen as creative and innovative. Managers reorganized work procedures and classified workers' skills. They categorized jobs held by women as requiring less skill — whether they did or not — and therefore deserving of lower wages. With male workers' jobs increasingly threatened by labor-saving machinery, unions usually agreed that women should receive lower wages to keep them from competing with men for scarce high-paying jobs. Like the managerial sector, a complex union bureaucracy had ballooned during World War I to help monitor labor's part in the war. Unions could mobilize masses of people, as evidenced by their actions against coups in Weimar Germany and by the general strike in Great Britain in 1926.

Restoring Society

Civilians met the returning millions of brutalized, incapacitated, and shell-shocked veterans with combined joy and apprehension — and that apprehension was often valid. Tens of thousands of German, central European, and Italian soldiers refused to disband; some British veterans vandalized university classrooms and assaulted women streetcar conductors and factory workers. Many veterans were angry that civilians had protested wartime conditions instead of enduring them. Patriotic when the war erupted, civilians, especially women, sometimes felt estranged from the returning warriors who had inflicted so much death and who had lived daily with filth, rats, and decaying human flesh. While women who had served on the front had seen the soldiers' suffering firsthand and could sympathize with them, many British suffragists, for instance, who had fought for equality in men's and women's lives before the war, now embraced separate spheres for men and women, so fearful were they of returning veterans.

For their part, veterans returned to a world that differed from the home they had left. They found that the war had blurred class distinctions, giving rise to expectations that

life would be fairer afterward. Despite their expectations, veterans often had few or no jobs open to them, and some found that their wives and sweethearts had abandoned them. Many found, too, that women's roles had gone through other changes: middle-class women did their own housework because former servants could earn more money in factories, and greater numbers of women worked outside the home. Women of all classes cut their hair short, wore sleeker clothes, smoked, and had money of their own because of war work.

Focusing on veterans' needs, governments tried to make civilian life as comfortable as possible to reintegrate men into society and reduce the appeal of communism. Politicians believed in the calming power of family life and supported social programs such as veterans' pensions and housing and benefits for out-of-work men. The new housing — "homes for heroes," as politicians called the program in Vienna, Frankfurt, Berlin, and Stockholm — provided common laundries, day-care centers, and rooms for socializing. Gardens, terraces, and balconies provided a soothing country ambience that offset the hectic nature of industrial life. Inside, they boasted modern kitchens and bathrooms, central heating, and electricity.

Despite government efforts to restore traditional family life, freer relationships and more open discussions of sex characterized the 1920s. Middle-class youths of both sexes visited jazz clubs and attended movies together. Revealing bathing suits, short skirts, and body-hugging clothing emphasized women's sexuality, seeming to invite men and women to join together and replenish the postwar population. British scientist Marie Stopes published the best seller *Married Love* in 1918, and Dutch author Theodor van de Velde produced the wildly successful *Ideal Marriage: Its Physiology and Technique* in 1927. Both authors described sex in glowing terms and offered precise information about birth control and sexual physiology. One Viennese reformer described working-class marriage as "an erotic-comradely relationship of equals" rather than the economic partnership of past centuries. Meanwhile, such writers as the Briton D. H. Lawrence and the American Ernest Hemingway glorified men's sexual vigor in, respectively, *Women in Love* (1920) and *The Sun Also Rises* (1926). Mass culture's focus on heterosexuality encouraged the return to normality after the gender disorder that had troubled the prewar and war years.

As images of men and women changed, people paid more attention to bodily improvement. The increasing use of toothbrushes and toothpaste, safety and electric razors, and deodorants reflected new standards for personal hygiene and grooming. A multibillion-dollar cosmetics industry sprang up almost overnight. Women went to beauty parlors regularly to have their short hair cut, dyed, straightened, or curled. They also tweezed their eyebrows, applied makeup, and even submitted to cosmetic surgery. Ordinary women "painted" their faces (something only prostitutes had done formerly) and competed in beauty contests. Instead of wanting to look plump and pale, people aimed to become thin and tan, often through exercise and playing sports. Consumers' new focus on personal health coincided with industry's need for a physically fit workforce.

As prosperity returned in the mid-1920s, people could afford to buy more consumer goods. Middle- and upper-class families snapped up sleek modern furniture, washing machines, and vacuum cleaners. Other modern conveniences such as electric

irons and gas stoves appeared in better-off working-class households. Installment buying, popularized from the 1920s on, helped people finance these purchases. Family intimacy increasingly depended on machines of mass communication like radios, phonographs, and even automobiles, which not only transformed private life but also brought changes to the public world of mass culture and mass politics.

> **REVIEW QUESTION** What were the major political, social, and economic problems facing postwar Europe, and how did governments attempt to address them?

Mass Culture and the Rise of Modern Dictators

Wartime propaganda had aimed to unite all classes against a common enemy. In the 1920s, new technology made the process of integrating diverse groups into a single Western or mass culture easier. The tools of mass culture — primarily radio, film, and newspapers — expanded their influence in the 1920s. Some intellectuals who wanted to use modern media and art to reach the masses saw their potential for creating an informed citizenry and thus strengthening democracy. At the same time, the media allowed authoritarian rulers and would-be dictators such as Benito Mussolini, Joseph Stalin, and Adolf Hitler to shape uniform political thought and to control citizens' behavior far beyond what previous rulers had been able to do.

Culture for the Masses

The media received a big boost from the war. Bulletins from the battlefront whetted the public's craving for news and real-life stories, and sales of nonfiction books soared. After years of deprivation, people were driven to achieve material success, and they devoured books about how to gain it. A biography of Henry Ford, telling his story of upward mobility and technological accomplishment, became a best seller in Germany. Phonographs, radio programs, and movies also widened the scope of national culture.

In the 1920s, film evolved from an experimental medium to a thriving international business in which large corporations set up theater chains and marketed movies worldwide. Films of literary classics and political events developed people's sense of a common heritage and were often sponsored by governments. Bolshevik leaders backed the inventive work of director Sergei Eisenstein, whose films *Potemkin* (1925) and *Ten Days That Shook the World* (1927–1928) presented a Bolshevik view of history to Russian and international audiences.

Films incorporated familiar elements from everyday life. The popular comedies of the 1920s made the flapper more visible to the masses, attracting some hundred million weekly viewers, the majority of them women. Films also played to postwar fantasies and fears. In Germany, the influential hit *The Cabinet of Doctor Caligari* (1919) depicted frightening events in an insane asylum as horrifying symbols of state power. Popular detective and cowboy films portrayed heroes who could restore wholeness to the disordered world of murder, crime, and injustice. The plight of gangsters appealed to veterans,

The Flapper
This modern workingwoman smoking her cigarette stood for all that had changed — or was said to have changed — in the postwar world. Women had worked and had money of their own, they were out in public and could vote in many countries, and they were liberated from old constraints on their sexual and other behavior. (Hulton Archive / Getty Images.)

who had been exposed to the cheap value of modern life in the trenches. Films featured characters from around the world and were often set in faraway deserts and mountain ranges; newsreels showed athletic, soldier-like bodies in sporting events such as boxing.

Like film, radio evolved from an experimental medium to an instrument of mass culture during the 1920s. Developed from the wireless technology of Italian inventor Guglielmo Marconi, the radio quickly became an affordable consumer item, allowing the public concert or lecture to penetrate the individual's private living space. Specialized programming for men (such as sports reporting) and for women (such as advice on home management) attracted listeners. Through radio, disabled veterans found ways to participate in public events and keep up-to-date. By the 1930s, radio helped politicians to reach the masses wherever they might be — even alone at home.

Cultural Debates over the Future

Cultural leaders in the 1920s either were obsessed with the horrendous experience of war or held high hopes for creating a fresh, utopian future that would have little relation to the past. German artists, especially, produced bleak or violent visions. The sculpture and woodcuts of German artist Käthe Kollwitz (1867–1945), whose son had died in

the war, portrayed bereaved parents, starving children, and other heart-wrenching anti-war images (see the chapter-opening image). Others thought that Europeans needed to search for answers in far-off cultures. Seeing Europe as decadent, some turned to the spiritual richness of Asian philosophies and religions. An "Asiatic fever" seemed to grip intellectuals, including the British writer Virginia Woolf, who drew on ideas of reincarnation in her novel *Orlando* (1928), and the filmmaker Sergei Eisenstein, who modeled new techniques of film shots (montage) on Japanese calligraphy.

Other artists used satire and contempt to express postwar rage at civilization's wartime failure. George Grosz (1893–1959), stunned by the war's carnage, produced works marked by nonsense and shrieking expressions of alienation. Grosz's paintings and cartoons of maimed soldiers and brutally murdered women reflected his self-proclaimed desire "to bellow back." In the postwar years, the modernist practice of shocking audiences became more savage while portrayals of seedy everyday life flourished in cabarets and theaters in the 1920s and reinforced veterans' beliefs in civilian decadence.

The art world itself became a battlefield, especially in defeated Germany, where it mirrored the Weimar Republic's contentious politics. Popular writers such as veteran Ernst Jünger glorified life in the trenches and called for the militarization of society. In contrast, Erich Maria Remarque, also a veteran, cried out for an end to war in his controversial novel *All Quiet on the Western Front* (1928). This international best seller depicted the shared life of enemies on the battlefield, thus aiming to overcome the national hatred aroused by wartime propaganda. Remarque's novel was part of a flood of popular, and often bitter, literature appearing on the tenth anniversary of the war's end. It coincided with an interest in "Great War tourism" such as visiting battlefields.

George Grosz, "Twilight" from the Series *Ecce Homo* (1922)

George Grosz's series of postwar art was named after a book by Friedrich Nietzsche, *Ecce Homo* (*Behold the Man*). The "man" to behold was the veteran, opportunistically called a hero by postwar politicians to get their votes but in fact living a grim reality, as Grosz saw it. Surrounded by prosperous businessmen, fashionable women, and strutting military officers, the veteran was pushed to the background, gray and lonely amid the colorful peacetime society. (bpk, Berlin / Kunstbibliothek, Staatliche Museen, Berlin, Germany / photo by Kund Petersen / Art Resource, NY / Art © Estate of George Grosz / Licensed by VAGA, New York, NY.)

The postwar arts produced many a utopian fantasy turned upside down; dystopias of life in a war-traumatized Europe multiplied. In the bizarre stories of Franz Kafka, who worked by day in a large insurance company in Prague, the world is a vast, impersonal machine. His novels *The Trial* (1925) and *The Castle* (1926) show the hopeless condition of individuals caught between the cogs of society's relentlessly turning gears. His theme seemed to capture for civilian life the helplessness that soldiers had felt at the front. As the prewar way of life collapsed in the face of political and technological innovation, other writers depicted the complex, sometimes nightmarish inner life of individuals.

Irish writer James Joyce portrayed this interior self built on memories and sensations, many of them from the war. Joyce's *Ulysses* (1922) illuminates the fast-moving inner lives of its characters in the course of a single day. In one of the most celebrated passages in *Ulysses*, a long interior monologue traces a woman's lifetime of erotic and emotional sensations. The technique of using a character's thoughts to propel a story was called stream of consciousness. Virginia Woolf, too, used this technique in her novel *Mrs. Dalloway* (1925). For Woolf, the war had dissolved the solid society from which absorbing stories and fascinating characters were once fashioned. Her characters experience fragmented conversations and incomplete relationships. Woolf's novel *Orlando* also reflected the postwar attention to women. In the novel, the hero Orlando lives hundreds of years and in the course of his long life is eventually transformed into a woman.

There was another side to the postwar story, however — one based on the promise of technology. Before the war, avant-garde artists had celebrated the new, the futuristic, the utopian. After the war, like Jules Amar crafting prostheses for shattered limbs, many postwar artists were optimistic that technology could make an entire wounded society whole. The aim of art, observed one of them, "is not to decorate our life but to organize it." German artists, calling themselves the Bauhaus (after the idea of a craft association, or *Bauhütte*), created streamlined office buildings and designed functional furniture and utensils, many of them inspired by forms from "untainted" East Asia and Africa. Russian artists, temporarily caught up in the communist experiment, optimistically wrote novels about cement factories and created ballets about steel.

Artists fascinated by technology and machinery were drawn to the most modern of all countries — the United States. Hollywood films, glossy advertisements, and the bustling metropolis of New York tempted careworn Europeans. They loved films and stories about the Wild West or the carefree "modern girl." They were especially attracted to jazz, the improvisational music developed by African Americans. Performers like Josephine Baker (1906–1975) and Louis Armstrong (1901–1971) became international sensations when they toured Europe's capital cities. Like jazz, the New York skyscraper pointed to the future, not to the grim wartime past.

The Communist Utopia

Communism also promised a shining future and a modern, technological culture. As the Bolsheviks met powerful resistance, however, they became ever more ruthless and authoritarian. In the early 1920s, peasant bands called Green Armies revolted against

the Bolshevik policy of war communism that confiscated their crops. Industrial production stood at only 13 percent of prewar levels, and millions of refugees clogged the cities and roamed the countryside. In the early spring of 1921, workers in Petrograd and sailors at the naval base at Kronstadt revolted, protesting the privileged standard of living that Bolshevik supervisors enjoyed. They called for "soviets without Communists" — that is, a worker state without elite leaders.

The Bolsheviks had many of the rebels shot, but the Kronstadt revolt pushed Lenin to institute reform. His New Economic Policy (NEP) returned parts of the economy to capitalist methods that allowed peasants to sell their grain and others to trade consumer goods freely. Although the state still controlled large industries and banking, the NEP encouraged people to produce and even, in the spirited slogan of one official, "get rich." As a result, consumer goods and more food became available; some peasants and merchants prospered. The rise of these wealthy "NEPmen," who bought and furnished splendid homes, broke the Bolshevik promise of a classless utopia.

Further protests erupted within Communist ranks. At the 1921 party congress, a group called the Worker Opposition objected to the party's takeover of economic control from worker organizations and pointed out that the NEP was not a proletarian program for workers. In response, Lenin suppressed the Worker Opposition and set up procedures for purging opponents — a policy that would become a deadly feature of Communist rule. Bolshevik leaders also worked to make the Communist revolution a cultural reality in people's lives and thinking. The Communist Party set up classes to improve the literacy rate — which had been only 40 percent on the eve of World War I. To create social equality between the sexes, which had been part of the Marxist vision of the future, the state made birth control, abortion, and divorce readily available. As commissar for public welfare, **Aleksandra Kollontai** (1872–1952) promoted birth-control education for adults and day care for children of working parents. To encourage literacy, she wrote simply-worded novels about love and work in the new socialist state for ordinary readers.

The bureaucracy swelled to promote modern ways, and *hygiene* and *efficiency* became watchwords, as they were in the rest of Europe. Agencies such as the Zhenotdel ("Women's Bureau") taught women about sanitary housekeeping, while efficiency experts aimed to replace backwardness with American-style technological modernity. The short-lived government agency Proletkult tried to develop proletarian culture through such undertakings as workers' universities, a workers' theater, and workers' publishing. Poet Vladimir Mayakovsky wrote verse praising his Communist passport and essays promoting toothbrushing, while composers punctuated their music with the sound of train or factory whistles. As with war communism, many resisted attempts to change everyday life and culture. In Islamic regions of central Asia, incorporated from the old Russian Empire into the new Communist one, Bolsheviks urged Muslim women to remove their veils and generally to become more "modern," but Muslims often attacked both Zhenotdel workers and women who followed their advice.

Lenin suffered a debilitating stroke in the spring of 1922, and amid ongoing cultural experimentation and factional fighting, this architect of the Bolshevik Revolution

died in January 1924. The party congress changed the name of Petrograd to Lenin-grad and elevated the deceased leader into a secular god. Joseph Stalin (1879–1953), who served in the powerful post of general secretary of the Communist Party, was the chief mourner at Lenin's funeral, using the occasion to hand out good jobs. He advertised his role in joining Russian and non-Russian regions into the Union of Soviet Socialist Republics (USSR) in 1923. Concerned with Stalin's influence and ruthlessness, Lenin in his last will and testament had asked that "the comrades find a way to remove Stalin." Stalin, however, prevented Lenin's will from being publicized and discredited his chief rival, Trotsky, as an unpatriotic internationalist. Simultaneously, Stalin organized the Lenin cult, which included the public display of Lenin's embalmed corpse — still on view today. By 1929, Stalin had achieved virtually complete control of the USSR.

Fascism on the March in Italy

In Italy, the rise to power of political journalist **Benito Mussolini** (1883–1945), who had turned from socialism to the radical right, kept the war alive. Italians raged when the Allies at Paris refused to honor the territorial promises of the Treaty of London, and peasants and workers protested their economic plight during the slump of the early 1920s. Many Europeans blamed parliaments and constitutions for their troubles, so Italians backed Mussolini when he gathered veterans and unemployed men into a personal army (the Black Shirts) to overturn parliamentary government. In 1922, his supporters, known as the Fascists, started a march on Rome, forcing King Victor Emmanuel III (r. 1900–1946) to make Mussolini prime minister.

Like the Bolsheviks, Mussolini promised an efficient military utopia and the restoration of men's warrior status. The Black Shirts attracted many young men who felt cheated of wartime glory and many veterans who missed the vigor of military life. The fasces, an ancient Roman symbol depicting a bundle of sticks wrapped around an ax with the blade exposed (representing both unity and force), served as the movement's emblem and provided its name: **fascism**. Unlike Marxism, fascism scoffed at coherent ideology: "Fascism is not a church," Mussolini announced. "It is more like a training ground." The Fascist Party was defined by deeds — specifically its promotion of male violence and its attacks on parliamentary rule.

Mussolini criminalized any criticism of the state and used violence against opponents in parliament. Bands of men from the Fascist Party attacked striking workers, using their favorite tactic of forcing castor oil (which caused diarrhea) down the throats of socialists, and even murdering rivals. Yet the sight of the Black Shirts marching through the streets like disciplined soldiers signaled to many Italians that their country was orderly and modern. Large landowners and businessmen approved the Fascists' attacks on strikers and therefore financed the movement. Their generous funding allowed Mussolini to build a large staff by hiring the unemployed, creating the illusion that the Fascists could rescue the economy when no one else could.

Mussolini and the Black Shirts, 1922
Mussolini always struck a tough military pose, even when not in uniform, as in this photo taken in 1922 with his Black Shirt supporters, many also without uniforms. Once in power, Mussolini continued the militarization of society that had begun during World War I, instilling a cult of obedience and submission to state authority that he viewed as more important than fancy theories of politics and government.

Like a wartime leader, Mussolini used mass propaganda to build support for a kind of military campaign to remake Italy. Peasant men huddled around radios to hear him call for a "battle of wheat" to enhance farm productivity. Peasant women adored him for appearing to value motherhood. In the cities the government launched avant-garde architectural projects and used public relations promoters to advertise its achievements. The modern city became a stage set for Fascist spectacles captured by newsreel cameras and broadcast by radio. Mussolini claimed that he made the trains run on time, and this triumph of modern technology fanned people's hopes that he could restore order, albeit violently.

Mussolini added traditional values and prejudices to his modern order. An atheist himself, he recognized the importance of Catholicism in Italian life. In 1929, the Lateran Agreement between the Italian government and the church made the Vatican an independent state under papal sovereignty. The government recognized the church's right to determine marriage and family policy; in return, the church ended its criticism of Fascist

tactics. Mussolini also outlawed labor unions, replacing them with organized groups of employers, workers, and professionals to settle grievances and determine conditions of work. Mussolini drew praise from business leaders and professionals when he announced cuts in women's wages and a ban on women in the professions. Mussolini aimed to confine women to low-paying jobs as part of his scheme for reinvigorating men.

Mussolini's numerous admirers across the West included Adolf Hitler, who throughout the 1920s had been building a paramilitary group of storm troopers alongside a political organization called the National Socialist German Workers' Party (the Nazi Party). During his brief stint in jail for the 1923 Beer Hall Putsch, Hitler wrote *Mein Kampf* (My Struggle); in the book, he expressed both his vicious anti-Semitism and his recipe for manipulating the masses. Hitler was fascinated by Mussolini's legal accession to power and his triumph over all opposition. Late in the 1920s, however, the conditions that had allowed Mussolini to rise to power in 1922 no longer existed in Germany. Although the Nazi Party was becoming a strong political instrument, Weimar democracy was functioning better as the decade wore on.

REVIEW QUESTION How did the postwar atmosphere influence cultural life and encourage the trend toward dictatorship?

Conclusion

The year 1929 was to prove just as fateful as 1914 had been. In 1914, World War I began an orgy of death, causing tens of millions of casualties and the destruction of major dynasties. For four years, the war promoted military technology, fierce nationalism, and the control of everyday life by bureaucracy. As dynasties fell, the Peace of Paris treaties of 1919–1920 left Germans bitterly resentful. In eastern and central Europe the creation of new states by the treaties failed to guarantee a peaceful future. Massive migrations produced additional chaos, as some new nations expelled minority groups.

War furthered the development of mass society. It leveled social classes on the battlefield and in the graveyard, standardized political thinking through wartime propaganda, and extended many political rights to women. Production techniques, improved during wartime, were used in peacetime for manufacturing consumer goods. Technological innovations from the prostheses built by Jules Amar to air transport, cinema, and radio transmission became available. Modernity in the arts intensified, probing the nightmarish war that continued to haunt the population.

By the end of the 1920s, the war had so militarized the population that strongmen had come to power in several countries, including the Soviet Union and Italy, with Adolf Hitler waiting in the wings in Germany. These strongmen and their followers kept alive the wartime commitment to violence. Many Westerners were impressed by the tough, modern efficiency of Fascists and Communists who made parliaments and citizen rule seem out of date, even effeminate. When the U.S. stock market crashed in 1929 and economic disaster circled the globe, authoritarian solutions and militarism continued to look appealing. What followed was a series of catastrophes even more devastating than those of World War I.

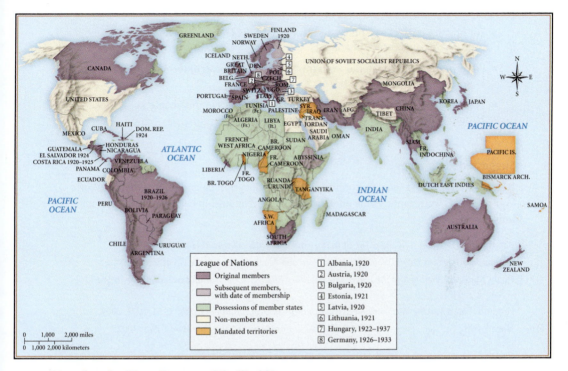

Mapping the West Europe and the World in 1929

The map reflects the partitions and nations that came into being as a result of war and revolution, while it obscures the increasing movement toward throwing off colonial rule. This was the true high point of empire: the drive for empire would diminish after 1929 except for Italy, which still craved colonies, and Japan, which continued searching for more land and resources to fuel its rapid growth. Observe the League of Nations membership as depicted in the map. What common bonds, if any, united these member nations?

Review Questions

1. In what ways was World War I a total war?
2. Why did people rebel during World War I, and what turned rebellion into outright revolution in Russia?
3. What were the major outcomes of the postwar peacemaking process?
4. What were the major political, social, and economic problems facing postwar Europe, and how did governments attempt to address them?
5. How did the postwar atmosphere influence cultural expression and encourage the trend toward dictatorship?

Making Connections

1. How did the experience of war shape postwar mass politics?
2. What social changes from World War I carried over into the postwar years, and why?
3. How did postwar artistic and cultural innovations build on the modern movements that developed between 1890 and 1914?
4. What changes did the war bring to relationships between European countries and their colonies?

- For practice quizzes and other study tools, visit the **Online Study Guide** at bedfordstmartins.com/huntconcise.

- For primary-source material from this period, see *Sources of the Making of the West*, Fourth Edition.

- For Web sites, images, and documents related to topics in this chapter, visit *Make History* at bedfordstmartins.com/huntconcise.

Suggested References

Readers of history and scholars continue to explore the gripping and tragic events of World War I. Hanna's work captures the often heartrending relationship between the battlefront and home front.

Barry, John. *The Great Influenza: The Epic Story of the Greatest Plague in History.* 2004.

Hanna, Martha. *Your Death Would Be Mine: Paul and Marie Pireaud in the Great War.* 2006.

Healy, Maureen. *Vienna and the Fall of the Habsburg Empire: Total War and Everyday Life in World War I.* 2004.

Holquist, Peter. *Making War, Forging Revolution: Russia's Continuum of Crisis, 1914–1921.* 2002.

Horne, John, ed. *State, Society, and Mobilization in Europe during the First World War.* 2002.

TIMELINE

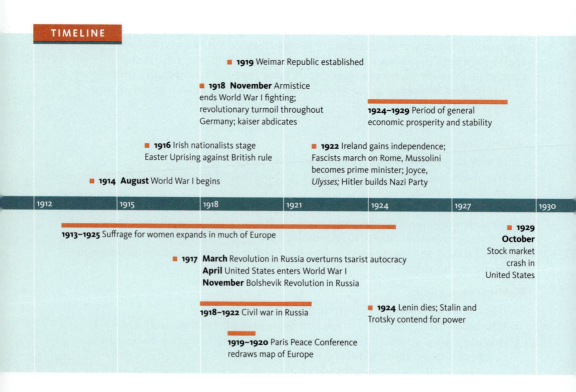

1919 Weimar Republic established

1918 November Armistice ends World War I fighting; revolutionary turmoil throughout Germany; kaiser abdicates

1924–1929 Period of general economic prosperity and stability

1916 Irish nationalists stage Easter Uprising against British rule

1922 Ireland gains independence; Fascists march on Rome, Mussolini becomes prime minister; Joyce, *Ulysses*; Hitler builds Nazi Party

1914 August World War I begins

| 1912 | 1915 | 1918 | 1921 | 1924 | 1927 | 1930 |

1913–1925 Suffrage for women expands in much of Europe

1929 October Stock market crash in United States

1917 March Revolution in Russia overturns tsarist autocracy
April United States enters World War I
November Bolshevik Revolution in Russia

1918–1922 Civil war in Russia

1924 Lenin dies; Stalin and Trotsky contend for power

1919–1920 Paris Peace Conference redraws map of Europe

Jensen, Eric N. *Body by Weimar: Athletes, Gender and German Modernity*. 2010.

Kent, Susan Kingsley. *Aftershocks: The Politics of Trauma in Britain, 1918–1931*. 2009.

Liulevicius, Vejas Gabriel. *War Land on the Eastern Front: Culture, National Identity and German Occupation in World War I*. 2000.

Makaman, Douglas, and Michael Mays, eds. *World War I and the Cultures of Modernity*. 2000.

Marks, Sally. *The Ebbing of European Ascendancy: An International History of the World*. 2002.

Northrup, Douglas. *Veiled Empire: Gender and Power in Stalinist Central Asia*. 2004.

Panchasi, Roxanne. *Future Tense: The Culture of Anticipation in France between the Wars*. 2009.

Robb, George. *British Culture and the First World War*. 2002.

Roshwald, Aviel. *Ethnic Nationalism and the Fall of Empires: Central Europe, Russia and the Middle East, 1914–1923*. 2001.

Scales, Rebecca. "Radio Broadcasting, Disabled Veterans, and Politics of National Recovery in Interwar France." *French Historical Studies*. 2008.

Weitz, Eric D. *Weimar Germany: Promise and Tragedy*. 2009.

*World War I Document Archive: http://www.lib.byu.edu/%7Erdh/wwi

Primary source.

The Great Depression and World War II

1929–1945

WHEN ETTY HILLESUM MOVED to Amsterdam from the Dutch provinces in 1932 to attend law school, an economic depression gripped the world. A resourceful young woman, Hillesum pieced together a living as a housekeeper and part-time language teacher so that she could continue her studies. Absorbed in her everyday life, she took little note of Adolf Hitler's spectacular rise to power in Germany, even when he demonized her fellow Jews as responsible for the economic slump and for virtually every other problem Germany faced. In 1939, the outbreak of World War II awakened her to the reality of what was happening. The German conquest of the Netherlands in 1940 led to the persecution of Dutch Jews, bringing Hillesum to note in her diary: "What they are after is our total destruction." The Nazis started relocating Jews to camps in Germany and Poland. Hillesum went to work for Amsterdam's Jewish Council, which was forced to organize the transport of Jews to these death camps. Changing from self-absorbed student to heroine, she did what she could to help other Jews and began carefully recording the deportations. When she and her family were captured and deported in turn, she smuggled out letters from the transit camps along the route to Poland, describing the inhumane conditions and brutal treatment of the Jews. "I wish I could live for a long time so that one day I may know how to explain it," she wrote. Etty Hillesum never got her wish: she died at Auschwitz in November 1943.

Nazis on Parade

By the time Hitler came to power in 1933, Germany was mired in the Great Depression. Hated by Communists, Nazis, and conservatives alike, the Weimar Republic had few supporters. Hitler took his cue from Mussolini by promising an end to democracy and tolerance and by using the visual power of Nazi soldiers marching through the streets during the depression to win support for overthrowing the government. (Hugo Jaeger / Time & Life Pictures / Getty Images.)

The economic recovery of the late 1920s came to a halt with the U.S. stock market crash in 1929, which launched a worldwide economic depression. Economic distress attracted many people to military-style strongmen for solutions to their problems. Among these dictators was Adolf Hitler, who called on the German masses to restore the national

glory that had been damaged by defeat in 1918. He urged Germans to scorn democratic rights and root out those he considered to be inferior people: Jews, Slavs, and Sinti and Roma (often called Gypsies), among others. Militaristic and fascist regimes spread to Spain, Poland, Hungary, Japan, and countries of Latin America, crushing representative institutions. In the Soviet Union, Joseph Stalin justified the killing of millions of citizens as necessary for the USSR's industrialization and the survival of communism. For millions of hard-pressed people in the 1930s, dictatorship had great appeal.

Elected leaders in the democracies reacted cautiously to both economic depression and the dictators' aggression. In an age of mass media, leaders following democratic principles appeared timid, while dictators dressed in uniforms looked bold and decisive. Only the German invasion of Poland in 1939 pushed the democracies to strong action, as World War II erupted in Europe. By 1941, the war had spread across the globe with the United States, Great Britain, the Soviet Union, and many other nations united in combat against Germany, Italy, Japan, and their allies. Tens of millions would perish in this war because both technology and ideology had become more deadly than they had been just two decades earlier. More than half the dead were civilians, among them Etty Hillesum, killed for being Jewish.

CHAPTER FOCUS What were the main economic, social, and political challenges of the years 1929–1945, and how did governments and individuals respond to them?

The Great Depression

The U.S. stock market crash of 1929 and economic developments around the world triggered the Great Depression of the 1930s. Rural and urban folk alike suffered as tens of millions lost their jobs and livelihoods. The whole world felt the depression's impact: commerce and investment in industry fell off, social life and gender roles were upset, and the birthrate plummeted. From peasants in Asia to industrial workers in Germany and the United States, the Great Depression shattered the lives of millions.

Economic Disaster Strikes

In the 1920s, U.S. corporations and banks as well as millions of individual Americans had not only invested all their money but also borrowed funds to invest in the soaring stock market. They used easy credit to buy shares in popular companies based on electric, automotive, and other new technologies. By the end of the decade, the Federal Reserve Bank — the nation's central bank, which controlled financial policy — tried to slow speculation by limiting credit availability and causing brokers to demand that their clients immediately pay back the money they had borrowed to buy stock. As stocks were sold to raise the necessary cash, the market collapsed. Between early October and mid-November 1929, the value of businesses listed on the U.S. stock exchange dropped from $87 billion to $30 billion. For individuals and for the economy as a whole, it was the beginning of catastrophe.

Unemployed in Germany (1932)

"I'm looking for work of any kind," this respectably dressed unemployed man announces on his sign. Germans were among those hardest hit by the Great Depression, and when demagogues pointed to such sights as evidence that democracy didn't work, it helped pull down the rule of constitutions, representative government, and guaranteed rights. (ullstein bild / The Granger Collection, NYC — All rights reserved.)

The crash helped bring on a global depression that unfolded over the course of several years. The United States had financed the international economic growth of the previous five years, so when the suddenly strapped U.S. banks cut back on loans and called in debts, they undermined businesses at home and abroad. Jobs dwindled and a decline in consumer buying slowed the world economy, including the young businesses of eastern Europe.

The Great Depression left no sector of the world economy unscathed, but government actions made the depression worse. To try to spur their economies, governments cut budgets and set high tariffs against foreign goods; these policies discouraged the consumer spending and international trade needed to spark the economy. Officials in charge of the flow of global money that fostered commerce desperately guarded their own supplies of gold. Unemployment soared: Great Britain — with its outdated textile, steel, and coal industries — had close to three million unemployed in 1932. By 1933, almost six million German workers, or about one-third of the workforce, had lost their jobs.

Agricultural prices had been declining for several years because of technological advances and abundant harvests around the world. With their incomes slashed, millions of small farmers had no money to buy the chemical fertilizers and motorized machinery they needed to remain competitive. Now creditors confiscated farms. Eastern and southern European peasants, who had pressed for the redistribution of land after World War I, could not afford to operate their newly acquired farms, and they, too, went under.

Social Effects of the Depression

The Great Depression had complex effects on society. First, life was not uniformly bleak, and despite the slump, modernization continued. Bordering English slums, one traveler in the mid-1930s noticed, were "filling stations and factories that look like exhibition buildings, giant cinemas and dance halls and cafés, bungalows with tiny garages, cocktail bars, Woolworth's [and] swimming pools." Municipal and national governments continued road construction and sanitation projects. New factories manufactured synthetic fabrics, automobiles, and electrical products such as stoves — all of them in demand. With government assistance, eastern European industry developed: Romanian industrial production, for example, increased by 55 percent between 1929 and 1939. Second, the majority of Europeans and Americans had jobs throughout the 1930s, and people with steady employment benefited from a drastic drop in prices. Service workers, managers, and business magnates often prospered. In contrast, towns with heavy industry often saw more than half the population out of work, spreading fear beyond the unemployed.

Economic catastrophe upset gender relations and weakened social ties. Women often found low-paying jobs doing laundry and cleaning house, while unemployed men sometimes stayed home all day and took over housekeeping chores. Some, however, felt that this "women's work" demeaned their masculinity, and as many women became breadwinners, albeit for low wages, men could be seen standing on street corners begging — a change in gender expectations that fed discontent. Young men in cities faced severe unemployment; with nothing to do but loiter in parks, they became ripe for movements like Nazism. Demagogues everywhere attacked democracy's failure to stop the collapse of traditional life, clearing the way for Nazi and Fascist politicians who promised to create jobs and thus restore male dignity.

Politicians drew attention to the declining birthrates. In difficult economic times, people chose to have fewer children than ever before. In addition, compulsory education, enforced more strictly after the war, reduced the income once earned by children, who now cost their families money while they went to school. Family-planning centers opened, receiving many clients, and knowledge of birth control spread across the working and lower middle classes. The situation, leaders believed, would lead to a national collapse in military readiness as "superior" peoples selfishly failed to breed and "inferior" peoples waited to take their place. This racism took a particularly violent form in eastern Europe, where political parties also blamed Jewish bankers for farm foreclosures and Jewish civil servants (of whom there were actually very few) for inadequate relief programs. Thus, population issues along with economic misery produced discord, especially in the form of ethnic hatred and anti-Semitism.

The Great Depression beyond the West

The depression spread discontent in European empires. World War I and postwar investment had produced economic growth, a rising population, and explosive urbanization in Asia, Africa, and Latin America. The depression, however, cut the demand for cop-

Gandhi Speaks to Women and Children

Mohandas K. Gandhi, an English-trained lawyer, was central to making the Indian independence movement a mass phenomenon. He made Indians see the superior values in their own culture in contrast to those of the West. The West, he maintained, including the United States, valued only money. Gandhi riveted his audiences, addressing women and children as well as men. (akg-images / Archiv Peter Rühe.)

per, tin, and other raw materials and for the finished products made in urban factories world-wide. Rising agricultural productivity drove down the price of foodstuffs like rice and coffee, a disaster for colonial peoples who had been forced to grow a single cash crop. Just as in Europe, however, the economic picture in the colonies was uneven. For instance, established Indian industries such as the textile business gained strength, with India no longer needing British cloth.

Economic distress led to anticolonial action. Colonial farmers withheld produce like cocoa from imperial trade, and colonial workers went on strike to protest the wage cuts imposed by imperial landlords. In India, millions of working people, including hundreds of thousands of veterans, joined with the upper-class Indians, who had organized to gain rights from Britain in the late nineteenth century. Mohandas K. Gandhi (1869–1948), called Mahatma ("great-souled"), emerged as the charismatic leader for Indian independence. Trained in England as a Western-style lawyer, Gandhi preached Hindu self-denial and rejected British love of material wealth. He wore simple clothing made of thread he had spun himself and advocated **civil disobedience** — deliberately but peacefully breaking the law — a tactic he claimed to have taken from the British suffragists and from the teachings of spiritual leaders like Jesus and Buddha. Gandhi aimed to end Indian deference to the British, who jailed Gandhi repeatedly and tried to split the Indian independence movement by promoting Hindu-Muslim antagonism. Instead, commitment to independence in India grew.

The end of the Ottoman Empire following World War I led to efforts to build modern, independent nations in the Middle East. Mustafa Kemal (1881–1938), who later took the name Atatürk ("first among Turks"), led the Turks to found an independent republic in 1923 and to craft a capitalist economy. In an effort to Westernize Turkish culture and promote the new Turkish state, Kemal moved the capital from Constantinople to Ankara in 1923, officially changed the name Constantinople to the Turkish name Istanbul in 1930, mandated Western dress for men and women, introduced the Latin alphabet, and abolished polygamy. In 1936, Turkish women received the vote and were

made eligible to serve in the parliament. Persia, which changed its name to Iran in 1935, similarly loosened the European grip on its economy by updating its government and by forcing the renegotiation of oil contracts to keep Western countries from taking the oil for virtually nothing.

Anticolonial activism thrived in French colonies, too, but the government made few concessions. Like all other imperial countries during the depression, France depended increasingly on the profits it could take from its empire; therefore, its trade with its colonies increased as trade with Europe lagged. France also depended on the growing colonial population for sheer numbers. One official estimated what colonial numbers meant for national security: "One hundred and ten million strong, France can stand up to Germany." Ho Chi Minh, founder of the Indochinese Communist Party, rallied his people to protest French imperialism, but in 1930 the French government brutally crushed the peasant uprising he led. Needing their empires, Britain and France increased the number of their troops stationed around the world. As a result, fascism spread largely unchecked in Europe during the 1930s.

REVIEW QUESTION How did the Great Depression affect society and politics?

Totalitarian Triumph

Representative government collapsed in many countries under the sheer weight of social and economic crisis. After 1929, Mussolini in Italy, Stalin in the USSR, and Hitler in Germany were able to mobilize vast support for their regimes. Desperate for economic relief, many citizens supported political violence as key to restoring well-being. Scholars have classified the Fascist, Nazi, and Communist regimes of the 1930s as totalitarian. The term *totalitarianism* refers to highly centralized systems of government that attempt to control society and ensure obedience through a single party and police terror. Born during World War I and gaining support in its aftermath, totalitarian governments broke with liberal principles of freedom and natural rights and came to wage war on their own citizens. But there were important differences among totalitarian states, especially between Fascist and Communist states. Whereas communism denounced private ownership of property and economic inequality, fascism supported them as crucial to national might.

The Rise of Stalinism

In the 1930s, **Joseph Stalin** (1879–1953) led the transformation of the USSR from a rural society into an industrial power. Stalin ended Lenin's New Economic Policy, which had allowed individuals to profit from trade and agriculture, and in 1929 laid out the first of several bold **five-year plans** for industrializing the country. Without an end to economic backwardness, Stalin warned, "the advanced countries . . . will crush us." He thus established economic planning — that is, government direction of the economy

used on both sides in World War I and increasingly implemented around the world. Between 1928 and 1940, the number of Soviet workers in industry, construction, and transport grew from 4.6 million to 12.6 million and factory output soared. Stalin's first five-year plan helped make the USSR a leading industrial nation.

A new bureaucratic elite implemented the plans, and despite limited rights to change jobs or even move from place to place, skilled workers benefited from the privileges that went along with their new industrial role. Communist officials received additional rewards such as country homes, good food, and luxurious vacations. New or unskilled workers enjoyed no such benefits, however. Newcomers from the countryside were herded into barracks or tents and subjected to dangerous factory conditions. Despite the hardships, many took pride in their new skills. "We mastered this profession — completely new to us — with great pleasure," a female lathe operator recalled. More often workers fresh from the countryside lacked the technical skills necessary to accomplish goals of the five-year plans, so official lying about productivity became part of the economic system. The attempt to turn an illiterate peasant society into an advanced industrial economy in a single decade brought intense suffering, but people tolerated hardship to achieve a Communist society.

Stalin demanded more grain from peasants both to feed the urban workforce and to provide exports whose sale abroad would finance industrialization. Some peasants resisted government demands by withholding produce from the market, prompting Stalin to demand a "liquidation of the kulaks." The word *kulak*, which literally means "fist," was a negative term for prosperous peasants, but in practice it applied to anyone who opposed Stalin's plans to end independent farming. Party workers began searching villages, seizing grain, and forcing villagers to identify the kulaks among them. One Russian remembered believing the kulaks were "bloodsuckers, cattle, swine, loathsome, repulsive: they had no souls; they stank." Denounced as "enemies of the state," whole families were robbed of their possessions, left to starve, or even murdered outright. Confiscated kulak land formed the basis for the new collective farms, or kolkhoz, where the remaining peasants were forced to share facilities. Traditional peasant life was brought to a violent end.

Failure across the economy followed. Factory workers, farmers, and party officials alike were too inexperienced with advanced industrialization to meet quotas. The experiment with collectivization, combined with the murder of farmers, resulted in a drop in the grain harvest from 83 million tons in 1930 to 67 million in 1934. Soviet citizens starved. Blaming failure on "wreckers" deliberately plotting against communism, Stalin instituted **purges** — that is, state violence in the form of widespread arrests, imprisonments in labor camps, and executions — to rid society of these "villains."

The purges touched all segments of society, beginning with engineers who were condemned for causing low productivity. Beginning in 1936, the government next charged prominent Bolshevik leaders with conspiring to overthrow Soviet rule. In a series of "show trials" — trials based on trumped-up charges, fabricated evidence, and coerced confessions — Bolshevik leaders were tortured and forced to confess in court.

Most of those found guilty were shot. Some of the top leaders accepted their fate, seeing the purges as good for the future of socialism. Just before his execution, one Bolshevik loyalist and former editor of the party newspaper *Pravda* wrote to Stalin praising the "great and bold political idea behind the general purge."

The spirit of purge swept through society: one woman poet described the scene in towns and cities: "Great concert and lecture halls were turned into public confessionals. . . . Beating their breasts, the 'guilty' would lament that they had 'shown political short-sightedness' and 'lack of vigilance' . . . and were full of 'rotten liberalism.'" In 1937 and 1938, military leaders were arrested and executed without public trials; some ranks were entirely wiped out. Although the massacre of military leaders appeared suicidal at a time when Hitler threatened war, thousands of high military posts became open to new talent. Stalin would not have to worry about an officer corps wedded to old ideas, as had happened in World War I. Simultaneously, the government expanded the system of prison camps, founded under Lenin, into an extensive network stretching several thousand miles from Moscow to Siberia. In the Gulag — an acronym for the government department that ran the camps — some one million died annually as a result of the insufficient food, inadequate housing, and twelve- to sixteen-hour days of crushing physical labor. Regular beatings and murders of prisoners rounded out Gulag life, which became another aspect of totalitarian violence.

As social and sexual experimentation disappeared in the 1930s, toleration in Soviet social life ended. The birthrate in the USSR, like that in the rest of Europe, declined rapidly. The Soviet Union needed to replace the millions of people lost since 1914. To meet this need, Stalin restricted access to birth-control information and abortion. Lavish wedding ceremonies came back into fashion, divorces became difficult to obtain, and the state made homosexuality a crime. Whereas Bolsheviks had once attacked the family as a capitalist institution, propaganda now referred to the family as a "school for socialism." At the same time, women in rural areas made gains in literacy and received improved health care. Positions in the lower ranks of the party opened to women as the purges continued, and more women were accepted into the professions.

Avant-garde experimentation in the arts also ended under Stalin. He called artists and writers "engineers of the soul" and, thus recognizing their influence, controlled their output through the Union of Soviet Writers. The union not only assigned housing, office space, equipment, and secretarial help but also determined the types of books authors could write. In return, the "comrade artist" adhered to the official style of "socialist realism," derived from the focus on the common worker as hero. Although some writers and artists went underground, others found ways to adjust their talents to the state's demands. The composer Sergei Prokofiev, for example, composed scores both for the delightful *Peter and the Wolf* and for Sergei Eisenstein's 1938 film *Alexander Nevsky*, a work that flatteringly compared Stalin to the medieval rulers of the Russian people. Aided by adaptable artists, workers, and bureaucrats, Stalin stood triumphant as the 1930s drew to a close. He was, as two different workers put it, "our beloved Leader" and "a god on earth."

Hitler's Rise to Power

A different but ultimately no less violent system emerged when **Adolf Hitler** and his followers put an end to democracy in Germany. Since the early 1920s, Hitler had harangued the German masses to destroy the Weimar Republic and drummed at a message of anti-Semitism and the rebirth of the German "race." When the Great Depression struck Germany in 1929, his Nazi Party began to outstrip its rivals in elections, thanks in part to financial support from big business. Film and press tycoon Alfred Hugenberg helped, constantly slamming the Weimar government as responsible for the disastrous economy and for the loss of German pride after World War I. Nazi supporters took to the streets, attacking young Communist groups who agitated just as loudly on behalf of the new Soviet experiment. Hugenberg's newspapers always reported such incidents as the work of Communist thugs who had assaulted blameless Nazis, thus building sympathy for the Nazis among the middle classes.

Parliamentary government practically ground to a halt during the depression, adding to unrest and the sense of disorder. The Reichstag, or German assembly, failed to approve emergency plans to improve the economy, first because its members disagreed over policies and second because Nazi and Communist deputies disrupted its sessions. Its failure to act discredited democracy among the German people. To make parliamentary government look incapable of providing basic law and order, Hitler's followers rampaged unchecked through the streets and attacked Jews, Communists, and Social Democrats. Many thought it was time to replace democratic government with a bold new leader who would take on these enemies military-style, without concern for constitutions, laws, or individual rights. It was time for war at home.

Every age group and class of people supported Hitler, though like Stalin, he especially attracted young people. In 1930, 70 percent of Nazi Party members were under forty and many thought of war as exciting, like the games they played as children during World War I. They believed that a better world was possible under Hitler's command. The largest number of supporters came from the industrial working class, but many white-collar workers and members of the lower-middle class also joined the party in percentages out of proportion with their numbers in the population. The inflation that had wiped out savings left them especially bitter and open to Hitler's rhetoric. In the deepening economic crisis, the Nazi Party, which had received little more than 2 percent of the vote in 1928, won almost 20 percent in the Reichstag elections of 1930 and more than twice that in 1932.

Hitler used modern propaganda techniques to build up his following. Nazi Party members passed out thousands of recordings of Hitler's speeches, and teenagers painted their fingernails with swastikas. Nazi rallies were carefully planned displays in which Hitler captivated the crowds, who saw him as their strong, vastly superior *Führer* ("leader"). In actuality, Hitler regarded the masses with contempt, and in *Mein Kampf* he discussed how to deal with them:

The receptivity of the great masses is very limited, their intelligence is small. In consequence of these facts, all effective propaganda must be limited to a

very few points and must harp on those in slogans until the last member of the public understands what you want him to understand.

Hitler's media techniques were so successful that they continue to influence political campaigns today, particularly in the use of simple messages often filled with hate or threats.

In the 1932 elections, both Nazis and Communists did very well, making the leader of one of these two parties the logical choice as chancellor. Influential conservative politicians loathed the Communists for their opposition to private property and favored Hitler as someone they could easily control. When Hitler was invited to become chancellor in January 1933, he accepted.

The Nazification of German Politics

Millions of Germans celebrated Hitler's ascent to power. "My father went down to the cellar and brought up our best bottles of wine. . . . And my mother wept for joy," one German recalled. "Now everything will be all right." Yet instead of being easy to control, Hitler took command brutally, quickly closing down representative government with an ugly show of force. Tens of thousands of his paramilitary supporters — the Stürmabteilung (SA), or "storm troopers" — paraded through the streets with blazing torches. When the Reichstag building was gutted by fire in February 1933, Nazis used the fire as the excuse for suspending civil rights, censoring the press, and prohibiting meetings of other political parties. Hitler had always claimed to hate democracy and diverse political opinions, declaring of parties other than his own: "I have set myself one task, namely to sweep those parties out of Germany."

The storm troopers' violence silenced democratic politicians but also made those who participated in the violence feel part of a glorious whole. At the end of March, intimidated Reichstag delegates let pass the **Enabling Act**, which suspended the constitution for four years and allowed Nazi laws to take effect without parliamentary approval. Solid middle-class Germans approved the Enabling Act as a way to advance the creation of a *Volksgemeinschaft* ("people's community") of like-minded, racially pure Germans — Aryans, the Nazis named them. Heinrich Himmler headed the elite Schutzstaffel (SS), Hitler's "protection squadron," and he commanded the Reich's political police system. These and the Gestapo, the secret police force run by Hermann Goering, had vast powers to arrest people and either execute them or imprison them in concentration camps, the first of which opened at Dachau, near Munich, in March 1933. The Nazis filled it and later camps with political enemies like socialists, and then with Jews, homosexuals, and others said to be enemies of the Volksgemeinschaft.

Hitler deliberately blurred authority in the government and his political party to encourage confusion and competition. He then settled disputes, often with violence. When Ernst Roehm, leader of the SA and Hitler's longtime collaborator, called for a "second revolution" to end the business and military elites' continuing influence on top Nazis, Hitler ordered Roehm's assassination. The bloody Night of the Long Knives

(June 30, 1934), during which hundreds of SA leaders and innocent civilians were killed, strengthened the support of the conservative upper classes for the Nazi regime. They saw that Hitler would deal ruthlessly with those favoring a leveling-out of social privilege. Nazism's terrorist politics served as the foundation of Hitler's Third Reich — a German empire grandly advertised as the successor to the First Reich of Charlemagne and the Second Reich of Bismarck and William II.

New economic programs, especially those putting people back to work, were crucial to the survival of Nazism. The Nazi government pursued **pump priming** — that is, stimulating the economy through government spending on tanks and airplanes and on public works programs such as building the Autobahn, or highway system. Unemployment declined from a peak of almost 6 million in 1932 to 1.6 million by 1936. The Nazi Party closed down labor unions, and government managers determined work procedures and set pay levels, rating women's jobs lower than men's regardless of the level of expertise required. Nazi programs produced large budget deficits, but Hitler was already planning to conquer and loot neighboring countries to cover the costs.

Nazi officials devised policies to control everyday life, including gender roles. In June 1933, a bill took effect that encouraged Aryans (those people defined as racially German) to marry and have children. The bill provided for loans to Aryan newlyweds, but only if the wife left the workforce. The loans were forgiven on the birth of the pair's fourth child. The ideal woman gave up her job, gave birth to many children, and completely surrendered her will to that of her husband, allowing him to feel powerful despite military defeat and economic depression. A good wife "joyfully sacrifices and fulfills her fate," as one Nazi leader explained.

The government also controlled culture, destroying the rich creativity of the Weimar years. Although 70 percent of households had radios by 1938, programs were severely censored. Books like Erich Maria Remarque's *All Quiet on the Western Front* were banned, and in May 1933 a huge book-burning ceremony rid libraries of works by Jews, socialists, homosexuals, and modernist writers. In the Hitler Youth, which boys and girls over age ten were required to join, children learned to report those adults they suspected of disloyalty to the Third Reich, even their own parents. People boasted that they could leave their bicycles out at night without fear of robbery, but their world was filled with informers — some 100,000 of them on the Nazi payroll. In general, the improved economy led many to see Hitler working an economic miracle while restoring pride in Germany and strengthening the Aryan community. For hundreds of thousands if not millions of Germans, however, Nazi rule in the 1930s brought anything but harmony and community.

Nazi Racism

The Nazis defined Jews as an inferior "race" dangerous to the superior Aryan "race" and responsible for most of Germany's problems, including defeat in World War I and the economic depression. The reasons for targeting Jews, Hitler declared in a 1938 speech, were "based on the greatest of scientific knowledge." Hitler attacked many ethnic and

social groups, but he took anti-Semitism to new and frightening heights. In the rhetoric of Nazism, Jews were "vermin," "abscesses," and "Bolsheviks." They were enemies, biologically weakening the race and plotting Germany's destruction — all of which, given scientific knowledge then and now, was of course utterly false. Thus Hitler's concept of building community also included making some members of the community enemies within. By branding Jews both as evil businessmen and as working-class Bolsheviks, Nazis fashioned an enemy for the population to hate.

Nazis insisted that terms such as *Aryan* and *Jewish* (a religious category) were scientific racial classifications that could be determined by physical characteristics such as the shape of the nose. In 1935, the government enacted the **Nuremberg Laws**, legislation that deprived Jews of citizenship and prohibited marriage between Jews and other Germans. Abortions and birth-control information were readily available to enemy outcast groups, including Jews, Slavs, Sinti and Roma, and mentally or physically disabled people, but were forbidden to women classified as Aryan. In the name of improving the Aryan race, doctors helped organize the T4 project, which used carbon monoxide poisoning and other means to kill large numbers of people — 200,000 handicapped and elderly — late in the 1930s. The murder of the disabled aimed to eliminate those whose "racial inferiority" endangered the Aryans. These murders prepared the way for even larger mass exterminations in the future.

Jews were forced into slave labor, evicted from their apartments, and prevented from buying most clothing and food. In 1938, a Jewish teenager, reacting to the harassment inflicted on his parents, killed a German official. In retaliation, Nazis and other Germans attacked some two hundred synagogues, smashed windows of Jewish-owned stores, ransacked apartments of known or suspected Jews, and threw more than twenty thousand Jews into prisons and camps. The night of November 9–10 became known as Kristallnacht, or the Night of Broken Glass. Faced with such relentless persecution, more than half of Germany's 500,000 Jews had emigrated by the outbreak of World War II in 1939.

REVIEW QUESTION What role did violence play in the Soviet and Nazi regimes?

Their enormous emigration fees helped finance Germany's economic recovery, while neighbors and individual Nazis used anti-Semitism to justify stealing Jewish property and taking the jobs Jews were forced to leave.

Democracies on the Defensive

Nazism, communism, and fascism offered bold new approaches to modern politics. These ideologies maintained that democracy was effeminate and that it wasted precious time in building consensus among citizens. Totalitarian leaders' military style made representative government and the democratic values of the United States, France, and Great Britain appear feeble — a sign that these societies were on the decline. Totalitarianism put democracies on the defensive as they aimed to restore prosperity while still upholding individual rights and the rule of law.

Confronting the Economic Crisis

As the depression wore on through the 1930s, some governments experimented with ways to solve social and economic crises in a democratic fashion. In the early days of the economic slump, U.S. president Herbert Hoover had opposed direct help to the unemployed and even ordered the army to drive away jobless veterans who had marched on Washington, D.C. With unemployment close to fifteen million, Franklin Delano Roosevelt (1882–1945), the wealthy governor of New York, defeated Hoover in the presidential election of 1932 on the promise of relief and recovery. Roosevelt, or FDR as he became known, pushed through a torrent of legislation: relief for businesses, price supports for hard-pressed farmers, and public works programs for the unemployed. The Social Security Act of 1935 set up a fund to which employers and employees contributed. It provided retirement benefits for workers, unemployment insurance, and payments to dependent mothers, their children, and people with disabilities.

A Fireside Chat with FDR
President Franklin Delano Roosevelt was a master of words, inspiring Americans during the depression and World War II. Aware of its growing power in making politicians look dynamic, the press never showed that Roosevelt was actually confined to a wheelchair (after being paralyzed by polio). Instead, FDR became a symbol of U.S. resolve and might. Here he addresses the nation over a radio hookup on August 23, 1938, while First Lady Eleanor Roosevelt and the president's mother, Sara, observe — a far different image from that of Hitler and Mussolini. (Hulton Archive / Getty Images.)

Programs such as these in the United States advanced a new kind of state taking shape across the West: the welfare state, in which the government guarantees a certain level of economic well-being for individuals and businesses. Although his "New Deal" angered businesspeople and the wealthy, Roosevelt maintained widespread support. Like other successful politicians of the 1930s, he was an expert at using the new mass media, especially in his broadcasts by radio. Unlike Mussolini and Hitler, however, Roosevelt's public statements promoted rather than attacked democratic rights and government. The participation of First Lady Eleanor Roosevelt sharply contrasted with the antiwoman ideology of Nazis and Fascists, and the Roosevelts insisted that human rights must not be surrendered in difficult times. "We Americans of today . . . are characters in the living book of democracy," FDR told a group of teenagers in 1939. "But we are also its author." Racial violence continued to cause great suffering in the United States, and the economy did not fully recover, yet Americans' faith in democracy was strong.

Sweden also developed a coherent program for solving economic and population problems, assigning the government a central role in promoting social welfare and economic democracy. Sweden devalued its currency to make Swedish exports more attractive on the international market, and addressed the population problem with government programs, but without the racism and coercion of Nazism. Alva Myrdal, a leading member of Sweden's parliament, believed that boosting childbirth depended both on the economy and on individual well-being. It was undemocratic, she maintained, that "the bearing of a child should mean economic distress" to parents. Acting on Myrdal's advice, the government introduced prenatal care, free childbirth in a hospital, a food relief program, and subsidized housing for large families. By the end of the decade, almost 50 percent of all mothers in Sweden received government aid, most effectively in the form of a **family allowance** to help cover the costs of raising children. Because all families — rural and urban, poor or prosperous — received these social benefits, there was widespread approval for developing a welfare state.

The most powerful democracy, the United States, had withdrawn from world leadership by refusing to participate in the League of Nations, leaving Britain and France with greater responsibility for international peace and well-being than their postwar resources could sustain. When the Great Depression hit, British prime minister Ramsay MacDonald, though leader of the Labour Party, reduced payments to the unemployed, and Parliament denied unemployment insurance to women even though they had contributed to the unemployment fund. To protect jobs, the government imposed huge tariffs on imported goods, but these only discouraged a revival of international trade and did not relieve British misery. Finally, in 1933, with the economy continuing to worsen, the government began to take effective steps with massive programs of slum clearance, new housing construction, and health insurance for the needy. British leaders rejected pump-priming methods of stimulating the economy as foolish and thus resorted to them only when all else had failed.

Depression struck later in France, but the country endured a decade of public strife in the 1930s. Deputies with opposing solutions to the economic crisis frequently came

to blows in the Chamber of Deputies, Parisians took to the streets to protest the government's budget cuts, and Nazi-style paramilitary groups flourished, attracting the unemployed, students, and veterans to the cause of ending representative government. In February 1934, the paramilitary groups joined Communists and other outraged citizens in riots around the parliament building. "Let's string up the deputies," chanted the crowd. "Let's beat in their faces, let's reduce them to a pulp." The right-wing enemies of democratic government, however, lacked both substantial support and a charismatic leader like Hitler or Mussolini.

Shocked into action by fascist violence, French liberals, socialists, and Communists established an antifascist coalition known as the **Popular Front**. Until that time, such a merging of groups had been impossible because Stalin had directed Communists across Europe not to cooperate with other political parties. As fascism attracted followers around the world, however, Stalin allowed Communists to join efforts to protect democracy. For just over a year in 1936–1937 and again briefly in 1938, the French Popular Front led the government, with the socialist leader Léon Blum as premier. Like the American New Dealers and the Swedish reformers, the Popular Front instituted social-welfare programs, including family subsidies. Blum appointed women to his government (though women in France were still not allowed to vote). In June 1936, the French government guaranteed workers two-week paid vacations, a forty-hour workweek, and the right to bargain collectively. Working people would long remember Blum as the man who improved their living standards and provided them with the right to vacations.

During its brief life, the Popular Front offered citizens a youthful but democratic political culture. "In 1936 everyone was twenty years old," one man recalled, evoking the atmosphere of idealism. To express their opposition to fascism, the French celebrated democratic holidays like Bastille Day with new enthusiasm. Not everyone liked the Popular Front, however. Bankers and industrialists sent their money out of the country in protest, leaving France financially strapped. "Better Hitler than Blum" was the slogan of the upper classes. Blum's government lost crucial support for refusing to aid the fight against fascism in Spain because of antiwar sentiment. The collapse of the antifascist Popular Front showed the difficulties that democratic societies had facing the revival of militarism during hard economic times.

Fledgling democracies in central Europe, hit hard by the depression, also struggled for economic survival and representative government, but with little success. In 1932, Engelbert Dollfuss came to power in Austria, dismissing the parliament and ruling briefly as a dictator. Despite his authoritarian stance, Dollfuss would not submit to the Nazis, who stormed his office and assassinated him in 1934 in an unsuccessful coup attempt. In Hungary, where outrage over the Peace of Paris remained intense, a crippled economy allowed right-wing general Gyula Gömbös to take over in 1932. Gömbös reoriented his country's foreign policy toward Mussolini and Hitler. He stirred up anti-Semitism and ethnic hatreds and left considerable pro-Nazi feeling after his death in 1936. In democratic Czechoslovakia, the Slovaks, who were poorer than the urbanized

Czechs, built a strong Slovak Fascist Party as the appeal of fascism grew during the Great Depression.

Cultural Visions in Hard Times

Responding to the hard times and political menace, cultural leaders captured the spirit of everyday struggle. Some sympathized with the situations of factory workers, home-makers, and shopgirls straining to support themselves and their families; others looked to interpret the lives of an ever-growing number of unemployed. Artists portrayed the inhuman, regimented side of modern life. In 1931, French director René Clair's film *Give Us Liberty* likened the routine of prison to work on a factory assembly line. In the film *Modern Times* (1936), the Little Tramp character created by **Charlie Chaplin** is a factory worker so molded by his monotonous job that he assumes anything he can see, even a coworker's body, needs mechanical adjustment.

Media portrayed women alternately as the cause and as the cure for society's prob-lems. *The Blue Angel* (1930), a German film starring Marlene Dietrich, contrasted a pow-erfully seductive woman with an impractical, bumbling professor, showing how mixed-up gender roles could destroy men — and civilization. Such films worked to strengthen fascist claims. In comedies and musicals, by comparison, heroines pulled their men out of the depths of despair. In such films as *Keep Smiling* (1938), the British comedienne Gracie Fields portrayed spunky working-class women who remained cheerful despite the challenges of living in hard times. To drive home their antifascist, pacifist, or pro-worker beliefs, writers created realistic studies of human misery and the threat of war that haunted life in the 1930s. The British writer George Orwell described the unem-ployed in the north of England and published an account of atrocities committed dur-ing the Spanish Civil War (1936–1939). German writer Thomas Mann, a Christian, was so outraged at Hitler's ascent to power that he went into voluntary exile. Mann's series of novels based on the Old Testament hero Joseph convey the struggle between humane values and barbarism. One volume praised Joseph's welfare state, in which the grana-ries were full and the rich paid taxes so that the poor might live decent lives. In *Three Guineas* (1938), one of her last works, English writer Virginia Woolf attacked militarism, poverty, and the oppression of women, claiming they were interconnected parts of a single, devastating ethos undermining Europe in the 1930s.

Scientists in research institutes and universities pointed out limits to human understanding — limits that seemed at odds with the rigid pronouncements of dicta-tors. Astronomer Edwin Hubble in California determined in the early 1930s that the universe was an expanding entity and thus an unpredictably changing one. Czech mathematician Kurt Gödel maintained that all mathematical systems contain some propositions that are undecidable. The German physicist Werner Heisenberg developed the uncertainty, or indeterminacy, principle in physics. Scientific observation of atomic behavior, according to this theory, itself disturbs the atom and thereby makes precise formulations impossible. Even scientists, Heisenberg asserted, had to settle for statisti-

cal probability. Approximation, probability, and limits to understanding were not concepts that military dictators welcomed.

Religious leaders helped foster a spirit of resistance to dictatorship among the faithful. Some prominent clergymen hoped for a re-Christianization of ordinary people so that they might choose religious values rather than fascist ones. The Swiss theologian Karl Barth encouraged opposition to the Nazis, teaching that religious people had to take seriously biblical calls for resistance to oppression. In his 1931 address to the world on social issues, Pope Pius XI (r. 1922–1939) condemned the failure of modern societies to provide their citizens with a decent, moral life. To critics, the proclamation seemed an endorsement of the heavy-handed intervention of the fascists. In Germany, nonetheless, German Catholics opposed Hitler, and religious commitment inspired many other individuals to oppose the rising tide of fascism and protect Jews and other fellow citizens whose lives were now threatened.

> **REVIEW QUESTION** How did the democracies' responses to the twin challenges of economic depression and the rise of fascism differ from those of totalitarian regimes?

The Road to Global War

The economic crash intensified competition among the major powers and made external colonies more important than ever. Governments did not let up on the collection of taxes in the colonies. As Britain, France, and other imperial powers guarded their holdings, Hitler, Mussolini, and Japan's military leaders believed that their nation's destiny was to rule a far larger territory. At first, statesmen in Britain and France hoped that sanctions imposed by the League of Nations would stop these aggressors. Other people, still traumatized by memories of the past war, wanted to turn a blind eye both to expansionism and to the fascist attack on the Spanish republic.

A Surge in Global Imperialism

The global imperialism of the 1930s ultimately produced a thoroughly global war. The French, Dutch, British, and Belgians increased their control over their colonies, while in Palestine European Jews continued to arrive and claim the area from local peoples especially as Hitler enacted his harsh anti-Jewish policies in 1933. Japan's military and business leaders longed to control more of the continent and saw China, the Soviet Union, and the Western powers as obstacles to the empire's prosperity and the fulfillment of its destiny.

Japan suffered from a weak monarchy in the person of Hirohito, just twenty-five years old when he became emperor in 1926, which led military and other groups to seek control of the government. Nationalists encouraged these leaders to pursue an expanded empire as key to pulling agriculture and small business from the depths of economic depression. A belief in racial superiority and in the right to take the lands of

"inferior" peoples led the Japanese army to swing into action. In 1931, Japanese officers blew up a train in the Chinese province of Manchuria, where Japanese businesses had invested heavily. The army made the explosion look like a Chinese plot and used it as an excuse to take over the territory, set up a puppet government, and push farther into China. Amid journalistic calls in Japan for aggressive expansion, Japan continued to attack China from 1931 on, angering the United States, on which Japan depended for natural resources and markets. Advocating Asian conquest as part of Japan's "divine mission," the military solidified its influence in the government. By 1936–1937, Japan was spending 47 percent of its budget on arms.

The situation in East Asia affected international politics. The League of Nations condemned the invasion of Manchuria but imposed no sanctions. The league's condemnation outraged Japanese citizens and goaded the government to ally with Hitler and Mussolini. In 1937, Japan attacked China again, justifying its offensive as a first step toward liberating the region from Western imperialism. Hundreds of thousands of Chinese were massacred in the Rape of Nanjing — an atrocity so named because of the Japanese soldiers' brutality, especially toward girls and women. President Roosevelt immediately announced a U.S. embargo on the exportation of airplane parts to Japan and later drastically cut the flow of the crucial raw materials that supplied Japanese industry. Nonetheless, the Western powers, including the Soviet Union, did not effectively resist Japan's territorial expansion.

Like Japanese leaders, Mussolini and Hitler called their countries "have-nots" and demanded land and resources more in line with the other imperial powers. Mussolini threatened "permanent conflict" to expand Italy's borders. Hitler's agenda included gaining **Lebensraum** ("living space"), to be taken from the "inferior" Slavic peoples and Bolsheviks, who would be moved to Siberia or would serve as slaves. The two dictators portrayed themselves as peace-loving men who resorted to extreme measures only to benefit their country and humanity. Their anticommunism appealed to statesmen across the West, and Hitler's anti-Semitism also had widespread support.

Germany and Italy now moved to plunder other countries openly. In the autumn of 1933, Hitler announced Germany's withdrawal from the League of Nations. In 1935, he loudly rejected the clauses of the Treaty of Versailles that limited German military strength. Germany had been rearming in secret for years, but now it started doing so openly. Mussolini chose in 1935 to invade Ethiopia, one of the few African states not overwhelmed by European imperialism. "The Roman legionnaires are again on the march," one soldier exulted. The poorly equipped Ethiopians resisted, but their capital, Addis Ababa, fell in the spring of 1936. Although the League of Nations voted to impose sanctions against Italy, Britain and France opposed an embargo with teeth in it — that is, one including oil — and thus kept the sanctions from being effective while also suggesting a lack of resolve to fight aggression. In March 1936, Hitler defiantly sent his troops into what was supposed to be a permanently demilitarized zone in the Rhineland bordering France. The inhabitants greeted the arrival with wild enthusiasm, and the French, whose security was most endangered by this action, protested to the League of Nations instead of occupying the region, as they had done in the Ruhr in 1923. The

British simply accepted the German military move. The Italian and German dictators thus appeared as powerful heroes, creating, in Mussolini's muscular phrase, a dynamic "Rome–Berlin Axis." Next to them, the politicians of France and Great Britain looked timid and weak.

The Spanish Civil War, 1936–1939

Spain seemed to be headed toward democracy when, in 1931, Spanish republicans over-threw the monarchy and the dictatorship that ruled in its name. For centuries, the Span-ish state had backed the domination of large landowners and the Catholic clergy in the countryside. These ruling elites kept an impoverished peasantry in their grip, making Spain a country of economic extremes. People in industrial cities reacted enthusiasti-cally to the end of the dictatorship and began debating the course of change, with con-stitutionalists, anarchists, Communists, and other splinter groups disagreeing on how to create a democratic nation. For republicans, the air was electric with promise. As one woman recalled: "We saw a backward country suddenly blossoming out into a modern state. We saw peasants living like decent human beings. We saw men allowed freedom of conscience."

With little political experience, however, the republic had a hard time putting in place a political program that would gain support in the countryside. Instead of building popular loyalty by enacting land reform, the various antimonarchist factions struggled among themselves to shape the new government. They wanted political and economic modernization, but they failed to mount a unified effort against their reactionary op-ponents. In 1936, growing monarchist opposition frightened the pro-republican forces into forming a Popular Front coalition to win elections and prevent the republic from collapsing.

In response to the Popular Front victory, a group of army officers led by General **Francisco Franco** (1892–1975) staged an uprising against the republic in 1936. The rebels, who included monarchist landowners, the clergy, and the fascist Falange Party, soon had the help of fascists in other parts of Europe. Pro-republican citizens — male and female — fought back, forming armed volunteer units. In their minds, citizen armies symbolized republicanism, while professional troops followed the aristocratic rebels against democracy. As civil war gripped the country, the republicans generally held Madrid, Barcelona, and other commercial and industrial areas. The right-wing rebels took the agricultural west and south (Map 26.1).

Spain became a training ground for World War II. Hitler and Mussolini sent mili-tary personnel in support of Franco, gaining the opportunity to practice the terror bombing of civilians. In 1937, German planes attacked the town of Guernica, mowing down civilians in the streets. This useless slaughter inspired Pablo Picasso's memorial mural to the dead, *Guernica* (1937), in which the intense suffering is starkly displayed. The Spanish republic appealed everywhere for assistance, but only the Soviet Union answered. Britain and France refused to provide aid despite the outpouring of popular support for the cause of democracy. Instead, a few thousand volunteers from a variety

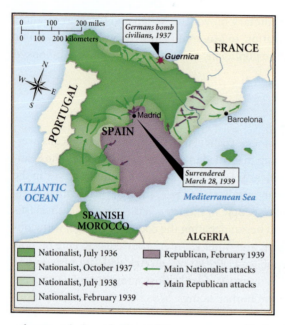

Map 26.1 The Spanish Civil War, 1936–1939
Republican and antirepublican forces bitterly fought one another to determine whether Spain would be a democracy or an authoritarian state. Germany and Italy sent military assistance to the rebels, notably airplanes to experiment with bombing civilians, while volunteers from around the world arrived to fight for the republic. Defeating the ill-organized republican groups, General Francisco Franco instituted a pro-fascist government that sent many to jail and into exile.

of countries — including many students, journalists, and artists — fought for the republic. "Spain was the place to stop fascism," these volunteers believed. The aid Franco received helped his professional armies defeat the republicans in 1939, strengthening the cause of military authoritarianism in Europe. Tens of thousands fled Franco's brutal revenge; remaining critics found themselves jailed or worse.

Hitler's Conquest of Central Europe, 1938–1939

The next step toward World War II was Germany's annexation of Austria in 1938. Many Austrians had actually wished for a merger, or *Anschluss,* with Germany after the Paris peace settlement stripped them of their empire. So Hitler's troops simply entered Austria, and the joy of Nazi sympathizers there made the Anschluss appear an example of the Wilsonian idea of self-determination by unifying so-called Aryan peoples into one nation. The Nazi seizure of Austria's gold marked an important step in financing German expansion, as Austria was declared a German province. Nazi thugs ruled once-cosmopolitan Vienna; an observer later commented on the scene:

> University professors were obliged to scrub the streets with their naked hands, pious white-bearded Jews were dragged into the synagogue by hooting youths and forced to do knee-exercises and to shout "Heil Hitler" in chorus.

Nazis gained additional support in Austria by attacking the stubborn problem of unemployment — especially among the young and out-of-work rural migrants to the cities. Factories sprang up overnight, and German policies eliminated some of the pain Austrians had suffered when their empire had been reduced to a small country after World War I.

Bombing of Barcelona, 1938
The Spanish Civil War gave fair warning that major wars to come would target civilians as well as soldiers.
The forces aiming to overthrow the republic, with the aid of their Fascist allies in Germany and Italy,
bombed cities large and small without regard to civilians. This indiscriminate bombing shocked the
democracies, though not enough for any of them to intervene. (AP Photo.)

With Austria firmly in his grasp, Hitler turned next to Czechoslovakia and its rich
resources. Conquering this democracy looked more difficult, however, because Czechoslovakia had a large army, strong border defenses, and efficient armament factories.
The Nazi propaganda machine swung into action, accusing Czechoslovakia of persecuting its German minority. By October 1, 1938, Hitler warned, Czechoslovakia would have
to grant autonomy (amounting to Nazi rule) to the German-populated border region,
the Sudetenland, or face German invasion.

Hitler gambled correctly that the other Western powers would choose **appeasement**,
the prevention of conflict by making concessions for grievances (in this case, the treatment of Germany in the Treaty of Versailles). As the October deadline approached,
British prime minister Neville Chamberlain, French premier Edouard Daladier, and
Mussolini met with Hitler at Munich and agreed not to oppose Germany's claim to the
Sudetenland. Appeasement was widely seen as positive at the time, and the Munich
Pact prompted Chamberlain to announce that he had secured "peace in our time." Having portrayed himself as a man of peace, Hitler waited until March 1939 to invade the
rest of Czechoslovakia (Map 26.2). Whether the Munich Pact bought Hitler time to
build his army and gave him the green light for further aggression or whether it wisely

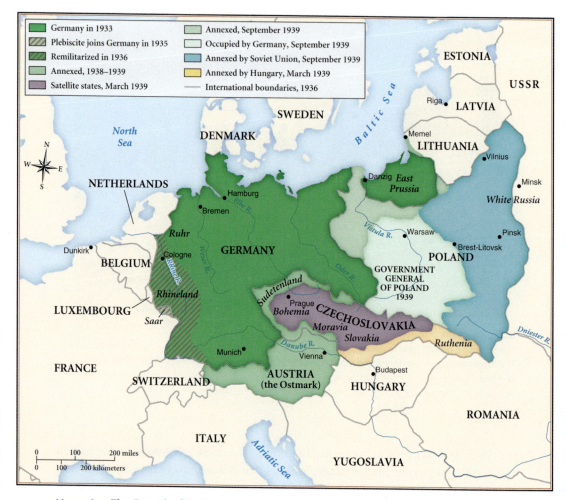

Map 26.2 The Growth of Nazi Germany, 1933–1939
German expansion was rapid and surprising, as Hitler's forces and Nazi diplomacy achieved the annexation of several new states of central and eastern Europe. Although committed to defending the independence of these states through the League of Nations, French and British diplomats were more concerned with satisfying Hitler in the mistaken belief that doing so would prevent his claiming more of Europe. In the process, Hitler acquired the human and material resources of adjacent countries to support his Third Reich. What is the relationship between Germany's expansion during the 1930s and the terms of the Treaty of Versailles after World War I?

provided France and Britain precious time to beef up their own armies is heatedly debated even today.

Stalin, excluded from the Munich deliberations, saw that the democracies were not going to fight to protect eastern Europe. He took action. To the astonishment of people in the West, on August 23, 1939, Germany and the USSR signed a nonaggression agreement. The **Nazi-Soviet Pact** provided that if one country became embroiled in war, the other country would remain neutral. Moreover, the two dictators secretly

agreed to divide Poland and the Baltic states — Latvia, Estonia, and Lithuania — at some future date. The Nazi-Soviet Pact ensured that, should war come, the democracies would be fighting a Germany that feared no attack on its eastern borders. The pact also allowed Stalin extra time to reconstitute his officer corps, which had been wiped out by the purges. In the belief that Great Britain and perhaps even France would continue not to resist, the Nazis now targeted Poland.

> **REVIEW QUESTION** How did the aggression of Japan, Germany, and Italy create the conditions for global war?

World War II, 1939–1945

World War II opened when Hitler launched an all-out attack on Poland on September 1, 1939. In contrast to 1914, no jubilation in Berlin accompanied the invasion; when Britain and France declared war two days later, the mood in those nations was similarly grim. Although Japan, Italy, and the United States did not join the battle immediately, their eventual participation spread the fighting and mobilized civilians around the world. By the time World War II ended in 1945, millions were starving; countries lay in ruins; and unparalleled atrocities, including genocide, had killed six million Jews and six million Slavs, Sinti and Roma, homosexuals, and other civilian targets of fascism.

The German Onslaught

German forces quickly defeated the ill-equipped Polish troops by launching a **Blitzkrieg** ("lightning war"), in which they concentrated airplanes, tanks, and motorized infantry with overpowering force and speed. Blitzkrieg suggested to Germans at home that the costs of gaining Lebensraum would be low. On September 17, 1939, the Soviets invaded Poland from the east. By the end of the month, the victors had divided the country according to the Nazi-Soviet Pact. Nazi propagandists frightened Germans into supporting the conflict because of the "warlike menace" of world Jewry that threatened the nation's very existence.

In April 1940, Blitzkrieg crushed Denmark and Norway; the battles of Belgium, the Netherlands, and France followed in May and June. On June 5, Mussolini, eyeing future gains for Italy, invaded France from the southeast. The French defense and its British allies could not withstand the German onslaught. Trapped on the beaches of Dunkirk in northern France, 370,000 French and British soldiers were rescued by an improvised fleet of naval ships, fishing boats, and pleasure craft. The French government surrendered on June 22, 1940, leaving Germany to rule the northern half of the country,

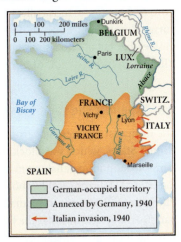

The Division of France, 1940

including Paris. In the south, named Vichy France after the spa town where the government sat, the aged World War I hero Henri Philippe Pétain was allowed to govern because of his and his administration's pro-Nazi values. Stalin used the diversion in western Europe to annex the Baltic states.

Britain now stood alone, installing as prime minister Winston Churchill (1874–1965), an early campaigner for resistance to Hitler. As Hitler ordered the bombardment of Britain in the summer of 1940, Churchill rallied the nation by radio to protect the ideals of liberty with "blood, toil, tears, and sweat." In the battle of Britain — or Blitz, as the British called it — the German Luftwaffe ("air force") bombed monuments, public buildings, weapons depots, and industry. In response, Britain poured resources into its highly successful code-breaking group called Ultra, further development of radar, and air weaponry, outproducing the Germans by 50 percent.

By the fall of 1940, German air losses compelled Hitler to abandon his plan for a naval invasion of Britain. Forcing Hungary, Romania, and Bulgaria to join the Axis powers, Germany gained access to more food, oil, and other resources. He then made his fatal decision to break the Nazi-Soviet Pact and attack the Soviet Union — the "center of judeobolshevism," he called it. In June 1941, three million German and other troops penetrated Soviet lines along a two-thousand-mile front; by July, they had rolled to within two hundred miles of Moscow. Using a strategy of rapid encirclement, German troops killed, captured, or wounded more than half the 4.5 million Soviet soldiers.

Amid success, Hitler blundered. Considering himself a military genius and the Slavic people inferior, he proposed attacking Leningrad, the Baltic states, and Ukraine simultaneously, even though his generals wanted to concentrate on Moscow. Driven by Stalin and local party members, the Soviet people fought back. The onset of winter turned Nazi soldiers into frostbitten wretches because Hitler had feared that equipping his army for Russian conditions would suggest to civilians that a long campaign lay ahead. Convinced of a quick victory in the USSR, he switched German production from making tanks and artillery to making battleships and airplanes for war beyond the Soviet Union. Consequently, Germany's poorly supplied armies fell victim not only to the weather but also to a shortage of equipment. As the war became worldwide, Germany still had an inflated view of its own power.

War Expands: The Pacific and Beyond

The militarist Japanese government decided to settle matters once and for all with the United States, which was blocking Japan's access to technology and resources in an attempt to stop its expansionism. On December 7, 1941, it launched an all-out attack on the United States at Pearl Harbor in Hawaii and then decimated a fleet of airplanes in the Philippines. Roosevelt immediately summoned the U.S. Congress to declare war on Japan. By the spring of 1942, the Japanese had conquered Guam, the Philippines, Malaya, Burma, Indonesia, Singapore, and much of the southwestern Pacific. Like Hitler's early conquests, the Japanese victories strengthened the military's confidence: "The era of de-

mocracy is finished," the foreign minister announced, marketing Emperor Hirohito as the monarch who would liberate Asians everywhere.

Germany quickly declared war on the United States; Mussolini followed suit. The United States was not prepared for a prolonged struggle at the time, partly because isolationist sentiment remained strong. Its armed forces numbered only 1.6 million, and no plan existed for producing the necessary guns, tanks, and airplanes. In addition, the United States and the Soviet Union mistrusted each other. Yet despite these obstacles to cooperation, Hitler's four enemies came together in the Grand Alliance of Great Britain, the Free French (an exile government in London led by General Charles de Gaulle), the Soviet Union, and the United States along with twenty other countries — known collectively as the Allies. Against the Axis powers — Germany, Italy, and Japan — the Allies had advantages: greater manpower and resources, access to goods from global empires, and Britain's traditional naval strength and its experience in combat on many continents. Allied leaders worked hard to wage effective war against the Axis powers, whose rulers were fanatically committed to global conquest at any price.

The War against Civilians

Far more civilians than soldiers died in World War II. The Axis powers and Allies alike bombed cities to destroy civilian will to resist: the Allied firebombings of Dresden and Tokyo killed tens of thousands of civilians, though Axis attacks were more widespread. The British people, not British soldiers, were the target of the battle of Britain, and in Poland and Ukraine, the Nazi SS murdered hundreds of thousands of Polish citizens. Confiscated Polish land and homes were given to "racially pure" Aryans from Germany and other central European countries. In the name of collectivization, Soviet forces perpetuated the same violence in the same area of eastern Europe, which has been called the "Bloodlands" for the millions who died in the battle for land and food.

Nazi and Soviet leaders saw literate people in the conquered areas as leading members of the civil society that they wanted to destroy. A ploy of the Nazis was to test captured people's reading skills, suggesting that those who could read would be given clerical jobs while those who could not would be relegated to hard labor. Those who could read, however, were lined up and shot. Because many in the German army initially rebelled at this inhuman mission, special Gestapo forces took up the charge of herding their victims into woods, to ravines, or even against town walls where they would be shot en masse. The Japanese did the same in China, in Southeast Asia, and on the islands in the Pacific. The number of casualties in China alone has been estimated at thirty million, with untold millions murdered elsewhere.

On the eve of war in 1939, Hitler had predicted "the destruction of the Jewish race in Europe." The Nazis' initial plan for reducing the Jewish population included driving Jews into urban ghettos and making them live on minimal rations until they died of starvation or disease. There was also direct murder. Around Soviet towns, the Nazis killed ten thousand or more at a time, often with the help of local anti-Semitic volunteers. In Jedwabne, Poland, some eight hundred citizens on their own initiative beat

Map 26.3 Concentration Camps and Extermination Sites in Europe
This map shows the major extermination sites and concentration camps in Europe, but the entire continent was dotted with thousands of lesser camps to which the victims of Nazism were transported. Some of these lesser camps were merely way stations on the path to ultimate extermination. In focusing on the major camps, historians often lose sight of the ways in which evidence of deportation and extermination blanketed Europe.

and burned their Jewish neighbors to death and took their property — evidence that the Holocaust was not simply a Nazi initiative. However, the "Final Solution" — the Nazis' plan to murder all of Europe's Jews systematically — was not yet fully under way.

An organized, technological system for transporting Jews to extermination sites had taken shape by the fall of 1941 and was formalized at a meeting in Wannsee, Germany, in January 1942. Although Hitler did not attend the meeting at Wannsee, his responsibility for the Holocaust is clear: he discussed the Final Solution's progress, issued oral directives for it, and had made violent anti-Semitism a basis for Nazism from the beginning. Scientists, doctors, lawyers, government workers, and Nazi officials took initiative in making the Holocaust work. Six camps in Poland were developed specifically for the purposes of mass murder (Map 26.3). Using techniques developed in the T4 project, which killed disabled and elderly people, the camp at Chelmno initially gassed Christian Poles and Soviet prisoners of war. Specially designed crematoria for the mass burning of corpses started functioning in 1943. By then, Auschwitz had the capacity to burn 1.7 million bodies per year. About 60 percent of new arrivals — particularly children, women, and old people — were selected for immediate murder in the gas chambers; the other 40 percent labored until, utterly used up, they too were gassed.

Victims from all over Europe were sent to extermination camps. In the ghettos of European cities, councils of Jewish leaders, such as the one in Amsterdam where Etty Hillesum worked, often chose those to be sent for "resettlement in the east" — a phrase used to mask the Nazis' true plans. For weakened, poorly armed ghetto inhabitants, open resistance meant certain death. When Jews bravely rose up against their Nazi captors in Warsaw in 1943, they were mercilessly butchered. The Nazis also took pains to cloak the purpose of the extermination camps. Bands played to greet incoming train-

Children in Concentration Camps, c. 1945
When Germany undertook the Holocaust and ethnic cleansing, children of outcast groups were generally automatic victims, unless they seemed useful for medical experiments. Great numbers of children
died of starvation in occupied and besieged areas or were killed when the Germans exacted reprisals
for acts of resistance. Teenagers were used as slave laborers; the children in this picture may be older
than they look because of starvation. (Mary Evans / Alinari Archives.)

loads of victims, and survivors later noted that the purpose of the camps was so unthink-
able that potential victims could not begin to imagine their fate. Those not chosen for
immediate murder had their heads shaved and were disinfected. So began life in "a living hell," as one survivor wrote.

The camps were scenes of struggle for life in the face of torture and death. Over-
worked inmates usually received less than five hundred calories per day, far below the
minimum needed to keep an adult in good health. As diseases swept through the camps,
doctors performed unbelievably cruel medical experiments with no anesthesia on pregnant women, twins, and other innocent people in the name of advancing "racial science." Despite the harsh conditions, however, some people maintained their spirit: prisoners forged new friendships, and women in particular observed religious holidays
and celebrated birthdays. Thanks to those sharing a bread ration, wrote the Auschwitz
survivor Primo Levi, "I managed not to forget that I myself was a man." In the end, six
million Jews, the vast majority from eastern Europe — along with an estimated five to
six million Slavs, Sinti and Roma (often called Gypsies), homosexuals, and countless

others — were deliberately murdered in the Nazi genocidal fury. This vast crime perpe-trated by apparently civilized people still shocks and outrages the world.

Societies at War

Even more than World War I, World War II depended on industrial productivity. The Axis countries remained at a disadvantage throughout the war despite their initial con-quests, for the Allies consistently outproduced them. For example, in 1942, Great Brit-ain and Russia produced collectively nearly 50,000 aircraft while Germany produced around 15,000. Even as Germany occupied the Soviet industrial heartland and besieged many of its cities, the USSR increased its production of weapons. Both Japan and Ger-many made the most of their lower output, especially in the use of Blitzkrieg. The use of vast quantities of stolen resources and of millions of slave laborers also helped, but both Japan's and Germany's belief in their racial superiority prevented them from accurately assessing the capabilities of an enemy they held in contempt.

Allied governments were overwhelmingly successful in mobilizing civilians, espe-cially women. In Germany and Italy, where government policy particularly exalted moth-erhood and kept women from good jobs, officials began to realize that women were desperately needed in the workforce. Nazis changed their propaganda to emphasize the need for everyone to take a job, but their messages were not effective enough to convince women to take the low-paid work offered them. In contrast, Soviet women constituted more than half their nation's workforce by war's end, and 800,000 volunteered for the military, even serving as pilots. As the Germans invaded, Soviet citizens moved entire factories eastward. In a dramatic about-face, the government encouraged devotion to the Russian Orthodox church as a way of boosting patriotism.

Even more than in World War I, civilians faced propaganda, censorship, and gov-ernment regulation. People were glued to their radios for war news, but much of it was tightly controlled. The totalitarian powers often withheld news of military defeats and large casualty numbers in order to keep civilian support. Wartime films focused on avia-tion heroes and infantrymen as well as on the self-sacrificing workingwomen and wives on the home front. In most countries, it was simply taken for granted that civilians would not receive what they needed to survive in good health. Soviet children and old people were at the greatest risk, a high proportion of them among the one million residents who starved to death during the siege of Leningrad. Government specialists regulated the production and distribution of food, clothing, and household products, all of which were rationed and generally of lower quality than before the war. With governments standardizing such items as food, clothing, and entertainment, World War II furthered the development of mass society.

On both sides, propaganda and government policies promoted racial thinking. Since the early 1930s, the German government had published ugly caricatures of Jews and Slavs. Similarly, Allied propaganda during the war depicted Germans as perverts and the "Japs" as insectlike fanatics. The U.S. government forced citizens of Japanese origin into internment camps, while Muslims and minority ethnic groups in the Soviet

Union were uprooted and relocated away from the front lines as potential Nazi collaborators. As in World War I, both sides drew colonized peoples into the war through forced labor and conscription into the armies. Some two million Indian men served the Allied cause, as did several hundred thousand Africans. As the Japanese swept through the Pacific and parts of East Asia, they, too, conscripted local men into their army.

From Resistance to Allied Victory

Resistance to fascism began early in the war. Having escaped from France to London in 1940, General Charles de Gaulle directed from a distance the Free French government and its forces — a mixed organization of troops of colonized Asians and Africans, soldiers who had escaped via Dunkirk, and volunteers from other occupied countries. Less well-known than the Free French, resisters in occupied Europe fought in Communist-dominated groups, some of which gathered information to aid the Allied invasion of the continent. Rural groups called partisans not only planned assassinations of traitors and German officers but also bombed bridges, rail lines, and military facilities. Although the Catholic church supported Mussolini in Italy and endorsed the Croatian puppet government's slaughter of a million Serbs, Catholic and Protestant clergy and their parishioners were among those who set up resistance networks, often hiding Jews and fugitives. The Polish resistance attacked imported German settlers; individuals such as Swedish diplomat Raoul Wallenberg saved thousands of Jews.

People also fought back through everyday activities. Homemakers circulated newsletters urging demonstrations at prisons where civilians were detained. In central Europe, hikers smuggled Jews and others over dangerous mountain passes. Danish villagers created vast escape networks, and countless thousands across Europe volunteered to be part of escape routes. Women resisters used stereotypes to good advantage, often carrying weapons to assassination sites in the correct belief that Nazis would rarely suspect or search them. "Naturally the Germans didn't think that a woman could have carried a bomb," explained one Italian resister. Resistance kept alive the liberal ideal of individual action in the face of tyranny.

Both subtle and dramatically visible resistance took place in the fascist countries. Couples in Germany and Italy limited family size in defiance of pro-birth policies. In July 1944, a group of German military officers, fearing their country's military humiliation, tried but failed to assassinate Hitler — one of several such attempts. Wounded and shaken, Hitler mercilessly tortured and killed hundreds of conspirators, innocent friends, and family members. Some ask whether the assassination attempt came too late in the war to count as resistance. However, some five million Germans alone, and millions more of other nationalities, lost their lives in the last nine months of the war. Had Hitler died even as late as the summer of 1944, the relief to humanity would have been considerable.

Amid civilian resistance, Allied forces turned the frontline war against the Axis powers beginning with the battle of Stalingrad in 1942–1943 (Map 26.4). The German army sought Soviet oil through capturing this city. Months of ferocious house-to-house

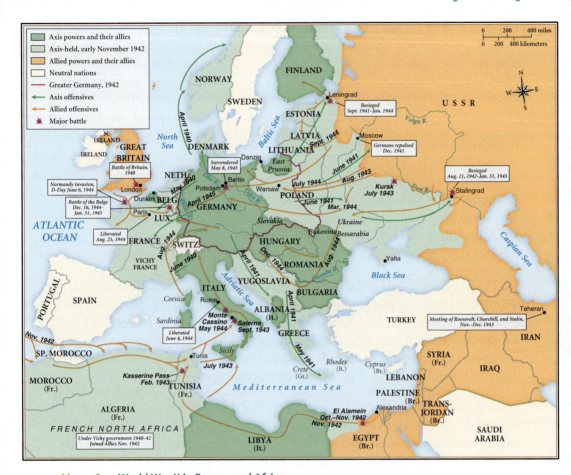

Map 26.4 World War II in Europe and Africa
World War II inflicted massive loss of life and destruction of property on civilians, armies, and all the infrastructure — including factories, equipment, and agriculture — needed to wage total war. Thus, the war swept the European continent as well as areas in Africa colonized by or allied with the major powers. Ultimately the Allies crushed the Axis powers by moving from east, west, and south to inflict a total defeat.

fighting ended when the Soviet army captured the ninety thousand German survivors in February 1943. Meanwhile, the British army in North Africa held against German troops under Erwin Rommel, a skilled practitioner of the new kind of mobile warfare. He aimed to capture the Suez Canal and thus gain access to Middle Eastern oil, but the Allies' code-breaking capacity ultimately helped them block the capture of Egypt and take Morocco and Algeria in the fall of 1942. After driving Rommel out of Africa, the Allies landed in Sicily in July 1943, provoking a German invasion. The slow, bitter fight for the Italian peninsula lasted until April 1945, when Allied forces finally triumphed. After Italy's liberation, partisans shot Mussolini and his mistress and hung their dead bodies for public display.

Fighting in the Streets of Budapest, 1945
House-to-house fighting characterized many battles in World War II (including Stalingrad) despite the "high-tech" nature of the war. As resisters saw the Allies undermining the Axis hold on their cities and towns, they shot from windows, threw bombs at enemy soldiers, and blew up or dismantled train tracks. The history of warfare from World War II to the present has thrown the invincibility of even the most powerful military forces into question. (© Sovfoto.)

The victory at Stalingrad marked the beginning of the Soviet drive westward, during which the Soviets bore the brunt of the Nazi war machine. From the air, Britain and the United States bombed German cities, but it was an invasion from the west that Stalin wanted from his allies. Finally, on June 6, 1944, known as D-Day, the combined Allied forces, under the command of U.S. general Dwight Eisenhower, attacked the heavily fortified French beaches of Normandy and then fought their way through the German-held territory of western France. In late July, Allied forces broke through German defenses and a month later helped liberate Paris. The Soviets meanwhile captured the Baltic states and entered Poland, pausing for desperately needed supplies. The Germans took advantage of the pause to put down an uprising of the Polish resistance in August 1944, which gave the Soviets a freer hand in eastern Europe after the war. Facing more than twice as many troops as on the western front, the Soviet army took Bulgaria and Romania at the end of August, then Hungary in 1945. British, Canadian, U.S., and other Allied forces simultaneously fought their way eastward to join the Soviets in squeezing the Third Reich to its final defeat.

As the Allies advanced, Hitler decided that Germans deserved to perish. He thus refused all negotiations that might have spared them further death and destruction. As the Soviet army took Berlin, Hitler and his wife, Eva Braun, committed suicide. Although

many soldiers remained loyal to the Third Reich, Germany finally surrendered on May 8, 1945.

The Allies had followed a "Europe first" strategy in conducting the war. In 1940 and 1941, Japan had ousted the Europeans from many colonial holdings in Asia, but the Allies turned the tide in 1942 by destroying some of Japan's formidable navy in battles at Midway Island and Guadalcanal (Map 26.5). Allied forces stormed one Pacific island after another, gaining bases from which to cut off the importation of supplies and to launch bombers toward Japan itself. Short of men and weapons, the Japanese military resorted to kamikaze tactics, in which pilots deliberately crashed their planes into Allied ships, killing themselves in the process. In response, the Allies stepped up their bombing of major cities, killing more than 100,000 civilians in their spring 1945 firebombing of Tokyo. The Japanese leadership still ruled out surrender.

Meanwhile a U.S.-based international team of more than 100,000 workers, including scientists and technicians, had been working on the Manhattan Project, the code name for a secret project to develop an atomic bomb. The Japanese practice of dying almost to the man rather than surrendering caused Allied military leaders to calculate that defeating Japan might cost the lives of hundreds of thousands of Allied soldiers (and even more Japanese). On August 6 and 9, 1945, the U.S. government therefore unleashed the new atomic weapons on Hiroshima and Nagasaki, killing 140,000 people instantly; tens of thousands later died from burns, wounds, and other afflictions. (See the illustration on page 874.) Hardliners in the Japanese military wanted to continue the war, but on August 14, 1945, Japan surrendered.

An Uneasy Postwar Settlement

Unlike World War I, this war saw neither a celebrated peace conference nor a formal agreement among all the Allies about the final terms for peace. Instead, wartime agreements among members of the Grand Alliance about the future reflected their differences while aiming to guide the postwar years. In 1941, Roosevelt and Churchill crafted the Atlantic Charter, which condemned aggression, endorsed collective security, and supported the right of all people to choose their governments. Not only did the Allies back these ideals, but so did colonized peoples to whom, Churchill said, the charter was not meant to apply. In October 1944, Churchill and Stalin agreed on the postwar distribution of territories. The Soviet Union would control Romania and Bulgaria, Britain would control Greece, and they would jointly oversee Hungary and Yugoslavia. These agreements went against Roosevelt's faith in collective security, self-determination, and open doors in trade. In February 1945, the "Big Three" — Roosevelt, Churchill, and Stalin — met in the Crimean town of Yalta. Roosevelt advocated for the formation of the United Nations to replace the League of Nations as a global peace mechanism, and he supported future Soviet influence in Korea, Manchuria, and the Sakhalin and Kurile Islands. The last meeting of the Allied leaders, with President Harry S. Truman replacing Roosevelt, who had died in April, took place at Potsdam, Germany, in the summer of

Map 26.5 World War II in the Pacific

As in Europe, the early days of World War II gave the advantage to the Axis power Japan as it took the offensive in conquering islands in the Pacific and territories in Asia — many of them colonies of European states. Britain countered by mobilizing a vast Indian army, while the United States, after the disastrous losses at Pearl Harbor and in the Philippines, gradually gained the upper hand by costly assaults, island by island. The Japanese strategy of fighting to the last person instead of surrendering when a loss was in sight was one factor in President Truman's decision to drop the atomic bomb in August 1945.

Hiroshima, 1945

This photo captures what little remained of the city of Hiroshima after the United States dropped an atomic bomb on August 6, 1945. Without the bomb, the U.S. military foresaw a long and costly struggle to defeat Japan, given that country's overall strategy of fighting to the last person and in the process inflicting the maximum number of enemy casualties. Some claim that the United States dropped the bomb to menace the Soviet Union, its opponent in the cold war that was just beginning. Others point to the fact that no such bomb was ever dropped on a Caucasian population. (The Everett Collection, Inc.)

1945. At Potsdam, the leaders agreed to give the Soviets control of eastern Poland, to transfer a large stretch of eastern Germany to Poland, and to finalize a temporary four-way occupation of Germany that would include France as one of the supervising powers.

These agreements could hardly undo the war's grim legacy. The Great Depression had inflicted global suffering, while the Second World War left up to 100 million dead, more than 50 million refugees without homes, and one of the most abominable moral legacies in human history. Conscripted into armies or into labor camps for war production, colonial peoples in Vietnam, Algeria, India, and elsewhere were in full rebellion or close to it. The war weakened and even destroyed standards of decency and truth. Democratic Europe had succumbed to continuous wartime values, and it was this Europe that George Orwell captured in his novel *1984* (1949). Orwell had worked for the wartime Ministry of Information (called the Ministry of Truth in the novel) and made

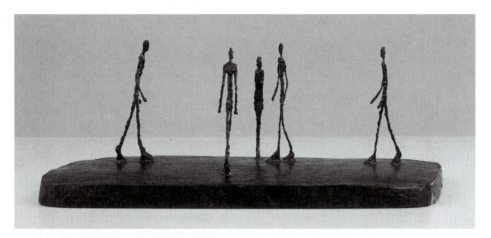

Alberto Giacometti, *The Square II* (1948–1949)
Swiss Artist Alberto Giacometti began making sculptures featuring thin, elongated figures in the 1940s. They appear to be moving forward, striving and active, but at the same time their spareness evokes the skeletal shape of concentration camp survivors. What kind of statement do you see Giacometti making about the times? (bpk, Berlin / Nationalgalerie, Museum Berggruen, Staatliche Museen, Berlin, Germany / Art Resource, NY / © 2012 Succession Giacometti / Licensed by the Artists Rights Society [ARS], New York / ADAGP, Paris; Licensed by VAGA, New York, NY.)

up phony war news and threats for civilian audiences. Truth hardly mattered, and words changed meaning during the war to sound better: *battle fatigue* substituted for *insanity*, and *liberating* a country could mean invading it and slaughtering its civilians. Hungry, careworn people walking in ragged clothing along grimy streets characterized both wartime London and Orwell's fictional state of Oceania. Millions cheered the demise of Nazi evil in 1945, but for Orwell, bureaucratic domination depended on continuing conflict. Indeed as Allied powers competed for territory at the war's end, a new struggle called the cold war was beginning.

REVIEW QUESTION How and where was World War II fought, and what were its major consequences?

Conclusion

The Great Depression, which brought fear, hunger, and joblessness to millions, created a setting in which dictators thrived because they promised to restore economic prosperity by destroying democracy and representative government. Desperate people believed the promises of these dynamic new leaders — Mussolini, Stalin, and Hitler — and often embraced the brutality of their regimes. In the USSR, Stalin's program of rapid industrialization cost the lives of millions as he inspired Communist believers to purge enemies — real and imagined. With the democracies preoccupied with economic recovery while preserving the rule of law and still haunted by memories of World War I, Hitler, Mussolini, and their millions of supporters went on to menace Europe unchallenged.

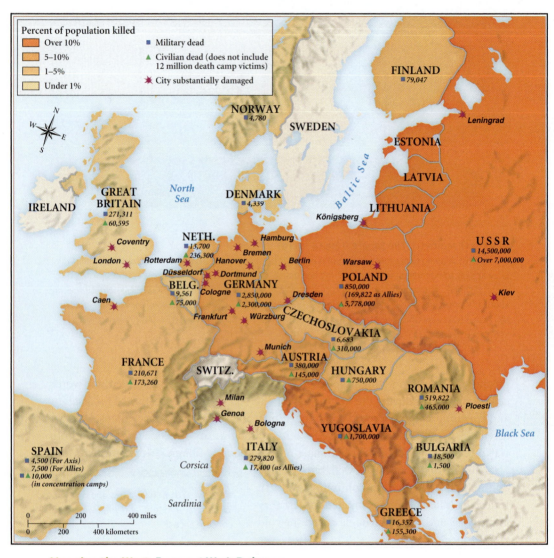

Percent of population killed

- Over 10%
- 5–10%
- 1–5%
- Under 1%

- ■ Military dead
- ▲ Civilian dead (does not include 12 million death camp victims)
- ✹ City substantially damaged

FINLAND
■ 79,047

Leningrad ✹

NORWAY
■ 4,780

SWEDEN

ESTONIA

LATVIA

North Sea

GREAT BRITAIN
■ 271,311
▲ 60,595

Coventry ✹

London ✹

IRELAND

DENMARK
■ 4,339

Königsberg ✹

LITHUANIA

Baltic Sea

USSR
■ 14,500,000
▲ Over 7,000,000

NETH.
■ 13,700
▲ 236,300

Hamburg ✹
Bremen ✹
Hanover ✹

Rotterdam ✹
Düsseldorf ✹
Dortmund ✹

Berlin ✹
Warsaw ✹

Kiev ✹

BELG.
■ 9,561
▲ 75,000

Cologne ✹
GERMANY
■ 2,850,000
▲ 2,300,000

Dresden ✹

POLAND
■ 850,000
(169,822 as Allies)
▲ 5,778,000

Caen ✹

Frankfurt ✹
Würzburg ✹

CZECHOSLOVAKIA
■ 6,683
▲ 310,000

FRANCE
■ 210,671
▲ 173,260

Munich ✹

SWITZ.

AUSTRIA
■ 380,000
▲ 145,000

HUNGARY
▲ 750,000

ROMANIA
■ 519,822
▲ 465,000

Ploesti ✹

Milan ✹
Genoa ✹

Bologna ✹

YUGOSLAVIA
■▲ 1,700,000

Black Sea

SPAIN
■ 4,500 (For Axis)
7,500 (For Allies)
■▲ 10,000
(in concentration camps)

Corsica

ITALY
■ 279,820
▲ 17,400 (as Allies)

BULGARIA
■ 18,500
▲ 1,500

Sardinia

GREECE
■ 16,357
▲ 155,300

0   200   400 miles
0   200   400 kilometers

N   W   E   S

Mapping the West   Europe at War's End, 1945

The damage of World War II left scars that would last for decades. Major German cities were bombed to bits, while the Soviet Union suffered an unimaginable toll of perhaps as many as forty-five million deaths due to the war alone. In addition to the vast civilian and military losses shown on this map, historians estimate that no less than twelve million people were murdered in the Nazi death camps. Everything from politics to family life needed rebuilding, adding to the chaos. (From *The Hammond Atlas of the Twentieth Century* [London: Times Books, 1996], 102.)

At the same time, Japan embarked on a program of conquest aimed at ending Western domination in Asia and taking more of Asia for itself. The coalition of Allies that finally formed to stop the Axis powers of Germany, Italy, and Japan was an uneasy alliance among Britain, Free France, the Soviet Union, and the United States. World War II ended European dominance. Europe's economies were shattered, its colonies were on the verge of independence, and its peoples were starving and homeless.

The costs of a bloody war — one waged against civilians as much as armies — taught the victorious powers different lessons. The United States, Britain, and France were convinced that a minimum of citizen well-being was necessary to prevent a recurrence of fascism. The devastation of the USSR's population and resources made Stalin increasingly obsessed with national security and compensation for the damage inflicted by the Nazis. Britain and France faced the end of their imperial might, underscoring Orwell's insight that the war had utterly transformed society. The militarization of society and the deliberate murder of millions of innocent citizens like Etty Hillesum were tragedies that permanently injured the West's claims to being an advanced civilization. Nonetheless, backed by vast supplies of sophisticated weaponry, the United States and the Soviet Union used their opposing views on a postwar settlement to justify threatening one another — and the world — with another horrific war.

Review Questions

1. How did the Great Depression affect society and politics?
2. What role did violence play in the Soviet and Nazi regimes?
3. How did the democracies' responses to the twin challenges of economic depression and the rise of fascism differ from those of totalitarian regimes?
4. How did the aggression of Japan, Germany, and Italy create the conditions for global war?
5. How and where was World War II fought, and what were its major consequences?

Making Connections

1. Compare fascist ideas of the individual with the idea of individual rights that inspired the American and French Revolutions.
2. What connections can you make between the Great Depression and the coming of World War II?
3. What are the major differences between World War I and World War II?
4. What explains the bleak view of writers like George Orwell after the Allied victory over the Axis powers?

- For practice quizzes and other study tools, visit the **Online Study Guide** at bedfordstmartins.com/huntconcise.

- For primary-source material from this period, see *Sources of the Making of the West*, Fourth Edition.

- For Web sites, images, and documents related to topics in this chapter, visit *Make History* at bedfordstmartins.com/huntconcise.

Suggested References

This grim period in human history has yielded an ever-growing crop of excellent books, some of them coldly examining the worst aspects of the Great Depression and World War II and others looking at resistance, survival, and intellectual breakthroughs.

Alvarez, Luis. *The Power of the Zoot: Youth Culture and Resistance during World War II*. 2008.

Clavin, Patricia. *The Great Depression in Europe, 1929–1939*. 2000.

Collingham, Lizzie. *The Taste of War: World War II and the Battle for Food*. 2011.

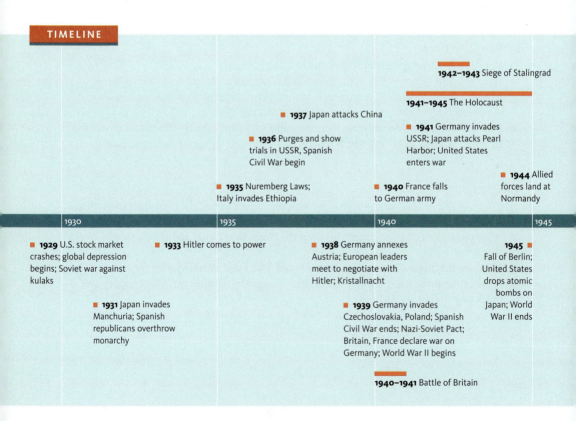

TIMELINE

1942–1943 Siege of Stalingrad

1941–1945 The Holocaust

1937 Japan attacks China

1941 Germany invades USSR; Japan attacks Pearl Harbor; United States enters war

1936 Purges and show trials in USSR, Spanish Civil War begin

1944 Allied forces land at Normandy

1935 Nuremberg Laws; Italy invades Ethiopia

1940 France falls to German army

1930   1935   1940   1945

1929 U.S. stock market crashes; global depression begins; Soviet war against kulaks

1933 Hitler comes to power

1938 Germany annexes Austria; European leaders meet to negotiate with Hitler; Kristallnacht

1945 Fall of Berlin; United States drops atomic bombs on Japan; World War II ends

1931 Japan invades Manchuria; Spanish republicans overthrow monarchy

1939 Germany invades Czechoslovakia, Poland; Spanish Civil War ends; Nazi-Soviet Pact; Britain, France declare war on Germany; World War II begins

1940–1941 Battle of Britain

Friedlander, Saul. *The Years of Extermination: Nazi Germany and the Jews, 1939–1945*. 2007.

Hellbeck, Jochen. *Revolution on My Mind: Writing a Diary under Stalin*. 2006.

Imlay, Talbot C. *Facing the Second World War: Strategy, Politics, and Economics in Britain and France 1938–1940*. 2003.

Kaplan, Marion. *Between Dignity and Despair: Jewish Life in Nazi Germany*. 1998.

Maas, Ad, and Hans Hooijijers, eds. *Scientific Research in World War II: What Scientists Did in the War*. 2009.

Miner, Steven Merritt. *Stalin's Holy War: Religion, Nationalism, and Alliance Politics, 1941–1945*. 2003.

Naimark, Norman M. *Stalin's Genocides*. 2010.

Seidman, Michael. *Republic of Egos: A Social History of the Spanish Civil War*. 2002.

Snyder, Timothy. *Bloodlands: Europe between Hitler and Stalin*. 2010.

Stoltzfus, Nathan, et al., eds. *Courageous Resistance: The Power of Ordinary People*. 2007.

Tierney, Robert T. *Tropics of Savagery: The Culture of Japanese Empire in Comparative Frame*. 2010.

Viola, Lynn, ed. *Contending with Stalinism: Soviet Power and Popular Resistance in the 1930s*. 2003.

Weinberg, Gerhard. *A World at Arms: A Global History of World War II*. 2005.

Wildt, Michel. *An Uncompromising Generation: The Nazi Leadership of the Reich Security Main Office*. 2009.

A LOVE CAUGHT IN THE FIRE OF REVOLUTION

Turbulent were the times and fiery was the love story of Zhivago, his wife... and the passionate, tender Lara.

METRO-GOLDWYN-MAYER PRESENTS A CARLO PONTI PRODUCTION

DAVID LEAN'S FILM OF BORIS PASTERNAKS

DOCTOR ZHIVAGO

STARRING
GERALDINE CHAPLIN · JULIE CHRISTIE · TOM COURTENAY
ALEC GUINNESS · SIOBHAN McKENNA · RALPH RICHARDSON
OMAR SHARIF [AS ZHIVAGO] ROD STEIGER · RITA TUSHINGHAM

WINNER OF 6 ACADEMY AWARDS!

SCREEN PLAY BY
ROBERT BOLT · DAVID LEAN   IN PANAVISION® AND METROCOLOR
DIRECTED BY

The Cold War and the Remaking of Europe

1945–1960s

L ATE IN 1945, WITH THE USSR still reeling from the devastation of World War II, Soviet poet Boris Pasternak began a new project — *Doctor Zhivago*, a novel about a thoughtful medical man caught up in the whirlwind of the Russian Revolution. Like others in the USSR, Pasternak expected the postwar era to usher in, as he put it, "a great renewal of Russian life." So he struggled on with his complex epic even as the cold war tensions between the United States and the USSR unfolded. In 1953, Joseph Stalin's sudden death raised Pasternak's hopes for his masterpiece to receive a warm reception; those hopes were dashed, however, when the Soviets forbade the book's publication.

A determined Pasternak bypassed the Soviet authorities and arranged for *Doctor Zhivago* to be published first in 1957 in Italy — now an anti-Soviet ally of the United States in the cold war. The book became a best seller, showing its readers that the Russian Revolution was far from perfect and so angering the Soviet leadership that Stalin's successor, Nikita Khrushchev, forced Pasternak to decline the Nobel Prize for Literature awarded him in 1958. But the cold war allowed *Doctor Zhivago* to live on when the famed Hollywood studio MGM turned it into a blockbuster film (1965), seen by tens of millions. By that time, however, Pasternak had died — a broken victim of cold war persecutions that haunted the world long after the calamitous years of war and genocide had ended.

Following World War II, people in Europe, Japan, and much of East and Southeast Asia were starving and homeless. Evidence of genocide and other inhumanity was everywhere; and nuclear annihilation menaced the world. The old international order was

***Doctor Zhivago* Poster**

As soon as Boris Pasternak's forbidden novel *Doctor Zhivago* was published in Italy in 1957, Hollywood's MGM studio went after the rights for the film. Finally completed in 1965, the movie was a cold war blockbuster — an epic of life and love in postrevolutionary Russia. The opening scene, invented for the movie, was a grim Soviet factory, while the story itself was more or less symbolized in this advertising poster highlighting two incredibly attractive people who fall in love and are torn apart by the crushing Bolshevik system. (MGM/The Kobal Collection at Art Resource, NY.)

gone, replaced by the rivalry of the United States and the Soviet Union for control of Europe, whose political, social, and economic order was shattered. The nuclear arsenals of these two superpowers — a term coined in 1947 — grew massively in the 1950s, but the enemies did not fight outright. Thus, their terrifying rivalry was called the **cold war**. The cold war divided the West and led to political persecution in many areas, even in the wealthy and secure United States.

At the same time, the defeat of Nazism inspired cautious optimism and a revival of thoughtful reflection like Pasternak's. Heroic effort had defeated fascism, and that defeat raised hopes that a new age would begin. Atomic science promised advances in medicine, and nuclear energy was seen as a replacement for coal and oil. The creation of the United Nations in 1945 heralded an era of international cooperation. Around the globe, colonial peoples won independence from European masters, while in the United States the civil rights movement grew in strength. The welfare state expanded, and by the end of the 1950s, economic rebirth had made much of Europe more prosperous than ever before. An "economic miracle" had occurred, bringing many Europeans and Americans the highest standard of living they had ever known, including quantities of new consumer goods and simple pleasures such as seeing films like *Doctor Zhivago*.

The postwar period became one of open redefinition as the experience of total war transformed both society and the international order. New terms arose in the 1950s, dividing the globe into the first world (the West, or capitalist bloc of countries); the second world (the East, or socialist bloc); and the third world (countries emerging from imperial domination). This last term, *third world,* was meant as a favorable comparison of emerging nations to the Third Estate — that is, the rising citizens of the French Revolution — but is now considered an insulting term.

As the world's people redefined themselves, the superpowers took the world to the brink of nuclear disaster. From the dropping of the atomic bomb on Japan in 1945 to the Cuban missile crisis of 1962, fear and personal anguish like that suffered by Pasternak gripped much of the world, even in the midst of prosperity and Europe's rebirth.

CHAPTER FOCUS How did the cold war shape the politics, economy, social life, and culture of post–World War II Europe?

World Politics Transformed

World War II ended Europe's global leadership. Many countries lay in ruins in the summer of 1945, and conditions would deteriorate before they improved. Though victorious, bombed and bankrupt Britain could not feed its people, and continuing turmoil destroyed the lives of millions in central and eastern Europe. In contrast, the United States, whose territory was virtually untouched in the war, emerged as the world's sole economic giant, while the Soviet Union, despite suffering immense devastation, retained formidable military might. Occupying Europe as part of the victorious alliance against Nazism and fascism, the two superpowers used Germany — at the heart of the continent and its politics — to divide Europe in two. By the late 1940s, the USSR had imposed Communist rule throughout most of eastern Europe as it gained control of the territory

that the Nazis had desired for German settlement. Western Europeans found themselves at least partially controlled by the very U.S. economic power that helped them rebuild, especially because the United States maintained air bases and nuclear weapons sites on their soil. The new age of bipolar world politics made Europe its testing ground.

Chaos in Europe

In contrast to the often stationary trench warfare of World War I, armies in World War II had fought a war of movement on the ground and in the air. Massive bombing had leveled thousands of square miles of territory, and whole cities were clogged with rubble. On the Rhine River, almost no bridge remained standing; in the Soviet Union, seventy thousand villages and more than a thousand cities lay in shambles. Everywhere people were suffering. In the Netherlands, the severity of Nazi occupation left the Dutch population close to death, relieved only by a U.S. airlift of food. To control scarce supplies, Italian bakers sold bread by the slice. Allied troops in Germany were almost the sole source of food: "To see the children fighting for food," remarked one British soldier handing out supplies, "was like watching animals being fed in a zoo." There were no mass uprisings as after World War I; until the late 1940s, people were too absorbed by the struggle for bare survival.

The tens of millions of refugees suffered the most, as they wandered a continent where the dangers of assault, robbery, and ethnic violence were great. An estimated thirty million Europeans, many of German ethnicity, were forcibly expelled from Poland, Czechoslovakia, and Hungary (Map 27.1). The USSR lobbied hard for the return of several million Soviet prisoners of war and forced laborers, and the Allies transported millions of Soviet refugees home. The Allies slowed the process when they discovered that Soviet leaders had ordered the execution of many of the returnees for being "contaminated" by Western ideas.

Survivors of the concentration camps discovered that their suffering had not ended with Germany's defeat. Many returned home diseased and disoriented, while others had no home to return to because their property had been confiscated. Anti-Semitism — official policy under the Nazis — lingered in popular attitudes, and people used it to justify their claim to Jewish property and to jobs vacated by Jews. In the summer of 1946, a vicious crowd in Kielce, Poland, assaulted some 250 Jewish survivors, killing at least 40. Survivors fled to the port cities of Italy and other Mediterranean countries, eventually leaving Europe for Palestine, where Zionists had been settling for half a century.

New Superpowers: The United States and the Soviet Union

Only two countries were still powerful in 1945: the United States and the Soviet Union. The United States was now the richest nation in the world. Its industrial output had increased by a remarkable 15 percent annually between 1940 and 1944. By 1947, the United States controlled almost two-thirds of the world's gold bullion and launched more than half of the world's commercial shipping. Continued spending on industrial and military

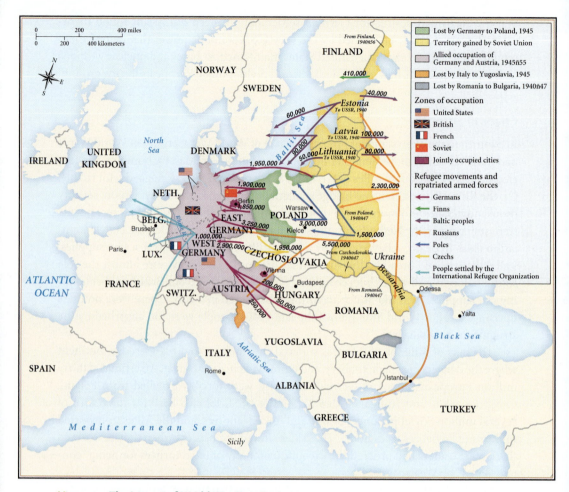

Map 27.1 The Impact of World War II on Europe
European governments, many of them struggling to provide food and other necessities for their populations, found themselves responsible for hundreds of thousands, if not millions, of new refugees. Simultaneously, millions of prisoners of war, servicemen, and slave laborers were returned to the Soviet Union, many of them by force. This situation unfolded amid political instability and even violence. What does the movement of peoples shown on the map suggest about social conditions in post–World War II Europe?

research added to postwar prosperity. In contrast to the post–World War I policy of isolationism, Americans embraced global leadership. Many had learned about the world while tracking the war's progress. Despite widespread fear of nuclear annihilation, a wave of suburban housing development and consumer spending kept the economy buoyant. A baby boom exploded from the late 1940s through the early 1960s in response to prosperity.

The Soviets also emerged from the war with a well-justified sense of accomplishment. Despite horrendous losses — as many as forty-five million lives lost in the war

itself — they had resisted the most massive onslaught ever launched against a nation. Indeed many Europeans and Americans gratefully acknowledged the Soviet contribution to Hitler's defeat. Ordinary Soviet citizens believed that the victory would lead to improvement in everyday conditions. Rumors spread among the peasants that the collective farms would be divided and returned to them as individual property. "Life will become pleasant," one writer prophesied. "There will be much coming and going, and a lot of contacts with the West." The Stalinist goals of industrialization and defense against Nazism had been won, and thus many Soviets, among them Boris Pasternak, anticipated an end to decades of hardship and repression.

Stalin took a different view and moved ruthlessly to reassert control. In 1946, his new five-year plan set increased production goals and mandated more stringent collectivization of agriculture. For him, rapid recovery meant more work, not less, and more order, not greater freedom. Stalin also turned his attention to the low birthrate, a result of wartime male casualties and women's long, arduous working days. He introduced an intense propaganda campaign emphasizing that women should hold down jobs and also fulfill their "true nature" by producing many children. A new round of purges began in which people were told that enemies among them were threatening the state. Jews were especially targeted, and in 1953 the government announced that doctors — most of them Jews — had long been assassinating Soviet leaders, murdering newborns and patients in hospitals, and plotting to poison water supplies. Hysteria gripped the nation, and people feared for their lives. "I am a simple worker and not an anti-Semite," one Moscow resident wrote, "but I say . . . it's time to clean these people out." With this rebirth of Stalinism, an atmosphere of fear returned to feed the cold war.

Origins of the Cold War

The cold war between the United States and the Soviet Union, which began in 1945, would afflict the world for more than four decades. No peace treaty officially ended World War II to document what went wrong, as in the Peace of Paris of 1919–1920. Therefore, the origins of the cold war remain a matter of debate, with historians faulting both sides for starting the dangerous rivalry. Some point to consistent U.S., British, and French hostility to the Soviets because of Communists' abolition of private property and Russia's withdrawal from World War I. Others stress Stalin's aggressive policies, notably the 1939 Nazi-Soviet Pact and Soviet expansionism.

Suspicion ran deep among the Allied leadership during the war: Stalin believed that Churchill and Roosevelt were deliberately letting the USSR bear the brunt of Hitler's rampage across the continent as part of their anti-Communist policy. He rightly viewed Churchill in particular as interested primarily in preserving Britain's imperial power, no matter what the cost in Soviet lives. At the time, some Americans believed that dropping the atomic bomb on Japan would also frighten the Soviets and discourage them from making any more land grabs. In addition, the new U.S. president, Harry Truman, cut off aid to the USSR almost the instant the last gun was fired, fueling Stalin's suspicions and leading to the takeover of eastern Europe as a permanent "buffer zone" of

The Cold War

1945–1949	USSR establishes satellite states in eastern Europe
1947	Truman Doctrine announces American commitment to contain communism; Marshall Plan provides massive aid to rebuild Europe
1948–1949	Soviet troops blockade Berlin; United States airlifts provisions to Berliners
1949	West Germany and East Germany formed; Western nations form North Atlantic Treaty Organization (NATO); Soviet bloc establishes Council for Mutual Economic Assistance (COMECON); USSR tests its first nuclear weapon
1950–1953	Korean War
1950–1954	U.S. senator Joseph McCarthy leads hunt for American Communists
1953	Stalin dies
1955	USSR and eastern-bloc countries form military alliance, the Warsaw Pact
1956	Khrushchev denounces Stalin in "secret speech" to Communist Party Congress; Hungarians revolt unsuccessfully against Soviet domination
1959	Fidel Castro comes to power in Cuba
1961	Berlin Wall erected
1962	Cuban missile crisis

dependent European states. Across the Atlantic, members of the U.S. State Department fueled U.S. fears by depicting Stalin as another in a long line of neurotic Asian tyrants thirsting for world domination.

The cold war thus became a series of moves and countermoves in the shared occupation of a rich European heartland that had fallen into chaos. In line with the view of its political needs, the USSR repressed democratic coalition governments of liberals, socialists, Communists, and peasant parties in central and eastern Europe between 1945 and 1949. It imposed Communist rule almost immediately in Bulgaria and Romania. In Romania, Stalin cited citizen violence in 1945 as the excuse to demand an ouster of all non-Communists from the civil service and cabinet. In Poland, the Communists fixed the election results of 1945 and 1946 to create the illusion of approval for communism.

The United States worried that Communist power would spread to western Europe. The Communists' promises of better conditions appealed to hungry workers in Europe, while memories of Communist leadership in the resistance to fascism gave it powerful appeal. In March 1947, Truman reacted by announcing the **Truman Doctrine**, the use of economic and military aid to block communism. The president requested $400 million in military aid for Greece and Turkey, where the Communists were also exerting pressure. Fearing that Americans would balk at backing an undemocratic Greece, the U.S. Congress said it would agree to the program only if, as one congressman put it, Truman would "scare the hell out of the country." Truman thus publicized the expensive aid program as a necessary first step to prevent Soviet conquest of the world. The show of American support made the Communists back off.

In 1947, the United States also devised the **Marshall Plan** — a program of massive economic aid to Europe — to relieve the daily hardships that were making communism attractive to Europeans. "The seeds of totalitarian regimes are nurtured by misery and want," Truman warned. Named after Secretary of State George C. Marshall, who proposed the plan, the program's direct aid would immediately improve everyday life, while its loans and financial credits would restart international trade. The government

Marshall Plan Poster

The Marshall Plan was a major factor in both western European recovery and the cold war. This poster in Italian advertises the plan as "Aid from America" and specifies that it includes "grain, coal, food, and medical supplies." Given both the image and the text, what would you judge the poster's effect to be? (Archivio GBB / CONTRASTO / Redux.)

claimed that the Marshall Plan was not directed "against any country or doctrine but against hunger, poverty, desperation, and chaos." By the early 1950s, the United States had sent Europe more than $12 billion in food, equipment, and services, reducing communism's appeal in the countries of western Europe that received the aid.

Stalin saw the Marshall Plan as a U.S. political trick because the devastated USSR had little aid to offer client countries in eastern and central Europe. He thus clamped down still harder on eastern European governments, preventing them from responding to the U.S. offer of assistance and eliminating the last scraps of democracy in Hungary, Poland, and Czechoslovakia. The populace accepted the change so passively that Communist leaders said the takeover was "like cutting butter with a knife."

The only exception to the Soviet sweep in eastern Europe came in Yugoslavia, under the Communist ruler known as Tito (Josip Broz, 1892–1980). During the war, Tito had led the powerful anti-Nazi Yugoslav "partisans." After the war, he drew on support from Serbs, Croats, and Muslims to mount a Communist revolution, but one explicitly meant to avoid Soviet influence. Eager for Yugoslavia to develop industrially rather than simply serve Soviet needs, Tito remarked, "We study and take as an example the Soviet system, but we are developing socialism in our country in somewhat different forms." Stalin was furious; in his eyes, commitment to communism meant obedience to him. Nonetheless, Yugoslavia emerged from its Communist revolution as a culturally diverse federation

Yugoslavia after the Revolution

of six republics and two independent provinces within Serbia that held together until Tito's death in 1980.

The Division of Germany

The superpower struggle for control of Germany took the cold war to a menacing level. The agreements reached at the Yalta and Potsdam conferences in 1945 provided for Germany's division into four zones, each of which was controlled by one of the four principal victors in World War II — the United States, the Soviet Union, Britain, and France. However, the superpowers disagreed on how to treat Germany. The U.S. occupation forces undertook to reprogram German attitudes by controlling the press and censoring all media in the U.S. zone to ensure that they did not express fascist values. In contrast, believing that Nazism was an extreme form of capitalism, Stalin confiscated the estates of wealthy Germans and redistributed them to ordinary people and supporters.

A second disagreement, concerning the economy, led to Germany's partition. According to the American plan for coordinating the various segments of the German economy, surplus crops from the Soviet-occupied areas would feed urban populations in the western zones; in turn, industrial goods would be sent to the USSR. The Soviets upset this plan. Following the Allied agreement that the USSR would receive reparations from German resources, the Soviets seized German equipment, shipping it all to the Soviet Union. They transported skilled German workers, engineers, and scientists to the USSR to work as forced laborers. The Soviets also manipulated the currency in their zone, enabling the USSR to buy German goods at unfairly low prices. In response, the western Allies agreed to merge their zones into a West German state, and the United States began an economic buildup of the western zone under the Marshall Plan. Notions of

Map 27.2 Divided Germany and the Berlin Airlift, 1946–1949
Berlin — controlled by the United States, Great Britain, France, and the Soviet Union — was deep in the Soviet zone of occupation and became a major point of contention among the former allies. When the USSR blockaded the western half of the city, the United States responded with a massive airlift. To stop movement between the two zones, the USSR built the Berlin Wall in 1961 and used troops to patrol it.

Map 27.3 European NATO Members and the Warsaw Pact in the 1950s

The two superpowers intensified their rivalry by creating large military alliances: NATO, formed in 1949, and the Warsaw Pact, formed in 1955 after NATO invited West German membership. International politics revolved around these two alliances, which faced off in the heart of Europe. War games for the two sides often assumed a massive war concentrated in central Europe over control of Germany.

a permanently weakened Germany ended as the United States enlisted many former Nazi officials as spies and bureaucrats to jump-start the economy and pursue the cold war.

On July 24, 1948, Stalin retaliated by using Soviet troops to blockade Germany's capital, Berlin. Like Germany as a whole, the city — located more than one hundred miles deep into the Soviet zone and thus cut off from western territory — had been divided into four occupation zones. The Soviets also refused to allow western vehicles to travel through the Soviet zone to reach Berlin. The United States responded decisively with the Berlin airlift — Operation Vittles, as U.S. pilots called it — flying in millions of tons of provisions to some two million isolated citizens (Map 27.2). Given the limited number of available transport planes, pilots kept the plane engines on to achieve a rapid turnaround that would ensure adequate delivery. The Soviets ended their blockade in May 1949, but the cold war rhetoric of good versus evil made the divided capital of Berlin an enduring symbol of the capitalist-communist divide.

The creation of competing military alliances added to cold war tensions (Map 27.3). A few months after the establishment of the West German state in 1948, the USSR formed an East German state. In 1949, the United States, Canada, and their allies in western Europe and Scandinavia formed the **North Atlantic Treaty Organization (NATO)**, which provided a unified military force for its member countries. In 1955, after the United States forced France and Britain to invite West Germany to join NATO, the Soviet Union retaliated by establishing with its satellite countries the military organization commonly called the **Warsaw Pact**. By that time, both the United States and the USSR had accelerated arms buildups: the Soviets had exploded their own atomic bomb in 1949, and both nations then tested increasingly powerful nuclear weapons, outstripping the individual might of the formerly dominant European powers.

REVIEW QUESTION What were the major events in the development of the cold war?

Political and Economic Recovery in Europe

The clash between the United States and the Soviet Union served as a background to the remarkable recovery that took place in Europe. The first two items on the political agenda were the eradication of the Nazi past and the establishment of stable governments. While western Europe revived its democratic political structures and productivity, eastern Europe was far less prosperous and far more repressive. Even to the east, however, the conditions of everyday life improved as peasant societies were forced to modernize and some consumer goods were restored. By 1960, people across the continent were enjoying a higher standard of living than ever before.

Dealing with Nazism

In May 1945, the goals of feeding civilians, dealing with millions of refugees, purging Nazis, and setting up peacetime governments all needed attention. Governments-in-exile returned to reclaim power, but they often ran up against occupying armies that were a law unto themselves. The Soviets were especially feared for inflicting rape and robbery on Germans — abuses they justified by pointing to the tens of millions of worse atrocities committed by the Nazis. Adding to the sense of disorder was the lively trade in sex for food among starving civilians and well-supplied soldiers in all armies. Employing swift vigilante justice, civilians released pent-up rage and punished collaborators for their participation in genocide and occupation crimes. In France, villagers often shaved the heads of women suspected of associating with Germans and made some of them parade naked through the local streets. Members of the resistance executed tens of thousands of Nazi officers and collaborators without trial.

Allied representatives undertook what they claimed to be a systematic "denazification" that ranged from forcing German civilians to view the death camps to bringing to trial suspected local collaborators. The trials conducted at Nuremberg, Germany, by the victorious Allies in the fall of 1945 used the Nazis' own documents to reveal a horrifying panorama of crimes by Nazi leaders. Although international law lacked any definition of genocide as a crime, the judges at Nuremberg found sufficient cause to impose death sentences on half of the twenty-four defendants, among them Hitler's closest associates, and to give prison terms to the remainder. The Nuremberg trials introduced today's notion of prosecution for crimes against humanity.

Allied prosecution of the Axis leadership was hardly thorough. Some of those most responsible for war crimes were not pursued, leaving many Germans skeptical about Allied intentions. As women in Germany faced violence at the hands of occupying troops, endured starvation, and were forced to do the rough manual labor of clearing rubble (see the illustration on page 892), Germans came to believe that they themselves were the main victims of the war. Distrust mounted when Allied officials, eager to restore government services and make western Europe more efficient than Soviet-controlled eastern Europe, began to hire former high-ranking Fascists and Nazis. Soon the new West German government proclaimed that the war's real casualties were the German prisoners of war still held in Soviet camps.

Polish Refugees

These refugees, a handful among millions, are waiting for a train that might carry them to a safer destination. The refugee situation was appalling, as ethnic Poles, Germans, Hungarians, Croats, Czechs, and others were driven from areas where in some cases their families had lived for centuries. The goal of many postwar governments was to "ethnically cleanse" regions along the line of thought that grew up with Wilson's Fourteen Points: that national ethnicities should determine the kind of society and government they would have. (Photo by Fred Ramage / Keystone / Getty Images.)

Rebirth of the West

Following the immediate postwar chaos, the first civilian governments in western Europe reflected the broad coalitions of the resistance movements and other opposition to the Axis powers. These reform-minded governments conspicuously emphasized democratic values to show their rejection of the totalitarian regimes that had earlier attracted so many Europeans. In France, the leader of the Free French, General Charles de Gaulle, governed briefly as chief of state, and the French approved a constitution in 1946 that established the Fourth Republic and finally granted the vote to French women. De Gaulle wanted a political system with a strong executive and, failing to achieve that, soon resigned in favor of centrist and left-wing parties. Meanwhile, Italy replaced its constitutional monarchy with a republic that also allowed women the vote for the first time. As in France, a resistance-based government was soon replaced by a coalition headed by the conservative **Christian Democrats**, descended from the traditional Catholic centrist parties of the prewar period. Other countries likewise saw the growing influence of Christian politicians because of their resistance to fascism.

Other voters in western Europe favored communist and labor parties. Symbol of the common citizen, the Soviet soldier was a hero to many western Europeans outside

Women Clearing Berlin
The amount of destruction caused by World War II was staggering, requiring the mobilization of the civilian population in Berlin, where women were conscripted to sort the rubble and clear it away. Scenes like this were ultimately used as propaganda in the cold war to make it seem as if the Germans were the victims rather than the perpetrators of the war. That German soldiers held in Soviet camps were only slowly repatriated added to the image of Soviet rather than German aggression in World War II. (akg-images.)

occupied Germany. People also remembered the hardships of the depression of the 1930s. Therefore, in Britain, despite the wartime successes of Winston Churchill's Conservative Party leadership, the government of Labour Party leader Clement Attlee — though not Communist — appeared most likely to fulfill promises to share prosperity better among the classes. The extreme difficulties of the immediate postwar years provided further support for governments that would represent the millions of ordinary citizens who had suffered, fought, and worked incredibly hard during the war.

In West Germany, however, with the Communist takeovers occurring directly to the east and with memories of the millions of German soldiers who had died at the hands of the Red Army, communism and the left in general had little appeal. In 1949, centrist politicians came to power in the new state, officially named the German Federal Republic, whose constitution aimed to prevent the emergence of a dictator and to guarantee individual rights. West Germany's first chancellor was the seventy-three-year-

old Catholic anti-Communist Konrad Adenauer, who allied himself with the economist Ludwig Erhard. Erhard stabilized the postwar German currency so that people would have enough confidence in its soundness to resume normal trade and manufacturing while Adenauer restored the representative government that Hitler had overthrown.

Paradoxically, given its leadership in the fight against fascism, the United States was a country in which individual freedom and democracy were imperiled after the war. Two events in 1949 — the Soviet Union's successful test of an atomic bomb and the Communist revolution in China — brought to the fore Joseph McCarthy, a U.S. senator fearing a reelection defeat. To win the election, McCarthy warned of a great conspiracy to overthrow the U.S. government. As during the Soviet purges, people of all occupations — including government workers, film stars, and union leaders — were called before U.S. congressional panels to confess, testify against friends, and say whether they had ever had Communist sympathies. The atmosphere was electric with confusion, for only five years before, the mass media had run glowing stories about Stalin and the Soviet system. By 1952, however, millions of Americans had been investigated, imprisoned, or fired from their jobs. McCarthy personally oversaw book burnings, and although the Senate finally voted to censure him in the winter of 1954, fearfulness and anticommunism had come to dominate political life.

Given the wartime destruction, the economic rebirth of western Europe was even more surprising than the revival of democracy. In the first weeks and months after the war, the job of rebuilding often involved menial physical labor that mobilized entire populations for such jobs as clearing the massive urban rubble by hand. Initially, governments diverted labor and capital into rebuilding transportation, communications, and industrial capacity instead of producing consumer goods. However, the scarcity of household goods sparked unrest. In the midst of this growing discontent, the Marshall Plan suddenly boosted recovery with American dollars; food and consumer goods became more plentiful; and demand for automobiles, washing machines, and vacuum cleaners accelerated economic growth.

The postwar recovery was helped by the continuation of military spending for the cold war and the adaptation of wartime technology to meet consumer needs. Civilian travel expanded as nations organized their own airlines based on improved airplane technology. Developed to relieve wartime shortages, synthetic goods such as nylon and a vast assortment of plastic products, ranging from pipes to rainwear, enriched civilian life. Governments also ordered bombs, fighter planes, tanks, and missiles, and sponsored military research. The outbreak of the Korean War in 1950 (see page 900) increased U.S. orders for manufactured goods to wage that war, further sustaining economic growth in Europe. Ultimately, the cold war prevented a repeat of the 1920s, when reduced military spending threw people out of jobs and fed the growth of fascism.

Large and small European states alike developed and redeveloped modern economies in short order. In the twelve principal countries of western Europe, the annual rate of economic growth had been 1.3 percent per inhabitant between 1870 and 1913. Those countries almost tripled that rate between 1950 and 1973, attaining an annual per capita growth rate of 3.8 percent. Among the larger powers, West Germany surprisingly became

the economic leader, achieving by the 1960s a stunning revival called the "economic miracle." The smaller Scandinavian countries also achieved a notable recovery: Sweden succeeded in the development of automobile, truck, and shipbuilding industries. Finland modernized its industry and agriculture, which in turn forced the surplus farm population to seek factory work. Scandinavian women joined the workforce in record numbers, which also boosted economic growth and expanded prosperity. The thirty years after World War II were a golden age of European economic revival.

The creation of the Common Market, which evolved over time to become the European Union, was the final ingredient in the postwar recovery. In 1951, Italy, France, West Germany, Belgium, Luxembourg, and the Netherlands took a major step toward cooperation when they formed the European Coal and Steel Community (ECSC) — an organization to manage the joint production of basic resources. According to the ECSC's principal architect, Robert Schuman, ties created by joint productivity and trade would keep France and Germany from another cataclysmic war. Then in 1957, the six ECSC members signed the Treaty of Rome, which provided for a more general trading partnership called the **European Economic Community (EEC)**, known popularly as the **Common Market**. The EEC reduced tariffs among the six partners, developed common trade policies, and brought under one cooperative economic umbrella more than two hundred million consumers. According to one of its founders, the EEC aimed to "prevent the race of nationalism, which is the true curse of the modern world." Increased cooperation produced great economic rewards for the six members, whose rates of economic growth soared.

Britain pointedly refused to join the partnership at first. Membership would have required it to surrender certain imperial trading rights among its Commonwealth partners such as Australia and Canada and, as one British politician put it, make Britain "just another European country." Even without Britain, the rising prosperity of a new western Europe joined in the Common Market was striking.

Economic planning and coordination by specialists (as developed during wartime) shaped the Common Market. Called technocrats, specialists working for the Common Market were to base decisions on expertise rather than on personal interest and on the goals of the organization as a whole rather than on the demands of any one nation. The aim was to reduce the potential for irrationality and violence in politics, both domestic and international. Administered by a commission of technocrats based in Brussels, Belgium, the Common Market transcended the borders of the nation-state and thus exceeded the power of elected politicians.

The Welfare State: Common Ground East and West

On both sides of the cold war divide, governments channeled new resources into state-financed programs such as pensions, disability insurance, and national health care. These social programs taken as a whole became known as the **welfare state**, indicating that states were no longer interested solely in maintaining order and augmenting their power.

The Welfare State in Action, 1947

The Danish creche, or day-care center, here shows the welfare state in action. Government programs to maintain the well-being of citizens became almost universally available in Europe, Canada, and (to a lesser extent) the United States. Children were seen as particularly important, given the loss of life in the war, so governments encouraged couples to reproduce through up-to-date health care systems, day-care centers, and generous family allowances to support family growth. (Hulton Archive / Getty Images.)

Veterans' pensions and programs were primary, but the welfare state extended beyond those who had sacrificed in wartime. Because the European population had declined during the war, almost all countries now desperately wanted to boost the birthrate and thus gave couples direct financial aid for having children. Imitating the social security programs initiated under Bismarck in Germany in the 1870s and the more sweeping Swedish programs of the 1930s, nations expanded or created family allowances, health care and medical benefits, and programs for pregnant women and new mothers.

Some welfare-state policies had a strong gender bias against women. Britain's maternity benefits and child allowances favored women who did not work outside the home by providing little coverage for workingwomen. The West German government passed strict legislation that forced employers to give women maternity leave, thus discouraging them from hiring women. It also cut back or eliminated pensions and benefits to married women. In fact, West Germans bragged about removing women from the workforce, claiming that doing so distinguished democratic practices from Communist ones. The refusal to build day-care centers or to allow stores to remain open in the evening so that workingwomen could buy food for their families led West Germany to have among the lowest rates of female employment of any industrial country. Another result of West Germany's discriminatory policies was a high rate of female poverty in old age.

By contrast, in eastern Europe and the Soviet Union, where wartime loss of life had been enormous, women worked nearly full-time and usually outnumbered men in the workforce. As in many western European countries, however, child-care programs, family allowances, and maternity benefits were designed to encourage pregnancies by

workingwomen. The scarcity of consumer goods and the lack of household conveniences discouraged workingwomen in Communist countries from having large families no matter what the government wanted. Because women bore the sole burden of domestic duties under such conditions on top of their paying jobs, birthrates in the eastern bloc stagnated.

Across Europe, welfare-state programs aimed to improve people's well-being. State-funded health care systems covered medical needs in most industrial nations except the United States. The combination of better material conditions and state provision of health care dramatically extended life expectancy and lowered rates of infant mortality. Contributing to the overall progress, vaccines greatly reduced the death toll from such diseases as tuberculosis, diphtheria, measles, and polio. In England, schoolchildren stood an inch taller, on average, than children the same age had a decade earlier.

State initiatives in other areas played a role in raising the standard of living. A growing network of government-built atomic power plants brought more thorough electrification of eastern Europe and the Soviet Union. Governments legislated more leisure time for workers; for example, Italian workers received twenty-eight paid holidays annually. To rebuild, postwar governments sponsored new suburbs around the edges of major urban areas in both East and West. Many buildings went up slapdash, but they dramatically improved living conditions for postwar refugees, workers, and immigrants.

Recovery in the East

To create a Soviet bloc according to Stalin's vision, Communists revived the harsh methods that had transformed peasant economies earlier in the century. In eastern Europe, Stalin not only continued to collectivize agriculture but also brought about badly needed industrialization through the nationalization of private property. The process was brutal, and people later looked back on the 1950s as dreadful. But some workers in the countryside felt that ultimately their lives and their children's lives had improved. "Before we peasants were dirty and poor, we worked like dogs. . . . Was that a good life? No sir, it wasn't. . . . I was a miserable sharecropper and my son is an engineer," said one Romanian peasant. Despite modernization, government investment in agriculture was never high enough to produce the bumper crops of western Europe, and even the USSR depended on produce from the small plots that enterprising farmers cultivated on the side.

Stalin admired American industrial know-how and prodded the Communist economies to match U.S. productivity. The Soviet Union formed regional organizations like those in the West, instituting the Council for Mutual Economic Assistance (COMECON) in 1949 to coordinate economic relations among the satellite countries of the USSR and Moscow. The terms of the COMECON relationship worked against the satellite states, however, for the USSR was allowed to buy goods from its clients at bargain prices and sell goods to them at exorbitant ones. Nonetheless, these formerly peasant states became oriented toward technology and industrial economies directed by bureaucrats, who touted the virtues of steel plants and modern transport. The Roman Catholic church of-

Propaganda for Collective Farming

Dramatic changes were in store for people in eastern Europe who fell under Communist control after World War II. Most objectionable was the policy of collective farming, which stripped farmers of their lands and forced them to farm state property as a group. The poster aims to show Czechs that farming will bring huge benefits, including personal satisfaction. How do you interpret this poster, and why does a woman figure so prominently? (German Poster Museum, Essen / Marc Charmet / The Art Archive at Art Resource, NY.)

OBILÍ JE BOHATSTVÍM VLASTI
ČESTNĚ SPLNÍME VÝKUP

ten protested the imposition of communism, but the government crushed it as much as possible or used agents to infiltrate it.

Culture, along with technology, was a building block of Stalinism in both the USSR and its satellite countries. State-instituted programs aimed to build loyalty to the modernizing regime; thus, citizens were obliged to attend adult education classes, women's groups, and public ceremonies. An intense program of de-Christianization and Russification forced non-Russian students in eastern Europe to read histories of the war that ignored their own country's resistance and gave the Red Army sole credit for fighting the Nazis. Rigid censorship resulted in what even one Communist writer in the USSR characterized as "a dreary torrent of colorless, mediocre literature." Stalin also purged prominent wartime leaders to ensure obedience and conformity. Marshal Zhukov, a popular leader of the Soviet armed forces, was shipped to a distant command, while Anna Akhmatova, a widely admired poet who championed wartime resistance to the Nazis, was confined to a crowded hospital room because she refused to glorify Stalin in her postwar poetry.

In March 1953, amid growing repression, Stalin died, and it soon became clear that the old ways would not hold. Political prisoners in the labor camps rebelled, leading to the release of more than a million people from the Gulag. In June 1953, workers in East German cities, many of them socialists and antifascist activists from before the war, protested the rise of privileged Communists in a series of strikes that spread like wildfire. At the other end of the social order, Soviet officials, despite enjoying luxury goods and plentiful food, had come to distrust Stalinism and now favored change. To calm protests across the Soviet bloc, governments stepped up the production of consumer goods — a

policy called goulash communism (after the Hungarian stew) because it resulted in more food for ordinary people.

In 1955, **Nikita Khrushchev** (1894–1971), an illiterate coal miner before the Bolshevik Revolution, outmaneuvered other rivals to become the undisputed leader of the Soviet Union — but he did so without the Stalinist practice of executing his opponents. Khrushchev then made the surprising move of attacking Stalin. At a party congress in 1956, he denounced the "cult of personality" Stalin had built about himself and announced that Stalinism did not equal communism. Khrushchev thus cleverly attributed problems with communism to a single individual. The "secret speech" was a bombshell. Debates broke out in public, and books appeared championing the ordinary worker against the party bureaucracy. The climate of relative tolerance for free expression after Stalin's death was called the thaw.

In early summer 1956, discontented Polish railroad workers struck for better wages, and angry Hungarians rebelled against forced collectivization in October 1956. As in Poland, economic issues (especially announcements of reduced wages) and reports of Stalin's crimes contributed to the outbreak of violence in Hungary. Soon targeting the entire Communist system, tens of thousands of protesters filled the streets of Budapest and returned a popular hero, Imre Nagy, to power. When Nagy announced that Hungary might leave the Warsaw Pact, however, Soviet troops moved in, killing tens of thousands and causing hundreds of thousands more to flee to the West. Nagy was hanged. Despite a rhetoric of democracy, the United States refused to intervene in Hungary, choosing not to risk World War III by challenging the Soviet sphere of influence.

The failure of eastern European uprisings overshadowed the significant changes that had taken place since Stalin's death. While defeating his rivals, Khrushchev ended the Stalinist purges, reformed the courts, and curbed the secret police. "It has become more interesting to visit and see people," Boris Pasternak said of the changes. "It has become easier to work." In 1957, the Soviets successfully launched the first artificial earth satellite, *Sputnik*, and in 1961 they put the first cosmonaut, Yuri Gagarin, in orbit around the earth. The Soviets' edge in space technology shocked the western bloc and motivated the creation of the U.S. National Aeronautics and Space Administration (NASA). For Soviet citizens, such successes indicated that the USSR had achieved Stalin's goal of modernization and might inch further toward freedom.

Khrushchev, however, was inconsistent, showing himself open to changes in Soviet culture at one moment and then bullying honest writers at another. After assaulting Pasternak because of his novel *Doctor Zhivago*, in 1961 he allowed the publication of Aleksandr Solzhenitsyn's *One Day in the Life of Ivan Denisovitch*. This chilling account of life in the Gulag was useful, however, in underscoring Stalin's crimes and excesses. Under the thaw, Khrushchev made several trips to the West and took steps to expand communism's appeal in the new nations of Asia, Africa, and Latin America. Despite the USSR's more relaxed posture, however, the superpowers moved closer to the nuclear brink.

REVIEW QUESTION What factors drove recovery in western Europe and in eastern Europe?

Decolonization in a Cold War Climate

After World War II, activists in colonized regions in Asia, Africa, and the Middle East used the postwar chaos and the cold war to achieve their long-held goal of liberation. At war's end, the colonial powers attempted to reimpose their control as if they were still dominant around the world. Yet colonized peoples had been on the front lines defending the West; and as in World War I, they had witnessed the full barbarism of Western warfare. Like African American soldiers in the U.S. army, they experienced discrimination even while saving the West and, returning home, did not receive the rights of citizenship promised them. Moreover, successive wars had allowed local industries in the colonies to develop, while industry in the imperial homelands fell into decline.

The path to independence — a process called **decolonization** — was paved with difficulties. In India, Hindus and Muslims battled one another even though they shared the goal of eliminating the British. In the Middle East and North Africa, pan-Arab and pan-Islamic movements — that is, those wanting to bring together all Arabs or all Muslims as the basis for decolonization — might seem to have been unifying forces. Yet many Muslims were not Arab, not all Arabs were Muslim, and Islam itself encompassed a range of beliefs. Differences among religious beliefs, ethnic groups, and cultural practices — many of them invented or promoted by the colonizers to divide and rule — worked against political unity. Despite these complications, various peoples in what was coming to be called the third world succeeded in overthrowing imperialism, while the United States and the Soviet Union rushed in to co-opt them for the cold war.

The End of Empire in Asia

At the end of World War II, leaders in Asia succeeded in mobilizing mass discontent to drive out foreign rulers. Declining from an imperial power to a small island nation, Britain was the biggest loser. In 1947, it parted with India, whose independence it had promised in the 1930s. Indian business leaders bought out British entrepreneurs short of cash, and armed with an effective military, Indians began to face off with the British in strikes and other protests. Britain quickly faced reality and decreed that two independent countries should emerge from the old colony. The partition of 1947 created India for Hindus and Pakistan (itself later divided into two parts) for Muslims, but political tensions exploded among opposing members of the two religions. Hundreds of thousands of people overall were massacred in the great shift of populations between India and Pakistan. In 1948, a radical Hindu assassinated Gandhi, who though a Hindu himself had continued to champion religious reconciliation. Elsewhere, as some half a billion Asians gained their independence, Britain's sole remaining Asian colony of note was Hong Kong.

In 1949, after prolonged fighting, a Communist takeover in China brought in a government led by Mao Zedong (1893–1976). Chinese communism in the new People's Republic of China emphasized above all that the country was no longer the plaything

The Korean War, 1950–1953

of the colonial powers as Mao instituted reforms such as civil equality for women and imposed Soviet-style collectivization and brutal repression of the privileged classes.

The United States and the Soviet Union were deeply interested in East Asia — the United States because of the region's economic importance, and the USSR because of its shared borders. The victory of the Chinese Communists spurred both to increase their involvement in Asian politics. The superpowers faced off first in Korea, which had been split at the thirty-eighth parallel after World War II. In 1950, the North Koreans, with the support of the Soviet Union, invaded U.S.-backed South Korea, whose agents had themselves been stirring up tensions with raids across the border. The United States maneuvered the Security Council of the United Nations into approving a "police action" against the North. After two and a half years of a horribly destructive stalemate, the opposing sides finally agreed to a settlement in 1953: Korea would remain split at the thirty-eighth parallel. As a result of the Korean War, the United States increased its military spending from almost $11 billion in 1948 to almost $60 billion in 1953. An Asian counterpart to NATO, the U.S.-backed Southeast Asia Treaty Organization (SEATO), was established in 1954. Another effect of the Korean War was the rapid reindustrialization of Japan to provide the United States with supplies.

The cold war then spread to Indochina (now modern Cambodia, Laos, and Vietnam) where the European-educated Ho Chi Minh (1890–1969) had built a powerful organization, the Viet Minh, to fight colonial rule. He advocated the redistribution of land held by big landowners, who possessed more than 60 percent of the land. In 1954, Viet Minh peasant guerrillas ultimately defeated the technologically superior French army, which was receiving aid from the United States. Later that year, the Geneva Conference carved out an independent Laos and divided Vietnam along the seventeenth parallel into North and South, each free from French control. The Communist-backed Viet Minh, under Ho Chi Minh as president, ruled in the north, while the United

Indochina, 1954

States supported the landowner-backed regime in the south. Continued superpower intervention undermined the peace agreement as the superpowers fought the cold war in small foreign nations — conflicts now referred to as proxy wars.

The Struggle for Identity in the Middle East

Independence struggles in the Middle East highlighted the world's growing need for oil and often showed the ability of small countries to maneuver between the superpowers. As in other regions dominated by the West, Middle Eastern peoples resisted attempts to reimpose imperial control after 1945. Weakened by the war, British oil companies wanted to tighten their grip on profits. By playing the Western countries against one another, however, Middle Eastern leaders gained their independence and simultaneously renegotiated higher payments for drilling rights.

The legacy of the Holocaust complicated the Middle Eastern political scene. Since early in the century Western backing for a Jewish settlement in the Middle East had stirred up Arabs' determination not to be pushed out of their ancient homeland. When World War II broke out, 600,000 Jewish settlers and twice as many Arabs lived, tensely, in British-controlled Palestine. In 1947, an exhausted Britain ceded Palestine to the newly created United Nations, which voted to partition Palestine into an Arab region and a Jewish one (Map 27.4). Hostility turned to open war, which Jewish military forces won, and on May 14, 1948, the state of Israel came into being. "The dream had come true," Golda Meir, the future prime minister of Israel, remembered, but "too late to save those who had perished in the Holocaust." Israel opened its gates to immigrants, pitting its expansionist ambitions against its Arab neighbors.

One of those neighbors, Egypt, gained its independence from Britain at the end of the war. Britain, however, still dominated shipping to Asia through its control of the Suez Canal.

Map 27.4 The Partition of Palestine and the Creation of Israel, 1947–1948 The creation of the Jewish state of Israel in 1948 against a backdrop of ongoing wars among Jews and indigenous Arab peoples turned the Middle East into a powder keg, a situation that has lasted until the present day. The struggle for resources and for securing the borders of viable nation-states was at the heart of these bitter contests, threatening to pull the superpowers into a third world war.

Emerging Nations in the Cold War
Emerging nations could be the playthings of the superpowers during the cold war, but they could also benefit from the rivalry. When Egyptian president Gamal Abdel Nasser refused U.S. military aid in the 1950s because of the supervision the U.S. demanded, Nasser turned to the Soviets and received not only military support but also a low-interest loan for the Aswan Dam — the kind of development project undertaken by emerging nations to provide power and water for both agriculture and industry. In 1964, Nasser (right), Soviet leader Nikita Khrushchev, and Algerian president Ahmed Ben Bella inaugurated the opening of the dam.

In 1952, Colonel Gamal Abdel Nasser (1918–1970) became Egypt's president on a platform of economic modernization and true national independence — meaning Egyptian control of the canal. In July 1956, Nasser nationalized the canal: "I am speaking in the name of every Egyptian Arab," he remarked in his speech explaining the takeover, "and in the name of all free countries and of all those who believe in liberty." Nasser became a heroic figure to Arabs in the region, especially when Britain, supported by Israel and France, attacked Egypt while the Hungarian Revolution (see page 898) was in full swing. The British branded Nasser another Hitler, but the United States, fearing that Egypt would turn to the USSR, made the British back down. Nasser's triumph inspired confidence that colonized peoples around the world could gain true independence.

New Nations in Africa

In sub-Saharan Africa, nationalist leaders roused their people to challenge Europe's increasing demands for resources and labor — demands that resulted in poverty for African peoples. "The European Merchant is my shepherd, and I am in want," went one African version of the Twenty-third Psalm. At the war's end, veterans returned home and protest mounted. Kwame Nkrumah (1909–1972), for example, led the inhabitants of the British-controlled West African Gold Coast in Gandhi-inspired civil disobedience, finally driving the British out and bringing the state of Ghana into being in 1957. Nigeria, the most populous African region, achieved independence in 1960, and many other African states also became free (Map 27.5).

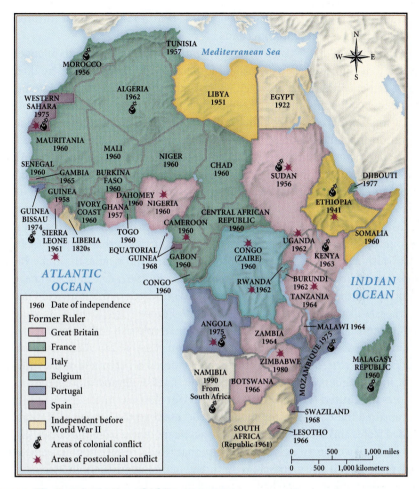

Map 27.5 The Decolonization of Africa, 1951–1990
The liberation of Africa from European rule was an uneven process, sometimes occurring peacefully and at other times demanding armed struggle to drive out European settlers, governments, and armies. The difficult — and costly — process of nation building following liberation involved setting up state institutions, including educational and other services. Creating national unity out of many ethnicities also took work, except where the struggle against colonialism had already brought people together.

In mixed-race territory with large settler populations, Europeans resisted giving up their control. In British East Africa, where white settlers ruled in splendor and where blacks lacked both land and economic opportunity, fighting erupted in the 1950s. African men formed rebel groups named Mau Mau but called by some the Land and Freedom Army. With women serving as provisioners, messengers, and weapon stealers, Mau Mau bands, composed mostly of war veterans from the Kikuyu ethnic group, tried to recover land from whites. In 1964, Mau Mau resistance helped Kenya gain formal independence, but only after the British had put hundreds of thousands of Kikuyus in

concentration camps — called a "living hell" and a "British gulag" by those tortured there. The British slaughtered tens of thousands more.

France followed the British pattern of granting independence with relatively little bloodshed to territories such as Tunisia, Morocco, and West Africa, where there were few white settlers. In Algeria, however, which had one million settlers of European descent, the French fought bitterly to keep control. In the final days of World War II, the French army massacred tens of thousands of Algerian nationalists seeking independence; however, the liberation movement resurfaced with new intensity in 1954 as the Front for National Liberation (FNL). The French dug in and savagely tortured Algerian Arabs; Algerian women, shielded from suspicion by gender stereotypes, planted bombs in European cafés and carried weapons to assassination sites. "The loss of Algeria," warned one statesman, defending French savagery, "would be an unprecedented national disaster," while the FNL, far less powerful and smaller in number, took its case to the court of world opinion. Reports of the French army's barbarous practices against Algeria's Muslim population prompted protests in Paris and around the globe, bringing wartime leader Charles de Gaulle to power in 1958. By 1962, de Gaulle had negotiated independence with the Algerian nationalists, and hundreds of thousands of Europeans in Algeria as well as their Arab supporters fled to France.

Violent resistance to the reimposition of colonial rule also ended the empires of the Dutch and Belgians. As newly independent nations emerged in Asia, Africa, and the Middle East, structures arose to promote international security and worldwide deliberations, including representation from the new states. Foremost among these organizations was the **United Nations (UN)**, convened for the first time in 1945. One notable change ensured the UN a greater chance of success than the League of Nations: both the United States and the Soviet Union were active members from the outset. The UN's charter outlined a collective global authority that would resolve conflicts and provide military protection if any members were threatened by aggression. In 1955, the Indonesian president Sukarno, who had succeeded in wrenching Indonesian independence from the Dutch, sponsored the Bandung Convention of nonaligned nations to set a common policy for achieving modernization and facing the superpowers. Newly independent countries viewed the future with hope but still had to contend with the high costs of nation building and problems left over from decades of colonial exploitation.

Newcomers Arrive in Europe

Amid the uncertainties of wars of independence, people from the former colonies began migrating to Europe — a reversal of the nineteenth-century trend of migration out of Europe. The first non-Europeans came from Britain's Caribbean territories right after the war. Next, labor shortages in Germany, France, Switzerland, and elsewhere drove governments to negotiate with southern European countries for temporary workers. The German situation was particularly dire; in 1950, the working-age population (people between the ages of fifteen and sixty-four) was composed of 15.5 million men and 18 million women. In an ideological climate that wanted women out of the workforce, the

Newcomers to Europe
World War II disrupted everyday life and patterns of trade not only in Europe but also around the globe. Some of the first people to immigrate to Europe in search of postwar opportunity were from the Caribbean (like these men photographed in London in 1956) and South Asia. An expanding welfare state hired some of them to do menial work in hospitals, clinics, and construction, no matter what their qualifications. Governments and businesses in western Europe needed these new laborers to rebuild after World War II, and though some objected, many of these workers — and their wives and children — became not only citizens but political, economic, and cultural leaders as well. (© Hulton-Deutsch Collection / Corbis.)

government desperately needed immigrants. Germany and France next turned to North African and then to sub-Saharan countries in the 1960s. Immigrants from around the world flocked to Scandinavia because of reportedly greater opportunity and social programs to integrate newcomers. By the 1980s, some 8 percent of the European population was foreign-born, compared with 6 percent in the United States.

According to negotiated agreements, immigrant workers would have only temporary resident status, with a regular process of return to their homeland. Turks and Algerians would arrive in Germany or France, for example, to work for a set period of time, return home temporarily to see their families, then head back to Europe for another period as guest workers. They were welcomed because they took few social services, not even needing education because they came as adults. For businesspeople, temporary workers made good economic sense; often their menial work was off the books. "As they are young," one French business publication added, "the immigrants often pay more in taxes than they receive in allowances." Most immigrants did jobs that people

in the West avoided: they collected garbage, built roads, and cleaned homes. Although men predominated among migrant workers, women performed similar chores for even less pay.

Immigrants came to see Europe as a land of relatively good government, wealth, and opportunity. Living conditions, too, seemed decent to many. The advantages of living in Europe, especially the higher wages, made many decide to stay and soon attracted clandestine workers to countries like Italy that had formerly exported labor. As empires collapsed, European populations became more diverse in terms of race, religion, ethnicity, and social life. Across Europe and North America, many newcomers eventually became citizens and their children achieved good positions in government, business, education, and the professions.

REVIEW QUESTION What were the results of decolonization?

Daily Life and Culture in the Shadow of Nuclear War

Both World War II and the cold war shaped postwar culture. People across Europe engaged in heated debates over who was responsible for Nazism and how to achieve ethnic and racial justice. Europeans also discussed the Americanization that seemed to accompany the influx of U.S. dollars, consumer goods, and cultural media. As Europeans examined their war-filled past and their newfound prosperity, the cold war menaced hopes for peace and stability. In 1961, the USSR demanded the construction of a massive wall that physically divided the city of Berlin in half. In October 1962, the world held its breath while the leaders of the Soviet Union and the United States nearly provoked nuclear conflagration over the issue of missiles on the island of Cuba. In hindsight, the existence of extreme nuclear threat in an age of unprecedented prosperity seems utterly bewildering, but for those who lived with the threat of global annihilation, the dangers were all too real.

Restoring "Western" Values

After the depravity of Nazism and fascism, cultural currents in Europe and the United States reemphasized universal values. Responding to what he saw as a crisis in faith caused by affluence and secularism, Pope John XXIII (r. 1958–1963) in 1962 convened the Second Vatican Council. Known as **Vatican II**, this council modernized the liturgy, democratized many church procedures, and at the last session in 1965 renounced church doctrine that condemned the Jewish people as guilty of killing Jesus. Vatican II promoted ecumenism — that is, mutual cooperation among the world's faiths — and outreach to the world without imperial designs.

In the early postwar years, people in the U.S. bloc emphasized the triumph of a Western heritage, a Western civilization, and Western values as they encountered "barbaric" forces, a concept that came to include nomadic tribes, Nazi armies, Communist agents, or national liberation movements in Asia and Africa. Many white Europeans looked

back nostalgically on their imperial history and produced exotic films and novels about conquest and its pageantry.

Readers around the world snapped up memoirs of the death camps and tales of the resistance. Rescued from the Third Reich in 1940, Nelly Sachs won the Nobel Prize for Literature in 1966 for her poetry about the Holocaust. Anne Frank's *Diary of a Young Girl* (1947), the moving record of a Jewish teenager hidden with her family in the back of an Amsterdam house, showed the survival of Western values in the face of Nazi persecution. Amid the menacing evils of Nazism, Frank, who died near the end of the war in the Bergen-Belsen camp, wrote that she never stopped believing that "people are really good at heart." Governments erected permanent plaques at spots where resisters had been killed, and organizations of resisters publicly commemorated their role in winning the war, hiding the fact of widespread collaboration. Many a politician with a Nazi past returned easily to the new cultural mainstream even as the stories of resistance took on mythical qualities.

At the end of the 1940s, **existentialism** became the rage among the cultural elites and students in universities. This philosophy explored the meaning of human existence in a world where evil flourished. Two of existentialism's leaders, Albert Camus and Jean-Paul Sartre, confronted the question of "being," given what they perceived as the absence of God and the tragic breakdown of morality. Their answer was that being, or existing, was not the automatic process either of God's creation or of birth into the natural world. One was not born with spiritual goodness in the image of a creator, but instead one created an "authentic" existence through action and choice. Sartre's writings emphasized political activism and resistance under totalitarianism. Even though they had never confronted the enormous problems of making choices while living under fascism, young people in the 1950s found existentialism compelling and made it the most fashionable philosophy of the day.

In 1949, **Simone de Beauvoir**, Sartre's lifetime companion, published the twentieth century's most important work on the condition of women, *The Second Sex*. Beauvoir believed that most women had failed to take the kind of action necessary to lead authentic lives. Instead, they lived in the world of biological necessity, devoting themselves exclusively to having children. Failing to create an authentic self through action and accomplishment, they had become its opposite — an object, or "Other." Moreover, instead of struggling to define themselves and assert their freedom, women passively accepted their lives as defined by men. Beauvoir's now classic book was a smash hit, and people wrote her thousands of letters asking for advice. Both Sartre and Beauvoir became celebrities, for the media spread the new commitment to humane values just as it had previously spread support for Nazism or for other political ideas.

People of color in Africa and Asia contributed new theories of humanity by exploring the topics of liberation and racial difference. During the 1950s, Frantz Fanon, a black psychiatrist from the French colony of Martinique, began analyzing liberation movements, gaining his insights from his participation in the Algerian war of liberation and other struggles at the time. He wrote that the mental functioning of the colonized person was "traumatized" by the brutal imposition of an outside culture. Ruled by

guns, the colonized person knew only violence and would thus naturally decolonize by means of violence. Translated into many languages, Fanon's *Black Skin, White Masks* (1952) and *The Wretched of the Earth* (1961) posed the question of how to decolonize one's culture and mind.

Simultaneously, the commitment to the cause of civil rights intensified in the 1950s. African Americans had fought in World War II to defeat the Nazi idea of white racial superiority; as civilians, they now hoped to advance that ideal in the United States. With its ruling in *Brown v. Board of Education* (1954), the U.S. Supreme Court declared that segregated education violated the U.S. Constitution. In December 1955, in Montgomery, Alabama, Rosa Parks, a seamstress and part-time secretary for the local branch of the National Association for the Advancement of Colored People (NAACP), boarded a city bus and took the first available seat in the "colored" section. When a white man found himself without a seat, the driver screamed at Parks, "Nigger, move back." She refused to move, and her studied use of civil disobedience led to widespread nonviolent disobedience among African Americans throughout the South. Talented leaders emerged, foremost among them the great orator Martin Luther King Jr. (1929–1968), a Baptist pastor from Georgia, who advocated "soulforce" — Gandhi's *satyagraha* ("holding to truth") — to counter aggression. The postwar culture of nonviolence shaped the early years of the U.S. civil rights movement until the influence of Fanon and other third world activists turned some toward more violent activism.

Cold War Consumerism and Shifting Gender Norms

Government spending on Europe's reconstruction and welfare after World War II helped prevent the kind of upheaval that had followed World War I. Meanwhile, the rising birthrate and bustling youth culture led to an upsurge in consumer spending that created jobs for veterans. Nonetheless, the war had affected men's roles and sense of themselves. Young men who had missed World War II adopted the rough, violent style of soldiers, and roaming gangs posed as tough military types. While Soviet youth admired aviator aces, elsewhere groups such as the "teddy boys" in England (named after their Edwardian style of dressing) and the *gamberros* ("hooligans") in Spain took their cues from pop culture in rock-and-roll music and film.

The leader of rock-and-roll style was the American singer Elvis Presley. Sporting slicked-back hair and an aviator-style jacket, Presley bucked his hips and sang sexual lyrics to screaming and devoted fans. Rock-and-roll concerts and movies galvanized youth across Europe, including the Soviet bloc, where teens demanded the production of blue jeans and leather jackets. In a German nightclub late in the 1950s, members of a British rock group of Elvis fans called the Quarrymen performed, yelling at and fighting with one another as part of their show. They would soon become known as the Beatles. Rebellious young American film stars like James Dean in *Rebel Without a Cause* (1955) created the beginnings of a postwar youth culture in which the ideal was to be a bad boy. The rebellious and rough masculine style appeared also in literature, for example in James Watson's autobiography, *The Double Helix* (1968), in which he described

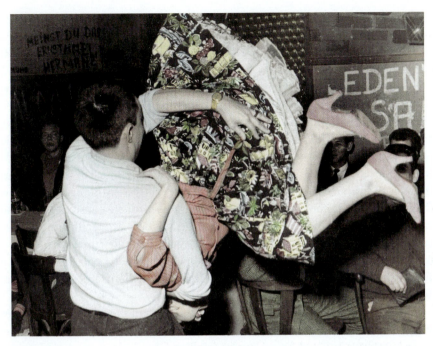

Rock and Roll
Rock and roll, born in the 1950s, swept cities around the world with unprecedented energy and speed. Teen women wore the voluminous skirts that the "new look" had made fashionable in the late 1940s, and young men sported hairdos like that of Elvis Presley. East and west, teens thronged and even rioted to attend rock concerts and would continue to do so despite public criticism and even police action against the movement. (ullstein bild / The Granger Collection, NYC — All rights reserved.)

how he and Francis Crick had discovered the structure of the DNA molecule by stealing other people's findings. American "beat" poets and writers vehemently rejected the traditional ideals of the upright male breadwinner, family man, and responsible achiever. The 1953 inaugural issue of the American magazine *Playboy,* and the hundreds of magazines that imitated it across Europe, presented the modern man as sexually aggressive and independent of dull domestic life — just as he had been in the war. The definition of men's citizenship had come to include not just political and economic rights but also sexual freedom outside the restrictions of marriage.

In contrast, Western society promoted a postwar model for women that differed from their wartime roles, adopting instead the fascist notion of women's inferiority. Rather than being essential workers and heads of families in the absence of their men, postwar women were to symbolize the return to normalcy by leading a domestic and submissive life at home. Late in the 1940s, the fashion house of Christian Dior launched a clothing style called the "new look." It featured pinched waists, tightly fitting bodices, and voluminous skirts. This restoration of the nineteenth-century female silhouette invited a renewal of clearly defined gender roles. Women's magazines publicized the new look and urged women to give up ambitions for themselves. Even in the hard-pressed

Soviet Union, domesticity flourished; recipes for homemade face creams, for example, passed from woman to woman, and beauty parlors did a brisk business. In the West, household products such as refrigerators and washing machines raised standards for housekeeping by giving women the means to be "perfect" housewives.

However, new-look propaganda did not necessarily mesh with reality or even with all social norms. Dressmaking fabric was still being rationed in the late 1940s; even in the next decade, women could not always get enough of it to make voluminous skirts. In Europe, where people had barely enough to eat, the underwear needed for new-look contours simply did not exist — although for many, unfortunately, the semistarved look was not achieved by choice. Moreover, European women continued to work outside the home after the war; indeed, mature women and mothers were working more than ever before — especially in the Soviet bloc. Across the Soviet sphere consumer goods were always in short supply, but opinion makers stressed to these women the importance of a tasteful and up-to-date domestic interior. East and West, the female workforce was going through a profound revolution as it gradually became populated by wives and mothers who would hold jobs all their lives despite being bombarded with images of nineteenth-century femininity.

The advertising business presided over the creation of these cultural messages as part of both the return of consumerism and the cold war. Guided by marketing experts, western Europeans imitated Americans by drinking Coca-Cola; using American detergents, toothpaste, and soap; and driving some forty million motorized vehicles, including motorbikes, cars, buses, and trucks. While many Europeans embraced American business practices, the cold war was ever present: the Communist Party in France led a successful campaign to ban Coca-Cola for a time in the 1950s, and tastemakers in the Soviet sphere initiated competing products and styles.

Radio remained the most influential medium in the 1950s, carrying much of the postwar consumer advertising and making the connection between cold war and consumerism. Even as the number of radios in homes grew steadily, television loomed on the horizon. In the United States, two-thirds of the population had TV sets in the early 1950s, while in Britain only one-fifth did. Only in the 1960s did television become an important consumer item for most Europeans. In radio and television, though, both East and West tried to exceed the other in advertising their values. Russian programs stressed a uniform Communist culture, often emphasizing the importance of family values and practical, if aesthetically pleasing, household tips for women. The United States, by contrast, promoted debate about current affairs and filled the airwaves with advertising for consumer goods. The cold war was thus a consumer as well as a military phenomenon.

The Culture of Cold War

Films, books, and other cultural productions also promoted the cold war even when they conveyed an antiwar message. Books like George Orwell's *1984* (1949) were claimed by both sides in the cold war as supporting their position. Ray Bradbury's popular *Fahrenheit 451* (1953), whose title refers to the temperature at which books would burn,

condemned restrictions on intellectual freedom on both sides of the cold war divide. In the USSR, official writers churned out spy stories, and espionage novels topped best-seller lists in the West. *Casino Royale* (1953), by the British author Ian Fleming, introduced the fictional British intelligence agent James Bond, who tested his wit and physical prowess against Communist and other political villains. So popular were such programs that Soviet pilots would not take off for flights when the work of Yulian Simyonov, the Russian counterpart of Ian Fleming, was playing on radio or television. Reports, fictional and real, of Soviet- and U.S.-bloc characters facing one another down became part of everyday life.

High culture also operated in a cold war climate. Europe's major cities rebuilt their war-ravaged opera houses and museums, and both sides tried to win the cold war by pouring vast sums of money into high culture. As leadership of the art world passed to the United States, art became part of the cold war. Abstract expressionists such as American artist Jackson Pollock produced nonrepresentational works by dripping and spattering paint; they also spoke of the importance of the artist's self-discovery in the process of painting. "If I stretch my arms next to the rest of myself and wonder where my fingers are, that is all the space I need as a painter," commented Dutch-born artist Willem de Kooning on his relationship with his canvas. Said to exemplify Western freedom, such painters were awarded commissions at the secret direction of the U.S. Central Intelligence Agency (CIA).

The USSR more openly promoted an official Communist culture. When a show of abstract art like Pollock's opened in the Soviet Union, Khrushchev yelled that it was "dog shit." Pro-Soviet critics in western Europe saw U.S.-style abstract art as "an infantile sickness" and supported socialist realist art with "human content," showing the condition of the workers and the oppressed races in the United States. The Italian filmmakers Roberto Rossellini, in *Open City* (1945), and Vittorio De Sica, in *The Bicycle Thief* (1948), developed the neorealist technique that challenged lush Hollywood-style sets and costumes by using ordinary characters living in devastated, impoverished cities. By depicting stark conditions, neorealist directors conveyed their distance both from middle-class prosperity and from fascist bombast. "We are in rags? Let's show everyone our rags," said one Italian director. Many of these left-leaning directors associated support for the suffering masses with the Communist cause, while on the pro-American side, the film *Doctor Zhivago* became a hit celebrating individualism and condemning the Communist way of life. Overtly or covertly, the cold war affected virtually all aspects of cultural life.

The Atomic Brink

The 1950s were a time of emotional terror for people at the center of the cold war. Radio bombarded the public with messages about the threat of nuclear annihilation at the hands of the villainous superpower enemy (meaning the United States or the USSR, depending). During the late 1940s and 1950s, the Voice of America, with its main studio in Washington, D.C., broadcast in thirty-eight languages from one hundred transmitters

and provided an alternative source of news as well as menacing messages for people in eastern Europe. Its Soviet counterpart broadcast in Russian around the clock but initially spent much of its wattage jamming U.S. programming. The public also heard reports of nuclear buildups and tests of emergency power facilities that sent them scurrying for cover. Children rehearsed at school for nuclear war, while at home families built bomb shelters in their backyards. Fear gripped people's emotions in these decades.

In this upsetting climate of cold war, **John Fitzgerald Kennedy** (1917–1963) became U.S. president in 1960. Kennedy represented American affluence and youth; he also confirmed the power of television. A war hero and an early fan of the fictional cold war spy James Bond, Kennedy participated in the escalating cold war over the nearby island of Cuba, where in 1959 Fidel Castro (1926–) had come to power. After being rebuffed by the United States, Castro aligned his new government with the Soviet Union. In the spring of 1961, Kennedy, assured by the CIA of success, launched an invasion of Cuba at the Bay of Pigs to overthrow Castro. The invasion failed miserably and humiliated the United States.

Cold war tensions increased. In the summer of 1961, the East German government directed workers to stack bales of barbed wire across miles of the city's east–west border. This was the beginning of the Berlin Wall, built to block the escape route by which some three million people had fled to the West. In October 1962, tensions came to a head in the **Cuban missile crisis**, when the CIA reported the installation of silos to house Soviet medium-range missiles in Cuba. Kennedy acted forcefully, ordering a naval blockade of ships headed for Cuba and demanding removal of the installations. For several days, the world stood on the brink of nuclear war. Then, between October 25 and 27, Khrushchev and Kennedy negotiated an end to the crisis. Kennedy spent the remainder of his short life working to improve nuclear diplomacy; Khrushchev did the same. In the summer of 1963, less than a year after the shock of the Cuban missile crisis, the United States and the Soviet Union signed a test-ban treaty outlawing the explosion of nuclear weapons in the atmosphere and in the seas. The treaty held out hope that the cold war and its culture would give way to something better.

REVIEW QUESTION How were everyday culture and social life part of the cold war?

Conclusion

Nikita Khrushchev was ousted in 1964 for his erratic policies and for the Cuban missile crisis. In his forced retirement, he expressed regret at his brutal treatment of Boris Pasternak: "We shouldn't have banned [*Doctor Zhivago*]. There's nothing anti-Soviet in it." But the postwar decades were grim times. Two superpowers — the Soviet Union and the United States — each controlling atomic arsenals, overshadowed European leadership and engaged in a menacing cold war, complete with the threat of nuclear annihilation. The cold war saturated everyday life, giving birth to bomb shelters, spies, purges, and witch hunts — all of them creating a culture of anxiety that kept people in constant fear of war. Cold war diplomacy divided Europe into an eastern bloc dominated by the

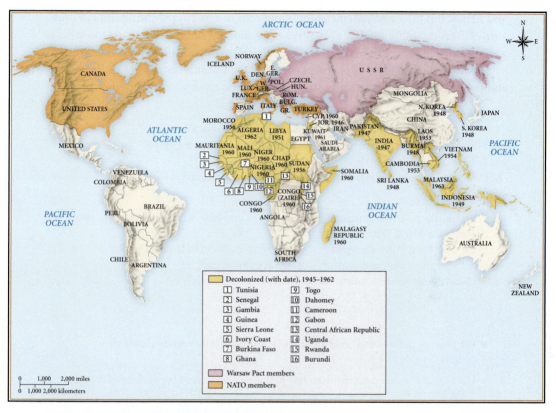

Mapping the West **The Cold War World, c. 1960**
Superpower rivalry between the United States and the Soviet Union resulted in the division of much of the industrial world into cold war alliances. Simultaneously, the superpowers vied for the allegiance of the newly decolonized countries of Asia and Africa by providing military, economic, and technological assistance. Wars such as those in Vietnam and Korea were also products of the cold war. How might this map be said to convey the idea that a first world, a second world, and a third world existed? How does this map differ from the map on page 763?

Soviets and a freer western bloc mostly allied with the United States. In this bleak atmosphere, starving, homeless, and refugee people joined the task of rebuilding a devastated Europe.

Despite the chaos at the end of 1945, both halves of Europe recovered almost miraculously in little more than a decade. Eastern Europe, where wartime devastation and ongoing violence were greatest, experienced less prosperity. In the West, wartime technology served as the basis for new consumer goods and welfare-state planning improved health. Spurred on by aid from the United States, western Europe formed the successful Common Market, which became the foundation for greater European unity in the future. As a result of World War II and the cold war, Germany recovered as two countries, not one. The war so weakened the European powers that they lost their colonies to thriving independence movements. Newly independent nations emerged in Asia

and Africa, but they were often caught in the cold war and faced the additional problems of creating stable political structures and a sound economic future. As the West as a whole grew in prosperity, its cultural life focused paradoxically on reviving Western values while enjoying the new phenomenon of mass consumerism. Above all, the West — and the rest of the world — had to survive the atomic rivalry of the superpowers.

Review Questions

1. What were the major events in the development of the cold war?
2. What factors drove recovery in western Europe and in eastern Europe?
3. What were the results of decolonization?
4. How were everyday culture and social life part of the cold war?

Making Connections

1. What was the political climate after World War II, and how did it differ from the political climate after World War I?
2. What were the relative strengths of the two European blocs in the cold war?
3. What were the main developments of postwar cultural life?
4. Why did decolonization follow World War II so immediately?

- For practice quizzes and other study tools, visit the **Online Study Guide** at bedfordstmartins.com/huntconcise.

- For primary-source material from this period, see *Sources of the Making of the West*, Fourth Edition.

- For Web sites, images, and documents related to topics in this chapter, visit *Make History* at bedfordstmartins.com/huntconcise.

TIMELINE

- **1949** Mao Zedong leads Communist revolution in China; Simone de Beauvoir publishes *The Second Sex*

- **1948** State of Israel established

- **1945** Cold war begins

- **1950** Korean War begins

- **1957** Boris Pasternak publishes *Doctor Zhivago*; USSR launches *Sputnik*; Treaty of Rome establishes European Economic Community (Common Market)

- **1956** Egypt's president Gamal Abdel Nasser nationalizes Suez Canal; uprising in Hungary against USSR

1945   1950   1955   1960   1965

- **1947** India and Pakistan win independence from Britain

- **1953** Stalin dies; Korean War ends

- **1954** *Brown v. Board of Education* prohibits segregated schools in the United States; Vietnamese forces defeat French

- **1958** Fifth Republic begins in France

- **1962** United States and USSR face off in the Cuban missile crisis

Suggested References

New nationhood and the postwar era are charted in exciting new books that study veterans, youth, and daily life in the aftermath of Nazism and an age of cold war. Historians are also focusing on the complexities of decolonization.

Chin, Rita, et al., eds. *After the Nazi Racial State: Difference and Democracy in Germany and Europe.* 2009.

De Grazia, Victoria. *Irresistible Empire: America's Advance through 20th-Century Europe.* 2005.

Edele, Mark. *Soviet Veterans of World War II: A Popular Movement in an Authoritarian Society, 1941–1991.* 2008.

Frommer, Benjamin. *National Cleansing: Retribution against Nazi Collaborators in Postwar Czechoslovakia.* 2005.

Gaddis, John. *George Kennan: An American Life.* 2011.

Grossman, Atina. *Jews, Germans, and Allies: Close Encounters in Occupied Germany, 1945–1949.* 2007.

Jobs, Richard I. *Riding the New Wave: Youth and the Rejuvenation of France after World War II.* 2007.

Milward, Alan S. *The United Kingdom and the Economic Community.* 2002.

Moeller, Robert. *War Stories: The Search for a Usable Past in the Federal Republic of Germany.* 2001.

Nord, Philip. *France's New Deal: From the Thirties to the Postwar Era.* 2010.

Pence, Katherine, and Paul Betts, eds. *Socialist Modern: East German Everyday Culture and Politics.* 2008.

Poiger, Uta. *Jazz, Rock, and Rebels: Cold War Politics and American Culture in a Divided Germany.* 2000.

Shepard, Todd. *The Invention of Decolonization: The Algerian War and the Remaking of France.* 2006.

Shipway, Martin. *Decolonization and Its Impact: A Comparative Approach to the End of the Colonial Empires.* 2008.

Smith, Mark B. *Property of Communists: The Urban Housing Program from Stalin to Khrushchev.* 2010.

The challenges posed by young reformers came at a bad time for the superpowers and other leading European states. An agonizing war in Vietnam weakened the United States, and China confronted the Soviet Union on its borders. In a dramatic turn of events, the oil-producing states of the Middle East reduced the export of oil to the leading Western nations in the 1970s, bringing on a recession. Despite their wealth and military might, the superpowers could not guarantee that they would emerge victorious in this age of increasingly global competition. As the USSR experienced decay in a climate of post-industrial innovation across the West, a reform-minded leader — Mikhail Gorbachev — initiated new policies of economic and political freedom. It was too late: in 1989, the Soviet bloc collapsed, an event brought about in part by countless acts of protest, not least of them the individual heroism of Jan Palach and his fellow human torches.

CHAPTER FOCUS How did technological, economic, and social change contribute to increased activism, and what were the political results of that activism?

The Revolution in Technology

The protests of the 1960s began in the midst of astonishing technological advances in all areas of life. These advances steadily boosted prosperity and changed daily life in the West, where people awoke to instantaneous radio and television news, worked with computers, and used new forms of contraceptives to control reproduction. Satellites orbiting the earth relayed telephone signals and collected military intelligence, while around the world nuclear energy powered economies. Smaller gadgets — electric popcorn poppers, portable radios and tape players, automatic garage door openers — made life more pleasant. The increased use of machines led one philosopher to insist that people were no longer self-sufficient individuals, but rather cyborgs — that is, humans who needed machines to sustain ordinary life processes.

The Information Age: Television and Computers

Information technology powered change in the postindustrial period that began in the 1960s, just as innovations in textile making and the spread of railroads had in the nineteenth century. This technology's ability to transmit knowledge, culture, and political information globally competed with mass journalism, film, and radio via television, computers, and telecommunications. Once-remote villages were linked to urban capitals on the other side of the world thanks to videocassettes, satellite television, and telecommunications. Because of technology, protests became media events worldwide.

Americans embraced television in the 1950s; between the mid-1950s and the mid-1970s, Europeans rapidly adopted television as a major entertainment and communications medium. In 1954, just 1 percent of French households had television; by 1974, almost 80 percent did. With the average viewer tuning in about four and a half hours a day, the audience for newspapers and theater declined. "We devote more . . . hours per

Postindustrial Society and the End of the Cold War Order

1960s–1989

I N JANUARY 1969, JAN PALACH, a twenty-one-year-old philosophy student, drove to a main square in Prague, doused his body with gasoline, and set himself ablaze. Before that, he had put aside his coat with a message in it demanding an end to Communist repression in Czechoslovakia. It promised more such suicides unless the government lifted state censorship. The manifesto was signed "Torch No. 1." Jan Palach's suicide stunned his nation. Black flags hung from windows, and close to a million people flocked to his funeral. In the next months, more Czech youth followed Palach's grim example and became torches for freedom.

Before his self-immolation, Jan Palach was an ordinary, well-educated citizen of an increasingly technological society. Having recovered from World War II, the West shifted from a manufacturing economy based on heavy industry to a service economy that depended on technical knowledge in such fields as engineering, health care, and finance. This new service economy has been labeled "postindustrial." To staff it, institutions of higher education sprang up at a dizzying rate and attracted more students than ever before. Young men like Jan Palach — along with women, minorities, and many other activists in the 1960s and 1970s — far from being satisfied with their rising status, struck out against war and cold war, inequality and repression, and even against technology itself. From Czechoslovakia to the United States and around the world, protesters warned that postindustrial nations in general and the superpowers in particular were becoming technological and political monsters. Before long, countries in both the Soviet and U.S. blocs were on the verge of political revolution.

Shrine to Jan Palach

Jan Palach was a martyr to the cause of an independent Czechoslovakia. His self-immolation on behalf of that cause roused the nation. As makeshift shrines sprang up and multiplied throughout the 1970s and 1980s, they served as common rallying points that ultimately contributed to the overthrow of Communist rule. Václav Havel, the future president of a liberated Czechoslovakia, was arrested early in the momentous year of 1989 for commemorating Palach's sacrifice at a shrine. In light of so many other deaths in the Soviet bloc, why did Jan Palach's death become so powerful a force? (© Marc Garanger / Corbis.)

The challenges posed by young reformers came at a bad time for the superpowers and other leading European states. An agonizing war in Vietnam weakened the United States, and China confronted the Soviet Union on its borders. In a dramatic turn of events, the oil-producing states of the Middle East reduced the export of oil to the leading Western nations in the 1970s, bringing on a recession. Despite their wealth and military might, the superpowers could not guarantee that they would emerge victorious in this age of increasingly global competition. As the USSR experienced decay in a climate of postindustrial innovation across the West, a reform-minded leader — Mikhail Gorbachev — initiated new policies of economic and political freedom. It was too late: in 1989, the Soviet bloc collapsed, an event brought about in part by countless acts of protest, not least of them the individual heroism of Jan Palach and his fellow human torches.

CHAPTER FOCUS How did technological, economic, and social change contribute to increased activism, and what were the political results of that activism?

The Revolution in Technology

The protests of the 1960s began in the midst of astonishing technological advances in all areas of life. These advances steadily boosted prosperity and changed daily life in the West, where people awoke to instantaneous radio and television news, worked with computers, and used new forms of contraceptives to control reproduction. Satellites orbiting the earth relayed telephone signals and collected military intelligence, while around the world nuclear energy powered economies. Smaller gadgets — electric popcorn poppers, portable radios and tape players, automatic garage door openers — made life more pleasant. The increased use of machines led one philosopher to insist that people were no longer self-sufficient individuals, but rather cyborgs — that is, humans who needed machines to sustain ordinary life processes.

The Information Age: Television and Computers

Information technology powered change in the postindustrial period that began in the 1960s, just as innovations in textile making and the spread of railroads had in the nineteenth century. This technology's ability to transmit knowledge, culture, and political information globally competed with mass journalism, film, and radio via television, computers, and telecommunications. Once-remote villages were linked to urban capitals on the other side of the world thanks to videocassettes, satellite television, and telecommunications. Because of technology, protests became media events worldwide.

Americans embraced television in the 1950s; between the mid-1950s and the mid-1970s, Europeans rapidly adopted television as a major entertainment and communications medium. In 1954, just 1 percent of French households had television; by 1974, almost 80 percent did. With the average viewer tuning in about four and a half hours a day, the audience for newspapers and theater declined. "We devote more . . . hours per

Suggested References

New nationhood and the postwar era are charted in exciting new books that study veterans, youth, and daily life in the aftermath of Nazism and an age of cold war. Historians are also focusing on the complexities of decolonization.

Chin, Rita, et al., eds. *After the Nazi Racial State: Difference and Democracy in Germany and Europe.* 2009.

De Grazia, Victoria. *Irresistible Empire: America's Advance through 20th-Century Europe.* 2005.

Edele, Mark. *Soviet Veterans of World War II: A Popular Movement in an Authoritarian Society, 1941–1991.* 2008.

Frommer, Benjamin. *National Cleansing: Retribution against Nazi Collaborators in Postwar Czechoslovakia.* 2005.

Gaddis, John. *George Kennan: An American Life.* 2011.

Grossman, Atina. *Jews, Germans, and Allies: Close Encounters in Occupied Germany, 1945–1949.* 2007.

Jobs, Richard I. *Riding the New Wave: Youth and the Rejuvenation of France after World War II.* 2007.

Milward, Alan S. *The United Kingdom and the Economic Community.* 2002.

Moeller, Robert. *War Stories: The Search for a Usable Past in the Federal Republic of Germany.* 2001.

Nord, Philip. *France's New Deal: From the Thirties to the Postwar Era.* 2010.

Pence, Katherine, and Paul Betts, eds. *Socialist Modern: East German Everyday Culture and Politics.* 2008.

Poiger, Uta. *Jazz, Rock, and Rebels: Cold War Politics and American Culture in a Divided Germany.* 2000.

Shepard, Todd. *The Invention of Decolonization: The Algerian War and the Remaking of France.* 2006.

Shipway, Martin. *Decolonization and Its Impact: A Comparative Approach to the End of the Colonial Empires.* 2008.

Smith, Mark B. *Property of Communists: The Urban Housing Program from Stalin to Khrushchev.* 2010.

year to television than [to] any other single artifact," one sociologist commented in 1969. As with radio, European governments funded television broadcasting with tax dollars and controlled TV programming to avoid what they perceived as the substandard fare offered by American commercial TV; instead they featured drama, ballet, concerts, variety shows, and news. The welfare state, in Europe at least, thereby gained more power to shape daily life.

The emergence of communications satellites and video recorders in the 1960s brought competition to state-sponsored television. Worldwide audiences enjoyed broadcasts from throughout the West as satellite technology allowed for the global transmission of sports broadcasts and other programming. Soap operas, game shows, and situation comedies (sitcoms) from the United States arrived dubbed in native languages. Feature films on videotape first became readily available to television stations; then, in 1969, competition increased when the Sony Corporation introduced the first affordable color videocassette recorder to the consumer market.

East and west, television exercised a powerful political and cultural influence. Even in a rural area of the Soviet Union, more than 70 percent of the inhabitants watched television regularly in the late 1970s. Educational programming united the far-flung population of the USSR by broadcasting shows designed to advance Soviet culture. At the same time, with travel impossible or forbidden to many, shows about foreign lands were among the most popular. Heads of state could usually bump regular programming. In the 1960s, French president Charles de Gaulle appeared frequently on television, using the grandiose gestures of an imperial ruler to stir patriotism. Increasingly, politicians needed media experts as much as they did policy experts.

Just as revolutionary as television, the computer reshaped work in science, defense, and ultimately industry. Computers had evolved dramatically since the first electronic ones, like the Colossus used by the British in 1943 to decode Nazi military and diplomatic messages. From the 1940s to the 1980s, computing machines shrank from the size of a gymnasium to that of an attaché case. They also became both far less expensive and fantastically more powerful, thanks to the development of increasingly sophisticated digital electronic circuitry implanted on tiny silicon chips, which replaced clumsy radio tubes. Within a few decades, the computer could perform hundreds of millions of operations per second and the price of the integrated circuit at the heart of computer technology would fall to less than a dollar.

Computers changed the pace and patterns of work not only by speeding up tasks but also by performing many operations that workers had once done themselves. Soon, like outworkers of the eighteenth century, people could also work for large industries at home, connected to a central mainframe. In 1981, the French phone company launched a public computer network, the Minitel (a forerunner of the World Wide Web), through which individuals could make travel reservations, perform stock transactions, and obtain information. Many observers believed that computers would profoundly expand mental capacity, providing, in the words of one scientist, "boundless opportunities . . . to resolve the puzzles of cosmology, of life, and of the society of man." Others countered

that computers programmed people, reducing human initiative and the ability to solve problems. Regardless of observers' opinions, positive or negative, the information revolution was under way.

The Space Age

The "space race" between the United States and the Soviet Union, also made possible by computers, began when the Soviets launched the satellite *Sputnik* in 1957. The competition led to increasingly complex space flights that tested humans' ability to survive the process of space exploration, including weightlessness. Astronauts walked in space, endured weeks (and later months) in orbit, docked with other craft, fixed satellites, and carried out experiments for the military and private industry. In addition, a series of unmanned rockets launched weather, television, intelligence, and other communications satellites into orbit around the earth. In July 1969, a worldwide television audience watched as U.S. astronauts Neil Armstrong and Edwin "Buzz" Aldrin walked on the moon's surface — the climactic moment in the space race.

The space race also influenced Western culture. Astronauts and cosmonauts were perhaps the era's most admired heroes: Yuri Gagarin, John Glenn, and Valentina Tereshkova — the first woman in space — topped the list. A whole new fantasy world developed. Children's toys and games revolved increasingly around space. Films such as *2001: A Space Odyssey* (1968) portrayed space explorers answering questions about life that were formerly the domain of church leaders. Polish author Stanislaw Lem's popular novel *Solaris* (1961), later made into a film, described space-age individuals engaged in personal quests that drew readers and ultimately viewers into a futuristic fantasy.

Valentina Tereshkova, Russian Cosmonaut
People sent into space became heroes, representing modern values of courage, strength, and well-honed skills. Insofar as the space age was part of the cold war race for superpower superiority, the USSR held the lead during the first decade. The Soviets trained both women and men, and the 1963 flight of Valentina Tereshkova — the first woman in space — supported Soviet claims of gender equality in contrast to the all-male superstar image of the early U.S. space program. (Hulton Archive / Getty Images.)

The space age grew out of cold war concerns, and advances in rocket technology not only launched vehicles into space but also powered destructive missiles. At the same time, the space age promoted and even depended on global cooperation. From the 1960s on, U.S. spaceflights often involved the participation of other countries. In 1965, an international consortium headed by the United States launched the first commercial communications satellite, *Intelsat I*—a feat envisioned since early in the postwar period. By the 1970s, some 150 countries were working together at more than four hundred stations worldwide to maintain global satellite communications. Although some 50 percent of satellites were for spying purposes, the rest promoted international communication and transnational collaboration.

Pure science flourished amid the space race. Astronomers used mineral samples from the moon to calculate the age of the solar system with unprecedented precision. Unmanned spacecraft provided data on cosmic radiation, magnetic fields, and infrared sources. Although the media depicted the space age as one of warrior astronauts conquering space, breakthroughs depended on the products of technology, including the radio telescope, which depicted space by receiving, measuring, and calculating nonvisible rays. These findings reinforced the so-called big bang theory of the origin of the universe, first outlined in the 1930s by American astronomer Edwin Hubble and given crucial support in the 1950s by the discovery of low-level radiation permeating the universe in all directions. The big bang theory proposes that the universe originated from the explosion of superdense, superhot matter some ten to twenty billion years ago.

The Nuclear Age

Scientists, government officials, and engineers put the force of the atom to economic use, especially in the form of nuclear power, and the dramatic boost in available energy helped continue postwar economic expansion into the 1960s and beyond. The USSR built the world's first civilian nuclear power station, in the town of Obninsk, in 1954; Britain and the United States soon followed suit. During the 1960s and 1970s, nuclear power for industrial and household use multiplied a hundredfold—a growth that did not include nuclear-powered submarines and aircraft carriers, which also multiplied in this period.

Because of the vast costs and complex procedures involved in building, supplying, running, and safeguarding nuclear reactors, governments provided substantial aid and even financed nuclear power plants almost entirely. "A state does not count," announced French president Charles de Gaulle, "if it does not . . . contribute to the technological progress of the world." The watchword for all governments building nuclear reactors was technological development—a new function for the modern state. The USSR sponsored plants throughout the Soviet bloc as part of the drive to modernize, but it was not alone—Western nations, too, funded nuclear power. In 2006, France produced some 80 percent of its energy, and the United States 20 percent, via nuclear power plants. More than thirty countries had substantial nuclear installations in the twenty-first century, with new ones under construction.

Revolutions in Biology and Reproductive Technology

A revolution in the life sciences brought about dramatic health benefits and ultimately changed reproduction itself. In 1952, scientists Francis Crick, an Englishman, and James Watson, an American, discovered the structure of deoxyribonucleic acid **(DNA)**, the material in a cell's chromosomes that carries hereditary information. Simultaneously, other scientists were working on "the pill" — an oral contraceptive for women that capped more than a century of scientific work in the field of birth control. Still other breakthroughs in biology lay ahead, including ones that revolutionized conception and made possible the scientific duplication of species (cloning).

Crick and Watson solved the mystery of biological inheritance when they demonstrated the structure of DNA. They showed how the double helix of the DNA molecule splits in cellular reproduction to form the basis of each new cell. This genetic material, biologists concluded, provides a chemical pattern for an individual organism's life. Beginning in the 1960s, genetics and the new field of molecular biology not only increased knowledge about viruses and bacteria but also effectively ended in the West such diseases as polio, mumps, measles, and tetanus through the development of new vaccines.

Other scientists used their understanding of DNA to alter the makeup of plants (for instance, to control agricultural pests) and to bypass natural animal reproduction in a process called cloning — obtaining the cells of an organism and dividing or reproducing them in an exact copy in a laboratory. In 1967, Dr. Christiaan Barnard of South Africa performed the first successful heart transplant. Other researchers later developed both immunosuppressants (to prevent rejection of the transplant) and an artificial heart. As major advances like these occurred, commentators began to ask whether the enormous cost of new medical technology to save a few people would be better spent on helping the many who lacked even basic medical care.

Technology also influenced the most intimate areas of human relations — sexuality and procreation. Matching family size to agricultural productivity no longer shaped sexual behavior in the industrialized and urbanized West. With reliable birth-control devices more readily available, young people began sexual relations earlier, with less risk of pregnancy. These trends accelerated in the 1960s when the birth-control pill, the result of research around the world, was first marketed in the United States. The pill was initially tested on American medical students in Puerto Rico and then on a larger scale among Puerto Rican nurses, many of whom were eager for reliable contraception. By 1970, the pill's use was spreading around the world. New techniques brought abortion, traditionally performed by amateurs, into the hands of medical professionals, making it a safe procedure for the first time.

Conception and childbirth were similarly transformed. Whereas only a small minority of Western births took place in hospitals in 1920, more than 90 percent did by 1970. Obstetricians now performed much of the work midwives had once done. As pregnancy and birth became medicalized, the number of medical interventions such as cesarean births rose. In 1978, the first "test-tube baby," Louise Brown, was born to an

The First Test-Tube Baby
The birth in Britain in 1978 of Louise Brown, the first baby conceived by in vitro fertilization, caused a sensation worldwide. The new procedure was just one of the many medical breakthroughs of the late twentieth century and gave hope to would-be parents around the world that science might make infertility a thing of the past. (Getty Images.)

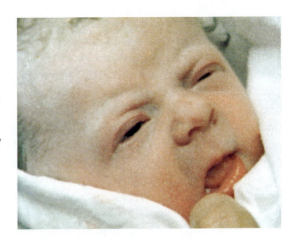

English couple. She had been conceived when her mother's eggs were fertilized with her father's sperm in a laboratory dish and then implanted in her mother's uterus — a complex process called **in vitro fertilization**. In reproductive technology, as in other areas, the revolution in biology was dramatically changing human life, improving health, and even making new life possible.

> **REVIEW QUESTION** What were the technological and scientific advances of the 1960s and 1970s, and how did they change human life and society?

Postindustrial Society and Culture

Soaring investments in science and the spread of technology put Western countries on what has been labeled a postindustrial course. Instead of being centered on manufacturing and heavy industry, a postindustrial economy emphasized the distribution of services such as health care and education. This meant that intellectual work, as well as industrial work, was central to creating jobs and profits. Moreover, all parts of society and industry interlocked, forming a system constantly in need of complex analysis, as in the nuclear industry. These characteristics of postindustrial society and culture would carry over into the twenty-first century.

Multinational Corporations

A major development of the postindustrial era was the growth of the **multinational corporation**. Multinationals produced goods and services for a global market and conducted business worldwide, but unlike older kinds of international firms, they established major factories and managerial centers in countries other than their home base. For example, of the five hundred largest businesses in the United States in 1970, more than one hundred did over a quarter of their business abroad, with business machine manufacturer IBM operating in more than one hundred countries. Although U.S.-based

corporations led the way, European and Japanese multinationals like Volkswagen, Shell, Nestlé, and Sony also had a broad global reach.

Some multinational corporations burst the bounds of the nation-state as they set up shop in whatever part of the world offered cheap labor. In the first years after World War II, multinationals preferred European employees, who constituted a highly educated labor pool and had well-developed consumer habits. Then, beginning in the 1960s, multinationals moved more of their operations to the emerging economies of formerly colonized states to reduce labor costs and avoid taxes. Although multinational corporations provided jobs in developing areas, profits usually went out of those areas to enrich foreign stockholders. Multinational corporations lacked the interest in the well-being of localities or nations that earlier industrialists had often shown. Thus, this system of business looked to some like imperialism in a new form.

Firms believed that they could stay competitive only by expanding, merging with other companies, or partnering with governments. They also increased their investment in research and used international cooperation to produce major new products. Beginning with its first commercial flight in 1976, the British-French Concorde supersonic aircraft flew from London to New York in under four hours. Another venture was the Airbus, a more practical series of passenger jets inaugurated in 1972 by a consortium of European firms. Both projects grew from the strong relationships among government, business, and science as well as from the international cooperation in manufacturing among members of the Common Market. Such relationships allowed European businesses to compete successfully with U.S.-based and other multinational giants.

The New Worker

In the early years of industry, workers often labored to exhaustion and lived in poor conditions. These conditions changed fundamentally in postwar Europe with the reduction of the blue-collar workforce and increased automation of industrial work. Manufacturing was simply cleaner and less dangerous than ever before. Meanwhile, a new working class of white-collar service personnel emerged. (See "Taking Measure," page 925.) Its rise undermined economic distinctions based on the way a person worked, for those who performed service work or had managerial titles were not necessarily better paid than blue-collar laborers. The ranks of service workers swelled with researchers, planners, health care and medical staff, and government functionaries. As emphasis on service grew, entire categories of employees such as flight attendants devoted much of their skill to the psychological well-being of customers. By 1969, the percentage of service-sector employees had surpassed that of manufacturing workers in several industrial countries: 61.1 percent versus 33.7 percent in the United States, and 48.8 percent versus 41.1 percent in Sweden.

Postindustrial work life differed somewhat in the Soviet bloc. There, the percentage of farmers remained higher than in western Europe. A huge difference between professional occupations and those involving physical work also remained in socialist countries because of declining investment in advanced machinery and cleaner work

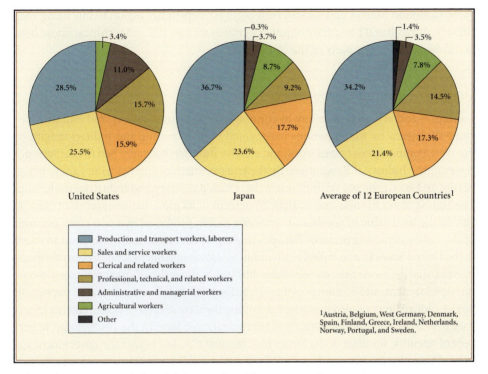

United States — Japan — Average of 12 European Countries[1]

Legend:
- Production and transport workers, laborers
- Sales and service workers
- Clerical and related workers
- Professional, technical, and related workers
- Administrative and managerial workers
- Agricultural workers
- Other

[1]Austria, Belgium, West Germany, Denmark, Spain, Finland, Greece, Ireland, Netherlands, Norway, Portugal, and Sweden.

Taking Measure Postindustrial Occupational Structure, 1984

Striking changes occurred in the composition of the workforce in the postwar period. Agriculture continued to decline as a source of jobs; by the 1980s, the percentage of agricultural workers in the most advanced industrial countries had dropped to well below 10 percent. The most striking development was the expansion of the service sector, which came to employ more than half of all workers. In the United States, the agricultural and industrial sectors (represented by production and transportation workers), which had dominated a century earlier, now offered less than a third of all jobs. (*Yearbook of Labour Statistics* [Geneva: International Labour Office, 1992], Table 2.7.)

processes. Men in both the U.S. and Soviet blocs generally earned higher pay and had better jobs than women. Uniquely in the Soviet bloc, however, women's badly paying jobs included street cleaning, garbage collection, heavy labor on farms, general medicine, and dentistry. Somewhere between 80 and 95 percent of women in socialist countries worked, mostly under difficult conditions.

Farming changed as well, consolidating and becoming more scientific. Small landowners sold family plots to corporations engaged in agribusiness — that is, vast acreage devoted to commercial rather than peasant farming. Governments, farmers' cooperatives, and planning agencies shaped the decision making of the individual farmer, while genetic research that yielded pest-resistant seeds and the skyrocketing use of pesticides, fertilizers, and machinery contributed to economic growth. For example, in the 1970s, a woman named Fernande Pelletier ran a hundred-acre farm in southwestern France, using the advice of a government expert to produce whatever foods might sell competitively

in the Common Market and joining with other farmers in her region to buy heavy machinery. Agricultural prosperity required as much managerial and technical know-how as did success in other parts of the economy.

The Boom in Education and Research

Education and research were key to running postindustrial society and had now become the means by which nations maintained their economic and military might. In the West, common sense, hard work, and creative intuition had launched the earliest successes of the Industrial Revolution. By the late twentieth century, a wide variety of expertise and ever-growing staffs of researchers fueled military and industrial leadership. The United States funneled more than 20 percent of its gross national product (a measure of the total value of goods and services a nation produced in a year) into research in the 1960s, attracting many of Europe's leading intellectuals and technicians to move to the United States in a so-called brain drain. Scientists and bureaucrats frequently made more crucial decisions than did elected politicians in the realm of space programs, weapons development, and economic policy. Here East–West differences became important: Soviet-bloc nations proved less adept at linking their considerable achievements in science to real-life applications because of bureaucratic red tape. In the 1960s, some 40 percent of scientific findings in the Soviet bloc became obsolete before the government approved them for application to technology. An invisible backsliding from superpower effectiveness and leadership had begun in the USSR — much of it due to the lack of systems coordination and cooperation.

The centrality of sophisticated knowledge to success in postindustrial society led to unprecedented growth in education, especially in universities and scientific institutes. The number of university students in Sweden rose by about 580 percent and in West Germany by 250 percent between 1950 and 1969. Great Britain established a network of technical universities to encourage the practical research that traditional elite universities often scorned. France set up schools to train future high-level experts in administration. The scientific establishment in the Soviet Union grew rapidly and some institutions of higher learning added courses in business management, information technology, and systems analysis designed for the new pool of postindustrial workers.

Changing Family Life and the Generation Gap

Just as education changed to meet the needs of postindustrial society, family structures and parent–child relationships shifted from what they had been a century earlier. Households became more varied: cohabiting couples, single-parent families, blended families, families headed by same-sex partners, and childless marriages all became more common. At the end of the 1970s, the marriage rate in the West had fallen by 30 percent from its 1960s level, and after almost two decades of baby boom, the birthrate dropped significantly. Belgian women, for example, bore 2.6 children on average in 1960 but only 1.8 by the end of the 1970s. In the Soviet bloc, the birthrate was even lower.

Daily life within the family also changed. Technological consumer items filled the home, with radio and television often forming the basis of the household's common social life. Appliances such as dishwashers, washing machines, and clothes dryers became more widespread, especially in the western bloc. More women worked outside the home during these years to pay for the prolonged economic dependence of children, and, in contrast with the past, the modern family seemed to have a primarily psychological mission, providing emotional nurturance for children who acquired their intellectual skills in school. Parents turned to psychologists, social workers, other experts, and the media for models of how to deal with life in postindustrial society.

Postindustrial society changed teenagers' lives most dramatically, creating strong differences between adolescents and adults. A century earlier, teens had been full-time wage earners like their parents; now, in the new knowledge-based society, most were students and some were financially dependent on their parents into their twenties. Despite teenagers' longer financial childhood, sexual activity began at an ever younger age, prompting the idea of a "sexual revolution." Youth simultaneously gained new roles as consumers, wooed with items associated with rock music — records, portable radios, and stereos. Rock music celebrated youthful rebellion against adult culture in scornful, critical, and often explicitly sexual lyrics. Sex roles for the young did not change, however: promoters focused on groups of male musicians, whom they depicted as heroic, surrounded by worshipping female "groupies." New models for youth such as the Beatles were themselves the products of advanced technology, marketing for mass consumption, and a unique youth culture separating the young from their parents — the so-called generation gap.

Art, Ideas, and Religion in a Technocratic Society

Cultural trends developed alongside the march of consumer society and technological breakthroughs. A new style in the visual arts was called **pop art**. It featured images from everyday life and employed the glossy techniques and products of what these artists called admass, or mass advertising. Like advertising itself, art leadership passed from Europe to the United States. U.S. pop artist Robert Rauschenberg, for example, made collages from comic strips, magazine clippings, and fabric to fulfill his vision that "a picture is more like the real world when it's made out of the real world." Maverick American artists such as Andy Warhol (1928–1987) made pop art a financial success with their parodies of modern commercialism. Through images of actress Marilyn Monroe and former first lady Jacqueline Kennedy, Warhol showed, for example, how depictions of women were used to sell everything mass culture had to offer in the 1960s and 1970s. He portrayed Campbell's soup cans as they appeared in advertisements and sold these works as elite artistic creations.

Swedish-born artist Claes Oldenburg (1929–) portrayed the grotesque aspects of ordinary consumer products in *Giant Hamburger with Pickle Attached* (1962) and *Lipstick Ascending on Caterpillar Tractor* (1967). Capturing this mocking world of art, German artist Sigmar Polke did cartoon-like drawings of products and of those who craved them. The Swiss sculptor Jean Tinguely used rusted parts of old machines — the junk of

Pop Art

Claes Oldenburg excelled in highlighting objects of everyday life, such as this hamburger (*Floor Burger*, 1962). He also modeled vacuum cleaners, shuttlecocks, telephones, and many other much-used things — a feature of pop art, which often contained humor in addition. Can you spot the humor in this creation? (Claes Oldenburg, *Floor Burger*, 1962 Canvas filled with foam rubber and cardboard boxes, painted with latex and Liquitex, 4 ft. 4 in. [1.32 m] high; 7 ft. [2.13 m] diameter. Collection Art Gallery of Ontario, Toronto, Canada, Purchase 1967. Photo courtesy the Oldenburg van Bruggen Studio. Copyright © 1962 Claes Oldenburg. Photo provided by The Bridgeman Art Library International.)

industrial society — to make fountains that could move. His partner Niki de Saint Phalle (1930–2002) then decorated them with huge, gaudy figures — many of them inspired by the folk traditions of the Caribbean and Africa. Their colorful, mobile fountains adorned main squares in Stockholm, Paris, and other cities.

The American composer John Cage (1912–1992) worked in a similar vein when he added to his musical scores sounds produced by such everyday items as combs, pieces of wood, and radio noise. Buddhist influence led Cage to incorporate silence in music and to compose by randomly tossing coins and then choosing notes by the corresponding numbers in the ancient Chinese *I Ching* (Book of Changes). These techniques continued the trend away from classical melody that had begun with modernism. Other composers, called minimalists, simplified music by featuring repetition and sustained notes instead of producing the lush melodies of nineteenth-century symphonies and piano music. Estonian composer Arvo Pärt wrote minimalist pieces in the 1970s using only three or four notes in total; he called this style "starvation" music to emphasize the lack of both freedom and goods in the Soviet bloc. Improved recording technology and mass marketing brought music of all varieties to a wider home audience than ever before.

The social sciences reached the peak of their prestige in the postindustrial era, often because of the increasing use of statistical models made possible by advanced electronic computations. Anthropology was among the most exciting of the social sciences, for it brought young university students information about societies that seemed untouched by modern technology and industry. Colorful ethnographic films revealed different lifestyles and seemingly exotic practices. While studying people who came to be called "the other," students had their sense of freedom reinforced by the vision of going back to nature. Whatever their discipline, social scientists announced that, like technicians and engineers, their specialized methods and factual knowledge were key to managing the complexities of postindustrial society and setting policy for developing nations.

At the same time, the social sciences undermined Enlightenment beliefs that individuals had true freedom. French anthropologist Claude Lévi-Strauss (1908–2009) developed a theory called structuralism, which insisted that all societies function within

controlling structures — kinship, for example. While challenging existentialism's claim that humans could create a free existence, structuralism also attacked the social sciences' faith in rationality. Lévi-Strauss's book *The Savage Mind* (1966) demonstrated that people outside the West, even though they did not use scientific methods, had their own effective systems of problem solving. In the 1960s and 1970s, the findings of some social scientists additionally echoed concerns that technology and highly managed bureaucratic systems were creating a society in which people lacked individuality and freedom.

Religious leaders and parishioners responded to the changing times in a variety of ways. Pope Paul VI (1963–1978) opposed artificial birth control as it became more prevalent, while also becoming the first pontiff to carry out the global vision of Vatican II by visiting Africa, Asia, and South America. In some places, grassroots religious fervor surged in the face of advancing science. Growing numbers of U.S. Protestants, for example, joined sects that denied the validity of scientific discoveries such as the age of the universe and the evolution of the species. In western Europe, however, Christian churchgoing remained at a low ebb. In the 1970s, for example, only 10 percent of the British population went to religious services — about the same number that attended live soccer matches. Most striking was the changing composition of the Western religious public, with immigration of people from former colonies and other parts of the world. Mosques, Buddhist temples, and shrines to other creeds appeared in a greater number of cities and towns.

> **REVIEW QUESTION** How did Western society and culture change in the postindustrial age?

Protesting Cold War Conditions

The United States and the Soviet Union reached new heights in the 1960s, but trouble was brewing for the superpowers. By 1965, the six-nation Common Market had temporarily replaced the United States as the leader in worldwide trade, and its members often acted in their own self-interest, not in the interests of the superpowers. In 1973, Britain's membership in the Common Market, followed by Ireland's and Denmark's, boosted the market's exports to almost three times those of the United States. The USSR faced challenges, too. Communist China, along with countries in eastern Europe, contested Soviet leadership, and by the mid-1960s, the United States was waging a devastating war in Vietnam in order to block the Communist independence movement there. Rising citizen discontent, sometimes expressed in dramatic acts of protest like that of Jan Palach, presented another serious challenge to the cold war order. From the 1960s until 1989, people rose up against technology-driven dehumanization, lack of fundamental rights, and the potential for nuclear holocaust.

Cracks in the Cold War Order

Across the social and political spectrum came calls to reduce cold war tensions in this age of unprecedented technological advance. In the Soviet Union, the new middle class of bureaucrats and managers demanded a better standard of living and a reduction in

the cold war hostility that made everyday life so menacing. In Germany, Social Democratic politicians had enough influence to shift money from cold war defense spending to domestic programs. Willy Brandt (1913–1992), the Socialist mayor of West Berlin, became foreign minister in 1966 and worked to improve frigid relations with Communist East Germany in order to open up trade. This anti–cold war policy, known as **Ostpolitik**, gave West German business leaders what they wanted: "the depoliticization of Germany's foreign trade," as one industrialist put it, and an opening of consumerism in the Soviet bloc. West German trade with eastern Europe grew rapidly, but it left the relatively poorer countries of the Soviet bloc strapped with mounting debt. Nonetheless, commerce began building bridges across the U.S.–Soviet cold war divide.

To break the superpowers' stranglehold on international politics, French president Charles de Gaulle poured huge sums into French nuclear development, withdrew French forces from NATO, and signed trade treaties with the Soviet bloc. However, de Gaulle protected France's good relations with Germany to prevent further encroachments from the Soviet bloc. At home, de Gaulle's government sponsored the construction of modern housing and ordered the exterior cleaning of all Parisian buildings — a massive project taking years — to wipe away more than a century of industrial grime and to demonstrate community, not cold war, values. With his haughty pursuit of French grandeur, de Gaulle offered the European public an alternative to obeying the superpowers.

Brandt's Ostpolitik and de Gaulle's independence had their echoes in Soviet-bloc reforms. After the ouster of Soviet premier Nikita Khrushchev in 1964, the new leadership of Leonid Brezhnev (1909–1982) and Alexei Kosygin (1904–1980) initially continued attempts at reform, encouraging plant managers to turn a profit and using consumer goods to alleviate the discontent of an increasingly educated and informed citizenry. The government also allowed more cultural and scientific meetings with Westerners, another move that relaxed the cold war atmosphere in the mid-1960s. Like the French, the Soviets set up "technopoles" — new cities devoted to research and technological innovation. The Soviet satellites in eastern Europe seized the economic opportunity presented by Moscow's relaxed posture. For example, Hungarian leader János Kádár introduced elements of a market system into the national economy by encouraging small businesses and trade to develop outside the Communist-controlled state network.

Soviet-bloc writers sought to break the hold of socialist realism on the arts and reduce their praise for the Soviet past. Dissident artists' paintings rejected brightly colored scenes and heroic figures and instead depicted Soviet citizens as worn and tired in grays and other monochromatic color schemes. East Berlin writer Christa Wolf challenged the celebratory nature of socialist art when she showed a couple tragically divided by the Berlin Wall in her novel *Divided Heaven* (1965). Repression of artistic expression returned in the later 1960s and 1970s, as the Soviet government took to bulldozing outdoor art shows. For their part, writers relied on **samizdat** culture, a form of protest activity in which individuals reproduced government-suppressed publications by hand and passed them from reader to reader, thus building a foundation for the successful resistance of the 1980s.

Other issues challenged U.S. leadership of the western bloc during the cold war. The assassination of President John F. Kennedy in November 1963 shocked the nation and the world, but only momentarily did it halt the escalating demands for civil rights for African Americans and other minorities. White segregationists murdered and brutalized those attempting to integrate lunch counters, register black voters, or simply march on behalf of freedom. In response to the murders and destruction, Kennedy had introduced civil rights legislation and forced the desegregation of schools and universities. Lyndon B. Johnson (1908–1973), Kennedy's successor, steered the Civil Rights Act through Congress in 1964. This legislation forbade racial segregation in public facilities and created the Equal Employment Opportunity Commission (EEOC) to fight job discrimination based on "race, color, national origin, religion, and sex." Southern conservatives had tacked on the provision outlawing discrimination against women in the vain hope that it would doom the bill. Modeling himself on his hero Franklin Roosevelt, Johnson envisioned what he called the Great Society, in which new government programs would improve the lot of the forty million Americans living in poverty. Johnson's many reform programs included Project Head Start for educating disadvantaged preschool children and the Job Corps for training youth. Black novelist Ralph Ellison called Johnson "the greatest American president for the poor and the Negroes."

Still, the cold war did not go away, and the United States became increasingly embroiled in Vietnam (Map 28.1). After the Geneva Conference of 1954, which divided Vietnam into North and South, the United States increased its support for the corrupt leaders of non-Communist South Vietnam. North Vietnam, China, and the Soviet Union backed the rebel Vietcong, or South Vietnamese Communists. By 1966, the United States had more than half a million soldiers in South Vietnam, yet the strength of the Vietcong seemed to grow daily. Despite massive bombings by the United States, the insurgents, who had struggled against colonialism for decades, rejected a negotiated peace.

The Growth of Citizen Activism

In the midst of cold war conflict and technological advance, a new activism emerged. Prosperity and the rising benefits of a postindustrial, service-oriented economy made people ever more eager for peace and justice. The U.S. civil rights movement broadened, as other minorities joined African Americans in demanding fair treatment. In 1965, César Chávez (1927–1993) led Mexican American migrant workers in the California grape agribusiness to strike for better wages and working conditions. Meanwhile, beginning in 1965, urban riots erupted across the United States out of African Americans' frustration in their struggle for equal rights. Some chose to celebrate their race under the banner "black is beautiful," and some urged a push for "black power" to reclaim rights forcefully instead of "begging" for them nonviolently. Separatism, not integration, became the goal of others. Small cadres of militants like the Black Panthers took up arms, believing that, like decolonizing peoples elsewhere, they needed to protect themselves against the violent whites around them.

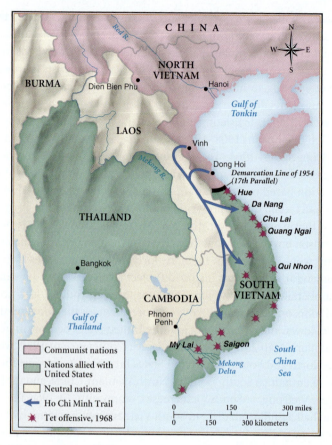

Map 28.1 The Vietnam War, 1954–1975
The local peoples of Southeast Asia had long resisted incursions by their neighbors. The Vietnamese beat the French colonizers in the battle of Dien Bien Phu in 1954. The Americans soon became involved, trying to stem what they saw as the tide of Communist influence behind the Vietnamese liberation movement. The ensuing war in Vietnam in the 1960s and 1970s spread into neighboring countries, making the region the scene of vast destruction.

From the 1950s on, homosexuals had also lobbied for the decriminalization of their sexual lives and practices. Some anti-gay propaganda equated male homosexuality with a lack of militaristic manliness needed to protect the nation-state on either side of the cold war divide. In June 1969, gay men in the Stonewall area of Greenwich Village, New York, rioted against the police and more general persecution, as had African Americans, both to assert their civil rights and to affirm their identity. The gay liberation movement born in that time came to span the globe and to include not only men but gay women, too.

As a result of the new turn in black efforts for change, white American university students who had participated in the early stages of the civil rights movement found themselves excluded from leadership positions in favor of an exclusively black leader-

ship. Many white students soon joined the swelling protests against technological change, consumerism, and the Vietnam War. European youth were also feverish for reform. In 1966, Prague students, chanting "The only good Communist is a dead one," held carnival-like processions to commemorate the tenth anniversary of the 1956 Hungarian uprisings. The "situationists" in France used shocking graffiti and street theater to call on students to wake up from the slumbering pace of consumer society.

Throughout the 1960s, students criticized the traditional university curriculum and flaunted their own countercultural values. They questioned how studying Plato or Dante would help them after graduation. "How to Train Stuffed Geese" was French students' satirical version of the teaching methods inflicted on them. Long hair, communal living, scorn for personal cleanliness, and ridicule for sexual chastity were part of students' rejection of middle-class values. Widespread use of the pill and open promiscuity made the sexual revolution explicit and public. Marijuana use became common among students, who had their own rituals, music, and gathering places. Hated by students, big business nonetheless made billions of dollars by selling everything from blue jeans to natural foods as well as by managing the rock stars of the counterculture.

Women's activism erupted, too. Working for reproductive rights, women in France helped end the nation's ban on birth control in 1965. Middle-class women eagerly responded to the international best seller *The Feminine Mystique* (1963), by American journalist Betty Friedan. Pointing to the stagnating talents of many housewives, Friedan helped organize the National Organization for Women (NOW) in 1966 "to bring women into full participation in the mainstream of American society now." NOW advocated equal pay for equal work and a variety of other legal and economic reforms. In Sweden, women lobbied to make tasks both at home and in the workplace less gender-segregated.

Women who engaged in the civil rights and student movements soon realized that many protest organizations devalued women just as society at large did. Male activists adopted the leather-jacketed machismo style of their film and rock heroes, but women in the movements were often judged by the status of their male protester lovers. "A woman was to 'inspire' her man," African American activist Angela Davis complained, adding that women seeking equality were accused of wanting "to rob [male activists] of their manhood." West German women students tossed tomatoes at male protest leaders in defiance of male domination of the movement and of standards set by society for ladylike behavior.

1968: Year of Crisis

Calls for reform finally boiled over in 1968. In January, on the first day of Tet, the Vietnamese New Year, the Vietcong and the North Vietnamese attacked more than one hundred South Vietnamese towns and American bases, inflicting heavy casualties and fueling the antiwar movement around the world. On April 4, 1968, a white racist assassinated civil rights leader Martin Luther King Jr. Riots erupted in more than a hundred cities in the United States as African Americans vented their anguish and rage. Rejecting

Second-Wave Feminists on the March

Like turn-of-the-century feminists, women in the 1960s and 1970s took to the streets to protest their condition. This march in Paris features signs showing a clock fixed at 7:30 and a list of chores including "breakfast for husband," "wake the children," and "hurry." For many citizens, the sight of "unladylike" women demonstrating in public was a shock—which was the point for many activists. (© Rue des Archives / AGIP / The Granger Collection, NYC—All rights reserved.)

King's policy of nonviolence, rioters rampaged through grim inner cities, chanting "Burn, baby, burn." On U.S. campuses, bitter clashes over the intertwined issues of war, technology, racism, and sexism closed down classes.

Similar student unrest erupted across the globe, most dramatically in France. In January, students at the university in Nanterre, outside of Paris, had gone on strike, invading administration offices to protest what they saw as a second-rate education. They called themselves a proletariat — an exploited working class — as worker activists had done for more than a century. They did not embrace Soviet communism but rather considered themselves part of the New Left, not the old Communist or Socialist left.

When students at the prestigious Sorbonne in Paris also took to the streets in protest, police assaulted them. French workers joined in the protest. Some nine million went on strike, occupying factories and calling not only for higher wages but also for participation in everyday decision making. The combined revolt of youth and workers looked as if it might spiral into another French revolution. President Charles de Gaulle sent tanks into Paris, and in June he announced a raise for workers. Many citizens, having grown tired of the street violence, the destruction of so much private property, and

the breakdown of services such as garbage collection, began to sympathize with the government instead of the students. The revolutionary moment had passed.

By contrast, the 1968 revolt in Prague began within the Czechoslovak Communist Party itself. At a party congress in the autumn of 1967, Alexander Dubček, head of the Slovak branch of the party, had called for more social and political openness, striking a chord among frustrated party officials, technocrats, and intellectuals. Czech citizens began to dream of creating a new society — one based on "socialism with a human face." Reform-minded party delegates elevated Dubček to the top position, and he quickly changed the Communist style of government by ending censorship, instituting the secret ballot for

Prague Spring, 1968

party elections, and allowing competing political groups to form. "Look!" one little girl in the street remarked as the new government took power. "Everyone's smiling today." The Prague Spring had begun as people bought uncensored publications, packed uncensored theater productions, and engaged in nonstop political debate.

Dubček faced the enormous problem of negotiating policies acceptable to both the USSR and reform-minded citizens. Fearing change, the Polish, East German, and Soviet regimes threatened the reform government daily. When Dubček failed to attend a meeting of Warsaw Pact leaders, Soviet threats intensified until finally, in August 1968, Soviet tanks rolled into Prague in a massive show of force. Citizens tried to halt the return to Communist orthodoxy through sabotage: they removed street signs to confuse invading troops, and merchants refused to sell food or other commodities to Soviet troops. The determined Soviet leadership gradually removed reformers from power, however. Jan Palach and other university students immolated themselves the following January, as governments around the world worked to stamp out criticism of the cold war order.

The protests of 1968 challenged the political direction of Western societies, but little turned out the way reformers hoped as governments turned to conservative solutions. In November 1968, the Soviets announced the Brezhnev Doctrine, which stated that reform movements, as a "common problem" of all socialist countries, would face swift repression. In the early 1970s, the hard-liner Brezhnev clamped down on critics, crushing the morale of dissidents in the USSR. "The shock of our tanks crushing the Prague Spring . . . convinced us that the Soviet colossus was invincible," explained one pessimistic liberal. In 1974, Brezhnev expelled author Aleksandr Solzhenitsyn from the USSR after the publication of the first volume of *The Gulag Archipelago* (1973–1976) in the U.S.-led bloc. Solzhenitsyn documented the story of the Gulag (the Soviet system of internment and forced-labor camps) with firsthand reports about the deadly conditions prisoners endured. More than any other single work, *The Gulag Archipelago* disillusioned loyal Communists around the world.

The USSR and other Communist countries used both persecution of ordinary citizens and the "soft" power of the new medium of television to reestablish order. Soviet

Invasion Puts Down the Prague Spring
When the Soviet Union and other Warsaw Pact members cracked down on the Prague Spring, they met determined citizen resistance. People refused assistance of any kind to the invaders and personally talked to them about the Czech cause. Despite the repression, protests small and large continued until the final fall of Communist rule two decades later. (© Bettmann / Corbis.)

psychologists, working with the government, certified the "mental illness" of people who did not play by the rules; thus, dissidents wound up as virtual prisoners in mental institutions. In a revival of tsarist Russia's anti-Semitism, Jews faced educational restrictions (especially in university admissions) and severe job discrimination. Soviet officials commonly accused Jews of being "unreliable." In Czechoslovakia, where by 1970 some 80 percent of households had TV, government writers created a new batch of soap operas featuring heroines who taught their families to replace activism in the public sphere with the contentment of private life. Heroes selflessly traveled to the West for their jobs, only to return disillusioned by its faults.

Despite these efforts, the brain drain of eastern European intellectuals to the West increased into the 1970s and beyond. The modernist composer György Ligeti had left Hungary in 1956, after which his work was celebrated in concert halls and in such classic films as *2001: A Space Odyssey*. From exile in Paris, Czech writer Milan Kundera enthralled audiences with *The Book of Laughter and Forgetting* (1979) and *The Unbearable Lightness of Being* (1984). Kundera claimed that the Soviet regime in Czechoslovakia depended on making people forget. The memory of fallen leaders was ruthlessly erased from history books, for instance, and individuals tried to block out grim reality by en-

gaging in lots of sexual activity. Like the migrants from fascist Germany and Italy in the 1930s, newcomers — from noted intellectuals to skilled craftspeople and dancers — enriched the culture of those countries that welcomed them.

In the United States, the reaction against activists was different, though restoring order ultimately succeeded there, too. Elected in 1968, President **Richard Nixon** (1913–1994) promised to bring peace to Southeast Asia, but in 1970 he ordered U.S. troops to invade Cambodia, the site of North Vietnamese bases. Campuses erupted again in protest, and on May 4 the National Guard killed four students and wounded eleven others at a demonstration at Kent State University in Ohio. Nixon called the victims "bums," and a growing reaction against the counterculture led many Americans to agree with one citizen who declared that the guardsmen "should have fired sooner and longer." In 1975, a determined North Vietnamese offensive defeated South Vietnam and its U.S. allies and forcibly reunified the country. A strong current of public opinion turned against activists, born of the sense that somehow they — not the war, government corruption, or the huge war debt — had brought down the United States. Both superpowers were being tested, almost to the limits.

> **REVIEW QUESTION** What were the main issues for protesters in the 1960s, and how did governments address them?

The Testing of Superpower Domination and the End of the Cold War

Protesters like Jan Palach left a lasting legacy that continued to motivate those seeking political change, particularly in the Soviet bloc. As order was restored, some disillusioned reformers in the West turned to open terrorism, and like every other political occurrence in these days, television broadcast the events. New forces also emerged from beyond Europe and the United States to challenge superpower dominance. Internal corruption, competition from the oil-producing states, and the pursuit of warfare beyond their borders all threw the superpowers and their allies off balance, allowing reform-minded heads of state to come to the fore. The two most famous innovators were Margaret Thatcher in Britain and Mikhail Gorbachev in the USSR, both of whom introduced drastic new policies in the 1980s to keep their economies moving forward. But in the Soviet bloc, refining the old system actually contributed to its collapse and thus to the end of the cold war in 1989.

A Changing Balance of World Power

Tested by protest at home, the superpowers found themselves facing a changing balance in world power. In the midst of turmoil, Henry Kissinger, Nixon's secretary of state and a believer — like Otto von Bismarck — in Realpolitik, decided to take advantage of the ongoing rivalry between the USSR and China. After the Communist Revolution in 1949, Mao Zedong, China's new leader, undertook foolish experiments in both manufacturing

and agriculture that caused famine and massive suffering. As internal problems grew in both the Soviet Union and China, the two Communist giants skirmished along their shared borders and in diplomatic arenas. In 1972, President Nixon visited China, linking two very different great nations both facing disorder at home. Within China, Nixon's visit helped slow the brutality and excesses of Mao's regime. It also advanced the careers of Chinese pragmatists who were interested in technology and relations with the West and who laid the groundwork for China's boom later in the century.

The diplomatic success of the visit led the Soviets to make their own overtures to the U.S.-led bloc, beginning a process known as détente (a relaxation of tensions). In 1972, the superpowers signed the first Strategic Arms Limitation Treaty (SALT I), which set a cap on the number of antimissile defenses each country could have. In 1975, in the Helsinki accords on human rights, the western bloc officially acknowledged Soviet territorial gains in World War II in exchange for the Soviet bloc's guarantee of basic human rights.

Despite these successes, the war in Vietnam left the United States billions of dollars in debt to other countries and the international currency system in collapse. In the face of the resulting global economic chaos, Common Market countries united to force the United States to relinquish its single-handed direction of Western economic strategy. Another blow to U.S. leadership followed when it was revealed that Nixon's office had threatened the U.S. system of free elections by authorizing the burglary and wiretapping of Democratic Party headquarters at Washington's Watergate building during the 1972 presidential campaign. The Watergate scandal forced Nixon to resign in disgrace in the summer of 1974 — one more weak spot in U.S. superpower status in the 1960s and 1970s.

The Middle East's oil-producing nations dealt Western dominance still another major blow. Tensions between Israel and the Arab world provided the catalyst. In 1967, Israeli forces, responding to Palestinian guerrilla attacks, quickly seized Gaza and the Sinai peninsula from Egypt, the Golan Heights from Syria, and the West Bank from Jordan. Israel's stunning victory in this action, which came to be called the Six-Day War, was followed in 1973 by a joint Egyptian and Syrian attack on Israel on Yom Kippur, the most holy day in the Jewish calendar. Israel, with material assistance from the United States, stopped the assault.

Having failed militarily, Arab nations in the **Organization of Petroleum Exporting Countries (OPEC)**, a relatively loose consortium before the Yom Kippur War, combined to quadruple the price of their oil and impose an embargo, cutting off all exports of oil to the United States and its allies because they backed Israel. For the first time since imperialism's heyday, the producers of raw materials — not the industrial powers — controlled the flow of commodities and set prices to their own advantage (Figure 28.1). As a result, unemployment rose by

Israel after the Six-Day War, 1967

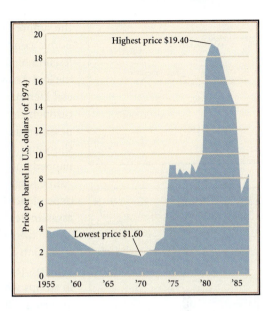

Figure 28.1 Fluctuating Oil Prices, 1955–1985
Colonization allowed the Western imperial powers to obtain raw materials at advantageous prices or even without paying at all. OPEC's oil embargo and price hikes of the 1970s were signs of change, which included the exercise of decolonized countries' control over their own resources. OPEC's action led to a decade of painful economic downturn, but it also encouraged some European governments to improve public transportation, encourage the production of fuel-efficient cars, and make individual consumers cut back their dependence on oil.

more than 50 percent in Europe and the United States and inflation soared. By the end of 1973, the inflation rate jumped to over 12 percent in France and 20 percent in Portugal. Eastern-bloc countries, dependent on Soviet oil, fared little better because the West could no longer afford their products and the Soviets boosted the price of their own oil. Skyrocketing interest rates discouraged both industrial investment and consumer buying. Prices, unemployment, and interest rates all rising created an unusual combination of economic conditions called **stagflation**. Western Europe drastically cut back on its oil dependence by undertaking conservation, enhancing public transportation, and raising the price of gasoline to encourage the development of fuel-efficient cars.

The U.S. bloc took further blows. In the late 1970s, students, clerics, shopkeepers, and unemployed men in Iran began an uprising that brought to power the Islamic ayatollah (a Shi'ite religious leader) Ruhollah Khomeini (1902–1989). Using the new medium of audiocassette recordings to spread his message, Khomeini called for a transformation of Iran into a truly Islamic society, which meant the renunciation of the Western ways advocated by the American-backed shah, who was overthrown. In the autumn of 1979, supporters of Khomeini took hostages at the U.S. embassy in Teheran even as images of the captives' stricken faces were sent around the globe via satellites. The United States was essentially paralyzed in the face of Islamic militancy, further OPEC price hikes, and a downwardly spiraling economy.

The Western Bloc Meets Challenges with Reform

As the 1980s opened, governments in the West had to put their economic houses in order and confront the growing phenomenon of terrorism — a trend that had actually begun in the West. In the 1970s, terrorist bands of young people in Europe responded to

Nationalist Movements of the 1970s

the suppression of activism and the worsening economic conditions with kidnappings, bank robberies, bombings, and assassinations. In West Germany, the Red Army Faction — eager to bring down the Social Democratic coalition that had led the country through the 1970s — assassinated prominent businessmen and public officials. Practiced in random shootings of pedestrians, Italy's Red Brigades kidnapped and then murdered the head of the dominant Christian Democrats in 1978. Advocates of independence for the Basque nation in northern Spain assassinated Spanish politicians and police officers.

In the 1970s, Catholics in Northern Ireland protested job discrimination and a lack of civil rights. With protest escalating, the British government sent in troops who on January 30, 1972 (which became known as Bloody Sunday), fired at demonstrators and killed thirteen, setting off a cycle of violence that left five hundred dead in that year alone. Protestants fearful of losing their dominant position combated a reinvigorated Irish Republican Army (IRA), which carried out bombings and assassinations to put an end to the oppression of Catholics.

Terrorists failed in their goal of overturning the existing democracies, and, battered as it was, parliamentary government scored a few important successes in the 1970s. Spain and Portugal, suffering under dictatorships since the 1930s, set out on a course of political openness and greater prosperity. The death of Spain's Francisco Franco in 1975 ended more than three decades of dictatorial rule. Franco's handpicked successor, King Juan Carlos, surprisingly steered his nation to Western-style constitutional monarchy, facing down threatened military coups. Portugal and Greece also ousted right-wing dictators, thus paving the way for their integration into western Europe. Despite these democratic advances, economic crisis and political terrorism weighed on the West.

More than anyone else, **Margaret Thatcher**, the leader of Britain's Conservative Party and prime minister from 1979 to 1990, reshaped the West's political and economic ideas to meet the crisis. Coming to power amid continuing economic decline, revolt in Northern Ireland, and labor unrest, the combative prime minister rejected the politics of consensus building. She believed that only business could revive the sluggish British economy, so she lashed out at union leaders, Labour Party politicians, and people who received welfare-state benefits, calling them enemies of British prosperity. In her view, business leaders were the key members of society. She characterized immigrants, whose low wages contributed greatly to business profits, as inferior. Under Thatcher, even workers blamed labor leaders or newcomers for Britain's troubles.

On the World Stage: Margaret Thatcher and Mohammed Anwar al-Sadat
Margaret Thatcher, Great Britain's conservative prime minister, and Egyptian president Mohammed Anwar al-Sadat met in London in August 1981, just two months before Sadat was assassinated for participating in the Egyptian-Israeli peace accord. Thatcher's term in office was as memorable as Sadat's: she went on to launch a new conservatism in politics and economics that would sweep the world in the 1980s and 1990s. (Mary Evans Picture Library / Marx Memorial Library.)

The policies of "Thatcherism" were based on monetarist, or supply-side, economic theory. According to monetarist theory, inflation results when government pumps money into the economy at a rate higher than the nation's economic growth rate. Monetarists believe that the government should keep a tight rein on the money supply to prevent prices from rising rapidly. Supply-side economists maintain that the economy as a whole flourishes when businesses grow and their prosperity "trickles down" throughout society. To implement these theories, the British government cut income taxes on the wealthy as a way of encouraging investment and increased sales taxes to compensate for the lost revenue. The result was a greater burden on working people, who bore the brunt of the higher sales tax. Thatcher also refused to prop up "outmoded" industries such as coal mining and slashed education and health programs. Her package of economic policies came to be known as **neoliberalism**.

In the first years of Thatcher's government, the British economy did not respond well to her shock treatment. The quality of universities, public transportation, highways, and hospitals deteriorated, and social unity fragmented as she pitted the lower classes against one another. In 1981, blacks and Asians rioted in major cities. Thatcher revived her sagging popularity with a nationalist war against Argentina in 1982 over ownership of the Falkland Islands off the Argentinian coast. Stagflation ultimately dissipated, and Thatcher's program became the standard for those facing the challenge of stagflation

and economic decline. Britain had been one of the pioneers of the welfare state, and now it pioneered in changing course.

In the United States, Ronald Reagan, who served as president between 1981 and 1989, followed a similar road to combat the economic crisis there. Dividing U.S. citizens into the good and the bad, Reagan vowed to promote the values of the "moral majority," which included commitment to Bible-based religion and unquestioned patriotism. He blasted so-called spendthrift and immoral "liberals" when introducing "Reaganomics" — a program of whopping income tax cuts for the wealthy combined with massive reductions in federal spending for student loans, school lunch programs, and mass transit. Funding social programs, he felt, only encouraged bad Americans to be lazy. In foreign policy, Reagan rolled back détente and demanded huge military budgets to counter the Soviets. The combination of tax cuts and military expansion had pushed the federal budget deficit to $200 billion by 1986. As in Britain, inflation was brought under control and business picked up.

Other western European leaders also limited welfare-state benefits in the face of stagflation, though without Thatcher's and Reagan's socially divisive rhetoric. West German leader Helmut Kohl, who took power in 1982, reduced welfare spending, froze government wages, and cut corporate taxes. Unlike Thatcher, Kohl did not fan the flames of class and racial hatreds. Such a strategy would have been particularly unwise in Germany, where terrorism on the left and on the right continued to flourish. Moreover, the legacy of Nazism loomed menacingly: for example, an unemployed German youth said of immigrant Turkish workers, "Let's gas 'em."

By 1981, stagflation had put more than 1.5 million people out of work in France, but the French took a different political path to deal with the economic crisis. They elected a Socialist president, François Mitterrand, who nationalized banks and certain industries and increased wages and social spending to stimulate the economy — the opposite of Thatcherism. New public buildings like museums and libraries arose along with new subway lines and improved public transport. When conservative Jacques Chirac succeeded Mitterrand as president in 1995, he adopted neoliberal policies. Socially divisive politics that had unfolded during hard economic times grew in appeal. From the 1980s on, the racist National Front Party won 10 percent and sometimes more of the French vote with promises to deport African and Middle Eastern immigrants.

At the same time, smaller European states without heavy defense commitments began to thrive, some of them by slashing welfare programs. Spain joined the Common Market in 1986 and used Common Market investment and tourist dollars to help rebuild its sagging infrastructure as in the southern cities of Granada and Córdoba. In Ireland, new investment in education for high-tech jobs combined with low wage rates attracted business to the country in the 1990s. Prosperity, along with the rising death toll from decades of violence, led to a political rapprochement between Ireland and Northern Ireland in 1999. Austria prospered, too, in part by reducing government pensions and aid to business.

Almost alone, Sweden maintained a full array of social programs. The government offered each immigrant a choice of subsidized housing in neighborhoods inhabited

primarily by Swedes or primarily by people from the immigrant's native land. Such programs were expensive, and Sweden dropped from fourth to fourteenth place among nations in per capita income by 1998. The Swedish welfare state came to seem extreme to many citizens, and, as elsewhere, immigrants were cast as the source of the country's problems — past, present, and future: "How long will it be before our Swedish children will have to turn their faces toward Mecca?" ran one politician's campaign speech in 1993.

Collapse of Communism in the Soviet Bloc

Beginning in 1985, reform came to the Soviet Union as well, but instead of fortifying the economy, it helped bring about the collapse of the Soviet bloc. The need for reform was evident. In 1979, the USSR became embroiled against Islam in Afghanistan when it supported a coup by a Communist faction against the government: casualties were 800,000 for the Soviets alone and 3 million for the Afghans. Further, global communications technology showed Soviet citizens that another way of life was possible. Citizens could see that the Soviet system of corrupt economic management produced a deteriorating standard of living. Shortages necessitated the three-generation household, in which grandparents took over tedious homemaking tasks from their working children and grandchildren, including waiting in long lines for basic commodities. "There is no special skill to this," a seventy-three-year-old grandmother and former garbage collector remarked. "You just stand in line and wait." One cheap and readily available product — vodka — pushed alcoholism to crisis levels, diminishing productivity and straining the nation's morale.

In 1985, a new leader, **Mikhail Gorbachev**, opened an era of change. The son of peasants, Gorbachev had risen through Communist Party ranks as an agricultural specialist and had traveled abroad to observe life in the West. At home, he saw the consequences of economic stagnation: in much of the USSR, ordinary people decided not to have children. The Soviet Union was forced to import massive amounts of grain because 20 to 30 percent of the grain produced in the USSR rotted before it could be harvested or shipped to market, so great was the inefficiency of the state-directed economy. Industrial pollution had reached scandalous proportions because state-run enterprises cared only about meeting production quotas. A massive and privileged party bureaucracy feared innovation and failed to achieve socialism's professed goal of a decent standard of living for working people. To match U.S. military growth, the Soviet Union diverted 15 to 20 percent of its gross national product (more than double the U.S. proportion) to armaments, further crippling the economy's chances of raising living standards.

Gorbachev knew from experience and from his travels to western Europe that the Soviet system was completely inadequate, and he quickly proposed several unusual programs. A crucial economic reform, **perestroika** ("restructuring"), aimed to reinvigorate the Soviet economy by improving productivity, increasing investment, encouraging the use of up-to-date technology, and gradually introducing such market features as prices and profits. The complement to economic change was the policy of **glasnost** (usually translated as "openness" or "publicity"), which called for "wide, prompt, and

Mikhail and Raisa Gorbachev
Mikhail Gorbachev and his wife, Raisa, gave a fresh look to Soviet politics. They traveled, made friends abroad, and were fashionable and modern. While the Gorbachevs became part of Western celebrity culture, however, average citizens back home in the USSR saw the Gorbachevs' privileged lifestyle as simply the continuation of the Communist government's disregard for ordinary people. (© Peter Turnley / Corbis.)

frank information" and for allowing Soviet citizens new measures of free speech. When officials complained that glasnost threatened their status, Gorbachev replaced more than a third of the Communist Party's leadership. The pressing need for glasnost became most evident after the Chernobyl catastrophe in 1986, when a nuclear reactor exploded and spewed radioactive dust into the atmosphere. Bureaucratic cover-ups delayed the spread of information about the accident, with lethal consequences for people living near the plant.

After Chernobyl, Communist Party meetings suddenly included complaints about the highest leaders and their policies. Television shows adopted the outspoken methods of American investigative reporting, and instead of publishing made-up letters praising the great Soviet state, newspapers were flooded with real ones complaining of shortages and abuse. One outraged "mother of two" protested that the cost-cutting policy of reusing syringes in hospitals was a source of AIDS, the deadly disease that had recently begun to spread worldwide. "Why should little kids have to pay for the criminal actions of our Ministry of Health?" she asked. Debate and factions arose across the political spectrum. In the fall of 1987, one of Gorbachev's allies, Boris Yeltsin, quit the government after denouncing perestroika as insufficient to produce real reform. Yeltsin's political daring inspired others to organize in opposition to crumbling Communist rule. In the

spring of 1989, in a remarkably free balloting in Moscow's local elections, not a single Communist was chosen.

Recognizing how severely the cold war arms race was draining Soviet resources, Gorbachev began scaling back missile production. His unilateral actions gradually won over Ronald Reagan. In 1985, the two leaders initiated a personal relationship and began defusing the cold war. "I bet the hard-liners in both our countries are bleeding when we shake hands," said Reagan at the conclusion of one meeting. In early 1989, Gorbachev withdrew the last of his country's forces from the debilitating war in Afghanistan, and the United States started to cut back its own vast military buildup.

As Gorbachev's reforms in the USSR started spiraling out of his control, dissent was rising across the Soviet bloc. In the summer of 1980, Poles had gone on strike to protest government-increased food prices; workers at the Gdańsk shipyards, led by electrician Lech Walesa and crane operator Anna Walentynowicz, created an independent labor movement called **Solidarity**. The organization soon embraced much of the adult population, including a million members of the Communist Party. Both intellectuals and the Catholic church, long in the forefront of opposition to antireligious communism, supported Solidarity workers as they occupied factories in protest against the deteriorating conditions of everyday life. The members of Solidarity waved Polish flags and paraded giant portraits of the Virgin Mary and Pope John Paul II — a Polish native.

Global media coverage encouraged Solidarity leaders. As food became scarce and prices rose, tens of thousands of women joined in with marches, crying "We're hungry!" They also protested working conditions, but as both workers and the only caretakers of home life, it was the scarcity of food that sent them into the streets. The Communist Party teetered on the edge of collapse, until the police and the army, with Soviet support, imposed a military government and in the winter of 1981 outlawed Solidarity. Using world communications networks, dissidents kept Solidarity alive and workers kept meeting, creating a new culture outside the official Soviet arts and newscasts. Poets read dissident verse to overflow crowds, and university professors lectured on such forbidden topics as Polish resistance in World War II. Activism in Poland and the news about it set the stage for communism's downfall across the Soviet bloc.

The year 1989 saw uprisings around the world — in Chile, the Philippines, Haiti, South Africa, and China, for example. In 1980 the global Cable News Network (CNN) was established, linking many individual movements for democratic change through its twenty-four-hour coverage of world events. The most widely covered of these was the attack on the Communist state in China. Inspired by Gorbachev's visit to Beijing, in the spring of 1989 thousands of Chinese students massed in the city's Tiananmen Square, the world's largest public square, to demand democracy. They used telex machines and e-mail to rush their messages to the international community, and they conveyed their goals through the cameras that Western television, broadcasting via satellite, trained on them. As workers began joining the pro-democracy forces, the government crushed the movement and executed as many as a thousand rebels.

News of the protests in Tiananmen Square was galvanizing to those in eastern Europe, who were inspired in their long-standing tradition of resistance. In June 1989, the

Polish government, weakened by its own bungling of the economy and lacking Soviet support for further repression, held free parliamentary elections. Solidarity candidates overwhelmingly defeated the Communists, and Walesa became president in early 1990. Gorbachev openly reversed the Brezhnev Doctrine, refusing to interfere in the political course of another nation. When it became clear that the Soviet Union would not intervene in Poland, the fall of communism repeated itself across the Soviet bloc.

Communism next collapsed in Poland; it then collapsed in Hungary, in part because Hungarians, too, had experimented with "market socialism" since the 1960s. Hungarian citizens were already protesting the government, lobbying, for example, against ecologically unsound projects like the construction of a new dam. They encouraged boycotts of Communist holidays, and on March 15, 1989, they boldly commemorated the anniversary of the Hungarian uprising. These popular demands for liberalization led the Parliament in the fall of 1989 to dismiss the Communist Party as the official ruling institution.

The most potent symbol of a divided Europe was the Berlin Wall, and East Germans had attempted to escape over it for decades. In the summer of 1989, crowds of East Germans flooded the borders to escape the crumbling Soviet bloc, and hundreds of thousands of protesters rallied throughout the fall against the regime. Satellite television brought them visions of postindustrial prosperity and of free and open public debate in West Germany. Crowds of demonstrators greeted Gorbachev, taken as a hero by many, when he visited the country in October. On November 9, guards at the Berlin Wall allowed free passage to the west, turning protest into a festive holiday. As they strolled freely in the streets, East Berliners saw firsthand the goods available in a successful postindustrial society. Soon thereafter, citizens — east and west — released years of frustration by assaulting the Berlin Wall with sledgehammers.

In Czechoslovakia people also watched televised news of glasnost expectantly. Persecuted dissidents had maintained their critique of Communist rule. In an open letter to the Czechoslovak Communist Party leadership, playwright Václav Havel accused Marxist-Leninist rule of making people materialistic and indifferent to public life. In 1977, Havel, along with a group of fellow intellectuals and workers, signed Charter 77, a public protest against the regime that resulted in the arrest of the signers. In the mid-1980s, they and the wider population heard Gorbachev on television calling for free speech. Protesters clamored for democracy, but the government turned the police on them, arresting activists in January 1989 for commemorating the death of Jan Palach. The turning point came in November 1989 when, in response to police beatings of students, Alexander Dubček, leader of the Prague Spring of 1968, addressed the crowds in Prague's Wenceslas Square with a call to oust the Stalinists from the government. Almost immediately, the Communist leadership resigned. Capping what became known as the "velvet revolution" for its lack of bloodshed, the formerly Communist-dominated parliament elevated Havel to the presidency.

From the mid-1960s on, Nicolae Ceaușescu had ruled Romania as the harshest dictator in Communist Europe since Stalin. In the name of modernization, he destroyed whole villages; to build up the population, he outlawed contraceptives and abortions, a

November 1989: East Germany Meets West Germany
The fall of the Berlin Wall and the "iron curtain" separating the Soviet from the western bloc was a joyous occasion across Europe, but nowhere more so than in Germany. Divided from one another into two countries after World War II, Germans would later find that reunification was a problem, bringing unemployment and social dislocation. In November 1989, however, West Germans lined up to welcome their fellow citizens traveling from the east to see what life was like beyond the Soviet sphere. (ullstein bild / Bildarchiv / The Granger Collection, NYC — All rights reserved.)

restriction that led to the abandonment of tens of thousands of children. He preached the virtues of a very slim body so that he could cut rations and use the savings for buying private castles and building himself an enormous palace in Bucharest. To this end, he tore down entire neighborhoods and dozens of historical buildings and crushed opponents of the gaudy project to make it appear popular. Yet in early December 1989, workers demonstrated against the dictatorial government, and the army turned on Ceauşescu loyalists. On Christmas Day, viewers watched on television as the dictator and his wife were tried by a military court and then executed. For many, the death of Ceauşescu meant that the very worst of communism was over.

> **REVIEW QUESTION** How and why did the balance of world power change during the 1980s?

Conclusion

The collapse of communism in the Soviet satellites surprised the world, for U.S.-bloc analysts had reported throughout the 1980s that the Soviet empire was in dangerously robust health. But no one should have been unaware of dissent or economic discontent.

Since the 1960s, rebellious youth, ethnic and racial minorities, and women had all been condemning conditions across the West, along with criticizing the threat posed by the cold war. By the early 1980s, wars in Vietnam and Afghanistan, protests against scarcity in the Soviet bloc, the power of oil-producing states, and the growing political force of Islam had cost the superpowers their resources and reputations. Margaret

Mapping the West The Collapse of Communism in Europe, 1989–1990

The 1989 overthrow of the Communist Party in the USSR satellite countries of eastern Europe occurred with surprising rapidity. The transformation began when Polish voters tossed out Communist Party leaders in June 1989, and then accelerated in September when thousands of East Germans fled to Hungary, Poland, and Czechoslovakia. Between October and December, Communist regimes were replaced in East Germany, Czechoslovakia, Bulgaria, and Romania. Within three years, the Baltic states would declare their independence, the USSR itself would dissolve, and the breakup of Yugoslavia would lead to war in the Balkans.

Thatcher in Britain and Ronald Reagan in the United States tried to put their post-industrial and cold war houses in order. Mikhail Gorbachev's policies of glasnost and perestroika in the Soviet Union — aimed at political and economic improvements — brought on collapse.

Glasnost and perestroika were supposed to bring about the high levels of prosperity enjoyed outside the Soviet bloc. Across the West, including the USSR, an unprecedented set of technological developments had transformed businesses, space exploration, and the functioning of government. Technological advances also had an enormous impact on everyday life. Work changed as society reached a stage called postindustrial, in which the service sector predominated. New patterns of family life, new relationships among the generations, and revised standards for sexual behavior also characterized these years. It was only in the United States and western Europe, however, that the full consumer benefits of postindustrialization reached ordinary people. The attainment of a thoroughgoing consumer, service, and high-tech society demanded levels of efficiency, coordination, and cooperation unknown in the Soviet bloc.

Many complained, nonetheless, about the dramatic changes resulting from postindustrial development. The protesters of the late 1960s addressed postindustrial society's concentrations of bureaucratic and industrial power (often enabled by technology), social inequality, and environmental degradation. In the Soviet sphere, protests were continuous but were little heeded until the collapse of Soviet domination of eastern Europe in 1989. Soon communism would be overturned in the USSR itself. However, the triumph of democracy in the former Soviet empire opened an era of painful adjustment for hundreds of millions of people. Amid this rapid change was the growing awareness — via technology's instantaneous coverage of events across the globe — that the world's peoples were more tightly connected than ever before.

Review Questions

1. What were the technological and scientific advances of the 1960s and 1970s, and how did they change human life and society?
2. How did Western society and culture change in the postindustrial age?
3. What were the main issues for protesters in the 1960s, and how did governments address them?
4. How and why did the balance of world power change during the 1980s?

Making Connections

1. What were the differences between industrial society of the late nineteenth century and postindustrial society of the late twentieth century?
2. Why were there so many protests, acts of terrorism, and uprisings across the West in the decades between 1960 and 1990?
3. What have been the long-term consequences of Communist rule in the Soviet bloc between 1917 and 1989?
4. How did technology shape politics over the course of the twentieth century?

■ For practice quizzes and other study tools, visit the **Online Study Guide** at bedfordstmartins.com/huntconcise.

■ For primary-source material from this period, see *Sources of the Making of the West*, Fourth Edition.

■ For Web sites, images, and documents related to topics in this chapter, visit *Make History* at bedfordstmartins.com/huntconcise.

Suggested References

The history-changing events of the 1960s to 1989 ran the gamut from life-changing technology to dramatic political upheavals — all of them chronicled in the innovative books below. The story of television in post-uprising Czechoslovakia illustrates that even dictatorships used this new technology to "soften" its control.

Bauer, Martin W., and George Gaskell, eds. *Biotechnology: The Making of a Global Controversy.* 2002.

Bren, Paulina. *The Greengrocer and His TV: The Culture of Communism after the 1968 Prague Spring.* 2010.

Carter, David. *Stonewall: The Riots that Sparked the Gay Rights Movement.* 2011.

Chaplin, Tamara. *Turning On the Mind: French Philosophers on Television.* 2007.

Fink, Carole, et al. *1968: The World Transformed.* 1998.

*Freedman, Estelle B. *The Essential Feminist Reader.* 2007.

TIMELINE

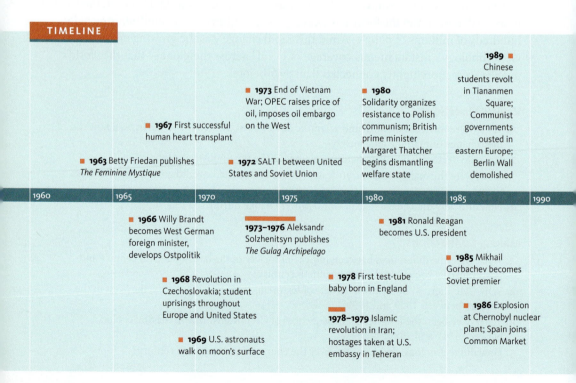

- **1963** Betty Friedan publishes *The Feminine Mystique*
- **1966** Willy Brandt becomes West German foreign minister, develops Ostpolitik
- **1967** First successful human heart transplant
- **1968** Revolution in Czechoslovakia; student uprisings throughout Europe and United States
- **1969** U.S. astronauts walk on moon's surface
- **1972** SALT I between United States and Soviet Union
- **1973** End of Vietnam War; OPEC raises price of oil, imposes oil embargo on the West
- **1973–1976** Aleksandr Solzhenitsyn publishes *The Gulag Archipelago*
- **1978** First test-tube baby born in England
- **1978–1979** Islamic revolution in Iran; hostages taken at U.S. embassy in Teheran
- **1980** Solidarity organizes resistance to Polish communism; British prime minister Margaret Thatcher begins dismantling welfare state
- **1981** Ronald Reagan becomes U.S. president
- **1985** Mikhail Gorbachev becomes Soviet premier
- **1986** Explosion at Chernobyl nuclear plant; Spain joins Common Market
- **1989** Chinese students revolt in Tiananmen Square; Communist governments ousted in eastern Europe; Berlin Wall demolished

1960   1965   1970   1975   1980   1985   1990

Green Parties Worldwide: http://www.greens.org

Hadley, Louisa, and Elizabeth Ho, eds. *Thatcher & After: Margaret Thatcher and Her Afterlife in Contemporary Culture.* 2011.

Harvey, Brian. *Europe's Space Program: To Ariane and Beyond.* 2003.

Horn, Gerd-Rainer. *The Spirit of 68: Rebellion in Western Europe and North America, 1956–1976.* 2007.

Kenney, Padraic. *Carnival of Revolution: Central Europe, 1989.* 2002.

Kotkin, Steven. *Armageddon Averted: Soviet Collapse, 1970–2000.* 2008.

Natalicchi, Giorgio. *Wiring Europe: Reshaping the European Telecommunications Regime.* 2001.

Ouimet, Matthew J. *The Rise and Fall of the Brezhnev Doctrine in Soviet Foreign Policy.* 2003.

Suri, Jeremy. *Power and Protest: Global Revolution and the Rise of Détente.* 2003.

Varon, Jeremy. *Bringing the War Home: The Weather Underground, the Red Army Faction, and Revolutionary Violence in the Sixties and Seventies.* 2004.

*Primary source.

A New Globalism

1989 to the Present

THÉRÈSE IS A CONGOLESE IMMIGRANT to France who arrived in Paris in the late 1970s with the help of a brother who worked for an airline. Thérèse had been well-known in Africa as the teenage girlfriend of pop singer Bozi Boziana, who wrote a hit song about her. But Congo's political instability had made her search for safety in Paris. Once there, Thérèse remained famous among African immigrants because she ran *nganda,* or informal bars, for them. Like Thérèse, the immigrants who frequent her nganda are often Congolese and other Africans who have settled in Paris, many of them illegally. They flock to her nganda because they like her stylish dress, the African food she cooks, the African music she plays, and the African products she sells. Many of Thérèse's small bars and eateries have flourished, only to be closed down by landlords who want more of her handsome profits or who object to her running an unlicensed café. Despite such obstacles, Thérèse keeps business going by moving her faithful clientele around her Paris neighborhood from basement to shop front to spare room. Thérèse is a new global citizen, counting on networks back home for supplies, constantly on the move because she lives on the margins of legality, and always striving to make a good living.

Thérèse's story is just one example of the ways in which people in the post–cold war world crossed national boundaries while maintaining crucial ties around the globe. The end of the cold war rivalry between the superpowers paved the way for a more intimately connected world. In the 1990s, globalization advanced further with the dramatic collapse of communism in Yugoslavia and then of the Soviet Union itself. The world was no longer divided in two by heavily guarded borders and hostile cold war propaganda, allowing nations and individuals more opportunity to trade and interact freely. The Common Market transformed itself into the European Union, which from 2004 on admitted many

Global Citizens

The world's migrants at the turn of the millennium sought safety, education, or jobs in the West's manufacturing and service occupations. Like these young immigrants from Senegal who are sharing a meal at a café in Paris, they also appreciated Western amenities. Children of immigrants were sometimes disillusioned, however, not wanting the life of extreme sacrifice that their parents had lived. Their frustrations at not being accepted as full citizens occasionally erupted into protest and even violence. (© Directphoto.org / Alamy.)

953

states from the former Soviet bloc. The telecommunication systems put in place in the 1960s advanced **globalization**, binding peoples and cultures together in an ever more complicated social and economic web. The World Wide Web and its offspring social networking even united them to enact stunning social and political change.

The global age brought the vast national and international migration of tens of millions of people, an expanding global marketplace, and rapid cultural exchange of popular music, books, films, and television shows. On the negative side, the new globalization also brought lethal disasters such as epidemic diseases, environmental deterioration, genocide, and terrorism. Nations in the West faced competition from the rising economic power of Asia and Latin America. International business mergers accelerated in the 1990s, advancing efficiencies but often threatening jobs. Millions of workers in this interlinked economy discovered that the global age was one of both opportunities and insecurities.

The end of superpower rivalry resulted in the dominance of a single power, the United States, in world affairs. As the United States sought to exercise global power through warfare, however, European states started to resist, just as the Soviet satellites had pulled away from the USSR. New forces, including the economic power of non-Western countries and the cultural might of Islam, created new centers of influence. Some observers predicted a huge "clash of civilizations" because of sharp differences between Western civilization and cultures beyond the West. Others, however, saw a different clash — one between a Europe reborn after decades of disastrous wars as a peace-seeking group of nations confronting an imperial United States that, like Europe in the nineteenth century, was increasingly at war around the world. Globalization in either of these scenarios could bring global splintering or even catastrophic warfare.

Such a dire future was not on most Westerners' minds, but globalization did bring economic struggles for many. Beginning in 2007, the global economy collapsed, resulting in widespread hardship. As Asia and other non-Western parts of the world recovered, it became apparent that a reenergizing of Western capacities was needed. Illegal immigrants began leaving Europe and the United States as unemployment climbed. Whether Thérèse was among them, we do not know.

CHAPTER FOCUS How has globalization been both a unifying and a divisive influence on the West in the twenty-first century?

Collapse of the Soviet Union and Its Aftermath

Following the fall of communist regimes in eastern Europe, rejection of communism spread in the 1990s, turning events in unpredictable, even violent directions. Yugoslavia and then the Soviet Union itself fell apart as ethnic groups began to demand independence. The USSR had held together more than one hundred ethnicities, and the five republics of Soviet Central Asia were home to fifty million Muslims. For more than a century, successive governments had attempted to instill Russian and Soviet culture, but the policy of Russification failed to build any heartfelt allegiance, leading to a swift collapse of the USSR. In Yugoslavia, Communist rulers had also enforced unity among

religious and ethnic groups, and intermarriage among them occurred regularly. Beginning in the unstable years of the early 1990s, however, ambitious politicians seeking to build a following whipped up ethnic hatreds, making it unclear whether peaceful, democratic nations would emerge.

The Breakup of Yugoslavia

In Yugoslavia, tensions erupted in 1990 after Serbia's president **Slobodan Milosevic** began to promote control of the entire Yugoslav federation by ethnic Serbs as a replacement for communism. Other ethnic groups in Yugoslavia resisted Milosevic's militant pro-Serb nationalism and called for secession. "Slovenians . . . have one more reason to say they are in favor of independence," warned one of them in the face of rising Serb claims to dominate the small republics that comprised Yugoslavia (Map 29.1). In the summer of 1991, two of these republics, Slovenia and Croatia, seceded. Croatia, however, lost almost a quarter of its territory when the Yugoslav army, eager to enforce Serbian supremacy, invaded. A devastating civil war broke out in Bosnia-Herzegovina when the republic's Muslim majority tried to create a multicultural and multiethnic state. With the covert military support of Milosevic's government, Bosnian Serb men formed a guerrilla army and gained the upper hand. A United Nations (UN) arms embargo prevented the Bosnian Muslims from equipping their forces even though the Serbs at the time were massacring them.

Relentless violence in the Balkans was inflicted on neighbors in the name of creating "ethnically pure" states in a region where ethnic mixture, not ethnic purity, was the norm. During the 1990s, civilians died by the tens of thousands as Serbs under Milosevic's leadership pursued a policy they called **ethnic cleansing** — that is, genocide — against non-Serb ethnicities. Serb men raped women to leave them pregnant with Serb babies as another form of conquest. In 1995, Croatian forces murdered Serbs who had helped seize land from Croatia. That same year, the Serbs retaliated by slaughtering eight thousand Muslim boys and men in the town of Srebrenica: "Kill the lot," the commander of the Serb forces ordered. Military units on all sides destroyed libraries and museums, architectural treasures like the Mostar Bridge, and cities rich with history such as Dubrovnik. Many in the West explained violence in the Balkans as part of "age-old" blood feuds typical of a backward, "almost Asian" society. Others saw using genocide to achieve national power as simply a modern political practice that had been employed by the imperial powers and by other politicians, including Adolf Hitler.

Peacekeepers were put in place, but they turned their backs on such atrocities as the Srebrenica massacre and let them proceed to their horrific end. Late in the 1990s, Serb forces moved to attack Muslims of Albanian ethnicity living in the Yugoslav province of Kosovo. From 1997 to 1999, crowds of Albanian Kosovars fled their homes as Serb militias and the Yugoslav army slaughtered the civilian population. North Atlantic Treaty Organization (NATO) pilots bombed the region to drive back the army and Serb militias, but people throughout the world felt that this intervention came far too late. After a new regime in Serbia emerged alongside the independent republics of Bosnia and

Map 29.1 The Former Yugoslavia, c. 2000
After a decade of destructive civil war, UN forces and UN-brokered agreements attempted to protect the civilians of the former Yugoslavia from the brutal consequences of post-Communist rule. Ambitious politicians, most notably Slobodan Milosevic, used the twentieth-century Western strategy of fostering ethnic and religious hatred as a powerful tool to build support for themselves while making those favoring peace look softhearted and unfit to rule. What issues of national identity does the breakup of Yugoslavia indicate?

Croatia, Milosevic was turned over to the International Court of Justice, or World Court, in the Netherlands to be tried for crimes against humanity. Across a fragmenting eastern Europe, hateful racial, ethnic, and religious rhetoric influenced political agendas in the post-Communist states.

The Soviet Union Comes Apart

In less than three years after the overthrow of communism in its eastern European satellites, the once powerful Soviet Union itself fell apart. Perestroika had failed to revitalize the Soviet economy; people confronted corruption and soaring prices, and

Mikhail Gorbachev's planned "transition to the market [economy]" satisfied no one. In 1991, the Russian parliament elected Boris Yeltsin over a Communist candidate as president of the Russian Republic — the last straw for a group of eight antireform hardliners, including the powerful head of the Soviet secret police, or KGB, who attempted a coup. As coup leaders held Gorbachev under house arrest, Yeltsin defiantly stood atop a tank outside the Russian parliament building and called for mass resistance. Residents of Moscow and Leningrad filled the streets, and units of the army defected. People used fax machines and computers to coordinate internal resistance and alert the world. Citizen action defeated the coup and prevented a return to the Communist past.

After the failed coup, the Soviet Union disintegrated. People tore down statues of Soviet heroes; Yeltsin outlawed the Communist Party newspaper, *Pravda,* and sealed the KGB's files. At the end of August 1991, the Soviet parliament suspended operations of the Communist Party itself. The Baltic states of Estonia, Latvia, and Lithuania declared their independence in September; other republics within the USSR followed their lead. Bloody ethnic conflicts and anti-Semitism revived as political tools. On December 31, 1991, the final agreements dissolved the USSR and twelve of the fifteen former Soviet republics banded together to form the Commonwealth of Independent States (CIS) (Map 29.2).

Weakened by the coup attempt, Gorbachev abandoned politics. Yeltsin stepped in and accelerated the change to a market economy, but the Russian economy entered an ever-deepening crisis. Yeltsin's political allies, the military, and bureaucrats bought up or simply confiscated national resources. A new class of super-wealthy Russians called oligarchs was born. Yeltsin's own family appeared to be deeply implicated in stealing the wealth once seen as belonging to all the people. Meanwhile social disorder prevailed as organized criminals interfered in the distribution of goods and services and assassinated legitimate entrepreneurs, legislators, and anyone who criticized them. Amid these scandals, Yeltsin resigned on December 31, 1999. He appointed a new protégé, **Vladimir Putin**, as interim president.

Putin was a little-known functionary in Russia's new security apparatus, which had evolved from the old KGB. In the presidential elections of spring 2000, Putin surprised everyone when the electorate voted him in. Though associated with the Yeltsin family corruption, he declared himself committed to legality. "Democracy," he announced, "is the dictatorship of law." With a solid mandate, Putin proceeded to drive from power the biggest figures in regional and central government, usually the henchmen of the oligarchs. Putin's popularity rose even higher when the government arrested the billionaire head of the Yukos Oil Company in 2003. The pillaging of the country — the source of ordinary citizens' recent suffering — was finally being punished. According to critics, however, Putin was merely transferring Russia's natural resources and other assets to himself and his own cronies. He also continued the destructive war that Yeltsin had started in Chechnya (a resource-rich province that sought independence), causing casualties, atrocities, disease, and the physical devastation of Chechen cities.

Map 29.2 Countries of the Former Soviet Union, c. 2000
Following an agreement of December 1991, twelve of the countries of the former Soviet Union formed the Commonwealth of Independent States (CIS). Dominated by Russia and with Ukraine often disputing this domination, the CIS worked to bring about common economic and military policies. As nation-states dissolved rapidly in the late twentieth century, regional alliances and coordination were necessary to meet the political and economic challenges of the global age.

Toward a Market Economy

Developing free markets and republican governments initially brought misery to Russia and the rest of eastern Europe. The conditions of everyday life grew increasingly dire as salaries went unpaid, food remained in short supply, and essential services disintegrated. In 1994, inflation soared at a rate of 14 percent a month in Russia, while industrial production dropped by 15 percent. Hotel lobbies became clogged with prostitutes because women were the first people fired as governments privatized industry and cut service jobs. Unpaid soldiers sold their services to the Russian Mafia. Ordinary citizens lined the sidewalks of major cities selling their household possessions. "Anything and everything is for sale," one critic noted at the time.

There were, of course, many pluses to the new system of government. People with enough money were able to travel freely for the first time, and the media were initially more open than ever before. Some workers, many of them young and highly educated, frequently emigrated to more prosperous parts of the world, further depleting the human resources of the former Communist states. At the same time, as the different republics that had once composed the Soviet Union became independent, the hundreds of thousands of ethnic Russians who had earlier been sent by the state to colonize these regions returned to Russia as refugees, putting further demands on the chaotic Russian economy.

Post-Soviet Shopping
The economy of the former Soviet bloc changed dramatically after the fall of communism. Insiders and Western firms bought up out-of-date factories and natural resources for very little money, often installing modern labor-saving equipment. As prosperity grew, megastores and luxury malls sprang up for eager consumers. The one above, converted from the old Soviet GUM store in Moscow, catered to the tastes of the very wealthy. (© TASS / Sovoto.)

For many in the former Soviet bloc, the first priority was getting their economies running again — but on new terms. Given the spiraling misery, however, many opposed the introduction of new market-oriented measures. With the collective farms up for sale, most farmers on them faced landlessness and starvation. The countries that experienced the most success were those in which farmers already sold their produce on the open market or in which independent entrepreneurs or even government factories dealt in international trade. Hungary and Poland thus emerged from the transition with less strain, because both had adopted some free-market practices early on. They set up business schools and worked to attract foreign capital, anchoring themselves securely to the world economy.

In contrast, the former Soviet Union itself became, in the words of one critic, a vast "kleptocracy" in the 1990s as the country's resources — theoretically the property of all the people — were stolen for individual gain. An economist described the new scene as "piratization" rather than privatization. In this regard, one Polish adviser noted, democracy and a successful economic transition went hand in hand, for without a powerful representative government, former officials would simply operate as criminals. Corruption fed on the Soviet system of off-the-books dealing, tax evasion, bribery, and outright theft. Additionally, because industry had not benefited from technological change or competition, free trade often meant closing factories and firing all the workers.

A region-wide brain drain followed in a rush of migration from eastern Europe to western Europe, often involving those with marketable skills. "I knew in my heart that communism would collapse," said one Romanian ex-dissident, commenting sadly on the exodus of youth from his country, "but it never crossed my mind that the future would look like this." The everyday advantages of living in western Europe included safe water, adequate housing, personal safety, and at least a minimal level of social services. Although western Europe was now on a firm neoliberal course of reducing spending on welfare-state programs, most benefits had disappeared entirely in former Communist countries. Day-care centers, kindergartens, and homes for the elderly closed their doors, and health care deteriorated. In these circumstances, the benefits of citizenship in western European countries were a powerful attraction.

International Politics and the New Russia

Although Gorbachev had pulled the Soviet Union out of its disastrous war with Afghanistan, his successors opened another war to prevent the secession of oil-rich Chechnya and to provide a nationalist rallying cry during the difficult transition. For decades, Chechens had been integrated into the Soviet bureaucracy and military, but in the fall of 1991, the National Congress of the Chechen People took over the government of the region from the USSR to gain the same kind of independence achieved by other former Soviet states. In June 1992, Chechen rebels got control of massive numbers of Russian weapons, including airplanes, tanks, and some forty thousand automatic weapons and machine guns.

Assassination in Moscow

In 2009, Russian citizens honored journalist and human rights activist Anna Politkovskaya, assassinated three years earlier in her Moscow apartment building. Politkovskaya relentlessly investigated the atrocities during the war in Chechnya as well as the corruption in the Putin government. Honest journalism in post-Soviet Russia was dangerous; scores of journalists were murdered in the twenty years following the collapse of communism, and many of Politkovskaya's collaborators were also killed. Several men were arrested, tried, and acquitted in the Politkovskaya case. (AP Photo / Pavel Golovkin.)

In December 1994, the Russian government invaded. An official defended the war: "We now need a small victorious war . . . [to] raise the President's rating." Despite the Russian population's opposition to the war, Chechnya's capital city of Grozny was pounded to bits. Casualties mounted not only among Chechen civilians but also among Russians. In 2002, Chechen loyalists took hundreds of hostages in a Moscow theater; Chechen suicide bombers blew up airplanes, buses, and apartment buildings as Putin pursued the Chechen war into the twenty-first century.

Putin expanded Soviet influence in Ukraine, Belarus, India, and China as well by taking advantage of the politics of energy. Russia had the commodities—especially oil and gas—needed to sustain the fantastic growth of emerging industries around the world, and by 2005 surging commodity prices were making Russia once again a real player in global politics—now because of its economic strength. Democratic values, however, were not put into practice. Critics of the government were mercilessly assassinated, and newspapers and broadcast media were closed down. Still, Putin's popularity remained steady, as the Russian government used its new wealth to refurbish cities and everyday life grew easier. Putin served as prime minister between 2008 and 2012 because the constitution forbade more than two consecutive terms as president. Despite calls for honest elections, he was returned to the presidency for a third term in 2012.

REVIEW QUESTION What were the major issues facing the former Soviet bloc in the 1990s and early 2000s?

The Nation-State in a Global Age

Although the end of the Soviet system fractured one large regional economy, it gave a boost to European unification. In the 1990s and early 2000s, the European Economic Community (Common Market), which renamed itself the European Community in 1993, was healthy and economically robust compared with other regions of the world, especially those plagued with civil wars and violence. The European Community's economic success provoked the formation of the North American Free Trade Agreement (NAFTA), which established a free-trade zone of the United States, Canada, and Mexico. The nationalist function of cities diminished as major urban areas like London and Paris became packed with people from other countries. Organizations for world governance grew in influence alongside the strength of large regional economic blocs. There was resistance to these trends from those who wanted to preserve their own traditions and who felt the loss of a secure, face-to-face, local way of life.

Europe Looks beyond the Nation-State

The Common Market changed dramatically after the demise of European communism. In 1992, the twelve countries of the Common Market ended national distinctions in certain business activities, border controls, and transportation, effectively closing down passport controls at their shared borders. Citizens of the member countries carried a uniform burgundy-colored passport, and governments, whether municipal or national, had to treat all member nations' firms the same. In 1994, by the terms of the **Maastricht Treaty**, the European Community became the **European Union (EU)**, and in 1999 a common currency — the **euro** — came into being, first for transactions among financial institutions and then in 2002 for general use by the public. Common policies governed everything from the number of American soap operas aired on television to pollution controls on automobiles to the health warnings on cigarette packages. The EU parliament convened regularly in Strasbourg, France, and with the adoption of a common currency, an EU central bank came into being to guide interest rates and economic policy.

The EU was seen as the key to a peaceful Europe. "People with the same money don't go to war with one another," said a French nuclear scientist about the introduction of the euro. Greece pushed for the admission of its traditional enemy Turkey in 2002 and 2003 despite the warnings of a former president of France that a predominantly Muslim country could never fit in with the Christian traditions of EU members. Both Greece and Turkey stood to benefit by having their disputes adjudicated by the larger body of European members, principally because they would be able to cut that part of their defense budget used for weapons directed against each other. Like the rivalry between Germany and France, that between Turkey and Greece, it was hoped, would dissolve if bound by the strong economic and political ties of the EU. As of 2012, however, Turkey was still awaiting progress on its application.

Drawbacks to EU membership remained. The EU enforced no common regulatory practices, and common economic policies such as limits on budget deficits were not al-

ways observed. Individual governments set up hurdles and barriers for businesses, obstructing, for example, transnational mergers they did not like. A government might block the acquisition of a company based on its own soil no matter what the advantages to shareholders, the economy, the workforce, or the consumers of unified Europe. Nonetheless, countries of eastern Europe clamored to join, working hard to meet not only the EU's fiscal requirements but also those pertaining to human rights and social policy (Map 29.3).

The collapse of the Soviet system advanced privatization of eastern European industry, and governments sold basic services to the highest bidder. Often, only companies in the wealthy western countries of the EU could afford to purchase eastern European assets. For example, the Czech Republic in 2001 sold its major energy distributor Transgaz and eight other regional distributors for 4.1 billion euros to a German firm. Lower wages

Map 29.3 The European Union in 2011
The European Union (EU) appeared to increase the economic health of its members despite the rocky start of its common currency, the euro. The EU helped end the traditional competition between its members and facilitated trade and worker migration by providing common passports and business laws, and open borders. But many critics feared a loss of cultural distinctiveness among peoples in an age of mass communications.

and costs of doing business in eastern Europe attracted foreign investment, especially to Poland, the Czech Republic, Hungary, and Slovenia — the most developed state spun off from Yugoslavia. For these reasons, membership in the EU became attractive to eastern Europe. There were hopes that membership would encourage further investment, advance modernization, and simultaneously protect national economies.

In 2004, the EU admitted ten new members — the Czech Republic, Cyprus, Estonia, Hungary, Latvia, Lithuania, Malta, Poland, Slovakia, and Slovenia — and in 2007 it welcomed Bulgaria and Romania. Just before its admission to the EU, Poland's standard of living was 39 percent of EU standards, up from 33 percent in 1995. The Czech Republic and Hungary were at 55 and 50 percent, respectively. In all three cases these figures masked the discrepancy between the ailing countryside and thriving cities. Citizens in eastern Europe were not always happy at the prospect of joining the EU. A retiree foresaw the cost of beer going up and added, "If I wanted to join anything in the West, I would have defected." Still others felt that having just established an independent national identity, they should not allow themselves to be swallowed up once again. People in older member states were having second thoughts, too: in the spring of 2005, a majority of voters in France and the Netherlands rejected a complex draft constitution that would have strengthened EU ties. Commentators attributed the rejection to popular anger at the EU bureaucracy's failure to consult ordinary people in this and other decision making.

Although still weak by comparison with most of western Europe, the economic life of eastern Europe had in fact picked up considerably by 2000. In contrast to the massive layoffs, soaring inflation, and unpaid salaries of the first post-Communist years, in 2002 residents of Poland, Slovenia, and Estonia had purchasing power some 40 percent higher than in 1989. Outsourcing by international companies began to flourish across the region, increasing opportunities for those with language and commercial skills. Even in countries with the weakest economies — Latvia, Bulgaria, and Romania — a greater number of residents enjoyed such modern conveniences as freezers, computers, and portable telephones. Shopping malls sprang up, mostly around capital cities, and superstores like the furniture giant IKEA and the electronics firm Electroworld became a consumer's paradise to those long starved of goods. "When Electroworld opened in Budapest [April 2002], it provoked a riot. Two hundred thousand people crowded to get in the doors," reported one amazed observer. Critics worried that eastern Europeans had fallen prey to "consumania," that is, uncontrolled materialism and frenzied shopping. For consumers, however, learning to read labels and to compare prices offered by superstores was a sign of belonging to a global community of those free and prosperous enough to consume. Many proudly believed they had left Communist poverty behind.

Globalizing Cities and Fragmenting Nations

After the collapse of communism, the West experienced the globalization of major cities. These were cities whose institutions, functions, and visions were overwhelmingly global rather than regional or national. They contained stock markets, legal firms, in-

surance companies, financial service organizations, and other enterprises that operated worldwide and that were linked to similar enterprises in other global cities. Within these cities, high-level decision makers set global economic policy and enacted global business. The presence of high-powered and high-income global businesspeople made urban life extremely costly, driving middle managers and engineers to lower-priced living quarters in the suburbs, which nonetheless provided good schools and other amenities for well-educated white-collar earners. Crowded into the slums of global cities and the poorer suburbs were the lowest paid of service providers — the maintenance, domestic, and other workers whose menial labor was essential around the clock to the needs and comfort of those at the top.

Global cities became centers for migration of highly skilled and more modest workers alike. Paris, London, Moscow, and New York were global spaces in direct and constant contact with institutions, businesses, and governments around the world. In contrast, citizens of more locally oriented cities took pride in maintaining a distinctive national culture or local sense of community and often denounced global cities as rootless. Critics also pointed out that the concentrated wealth of such cities came at the expense of poorer people in southern countries, and that their citizens lacked patriotic focus on national causes. Global cities were often the base for diasporas of prosperous migrants, such as the estimated ninety thousand Japanese in England in the mid-1990s who staffed Japan's thriving global businesses. Because these migrants did not aim to become citizens, global cities were said to produce a "deterritorialization of identities" — meaning that many city dwellers lacked both a national and a local sense of themselves, so much did they travel the world or deal worldwide.

Ironically, as globalization took hold economically and culturally, there came to be more nation-states in Europe in 2000 than there had been in 1945. Claims of ethnic distinctiveness caused individual nation-states to break apart and separatist movements — like that in Chechnya — to grow. Despite two centuries aimed at unification of the Slavs, for example, Slavs separated themselves from one another in the 1990s and early twenty-first century. Yugoslavia came apart into several states (as discussed on page 955), and in 1993, Czechoslovakia split into the Czech Republic and Slovakia (Map 29.3, page 963).

Activists also launched movements for regional independence in France, Italy, and Spain. Some Bretons (residents of the historical French province of Brittany) and Corsicans demanded independence from France, the Corsicans violently attacking national officials. Sharp cultural differences threatened to split Belgium in two. Basque nationalists in northern Spain assassinated tourists, police, and other public servants in an effort to gain autonomy, and although in 2005 they publicly renounced terrorism, violence often resurfaced. The push for an independent northern Italy began somewhat halfheartedly, but when politicians saw its attractiveness to voters, they loudly publicized the urgent need for secession. As cities globalized and nations fragmented, new combinations of local, national, and global identities took shape. Such changing identities, plus the overall expansion of the EU, called the nation-state into question.

Global Organizations

Supranational organizations, some of them regulating international politics and others addressing finance and social issues, became more plentiful and influential. The World Bank, the International Monetary Fund (IMF), and the World Trade Organization (WTO) raised money from national governments and dealt, for example, with the terms of trade among countries and the economic well-being of individual peoples. The IMF made loans to developing countries on the condition that those countries restructure their economies according to neoliberal principles. Other supranational organizations were charitable foundations, think tanks, or service-based organizations acting independently of governments, many of them based in Europe and the United States; they were called **nongovernmental organizations (NGOs)**. Because some of these groups — the Rockefeller Foundation, the Ford Foundation, and the Open Society Foundation, for example — controlled so much money, NGOs often had considerable international power. Some charitable and activist NGOs, like the French-based Doctors Without Borders, depended on global contributions and used them to provide medical attention in such places as the former Yugoslavia, where people facing war had no other medical help. Small, locally based NGOs excelled at inspiring grassroots activism, while the larger NGOs were often criticized for influencing government policies with no regard for democratic processes.

Not everyone supported or was pleased with the process of globalization; some people formed activist groups to attack globalization or to influence its course. In 1998, the Association for the Taxation of Financial Transactions and Aid to Citizens (ATTAC) worked to block the control of globalization by the forces of high finance, declaring: "Commercial totalitarianism is not free trade." ATTAC had as its major policy goal to tax international financial transactions (just as the purchase of household necessities was taxed) and to create with the tax a fund for people living in poor countries. Some governments began to suggest such a tax themselves with the aim of raising much-needed revenue, not to help the poor. Another globally known opponent, French farmer José Bové, protested the opening of McDonald's chains in France and destroyed stocks of genetically modified seeds: "The only regret I have now," Bové claimed at his trial in 2003, "is that I didn't destroy more of it." Bové went to jail, but he remained a hero to antiglobalism activists who saw him as an enemy of standardization and an honest champion, in his own words, of "good food."

REVIEW QUESTION What trends suggest that the nation-state was a declining institution at the beginning of the twenty-first century?

An Interconnected World's New Challenges

The rising tide of globalization ushered in as many challenges as opportunities. First, the health of the world's peoples and their environment came under a multipronged attack from nuclear disaster, acid rain, and surging population. Second, economic prosperity and physical safety continued to elude great masses of people, especially in the

southern half of the globe. Third, as suprastate organizations developed, transnational allegiances and religious and ethnic movements vied for power and influence. Finally, a devastating economic crisis that rippled from Wall Street across the globe challenged the traditional economic leadership of the United States and Europe even as Asia, the Middle East, and Latin America grew more prosperous.

The Problems of Pollution

By the early years of the twenty-first century, industrial growth continued to threaten the environment. The 1986 nuclear explosion at Chernobyl killed thirty-one people instantly; in the aftermath, levels of radioactivity rose for hundreds of miles in all directions and some fifteen thousand people perished over time from the effects of radiation. Moreover, as Russia opened up, it became clear that Soviet managers and officials had thrown toxic waste into thousands of square miles of lakes and rivers. Used nuclear fuel had been dumped in neighboring seas, and many nuclear and other tests had left entire regions of Asia unfit for human, animal, and plant life.

Other environmental problems had devastating global effects. Pollutants from fossil fuels such as natural gas, coal, and oil mixed with atmospheric moisture to produce acid rain, a poisonous brew that destroyed forests in industrial areas. In eastern Europe, the unchecked use of fossil fuels turned trees into brown skeletons and inflicted ailments such as chronic bronchial disease on children. In other areas, clearing the world's rain forests to develop the land for cattle grazing or for cultivation of cash crops depleted the global oxygen supply. By the late 1980s, scientists determined that the use of chlorofluorocarbons (CFCs), chemicals found in aerosol and refrigeration products, had blown a hole in the earth's ozone layer, the part of the blanket of atmospheric gases that prevents harmful ultraviolet rays from reaching the planet.

Simultaneously, automobile and industrial emissions of chemicals were infusing that thermal blanket. The buildup of CFCs, carbon dioxide, and other atmospheric pollutants produced what is known as a greenhouse effect that results in **global warming**, an increase in the temperature of the earth's lower atmosphere. Already in the 1990s, the Arctic pack ice was breaking up, and scientists predicted that global ice melting would raise sea levels by more than ten inches by 2100, flooding coastal areas, disturbing fragile ecosystems, and harming the freshwater supply. Already in 2012 important island nations such as the Maldives were menaced with disappearance because of rising water levels. Other results of the greenhouse effect included climatic extremes such as drought, drenching rain, and increasingly catastrophic weather events such as deadly storms.

Activism against unbridled industrial growth took decades to develop as an effective political force. Rachel Carson's powerful critique *Silent Spring* (1962) advocated the immediate rescue of rivers, forests, and the soil from the ravages of factories and chemical farming in the United States. In West Germany, environmentalism united members of older and younger generations around a political tactic called citizen initiatives, in which groups of people blocked plans for urban growth that menaced forests and

Smart Cars in Europe
The havoc caused by the oil crisis of the 1970s and the growing awareness of climate change in the latter part of the twentieth century spurred many European states to encourage the development of alternate sources of energy and transportation. Thus, by the twenty-first century, the landscape was dotted not only with windmills but also with tiny, highly fuel-efficient automobiles like the Smart car shown here. European governments also heavily taxed gasoline with the result that it cost twice as much or more than in the United States, thus further encouraging people to buy the Smart car rather than an SUV — a far rarer sight in Europe than in the United States. (© David Cooper / Toronto Star / ZUMA / Corbis.)

farmland. In 1979, the **Green Party** was founded in West Germany; soon the emergence of Green Party candidates across Europe forced other politicians to voice their concern for the environment.

Spurred by successful Green Party campaigns, Europeans attacked environmental problems on local and global levels. Some European cities — Frankfurt, for example — developed car-free zones, and in Paris, whenever automobile emissions reached dangerous levels, cars were banned from city streets until the emission levels receded. The Smart car, a very small car using reduced amounts of fuel, became fashionable in Europe. European cities also developed bicycle lanes on major city streets, and some cities in the United States followed their lead. To reduce dependence on fossil fuels, parts of Europe developed wind power to such an extent that 20 percent of some countries' electricity was generated by wind. Many cities in the West undertook extensive recycling of waste materials. By 1999, some eighty-four countries, including EU members, had signed the Kyoto Protocol, an international treaty whose signatories agreed to reduce their levels of emissions and other pollutants to specified targets. However, the United States, the world's second leading polluter after China, failed to ratify this agreement, suggesting that the West was fragmenting around basic values.

Population, Health, and Disease

The issue of population was as difficult in the early twenty-first century as it had been in the 1930s. Nations with less-developed economies struggled with the pressing problem of surging population, while Europe experienced more deaths than births after 1995. The less industrially developed countries accounted for 98 percent of worldwide population growth, in part because the spread of Western medicine enabled people there to live much longer than before. By late 1999, the earth's population had reached six billion, with a doubling forecast for 2045 (see "Taking Measure," below). Yet many European countries were facing problems related to an aging citizenry and a shortage of younger people to bring new ideas and promote change. In fact, Europe as a region had the lowest fertility in the world. The fertility rate in Italy and Spain was only 1.3 children per woman of reproductive age, far below the replacement level of 2.1 needed to maintain a steady population number. As a consequence, fewer young workers paid into the social security system to fund retirees' pensions and health care.

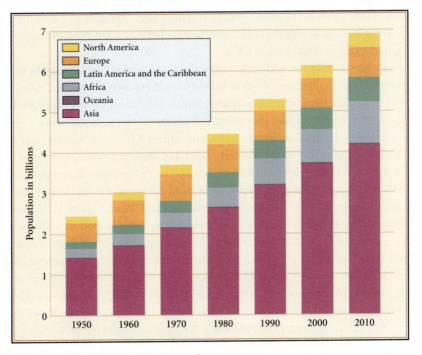

Taking Measure **World Population Growth, 1950–2010**

A major question in the twenty-first century is whether the global environment can sustain billions of people indefinitely. In the early modern period, local communities had lived according to unwritten rules that balanced population size with the productive capacities of individual farming regions. Centuries later, the same need for balance had reached global proportions. As fertility dropped around the planet because of contraception, population continued to grow because of improved health.

Population problems were especially urgent in Russia, where life expectancy was declining at a catastrophic rate from a peak of seventy years for Russian men in the mid-1970s to fifty-one years at the beginning of the twenty-first century. Heart disease and cancer were the leading causes of male death, and these stark death rates were generally attributed to increased drinking (one in seven men was an alcoholic in Russia), smoking, drug use, poor diet, and general stress. Between 1992 and 2010, the Russian population declined from 149 to 142 million. Meanwhile, fertility rates in the former Soviet bloc were also declining: the lowest levels of fertility in 2003 were in the Czech Republic and Ukraine (1.1 children per woman of reproductive age), and children in eastern Europe lived on average twelve years less than their counterparts in western Europe.

Good health was spread unevenly around the world. Western medicine brought better health to many in the less-developed world through the increased use of vaccines and drugs for diseases such as malaria and smallpox. However, half of all Africans lacked the basic requirements of well-being such as safe drinking water. Drought and poverty, along with the corruption of politicians in some cases, spread famine in Sudan, Somalia, Ethiopia, and elsewhere. Around the world, the poor and the unemployed suffered more chronic illnesses than those who were better off, but they received less care. Whereas in many parts of the world people still died from malnutrition and infectious diseases, in the West noncontagious illnesses (heart disease, autoimmune diseases, stroke, cancer, and depression) were more lethal.

Disease, like population and technology, operated on a global terrain. In the early 1980s, both Western values and Western technological expertise were challenged by the spread of a global epidemic disease: acquired immunodeficiency syndrome (AIDS). An incurable, highly virulent killer that effectively shuts down the body's entire immune system, AIDS initially afflicted heterosexuals in central Africa; the disease later turned up in Haitian immigrants to the United States and in homosexual men worldwide. Within a decade, AIDS became a global epidemic. The disease spread especially quickly and widely among the heterosexual populations of Africa and Asia, passed mainly by men to and through women, but in 2010 the U.S. capital, Washington, D.C., had a rate of infection as high as that in Africa. Protease-inhibiting drugs helped alleviate the symptoms, but the mounting global death toll made some equate AIDS with the Black Death of the fourteenth century. Treatment was often not provided to poor people living in sub-Saharan Africa and the slums of Asian cities. In addition to the AIDS pandemic, the deadly Ebola virus, severe acute respiratory syndrome (SARS), swine flu, and dozens of other viruses smoldered like a global conflagration in the making. Diseases as much as environmental dangers underscored the interconnectedness of the world's peoples.

North versus South?

During the 1980s and 1990s, world leaders tried to address the differences between the earth's northern and southern regions. Other than Australians and New Zealanders, southern peoples generally suffered lower living standards and measures of health than northerners. Emerging from colonial rule, environmental degradation, and economic

exploitation by northerners, citizens in the southern regions could not yet count on their governments to provide welfare services or education. Although organizations like the World Bank and the International Monetary Fund provided loans for economic development, the conditions tied to those loans, such as cutting government spending for education and health care, led to criticism.

Southern regions of the world experienced other barriers to economic development. Latin American nations grappled with government corruption, multibillion-dollar debt, widespread crime, and grinding poverty, though some countries — prominent among them Brazil — began to strengthen their economies by marketing their oil and other natural resources more effectively and by building administrative expertise among government officials. In contrast, Africa suffered from drought, famine, and civil war. In countries such as Rwanda, Somalia, and Sudan, the military rule, factionalism, and ethnic antagonism encouraged under imperialism produced a lethal mixture of conflict and genocide in the 1990s and early 2000s. Millions of people perished; others were left starving and homeless due to kleptocracies that drained revenues. In the face of these conditions, African nations began turning away from violence and dictatorship toward constitutional government and economic sustainability.

Radical Islam Meets the West

North–South antagonisms became evident in the rise of radical Islam, which often flourished where democracy and prosperity for the masses were missing. The Iranian hostage crisis that began in 1979 revealed nationalism and a strong anti-Western sentiment among Islamic fundamentalists. The charismatic leaders of the 1980s and 1990s — the ayatollah Ruhollah Khomeini in Iran, Libya's Muammar Qaddafi, Iraq's Saddam Hussein, and **Osama bin Laden**, a Saudi Arabian by birth and leader of the transnational terrorist organization al-Qaeda — variously promoted a pan-Islamic or (outside Iran) pan-Arabic world order that gathered increasing support. Khomeini's program — "Neither East, nor West, only the Islamic Republic" — had wide appeal. Renouncing the Westernization that had flourished under the shah, Khomeini's regime in Iran (whose population is predominantly Persian, not Arabic) required women once again to cover their bodies almost totally in special clothing, restricted their access to divorce, and eliminated a range of other rights for men and women alike. Buoyed by the prosperity that oil had brought, Islamic revolutionaries aimed to restore the pride and Islamic identity that imperialism had stripped from Middle Eastern men. Khomeini built widespread support among Shi'ite Muslims who, although they were numerous, had long been discriminated against by the Sunnis.

Power in the Middle East remained fragmented, however, as war plagued the region. In 1980, Saddam Hussein, fearing a rebellion from Shi'ites in Iraq, attacked Iran, in hopes of channeling Shi'ite discontent into a patriotic crusade against non-Arab Iranians. The United States provided Iraq with massive aid in the struggle against Iran, but eight years of combat, with extensive loss of life on both sides, ended in stalemate. In 1990, Saddam tested the post–cold war waters by invading neighboring Kuwait in hopes of annexing

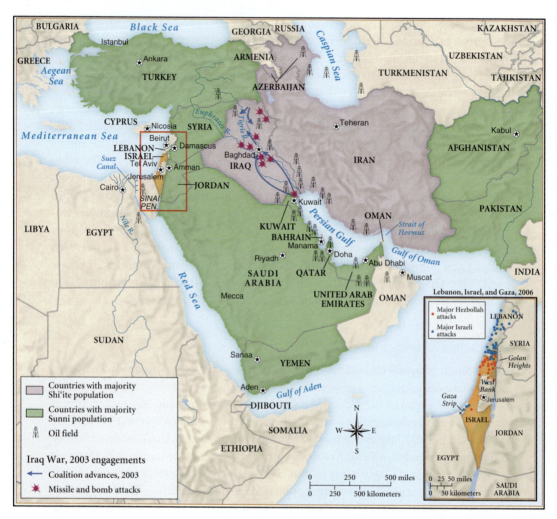

Map 29.4 The Middle East in the Twenty-First Century
Tensions among states in the Middle East, especially the ongoing conflict between the Palestinians
and Israelis and animosities among Shi'ites and Sunnis, became more complicated from the 1990s on.
The situation in the Middle East grew more uncertain in 2003 when a U.S.- and British-led invasion of
Iraq deteriorated into escalating violence among competing religious and ethnic groups in the country.
Additionally, for thirty-four days in the summer of 2006, Israel bombed Lebanon, including its capital
city and refugee camps, with fire returned by Hezbollah and Hamas forces in the region.

the oil-rich country to debt-ridden Iraq. A United Nations coalition led by the United
States stopped the invasion and defeated the Iraqi army, but discontent mounted in the
region (Map 29.4).

To the east, the Taliban — a militant Islamic group initially funded by the United
States, China, Saudi Arabia, and Pakistan during the cold war — took over the govern-

ment of Afghanistan in the late 1990s. Its leaders imposed a regime that forbade girls from attending schools and women from leaving their homes without a male escort and demanded from men strict adherence to its rules for dress.

To the west, conflict between the Israelis and the Palestinians continued. As Israeli settlers took more Palestinian land, Palestinian suicide bombers began murdering Israeli civilians in the late 1990s. The Israeli government retaliated with missiles, machine guns, and tanks, often killing Palestinian civilians in turn. In 2006, the Israelis, responding to the political militia Hezbollah's kidnapping of Israeli soldiers, attacked Lebanon, destroying infrastructure, sending missiles into its capital city of Beirut, and killing hundreds of civilians. Beginning in the 1980s and continuing into the 2000s, terrorists from the Middle East and North Africa planted bombs in European cities, blew airplanes out of the sky, and bombed the Paris subway system. These attacks were said to be punishment for the West's support both for Israel and for Middle Eastern dictatorships.

On September 11, 2001, the ongoing terrorism in Europe and around the world caught the full attention of the United States when Muslim militants hijacked four planes in the United States and flew two of them into the World Trade Center in New York City and one into the Pentagon in Virginia. The fourth plane, en route to the Capitol, crashed in Pennsylvania when passengers forced the hijackers to lose control of the aircraft. The hijackers, most of whom were from Saudi Arabia, were inspired by the wealthy radical leader of al-Qaeda, Osama bin Laden, who sought to end the presence of U.S. forces in Saudi Arabia. They had trained in bin Laden's terrorist camps in Afghanistan and learned to pilot planes in the United States. The loss of more than three thousand lives led the United States to declare a "war against terrorism." In the wake of the September 11 attacks, the administration of U.S. president George W. Bush forged a multinational coalition, which included the vital cooperation of Islamic countries such as Pakistan, with the main goal of driving the ruling Taliban out of Afghanistan.

At first, the September 11 attacks and other lethal terrorist attacks around the world promoted global cooperation. European countries rounded up suspected terrorists and conducted the first successful trials of them in the spring of 2003. Ultimately, however, the West became divided when the United States claimed that Saddam Hussein was concealing weapons of mass destruction in Iraq and suggested ties between him and bin Laden's terrorist group. Great Britain, Spain, and Poland were among those who joined the coalition of invading forces, but some powerful European states — including Germany, Russia, and France — refused, sparking the anger of many Americans, some of whom sported bumper stickers with the demand "First Iraq, Next France" or participated in happy hours devoted to "French bashing."

U.S. war fever mounted with the suggestion that Syria and Iran should also be invaded, while the rest of the world condemned what seemed a sudden American blood lust. Europeans in general, including the British public, accused the United States of becoming a world military dictatorship in order to preserve its only remaining value — wasteful consumerism. The United States countercharged that the Europeans were too selfishly enjoying their democracy and creature comforts to help fund the military

Europeans React to September 11 Terror Attacks
On September 11, 2001, terrorists killed thousands of people from dozens of countries in airplane attacks on the World Trade Center and the Pentagon. Throughout the world, people expressed their shock and sorrow in vigils, and like this British tourist in Rome, they remained glued to the latest news. Terrorism, which had plagued Europeans for several decades, easily traveled the world in the days of more open borders, economic globalization, and cultural exchange. (© Alberto Pizzoli / Corbis-Sygma.)

defense of freedom under attack. The Spanish withdrew from the U.S. occupation of Iraq after terrorists linked to al-Qaeda bombed four Madrid commuter trains on March 11, 2004. The British, too, reeled when terrorists exploded bombs in three subway cars and a bus in central London in July 2005. Barack Obama, who was elected the first African American U.S. president in 2008, brought home all the troops from Iraq in 2012, though the United States maintained a presence there of military advisers. As for al-Qaeda, the United States weakened the organization by assassinating top leaders, including Osama bin Laden in 2011.

The Promise and Problems of a World Economy

Amid the violence, an incredible rise in industrial entrepreneurship and technological development took place outside the West. In 1982, the Asian-Pacific nations accounted for 16.4 percent of global gross domestic product, a figure that had doubled since the 1960s. By 1989, East Asia's share of world production had grown to more than 25 percent as that of the West declined. By 2006, China alone was achieving economic growth rates of more than 10 percent per year, and in 2010 it overtook Japan as the second largest national economy after the United States, with Germany falling to fourth place.

South Korea, Taiwan, Singapore, and Hong Kong were popularly called **Pacific tigers** for the ferocity of their growth in the 1980s and 1990s. By the 1990s, China, pursuing a policy of economic modernization and market orientation, had surpassed all the others. Japan, however, led the initial charge of Asian economies with investment in high-tech consumer industries driving the Japanese economy. For example, in 1982, Japan had thirty-two thousand industrial robots in operation; western Europe employed only nine thousand, and the United States had seven thousand. In 1989, the Japanese government and private businesses invested $549 billion to modernize industrial capacity, a full $36 billion more than in the United States. As buyers around the world snapped up automobiles, televisions, videocassette recorders, and computers from Asian-Pacific companies, the United States poured vast sums into its wars and Asian and Middle Eastern governments financed America's ballooning national debt. By 2000, China had become the largest creditor of the United States.

Tigers of the Pacific Rim, c. 1995

Despite rising national prosperity, individual workers, particularly outside of Japan, often paid dearly for this newly created wealth. For example, safety standards in China were abominable, leading to horrendous mining disasters among other catastrophes. Women in South Korea, Taiwan, and Central America labored in sweatshops to produce clothing for U.S.-based companies. Using the lure of a low-paid and docile female workforce, governments were able to attract electronics and other industries. However, educational standards rose, along with access to birth control and other medical care for these women, and many valued the escape from rural poverty.

Other emerging economies in the Southern Hemisphere as a whole continued to increase their share of the world's gross domestic product during the 1980s and 1990s, and some achieved political gains as well. In South Africa, native peoples began winning the struggle for political rights when, in 1990, the moderate government of F. W. de Klerk released political leader Nelson Mandela, imprisoned for almost three decades because of his antiapartheid activism. After holding free elections in 1994, which Mandela won, South Africa — like Brazil, Russia, Iran, Saudi Arabia, Nigeria, and Chile — profited from the need for vast quantities of raw materials such as oil and ores to feed global expansion. India made strides in education and women's rights and calmed bitter local rivalries, but the assassination of two successive Indian prime ministers in 1984 and 1991 raised the question of whether India would be able to attract investment and thus continue modernization. After the brief rule of a Hindu nationalist government that often opposed development, India's economy also achieved soaring growth early in the

Protesting Reform amid Economic Crisis
By 2010 and 2011, global economic crisis and the attempts to repair the damage had led to massive government debt. To remedy the situation, governments cut back on jobs, benefits, and services while giving
banks and businesses huge bailouts. Here, on the island of Cyprus, unions and NGOs sponsored this
demonstration against the policy of simultaneously heaping money on banks and taking it from ordinary
citizens. (EPA / Katia Christodouloul / Landov.)

twenty-first century, taking business from Western firms and making global acquisitions
that gave it, for example, the world's largest steel industry.

There was a downside to global economic interconnectedness. Beginning in 1997,
when speculators brought down the Thai baht, and continuing with the collapse of the
Russian ruble in 1998 and the bursting of the technology bubble in the early 2000s, the
global economy suffered a series of shocks. Then in 2008, the real estate bubble burst in
the United States, setting in motion a financial crisis of enormous proportions. For several years, lenders had been making home mortgages available to U.S. consumers who
could not afford them. The boom in housing made the economy as a whole look robust.
Bankers then sold their bad housing debt around the world to those who hoped to make
handsome profits based on rate increases written into the mortgage contracts. When
people were unable to make their monthly mortgage payments and pay their credit
card debt, a credit collapse followed, just as it had in the stock market crash of 1929.
Beginning in the United States and continuing around the world, banks and industries
became insolvent, forcing governments to set common policies to prop up failing banks
with billions of dollars, which in turn added to government debt. Unemployment rose
as businesses and consumers alike stopped purchasing goods.

By 2011, their more prudent management helped Asian economies as well as that
of Brazil recover, even as governments in the West faced bankruptcy and horrific rates

of unemployment — more than 20 percent in Spain. It looked to some as if the European Union itself might collapse as the richer nations such as Germany and France were threatened by backing the debt of the poorer ones such as Greece, Ireland, Portugal, and even Italy. The globalization of economic crises was another of the perils faced by the world's population.

> **REVIEW QUESTION** What were the principal challenges facing the West at the beginning of the twenty-first century?

Global Culture and Society in the Twenty-First Century

Amid warfare, booms, and crises, increased migration and growing global communications were changing culture and society, prompting many to ask what would become of national cultures and Western civilization itself. Would the world become a homogeneous mass with everyone wearing the same kind of clothing, eating the same kind of food, watching the same films, and communicating with the same smartphones? Some critics predicted a clash of civilizations in which increasingly incompatible religions and cultures would lead to a global holocaust. The information revolution and the global sharing of culture argued against the cultural purity of any group, Western or otherwise. "Civilizations," Indian economist and Nobel Prize winner Amartya Sen wrote after the terrorist attacks of September 11, "are hard to partition . . . given the diversities within each society as well as the linkages among different countries and cultures."

Through global communication and migration, Western society changed even more rapidly in the 1980s and 1990s than it had hundreds of years earlier when it came into intense contact with the rest of the globe. Culture knew no national boundaries, as East, West, North, and South became saturated with one another's cultural products via satellite television, films, telecommunications, and computer technology. Consequently some observers labeled the new century an era of denationalization — meaning that national cultures as well as national boundaries were becoming less distinct. There is no denying that even while the West absorbed peoples and cultures, it continued to exercise not only economic but also cultural influence over the rest of the globe. Yet Western influence was also being contested as Westerners absorbed the cultures of other regions.

Redefining the West: The Impact of Global Migration

The global movement of people was massive in the last third of the twentieth century and into the twenty-first. Uneven economic development, political persecution, and warfare (which claimed more than 100 million victims after 1945) sent tens of millions in search of opportunity and safety. By 2010, France had between five and eight million Muslims within its borders, and Europe as a whole had between thirty-five and fifty million. Other parts of the world were as full as the West of migrants from other cultures. The oil-producing nations of the Middle East employed millions of foreign workers, who generally constituted one-third of the labor force. Wars in Afghanistan increased the number of refugees to Iran to nearly two million in 1995, while the Iraq-Iran War and the

Headscarf Controversy in Germany
Western countries have long debated the relationship between religion and the nation-state, especially in public education. In an age of global migration, the issue of religion in the schools resurfaced, this time focusing on the headscarves worn by many Muslim women. In 2003, a German court upheld the right of teacher Fereshta Ludin, pictured here, to wear her headscarf while teaching on the grounds of religious freedom. Note the justices' own different clothing. (© Vincent Kessler / Reuters / Corbis.)

U.S. invasion of Iraq in 2003 sent millions more fleeing. In 2010, there were more than 200 million migrants worldwide, with many of them headed to the West.

Migrants from countries as different as the Yugoslav republics, Egypt, Spain, Mexico, and Pakistan sent money home from abroad that constituted up to 60 percent of national income. Sometimes migration was coerced: many eastern European and Asian prostitutes were held in international sex rings that controlled their passports, wages, and lives. Others came to the West voluntarily, seeking opportunity and a better life: "I do not want to go back to China," said one woman restaurant owner in Hungary in the 1990s. "Some of my relatives there also have restaurants . . . and sometimes they have to bribe somebody. . . . I would not be happy living like that." Like the illegal Congolese café proprietor Thérèse, whose story opens this chapter, many lived on the margins of the law, maintaining global ties with families from a new base in the West.

Foreign workers were often scapegoats for native peoples suffering from economic woes such as unemployment caused by downsizing. On the eve of EU enlargement in 2004, the highly respected weekly magazine *The Economist* included an article entitled "The Coming Hordes," which warned of Britain's being overrun by Roma (Gypsies) from eastern Europe. The Moscow rock band Corroded Metals campaigned for anti-immigrant politicians with hate-filled songs and chants in English of "Kill, kill, kill, kill the bloody foreigners" running in the background. Even citizens of immigrant descent often had a difficult time being accepted. Thriving anti-immigrant and white supremacist politicians challenged centrist parties, and in Austria and the Netherlands, anti-immigration candidates were elected to head the government. Nonetheless, because em-

ployers sought out illegal immigrants for the low wages they could be paid, the West remained a place of opportunity.

Global Networks and Social Change

Like migration, rapid technological change also weakened traditional political, cultural, and economic borders and to some extent even made borders obsolete. In 1969, the U.S. Department of Defense began to develop a computer network to carry communications in case of nuclear war. This system and others like it in universities, government, and business grew into an unregulated system of more than ten thousand networks worldwide. These came to be known as the Internet — shorthand for *internetworking*. By 1995, users in more than 137 countries were connected to the Internet, creating new "communities" via the World Wide Web that transcended common citizenship in a particular nation-state. By 2011, some two billion people — one-third of the world's population — used the Internet, creating an online marketplace that offered goods and services ranging from advanced weaponry to organ transplants. Critics charged that communications technology favored elites and disadvantaged those without computer skills or the financial resources needed to access computers. In fact, wealthy North America, Europe, and Australia/Oceania had the highest percentage of users.

The Internet had brought service jobs to countries that had heretofore suffered unemployment and real poverty. One of the first countries to recognize the possibilities of computing and help-desk services was Ireland, which pushed computer literacy to attract business. In 2003, U.S. firms spent $8.3 billion on outsourcing to Ireland and $7.7 billion on outsourcing to India. In that same year, the United States bought $77.38 billion in services from foreign countries and sold $131.01 billion to them, meaning in fact that more was insourced than outsourced. Thus, the Internet allowed for jobs to be apportioned anywhere. Moroccans did help-desk work for French or Spanish speakers, and in the twenty-first century Estonia, Hungary, and the Czech Republic as well as India and the Philippines were rebuilding their economies successfully by providing call-center and other business services. The Internet allowed service industries to globalize just as the manufacturing sector had done much earlier through multinational corporations.

Globalization of the economy via the Internet and other technology affected the West in complex ways. Benefiting from the booming global economy of the 1990s, the Irish and eastern Europeans became integrated into the Western consumer economy, and by the 2000s Asians and South Americans were integrated, too. By purchasing automobiles, CD players, and personal computers, non-Westerners may have taken jobs from the West, but they often sent funds back via their new purchasing power. For example, a twenty-one-year-old Indian woman, working for a service provider in Bangalore under the English name Sharon, used her salary to buy Western consumer items such as a cell phone from the Finnish company Nokia. "As a teenager I wished for so many things," she said. "Now I'm my own Santa Claus." Ordinary Western workers often found this global revolution threatening, as it redistributed jobs across the West and worldwide.

On the positive side, digital media have enabled widespread information sharing, and allowed individuals and organizations to spread awareness of the daunting problems of contemporary life — population explosion, scarce resources, North–South inequities, global pollution, ethnic hatred, and global terrorism — which demand, more than ever, the exercise of humane values and rational thought. Positive social change has occurred, thanks in part to digital media. In 2011, governments were overturned relatively peacefully in Tunisia and Egypt because Facebook, Twitter, and other electronic media brought protesters together with a common purpose, using communication to coordinate change rather than having change accompanied by escalating expressions of public violence. Evidence from the recent past gives hope that an era of even more instantaneous news feeds and digital communications will ease tensions, advance democracy, and make violence less likely.

A New Global Culture?

Despite the sense that national boundaries are weakening, cultural exchange flowing in many directions goes back millennia. In the ancient world, Greek philosophers and traders knew of distant Asian religious beliefs, and Middle Eastern religions such as Judaism and Christianity were influenced by them and then spread these beliefs to Europe. Chinese students in Tiananmen Square in 1989 testified to the global power of the West when in the name of freedom they rallied around their own representation of the Statue of Liberty (which itself was a gift from France to the United States). In Japan, businesspeople wore Western-style clothing and watched soccer, baseball, and other Western sports using English terms, while Europeans and Americans wore flip-flops, carried umbrellas, and practiced yoga — all imports from beyond the West.

Remarkable innovations in communications integrated cultures, possibly giving them a Western flavor. Videotapes and satellite-beamed telecasts transported American television shows to Hong Kong and Japanese movies to Europe and North America. American rock music sold briskly in Russia and elsewhere in the former Soviet bloc. More than 100,000 Czechoslovakian rock fans, including President Václav Havel, attended a Rolling Stones concert in Prague in 1990, showing that despite half a century of supposed isolation under communism they had been well tuned in to the larger world. Young black immigrants forged transnational culture when they created hip-hop and other pop music styles by combining elements of Africa, the Caribbean, Afro-America, and Europe. Athletes like the Brazilian soccer player Ronaldo and Japanese baseball star Ichiro Suzuki became better known to countless people than their own national leaders were. Even today's moral leaders — the Nobel Peace Prize winners Nelson Mandela, former president of South Africa; the Dalai Lama, the spiritual leader of Tibet; and Aung San Suu Kyi, opposition leader in Burma — are global figures.

As it had done for centuries, the West continued to devour material from other cultures — whether Hong Kong films, African textiles, Indian music, or Latin American pop culture. One of the most important influences in the West came from what was called the boom in Latin American literature. Latin American authors developed a style

Tourism, Migration, and the Mixing of Cultures
Tourism was a major economic boon to the West, and Western countries were the top tourist destinations in the world. Spreading prosperity allowed for greater leisure and travel to distant spots. Curiosity grew about other cultures. This Scottish bagpiper in London clearly arouses the interest of passersby, whether visitors from afar or citizens of his own country. (© Will van Overbeek. All Rights Reserved.)

known as magical realism, which melded everyday events with Latin American history and geography and with elements of myth, magic, and religion. The novels of Colombian-born Nobel Prize winner Gabriel García Márquez were translated into dozens of languages. His lush fantasies, including *One Hundred Years of Solitude* (1967), *Love in the Time of Cholera* (1988), and many later works, portray people of titanic ambitions and passions who endure war and all manner of personal trials. García Márquez narrated the tradition of dictators in Latin America, but he also paid close attention to the effects of global business. *One Hundred Years of Solitude,* for example, closes with the machine-gunning in 1928 of thousands of workers for the American-owned United Fruit Company because they asked for one day off per week and breaks to use the toilet. Wherever they lived, readers snapped up the book, which sold thirty million copies worldwide. García Márquez's work inspired a host of other outstanding novels in the magical realism tradition, including Laura Esquivel's *Like Water for Chocolate* (1989). In the 1990s,

the work was translated into two dozen languages and became a hit film because of its setting in a Mexican kitchen during the revolution of 1910, where cooking, sexuality, and brutality are intertwined. Innumerable authors in the West adopted aspects of this style.

Magical realism influenced a range of Western writers, including those migrating to Europe. British-born Zadie Smith, daughter of a Jamaican mother, became a prizewinning author with her novel *White Teeth* (2000), which describes postimperial Britain through the lives of often bizarre and larger-than-life characters from many ethnic backgrounds. Odd science fiction technology, deep emotional wounds, and weird but hilarious situations guide a plot full of heartbreak. Equally drawn to aspects of the magical realist style, Indian-born immigrant **Salman Rushdie** published the novel *The Satanic Verses* (1988), which outraged Muslims around the world because it appeared to blaspheme the Prophet Muhammad. From Iran, the ayatollah Khomeini issued a fatwa (decree) promising both a monetary reward and salvation in the afterlife to anyone who would assassinate the writer. Rushdie's Italian and Japanese translators were murdered, while his Norwegian publisher survived an assassination attempt.

As groups outside the accepted circles engaged in artistic production, battles over culture erupted. U.S. novelist **Toni Morrison** became, in 1993, the first African Ameri-

Toni Morrison, Recipient of the Nobel Prize
Toni Morrison, shown here receiving the Nobel Prize in Literature in 1993, was the first African American woman to receive the Nobel Prize. Morrison uses her literary talent to depict the condition of blacks under slavery and after emancipation. She also publishes insightful essays on social, racial, and gender issues. (AP Photo.)

can woman to win the Nobel Prize for Literature. In works such as *Beloved* (1987), *A Mercy* (2008), and *Home* (2012), Morrison describes the nightmares, daily experiences, achievements, and dreams of those who were brought as slaves to the United States and their descendants. But some parents objected to the inclusion of Morrison's work in school curricula. Critics charged that unlike Shakespeare's universal Western truth, the writing of African Americans, Native Americans, and women represented only propaganda, not great literature. In both the United States and Europe, politicians on the right saw the presence of multiculturalism as a sign of national decay similar to that brought about by immigration.

In the former Soviet bloc, artists and writers faced unique challenges. After the Soviet Union collapsed, celebrated writers like Mikhail Bulgakov (1891–1940), famous in the West for his novel *The Master and Margarita* (published posthumously in 1966–1967), became known in his homeland. At the same time, the collapse put literary dissidents out of business. In helping bring down the Soviet regime, they had lost their subject matter — the critique of a tyrannical system. State-supported authors suddenly lost their jobs. Eastern-bloc writers who formerly found both critical and financial success in the West seemed less heroic — and less talented — in the wide-open post-Soviet world. To make matters worse, there was no idea of what the post-Communist arts should be.

New literature aimed at rethinking the communist experience and eastern Europe's cultural relationship to western Europe and the West more generally. Andrei Makine, an expatriate Russian author, described the attraction of western European culture and the role of the war and the Gulag on the imaginations of eastern-bloc people, including teenagers. Both *Dreams of My Russian Summers* (1995) and *Once Upon the River Love* (1994) describe young people bred to fantasize about the wealth, sexiness, and material goods of western Europe and America. Victor Pelevin wrote more satirically and bitingly in such works as *The Life of Insects* (1993), in which insect-humans buzz around Russia trying to discover who they are in the post-Soviet world. Pelevin, a Buddhist and former engineer, wrote hilarious send-ups of politicians and the almost sacred Soviet space program, depicting it as a media sham run from the depths of the Moscow subway system in which hundreds of cosmonaut-celebrities are killed to prevent the truth from getting out. For him, "any politician is a TV program," as he showed in his novel *Homo Zapiens* (1999), in which politicians are all "virtual" — that is, produced by technical effects, clothing, and scriptwriters.

In music and the other arts, much energy was spent on recovering and absorbing all the underground works that had been hidden since 1917. For example, music lovers were astonished as the work of first-rate composers emerged. Those composers had written their classical works in private for fear that they might contain phrasings, sounds, and rhythms that would be called subversive. Meanwhile, they had often earned a living writing for films, as did Giya Kancheli, who wrote immensely popular music for more than forty films but was in addition a gifted composer of classical music. Alongside great artists, ordinary people in eastern Europe rethought the past, creating

ceremonies honoring victims of the Gulag and of Stalin's purges, all the while trying to sort out what communism had meant to their lives and to history.

In contrast to post-Soviet cultural reflection, the United States' success in marketing its culture, along with the legacy of British imperialism, helped make English the dominant international language by the end of the twentieth century. Such English words as *stop, shopping, parking, okay, weekend,* and *rock* infiltrated dozens of non-English vocabularies. Across Europe, English served as the main language of higher education, science, and tourism. Already in the 1960s, French president Charles de Gaulle, fearing the corruption of the French language, had banned such new words as *computer* in government documents, and succeeding administrations followed his path. The ban did not stop the influx of English into daily life, even though the EU's parliament and national cultural ministries regulated the amount of American programming on television and in cinemas.

American influence in film was dominant: films such as *The Matrix Reloaded* (2003) and *Avatar* (2009) earned hundreds of millions of dollars from global audiences. Simultaneously, however, the United States itself welcomed films from around the world — whether the Mexican *Y Tu Mamá También* (2001) or the British *Slumdog Millionaire* (2009). "Bollywood" films — happy, lavish films from the Indian movie industry — had a huge following in all Western countries, even influencing the plots of some American productions. The fastest-growing television market in the United States in the twenty-first century was Spanish-language programming, just one more indication that even in the United States culture was based on mixture and global exchange.

Some have called the global culture of the late twentieth and early twenty-first centuries **postmodernism**, defined in part as intense stylistic mixing in the arts without following an elite set of standards. Striking examples of postmodern art abound in Western society, including the AT&T Building (now known as the Sony Building) in New York City, which looks sleek and modern. Its entryway, however, is a Roman arch, and its cloud-piercing top suggests eighteenth-century Chippendale furniture. The Guggenheim Museum in Bilbao, Spain, designed by American Frank Gehry and considered bizarre by classical or even modern standards, includes forms, materials, and perspectives that, by rules of earlier decades, do not belong together. Architects working in a variety of hybrid styles completed the postunification rebuilding of the Reichstag in Berlin, whose traditional facade was given a modern dome of glass and steel. To add to the changing reality, all of these postmodern buildings could be visited virtually on the World Wide Web.

Some intellectuals defined postmodernism in political terms as part of the decline of the eighteenth-century Enlightenment ideals of human rights, individualism, and personal freedom, which were seen as modern. This political postmodernism included the decline of the Western nation-state. A structure like the Bilbao Guggenheim was simply an international tourist attraction rather than an institution reflecting Spanish traditions or national purpose. It embodied consumption, global technology, mass communications, and international migration rather than citizen-

The German Reichstag: Reborn and Green

Nothing better symbolizes the end of the postwar era and the new millennium than the restoration of the Reichstag, the parliament building in Berlin. Like other manifestations of postmodernism, the restoration — designed by a British architect — preserves the old, while adding a new dome of glass, complete with solar panels that make the building self-sufficient in its energy needs. Visitors can walk around the glass dome, looking at their elected representatives deliberating below. (© Svenja-Foto / Corbis.)

ship, nationalism, and rights. These qualities made it a rootless structure, unlike the Louvre in Paris, for example, which was built by the French monarchy to serve its own purposes. Critics saw the Bilbao Guggenheim as drifting, more like the nomadic businesswoman Thérèse, who moved between nations and cultures with no set identity. Cities and nations alike were losing their function as places providing social roots, personal identity, or human rights. For postmodernists of a political bent, computers had replaced the autonomous, free self and bureaucracy had rendered representative government obsolete.

REVIEW QUESTION What social and cultural questions has globalization raised?

Conclusion

Postmodernist thinking has not eclipsed humane values in the global age. The urge to find practical solutions to the daunting problems of contemporary life — population explosion, scarce resources, pollution, global warming, ethnic hatred, North–South inequities, and terrorism — through the careful assessment of facts still guides public policy. Some of these global problems were briefly overshadowed by the collapse of the Soviet empire, which initially produced human misery, rising criminality, and the flight of population during the 1990s and even into the 2000s. Reformers who sought improved conditions of life by bringing down Soviet and Yugoslav communism saw unexpected bloodshed and even genocide. What appeared an economic boom resulting from globalization and the collapse of communism itself had disadvantages, as a series of crises beginning in Thailand in 1997 and finally exploding in the more sustained crisis from 2007 on cost jobs and harmed human well-being.

Yet the past twenty-five years have also seen great improvements. Events in South Africa, the Middle East, and Latin America, for example, indicated that there could be progress toward democracy, prosperity, and an end to oppression. Human health gradually improved even as scientists sought to cure the victims of global pandemics and even to prevent such ravages altogether. The global age ushered in by the Soviet collapse unexpectedly brought denationalization to many regions of the world, leading to weakening of borders and cooperation among former enemies. The expansion of the European Union and the tightening of relationships within it are the best example of this development.

Some consequences of increasing globalization are still being determined. The Internet and migration suggest that people's empathy for one another grew worldwide. One commentator claimed that there was little bloodshed in the collapse of the Soviet empire because fax machines and television circulated images of events globally, which discouraged the excessive violence often associated with political revolution. At the same time, militants from Saudi Arabia, Egypt, Indonesia, the Philippines, North Africa, Britain, and elsewhere unleashed unprecedented terrorism on the world in an attempt to push back global forces. Nor did powerful countries hesitate to wage wars against Chechnya, Kuwait, Iraq, Afghanistan, Lebanon, or against their own people as in Libya and Syria. On a different level, even as globalization raised standards of living and education in many parts of the world, in other areas — such as poorer regions in Africa and Asia — people faced disease and the dramatic social and economic crises specifically associated with the global age. In contrast, the most hopeful developments in recent globalization were communication in the arts and in culture more generally — most visible in the exchange of books, music, and ideas around the world — and the cooperation that nations undertook with one another in the realm of health, economics, and politics. Social media via the World Wide Web offered people in families, localities, nations, and the world a new way of communicating. Events from the recent past thus show that both opportunities and challenges lie ahead for citizens of the West and of the world as they make the transition to what some are calling the Digital Age.

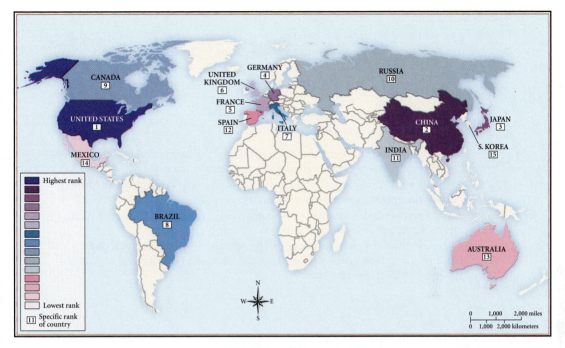

Mapping the West The World's Top Fifteen Economies as of 2010

From the nineteenth to the twenty-first centuries, the comparative economic strength of individual nations changed considerably. In the nineteenth century, India and China had the largest economies; they were eclipsed by the European powers as the Industrial Revolution progressed. The European powers in turn were eventually overtaken by the United States. By the end of the twentieth century, the reemergence of non-Western economic powerhouses marked another transformation. How would you describe economic dynamism in the twenty-first century as shown in the map?

Thus the challenge to the making of the West today involves the inventive human spirit. Over the past five hundred years, the West has benefited from its scientific and technological advances and perhaps never more so than in the Digital Age. Although communication and information technology have brought people closer to one another than ever before, the use of technology has made the period from 1900 to the present one of the bloodiest eras in human history — and one during which the use of technology has threatened, and still threatens, the future of the earth as a home for the human race. While technology has enhanced daily life, it has also facilitated war, genocide, terrorism, and environmental deterioration, all of which pose great challenges to the West and to the world; the use of digital media to promote violent causes, inflame others, and network with and recruit new followers has made some of these challenges even more significant. The question is, How will the human race adapt to the creativity the Digital Age has unleashed? How will the West and the world manage both the promises and the challenges of Digital Age technology to protect the human race in the years ahead?

Review Questions

1. What were the major issues facing the former Soviet bloc in the 1990s and early 2000s?
2. What trends suggest that the nation-state was a declining institution at the beginning of the twenty-first century?
3. What were the principal challenges facing the West at the beginning of the twenty-first century?
4. What social and cultural questions has globalization raised?

Making Connections

1. In what ways were global connections at the beginning of the twenty-first century different from the global connections at the beginning of the twentieth century?
2. How did the Western nation-state of the early twenty-first century differ from the Western nation-state at the opening of the twentieth century?
3. Migration has been a major factor across the human past. How has it affected the West differently in the twenty-first century?
4. Economic crises caused by changes in weather, the spread of disease, and trade and financial disturbances have been constants throughout history. How does the economic crisis that began in 2007 compare to earlier crises?

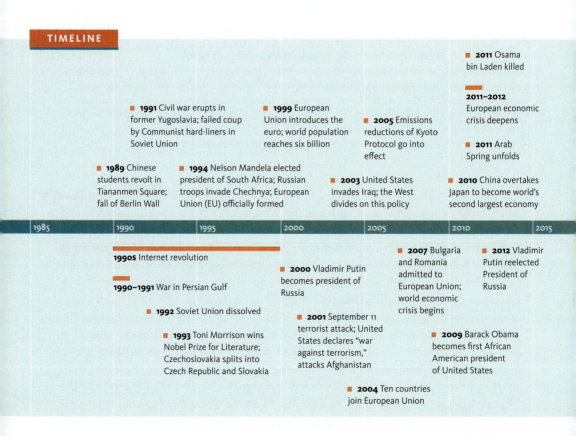

TIMELINE

- **2011** Osama bin Laden killed

- **1991** Civil war erupts in former Yugoslavia; failed coup by Communist hard-liners in Soviet Union
- **1999** European Union introduces the euro; world population reaches six billion
- **2005** Emissions reductions of Kyoto Protocol go into effect
- **2011–2012** European economic crisis deepens
- **2011** Arab Spring unfolds

- **1989** Chinese students revolt in Tiananmen Square; fall of Berlin Wall
- **1994** Nelson Mandela elected president of South Africa; Russian troops invade Chechnya; European Union (EU) officially formed
- **2003** United States invades Iraq; the West divides on this policy
- **2010** China overtakes Japan to become world's second largest economy

1985   1990   1995   2000   2005   2010   2015

- **1990s** Internet revolution
- **1990–1991** War in Persian Gulf
- **1992** Soviet Union dissolved
- **1993** Toni Morrison wins Nobel Prize for Literature; Czechoslovakia splits into Czech Republic and Slovakia
- **2000** Vladimir Putin becomes president of Russia
- **2001** September 11 terrorist attack; United States declares "war against terrorism," attacks Afghanistan
- **2004** Ten countries join European Union
- **2007** Bulgaria and Romania admitted to European Union; world economic crisis begins
- **2009** Barack Obama becomes first African American president of United States
- **2012** Vladimir Putin reelected President of Russia

- For practice quizzes and other study tools, visit the **Online Study Guide** at bedfordstmartins.com/huntconcise.

- For primary-source material from this period, see *Sources of the Making of the West*, Fourth Edition.

- For Web sites, images, and documents related to topics in this chapter, visit *Make History* at bedfordstmartins.com/huntconcise.

Suggested References

Studies of the globalized world describe both hopeful efforts to cure disease and survive migration and devastating effects of terrorism and ethnic conflict. Interesting works portray politics and everyday life in post-Soviet Russia and eastern Europe.

Bass, Gary J. *Freedom's Battle: The Origins of Humanitarian Intervention*. 2008.

Bess, Michael. *The Light-Green Society: Economic and Technological Modernity in France*. 2003.

Brier, Jennifer. *Infectious Ideas: U.S. Political Response to the AIDS Crisis*. 2009.

Bucur, Maria. *Heroes and Victims: Remembering the War in Twentieth-Century Romania*. 2009.

Burleigh, Michael. *Blood and Rage: A Cultural History of Terrorism*. 2008.

Burrett, Tina. *Television and Presidential Power in Putin's Russia*. 2010.

Gleich, James. *The Information: A History, A Theory, A Flood*. 2011.

*Gorbachev, Mikhail. *Memoirs*. 1996.

Hsu, Roland, ed. *Ethnic Europe: Mobility, Identity, and Conflict in a Globalized World*. 2010.

Humphrey, Caroline. *The Unmaking of Soviet Life: Everyday Economies after Socialism*. 2002.

Kavoori, Anandam P., and Aswin Punathambekar, eds. *Global Bollywood*. 2008.

Kenney, Padraic. *The Burdens of Freedom: Eastern Europe since 1989*. 2006.

MacGaffey, Janet, et al. *Congo-Paris: Transnational Traders on the Margins of the Law*. 2000.

Osumare, Halifu. *The Africanist Aesthetic in Global Hip-Hop: Power Moves*. 2007.

Ried, T. R. *The United States of Europe: The New Superpower and the End of American Supremacy*. 2005.

Sinno, Abdulkader H., ed. *Muslims in Western Politics*. 2008.

United Nations population data: http://www.unfpa.org/swp/swpmain.htm

*Primary source.

Glossary of Key Terms and People

This glossary contains definitions of terms and people that are central to your understanding of the material covered in this textbook. Each term or person in the glossary is in **boldface** in the text when it is first defined. We have also included the page number on which the full discussion of the term or person appears so that you can easily locate the complete explanation to strengthen your historical vocabulary.

For words or names not defined here, two additional resources may be useful: the index, which will direct you to many more topics discussed in the text, and a good dictionary.

Abbasids (A buh sihds) (275): The dynasty of caliphs that, in 750, took over from the Umayyads in all of the Islamic realm except for Spain (al-Andalus). From their new capital at Baghdad, they presided over a wealthy realm until the late ninth century.

abolitionists (567): Advocates of the abolition of the slave trade and of slavery.

absolutism (493): A system of government in which the ruler claims sole and uncontestable power.

agora (AH gore uh) (83): The central market square of a Greek city-state, a popular gathering place for conversation.

agricultural revolution (538): Increasingly aggressive attitudes toward investment in and management of land that increased production of food in the 1700s.

Alexander II (699): Russian tsar (r. 1855–1881) who initiated the age of Great Reforms and emancipated the serfs in 1861.

Alexander the Great (115): The fourth-century B.C.E. Macedonian king whose conquest of the Persian Empire led to the greatly increased cultural interactions of Greece and the Near East in the Hellenistic Age.

Alexius I (Alexius Comnenus) (324): The Byzantine emperor (r. 1081–1118) whose leadership marked a new triumph of the *dynatoi*. His request to Pope Urban II for troops to fight the Turks turned into the First Crusade.

Alfred the Great (295): King of Wessex (r. 871–899) and the first king to rule over most of England. He organized a successful defense against Viking invaders, had key Latin works translated into the vernacular, and wrote a law code for the whole of England.

Anabaptists (445): Sixteenth-century Protestants who believed that only adults could truly have faith and accept baptism.

anarchism (717): The belief that people should not have government; it was popular among

some peasants and workers in the last half of the nineteenth century and the first decades of the twentieth.

apostolic (ah puh STAH lihk) **succession** (191): The principle by which Christian bishops traced their authority back to the apostles of Jesus.

appeasement (861): Making concessions in the face of grievances as a way of preventing conflict.

apprentices (309): Boys (and occasionally girls) placed under the tutelage of a master craftsman in the Middle Ages. Normally unpaid, they were expected to be servants of their masters, with whom they lived, at the same time as they were learning their trade.

areté (ah reh TAY) (49): The Greek value of competitive individual excellence.

Arianism (215): The Christian doctrine named after Arius, who argued that Jesus was "begotten" by God and did not have an identical nature with God the Father.

Aristotle (113): Greek philosopher famous for his scientific investigations, development of logical argument, and practical ethics.

art nouveau (777): An early-twentieth-century artistic style in graphics, fashion, and household design that featured flowing, sinuous lines, borrowed in large part from Asian art.

asceticism (uh SEH tuh sih zuhm) (217): The practice of self-denial, especially through spiritual discipline; a doctrine for Christians emphasized by Augustine.

Atlantic system (529): The network of trade established in the 1700s that bound together western Europe, Africa, and the Americas. Europeans sold slaves from western Africa and bought commodities that were produced by the new colonial plantations in North and South America and the Caribbean.

Augustine (212): Bishop in North Africa whose writings defining religious orthodoxy made him the most influential theologian in Western civilization.

Augustus (171): The honorary name meaning "divinely favored" that the Roman Senate bestowed on Octavian; it became shorthand for "Roman imperial ruler."

Avignon (AH vee NYAW) **papacy** (388): The period (1309–1378) during which the popes ruled from Avignon rather than from Rome.

baroque (buh ROHK) (487): An artistic style of the seventeenth century that featured curves, exaggerated lighting, intense emotions, release from restraint, and even a kind of artistic sensationalism.

Basil II (274): The Byzantine emperor (r. 976–1025) who presided over the end of the Bulgar threat (earning the name Bulgar-Slayer) and the conversion of Kievan Russia to Christianity.

battle of Hastings (329): The battle of 1066 that replaced the Anglo-Saxon king with a Norman one and thus tied England to the rest of Europe as never before.

battle of Waterloo (641): The final battle lost by Napoleon; it took place near Brussels on June 18, 1815, and led to the deposed emperor's final exile.

Beauvoir, Simone de (see MAWN duh bohv WAHR) (907): Author of *The Second Sex* (1949), a globally influential work that created an interpretation of women's age-old inferior status from existentialist philosophy.

Beethoven, Ludwig van (649): The German composer (1770–1827) who helped set the direction of musical romanticism; his music used recurring and evolving themes to convey the impression of natural growth.

bin Laden, Osama (971): Wealthy leader of the militant Islamic group al-Qaeda, which executed terrorist plots, including the September 11, 2001, attacks on the United States, to end the presence of U.S. forces in his home country, Saudi Arabia.

Bismarck, Otto von (705): 1815–1898. Leading Prussian politician and German prime minister who waged war in order to create a united German Empire, which was established in 1871.

Black Death (400): The term historians give to the disease that swept through Europe in 1347–1352.

Blitzkrieg (863): Literally, "lightning war"; a strategy for the conduct of war (used by the Germans in World War II) in which motorized firepower quickly and overwhelmingly

attacks the enemy, leaving it unable to resist psychologically or militarily.

blood libel (374): The charge that Jews used the blood of Christian children in their Passover ritual; though false, it led to massacres of Jews in cities in England, France, Spain, and Germany in the thirteenth century.

Bolívar, Simón (652): 1783–1830. The Venezuelan-born, European-educated aristocrat who became one of the leaders of the Latin American independence movement in the 1820s. Bolivia is named after him.

Bolshevik Revolution (813): The overthrow of Russia's Provisional Government in the fall of 1917 by V. I. Lenin and his Bolshevik forces.

Bonaparte, Louis-Napoleon (685–86): 1808–1873. Nephew of Napoleon I; he was elected president of France in 1848, declared himself Emperor Napoleon III in 1852, and ruled until 1870.

Bonaparte, Napoleon (628): The French general who became First Consul in 1799 and emperor (Napoleon I) in 1804; after losing the battle of Waterloo in 1815, he was exiled to the island of St. Helena.

Boniface VIII (386): The pope (r. 1294–1303) whose clash with King Philip the Fair of France left the papacy considerably weakened.

buccaneers (535): Pirates of the Caribbean who governed themselves and preyed on international shipping.

bureaucracy (498): A network of state officials carrying out orders according to a regular and routine line of authority.

Calvin, John (442): French-born Christian humanist (1509–1564) and founder of Calvinism, one of the major branches of the Protestant Reformation; he led the reform movement in Geneva, Switzerland, from 1541 to 1564.

Capetian (kuh PAY shuhn) **dynasty** (297): A long-lasting dynasty of French kings, taking their name from Hugh Capet (r. 987–996).

capital-intensive industry (743): A mid- to late-nineteenth-century development in industry that required great investments of money for machinery and infrastructure to make a profit.

capitalism (310): The modern economic system characterized by an entrepreneurial class of property owners who employ others and produce (or provide services) for a market in order to make a profit.

Carolingian (280): The Frankish dynasty that ruled a western European empire from 751 to the late 800s; its greatest vigor was in the time of Charlemagne (r. 768–814) and Louis the Pious (r. 814–840).

castellan (KAS tuh luhn) (293): The holder of a castle. In the tenth and eleventh centuries, castellans became important local lords. They mustered men for military service, collected taxes, and administered justice.

Cavour, Camillo di (702): Prime minister (1852–1861) of the kingdom of Piedmont-Sardinia and architect of a united Italy.

chansons de geste (shahn SOHN duh ZHEST) (356): Epic poems of the twelfth century about knightly and heroic deeds.

Chaplin, Charlie (856): Major entertainment leader, whose sympathetic portrayals of the common man and satires of Hitler helped preserve democratic values in the 1930s and 1940s.

Charlemagne (SHAR luh mayn) (281): The Carolingian king (r. 768–814) whose conquests greatly expanded the Frankish kingdom. He was crowned emperor on December 25, 800.

Charles V (441): Holy Roman Emperor (r. 1519–1556) and the most powerful ruler in sixteenth-century Europe; he reigned over the Low Countries, Spain, Spain's Italian and New World dominions, and the Austrian Habsburg lands.

Chartism (683): The British movement of supporters of the People's Charter (1838), which demanded universal manhood suffrage, vote by secret ballot, equal electoral districts, and other reforms.

chivalry (357): An ideal of knightly comportment that included military prowess, bravery, fair play, piety, and courtesy.

Christ (186): Greek for "anointed one," in Hebrew *Mashiach* or in English *Messiah;* in apocalyptic thought, God's agent sent to conquer the forces of evil.

Christian Democrats (891): Powerful center to center-right political parties that evolved in the late 1940s from former Catholic parties of the pre–World War II period.

Christian humanism (438): A general intellectual trend in the sixteenth century that coupled love of classical learning, as in Renaissance humanism, with an emphasis on Christian piety.

Cicero (SIH suh roh) (156): Rome's most famous orator and author of the doctrine of *humanitas*.

city-state (8): An urban center exercising political and economic control over the surrounding countryside.

Civil Code (632): The French legal code formulated by Napoleon in 1804; it ensured equal treatment under the law to all men and guaranteed religious liberty, but it curtailed many rights of women.

civil disobedience (845): The act of deliberately but peacefully breaking the law, a tactic used by Mohandas Gandhi in India and earlier by British suffragists to protest oppression and obtain political change.

civilization (3): A way of life based in cities with dense populations organized as political states, large buildings constructed for communal activities, the production of food, diverse economies, a sense of local identity, and some knowledge of writing.

classicism (519): A seventeenth-century style of painting and architecture that reflected the ideals of the art of antiquity; in classicism, geometric shapes, order, and harmony of lines took precedence over the sensuous, exuberant, and emotional forms of the baroque.

cold war (882): The rivalry between the United States and the Soviet Union from 1945 to 1989 that led to massive growth in nuclear weapons on both sides.

coloni (kuh LOH ny) (208): Literally, "cultivators"; tenant farmers in the Roman Empire who became bound by law to the land they worked and whose children were legally required to continue to farm the same land.

Colosseum (179): Rome's fifty-thousand-seat amphitheater built by the Flavian dynasty for gladiatorial combats and other spectacles.

Columbus, Christopher (433): An Italian sailor (1451–1506) who opened up the New World by sailing west across the Atlantic in search of a route to Asia.

commercial revolution (306): A term for the western European development (starting around 1050) of a money economy centered in urban areas but affecting the countryside as well.

common law (347): Begun by Henry II (r. 1154–1189), the English royal law carried out by the king's justices in eyre (traveling justices). It applied to the entire kingdom and thus was "common" to all.

commune (311): In a medieval town, a sworn association of citizens who formed a legal corporate body. The commune appointed or elected officials, made laws, kept the peace, and administered justice.

communists (682): Those socialists who after 1840 (when the word was first used) advocated the abolition of private property in favor of communal, collective ownership.

Concordat of Worms (317): The agreement between pope and emperor in 1122 that ended the Investiture Conflict.

Congress of Vienna (641): Face-to-face negotiations (1814–1815) between the great powers to settle the boundaries of European states and determine who would rule each nation after the defeat of Napoleon.

conservatism (645): A political doctrine that emerged after 1789 and took hold after 1815; it rejected much of the Enlightenment and the French Revolution, preferring monarchies over republics, tradition over revolution, and established religion over Enlightenment skepticism.

constitutionalism (493): A system of government in which rulers share power with parliaments made up of elected representatives.

consumer revolution (537): The rapid increase in consumption of new staples produced in the Atlantic system as well as of other items of daily life that were previously unavailable or beyond the reach of ordinary people.

Continental System (638): The boycott of British goods in France and its satellites ordered by Napoleon in 1806; it had success but was later undermined by smuggling.

Corn Laws (680): Tariffs on grain in Great Britain that benefited landowners by preventing the import of cheap foreign grain; they were repealed by the British government in 1846.

cortes (kawr TEHZ) (385): The earliest European representative institution, called initially to consent to royal wishes; first convoked in 1188 by the king of Castile-León.

Cortés, Hernán (435): The Spanish explorer (1485–1547) who captured the Aztec capital, Tenochtitlán (present-day Mexico City), in 1519.

Council of Trent (449): A general council of the Catholic church that met at Trent between 1545 and 1563 to set Catholic doctrine, reform church practices, and defend the church against the Protestant challenge.

Cuban missile crisis (912): The confrontation in 1962 between the United States and the USSR over Soviet installation of missile sites off the U.S. coast in Cuba.

cult (56): In ancient Greece, a set of official, publicly funded religious activities for a deity overseen by priests and priestesses.

cult of the offensive (806): A military strategy of constantly attacking the enemy that was believed to be the key to winning World War I but that brought great loss of life while failing to bring decisive victory.

cuneiform (kyoo NEE uh form) (11): The earliest form of writing, invented in Mesopotamia and done with wedge-shaped characters.

curials (KYUR ee uhls) (208): The social elite in the Roman Empire's cities and towns, most of whom were obliged to serve as decurions on municipal Senates and collect taxes for the imperial government, paying any shortfalls themselves.

Cyrus (42): Founder of the Persian Empire.

Darwin, Charles (723): The English naturalist (1809–1882) who popularized the theory of evolution by means of natural selection and thereby challenged the biblical story of creation.

debasement of coinage (195): Putting less silver in a coin without changing its face value; a failed financial strategy during the third-century C.E. crisis in Rome.

de-Christianization (610): During the French Revolution, the campaign of extremist republicans against organized churches and in favor of a belief system based on reason.

Declaration of the Rights of Man and Citizen (602): The preamble to the French constitution drafted in August 1789; it established the sovereignty of the nation and equal rights for citizens.

decolonization (899): The process — whether violent or peaceful — by which colonies gained their independence from the imperial powers after World War II.

decurions (dih KYUR ee uhns) (182): Municipal Senate members in the Roman Empire responsible for collecting local taxes.

deists (566): Those who believe in God but give him no active role in human affairs. Deists of the Enlightenment believed that God had designed the universe and set it in motion but no longer intervened in its functioning.

Delian (DEE lee un) **League** (79): The naval alliance led by Athens in the Golden Age that became the basis for the Athenian Empire.

demes (DEEMZ) (67): The villages and city neighborhoods that formed the constituent political units of Athenian democracy in the late Archaic Age.

Diaspora (die ASS por a) (47): The dispersal of the Jewish population from their homeland.

DNA (922): The genetic material that forms the basis of each cell; the discovery of its structure in 1952 revolutionized genetics, molecular biology, and other scientific and medical fields.

domesticity (675): An ideology prevailing in the nineteenth century that women should devote themselves to their families and the home.

dominate (205): The openly authoritarian style of Roman rule from Diocletian (r. 284–305) onward; the word was derived from *dominus* ("master" or "lord") and contrasted with *principate*.

Dual Alliance (760): A defensive alliance between Germany and Austria-Hungary created in 1879 as part of Bismarck's system of alliances to prevent or limit war. It was joined by Italy in 1882 as a third partner and then called the Triple Alliance.

dualism (113): The philosophical idea that the human soul (or mind) and body are separate.

dual monarchy (709): The shared power arrangement between the Habsburg Empire and Hungary after the Prussian defeat of the Austrian Empire in 1866–1867.

Duma (790): The Russian parliament set up in the aftermath of the outbreak of the Revolution of 1905.

dynatoi (DY nuh toy) (273): The "powerful men" who dominated the countryside of the Byzantine Empire in the tenth and eleventh centuries, and to some degree challenged the authority of the emperor.

Edict of Milan (209): The proclamation of Roman co-emperors Constantine and Licinius decreeing free choice of religion in the empire.

Edict of Nantes (463): The decree issued by French king Henry IV in 1598 that granted the Huguenots a large measure of religious toleration.

Einstein, Albert (775): Scientist whose theory of relativity (1905) revolutionized modern physics and other fields of thought.

Eliot, George (719): The pen name of English novelist Mary Ann Evans (1819–1880), who described the harsh reality of many ordinary people's lives in her works.

Elizabeth I (467): English queen (r. 1558–1603) who oversaw the return of the Protestant Church of England and, in 1588, the successful defense of the realm against the Spanish Armada.

empire (12): A political state in which one or more formerly independent territories or peoples are ruled by a single sovereign power.

Enabling Act (850): The legislation passed in 1933 suspending constitutional government for four years in order to meet the crisis in the German economy.

enlightened despots (580): Rulers — such as Catherine the Great of Russia, Frederick the Great of Prussia, and Joseph II of Austria — who tried to promote Enlightenment reforms without giving up their own supreme political power; also called enlightened absolutists.

Enlightenment (554): The eighteenth-century intellectual movement whose proponents believed that human beings could apply a critical, reasoning spirit to every problem.

Entente Cordiale (793): An alliance between Britain and France that began with an agreement in 1904 to honor colonial holdings.

Epicureanism (eh puh KYUR ee uh nizm) (127): The philosophy founded by Epicurus of Athens to help people achieve a life of true pleasure, by which he meant "absence of disturbance."

epigrams (125): Short poems written by women in the Hellenistic Age; many were about other women and the writer's personal feelings.

equites (EHK wih tehs) (159): Literally, "equestrians" or "knights"; wealthy Roman businessmen who chose not to pursue a government career.

Estates General (599): A body of deputies from the three estates, or orders, of France: the clergy (First Estate), the nobility (Second Estate), and everyone else (Third Estate).

ethnic cleansing (955): The mass murder — genocide — of people according to ethnicity or nationality; it can also include eliminating all traces of the murdered people's past. Examples include the post–World War I elimination of minorities in eastern and central Europe and the rape and murders that resulted from the breakup of Yugoslavia in the 1990s.

euro (962): The common currency in seventeen member states of the European Union (EU) and of EU institutions. It went into effect gradually, used first in business transactions in 1999 and entering public circulation in 2002.

European Economic Community (EEC or Common Market) (894): A consortium of six European countries established in 1957 to promote free trade and economic cooperation among its members; its membership and activities expanded over the years,

and it later evolved into the European Union (EU).

European Union (EU) (962): Formerly the European Economic Community (EEC, or Common Market), and then the European Community (EC); formed in 1994 by the terms of the Maastricht Treaty. Its members have political ties through the European parliament as well as long-standing common economic, legal, and business mechanisms.

existentialism (907): A philosophy prominent after World War II developed primarily by Jean-Paul Sartre to stress the importance of action in the creation of an authentic self.

family allowance (854): Government funds given to families with children to boost the birthrate in democratic countries (e.g., Sweden during the Great Depression) and totalitarian ones alike.

fascism (834): A doctrine that emphasizes violence and glorifies the state over the people and their individual or civil rights; in Italy, the Fascist Party took hold in the 1920s as Mussolini consolidated power.

Fatimids (FAT ih mihds) (277): Members of the tenth-century Shi'ite dynasty who derived their name from Fatimah, the daughter of Muhammad and wife of Ali; they dominated in parts of North Africa, Egypt, and even Syria.

feudalism (290): The whole complex of lords, vassals, and fiefs (from the Latin *feodum*) as an institution. The nature of that institution varied from place to place, and in some regions it did not exist at all.

fiefs (290): Grants of land, theoretically temporary, from lords to their noble dependents (*fideles* or, later, vassals) given in recognition of services, usually military, done or expected in the future; also called *benefices*.

First Consul (629): The most important of the three consuls established by the French Constitution of 1800; the title, given to Napoleon Bonaparte, was taken from ancient Rome.

First Crusade (324): The massive armed pilgrimage to Jerusalem that lasted from 1096 to 1099. It resulted in the massacre of Jews in the Rhineland (1095), the sack of Jerusalem (1099), and the setting up of the crusader states.

First Triumvirate (162): The coalition formed in 60 B.C.E. by Pompey, Crassus, and Caesar. (The word *triumvirate* means "group of three.")

Five Pillars of Islam (243): The five essential practices of Islam, namely, the *zakat* (alms); the fast of Ramadan; the *hajj* (pilgrimage to Mecca); the *salat* (formal worship); and the *shahadah* (profession of faith).

five-year plans (846): Centralized programs for economic development begun in 1929 by Joseph Stalin and copied by Adolf Hitler; these plans set production priorities and gave production targets for individual industries and agriculture.

Fourteen Points (812): U.S. president Woodrow Wilson's World War I peace proposal; based on settlement rather than on conquest, it encouraged the surrender of the Central Powers.

Fourth Crusade (360): The crusade that lasted from 1202 to 1204; its original goal was to recapture Jerusalem, but the crusaders ended up conquering Constantinople instead.

Fourth Lateran Council (370): The council that met in 1215 and covered the important topics of Christianity, among them the nature of the sacraments, the obligations of the laity, and policies toward heretics and Jews.

Franciscans (357): The religious order founded by St. Francis (c. 1182–1226) and dedicated to poverty and preaching, particularly in towns and cities.

Franco, Francisco (859): 1892–1975. Right-wing general who in 1936 successfully overthrew the democratic republic in Spain and instituted a repressive dictatorship.

Frederick I (Barbarossa) (351): King of Germany (r. 1152–1190) and emperor (crowned 1155) who tried to cement the power of the German king through conquest (for example, of northern Italy) and the bonds of vassalage.

Frederick II (381): The grandson of Barbarossa who became king of Sicily and Germany, as well as emperor (r. 1212–1250), who allowed the German princes a free hand as he battled the pope for control of Italy.

Frederick William of Hohenzollern (514): The Great Elector of Brandenburg-Prussia (r. 1640–1688) who brought his nation through the end of the Thirty Years' War and then succeeded in welding his scattered lands into an absolutist state.

Freemasons (575): Members of Masonic lodges, where nobles and middle-class professionals (and even some artisans) shared interest in the Enlightenment and reform.

Freud, Sigmund (773): Viennese medical doctor and founder, in the late nineteenth century, of psychoanalysis, a theory of mental processes and problems and a method of treating them.

Gladstone, William (756): 1809–1898. Liberal politician and prime minister of Great Britain who innovated in popular campaigning and who criticized British imperialism.

glasnost (943): Literally "openness" or "publicity"; a policy instituted in the 1980s by Soviet premier Mikhail Gorbachev calling for greater openness in speech and in thinking, which translated to the reduction of censorship in publishing, radio, television, and other media.

globalization (954): The interconnection of labor, capital, ideas, services, and goods around the world. Although globalization has existed for hundreds of years, the late twentieth and early twenty-first centuries are seen as more global because of the speed with which people, goods, and ideas travel the world.

global warming (967): An increase in the temperature of the earth's lower atmosphere resulting from a buildup of chemical emissions.

Glorious Revolution (507): The events of 1688 when Tories and Whigs replaced England's monarch James II with his Protestant daughter, Mary, and her husband, Dutch ruler William of Orange; William and Mary agreed to a Bill of Rights that guaranteed rights to Parliament.

Golden Horde (390): The political institution set up by the Mongols in Russia, lasting from the thirteenth to the fifteenth century.

Gorbachev, Mikhail (943): Leader of the Soviet Union (1985–1991) who instituted reforms such as glasnost and perestroika, thereby contributing to the collapse of Communist rule in the Soviet bloc and the USSR.

Gothic architecture (342): The style of architecture that started in the Île-de-France in the twelfth century and eventually became the quintessential cathedral style of the Middle Ages, characterized by pointed arches, ribbed vaults, and stained-glass windows.

Great Famine (390): The shortage of food and accompanying social ills that besieged northern Europe between 1315 and 1322.

Great Fear (602): The term used by historians to describe the French rural panic of 1789, which led to peasant attacks on aristocrats or on seigneurial records of peasants' dues.

Great Persecution (209): The violent program initiated by Diocletian in 303 to make Christians convert to traditional religion or risk confiscation of their property and even death.

Great Schism (409): The papal dispute of 1378–1417 when the church had two and even (between 1409 and 1417) three popes. The Great Schism was ended by the Council of Constance.

Green Party (968): A political party first formed in West Germany in 1979 to bring about environmentally sound policies. It spread across Europe and around the world thereafter.

Gregorian reform (315): The papal movement for church reform associated with Gregory VII (r. 1073–1085); its ideals included ending three practices: the purchase of church offices, clerical marriage, and lay investiture.

Gregory of Tours (255): Bishop of Tours (in Gaul) from 573 to 594, the chief source for the history and culture of the Merovingian kingdoms.

Gregory the Great (260): The pope (r. 590–604) who sent missionaries to Anglo-Saxon England, wrote influential books, tried to reform the church, and had contact with the major ruling families of Europe and Byzantium.

guild (309): A trade organization within a city or town that controlled product quality

and cost and outlined members' responsibilities. Guilds were also social and religious associations.

Hammurabi (ha muh RAH bee) (14): King of Babylonia in the eighteenth century B.C.E., famous for his law code.

Hanseatic League (419): A league of northern European cities formed in the fourteenth century to protect their mutual interests in trade and defense.

heliocentrism (482): The view articulated by Polish clergyman Nicolaus Copernicus that the earth and other planets revolve around the sun.

Hellenistic (118): An adjective meaning "Greek-like" that is today used as a chronological term for the period 323–30 B.C.E.

helot (62): A slave owned by the Spartan city-state; such slaves came from parts of Greece conquered by the Spartans.

Henry II (345): King of England (r. 1154–1189) who ended the period of civil war there and affirmed and expanded royal powers. He is associated with the creation of common law in England.

Henry IV (315): King of Germany (r. 1056–1106), crowned emperor in 1084. From 1075 until his death, he was embroiled in the Investiture Conflict with Pope Gregory VII.

Henry VIII (443): The English king (r. 1509–1547) who first opposed the Protestant Reformation and then broke with the Catholic church, naming himself head of the Church of England in the Act of Supremacy of 1534.

Heraclius (her uh KLY uhs) (247): The Byzantine emperor who reversed the fortunes of war with the Persians in the first quarter of the seventh century.

heresy (191): False doctrine; specifically, the beliefs banned for Christians by councils of bishops.

hetaira (heh TYE ruh) (89): A witty and attractive woman who charged fees to entertain at a symposium.

hierarchy (4): The system of ranking people in society according to their status and authority.

hieroglyphic (18): The ancient Egyptian pictographic writing system for official texts.

Hijra (HIJ ruh) (242): The emigration of Muhammad from Mecca to Medina. Its date, 622, marks the year 1 of the Islamic calendar.

Hitler, Adolf (849): 1889–1945. Chancellor of Germany (1933–1945) who, with considerable backing, overturned democratic government, created the Third Reich, persecuted millions, and ultimately led Germany and the world into World War II.

Homer (49): Greece's first and most famous author, who composed *The Iliad* and *The Odyssey*.

home rule (757): The right to an independent parliament demanded by the Irish and resisted by the British from the second half of the nineteenth century on.

hoplite (57): A heavily armed Greek infantryman. Hoplites constituted the main strike force of a city-state's militia.

hubris (HYOO bris) (98): The Greek term for violent arrogance.

humanism (412): A literary and linguistic movement cultivated in particular during the Renaissance (1350–1600) and founded on reviving classical Latin and Greek texts, styles, and values.

humanitas (156): The Roman orator Cicero's ideal of "humaneness," meaning generous and honest treatment of others based on natural law.

Hundred Years' War (404): The long war between England and France, 1337–1453 (actually 116 years); it produced numerous social upheavals yet left both states more powerful than before.

hunter-gatherers (5): Human beings who roam to hunt and gather food in the wild and do not live in permanent, settled communities.

iconoclasm (251): Literally, "icon breaking"; referring to the destruction of icons, or images of holy people. Byzantine emperors banned icons from 726 to 787; a modified ban was revived in 815 and lasted until 843.

icons (250): Images of holy people such as Jesus, Mary, and the saints. Controversy arose in

Byzantium over the meaning of such images. The iconoclasts considered them "idols," but those who adored icons maintained that they manifested the physical form of those who were holy.

ideology (660): A word coined during the French Revolution to refer to a coherent set of beliefs about the way the social and political order should be organized.

imperialism (676): European dominance of the non-West through economic exploitation and political rule; the word (as distinct from *colonialism,* which usually implied establishment of settler colonies, often with slavery) was coined in the mid-nineteenth century.

impressionism (752): A mid- to late-nineteenth-century artistic style that captured the sensation of light in images, derived from Japanese influences and in opposition to the realism of photographs.

indulgence (409): A step beyond confession and penance, an indulgence (normally granted by popes or bishops) lifted the temporal punishment still necessary for a sin already forgiven. Normally, that punishment was said to take place in purgatory. But it could be remitted through good works (including prayers and contributing money to worthy causes).

Industrial Revolution (660): The transformation of life in the Western world over several decades in the late eighteenth and early nineteenth centuries as a result of the introduction of steam-driven machinery, large factories, and a new working class.

Innocent III (370): The pope (r. 1198–1216) who called the Fourth Lateran Council; he was the most powerful, respected, and prestigious of medieval popes.

Investiture Conflict (316): The confrontation between Pope Gregory VII and Emperor Henry IV that began in 1075 over the appointment of prelates in some Italian cities and grew into a dispute over the nature of church leadership. It ended in 1122 with the Concordat of Worms.

in vitro fertilization (923): A process developed in the 1970s by which human eggs are fertilized with sperm outside the body and then implanted in a woman's uterus.

Jacobin Club (606): A French political club formed in 1789 that inspired the formation of a national network whose members dominated the revolutionary government during the Terror.

Jacquerie (zhah kuh REE) (407): The 1358 uprising of French peasants against the nobles amid the Hundred Years' War; it was brutally put down.

Jesuits (449): Members of the Society of Jesus, a Catholic religious order founded by Ignatius of Loyola (1491–1556) and approved by the pope in 1540. Jesuits served as missionaries and educators all over the world.

jihad (242): In the Qur'an, the word means "striving in the way of God." This can mean both striving to live righteously and striving to confront unbelievers, even as far as holy war.

Joan of Arc (405): A peasant girl (1412–1431) whose conviction that God had sent her to save France in fact helped France win the Hundred Years' War.

journeymen/journeywomen (309): Laborers in the Middle Ages whom guildmasters hired for a daily wage to help them produce their products.

Julian the Apostate (211): The Roman emperor (r. 361–363) who rejected Christianity and tried to restore traditional religion as the state religion. *Apostate* means "renegade from the faith."

Julio-Claudians (178): The ruling family of the early principate from Augustus through Nero, descended from the aristocratic families of the Julians and the Claudians.

Justinian and Theodora (227): Sixth-century emperor and empress of the eastern Roman Empire, famous for waging costly wars to reunite the empire.

Kennedy, John Fitzgerald (912): U.S. president (1961–1963) who faced off with Soviet leader Nikita Khrushchev in the Cuban missile crisis.

Khrushchev, Nikita (nyih KEE tuh kroosh CHAWF) (898): Leader of the USSR from c. 1955 until his dismissal in 1964; known for his speech denouncing Stalin, creation of the "thaw," and participation in the Cuban missile crisis.

Koine (koy NAY) (130): The "common" or "shared" form of the Greek language that became the international language in the Hellenistic period.

Kollontai, Aleksandra (833): A Russian activist and minister of public welfare in the Bolshevik government who promoted social programs such as birth control and day care for children of working parents.

Kulturkampf (722): Literally, "culture war"; a term used in the 1870s by German chancellor Otto von Bismarck to describe his fight to weaken the power of the Catholic church.

ladder of offices (148): The series of Roman elective government offices from quaestor to aedile to praetor to consul.

laissez-faire (LEH say FEHR) (569): French for "leave alone"; an economic doctrine developed by Adam Smith that advocated freeing the economy from government intervention and control.

lay investiture (313): The installation of clerics into their offices by lay rulers.

League of Nations (819): The international organization set up following World War I to maintain peace by arbitrating disputes and promoting collective security.

Lebensraum (858): Literally, "living space"; the land that Hitler proposed to conquer so that the people he defined as true Aryans might have sufficient space to live their noble lives.

Lenin, V. I. (813): Bolshevik leader who executed the Bolshevik Revolution in the fall of 1917, took Russia out of World War I, and imposed communism in Russia.

Leopold II (733): King of Belgium (r. 1865–1909) who sponsored the takeover of the Congo in Africa, which he ran with great violence against native peoples.

Lepanto (465): A site off the Greek coast where, in 1571, the allied Catholic forces of Spain's king Philip II, Venice, and the papacy defeated the Ottoman Turks in a great sea battle; the victory gave the Christian powers control of the Mediterranean.

leprosy (374): A bacterial disease that causes skin lesions and attacks the peripheral nerves. In the later Middle Ages, lepers were isolated from society.

Levellers (503): Disgruntled soldiers in Oliver Cromwell's New Model Army who in 1647 wanted to "level" social differences and extend political participation to all male property owners.

liberalism (680): An economic and political ideology that — tracing its roots to John Locke in the seventeenth century and Enlightenment philosophers in the eighteenth — emphasized free trade and the constitutional guarantees of individual rights such as freedom of speech and religion; its adherents stood between conservatives on the right and revolutionaries on the left in the nineteenth century.

limited liability corporation (744): A legal entity, such as a factory or other enterprise, developed in the second half of the nineteenth century whose owners were liable for only restricted (limited) amounts of money owed to creditors in the case of financial failure.

Linear B (32): The Mycenaeans' pictographic script for writing Greek.

Lombards (248): The people who settled in Italy during the sixth century, following Justinian's reconquest. A king ruled the north of Italy, while dukes ruled the south. In between was the papacy, which felt threatened both by Lombard Arianism and by the Lombards' geographical proximity to Rome.

Louis IX (382): A French king (r. 1226–1270) revered as a military leader and a judge; he was declared a saint after his death.

Louis XIV (494): French king (r. 1643–1715) who in theory personified absolutism but in practice had to gain the cooperation of nobles, local officials, and even the ordinary subjects who manned his armies and paid his taxes.

Louis XVI (598): French king (r. 1774–1792) who was tried for treason during the French Revolution; he was executed on January 21, 1793.

Luther, Martin (440): A German monk (1483–1546) who started the Protestant Reformation in 1517 by challenging the practices and doctrines of the Catholic church and advocating salvation through faith alone.

Lyceum (113): The school for research and teaching in a wide range of subjects founded by Aristotle in Athens in 335 B.C.E.

Maastricht Treaty (962): The agreement among the members of the European Community to have a closer alliance, including the use of common passports and eventually the development of a common currency; by the terms of this treaty, the European Community became the European Union (EU) in 1994.

Maat (MAH aht) (20): The Egyptian goddess embodying truth, justice, and cosmic order. (The word *maat* means "what is right.")

Magna Carta (349): Literally "Great Charter"; the charter of baronial liberties that King John was forced to agree to in 1215. It implied that royal power was subject to custom and law.

mandate system (821): The political control over the former colonies and territories of the German and Ottoman Empires granted to the victors of World War I by the League of Nations.

Marie-Antoinette (598): Wife of Louis XVI and queen of France who was tried for treason during the French Revolution and executed in October 1793.

Marshall Plan (886): A post–World War II program funded by the United States to get Europe back on its feet economically and thereby reduce the appeal of communism. It played an important role in the rebirth of European prosperity in the 1950s.

martyr (189): Greek for "witness," the term for someone who dies for his or her religious beliefs.

Marxism (718): A body of thought about the organization of production, social inequality, and the processes of revolutionary change as devised by the philosopher and economist Karl Marx.

masters (309): Men (and occasionally women) who, having achieved expertise in a craft, ran the guilds in the Middle Ages. They had to be rich enough to have their own shop and tools and to pay an entry fee into the guild. Often their positions were hereditary.

materialism (127): A philosophical doctrine of the Hellenistic Age that denied metaphysics and claimed instead that only things consisting of matter truly exist.

Mazzini, Giuseppe (679): An Italian nationalist (1805–1872) who founded Young Italy, a secret society to promote Italian unity. He believed that a popular uprising would create a unified Italy.

Medici (MEH dih chee) (423): The ruling family of Florence during much of the fifteenth to the seventeenth centuries.

Médicis, Catherine de (462): Italian-born mother of French king Charles IX (r. 1560–1574); she served as regent and tried but failed to prevent religious warfare between Calvinists and Catholics.

Mediterranean polyculture (29): The cultivation of olives, grapes, and grains in a single, interrelated agricultural system.

Mehmed II (407): The sultan under whom the Ottoman Turks conquered Constantinople in 1453.

mercantilism (498): The economic doctrine that governments must intervene to increase national wealth by whatever means possible.

Merovingian (mehr oh VIN jian) **dynasty** (252): The royal dynasty that ruled Gaul from about 486 to 751.

mestizo (535): A person born to a Spanish father and a native American mother.

metaphysics (112): Philosophical ideas about the ultimate nature of reality beyond the reach of human senses.

Methodism (573): A religious movement founded by John Wesley (1703–1791) that broke with the Church of England and insisted on strict self-discipline and a "methodical" approach to religious study and observance.

metic (87): A foreigner granted permanent residence status in Athens in return for paying taxes and serving in the military.

Metternich, Klemens von (KLAY mehnts fawn MEH tur nihk) (643): An Austrian prince (1773–1859) who took the lead in devising the post-Napoleonic settlement arranged by the Congress of Vienna (1814–1815).

Milosevic, Slobodan (955): President of Serbia (1989–1997) who pushed for Serb control of post-Communist Yugoslavia; in 2002, he was tried for crimes against humanity in the ethnic cleansing that accompanied the dissolution of the Yugoslav state.

mir (mihr) (700): A Russian farm community that provided for holding land in common and regulating the movements of any individual by the group.

Mitteleuropa (miht el oy ROH pah) (794): Literally, "central Europe," but used by military leaders in Germany before World War I to refer to land in both central and eastern Europe that they hoped to acquire.

modernism (774): Artistic styles around the turn of the twentieth century that featured a break with realism in art and literature and with lyricism in music.

moral dualism (43): The belief that the world is the arena for an ongoing battle for control between divine forces of good and evil.

Morrison, Toni (982): The first African American woman to win the Nobel Prize for Literature; her works include *Beloved* (1987), *Jazz* (1992), and *A Mercy* (2008).

mos maiorum (140): Literally, "the way of the elders"; the set of Roman values handed down from the ancestors.

Muhammad (240): The prophet of Islam (c. 570–632). He united a community of believers around his religious tenets, above all that there was one God whose words had been revealed to him by the angel Gabriel. Later, written down, these revelations became the Qur'an.

multinational corporation (923): A business that operates in many foreign countries by sending large segments of its manufacturing, finance, sales, and other business components abroad.

Mussolini, Benito (834): Leader of Italian fascist movement and, after the March on Rome in 1922, dictator of Italy.

mystery cults (87): Religious worship that provided initiation into secret knowledge and divine protection, including hope for a better afterlife.

nationalism (678): An ideology that arose in the nineteenth century and that holds that all peoples derive their identities from their nations, which are defined by common language, shared cultural traditions, and sometimes religion.

nation-state (702): An independent political unit of modern times based on representing a united people.

Nazi-Soviet Pact (862): The agreement reached in 1939 by Germany and the Soviet Union in which both agreed not to attack the other in case of war and to divide any conquered territories.

neoliberalism (941): A theory first promoted by British prime minister Margaret Thatcher, calling for a return to liberal principles of the nineteenth century, including the reduction of welfare-state programs and the cutting of taxes for the wealthy to promote economic growth.

Neoplatonism (193): Plotinus's spiritual philosophy, based mainly on Plato's ideas, which was very influential for Christian intellectuals.

new unionism (755): A nineteenth-century development in labor organizing that replaced local craft-based unions with those that extended membership to all kinds of workers.

new woman (771): A woman who, from the 1880s on, dressed practically, moved about freely, and often supported herself.

Nicene Creed (215): The doctrine agreed on by the council of bishops convened by Constantine at Nicaea in 325 to defend orthodoxy against Arianism. It declared that God the Father and Jesus were *homoousion* ("of one substance").

Nicholas II (782): Tsar of Russia (r. 1894–1917) who promoted anti-Semitism and resisted reform in the empire.

Nietzsche, Friedrich (775): Late-nineteenth-century German philosopher who called for a new morality in the face of God's death at the hands of science and whose theories were reworked by his sister to emphasize militarism and anti-Semitism.

Nightingale, Florence (699): The Englishwoman who in the nineteenth century pioneered

the professionalization of nursing and the use of statistics in the study of public health and the well-being of the military.

Nixon, Richard (937): U.S. president (1969–1974) who escalated the Vietnam War, worked for accommodation with China, and resigned from the presidency after trying to block free elections.

nongovernmental organizations (NGOs) (966): Charitable foundations and activist groups such as Doctors Without Borders that work outside of governments, often on political, economic, and relief issues; also, philanthropic organizations such as the Rockefeller, Ford, and Open Society Foundations that shape economic and social policy and the course of political reform.

North Atlantic Treaty Organization (NATO) (889): The security alliance formed in 1949 to provide a unified military force for the United States, Canada, and their allies in western Europe and Scandinavia.

Nuremberg Laws (852): Legislation enacted by the Nazis in 1935 that deprived Jewish Germans of their citizenship and imposed many other hardships on them.

Opium War (677): War between China and Great Britain (1839–1842) that resulted in the opening of four Chinese ports to Europeans and British sovereignty over Hong Kong.

optimates (op tee MAH tehs) (159): The Roman political faction supporting the "best," or highest, social class; established during the late republic.

orders (148): The two groups of people in the Roman republic — **patricians** (aristocratic families) and **plebeians** (all other citizens).

Organization of Petroleum Exporting Countries (OPEC) (938): A consortium that regulated the supply and export of oil and that acted with more unanimity after the United States supported Israel against the Arabs in the wars of the late 1960s and early 1970s.

orthodoxy (191): True doctrine; specifically, the beliefs defined for Christians by councils of bishops.

Ostpolitik (930): A policy initiated by West German foreign minister Willy Brandt in the late 1960s in which West Germany sought better economic relations with the Communist countries of eastern Europe.

ostracism (AHS truh sizm) (81): An annual procedure in Athenian radical democracy by which a man could be voted out of the city-state for ten years; its purpose was to prevent tyranny.

Ottonian (ah TOH nee uhn) **kings** (297): The tenth- and early-eleventh-century kings of Germany; beginning with Otto I (r. 936–973), they claimed the imperial crown and worked closely with their bishops to rule a vast territory.

outwork (741): The nineteenth-century process of having some aspects of industrial work done outside factories in individual homes.

Pacific tigers (975): Countries of East Asia so named because of their massive economic growth, much of it from the 1980s on; foremost among these were Japan and China.

palace society (28): Minoan and Mycenaean social and political organization centered on multichambered buildings housing the rulers and the administration of the state.

Pankhurst, Emmeline (780): 1858–1928. Organizer of a militant branch of the British suffrage movement, working actively for women's right to vote.

Pan-Slavism (709): The nineteenth-century movement calling for the unity of all Slavs across national and regional boundaries.

Parnell, Charles Stewart (757): Irish politician (1846–1891) whose advocacy of home rule was a thorn in the side of the British establishment.

Parthenon (PAR thuh non) (83): The massive temple to Athena as a warrior goddess built atop the Athenian acropolis in the Golden Age of Greece.

partition of Poland (582): Division of one-third of Poland-Lithuania's territory between Prussia, Russia, and Austria in 1772.

patria potestas (PAH tree uh po TEHS tahs) (142): Literally, "father's power"; the legal power a Roman father possessed over the children and slaves in his family, including owning all their property and having the right to punish them, even with death.

patriarchy (10): Dominance by men in society and politics.

patrilineal (294): Relating to or tracing descent through the paternal line (for example, through the father and grandfather).

patron-client system (141): The interlocking network of mutual obligations between Roman patrons (social superiors) and clients (social inferiors).

Pax Romana (170): Literally "Roman Peace"; the two centuries of relative peace and prosperity in the Roman Empire under the early principate begun by Augustus.

Peace of Augsburg (456): The treaty of 1555 that settled disputes between Holy Roman Emperor Charles V and his Protestant princes. It recognized the Lutheran church and established the principle that all Catholic or Lutheran princes enjoyed the sole right to determine the religion of their lands and subjects.

Peace of God (294): A movement begun by bishops in the south of France around 990, first to limit the violence done to property and to the unarmed, and later, with the Truce of God, to limit fighting between warriors.

Peace of Paris (819): The series of peace treaties (1919–1920) that provided the settlement of World War I. The Treaty of Versailles with Germany was the centerpiece of the Peace of Paris.

Peace of Westphalia (472): The settlement (1648) of the Thirty Years' War; it established enduring religious divisions in the Holy Roman Empire by which Lutheranism would dominate in the north, Calvinism in the area of the Rhine River, and Catholicism in the south.

perestroika (943): Literally, "restructuring"; an economic policy instituted in the 1980s by Soviet premier Mikhail Gorbachev calling for the introduction of market mechanisms and the achievement of greater efficiency in manufacturing, agriculture, and services.

Pericles (PEHR uh kleez) (81): Athens's political leader during the Golden Age.

Peter the Great (549): Russian tsar Peter I (r. 1689–1725), who undertook the Westernization of Russia and built a new capital city named after himself, St. Petersburg.

Petrarch, Francis (413): An Italian poet (1304–1374) who revived the styles of classical authors; he is considered the first Renaissance humanist.

Philip II (465): King of Spain (r. 1556–1598) and the most powerful ruler in Europe; he reigned over the western Habsburg lands and all the Spanish colonies recently settled in the New World.

Philip II (Philip Augustus) (349): King of France (r. 1180–1223) who bested the English king John and won most of John's continental territories, thus immeasurably strengthening the power of the Capetian dynasty.

philosophes (fee luh SAWF) (564): French for "philosophers"; public intellectuals of the Enlightenment who wrote on subjects ranging from current affairs to art criticism with the goal of furthering reform in society.

Pietism (544): A Protestant revivalist movement of the early eighteenth century that emphasized deeply emotional individual religious experience.

plantation (530): A large tract of land that produced staple crops such as sugar, coffee, and tobacco; was farmed by slave labor; and was owned by a colonial settler.

Plato (112): A follower of Socrates who became Greece's most famous philosopher.

plebiscites (PLEH buh sites) (150): Resolutions passed by the Plebeian Assembly; such resolutions gained the force of law in 287 B.C.E.

polis (52): The Greek city-state, an independent community of citizens not ruled by a king.

politiques (poh lih TEEK) (463): Political advisers during the sixteenth-century French Wars of Religion who argued that compromise in matters of religion would strengthen the monarchy.

polytheism (10): The belief in and worship of multiple gods.

pop art (927): A style in the visual arts that mimicked advertising and consumerism and that used ordinary objects as a part of paintings and other compositions.

popolo (388): Literally, "people"; a communal faction, largely made up of merchants, that demanded (and often obtained) power in thirteenth-century Italian cities.

populares (poh poo LAH rehs) (159): The Roman political faction supporting the common people; established during the late republic.

Popular Front (855): An alliance of political parties (initially led by Léon Blum in France) in the 1930s to resist fascism despite philosophical differences.

positivism (724): A theory developed in the mid-nineteenth century that the study of facts would generate accurate, or "positive," laws of society and that these laws could, in turn, help in the formulation of policies and legislation.

postmodernism (984): A term applied in the late twentieth century to both an intense stylistic mixture in the arts without a central unifying theme or elite set of standards and a critique of Enlightenment and scientific beliefs in rationality and the possibility of certain knowledge.

praetorian guard (172): The group of soldiers stationed in Rome under the emperor's control; first formed by Augustus.

predestination (442): John Calvin's doctrine that God preordained salvation or damnation for each person before creation; those chosen for salvation were considered the "elect."

primogeniture (293): An inheritance practice that left all property to the oldest son.

principate (171): Roman political system invented by Augustus as a disguised monarchy with the *princeps* ("first man") as emperor.

proletarians (160): In the Roman republic, the mass of people so poor they owned no property.

Pugachev (poo guh CHAWF) rebellion (587): A massive revolt of Russian Cossacks and serfs in 1773 against local nobles and the armies of Catherine the Great; its leader, Emelian Pugachev, was eventually captured and executed.

pump priming (851): An economic policy used by governments, including the Nazis in Germany, to stimulate the economy through public works programs and other infusions of public funds.

purges (847): The series of attacks on citizens of the USSR accused of being "wreckers," or saboteurs of communism, in the 1930s and later.

Puritans (467): Strict Calvinists who in the sixteenth and seventeenth centuries opposed all vestiges of Catholic ritual in the Church of England.

Putin, Vladimir (957): President of Russia from 2000 to 2008; prime minister 2008–2012; reelected president in 2012. He has worked to reestablish Russia as a world power through control of the country's resources and military capabilities.

Qur'an (kur AN/koo RAHN) (241): The holy book of Islam, considered the word of Allah ("the God") as revealed to the Prophet Muhammad.

radical democracy (81): The Athenian system of democracy established in the 460s and 450s B.C.E. that extended direct political power and participation in the court system to all adult male citizens.

raison d'état (ray ZOHN day TAH) (475): French for "reason of state," the political doctrine, first proposed by Cardinal Richelieu of France, which held that the state's interests should prevail over those of religion.

rationalism (69): The philosophic idea that people must justify their claims by logic and reason, not myth.

Razin, Stenka (517): Leader of the 1667 rebellion that promised Russian peasants liberation from noble landowners and officials; he was captured by the tsar's army in 1671 and publicly executed in Moscow.

realism (719): An artistic style that arose in the mid-nineteenth century and was dedicated to depicting society realistically without romantic or idealistic overtones.

Realpolitik (ray AHL poh lih teek) (695): Policies developed after the revolutions of 1848 and initially associated with nation building; they were based on realism rather than on the romantic notions of earlier nationalists.

The term has come to mean any policy based on considerations of power alone.

reconquista (ray con KEE stuh) (315): The collective name for the wars waged by the Christian princes of Spain against the Muslim-ruled regions to their south. These wars were considered holy, akin to the crusades.

redistributive economy (10): A system in which state officials control the production and distribution of goods.

Reform Act of 1884 (756): British legislation that granted the right to vote to a mass male citizenry.

Reform Bill of 1832 (655): A measure passed by the British Parliament to increase the number of male voters by about 50 percent and give representation to new cities in the north; it set a precedent for widening suffrage.

res publica (REHS POOB lih kuh) (146): Literally, "the people's matter" or "the public business"; the Romans' name for their republic and the source of our word *republic*.

restoration (643): The epoch after the fall of Napoleon, in which the Congress of Vienna aimed to "restore" as many regimes as possible to their former rulers.

revocation of the Edict of Nantes (498): French king Louis XIV's 1685 decision to eliminate the rights of Calvinists granted in the edict of 1598; Louis banned all Calvinist public activities and forced those who refused to embrace the state religion to flee.

Robespierre, Maximilien (roh behs PYEHR) (607): A lawyer from northern France who, as leader of the Committee of Public Safety, laid out the principles of a republic of virtue and of the Terror; his arrest and execution in July 1794 brought an end to the Terror.

rococo (542): A style of painting that emphasized irregularity and asymmetry, movement and curvature, but on a smaller, more intimate scale than the baroque.

Romanesque (341): An architectural style that flourished in Europe between about 1000 and 1150. It is characterized by solid, heavy forms and semicircular arches and vaults. Romanesque buildings were often decorated with fanciful sculpture and wall paintings.

Romanization (182): The spread of Roman law and culture in the provinces of the Roman Empire.

romanticism (571): An artistic movement of the late eighteenth and early nineteenth centuries that glorified nature, emotion, genius, and imagination.

Rousseau, Jean-Jacques (zhahn zhahk roo SOH) (569): One of the most important philosophes (1712–1778); he argued that only a government based on a social contract among the citizens could make people truly moral and free.

ruler cults (131): Cults that involved worship of a Hellenistic ruler as a savior god.

Rushdie, Salman (982): Immigrant British author whose novel *The Satanic Verses* (1988) led the ayatollah Ruhollah Khomeini of Iran to issue a fatwa calling for Rushdie's murder.

Russification (702): A program for the integration of Russia's many nationality groups that involved the forced learning of the Russian language and the practice of Russian Orthodox religion as well as the settlement of ethnic Russians among other nationality groups.

sacraments (318): In the Catholic church, the institutionalized means by which God's heavenly grace is transmitted to Christians. Examples of sacraments include baptism, the Eucharist (communion), and marriage.

salon (522): An informal gathering held regularly in a private home and presided over by a socially eminent woman; salons spread from France in the seventeenth century to other countries in the eighteenth century.

samizdat (930): A key form of dissident activity across the Soviet bloc in which individuals reproduced government-suppressed publications by hand and passed them from reader to reader, thus building a foundation for the successful resistance of the 1980s.

Sand, George (672): The pen name of French novelist Amandine-Aurore-Lucile Dupin Dudevant (1804–1876), who showed her independence in the 1830s by dressing like a man and smoking cigars. The term *George-Sandism* became an expression of disdain for independent women.

Sappho (SAF oh) (68): The most famous woman lyric poet of ancient Greece, a native of Lesbos.

Schlieffen Plan (806): The Germans' strategy in World War I that called for attacks on two fronts — concentrating first on France to the west and then turning east to attack Russia.

scholasticism (375): The method of logical inquiry used by the scholastics, the scholars of the medieval universities; it applied Aristotelian logic to biblical and other authoritative texts in an attempt to summarize and reconcile all knowledge.

scientific method (482): The combination of experimental observation and mathematical deduction used to determine the laws of nature; first developed in the seventeenth century, it became the secular standard of truth.

Scott, Sir Walter (649): A prolific author (1771–1832) of popular historical novels; he also collected and published traditional Scottish ballads and wrote poetry.

Sea Peoples (33): The diverse groups of raiders who devastated the eastern Mediterranean region in the period of violence 1200–1000 B.C.E.

Second International (755): A transnational organization of workers established in 1889, mostly committed to Marxian socialism.

secularization (481): The long-term trend toward separating state power and science from religious faith, making the latter a private domain; begun in the seventeenth century, it prompted a search for nonreligious explanations for political authority and natural phenomena.

Seven Years' War (580): A worldwide series of battles (1756–1763) between Austria, France, Russia, and Sweden on one side and Prussia and Great Britain on the other.

Shi'ite (244): A Muslim of the "party of Ali" and his descendants. Shi'ites are thus opposed to the Sunni Muslims, who reject the authority of Ali.

simony (SY muh nee) (313): The sin of giving gifts or paying money to get a church office.

social contract (508): The doctrine, originated by Hugo Grotius and argued by both Thomas Hobbes and John Locke, that all political authority derives not from divine right but from an implicit contract between citizens and their rulers.

socialism (681): A social and political ideology, originating in the early nineteenth century, that advocated the reorganization of society to overcome the new tensions created by industrialization and restore social harmony through communities based on cooperation.

Socratic method (94): The Athenian philosopher Socrates' method of teaching through conversation, in which he asked probing questions to make his listeners examine their most cherished assumptions.

Solidarity (945): A Polish labor union founded in 1980 by Lech Walesa and Anna Walentynowicz that contested Communist Party programs and eventually succeeded in ousting the party from the Polish government.

Solon (66): Athenian political reformer whose changes promoted early democracy.

Sophists (SAH fists) (91): Competitive intellectuals and teachers in ancient Greece who offered expensive courses in persuasive public speaking and new ways of philosophic and religious thinking beginning around 450 B.C.E.

South African War (786): The war (1899–1902) between Britain and the Boer (originally Dutch) inhabitants of South Africa for control of the region; also called the Boer War.

soviets (813): Councils of workers and soldiers first formed in Russia in the Revolution of 1905; they were revived to represent the people in the early days of the 1917 Russian Revolution.

stagflation (939): The combination of a stagnant economy and soaring inflation; a period of stagflation occurred in the West in the 1970s as a result of an OPEC embargo on oil.

Stalin, Joseph (846): Leader of the USSR who, with considerable backing, formed a brutal dictatorship in the 1930s and forcefully converted the country into an industrial power.

St. Bernard (320): The most important Cistercian abbot (early twelfth century) and the chief preacher of the Second Crusade.

Stoicism (127): The Hellenistic philosophy whose followers believed in fate but also in pursuing excellence (virtue) by cultivating good sense, justice, courage, and temperance.

Suleiman the Magnificent (452): Sultan of the Ottoman Empire (r. 1520–1566) at the time of its greatest power.

Synod of Whitby (261): The meeting of churchmen and King Oswy of Northumbria in 664 that led to the adoption of the Roman brand of Christianity in England.

Terror (607): The policy established under the direction of the Committee of Public Safety during the French Revolution to arrest dissidents and execute opponents in order to protect the republic from its enemies.

tetrarchy (205): The "rule by four," consisting of two co-emperors and two assistant emperors/designated successors, initiated by Diocletian to subdivide the ruling of the Roman Empire into four regions.

Thatcher, Margaret (940): Prime minister of Britain (1979–1990) who set a new tone for British politics by promoting neoliberal economic policies and criticizing poor people, union members, and racial minorities as worthless, even harmful citizens.

theme (249): A military district in Byzantium. The earliest themes were created in the seventh century and served mainly defensive purposes.

Themistocles (thuh MIST uh kleez) (77): Athens's leader during the great Persian invasion of Greece.

Theodora — *See* Justinian.

Theodosius I (211): The Roman emperor (r. 379–395) who made Christianity the state religion by ending public sacrifices in the traditional cults and closing their temples. In 395, he also divided the empire into western and eastern halves to be ruled by his sons.

Thermidorian Reaction (615): The violent backlash against the rule of Robespierre that dismantled the Terror and punished Jacobins and their supporters.

Third Republic (757): The French government that succeeded Napoleon III's Second Empire after its defeat in the Franco-Prussian War of 1870–1871. It lasted until France's defeat by Germany in 1940.

Torah (45): The first five books of the Hebrew Bible, also referred to as the Pentateuch. It contains early Jewish law.

total war (804): A war built on the full mobilization of soldiers, civilians, and technology of the nations involved. The term also refers to a highly destructive war of ideologies.

Treaty of Verdun (285): The treaty that, in 843, split the Carolingian Empire into three parts; its borders roughly outline modern western European states.

triremes (TRY reems) (80): Greek wooden warships rowed by 170 oarsmen sitting on three levels and equipped with a battering ram at the bow.

troubadours (355): Vernacular poets in southern France in the twelfth and early thirteenth centuries who sang of love, longing, and courtesy.

Truman Doctrine (886): The policy devised by U.S. president Harry Truman to limit communism after World War II by countering political crises with economic and military aid.

Twelve Tables (148): The first written Roman law code, enacted between 451 and 449 B.C.E.

Umayyad caliphate (oo MAH yuhd KAY luhf ayt) (245): The caliphs (successors of Muhammad) who traced their ancestry to Umayyah, a member of Muhammad's tribe. The dynasty lasted from 661 to 750.

United Nations (UN) (904): An organization set up in 1945 for collective security and for the resolution of international conflicts through both deliberation and the use of force.

Urban II (324): The pope (r. 1088–1099) responsible for calling the First Crusade in 1095.

urbanization (666): The growth of towns and cities due to the movement of people from rural to urban areas, a trend that was encouraged by the development of factories and railroads.

Vatican II (906): A Catholic Council held between 1962 and 1965 to modernize some aspects of church teachings (such as condemnation of Jews), to update the liturgy, and to promote cooperation among the faiths (i.e., ecumenism).

Visigoths (222): The name given to the barbarians whom Alaric united and led on a military campaign into the western Roman Empire to establish a new kingdom; they sacked Rome in 410.

Voltaire (556): The pen name of François-Marie Arouet (1694–1778), who was the most influential writer of the early Enlightenment.

Walpole, Robert (548): The first, or "prime," minister (1721–1742) of the House of Commons of Great Britain's Parliament. Although appointed initially by the king, through his long period of leadership he effectively established the modern pattern of parliamentary government.

war guilt clause (819): The part of the Treaty of Versailles that assigned blame for World War I to Germany.

War of the Austrian Succession (552): The war (1740–1748) over the succession to the Habsburg throne that pitted France and Prussia against Austria and Britain and provoked continuing hostilities between French and British settlers in the North American colonies.

Warsaw Pact (889): A security alliance of the Soviet Union and its allies formed in 1955, in retaliation for NATO's admittance of West Germany.

Weimar Republic (818): The parliamentary republic established in 1919 in Germany to replace the monarchy.

welfare state (894): A system (developed on both sides during the cold war) comprising government-sponsored social programs to provide health care, family allowances, disability insurance, and pensions for veterans and retired workers.

wergild (226): Under Frankish law, the payment that a murderer had to make as compensation for the crime, to prevent feuds of revenge.

Westernization (549): The effort, especially in Peter the Great's Russia, to make society and social customs resemble counterparts in western Europe, especially France, Britain, and the Dutch Republic.

William, prince of Orange (506): Dutch ruler who, with his Protestant wife, Mary (daughter of James II), ruled England after the Glorious Revolution of 1688.

wisdom literature (22): Texts giving instructions for proper behavior by officials.

Zionism (786): A movement that began in the late nineteenth century among European Jews to found a Jewish state.

Index

A note about the index:

Names of individuals appear in boldface.

Letters in parenthesis following pages refer to:

(i) illustrations, including photographs and artifacts

(f) figures, including charts and graphs

(m) maps

Aachen, 281, 283*(i)*. *See also* Aix-la-Chapelle

Abbasid caliphate, 270, 275–276, 286, 324

Abbesses, Merovingian, 259

Abd al-Rahman I (caliph of Córdoba), 277

Abd al-Rahman III (caliph of Córdoba), 278, 279*(i)*

Abdul Hamid II (Ottoman sultan), 792

Abelard, Peter, 339, 375

Abgar (Osrhoëne king), 216*(i)*

Abolitionism, 509, 567, 590, 659, 676

Abortion, 769, 922
in Byzantine Empire, 248
in France, 825
Nazi Germany and, 852
Romania and, 946
in Soviet Union, 833

Abraham (Hebrew patriarch), 44

Absolutism, 493
in Austria, 708
Bodin and, 485
in Brandenburg-Prussia, 514–515
in central and eastern Europe, 513, 514–518
Hobbes and, 508
Locke and, 508–509

Louis XIV and, 493, 494–501, 502
in Russia, 517–518

Abstract painting, 777, 911

Academies, 576
in Athens, 112, 233
of Louis XIV, 496
Royal Academy of Sciences (France), 521
of Sciences (Russia), 549, 550

Acid rain, 967

Acquired immunodeficiency syndrome (AIDS), 944, 970

Acropolis (Athens), 83*(i)*, 84*(i)*, 97. *See also* Parthenon (Athens)

Actium, battle of, 171

Activism. *See also* specific movements
in 1960s and 1970s, 917, 931–933
anticolonial, 845, 846
citizen, 931–933
collective, 754–755
environmental, 967–968
Irish, 757
in Poland, 945–946
student, 933, 934–935
by women, 823, 933, 934*(i)*
World War I and, 810

Act of Supremacy (England, 1534), 444

Act of Union (Britain)
in 1707, 547–548
in 1801, 680

Adam, Robert, 576*(i)*

Adam and **Eve,** 217

Adams, John, on French Revolution, 619

Addis Ababa, Ethiopia, 858

Addison, Joseph, 542

Adenauer, Konrad, 893

Administration. *See also* Bureaucracy; Government; specific locations
of England, 296
of France, 604*(m)*
Hellenistic, 120–121
of Russia, 701

Adoption, in Rome, 186

Adrianople, Treaty of, 652

Adultery, 174, 579

Advancement of Learning, The (Bacon), 484

Advertising, culture and, 910, 927

Aediles (Rome), 149

Aegean Sea region, 25, 26*(m)*, 33, 79, 80

Aeneas (mythological character), 161*(i)*

Aeneid, The (Virgil), 176

Aeschylus (Athens), 97
Affair of the Placards (1534), 442,
    455
Afghanistan
    Alexander the Great in, 117
    refugees from, 977
    Russia and, 736, 737(*m*)
    Soviet Union and, 943, 945,
        960
    Taliban in, 972–973
Africa. *See also* Egypt (ancient);
        Imperialism; North Africa;
        South Africa; specific
        locations
    c. 1890, 734(*m*)
    AIDS in, 970
    Catholic discrimination in,
        449–450
    colonization in, 536, 676,
        731–736, 734(*m*), 739, 742,
        787(*m*), 788, 904
    conflict and genocide in, 971
    decolonization in, 899,
        902–904, 903(*m*)
    immigrants from, 952(*i*), 953
    imperialism in, 731–732,
        733–736, 742, 787(*m*), 788,
        792–793, 826
    missionaries and, 739–740
    public health in, 970
    slavery and, 434–435, 511–512,
        531, 643
    violence in, 735(*i*)
    white settlements in, 536
    World War I and, 806, 808
    World War II and, 869, 870(*m*)
Africa (Carriera), 537(*i*)
African Americans, 832
    literature by, 982–983
    rights for, 711, 908, 931
    as U.S. president, 974
    violence after King's death,
        933–934
African people
    European attitudes toward,
        735–736
    in North American colonies,
        480
    in World War I, 811
Afterlife
    Egyptian belief in, 2(*i*)
    Paleolithic, 5
Agamemnon, 97, 98(*i*)
    Schliemann on, 30–31
Agora, in Athens, 83, 83(*i*)
Agribusiness, 925, 931

Agriculture. *See also* Farms and
        farming; Irrigation; Land
    in early 19th century, 668–670
    in Africa, 736
    ancient, 4
    Black Death and, 402–403
    Byzantine, 249
    Dutch, 538–539
    economic activity and, 256–257
    Egyptian, 18, 733
    Flemish, 538–539
    genetic research in, 925
    in Great Depression, 843, 845
    Hellenistic, 122
    industrial innovation in, 742
    Mediterranean, 29
    Mesopotamian, 8
    reforms in, 585
    revolution in, 538–540, 661
    Roman, 197
    in western Europe, 305–306
    workers in, 540, 664, 665
    yield ratios (1400 to 1800),
        539(*f*)
Ahriman (god), 43
Ahura Mazda (god), 43
Aïda (Verdi), 694(*i*), 716
AIDS. *See* Acquired
        immunodeficiency
        syndrome
Ai-Khanoum, Afghanistan, 129
Airbus, 924
Air force, Luftwaffe, 864
Airline industry, international
        ventures in, 924
Airplanes
    World War I and, 816
    World War II and, 863
Aix-la-Chapelle. *See also* Aachen
    Peace of (1748), 553
    Treaty of, 499
Akhenaten (Amenhotep IV,
        Egypt), 24
Akhmatova, Anna, 897
Akkadian Empire, 12–13, 12(*m*)
al-Andalus (Spain). *See also* Spain
    Charlemagne and, 281
    Muslims in, 278, 361(*m*), 362(*m*)
Alaric (Visigoth), 222
Albania, 794
Albanian Kosovars, 955
Albert (England), 709, 710, 712
Alberti, Leon Battista, 414, 414(*i*)
Albigensian Crusade, 364, 364(*m*)
Albigensians, 359
Alchemy, 487

Alcibiades (Athens), 102–103
Alcohol and alcoholism, 668, 943,
        970
Alcuin, 284
Aldrin, Edwin "Buzz," 920
Alemanni people, 225
Alexander I (Russia), 640, 651
    Holy Alliance and, 643
    Poland and, 654
    reforms of, 638, 720
Alexander II (Russia), 699, 700,
        702, 761, 762(*i*)
Alexander III (Russia), 761–762
Alexander VI (Pope), 434
Alexander the Great (Macedonia),
        109–110, 116–118, 116(*i*),
        117(*m*). *See also* Hellenistic
        world
Alexandria, Egypt, 121, 124–125
    Neoplatonist school at, 234
    Rome and, 182
Alexei (Russia, son of Peter the
        Great), 550
Alexei I (Russia), 517, 518
Alexius I (Alexius Comnenus,
        Byzantine Empire), 324,
        325, 328
Alfonso IX (Castile-León), 385
Alfonso X (Castile-León), 385
Alfred the Great (Wessex),
        295–296, 295(*m*)
Algebra, 15
Algeria, 870, 872
    France and, 669, 676, 698, 716,
        904
Ali (caliph), 244, 277
Allah, 241
Alliances. *See also* Allies; specific
        alliances
    Athenian, 79–81
    in cold war, 889, 889(*m*)
    against France, 500
    Peloponnesian League as, 100
    in Seven Years' War, 580
    Spartan, 79
    World War I and, 793, 804–806,
        822
    before World War II, 858,
        862–863
Allies
    at Congress of Vienna,
        642–644
    in Crimean War, 698(*m*)
    Greek, 77–80, 90–91, 100, 102,
        103, 106, 114–115
    in Napoleonic wars, 640–641

Roman, 160
World War I and, 804, 805–806, 807, 810, 814, 816, 819
World War II and, 865, 868, 869, 870, 870(m), 871, 872, 883
All Quiet on the Western Front (Remarque), 831, 851
Almourol Castle, 363(i)
Alphabets, 15. *See also* Languages; Writing
Cyrillic, 274
Latin, 845
Mesopotamian, 15
Sumerian writing and, 11
al-Qaeda organization, 971, 973, 974
Alsace
France and, 472, 819
Germany and, 707, 742
World War I and, 819
Amar, Jules, 803, 809, 823, 832
Ambrose (bishop of Milan), 216, 233
American Indians, 450, 480
Columbus and, 434
conversion of, 431
European diseases and, 436
forced labor of, 454
Americanization, of culture, 906
American Revolution. *See* American War of Independence
American Temperance Society, 674
American War of Independence, 509, 582, 586, 588–590, 596
Americas. *See also* Exploration; New World; Portugal; Spain; specific locations
colonies in, 480–481, 480(m), 511–512, 535–537
Dutch trade with, 549
Mongol invasions and, 390
settlement of, 535
slavery in, 435, 511–512
slave trade and, 435, 532–535, 532(f), 533(f)
travel to, 557
Amiens, Treaty of, 635
Amnesty, after Peloponnesian War, 104
Amritsar massacre (1919), 826
Amsterdam, 467, 510, 570, 596
Amun (Amen, god), 24
Amun-Re (god), cult of, 24

Anabaptists, 445–447
Anacletus, 386(i)
Anarchists and anarchism, 717–718, 755, 776, 779
Anatolia, 4, 525(m). *See also* Turkey
Attalids in, 119
Greece and, 114
Hellenistic Greeks and, 121
Hittites and, 25–28
Ottomans in, 407
Seljuk Turks in, 333(m)
Anatomy, 130, 483
Anaximander of Miletus, 69
Angevin dynasty (England), 345
Angles, 224
Anglican church. *See* Church of England
Anglo-Saxon (Old English) language, 262, 295–296
Anglo-Saxon people and culture
in Britain, 260, 261, 329, 347
Roman Empire and, 224
Angola, 536
Animals. *See also* Hunting
domestication of, 4, 6
human treatment of, 578, 674
Anjou, France and, 349
Ankara, Turkey, 845
Anna Karenina (Tolstoy), 760–761
Annals (Ennius), 155
Annam, 736
Anne (England), 547
Anne of Austria, 494, 495
Annunciation, The (Leonardo da Vinci), 415, 416(i)
Anschluss (merger), 860
Anselm (Saint), 322, 330
Antarctica, 567
Anthony, Susan B., 780
Anthropology, in postindustrial society, 928
Anticlericalism, 639
Anticommunism, 885
of Hitler and Mussolini, 858
of McCarthy, 893
Anti-Corn Law League (England), 680
Antifascism, in 1930s, 855, 859–860
Antigone (Sophocles), 98
Antigonus (Macedonia), 119, 131
Anti-immigrant sentiment, 978
Antioch, 182, 325, 326
Antiochus I (Seleucids), 119
Antiochus II (Seleucids), 132
Antiochus IV (Seleucids), 186

Anti-Semitism, 513. *See also* Holocaust; Jews and Judaism; Nazis and Nazism
in Austria, 855
in Austria-Hungary, 784
in Dreyfus Affair, 782–783
in eastern Europe, 957
in France, 757, 782–783
Freud and, 773(i)
in Germany, 783–784, 849
in Great Depression, 844
of Hitler, 836, 852
in mass politics, 782–784
of Nazis, 851–852, 865–868
in Russia, 748, 782
in Soviet Union, 885, 936
World War I and, 811
World War II and, 865–868, 883
Antiseptics, 554
Antislavery movement, 567, 676
Antiwar sentiment, in Vietnam War, 933, 937
Antoninus Pius (Rome), 180
Antony (Christian ascetic), 218
Antony, Mark (Rome), 124, 170–171
Antwerp, Spanish sack of, 460(i), 461
Apartheid, 975
Aphrodite (goddess), 55, 126, 126(i)
Apocalyptism, 46, 133, 186
Apollo (god), 55
Apollonis (Attalid queen), 123
Apostate, 211
Apostles, 187, 191
Apostolic succession, 191
Appeasement, 861
Appliances. *See* Consumer goods
Apprentices, in guilds, 309
April Theses (Lenin), 813
Apuleius (Rome), 183–184, 192
Aqueducts, Roman, 151, 152(i)
Arabic language, 278
Arabic numerals, 549
Arab-Israeli wars (1967, 1973), 938, 938(m)
Arabs and Arab world. *See also* Caliphs and caliphates; Islam; Muhammad; specific leaders
Palestine and, 901
Spain and, 263
Aragon, 360, 362(m), 419–420
Aramaic language, 41

Arawak Indians, 434
Arc de Triomphe, 630
Archaic Age (Greece), 38(i). See
        also Greece (ancient);
        specific locations
    city-state in, 52–67
    intellectual thought in, 67–70
Archilochus of Paros (Greek poet),
        68–69
Archimedean screw, 129
Archimedes of Syracuse, 129
Architecture. See also Building;
        Housing; specific buildings
    in Athens, 82–86, 84(i)
    baroque, 487
    Bauhaus and, 832
    Egyptian, 16–17, 20–21, 20(i)
    Gothic, 336(i), 337, 341,
        342–343
    in Greek Dark Age, 48
    neoclassical, 576, 576(i)
    postmodern, 984, 985(i)
    Renaissance, 414
    Roman, 173–174
    Romanesque, 341–342, 342(i),
        343(i)
Arctic region, pack ice melting in,
        967
Areopagitica (Milton), 518
Areopagus Council (Athens), 66,
        81
Aretê (excellence), 49, 94
Argentina, 941
Argument, Aristotle on, 114
Arianism
    of Theodoric, 215, 224–225
    of Visigoths, 262
Ariosto, Ludovico, 451, 522
Aristarchus, 129
Aristides, 79, 81–82
Aristocracy, 485. See also Elites;
        Nobility; specific locations
    after 1848 revolutions, 689
    in Britain, 747
    Carolingian, 286
    in England, 329
    in France, 496, 602, 605, 614
    in Germany, 708
    in Merovingian society,
        257–260
    in Rome, 141
    special privileges of, 574
Aristophanes, 92, 95, 99
Aristotle, 54, 113–114, 127, 481
    Alexander the Great and, 118
    Christianization of, 368(i)

On the Length and Shortness of
        Life, 368(i), 369
    scholastics and, 375
    translations of, 339
Arius, 215
Armada (Spain), 468, 468(m)
Armed forces. See also Navies;
        Soldiers; Warriors; Wars
        and warfare; specific battles
        and wars
    in 17th century, 514(f)
    of Brandenburg-Prussia,
        514–515
    Byzantine, 249, 270, 271
    in Egypt, 21
    in First Crusade, 324–325, 325(i)
    in France, 499, 605, 609,
        616–618, 628–629,
        635–637, 758, 782–783
    Greek, 76–77, 79
    Hellenistic, 120
    Hittite, 27
    in India, 537, 677
    in Japan, 858
    Macedonian, 115
    medieval, 293
    in Napoleonic France, 635–637,
        640, 641
    in Prussia, 552, 580, 582,
        637–638
    of Romanus IV, 324
    in Rome, 148, 151, 153, 160,
        163, 172, 194, 195–196
    in Russia, 518, 550, 551, 701
    Spartan, 61–62
    in Wessex, 295
    after World War I, 819
Armenia, Christianity in, 215
Armenian people, 789–790
Armistice, of 1918, 803, 817, 819
Arms and armaments. See
        Weapons
Arms race
    in cold war, 945
    before World War I, 793,
        794–795, 796, 797(f)
Armstrong, Louis, 832
Armstrong, Neil, 920
Arouet, François-Marie. See
        Voltaire
Arsinoe II (Egypt), 122–123
Art(s). See also Architecture;
        Drama; Renaissance;
        Sculpture; specific types
    in 1920s, 830–832
    in 1930s, 856

    in Age of Crisis, 486–487
    Asian influence on, 752–753,
        831
    baroque, 487, 519, 519(i)
    black-figure painting, 38(i)
    in Carolingian renaissance, 284,
        284(i)
    Christian, 189(i)
    classicism in, 519, 520(i)
    in cold war, 911
    Dutch and, 510
    in Egypt, 21–22
    freedom and order in,
        518–520
    globalization and, 986
    Gothic, 378–380
    Greek, 48, 61, 67–69, 86
    Hellenistic, 124–126, 125(i),
        126(i)
    Louis XIV and, 496–497, 519
    Mesopotamian, 13
    Minoan, 29, 29(i)
    Minoan influence on
        Mycenae, 31
    modern, 776–777
    in Nazi Germany, 851
    neoclassical, 576, 576(i)
    politics and, 588, 776–777
    pop, 927–928, 928(i)
    postmodernism in, 984–985
    realism in, 719–722, 721(i)
    red-figure painting, 55(i), 68(i),
        74(i)
    in Renaissance, 414–418,
        450–451
    rococo, 537(i), 542–543, 542(i),
        577
    romanticism in, 571–573,
        646–650, 670–671
    rustic styles in, 752
    in Soviet bloc, 897, 930
    in Soviet Union, 848
    state power and, 474(i)
    in Venice, 423, 424(i)
    vernacular culture and,
        354–357
    World War II and, 874–875,
        875(i)
Artemia (mother of Nicetius),
        259
Artemis (goddess), 55
Arthur (legendary English king),
        357, 377
Arthur Tudor, 444
Articles of Confederation (U.S.),
        590

Artisans, 541, 717, 748
Art nouveau, 777
Art of Love (Ovid), 177
Arts and crafts style, 752
Aryans
    in Nazi Germany, 850, 851, 852, 865
    unification of, 860
Asceticism, Christian, 217. *See also* Monasticism and monasteries; Monks
Ascetics, Skeptics and, 128
Asclepius (Greek god), 133(*i*), 144
Ashoka (Afghanistan), 130
Asia. *See also* specific locations
    art influences from, 752–753, 831
    cold war in, 899–901
    decolonization in, 899–901
    global economic crisis and, 976
    Great Depression in, 845, 846
    health in, 970
    imperialism in, 715–717, 736–738, 736(*m*), 737(*m*), 788, 789(*m*)
    Japan and, 788, 857–858
    missionaries in, 450
    Mongols in, 389–390, 389(*i*)
    Pacific nations in, 974–975
    Russian expansion in, 698, 715, 736–737, 737(*m*)
    western consumer economy and, 979
    white settlements in, 536–537
    World War I and, 808
    World War II and, 872, 873(*m*)
    after World War II, 881–882
Asia Minor
    Christianity in, 190(*m*)
    Rome and, 155
    Turks in, 324
Aspasia (Miletus), 89–90, 95
Assassinations. *See also* specific individuals
    by anarchists, 779
    terrorism and, 940
Assemblies. *See also* National Assembly (France); specific locations
    in Athens, 80, 82
    in France, 387
    in Germany, 708
    in Rome, 150
    in Spain, 385
Assembly of Notables (France), 599

Assembly of the Land (Russia), 517, 518
Assignats (paper money), 603
Association for the Taxation of Financial Transactions and Aid to Citizens (ATTAC), 966
Assyria, 13–14
    Hittites and, 28
    Jewish deportation to, 46
    Neo-Assyrian Empire and, 40, 41
Astarte figurines, 47(*i*)
Astell, Mary, 558–559
Astrologia (Gole), 555(*i*)
Astrology, 15, 131, 487
Astronauts, 920
Astronomy, 856
    Mesopotamian, 15
    Neo-Babylonian, 42
    revolution in, 481–483
    space exploration and, 921
Aswan Dam, 902(*i*)
Athaulf (Visigoths), 225
Atheism, 566, 610
Athena (goddess), 55, 144
Athenian Empire, 79–81
Athens, 54. *See also* Allies, Greek; Greece (ancient); Philosophy; specific philosophers
    acropolis of, 83(*i*), 84(*i*)
    citizenship in, 82
    coins of, 111(*i*)
    Delian League and, 79–81
    democracy in, 61, 65–67, 80, 81–82
    drama in, 86, 96–100
    in Greek Golden Age, 79–106
    homosexual behavior in, 91
    intellectual thought in, 67–70, 90–100
    Macedonians and, 115–116
    Peloponnesian War and, 100–104, 110–112
    Persian Wars and, 76, 79
    rebuilt city of, 111(*m*)
    slaves in, 90
    Sparta and, 75, 82, 114–115
    theater at, 97
    women in, 87–90
Athletes
    male, 750, 751(*i*)
    women as, 226(*i*)
Athletics. *See* Sports
Atlantic Charter, 872

Atlantic Ocean region. *See also* specific locations
    division between Portugal and Spain, 434
    slave trade and, 591(*m*)
Atlantic revolutions, 596
Atlantic system
    settlement and, 535–537
    slave trade in, 512, 530–535
    trade and expansion in, 529
Atomic bomb, 776, 872, 874(*i*), 882, 889, 893. *See also* Nuclear weapons
Atomic theory, 92–93, 775
ATTAC. *See* Association for the Taxation of Financial Transactions and Aid to Citizens
Attalid kingdom, 119, 159
Attila (Huns), 222
Attlee, Clement, 892
Atum (god), 21
Augsburg
    League of, 500
    Peace of (1555), 456, 461, 462, 470
Augustine (archbishop of Canterbury), 260
Augustine of Hippo (Saint), 212, 216–217, 263–264, 295
Augustinus (Jansen), 497
Augustus (**Octavian,** Rome), 164(*i*), 166(*m*), 170, 177(*i*), 181(*m*)
    principate under, 171–177
    succession to, 177–178
    title of, 171
Aung San Suu Kyi, 980
Aurelian (Rome), 197
Auschwitz-Birkenau concentration camp, 841, 866
Austerlitz, battle of, 636
Australia, 567, 748, 894
Austrasia, 252(*m*), 259
Austria, 456, 663, 978. *See also* Austria-Hungary
    Balkan region and, 794
    Congress of Vienna and, 642, 643
    Crimean War and, 698
    dissent in, 651
    France and, 580, 605, 608, 636, 637, 698
    in Great Depression, 855
    Habsburgs in, 473, 515–516
    Hungary and, 515–516, 552(*m*)

Austria (continued)
    Italy and, 654, 686, 687,
        703–704, 705
    merger with Germany, 860
    Napoleon and, 628, 635, 636
    Poland and, 618, 618(m)
    Poland-Lithuania and, 552, 580
    prosperity in, 942
    Prussia and, 705–706
    Social Democratic Party in, 755
    suppression of revolutionary
        movements by, 650–651
    War of the Polish Succession
        and, 552
    World War I and, 796–798, 819
Austria-Hungary, 708–709, 709(m),
    768, 779. See also Austria;
    Hungary
    anti-Semitism in, 784
    Balkan region and, 794
    in Dual Alliance, 760
    industry in, 743
    liberalism in, 759
    nationalism in, 784
    in Three Emperors' League, 758
    in Triple Alliance, 760, 793
    World War I and, 796–798,
        804–805, 812
Austrian Empire, 553. See also
    Austria; Austria-Hungary
    1848 revolution in, 687–688
    industrialization in, 664
    nationalism in, 678–679
Austrian Netherlands, 540, 546(m),
    553, 596, 597, 609, 616,
    629, 643
Authoritarianism, 696
    Napoleon I and, 628
    Napoleon III and, 697
    in Russia, 815
    in Soviet Union, 832–834
Authority. See also Government;
    Political power
    clerical, 449
    growth of state, 474–475
    Hobbes on, 508
    Locke on, 508–509
    in Merovingian dynasty, 259
Authors. See Literature; specific
    works and authors
Autobahn, 851
Automation, 924
Automobiles, 740, 826, 967, 968,
    968(i)
Avaris (Hyksos capital), 22
Avars, 248, 281

Aviation. See Airplanes
Avicenna. See Ibn Sina (Avicenna)
Avignon papacy, 388, 400,
    408–409
Axis powers, 864, 865, 868, 870(m),
    890
Aztecs, 435

Baby boom, 884, 926
Babylonia, 13–15
    Judah and, 46
    Neo-Babylonian Empire and,
        41–42
Babylonian captivity, of Roman
    Catholic Church, 388, 413
Babylonian exile, of Jews, 46
Bacchus (god). See Dionysus (god)
Bacon, Francis (scientist), 484
Bacteria, 712, 713
Bactria, 117, 119, 120(i)
Badr, battle of, 242
Bagatelle, battle at, 809(i)
Baghdad
    Abbasid capital in, 270,
        275–276
    Seljuk Turks in, 324
Bahamas, Columbus in, 434
Bailouts, in global economic crisis,
    976(i)
Baker, Josephine, 832
Baker Arent Oostward and His
    Wife, The (Steen), 511(i)
Bakunin, Mikhail, 717
Baku region, 789
Balance of power. See also
    Diplomacy
    1750–1775, 580
    Crimean War and, 698
    diplomacy and, 553
    in eastern Europe, 551
    economic, 479–481
    French expansion and, 622(m)
    superpowers and, 937–939
    Thirty Years' War and,
        470–475
    War of the Spanish Succession
        and, 545
    after World War I, 826
Baldwin of Flanders, 360
Balkan region, 274, 525(m)
    in c. 1878, 761(m)
    in 1908–1914, 795(m)
    Bulgars in, 248
    Byzantine Empire and, 248,
        271(m), 274
    Germany and, 794

nationalism in, 651–652,
    651(m), 792
Ottomans in, 400, 407, 469, 516
Roman Empire and, 206
World War I and, 810
Balkan Wars, 794
Ballet, 777
Ballot Act (Britain), 756
Baltic region
    balance of power in, 551
    cities and towns of, 362–363
    Dutch trade in, 549
    Great Northern War and, 551,
        551(m)
    Hanseatic League and, 419
    independence in, 957
    Northern Crusades and,
        362–364
    Soviet annexation of, 864
    World War II and, 863, 871
Balzac, Honoré de, 671
Bandung Conference, 904
Bankruptcy, 474, 744
Banks and banking
    Bank of England, 548
    in Dutch Republic, 596
    economic crisis (2008–) and,
        976
    EU, 962
    in France, 547, 630
    Fugger family and, 454, 455
    in Germany, 758
Baptism, Christian, 191, 318, 445
Baptists, 504
Barbados, 512
Barbarians, 204, 220. See also
    specific groups
Barbarossa. See Frederick I
    Barbarossa (Germany)
Barcelona, bombing in, 861(i)
Barnard, Christiaan, 922
Barons (England), 330, 349, 385
Baroque arts, 476, 576
Barth, Karl, 857
Basil I (Byzantine Empire), 272
Basil II (Byzantine Empire), 274
Basil of Caesarea ("the Great"),
    218–219
Basket case, use of term, 823
Basques, 940, 940(m), 965
Bastille Day (France), 855
Bastille (Paris), fall of, 600(i), 601
Bathing, 554, 713
Baths. See Roman baths
Battle of the Nations (1813), 640
Battles. See specific battles and wars

Baudelaire, Charles-Pierre, 720
Bauhaus, 832
Bavaria, 618(m)
Bayeux Tapestry, 329, 330(i)
Bayle, Pierre, 523, 555–556
Bay of Pigs invasion, 912
Beatles, 908, 927
Beat poets, 909
Beatrice of Burgundy, 351
Beauharnais, Eugène de, 631
Beaumarchais, Pierre-Augustin Caron de, 588
Beauvoir, Simone de, 907
Beccaria, Cesare, 583, 649
Becket, Thomas, 348, 348(i)
Beckford, William, 534
Becquerel, Antoine, 775
Bede (English monk), 261, 262
Bedouins, 240
Beer Hall Putsch, 825, 836
Beethoven, Ludwig van, 649
Beguines, 358, 359(i), 373
Behn, Aphra, 523
Beijing, Tiananmen Square protests in, 945
Beirut, 973
Béla III (Hungary), 353
Belarus, Russia and, 961
Belgium, 641, 689, 757, 819. *See also* Austrian Netherlands
    birthrate in, 926
    after Charlemagne, 285
    decolonization and, 904
    in ECSC, 894
    German invasion of, 863
    imperialism of, 733, 735(i)
    independence and, 597, 654, 965
    railroads in, 662
    revolt in, 654
    steam engines in, 664
    urbanization in, 748
    World War I and, 798, 806, 821
Belgrade, 552
Bellini, Gentile, 398(i), 423
Beloved (Morrison), 983
Ben Bella, Ahmed (Algeria), 902(i)
Benedict Biscop. *See* Biscop, Benedict
Benedictine rule, 219
Benedictines, 313
Benedict of Nursia (Saint), 219, 321
Benefits, after World War I, 828
Benevento, duchy of, 263, 264
Bentham, Jeremy, 680
Benz, Karl, 740
Berbers, in Africa, 235(m)

Bergen-Belsen camp, 907
Berlin, 687, 758
    airlift in, 888(m), 889
    blockade of, 888(m), 889
    cold war in, 892(i)
    Congress of, 760
    expansion to 1914, 759(m)
    population growth in, 540
    postmodern architecture in, 984, 985(i)
    reuniting of, 946, 947(i)
    World War II and, 871
Berlin conference (1884–1885), 733–735, 788
Berlin Wall, 888(m), 906, 912, 946, 947(i)
Bernadette (Saint). *See* Soubirous, Bernadette
Bernard (Franks), 269
Bernard of Clairvaux (St. Bernard), 320, 327, 346
Bernini, Gian Lorenzo, 519, 519(i)
Berthold (Franciscan preacher), 372
"Best circles," upper classes as, 746–747
Betrothed, The (Manzoni), 649
Bible
    Christian New Testament, 47, 188
    Darwin and, 724
    Enlightenment challenges to, 556
    Erasmus and, 438
    Hebrew Old Testament, 40, 44–45, 47, 188
    Latin, 438
    Latin Vulgate, 284, 449
    translations of, 447, 448(i)
Bicycle, 740, 750, 751
Big bang theory, 921
Big business, 933
"Big Three," at Yalta (1945), 872
Bildung (importance of education), 779
Bill of Rights
    in England, 1689, 507
    in United States, 1791, 590
Bin Laden, Osama, 971, 973, 974
Biology
    Darwin and, 723–724
    research on reproduction, 724
    revolution in, 922–923
Bipolar world politics, 883
Birth, out of wedlock, 479, 578, 667–668

Birth control, 479, 750, 769, 975
    in early 19th century, 669
    in 1960s, 922
    France and, 825
    Great Depression and, 844
    in Nazi Germany, 852
    Romania and, 946
    in Rome, 186
    in Soviet Union, 833, 848
Birth-control pill, 922
Birth of the Virgin (Giotto), 380(i)
Birth of Venus, The (Botticelli), 415, 416(i)
Birthrate
    in 1960s and 1970s, 926
    decline in, 768, 769, 926
    in eastern bloc, 896
    in Great Depression, 842, 844
    rise in, 908
    Soviet, 848, 885
    U.S. baby boom and, 884
    World War II and, 869, 895
Biscop, Benedict (England), 261
Bishops
    of Alexandria, 215
    Byzantine, 250
    Christian, 191, 212
    German, 298
    medieval, 294
    monasteries and, 220
    power of, 258
    of Rome, 187, 212–213, 215
    in Spain, 262–263
Bismarck, Otto von, 692, 696, 778, 793
    Africa and, 733
    Congress of Berlin and, 760
    German unification and, 705–708
    Kulturkampf and, 722
    power politics and, 695, 758–759
Black and Tans, 825
Black codes, 512
Black Death, 399–404, 401(f). *See also* Plague
Black-figure painting, 38(i), 68(i), 89(i)
Black monks, 319–320
Black Panthers, 931
Black power, 931
Black Sea, 699
Black Shirts (Italy), 834, 835(i)
Black Skin, White Masks (Fanon), 908
Blanc, Louis, 682

Blanche of Castile, 383(i)
Blenheim, battle of, 545
Blitz (battle of Britain), 864
Blitzkrieg ("lightning war"), 863,
    868
Blockade
    of Berlin, 888(m), 889
    in Cuban missile crisis, 912
    in World War I, 807
Blood libel, 374
Blood sports, 674
Bloody Sunday
    in Northern Ireland, 940
    Russia, 1905, 790
Blue-collar workers, 924
"Blue Rider" artists, 777
Blues (faction), 228, 231
Blum, Léon, 855
Bodin, Jean, 485, 487, 558
Boers, 735
Boer War, 786
Bohemia, 418, 470, 472, 515, 743,
    759
    Christianity in, 299
    Hus and, 411
    after Peace of Westphalia, 473
Boleslaw the Brave (Poland), 299
Boleyn, Anne, 444, 455
Bolívar, Simón, 652–653, 652(i)
Bolivia, 653
Bollywood films, 984
Bologna, university in, 338, 339, 341
Bolshevik Revolution (Russia), 813
Bolsheviks, 779, 813, 818, 829, 832
Bombs and bombings. See also
    Atomic bomb; Nuclear
    weapons
    anarchist, 755, 779
    in Ireland, 940
    of Pearl Harbor, 864
    in Spanish Civil War, 859,
        861(i)
    terrorist, 973
    in Vietnam, 931
    World War I and, 806
    World War II and, 865, 871,
        872, 874(i)
Bomb shelter, 912
Bonald, Louis de, 645
Bonaparte family. See also
        Napoleon I Bonaparte;
        Napoleon III
    Caroline, 631
    Jerome, 637
    Joseph, 631, 638, 641
    Louis, 631, 637

Bonhomme, Jacques (name for
    peasants), 407
Boniface (Bishop), 262, 280
Boniface VIII (Pope), 384,
    386–388
Book of Common Prayer
    (Anglican), 504, 506
Book of Hours, 410, 410(i)
*Book of Laughter and Forgetting,
    The* (Kundera), 936
Book of Psalms (Psalter), 249
Book of the Dead (Egypt), 2(i), 3, 25
Books, 437–438, 437(i), 542
    burning by Nazis, 851
    for children, 577
    in Christian Britain, 261
    in Enlightenment, 563,
        570–571, 571(f), 577
    in France, 570–571
    in late Roman Empire, 233,
        234(i)
    novels, 523, 544, 671–672
Bordeaux, 404
Borders. See Frontiers
Borodino, battle at, 640
Bosnia, 955
Bosnia-Herzegovina, 759, 794, 796,
    955
Bossuet, Jacques-Bénigne
    (Bishop), 497, 556
Boston Tea Party, 589
Botticelli, Sandro, 415, 416(i), 424
Boucher, François, 543(i)
Boudica (Britain), 179
Boulanger, Georges, 757
Boulton, Matthew, 660
Boundaries. See also Frontiers
    of Egypt, 22
    of Roman Empire, 231
Bourbon dynasty, in France, 462,
    657(m)
Bourgeoisie, 575, 683. See also
    Middle class
Bourges, cathedral of, 343(i),
    378(i)
Bouvines, battle of, 349
Bové, José, 966
Boxer Uprising (China), 791–792
Boys. See also Men
    Spartan, 62–63, 63(i)
Boziana, Bozi, 953
Bracciolinus, Poggius, 412
Bradbury, Ray, 910–911
Brahe, Tycho, 482, 487
Brain drain, 926, 936–937, 960
Brandenburg, 473, 514

Brandenburg-Prussia, 514–515,
    516(m). See also Prussia
Brandt, Willy, 930
Braque, Georges, 776
Brasides, 102
Braun, Eva, 871
Brazil, 971, 976
    Napoleon and, 638
    Portugal and, 434
    slavery in, 435, 530, 643, 676
Brest-Litovsk, Treaty of, 813–814
Brethren of the Common Life,
    409–410, 438
Bretons, 965
Brezhnev, Leonid, 930
Brezhnev Doctrine, 935, 946
Britain, 260(m). See also England;
        Ireland; Scotland; specific
        leaders
    agriculture in, 538–540
    American Revolution and,
        588–590
    Anglo-Saxons in, 224, 260
    Balkan region and, 760
    banking in, 548
    battle of, 864, 865
    Boer War and, 786
    Canada and, 711
    Chartism in, 683, 689
    China and, 677
    Christianity in, 260–262
    colonies of, 535, 591(m), 677,
        846
    Common Market and, 894, 929
    Congress of Vienna and, 642,
        643
    Crimean War and, 698–699
    decolonization and, 899,
        902–903, 903–904
    Dutch and, 505, 511, 547, 596
    education in, 715, 926
    Egypt and, 733, 793, 901, 902
    enclosure and, 539–540
    Enlightenment and, 570
    in Entente Cordiale, 793
    Falklands war and, 941
    foreigners in, 978
    formation of Great Britain, 547
    France and, 608
    German occupation by, 874,
        888–889
    government of, 892
    in Great Depression, 843, 854
    Hitler and, 864, 865
    imperialism by, 715–716, 733,
        735, 736, 738, 826

industrialization in, 660–661, 741, 742

Iraq War and, 972(m)

Ireland and, 679, 680, 781, 812, 825–826, 940

liberalism in, 680–681, 781

Liberal Party in, 756

manufacturing in, 663–664

Middle East and, 901–902

Monroe Doctrine and, 653

Napoleon and, 628–629, 635, 638, 640

navy of, 581–582, 636, 796

political participation in, 756–757

poor laws in, 674–675

Prussia and, 580

reforms in, 709–710

religious revival in, 646

rise of, 548

Rome and, 180, 182

St. Domingue and, 619

slave trade and, 531, 643, 676

southern Africa and, 735

suffragists in, 780–781

terrorism in London and, 974

Thatcher in, 940–942

urbanization in, 666, 748

Vikings and, 288

voting rights in, 655

War of the Austrian Succession and, 553

water in, 667

welfare state and, 942

World War I and, 798, 804, 806, 818, 821, 825

World War II and, 863, 877

after World War II, 882

British East Africa, 903

British East India Company, 535

Brittany, 965

Brontë, Charlotte, 672

Bronze, 12, 22, 48

Bronze Age, in Greece, 30

Brown, Louise, 922–923, 923(i)

Browning, Elizabeth Barrett, 670

Brown Shirts (Germany), 825

Brown v. Board of Education (1954), 908

Bruno, Giordano, 482

Bruno of Cologne, 320

Brussels, Common Market in, 894

Brutus, Marcus Junius, 164

Bubonic plague. *See* Black Death; Plague

Buccaneers, 535–536

Budapest, 784, 871(i)

Buddha, Greek-style, 131(i)

Buddhism, 929

Building. *See also* Architecture; specific buildings

   Egyptian, 20–21, 20(i)

   Greek, 83–85, 84(i)

   Roman, 151–152

Bulgakov, Mikhail, 983

Bulgaria, 270, 794, 964

   Byzantines and, 274

   cold war and, 886

   migration from, 824

   Ottoman Empire and, 759

   Russia and, 760

   Soviets and, 872

   World War II and, 864, 871

Bulgarians, nationalism of, 792

Bulgars, 246, 248

Bulls (papal). *See* Papal bulls

Bundesrat (Germany), 708

Burden, The (Daumier), 721(i)

Bureaucracy

   Byzantine, 248

   expansion of, 713–714

   of Louis XIV, 498–499

   in Rome, 179, 181–182

   Russian, 810

   Soviet, 833, 847, 943, 944

   Thirty Years' War and, 475

Burgundian people, 225

Burgundy, 252(m), 259, 456

   in 15th century, 419

   duchy of, 404–406, 405(m)

   Germany and, 351

Burials

   at Mycenae, 30, 31

   Paleolithic, 5

Burke, Edmund, 645

Burma, 736, 736(m), 864

Burschenschaften (student societies), 651

Bush, George W., 973

Business. *See also* Commerce; Trade

   in 1870s and 1880s, 743–744

   commercial revolution and, 306–312

   forms of, 310

   in France, 632, 743

   in Germany, 743

   in Great Depression, 842, 843

   Mesopotamian, 15

   multinational corporations and, 923–924

   revolution in, 744–746

Byron, George Gordon (Lord), 647, 652

Byzantine Empire, 240, 270–274. *See also* Eastern Roman Empire

   in c. 600, 247(m)

   in 1025, 271(m)

   in 12th century, 353–354

   in c. 1215, 365(m)

   Comnenian dynasty in, 328

   dynatoi in, 273–274, 276, 324

   eastern Roman Empire as, 227

   emperors in, 353

   fall of, 399

   government in, 249, 353–354

   icons and iconoclasm in, 250–251

   Macedonian renaissance in, 272–274

   Muslims in, 243

   religion in, 250–251

   renaissance in, 270

   Roman Catholicism and, 264

   Russia and, 274–275

   scholars in, 279

   Seljuk Turks and, 324

   warfare in, 246–248

   women in, 249

Byzantium (Constantinople), 240. *See also* Byzantine Empire

Cabet, Étienne, 682

Cabinet of Doctor Caligari, The (movie), 829

Cable News Network (CNN), 945

Cabral, Pedro Alvares, 434

Cádiz, 434

Caesar, Julius (Rome), 140, 161(i), 162–164, 166(m), 170

Caesarion (Egypt and Rome), 164

Cafés, 538

Cage, John, 928

Cairo, 733

Calas, Jean, 567

Calculus, 520

Calcutta, 664

Calendar

   in Egypt, 24

   in French Republic, 611

   in Rome, 164

   in Russia, 549, 812

Calico, from India, 537

Calicut, India, 433

California, 710

Caligula (Rome), 178–179

Caliphs and caliphates (Islamic),
    240, 243–245
  Abbasid, 270, 275–276
  of Córdoba, 278
  dissolution of, 278–279
  Umayyad, 241(i), 244,
    245–246
Call centers, 979
Calvin, John, and Calvinism,
    442–443, 470. See also
    Puritanism
  in c. 1648, 489(m)
  in France, 455, 462–464, 498,
    567
  in Germany, 515
  in Netherlands, 466–467
  Peace of Augsburg and, 456, 462
  after Peace of Westphalia, 473
  in Scotland, 456, 468
Cambodia, 736, 900, 937
Cambridge University, 484, 715
Cameroon, 733, 788, 819
Camus, Albert, 907
Canaan, 15, 44, 48
Canada, 871, 894
  cession to Britain, 546(m), 582
  emigration to, 749(f)
  French, 436, 480–481, 499
  NAFTA and, 962
  self-determination for, 677
  United States and, 711
Canals
  Mesopotamian, 8
  Suez, 698, 716, 733, 870, 901
Cannae, battle at, 154
Cannons, 406
Canon (church) law, reforms of,
    319
Canon of Medicine (Ibn Sina), 279
Canossa, Investiture Conflict and,
    316, 317(i)
Canterbury, Becket at, 348(i)
Cantons, Swiss, 616
Cape Colony, 786
Cape Horn, 433(m)
Cape of Good Hope, 432–433, 536
Capetian dynasty (France),
    296–297, 364
Capital cities, 712. See also specific
    cities
Capital-intensive industry, 743
Capitalism, capitalists, 310, 681
  Marxists on, 755
Caporetto, battle at, 816
Caracalla (Rome), 196, 196(i)
Caravels, 432

Carbonari, 638, 650, 651
Cardinals, papacy and, 408–409
Caribbean region
  colonization of, 480, 480(m),
    481, 591(m), 596, 618–619,
    635–636, 661, 664, 676
  exploration of, 424
  French in, 618–619, 635–636
  immigrants to Europe from,
    904, 905(i)
  pirates (buccaneers) in, 535–536
  slavery in, 436, 481, 511, 531,
    533–534
Carib people, 434, 481, 535
Carlsbad Decrees (1819), 651
Carnegie, Andrew, 742
Carnival, 524
Caroline minuscule, 285
Carolingian Empire, 260, 270,
    280–289, 282(m)
  capital at Aachen, 281, 283(i)
  end of, 297
  local rule after, 289–299
  Roman Catholicism and, 281
Carolingian renaissance, 284–285
Carpaccio, Vittore, 424
Carpathian Mountains, 807
Carrier, Jean-Baptiste, 612, 615
Carriera, Rosalba, 537(i)
Cars. See Automobiles
Carson, Rachel, 967
Cartels, 744
Carthage
  Phoenicians in, 53
  Punic Wars and, 152–155
  Rome and, 150
  Syracuse and, 78
Carthusian order, 320
Cartwright, Edmund, 660
Casino Royale (Fleming), 911
Cassatt, Mary, 753, 753(i)
Cassiodorus, 227
Castellans, 293, 294
Castiglione, Baldassare, 451
Castile, 360, 362(m), 385, 420
Castile-León, cortes of, 385
Castle, The (Kafka), 832
Castlereagh, Robert, 643, 644
Castles, 292–293, 306–307, 308
Castro, Fidel, 912
Casualties
  in Afghanistan, 943
  in Chechnya, 961
  in Crimean War, 699
  in Napoleonic wars, 640, 641
  in Seven Years' War, 582

  in War of the Spanish
    Succession, 545
  in World War I, 803, 806, 807,
    816, 817
  in World War II, 864, 865, 867,
    872, 876(m), 884
Catacombs, Christian, 189(i)
Çatalhöyük, housing at, 7(i)
Catalonia, 472
Catasto (Italian census), 425
Cateau-Cambrésis, Treaty of, 452
Cathars, 359, 364
Cathedrals, 253. See also specific
    cathedrals
  Gothic, 336(i), 337, 341, 379,
    414
  schools in, 338
Catherine II (the Great, Russia),
    562(i), 563, 574, 580, 581,
    638
  law code reforms and, 583
  Poland and, 597, 618
  Pugachev uprising and, 587
Catherine de Médicis, 462
Catherine of Alexandria, 219(i)
Catherine of Aragon, 443–444
Catholicism. See Roman
    Catholicism
Catholic League, 463
Cato, Marcus Porcius, 143, 155
Cavaliers (England), 503
Cavendish, Margaret, 521
Cavour, Camillo di, 695, 702–703,
    704
Ceauçescu, Nicolae, 946–947
Celibacy, Christian clerical, 191,
    319, 340, 358, 448
Celtic peoples. See also Gauls
    (Celts)
  Anglo-Saxons and, 224
  in Britain, 260
Censorship
  by Catholic Church, 449
  in France, 496, 556, 599, 630,
    633, 653
  in German states, 438, 651
  in Nazi Germany, 850, 851
  in Russia, 790
  in Soviet bloc, 897
  in World War II, 868
Census, 713
  Domesday survey as, 330,
    331(f)
  Italian catasto as, 425
  in Rome, 153(f)
Central America, 511, 975

Central Europe. *See also* specific locations
  1848 revolutions in, 687–688
  absolutism in, 513, 515–516
  in Great Depression, 855–856
  Hitler and, 860–863
  Jews in, 784–785
  monarchies in, 297–299
  Peace of Augsburg in, 456
  power politics in, 758–759
  Thirty Years' War in, 470–475, 473(m), 476
Central Intelligence Agency (CIA), 911, 912
Centralization
  in England, 296
  by Napoleon, 630
Central planning, 854
Central Powers (World War I), 804–805, 810, 812, 816
Central Short Time Committee (Britain), 665–666
Centuriate Assembly (Rome), 150
Ceramics, Greek, 48
Cervantes, Miguel de, 468, 544
Cézanne, Paul, 776
CFCs. *See* Chlorofluorocarbons
Chaeronea, battle of, 115–116
Chalcedon, Council of, 216, 232
Chaldeans, 41
Chamberlain, Neville, 862
Chamber of Deputies (France), 645, 757, 855
Chamber of Peers (France), 645
Champagne, France, fairs in, 306
Chansons de geste, 356
Chaplin, Charlie, 856
Chariots, 168(i)
  Byzantine, 228
  Hittite, 27
  Hyksos, 22
  Mycenaean, 32
Charity(ies), 448, 578, 674, 750
Charlemagne (Frankish king), 270, 276, 280, 283(i)
  Carolingian Empire of, 281–284
Charles I (England), 502–503, 504, 607
Charles II (England), 506, 508
Charles II (Spain), 500
Charles IV (Spain), 638, 639
Charles V (Holy Roman Empire, Charles I of Spain), 435, 439, 441, 443, 448, 450, 464
  Habsburg-Valois-Ottoman wars and, 452–453, 453(i)

resignation of, 456
Schmalkaldic League and, 456
Charles VI (Holy Roman Empire), 552
Charles VII (France), 405
Charles IX (France), 462, 463, 465
Charles X (France), 653
Charles Albert (Piedmont-Sardinia), 650, 686
Charles Martel (Franks), 280
Charles of Anjou, 382
Charles the Bald (Carolingians), 269, 285
Charles the Bold, 406, 420
Charles the Great. *See* Charlemagne
Charles the Simple (Charles the Straightforward, Frankish king), 288
Charter 77 (Czechoslovakia), 946
Charter of the Nobility (Russia), 574, 587
Chartism, 683, 689
Chartres cathedral, 336(i), 337–338
Chastity. *See also* Celibacy
  Augustine on, 217
Chateaubriand, François-René de, 633
Châtelet, Émilie du, 565
Chávez, César, 931
Chechnya, 957, 960, 961, 965
Cheka (secret police), 815
Chelmno concentration camp, 866
Cheops (Khufu, Egypt), 21
Chernobyl catastrophe (1986), 944, 967
Chevet (apse), in churches, 342
Chiefdoms, barbarian, 221
Childbirth, 479, 669, 713
  in Greece, 87
  medicalization of, 922
  in Rome, 185–186
  in Sweden, 854
  test-tube babies and, 922–923, 923(i)
Child labor, 665, 666(i), 689
Children. *See also* Child labor; Education; Infant exposure
  in Britain, 896
  in cold war, 912
  in concentration camps, 866, 867(i)
  financial aid for, 895
  government support for, 771
  in Great Depression, 844
  in Greece, 87

illegitimate, 667–668
  of immigrants, 952(i)
  of middle and upper classes, 580, 745
  mortality of, 479
  in Nazi Germany, 851
  in postindustrial society, 927
  in Romania, 947
  in Rome, 142, 174
  sexuality of, 579, 774
  upper class, 747
  welfare state and, 895, 895(i)
  working class, 674, 750
  World War II and, 868
Chile, 435, 945
China, 538
  Boxer Uprising in, 791–792
  Communists in, 899–900, 937–938
  economy in, 974, 975
  European imperialism in, 717
  foreigners in, 536
  Japan and, 788, 791, 858
  missionaries in, 536, 557(i), 717, 791
  Mongols in, 389–390, 389(m)
  Nixon in, 938
  opium in, 677, 677(m)
  resistance to colonialism in, 791–792
  revolution in (1949), 893, 937
  Russia and, 736, 961
  Soviet Union and, 918, 929, 938
  Tiananmen Square protest in, 945, 980
  as U.S. creditor, 975
  Vietnam and, 931
  World War II and, 865
Chingiz (Genghis) Khan, 389
Chirac, Jacques, 942
Chivalry, 357, 406
Chlorofluorocarbons (CFCs), 967
Cholera, 667, 668(m), 712
Chopin, Frédéric, 672
Choricius (rhetoric professor), 233
Chosen people, 45
Chosroes II (Sasanid), 247
Christ. *See also* Jesus
  meaning of term, 186
Christian IV (Denmark), 470
Christian Bible. *See* Bible
Christian Democrats
  in Germany, 940
  in Italy, 891
Christian humanism, 438–439, 440, 443

Christianity. *See also* Crusades; Great Schism; specific groups
  in Americas, 431
  Arian, 215, 224
  in Britain, 260–262
  Byzantines and, 274
  in China, 717, 791
  of Clovis, 225
  competing beliefs about, 191–193, 214–217
  Constantine and, 203
  conversion to, 431
  Coptic, 215
  deist criticisms of, 566–567
  in Denmark, 288–289
  in eastern Roman Empire, 230, 232
  in England, 260
  in Germany, 299
  growth of, 188–191
  Hellenistic world and, 133
  hierarchy in, 190–191, 212–213
  imperialism and, 739–740
  in Islamic Spain, 277–278
  Jews in society of, 373–374
  lay piety and, 372–373
  in Lithuania, 419
  martyrs to, 169
  polytheism and, 211–213
  population of, 190(*m*)
  Roman, 170, 186–193, 204, 209–213, 261, 262
  in Russia, 275
  scripture in, 47
  Spanish reconquista and, 315, 360
  spread of, 213(*m*)
  of Vikings, 288
  women in, 212
Christine de Pisan, 413
Church(es). *See also* specific religions
  in cities, 308
  during cold war, 906
  decline in attendance, 722, 929
  Gothic, 336(*i*), 337, 341, 342–344, 343(*i*), 344(*i*), 378(*i*), 379
  government control of, 583
  Hagia Sophia as, 231
  hierarchy of Christian, 190–191
  music sponsored by, 418
  reform of, 312–322, 440–444
  Romanesque, 341–342, 342(*i*), 343(*i*)

Church and state, Investiture Conflict and, 315–318, 332
Church fathers, 216
  writings of, 261, 369
Churchill, Jeanette Jerome, 747
Churchill, Randolph, 747
Churchill, Winston, 747, 864, 872, 885, 892
Church of England (Anglican Church), 443–444, 506, 781
  Charles I and, 502–503
  under Elizabeth I, 455, 467–468
  on family limitation, 769
  Puritans and, 467
  Wesley and, 573, 646
Church of the Holy Wisdom. *See* Hagia Sophia
CIA. *See* Central Intelligence Agency
Cicero, Marcus Tullius, 142, 144, 156, 175, 233, 412
Cimon (Athens), 83
Cincius Romanus, 412
Ciompi Revolt, 423
CIS. *See* Commonwealth of Independent States
Cisalpine Republic, 616
Cistercians, 320–322, 321(*f*), 322(*i*), 362
Cîteaux, monastery of, 320
Cities and towns. *See also* Urban areas; Urbanization; Walled cities; specific locations
  in 1050–1150, 305–306
  in mid-1800s, 712–713
  Athens as, 83–86
  Babylonian, 14–15
  along Baltic coast, 362–363
  bombings of, in World War II, 865, 871, 872, 874(*i*)
  Byzantine, 248–249
  characteristics of, 308
  commerce in, 306–307
  in Egypt, 16
  electricity in, 741
  in Frankish kingdoms, 253
  globalization of, 964–965
  government of, 310–311
  in Great Famine, 392
  as Hanse, 419
  Hellenistic, 121
  industrialization and, 667
  Jews in, 307–308
  in Mesopotamia, 8–12
  movement to, 578, 748
  nation building and, 712–713

  poor in, 667–668
  population growth and, 537, 540, 666–667
  religious orders in, 357–359
  Roman, 182
  sanitation and health in, 553–554, 667
  social life in, 540–542
  technopoles and, 930
  after World War II, 896
Citizen initiatives (political tactic), 967–968
Citizens and citizenship. *See also* Democracy; Voting and voting rights
  in Athens, 65, 81–82
  global, 952(*i*), 953
  in Greece, 40, 48, 50, 53–61, 76
  for Greek women, 59, 87
  Jews and, 307–308
  of non-European immigrants, 905(*i*), 906
  in Rome, 139, 152, 160, 174, 180, 196
  in Sparta, 62
City of God, The (Augustine of Hippo), 216, 217
City-states. *See also* Citizens and citizenship; Polis; specific locations
  democratic, 65–67
  Greek, 40, 50, 52–61, 76, 114–115
  Mesopotamian, 8, 10
  organization of Greek, 61–70
Civil cases, in England, 347
Civil Code (Napoleonic), 628, 632, 637, 645, 675
Civil Constitution of the Clergy (France, 1790), 603, 604
Civil disobedience
  in Gold Coast, 902
  in India, 845
  in U.S. civil rights movement, 908
Civilians
  World War I and, 809–811, 819, 827
  World War II and, 842, 859, 861(*i*), 865–868, 872
Civilization(s). *See also* Culture; Geography; West, the; specific societies
  in Anatolia, 25–28
  ancient, 3–35
  defined, 3–4

Egyptian, 15–25
Greek, 47–51
Mediterranean, 70(m)
in Mesopotamia, 8–15
violent end to, 32–35
Civilizing, through imperialism, 739
Civil rights
in France, 567, 584
in Nazi Germany, 850
in U.S., 882, 908, 931
Civil Rights Act (U.S., 1964), 931
Civil service. See Bureaucracy
Civil service law (Britain, 1870), 714
Civil war(s)
in Bosnia-Herzegovina, 955
in China, 717
in England, 330, 421–422, 503
between French Catholics and Huguenots, 462–464
in French Revolution, 612
in Rome, 158–164, 170–171, 179, 196–197
in Russia, 275, 814–816, 815(m), 824
in Spain, 856, 859–860
in United States, 700(i), 710
in Ur III kingdom, 13
Clairvaux, 320
Clandestine workers, in Europe, 906
Clans, non-Roman, 221, 222
Clare (13th century), 358
Classes, 265–266. See also Aristocracy; Estates (French classes); specific classes
in cities, 668
in England, 422, 710, 941
in feudal society, 290–291
in France, 463, 685, 855
in Italy, 388–389, 686
Marx on, 718
in Rome, 148–150, 184, 208–209
in Russia, 517
in Venice, 422
World War I and, 808
Classical culture. See also Classical Greece; Literature
in late Roman Empire, 232–234
in Renaissance, 411–412, 414
Classical Greece. See also Golden Age; specific locations
end of, 115–118
after Peloponnesian War, 110–115

Classical music, 577
Classicism
in French arts, 519, 520(i)
vs. romanticism, 647
Claudius (Rome), 179
Cleisthenes (Athens), 66
Clemenceau, Georges, 818
Clement VII (Pope), 409, 444
Clement XIV (Pope), 583
Cleon, 99, 102
Cleopatra VII (Egypt), 124, 134, 163, 164(i), 171
Clergy. See also Monasticism and monasteries; specific types
Byzantine, 250
celibacy of, 191, 319, 340, 358, 448
church reform and, 449
education and, 409–410
in England, 599
in France, 603–604, 614
in Germany, 298
in Great Famine, 392
Luther on, 441
masters and students as, 341
medieval, 290, 294
in Prussia, 722
taxation of, 387–388, 478
Clermont, Council of, Urban II and, 324
Client republics, of Napoleon, 628
Clients, in Rome, 141–142, 155, 173
Climate
in Egypt, 22
global warming and, 967
Great Famine and, 390–391
of Mesopotamia, 8
Paleolithic, 5
Clito, William, 311
Cloning, 922
Cloth and clothing, 310
in 1920s, 828
Assyrian trade and, 13
gender roles and, 675
industrialization and, 660, 661
new look in, 909, 909(i)
of new woman, 771
of rock-and-roll culture, 908, 909
in Russia, 549, 550
social status and, 542
of upper classes, 747
Clotilda (Franks), 225
Clouds, The (Aristophanes), 95
Clovis (Franks), 225, 262
law code under, 225–226
Cluniac monks, 313

Cluny, Benedictine monastery of, 313, 320(i), 341
Cnut (Canute), 289, 296
Coal and coal industry, 660, 662, 665, 666(i), 740, 744, 825
Coalitions
anti-Spartan, 114
anti-Swedish, 551
English-Dutch, 622(m)
Greek, 77–78
in Iraq War, 973
in Rome, 162
in Seven Years' War, 580–581
Cochin China, 716, 737. See also Indochina; Vietnam
Codes (Christian monastic), 219
Codes (secret), in World War II, 864, 870
Codes of law. See Law(s); Law codes
Codex (Justinian), 232
Coffee (kavah), 529
Coffeehouses, 528(i), 537–538, 542, 563
Coins, 195, 454
from Athens, 111(i)
from Bactria, 120(i)
debasement of, 195, 195(i)
devaluation, 454
Roman, 161(i), 165(i), 172, 195, 195(i)
Coitus interruptus, 769
Colbert, Jean-Baptiste, 498–499, 521
Cold war, 875, 881, 882, 886(f)
in Asia, 900–901
culture of, 906–911
decolonization during, 899–906
détente and, 938, 942
division of Germany and, 882, 888–889, 888(m)
emerging nations in, 902(i)
end of, 953, 954
military spending during, 893
origins of, 885–888
space exploration and, 898, 921
world during (1960), 913(m)
"Cold war," before World War I, 793
Cole, Thomas, 670
Collaborators, in World War II, 890
Collection in 74 Titles, 314
Collective action, by workers, 754
Collective security. See also Alliances; specific alliances
Hobbes on, 508
Little Entente for, 822

Collective security *(continued)*
  after World War I, 822
  World War II and, 872
Collectivization, 865
  in China, 900
  in Soviet bloc, 896, 897*(i)*
  in Soviet Union, 847, 885
Colleges. *See* Universities
Colloquy of Marburg, 442
Coloni (tenant farmers), 208, 254
Colonialism, compared to
    imperialism, 676
Colonies and colonization. *See also*
    Empire(s); Imperialism;
    specific locations
  in Africa, 536, 676, 731–736,
    734*(m)*, 739, 742, 787*(m)*,
    788, 904
  in Americas, 479–481, 480*(m)*,
    499, 535–537
  black slavery and, 511–512
  British, 481, 509, 512, 535, 677
  British North American, 480,
    535, 553, 588–590
  in Caribbean region, 480,
    480*(m)*, 481, 591*(m)*, 596,
    618–619, 635–636, 661,
    664, 676
  criticism of, 567
  decolonization and, 899–906
  Dutch, 511
  European attitudes toward,
    735–736, 738–740
  French, 480–481, 499, 500, 553,
    618–619, 676
  French and Indian War and,
    580
  in Great Depression, 845–846
  Greek, 52–53
  imperialism and, 731–740
  independence movements in,
    899
  literature on, 907–908
  nation building and, 715–717
  resistance to, 789–793
  Roman, 151, 163
  slave trade and, 476, 511–512,
    531–535
  Spanish, 464–465, 481
  World War I and, 806, 807, 811,
    811*(i)*
  after World War I, 820–821,
    820*(m)*, 826
  World War II and, 857, 869,
    872
  after World War II, 882

Colosseum (Rome), 179
Colossus (computer), 919
Columbanus (Saint), 258
Columbian exchange, 431, 436
Columbus, Christopher, 431,
    433–434
COMECON. *See* Council for
    Mutual Economic
    Assistance
Comedy (drama)
  Greek, 99–100
  Hellenistic, 125–126
  of manners, 522
  Roman, 155
"Coming Hordes, The" *(The
    Economist),* 978
Commerce. *See also* Business;
    Commercial revolution;
    Economy; Seaborne
    commerce; Trade
  Assyrian, 13
  cold war and, 930
  with colonies, 480
  crafts and, 309–310
  Dutch, 467, 509–510, 510*(m)*
  Egyptian, 18
  fairs and, 306–307
  Islamic, 278
  in Mycenae, 31
  Napoleon and, 638
  railroads and, 662*(f)*
Commercial revolution, 306–312
Committee of Public Safety
    (France), 607, 608, 610,
    614
Common land, 539–540
  conversion to private property,
    668
Common law (England), 347–348
Common Market, 894, 924, 926,
    929, 938, 962
  European Union and, 953–954
Common people
  in France, 599
  political power and, 408
  in Rome, 184–185
Commonwealth, British, 806, 894
Commonwealth of Independent
    States (CIS), 957, 958*(m)*
Communal values
  in Athens, 66
  in Rome, 209
Communards, 719
Communes. *See also* Paris
    Commune
  in Italy, 311, 318, 350

  in Middle Ages, 311
  in Paris (1871), 718–719, 725,
    755
Communication(s). *See also*
    Writing
  global, 945, 954, 979–980
  global culture and, 977, 980
  information age and, 918–920
  mass journalism and, 756, 918
  papal, 254*(f)*
  in Persian Empire, 42
  society and, 987
  telecommunications and, 919
  Tiananmen Square protests
    and, 945
Communications satellites, 919,
    921
Communion (Christian), 191
Communism, 682–683, 804, 846
  in China, 899–900
  cold war and, 885–888
  collapse of, 943–947, 948*(m)*,
    953
  in Czechoslovakia, 887, 935,
    946
  in eastern Europe, 882–883,
    886, 887, 896–898
  of English Diggers, 504
  in Germany, 825, 849
  Marshall Plan and, 887
  New Left and, 934
  in North Vietnam, 931
  in Soviet Union, 832–834,
    846–848
  war, 815, 833
  in World War II resistance, 869
Communist China. *See* China
Communist International
    (Comintern), 815
Communist Manifesto, The (Marx
    and Engels), 683
Communist Party
  in Czechoslovakia, 935
  in France, 855, 910
  in Hungary, 946
  in Poland, 945
  in Soviet Union, 813, 834, 944,
    957
  in western Europe, 891–892
Communities
  Christian, 212
  Internet, 979
  socialist, 681–682
  worker activities in, 755–756
Comnenian dynasty (Byzantine
    Empire), 328

Compendium of Witches, The (Guazzo), 488(*i*)
Competition
  control of, 744
  globalization and, 954
  among great powers, 793
  superpowers and, 918
Composers, 487, 543, 777–778, 928. *See also* specific individuals
Compulsory labor services, serfdom and, 540
Computers, 918
  evolution of, 919–920
  networks for, 919, 979
Comte, Auguste, 675, 724
Concentration camps
  Armenians in, 810
  in Boer War, 786
  in Kenya, 903–904
  Nazi, 841, 851, 866–868, 866(*m*)
  survivors of, 867, 883
Concert of Europe, 642, 696–697, 702, 760
Conciliar movement, 409
Concordat of Worms (1122), 317, 332, 351, 352
Concorde (aircraft), 924
Condition of the Working Class in England, The (Engels), 683
Condoms, 669, 769
Confederate States of America, 710
Confederation of the Rhine, 637, 641, 642
Confessions (Augustine of Hippo), 217
Confraternities, 524
Congo region
  Belgium and, 733, 735(*i*)
  immigrants from, 953
Congregationalism, in England, 503
Congress of Berlin, 760
Congress of Vienna, 641–644, 642(*i*), 644(*m*), 654
  France and, 642, 698, 699
Conrad III (Germany), 326–327, 332
Conscription. *See* Military draft
Conservation, oil embargo and, 939
Conservatism, 641, 644–645, 679, 680, 685, 689
  after 1968 protests, 935–936
  Nazis and, 851

Conservative Party (Britain), 709, 757, 796, 892, 940
Constance, Council of, 409, 411, 412
Constantine (Rome), 199, 204, 206, 210(*i*)
  conversion to Christianity, 203, 209
  Council of Nicaea and, 215
  as emperor, 205
  Roman Empire divided by, 207
Constantine (Russia), 651
Constantine Porphyrogenitos (Byzantine Empire), 273(*i*)
Constantinople, 207, 210, 246, 328, 399. *See also* Justinian (Byzantine Empire)
  Black Death in, 401
  as Byzantium, 240
  in Fourth Crusade, 360
  as Istanbul, 207, 845
  Ottoman conquest of (1453), 407–408
  patriarch of, 250
  sack of (1204), 354
  siege of (1453), 407(*m*)
Constantius (Roman Empire), 205
Constitution(s)
  EU and, 964
  in Florence, 424
  in France, 602–604, 605, 615, 629, 685, 757, 891
  in Germany, 687, 708
  in Japan, 737–738
  in Poland, 597, 654
  in Russia, 651
  in United States, 590
  in West Germany, 892
Constitutionalism, 462, 493–494, 508
  in Dutch Republic, 509–511
  in England, 493–494, 502–509, 548
  in English North America, 509, 512
  Enlightenment and, 570
  natural law, natural rights, and, 486
  in Poland-Lithuania, 513–514
Constitutional monarchy
  in Belgium, 654
  in Britain, 643
  in France, 602, 603, 654
  in Italy, 781, 891
  in Spain, 940
Consulate, in France, 629

Consuls
  in Milan, 311
  in Rome, 148–149, 150, 159–160, 162
Consumer economy, 979
Consumer goods
  in 1920s, 828–829, 833
  in eastern Europe, 964
  in postindustrial society, 927
  in Soviet bloc, 896, 897–898, 910, 930
  after World War II, 893
Consumerism
  empire and, 746
  gender norms and, 908–910
  in Soviet bloc, 930
Consumer revolution (1600s and 1700s), 537–538
Consumption
  agricultural revolution and, 538
  conspicuous, 540
  industrial growth and, 743–744, 745–746
  mass, 927
  patterns of, 436, 534
Contado (countryside), 311, 423
Continental Europe. *See also* Europe; specific locations
  industrialization in, 664
  labor movement in, 683
  liberalism in, 681
  workday in, 666
Continental System, 638
Contraception. *See* Birth control
Contracts, 310
Convention, the. *See* National Convention (France)
Convents, 259, 290
Conversion, to Christianity, 188, 203, 209, 431
Conversos (Spain), 425
Cook, James, 567
Cooperatives
  farmers', 925
  producer and consumers', 682
Copernicus, Nicolaus, 482
Copper, 12
Coptic alphabet, 19(*f*)
Coptic Christians, 215
Corday, Charlotte, 612
Córdoba, 277, 278, 279
Corinne (Staël), 633
Corinth, 79, 100, 155
  black-figure vase from, 38(*i*)
  tyranny in, 64–65
Corinthian style, 85, 85(*f*)

Corneille, Pierre, 496–497, 522
Cornelia (Rome), 143
Corn Laws (Britain), repeal of, 680
Coronation, of Charlemagne, 283
Coronation of Napoleon and
    Josephine, The (David),
    631(i)
Corporations, 310, 744
Corruption
    in former Soviet Union, 960
    in Italy, 781, 782
Corsica and Corsicans, 628, 965
Cortes (Spain), 385, 420
Cortés, Hernán, 430(i), 435
Corvée labor, 21
Cosimo de' Medici, 424
Cosmetics industry, in 1920s, 828
Cosmonauts, 898
    female, 920, 920(i)
Cosmos, 69
Cossacks, 513, 587
Cotton and cotton industry
    from India, 536(i), 537
    industrialization and, 661
    slavery and, 664
Council for Mutual Economic
    Assistance (COMECON),
    896
Council of Fifteen (England), 386
Council of Five Hundred (Athens),
    67, 81, 91
Council of Four Hundred
    (Athens), 67
Council of State (England), 504
Council of State (France), 629
Council of the Areopagus (Athens),
    66, 81
Councils, government and, 385. See
    also Senate
Councils (Christian)
    in 430 and 431, 215
    of Chalcedon, 216, 232
    of Clermont, 324
    of Constance, 409, 411, 412
    Fourth Lateran, 370–372
    of Lyon, 382
    of Nicaea, 215
    of Pisa, 409
    of Soissons, 340
    Third Lateran, 374
Counterculture, 937
Counter-Reformation, 445, 448–450
Counterrevolutionaries
    in French Revolution, 605
    in Russian civil war, 814
Countryside. See Rural areas

Coups
    in Germany, 825
    in Russia, 957
Courbet, Gustave, 720
Courtier, The (Castiglione), 451
Courtly love, 355
Courtly manners, 522
Court of Star Chamber (England),
    502, 503
Courts (law)
    in England, 348–349
    in France, 494, 585, 608
    in Rome, 150
    in Russia, 701
Courts (papal), 314
Courts (royal)
    culture of, 450–452
    of Louis XIV, 493, 495–497
    music in, 417–418
Covenant, Hebrew, 45, 47
Cracow University, 404
Craft-based unions, 754
Crafts
    in Crete, 30
    in Middle Ages, 309–310
Cranach, Lucas, 447(i)
Cranmer, Thomas, 444
Crassus, Marcus Licinius, 162
Creation myths, 51
Credit
    collapse of, 976
    Great Depression and, 842
Crete, 22, 25
    Minoans in, 28–30
    Mycenaeans and, 32
Crick, Francis, 909, 922
Crime. See also Punishment
    in cities, 668
    in England, 654
    in former Soviet Union, 957
    in Greece, 55–56
Crime and Punishment
    (Dostoevsky), 720
Crimean War, 696–697, 698–699,
    698(m), 700(i), 716
Crimes against humanity, by
    Milosevic, 956
Critias (Greek tyrant), 104
Critique of Pure Reason, The (Kant),
    571, 571(f)
Croatia, 515, 679, 955, 956
Croats (Croatians), 887
    in Austrian Empire, 679
    nationalism of, 784
    Serb massacre by, 955
    World War I and, 810

Cromwell, Oliver, 503, 504,
    505–506, 505(i)
Cromwell, Thomas, 444
Crop rotation, Carolingian,
    286–287
Crops. See also Agriculture; specific
        crops
    fertilizers and, 742
    fodder, 539
    in Great Famine, 391, 392(i)
    in Greece, 52
    harvests and seed used, 539(f)
    New World, 431
    plague and, 403
Crossbows, 406
Cross-cultural connections. See
        Culture; specific cultures
        and locations
Cross in the Mountains (Friedrich),
    648
Crucifixion, of Jesus, 187
Crusader states, 323, 325–326,
    326(m), 333(m), 359–360
Crusades, 322–327
    First, 322, 323–326, 323(m),
        327, 373
    Second, 325, 326–327, 361–362,
        373
    Third, 349, 359–360
    Fourth, 354, 360, 370
    Albigensian, 364, 364(m)
    anti-heretic campaigns and,
        361(m)
    in Europe, 360–364
    impact of, 327
    Jews during, 373
    Louis IX (France) and, 384
    Northern, 362–364
"Cry of the Children, The"
    (Browning), 670
Crystal Palace exhibition (London),
    689, 690(i)
Ctesibius, 129
Ctesiphon, 247
Cuba, 653
    slavery in, 676
    U.S. and, 788, 912
Cuban missile crisis, 882, 906, 912
Cubism, 776, 777
Cult(s)
    of Asclepius, 144
    of dukes of Burgundy, 420
    Egyptian, 24
    Greek, 56, 59, 60, 87, 130–131
    imperial (Rome), 179
    of Lenin, 834

of personality (Soviet Union),
898
Roman, 191–192
ruler, 131
of Vesta, 144
of Virgin Mary, 524
Cultivation. *See* Agriculture; Crops;
Farms and farming
Cult of Reason, 610
Cult of the offensive, in World War
I, 806
Cult of the Supreme Being, 610
Culture. *See also* Art(s); Classical
culture; Intellectual
thought; Society; specific
cultures
in mid-19th century, 696
in 1920s, 829–832
in 1930s, 856–857
Americanization of, 906
of Anglo-Saxons in England,
329
in Byzantine Empire, 249
Carthaginian, 155
in cold war, 906–911, 912
counterculture and, 937
courtly, 450–452
in Egypt, 18–21, 22–23
during Enlightenment,
573–580
Etruscan, 147–148
French, in Vietnam, 716
of French court, 494–497
globalization and, 954,
980–985
Greek, 48
Greek impact on Rome,
155–156
Greek in Near East, 109–110
Hellenistic, 124–133
imperialism and, 739, 746–753
interactions in Mediterranean
region, 31–32
Irish, 781
in later Roman Empire, 203,
232–234
mass (in 1920s), 828, 829–832
in Nazi Germany, 851
Neo-Assyrian, 41
non-Roman kingdoms and,
220, 225–227
peasant, 523–524
popular, 518–521, 523–524
postindustrial, 923–929
proletarian, 833
in Renaissance, 450–452

of rock-and-roll, 908, 909(*i*)
Roman, 135, 147, 151, 182
in Russia, 549
samizdat, 930
social order and, 719–725
Soviet, 898, 911
space race and, 920
Stalinism and, 897
in United States, 984
vernacular, 354–357
in western Roman Empire,
225–227
youth, 908, 917
Cuneiform, 11, 11(*i*)
Curials (urban social elite),
208–209, 249
Curie, Marie, 775, 776
Curie, Pierre, 775
Curius, Manius, 158
Currency, euro as, 962
Curriculum
common (France), 758
university, 341, 933
Cynics, 128, 128(*i*)
Cyprus, 469, 964
Cypselus, 64–65
Cyrillic alphabet, 274
Cyrus (Persian Empire), 42, 43(*m*),
46, 78(*m*)
Czartoryska, Zofia, 566
Czechoslovakia, 819, 824, 936
breakup of, 965
collapse of communism in, 946
in Great Depression, 855–856
in Little Entente, 822
Nazi invasion of, 861
Prague Spring in, 935, 935(*m*)
protests in, 916(*i*), 917, 946
refugees from, 883
Soviets and, 887
Czech people
in Austria-Hungary, 709, 759,
784
in Austrian Empire, 679
family size of, 770(*i*)
Hus and, 411, 441
independence of, 817
as Roman Catholics, 299
in Thirty Years' War, 470
World War I and, 810
Czech Republic, 962, 963, 964, 965,
970

Dachau concentration camp, 850
Dacia (Romania), 180
Da Gama, Vasco, 433

Daguerre, Jacques, and
daguerreotypes, 673, 673(*i*)
Daily life. *See* Lifestyle
Daladier, Edouard, 861
Dalai Lama, 980
Damascus, 244(*m*), 245, 270, 275
Great Mosque at, 245(*i*)
in Second Crusade, 327
Dance, modern, 777
"Dance of Death," 403(*i*), 419
Danelaw, 288
Danes. *See* Vikings
Dante Alighieri, 376–377
Danton, Georges-Jacques, 610,
614
Danube River region, 180, 194, 222,
681
Danubian principalities, Russian
protectorate over, 652
Dardanelles, Strait of, 699
Darius I (Persia), 42, 43(*m*), 75,
78(*m*)
Dark Age(s)
in Greece, 38(*i*), 47–49
in Mediterranean region,
35, 40
use of term, 40
Darwin, Charles, 723–724, 723(*i*),
751
Das Kapital (Marx), 718
**D'Aubigné, Françoise (marquise
de Maintenon),** 496
Daumier, Honoré, 721(*i*)
David (Israelite), 46, 272(*i*), 273,
284(*i*)
David (Michelangelo), 450
David, Jacques-Louis, 610, 626(*i*),
631(*i*)
Davis, Angela, 933
Dawes Plan (1924), 821
Day care, welfare state and, 895,
895(*i*)
D-Day (June 6, 1944), 871
Dean, James, 908
Death. *See also* Relics and
reliquaries
in Egypt, 21, 25
Paleolithic, 5
Death rate
decline in, 537
infant and child, 578, 665, 669
Debasement of coinage, 195, 195(*i*)
Debt
dynastic wars and, 454–455
global economic crisis and, 976,
976(*i*)

Debt (continued)
    of peasants, 478
    of United States, 938, 975
Debussy, Claude, 778
Decembrist Revolt (1825), 651, 674
De-Christianization
    in revolutionary France, 610
    in Soviet bloc, 897
Decius (Rome), 197
Declaration of Independence
        (United States, 1776), 564,
        589
Declaration of Indulgence
        (England, 1673), 506
Declaration of the Rights of Man
        and Citizen (France),
        602–603
Declaration of the Rights of
        Woman (Gouges), 603
Decolonization. See also specific
        locations
    in Africa, 899, 902–904,
        903(m)
    in Asia, 899–901
    during cold war, 899–906
    literature on, 907–908
    in Middle East, 899, 901–902
Decretum (Gratian), 319
Decurions, 182, 184, 209
Deductive reasoning, 484
Defender of the Peace, The
        (Marsilius), 408
Defense. See also Military
        spending
    Roman, 181
    spending before World War I,
        795
Defense Department (U.S.),
        computer network of, 979
Deficits
    French, 500, 685
    trade, 743
    in United States, 942
Defoe, Daniel, 544
De Gaulle, Charles, 891, 919, 921,
        930, 984
    Algerian independence and,
        904
    student and workers' protest
        and, 934
    World War II and, 865, 869
Degeneration (Nordau), 773
De Genlis, Stéphanie, 577, 580
Deists, 566–567, 610
Deities. See Gods and goddesses;
        specific deities

De Klerk, F. W., 975
De Kooning, Willem, 911
Delacroix, Eugène, 648, 649(i)
Delhi, British in, 716
Delian League, 79–81, 82, 100–101
Deluge (Poland-Lithuania), 513
Demagogues, in Great Depression,
        843(i), 844
Demes (political units), 67, 83(i)
Demeter (goddess), cult of, 55,
        60, 87
Demetrius (Macedonia), 131
Democracy(ies), 61, 485. See also
        specific locations
    in 1930s, 842
    Aristotle on, 113–114
    in Athens, 61, 65–67, 80, 81–82,
        104
    economic, 823–824, 854
    in Europe, 564
    Great Depression in, 844,
        852–857
    in Greece, 40, 54–55
    Plato on, 113
    Rousseau and, 569–570
    terrorism against, 940
    totalitarianism and, 852
    in United States, 564, 590
    after World War II, 891–894
Demographics. See Population;
        Wealth; specific locations
Demoiselles d'Avignon, Les
        (Picasso), 776
Demotic script, 19(f), 108(i)
Denationalization, era of, 977, 986
Denazification, World War II and,
        890
D'Enghien, duke, 630
Denmark, 551, 929
    Angles from, 224
    Christian kingdom of, 288–289
    Northern Crusades and, 362
    Prussia and, 705
    slave trade and, 531
    in Thirty Years' War, 470
    welfare state in, 895(i)
    World War II and, 863
Department stores, 745–746
Dépôts de mendicité, 578
Depression (economic), in 1873,
        743–744. See also Great
        Depression
Descartes, René, 484
Deserts, in Egypt, 17–18
De Sica, Vittorio, 911
Desprez, Josquin, 417–418

Détente policy, 938, 942
Devaluation, of coinage, 454
Deventer, school at, 410
Dhuoda (Franks), 269, 285, 286
Dia, Contessa de, 355
Diamonds, in Africa, 735
Diaphragm, for birth control, 750,
        769
Diary of a Young Girl (Frank), 907
Diaspora, Jewish, 47
Dickens, Charles, 672, 719
Dictators (Rome), Caesar as, 163
Dictatorships
    in 1930s, 841–842
    in 1970s, 940
    in Africa, 971
Diderot, Denis, 564–565, 570, 579(i)
Dien Bien Phu, battle of, 932(m)
Diet (assembly), in Hungary,
        515–516
Diet (food). See also Food(s)
    in concentration camps, 867
    of Paleolithic peoples, 5
Diet of Worms, 441
Dietrich, Marlene, 856
Digest (Justinian), 232
Diggers (England), 504
Digital Age, 986, 987
Dioceses, in Rome, 205
Diocletian (Rome), 199, 203,
        204–206
    Christian persecution by, 209
    division of Rome by, 205–206,
        206(m)
Diogenes (Sinope), 128, 128(i)
Dionysus (god), 55, 96, 132
Dior, Christian, 909
Diphtheria, 896
Diplomacy, 530. See also Balance of
        power
    in 18th century, 553
    Bismarck and, 758, 760, 762
    cold war, 912–913
    Egyptian, 23
    after Napoleon, 641–644
    after World War I, 821–823
Diplomatic congress, after Thirty
        Years' War, 472
Diplomatic Revolution, 580
Directory (France), 613, 615, 616,
        628, 629
Disabilities, in Nazi Germany, 852,
        866
Disability insurance, 894
Disarmament, after World War I,
        821–822

Discourse on Method (Descartes), 484
Discovery of Achilles on Skyros (Poussin), 520(i)
Discrimination
    against Jews, 373
    legislation against, 931
    racial, 449–450
Diseases
    in 14th century, 400–404
    carried to New World, 436
    cholera as, 667, 668(m)
    in cities, 667, 712–713
    environmental causes of, 553
    food shortages and, 461
    global health and, 970
    Indians and, 431, 436, 476
    inoculation, vaccines, and, 554, 896
    World War II and, 867
Disraeli, Benjamin, 709, 760
Dissection, medical, 483, 554
Dissent
    in Austria, 651
    in France, 607, 608
    in Soviet bloc, 945
Dissidents, Soviet, 935, 936, 983
Distribution of goods, 744
Diversity
    in Austrian Empire, 678–679
    in Dutch Republic, 466–467
    in Hellenistic kingdoms, 124, 135
    linguistic, 678(m)
    in Muslim world, 276–278
    Roman, 151, 180
Dives (Bible, rich man), 304(i), 305
Divided Heaven (Wolf), 930
Divine Comedy (Dante), 377
Divine right of monarchs
    Hobbes on, 508
    James I (England) on, 475
    Locke on, 508
Divinity, concept of, 3. *See also* Gods and goddesses
Division of labor
    in barbarian society, 221
    by gender, 8
    Smith on, 569
Divorce, 449, 518, 710, 768
    in Byzantine Empire, 249
    in France, 611, 632, 771
    in Hammurabi's code, 14
    Protestantism and, 448
    in Rome, 143–144
    in Soviet Union, 833, 848

DNA, 909, 922
Doctors, 554, 713, 714, 885. *See also* Medicine
    in Rome, 185–186
Doctors Without Borders, 966
Doctor Zhivago (novel and movie), 880(i), 881, 898, 911
Doctrine (Christian), 440, 449
Dollfuss, Engelbert, 855
Doll's House, A (Ibsen), 752
Dome of the Rock (Jerusalem), 238(i), 245
Domesday survey (England), 330, 331(f)
Domestication, of animals, 4, 6
Domesticity
    ideology of, 659, 675
    in postwar society, 909–910
Domestic service, women in, 478, 541, 578. *See also* Servants
Domestic system, of manufacturing, 661
Dominate (Rome), 205–210
Dominic (Saint), 364
Dominicans, 364, 375
Dominions, British, 711
Domitian (Rome), 179, 180, 194, 223(m)
Donation of Constantine, 282
Donation of Pippin, 280–281
Donatist Christianity, 215–216
Donatus, 216
Don Quixote (Cervantes), 468, 544
Dorian Greeks, 35
Doric style, 85, 85(f)
Dostoevsky, Fyodor, 720, 760, 761
Double Helix, The (Watson), 908–909
Double monasteries, 259
Downsizing, 978
Dowry
    barbarian, 221
    in Greece, 60, 88
    Merovingian, 257–258
Draco, 65
Draft. *See* Military draft
Drama. *See also* Comedy (drama)
    Greek, 86, 96–100
    Hellenistic, 125
    Roman, 155, 184(i)
Dreadnought, HMS (ship), 796
Dream of Philip II, The (El Greco), 466(i)
Dreams of My Russian Summers (Makine), 983
Dresden, World War II and, 865

Dreyfus, Alfred, 782, 783(i)
Dreyfus Affair (France), 782–783
Drinking water, 667, 970
Drought, in Africa and Asia, 742
Dual Alliance, 760
Dualism
    concept of, 113
    as heresy, 358–359
    Plato on, 113
Dual monarchy, 709, 784, 794. *See also* Austria-Hungary
Dubček, Alexander, 935, 946
Dublin, 812
Duchies
    of Burgundy, 404–406
    in Germany, 297
Dukes (Burgundy), personal cult of, 420
Duma (Russia), 790, 813
Duncan, Isadora, 777
Dunkirk, 863
Duns Scotus, John, 376
Dürer, Albrecht, 439(i)
Dutch. *See also* Dutch Republic; Netherlands
    in Africa, 735
    agriculture of, 538–539
    decolonization and, 904
    England and, 505, 506, 508, 511
    independence of, 466, 473
    revolts against Spain, 465, 466
    in southern Africa, 735, 786
    Thirty Years' War and, 477
    trade and, 509–510, 510(m), 536
    after World War I, 826
Dutch East India Company, 510(m)
Dutch Republic, 465, 466, 477, 483, 484, 525(m), 547. *See also* Dutch; Netherlands
    agriculture in, 540
    commerce of, 467, 509–510, 510(m)
    Congress of Vienna and, 643
    constitutionalism in, 509–511
    decline of, 511, 548–549
    England and, 589
    France and, 499, 511, 608, 616, 641
    homosexuals in, 579
    literacy in, 511, 578
    political reform and, 590
    Prussia and, 596
    religious toleration and, 556
    revolts in, 596–597
    slave trade and, 531

Dutch War, 499–500
Dynamite, 796
Dynasties. *See* Kings and
    kingdoms; Monarchs and
    monarchies; specific
    dynasties and rulers
Dynatoi (Byzantine Empire),
    273–274, 276, 324

Earth. *See* Astronomy
East, the, 882
East Africa, 731, 733, 788, 792–793,
    903
East Anglia, 296
East Asia, 717, 858, 869, 900, 974
Easter, dating of, 260
Eastern Christianity. *See* Greek
    Orthodox Church;
    Orthodox Christianity
Eastern Europe, 299. *See also*
    specific locations
    1848 revolutions in, 687–688
    1989 revolutions in, 945–947
    in 1990s, 979
    absolutism in, 515–518
    brain drain from, 936–937
    after Charlemagne, 285
    cold war in, 885–886
    collapse of communism in, 937,
        943–947, 948(m), 956
    communism in, 882–883, 886,
        896–898
    eastern Roman Empire as,
        239–240
    empires in, 469
    in EU, 963–965
    formation of, 274–275
    governments in, 353–354
    Great Depression in, 844
    Huns in, 222
    industrialization in, 664
    Jews in, 784–785, 844
    life expectancy in, 970
    literature in, 983
    migration from, 936–937
    peasants in, 540
    political formations in, 419
    pollution in, 967
    power in, 418
    power politics in, 759–760,
        762
    religion in, 274, 469
    serfdom in, 479–480
    social welfare in, 895–896
    Soviet Union and, 871, 887,
        896–898, 929

women in, 771, 895–896
    after World War I, 824
    World War II and, 865
Eastern front, World War I and,
    807
Eastern Orthodox Church. *See*
    Greek Orthodox Church;
    Orthodox Christianity
Eastern Roman Empire, 204,
    227–234. *See also* Byzantine
    Empire; Roman Empire;
    Western Roman Empire
    in c. 600, 235(m)
    Christianity in, 230
    as eastern Europe and Turkey,
        239–240
    separation from western
        Roman Empire, 206–207,
        207(m)
East Germany, 889, 897, 912, 930,
    946
East India Company (Britain), 677,
    715, 716
East Indies, 434, 536
East Prussia, 514, 807, 819
Ebert, Friedrich, 818, 819
Ebla, Syria, 12
Ebola virus, 970
Ecce Homo (Nietzsche), 831(i)
Economic democracy, 823–824, 854
Economics
    laissez-faire, 759
    liberalism in, 680–681
    monetarist (supply-side), 941
    Smith, Adam, on, 568–570
Economic shocks, 976
Economist, The (periodical), 680,
    978
Economy. *See also* Agriculture;
        Farms and farming;
        Global economy; Great
        Depression; Labor; Trade;
        Wealth
    in 1920s, 826–827
    in Athens, 65, 111–112
    balance of power and, 479–481
    boom and bust cycles in, 824
    in Britain, 941–942
    Carolingian, 286
    collapse of global economy,
        954, 976–977, 986
    commercial, 306–312
    crisis in 1870s and 1880s,
        743–744
    in Dutch Republic, 467
    dynastic wars and, 453–455

in eastern Europe, 963–964
    in Egypt, 733
    emerging, 975–976
    in England, 348, 349, 709
    in former Soviet bloc, 959(i), 960
    in former Soviet Union, 957,
        959–960
    in France, 942
    in Germany, 851, 888–889, 942
    in global south, 971
    in Great Depression, 841,
        842–843, 844, 845
    in Hellenistic kingdoms, 122
    Hittite, 27–28
    Marx on, 718
    Mesopotamian, 8, 10, 13
    Minoan, 30
    money economy, 305–306
    in non-Roman kingdoms, 223
    oil and, 918, 938–939
    in peasant society, 256–257
    postindustrial, 917, 923
    in Rome, 181–182, 181(m),
        194–195, 207–209
    in Russia, 699, 957
    serfdom and, 480
    service, 917
    Soviets and, 833, 846–847, 896,
        943–944
    Thirty Years' War and, 475–481
    in United States, 883–884, 942
    in western Europe, 305–306,
        893–894
    world's top fifteen economies
        (2010), 987(m)
    after World War I, 821, 824
    after World War II, 883–884,
        893–899
ECSC. *See* European Coal and Steel
        Community
Ecstasy of St. Teresa of Ávila
    (Bernini), 519
Ecumenism, Vatican II and, 906
Edessa
    crusaders and, 325–326
    mosaic of family from, 216(i)
Edgar (England), 296
Edict of Milan, 209–210
Edict of Nantes, 463
    revocation of, 498, 515, 530
Edict of Restitution, 470
Education, 579. *See also* Higher
        education; Learning;
        Schools
    Black Death and, 403–404
    Byzantine, 249

in France, 610, 758, 782
in Germany, 742, 779
Great Depression and, 844
in Greek Golden Age, 90
Islamic, 279
Jesuit, 449
literacy and, 542
Locke and, 509
in Merovingian society, 258
Napoleonic, 632
for nation building, 714–715
in postindustrial society, 926, 927
reforms of, 584, 674
in Rome, 144, 175–176
school attendance and, 714–715
segregation in, 908
for women, 298–299, 715, 758, 771, 779, 975
of workers, 714–715, 778
Edward (the Confessor, England), 328
Edward I (England), 386, 387
Edward III (England), 404, 404(f)
Edward VI (England), 444, 455
EEC. *See* European Economic Community
Ego, id, and superego, Freud on, 774
Egypt (ancient), 15–25, 16(m). *See also* Ptolemaic rulers
Abbasids and, 276
Alexander the Great and, 117
Caesar in, 163
Christianity in, 215
Cleopatra VII in, 124, 134, 163, 164(i), 171
decline of, 33
Hyksos people in, 22
Islam and, 243
Israelites and, 45
Middle Kingdom in, 22
monks in, 218
New Kingdom in, 22–25
Old Kingdom in, 16–22
peoples of, 18
Persia and, 82
religion in, 2(i), 3, 18–19, 24
in Roman Empire, 166(m)
Sasanids in, 247
society in, 18–19
trade in, 18–19
unification of, 15–16
writing and spelling in, 18, 19(f)

Egypt (modern), 870, 938
Britain and, 733, 793
digital media and government in, 980
Fatimids in, 277
imperialism in, 733
independence for, 901–902
Israeli peace accords with, 941(i)
Napoleon in, 628–629
nationalism in, 792
revolt in (1920s), 826
Suez Canal and, 698, 716, 733
Eiffel Tower, 740
Einstein, Albert, 774, 775–776
Eisenhower, Dwight, 871
Eisenstein, Sergei, 829, 831, 848
Elba, Napoleon on, 641
Elderly
in concentration camps, 866
in Nazi Germany, 852, 866
poverty of, 895
Elders, in Sparta, 62
Eleanor of Aquitaine, 327, 345–346, 347(i)
Elect, in Calvinism, 443, 468
Elections
in Poland, 946
in Rome, 148–150
in Soviet Union, 945
Electoral system, in Germany, 708
Electors
of Brandenburg, 473, 514
of Holy Roman Emperor, 470
of Saxony, 456
Electricity, 740, 741(i)
atomic power plants for, 896
from wind power, 968
Elements of the Philosophy of Newton (Voltaire), 556
El Greco, 466(i), 487
Eliezer, Israel ben, 572–573
Eliot, George (Mary Ann Evans), 719–720
Elisabeth de Valois, 465
Elisabeth of Hungary, 373
Elites. *See also* Aristocracy; Nobility
in Byzantine Empire, 270–275
in eastern Roman Empire, 231–232
in England, 504
English in North America, 512
French Revolution and, 620
Greek, 49, 88
in Hellenistic kingdoms, 121

in Italy, 289
Merovingian, 255, 257–260
middle-class, 553, 574, 575–577
native in India, 147, 736
in Roman military, 157–158
in Rome, 178, 182, 184
socialist, 779
social order and, 669–670
working class and, 674
Elizabeth (Russia), 591
Elizabeth I (England), 444, 455, 462, 467–468, 467(i)
Ellis, Havelock, 772
Ellison, Ralph, 931
Elpinike (Athens), 90
E-mail, 945
Emancipation
of Russian serfs, 700–701, 701(i)
of U.S. slaves, 710
Embargo
oil, 938–939
by U.S. against Japan, 858
Embassies
diplomacy and, 553
U.S. in Iran, 939
Emerging economies, 924, 975
Emerging nations, in cold war, 902(i)
Emigration. *See also* Immigrants and immigration; Migration
to Americas, 535–536
from Europe, 669
from former Soviet Union, 959
from French Revolution, 614
Greek, 53
from Ireland, 684
from Nazi Germany, 852
Emir (commander), 277
Emissions controls, 968
Emperors. *See also* Holy Roman Empire; specific empires and rulers
Byzantine, 353
in central and eastern Europe, 470
Charlemagne as, 283–284
church reform and, 314
German kings as, 352
Empire(s), 12. *See also* Imperialism; specific empires and rulers
competition before World War I, 793
decolonization and, 899–901
economies and technology of, 740–746

Empire Day (Britain), 739(i)
Empiricism, 571
Employment. See also Labor
    after World War I, 827, 828
Enabling Act (Germany, 1933), 850
Enclosure, 539–540
Encyclopedia (Diderot, ed.),
    564–565, 585
Energy
    alternative sources, 968, 968(i)
    Einstein's theory of, 775–776
    from nuclear power, 921
    politics of, 961
Engels, Friedrich, 682–683
Engineering. See Inventions;
    Technology; Weapons
England. See also Britain; specific
    rulers
    in 15th century, 419
    Alfred the Great in, 295–296,
        295(m)
    black slavery and, 511, 531
    Calvinism in, 461
    civil wars in, 330, 421–422, 502,
        503
    classes in, 422
    colonies of, 480, 480(m)
    constitutionalism in, 493–494,
        502–509
    Domesday survey in, 330, 331(f)
    Dutch and, 505, 506, 508, 511,
        547
    economy in, 349, 477
    finances in, 348
    France and, 349–350, 383, 499,
        582, 620, 621(i)
    gentry in, 422, 574
    Glorious Revolution in, 507
    house of Hanover and, 547
    human capital in, 553
    Hundred Years' War and,
        404–407
    Industrial Revolution in,
        660–661, 741
    Ireland and, 505, 548, 679–680,
        710
    Jews in, 373, 374
    kingdom in, 251
    literacy in, 542, 578
    Luddite riots in, 661
    Magna Carta and, 349
    in Middle Ages, 345–349
    naming of, 260
    nobility in, 574
    Normans in, 328–330, 329(m),
        330(i)

Parliament in, 502
peasant rebellion in, 407
Peterloo massacre in, 654
plague in, 506
playwrights in, 469, 486
political reforms in, 756–757
political system in, 295–296
Protestantism in, 443–444,
    467–469
published materials in, 543
railroads in, 659, 661–662
reform societies in, 620, 674
religious divisions in, 455
representative government in,
    385–386
Restoration in, 506–508
St. Domingue and, 619
Scotland and, 505, 547–548
Spanish Armada and, 468
theaters in, 486
vernacular language in,
    295–296
Vikings in, 289, 296
Wessex in, 295
working class in, 654, 665, 778
English language, 295–296, 330
    as dominant international
        language, 984
Enheduanna (Akkad), 12
Enlightened despots (absolutists),
    580, 585
Enlightenment, 530, 554–559,
    564–580
    conservative thinkers on, 645
    Declaration of Independence
        and, 564, 589
    in France, 556, 570–571, 602
    Freemasonry and, 575–576
    in Germany, 571
    philosophes in, 564–566,
        566(i)
    society and culture during,
        573–580
    state power in, 580–590
    women in, 555(i), 558–559,
        565–566, 577
Enlil (god), 12
Entente Cordiale, 793, 794, 804
Entertainment. See also Drama;
    Leisure; Sports
    in eastern Roman Empire, 228
    for peasants, 578
    Roman, 175, 184(i)
Entrepreneurs
    industrial, 974
    in United States, 742

Environment
    globalization and, 954,
        967–968
    of Greece, 52
    of Near East, 5
Ephors, in Sparta, 62
Epic literature, 155. See also
    Homer; specific works
    in Middle Ages, 356
    Roman, 155
    Theogony (Hesiod) as, 51
Epic of Creation (Mesopotamia), 10
Epic of Gilgamesh, 10, 41
Epicureanism, 127
Epicurus, 127
Epidemics. See also Black Death;
    Diseases; specific diseases
    in mid-19th century, 667,
        668(m)
    AIDS as, 970
    among Amerindians, 436
    in cities, 712
    in eastern Roman Empire, 231
    globalization and, 954
    influenza pandemic and,
        816(f), 817
Epigrams, 125
Equal Employment Opportunity
    Commission (EEOC), 931
Equality
    in Athens, 66
    in French Revolution, 602, 603
    in Greece, 56–57, 58
    in marriage, 770–771
    in Russia, 701
Equiano, Olaudah, 567
Equites (Roman equestrians,
    knights), 159
Erasmus, Desiderius, 438–439,
    443
Eratosthenes, 129
Erhard, Ludwig, 893
Eridu (Mesopotamian city-state), 8
Eriksen, Vigilius, 562(i)
Ermengard (wife of Louis the
    Pious), 285
Esquivel, Laura, 981
Essay Concerning Human
    Understanding (Locke), 509
Estates (French classes), 599. See
    also specific estates
    in Hundred Years' War, 406
Estates (land), expansion of, 668
Estates General
    in Dutch Republic, 509
    in France, 385, 387, 599, 600

Este, Isabella d', 418
Esterházy family, Haydn and, 577
Estonia, 863, 928, 957, 964
Ethics
    Aristotle on, 114
    Christianity and, 188, 233
    Socrates on, 94
Ethiopia, 970
    Christianity in, 215
    European struggle for (1896),
        781, 786(m)
    Italy and, 781, 858
Ethnic cleansing, 891(i), 955
Ethnic groups. See also specific
        groups and countries
    in Africa, 734(m)
    in Austria-Hungary, 709, 784
    in Austrian Empire, 678–679
    in Balkan region, 759–760, 794
    in former Soviet Union, 957
    in Germany, 687
    in Holy Roman Empire, 470
    in Hungary, 687, 709, 784
    among non-Romans, 221
    in Persian Empire, 42
    in Poland, 819, 824, 824(m)
    in Russia, 702, 761–762,
        789–790
    in Soviet Union, 954
    after World War I, 824
    in Yugoslavia, 954–955
Ethnography, 928
Etruscans, 53, 138(i), 146(m),
        147–148, 147(i), 156
EU. See European Union
Euboea, 49
Eucharist, 318, 410
    Jewish rituals and, 374
    transubstantiation and, 371,
        441–442, 449
Euclid, 129
Eugenics, 770
Eugénie (France), 697, 697(i)
Eulalius (Count), 259
Euphrates River region, 4, 8
Euripides (Athens), 87, 97
Euro, 962
European Coal and Steel
        Community (ECSC), 894
European Community (EC), 962
Europe and Europeans. See also
        specific locations, wars, and
        issues
    in 400 B.C.E., 105(m)
    in c. 1050, 300(m)
    in c. 1150, 333(m)

in 1150–1190, 346(m)
in c. 1215, 365(m)
in c. 1340, 394(m)
in 1492, 426(m)
c. 1715, 546(m)
in 1750, 561(m)
in c. 1780, 591(m)
in 1799, 622(m)
in 1830, 657(m)
in 1850, 691(m)
in 1871, 727(m)
in 1929, 837(m)
in Africa, 735–736, 903–904
Black Death in, 401
cholera in, 667, 668(m)
collapse of communism in,
        948(m)
Common Market in, 894
Congress of Vienna and,
        641–644, 644(m)
crusades in, 364
economy in, 475–481
emigration and (1870–1890),
        749(f)
emigration from, 669, 747–748
foreign-born population in,
        904–906
imperialist expansion by,
        715–717, 731–732,
        733–740
industrialization in, 663(m)
Iraq War and, 973–974
languages of (19th century),
        678(m)
migration from eastern to
        western, 960
migration from rural areas to
        cities, 748
Muslims in, 977
Napoleon and, 634–635,
        634(m)
at outbreak of World War I,
        799(m)
papacy and, 280
after peace settlements
        (1919–1920), 820(m)
population in, 577, 969, 969(f)
post-invasion society in, 289
postwar recovery in, 890–898
recovery in 1920s, 823–829
Reformation in (c. 1560),
        457(m)
religious divisions of (c. 1648),
        489(m)
Russia as power in, 549–552
scholars in, 279

terrorism in, 973
totalitarianism in, 846–852
trade patterns of (c. 1740),
        531(m)
unification of, 962–964
urbanization in (1750–1800),
        575(f)
after World War I, 817–818
World War II and, 842,
        863–864, 869–872, 870(m)
after World War II, 876(m),
        881–882, 882–883, 884(m)
European Economic Community
        (EEC, Common Market),
        894, 962
European Union (EU), 953–954,
        962–964, 965, 986
    in 2011, 963(m)
    global economic crisis and,
        977
    members of, 962, 964
    parliament of, 962, 984
"Europe first" strategy, in World
        War II, 872
Evangelicals, 440
Evans, Arthur, 28
Evelyn, John, 507(i)
Evolution, Darwin on, 723–724
Exarchate of Ravenna, 248, 264
Exchequer (England), 348
Exclusion Crisis (England, 1678),
        506, 508
Excommunication
    of Henry IV, 316–317
    Roman Catholic–Greek
        Orthodox schism and, 315
Executions, in French Revolution,
        607, 608, 614, 615
Existentialism, 907, 929
Exodus (Ezechiel), 126
Expansion. See also Crusades
    of France, 499, 616–618,
        617(m)
    of Greece, 54(m)
    imperialist, 715–717
    by Nazi Germany, 858–859,
        860–863, 862(m)
    Ottoman, 407–408, 407(m)
    of Persian Empire, 43(m)
    Phoenician, 54(m)
    Roman, 140, 145–146, 151–152,
        153–155, 154(m), 166(m),
        180, 181(m)
    Russian, 469, 698, 715,
        736–737, 737(m)
    before World War II, 857

Exploration. *See also* Invasions
　Enlightenment and, 567
　by France, 499
　by Portugal, 431, 432–433
　space exploration, 898,
　　920–921
　by Spain, 431, 433–434, 435
Exports. *See* Trade; specific
　locations
Expressionism, 777, 911
Extermination camps, World War
　II and, 866–868, 866(*m*)
Eylau, battle of, 636(*i*)
Eyres, in England, 347
Ezechiel (Jew in Alexandria), 126

Fabian Society, 750
Factories, 661
　child labor in, 665
　in Great Depression, 844
　Soviet, 847
　workers in, 664–665, 748
　working class and, 665
Factory Act (Britain, 1833), 665
Factory system, 741
Fahrenheit 451 (Bradbury),
　910–911
Fairs, 522
　commerce and, 306–307
Faith
　Council of Trent on, 449
　Luther on, 440–441
Falange Party (Spain), 859
Falkland Islands, 941
Families
　in Athens, 111–112
　in barbarian society, 221
　in Byzantine Empire, 249
　Civil Code of Napoleon and,
　　632
　corporations of, 310
　economy and, 479
　in factories, 665
　in France, 293–294, 611
　in Greece, 57(*f*), 87
　of helots, 62
　in Italy, 295
　medieval patrilineal, 293–294
　middle class, 745
　neoclassical depictions of, 577
　in postindustrial society,
　　926–927
　in Rome, 142–144
　rural, 669
　sizes of, 479, 750, 769, 770(*i*),
　　869

　in Soviet Union, 848, 896
　in Sweden, 854
Family allowance, in Sweden, 854
Family planning centers, 844
Famines, 461, 475, 476, 684. *See
　also* Starvation
　of 1846–1851, 684, 691(*m*)
　in Africa and Asia, 742, 970
　Great Famine, 390–393
　in Ireland, 684
　in World War I, 810
Fanon, Frantz, 907–908
Farming package, 6–7
Farms and farming, 769. *See also*
　　Agriculture; Irrigation;
　　Peasants; Rural areas; Serfs
　　and serfdom
　British, 539–540
　Byzantine, 249
　Carolingian, 286–288
　collectivization of, 847, 865,
　　885, 896, 897(*i*)
　in Egypt, 18
　enclosure and, 539–540
　in former Soviet bloc, 960
　in Great Depression, 843
　industrial innovation in, 742
　medieval, 292
　Mesopotamian, 8
　in postindustrial age, 925–926
　in Rome, 158, 208
　tenant farmers and, 540, 757
Fasces, 148
Fascism, 804, 844, 846, 882, 890.
　　See also Nazis and Nazism
　　(Germany)
　in Italy, 834–836
　resistance to, 855, 857
　in Spain, 842, 855, 859–860
Fashoda, Sudan, 793
Fathers. *See* Families; Men
Fathers and Sons (Turgenev), 720
Fatihah (Qur'an), 241
Fatimah (Islam), 244, 277
Fatimids, 277, 278(*i*), 324
Fawcett, Millicent Garrett, 780
Federal Reserve Bank (U.S.), 842
Feminine Mystique, The (Friedan),
　　933
Feminism, 770. *See also* Women
　in France, 689
　nationalism and, 792
　women's rights and, 933, 934(*i*)
　in World War I, 809
Ferdinand I (Austrian Empire),
　　687, 688

Ferdinand I (Holy Roman
　　Empire), 456
Ferdinand II (Aragon), 419, 425,
　　434, 436, 443
Ferdinand II (Holy Roman
　　Empire), 456, 470, 471
Ferdinand VII (Spain), 639, 650
Fertile Crescent, 5, 7
Fertilizers, chemical, 742, 925
Festivals, 522
　in Athens, 86–87
　in France, 610
Feudal society, relationships in,
　　290–293
Fidelity, oaths of, 268(*i*)
Fiefs, 290
Fields, Gracie, 856
Fighting "Téméraire" . . . (Turner),
　　671, 671(*i*)
Films. *See* Movies
"Final Solution," World War II and,
　　866. *See also* Holocaust
Finances. *See* Economy
Finland, 469, 780, 780(*i*)
Fireside chats, by Roosevelt, F. D.,
　　853(*i*)
First Balkan War (1912), 794
First Consul, Napoleon as, 629–630
First Crusade, 322, 323–326,
　　323(*m*), 327, 373
First Estate (clergy), in France, 599
First International, 755
First Moroccan Crisis (1905), 794
First Punic War, 153–154, 153(*f*)
First Triumvirate (Rome), 162–163
First world (capitalist bloc), 882
First World War. *See* World War I
Five good emperors (Rome), 180
Five Pillars of Islam, 243
Five-year plans, Soviet, 846–847, 885
Flaccus, Valerius, 412
Flagellants, 401
Flanders, 306, 311, 406
Flappers, 829, 830(*i*)
Flaubert, Gustave, 719, 720
Flavian emperors (Rome), 179
Fleming, Ian, 911
Flemish people, agriculture of,
　　538–539
Fleurs du mal, Les (Baudelaire), 720
Fleury, Hercule de, 547
Floods
　in *Epic of Gilgamesh*, 10–11
　Mesopotamian, 8
　by Nile River, 18, 24
　Noah and, 11

Florence, 392(i), 422, 423–424, 450
Flour War (France, 1775), 586–587
Flu. *See* Influenza pandemics
Flying buttresses, 343
Flying shuttle, 660
Food(s). *See also* Agriculture;
    Crops; Diet (food)
    in Greece, 52
    increased production, 577
    of Paleolithic peoples, 5
    prices of, 539
    shortages of, 461, 599, 684, 811
Food riots
    in Britain, 586
    in France, 586–587
Forced labor. *See also* Slaves and
    slavery
    Nazis and, 852, 866, 867(i)
    Soviet, 888
Ford, Henry, 827, 829
Ford Motor Company, 827
Foreign aid, Marshall Plan and,
    886–887
Foreigners, anger against, 978
Foreign policy. *See* specific
    locations
Forging, 310
Formosa. *See* Taiwan
Forms, Plato's theory of, 113, 114
Forts, Portuguese, 432, 433,
    433(m)
Forum, of Augustus, 172–173,
    172(i)
Fossil fuels, 967, 968
Fouché, Joseph, 630
Foundling hospitals, 578
Fourier, Charles, 682
Fourteen Points (1918), 812,
    818–819
Fourth Crusade, 354, 360, 370
Fourth Lateran Council, 370–372
Fourth Republic (France), 891
France, 452. *See also* French
    Revolution; Napoleon I
    Bonaparte; Paris; Second
    Empire; specific rulers
    in 12th century, 331
    in 15th century, 419
    African decolonization and,
    904
    Algeria and, 669, 676, 716, 904
    American Revolution and, 589
    American settlement by, 535
    Austria and, 552, 553, 605, 698
    authority of state in, 498–501
    birthrate in, 769

Bourbon restoration in, 641,
    643, 645
Breton and Corsican
    independence and, 965
Burgundy in, 420
Calvinism in, 461, 462, 567
Canada and, 582
Capetian dynasty in, 296–297
    after Charlemagne, 285
colonies of, 480–481, 480(m),
    669, 739, 846
Congress of Vienna and, 642,
    643, 698
constitutional monarchy in,
    602, 603, 654
constraints on power of, 545
Crimean War and, 698, 699
crusades in, 364
de Gaulle in, 904, 930
diplomacy in, 553
division of (1940), 863(m)
divorce in, 771
Dreyfus Affair in, 782–783
Dutch and, 499, 511, 608, 616
economic crises in, 942, 977
in ECSC, 894
education in, 674, 926
Egypt and, 733
England and, 349–350, 383,
    546(m)
in Enlightenment, 556,
    570–571
in Entente Cordiale, 793
expansion of, 499, 616–618,
    617(m), 622(m), 716
families in, 293–294
feminism in, 934(i)
Germany and, 793–794, 821,
    888–889
global economic crisis and,
    977
government in, 381, 891
Grand Army in, 635–637
in Great Depression, 854–855
Hitler and, 858
Huguenots (Calvinists) in,
    462–464, 515
Hundred Years' War and,
    404–407
Huns in, 222
imperialism by, 500, 716, 733,
    736–737, 826
Indochina and, 736–737, 793,
    900
industry in, 743
inflation in, 939

Iraq War and, 973
Italian unification and, 704,
    705
Jews in, 373–374, 384
July revolution in, 653
June Days in, 685–686
liberalism in, 681
literacy in, 542, 578
in Middle Ages, 349–350
middle class in, 575
Milan and, 420–421
monarchy in, 493, 494–501,
    602, 604–607, 645
Morocco and, 793, 794
Muslims in, 977
Naples and, 420–421
Navarre and, 362(m)
non-Europeans in, 904, 905
Peace of Westphalia and, 472,
    473(m)
peasants in, 599, 602
plague epidemic in, 477
political system in, 296–297
Protestants in, 442
Prussia and, 605–606, 705,
    706–707
railroads in, 698
reforms in, 585, 586
regional departments in, 603,
    604(m)
religious toleration in, 455
republics in, 606, 615, 684–685,
    757–758, 782–783
revolution and civil war in
    (1870–1871), 718–719
Rome and, 155
Russia and, 696, 698–699, 793
Second Empire in, 686, 707,
    757
Seven Years' War and, 580–582,
    581(m)
slavery and, 511, 531, 676
socialism in, 682
Spain and, 499, 545, 650
student strike in, 934
Suez Canal and, 698, 716
taxation in, 474, 498, 500, 598,
    602, 603
Thirty Years' War and,
    471–472
Tunisia and, 733
United States and, 590
urbanization in, 748
Vichy France in, 864
Vietnam and, 716
voting in, 599, 600, 654

France (continued)
    War of the Polish Succession
        and, 552
    War of the Spanish Succession
        and, 545
    wars of religion in, 462–464, 568
    woman suffrage in, 823, 823(f)
    women in, 632, 933
    World War I and, 798, 804,
        805–806
    after World War I, 818, 819,
        821, 823, 825
    World War II and, 863–864,
        871, 874, 877, 890
Franche-Comté, 500
Francia, Gaul as, 225
Francis (Saint), 357
Francis (son of Henry II, France),
    455, 462
Francis I (France), 451, 451(i), 452,
    453(i), 454
Francis I (Holy Roman Empire),
    553
Franciscans, 357–358, 375
Francis Ferdinand (Austria), 796,
    798(i)
Francis Joseph (Austrian Empire),
    688, 698, 706, 708, 709, 712
Francis Xavier, 450
Franck, Hans Ulrich, 471(i)
Franco, Francisco, 859, 940
Franco-Prussian War, 707–708,
    718, 742, 758, 793, 805–806
Frank, Anne, 907
Frankenstein (Shelley), 627, 647
Frankfurt, 968
Frankfurt parliament (1848), 687,
    688
Frankish kingdoms, 252–256,
    259–260, 270, 280. See also
    Carolingian Empire
Franks, 225, 254. See also
    Carolingian Empire;
    Frankish kingdoms
    under Hugh Capet, 296–297,
    296(m)
Frederick I (Brandenburg-Prussia),
    515
Frederick I Barbarossa
    (Germany), 332, 346(m),
    351, 352–353, 352(i)
    Third Crusade and, 359
Frederick II (Sicily, Germany, Holy
    Roman Empire), 381–382
Frederick II (the Great, Prussia),
    553, 574, 577, 580, 581, 582

Freemasonry and, 575
    reforms by, 583, 584, 585
Frederick V (Palatinate), 470
Frederick the Wise (elector of
    Saxony), 441
Frederick William I (Prussia),
    551–552
Frederick William II (Prussia),
    596
Frederick William III (Prussia),
    637–638
Frederick William IV (Prussia),
    687
Frederick William of
    Hohenzollern (Great
    Elector of Brandenburg-
    Prussia), 514–515
Free Companies, 406, 407
Free Corps (Dutch Republic), 597
Freedom(s). See also Rights
    in cities and towns, 310–311
    in Greece, 58, 59–60
    philosophes on, 564, 565
    religious, 584
    for slaves, 59
    of Spartan women, 64
Freedom of a Christian (Luther),
    440–441
Free French, 865, 869, 891
Free markets. See also Market(s)
    physiocrats and, 585, 586
    Smith, Adam, on, 568, 586
Freemasons, 575. See also Masons
    and Masonic lodges
Free peasants, 293
Free people
    in England, 347, 349
    in Greece, 40
Free trade, 586
    in 19th century, 680, 681, 697,
        744
    in former Soviet Union, 960
    NAFTA and, 962
    Smith, Adam, on, 569
Free Woman, The (newspaper), 682
Freikorps, 818
French Academy of Science, 776
French and Indian War. See Seven
    Years' War
French East India Company, 535
French Empire, 615, 627
French Indochina. See Indochina
French Revolution (1787–1800),
    595–596, 602–604. See also
    Napoleon I Bonaparte
    conservative thinkers on, 645

Directory in, 613, 615, 616,
    628–629
education during, 610
fall of Bastille and, 600(i), 601
family life in, 611
Freemasonry and, 576
major events of, 613(f)
monarchy in, 602, 604–607
origins of, 597–602
Paris in, 601, 606, 608–609,
    614–615
Republic of Virtue during, 607,
    609–611
resistance to, 611–612
Rousseau and, 569
Terror in, 607–615
Vendée Rebellion and, 612, 615
wars during, 605, 607, 608–609,
    614, 615–619, 617(m)
women in, 594(i), 595, 603, 612
worldwide reaction to, 619–621
French Wars of Religion, 462–464,
    568
Freud, Sigmund, 767, 768, 769,
    773–774, 773(i), 785
Friars
    Dominican, 364
    Franciscan, 357–358
Friedan, Betty, 933
Friedland, battle at, 636
Friedrich, Caspar David, 647–648
Friends of Blacks, 618
Froissart, Jean, 406
Fronde, The (France), 494–495, 496
Front for National Liberation (FNL,
    Algeria), 904
Frontiers. See also Boundaries;
    Invasions
    Byzantine, 246
    of Carolingian Empire, 281, 285
    Christianity along, 361–362
    Congress of Vienna and, 642,
        643, 644(m)
    of Roman Empire, 194
Fugger family, 455
    Jakob, 454
Führer, Hitler as, 849
Fulbert (cleric), 339
Fur trade, 481, 499
Fuseli, Johann Heinrich, 648(i)

Gaelic language, 680
Gagarin, Yuri, 898, 920
Gaius. See Caligula
Gaius Gracchus. See Gracchus
    family

Galatians. *See* Gauls (Celts)
Galen, 483
Galerius (Roman Empire), 205
Galicia, 679, 807
Galileo Galilei, 482–483, 483*(i)*
Gallia (Gaul), 298*(i)*
Gallicanism, 421
Gallienus (Rome), 197
Gallo-Romans, 254
Gambling, 578
Game laws, in England, 574
Gandhi, Mohandas ("Mahatma"), 845, 845*(i)*, 899, 908
García Márquez, Gabriel, 981
Garibaldi, Giuseppe, 686, 704, 705
Gas (poison), in World War I, 806
Gas chambers, in World War II, 866
Gasoline engine, 740
Gaul. *See also* France
    kingdom in, 251
    Magyars in, 289
    monasteries in, 258
    Romanization of, 182
    Rome and, 151, 154*(m)*, 155, 222
    Visigoths and, 222, 262
Gauls (Celts), 151
Gay liberation movement, 932
Gays. *See* Homosexuals and homosexuality
Gaza, 938, 938*(m)*
Gender and gender issues. *See also* Homosexuals and homosexuality; Men; Women
    changing norms and, 908–910
    division of labor and, 8
    in Egypt, 21
    in Great Depression, 844
    in Nazi Germany, 851
    in postwar society, 909–910
    in protest movements, 933
    religion and, 722–723
    social distinctions in mid-19th century, 675–676
    social roles and, 12, 511, 579, 768, 769, 810, 927
    wages and, 752, 755, 827, 925
    in welfare state, 895
General Maximum (France), 608
General School Ordinance (Austria), 584
General strike
    in England (1926), 825, 827
    in Germany, 818

General will, Rousseau on, 569–570
Generation gap, 927
Genetics, 724, 922, 925
Geneva, Calvin in, 442–443
Geneva Conference (1954), 900, 931
Genghis Khan. *See* Chingiz (Genghis) Khan
Genius of Christianity (Chateaubriand), 633
Genoa, Black Death in, 400–401
Genocide. *See also* Holocaust
    in Africa, 971
    ethnic cleansing as, 955
    World War II and, 863, 881
Gentiles, 188
Gentilhomme, 522
Gentry, in England, 422, 574
Geocentrism, 129
Geoffrey of Anjou, 345
Geoffrin, Marie-Thérèse, 565–566, 566*(i)*
Geography. *See also* specific locations
    of Greece, 26*(m)*, 48, 52
    mathematical, 129
    Paleolithic, 5
Geology, 556
Geometry, Euclid and, 129
George I (England), 547, 548
George II (England), 548
George III (England), 587
George V (England), 807
German Confederation, 643, 706
German Democratic Party, 822*(i)*
German Federal Republic. *See* West Germany
Germania (Germany), 253*(i)*, 298*(i)*
Germanic peoples and kingdoms. *See* Barbarians; specific groups
German people
    in Austria-Hungary, 759, 784
    in Austrian Empire, 678–679
    in Baltic region, 362–363
    as refugees, 883
Germany. *See also* East Germany; Nazis and Nazism (Germany); West Germany; World War I; World War II; specific leaders
    anti-Semitism in, 783–784
    antisocialist laws in, 778
    birthrate in, 769

Bismarck in, 758–759, 760, 762
after Charlemagne, 285
colonies of, 739, 788, 820–821, 826
division of, 882, 888–889, 888*(m)*
in Dual Alliance, 760
duchies in, 297
economy in, 742, 824, 974
empire in, 381–382
in Enlightenment, 571
France and, 621, 821
global economic crisis and, 977
government of, 350–353
Great Depression in, 843*(i)*, 849
imperialism by, 731, 733, 788
industry in, 742
Investiture Conflict and, 312–313, 312*(m)*, 318, 328, 332
Jews in, 401, 784
Kulturkampf in, 722
in League of Nations, 822
literary works in, 672–673
Magyars in, 289
in Middle Ages, 350–353
Morocco and, 793–794
Muslims in, 978*(i)*
Napoleon and, 637, 638, 640–641
nationalism in, 621
non-European immigrants to, 904–905
occupation of, 874
Pietism in, 572, 646
Poland and, 874
princes in, 352–353
principalities in, 381
Realpolitik in, 705–708
reparations after World War I, 819, 821
republic in, 817
reuniting of, 947*(i)*
Russian Revolution and, 813
Saxons from, 224
Schmalkaldic League and, 456
settlers in Poland from, 419
Social Democratic Party in, 755
socialism in, 930
in Thirty Years' War, 470, 471
in Three Emperors' League, 758
in Triple Alliance, 793
unification and, 514, 687, 705–708, 707*(m)*, 758
urbanization in, 748
war guilt of, 819

Germany (continued)
women in, 779, 851, 890, 892(i)
workhouses in, 578
working class in, 758–759
Zollverein in, 679
Germ theory, 713
Gerome, Jean-Léon, 697(i)
Gestapo, 850, 865
Geta (Rome), 196(i)
Ghana, state of, 902
Ghettos, Jews in, 762, 785, 865
Ghibellines, 350
Ghiberti, Lorenzo, 414, 415(i)
Giacometti, Alberto, 875(i)
Gibbon, Edward, 570
Gibraltar, 500–501
Gift economy, in western Europe,
256–257
Gilgamesh (Mesopotamian
hero), 10
Gillray, James, 621(i)
Giolitti, Giovanni, 781–782
Giotto, 380, 380(i)
Girls. See Gender; Women
Girondins (France), 606–607, 608,
612, 614
Girton (women's college), 715
Giza, pyramids at, 20(i), 21
Gla, palace at, 34
Gladiators (Rome), 175, 176(i)
Gladstone, William, 756
Glanvill, 348
Glasnost (openness), 943–944, 949
Glenn, John, 920
Global citizens, 952(i), 953
Global economy, 974–977
Atlantic system in, 529,
530–538
collapse of, 954, 976–977, 986
Internet and, 979–980
Russia in, 961
shocks in, 976
Globalization, 953. See also
Immigrants and
immigration; Market(s);
Market economy;
Migration; specific issues
attacks on, 966
of cities, 964–965
of communications, 945
of culture and society, 977–985
immigrants and, 952(i), 953
nation-states and, 961–966
pollution, environmentalism,
and, 967–968

population growth and,
969–970
telecommunication systems
and, 954
Global markets, 923
Global organizations, 966
Global warming, 967
Glorious Revolution (England,
1688), 507
Goddess figurines, from Judah,
47(i)
Gödel, Kurt, 856
Gods and goddesses. See also
Cult(s); Polytheism;
Religion(s); specific deities
Egyptian, 19–20, 24, 25
Greek, 54–55, 85–86
Hellenistic rulers as, 131–132
Mesopotamian, 10
Mycenaean, 32
Roman, 144–145, 197
Goering, Hermann, 850
Goethe, Johann Wolfgang von,
571–572, 647
Golan Heights, 938, 938(m)
Gold, from New World, 431, 435,
454, 465, 475
Gold Coast (Africa), 735, 902
Golden Age
in Greece, 75–76, 79–106
of Latin literature (Rome),
176–177
in Rome, 180–186, 196
Golden Ass, The (Apuleius),
183–184, 192
Golden Horde, 390
Gole, Jacob, 555(i)
Gömbös, Gyula, 855
Gonne, Maud, 781
Good Emperors. See Five Good
Emperors
Gorbachev, Mikhail, 918, 937,
943–945, 944(i), 946, 957,
960
Gorbachev, Raisa, 944(i)
Gordon, George, 588
Gordon riots (London, 1780), 588
Gospels, Christian, 440
Gothic arts and architecture, 338,
342–344, 343(i), 344(i),
378–380
cathedral elements, 337, 341,
378(i), 414
in Venice, 423
Gouges, Olympe de, 603, 608

Government. See also
Administration; Authority;
Kings and kingdoms; Law
codes; Politics; Society;
State (nation); specific
locations and rulers
of barbarian tribes, 222
in Byzantine Empire, 249,
353–354
after Carolingians, 289–299
of cities and towns, 310–311
of city-states, 8
constitutionalism and, 493–494
of Dutch Republic, 509
in eastern Europe, 353–354
in eastern Roman Empire, 230
economy and, 569
of Egypt, 18, 20
of England, 296, 329, 345–349,
385–386, 493–494, 548, 892
of English North American
colonies, 512
of France, 349–350, 493, 570,
612–613, 718–719, 855
of Germany, 299, 350–353
in Great Depression, 843, 844,
849
of Greece, 61–67, 76
of Hellenistic kingdoms,
120–121
Hobbes on, 508
as institution, 344–354
intervention in society by,
674–675, 750
of Italy, 352
of Japan, 717, 737
labor strikes and, 754
Locke on, 508–509
in Middle Ages, 380–393
under Napoleon, 630–631
nation-states and, 696
parliamentary (Britain), 548
of Persian Empire, 42
Plato on, 113
popolo in, 388–389
reforms after Seven Years' War,
583–586
representative, 385–386, 512
of Roman dominate, 205–207
of Roman provinces, 158,
226–227
of Rome, 161–164, 170–171
Smith, Adam, on role of, 569
of Spain, 385
of United States, 590

of Venice, 423
of Wessex, 295
in West Germany, 892–893
in World War I, 809–810
World War II and, 868–869, 890
Goya y Lucientes, Francisco Jose de, 639(i)
Gracchus family
Gaius Sempronius, 143, 158, 159
Tiberius, 143, 158–159
Grain, 477, 585
in Great Famine, 391–392, 391(f)
Soviet imports of, 943
Granada, Spain, 436
Grand Alliance. See Allies, World War II and
Grand Army (France), 635–637
retreat from Moscow by, 640
Grand tours, of Europe, 576
Gratian (church reformer), 319
Great Awakening, 572, 572(i), 646
Great Britain. See Britain; England
Great Charter. See Magna Carta
Great Council (Venice), 423
Great Depression (1930s), 841, 872
in Britain, 843, 854
in central Europe, 855–856
culture during, 856–857
in democracies, 852–857
in France, 854–855
in non-Western countries, 844–846
society and, 844
in Sweden, 854
totalitarianism during, 841–842, 846–852
in United States, 853–854
Great Famine, 390–393, 391(f)
Great Fear, in rural France, 602
Great Fire (London), 506, 507(i)
Great Khan (Mongols), 390. See also Chingiz (Genghis) Khan
Great King (Persia), 44(i)
Great men, in Rome, 158, 164
Great Mosque (Damascus), 245(i)
Great Northern War, 551, 551(m)
Great Persecution, of Christians, 209–210
Great powers, 580
Britain as, 548
at Congress of Vienna, 642

Great Pyramid (Giza), 17(i), 20(i), 21
Great Reforms (Russia), 700
Great Schism, 400
of 1054, 319
of 1378–1417, 408–411
Great Society, 931
Great Sphinx, 16–17, 17(i), 20
Great War. See World War I
Greece (ancient), 25–26, 26(m), 105(m). See also Athens; Hellenistic world; Ionia; Minoan Greece; Mycenaean civilization; Sparta; specific cities and towns
Bactria and, 119
citizenship in, 53–61
city-states in, 40, 50, 52–61
civilization in, 47–51
colonization by, 53
cross-cultural contacts in, 39–40, 130
expansion of, 54
family size and agricultural labor in, 57(f)
geography of, 26(m), 48, 52
Golden Age in, 75–76, 79–106
hoplites in, 57–58
Macedonia and, 115–118
Minoan impact on, 28–30
Mycenaeans and, 30–32
Near Eastern culture and, 109–110
Olympic Games in, 49–51
organization of city-states in, 61–70
Peloponnesian War and, 100–104
Persia and, 74(i), 75, 76–79
philosophy in, 69–70, 86, 90–96
political disunity in, 114–115
red-figure painting in, 55(i)
religion in, 54–55, 86–87
Rome and, 140, 147, 155–156, 163
scientific thought in, 92–93
violence in, 33–34
Greece (modern), 794, 977
Byzantine Empire and, 274
in cold war, 886
democracy in, 940
in EU, 962
independence of, 651–652
migration from, 824

Turks and, 651–652
World War II and, 872
Greek fire, 249
Greek language, 30
classical, 233
in eastern Roman Empire, 229
Rome and, 183
Greek Orthodox Church, 469, 489(m)
separation from Catholic church, 315
in Sicily, 300(m)
Green Armies, 832–833
Greenhouse effect, 967
Greenland, Vikings and, 288
Green Party, 968
Greens (faction), 228, 231
Gregoras, Nicephorus, 400
Gregorian calendar, 549, 812
Gregorian reform, 315–316
Gregory VII (Pope), 312, 314, 315–317, 317(i), 358
Gregory XI (Pope), 408
Gregory of Tours (Bishop), 255, 256, 259
Jews, commerce, and, 257
power of bishops and, 258
Gregory the Great (Pope), 260, 263, 295
Greuze, Jean-Baptiste, 579(i)
Gros, Antoine-Jean, 636(i)
Grosz, George, 831, 831(i)
Grotius, Hugo, 485–486
Grozny, Chechnya, 961
Guadalcanal, battle at, 872
Guam, 788, 864
Guangzhou, China, foreigners in, 536, 677
Guardianship
of children, 770
in Rome, 142
Guazzo, Francesco Maria, 488(i)
Guelphs, 350
Guernica (Picasso), 859
Guest workers, 905
Guggenheim Museum (Bilbao), 984–985
Guilds, 309, 585
Byzantine, 271
universities as, 341
Guillotin, J. I., 607(i)
Guillotine, 607, 607(i), 608
Guise family, 462, 463
Guizot, François, 674
Gulag, 848, 897, 898

Gulag Archipelago, The
    (Solzhenitsyn), 935
Gunpowder, 406
Gustavus Adolphus (Sweden), 471
Gutenberg, Johannes, 437, 438
Guyenne, 404
Guyon, Jeanne Marie, 544
Gypsies
    in Britain, 978
    Nazis and, 842, 852, 867

Habsburg dynasty, 382, 516*(m)*.
    See also Dual monarchy;
    Holy Roman Empire
    in Austria, 473, 708
    in Austro-Hungarian
        Monarchy, 709
    Balkan region and, 794
    challenges to, 810
    France and, 500
    German unification and,
        707*(m)*
    in Holy Roman Empire, 470,
        471, 515–516, 552–553
    Peace of Westphalia and,
        472–473
    wars with Valois and Ottomans,
        452–453
    World War I and, 796–797, 819
Hadith literature, 245–246
Hadrian (Rome), 180
Hagia Sophia, 231, 408
Hague, The, women's peace
    meeting in, 810
Haiti. *See* St. Domingue
Hajj (pilgrimage), 243
Hamas, 972*(m)*
Hamlet (Shakespeare), 469, 486
Hammurabi (Babylon), laws of, 14
Handbook of the Militant Christian
    (Erasmus), 439, 439*(i)*
Handel, George Frideric, 543
Handguns, 406
Hannibal (Carthage), 154, 155
Hanover, house of, 547
Hanseatic League, 419
Harald Hardrada (Norway), 328,
    329
Hard Times (Dickens), 719
Harold (Wessex), 328, 329
Harun al-Rashid (Abbasid caliph),
    276
Harvey, William, 483
Hashim clan, 244
Hasidism, 572–573
Hatshepsut (Egypt), 23–24, 23*(i)*

Hattusas (Hittite capital), 33
Haussmann, Georges-Eugène,
    712, 713
Havel, Václav, 916*(i),* 946, 980
Hawaii, 788
Haydn, Franz Joseph, 577
Haywood, Eliza, 544
Headscarf, controversy over, 978*(i)*
Health, 742. *See also* Diseases;
        Health care
    air quality and, 553
    as global issue, 970
    healing by gods and, 132
    in Rome, 173
Health care, 715, 749, 894, 895, 896,
    960
Hebrew Bible. *See* Bible
Hebrews. *See* Jews and Judaism
Heisenberg, Werner, 856–857
Heliocentrism, 129, 482
Hellenistic world, 109–110,
        118–124
    arts in, 124–126, 125*(i),* 126*(i)*
    culture in, 124–133
    fall of, 124
    Jews in, 121, 124, 132
    kingdoms in, 119–122
    Macedonia and, 115–118
    philosophy in, 126–129
    religions in, 130–131
    Rome and, 124, 134*(m),* 182
    science in, 129–130
    society in, 122–123
Heloise, 339–340
Helots (Greek slaves), 62
Help-desk services, 979
Helsinki accords, on human rights,
    938
Hemingway, Ernest, 828
Henry I (England), 330
Henry I (Saxony), 297
Henry II (England), 327, 345–349,
    346*(m),* 347*(i)*
Henry II (France), 455, 462
Henry III (England), 382, 383,
    385–386
Henry III (France), 463, 465
Henry III (Holy Roman Empire),
    314, 316
Henry IV (Germany), 312,
    315–317, 317*(i),* 332
Henry IV (Henry of Navarre,
    France), 462, 463–464, 498
Henry V (Germany), 317, 332, 350
Henry VI (Holy Roman Empire),
    381

Henry VII (England), 421
Henry VIII (England), 443–444,
    447, 450, 455
Henry of Anjou. *See* Henry II
    (England)
Henry of Navarre. *See* Henry IV
    (France)
Henry the Lion (Saxony and
    Bavaria), 352–353, 362
Henry the Navigator (Portugal),
    432
Henry the Younger (England),
    347
Hephaestus (god), 55
Hera (goddess), 55, 144
Heraclius (Byzantine Empire), 247
Herculaneum, Italy, 174*(i),* 576
Heredity principles, 724
Heresy, 215, 358–359. *See also*
        Inquisition
    anti-heretic campaigns and,
        230, 361*(m)*
    Cathars and, 359
    Fourth Lateran Council on, 371
    Lollards and, 410–411
Hermes (god), 55
Hermit monks, 320
Hero cults, 87
Herodotus of Halicarnassus,
    42, 95
Hero of Alexandria, 129
Herzen, Alexander, 681
Herzl, Theodor, 786
Hesiod, 51, 52, 61
Hetaira (companion), 89
Heterosexuality, 828, 970
Hezbollah, 972*(m),* 973
Hierarchy. *See also* Classes
    in Christian churches, 190–191,
        212–213, 312, 358
    Mesopotamian, 9–10
    Neolithic, 7–8
    Paleolithic, 5
    in Rome, 148–150, 184
    social, 4, 265, 290–291
Hieroglyphs (Egypt), 18, 19*(f),*
    108*(i)*
High culture
    during cold war, 911
    in vernacular, 354–357
Higher education, 675, 702, 715,
    917, 984. *See also*
        Universities
High schools, in France, 758
High-tech industries, in Japan, 975
Hijra, 242

Hildebrand, 314. *See also*
    Gregory VII
Hillel (*Rabbinic teacher*), 187
Hillesum, Etty, 841, 842, 866, 872
Himmler, Heinrich, 850
Hindenburg, Paul von, 807
Hindus, 536, 715–716, 792, 845,
    899
Hipparchia, 128
Hippias (*Athens*), 67
Hippocrates of Cos, 96
Hirohito (*Japan*), 857, 864
Hiroshima, bombing of, 872, 874*(i)*
Hispaniola, 534, 619
Historical and Critical Dictionary
    (Bayle), 556
Histories (Gregory of Tours), 255
Histories (Herodotus), 95
History of the Decline and Fall of the
    Roman Empire, The
    (Gibbon), 570
History of the Peloponnesian War
    (Thucydides), 95–96
Hitler, Adolf, 640, 825, 829,
    841–842, 854
    anti-Semitism of, 836, 852, 857
    assassination attempt against,
        869
    in central Europe, 860–863
    expansion by, 858–859
    Final Solution and, 866
    Munich Pact and, 861–862
    Mussolini and, 836
    Spain and, 859
    suicide of, 871
    totalitarianism of, 849–852
    World War II and, 864
Hitler Youth, 851
Hittites, 25–28
Hobbes, Thomas, 494, 508, 569
Ho Chi Minh, 846, 900
Hohenstaufen dynasty, 350
Hohenzollern family, 473
Holbein, Hans, 450
Holland. *See* Dutch Republic
Holocaust, 865–868, 866*(m)*, 901
Holstein, 705, 706
Holy Alliance (1815), 643–644
Holy communion. *See* Eucharist
Holy Land. *See* Crusader states;
        Crusades; Israel; Jerusalem;
        Middle East; Palestine
Holy Roman Emperor
    election of, 514
    as emperor of Austria, 637
    use of title, 382

Holy Roman Empire, 327, 328,
    394, 404, 406, 418, 419,
    458, 461, 470. *See also*
    Hapsburg dynasty;
    Ottonian kings
    Brandenburg-Prussia and, 515
    Burgundy and, 406, 420
    France and, 500
    German Confederation after,
        643
    Luther and, 440, 441
    Otto I and, 297
    Peace of Westphalia and,
        472–474, 473*(m)*
    Thirty Years' War and, 470–472,
        473*(m)*, 476
    weakening of, 381–382, 515
Holy Synod, 551
Holy wars, crusades as, 323
Home (Morrison), 983
Home front, in World War I,
    809–811
Homelessness. *See also* Refugees
    in cities, 541
    and economic crisis (17th
        century), 478
    in Rome, 157
Homer (*Greek poet*), 39, 49, 51,
    155
Home rule
    for Ireland, 757, 781
    for Magyars, 687
Homo sapiens, 4–5
Homosexuals and homosexuality,
    579
    activism by, 932
    AIDS and, 970
    in Athens, 91
    in eastern Roman Empire, 232
    Nazis and, 850, 867
    persecution of, 772
    in Soviet Union, 848
    Spartan boys and, 63–64
    as "third sex," 772
Homo Zapiens (Pelevin), 983
Hong Kong, 677, 899, 975, 975*(m)*
Honorius (*western Roman*
    Empire), 207, 222
Hoover, Herbert, 853
Hoplites, in Greece, 57–58, 58*(i),*
    74*(i),* 76
Horace, 124, 176
Hospitals, 554, 699, 922
Hostage crisis (Iran), 939, 971
Hotchkiss machine guns, 796
House, Edward, 793

Households
    Greek, 88
    in postindustrial society, 926
    in Rome, 143, 145
House of Commons (England),
    503, 548
House of Lords (England), 504, 655
Housing
    in 1920s, 828
    at Çatalhöyük, 7*(i)*
    in cities, 541, 712
    in Frankish villages, 255
    Mesopotamian, 8
    postwar boom in, 173–174
    in Rome, 157*(i),* 173
    urbanization and, 667
    after World War II, 896
Howitzers, 796, 806
Hubble, Edwin, 856, 921
Hubris (arrogance), 98
Hudson Bay region, 500
Hugenberg, Alfred, 849
Hugh (*abbot of Cluny*), 317*(i),* 320
Hugh Capet (*France*), 297
Hugh of St. Victor, 318
Huguenots, 462–464, 498, 515. *See*
    also Protestantism
Human capital, 553
Humanism
    Christian, 438–439
    in Renaissance, 412–413
Human origins, 4–5
Human rights, 486, 854, 938
Humbert of Silva Candida,
    314–315
Hume, David, 566, 571*(f)*
Hundred Days (France), 641, 643
Hundreds (government units), 296
Hundred Years' War, 400, 404–407,
    405*(m)*
Hungarian Revolution (1956), 898,
    902, 946
Hungary, 525*(m),* 842, 964. *See also*
    Magyars
    after 1529, 426*(m)*
    1848 revolution in, 687–688
    Austria and, 515–516, 552,
        552*(m)*
    in Austria-Hungary, 709,
        709*(m)*
    bureaucracy in, 713–714
    communism in, 887, 946
    economy in, 930, 946
    government in, 353
    in Great Depression, 855
    Huns in, 222

Hungary (continued)
    liberalism in, 681
    Magyars in, 299, 687, 709, 824
    Mongols in, 389, 390
    nationalism in, 784
    after Peace of Westphalia, 473
    refugees from, 883
    Social Democratic Party in, 755
    after Soviet Union, 960
    Turks and, 552
    after World War I, 818, 819, 824
    World War II and, 864, 871, 872
Hunger. See Famines
Huns, 221, 222, 223(m)
Hunter-gatherers, 3
Hunting, 747
Hus, Jan, 411, 441
Husbands, in Rome, 142. See also
    Men
Huskisson, William, 659
Hussein, Saddam, 971–972, 973
Hussites, 411
Hydrostatics, 129
Hygiene, 828, 833
Hyksos people, in Egypt, 22
Hyperinflation, in Rome, 197, 207

Iberian peninsula, 419–420. See
    also Portugal; Spain
IBM, 923
Ibn Sina (Avicenna), 279
Ibsen, Henrik, 752
Iceland, Vikings in, 288
Iconoclasm, 251, 284
Icons, 250–251, 250(i), 272
Idealism, Kant and, 571
Ideal Marriage: . . . (van de Velde),
    828
Ideas, modernity and, 774–778
Identity
    Greek, 50
    Jewish, 47
    sexual, 768
Ideologies, 328, 660, 675, 677. See
    also specific ideologies
Ides of March, 164, 165(i)
Ignatius (bishop of Antioch),
    189–190
Ignatius of Loyola, 449
Île-de-France, 297, 331
Iliad, The (Homer), 30, 39, 49
Illegal immigrants, 953, 954, 978,
    979
Illegitimate children, 535, 667–668
Illiteracy, 542, 714. See also
    Literacy

Illness. See Diseases; Health;
    Medicine
Illuminated manuscripts, 368(i),
    369
Illyria, 115
Imam, 244, 277
Immaculate Conception doctrine,
    723
Immigrants and immigration. See
    also Migration
    French racism and, 942
    illegal, 953, 954, 978, 979
    industrialization and, 667
    motivation for, 747–748
    non-European to Europe,
        904–906
    religion and, 929
    in Sweden, 942–943
    to Western Hemisphere, 730(i)
Imperial cult (Rome), 179
Imperial Diet of Worms (1521),
    441
Imperialism
    in Africa, 731, 733–736,
        734(m), 735(i), 786,
        787(m)
    in Asia, 715–717, 736–738,
        736(m), 737(m), 788,
        789(m)
    in Athenian Golden Age,
        81–82
    British, 715–716, 733, 735
    in China, 717, 791–792
    "civilizing mission" of, 739
    compared to colonialism, 676
    French, 500, 716, 733,
        736–737
    German, 731
    Japanese, 738, 857–858
    missionaries and, 646, 717,
        739–740
    multinationals and, 924
    new imperialism, 732–740
    Roman, 150–158, 154(m),
        156–158
    after World War I, 826
    World War II and, 857–859
Imports
    Dutch, 509–510
    of New World gold and silver,
        476
    slave, 533(f)
Impressionism, 752–753, 753(i)
Inanna (Ishtar, goddess), 10
Incas, 435, 524
Income tax, in Britain, 941

Indentured servants, 531, 535
Independence. See also specific
    locations
    in Africa, 902–904, 903(m)
    of Austrian Netherlands, 597
    of Czechs, 470
    Dutch, 466, 473, 509
    of Greece, 651–652
    of India, 845, 899
    of Ireland, 812, 825
    in Latin America, 652–653,
        653(m)
    in Middle East, 901–902
    of Portugal, 472
    regional, 965
    of Serbs, 651
    in Soviet bloc, 957
    of United States, 590
Independence movements. See also
    specific locations
    in 1820s, 650(m)
    decolonization and, 899
Independents (England), 503, 504
Index of forbidden books (Vatican),
    449, 558
India
    Amritsar massacre in, 826
    Britain and, 664, 677, 715–716,
        736, 845
    decolonization in, 899
    economy in, 975–976
    Europeans and, 433, 536–537
    French Revolution and, 619
    Gandhi in, 845, 845(i)
    in Great Depression, 845
    independence for, 899
    Mesopotamian trade with, 8
    nationalism in, 716
    outsourcing to, 979
    partition of, 899
    railroads in, 662
    resistance to colonialism in,
        792
    Russia and, 736, 961
    sati in, 646, 716
    Seven Years' War in, 580, 581
    textiles in, 664
    War of the Austrian Succession
        and, 553
    World War I and, 806
    World War II and, 869, 872
Indian National Congress, 736,
    792
Indian Ocean region, 433(m), 716
Indian Rebellion (1857), 716
Indians. See American Indians

Indigenous peoples
    in Americas, 435
    Catholic missionaries and,
        449–450
Individuals, roles in society,
    568–570
Indochina. *See also* Cochin China;
        Vietnam
    in 1954, 900(*m*)
    cold war in, 900–901
    France and, 736–737, 793
Indochinese Communist Party, 846
Indo-European languages
    in Greece, 30
    of Hittites, 27
Indonesia, 826, 864, 904
Inductive reasoning, 484
Indulgences, 409, 440, 449
Industrialism/industrialist,
        Saint-Simon on, 682
Industrialization. *See also* Factories
    in Austria-Hungary, 743
    birthrates and, 769
    in Britain, 660–661, 741, 742
    in eastern Europe, 664, 896
    in Europe (c. 1850), 663(*m*)
    in Germany, 742
    in Great Depression, 844
    Marx and Engels on, 683
    railroads and, 659, 661–662
    roots of, 660–661
    in Russia, 664, 743, 789
    in Scandinavia, 743
    in Soviet Union, 846–847
    in Spain, 743
    in United States, 742, 883–884
    working class and, 665
Industrial Revolution, 659,
        660–670. *See also*
        Industrialization
    in England, 660–661
    liberal thinkers and, 681
    second, 741
Industry
    colonization and, 732
    in eastern Europe, 963–964
    emissions from, 967
    in former Soviet Union, 959
    in France, 743
    in Great Depression, 844
    home, 741
    innovation in, 740–743
    in Japan, 737, 975
    management of, 744, 827
    outwork and, 749
    service, 979

after World War I, 827
World War II and, 868
"I Never Died for Love"
        (troubadour song), 356(*f*)
Infant exposure, 90, 123
Infanticide, 123, 579, 668
Infant mortality, 578, 665, 896
Infantry. *See also* Armed forces;
        Soldiers
    Athenian, 77
    Roman, 151, 194
    in Sparta, 61–62
Inflation, 435, 574, 942
    in 17th century, 475–476
    in former USSR, 959
    in Germany, 821, 822(*i*), 849
    oil and, 939
    in Rome, 195, 207
Influenza pandemics, 816(*f*), 817
Information, sharing of, 980
Information age, 918–920
Information revolution, 977
Infrastructure, in Rome, 227
Inheritance
    in Greece, 88
    medieval patrilineal, 293–294
    of monarchy, 8–9
    in non-Roman tribes, 221
    in revolutionary France, 611
Inner light, religious, 504
Innocent III (Pope), 370–372, 381
Innovation. *See* Intellectual thought;
        Inventions; specific types
Inoculation, 554
*Inquiry into the Nature and Causes
        of the Wealth of Nations, An*
        (Smith), 568, 571(*f*)
Inquisition, 371, 372, 449
    Galileo and, 482–483
    in Spain, 425–426, 450
Installment buying, 829
Institutes (Justinian), 232
Institutes of the Christian Religion
        (Calvin), 442
Institutions (Cassiodorus), 227
Instruction (Catherine II, Russia),
        583
Instructions for Merikare (Egypt), 3
Insurance, in Germany, 759
Intellectual thought. *See also*
        Philosophy; Renaissance;
        Scholars and scholarship;
        Schools; Universities;
        specific issues and thinkers
    in Balkans, 761(*m*)
    brain drain and, 936–937

Byzantine, 272–273
    in cold war, 907–908, 911
    in Enlightenment, 530,
        554–559, 563–571
    Erasmus and, 438–439
    in Germany, 621, 638
    in Greece, 40, 67–70, 90–100
    Hellenistic, 124–125, 126–130
    Mesopotamian, 15
    modernism in, 774–778
    Napoleon and, 632–633
    in Near East, 40
    politics and, 485–486
    on postmodernism, 984–985
    revolutions of 1848 and, 670
    in sciences, 461–462,
        481–484
    Social Darwinism, 724
    on social order, 719
Intelligentsia (Russia), 790
Intelsat I (satellite), 921
Intendants (France), 498
*Interesting Narrative of the Life of
        Olaudah Equiano, The,* 567
Interest payments, in Middle Ages,
        310
Intermarriage
    in American colonies, 535
    in Yugoslavia, 955
International Court of Justice. *See*
        World Court
International law, Nazi trials and,
        890
International Monetary Fund, 966,
        971
International organizations. *See*
        specific organizations
International politics. *See* Global
        entries; specific locations
Internationals, Marxist, 755, 756,
        779, 815
International trade. *See* Trade
International Woman Suffrage
        Association, 780
International Women's Day, 812
International Zionist Congress
        (Basel), 786
Internet, 979–980
Interpretation of Dreams, The
        (Freud), 773
Interventionism, by U.S., 886
Invasions. *See also* specific
        locations
    of 4th and 5th centuries, 223(*m*)
    c. 790–955, 288–289
    Magyar, 289, 297

Invasions (continued)
  Mongol, 389–390, 389(m)
  Muslim, 289
  Persian, 77–78
  Viking, 288–289
Inventions, industrial, 740–743. See
    also Technology; specific
    inventions
Investiture
  of German bishops, 298
  lay, 313
Investiture Conflict, 312–313,
    312(m), 315–318, 328, 332,
    350
Investment
  Assyrian, 13
  in eastern Europe, 964
  in railroads, 662
  in research, 924, 926
  in Soviet bloc, 924
  in United States, 842
Invisible hand, Adam Smith on, 568
In vitro fertilization, 923, 923(i)
Ionia, 69, 76
Ionic style, 85, 85(f)
Iran, 977. See also Khomeini,
    Ayatollah Ruhollah; Persia;
    Persian Empire
  hostage crisis in, 939, 971
  Mongols in, 389(m)
  Persia as, 42, 846
Iraq, 972(m). See also Babylonia;
    Baghdad; Iraq War;
    Mesopotamia
Iraq-Iran war, 971, 973–974,
    977–978
Iraq War, 972(m), 978
Ireland, 224, 260, 977
  Christianity in, 260, 261
  in Common Market, 929
  Easter protests in (1916), 812
  education for high-tech jobs in,
    942
  England and, 503, 505, 508,
    548, 620, 679, 680, 710, 781
  famine in, 684
  France and, 620
  in Great Britain, 505, 547
  home rule for, 757, 781
  immigrants from, 748
  independence for, 812, 825
  nationalism in, 679–680
  Northern, 825–826, 826(m),
    940, 942
  outsourcing to, 979
  protests in, 757, 940, 940(m)

Irish Free State, 825, 826(m)
Irish National Land League, 757
Irish Republican Army (IRA), 940
Iron and iron industry, 12, 740
  in Greece, 48
  in Middle Ages, 310
  railroads and, 662–663
  weapons from, 27
Iroquois Indians, 499
Irrigation
  Egyptian, 16(m)
  Mesopotamian, 8, 13
Isabella of Castile, 419, 425, 434,
    436, 443
Isabelle (Bavaria), 413
Isis (goddess), cult of, 132, 192
Islam, 240–246, 265(m), 899, 954.
    See also Arab-Israeli wars;
    Middle East; Muslims
  c. 1000, 277(m)
  Abbasid caliphate in, 270,
    275–276
  Black Death in, 401
  commerce in, 278
  expansion to 750, 244(m)
  in Holy Land, 359–360
  languages in, 278
  in Ottoman Empire, 792
  Qur'an and, 241, 241(i)
  regional lords in, 276
  renaissance in, 278–279
  in Roman Empire, 239
  scholars in, 279
  scripture in, 47
  Soviet Union and, 833
  in Spain, 277
  West and, 971–974
Israel. See also Jews and Judaism;
    Palestine
  Arab wars with (1967, 1973),
    938, 938(m)
  creation of, 901, 901(m)
  as Judaea, 186
  Palestinians and, 938, 972(m),
    973
  peace accords with Egypt,
    941(i)
  separation from Judah, 46
Israelites, 42, 44–47
Istanbul, 207, 399, 408, 845. See
    also Constantinople
Italian language, Dante's Divine
    Comedy in, 377
Italian people, in Austrian Empire,
    679
Italian Wars (1494), 452

Italy, 757, 779, 818, 896, 977. See
    also Papacy; Roman
    Empire; Rome; Sicily;
    specific rulers
  in 13th century, 381(m)
  ancient (500 B.C.E.), 146(m)
  Austria and, 546(m), 654, 686,
    687
  Black Death in, 401
  Carolingians and, 281
  after Charlemagne, 285
  city-states in, 422–423
  communes in, 311, 318, 350
  divisions of (1848), 686(m)
  in ECSC, 894
  education in, 714
  Ethiopia and, 781, 858
  families in, 295
  fascism in, 834–836
  fertility rate in, 969
  France and, 635
  Frederick Barbarossa in, 351
  government of, 289, 352, 891
  Huns in, 222
  industry in, 743
  after Investiture Conflict, 318,
    332
  Jewish commerce in, 307
  kingdom in, 251
  Lombards in, 248, 263(m)
  Magyars in, 289
  major powers in, 418
  monasteries in, 258
  Napoleon and, 628, 635, 637, 638
  nationalism in, 679
  nationalist revolution in (1848),
    686
  Normans and, 315, 333(m)
  northern independence
    movement in, 965
  Ostrogoths in, 224
  Otto in, 297
  papacy and, 381
  at Peace of Lodi, 422(m)
  political system in, 295
  pope and, 281
  railroads in, 658(i)
  Roman expansion in, 151–152
  Rome in, 147, 708
  signori in, 381, 388–389
  Spain and, 500
  terrorism in, 940
  trade and, 307
  in Triple Alliance, 760, 793
  unification of, 686, 702–705,
    703(m), 781

women in, 835, 836, 868
World War I and, 804, 806
World War II and, 870
Ivan III (Russia), 469
Ivan IV (**the Terrible,** Russia), 462, 469
Ivanhoe (Scott), 650
Iwasaki Yataro, 737

J'accuse (Zola), 783
Jacob (Israelites), 44
Jacobin Clubs (France), 606, 615, 616
Jacobite rebellion (Scotland), 548
Jacobitism, 547
Jacobs, Aletta, 750, 810
Jacquerie, 407
Jadwiga (Poland), 419
James I (England), 456, 468, 469, 475, 502, 547
James II (England), 506–507, 508, 547, 548
James V (Scotland), 455
James Edward (England), 547
Jane Eyre (Brontë), 672
Jansen, Cornelius, 497
Jansenism, 497–498, 544–545
Japan, 842
    art influences from, 753, 831
    atomic bombing of, 872, 874(i)
    China and, 788, 791
    economy in, 974
    European imperialism and, 717
    high-tech industries in, 975
    imperialism by, 738, 788, 857–858
    Jesuits in, 450
    modernization in, 737–738, 738(i), 975
    reindustrialization of, 900
    Russia and, 786, 788, 789, 789(m), 816
    World War I and, 804
    after World War I, 826
    World War II and, 864–865, 872, 873(m)
    after World War II, 881–882
Japanese Americans, internment camps for, 868
Java, Europeans in, 529, 536
Jazz, 828, 832
Jedwabne, Poland, 865–866
Jefferson, Thomas
    Declaration of Independence and, 589

on French Declaration of Rights, 602–603
    on French Revolution, 619
Jena, battle at, 636
Jenner, Edward, 554
Jerome (Saint), 216, 220
Jerome, Jeanette. *See* Churchill, Jeanette Jerome
Jerusalem
    Antiochus and, 132
    crusades and, 322–327
    Dome of the Rock in, 238(i), 245
    Jesus in, 187
    Jewish temple in, 46, 132–133, 188, 326
    Rome and, 179
    Saladin in, 359
    Sasanids in, 247
    Turks in, 324
Jesuits, 449, 450, 481, 557(i), 583, 646, 722
Jesus (Christ), 186–188
    mosaic as Sun God, 214(i)
    nature of, 215
Jesus movement, 186, 187
Jews and Judaism. *See also*
        Anti-Semitism; Holocaust; Israel; Israelites; Nazis and Nazism
    assimilation of, 784
    Babylonian exile of, 46
    Black Death blamed on, 401–402
    Christian impact on art of, 372(i)
    Christianity and, 186, 187–188, 373–374, 443
    crusades and, 325
    diaspora and, 47
    differences within, 187
    in Dutch Republic, 467, 511, 556
    in eastern Europe, 784–785
    in England, 373, 374, 504
    Enlightenment and, 566, 571
    Fourth Lateran Council on, 371
    in France, 373–374, 757
    in Germany, 401, 784, 825
    Greek influence on, 132
    Hellenistic, 121, 132
    Holocaust against, 865–868
    impact on West, 44
    Islam and, 242, 278
    lifestyle of, 307–308
    Louis IX (France) and, 384

in Merovingian world, 257
    migration from Europe, 748, 785, 785(m), 852
    monotheism of, 44, 46, 47
    Napoleon and, 637
    nationalism of, 785–786
    Nazis and, 841, 842, 850, 851–852
    Nietzsche and, 775
    origins of term, 46
    Palestine and, 786, 857, 901
    in Poland, 419
    in Poland and Lithuania, 513
    religion and, 723
    religious toleration and, 584–585
    revivalism and, 572–573
    rights of, 722
    in Rome, 211–212
    Rome and, 179
    in Russia, 762, 762(i), 782
    in Soviet Union, 885, 936
    in Spain, 425–426, 436
    Spinoza and, 511
    trade and, 307
    Vatican II and, 906
    World War I and, 809, 811
    after World War II, 883
    Zoroastrianism and, 46
Jihad, 242
Joan of Arc, 405
Job Corps, 931
Jobs. *See also* Employment
    in Great Depression, 844
    service, 924, 979
    white-collar, 771
    worldwide apportionment of, 925(f)
    worldwide redistribution of, 979
Jogailo (Lithuania), 419
John (England), 348–349
John II (France), 406
John II (Portugal), 432
John XXIII (antipope), 409
John XXIII (Pope), 906
John Paul II (Pope), 945
Johnson, Lyndon B., 930
John the Baptist, 187
Joint-stock companies, 480
Jolliet, Louis, 499
Jordan, Israel and, 938
Joseph (Israelites), 44–45
Joseph II (Austria and Holy Roman Empire), 582(i), 583, 584, 585, 597

Josephine (France), 631, 631(i)
Joshua (Syrian monk), 239
Journalism
    mass, 756, 918
    in post-Soviet Russia, 961(i)
Journeymen and journeywomen,
    309, 541
Joyce, James, 832
Juan Carlos (Spain), 940
Judaea, 179, 186
Judah, 46, 47(i)
Judah the Maccabee, 133
Judaism. See Jews and Judaism
Judas, 268(i)
Judges (Israelite), 46
Judiciary. See also Courts; Law(s)
    in Athens, 66
    in Rome, 150
Judith (wife of Louis the Pious),
    285
Julia (Rome, daughter of
    Augustus), 178
Julia (Rome, daughter of Julius
    Caesar), 162–163
Julia Domna (Rome), 196(i)
Julian calendar, in Russia, 549,
    812
Julian the Apostate, 211
Julius II (Pope), 444
Julius Caesar (Shakespeare), 778
July revolution (Paris), 653
June Days (Paris), 685–686, 689
Jünger, Ernst, 831
Junkers, 514, 515, 585, 705
Juno (goddess), 144
Jupiter (god), 144, 192
Juries
    in Athens, 81
    in Rome, 150
Justice
    in Athens, 91
    in Carolingian Empire, 281
    divine, in Greek myth, 51
    in England, 347
    in Hammurabi's code, 14
    Israelite, 45
    Socrates on, 93–94
Justices of the peace, 447
Justinian (Byzantine Empire),
    219(i), 225, 229(i), 246
    eastern Roman Empire under,
    227, 230–232
    law code of, 232
Jutland, battle at, 807
Juvenal (Rome), 183

Ka'ba, 241, 242
Kádár, János, 930
Kadesh, battle of, 28
Kafka, Franz, 832
Kaiser. See William I (Prussia and
    Germany); William II
    (Germany)
Kamikaze tactics, World War II
    and, 872
Kanchei, Giya, 983
Kandinsky, Wassily, 777
Kant, Immanuel, 564, 570, 571(f),
    621
Karlowitz, Treaty of, 515
Kay, John, 660
Kazakhstan, 276
Kellogg-Briand Pact, 822
Kemal, Mustafa (Atatürk), 845
Kennedy, John F., 912, 931
Kent State University, 937
Kenya, 903–904
Kepler, Johannes, 483, 484
Kerensky, Aleksandr, 813
Khadija, 241
Khagan, 274
Khomeini, Ruhollah (Ayatollah),
    939, 971, 982
Khrushchev, Nikita, 881, 898,
    902(i), 911, 912, 930
Khufu (Cheops, Egypt), 21
Kiev (city), 274, 390, 513
Kievan Rus, 272, 274–275
Kikuyu people, 903
King, Martin Luther Jr., 908,
    933–934
Kingdom of Naples, 631, 650
Kingdom of the Serbs, Croats, and
    Slovenes, 819. See also
    Yugoslavia
King Lear (Shakespeare), 469
King Philip. See Metacomet (King
    Philip)
Kings and kingdoms. See also
    Empire(s); specific kings
    and kingdoms
    in 15th century, 419–422
    in Egypt, 16, 18, 20
    in England, 296
    European, 265(m)
    Frankish, 252–256
    German, 299, 350
    Hellenistic, 118–132
    Hittite, 26–28
    Israelite, 46
    Merovingian, 259

in Mesopotamia, 9–10
in Middle Ages, 344–353
non-Roman in West, 220–227
Persian, 42
post-Carolingian, 289–290
in Rome, 140
in Spartan oligarchy, 62
in western Europe, 251–264
King's Peace (Greece), 114
Kinship, barbarian, 221
Kipling, Rudyard, 788
Kissinger, Henry, 937
Kleptocracies, 960, 971
Knight, Death, and the Devil, The
    (Dürer), 439(i)
Knights. See also Warriors
    chivalry and, 357
    in crusades, 326
    epic poems and, 356
    in Hundred Years' War, 406
    in medieval society, 290, 293
    as mercenaries, 439(i)
Knights Templar, 326, 363(i)
Knossos, Crete, 28–29, 29(i)
Kohl, Helmut, 942
Koine language, 130
Kolkhoz (collective farms), 847
Kollontai, Aleksandra, 833
Köllwitz, Kaethe, 802(i), 830–831
Kore (goddess). See Persephone
    (goddess)
Korea
    Japan and, 788
    World War II and, 872
Korean War, 893, 900, 900(m)
Kościuszko, Tadeusz, 618
Kosovo, Albanians in, 955
Kossuth, Lajos, 681, 687
Kosygin, Alexei, 930
Kotzebue, August, 657
Kristallnacht, 852
Kronstadt revolt (1921), 833
Kulak, in Russia, 847
Kulturkampf (culture wars), in
    Germany, 722, 758
Kundera, Milan, 936
Kuril Islands, World War II and, 872
Kuwait, Iraq invasion of, 972
Kyoto Protocol, 968

Labor. See also Poverty; Slaves and
    slavery; Women; Workers;
    Working class
    agricultural, 664, 665
    colonists as, 806, 811, 811(i)

of concentration camp prisoners, 866
corvée, 21
in Egypt, 24–25
in England, 540
in Greece, 57(*f*)
for multinationals, 924
non-Europeans as, 904–906
political power of, 778–779
slave, 58–59, 531
in World War II, 868
Labor-intensive production, 743
Labor strikes. *See* Strikes
Labor unions, 665, 717, 754–755, 778. *See also* Strikes
in 1920s, 827
in England, 654
Mussolini and, 836
in Nazi Germany, 851
new unionism and, 755
women in, 755
Labour Party (England), 750, 755, 781, 825, 854, 892, 940
Ladder of offices (Rome), 148–149
Lady of the Lake, The (Scott), 650
Lafayette, Madame de (Marie-Madeleine de la Vergne), 496, 522
Lafayette, Marie-Joseph (Marquis de), 602, 606
Laissez-faire, 569, 715, 759
Laity, 313, 409–410, 449
Lakshmibai (India), 716
Lamb, Ann, 675
Land
in Byzantine Empire, 273–274
in Carolingian Empire, 286–288
commerce and, 311–312
in England, 539–540
in Frankish kingdoms, 254
Jews and, 307
native Americans and, 512
peasants and, 478, 540, 843
in Rome, 157, 158, 162
in Russia, 700–701, 847
Land and Freedom Army (British East Africa), 902
Land and Liberty (Russia), 760
Landlords, in Ireland, 757
Landowners, 256
agricultural changes and, 539–540
expansion of estates, 668
papacy as, 263

in Russia, 701
in western Europe, 257, 293
Languages. *See also* Latin language; Writing; specific languages
of 19th-century Europe, 678(*m*)
Anglo-Saxon (Old English), 262
Arabic, 278
Aramaic, 41
from battlefield, 823
Celtic, 224
Chinese, 437
in eastern Roman Empire, 229
English, 330
of Franks, 255
French, 378, 611
Gaelic, 680
Greek, 130
Irish Gaelic, 781
in Islam, 278
Italian, 377, 703(*m*), 704
Koine, 130
Latin, 151
letters in, 15
Magyar, 687
in Merovingian society, 258
Minoan, 28
of Roman Empire, 183(*m*)
Semitic, 8
Languedoc, 358–359, 364, 383
Laodice (Seleucids), 123
Laon, convent at, 259
Laos, 737, 900
Larrey, Dominique-Jean, 633
La Salle, René Robert Cavelier (Sieur de), 499
Las Casas, Bartolomé de, 435
Las Meninas (Velázquez), 474(*i*)
Las Navas de Tolosa, battle at, 361
Last Judgment, 378(*i*), 379
Lateen (triangular) sail, 432
Lateran Agreement (1929), 835
Lateran Councils. *See* Councils (Christian)
Latifundia (farms), in Rome, 158
Latin America, 842
economic development in, 971
independence in, 652–653, 653(*m*)
literature from, 980–982
Latin language, 151, 183
classical, 233
in eastern Roman Empire, 229
in Frankish kingdoms, 255

Greek literature in, 155
law code in, 226
in Merovingian society, 258
scholarship and, 233
Latin peoples, 146(*m*), 151
Latvia, 863, 957, 964
Laud, William, 502, 503
Law(s). *See also* Law codes; Legislation; specific acts
in Athens, 66
Byzantine, 248
church, 370–371
in England, 347–348
Frederick Barbarossa and, 351
of Hammurabi, 14
Hebrew, 45, 46
to improve marriage, 770–771
in Mesopotamia, 13–14
natural, 486–487
Roman, 148, 182, 184, 205, 225–226
schools of, 339
scientific, 482, 484
in Sparta, 62
of universal gravitation, 484
Law, John, 547
Law codes
in Austria, 583
Civil Code of Napoleon as, 628, 632
in England, 296
of Hammurabi, 14
of Justinian, 232
Roman, 222, 225–226
in Russia, 517, 583
of Ur III rulers, 13
Lawrence, D. H., 828
Laws of War and Peace, The (Grotius), 485
Lay investiture, 313–314
Lay piety, in Middle Ages, 372–373
Lazarus (Bible), 304(*i*), 305
Leadership
in Athenian radical democracy, 81
Hesiod on, 51
League of Augsburg, 500
League of Nations, 642, 819–821, 826, 857, 872, 904
Germany and, 819–820, 822, 858
Italian aggression and, 858
Japanese expansionism and, 858

League of Nations *(continued)*
    mandate system of, 821
    membership in, 819–820,
        837*(m)*
    United States and, 819, 854
Learning. *See also* Education;
        Intellectual thought
    in Germany, 298–299
    traditional, 484
Lebanon, Israeli attack on, 972*(m)*,
    973
Lebensraum (living space), 858,
    863
Lechfeld, battle of, 289, 297
Legal systems, reforms of, 583
Legion of Honor, 631, 633
Legislation. *See also* Law(s);
        specific acts
    to protect women, 750
    in Sparta, 62
Legislature. *See also* Assemblies;
        Councils; Senate; specific
        bodies and countries
    in France, 605
Legnano, battle of, 352
Leibniz, Gottfried Wilhelm, 520,
    565
Leisure, 747, 750–751, 896
Lem, Stanislaw, 920
Lenin, V. I., 779, 813–814, 814*(i)*,
    815, 833–834
Leningrad, 834. *See also* Petrograd;
        St. Petersburg
    siege of, 864, 868
Le Nôtre, André, 496
Leo III (Pope), 282–283
Leo III the Isaurian (Byzantine
        Empire), 251
Leo IX (Pope), 314, 314*(i)*
Leo X (Pope), 443
Leo XIII (Pope), 722
León, 362*(m)*
Leonardo da Vinci, 415, 416*(i)*
Leopold (Austria, 12th century),
    359
Leopold I (Austria, 18th century),
    500
Leopold I (Belgium), 654
Leopold I (Holy Roman Emperor),
    474*(i)*, 515–516
Leopold II (Belgium), 733, 735*(i)*
Leopold II (Holy Roman Empire),
    584*(i)*, 585, 597, 605
Leovigild (Visigoths, Spain), 262
Lepanto, battle of, 465, 465*(i)*, 469
Lepidus (Rome), 170–171

Leprosy, in medieval society,
    374–375
Lesbia, 156
Lesbians. *See* Homosexuals and
        homosexuality
Lessing, Gotthold, 571
Letter, The (Cassatt), 753, 753*(i)*
Letters (alphabetic), 15
*Letters Concerning the English
        Nation* (Voltaire), 556
Levellers (England), 503–504, 588
Levi, Primo, 867
Leviathan (Hobbes), 508
Lévi-Strauss, Claude, 928–929
Liberal arts, 338–339
Liberalism, 680, 782. *See also*
        Neoliberalism
    in Austria, 708
    in Britain, 680–681, 781
    economic, 758
    in Germany, 708, 758
    in Hungary, 681
    in Prussia, 705
    in Russia, 681
Liberal Party (Britain), 709, 756,
        757, 781
Liberation movements
    in Algeria, 904
    in Asia, 789*(m)*, 932*(m)*
    Fanon on, 907–908
Liberty, representation of, 609–610,
        609*(i)*
Libido, Freud on, 774
Libraries, 577
    at Alexandria, 124–125
    in Christian Britain, 261
Libya, Italy and, 788
Licinius (Rome), 209
Liebknecht, Karl, 818
Liège, baptismal font at, 309*(i)*
*Life and Martyrdom of St. William
        of Norwich, The* (Thomas of
        Monmouth), 374
Life expectancy
    in Russia, 970
    in welfare state, 896
Life of Insects, The (Pelevin), 983
Lifestyle. *See also* Society
    in Athens, 111–112
    during cold war, 906–910
    disposable income and,
        529–530, 538
    in eastern Roman Empire,
        227–230
    in former Soviet Union, 957,
        959

    in Germany, 825
    in global cities, 964–965
    in Greece after Peloponnesian
        War, 110–115
    Greek, 48
    in Hellenistic kingdoms,
        122–123
    in medieval cities, 308
    of middle class, 747
    Minoan, 28–29
    of nobility, 574
    plague and, 403
    in postindustrial society, 927
    in recession of 17th century,
        477–479
    religion and, 372–373, 410
    in Rome, 162, 173–175,
        180–186
    rural, 668–670
    of slaves, 532–533
    Spartan, 2
    in Stone Age, 4–8
    of students, 933
    of upper class, 746–747
    urban, 540–542, 667–668
    of women, 541, 771–772
    of working class, 667–668,
        747–749
Ligeti, Gyorgy, 936
Like Water for Chocolate (Esquivel),
        981–982
Limited liability corporation, 744
Lincoln, Abraham, 710
Lindisfarne Gospels, 261*(i)*
Linear A script, 28
Linear B script, 32, 33, 48
*Lipstick Ascending on Caterpillar
        Tractor* (Oldenburg), 927
Lister, Joseph, 713
Literacy, 438, 538, 671. *See also*
        Illiteracy
    of Beguines, 359*(i)*
    computer, 979
    in Dutch Republic, 511
    in lower classes, 542, 578
    in public sphere, 756
    social reality and, 719
    social status and, 542
    Soviet, 833
Literature. *See also* Classical
        culture; Epic literature;
        Poets and poetry; specific
        works and authors
    in 1920s, 831–832
    in 1930s, 856
    in cold war, 907–908, 910–911

Enlightenment, 555–556,
    558–559, 565, 571(*f*)
epic, 356
existential, 908
globalization and, 980–983
hadith, 245
of Holocaust, 908
humanist, 412–413
Latin American, 980–982
Mesopotamian, 13, 41–42
novels and, 523, 544, 671–672
realist, 719–720
Roman, 151, 155–156, 176–177
romance, 357
romanticism in, 571–572,
    649–650
Russian, 760–761
Soviet, 848, 897, 898, 911, 930
space race and, 920
Sumerian, 13
travel, 557–558
vernacular, 354–357, 376
wisdom literature, 22, 42, 46
by women, 125, 522–523,
    558–559, 672, 832, 908,
    982–983
World War II and, 874–875
Lithography, 670, 672(*i*), 690(*i*)
Lithuania, 419, 583, 618, 863, 957,
    964. *See also* Poland-
    Lithuania
    Northern Crusades and, 364
Little Entente, 822
Liverpool and Manchester Railway,
    659
Livestock, 539
Livia (wife of Augustus, Rome),
    171–172, 177(*i*)
Livy, 153(*f*), 177, 412
Lloyd George, David, 818
Loans
    contracts for, 310
    for economic development,
        971
Locarno, Treaty of, 822
Locke, John, 494, 556, 569, 680,
    718
Locomotives, 662, 740
Logic, 114, 339
Lollards, 410–411
Lombard League, 352
Lombards, 246, 247(*m*), 248
    in Italy, 263(*m*), 281
    Otto I and, 297
    popes and, 264, 280
Lombardy, 382, 679, 703, 704

London, 570, 667, 689, 712, 741,
    965
    coffeehouses in, 528(*i*)
    exhibition in (1851), 689,
        690(*i*)
    Great Fire (1666) in, 506, 507(*i*)
    population of, 540–541
    servants in, 541
    strikes in, 754
    terrorism in, 974
    Treaty of, 806, 818, 834
Long-distance trade. *See* Trade;
    specific locations
Looms, mechanized, 660
Lord Protector, Cromwell as, 506
Lords. *See also* Nobility
    in Germany, 352–353
    in post-Carolingian society,
        289
Lorentz, Alcide, 672(*i*)
Lorenzo de Medici (the
    Magnificent), 424
Lorrain, Claude, 519
Lorraine
    France and, 500, 552, 819
    Germany and, 707, 742
    World War I and, 819
Lothar I (Carolingians), 285
Lothar III (Germany), 332
Louis, A., guillotine and, 607(*i*)
Louis VI (Louis the Fat, France),
    331
Louis VII (France), 326–327,
    345–346
Louis IX (St. Louis, France), 381,
    382–384, 383(*i*), 384(*m*)
Louis XI (France), 420–421
Louis XIII (France), 471, 472, 475,
    494
Louis XIV (France), 472, 492(*i*),
    495(*i*), 515, 530
    as absolute ruler, 494–501, 502
    acquisitions of, 501(*m*)
    black code of, 512
    Charles II and, 506
    death of, 501, 545, 547
    Fronde and, 494–495, 496
    League of Augsburg against,
        500
    wars of, 499–500, 500(*f*), 545
Louis XV (France), 547, 552, 585
Louis XVI (France), 584, 585,
    598–599, 600–601, 641
    execution of, 607, 608
    flight of, 604–605
Louis XVII (France), 598(*i*), 641

Louis XVIII (France), 641, 643,
    645, 653
Louisiana, 499
Louisiana Territory, 636
Louis-Napoleon Bonaparte. *See*
    Napoleon III
Louis-Philippe (France), 653, 676,
    681, 684
Louis the German (Carolingians),
    285
Louis the Pious (Carolingians),
    285
Lourdes, shrine at, 723
Louvre Palace (Paris), 497, 985
Love, courtly, 355
Love Affairs (Ovid), 177
Love Feasts, 188
Love in the Time of Cholera (García
    Márquez), 981
Low Countries. *See also* Belgium;
    Luxembourg; Netherlands
    agriculture in, 540
    Brethren of the Common Life
        in, 409–410
Lower classes, 563, 573, 667–668.
    See also Classes; Working
    class
    Enlightenment thinkers on,
        568
    in Hundred Years' War, 406
    literacy in, 542, 578
Lower Egypt, 16, 16(*m*)
Loyalty, 268(*i*), 269–270
Loyola. *See* Ignatius of Loyola
Lübeck, 352
Lucian, 182
Lucilius, 140–141
Lucretius, 156
Ludd, Ned, 661
Luddites, 661
Ludendorff, Erich, 807, 825
Ludin, Fereshta, headscarf of,
    978(*i*)
Ludwig (Bavaria), 652
Lueger, Karl, 784
Luftwaffe, 864
Lully, Jean-Baptiste, 496
Luncheon, The (Boucher), 543(*i*)
Lupercalia festival, 145
Lusitania (ship), 807
Luther, Martin, 430(*i*), 432, 436,
    439, 441–442, 443
    Bible translation by, 447,
        448(*i*)
    Peasants' War of 1525 and, 445
    theology of, 440–441

Lutheranism
  in c. 1648, 489(m)
    Peace of Augsburg and, 456, 462
    after Peace of Westphalia, 473
Lützen, battle of, 471
Luxembourg, 285, 806, 894. See
    also Austrian Netherlands
Luxemburg, Rosa, 818
Luxuries, in Rome, 158, 174
Lycées, 632, 715
Lyceum (Athens), 113–114
Lydia (Christian woman), 188
Lyon, Council of, 382
Lysias, 104
Lysimachus (Macedonia), 123
Lysistrata (Aristophanes), 99–100

Maastricht Treaty (1994), 962
Maat (goddess), 20
Maat (truth, justice), 23(i)
Mabuse, Peter, 690(i)
Macaulay, Catherine, 577
Macaulay, Thomas, 655
Macbeth (Shakespeare), 469
Maccabees, 133
MacDonald, Ramsay, 825, 854
Macedonia, 794. See also
    Hellenistic world
    Alexander the Great of, 109–110
    rise of, 115–118
    Rome and, 154, 155
Macedonian renaissance
    (Byzantine Empire),
    272–274
Macedonians, nationalism of, 792
Machiavelli, Niccolò, 451–452,
    485, 508
Machine gun, 806
Machines, 918
    farm, 925
    in World War I, 806
Macrina, 219
Madame Bovary (Flaubert), 720
Madame Butterfly (Puccini), 778
Madrasa (Islamic school), 279
Madrid, 547, 974
Mafia, Russian, 959
Magazines, 542, 909
Magic, 25, 481, 487–488
Magical realism, in literature,
    981–982
Magna Carta (England), 349, 385
Magyarization, in Hungary, 784
Magyars
    in Austria-Hungary, 709
    in Austrian Empire, 679, 687

in Hungary, 299, 824
    invasions by, 289, 297
    nationalism and, 687
Mahdi (messiah), 277
Mail-order catalogs, 746
Maine, France and, 349
Maintenon, marquise de
    (Françoise d'Aubigné), 496
Mainz, Jews in, 325
Maize (corn), 478
Majority rule, in democracy, 82
Makine, Andrei, 983
Malaria, 742, 970
Malaya, 864
Malay peninsula, British in, 736,
    736(m)
Maldives, rising water levels and, 967
Malnutrition, 477, 479, 970
Malplaquet, battle of, 545
Malta, 20, 964
Mamelukes, 639(i)
Mamluks, 276
Management
    industrial, 744, 827
    postindustrial, 924
Manchester, England, 665, 780
Manchuria
    Japan and, 858
    railroad through, 788
    World War II and, 872
Mandate system, 821, 826
Mandela, Nelson, 975, 980
Manet, Édouard, 720, 721(i)
Manhattan Project, 872
Mani (prophet), 203
Manichaeans, 203
Mann, Thomas, 856
Mannerism, 486–487
Manners
    comedies of, 522
    women and, 521–523
Manors
    Carolingian, 286–288, 287(f)
    fees on, 292–293
Manses, 254, 312
Mantinea, battle of, 114–115
Mantua, duke of, 418
Manufacturing, 568, 924
    domestic system of, 661
    in England, 663–664
    industrialization and, 660, 740
    World War I and, 826–827
Manuscript(s), Byzantine, 272(i)
Manuscript illumination
    of Aristotle, 368(i)
    Gothic, 379–380

Manzikert, battle at, 324, 328
Manzoni, Alessandro, 649
Mao Zedong, 899, 900, 937–938
Maps, 430(i)
    Babylonian, 15
Marat, Jean-Paul, 608, 612
Marathon, battle of, 76–77
Marathon race, 77
Marburg, Colloquy of, 442
Marcel, Étienne, 406
March on Rome, 834
Marconi, Guglielmo, 830
Marcus Aurelius (Rome), 180, 192,
    194
Mardi Gras, 524
Marengo, battle at, 635
Margarita (Spain), 474(i)
Marguerite de Valois, 462
Maria Carolina (Naples), 584(i)
Maria Theresa (Austria), 552–553,
    582, 583, 584(i)
Marie-Antoinette (France), 584(i),
    598, 598(i), 605, 608
Marie-Louise (Austria), 631, 641
Marijuana, 933
Maritime commerce. See Seaborne
    commerce
Maritime powers. See Navies;
    specific locations
Marius, Gaius (Rome), 158,
    159–160, 161
Market(s)
    in cities, 308
    colonies and, 480
    commercial development and,
    306–307
    free, 568, 585, 586
    imperialism and, 732
    prices and, 586
    in rural areas, 311
Market economy
    in former Soviet Union, 957,
    959–960
    market socialism in Hungary,
    946
Marquette, Jacques, 499
Marriage
    in early 19th century, 669
    in 1960s and 1970s, 926
    of bishops, 258
    child, in India, 716
    church on, 371
    civil ceremony for, 722
    clerical, 319
    in colonies, 535
    in France, 611

in Greece, 60
Hellenistic, 123
medieval, 294
in Merovingian society, 257–258
in Nazi Germany, 851
postponement of, 479, 669
reforms of, 448, 768, 770–771
in Rome, 142, 185
in rural eastern Europe, 771
as sacrament, 318
Spartan, 64
working-class, 828
Marriage of Figaro, The (Beaumarchais), 588
Married Love (Stopes), 828
Married Women's Property Act (England, 1870), 710
"Marseillaise, La" (French anthem), 609
Marshall, George C., 886
Marshall Plan (1947), 886–887, 887(i), 888, 893
Marsilius of Padua, 408
Martial law
in Hungary, 688
in Rome, 158
Martin (Saint), 255
Martin V (Pope), 409
Martyrs, Christian, 189–190
Marx, Karl, 569, 682–683, 718, 813
Marxism, 718, 779
in Poland, 818
Russian, 779
Social Democratic Parties and, 755
Marxism-Leninism, 946
Mary. *See* Virgin Mary
Mary I (Mary Tudor, England), 443, 444, 455, 465, 467
Mary II (England), 506–507, 512, 547
Mary of Guise (Scotland), 455, 456
Mary of Oignies, 358
Mary Stuart (Mary, Queen of Scots, Scotland), 455–456, 468
Masons and Masonic lodges, 573, 575–576
Mass (Christian), 319, 378, 411
Massacre at Chios (Delacroix), 649(i)
Massacres. *See* specific massacres
Mass culture, in 1920s, 828, 829–832
Masses (common people), in Athens, 65

Mass journalism, 756, 918
Mass media. *See also* Media
dictators and, 842
Roosevelt, F. D., and, 854
Mass politics, 753–762. *See also* Mass media; Politics
anti-Semitism in, 782–784
tensions in, 778–786
Mass production. *See* Industrialization; Industry; Production
Mass society, World War II and, 868
Master and Margarita, The (Bulgakov), 983
Masters, 309–310
Mastersingers of Nuremberg, The (Wagner), 722
Masturbation, 579
Materialism, 127, 679, 718, 964
Maternity leave, 895
Mathematical geography, 129
Mathematics. *See also* Science
in 1930s, 856
in Enlightenment, 555
Euclid and, 129
Mesopotamian, 15
Matilda (Tuscany), 316, 317(i)
Matrimonial Causes Act (England), 710
Mau Mau, 903
Maurice (Saint), 256(i)
Mauser rifles, 796
Maximian (Roman Empire), 205
Maximianus (bishop of Ravenna), 229(i)
Maximilian (Austria), in Mexico, 698
Maximilian I (Holy Roman Empire), 454
Maximilla, 191
Mayakovsky, Vladimir, 833
Mayflower (ship), 480
Mayor of the palace, 259–260
Mazarin, Jules (Cardinal), 472, 494, 495
Mazzini, Giuseppe, 679, 686
McCarthy, Joseph, and McCarthyism, 893
McDonald's, protests against, 966
Measles, 896
Mecca, 242
Mechanics, Archimedes and, 129
Mechanization
in farming, 742
Luddite protests against, 661

Medea (Euripides), 87
Medes, 41
Media. *See also* Mass media; specific types
authoritarianism and, 829
digital, 980, 986
Hitler and, 849, 850
Roosevelt, F. D., and, 854
World War I and, 829
Medici family (Florence), 423–424
Catherine de Médicis, 462
Cosimo de', 423–424
Lorenzo the Magnificent, 424
Medicine
in 1960s, 922
breakthroughs in, 482, 483
childbirth and, 713, 923
in concentration camps, 867
in Egypt, 25
global health and, 970
health care and, 554, 896
Hellenistic, 130
Hippocrates and, 96
as profession, 714
in Rome, 185–186
schools of, 339
women in, 715
Medieval period. *See* Middle Ages
Medina, Hijra to, 242
Meditations (Marcus Aurelius), 192
Mediterranean polyculture, 29
Mediterranean region, 16(m), 476, 479, 546(m)
in 240 B.C.E., 119(m)
in c. 1050, 300(m)
in c. 1150, 333(m)
in 1871, 727(m)
Akkad in, 12
civilizations of, 34(m), 70(m)
cultural interactions in, 31–32
Dark Age in, 35, 40
Europeans in, 716
Jews of, 307
Muslim invasions and, 289
Rome and, 150, 155, 162
Megara, 100
Megarons (rooms), in Mycenaean palaces, 32
Mehmed II ("Mehmet the Conqueror," Ottomans), 398(i), 407, 423
Meiji Restoration (Japan), 717
Mein Kampf (Hitler), 836, 849–850
Meir, Golda, 901
Melos, 102–103
Memphis, Egypt, 16

Men. *See also* Boys; Gender
  education of, 675
  in Egypt, 21
  emigration to Americas, 535
  in Great Depression, 844
  homosexuality and, 932
  Paleolithic, 5
  in postwar society, 908–909
  in Rome, 141
Menander, 125–126, 155
Mendel, Gregor, 723
Mendelssohn, Moses, 571
Mendicant orders, 358, 373
Menes (Narmer, Egypt), 16
Mennonites, 447
Mensheviks (Russia), 779
Mental illness, 767
  Nazis and, 852
  Soviets and, 936
Mercantilism
  Colbert and, 498–499
  in England, 505
  Smith, Adam, on, 579
Mercenaries, 406, 452, 515
  knights as, 439(i)
  in Thirty Years' War, 470
Merchants, Dutch, 548
Mercia, 296
Mercy, A (Morrison), 983
Mergers, 954, 963
Merian, Maria Sibylla, 520,
  521(i)
Merovech (Franks), 225
Merovingian society, 225, 280
  in 7th century, 252(m)
  aristocracy in, 257–260
  elites in, 257–260
  gift economy in, 255–256
  law code in, 225–226
Mesopotamia, 4. *See also*
  Babylonia; Sumer
  Akkad and, 12
  civilizations in, 8–15
  commerce in, 13
  economy in, 8, 10
  intellectual thought in, 15
  irrigation in, 8, 13
  law in, 13–14
  mythology in, 10–11
  Neo-Assyrian Empire in, 40, 41
  polytheism in, 10
  Rome and, 180
  slavery in, 9
  writing in, 11
Messenia, helots in, 62
Messiah, 186, 187–188

Messiah (Handel), 543
Mestizos, 450, 535
Metacomet (King Philip), 512
Metals and metallurgy, 4. *See also*
  Gold; Silver
  17th century inflation and,
    475–476
  in Egypt, 18
  in Greece, 48
  in Mesopotamia, 12–13
  and Spanish colonies
    (1550–1800), 476(f)
Metamorphoses (Ovid), 177
Metaphysics, 112
Methodism, 573, 646
Metics (foreigners in Greece),
  87, 90
Metric system, in France, 611
Metternich, Klemens von, 643,
  651, 654, 679
Metz, Jews in, 576
Mexican Americans, as migrant
  workers, 931
Mexican Ecclesiastical Provincial
  Council (1555), 449–450
Mexico, 652
  Maximilian in, 698
  NAFTA and, 962
  societies of, 435
  U.S. war with, 710
Michael Romanov (Russia), 469
Michelangelo Buonarroti, 424, 450
Mickiewicz, Adam, 679
Middle Ages, 337–338. *See also*
  Renaissance
  beginning of, 240
  castles in, 292–293
  church in, 370–375
  classes in, 290–293
  commercial revolution of,
    306–312
  crafts in, 309–310
  England in, 345–349
  feudalism in, 290
  France in, 349–350, 599
  Germany in, 350–353
  governments in, 344–354
  interest payments in, 310
  peasants in, 291–292
  political power in, 290–293,
    380–393
  schools in, 338–341
  society in, 290–291
  synthesis in, 369–370
  universities in, 338–341
  warriors in, 293–294

Middle class, 681, 683. *See also*
  Bourgeoisie; Classes;
  specific locations
  Enlightenment and, 563, 570,
    573, 575–577
  expansion of, 747
  lifestyle of, 540–541
  literacy of, 542
  music and, 577
  and nobility, 576
  use of term, 575
  women in, 659, 675, 745, 769,
    780, 933
Middle-Class Gentleman, The
  (Molière), 522
Middle East. *See also* Near East;
  specific peoples and states
  in 1919–1920, 820(m)
  in 21st century, 972(m)
  in Arab world, 239
  Byzantine trade with, 272
  crusades and, 327
  decolonization in, 899,
    901–902
  foreign workers in, 977
  Great Depression and, 845–846
  imperialism in, 826
  Islam and, 971–974
  oil policy and, 918, 938–939
  Russian expansion in, 698
  Suez Canal and, 698, 716
  World War I in, 806
Middle Kingdom
  in Egypt, 22
  in Europe, 285, 297
Middlemarch (Eliot), 719
Midrash, 212
Midway Island, battle at, 872
Midwives, 185(i), 922
Mieszko I (Poland), 299
Migrant workers
  Mexican Americans as, 931
  money sent home by, 978
Migration. *See also* Immigrants and
  immigration; specific
  groups
  in 4th and 5th centuries,
    223(m)
  to colonies, 731–732
  from eastern to western
    Europe, 960
  to global cities, 965
  globalization and, 954,
    977–979
  internal, 748
  international, 747–748

of Jews, 785, 785(*m*), 786
in newly independent
   countries, 904–905
non-Roman into western
   Roman Empire, 221
into Rome, 226
society and, 977
by working people, 747–748
after World War I, 824
Milan, 420–421, 422, 686, 782
Militance. *See also* Activism;
   specific groups
black, 931
Islamic, 939
Military. *See* Armed forces
Military draft
in France, 607, 609, 629
Napoleonic, 635, 637
World War I and, 795, 806, 810
World War II and, 869, 872
Military spending
for cold war, 893
Korean War and, 893, 900
under Reagan, 942
in Soviet Union, 943
in U.S., 883–884
Military technology, 453–454. *See also* Weapons
of Alexander the Great,
   116–117
Hellenistic, 130
Militia. *See* Armed forces
Mill, Harriet Taylor, 725, 780
Mill, John Stuart, 725, 780
Mill on the Floss, The (Eliot), 719
Mills, water, in Middle Ages, 310
Milosevic, Slobodan, 955, 956
Miltiades (Athenian general), 233
Milton, John, 518–519
Milvian Bridge, battle of, 209
Mind-body dualism, 113
Minerva (goddess), 144, 192
Minimalist composers, 928
Mining, 454, 665, 666(*i*)
Ministerials, 299
Minitel (computer network), 919
Minnesingers (love singers), 355
Minoan Greece, 25, 26(*m*),
   28–30, 31
Minorities. *See also* Ethnic groups;
   specific groups
activism of, 917
in Poland, 824, 824(*m*)
in Russia, 702
Minos (King), 28
Minotaur (mythical creature), 28

Mir (Russian community), 700,
   743, 790
Mishnah, 212
Missi dominici, 281
Missiles, 921, 945
Missions and missionaries, 481. *See also* specific orders
in Africa, 739–740
in Asia, 450, 716, 739–740
in China, 557(*i*), 717, 791
European imperialism and, 646
in India, 646
in Ireland, 260
Jesuit, 449, 481
in New World, 431, 481
in Scandinavia, 288–289
Mithras (god), cult of, 192, 193(*i*)
Mithridates VI (Pontus), 160
Mitteleuropa, 794, 798
Mitterrand, François, 942
Mobile warfare, 870
Mobility
labor, 664
women and, 578
Mobilization
World War I and, 804
World War II and, 868
Modern, use of term, 768
Modern art, 776–777
Modernism, 774
Modernity, 568, 768, 800
Modernization
in China, 975
in eastern Europe, 896
Great Depression and, 844
in Japan, 717, 737–738, 738(*i*),
   975
Napoleon III and, 697–698
Mohács, battle at, 452
Moldavia, 699
Molière (Jean-Baptiste Poquelin),
   496, 522, 523
Monarchs and monarchies, 485. *See also* French Revolution;
   Kings and kingdoms;
   Queens; specific kingdoms
   and rulers
in Byzantine Empire, 328
in central Europe, 297–299
in England, 328–330, 345–349,
   444, 502–504, 506–508, 710
in France, 331, 349–350, 493,
   494–501, 602, 604–607, 645
in Germany, 332, 350–353
Hellenistic, 131–132
Israelite, 46

in Mesopotamia, 9–10
in Middle Ages, 338, 344–353
in northeastern Europe, 419
Ottoman, 408
reforms by, 583–586
revival of, 328–332
in Rome, 145–148
ruler cults and, 131
in western Europe, 418
Monasticism and monasteries,
   218–220, 219(*i*). *See also*
   Clergy; Convents; Religious
   orders
Augustianian Order, 438, 439
Benedictine, 313
Boniface and, 280
Carthusian, 320
Cistercian, 320–322, 321(*f*),
   322(*i*)
Columbanus and, 258
commercial centers near,
   306–307
conduct in, 219
in French Revolution, 603
orders of poverty and,
   319–322
Monet, Claude, 752, 753
Monetarist theory, 941
Money. *See also* Coins
euro as, 962
Money economy, in 1050–1150,
   305–306
Moneylending, by Jews, 373, 374
Mongols and Mongol Empire
invasions by, 389–390, 389(*m*)
in Poland, 419
Monks. *See also* Monasticism and
   monasteries; specific orders
black, 319–320
Christian, 218–220
white, 321
Monogamy, in Greece, 60
Mono no aware (Japan), 753
Monophysite Christianity, 216,
   219(*i*), 232, 243–244
Monopolies, in Assyria, 13
Monotheism, 239–240
of Islam, 242
of Israelites, 44, 46, 47
of Jews, 186
Monroe, James, 653
Monroe Doctrine, 653
Montagu, Mary Wortley, 554
Montaigne, Michel de, 463, 484,
   487–488
Montenegro, 759, 794

Montesquieu (**Charles-Louis de Secondat,** baron of), 558, 583
Montessori, Maria, 771–772, 771(i)
Monteverdi, Claudio, 487
Montgolfier brothers, 565(i)
Montpellier, university in, 338, 339
Moral dualism, in Zoroastrianism, 43
Moralistic family paintings, 577, 579(i)
Morality
    Hebrew, 45
    Plato and Aristotle on, 134
    in Rome, 140–141
Moral majority (U.S.), 942
Moral relativism, 92
Moravia, 515
More, Thomas, 443
Moriscos, 466
Morocco, 465, 793–794, 870, 904
Morris, William and **May,** 752
Morrison, Toni, 982–983, 983(i)
Mortality
    decline in, 537
    infant and child, 578, 665, 669
Mosaics
    Byzantine, 245(i)
    of Christ as Sun God, 214(i)
    of family from Edessa, 216(i)
    in Ravenna, 228(i), 229(i)
    Roman, 168(i)
    of women exercising (Sicily), 226(i)
Moscow, 640, 790, 813, 965
Moses, 45
Mos maiorum (the way of the ancestors), in Rome, 150
Mosques
    Dome of the Rock as, 238(i), 245
    in western Europe, 929
Mostar Bridge, destruction of, 955
Motet, 377(i), 378
Mothers. See Families; Women
Mountain, the (faction in France), 606–607, 608
Mount Olympus, 55
Mount Sinai, monastery at, 219(i)
Movable type, 436, 437
Movies, 829, 918
    in 1920s, 829–830
    in 1930s, 856
    during cold war, 880(i), 881
    ethnographic, 928
    globalization and, 984

neorealist, 911
    about space, 920
    in United States, 984
    World War II and, 868
    youth culture in, 908
Mozarabs, 277, 360
Mozart, Wolfgang Amadeus, 577
Mrs. Dalloway (Woolf), 832
Muhammad, 239, 240, 241–243. See also Islam
    successors to, 244–245
Mühlberg, battle at, 456
Mulattoes, 450
Multiculturalism, 983
Multiethnicity. See also Diversity
    of Alexander the Great's empire, 118
    of non-Roman kingdoms, 220
Multinational corporations, 923–924, 979
Multinationalism
    in Austria-Hungary, 784
    in Soviet Union, 816
Mummies, 21, 25
Munch, Edvard, 766(i), 777
Munich Pact (1938), 861–862
Münster, Anabaptists in, 447
Münter, Gabriele, 777
Müntzer, Thomas, 445
Murat, Joachim, 631
Mursili II (Hittites), 27
Muscovy, 469
Museum(s), 125, 672, 911
Music. See also Opera
    baroque, 577
    Beethoven symphonies as, 649
    Enlightenment and, 577
    in former Soviet bloc, 983–984
    globalization of, 980
    jazz, 828, 832
    minimalists and, 928
    modern, 777–778
    oratorios, 543
    orchestral, 577
    in postindustrial society, 928
    public concerts, 543
    Renaissance, 417–418
    rock, 927
    rock-and-roll culture and, 908, 909(i)
    romantic, 649
    sacred and secular, 377–378
    "starvation music" (Arvo Pärt), 928
    troubadours and, 355

Muslim League, 792
Muslims. See also Crusades; Islam; Ottoman Empire; Shi'ite Muslims; Sunni Muslims
    in Algeria, 904
    in Bosnia-Herzegovina, 955
    Byzantine Empire and, 246
    crusades and, 323–324, 325–326, 327
    in EU, 962
    in India, 536, 715–716, 845, 899
    invasions by, 288, 289
    in Jerusalem, 324
    Moriscos and, 466
    in Morocco, 465
    in Sicily, 300(m)
    in Soviet Union, 833, 868–869, 954
    in Spain, 243, 315, 360–361, 426, 436, 450, 462, 481, 547
    Sunni/Shi'ite split in, 276
    in Third Crusade, 359–360
    in Yugoslavia, 887
Mussolini, Benito, 829, 834–836, 854, 870
    Black Shirts and, 834, 835(i)
    expansion by, 858
    France and, 863
    Munich Pact and, 861
    Spain and, 859
Mutiny, in World War I, 812
Mycenaean civilization, 26, 30–32, 31(i), 34–35
Myrdal, Alva, 854
Mystery cults, 87, 132
Myth, science vs., 69–70
Mythology
    Egyptian, 3
    Greek, 39, 51, 55
    Mesopotamian, 10–11

NAFTA. See North American Free Trade Agreement
Nagasaki, bombing of, 872
Nagy, Imre, 898
Names (personal), in French Revolution, 611
Nanking, Treaty of, 677
Nantes, Edict of, 463
Naples, 621, 658(i), 704
    France and, 420–421
    as French satellite kingdom, 637
    kingdom of, 631, 650–651, 654

Napoleon I Bonaparte (France),
572, 615–616, 623, 626(i).
See also specific locations
conquests by, 634–641
coronation of, 630, 631(i)
in Egypt, 628–629
empire of, 634–635, 634(m),
640
Europe after, 641–646, 644(m)
fall of, 640–641
religion and, 629–630
retreat from Russia by, 640
rise of, 627, 628–633
Rosetta stone and, 108(i), 629
Russian invasion by, 640
slavery and, 619
Napoleon III (France), 672(i),
685–686, 696–697,
697–698, 697(i), 718
Crimean War and, 698, 699
Germany and, 707
Italian unification and, 686, 704
Suez Canal and, 698, 716
*Napoleon Crossing the Alps at St.
Bernard* (David), 626(i)
Napoleonic Code, 628, 632, 637,
645
Napoleonic wars and, 635–641
Naram-Sin (Akkad), 12
Narmer (**Menes,** Egypt), 16, 17–18
Naseby, battle of, 503
Nasser, Gamal Abdel, 902, 902(i)
Nation. *See* State (nation)
National Aeronautics and Space
Administration (NASA),
898
National Assembly (France),
600–601, 602–604, 685
National Association for the
Advancement of Colored
People (NAACP), 908
National Congress of the Chechen
People, 960
National Convention (France), 606,
607, 608, 610, 611, 614–615,
619
clubs, societies, and, 613–614
National debt, in United States,
938, 975
National Front Party (France), 942
National Guard
in France, 602, 615, 718
in United States, 937
National health care, 894
National Insurance Act (England,
1911), 764, 781

Nationalism
artists and, 777
in Austria-Hungary, 784
in Austrian Empire, 678–679
in Balkans, 651–652, 651(m),
759–760
Basque, 940(m)
Common Market and, 894
ethnic, 955
French Revolution and, 609
of German peoples, 679
in Germany, 708
growth of, 702
in Hungary, 687
ideology of, 677, 678
in India, 716, 792
in Ireland, 679–680, 940(m)
of Islamic fundamentalists, 971
in Italy, 638, 679, 704
Jewish, 785–786
Napoleon and, 639
in Ottoman Empire, 651(m),
792
in Poland, 679
revolutionary, 792
after revolutions of 1848,
688–689
romanticism and, 649
in Russia, 679
World War I and, 799, 809
Nationalist Party (China), 792
Nationalities. *See also* Ethnic
groups; Minorities
in Austria-Hungary, 759
National Organization for Women
(NOW), 933
National Socialists (Germany). *See*
Nazis and Nazism
National workshops (France), 685,
718
Nation building. *See also*
Imperialism; Unification
cities and, 712–713
education and, 714–715
social order for, 712–719
spread beyond West, 717–719
in United States, 710–711
warfare and, 696, 702–711
Nation-states, 696, 702. *See also*
Nation building; State
(nation)
future of, 965
in global age, 961–966
protests in Europe against,
717–719
religion and, 722–723

Native Americans, 710, 711(m),
788
discrimination against,
449–450
disease and, 476, 512
Europeans and, 435, 512, 535
literature by, 983
missionaries and, 431, 449–450
NATO. *See* North Atlantic Treaty
Organization
Natural harmonization, Adam
Smith on, 568
Natural History of Religion, The
(Hume), 566, 571(f)
Natural law, 486–487, 565
Natural resources, in United States,
742
Natural rights, 486, 565, 567, 569
Natural science, in 19th century,
723–724
Natural selection, 724
Nature
laws of, 481
romanticism and, 571, 647
Navarino Bay, battle at, 652
Navarre, 362(m), 420
Navies
Athenian, 77, 79–80, 80(i), 82,
114
British, 581–582, 636, 796
in England, 295
German, 796, 819
Persian, 76–78, 79
Roman, 153
Russian, 550
Spartan, 104
Washington Conference (1921)
and, 822
World War I and, 807
World War II and, 872
Navigation. *See* Exploration
Navigation Act (England), 505
Nazis and Nazism (Germany),
840(i), 844. *See also*
Fascism
Austria and, 855, 860
central European conquests by,
860–863
denazification program and,
890
emigration from, 852
expansion by, 858–859,
860–863
growth of, 862(m)
Hitler and, 836, 849–852
Holocaust by, 865–868, 866(m)

Nazis and Nazism (continued)
    Jews and, 773(i), 851–852
    Nuremberg trials and, 890
    religious opposition to, 857
    resistance to, 855
    totalitarianism of, 846,
        849–852
    West Germany and, 890, 942
Nazi-Soviet Pact (1939), 862–863,
    885
Near East, 4. See also Hellenistic
    world; Mesopotamia;
    Middle East; specific
    locations
    ancient, 3–35, 6(m)
    Dark Age in, 40
    defined, 5
    environment of, 5
    Greek culture and, 109–110
    Hellenistic Greeks and, 121
    myths from, 39
Necker, Jacques, 601, 633
Neferkare Pepy II (Egypt), 21
Nelson, Horatio, 629, 636
Neo-Assyrian Empire, 40, 41
Neo-Babylonian Empire, 41–42
Neoclassical style, 576, 576(i)
Neoliberalism, 941, 942, 960
Neolithic (New Stone) Age, 5, 6–8
Neoplatonism, 193, 234
Neorealism, in movies, 911
NEPmen, in Soviet Union, 833
Nero (Rome), 179, 188–189
Nerva (Rome), 180
Nestlé, 827
Nestorian Christianity, 215
Nestorius, 215, 216
Netherlands, 456, 642, 689, 978.
        See also Dutch; Dutch
        Republic
    Austrian, 540, 546(m), 553,
        596
    Belgium and, 654
    Calvinism in, 461, 462
    after Charlemagne, 285
    in ECSC, 894
    France and, 635
    kingdom of, 643
    male suffrage in, 758
    Nazi conquest of, 841
    Spain and, 466, 471, 500
    urbanization in, 748
    World War II and, 863, 883
Networks, global communication,
    979–980

Neustria, 252(m), 259
Neutrality, of Belgium, 654
Newcastle-upon-Tyne, England,
    310
New Deal (U.S.), 854
New Economic Policy (NEP), 833,
    846
New England, blacks in, 533
Newfoundland, 500
New France. See Canada
New Harmony, 681–682
New imperialism, 732–740
New Kingdom (Egypt), 22–25, 33
New Lanark, Scotland, 681
New Left, in France, 934
New man, in Rome, 159–160, 175
New Model Army (England), 503
New Netherland, 511
Newnham (women's college), 715
New Plymouth Colony, 480
New right, in Germany, 783–784
News from the Republic of Letters
    (Bayle), 555
New Spain, 435
Newspapers, 542, 549, 577, 587,
    600, 673, 944
    mass culture and, 829
    mass politics and, 756
New Stone Age. See Neolithic Age
New Testament. See Bible
Newton, Isaac, 482, 484, 485, 487,
    520, 556, 565, 566
New unionism movement, 755
New woman, 771–772, 783, 810
New World, 431, 475. See also
        Americas; Colonies and
        colonization
    Dutch trade with, 549
    slave trade and, 435, 532–535
New York, 730(i), 832, 965
    September 11, 2001, attacks on,
        973, 974(i)
New Zealand, 567, 677, 748
NGOs. See Nongovernmental
        organizations
Nicaea
    Council of, 215
    in crusades, 325
Nice, France, 453, 704
Nicene Creed, 215
Nicephorus I (Byzantine Empire),
    274
Nicephorus II Phocas (Byzantine
    Empire), 273
Nicetius (bishop), 259

Nicholas I (Russia), 651, 654, 674,
    689, 698, 699
    Austria and, 688
    liberalism and, 681
Nicholas II (Russia), 782, 790
    Russian Revolution and, 812,
        813
    World War I and, 798, 810
Nicholas III (Pope), 386(i)
Nietzsche, Friedrich, 772, 775,
    831(i)
Nigeria, 902
Nightingale, Florence, 699, 713
Nightmare, The (Fuseli), 648(i)
Night of the Long Knives (Nazi
    Germany), 850–851
Nihilism, in Russia, 702, 720
Nijmegen, Treaty of, 500
Nika Riot, 231
Nile River region, 15–16, 16(m),
    18, 24. See also Egypt
    (ancient)
Nîmes, France, aqueduct at, 152(i)
1984 (Orwell), 874–875
Ninety-five theses (Luther), 440
Nixon, Richard, 937, 938
Nkrumah, Kwame, 902
Noah, biblical account of, 11
Nobel, Alfred, 780, 796
Nobel Prize, 980, 981
Nobility. See also Aristocracy
    as ambassadors, 553
    in Austria, 515, 585
    in Brandenburg-Prussia, 514,
        515
    Byzantine, 328
    in England, 329–330, 422
    in Enlightenment, 573–574
    in France, 331, 350, 455, 463,
        585, 586, 599, 614, 631, 641
    Hittite, 27
    lifestyle of, 540
    middle class and, 576
    in Ostrogothic Italy, 224
    in Russia, 517, 550–551, 574,
        681, 699, 700, 701–702
    women of, 298–299
Nobility of the robe (France), 463
Nomads
    Bedouins as, 240
    Islam and, 241
    Russian control of, 715
Nonaggression pact, Nazi-Soviet,
    862–863
Nonaligned nations, 904

Non-Christian religions, 929
Nongovernmental organizations
(NGOs), 966
Nonviolent resistance, civil rights
movement and, 908
Nordau, Max, 773
Normandy, 288, 300(m), 349, 350,
871
Normans
Byzantine Empire and, 328
in England, 328–330, 329(m),
330(i), 347
power of, 315
in Sicily, 300(m), 323
North (global), 970
North (U.S.), 710, 711
North Africa. *See also* Carthage;
specific locations
Arab world and, 239
Christianity in, 215–216
decolonization in, 899
Fatimids in, 277
France and, 435–436, 794
immigrants from, 905
Justinian and, 235(m)
Phoenicians in, 53
Romanization of, 182
Rome and, 152–155
terrorists from, 973
Vandals in, 224
World War II and, 870, 870(m)
North America. *See also* specific
locations
colonies in, 480–481
French cession of, 500, 546(m)
Great Awakening in, 572
migration to, 748
revolution in, 588–590
Seven Years' War in, 580
slaves in, 435, 532–535
Vikings in, 288
War of the Austrian Succession
in, 553
North American Free Trade
Agreement (NAFTA), 962
North Atlantic Treaty Organization
(NATO), 889, 889(m), 955
North Briton (newspaper), 587
Northern Crusades, 362–364
Northern Ireland, 825–826,
826(m), 940, 942
North German Confederation, 706
North Korea, 900. *See also* Korea
Northmen. *See* Vikings
Northumbria, 296

North Vietnam, 931, 937. *See also*
Vietnam
Northwest passage, search for,
435–436
Norway, 289, 523
Notke, Bernt, 419
Notre Dame cathedral, 610
Nova Scotia, 500
Novels, 523, 856. *See also*
Literature; specific works
realist, 719–720
society and, 544, 671–672
Nubia, 17, 18
Nuclear family, in Greece, 60
Nuclear power, 775, 882, 918
Chernobyl catastrophe and,
944, 967
power plants for, 921
Nuclear weapons
atomic bomb and, 776, 872,
874(i), 889, 893
cold war and, 912
Soviet, 889, 893
test-ban treaty and, 912
World War II and, 872
Numidia, Carthage and, 154
Nuns. *See* Convents; Monasticism
and monasteries; specific
orders
Nur al-Din (Seljuk Empire), 359
Nuremberg Laws (Germany, 1935),
852
Nuremberg trials, 890
Nursing, in Crimean War, 699,
700(i)
Nutrition. *See* Diet (food)

Oases, 22–23
Obama, Barack, 974
Oblation, 220
Occitan (language), 354, 355
Occupation (military), of Germany,
874, 888–889, 888(m)
Occupations (jobs)
postindustrial structure of
(1984), 925(f)
in Rome, 208
Oceans. *See also* specific ocean
regions
global warming and, 967
Ockeghem, Johannes, 418
Ockham's razor, 408
O'Connell, Daniel, 680
Octavian (Augustus). *See* Augustus
(Octavian)

Odoacer (Germanic general), 224
Odyssey, The (Homer), 49, 53
Ogodei (Mongols), 390
Oil and oil industry, 939(f)
in Latin America, 971
in Middle East, 826, 870, 901,
938–939
Olaf (Saint), 523
Old Believers (Russia), 518
Old Curiosity Shop, The (Dickens),
672
Oldenburg, Claes, 927, 928(i)
Old English language, 262,
295–296
Old Kingdom (Egypt), 16–22
Old Stone Age. *See* Paleolithic Age
Old Testament. *See* Bible
Oligarchs, in Russia, 957
Oligarchy, in Sparta, 61–64
Olympia (Manet), 720, 721(i)
Olympic Games, in Greece,
49–51, 87
Olympus, Mount, 55
On Agriculture (Cato), 155
Once Upon the River Love
(Makine), 983
On Crimes and Punishments
(Beccaria), 583
*One Day in the Life of Ivan
Denisovitch* (Solzhenitsyn),
898
One Hundred Years of Solitude
(García Márquez), 981
On Germany (Staël), 633
On Liberty (Mill), 725
*On the Babylonian Captivity of the
Church* (Luther), 441
*On the Construction of the Human
Body* (Vesalius), 483
On the Length and Shortness of Life
(Aristotle), 368(i), 369
On the Nature of Things (Lucretius),
156
On the Origin of Species (Darwin),
723
*On the Revolution of the Celestial
Spheres* (Copernicus), 482
On the Rivers of Europe, 125
On the Solitary Life (Petrarch), 413
OPEC. *See* Organization of
Petroleum Exporting
Countries
Opera, 487, 496, 543, 577, 654,
694(i), 695, 722
Operation Vittles, 889

Opium, 677
Opium War, 677, 677(m), 717
Optimates (Rome), 159, 160, 161
Oral culture
    of Anglo-Saxons and Irish
        Celts, 261
    Greek, 48, 91
Oral literature, in Mycenae, 31
Orange, princes of, 467, 509, 596,
    641
Orange Free State, 786
Oration on the Dignity of Man
    (Pico), 413
Oratorios, 543
Order of the Sisters of St. Francis,
    358
Order of the Templars, 326
Orders (classes), in Rome, 148, 184
Oresteia (Aeschylus), 97
Orfeo (Monteverdi), 487
Organization of Labor (Blanc), 682
Organization of Petroleum
        Exporting Countries
        (OPEC), 938
Organizations, global, 966. See also
    specific organizations
Origen, 192–193
Original sin, 217
Origins, The (Cato), 155
Orlando (Woolf), 831, 832
Orlando Furioso (Ariosto), 451,
    522
Orléans, Philippe II (duke of),
    547
Oroonoko (Behn), 523
Orsanmichele, Florence, 392(i)
Orthodox Christianity, 232, 760.
        See also Greek Orthodox
        Church
    in Russia, 722
Orthodoxy (Christian true
        doctrine), 215, 358
Orwell, George, 856, 874–875, 910
Osiris (god), 192
Osman I (Ottomans), 407
Osrhoëne, kingdom of, 216
Ostia, 185(i)
Ostpolitik, 930
Ostracism, 81–82
Ostrogoths, 224, 231
Oswy (Northumbria), 260–261
Otto I (Germany), 289, 297
Otto I (Greece), 652, 654
Otto II (Ottonian Empire), 297
Otto III (Ottonian Empire), 297,
    298(i)

Ottoman Empire, 418, 433(m),
    525(m), 591(m), 788. See
    also Turkey
    Armenians in, 810
    Congress of Berlin and, 760
    Constantinople conquered by,
        407–408
    Crimean War and, 698–699,
        698(m)
    end of, 819
    expansion of, 516, 516(m)
    former colonies of, 820–821
    Habsburgs, Valois wars, and,
        452–453
    in Hungary, 515
    Lepanto and, 465, 469
    Middle East after, 826, 845–846
    nationalism in, 651–652,
        759–760, 792
    Russia and, 736, 760
    before World War I, 794
    World War I and, 804
Ottoman Turks, 399, 432, 452–453.
        See also Ottoman Empire
    Austria, Hungary, and, 552
    after Congress of Vienna,
        651–652
    Greece and, 651–652
    Russia and, 469, 597
    Spain and, 462, 465
    Venice and, 423
Ottonian kings (Germany), 297–299
Outsourcing, 964, 979
Outwork, 684, 741, 749
Ovid, 177
Ovism doctrine, 559
Owen, Robert, 681–682
Oxford University, 341, 715
Ozone layer, 967

Pärt, Arvo, 928
Pacific Ocean region. See also
        specific locations
    economic growth in, 974–745
    World War II in, 864–865, 872,
        873(m)
Pacific tigers, 975, 975(m)
Pacifism
    Christian, 439
    as women's cause, 779–780
Paestum, Italy, 576
Pagans and paganism
    religious campaigns against,
        523–524
    use of term, 190(m)
    Vikings and, 288

Painting. See also Art(s); specific
        works and artists
    in 1920s, 830–831, 831(i)
    abstract, 777
    abstract expressionism in, 911
    black-figure style, 38(i), 68(i),
        89(i)
    dissident, 930
    Dutch, 511(i)
    expressionism in, 777
    Gothic, 379–380
    gouache, 528(i)
    Hellenistic, 126
    impressionism in, 752–753,
        753(i)
    mannerism in, 486–487
    middle class and, 577
    Minoan, 29(i)
    modern, 776–777
    moralistic family scenes in, 577,
        579(i)
    neoclassical, 576
    realism in, 720, 721(i)
    red-figure style, 55(i), 68(i)
    rococo, 537(i), 542, 542(i)
    romanticism in, 647–648,
        648(i), 670–671, 671(i)
Pakistan, 899
Palaces. See also specific locations
    at Gla, 34
    Mesopotamian, 10
    Minoan, 28–29
    Mycenaean, 32, 33
Palace society, in Crete, 28
Palach, Jan, 916(i), 917, 918, 929,
    935, 937, 946
Pale of Settlement, for Russian
    Jews, 762
Paleolithic ("Old Stone") Age, 5
Palermo, 654, 686
Palestine
    Canaan as, 15
    Israel and, 938, 972(m), 973
    Jews and, 132–133, 786, 857,
        883, 901
    as Judaea, 186
    partition of, 901, 901(m)
    Roman Empire and, 212
    after World War I, 821
Palmyra, 197
Pan-African movement, 787(m)
Pan-Arabic world, 971
Pan-Arab movements, 899
Pandemics, influenza, 816(f), 817
Pandora (Greek mythology), 61
Pan-Islamic movements, 899

Pan-Islamic world, 971
Pankhurst, Christabel, 809
Pankhurst, Emmeline, 780–781, 809
Pan-Slavism, 709, 759–760
Papacy. *See also* Great Schism; Popes; specific popes
in Avignon, 388, 400, 408–409
Carolingians and, 280
criticisms of, 408
Freemasonry and, 575–576
Germany and, 350, 381
Great Schism and, 400, 408–411
Investiture Conflict and, 315–317
in Italy, 708
in Middle Ages, 381
Normans and, 315
payment for, 319
power of, 263–264, 319, 382, 386–388
Papal bulls
Louis XIV and, 498
Unam Sanctam, 387
Papal curia (government), 319
Papal inquisition. *See* Inquisition
Papal primacy, 315
Papal States, 381, 577, 616
Paper, in Islam, 279
Papermaking, 437
Paradise Lost (Milton), 519
Parchment, books on, 233, 437
Paris, 259, 297, 331, 570, 871, 930, 965. *See also* France; Peace of Paris
French Revolution and, 601
Haussmannization in, 712
immigrants in, 953
July revolution in, 653
parlement of, 383
protests in (1968), 934–935
rebuilding of, 697
sanitation in, 713
siege of (1870–1871), 707, 718
terrorism in, 973
university in, 338, 341
uprising in (1848), 684–686
Paris, Treaty of (1763), 582
Paris Commune (1871), 718–719, 725, 755
Paris Peace Conference, 818–821
Parks, Rosa, 908
Parlement of Paris, 383, 599
Parlements (France), 385, 494, 498, 585, 587

Parliament (England), 385–386, 444, 502, 504, 505, 548, 587–588, 709
Charles I and, 502–503
Irish representatives in, 757, 826
reform of, 654–655
Parliament(s)
in EU, 962
in Finland, 780
in France, 645
in Hungary, 709, 946
in Russia, 957
Parnell, Charles Stewart, 757
Pärt, Arvo, 928
Parthenon (Athens), 83–85, 84*(i),* 211
Parthian Empire, 119*(m),* 177*(i),* 194
Partisans, World War II and, 887
Partitions. *See* Germany; Poland; Zones of occupation
Partnerships, 310
Pascal, Blaise, 497, 518
Pasternak, Boris, 880*(i),* 881, 882, 885, 898, 912
Pasteur, Louis, 713
Pasteurization, 713
Pastoral Rule (Gregory the Great), 264
Paternalism, Napoleonic, 632
Patria potestas (father's power, Rome), 142
Patriarch
of Constantinople, 250
of Greek Orthodox Church, 652
of Russian Orthodox Church, 551
Patriarchy
in barbarian society, 221
Islamic, 243
in Mesopotamia, 10
Patricians (Rome), 148, 149
Patrick (Saint), 260
Patrilineal inheritance, 293–294, 297
Patriotism
during French Revolution, 610
in World War II, 868
Patriots
in Dutch Republic, 596–597
in Poland, 597, 618
Patristic authors, 216
Patron-client system, in Rome, 141–142, 155, 173. *See also* Clients
Paul III (Pope), 448
Paul VI (Pope), 929

Paul of Tarsus (Saint Paul), 186, 187–188
Pavia, Italy, 263, 452
Pax Romana, 170, 194
Paxton, Joseph, 690*(i)*
Peace. *See also* specific treaties
diplomacy and, 553, 758
World War I and, 810, 821–823
Peacekeeping, in former Yugoslavia, 955
Peace of Aix-la-Chapelle, 553
Peace of Augsburg, 456, 461, 462, 470
Peace of God movement, 294–295
Peace of Lodi, 422–423, 422*(m)*
Peace of Paris
of 1856, 699
of 1919–1920, 819, 820*(m),* 821, 836, 855, 885
Peace of Rijswijk, 500
Peace of Utrecht, 500, 553
Peace of Westphalia, 472–474, 473*(m),* 553
Pearl Harbor, Japanese attack on, 864
Peasants. *See also* Serfs and serfdom
in Austrian Empire, 688
in Austrian Netherlands, 597
in Byzantine Empire, 249
in Carolingian Empire, 286–287
commerce and, 306–307, 311
culture of, 523–524
in eastern Europe, 540
economic activity and, 256–257, 477–478
in England, 329, 540
in Enlightenment, 574, 577–579
entertainment for, 578
as factory workers, 664
famine and, 477
in France, 599, 602, 668
in Frankish kingdoms, 254
in Great Depression, 843
Hundred Years' War and, 406, 407
illiteracy of, 542
Irish, 684
lifestyle of, 574
as medieval class, 291
plague and, 403, 477
in Prussia, 515, 637
revolts by, 393, 472, 586–587
in Rome, 208*(f)*
in Russia, 517, 621, 674, 699, 700–701, 736, 743, 779, 789, 790, 813

Peasants (continued)
  as serfs, 480
  in Soviet bloc, 896
  in Soviet Union, 847
  after Thirty Years' War, 472
  uprising in Greece, 651
Peasants' War (1525), 445, 445(i),
  446(m)
Pedagogues, 144
Peel, Robert, 654, 680
Peers (England), 540, 574. See also
  Nobility
Peisistratus (Athens), 66–67
Pelevin, Victor, 983
Pelletier, Fernande, 925–926
Peloponnese region, 33
  Byzantines and, 274
  Corinth and, 64–65
  Mycenae in, 30
  Sparta in, 62
Peloponnesian League, 100
Peloponnesian War, 76, 100–104,
  101(m), 103(f)
  Classical Greece after, 110–115
Penance, sacrament of, 440
Pensées (Pascal), 518
Pensions, 969
  veterans, 828, 895
  in welfare states, 894
Pentagon, terrorist attack on, 973,
  974(i)
Pentateuch. See Torah
People, the. See Common people
People's Charter, 683
People's Crusade, 325
People's Republic of China. See
  China
People's Will (Russia), 761
Perestroika (restructuring), 943,
  944, 949, 956
Pergamum, 119
Pericles (Athens), 81–82, 89–90,
  99, 101–102
Periodicals, 542, 672–673
Perpetua, Vibia, 169, 189
Persecution
  of Christians, 189, 197, 209
  political, 779
  of witches, 487–488
Persephone (goddess), 87
Persia. See also Iran; Persian
  Empire; specific dynasties
  Great King of, 44(i)
  as Iran, 42
  Islam and, 243
  nationalism in, 846

Rome and, 205
Russia and, 736
Sasanids and, 247
Persian Empire, 42–44
  Alexander the Great and,
    109–110, 116
  Athens and, 79–80
  expansion of, 43(m)
  Jews in, 46
  Peloponnesian War and,
    101(m), 103–104
  Philip II (Macedonia) and, 115
Persian Letters (Montesquieu), 558
Persian people
  in India, 536
  in Iran, 971
Persian Wars, 74(i), 75, 76–79, 78(m)
Peru, 435, 524
Pesticides, 925
Pétain, Henri Philippe, 864
Peter (Saint), 187, 213, 261, 268(i)
  "republic" of, 281
Peter I (the Great, Russia),
  549–550, 550(i)
Peter III (Russia), 562(i), 581
Peterloo massacre, 654
Peters, Carl, 731, 732, 733, 763
Peter the Chanter, 339, 340, 375
Peter the Hermit, 325
Petition of Right (England), 502
Petrarch, Francesco, 413
Petrograd, 810, 813, 833. See also
  St. Petersburg
Petty, William, 553
Peugeot, Armand, 740
Pharaohs (Egypt), 23, 24, 45
Pharisees, 187
Pharsalus, battle of, 163
Philanthropy. See Charity(ies)
Philip II (Augustus, France),
  349–350, 359, 383
Philip II (Macedonia), 115–116
Philip II (Spain), 456, 462, 463,
  464–466, 464(m), 466(i),
  467, 468
Philip III (France), 466
Philip IV (the Fair, France),
  386–387
Philip IV (Spain), 474(i)
Philip V (Spain), 500, 545
Philip VI (France), 404
Philip of Hess, 456
Philippines, 481, 788, 864, 945
Philip the Bold (Burgundy), 413
Philip the Good (Burgundy), 420,
  421(i)

Philoponus, John, 234
Philosopher-kings, Plato on, 113
Philosophes, 564–566, 566(i), 570,
  571, 584–585
Philosophical and Political History
  of European Colonies and
  Commerce in Two Indies
  (Raynal), 567, 571(f)
Philosophical Dictionary (Voltaire),
  567, 571(f)
Philosophy. See also specific
  philosophers
  existential, 907
  Greek, 54, 69–70, 86, 90–96,
    112–114
  Hellenistic, 126–129
  positivism and, 774–775
  Romans and, 192
Phocas family (Byzantine Empire),
  273
Phoenicians, 53, 54(m). See also
  Carthage; Punic Wars
Photography, 670, 673, 752
Physical fitness, of workers, 756
Physically disabled. See Disabilities
Physicians. See Doctors; Medicine
Physics, 485, 774, 775–776, 856
Physiocrats, 585
Piacenza, 308(m), 388–389
Picasso, Pablo, 776, 859
Pico della Mirandola, Giovanni,
  413
Pictographs. See Writing
Piedmont, 628, 654, 695, 703,
  703(m)
Piedmont-Sardinia, 650–651, 702,
  704
Pietas (piety), in Rome, 145
Pietism, 544, 572, 646
Pilate, Pontius (Judaea), 187
Pilgrimage of Grace, 444
Pilgrimages
  church regulation of, 524
  to Lourdes, 723
  to Mecca, 243
Pilgrims, in American colonies,
  480
Pill, the, 822
Pilsudski, Jozef, 824
Pinsker, Leon, 784–785
Pipe Rolls (England), 348
Pippin (son of Louis the Pius), 285
Pippin III (the Short,
  Carolingians), 264, 280
Piracy, 162, 535–536
Pisa, Council of, 409

Pistoia, Italy, Black Death in, 401
Pitt, William, 608–609
Pius V (Pope), 466(i)
Pius VI (Pope), 604
Pius VII (Pope), 629, 631(i)
Pius IX (Pope), 686, 722
Pius XI (Pope), 857
Pizarro, Francisco, 435
Plague, 399–400, 477, 506, 537. See
    also Black Death; Epidemics
Planck, Max, 775
Planetary motion, 461–462, 482
Plantagenet dynasty, 345
Plantation(s)
    described, 530
    slavery on, 530, 531
Plantation economy, 481, 532
Plato, 94, 112–113, 233
Playboy magazine, 909
Playwrights, 486, 496. See also
    Drama; Theater(s); specific
    writers
Plebeian Assembly (Rome), 150,
    159
Plebeians (Rome), 148, 149
Plebiscites
    in France, 629, 630
    in Rome, 150
Plenary indulgence. See
    Indulgences
Pliny (Rome), 189
Pliska, Bulgaria, 274
Plotinus, 193
Plows, 8
Plutarch, 182
Poets and poetry. See also specific
    poets
    in Akkad, 12
    "beat," 909
    Bedouin, 241
    epics and, 451
    Greek, 68–69
    Hellenistic, 125
    Islamic, 245–246
    realist, 720
    romanticism in, 647, 670
    Soviet, 897
    of troubadours, 355
    vernacular culture and,
        354–357
Pogroms, against Jews, 325, 748,
    762, 782
Poitiers, battle at
    of 732, 280
    of 1358, 406
Poitou, 349, 383

Poland, 299, 551, 863, 964. See also
    Poland-Lithuania
    in 14th century, 419
    agriculture in, 540
    cold war and, 886, 887
    communism in, 886, 898, 945,
        946
    concentration camps in, 866,
        866(m)
    duchy of Warsaw and, 643
    ethnic minorities in, 824,
        824(m)
    German invasion of (1939),
        842, 863
    Holocaust in, 865–866
    Jews in, 401
    Mongols in, 389
    nationalism in, 679
    partitions of, 582–583, 582(i),
        582(m), 597, 618, 618(m)
    refugees from, 883
    reunification of, 824
    revolts in, 596, 597, 654,
        945–946
    Russia and, 618, 618(m), 654,
        702
    Solidarity movement in, 945,
        946
    Soviet invasion of, 863
    after Soviet Union, 960
    succession in, 552
    Sweden and, 551
    after World War I, 818, 819, 822
    World War II and, 842, 863,
        865, 869, 871, 874
Poland-Lithuania, 419, 462, 469,
    513(m), 525(m), 552, 566.
    See also Lithuania; Poland
    constitutionalism in, 513–514
    government system in, 513
    partitions of, 580, 582–583,
        582(i)
Polanians (Slavic tribe), 299
Police
    in Austrian Empire, 679
    Cheka, 815
    in London, 654
    in Russia, 651, 760, 790
Polio, 853(i), 896
Polis (Greek city-state), 40, 56–57.
    See also City-states
Polish Corridor, 819
Polish Legion, 679
Polish people
    in Austrian Empire, 679
    as refugees, 891(i)

Politianus, Bartholomaeus, 412
Political Arithmetick (Petty), 553
Political life. See also Authority;
    Government; Political
    power
    Great Depression and, 844, 849
    Greek disunity in, 114–115
    Islam and, 242
    religion and, 523–524
    World War II and, 891–893
Political parties. See also specific
    parties and locations
    Green, 968
    right-wing in Germany, 825
    women in, 755
    working-class, 755, 758–759,
        778–779
    World War I and, 809
Political power. See also Authority;
    specific locations and types
    in 15th-century republics,
        422–424
    in Athens, 81
    in Carolingian Empire,
        286–288
    in central Europe, 299
    consolidation of, 418–426
    European state system and,
        545–547
    in feudal society, 290–293
    of labor, 778–779
    Machiavelli on, 452
    in Merovingian society,
        257–260
    of papacy, 263–264, 319, 382,
        386–388
    people as source of, 408
    rebellions against state,
        586–590
    in Rome, 146
    of rural elites, 669–670
    of state (18th century), 580–586
    tools of, 424–426
Political science, 451–452, 494
Political structure. See
    Government; specific types
Politics. See also Conservatism;
    Government; Liberalism;
    specific locations
    anti-Semitism in, 782–785
    artists and, 776–777
    Catholicism and, 722
    democratic, 40
    in England, 655, 709–710
    in Ireland, 781
    mass, 753–762, 778–786

Politics *(continued)*
  in Middle Ages, 380–393
  natural law and, 485
  Nazification of German,
    850–851
  Realpolitik in, 695
  in Rome, 158–159, 177–180
  Russia and, 960–961
  television and, 919
  after World War I, 823–826
  after World War II, 882–889
Politiques, 463, 474
Politkovskya, Anna, 961*(i)*
Poliziano, Angelo, 415, 424
Polke, Sigmar, 927–928
Pollock, Jackson, 911
Pollution
  from factories, 665
  globalization and, 967–968
  in Soviet Union, 943
Polo, Marco, 390
Polo team, Anglo-Indian, 751*(i)*
Poltava, battle of, 551
Polyculture, Mediterranean, 29
Polygyny, 240
Polytheism
  in Arabia, 240
  in Canaan, 44
  Christianity and, 190*(m),*
    191–192, 211–213
  Greek, 130
  Mesopotamian, 10
  Roman, 209
Pompeii, 174*(i),* 576
Pompey, Gnaeus (Rome), 154*(m),*
    162–163
Poniatowski, Stanislaw August
    (Poland), 597
Pontifex maximus (chief Roman
    priest), 145, 210, 211
Poor people. *See also* Poverty
  attitude toward, 524
  in cities, 541, 542, 667–668
  in Enlightenment, 578
  as Greek citizens, 57–58
  in Hellenistic world, 123
  relief for, 447–448
  in Rome, 158–159, 162
Pop art, 927–928, 928*(i)*
Popes. *See also* Great Schism;
    Papacy; specific popes
  expansion of power by,
    263–264
  German kings and, 298
  in Italy, 263–264, 686
  letters sent by, 254*(f)*

multiple (1046), 314
Napoleon and, 629–630
taxation of clergy by, 387–388
Popolo (people), 388–389
Popular culture. *See also* Art(s);
    Culture; Mass media
  in 18th century, 518–521,
    523–524
Populares (Rome), 159
Popular Front
  in France, 855
  in Spain, 859
Population. *See also* Agriculture;
    Food(s)
  birthrate decline and, 768
  Black Death and, 401*(f)*
  of Britain, 553
  Christian (3rd century), 190*(m)*
  in cities, 537, 540, 666–667
  Dutch, 548–549
  of Egypt, 18
  famine and, 684
  foreign-born in Europe, 905
  of French colonies, 846
  as global issue, 969–970
  of Greek slaves, 58
  growth of, 475, 537, 577, 769
  of Rome, 147, 162, 185
  of Sparta, 64
  after Thirty Years' War, 472,
    476, 479
  worldwide growth of, 969*(f)*
Populists (Russia), 760
Pornography, 570–571
Porphyry (Greek philosopher),
    211
Porta Nigra (Trier), 253, 253*(i)*
Port Arthur, battle at, 788
Portugal, 362*(m),* 940, 977
  African trading posts of, 536
  American settlement by, 431,
    535
  Brazil and, 434, 653
  explorations by, 431, 432–433
  inflation in, 939
  Napoleon and, 638, 640
  reconquista as crusade and,
    363*(i)*
  slave trade and, 435, 530, 531,
    643, 676
  Spain and, 360, 458, 465, 472
Poseidon (god), 55
Positivism, 724, 774–775
Possessed, The (Dostoevsky), 761
Postindustrialism, society, culture,
    and, 917–947

Postmodernism, 984–985
Potatoes, 684
Potemkin (movie), 829
Potemkin mutiny, 790
Potocki family (Polish Ukraine),
    540
Potosí, 435
Potsdam, World War II meeting at,
    872–874, 888
Pottery. *See* Art(s); Black-figure
    painting; Red-figure
    painting; specific works
    and types
Poulain de la Barre, François, 523
Poussin, Nicolas, 519, 520*(i)*
Poverty. *See also* Poor people
  in Africa, 902
  of Cistercian churches, 321
  in Enlightenment, 577–578
  of factory workers, 665
  female, 895
  health and, 970
  religious orders of, 319–322
  in Rome, 156–157, 208*(f)*
Power (political). *See* Political
    power
Power politics. *See* Realpolitik
Praetor (Rome), 149
Praetorian guard (Rome), 172, 178
Pragmatic Sanction (Austria),
    552–553
Pragmatic Sanction of Bourges,
    421
Pragmatists, 775
Prague, 404, 688, 935
Prague Spring, 935, 935*(m),* 936*(i),*
    946
Praise of Folly, The (Erasmus), 439
Pravda (Soviet newspaper), 848,
    957
Praxiteles, 126, 126*(i)*
Predestination, 442–443
Pregnancy. *See also* Abortion; Birth
    control
  birth control and, 750
  out of wedlock, 580
  social legislation and, 895–896
Premarital intercourse, 479
Presbyterians and Presbyterianism,
    468, 503, 504
Presley, Elvis, 908
Press. *See also* Newspapers
  Milton on freedom of, 518
Price, Richard, 620
Priests, 410. *See also* Clergy
  in Hellenistic kingdoms, 122

Primary school systems, 674, 714
Prime ministers, 475
    in England, 548, 825, 940–942
    in France, 757
    in Italy, 781–782
Primogeniture, 293–294
Prince, The (Machiavelli), 452
Princeps (Rome), 205
Princes. See also specific rulers
    courts of, 450
    in Germany, 350, 352–353
Princess of Cleves, The (Madame de
    Lafayette), 496, 522
Princip, Gavrilo, 796–797, 798(i)
Principalities, in Germany, 381
Principate (Rome), 171–173, 182,
    196–197, 204, 205
Principia Mathematica (Newton),
    484
Printing
    innovations in, 756
    invention of press, 437–438,
    437(i)
Prisca, 191
Prison camps, Soviet, 848, 897
Prisoners, in concentration camps,
    866–868, 867(i)
Prisoners of war
    German, 890
    Grotius on, 485
    Soviet, 883, 884(m)
Production. See also Agriculture;
    Industry
    in 1870s and 1880s, 743–744
    World War II and, 868
Productivity, in 1920s, 827
Professions
    in 19th century, 714
    middle class in, 575, 747
    women in, 715
Profits
    in money economy, 305–306
    from slave trade, 435
Project Head Start, 931
Prokofiev, Sergei, 848
Proletarians, in Rome, 160
Proletariat, 683, 755, 934
Prometheus (Greek mythology),
    61, 647
Propaganda
    during cold war, 911–912
    in fascist Italy, 835
    Hitler's use of, 849
    in World War I, 810, 819, 829
    World War II and, 861,
    868–869

Property. See also Inheritance
    church (France), 603
    in Hammurabi's code, 14
    in Napoleonic code, 632
    private, 569, 682
    in Rome, 143–144, 209
    slaves as, 59
    of women, 291(f), 710, 770–771
Prophets
    Greek, 56
    Jewish, 46
Prosperity
    in 1920s, 828–829
    after World War II, 884, 894,
    906
Prostitutes and prostitution, 175,
    524, 579, 978
    in cities, 668
    in former Soviet Union, 959
    international sex rings and, 978
    regulation of, 713
    in Rome, 144, 157
    women's work against, 659, 674
Protagoras (Athens), 92
Protectorates, French, 676
Protest(s). See also Strikes; specific
    movements
    from 1960s to 1989, 929–937,
    945–947
    in China (1989), 945
    in Czechoslovakia, 916(i), 917,
    935, 946
    in Ireland, 757, 940
    in Italy, 782
    labor, 754
    against nation-state, 717–719
    in Rome, 175
    in Russia, 789–790
    by students, 932–933, 934–935,
    937, 945
    technology and, 918, 945, 957
    by women, 933, 934(i)
    in World War I, 812
    after World War I, 817–818
Protestantism, 432, 458, 513. See
    also Calvin, John, and
    Calvinism; Luther, Martin;
    Lutheranism; specific groups
    in c. 1648, 489(m)
    in Dutch Republic, 556
    Edict of Nantes and, 463, 498,
    567
    in England, 443–444, 455,
    467–469, 507, 547
    in France, 455, 462–464, 498,
    567, 584, 610, 630

    in Holy Roman Empire, 470
    in Ireland, 826, 940
    paganism and, 523
    in postindustrial society, 929
    reform societies and, 673–674
    revivalism and, 438, 544, 572,
    573, 646
    Schmalkaldic League and, 456
    in Scotland, 456, 547–548
    spread of, 441–444
Protestant Reformation, 440–443,
    442(f), 445–448, 455,
    457(m). See also Calvin,
    John, and Calvinism;
    Luther, Martin; specific
    groups
Proto-industrialization, 661
Proudhon, Pierre-Joseph, 682, 717
Provence, Germany and, 351
Provinces, Roman, 153, 158, 182,
    226–227
Provincial Letters (Pascal), 497
Provisional Government (Russia),
    813
Proxy wars, 901
Prussia, 650, 679. See also Junkers
    agriculture in, 540
    aristocracy in, 574
    armed forces in, 552, 580
    Bismarck and, 705–706
    clergy in, 722
    Congress of Vienna and, 642
    Dutch Republic and, 596
    education in, 584
    France and, 605–606, 608, 718
    German unification and,
    705–708, 707(m)
    Great Britain and, 580
    after Great Northern War,
    551–552
    industrialization in, 664
    Napoleon and, 636–637
    Pietism in, 544
    Poland and, 618, 618(m)
    Poland-Lithuania and, 514, 552,
    580
    reforms in, 637–638
    revolutionary movement in, 687
    Seven Years' War and, 582
    slave trade and, 531
    War of the Austrian Succession
    and, 553
    War of the Polish Succession
    and, 552
Psalters, 249, 273, 359(i)
Psychoanalysis, 767, 773, 774

Psychology, 773, 927
Ptolemaic rulers (Egypt), 119, 121, 122–123, 124, 131
   Ptolemy I, 119
   Ptolemy II, 123
   Ptolemy III, 131
   Ptolemy V, 108(i)
Ptolemy (astronomer), 481, 482
Public health, 554, 559, 668(m), 713, 970
Public life. See also Lifestyle
   arts in, 542–543
   in Athens, 82–83
   coffeehouses and, 528(i)
   in Rome, 172–173, 172(i)
Public opinion, 587–588
Public policy, 986
Public speaking, in Rome, 144
Public works
   in Great Depression, 853
   of Louis XIV, 497
   in Rome, 227
Publishing, in France, 570
Puccini, Giacomo, 778
Puerperal fever, 713
Puerto Rico, 653, 788
Pugachev, Emelian, 587
Pugachev rebellion, 587, 587(m)
Pump priming, 851, 854
Punch, 669(i)
Punic Wars, 152–155
Punishment
   in Hammurabi's code, 14
   by Hebrews, 45
   in Persia, 42
   in Rome, 205
   of slaves, 59, 533
   torture and, 486
   wergeld as, 226
Purges
   Lenin and, 833
   by Stalin, 847–848, 885, 897
Puritanism. See also Calvin, John, and Calvinism
   in England, 467–468, 502–503, 504
   paganism and, 523
Putin, Vladimir, 957, 961
Putting-out system, 661, 664
Pylos, 33, 102
Pyramids, in Egypt, 20–21, 20(i)
Pyxis, 279(i)

Qaddafi, Muammar, 971
Qing dynasty (China), 717, 789(m), 791, 792

Quakers, 504, 676
Quantum theory, 775
Quebec, 499
Queens. See also Kings and kingdoms; Monarchs and monarchies; specific rulers
   in Egypt, 23–24, 23(i), 124, 134, 163, 164(i), 171
   Hellenistic, 122–123
   in Sumer, 10
Quest of the Holy Grail, 377
Quietism, 544
Quinine, Africa and, 733
Quirini, Lauro, 413, 423
Qur'an, 47, 241–242, 241(i), 243, 245
Quraysh tribe, 241, 242

Race and racism
   in Catholic church in Americas and Africa, 449–450
   in colonies, 535
   Darwin and, 724
   decline in fertility and, 769–770
   in France, 942
   in Great Depression, 844
   imperialism and, 731, 735
   in Nazi Germany, 851–852
   in United States, 854, 931
   World War I and, 808
   World War II and, 868–869
Racine, Jean-Baptiste, 496–497, 522
Radical democracy, in Athens, 81–82, 91, 103
Radicalism
   France and, 685
   Islamic, 971
   Russia and, 760–761
   after World War I, 817–818
Radical right, 782
Radio, 829, 830, 835, 851, 854, 854(i), 868, 910, 911–912, 918, 926
Radioactivity, 775, 967
Radio telescope, 921
Railroads, 690, 699, 740
   in Asia and Africa, 662
   in Belgium, 662
   in England, 659, 661–662
   in Hungary, 681
   in Italy, 658(i), 704
   lines, 662(f)
   in Russia, 670, 743
   state power and, 662
   in United States, 662

Rain, Steam, and Speed: . . . (Turner), 670
Rainforests, clearing of, 967
Raison d'état, 475
Rákóczi, Ferenc, 552
Ramadan, 242–243
Ranters (England), 504
Rape, 578, 890, 955
Rape of Nanjing, 858
Rational investigation, Bayle on, 556
Rationalism, 69, 679, 929
Rationing
   in World War I, 811
   in World War II, 868
Rauschenberg, Robert, 927
Ravenna
   Aachen and, 281
   Exarchate of, 248, 264
   Justinian in, 229(i)
   Theodora in, 228(i)
   as western Roman capital, 207
Raw materials. See also specific materials
   from Africa, 732, 733
   from Asia, 732, 736
   global need for, 975
   natural resources in U.S. and, 742
Raymond d'Aguiliers, 326
Raynal, Guillaume (Abbé), 566(i), 567, 571(f)
Razin, Stenka, 517, 517(i)
Reading, 542, 577. See also Literacy
Reagan, Ronald, 942, 945
Reaganomics, 942
Real estate bubble, 976
Realism
   in arts, 719–722, 721(i)
   Roman, 156
Realpolitik, 695, 702, 705–708, 710, 722, 937
Reason. See also Logic; Rationalism
   Descartes on, 484
   Enlightenment and, 564, 568, 571
   faith and, 369–370
   limits of, 571–573
   scholastics and, 376
   Socrates and, 94
Rebellions. See Revolts and rebellions
Rebel Without a Cause (movie), 908
Reccared (Visigoths, Spain), 262

Receipt Rolls (England), 348

Recessions
in 17th century, 476–479, 479–480
oil and, 918

Reconquista (Spain), 315, 360–361, 362(m), 363(i)

Recovery
in Europe (1920s), 823–829
after financial crisis (2008), 976–977
after World War II, 890–898, 913

Recycling, 968

Red Army (Soviet), 814(i), 815, 818, 892, 897

Red Army Faction, 940

Red Brigades, 940

Red-figure painting, 55(i), 68(i), 74(i)

Redistributive economy, 10, 13, 30

Reds (faction), in Russian civil war, 814

Red Sea, 716

Red Shirts (Italy), 704, 704(i), 705

Red Terror (Jacobin France), 615

Reflections upon Marriage (Astell), 558–559

Reform(s). *See also* specific reforms and locations
in agriculture, 585
British parliamentary, 587–588
in Czechoslovakia, 935
Diocletian and, 204
educational, 674, 714–715
in England, 295–296, 347, 503, 654–655, 757
Enlightenment and, 563–564, 565, 567–568, 570
in France, 585, 586, 684–685
Gregorian, 315–316
industrialization and, 659
in Japan, 717
of popular culture, 523–524
in Prussia, 637–638
religion and, 24, 432, 440–444, 445–447, 673–674, 750
in Roman Catholic church, 312–322, 445, 448–450
in Rome, 158–159
in Russia, 638, 699–702, 790
social, 673–676, 749–750
in Soviet Union, 833, 930, 943–945
state-sponsored, 583–586
in urban areas, 667–668
in West, 940–943

Reform Act (England, 1884), 756–757

Reformation
Catholic Counter-Reformation, 445, 448–450, 457(m)
Protestant, 440–443, 442(f), 445–448, 457(m)

Reform Bills (England)
in 1832, 655, 689
in 1867, 709

Reformed church, 443

Refrigeration, 742

Refugees
from Afghanistan wars, 977
from former Soviet bloc, 959
after World War I, 824
after World War II, 883, 884(m), 891(i)

Regents, in Dutch Republic, 467, 509

Regional departments, in France, 603, 604(m)

Regional nationalism, 965

Regulus, Marcus Atilius (Rome), 156–157

Reichstag (Germany), 708, 778, 812, 849, 850
postmodern style of, 984, 985(i)

Reims, 338

Reinsurance Treaty, 760, 762

Relativists, 775

Relativity theory, 776

Relics and reliquaries (Christian), 218, 251, 255–256, 256(i)

Relief. *See also* Social welfare; Welfare state
organizations for, 673
for poor, 447–448
in World War I, 810

Religion(s). *See also* Caliphs; Crusades; Gods and goddesses; Monotheism; Polytheism; Reformation; specific religions
in 19th century, 722–723
in 1930s, 857
Black Death and, 401–402
in Byzantine Empire, 250–251, 274
in cities, 357–359
civilization and, 4
during cold war, 906
decolonization and, 899
in Dutch Republic, 466–467
education and, 714
in Egypt, 2(i), 18–19

in England, 455, 502–503
Enlightenment and, 555–556, 563, 564, 566–568
in Europe (c. 1648), 489(m)
in France, 455, 462–464, 497–498, 610
Greek, 54–55, 86–87
Hellenistic, 130–131
Hittite, 27
Holy Alliance and, 643–644
in homes, 410
humanism and, 438–439
independence movements and, 899
Israelites and, 44–47
Mesopotamian, 10
Mycenaean, 32
Napoleon and, 629–630, 633
Neo-Assyrian, 41
paganism and, 523–524
after Peace of Westphalia, 473
Persian, 43–44
in postindustrial society, 929
reforms and, 432, 440–444, 445–447, 673–674, 750
revivals in, 438, 544–546, 572–573, 646
in Rome, 144–145, 169–170
in schools, 978(i)
secular worldview vs., 481–488
Sophists on, 92
in Spain, 425–426
Thirty Years' War and, 470–475
wars of, 455, 462–464, 502, 568
in Wessex, 295–296

Religious orders. *See also* Monasticism and monasteries; specific orders
in Middle Ages, 357–358, 364
poverty, 319–322
for women, 358, 373, 723

Religious Society of Friends. *See* Quakers

Religious toleration. *See also* Anti-Semitism
Charles V and, 456
in Dutch Republic, 466–467, 556
in Enlightenment, 555–556, 564, 567, 571
in France, 455, 463, 584, 632
by Joseph II (Austria), 584
by Ottoman Turks, 469
in Persian Empire, 42

Remarque, Erich Maria, 831, 851

Renaissance, 411–418, 450
    arts in, 414–418
    Byzantine, 270, 272–274
    humanism in, 412–413
    Islamic, 278–279
    Italian, 412–418
Reparations
    after World War I, 819, 821
    World War II and, 888
Representative government
    in England, 385–386
    in English North American
        colonies, 512
    in Spain, 385
Repression
    in France, 681
    in Russia, 762
    in Soviet bloc, 930
Reproduction
    Aristotelian view of, 559
    biological research on, 724
    ovism doctrine and, 559
    technology for, 922–923
Reproductive rights, 933
Republic(s). See also Roman
        republic; specific locations
    in 15th century, 422–423
    in former Soviet Union, 957,
        958(m)
    in France, 606, 611, 615,
        684–685, 757, 782–783, 891
    in Italy, 686
    Rousseau on, 569
    in Spain, 859
Republic, The (Plato), 113
Republicanism (Spain), 859
Republican Party (U.S.), 710
Republic of letters, 564
Republic of Virtue (France), 607,
    609–611
Research
    genetic, 922, 925
    investments in, 924, 926
    military, 883–884, 893
    scientific, 484
Resistance. See also Protest(s);
        Revolts and rebellions;
        specific locations
    to imperialism, 736
    movements in World War II,
        869, 870, 890, 891, 907
Res publica (Rome), 146
Restoration
    in England, 506–508
    of European regimes, 643, 645,
        650

Reunification
    of Germany, 947
    of Poland, 824
Revenue. See Economy
Revisionism, in socialism, 779
Revivals, religious, 438, 544–546,
    572–573, 646
Revolts and rebellions. See also
        Protest(s)
    in 1820s, 650–653, 650(m)
    in 1830s, 628, 653–654
    in Austrian Netherlands, 597
    against British in India,
        715–716
    Decembrist Revolt, 651, 674
    Dutch, 465, 466, 596–597
    in eastern Europe, 898
    in France, 406, 494–495, 500,
        586–587, 612, 615,
        718–719
    in Greece, 59, 651–652
    in Ionia, 76
    in Italy, 686
    Jacobite, 548
    Jacquerie, 407
    by Jews, 186, 188
    in Neo-Assyrian Empire, 41
    in Ottoman Empire, 759–760,
        792
    Paris Commune and, 718–719
    by peasants, 393, 472, 586–587
    in Poland, 597
    Pugachev Rebellion, 587,
        587(m)
    in Russia, 669–670
    in St. Domingue, 619, 619(m)
    in Soviet Union (1921), 833
    in Spain, 472, 638–640
    against state power, 586–590
    Wat Tyler's Rebellion, 407
Revolution(s). See also specific
        locations and types
    of 1830s, 628, 653–654
    of 1848, 684–689, 688(f),
        691–692
    English, 588
    suppression of movements,
        651–652
    in technology, 918–923
    World War I and, 812–814
Revolutionary Tribunal (France),
    608, 614, 615
Revolutionary War in America. See
    American War of
    Independence

Rhetoric, Roman training in, 144
Rhineland
    demilitarization of, 822
    German invasion of, 858–859
    Jews in, 325
Rhine River region
    cities in, 307
    as Roman frontier, 194
    after World War I, 819
    after World War II, 883
Rhodes, Cecil, 735, 786
Rhône River region, 253
Richard I (the Lion-Hearted,
        England), 348–349, 355,
        359
Richelieu, Armand-Jean du
        Plessis (Cardinal), 471, 472,
        475, 494
Rich people. See Wealth
Riga, 748
Rights. See also specific groups
    civil rights movement and, 882,
        908, 931
    in France, 645
    of Jews, 722
    in Magna Carta, 349
    in Nazi Germany, 850
    of women, 675, 725, 770–771,
        779–781, 933
Right wing (political), 825, 855
Rijswijk, Peace of (1697), 500
Ring of the Nibelung, The (Wagner),
    722
Riots. See also Revolts and
        rebellions
    in Britain (1981), 941
    food shortages and, 585,
        586–587
    Gordon, 588
    Nika, 231
    urban, 931, 933–934
Rite of Spring, The (Stravinsky), 777
Rivers. See Transportation; specific
    river regions
Roads and highways
    in 12th century, 308
    Autobahn and, 851
    in Greece, 52
    Ottoman, 408
    Roman, 151(m)
Roaring Twenties, 804, 823
Robber-knights, 439(i)
Robespierre, Maximilien, 607,
        608, 610, 612, 614–615
Robinson Crusoe (Defoe), 544
Robots, in Japan, 975

Rob Roy (Scott), 650
Rockefeller, John D., 742, 744
Rockefeller Foundation, 966
Rocket (railroad engine), 659, 660
Rock music, 908, 909(*i*), 927, 980
Rococo style, 537(*i*), 542–543,
    543(*i*), 570, 577
Roehm, Ernst, 850
Roger I (Norman), 315
Roland, Jeanne, 606, 608
Rolin, Nicolas, 415–417
Rolling Stones, 980
Rollo (Vikings), 288
Roma. *See* Gypsies
Roma (Rome), 298(*i*)
Roman baths, 173
Roman Catholicism, 261, 262, 929.
    See also Councils
    (Christian); Inquisition;
    Investiture Conflict; Papacy;
    Popes; specific orders
    in c. 1648, 489(*m*)
    in Austria, 583, 708
    Babylonian captivity of church,
    388
    Byzantium and, 264
    Carolingian dynasty and, 281
    Concordat of Worms and, 317,
    332
    Counter-Reformation of, 445,
    448–450
    in Dutch Republic, 556
    in eastern Europe, 275
    in England, 443, 455, 467,
    502–503, 504, 506, 507–508,
    588, 655
    in France, 462–464, 497–498,
    570, 599, 603–604, 610, 646
    Galileo and, 482–483
    in Germany, 299, 857
    Greek Orthodox church and,
    315
    hierarchy in, 358
    in Holy Roman Empire, 470
    in Hungary, 299
    of Indians, 431
    in Ireland, 548, 781, 940
    in Italy, 835–836
    Luther and, 440–441
    of Magyars, 289
    mission in Middle Ages,
    370–375
    Napoleon and, 628
    paganism and, 523–524
    Philip II (Spain) and, 465
    politics and, 722

    Protestant Reformation and,
    440–444
    reforms of, 312–322, 432, 906
    religious orders of poverty and,
    319–322
    revival of, 544–545, 646
    in Scotland, 455–456
    social reform and, 673–674
    in Soviet bloc, 896–897
    in Spain, 262, 547, 639, 758
    Zwingli and, 441–442
Romance literature, 357
Roman Empire, 140. *See also*
    Byzantine Empire; Cult(s);
    Eastern Roman Empire;
    Holy Roman Empire; Pax
    Romana; Roman republic;
    Rome; Western Roman
    Empire
    in 284 C.E., 198(*m*)
    in 3rd century C.E., 194–197,
    197(*m*)
    under Augustus, 164(*i*),
    166(*m*), 170, 171–178,
    177(*i*), 181(*m*)
    barbarians in, 204
    Charlemagne and, 283
    Christianity in, 170, 186–193,
    208–209, 210–213, 213(*m*)
    culture of, 135
    division of, 205, 206–207,
    206(*m*), 207(*m*)
    dominate in, 205–210
    economy in, 207–209
    expansion of, 180, 181(*m*)
    features and languages of, 183(*m*)
    Frankish kingdoms and, 252
    Golden Age in, 180–186
    heirs to (c. 750), 265(*m*)
    Islam in, 239
    loyalty in, 169–170
    politics in, 177–180
    Vandals and, 224
Romanesque architecture, 341–342,
    342(*i*), 343(*i*)
Romania, 180, 699, 794, 824, 964
    abandoned children in, 947
    cold war and, 886
    collapse of communism in,
    946–947
    in Little Entente, 822
    Soviets and, 872
    World War II and, 864, 871
Romanian people, 679, 784
Romanization, 182
Roman law, 148, 182, 184, 205, 225

Romanov dynasty, 813. *See also*
    specific tsars
Roman republic, 166(*m*). *See also*
    Roman Empire; Rome
    civil wars in, 158–164
    downfall of, 161–164
    early, 140, 148–150
    imperialism by, 150–158
    Punic Wars and, 152–155
Romanticism, 571–573, 646–650
Romanus IV (Byzantine Empire),
    324
Rome, 149(*m*), 151, 205–206, 705,
    708. *See also* Papacy;
    Roman Empire; Roman
    republic; Wars and warfare;
    specific wars
    armed forces in, 148, 151, 153,
    160, 163, 172
    bishops of, 187, 212–213
    census in, 153(*f*)
    citizenship in, 152
    civil wars in, 158–164, 170–171,
    179, 196–197
    coins in, 161(*i*), 165(*i*), 172,
    195, 195(*i*)
    culture of, 151
    economy in, 181–182, 181(*m*),
    194–195
    education in, 144, 175–176
    entertainment in, 175
    Etruscans and, 146(*m*),
    147–148, 147(*i*)
    expansion of, 140, 145–146,
    151–152, 153–155, 154(*m*),
    180
    families in, 142–144
    five good emperors in, 180
    founding of, 138(*i*), 139, 145
    Greek culture and, 140, 147,
    155–156
    Hellenistic kingdoms and, 124,
    134(*m*)
    housing in, 157(*i*)
    law in, 148, 182, 184, 205,
    225–226
    lifestyle in, 173–175, 180–186
    literature in, 151, 176–177
    monarchy in, 145–148
    patron-client system in,
    141–142
    provincial government by, 158
    religion in, 144–145
    republic of, 686
    society in, 140–144, 156–158
    women in, 156

Rome (city), sacks of, 151, 222, 452
Rome, Treaty of, 894
Rome-Berlin Axis, 859
Rommel, Erwin, 870
Romulus and **Remus,** 138(i), 139, 145
Romulus Augustulus (Rome), 224
Roosevelt, Eleanor, 853(i), 854
Roosevelt, Franklin Delano, 853–854, 853(i), 858, 864, 872, 885
Roosevelt, Sarah, 853(i)
Rosetta stone, 108(i), 629
Rossbach, battle at, 581
Rosselini, Roberto, 911
Rotten boroughs (England), 588
Roundheads (England), 503
Rousseau, Jean-Jacques, 565, 566(i), 568, 569–570, 571, 571(f), 576, 580, 610
Roxane (wife of Alexander the Great), 117, 118
Royal Academy of Sciences (France), 521
Royal African Company (England), 509
Royal courts. See Courts (law); Courts (royal)
Royal Dutch Shell, 827
Royalists
    in England, 503, 504
    in France, 615, 630, 633, 645
Royal Society (London), 521, 557
Royalty. See Kings and kingdoms; Monarchs and monarchies; Queens; specific kingdoms and rulers
Rubber, vulcanization of, 669, 769
Rubicon River, Caesar at, 163
Ruble (Russia), 976
Rudolf (Habsburgs, Germany), 382
Ruhr basin, World War I and, 821, 825
Ruler cults, 131
Rump Parliament (England), 504, 506
Runnymede, Magna Carta and, 349
Rural areas. See also Farms and farming
    arts and customs from, 752
    Byzantine, 249
    commercial revolution in, 311–312
    in France, 602
    industrialization and, 667
    migration from, 748

peasants in, 292
in Soviet bloc, 896
television in, 919
Rus, 270. See also Russia
Rushdie, Salman, 982
Russia, 270, 650, 754. See also Russian Republic; Russian Revolution; Soviet Union; World War II; specific rulers
    1848 revolutions and, 689
    absolutism in, 517–518
    agriculture in, 540
    Balkan region and, 275, 759–760, 794
    Baltic region and, 551
    Black Death in, 401
    Britain and, 793
    Byzantines and, 274–275
    Chechnya invasion by, 960–961
    civil war in, 814–816, 815(m), 824
    Crimean War and, 698–699
    Danubian principalities and, 652
    Decembrist Revolt in, 651
    domestic problems in, 760–762
    education in, 674, 689
    Enlightenment and, 570
    epidemics in, 667
    as European power, 549–552
    France and, 696, 698, 793
    Franco-Austrian alliance and, 580
    Great Northern War and, 551, 551(m)
    Huns in, 222
    imperialism of, 698, 715, 736–737, 737(m)
    industrialization in, 664, 743, 789
    Jews in, 762, 762(i), 782
    landowners in, 702
    liberalism in, 681
    Lithuania and, 419, 583
    minorities in, 702
    Mongols in, 389, 389(m), 390
    Muscovy and, 469
    Napoleon I and, 636–637, 640
    nationalism in, 679
    nobility in, 517, 550–551, 574, 681, 699, 700, 701–702
    Orthodox Christianity in, 462
    Ottoman Empire and, 760
    Pan-Slavism and, 709, 759
    peasants in, 587, 621

Poland and, 618, 618(m), 643, 654, 702
Poland-Lithuania and, 552, 580, 583
    political persecution in, 779
    population decline in, 970
    realist literature in, 720
    reforms in, 638, 699–702, 790
    revolts against, 654
    serfs in, 517, 550, 574, 587, 638, 669–670
    Seven Years' War and, 581
    Slavophiles in, 679
    social order in, 715
    threats to empire of, 789–790
    in Three Emperors' League, 758
    Time of Troubles in, 469
    Turks and, 652
    Ukraine and, 513
    Westernization of, 549–552, 679
    women in, 550, 702, 790
    World War I and, 798, 804, 805, 807
Russian Academy of Sciences, 549, 550
Russian Mafia, 959
Russian Orthodox Church, 401, 462, 469, 518, 551, 722
Russian people, migration from former Soviet bloc, 959
Russian Republic, 957. See also Russia; Soviet Union (former)
Russian Revolution
    of 1905, 789–790
    of 1917, 779, 812–814, 881
Russification, 789, 790
    under Alexander II (Russia), 702
    in eastern Europe, 897
Russo-Japanese War, 786, 788, 789(m), 792, 796
Russo-Polish war, 513
Ruthenians, in Hungary, 784
Rwanda, 971

SA (Stürmabteilung), 850, 851
Saar basin, after World War I, 819
Sabines, 139
Sachs, Nelly, 907
Sacks
    of Constantinople, 354
    of Rome, 151, 222, 452
Sacraments (Christian), 191, 318–319, 440
    Fourth Lateran Council on, 371

Sacred music, 377–378
Sacred texts, 47
Sacrifice of Isaac, The (Ghiberti), 415, 415(i)
Sacrifices
    in Greece, 56, 86, 87
    polytheist, in Rome, 211
Sadat, Mohammed Anwar al-, 941(i)
Saddam Hussein. *See* Hussein, Saddam
Saducees, 187
Sahara region, 15
Saigon, 716
Sailors. *See also* Navies; Ships and shipping
    Kronstadt revolt by, 833
Saint(s). *See also* specific individuals
    relics of, 218, 251, 255–256, 256(i)
St. Bartholomew's Day Massacre (1572), 463
St. Catherine at Mount Sinai, monastery of, 219(i), 306
Saint-Denis, church of, 331
St. Domingue, 534, 619, 619(m), 636, 945
Saint-Germain-des-Prés (monastery), 286
St. Giles (London), 667
St. Helena, Napoleon on, 641
St. Paul's Outside the Walls (Rome), 386(i)
St. Peter's Basilica (Rome), 519
St. Petersburg, 549–550, 790. *See also* Leningrad; Petrograd
St. Peter's Fields, Peterloo massacre at, 654
Saint Phalle, Niki de, 928
Saint-Savin-sur-Gartempe, church of, 343(i)
Saint-Simon, Claude Henri de, 682
Saint-Simon, Louis de Rouvroy (duke of), 501
Sakhalin Islands, World War II and, 872
Saladin (Seljuk Empire), 359
Salamis, battle at, 79
Salem, Massachusetts, witchcraft trials in, 488
Sales taxes, in Britain, 941
Salian dynasty (Germany), 299
Salisbury, earl of, 413
Salons, 522, 565–566, 566(i), 575

Salt, taxation on, 574
SALT I. *See* Strategic Arms Limitation Treaty
Salvation, 449
    in Calvinist doctrine, 442
    in Christianity, 188
    by faith alone, 440–441
    Jansenists on, 497
    of Jews, 46
    Mass and, 319
    mystery cults for, 132
Same-sex households, 926
Samizdat culture, 930
Samurai (Japan), 738
Sand, George (Amandine-Aurore-Lucile Dupin Dudevant), 672, 672(i)
Sanitation
    in cities, 14, 553–554, 712, 713
    in Crimean War, 699, 700(i)
    in Rome, 173
    in Soviet Union, 833
    urbanization and, 667
Sans-culottes (French workers), 599, 600, 606, 614
Sanssouci (palace of Frederick II), 577
San Stefano, Treaty of, 760
Santa Maria Novella, 414, 414(i)
Sant'Andrea, church of (Vercelli), 344, 344(i)
San Vitale (Ravenna), 281
Sappho, 68
Saracens, Muslims as, 276
Sarajevo, Francis Ferdinand assassination in, 796
Sardinia, 153, 552, 608, 695, 703(m). *See also* Piedmont-Sardinia
Sargon (Akkad), 12
Sartre, Jean-Paul, 907
Sasanid Empire
    c. 600, 243, 247(m)
    Byzantine Empire and, 247, 247(m)
    Muslims in, 243
    Rome and, 197, 205
Satanic Verses, The (Rushdie), 982
Satellite kingdoms, of Napoleon, 637
Satellite republics, of Revolutionary France, 616
Satellites (artificial)
    in 1960s, 918
    communications, 918, 920, 921
    Sputnik, 898, 920

Satellite states. *See* Soviet bloc; Soviet Union
Satellite television, 918
Sati, in India, 646, 716
Satire
    in 1920s, 831
    by Erasmus, 439
Satraps (regional governors), in Persian Empire, 42
Satyagraha (Gandhi), 908
Saudi Arabia, 973
Savage Mind, The (Lévi-Strauss), 929
Savoy, 704
Saxons, 224, 281
Saxony, 441, 456, 551, 580, 642
Scandinavia, 288. *See also* Baltic region; Vikings; specific locations
    economy in, 894
    England and, 289, 296
    immigrants to, 905
    industrialization in, 743
    Lutheranism in, 441
Schiller, Friedrich, 649
Schism. *See* Great Schism
Schleswig, 705, 706
Schlieffen Plan, 806, 807
Schliemann, Heinrich, 30
Schmalkaldic League, 456
Schoenberg, Arnold, 778
Scholars and scholarship. *See also* Intellectual thought; specific disciplines and individuals
    in 12th century, 338–339
    Byzantine, 272–273
    in Carolingian renaissance, 284–285
    Islamic, 279
    Jewish, 212
    in late Roman Empire, 233
    Latin, 233
    printing and, 438
Scholastica (sister of Benedict of Nursia), 219
Scholasticism, 375–376
Schools, 542. *See also* Education
    in 12th and 13th centuries, 337
    attendance in, 714–715
    in Byzantine Empire, 249
    Christianity and, 438
    classical, 233–234
    in France, 610, 632
    Islamic, 279
    in Middle Ages, 338–341
    reforms of, 584, 674

Schools *(continued)*
　religion and, 978*(i)*
　in Rome, 175
Schuman, Robert, 894
Science, 462. *See also* Astronomy;
　　Medicine; Scientific
　　revolution; Technology;
　　specific fields
　in 1930s, 856–857
　Aristotle and, 114
　brain drain and, 926
　in Enlightenment, 555–557
　experimental, 129
　gender stereotypes and, 675
　Greek philosophy and, 69–70,
　　92–93
　Hellenistic, 129–130
　of the mind, 773–774
　Napoleon and, 632–633
　paradigm shift in, 776
　physics and, 774, 775–776,
　　856–857
　in postindustrial society,
　　920–923
　revolution in, 775–776
　space race and, 921
　training in, 715
　women in, 521, 522, 775, 776
Scientific method, 482, 484, 555
　social laws uncovered by, 750,
　　774
Scientific research, 484
Scientific revolution, 481–485
Scientific societies, 520
Sclavinia (Slavic lands), 298*(i)*
Scotland
　Calvinism in, 462
　Christianity in, 260, 261
　England and, 503
　in Great Britain, 505
　literacy in, 542
　Protestant and Catholic
　　divisions in, 455–456
Scott, Walter, 649–650
Scottish Parliament, 547
Scotus, John Duns. *See* Duns
　　Scotus, John
Scream, The (Munch), 766*(i)*, 777
Scribes
　Mesopotamian, 11*(i)*
　Roman, 233, 234*(i)*
Script. *See* Writing
Scriptures, Hebrew, 47, 187
Sculpture
　baroque, 519*(i)*
　Gothic, 379, 380

Greek, 85–86, 131*(i)*
　Hellenistic, 125*(i)*, 126*(i)*
　in Parthenon, 85
　Roman, 177, 177*(i)*
Scutage (tax), 349
Seaborne commerce
　Dutch and, 467
　Egyptian, 18
　Greek, 48, 52–53
Sea Peoples, 33, 34, 34*(m)*
Secondary education, 715
Second Balkan War, 794
Second Continental Congress, 589
Second Crusade, 325, 326–327,
　　361–362, 373
Second Empire (France), 686, 707,
　　757
Second Estate (France), 599
Second Great Awakening, 646
Second Industrial Revolution, 741
Second Intermediate Period
　　(Egypt), 22
Second International, 755, 756, 779
Second Moroccan Crisis, 794
Second of May, 1808, The (Goya),
　　639*(i)*
Second Punic War, 153*(f)*, 154
Second Reform Bill (England), 709
Second Republic (France), 686
Second Sex, The (Beauvoir), 907
Second Triumvirate (Rome),
　　170–171
Second Vatican Council (Vatican
　　II), 906
Second world (socialist bloc), 882
Second World War. *See* World
　　War II
Secret ballot, 756, 757
Secret police
　in Russia, 760, 790
　Soviet (KGB), 898, 957
Secret societies, in 1820s, 650
"Secret speech," of Khrushchev, 898
Sects. *See also* Religion(s); specific
　　groups
　English religious, 504
　Protestant, 929
Secularism
　Catholic church and, 312
　in French Revolution, 610
　religion and, 723
Secularization
　Enlightenment and, 568
　nonreligious foundations and,
　　481
Secular music, 377–378

Sedition laws, 810
Seekers (England), 504
Segregation, civil rights movement
　　and, 931
Seigneurial dues, 574, 599, 602
Selective breeding, 539
Seleucid kingdom, 119, 122, 131,
　　132, 162
Seleucus, 119
Self-determination
　for Canada, 677
　of Czechs, 810
　of ethnic groups in Germany,
　　687
　World War II and, 860, 872
Self-government, for cities and
　　towns, 310–311
Self-interest, Adam Smith on, 568
Seljuk Turks, 328
　in Anatolia, 333*(m)*
　First Crusade and, 323–324
　Third Crusade and, 359
Semitic languages, 8
Semitic peoples
　Chaldeans as, 41
　Hyksos as, 22
Sen, Amartya, 977
Senate
　in France, 641
　in Rome, 146, 149, 155, 159,
　　161, 172, 177–178
Senatorial order (Rome), 184, 208
Sensationalist press, 756
Separate spheres, 675–676, 827
Separatist movements, 965
September 11, 2001, terrorist
　　attacks, 973, 974*(i)*
"September massacres" (French
　　Revolution), 606
Septuagint, 132
Serbia, 270, 274, 759, 794, 796–797,
　　798, 888, 955
Serbs, 887
　in Austrian Empire, 679
　Bosnian, 955
　nationalism of, 784, 792, 955
　revolt against Turks, 651
　Srebrenica massacre by, 955
　World War I and, 810
　World War II and, 869
Serfs and serfdom. *See also*
　　Peasants; Slaves and slavery
　compulsory labor services and,
　　540
　in eastern Europe, 479–480
　in England, 407

in France, 602
industrialization and, 664
Joseph II and, 585
medieval, 291
in Poland, 618
in Prussia, 585, 637
in Russia, 517, 550, 574, 587, 638, 669–670
Russian emancipation of, 700–701, 701(i), 743
Serious Proposal to the Ladies, A (Astell), 558
Servants, 478, 531, 541, 578, 747
Servetus, Michael, 443
Service economy, 917
Service industries, Internet and, 979
Service workers, 924
Settlements. *See also* Cities and towns; Villages; specific locations
    Greek, 53
    oases as, 22–23
    permanent, 6–7
    world trade and, 535–537
Seurat, Georges, 752
Sevastopol, siege of, 699
Seven Years' War, 580–583, 581(m), 589
    France after, 597–598
    reforms after, 583–586
Severe acute respiratory syndrome (SARS), 970
Severus, Septimius (Rome), 195, 196
Seville, 434
Sex and sexuality. *See also* Homosexuals and homosexuality
    in 17th century, 479
    in 1920s, 828
    in Athens, 89, 91
    bishops and, 258
    Christian doctrine on, 217
    Freud on, 774
    in Greece, 60
    men and, 908–909
    patterns of, 578
    pill and, 922
    in postindustrial society, 927, 933
    reproductive technology and, 922–923
    sexual identity and, 768, 772, 774
    in Sparta, 63–64

urbanization and, 667–668
women and, 230, 748, 772
Sexism, Marie Curie and, 776
"Sexology," 772
Sex rings, international, 978
Sexual harassment, 755
Sexual Inversion (Ellis), 772
Sexual revolution, 927, 933
Shahadah (profession of faith), 243
Shakespeare, William, 182, 469, 486, 778
Shapur I (Sasanids), 197
Shelley, Mary, 627, 647
Sheriffs, in England, 347
Shi'at Ali, 244
Shi'ite Muslims, 244–245, 275, 276, 324, 327, 971, 972(m)
Ship money, 502
Ships and shipping, 153, 796
    convoy system of, 812
    lateen sail and, 432
    technology of, 432
    transatlantic, 480
    triremes and, 80, 80(i)
Shires (England), 298, 329
Shock treatment (economic), 941
Shopkeepers, 541
Show trials, 847
Shtetls, 513
Siberia, 681, 736, 737(m), 816
Sic et Non (Abelard), 339
Sicily, 103, 146(m), 686, 704
    Byzantines in, 248
    Frederick II in, 381–382
    governing of, 382
    immigration from, 748
    Muslims in, 300(m)
    Normans in, 300(m), 323, 333(m)
    Roger I and, 315
    Rome and, 153
    World War II and, 870
Sickingen, Franz von, 439(i)
Sidonius Apollinaris (Rome), 223
Sieyès, Emmanuel-Joseph, 599
Sigismund (Holy Roman Empire), 411, 419
Signori (Italy), 381, 388–389, 423
Sikhs, 536
Silent Spring (Carson), 967
Silesia, 515, 553, 581
Silver, 111(i), 431, 435, 454, 465
Simeon (hermit), 253
Simon de Montfort (England), 386
Simon Magus, 313
Simons, Menno, 447

Simony, 313, 314
Simyonov, Yulian, 911
Sin
    indulgences for, 409
    original, 217
Sinai, 16(m), 938, 938(m)
Singapore, 677, 864, 975, 975(m)
Sinn Fein (Ireland), 718
Sino-Japanese War, 788
Sinope, 699
Sinti people, 842, 852, 867
Sister republics, of France, 616, 617(m), 627
Sistine Chapel, 450
Six Acts (England), 654
Six Books of the Republic, The (Bodin), 485
Six-Day War, 938, 938(m)
Skepticism, doctrine of, 463
Skeptics, 128
Skin color, in Egypt, 18
Slav congress, 688
Slave code (Barbados), 512
Slaves and slavery. *See also* Forced labor; Serfs and serfdom; Slave trade
    from Africa, 434–435, 511–512, 530, 531
    Africa–New World system of, 431
    in American colonies, 511–512, 532–535
    in Athens, 90
    in Caribbean region, 436, 512, 618
    cotton industry and, 664
    criticism of, 435, 567
    in Egypt, 21
    before European voyages, 434
    France and, 511, 618
    in Greece, 58–59, 62
    Hebrews and, 45
    in Hellenistic kingdoms, 122
    justification of, 534–535
    lifestyle of, 532–533
    Locke and, 509
    Portuguese and, 434–435, 676
    Rome and, 174, 175
    Rousseau on, 569
    in Russia, 517
    Spain and, 434, 676
    in Sparta, 64
    in Sumer, 9
    treatment of, 533–534
    in United States, 590, 676, 710, 711

Slave trade, 434, 511, 591(m), 643.
    See also Africa; Slaves and
    slavery
  abolition of, 676
  in Atlantic system, 512, 529,
    530–535
  denunciation of, 567
  in European colonies, 532(f),
    533(f)
  growth of, 476, 512
  patterns of, 436
  slave ships in, 532, 534(i)
Slavophiles, in Russia, 679
Slavs, 274, 299
  in Austrian Empire, 679
  in Balkan region, 794
  Byzantine Empire and, 246,
    248, 270
  Christianity among, 275
  in concentration camps, 867
  nationalism of, 784
  in Nazi Germany, 842, 852
  Northern Crusades and, 363
  in Ottoman Empire, 759
  Pan-Slavism and, 709
  separate states of, 965
Slovak Fascist Party, 856
Slovakia, 964, 965
Slovaks, 855–856
  in Austro-Hungarian Empire,
    784
  independence of, 817
  nationalism of, 784
Slovenes (Slovenians), 810, 955
Slovenia, 955, 964
Slumdog Millionaire (movie), 984
Slums
  of global cities, 965
  in Rome, 162
Smallpox, 436, 554, 970
Smart car, 968, 968(i)
Smelting, 12
Smith, Adam, 568–569, 570, 571,
    571(f)
Smith, Zadie, 982
Smuggling, British, 638
Sobieski, Jan (Poland-Lithuania),
    513–514
Social classes. See Classes
Social Contract, The (Rousseau),
    569–570, 571(f)
Social contract theory, 508–509,
    590
Social Darwinism, 724, 725, 735,
    747, 773

Social Democratic Parties, 755,
    758–759, 778, 782, 796, 817,
    818, 930, 940
Social hierarchies. See Classes
Socialism, 681–683, 792
  divisions in, 778–779
  in France, 682, 942
  Nazis and, 850
  World War I and, 809, 817–818
Socialist Parties, in France, 755
Socialist realism, 848, 930
Socialist Revolutionaries (Russia),
    779
Social laws, 774
Social media, 986
Social networking, 954
Social order
  conservatism and, 645
  culture of, 719–725
  for nation building, 712–719
  reform of, 670–677
  rural, 669–670
  World War I and, 810–811
Social programs. See also Social
    welfare
  Reagan on, 942
  after World War I, 828
Social question, cultural responses
    to, 670–673
Social sciences
  in 19th century, 724–725
  Enlightenment and, 928–929
  in postindustrial society,
    928–929
Social Security Act (U.S., 1935),
    853
Social status
  in cities, 541–542
  clothing and, 542
  of rich, 574
Social War (Rome), 160
Social welfare. See also Welfare
    state
  Britain and, 674–675, 941
  in France, 641, 855
  global south and, 971
  in smaller states, 942
  in Sweden, 854, 942–943
  in United States, 942
Social work and social workers,
    774, 927
Societies (organizations). See also
    Academies
  women's reform, 674
  workers', 755–756

Society. See also Art(s); Culture;
    Lifestyle; Religion(s);
    specific locations
  in 1920s, 827–829
  agricultural revolution and,
    538–540
  arts and, 719–722
  barbarian, 221–227
  Byzantine, 248–249, 273–274
  capitalist, 568
  Christian, 212
  in cities, 540–542
  consumer, 537–538
  Dutch, 510–511
  Egyptian, 18–19
  in England, 540, 675, 709–710
  during Enlightenment,
    573–580
  European, 289
  feudal, 290–293
  in Great Depression, 844
  in Greece, 49, 58–61
  Hellenistic, 122–123
  hierarchy in, 4
  imperialism and, 746–753
  individuals and, 568–570
  Jews in Middle Ages, 373–374
  leprosy in, 374–375
  manners in, 521–523
  Marx on, 718
  medieval, 290–291
  under Napoleon, 633
  Neo-Assyrian, 41
  Neolithic, 7–8
  Paleolithic, 5–6
  peasant, 256–257
  reforms of (mid-19th century),
    673–676
  religion and, 444–450, 722–723
  Roman, 140–144, 146–148,
    148–150, 156–158, 174,
    184–185, 208–209, 225–227
  rural, 668–670
  scientific approach to problems
    of, 750
  socialists on, 681–682
  Soviet, 848
  Sumerian, 8–9
  in World War I, 804, 809–811,
    812
  after World War I, 823
  World War II and, 868–869
Society for the Prevention of
    Cruelty to Animals, 674
Society of Jesus (Jesuits). See Jesuits

Society of Revolutionary
    Republican Women, 613
Society of Supporters of the Bill of
    Rights, 588
Society of United Irishmen, 620
Sociology, 724
Socrates (Athens), 86, 90, 93–95,
    93(i), 112
Socratic method, 94
Sodomy, 579
Soissons, Council of, 340
Solaris (Lem), 920
Solar system
    age of, 921
    Aristarchus and, 129
Soldiers. *See also* Armed forces;
        Veterans; specific battles
        and wars
    as Christians, 212
    in crusades, 324–325, 325(i)
    in French revolutionary army,
        616
    Hellenistic, 120
    mercenaries as, 406
    in Napoleonic army, 640
    permanent army and, 406
    poverty of, 156–157
    Roman, 151, 163, 194
    in Russia, 812
    Soviet, 891–892
    in Thirty Years' War, 472
    in World War I, 806, 807–809,
        809(i), 817
    after World War I, 817, 824,
        827, 828
    in World War II, 864, 869
Solidarity movement, 945, 946
Solomon (Israelite), 46
Solon (Athens), 66, 68
Solzhenitsyn, Aleksandr, 898, 935
Somalia, 970, 971
Somme region, battle at, 807
Sony Corporation, 919
Sophia (Russia), 518
Sophie (Austria), 796
Sophists, 86, 90. 91, 92
Sophocles (Athens), 97, 98
Sorbonne, student riots at, 934
Sorrows of Young Werther, The
    (Goethe), 571–572
Soubirous, Bernadette (St.
    Bernadette of Lourdes),
    723
South (global), 970–971
South (U.S.), 710, 711

South Africa, 735, 786, 945, 975
South African War (Boer War),
    786, 796
South America
    colonization of, 480, 511, 535
    migration to, 748
    slavery in, 511
    western consumer economy
        and, 979
South Asia, immigrants from,
    905(i)
South Carolina, blacks in, 533
Southeast Asia, 432
    France and, 698
Southeast Asia Treaty Organization
    (SEATO), 900
Southern Africa, imperialism in,
    735
Southern Europe, economies of,
    479
Southern Hemisphere, emerging
    economies in, 975–976
South Korea, 900, 975, 975(m)
South Vietnam, 931, 937. *See also*
    Vietnam
Southwest (U.S.), 710
Southwest Africa, 788
Sovereignty, types of, 485
Soviet bloc, 889, 939
    birthrate in, 896, 926
    collapse of, 937, 943–947,
        948(m)
    dissent in, 897–898
    postindustrial work life in,
        924–925
    recovery in, 896–898
    reforms in, 930
    refugees from, 959
    revolutions of 1989 in, 945–947
    scientific findings in, 926
    Stalinism and, 896–897
    "starvation music" (Arvo Pärt)
        in, 928
    women in, 910
    youth in, 908
Soviet republics, after World War I,
    818
Soviets (councils), 790, 813
Soviet Union. *See also* Russia;
        Soviet Union (former)
    in 1920s, 832–834
    Afghanistan and, 943, 945
    Berlin and, 889
    Chernobyl catastrophe in, 944
    China and, 918, 938

in cold war, 885–888, 900, 931
collapse of, 918, 944–945,
    948(m), 954, 956–957
Cuba and, 912
Czech protests and, 917, 935
détente and, 938, 942
dissidents in, 935, 936
eastern Europe and, 896–898,
    946
effects of collapse of, 954–961
German occupation by, 874,
    888–889
Gorbachev in, 918, 943–945
under Khrushchev, 881, 898,
    911, 912
naming of, 834
Nazi attack on, 864
Nazi-Soviet Pact and, 862–863
nuclear power in, 921
oil and, 939
Poland and, 863
purges in, 833, 847–848, 885
Reagan and, 945
reforms in, 833, 930, 943–945
scientific establishment in, 926
social welfare in, 895–896
Spanish Civil War and, 859
Stalin in, 842, 846–848
as superpower, 882, 884–885
television in, 919
women in, 848, 868, 885,
    895–896, 910
World War II and, 864,
    868–869, 869–870, 871,
    883, 884–885
Soviet Union (former). *See also*
    Commonwealth of
    Independent States; Russia
artists and writers in, 983
Chechnya and, 957, 960–961
consequences of Soviet collapse
    and, 956–957
corruption in, 960
countries of (c. 2000), 958(m)
international politics and,
    960–961
market economy in, 957,
    959–960
Space exploration, 898, 920–921
Spain, 456, 552, 757, 977. *See also*
    Cortes (Spain); Spanish
    Civil War; specific rulers
    in 15th century, 419
    American settlement by, 535
    baroque churches of, 487

Spain (continued)
  Basque nationalists in, 940,
    940(m), 965
  in Common Market, 942
  constitutional monarchy in, 940
  creation of, 418
  crusades in, 360–361
  decline of, 545
  Dutch and, 465, 466, 509
  empire of, 464–465, 464(m),
    466
  England and, 467, 468, 588
  Enlightenment and, 570
  explorations by, 432, 434
  fascism in, 842, 855, 859–860
  fertility rate in, 969
  France and, 499, 545–547,
    546(m), 608, 621
  as global power, 458
  gold imports by, 435
  industry in, 743
  Inquisition in, 425–426
  Jews in, 307, 425–426
  kingdom in, 251
  Latin American independence
    from, 652–653
  Muslims and, 243, 315, 426, 462
  Napoleon and, 631, 638–640
  Ottoman Turks and, 462
  Peace of Utrecht and, 500–501
  Peace of Westphalia and,
    472–473
  peasant revolt in, 472
  property of women in, 291(f)
  reconquista in, 315, 360–361,
    362(m)
  religious uniformity in,
    425–426
  representative government in,
    385
  revolts in, 650, 650(m)
  Roman Catholicism in, 262,
    547
  Rome and, 155, 163
  St. Domingue and, 619
  slave trade and, 434, 676
  succession in, 545–547
  terrorism in Madrid, 974
  theaters in, 486
  in Thirty Years' War, 471–472
  Umayyads in, 277
  unity in early medieval,
    262–263
  Visigoths in, 223, 262
  War of the Polish Succession
    and, 552

Spanish-American War (1898),
    788
Spanish Civil War, 856, 859–860,
    860(m), 861(i)
Spanish Empire, 435
Spanish Fury, 460(i), 461, 466
Spanish-language television, 984
Spanish Netherlands, 499
Sparta, 54. See also Allies, Greek
  Athens and, 75, 82, 114–115
  oligarchy in, 61–64
  Peloponnesian War and,
    100–104
  slaves in, 59
  at Thermopylae, 79
Spartacists, 818
Spartacus, 162
Spectator, The, 542
Spencer, Herbert, 724
Spending
  on education and research, 926
  on military, 795, 883–884, 893,
    900, 942, 943
  in Rome, 195–196
Speyer, Germany, Jews of, 325
Sphinx, 16–17, 17(i), 20
Spices, 432, 433
Spinning jenny, 660
Spinoza, Benedict, 511
Spirit of the Laws, The
  (Montesquieu), 558
Spoleto, duchy of, 263, 264
Spontaneous ovulation, 724
Sports, 750–751
  blood sports, 674
  in Greece, 49–51, 50(i)
Sputnik, 898, 920
Square II, The (Giacometti), 875(i)
Srebrenica, massacre in, 955
SS (Schutzstaffel), 850
Stadholder (Dutch official), 509,
    547, 548, 596, 643
Staël, Anne-Louise Germaine de,
    633, 633(i), 639
Stagflation, 939, 941, 942
Stained-glass windows, 337, 378(i),
    379
Stalin, Joseph, 829, 834, 842, 888
  cold war and, 885, 886
  death of, 881, 897
  eastern Europe and, 887,
    896–897
  Hitler and, 862–863
  totalitarianism of, 846–848, 885
  World War II and, 872, 877
Stalingrad, battle of, 869–870, 871

Stalinism, 885, 896–897, 898
Stamp Act (1765), 589
Standard of living. See also Lifestyle
  in Africa, 736
  of Dutch, 510(m)
  of EU members, 964
  in global south, 971
  medieval, 292
  plague and, 403
  in Soviet Union, 943
  welfare state and, 896
  after World War II, 882, 890
Standard Oil Trust, 744
Starvation. See also Famines; Great
    Famine
  in Crimean War, 699
  in Soviet Union, 847
  World War II and, 867(i), 868
Starvation Act (1834), 674
State (nation). See also Church and
    state; Nation-states; specific
    states
  in 18th century, 580–586
  bureaucratic growth and,
    713–714
  European system of, 545–554
  growth after Thirty Years' War,
    474–475
  power of, 662
  rebellions against power of,
    586–590
State of nature, Hobbes on, 508
Statue of Liberty, 609(i)
Statues. See Sculpture
Status. See Classes; Hierarchy;
    Social status; specific classes
Staufer clan, 350, 351
Steamboats, 664, 681, 742
Steam engines, 660, 661–662, 664
Steel, 740, 976
Steele, Richard, 542
Steen, Jan, 511(i)
Stephen I (Saint, Hungary), 299
Stephen II (Pope), 264
Stephenson, George, 659, 660, 661
Sterilization, 770
Stilicho (Vandals), 202(i)
Stock market, 744
  crash in 1929, 836, 841, 842
Stoicism, 127–128, 191, 192
Stolypin, Pyotr, 790
Stone Age, 3, 4–8. See also Neolithic
    Age; Paleolithic Age
Stonewall riot, 932
Stopes, Marie, 828
Stores, department, 745–746

Storm troopers (SA, Stürmabteilung), 850
Story of My Misfortunes, The (Abelard), 339
Story of Sinuhe, The (Egypt), 22
Strasbourg, seizure of, 500
Strategic Arms Limitation Treaty (SALT I, 1972), 938
Strategos (general), 249
Strauss, Richard, 778
Stravinsky, Igor, 777
Stream of consciousness technique, in literature, 832
Strikes, 654, 754–755. *See also* Labor; Labor unions
  in British coal industry (1926), 825
  in colonies, 845
  in France, 934
  in London, 754
  in Russia, 789–790
  in Soviet bloc, 897
  in U.S., 931
  in World War I, 812
  after World War I, 825
Structuralism, 928–929
Struggle of the orders (Rome), 148
Stuart family (Scotland), 548
Students
  activism by, 687, 932–933, 934–935, 937, 945
  as clerics, 341
  nationalistic, 651
Styria, 515, 743
Subjection of Women, The (Mill), 725
Subjectivism, 92
Submarines, in World War I, 806, 807, 812
Sub-Saharan Africa, 733, 806, 902, 905
Subsistence agriculture, 540
Subsistence economy, 538
Suburbs, 884, 896, 965
Succession
  in Christian church, 191
  in England, 506, 547
  in French Valois dynasty, 404(*f*)
  to Muhammad, 244–245
  in Rome, 177–178
  in Spain, 545–547
Sudan, 970, 971
Sudetenland, 861
Suetonius (Rome), 284
Suez Canal, 698, 716, 733, 870, 901

Suffrage
  in Britain, 548, 588, 655, 689, 756–757
  in France, 606, 684
  in Germany, 708, 754
  for men, 606, 655, 753–754, 758, 782
  universal, 813
  for women, 780–781, 823, 823(*f*)
Suffragists, in Britain, 780–781, 827
Sugar and sugar industry
  in Caribbean region, 481
  slavery in, 435, 481, 533
  as standard food item, 534
Suger (abbot of Saint-Denis), 331, 344
Suicide bombers, 973
Sukarno, Achmed, 904
Suleiman I (the Magnificent, Ottoman Empire), 452–453, 453(*i*)
Sulla, Lucius Cornelius (Rome), 140, 160–161
Sultans, Ottoman, 398(*i*), 516
Sumer and Sumerians, 8, 9(*i*), 10, 11, 13. *See also* Mesopotamia
Summa, 375
Summa Theologiae (Thomas Aquinas), 376
Sun Also Rises, The (Hemingway), 828
Sunday, naming of, 210
Sunday school movement, 674
Sun King, Louis XIV as, 496
Sunna, 245
Sunni Muslims, 245, 276, 327, 972(*m*)
  crusades and, 323–324
Sun Yat-sen (China), 789(*m*), 792
"Superman," Nietzsche on, 775
Superpowers, 917, 918. *See also* Soviet Union; United States
  balance of power and, 937–939
  cold war and, 912, 937–939
  U.S. as dominant power and, 954
  World War II and, 882, 883–885
Superstition, religion and, 523–524, 556
Superstores, 964
Supply-side economics, 941
Supranational organizations, 966
Supreme Court (U.S.), 908

Suras, 241, 241(*i*)
Surgery, Hammurabi's code on, 14
Surplus, agricultural, 256
Surplus food, in Crete, 30
Suttner, Bertha von, 779–780
Swabia, 351, 382
Sweden, 499, 513
  balance of power and, 551
  birthrate in, 769
  Danes in, 289
  economy in, 894
  education in, 926
  Franco-Austrian alliance and, 580
  in Great Depression, 854
  Great Northern War and, 551, 551(*m*)
  migration from, 748
  Peace of Westphalia and, 472, 473(*m*)
  Russia and, 469, 549, 551
  service-sector employees in, 924
  Social Democratic Party in, 755
  social welfare in, 854, 942–943
  in Thirty Years' War, 470
  women in, 770–771, 894, 933
Swift, Jonathan, 553–554
Swine flu, 970
Swiss Confederation, 418, 422
Switzerland, 422
  after Charlemagne, 285
  education in, 542
  non-Europeans in, 904
Syllabus of Errors, The, 722
Symeon (monk), 218
Symmachus (Rome), 211
Synagogues, 307(*i*), 308, 467. *See also* Temples
Syndicalists, 779
Synods
  Henry IV excommunicated by, 316
  of Sutri (1046), 314
  of Whitby (664), 261, 262
Synthetics, 893
Syphilis, 436, 713, 779
Syracuse, 77–78
Syria, 820, 938
  Abbasids and, 276
  Christianity in, 215
  Fatimids in, 277
  Islam and, 243
  nationalism in, 792
  Rome and, 154(*m*), 162
  Sasanids in, 197, 247
Széchenyi, Stephen, 681, 687

Taaffe, Edouard von, 759
Table of Ranks (Russia, 1772),
    550–551
Tabula rasa, 509
Tacitus, 173, 183
Tagmata (mobile armies), 270
Tahiti, as French protectorate, 676
Taifas (independent regions), 278,
    315
Taiping ("Heavenly Kingdom"
    movement), 717
Taiwan, as Pacific Tiger, 975,
    975*(m)*
Taliban, 972–973
Talking cure, of Freud, 774
Talleyrand, Charles Maurice de,
    643
Talmud, Palestinian and
    Babylonian, 212
Tanks, in World War I, 806, 816
Tariffs
    in Britain, 680, 854
    in Germany, 759
    in western Europe, 894
Tartuffe (Molière), 496
Tatars (Tartars), 389, 761, 789–790.
    See also Mongols and
    Mongol Empire
Taxation
    of clergy, 387–388
    in colonies, 589, 738
    in Egypt, 21
    in England, 349, 502, 505–506,
        941
    in France, 474, 498, 500, 598,
        602, 603
    of gasoline, 968*(i)*
    in Germany, 821
    Hellenistic, 121
    income, 941
    of Jews, 373–374
    by Justinian, 230
    in Mesopotamia, 10
    of peasants, 474–475, 478, 574
    representation and, 588
    in Rome, 181–182, 196,
        207–208
    in Russia, 550, 574, 789
    in Spain, 420, 448
    tithe as, 292, 478
    in United States, 942
Taylor, Frederick, 827
Tea Act (1773), 589
Teachers, women as, 674, 715
Team sports, 750

Technocrats, 894
Technology, 715, 897, 974. *See also*
    Metals and metallurgy;
    Science; Weapons
    in 1920s, 832
    in Britain, 742
    bubble in, 976
    in Crimean War, 699
    Einstein's theories applied to,
        775
    impact of, 949, 987
    imperialism and, 742
    information technology,
        918–920, 987
    medical, 922
    metallurgy and, 12, 48
    military, 453
    nuclear, 921
    Paleolithic, 5
    recording, 928
    reproductive, 922–923
    space, 898, 921
    voyages of discovery and, 432
    in World War I, 806, 809
Technopoles, 930
Teenagers, in postindustrial society,
    927. *See also* Young people
Teheran, U.S. embassy hostages in,
    939
Telecommunications, 918, 954
Telegraph, 699
Telephone, 740, 745*(i),* 756, 918
Telescope, 482, 921
Television, 776, 918, 935, 937, 946,
    947
    in 1950s and 1960s, 910
    in 1960s and 1970s, 918–919,
        927
    satellite-beamed telecasts on,
        980
    Soviet, 944
    Spanish-language, 984
Telex machines, 945
Tell el-Amarna, 24
Temperance, 659, 674
Temperatures, global warming and,
    967
Templars, 326, 363*(i)*
Temples. *See also* Synagogues
    Egyptian, 20, 24
    Jewish, in Jerusalem, 46,
        132–133, 188, 326
    in Malta, 20
Temporary workers, foreign,
    905–906

Tenant farmers
    coloni as, 208, 254
    in England, 540
    in Hellenistic kingdoms, 122
    in Ireland, 757
Ten Commandments, 45
Ten Days That Shook the World
    (movie), 829
Tennis court oath, 600
Tennyson, Alfred (Lord), 675
Tenochtitlán (Mexico City), 435
Tereshkova, Valentina, 920, 920*(i)*
Terror, the (France), 607–615
Terrorism, 937, 939–940
    in Algeria, 904
    al-Qaeda and, 971
    by anarchists, 779
    in Europe, 973
    as global issue, 954, 973–974,
        986
    in Ireland, 825
    in London, 974
    in Madrid, 974
    Middle East and, 973
    in Nazi Germany, 850–851
    on September 11, 2001, 973,
        974*(i)*
    at U.S. embassy in Iran, 939
    war against, 973
    in West Germany, 940, 942
Tertullian, 189
Test Act (England), 506
Test-ban treaty (1963), 912
Test-tube babies, 922–923, 923*(i)*
Tet offensive, 933
Tetradia, 258–259
Tetrarchy, 205, 206
Tetzel, Johann, 440
Texas, 710
Textile industry
    in Britain, 664, 780
    Dutch, 549
    in India, 664
    industrialization of, 660–661
T4 project, 852, 866
Thailand, 976, 986
Thales of Miletus, 69
Thatcher, Margaret, 937, 940–942,
    941*(i)*
Theater(s), 672. *See also* Drama
    professional, 486, 522
    in Russia, 518
Thebes, 114
    Egypt reunited by, 22–23
    Macedonians and, 115–116

Themes (Byzantine military districts), 249, 270, 274
Themistocles (Athens), 77, 79
Theocracy
    in Geneva, 443
    Mesopotamian, 10
Theocritus, 125
Theodora (Byzantine empress), 227, 228(i), 230, 231
Theodoric (Ostrogoths), 224
Theodorus the Atheist, 128
Theodosius I (Rome), 204, 206, 211, 222
Theogony (Hesiod), 51
Theology. *See also* Religion(s); specific groups
    of Calvin, 442–443
    Christian, 191–193
    Enlightenment and, 568
    of Jansenists, 497–498
    of Luther, 440–441
    of Peter the Chanter, 340
    schools of, 339
Thermidorian Reaction, 615
Thermopylae, battle at, 79
Third Crusade, 349, 359–360
Third Estate (general populace), in France, 599, 600, 601(i)
Third Lateran Council, 374
Third Punic War, 154–155
Third Reich (Germany), 851, 871, 872
Third Republic (France), 757–758
    Dreyfus Affair in, 782–783
Third Section (political police), 651
Third world, 882, 899
Thirty-Nine Articles of Religion, 468
Thirty Tyrants (Athens), 104, 112
Thirty Years' War, 461, 470–475, 471(i), 473(m), 477–478, 515, 551
Tholos tombs, 31
Thomas Aquinas (Saint), 376, 408
Thomas of Norwich, 374
Thoronet, Le (Cistercian monastery), 322(i)
Thrace, 78(m)
Three Emperors' League, 758
Three-field system, 286, 287(f), 292
Three Guineas (Woolf), 856
Thucydides of Athens, 95
    on Peloponnesian War, 95–96, 101–102
Thuringia, Peasants' War in, 445

Tiananmen Square, protests in, 945, 980
Tiberius (Rome), 178, 182
Tiberius Gracchus. *See* Gracchus family
Tigris River region, 4, 8
Tilak, B. G., 792
Tilsit, Treaties of, 637
Time of Troubles (Russia), 469
Tin, 742
"Tintern Abbey" (Wordsworth), 647
Tipu Sultan, 619
Tithe, 292, 478, 574, 599
Tito (Josip Broz), 887
Titus (Rome), 179
Tobacco, 481, 534
Tocqueville, Alexis de, 665
Togo, 820
Togoland, 788
Toilets, public, 713
Tokyo, World War II and, 865, 872
Toledo, Spain, 262
Tolerance. *See* Religion(s); Religious toleration
Toleration Act (England), 507
Tolstoy, Leo, 760
Tombs. *See* Burials
To Myself (*Meditations,* Marcus Aurelius), 192
Tonkin, 736
Tools, 4, 12, 48
Topkapi Saray, 399
Torah, 45
Tordesillas, Treaty of, 433(m), 434
Tories (Britain), 506, 548, 655, 709
Torture
    efforts to abolish, 563, 567
    natural law and, 486
    of witches, 488
Totalitarianism. *See also* Authoritarianism; Dictatorships
    in Europe, 846–852
    French Revolution and, 595
Total war, World War I as, 804, 809, 818
To the Nobility of the German Nation (Luther), 441
Touraine, France and, 349
Tour de France, 750
Tourism
    battlefield, 823
    Great War, 831
    in West, 981(i)

Tours, 255, 255(m)
Toussaint L'Ouverture, François-Dominique, 619, 620(i)
Towns. *See* Cities and towns; Urban areas; Villages; specific locations
Trade, 5, 872. *See also* Commerce; Economy; Free trade
    in 1050–1150, 305–306
    Alexander the Great and, 118
    in ancient Near East, 6(m)
    Assyrian, 13
    Atlantic system of, 529, 530–535, 535–537
    in Baltic region, 362–363
    Byzantine, 271–272, 274–275
    Carolingian, 286
    with China, 390
    Common Market and, 894, 929
    Congress of Vienna and, 643
    Dutch, 505, 509–510, 510(m), 549
    economy and, 476
    Egyptian, 18
    European imperialism and, 763(m)
    European patterns of (c. 1740), 531(m)
    in former Soviet Union, 960
    by France, 499, 577
    in Great Depression, 846, 854
    Greek, 48, 52–53
    Hanseatic League and, 419
    Hittite, 27–28
    international, 886
    Islamic networks of, 278
    Jews in, 307
    Mesopotamian, 8
    Neolithic, 7
    by nobility, 574
    Ottoman, 408
    Paleolithic, 5
    Roman, 147, 186
    Suez Canal and, 716
    in western Europe, 257, 894
Trade routes, 432–433, 434
Trade unions, 683, 779. *See also* Labor unions
Trading companies, French, 499, 547. *See also* specific companies
Trafalgar, battle of, 636
Tragedy (drama)
    Greek, 96–99
    of Shakespeare, 486

Trajan (Rome), 180, 181, 181(*m*)

Transportation. *See also* Canals;
    Travel; specific types
    in 12th century, 308
    of food, 742
    in Greece, 52

Trans-Siberian Railroad, 736, 743,
    788

Transubstantiation, 371

Transvaal, 786

Transvestitism, 772

Transylvania, 552, 679

Trasformismo policy (Italy), 782

Travel
    civilian, 893
    literature about, 557–558
    Montesquieu on, 558
    in Rome, 252–253

Travels in Icaria (Cabet), 682

Treasury of Atreas (Mycenaean
    domed tomb), 33

Treaties. *See also* specific treaties
    after War of the Spanish
        Succession, 545–547
    after World War I, 819

Trench warfare, in World War I,
    796, 805(*m*), 807, 808,
    809(*i*)

Trent, Council of, 448–449

Trial, The (Kafka), 832

Trials
    of Galileo, 483(*i*)
    of Nazis, 890
    of terrorists, 973
    of witches, 487–488

Tribal Assembly (Rome), 150

Tribes. *See also* specific groups
    barbarian, 220–221
    Hebrew, 46

Tribunes (Rome), 149

Tricolor (French flag), 611

Triennial Act (Great Britain), 548

Trier, as Roman city, 252, 253

Trinity (Christian), 215, 443

Triple Alliance, 760, 762, 793, 804

Triremes (warships), 80, 80(*i*)

Tristan, Flora, 682

Trivium, 339

Trojan War, 30, 33, 39, 49, 97–98

Tromboncino, Bartolomeo, 418

Troops. *See* Armed forces; Soldiers

Trotsky, Leon, 814–815, 814(*i*),
    834

Troubadours, 354–355, 356(*f*)

Trouvères (singers), 355

Troy, 30–31, 49, 97–98, 161(*i*)

Truce, in Peloponnesian War, 104

Truce of God movement, 294–295,
    323

Truce of Nice (1538), 453(*i*)

Truman, Harry S., 872, 885

Truman Doctrine, 886

Trusts (business), 744

Truth, Protagoras on, 92

Tsars (Russia), as absolutists, 517.
    See also specific individuals

Tsushima Strait, battle of, 788

Tuberculosis, 896

Tudor monarchs (England),
    421–422, 443, 444. *See also*
    specific monarchs

Tullia (Rome), 142–143

Tunis. *See* Carthage

Tunisia. *See also* Carthage
    digital media and government
        change in, 980
    Fatimids in, 277
    France and, 733
    independence for, 904

Turgenev, Ivan, 720

Turgot, Jacques, 585, 587

Turkey. *See also* Anatolia; Ottoman
    Empire
    Armenians in, 810
    in cold war, 886
    in eastern Roman Empire,
        239–240
    in EU, 962
    Germany and, 794
    gods worshipped in, 5
    Kemal Atatürk in, 845
    migration from, 824
    nationalism in, 792
    Russian war with, 760

Turks. *See also* Ottoman Empire;
    Ottoman Turks
    Mamluks as, 276
    Ottoman, 399, 452–453
    Seljuk, 323–324, 328, 359

Turner, Joseph M. W., 648,
    670–671, 671(*i*)

Tustari brothers (merchants), 278

Twelve Tables (Rome), 148

Twilight (Grosz), 831(*i*)

2001: A Space Odyssey (movie),
    920, 936

Two Treatises of Government
    (Locke), 508

Tychê (Chance, god), 131, 132

Type, 285

Typewriter, 740

Typhoid, 712, 713

Tyrants and tyranny, 61
    in Athens, 104
    in Corinth, 64–65

Tyre, 116–117

Tyrol, 515

Tz'u-hsi (Cixi), 791

U-boats. *See* Submarines

Ukraine
    Cossacks in, 513
    fertility in, 970
    land in, 540
    Russia and, 513, 961
    World War II and, 864, 865

Ulm, Bavaria, Napoleon in, 636

Ulster, 505

Ultra code-breaking group, 864

Ultrarevolutionaries (France), 614

Ulysses (Joyce), 832

Umayyads, 241(*i*), 244(*m*), 245(*i*)
    caliphate of, 244, 245–246, 270,
        275
    in Spain, 277

Ummah, 242, 243, 244(*m*)

UN. *See* United Nations

Unam Sanctam (papal bull), 387

Unbearable Lightness of Being, The
    (Kundera), 936

Uncertainty (indeterminacy)
    principle, 856

Unconscious, Freud on, 773

Unemployment
    in mid-19th century, 684
    assistance, 781
    in Britain, 843, 854
    in depression of 1873, 743
    in France, 599, 942
    in Germany, 843, 843(*i*), 851
    in global economic crisis, 976,
        976(*i*), 977
    in Great Depression, 842, 843,
        843(*i*), 853
    oil embargo and, 938–939
    after World War I, 824

Unification, 692. *See also* Berlin;
    Germany; Reunification
    of Egypt, 15–16
    of Europe, 962–964
    of Germany, 687, 705–708,
        707(*m*)
    of Italy, 686, 702–705, 703(*m*)

Unified law code, in Austria, 583

Union of Soviet Socialist Republics
    (USSR). *See* Soviet Union

Union of Soviet Writers, 848

Unions. *See* Labor unions

United Kingdom. *See* Britain; England
United Nations (UN), 872, 882
  in former Yugoslavia, 955
  Korean War and, 900
  Kuwait invasion and, 972
  newly independent nations in, 904
  Palestine partition and, 901
United States, 779. *See also* Iraq War; specific presidents
  American Revolution and, 588–590
  artists in 1920s, 832
  Canada and, 711
  cholera in, 667
  civil rights in, 882, 908, 931
  Civil War in, 700(*i*), 710
  in cold war, 883, 885–888, 900–901, 912, 931
  culture in, 984
  détente policy and, 938
  as dominant world power, 954
  economy in, 742, 827, 974
  emigration to, 669, 748, 749(*f*)
  environment and, 968
  expansion of, 710, 711(*m*)
  France and, 636
  French Revolution and, 619
  German occupation by, 874, 888–889
  Great Depression in, 853–854
  health care in, 896
  imperialism by, 788
  industry in, 742
  Iraq War and, 972(*m*), 973–974
  Jewish migration to, 785
  McCarthy in, 893
  Monroe Doctrine and, 653
  NAFTA and, 962
  national debt in, 938, 975
  railroads in, 662
  real estate bubble in, 976
  reform societies in, 674
  research funding by, 926
  second Great Awakening in, 646
  service-sector employees in, 924
  slavery in, 590, 676, 710, 711
  social protests and, 931–933, 933–934, 937
  stock market and (1929), 836, 841, 842
  as superpower, 882, 883–884, 954
  television in, 910, 918, 919
  terrorist attack on, 973, 974(*i*)
  Vietnam and, 900–901, 931, 937
  Watergate scandal in, 938
  women in, 780
  World War I and, 812
  World War II and, 864–865, 868, 877
United States of Belgium, 597
Universal Exhibition (Manet), 720
Universal Exposition (1889), 740
Universal gravitation, law of, 484
Universal male suffrage, 758
  in France, 606
  in Germany, 708
Universe, 92, 856, 921. *See also* Astronomy
Universities. *See also* Education; Higher education
  Black Death and, 404
  Dutch, 511
  Great Awakening and, 572
  growth of, 926
  as guilds, 341
  Jesuit, 449
  in Middle Ages, 337, 338–341
Upper classes, 522, 542, 550, 553, 554, 599, 746–747. *See also* Aristocracy; Classes; Elites; Lords
  in rural areas, 668, 669
  women in, 675
  in World War I, 811
Upper Egypt, 16, 16(*m*)
Ur (Mesopotamian city-state), 8, 9(*i*), 10, 12–13
Ur III dynasty (Sumer), 13, 14
Urban II (Pope), 324
Urban VI (Pope), 408–409
Urban areas. *See also* Cities and towns; specific locations
  Byzantine, 248–249
  charity in, 578
  factories in, 664–665
  Hellenistic, 121
  industrialization and, 659, 667
  social life in, 540–542
  after World War II, 896
Urbanization. *See also* Cities and towns; specific locations
  birthrates and, 667, 769
  in Britain, 666
  in Dutch Republic, 511
  European (1750–1800), 575(*f*)
  industrialization and, 660, 666–668
  internal migration and, 540, 748
Urbino, 451
Uruk (Mesopotamian city-state), 8, 10
USSR. *See* Soviet Union
Usury, 310
Uthman (Umayyad), 244
Utilitarianism, 680
Utopia, communist, 832–834
Utrecht
  occupation of, 596
  Peace of, 500, 553
Uzbekistan, Alexander the Great in, 117

Vacations, 896
Vaccines, 896, 970
Václav (Bohemia), 299
Valens (Rome), 215, 222
Valerian (Rome), 197
Vallain, Jeanne-Louise, 609(*i*)
Valois dynasty (France), 404, 404(*f*), 452–453, 462
Values
  postmodernism and, 986
  in Rome, 140–141, 161, 164, 209, 226
  in Sparta, 62–63
  during World War II, 874–875
Vandals, 202(*i*), 224, 226, 231
Van de Velde, Theodor, 828
Van de Venne, Adriaen Pietersz, 478(*i*)
Van Eyck, Jan, 417, 417(*i*)
Van Gogh, Vincent, 752, 753
Varro (writer), 412
Vassals and vassalage
  Carolingian, 285
  in England, 329, 349
  in France, 297
  medieval, 290–291, 293
Vassilacchi, Antonio, 465(*i*)
Vatican, as independent state, 835. *See also* Roman Catholicism; Sistine Chapel
Vatican II, 906, 929
Vauxhall Gardens, London, 541(*i*)
Vega, Lope de, 486
Veii (Etruscan town), 151
Velázquez, Diego, 474(*i*)
Vellum, 437
Velvet revolution, in Czechoslovakia, 946

Vendée rebellion, 612, 615
Venereal disease, 713
Venetia, 679, 703, 705
Venice, 422, 686
    arts in, 423, 424(i)
    Asian trade by, 390
    Byzantine trade and, 272
    crusaders in, 360
Ventris, Michael, 32
Verbiest, Ferdinand, 557(i)
Verdi, Giuseppe, 694(i), 695, 704,
    716, 722
Verdun
    battle at, 807
    Treaty of (843), 282(m), 285,
    297
Vernacular languages
    courtly culture in, 354–357
    in England, 295–296
    medieval literature in, 376–377
Versailles, 493, 496, 497
    Estates General at, 600
    women's march to, 594(i), 595,
    603
Versailles Treaty, 819, 823, 858,
    861
Vesalius, Andreas, 483
Vespasian (Rome), 179
Vespucci, Amerigo, 434
Vesta (goddess), cult of, 144
Vestal Virgins (Rome), 144
Vesuvius, eruption of, 174(i)
Veterans, 823, 827–828, 895, 902,
    903, 908
Veto
    absolute power of, 513
    in Rome, 149
Veturia (Rome), 185
Vichy France, 864
Victor Emmanuel II (Italy), 695,
    703, 704
Victor Emmanuel III (Italy), 834
Victoria (England), 675, 689, 709,
    710, 712, 716
Victorian society, 675, 709–710
Videocassette recorders, 918, 919
Videotape, 919, 980
Vienna, 636, 687, 688, 743, 860. See
    also Congress of Vienna
    Jews in, 784
    Ottoman siege of, 452–453,
    453(i)
    rebuilding of, 712
    siege of, 513
    university at, 404
Vietcong, 931, 933

Viet Minh, 900
Vietnam, 872. See also Indochina;
    Vietnam War
    in cold war, 900–901
    division of, 900, 931
    France and, 736–737
Vietnam War, 918, 929, 931,
    932(m), 937
    protests against, 933, 937
    Tet offensive in, 933
Vigée-Lebrun, Marie-Louise-
    Élizabeth, 598(i), 633(i)
Vikings
    in England, 289, 296
    invasions by, 288
    Kievan Rus and, 274
Villages. See also Cities and towns
    forms of justice in, 524
    Frankish, 255
    medieval, 292
Villeneuve Saint-Georges (manor),
    286–287
Violence. See also Wars and
    warfare; specific locations
    by anarchists, 755, 779
    decolonization and, 908
    in early Western civilization,
    32–35, 34(m)
    by fascists, 834
    medieval, 294–295
    in nation building, 696
    by suffragists, 781
    in Thirty Years' War, 471(i)
Vipsania (Rome), 178
Virgil (Rome), 176–177, 284, 377
Virginia, African slaves in, 476, 533
Virginity, in Christianity, 217
Virgin Mary, 524
Virgin of Chancellor Rolin, The (Van
    Eyck), 417(i)
Virtue(s)
    of Merovingian warriors, 257
    of Roman women, 143
    in Rome, 140
    Socrates on, 105
Viruses, 970
Visigoths, 222, 223–224, 225
Visual arts, 481. See also Art(s);
    Painting; Sculpture
    realism in, 720, 721(i)
    in technocratic society,
    927–928
Vladimir (Kiev and Russia), 275
Voice of America, 911–912
Volksgemeinschaft, in Germany,
    850

Voltaire (François-Marie Arouet),
    556–557, 565, 567, 571(f),
    645
    Catherine II and, 563
    persecution of, 556, 570
Von Bülow, Frieda, 731, 732, 733,
    763
Voting and voting rights
    in 19th century, 754
    in Britain, 548, 588, 655, 689,
    709, 756–757
    in France, 599, 600, 603, 629,
    645, 685–686
    in Germany, 708
    in Italy, 782
    in Russia, 779
    universal male suffrage and,
    606, 708, 758
    for women, 780–781, 813,
    845–846, 891
Voyages of exploration, 431,
    432–434, 433(m)
Vulcanization, of rubber, 669, 769
Vulgate Bible, 284, 449

Wage and price controls, under
    Diocletian, 208–209
Wages, 476, 578, 963–964
    by gender, 827, 925
    for women, 745, 755, 844
Wagner, Richard, 722
Walentynowicz, Anna, 945
Wales, 224, 666
Walesa, Lech, 945, 946
Wallachia, 699
Walled cities
    commerce and, 307
    Frankish, 255
    Greek, 34
    Piacenza as, 308(m)
    Rome as, 152
Wallenstein, Albrecht von, 470
Walpole, Robert, 548
Wannsee, Germany, 866
War against terrorism, 973
War and Peace (Tolstoy), 760
War communism, in Russia, 815,
    833
War debts, German, 821
War guilt clause, 819
Warhol, Andy, 927
Warinus (abbot), 314(i)
War ministries, in World War I, 810
War of the Austrian Succession,
    552–553, 561(m), 581
War of Devolution, 499

War of Independence (United
   States). *See* American War
   of Independence
War of Italian Unification, 698
War of the League of Augsburg
   (Nine Years' War), 500
War of the Polish Succession, 552
War of the Spanish Succession, 500,
   515, 545–547, 546(*m*)
Warriors. *See also* Armed forces;
   Soldiers
   Greek, 58(*i*)
   medieval, 293–294
   Merovingian, 257
   pharaohs as, 23
   in post-Carolingian society, 289
Wars and warfare. *See also* Armed
   forces; Crusades;
   Mercenaries; Weapons;
   specific battles and wars
   advantages to, 800
   in Assyrian culture, 41
   Bismarck and, 705–707
   in Byzantine Empire, 246–248
   dynastic, 452–453
   during French Revolution, 605,
      607, 608–609, 614, 615–619,
      617(*m*)
   French wars of religion,
      462–464
   in Greece, 75, 76–79
   Hittite, 27
   Hundred Years' War and, 406
   of Louis XIV, 499–500, 500(*f*),
      501(*m*)
   medieval, 293–294
   mobile, 870
   Mycenaean, 32
   Napoleonic, 635–641
   nation building and, 696,
      702–711
   Roman, 151, 152–155
   technology in, 699, 796
   troubadour poetry about, 355
Warsaw, duchy of, 637, 642, 643
Warsaw (city), 540
Warsaw ghetto, Jewish uprising in,
   866
Warsaw Pact, 889, 889(*m*), 935
Wars of the Roses, 421–422
Washington Conference (1921),
   822
Wastes, urbanization and, 667
Water
   in Africa, 970
   in Babylonian cities, 14

   in Rome, 151
   in urban areas, 667, 713
Watergate scandal, 938
Waterloo, battle at, 641
Water mills, 310
Waterways, commerce and, 308.
      See also specific river
      regions
Watson, James, 908–909, 922
Watt, James, 660
Watteau, Antoine, 537(*i*)
Wat Tyler's Rebellion, 407
Wealth. *See also* Upper classes
   in 12th century, 305
   in Asian-Pacific countries, 975
   Carolingian, 286
   in cities, 540
   from colonies, 732
   Egyptian, 23–24
   gap with poor, 478
   in Greece, 90
   in Hellenistic world, 121, 123,
      124
   human capital and, 553
   of nobility, 574
   in Rome, 152
   of Russian oligarchs, 957
Wealth of Nations (Smith), 568,
   571(*f*)
Weapons, 4. *See also* Arms race;
      Military technology;
      Nuclear weapons
   bronze, 12
   in Crimean War, 699
   flintlock muskets, 580
   Germany and, 819
   Hellenistic, 120
   Hittite, 27
   in Hundred Years' War, 406
   imperialism and, 742
   of mass destruction, 973
   World War I and, 796, 806
   World War II and, 863
Weather, 5. *See also* Climate
   global warming and, 967
Weaving, mechanization of, 660
Weber, Max, 774–775
Weddings, 60, 848. *See also*
      Marriage
Wedgwood, Josiah, 576
Wedgwood pottery, 576
Weimar Republic, 818, 825, 827,
   831, 836, 849
Welfare state, 894–896, 942. *See
   also* Social welfare
   in eastern Europe, 895–896

   foundations for, 771
   New Deal and, 854
   non-European workers and,
      905, 905(*i*)
   standard of living and, 896
   television and, 919
   in western Europe, 895, 942
   after World War I, 823
   after World War II, 882
Welfs (Germany), 350, 351
Wellington, Arthur Wellesley
   (duke of), 641, 655, 659
Wells, H. G., 767, 808(*i*)
Wergild, 226
Wesley, John, 573, 646
Wesleyans. *See* Methodism
Wessex, 295–296
West, the. *See also* World War I;
      World War II
   China and, 717
   cities in, 964–965
   cold war and, 882
   concept of, 4
   cross-cultural contact in, 40
   Europe and (c. 1340), 394(*m*)
   global economic crisis in,
      976–977
   global migration and,
      977–979
   Great Depression beyond,
      844–846
   immigrants in, 730(*i*), 977,
      978–979
   Khrushchev in, 898
   non-West cultural influences
      in, 980–982
   population growth in, 769
   postwar recovery in, 891–894
   religions in, 978(*i*)
   spread of national power and
      order from, 717–719
   violent ends to civilizations of,
      32–35, 34(*m*)
   and world (c. 1890), 763(*m*)
West Africa. *See also* Gold Coast
   decolonization in, 904
   Portugal and, 432–433, 434
   slave trade and, 531, 532
West Bank, 938, 938(*m*)
West Berlin, 930
Western civilization. *See* West, the
Western Europe. *See also* specific
      locations
   in c. 600, 235(*m*)
   by 1050, 270
   in 15th century, 419–422

Western Europe (continued)
   in 17th century, 525(m)
   in 1750, 561(m)
   Byzantine trade with, 272
   after Charlemagne, 285
   communist parties in, 891–892
   economy in, 305–306, 893–894
   governments in, 891–893
   Jews in, 784
   kingdoms in, 251–264
   lifestyle in, 960
   male suffrage in, 753–754
   monarchies in, 418
   nobility in, 574
   oil conservation in, 939
   political participation in,
      756–758
   religious conflict in, 461,
      462–469
   revival of democracy in, 891
   state power in, 464–469,
      545–547
   subsistence agriculture in, 540
   U.S. and, 883, 887
   western Roman Empire as,
      239–240
Western front, in World War I,
      805(m), 806–807, 816
Westernization
   in Iran, 971
   Russia and, 549–552, 550(i),
      679
   of Turkey, 845
Western Roman Empire, 204. See
      also Eastern Roman
      Empire; Roman Empire
   barbarians in, 204, 220
   Franks in, 225
   non-Roman kingdoms in,
      220–227
   separation from eastern empire,
      206–207, 207(m)
   society and culture in, 225–227
   as western Europe, 239–240
West Germany, 888, 946, 967–968
   economy of, 893–894
   in ECSC, 894
   former fascists and Nazis in,
      890
   Green Party in, 968
   policy changes in, 930
   postwar politics in, 892–893
   terrorism in, 940
   university students in, 926, 933
   welfare state and, 895, 942
West Indies, 481, 580

Westphalia
   kingdom of, 637
   Peace of, 472–474, 473(m), 553
Wetlands, draining of, 540
What Is Property? (Proudhon), 682
What Is the Third Estate? (Sieyès),
      599
Whigs (England), 506, 548, 588,
      655, 709
Whitby, Synod of, 261, 262
White-collar jobs, 771
White-collar service workers, 744,
      745, 924
Whitefield, George, 572(i), 646
White monks, 321
White Mountain, battle of, 470
White people
   in Africa, 735
   civil rights movement and, 931
Whites (faction), in Russia, 814, 824
White supremacists, anti-
      immigrant sentiment of,
      978
White Teeth (Smith), 982
"White Terror" (France), 615
Why God Became Man (Anselm),
      322, 330
Widows
   in Athens, 110–111
   in England, 349
   in recession (17th century), 478
   in Rome, 212
Wilde, Oscar, 772, 772(i)
Wilkes, John, 587–588
"Wilkes and Liberty" campaign,
      588, 589, 590–591
William (child, England), killing
      of, 374
William (Franks, 9th century), 269,
      285
William I (the Conqueror,
      England), 328–330, 330(i)
William I (Netherlands), 654
William I (Prussia and Germany),
      705, 706(i), 707
William II (Germany), 762, 772,
      778, 793–794
   World War I and, 797, 807, 809,
      817
William III (Prince of Orange and
      king of England and
      Scotland), 506–507, 512,
      547, 548
William IX of Aquitaine, 354
William of Ockham, 408
William of Orange (d. 1584), 466

Will to power, Nietzsche on, 775
Wilson, Woodrow, 793, 807
   Fourteen Points of, 812,
      818–819
Windischgrätz, Alfred von, 688
Wind power, 968, 968(i)
Windsor, house of, 547
Winfrith (Boniface), 262
Winter Palace (St. Petersburg), 790
Wisdom literature, 22, 42, 46
Witches and witchcraft, 481,
      487–488, 488(i), 556
Wives
   in Greece, 88
   in Napoleonic Code, 632
Wladyslaw II Jagiello (Lithuania-
      Poland), 419
Wolf, Christa, 930
"Wolf-Man" (Freud's patient), 767,
      768, 773, 796
Wolsey, Thomas, 443, 444
Woman suffrage, 780–781, 823,
      823(f)
Women. See also Feminism;
      Gender; Woman suffrage;
      Women's rights
   in 1920s, 827, 828
   as abbesses, 259
   activism of, 933, 934(i)
   in Afghanistan, 973
   Aristotle on, 114
   in arts, 68, 125, 753
   in Athens, 87–90
   as athletes, 226(i)
   as authors, 522–523, 544
   in barbarian society, 221
   Beauvoir and, 907
   birth control and, 750, 769
   in Byzantine Empire, 249
   Carolingian peasant, 287–288
   as Cathars, 359
   charitable work by, 674, 675
   in China, 900
   Christian, 191, 212
   in concentration camps, 866
   in confraternities, 524
   as consumers, 746
   in convents, 290
   in domestic service, 478, 541,
      578
   in Dutch society, 510–511
   in eastern Roman Empire, 230
   education for, 715, 758, 975
   in Egypt, 22
   emigration to Americas, 535
   in England, 646, 710

in Enlightenment, 555(i),
    558–559, 565–566, 577
in factories, 665
food riots and, 586
in former Soviet Union, 959
in France, 632, 855, 890
in French Revolution, 594(i),
    595, 603, 612, 613–614
in Germany, 298–299, 779, 851,
    890, 892(i)
in Great Depression, 844
Greek, 40, 49, 55(i), 59–60, 61
Hellenistic, 123
Hittite, 27
as indentured servants, 535
in Iran, 971
in Islam, 243
Israelite, 45
in Italy, 835, 836, 868
in labor unions, 755
lifestyle of, 541, 771–772
in Lysistrata, 99–100
march to Versailles by, 594(i),
    595
Masonic lodges of, 575
medieval schools and, 339
as medieval vassals, 290
Merovingian aristocratic,
    258–259
monastic communities for,
    219–220
nation building and, 704(i)
in Nazi Germany, 851, 868
Neo-Assyrian, 41
Neolithic, 8
new woman and, 771–772
as nurses, 699, 700(i)
outwork by, 749
paintings by, 537(i), 753, 753(i)
Paleolithic, 5
in Paris Commune, 718, 719
patrilineal inheritance and, 294
in Plato's Republic, 113
as political activists, 685, 754,
    755
portrayed in arts, 856
in postwar society, 909–910
as prime minister, 940–942
in professions, 715
protective legislation for, 750
protests by, 933, 934(i), 945
reading by, 542
in realist art, 721(i)
in recession (17th century), 478
reform and, 659, 674
religion and, 723

in religious orders, 358, 373
Roman, 141, 142–144, 143(i),
    156
in Russia, 550, 702
as salon hostesses, 522, 565–566
in sciences, 521, 522, 775, 776
scientific theories about, 724
separate spheres and, 675–676
sexuality and, 578, 774
social and legal status of, 675
socialism and, 682, 683
social manners and, 521–523
Soviet, 833, 848, 885
in space exploration, 920,
    920(i)
Spartan, 64
sports and, 751
in sweatshops, 975
in Turkey, 845–846
upper-class, 675, 747
wealth of, 291(f)
welfare-state policies and, 895
witch trials and, 488
in workforce, 689, 745, 748,
    824, 894, 895–896, 925, 927
working class, 675–676
in World War I, 810, 811(i)
after World War I, 823, 823(f)
World War II and, 868, 869
Women in Love (Lawrence), 828
Women's Paradise (Zola), 752
Women's rights, 632, 675, 725,
    770–771, 779–781, 933
Women's Social and Political Union
    (WSPU), 781
Wonders of the World, The, 125
Woolf, Virginia, 831, 832, 856
Wordsworth, William, 647
Workday, industrial, 665, 666
Worker Opposition (Soviet Union),
    833
Workers, 541. See also Labor
    Chartists and, 683, 689
    community activities of,
        755–756
    computers and, 919–920
    in England, 654, 941
    in factories, 664–665, 748
    foreign, 904–906, 977, 978–979
    in France, 542, 599, 600, 606,
        685, 855
    globalization and, 954
    in Great Depression, 843,
        843(i)
    guest, 905
    labor unions and, 665, 754–755

in medieval crafts, 309–310
migrant, 931
migrations by, 747–748
in multinationals, 924
in Napoleonic Code, 632
in Nazi Germany, 851
outworkers as, 648, 741, 749
in postindustrial age, 924–926
protests by, 934
Roman women as, 143–144
in Russia, 779, 789, 790
sans-culottes as, 559, 600
in service industries, 924
in Soviet bloc, 897, 945
in Soviet Union, 847
in textile industry, 661
women as, 745, 745(i), 748, 749,
    824, 827, 868, 894, 895–896,
    910, 925
workplace conditions and,
    665–666
World War I and, 810–811
after World War I, 817, 818, 827
Workhouses, 578, 674–675
Working class, 674, 781. See also
    Workers
education and, 714–715, 778
intervention in lives of,
    674–675, 750
lifestyle of, 667–668, 747–749
political parties of, 755,
    758–759, 778–779
protests by, 717–719
socialism and, 682
sports, leisure, and, 749–751
use of term, 665
white-collar service personnel
    in, 924
women in, 675–676, 780
World War I and, 809
Works and Days (Hesiod), 51
World Bank, 966, 971
World Court, Milosevic and, 956
World economy. See Global
    economy
World Trade Center, destruction of,
    973, 974(i)
World Trade Organization, 966
Worldview, secular vs. religious,
    481–488
World War I, 802(i)
    alliances before, 793–794
    alliances in, 804–806
    arms for, 796
    Balkan region and, 794
    battles in, 806–809

World War I *(continued)*
  colonial troops in, 806, 807
  ending of (1918), 816–817
  Europe after, 817–818,
    823–829
  Europe at outbreak of, 799*(m)*
  events leading to, 793–798
  fronts in, 805*(m)*
  home front in, 809–811
  Ireland and, 812
  mandate system after, 821
  mobilization for, 798
  outbreak of, 796–798, 799*(m)*
  peace after, 818–821
  protests against, 812
  Russian withdrawal from,
    813–814
  trench warfare in, 796, 805*(m)*,
    807, 808, 809*(i)*
  United States in, 812
  women in, 810, 811*(i)*
World War II
  in Africa, 869, 870, 870*(m)*
  alliances before, 858
  civilians in, 842, 859, 861*(i)*,
    865–868, 872
  colonized peoples in, 869
  in Europe, 842, 863–864,
    869–872, 870*(m)*
  Europe after, 876*(m)*, 881–882,
    882–883, 884*(m)*
  events leading to, 857–863
  genocide in, 865–868, 881
  German surrender in, 872
  Holocaust during, 865–868
  home front in, 868–869
  imperialism preceding,
    857–859
  Japanese surrender and, 872
  outbreak of, 841, 842, 863–864
  in Pacific region, 864–865,
    873*(m)*
  postwar settlement and,
    872–875
  resistance in, 869, 870

  Spain as training ground for,
    859–860
  wartime agreements in,
    872–874, 888
  weapons in, 863, 868
World Wide Web, 919, 954, 979,
    986
Worms
  Concordat of (1122), 317, 332,
    351, 352
  Imperial Diet of (1521), 441
  Jews of, 325
  synagogue in, 307*(i)*
Wretched of the Earth, The (Fanon),
    908
Writing
  alphabet and, 15
  cuneiform, 11, 11*(i)*
  Egyptian, 16, 18, 19*(f)*
  Linear A, 28
  Linear B, 32, 33
  in Mycenae, 31
  Rosetta stone and, 108*(i)*
  social status and, 542
  travel, 557–558
  in vernacular, 376–377
Wycliffe, John, 410, 443

Xenophanes of Colophon, 70
Xerxes I (Persia), 77–79
Xhosa people, 735

Yahweh (Hebrew deity), 45
Yalta meeting (1945), 872, 888
Yeats, William Butler, 781
Yehud (kingdom), 46
Yeltsin, Boris, 944, 957
Yeomanry, in England, 422
Young Bosnians, 798*(i)*
Young Ireland movement, 679–680
Young Italy, 679
Young people. *See also* Students
  in 1920s, 828
  activism by, 687, 932–933,
    934–935, 937

  in former Soviet bloc, 960
  generation gap and, 927
  in Great Depression, 844
  in Nazi Germany, 849, 851
  postwar youth culture and, 908
  in Russia, 701–702
  sexuality and, 922
  social reform and, 749
Young Plan (1929), 821
Young Turks, 792, 794
Youth culture, 908, 927
Ypsilanti, Alexander, 651
Y Tu Mamá También (movie), 984
Yugoslavia, 819, 824, 853
  breakup of, 955–956, 956*(m)*,
    965
  ethnic groups in, 954–955
  former (c. 2000), 956*(m)*
  in Little Entente, 822
  resistance to Soviets in,
    887–888
  World War II and, 872
Yukos Oil Company (Russia), 957

Zachary (Pope), 264, 280
Zakat (tax), 242
Zama, battle of, 154
Zara, Dalmatia, 360
Zasulich, Vera, 760
Zemstvos (Russian councils), 701,
    790
Zeno (eastern Roman Empire), 224
Zenobia (Palmyra), 197
Zeus (god), 51, 55, 144
Zhukov, Marshal, 897
Ziggurats, in Sumer, 9*(i)*, 10
Zionism, 786, 883
Zola, Émile, 752, 783
Zollverein (customs union), 679
Zones of occupation, in Germany,
    888, 888*(m)*
Zoroastrianism, 43, 46
Zulu people, 735
Zurich, Zwingli in, 441–442, 445
Zwingli, Huldrych, 441–442

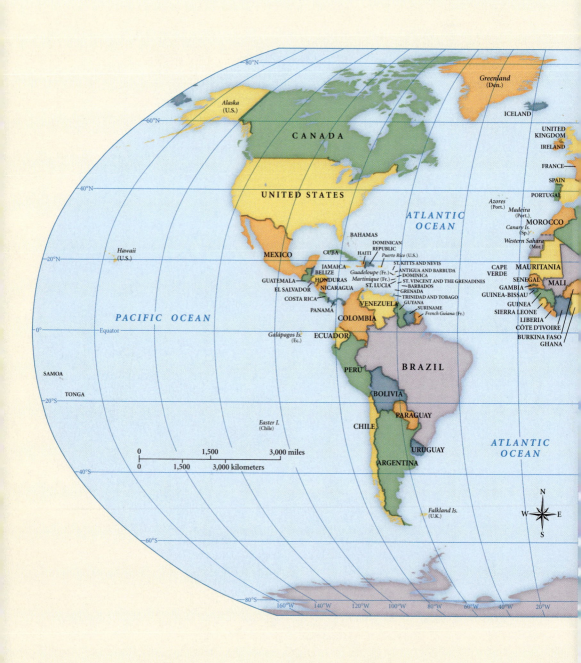

80°N

Greenland
(Den.)

Alaska
(U.S.)

ICELAND

60°N

UNITED
KINGDOM

CANADA

IRELAND

FRANCE

SPAIN

40°N

PORTUGAL

Azores
(Port.)

ATLANTIC
OCEAN

Madeira
(Port.)

MOROCCO

Canary Is.
(Sp.)

BAHAMAS

UNITED STATES

Western Sahara
(Mor.)

20°N

DOMINICAN
REPUBLIC

Hawaii
(U.S.)

CUBA

HAITI

Puerto Rico (U.S.)

CAPE
VERDE

MAURITANIA

MEXICO

ST. KITTS AND NEVIS

ANTIGUA AND BARBUDA

JAMAICA

Guadeloupe (Fr.)

DOMINICA

SENEGAL

BELIZE

Martinique (Fr.)

ST. VINCENT AND THE GRENADINES

GAMBIA

MALI

GUATEMALA

HONDURAS

ST. LUCIA

BARBADOS

GUINEA-BISSAU

EL SALVADOR

NICARAGUA

GRENADA

GUINEA

COSTA RICA

TRINIDAD AND TOBAGO

SIERRA LEONE

PANAMA

VENEZUELA

GUYANA

LIBERIA

PACIFIC OCEAN

COLOMBIA

SURINAME

CÔTE D'IVOIRE

French Guiana (Fr.)

BURKINA FASO

0°

Equator

GHANA

Galápagos Is.
(Ec.)

ECUADOR

SAMOA

PERU

BRAZIL

TONGA

20°S

BOLIVIA

Easter I.
(Chile)

PARAGUAY

CHILE

ATLANTIC
OCEAN

URUGUAY

0   1,500   3,000 miles

0   1,500   3,000 kilometers

ARGENTINA

40°S

Falkland Is.
(U.K.)

N

W   E

S

60°S

80°S

160°W   140°W   120°W   100°W   80°W   60°W   40°W   20°W

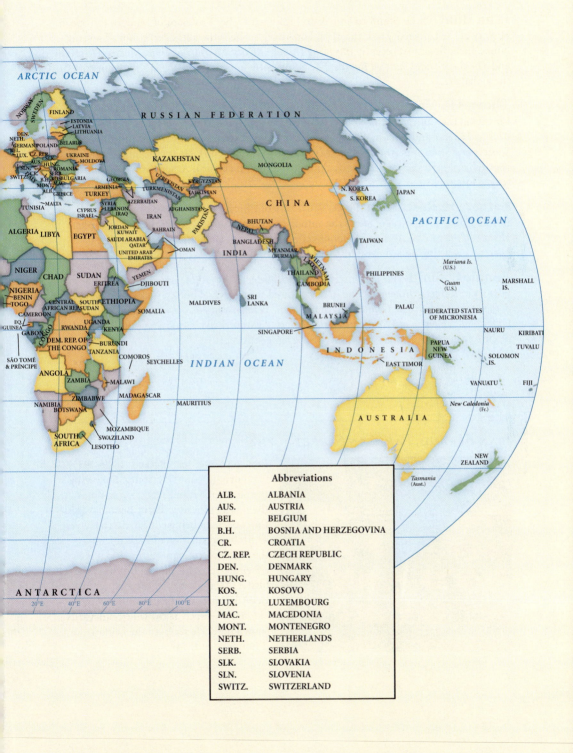

ARCTIC OCEAN

NORWAY
SWEDEN
FINLAND
ESTONIA
LATVIA
LITHUANIA
DEN.
NETH.
GERMAN POLAND
BEL.
LUX. CZ. REP. BELARUS
SLN. HUNG. UKRAINE
SWITZ. ROMANIA MOLDOVA
MONT. SERB.
B.H. MAC.
ALB. BULGARIA
GREECE GEORGIA
TUNISIA MALTA ARMENIA
CYPRUS TURKEY AZERBAIJAN
ISRAEL LEBANON
SYRIA

RUSSIAN FEDERATION

KAZAKHSTAN
MONGOLIA
UZBEKISTAN KYRGYZSTAN
TURKMENISTAN TAJIKISTAN
CHINA
N. KOREA
S. KOREA JAPAN

PACIFIC OCEAN

ALGERIA LIBYA EGYPT
NIGER CHAD SUDAN
NIGERIA
BENIN
TOGO
CENTRAL SOUTH
AFRICAN REP SUDAN ETHIOPIA
CAMEROON
EQ.
GUINEA
GABON
CONGO RWANDA
DEM. REP. OF BURUNDI
THE CONGO TANZANIA
SÃO TOMÉ
& PRÍNCIPE
ANGOLA ZAMBIA MALAWI
ZIMBABWE
NAMIBIA
BOTSWANA MADAGASCAR
SOUTH
AFRICA SWAZILAND
LESOTHO

AFGHANISTAN
IRAN
JORDAN
KUWAIT BAHRAIN
SAUDI ARABIA
QATAR
UNITED ARAB OMAN
EMIRATES
YEMEN
ERITREA
DJIBOUTI
SOMALIA
UGANDA
KENYA
COMOROS
SEYCHELLES

PAKISTAN
NEPAL BHUTAN
INDIA BANGLADESH
MYANMAR
(BURMA)
THAILAND LAOS VIETNAM
CAMBODIA
MALDIVES
SRI
LANKA

INDIAN OCEAN

MAURITIUS
MOZAMBIQUE

TAIWAN

Mariana Is.
(U.S.)
Guam
(U.S.)

PHILIPPINES

BRUNEI
MALAYSIA
SINGAPORE
INDONESIA
EAST TIMOR
PALAU

MARSHALL
IS.

FEDERATED STATES
OF MICRONESIA

NAURU KIRIBATI
TUVALU
PAPUA
NEW SOLOMON
GUINEA IS.

VANUATU FIJI

New Caledonia
(Fr.)

AUSTRALIA

NEW
ZEALAND

Tasmania
(Aust.)

ANTARCTICA

20°E 40°E 60°E 80°E 100°E

Abbreviations	
ALB.	ALBANIA
AUS.	AUSTRIA
BEL.	BELGIUM
B.H.	BOSNIA AND HERZEGOVINA
CR.	CROATIA
CZ. REP.	CZECH REPUBLIC
DEN.	DENMARK
HUNG.	HUNGARY
KOS.	KOSOVO
LUX.	LUXEMBOURG
MAC.	MACEDONIA
MONT.	MONTENEGRO
NETH.	NETHERLANDS
SERB.	SERBIA
SLK.	SLOVAKIA
SLN.	SLOVENIA
SWITZ.	SWITZERLAND

About the authors

Lynn Hunt (Ph.D., Stanford University) is Eugen Weber Professor of Modern European History at the University of California, Los Angeles. She is the author or editor of several books, including most recently *Inventing Human Rights*; *Measuring Time, Making History*; and *The Book That Changed Europe*. She is currently finishing a book on writing history in the global era.

Thomas R. Martin (Ph.D., Harvard University) is Jeremiah O'Connor Professor in Classics at the College of the Holy Cross. He is the author of *Sovereignty and Coinage in Classical Greece* and *Ancient Greece* and is one of the originators of *Perseus: Interactive Sources and Studies on Ancient Greece* (www.perseus.tufts.edu). He is currently conducting research on the career of Pericles as a political leader in classical Athens as well as on the text of Josephus's *Jewish War*.

Barbara H. Rosenwein (Ph.D., University of Chicago) is professor of history at Loyola University Chicago. She is the author or editor of several books, including *A Short History of the Middle Ages* and *Emotional Communities in the Early Middle Ages*. She is currently working on a general history of the emotions in the West.

Bonnie G. Smith (Ph.D., University of Rochester) is Board of Governors Professor of History at Rutgers University. She is author or editor of several books, including *Ladies of the Leisure Class*; *The Gender of History: Men, Women and Historical Practice*; and *The Oxford Encyclopedia of Women in World History*. Currently she is studying the globalization of European culture and society since the seventeenth century.

About the cover image

Jean Béraud, *Parisian Street Scene*

French painter Jean Béraud (1849–1935) was born in Saint Petersburg. Following the death of Béraud's father, a sculptor, the family moved to Paris. Béraud was in the process of being educated as a lawyer until the occupation of Paris during the Franco-Prussian war in 1870. Like other artists of his day, he captured the bustle of Parisian daily life during the Belle Époque and the innovations in the city itself — such as the wide boulevards shown here. He received the Légion d'honneur in 1894.